Fodor's 2014

FRANCE

WELCOME TO FRANCE

Famed artists, writers, gourmands, and bon vivants have all been put under France's intoxicating spell. And travelers can still relish the same enchanting attractions, from Matisse's coastal villages to Hemingway's Parisian cafés to Marie Antoinette's pastoral escape inside Versailles. France is a gastronomic wonderland, an artistic mecca, and a historical pop-up book. Vineyards blanket the wine regions, cathedrals crown the cities, and sandy beaches drape the coastline. With all these riches, you may start plotting your return visit before you even return home.

TOP REASONS TO GO

★ **Marvelous Food:** From the humble café to haute cuisine, the French know how to eat.

★ **Fairytale Castles and Châteaux:** The elegance and majesty of France's past endure.

★ **Shopping:** Parisian luxuries, famed street markets, and handicrafts all beckon.

★ **Wineries and Vineyards:** White to red, you can sip your way across the countryside.

★ **Awesome Art:** From the grand, sprawling Louvre to the intimate Atelier Cézanne.

★ **Charming Villages:** Countryside hamlets with pretty cottages are plentiful.

Fodor's FRANCE 2014

Publisher: Amanda D'Acierno, *Senior Vice President*

Editorial: Arabella Bowen, *Executive Editorial Director*; Linda Cabasin, *Editorial Director*

Design: Fabrizio La Rocca, *Vice President, Creative Director*; Tina Malaney, *Associate Art Director*; Chie Ushio, *Senior Designer*; Ann McBride, *Production Designer*

Photography: Melanie Marin, *Associate Director of Photography*; Jessica Parkhill and Jennifer Romains, *Researchers*

Maps: Rebecca Baer, *Map Editor*; Mark Stroud, Moon Street Cartography; David Lindroth; Ed Jacobus; Mapping Specialists *Cartographers*

Production: Linda Schmidt, *Managing Editor*; Evangelos Vasilakis, *Associate Managing Editor*; Angela L. McLean, *Senior Production Manager*

Sales: Jacqueline Lebow, *Sales Director*

Marketing & Publicity: Heather Dalton, *Marketing Director*; Katherine Fleming, *Senior Publicist*

Business & Operations: Susan Livingston, *Vice President, Strategic Business Planning*; Sue Daulton, *Vice President, Operations*

Fodors.com: Megan Bell, *Executive Director, Revenue & Business Development*; Yasmin Marinaro, *Senior Director, Marketing & Partnerships*

Copyright © 2014 by Fodor's Travel, a division of Random House, Inc.

Writers: Jennifer Ditsler-Ladonne, Linda Hervieux, Nancy Heslin, Christopher Mooney, Lyn Parry, Bryan Pirolli, Avery Sumner, Victoria Tang, Jack Vermee

Editors: Susan MacCallum-Whitcomb, Maria Teresa Hart, Jacinta O'Halloran
Production Editor: Elyse Rozelle

ISBN 978–0–7704–3241–6

ISSN 0532–5692

SPECIAL SALES

This book is available at special discounts for bulk purchases for sales promotions or premiums. For more information, e-mail specialmarkets@randomhouse.com

PRINTED IN COLOMBIA

10 9 8 7 6 5 4 3 2 1

CONTENTS

ABOUT
THIS GUIDE

Fodor's Ratings

Everything in this guide is worth doing—we don't cover what isn't—but exceptional sights, hotels, and restaurants are recognized with additional accolades. **Fodor's**Choice ★ indicates our top recommendations, and **Best Bets** call attention to notable hotels and restaurants in various categories. Care to nominate a new place? Visit Fodors.com/contact-us.

Trip Costs

We list prices wherever possible to help you budget well. Hotel and restaurant price categories from **$** to **$$$$** are noted alongside each recommendation. For hotels, we include the lowest cost of a standard double room in high season. For restaurants, we cite the average price of a main course at dinner or, if dinner isn't served, at lunch. For attractions, we always list adult admission fees; discounts are usually available for children, students, and senior citizens.

Hotels

Our local writers vet every hotel to recommend the best overnights in each price category, from budget to expensive. Unless otherwise specified, you can expect private bath, phone, and TV in your room. For expanded hotel reviews, facilities, and deals visit Fodors.com.

Restaurants

Unless we state otherwise, restaurants are open for lunch and dinner daily. We mention dress code only when there's a specific requirement and reservations only when they're essential or not accepted. To make restaurant reservations, visit Fodors.com.

Credit Cards

The hotels and restaurants in this guide typically accept credit cards. If not, we'll say so.

Top Picks
★ **Fodor's**Choice

Listings
⊠ Address
⊠ Branch address
☎ Telephone
🖷 Fax
⊕ Website
✉ E-mail
🎫 Admission fee
🕐 Open/closed times
Ⓜ Subway
⌖ Directions or Map coordinates

Hotels & Restaurants
🏨 Hotel
🛏 Number of rooms
🍴 Meal plans
✕ Restaurant
🖋 Reservations
👔 Dress code
☰ No credit cards
$ Price

Other
⇨ See also
☞ Take note
⛳ Golf facilities

1

EXPERIENCE FRANCE

FRANCE TODAY

It may be a cliché to say the French fret over their place in the world, but they do. Faced with the ever-dominant Anglo-American axis and hobbled by the global economic crisis, the French are rallying to protect their institutions, their language, and, above all, *la vie française*—their treasured lifestyle. Still, polls show the French are optimistic about the future—and there's plenty of good news.

Tourism is thriving, with France maintaining its rank as the world's top tourist destination, with more than 80 million visitors each year. The French remain leaders in science and technology. France is the world's leading producer of luxury goods, and fashion remains the nation's birthright. Dining in Paris has never been better, with the city experiencing a vibrant emergence of smaller, lower-priced bistros concentrating on quality and terroir, the local bounty that France is famous for.

Gastro-Bistrot

There's a certain amount of schadenfreude in the fashionable proclamation that French gastronomy is in decline. True, it's been a full 40 years since a French chef has rocked the culinary world like Paul Bocuse did in the early '70s, spawning the nouvelle cuisine movement and ushering in the era of celebrity chefs. With the ascendance of Spaniard Ferran Adria's molecular cuisine and Rene Redzepi's radically locavore outpost Noma, in Copenhagen, France has finally had to share the limelight, leading to a sort of identity crisis and a reevaluation of culinary values.

In the last decade, several of France's acclaimed chefs, including Alain Senderens and Olivier Roellinger, have handed in their Michelin stars and bowed out of the fast track in favor of smaller, less formal settings. The global crisis and changing lifestyles have deeply influenced a new generation of chefs seeking a more modern approach to cooking, yet still eager to strut their stuff for an educated, ever-appreciative audience. All of these trends have culminated in a movement that's taken France by storm—bistronomie.

Well underway since the late '90s, the bistronomie movement is now in full swing, with exciting new restaurants opening in Paris every month. A hybrid of "bistrot" and "gastronomy," bistronomie broadly defines a new breed of bistro, run by ambitious young chefs who combine rigorous haute cuisine training with a more laid-back, individual, and creative approach. As the irreverent foodie publications *Omnivore* and *Le Fooding*—viewed as little more than cheeky upstarts when they appeared a decade ago—have evolved into major forces behind the movement, people have taken notice.

Bistronomie dovetails with other popular movements—like the locavores, who advocate the use of fresh, local ingredients, and the trend toward natural and biodynamic wines, which are grown without the use of chemical fertilizers and produced with less sulfites. An international roster of passionate young chefs has also invigorated the movement, with no single approach stealing the limelight.

What else defines bistronomie? A convivial atmosphere, fresh, innovative yet accessible cuisine, adventurous wines, and affordable prices. With all this to offer, naysayers may want to think again—or catch the next flight to Paris!

Madame–Mademoiselle

The French government made a long-overdue concession to French feminists, finally enforcing a law that excises the honorific Mademoiselle from official forms, and advising that all women now be referred to as Madame regardless of marital status. What took France so long?

A deep ambivalence on the part of both men and women regarding gender roles certainly plays a part. As does the kind of entrenched inequality that puts France at a surprising number 46 on the World Economic Forum's Global Pay Gap survey—well behind Britain, Germany, and even Kazakhstan—with men earning wages an average of 12% to 20% higher than women. Attitudes here are slow to change, and with so few female legislators, another area where France lags behind other nations, it seems that French women have their work cut out for them.

Driving Smart

Paris has taken another big step toward mitigating the noise, pollution, and congestion caused by the city's automobile traffic. The dapper four-seat, fully electric Bluecar has finished its test run and is now available at 500 stations around the city.

Based on the successful Velib' bicycle exchange, which boasts more than 20,000 bicycles and is still growing, the Autolib' program allows cars to be taken from one of the semicircular metal-and-glass stations to any point in Paris, and 56 suburban destinations. After a nominal subscription rate, each ride is paid for in half-hour increments, costing €4–€8.

Pity the Rich

French millionaires can relax—for now. In December, France's Constitutional Council struck down incoming president François Hollande's proposed 75% tax on individuals earning more than €1 million just days before it was to take effect. Hollande may have clinched the Presidential office with the election promise of pushing through this tax, and he's refused to back down that pushing the tax through could result in a mass exodus of wealthy tax evaders. Already, two prominent Parisians, Gérard Depardeau, France's most famous actor, and Bernard Arnault, its richest citizen and chairman of the French LVMH luxury group, are preparing to jump ship. Depardieu, courted by none other than Russia's Vladimir Putin, put his 20,000-square-foot mansion in Paris's elegant 7th arrondissement up for sale, and Arnault has requested citizenship from neighboring Belgium. Even the ex-president has been implicated in the *scandale*. Nicholas Sarkozy set France abuzz when his plan to vacate Paris and start up a hedge fund with a group of wealthy investors in London was uncovered during a police raid on the scandal-ridden former president's property.

From a distance, an income tax this steep may seem like madness. But the French have long reconciled themselves to higher taxes in the interest of a fundamental French value, égalité, reaping the benefits in the form one the world's best health care systems, low-cost education, universal child care, and a plethora of social safety nets. With the global crisis, however, preserving the French quality of life is an ever more delicate balancing act. Whether President Hollande is up to the task remains to be seen and this battle, which will be revisited in 2014, may be a decisive one.

WHAT'S WHERE

Numbers refer to chapters.

2 Paris. A quayside vista that takes in the Seine, a passing boat, Notre-Dame, the Eiffel Tower, and mansard roofs all in one generous sweep is enough to convince you that Paris is indeed the most beautiful city on Earth.

3 Ile-de-France. Appearing like all France in miniature, the Ile-de-France region is the nation's heartland. Here Louis XIV built vainglorious Versailles, Chartres brings the faithful to their knees, and Monet's Giverny enchants all.

4 Loire Valley. Chenonceaux, Chambord, and Saumur—the parade of royal and near-royal châteaux magnificently captures France's golden age of monarchy in an idyllic region threaded by the Loire River.

5 Normandy. Sculpted with cliff-lined coasts, Normandy has been home to saints and sculptors, with a dramatic past marked by Mont-St-Michel's majestic abbey, Rouen's towering cathedral, and the D-Day beaches.

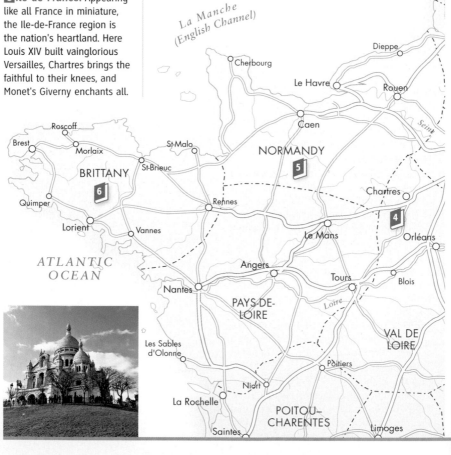

La Manche
(English Channel)

Boulogne

Dieppe

Cherbourg

Le Havre

Rouen

Seine

Caen

NORMANDY

5

Chartres

Roscoff

Brest

Morlaix

St-Malo

St-Brieuc

BRITTANY

6

Quimper

Lorient

Vannes

Rennes

Le Mans

4

Orléans

ATLANTIC
OCEAN

Angers

Tours

Blois

VAL DE
LOIRE

Nantes

PAYS-DE-
LOIRE

Loire

Les Sables
d'Olonne

Poitiers

Niort

La Rochelle

POITOU–
CHARENTES

Limoges

Saintes

6 **Brittany.** A long arm of rocky land stretching into the Atlantic, Brittany is a place unto itself, with its own language and time-defying towns such as Gauguin's Pont-Aven and the pirate haven of St-Malo.

7 **Champagne Country.** The capital of bubbly is Reims, set near four great Gothic cathedrals and the beginning of the scenic Route de Champagne.

8 **Alsace-Lorraine.** Although this region bordered by the Rhine often looks German and sounds German, its main sights—18th-century Nancy, medieval Strasbourg, and the lovely Route du Vin—remain proudly French.

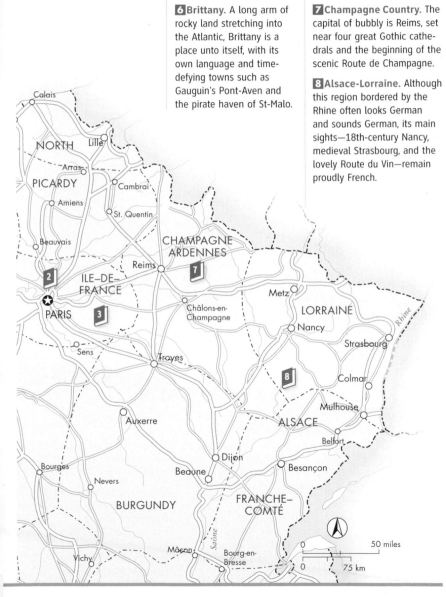

WHAT'S WHERE

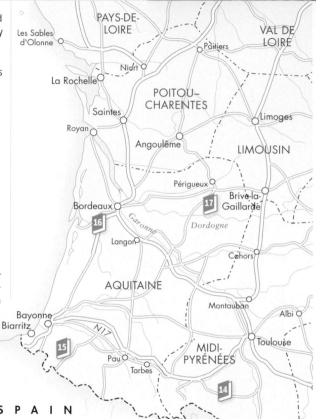

9 Burgundy. Hallowed ground for wine lovers, Burgundy hardly needs to be beautiful—but it is. Around the gastronomic hub of Dijon, the region is famed for its verdant vineyards and Romanesque churches.

10 Lyon and the Alps. Local chefs rival their Parisian counterparts in treasure-filled Lyon, heart of a diverse region where you ski down Mont Blanc or take a heady trip along the Beaujolais Wine Road.

11 Provence. Famed for its Lavender Route, the honey-gold hill towns of the Luberon, and vibrant cities like Aix and Marseilles, this region was dazzlingly abstracted into geometric daubs of paint by Van Gogh and Cézanne.

12 French Riviera (Côte d'Azur). From glamorous St-Tropez through beauteous Antibes to sophisticated Nice, this sprawl of pebble beaches and zillion-dollar houses has always captivated sun lovers and socialites.

13 Corsica. Corsica's gifts of artistic and archaeological treasures, crystalline waters, granite peaks, and pine forests add up to one of France's most unspoiled sanctuaries.

14 Midi-Pyrénées and Languedoc-Roussillon. Rose-hue Toulouse, once-upon-a-time-ified Carcassone, and the Matisse-beloved Vermillion Coast are among southwest France's most colorful sights.

15 Basque Country, Gascony, and the Hautes-Pyrénées. Whether you head for Bay of Biscay resorts like Biarritz, coastal villages such as St-Jean-de-Luz, or the Pyrenean peaks, this region will cast a spell.

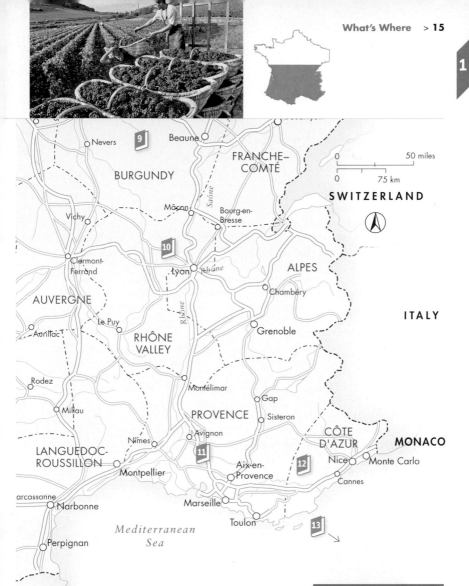

Nevers **9** Beaune

BURGUNDY

FRANCHE–
COMTÉ

0 _____ 50 miles
0 _____ 75 km

SWITZERLAND

Mâcon Bourg-en-
Bresse

Saône

Vichy

10

Clermont-
Ferrand

Lyon Rhône

ALPES

Chambéry

AUVERGNE

Le Puy

Rhône

Aurillac

RHÔNE
VALLEY

Grenoble

ITALY

Rodez

Montélimar

Gap

Millau

PROVENCE

Sisteron

Avignon

Nîmes

11

CÔTE
D'AZUR

MONACO

LANGUEDOC-
ROUSSILLON

Montpellier

Aix-en-
Provence

12

Nice Monte Carlo

Cannes

arcassonne

Narbonne

Marseille

Toulon

13

Perpignan

*Mediterranean
Sea*

16 **Bordeaux and the Wine
Country.** The wines of Bordeaux tower as a standard
against which others are
measured, and they made
the city of Bordeaux rich and
owners of its vineyards—like
Château Mouton-Rothschild—
even richer.

17 **The Dordogne.** One of the
hottest destinations in France,
the Dordogne is a stone-
cottage pastorale studded
with fairy-tale castles, storybook villages, and France's
top prehistoric sights.

FRANCE PLANNER

When to Go

Summer is the most popular (and expensive) season. July in Paris is crowded and can be hot, although the Paris Plage, the "beach" on the banks of the Seine, is popular with locals and tourists alike.

The Riviera sparkles in August—but the notorious *embouteillages* (traffic jams) on the drive south from Paris can make you wish you stayed home.

Famously fickle weather means you never know what to expect in Normandy and Brittany, where picture-postcard villages and languorous sandy beaches are never jam-packed.

September is gorgeous, with temperate weather, saner airfares, and cultural events scheduled specifically for the return from summer vacation, an institution that even has its own name: *la rentrée.*

Another good time to visit is in late spring, just before the masses arrive, when the sun sets after 9 pm and cafés are abuzz.

Unless you're skiing in the Alps, winter is the least appealing time to come, though it's the best time to find less expensive airfares and hotel deals—and escape the crowds.

Transportation Basics

There are two major gateway airports to France just outside the capital: Orly, 16 km (10 miles) south of Paris, and Charles de Gaulle, 26 km (16 miles) northeast of the city. At Charles de Gaulle, also known as Roissy, there's a TGV (*train à grande vitesse*) station at Terminal 2, where you can connect to high-speed trains going all over the country.

Once in France, the best way to travel is by train, either high-speed TGV or regional train. A France Rail Pass allows three days of unlimited train travel in a one-month period. With train service efficient and enjoyable, long-distance bus service is rarely used, though there are some regional buses that cover areas where train service is spotty.

If you're traveling by car, there are excellent links between Paris and most French cities, and more meandering ones between the provinces. For the fastest route between two points, look for roads marked for *autoroute*. A *péage* (toll) must be paid on most expressways: the rate varies, but can be steep. Note that gas prices are also steep, upward of €1.40 a liter, or about $6.90 a gallon.

Although renting a car is about twice as expensive as in the United States, it's the best way to see remote corners of the lovely French countryside. To get the best rate, book a rental car at home, and well in advance if you're planning a trip in summer and early fall. If you want automatic transmission, which is more expensive, be sure to ask for it when you reserve.

Here's a good tip: if you're traveling from Paris, a practical option is to take the TGV to another large city, such as Avignon or Nice, and rent a car there.

Hours

In Paris and larger cities, store hours are generally 10 am to 7:30 pm; smaller shops may open later. Elsewhere, expect stores to close in the afternoon, usually 2–4. Museums are closed one day a week, often Tuesday. As a general rule, shops close on Sunday, though many food stores and markets are open in the morning.

Tips on Eating and Staying

Restaurants follow French mealtimes, serving lunch from noon to 2 or 2:30 and dinner from 7:30 or 8 on. Some cafés and brasseries in larger cities serve food all day long. Always reserve a table for dinner, as top restaurants book up to months in advance. You must ask for the check (it's considered rude to bring it unbidden) except in cafés, where a register slip often comes with your order.

Gratuities (*servis*) are included in the bill, but leave some small change on the table: a few cents for drinks, €1 for lunch, or €3 at dinner. You can leave more at a top restaurant, but note that more than 10% is considered extremely generous.

To save money on food, take advantage of France's wonderful outdoor markets and chain supermarkets. Just about every town has its own market once or a couple of times a week. Ask the people at the front desk of wherever you're staying to find out when market days are. For supermarkets, the largest chain is Monoprix.

Some of the bigger stores have cafés where you can sit down and eat whatever you buy, as well as mini department stores that sell everything from clothing to children's toys to toiletries.

French cities generally have good hotel options at decent prices. There are several options in Paris, including furnished apartments, at all price levels.

In the countryside, seek out *chambres d'hôtes* (bed-and-breakfasts), which can mean anything from a modest room in a host's home to a grand suite in a Norman château or Provençal farmhouse. Or rent a *gîte rural*, a furnished apartment, often on a farm or a larger property.

⇨ *For more information on accommodations, see the France Lodging Primer in this chapter, as well as the Travel Smart chapter.*

Fête-ing It Up

Spring. Spot your favorite star at the Cannes Film Festival in May (⊕ *www.festival-cannes.fr*). The French Open kicks off the last week of May in Paris (⊕ *www.rolandgarros.com*).

Love *grand cru*? Head to Bordeaux for the wine festival in late June (⊕ *www.bordeaux-fete-le-vin.com*).

Summer. Avignon sparkles in July during the monthlong theater and arts festival (⊕ *www.festival-avignon.com*). French cities and towns celebrate le 14 juillet (July 14, Bastille Day), marking the start of the French Revolution (⊕ *www.14-juillet.cityvox.com*).

The popular Paris Plage transforms the Seine's banks into a "beach" in mid-July with palm trees, sand, and lounge chairs (⊕ *www.paris.fr*).

Fall. Tour France's most beautiful buildings on the Journée du Patrimoine (Patrimony Day), usually the third Sunday in September (⊕ *www.journeesdupatrimoine.culture.fr*).

Paris has cultural events throughout September for *la rentrée* (the return) from summer vacation (⊕ *www.paris.fr*).

Winter. The Carnaval de Nice rocks Lent for three weeks in February (⊕ *www.nicecarnaval.com*). Strasbourg's famous Marchés de Noël (Christmas Markets) runs from late November to early January (⊕ *www.noel-strasbourg.com*).

GETTING AROUND

Bus Travel

Because France has invested so dearly in its highly organized national rail network and well-connected highway system, nationwide bus service simply doesn't exist.

Eurolines offers only international routes, so you can get in or out of the country, but there are no routes connecting the big cities within France.

Happily, domestic bus travel is managed regionally, usually serving small rural communities or replacing SNCF train routes that are no longer commercially viable.

These bus routes, however, tend to be slow, with confusing schedules posted online (and rarely in English). Still, they can often be a cheap and direct way to travel short distances.

The Getting Around section at the start of each of our chapters has handy local information about useful bus routes.

Remember that it is always useful to visit the local tourism office or the central bus depot for schedules and tickets.

Car Travel

Although the French train network is quite vast, smaller towns—especially in harder-to-reach mountainous regions—may have only limited schedules. And because many route hubs are in major cities such as Paris, there's often a lack of direct routes in between these smaller towns, requiring a circuitous trajectory to cover a relatively short distance. This isn't a big deal for visitors with plenty of extra time who are flexible in their travel plans.

But if you're seeking the maximum amount of freedom to explore France off the beaten path, then a rental car could be your best option.

France's highways, or autoroutes (A), are well maintained, and generally traffic-free outside certain holidays and metropolitan areas during rush hour, but with so much natural beauty, charming villages, and interesting sights along the way, we would recommend sticking to the national trunk roads, or Routes Nationales (RN), which allow you to easily stop to see a local site, pick up some fresh produce at a farm, or pull over for a picnic at a lakeside park.

Of course, driving in France requires a valid license from your home country, a bit of talent with a map (as a backup to any GPS system), and enough knowledge about the local road rules to stay out of trouble.

Although there are many pluses to driving a car, there are important minuses. One of the biggest expenses of your trip can wind up being the gasoline, which has been hovering around €1.40/liter (or €6.90 gallon) at this writing. In addition, signage in France can be spotty—we've heard plenty of horror stories about half-hour trips turning into two-hour ordeals.

Finally, there is the obstacle course that is parking, with travelers to French cities having to run the gauntlet of meters, parking-ticket machines, parking cards (*cartes de stationnements*), chaotic rush-hour traffic, and the eternal search for an overnight garage.

If you're determined to drive, however, see our Travel Smart chapter for more tips for renting and driving a car in France.

Train Travel

The next best thing to flying, and sometimes more convenient, is traveling by France's efficient railways, from regional trains connecting small towns and villages all over the country to the high-speed TGVs serving major cities.

The best thing about the trains is that the stations are usually right in the center of town, and in the case of Paris, connected to the métro. This means that backpackers can find a hotel within walking distance of the train station without worrying about long taxi rides to and from the airport.

Traveling by train also eliminates long security checks and excess baggage fees, and you get to enjoy the scenery as you travel.

Managed by the SNCF, trains reach almost every corner of France, including about 60 cities by TGV, and thousands more under the regional rail lines including Téoz (Paris, Bordeaux, Nice, Perpignan, and Clermont-Ferrand), the Lunéa sleeper trains (which have first-class, second-class, and reclining-seat options starting at €17), iDTGV theme trains (choose "zen-," "games-," or "nightclub"-themed atmospheres on 20 routes), and the "TER" (Transport Express Régional) medium-distance trains serving the different French regions.

For instance, the Ile-de-France département surrounding Paris is served by the Transilien network, which links to the suburban Paris commuter rail known as the "RER" (Réseau Express Régional) and the Paris Métropolitan, or métro.

Aside from these Paris networks, which are part of the Parisian Transportation Authority known as the "RATP" (Régie Autonome des Transports Parisiens), all trains in France are managed by the French National Railway, or "SNCF" (Société Nationale des Chemins de Fer Français).

This makes it a lot easier for travelers to find the best ticket whether it's by TGV or by regional TER, either by the official French site (⊕ www.voyages-sncf.com) or via Rail Europe (⊕ www.raileurope.com), which lets you search in your home country's language and currency before you arrive in France.

If you want to remain flexible even after you've arrived in France, sign up for its "Anywhere Anytime France e-tickets" for the convenience of ordering your tickets online and printing them at any train station up to an hour before departure time.

Read our Travel Smart chapter for the different discount options when traveling by train, including Eurail Passes and student/senior rates.

Air Travel

With a landmass about four-fifths that of Texas, France presents its own set of transportation challenges when confronting the big question: what's the best way to get around? Fact is, the quickest and often least expensive option—thanks to budget airlines and competitive rates on Air France—is flying. You can fly in one hour from Paris into Nice Airport (plus 15 minutes by bus into town) on easyJet from Orly Airport (15 minutes south of Paris) from about €50 one way (without checked bags). But factor in the extra hour at the airport for security, the baggage restrictions, and out-of-town location of airports—budget lines use smaller airports far from city centers. An Air France flight from Paris Orly to Marseille costs €59–€72 if booked well in advance, while a RyanAir flight starts at just €33 but flies from Beauvais Airport (an hour north of Paris by bus) plus plenty of extra fees. But flying is often the best option if you have little luggage, less time, and travel to major cities.

FRANCE
TOP ATTRACTIONS

Louvre, Paris
(A) Home to art's most photogenic beauties—the *Venus de Milo*, the *Winged Victory*, and the *Mona Lisa*—this is not only the largest palace in France but also the most important museum in the world.

Chartres, Ile-de-France
(B) Triply famous for its peerless stained-glass windows, as the resting place for an important relic of the Virgin Mary, and as the birthplace of High Gothic, Chartres is more than a cathedral—it's a spiritual experience.

Versailles, Ile-de-France
(C) A palace and then some, this prime example of royals-gone-wild Baroque style served as backdrop for the rise to power of King Louis XIV. To escape all his bicep-flexing grandeur visit the park to see Marie-Antoinette's fairy-tale farm.

Monet's Garden, Giverny, Ile-de-France
(D) An 8-acre "Monet," these lush gardens were works of art the Impressionist master spent years perfecting before he began re-creating them on canvas. The colors radiate best on sunny spring days.

Chenonceau, Loire Valley
Half bridge, half pleasure palace, this "queen of the châteaux" was presided over by six remarkable women. It was Catherine de' Medici who brilliantly enlarged it to span the River Cher in homage to the Ponte Vecchio of her native Florence.

Lyon, Rhône-Alps
The second-largest city in France, Lyon vies with Paris as the country's true gastronomic capital—gourmands flock here for its galaxy of multistar superchefs and cozy *bouchons* (taverns).

Mont-St-Michel, Normandy

(E) Once seen, never forgotten, this Romanesque abbey rises from its bay like a shimmering apparition, becoming an island at high tide. French and English fought to dominate the "rock" until the 13th century, when it was crowned with a splendid Gothic church.

Strasbourg, Alsace-Lorraine

(F) The cosmopolitan seat of Europe's Parliament, this fascinating mix of half-timber houses and modern glass buildings was fought over by France and Germany—a battle that resulted in a rich intertwining of cultures.

Beaune, Burgundy

At the heart of some of the world's most esteemed vineyards, this atmospheric town is inextricably linked with the wine trade, especially during the annual auction at Beaune's beautiful 15th-century Hôtel-Dieu.

Èze, the French Riviera

Spectacularly perched atop a rocky promontory, this watercolor-pretty village has some of the most breathtaking views in la belle France.

St-Tropez, the French Riviera

(G) Single-handedly propelled from sleepy hamlet to glamorous resort by Brigitte Bardot, St-Trop today heaves with crowds of petulant glitterati. Chill out in the quiet pastel-hue alleys of La Ponche quarter.

Aix-en-Provence, Provence

(H) With sun-dappled squares, luxuriant fountains, and Paul Cézanne's hallowed studio, this captivating town is just the spot for those who consider café-sitting, people-watching, and boutique shopping a way of life.

TOP EXPERIENCES

How will you experience France? Will you while away the hours in the shops and cafés of Paris? Will you dine at the temples of gastronomy in Lyon? Will you play feudal lord among the châteaux of the Loire Valley? Or will you simply throw away your map and chance upon nestled-away villages of the Côte d'Azur or fairy-tale hamlets of the Dordogne? These suggestions, and the following, await you as memorable experiences for your next trip to France.

Walk Like a Parisian

Paris was made for wandering, and the French have coined a lovely word for a person who strolls, usually without a destination in mind: *le flâneur*. In Paris, no matter how aimlessly you wander, chances are you'll end up somewhere magical. Why not first head to the most beautiful spot on the Right Bank: the Palais Royal gardens?

Go Glam in Paris

Break out your bling in this capital of luxury with a stroll down the rue Saint-Honoré to window-shop—the French call it *lèche-vitrine* (or "licking the windows")—from Chanel and Hermès to Chloé. Then do some real feasting at one of Paris's gastronomic temples, L'Arpège (lunch main courses are around €130) or L'Astrance.

Rendezvous with the Phantom

Want to feel like a Rothschild for no money at all? Promenade the fabulously opulent lobby and theater of the 19th-century Palais Garnier (⊕ *www.opera-de-paris.fr*)—haunt of the Phantom and Degas's immortal dancers—daily 10 to 4:30 for free, or get tickets for an evening performance.

Pique-Nique at Place des Vosges

No restaurant can beat the "decor" of Paris's most beautiful square, the 17th-century place des Vosges, so pull up a bench and enjoy your own foodie fixings. Get them at the nearby Marché d'Aligre market, off rue du Faubourg Saint-Antoine. It beats those drab *supermarchés!*

Step into an 8-Acre Monet

It doesn't matter how many posters, photos, or T-shirts you've seen emblazoned with Monet's famous water lilies, nothing beats a visit to Giverny. Savor the Impressionist painter's famous house and gardens (⊕ *www.giverny.org*) in person.

Trip the Light Fantastique at Versailles

Exquisitely choreographed pyrotechnical shows are held each summer and fall in Versailles's immense château gardens (⊕ *www.chateauversailles.fr*). Accompanied by son-et-lumière music and dance performances, these evenings are fit for the Sun King himself.

Plan an Ascent on Heaven at Mont-St-Michel

Keep the faith with a climb to the top and get a God's View of this fabled Benedictine abbey (⊕ *mont-saint-michel.monuments-nationaux.fr*), whose fortified medieval village is the crowning glory of the Normandy coastline.

Become Scott and Zelda on the Riviera

Channel F. Scott Fitzgerald and his wife at their old haunts and discover their side of paradise: stay at their Les Belles Rives hotel in Juan-les-Pins, visit hangouts like the Villa Eilenroc at Cap d'Antibes (⊕ *www.antibes-juanlespins.com*), or dine with superstars at the Hôtel du Cap-Eden Roc.

Rate the Best of Alsace's Würsts

As you head down Alsace's famous Wine Road, Hansel and Gretel villages pop up every few miles, and each has *winstubs* (wine bistros) that cook up delicious dishes of *choucroute garnie*. The inns in Riquewihr and Ribeauvillé (⊕ *www.ribeauville-riquewihr.com*) are supposed to serve the best.

Pop Your Cork along the Champagne Road

The famous Route du Champagne (⊕ *www.tourisme-en-champagne.com*) leads fans of the famous bubbly to the prestigious Champagne houses of Épernay and Reims (including Mumm and Taittinger) plus smaller, family-run estates for tours and tastings.

Que la Fête Commence at Nice's Carnaval

February is festival time on the Côte d'Azur, with boisterous street processions and a celebratory bonfire for the Mardi-Gras Carnaval de Nice (⊕ *www.nicecarnaval.com*). Or march along the citrus-decked parade floats of Menton's Fête du Citron (⊕ *www.feteducitron.com*).

Go Castle-Hopping on a Loire Valley Bike Tour

From Orléans to Angers, bike with VBT Tours (⊕ *www.vbt.com*) along the meandering Loire River past royal châteaux and bountiful gardens, and discover quirky cliff-side troglodyte dwellings that house wine caves and mushroom growers.

Submerge Yourself in Hip-Deep Purple along the Lavender Route

Join the lavender-happy crowds from June to mid-July and travel the Route de la Lavande (⊕ *www.routes-lavande.com*), a wide blue-purple swath that connects major sights like the Abbaye Notre-Dame de Sènaque, Coustellet's Musée de la Lavande, and Forcalquier's famous market.

Après-Ski the Day Away in the French Alps

As home to the first Winter Olympic games in 1924, the ski station of Chamonix (⊕ *www.chamonix.com*), set at the foot of Mont Blanc, provides an ideal backdrop for all winter outdoor activities.

Ride Shotgun on Picasso's Road to St-Paul-de-Vence

Use Aix-en-Provence, Arles, or Antibes as a base for touring the Modern Art Road. Explore picture-perfect villages immortalized by Cézanne and Van Gogh and pose oh-so-casually under the Picassos on view at the Colombe d'Or inn (⊕ *www.la-colombe-dor.com*).

Play Once-Upon-a-Time in Carcassonne

Protected by a double ring of ramparts and 53 towers, this perfectly preserved fortified city (⊕ *www.carcassonne.org*) of the Languedoc-Roussillon region is considered to be one of the most romantic medieval settings in France.

Attend the Festival d'Avignon

This internationally renowned summer theater festival (⊕ *www.festival-avignon.com*) features nearly a thousand performances throughout the city, plus hundreds more in the "unofficial" Avignon Off festival.

Track the Tour de France

No tickets are required to watch this famed cycling competition (⊕ *www.letour.fr*) as it winds through some of the country's most dramatic scenery. Why not enjoy a picnic anywhere along the route as the riders race past?

QUINTESSENTIAL FRANCE

Café Society

Along with air, water, and wine, the café remains one of the basic necessities of life in France. You may prefer a posh perch at a renowned Paris spot such as the Deux Magots on boulevard St-Germain or opt for a tiny *café du coin* (corner café) in Lyon or Marseilles, where you can have a quick cup of coffee at the counter. Those on Paris's major boulevards (such as boulevard St-Michel and the Champs-Élysées) will almost always be the most expensive and the least interesting.

In effect, the more modest establishments (look for nonchalant locals) are the places to really get a feeling for French café culture.

And we do mean culture—not only the practical rituals of the experience (perusing the posted menu, choosing a table, unwrapping your sugar cube) but an intellectual spur as well.

You'll see businesspeople, students, and pensive types pulling out notebooks for intent scribblings. In fact, some Paris landmarks like the Café de Flore host readings, while several years ago a trend for *cafés philos* (philosophy cafés) took off.

And there's always the frisson of history available at places like La Closerie des Lilas, where an expensive drink allows you to rest your derrière on the spots once favored by Apollinaire, Picasso, and Henry Miller.

Finally, there's people-watching, which goes hand in glove with the café lifestyle—what better excuse to linger over your *café crème* or Lillet? So get ready to settle in, sip your *pastis*, and pretend your travel notebook is a Hemingway story in the making.

If you want to get a sense of contemporary French culture, and indulge in some of its pleasures, start by familiarizing yourself with the rituals of daily life. These are a few highlights—things you can take part in with relative ease.

Street Markets

Browsing through the street markets and *marchés couverts* (covered markets) of France is enough to make you regret all the tempting restaurants around. But even though their seafood, free-range poultry, olives, and produce cry out to be gathered in a basket and cooked in their purest forms, you can also enjoy them as a simple visual feast.

Over at flea and *brocante* (collectibles) markets, food plays second fiddle. With any luck, you'll find a little 18th-century engraving that makes your heart go *trottinant*.

Bistros and Brasseries

The choice of restaurants in France is a feast in itself. Of course, at least once during your trip you'll want to indulge in a luxurious meal at a great haute-cuisine restaurant—but there's no need to get knee-deep in white truffles at Paris's Alain Ducasse to savor the France the French

eat. For you can discover the most delicious and indulgent food with a quick visit to a city neighborhood bistro.

History tells us that bistros served the world's first fast food—after the fall of Napoléon, the Russian soldiers who occupied Paris were known to cry *bistro* ("quickly" in Russian) when ordering.

Here, at zinc-top tables, you'll find the great delights of *cuisine traditionelle*, like *grand-mère's* lamb with white beans.

Today the bistro boom has meant that many are designer-decorated and packed with trendsetters. If you're lucky, the food will be as witty and colorful as the clientele.

Brasseries, with few exceptions, remain unchanged—great bustling places with white-aproned waiters and hearty, mainly Alsatian, food, such as pork-based dishes, *choucroute* (sauerkraut), and beer (*brasserie* also means brewery). *Bon appétit!*

IF YOU LIKE

Great Food

Forget the Louvre or the Château de Chenonceau—the real reason for a visit to France is to dine at its famous temples of gastronomy. Once you dive into Taillevent's lobster soufflé, you'll quickly realize that food in France is far more than fuel. The French regard gastronomy as essential to the art of living, so don't feel guilty if your meal at Paris's Pierre Gagnaire takes as long as your visit to the Musée d'Orsay: two hours for a three-course menu is par, and you may, after relaxing into the routine, feel pressured at less than three. Gastronomads—those who travel to eat—won't want to miss a pilgrimage out to La Colle-sur-Loup to witness the culinary fireworks of chef Alain Llorca, whose name reveals his Basque roots. So plan on treating dining as religiously as the French do—at least once.

Alain Llorca Restaurant-Hôtel, La Colle sur Loup, near St-Paul-de-Vence, the Riviera. Master chef Alain Llorca marries grand cuisine with humble Provençal touches—don't be surprised to find octopus in your bouillabaisse.

Le Grand Véfour, Paris. Guy Martin's Savoyard creations are extraordinaire, but the 18th-century decor is almost more delicious.

Le Louis XV, Monaco. If you're going to feast like a king, this Alain Ducasse outpost is the place to do it.

L'Auberge de L'Ill, Illhaeusern, near Ribeauville, Alsace. Gourmands worship at this culinary temple where the Haeberlin family create a brave nouvelle world by fusing Alsatian and Asian fixings to the hautest cuisine.

La Vie de Châteaux

From the humblest feudal ruin to the most delicate Loire Valley spires to the grandest of Sun King spreads, the châteaux of France evoke the history of Europe as no museum can. It is easy to slip into the role of a feudal lord standing on his castellated ramparts and scrambling to protect his patchwork of holdings from kings and dukes. The lovely landscape takes on a strategic air and you find yourself role-playing thus, whether swanning aristocratically over Chenonceau's bridgelike *galerie de bal* spanning the River Cher or curling a revolutionary lip at the splendid excesses of Versailles. These are, after all, the castles that inspired Charles Perrault's "Sleeping Beauty" and "Beauty and the Beast," and their fairy-tale magic—rich with history and Disney-free—still holds true. Better yet, enjoy a "queen-for-a-stay" night at one of France's many châteaux-hotels. Many are surprisingly affordable.

Chambord, Loire Valley. This French Renaissance extravaganza—all 440 rooms and 365 chimneys—will take your breath away. Be sure to go up the down staircase designed by Leonardo da Vinci.

Château de la Bourdaisière, Loire Valley. Not one but *two* princes de Broglie welcome you to this idyllic and elegant neo-Renaissance hotel.

Château d'Ussé, Loire Valley. Step into a fairy tale at Sleeping Beauty's legendary home.

Vaux-le-Vicomte, Ile-de-France. Louis XIV was so jealous when he saw this 17th-century Xanadu that he commissioned Versailles.

Beautiful Villages

Nearly everyone has a mind's-eye view of the perfect French village. Oozing half-timber houses and roses, these once-upon-a-time villages have a sense of tranquillity not even tour buses can ruin. The Loire Valley's prettiest village, Saché, is so small it seems your own personal property—an eyebrow of cottages, a Romanesque church, a 17th-century *auberge* (inn), and a modest château. Little wonder Honoré de Balzac came here to write some of his greatest novels. Auvers-sur-Oise, the pretty riverside village in the Ile-de-France, inspired some of Van Gogh's finest landscapes. In the Dordogne region, hamlets have a Disney-like quality, right down to Rapunzel windows, flocks of geese, and storks'-nest towers. Along the Côte d'Azur you'll find the sky-kissing, hilltop *villages perchés*, like Èze. All in all, France has an *embarras de richesses* of nestled-away treasures—so just throw away the map. After all, no penciled itinerary is half as fun as stumbling upon some half-hidden Brigadoon.

Haut-de-Cagnes, French Riviera. This perfect example of the eagle's-nest village near the coast is nearly boutique-free, was once adored by Renoir, and remains ancient in atmosphere.

La Roque-Gageac, Dordogne. Lorded over by its immense rock cliff, this centuries-old riverside village is the perfect backdrop for a beautiful *pique-nique*.

Riquewihr, Alsace. Full of storybook buildings, cul-de-sac courtyards, and stone gargoyles, this is the showpiece of the Alsatian Wine Route.

Monet, Manet, and Matisse

It is through the eyes of its artists that many first get to know France. No wonder people from across the globe come to search for Gauguin's bobbing boats at Pont-Aven, Monet's bridge at Giverny, and the gaslit Moulin Rouge of Toulouse-Lautrec—not hung in a museum but alive in all their three-dimensional glory. In Arles you can stand on the spot where Van Gogh painted and compare his perspective to a placard with his finished work; in Paris you can climb into the garret-atelier where Delacroix created his epic canvases, or wander the redolent streets of Montmartre, once haunted by Renoir, Utrillo, and Modigliani. Of course, an actual trip to France is not necessary to savor this country: a short visit to any major museum will probably just as effectively transport the viewer—by way of the paintings of Pisarro, Millet, Poussin, Sisley, and Matisse—to its legendary landscapes. But go beyond museums and discover the actual towns that once harbored these famed artists.

Céret, Languedoc-Roussillon. Pack your crayons for a trip to Matisse Country, for this is where the artist fell in love with the *fauve* (savage) hues found only in Mother Nature.

Giverny, Ile-de-France. Replacing paint and water with earth and water, Monet transformed his 5-acre garden into a veritable live-in Impressionist painting.

St-Paul-de-Vence, Côte d'Azur. Pose oh-so-casually under the Picassos at the famed Colombe d'Or inn, once favored by Signac, Modigliani, and Bonnard.

Le Shopping

Although it's somewhat disconcerting to see Gap stores gracing major street corners in Paris and other urban areas in France, if you take the time to peruse smaller specialty shops, you can find rare original gifts—be it an antique brooch from the 1930s or a modern vase crafted from Parisian rooftop-tile zinc. It's true that the traditional gifts of silk scarves, perfume, and wine can often be purchased for less in the shopping mall back home, but you can make an interesting twist by purchasing a vintage Hermès scarf, or a unique perfume from an artisan perfumer. Bargaining is traditional in outdoor and flea markets, antiques stores, small jewelry shops, and craft galleries, for example. If you're thinking of buying several items, or if you're simply in love with something a little bit too expensive, you've nothing to lose by cheerfully suggesting to the proprietor, "Vous me faites un prix?" ("How about a discount?") The small businessperson will immediately size you up, and you'll have some good-natured fun.

Colette, Paris. Wiggle into something sleek and chic at this fashionista shrine.

Grain de Vanille, Cancale. These sublime tastes of Brittany—salted butter caramels and rare honeys—make great gifts, *non*?

L'Isle-sur-la-Sorgue, Provence. This canal-laced town becomes a Marrakech of marketeers on Sunday, when dazzling brocante (collectibles) dealers set up shop.

Gothic Churches and Cathedrals

Their extraordinary permanence, their everlasting relevance even in a secular world, and their transcendent beauty make the Gothic churches and cathedrals of France a lightning rod if you are in search of the essence of French culture. The product of a peculiarly Gallic mix of mysticism, exquisite taste, and high technology, France's 13th- and 14th-century "heavenly mansions" provide a thorough grounding in the history of architecture (some say there was nothing new in the art of building between France's Gothic arch and Frank Lloyd Wright's cantilevered slab). Each cathedral imparts its own monumental experience—knee-weakening grandeur, a mighty resonance that touches a chord of awe, and humility in the unbeliever. Even cynics will find satisfaction in these edifices' social history—the anonymity of the architects, the solidarity of the artisans, and the astonishing bravery of experiments in suspended stone.

Chartres, Ile-de-France. Get enlightened with France's most beautiful stained-glass windows and famous labyrinth.

Mont-St-Michel, Normandy. From its silhouette against the horizon to the abbey and gardens at the peak of the rock, you'll never forget this awe-inspiring sight.

Notre-Dame, Paris. Make a face back at the gargoyles high atop Quasimodo's home.

Reims, Champagne. Tally up the 34 VIPs crowned at this magnificent edifice, the age-old setting for the coronations of French kings.

L'Esprit Sportif

Though the physically inclined would consider walking across Scotland or bicycling across Holland, they often misconstrue France as a sedentary country where one plods from museum to château to restaurant. But it's possible to take a more active approach: imagine pedaling past barges on the Saône River or along slender poplars on a *route départementale* (provincial road); hiking over Alpine meadows near Megéve; or sailing the historic ports of Honfleur or Antibes. Experiencing this side of France will take you off the beaten path and into the countryside. As you bike along French country roads or along the extensive network of *Grandes Randonnées* (Lengthy Trails) crisscrossing the country, you will have time to tune into the landscape—to study crumbling garden walls, smell the honeysuckle, and chat with a farmer in his *potager* (vegetable garden).

Sentier des Cascades, Haute-Pyrénées. Near Cauterets is the GR10 walk, which features stunning views of the famous waterfalls and abundant *marmottes* (Pyrenean groundhogs).

Tracking the Camargue Reserve, Provence. Take an unforgettable *promenade équestre* (horseback tour) of this amazing nature park, home to bulls and birds— 50,000 flamingos, that is.

The VBT Loire Biking Tour. Stunning châteaux-hotels, Pissarro-worthy riverside trails, and 20 new best friends make this a *fantastique* way to go "around the whirl."

Clos Encounters

Bordeaux or Burgundy, Sauternes or Sancerre, Romanée-Conti or Côte du Rhône—wherever you turn in France, you'll find famous Gallic wine regions and vineyards, born of the country's curvaceous landscape. Speckled unevenly with hills, canals, forests, vineyards, châteaux, and the occasional cow clinging to 30-degree inclines, the great wine regions of France attract hordes of travelers more interested in shoving their noses deep into wine glasses than staring high into the stratosphere of French cathedral naves. Fact is, you can buy the bottles of the fabled regions—the Côte d'Or, the Rhône Valley, or that oenophile's nirvana, Bordeaux—anywhere, so why not taste the lesser-known local crus from, say, the lovely vineyards in the Loire Valley. Explore the various *clos* (enclosures) and *côtes* (hillsides) that grow golden by October, study the *vendangeur* (grape pickers), then drive along the wine routes looking for those "Dégustation" signs, promising free sips from the local vintner. Pretty soon you'll be an expert on judging any wine's aroma, body, and backwash.

The Alsace Route de Vin. Between Mulhouse and Strasbourg, many picture-book villages entice with top vintners.

Clos de Vougeot, Burgundy. A historic wine-making barn, 13th-century grape presses, and its verdant vineyard make this a must-do.

Mouton-Rothschild, Route de Médoc. Baron Philippe perfected one of the great five premiers crus here—and there's an excellent visitor center.

HISTORY YOU CAN SEE

France has long been the standard-bearer of Western civilization—without her, neither English liberalism nor the American Constitution would exist today. It has given us Notre-Dame, Loire châteaux, Versailles, Stendhal, Chardin, Monet, Renoir, and the most beautiful city in the world, Paris. So it is no surprise that France unfolds like a gigantic historical pop-up book. To help you understand the country's masterful mélange of old and new, here's a quick overview of La Belle France's stirring historical pageant.

Ancient France

France's own "Stonehenge"—the megalithic stone complexes at Carnac in Brittany (circa 3500 BC)—were created by the Celts, who inhabited most of northwest Europe during the last millennia BC. In the 1st century BC, Julius Caesar conquered Gaul, and the classical civilizations of the Mediterranean soon made artistic inroads. The Greek trading colonies at Marseille eventually gave way to the Roman Empire, with the result that ancient Roman aesthetics left a lasting impression: it is no accident that the most famous modern example of a Roman triumphal arch—the **Arc de Triomphe**—should have been built in Paris.

What to See: France possesses examples of ancient Roman architecture that even Italy cannot match: Provence, whose name comes from the Latin, had been one of the most popular places to holiday for the ancient Romans. The result is that you can find the best-preserved **Roman arena in Nîmes** (along with the **Maison Carrée**), the best preserved **Roman theater at Orange**, and the best preserved Roman bridge aqueduct, the **Pont du Gard**.

The Middle Ages: From Romanesque to Gothic

By the 7th century AD, Christianity was well established throughout France. Its interaction with an inherited classical tradition produced the first great indigenous French culture, the Frankish or Merovingian, created by the Franks (who gave their name to the new nation), Germanic tribes who expelled the Romans from French soil. Various French provinces began to unite as part of Charlemagne's new Holy Roman Empire and, as a central core of European Catholicism, France now gave rise to great monastic centers—**Tours, Auxerre, Reims, and Chartres**—that were also cultural powerhouses. After the Crusades, more settled conditions led to the flowering of the Romanesque style developed by

58–51 BC	Caesar's conquest of Gaul	1580–87	Montaigne's *Essays*
800 AD	Charlemagne made Holy Roman Emperor	1678	Louis XIV adds the Hall of Mirrors to Versailles
1066	William of Normandy invades England with victory at the Battle of Hastings	18th century	Zenith of French enlightenment and influence, thanks to Molière, Racine, Voltaire, Diderot, and Rousseau
12th–13th centuries	Cathedrals of Notre Dame and Chartres	1789–92	The French Revolution
1431	Joan of Arc burned; from lowest point, French nation revived	1793	Queen Marie-Antoinette is guillotined on Paris's Place de la Concorde
1572	St. Bartholomew Massacre of Protestants		

reformist monastic orders like the Benedictines at Cluny. This then gave way to the Gothic, which led to the construction of many cathedrals—perhaps the greatest architectural achievement created in France—during the biggest building spree of the Middle Ages. Under the Capetian kings, French government became more centralized. The most notable king was Louis IX (1226–70), known as Saint Louis, who left important monuments in the Gothic style, which lasted some 400 years and gained currency throughout Europe.

What to See: The Romanesque style sprang out of the forms of classical art left by the Romans; its top artistic landmarks adorn Burgundy: the giant transept of **Cluny,** the sculptures of Gislebertus at **Autun's Cathèdrale St-Lazare,** and the amazing tympanum of the **Basilique Ste-Madeleine at Vézelay.** Another top Romanesque artwork is in Normandy: the **Bayeux Tapestry** on view in Bayeux. The desire to span greater area with stone and to admit more light led to the development of the new Gothic style. This became famed for its use of the pointed arch and the rib vault, resulting in an essentially skeletal structure containing large areas of glass.

First fully developed at **Notre-Dame,** Paris (from 1163), **Chartres** (from 1200), **Reims** (from 1211), and **Amiens** (from 1220), the Gothic cathedral contains distinctive Gothic forms: delicate filigree-like rose windows of stained glass, tall lancet windows, elaborately sculpted portails, and flying buttresses. King Louis IV commissioned **Paris's Sainte-Chapelle** chapel in the 1240s and it remains the most beautiful artistic creation of the Middle Ages.

The Renaissance

France nationalism came to the fore once the tensions and wars fomented by the Houses of Anjou and Capet climaxed in the Hundred Years' War (1328–1453). During this time, Joan of Arc helped drive English rulers from France with the Valois line of kings taking the throne. From the late 15th century into the 16th, the golden light of the Italian Renaissance then dawned over France. This was due, in large measure, to King François I (accession 1515), who returned from wars in Italy with many Italian artists and craftsmen, among them Leonardo da Vinci (who lived in Amboise from 1507). With decades of peace, fortresses soon became châteaux and the picture palaces of the Loire Valley came into

1799–1804	Napoléon rules as First Consul of the Consulate	1870	Franco-Prussian War; France defeated, but Flaubert's and Baudelaire's writings soar
1805–12	Napoléon conquers large parts of Europe but is defeated in Russia	1871	Alsace-Lorraine ceded to Germany
1815	Napoléon loses battle at Waterloo to England's Duke of Wellington	1940	France surrenders to Germany during World War II: Paris falls
1848–70	The Second Empire, ruled by Emperor Napoléon III, with colonial expansion into Indochina, Syria, and Mexico	1958	General de Gaulle elected president
1863	Impressionists show at the Salon des Refusés in Paris	1969	Student riots in Paris; government is subsequently stabilized through presidents including Georges Pompidou, François Mitterand, and Nicolas Sarkozy

being. The grandest of these, Fontainebleau and Chambord, reflected the growing centralization of the French court and were greatly influenced by the new Italian styles.

What to See: An earnest desire to rival and outdo Italy in cultural pursuits dominated French culture during the 15th and 16th centuries. For the decoration of the new **Palace of Fontainebleau** (from 1528) artists like **Cellini, Primaticcio,** and **Rosso** used rich colors, elongated forms, and a concentration upon allegory and eroticism to help cement the Mannerist style. Gothic and vernacular forms of architecture were now rejected in favor of classical models, as could be seen in the châteaux in the Loire Valley such as **Blois** (from 1498), **Chambord** (from 1519, where design elements were created by **Leonardo**), and **Chenonceau,** which was commissioned by the king's mother, Catherine de' Medici. The rebuilding of Paris's **Louvre,** begun in 1546, marked the final assimilation of Italian classical architecture into France.

Royal Absolutism and the Baroque Style

Rising out of the conflicts between Catholic and Protestant (thousands of Huguenots were murdered in the St. Bartholomew's Day massacre of 1572), King Henry IV became the first Bourbon king and fomented religious tolerance with the Edict of Nantes (1598). By the 17th century architecture still had an Italianate flavor, as seen in the Roman Baroque forms adorning Parisian churches. The new Baroque architectural taste for large-scale town planning gave rise to the many squares that formed focal points within cities. King Louis XIV, the Sun King, came to the throne in 1643, but he chose to rule from a new power base he built outside

Paris: Versailles soon became a symbol of the absolutist court of the Sun King and the new insatiable national taste for glory. But with Louis XIV, XV, and XVI going for broke, a reaction against extravagance and for logic and empirical reason took over. Before long, writers like Jean-Jacques Rousseau argued for social and political reform—the need for revolution.

What to See: To create a more carefully ordered aristocratic bureaucracy, courtiers were commanded to leave their family châteaux and take up residence in the massive new **Versailles** palace. A golden age for art began. The palaces of the **Louvre** (1545–1878) and **Versailles** (1661–1756) bear witness to this in their sheer scale. "After me, the deluge," Louis XIV said, and early-18th-century France was on the verge of bankruptcy. In turn, the court turned away from the over-the-top splendor of Versailles and Paris's **Luxembourg Palace** to retreat to smaller, more domestic houses in Paris, seen in such hôtel particuliers as the **Musée Nissim de Camondo** and the charming **Hameau** farm created for Marie-Antoinette in Versailles's park. Bombastic Baroque gave way to the Rococo style, as the charming, feminine paintings of **Watteau, Boucher,** and **Fragonard** provided cultural diversions for an aristocracy withdrawn from the stage of power politics. Find their masterpieces at the Louvre, **Carnavalet,** and other museums.

Revolution and Romanticism

The end of Bourbon rule came with the execution of **Louis XVI and Marie-Antoinette.** The French Revolution ushered in the First Republic (1792–1804). After a backlash to the Terror (1793–94), in which hundreds were guillotined, **Napoléon** rose to power from the ashes of

the Revolutionary **Directoire**. With him a new intellectual force and aesthetic mode came to the fore—**Romanticism**. This new style focused on inner emotions and the self, leading to the withdrawal of the artists from politics, growing industrialization, and urbanization into a more subjective world. Napoléon's First Empire (1804–14) conquered most of Europe, but after the disastrous Russian invasion the Bourbon dynasty was restored with the rule of Charles X and Louis-Philippe. The latter, known as the Citizen King, abdicated in 1848 and made way for the Second Republic and the return of Napoleonic forces with Napoléon III's Second Empire (1852–70).

What to See: As often happens, art is one step ahead of history. The design of Paris's **Panthéon** by Soufflot, Gabriel's refined **Petit Trianon** at Versailles (1762), and the paintings of **Greuze** (1725–1805) and **David** (1745–1825), on view at the Louvre, display a conceit for moral order in great contrast to the flippancies of Fragonard. A renewed taste for classicism was seen in the Empire style promulgated by Napoléon; see the emperor's Paris come alive at the Left Bank's charming **Cour du Commerce St-André** and his shrine, **Les Invalides.** But the rigidly formal Neoclassical style soon gave way to Romanticism, whose touchstones are immediacy of technique, emotionalism, and the ability to convey the uncertainties of the human condition. Go to Paris's **Musée Delacroix** to get an up-close look at this expressive, emotive master of Romanticism.

The Modern Age Begins

Napoléon III's Second Empire lead to the vast aggrandizement of France on the world stage, with colonies set up across the globe, a booming economy, and the capital city of Paris remade into Europe's showplace thanks to **Baron Haussman.** After the Prussians invaded, France was defeated and culture was shattered and reformed. Romanticism became **Realism,** often carrying strong social overtones, as seen in the works of **Courbet.** The closer reexamination of reality by the **Barbizon School** of landscape painters lead to **Impressionism,** whose masters approached their subjects with a fresh eye, using clear, bright colors to create atmospheric effects and naturalistic observation. By 1870 French rule was reinstated with the **Third Republic,** which lasted until 1940.

What to See: Thanks to Haussman, Paris became the City of Light, with new large boulevards opening up the dark urban city, an outlook culminating in the **Eiffel Tower,** built for the Paris Exposition of 1889. Taking modern life as their subject matter, great Impressionist masters like **Monet** (1840–1926), **Renoir** (1841–1919), and **Degas** (1834–1917) proceeded to break down visual perceptions in terms of light and color, culminating in the late series of *Water Lilies* paintings (from 1916) done at **Monet's Giverny estate.** Along with masterpieces by **Degas, Gauguin, Van Gogh,** and **Cézanne,** the most famous Impressionist and Postimpressionist paintings can be seen at Paris's famed **Musée d'Orsay.** These artists began the myth of the Parisian bohemian artist, the disaffected idealist kicking at the shins of tradition, and they forged the path then boldly trod by the greatest artist of the 20th century, **Picasso,** whose works can be seen at Paris's **Musée Picasso** and **Centre Beaubourg.**

GREAT ITINERARIES

THE GOOD LIFE

Beginning in château country, head south and west, through Cognac country into wine country around Bordeaux. Then lose yourself in the Dordogne, a landscape of rolling hills peppered with medieval villages, fortresses, and prehistoric caves.

Loire Valley Châteaux

3 or 4 days. Base yourself at the crossroads of Blois, starting with its multi-era château. Then head for the huge château in Chambord. Amboise's château echoes with history, and the neighboring manor, Clos Lucé, was Leonardo da Vinci's final home—or instead of this "town" château, head west to the tiny village of Rigny-Ussé for the Sleeping Beauty castle of Ussé. Heading southeast, finish up at Chenonceau—the most magical one of all—then return to the transportation hub city of Tours. ⇨ *The Loire Valley in Chapter 4*

Bordeaux Wine Country

2 days. Pay homage to the great names of Médoc, north of the city of Bordeaux, though the hallowed villages of Margaux, St-Julien, Pauillac, and St-Estèphe aren't much to look at. East of Bordeaux, via the prettier Pomerol vineyards, the village of St-Émilion is everything you'd want a wine town to be, with ramparts and medieval streets. ⇨ *Bordeaux in Chapter 16*

Dordogne and Périgord

2 or 3 days. Follow the famous Dordogne River east to the half-timber market town of Bergerac. Wind through the green, wooded countryside into the region where humans' earliest ancestors left their mark, in the caves in Les Eyzies-de-Tayac and the famous Grotte de Lascaux. Be sure to sample the region's culinary specialties: truffles, foie gras, and preserved duck. Then travel south to the stunning and sky-high village of Rocamadour. ⇨ *The Dordogne in Chapter 17*

By Public Transportation

It's easy to get to Blois and Chenonceaux by rail, but you'll need to take a bus to visit other Loire châteaux. Forays farther into Bordeaux country and the Dordogne are difficult by train, involving complex and frequent changes (Limoges is a big railway hub). Further exploration requires a rental car or sometimes-unreliable bus routes.

FRANCE FROM NORTH TO SOUTH

Zoom from Paris to the heart of historic Burgundy, its rolling green hills traced with hedgerows and etched with vineyards. From here, plunge into the arid beauty of Provence and toward the spectacular coastline of the Côte d'Azur.

Burgundy Wine Country

2 to 3 days. Base yourself in the market town of Beaune and visit its famous hospices and surrounding vineyards. Make a day trip to the ancient hill town of Vézelay, with its incomparable basilica, stopping in Autun to explore Roman ruins and its celebrated Romanesque cathedral. For more vineyards, follow the Côte d'Or from Beaune to Dijon. Or make a beeline to Dijon, with its charming Vieille Ville and fine museums. From here it's a two-hour drive to Lyon, where you can feast on this city's famous earthy cuisine. Another three hours' push takes you deep into the heart of Provence. ⇨ *Burgundy in Chapter 9 and Lyon in Chapter 10*

Arles and Provence

2 to 3 days. Arles is the atmospheric, sun-drenched southern town that inspired Van Gogh and Gauguin. Make a day trip into

grand old Avignon, home to the 14th-century rebel popes, to view their imposing palace. And make a pilgrimage to the Pont du Gard, the famous triple-tiered Roman aqueduct west of Avignon. From here two hours' drive will bring you to the glittering Côte d'Azur. ⇨ *Arles, Avignon, and Pont du Gard in Chapter 11*

Antibes and the French Riviera

2 to 3 days. This historic and atmospheric port town is well positioned for day trips. First, head west to glamorous Cannes. The next day head east into Nice, with its exotic Vieille Ville and its bounty of modern art. There are ports to explore in Villefranche and St-Jean-Cap-Ferrat, east of Nice. Allow time for a walk out onto the tropical paradise peninsula of Cap d'Antibes, or for an hour or two lolling on the coast's famous pebble beaches. ⇨ *Cannes, Nice, Villefranche-sur-Mer, St-Jean-Cap-Ferrat, and Cap d'Antibes in Chapter 12*

By Public Transportation

The high-speed TGV travels from Paris through Burgundy and Lyon, then zips through the south to Marseille. Train connections to Beaune from the TGV are easy; getting to Autun from Beaune takes up to two hours, with a change at Chagny. Vézelay can be reached by bus excursion from Dijon or Beaune. Rail connections are easy between Arles and Avignon; you'll need a bus to get to the Pont du Gard from Avignon. Antibes, Cannes, and Nice are easily reached by the scenic rail line, as are most of the resorts and ports along the coast. To squeeze the most daytime out of your trip, take a night train or a plane from Nice back to Paris.

FRANCE AVEC FAMILLE

Make your way through Normandy and Brittany, with enough wonders and evocative topics to inspire any child to put down the iPhone games and gawk.

Paris

2 days. Paris's major museums, like the Louvre, can be as engaging as they are educational—as long as you keep your visits short. Start out your Paris stay by giving your kids an idea of how the city was planned by climbing to the top of the Arc de Triomphe. From here work your way down the Champs-Élysées toward place de la Concorde. Stop for a puppet show at the Marionettes des Champs-Élysées,

at avenues Matignon and Gabriel, half-way down the Champs. Continue walking down the Champs, to the Jardin des Tuileries, where kids can sail boats on a small pond. Then taxi or hike over to the Louvre for an afternoon visit. Your reward? Stop in at Angélina (on rue de Rivoli, across the street), a tearoom famous for its thick hot chocolate. If you want to see the puppet show, do this on a Wednesday, Saturday, or Sunday. The next morning, head to the Eiffel Tower for a bird's-eye view of the city. After you descend, ride on one of the Bateaux Mouches at place de l'Alma, nearby. Then take the métro to the hunchback's hangout, Notre-Dame Cathedral. Finish up your Paris visit by walking several blocks over, through the center of the Ile de la Cité, to Paris's most storybook sight—the Sainte-Chapelle, a fairy-tale, stained-glass chapel that looks like a stage set for Walt Disney's *Sleeping Beauty*. ⇨ *Paris in Chapter 2*

Versailles

1 day. Here's an opportunity for a history lesson: with its amazing Baroque extravagance, no other monument so succinctly illustrates what inspired the rage of the French Revolution. Louis XIV's eye-popping château of Versailles pleases the secret monarch in most of us. ⇨ *Western Ile-de-France in Chapter 3*

Honfleur

1 day. From this picture-book seaport lined with skinny half-timber row houses and salt-dampened cobblestones, the first French explorers set sail for Canada in the 15th century. ⇨ *Honfleur to Mont-St-Michel in Chapter 5*

Bayeux

2 days. William the Conqueror's extraordinary invasion of England in 1066 was launched from the shores of Normandy.

The famous Bayeux tapestry, showcased in a state-of-the-art museum, spins the tale of the Battle of Hastings. From this home base you can introduce the family to the modern saga of 1944's Allied landings with a visit to the Museum of the Battle of Normandy, then make a pilgrimage to Omaha Beach. ⇨ *Honfleur to Mont-St-Michel in Chapter 5*

Mont-St-Michel

1 day. Rising majestically in a shroud of sea mist over vacillating tidal flats, this mystical peninsula is Gothic in every sense of the word. Though its tiny, steep streets are crammed with visitors and tourist traps, no other sight gives you a stronger sense of the worldly power of medieval monasticism than Mont-St-Michel. ⇨ *Honfleur to Mont-St-Michel in Chapter 5*

St-Malo

1 day. Even in winter you'll want to brave the Channel winds to beachcomb the shores of this onetime pirate base. (Yes, kids, *pirates!*) In summer, of course, it's mobbed with sun seekers who stroll the old streets, restored to quaintness after World War II. ⇨ *Northeast Brittany and the Channel Coast in Chapter 6*

Chartres

1 day. Making a beeline on the autoroute back to Paris, stop in Chartres to view the loveliest of all of France's cathedrals. ⇨ *Western Ile-de-France in Chapter 3*

By Public Transportation

Coordinating a sightseeing tour like this with a limited local train schedule isn't easy, and connections to Mont-St-Michel are especially complicated. Versailles, Chartres, and St-Malo are easy to reach, and Bayeux and Honfleur are doable, if inconvenient. But you'll spend a lot of vacation time waiting along train tracks.

FRANCE LODGING PRIMER

If your France fantasy involves staying in a historic hotel with the smell of fresh-baked croissants gently rousing you in the morning, here's some good news: you need not be Ritz-rich to realize it. Throughout the country, you'll find stylish lodging options—from charming hotels and intimate B&Bs to regal apartments and grand country houses—in all price ranges.

Hotels

Rates are always by room, not per person. Sometimes a hotel in a certain price category will have a few less-expensive rooms; it's worth asking about. In the off-season—usually November to Easter (except for southern France)—tariffs may be lower. Always inquire about promotional specials and weekend deals. Rates must be posted in all rooms, with extra charges clearly indicated.

Hotel rooms have telephones, television, and private bath unless otherwise noted. When making your reservation, state your preference for shower (*douche*) or tub (*baignoire*)—the latter always costs more. Also when booking, ask for a *grand lit* if you want a double bed.

Apartment and House Rentals

If you want more spacious accommodations with cooking facilities, consider a furnished rental. These can save you money, especially if you're traveling with a group.

Renting a *gîte rural*—furnished house in the country—for a week or month can also save you money. Gîtes are nearly always maintained by on-site owners, who greet you on your arrival and provide information on groceries, doctors, and nearby attractions.

The national rental network, the Fédération Nationale des Gîtes de France, rents all types of accommodations rated by ears of corn (from one to four) based on comfort and quality criteria.

You can find listings for fabulous renovated farmhouses with swimming pools or simple cottages in the heart of wine country. Besides country houses, Gîtes de France has listings for B&Bs, lodges, hostels, and campsites.

Bed-and-Breakfasts

Chambres d'hôtes (bed-and-breakfasts) range from simple lodgings with breakfast in a humble home to beautiful rooms in a château with gourmet food. Chambres d'hôtes are most common in rural France, though they are becoming more popular in Paris and other major cities.

Check with local tourist offices or private reservation agencies like Hôtes Qualité Paris. Often *table d'hôte* dinners (meals cooked by and eaten with the owners) can be arranged for a nominal fee.

Note that your hosts at B&Bs, unlike those at hotels, are more likely to speak only French.

Hostels

Hostels offer bare-bones lodging at low, low prices—often in shared dorm rooms with shared baths—to people of all ages, though the primary market is students. Most hostels serve breakfast; dinner and/or shared cooking facilities may also be available.

In some hostels you aren't allowed to be in your room during the day, and there may be a curfew at night. Nevertheless, hostels provide a sense of community, with public rooms where travelers often gather to share stories.

For resources and booking information, see the Travel Smart chapter.

WHEN TO GO

Keep in mind that French schoolchildren have *five* holidays a year: one week at the end of October, two weeks at Christmas, two weeks in February, two weeks in April, and the two full months of July and August. During these times travel in France is truly at its peak season, which means that prices are higher, highways are busier, the queues for museums are long, and transportation is at its most expensive. Your best bet for quality and calm is to travel off-season. June and September are the best months to be in France, as both are free of the midsummer crowds. Try to avoid the second half of July and all of August, when almost everyone in France goes on vacation. July and August in southern France can be stifling. Paris can be stuffy and uncomfortable in August. Many restaurants, theaters, and small shops close, but enough stay open these days to make a low-key, unhurried visit a pleasure. Anytime between March and November will offer you a good chance to soak up the sun on the Côte d'Azur. If Paris and the Loire are among your priorities, remember that the weather is unappealing before Easter. If you're dreaming of Paris in the springtime, May is your best bet, not rainy April. But the capital remains a joy during midwinter, with plenty of things to see and do.

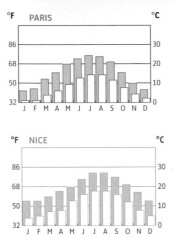

PARIS

WELCOME TO PARIS

TOP REASONS TO GO

★ **Masterpiece Theater:** There will always be something new to see at the Louvre—after all, the Mona Lisa is just one of 800,000 treasures.

★ **Feasting at Le Grand Véfour:** Back when Napoléon dined here, this was the most beautiful restaurant in Paris. Guess what? It still is.

★ **Quasimodo's Notre-Dame:** Get to know the stone gargoyles high atop this playground of Victor Hugo's hunchback, then savor the splendor inside this great Gothic cathedral.

★ **Café Society:** Whether you prefer a posh perch at Les Deux Magots or just the corner café *du coin*, be sure to Hemingway an afternoon away over two café filtrés.

★ **Spend Time on the Seine:** Take a leisurely stroll along the Rive Droite and the Rive Gauche, making sure to carve out time to visit the oldest part of Paris—Ile de la Cité and Ile St-Louis.

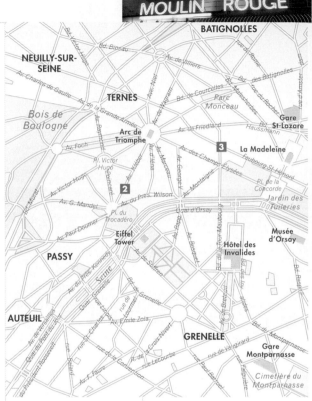

1 **From Notre-Dame to the Place de la Concorde.** Spend time wandering around the lovely Ile-de-la-Cité, home of Notre-Dame, and relaxing in the Tuileries before and after tackling the Louvre.

2 **From the Tour Eiffel to the Arc de Triomphe.** You won't be able to cover this whole area in one day, but plan lots of time for what could be called "monumental" Paris. In addition to the Eiffel Tower, the Champs-Élysées, and the Arc de Triomphe, there are several excellent museums worth planning your days around.

3 **The Faubourg St-Honoré to Les Halles.** Chic spots in cities come and go, but the Faubourg's always had it and probably always will, while trend-spotters are betting on the up-and-coming Les Halles neighborhood.

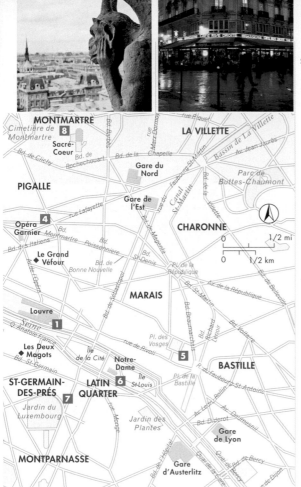

GETTING ORIENTED

Paris is divided into 20 *arrondissements* (or neighborhoods) spiraling out from the center of the city. The numbers reveal the neighborhood's location, and its age: the 1st arrondissement at the city's heart being the oldest. The arrondissements in central Paris—the 1st to 8th—are the most visited. If you want to figure out what arrondissement something is in, check the zip code. The first three digits are always 750 for Paris, and the last two identify the arrondissement.

It's worth picking up a copy of *Paris Pratique,* the essential map guide, available at bookstores, newsstands, and souvenir shops.

4 The Grands Boulevards. Use the Opéra Garnier as your orientation landmark and set out to do some power shopping. There are some intriguing small museums in the neighborhood, too, if you want a dose of culture.

5 The Marais, the Bastille, and the Canal St-Martin. The Marais is Paris's most popular lazy-Sunday-afternoon neighborhood, where you can while away the day at the place des Vosges, and shop to your heart's content. Or hang with the hipsters in the Bastille or along the Canal St-Martin.

6 Ile St-Louis and the Quartier Latin. Ile St-Louis is tiny, and one of the most romantic spots in Paris. Leave yourself lots of time to wander the Latin Quarter, a 'hood known for its vibrant student life.

7 From Orsay to St-Germain-des-Pres. Fabulous cafés and two of the city's most fabulous museums are found here, on the Left Bank, but make sure you also leave yourself time to wander the Jardins du Luxembourg.

8 Montmartre. Like a small village inside a big city, charming Montmartre feels distinctly separate from the rest of Paris.

Updated by
Jennifer Ditsler-
Ladonne,
Linda Her-
vieux, Bryan
J. Pirolli, and
Victoria Tang

If there's a problem with a trip to Paris, it's the embarrassment of riches that faces you. No matter which aspect of Paris you choose—touristy, historic, fashion-conscious, pretentious-bourgeois, thrifty, or the legendary bohemian arty Paris of undying attraction—one thing is certain: you will carve out your own Paris, one that is vivid, exciting, ultimately unforgettable.

Wherever you head, your itinerary will prove to be a voyage of discovery. But choosing the Paris of your dreams is a bit like choosing a perfume or cologne. Do you want something young and dashing, or elegant and worldly? How about sporty, or perhaps strictly glamorous? No matter: they are all here—perfumes, famous museums, legendary churches, or romantic cafés. Whether you spend three days or three months in this city, it will always have something new to offer you, which may explain why the most assiduous explorers of Paris are the Parisians themselves.

Veterans know that Paris is a city of vast, noble perspectives and intimate, ramshackle streets, of formal *espaces vertes* (green open spaces) and quiet squares. This combination of the pompous and the private is one of the secrets of its perennial pull. Another is its size: Paris is relatively small as capitals go, with distances between many of its major sights and museums invariably walkable.

For the first-timer there will always be several must-dos at the top of the list, but getting to know Paris will never be quite as simple as a quick look at Notre-Dame, the Louvre, and the Eiffel Tower. You'll discover that around every corner, down every *ruelle* (little street) lies a resonance-in-waiting. You can stand on the rue du Faubourg St-Honoré at the very spot where Edmond Rostand set Ragueneau's pastry shop in *Cyrano de Bergerac*. You can read the letters of Madame de Sévigné in her actual *hôtel particulier*, or private mansion, now the Musée Carnavalet. You can hear the words of Racine resound in the ringing, hair-raising diction of the Comédie Française. You can breathe in the fumes of hubris before the extravagant onyx tomb Napoléon designed for himself. You can gaze through the gates at the school where Voltaire honed his wit, and you can add your own pink-lipstick kiss to Oscar Wilde's bedecked grave at Père-Lachaise Cemetery.

If this is your first trip, you may want to take a guided tour of the city— a good introduction that will help you get your bearings and provide you with a general impression before you return to explore the sights that particularly interest you. To help track those down, this chapter's exploration of Paris is divided into eight neighborhood walks. Each *quartier*, or neighborhood, has its own personality, which is best discovered by foot power. Ultimately, your route will be marked by your preferences, your curiosity, and your state of fatigue. You can wander for hours without getting bored—though not, perhaps, without getting lost. By the time you have seen only a few neighborhoods, drinking in the rich variety they have to offer, you should not only be culturally replete but downright exhausted—and hungry, too. Again, take your cue from Parisians and think out your next move in a sidewalk café. So you've heard stories of a friend who paid $8 for a coffee at a café. So what? What you're paying for is time, and the opportunity to watch the intricate drama of Parisian street life unfold. Hemingway knew the rules; after all, he would have remained just another unknown sportswriter if the waiters in the cafés had hovered around him impatiently.

PLANNING

WHEN TO GO

The City of Light is magical all year round, but it's particularly gorgeous in June, when the long days (the sun doesn't set until 10 pm) stretch sightseeing hours and make it ideal to linger in the cafés practicing the city's favorite pastime—people-watching. Winter can be dark and chilly, but it's also the best time to find cheap airfares and hotel deals. April in Paris, despite what the song says, is often rainy. Summer is the most popular (and expensive) season, and at the height of it, in July, Paris can feel like a city under siege, bursting at the seams as crowds descend en masse.

Keep in mind that, like some other European cities, Paris somewhat shuts down in August—some restaurants are closed for the entire month, for example—though there are still plenty of fun things to do, namely, free open-air movies and concerts, and the popular Paris plage, the "beach" on the right bank of the Seine. September is gorgeous, with temperate weather, saner airfares, and cultural events timed for the *rentrée* (or return), signifying the end of summer vacation.

THE BIG PICTURE

As world capitals go, Paris is surprisingly compact. The city is divided in two by the River Seine, with two islands (Ile de la Cité and Ile St-Louis) in the middle. Each bank of the Seine has its own personality; the Rive Droite (Right Bank), with its spacious boulevards and formal buildings, generally has a more genteel, dignified feel than the carefree and chic Rive Gauche (Left Bank), to the south. The east–west axis from Châtelet to the Arc de Triomphe, via the rue de Rivoli and the Champs-Élysées, is the Right Bank's principal thoroughfare for sightseeing and shopping.

RULES OF THE RUE: ETIQUETTE

Simply put, the French like to look at people, so get used to being stared at. Flirting is as natural here (at all ages) as breathing. The French don't smile at strangers, and doing so can be taken as an invitation for something more. Are the French rude? In a word: *Non.* In France, *politesse* is highly prized, as well as good manners. For example, failing to say *bonjour* (hello) when entering a shop—and *au revoir* (good-bye) on the way out—is considered rude.

In fact, Parisians are sticklers for politesse and exchanging formal greetings is the rule. Informal American-style manners are considered impolite. Beginning an exchange with a simple "Do you speak English?" will get you on the right foot. Learning a few key French words will take you far. Offer a hearty *bonjour* (bohn-zhoor) when walking into a shop or café and an *au revoir* (o ruh-vwahr) when leaving, even if nobody seems to be listening (a chorus may reply). When speaking to a woman over age 16, use *madame* (ma-dam), literally "my lady." For a young woman or girl, use *mademoiselle* (mad-mwa-zel). A man of any age goes by *monsieur* (murh-syur). Always say please, *s'il vous plaît* (seel-voo-play), and thank you, *merci* (mehr-see).

PLANNING YOUR TIME

Paris is one of the world's most visited cities—with crowds to prove it—so it pays to be prepared. Buy tickets online when you can: most cultural centers and museums offer advance-ticket sales, and the small service fee you'll pay is worth the time saved waiting in line. Investigate alternative entrances at popular sites (there are three at the Louvre, for example), and check when rates are reduced, often during once-a-week late openings. Also, national museums are free the first Sunday of each month. There are many within Paris, including the Louvre, Musée d'Orsay, and Centre Pompidou.

A Paris Museum Pass can save you money if you're planning serious sightseeing, but it might be even more valuable because it allows you to bypass the lines. It's sold at the destinations it covers and at airports, major métro stations, and the tourism office in the Carrousel du Louvre (two-, four-, or six-day passes are €32, €48, and €64, respectively; for more info visit ⊕ *www.parismuseumpass.com*).

Stick to the omnipresent ATMs for the best exchange rates; exchanging cash at your hotel or in a store is never going to be to your advantage.

GETTING HERE AND AROUND

Paris is without question best explored on foot, and thanks to Baron Haussmann's mid-19th-century redesign, the City of Light is a compact wonder of wide boulevards, gracious parks, and leafy squares. When you want a lift, though, public transportation is easy and inexpensive. The métro (subway) goes just about everywhere you're going for €1.70 a ride (a *carnet*, or pack, of 10 tickets is €12); tickets also work on buses and trams, and the RER train line within Paris.

Paris is divided into 20 arrondissements (or neighborhoods) spiraling out from the center of the city. The numbers reveal the neighborhood's location and its age, the 1er arrondissement at the city's heart being the oldest. The arrondissements in central Paris—the 1er to 8e—are the most visited.

It's worth picking up a copy of *Paris Pratique*, the essential map guide, available at newsstands and bookstores.

AIR TRAVEL

Major airports in the Ile-de-France area are Charles de Gaulle (☎ *01–48–62–22–80 ⊕ www.adp.fr*), commonly known as Roissy, 25 km (16 miles) northeast of Paris, and Orly (☎ *01–49–75–15–15 ⊕ www.adp.fr*), 16 km (10 miles) south. Shuttle buses link Disneyland to the airports at Roissy, 56 km (35 miles) away, and Orly, 50 km (31 miles) distant; buses take 45 minutes and run every 45 minutes from Roissy, every 60 minutes from Orly (less frequently in low season), and cost €18.

GETTING INTO PARIS FROM CHARLES DE GAULLE AIRPORT

The RER-B, the suburban commuter train, beneath Terminals 2 and 3, has trains to central Paris every 15 minutes; the fare is €9.40, and takes about 45 minutes. Important: remember to hold onto your ticket because you'll need it to exit the tricky turnstiles at the end of your trip.

Coaches operated by Air France (you need not have flown with the airline) (☎ *08–92–35–08–20 recorded information in English ⊕ www. cars-airfrance.com*) run about every 20 minutes between Roissy and western Paris (Porte Maillot and the Arc de Triomphe, or Gare de Lyon and Gare Montparnasse). The fare is €15 or €16.50, and it takes about 60 minutes. The Roissybus, operated by the RATP (☎ *32–46 [€0.34 per min] ⊕ www.ratp.com*), runs directly between Roissy and rue Scribe by the Opéra every 15 minutes and costs €9.40. Tickets for both bus lines can be purchased in the terminals or from the driver.

Taxis are readily available; the fare will be around €40–€70, depending on traffic.

GETTING INTO PARIS FROM ORLY AIRPORT

There are several options to get to Paris from Orly Airport. Take the free OrlyVal shuttle train, departing every seven minutes, to the Antony station; then take the RER-B line into Paris. The fare is €10.25 and it takes about 25 minutes. Or, take the airport shuttle bus to the RER-C line station; trains leave every 15 minutes. The fare is €2.60 (Shuttle) plus €3.80 (RER), and journey time is about 35 minutes.

Air France buses run every 12 minutes between Orly and Montparnasse station, Les Invalides and L'Etoile/Arc de Triomphe. The fare is €11.50, and the trip can take from 30 to 45 minutes, depending on traffic. RATP also runs the Orlybus between the Denfert-Rochereau métro station and Orly every 15 minutes, and the trip costs €6.60.

BOAT TRAVEL (SEINE TOURS)

Bateaux Mouches. If you want to view Paris in slow motion, hop on one of these famous motorboats, which set off on their hour-long tours of the city waters regularly (every half hour in summer) from place de l'Alma. Their route heads east to the Ile St-Louis and then back west, past the Tour Eiffel, as far as the Allée des Cygnes and its miniature version of the Statue of Liberty. It departs from the Pont de l'Alma (Right Bank) April to September, daily, every 20, 30, or 45 minutes, from 10:15 am to 11 pm; October through March, daily, approximately every hour from 11 am to 9 pm. ⊠ *Pl. de l'Alma, Trocadéro* ☎ *01–42–25–96–10* ⊕ *www.bateaux-mouches.fr* Ⓜ *Alma-Marceau.*

Batobus. For those who wish to enjoy a little cruise along Paris's Seine in peace and quiet, opt for the city-run Batobus, which has no commentary and allows you to get on and off at its various quayside stops. It departs from eight locations: Eiffel Tower, Champs-Élysées, Musée d'Orsay, Louvre, St-Germain-des-Pres, Notre-Dame, Hotel de Ville, and Jardin des Plantes. There is no service early January through early February. ⊠ *Port de la Bourdonnais, Eiffel Tower* ☎ *08–25–05–01–01* ⊕ *www.batobus.com.*

Vedettes du Pont Neuf. Instead of the famed Bateaux Mouches, some travelers prefer to take take a cruise on the Seine in Paris using the smaller Vedettes du Pont Neuf, which depart from square du Vert-Galant on the Ile de la Cité. A top selling point: the Vedettes have a guide giving commentary in French and English, while the Bateaux Mouches have a loud recorded spiel in several languages. ⊠ *Sq. du Vert-Galant on the Ile de la Cité* ☎ *01–46–33–98–38* ⊕ *www.vedettesdupontneuf.com.*

BUS TRAVEL

The Paris bus system (⊠ *54 quai de la Rapée* ☎ *32–46 [€0.34 per min]* ⊕ *www.ratp.com*) is user-friendly and a great way to see the city. With dedicated lanes throughout the city allowing buses and taxis to whiz past traffic jams, taking the bus can be a pleasant way to get around. Buses are marked with the route number and destination in front and with major stopping places along the sides. The brown bus shelters contain timetables and route maps, and electronic boards tell you when the next bus will arrive. Maps are also found on each bus. To get off, press one of the red buttons mounted on the silver poles that run the length of the bus and the *arrêt demandé* (stop requested) light directly above the driver will light up. Use the rear door to exit (some require you to push a silver button to open the door). You can use your métro ticket on buses; if you have individual tickets (as opposed to weekly or monthly tickets), be prepared to punch your ticket in the gray machines on board the bus. The best bet is to buy a carnet of 10 tickets for €12 at any métro station, or you can buy a single ticket on board for €1.80 (though the drivers may gripe about selling you one, so have exact change ready).

CAR TRAVEL

Driving is not recommended within Paris. Parisian drivers are aggressive behind the wheel and it's often very difficult to park. Should you be driving into the city from elsewhere in Ile de France, the major ring road encircling the city is called the *périférique,* with the *périférique intérieur* going counterclockwise around the city, and the *périférique extérieur,* or the outside ring, going clockwise. Five lanes wide, the périférique is a highway from which *portes* (gates) connect Paris to the major highways of France. The highway names function on the same principle as the métro, with the final destination used as the route "name."

2

MÉTRO TRAVEL

The métro is by far the quickest and most efficient way to get around and tickets cost €1.80 each; a carnet (10 tickets for €12 is a better value). Trains run from 5:30 am until 1 am, and 2 am on Friday and Saturday (and be forewarned—this means the famous "last métro" can pass your station anytime after 12:30 am on weekdays). Stations are signaled either by a large yellow M within a circle or by their distinctive curly green Art Nouveau railings and archway entrances bearing the subway's full title (Métropolitain).

It's essential to know the name of the last station on the line you take, as this name appears on all signs. You can make as many connections as you wish on one ticket. Very important: keep your ticket during your journey as you will need it to pass through the turnstiles and exit from the RER system at the end of your trip (also retain your tickets to avoid being fined, as inspectors appear regularly). In general, the métro is safe, although try to avoid the larger, mazelike stations at Châtelet-Les Halles and République if you're alone late at night. Parisian pickpockets are famously discreet, so be aware of your surroundings, *most especially* as you go through the subway turnstiles, as they like to rush you through and, in the confusion, manage to steal things from confused travelers.

TAXI TRAVEL

On weekend nights after 11 pm, and during the morning rush, it's nearly impossible to find a taxi—you're best off asking hotel or restaurant staff to call you one, but, be forewarned: you'll have to pay for them to come get you and, depending on where they are, the fare can quickly add up. If you want to hail a cab on your own, look for the taxis with their signs lighted up—their signs will be glowing green (white for older taxis) as opposed to the taxis that are already taken whose signs will glow red (dull orange for older taxis). There are taxi stands on almost every major street corner but again, expect a wait if it's a busy weekend night. Taxi stands are marked by a square dark blue sign with a white T in the middle.

There's a basic hire charge of €2.20 for all rides, and a minimum voyage charge of €5.60. Expect a €1 supplement per bag after the second piece, a €0.70 supplement if you're picked up at an SNCF (the French rail system) station, and a €2.95 supplement for a fourth person. Taxi G7 (☎ 01–47–39–47–39) is one of the most reliable taxi companies in Paris.

TRAIN TRAVEL

Paris has six international train stations run by the SNCF: (☎ 36–35; 00338–92–35–35–35 [€0.34 per min] outside of France ⊕ www.sncf. fr). Gare du Nord, Gare St-Lazare, Gare de l'Est, Gare de Lyon, Gare Montparnasse, and Gare d'Austerlitz. Trains heading outside of Ile-de-France are usually referred to as *Grandes Lignes* and include the high-speed TGV (or Trains à Grande Vitesse) while regional train service is referred to as *trains de banlieue,* or *Le Transilien.*

RER (☎ 32–46 [€0.34 per min] ⊕ www.ratp.com) trains travel between Paris and the suburbs and are operated by the RATP. When they go through Paris, they act as a sort of baby métro—they connect with the métro network at several points—and can be great time-savers. Access to RER platforms is through the same type of automatic ticket barrier (if you've started your journey on the métro, you can use the same ticket), but you'll need to have the same ticket handy to put through another barrier when you leave the system.

HOTELS

Hotel prices are for a standard double room in high season, including tax (19.6%) and service charge. Unless stated in the review, hotels have elevators, and all guest rooms have TV, telephone, and a private bathroom. Recently, more and more hotels have standard air-conditioning, something that makes a summer stay much more bearable. Tubs don't always have shower curtains or showerheads. (How the French mange to scrub up without flooding the bathroom remains a cultural mystery.) If you book a budget hotel, be sure to confirm whether the bathroom is shared or not.

HOURS

Paris is by no means a 24/7 city, so planning your days beforehand can save you aggravation. Museums are closed one day a week, usually Tuesday, and most stay open late at least one night each week, which is also the least crowded time to visit. Store hours are generally 10 am to 7:30 pm, though smaller shops may not open until 11 am, only to close for several hours during the afternoon. Retailers now have the option of doing business on Sunday, although your best bets are department stores, the shops along the Champs-Élysées, the Carrousel du Louvre, and around the Marais, where most boutiques open at 2 pm.

RESTAURANTS

Restaurants follow French mealtimes, serving lunch from noon to 2:30 pm and dinner from 7:30 or 8 pm. Some cafés serve food all day long. Always reserve a table for dinner, as top restaurants book up months in advance. When it comes to the check, you must ask for it (it's considered rude to bring it unbidden). In cafés you'll get a register receipt with your order. *Servis* (gratuity) is always included in the bill, but it's good form to leave something extra if you're satisfied with the service: a few cents for drinks, €1 for lunch, €3 at dinner; leave 5% of the bill only in higher-end restaurants.

Brasseries often have nonstop service; some are open 24 hours. Assume a restaurant is open every day, unless otherwise indicated. Surprisingly, many prestigious restaurants close on weekends and sometimes Monday. July and August are the most common months for annual closings, although Paris in August is no longer the wasteland it once was.

Restaurant prices are per person for a main course at dinner, including tax (5.5%) and service; note that if a restaurant offers only prix-fixe (set-price) meals, it has been given the price category that reflects the full prix-fixe price.

VISITOR INFORMATION

Paris is without question best explored on foot and, thanks to Baron Haussmann's mid-19th-century redesign, the City of Light is a compact wonder of wide boulevards, gracious parks, and leafy squares. Happily and conveniently, there are a half dozen branches of the Paris tourist office located at key points in the capital:

Office du Tourisme de la Ville de Paris Pyramides ⊠ *25 rue des Pyramides, 1er, Pyramides* ⊕ *www.parisinfo.com* Ⓜ *Pyramides.*

TOUR OPTIONS

For full information about escorted city bus tours, see our box on "Touring Paris by Bus" in this chapter.

WHAT TO WEAR

When it comes to clothing, the standard French look is dressier than the American equivalent. Athletic clothes are reserved for sports. Sneakers are not usually worn by adults but if you pack yours, keep them for daytime only. Neat jeans are acceptable everywhere except at higher-end restaurants; check to see whether there's a dress code.

EXPLORING PARIS

FROM NOTRE-DAME TO THE PLACE DE LA CONCORDE

Updated by Linda Hervieux and Bryan J. Pirolli

In the center of Paris, nestled in the River Seine are the two celebrated islands, the Ile de la Cité and the Ile St-Louis. Of the two, it's the Ile de la Cité that forms the historic ground zero of Paris. It was here that the earliest inhabitants of Paris, the Gaulish tribe of the Parisii, settled in about 250 BC, calling their home Lutetia, meaning "settlement surrounded by water." Today it's famed for the great, brooding cathedral of Notre-Dame, the haunted Conciergerie, and the dazzling Sainte-Chapelle. If Notre-Dame represents Church, another major attraction of this walk—the Louvre—symbolizes State. A succession of French rulers was responsible for filling this immense structure with the world's greatest paintings and works of art. It's the largest museum in the world, as well as one of the easiest to get lost in. Beyond the Louvre lie the graceful Tuileries Gardens, the grand place de la Concorde—the very hub of the city—and the Belle Époque splendor of the Grand Palais and the Pont Alexandre III. All in all, this area comprises some of the most historic and beautiful sights to see in Paris.

TOP ATTRACTIONS

Grand Palais. With its curved-glass roof and gorgeously restored Belle Époque ornamentation, you can't miss the Grand Palais whether you're approaching from the Seine or the Champs-Élysées. It forms an elegant duo with the Petit Palais across avenue Winston Churchill: both stone buildings, adorned with mosaics and sculpted friezes, were built for the 1900 World's Fair, and, like the Eiffel Tower, were not intended to be permanent. The exquisite main exhibition space called le Nef (or nave) plays host to large-scale shows that might focus on anything from jewelry to cars. The art-oriented shows staged here are some of the hottest tickets in town. Previous must-sees included an Edward Hopper retrospective, "Marie Antoinette," and "Picasso and the Masters." To skip the long lines, it pays to book an advance ticket online, which will cost you an extra euro. ⊠ *Av. Winston Churchill, Champs-Élysées* ☎ *01–44–13–17–17* ⊕ *www.grandpalais.fr, www.rmn.fr for reservations* 🎫 *€12 (can vary)* ⊙ *Wed.–Mon. 10–8 or 10–10, depending on the exhibit; closed Tues.* Ⓜ *Champs-Élysées–Clemenceau.*

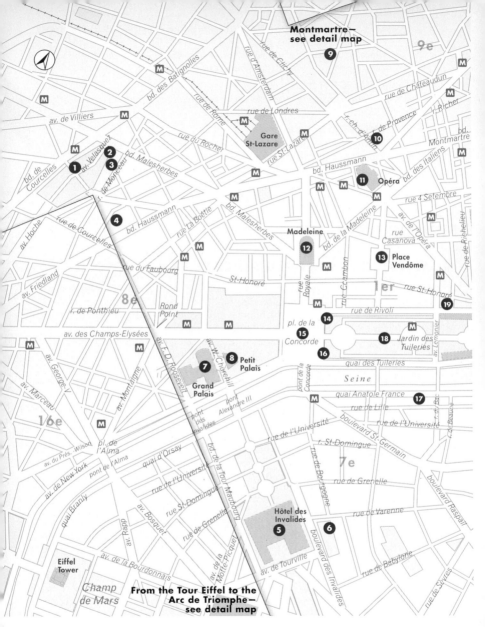

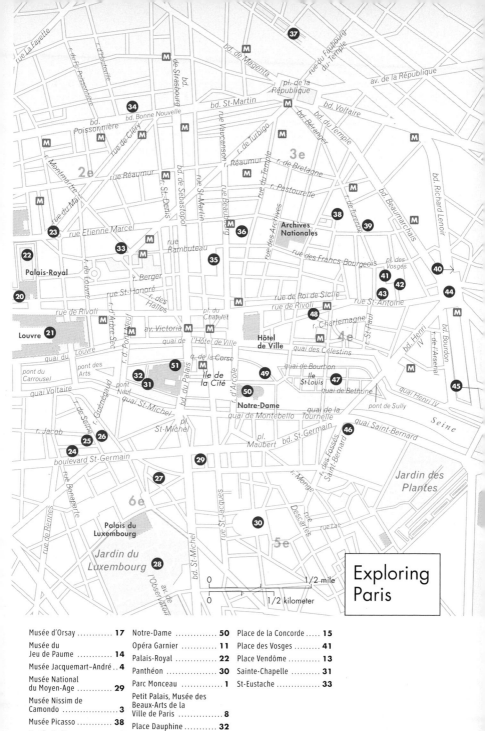

Exploring Paris

FAMILY
Fodor's Choice
★

Jardin des Tuileries. The quintessential French garden, with its verdant lawns, manicured rows of trees, and gravel paths, was designed by André Le Nôtre for Louis XIV. After the king moved his court to Versailles, in 1682, the Tuileries became *the* place for stylish Parisians to stroll. (Ironically, the name derives from the decidedly unstylish factories which once occupied this area: they produced *tuiles,* or roof tiles, fired in kilns called *tuileries.*) Monet and Renoir captured the garden with paint and brush, and it's no wonder the Impressionists loved it— the gray, austere light of Paris's famously overcast days make the green trees appear even greener.

The garden still serves as a setting for one of Paris's loveliest walks. Laid out before you is a vista of must-see monuments, with the Louvre at one end and the place de la Concorde at the other. The Tour Eiffel is on the Seine side, along with the Musée d'Orsay, reachable across a footbridge in the center of the garden. A good place to begin is at the Louvre end, at the Arc du Carrousel, a stone-and-marble arch ordered by Napoléon to showcase the bronze horses he stole from St. Mark's Cathedral in Venice. The horses were eventually returned and replaced here with a statue of a *quadriga,* a four-horse chariot. On the place de la Concorde end, twin buildings bookend the garden. On the Seine side, the former royal greenhouse is now the exceptional Musée de l'Orangerie, home to the largest display of Monet's lovely *Water Lilies* series, as well as a sizable collection of early-20th-century paintings. On the opposite end is the Musée du Jeu de Paume, which has some of the city's best temporary photography exhibits.

■ TIP➔ Garden buffs will enjoy the small bookstore at the place de la Concorde entrance, open 10 am to 7 pm. Aside from volumes on gardening and plants (including some titles in English), it has gift items, knickknacks, and toys for the junior gardener. The Tuileries is one of the best places in Paris to take kids if they're itching to run around. There's a carrousel (€2.50), trampolines (€2) and, in summer, an amusement park. If you're hungry, look for carts serving gelato from Amorino or sandwiches from the chain bakery Paul. Also, there are four cafés with terraces in the center of the garden. The two closer to place de la Concorde—Café Renard and Le Médicis—serve fare a bit more upscale. ✉ *Bordered by quai des Tuileries, pl. de la Concorde, rue de Rivoli, and the Louvre, Louvre/Tuileries* ☎ *01–40–20–90–43* ✆ *Free* ☉ *June, July, and Aug., daily 7 am–11 pm; Apr., May, and Sept., daily 7:30 am–9 pm; Oct.–Mar., daily 7:30–7:30* Ⓜ *Tuileries or Concorde.*

Fodor's Choice
★

The Louvre. The most recognized symbol of Paris is the Tour Eiffel, but the ultimate traveler's prize is the Louvre. This is the world's greatest art museum—and the largest, with 675,000 square feet of works from almost every civilization on Earth. The three most popular pieces here are, of course, the *Mona Lisa,* the *Venus de Milo,* and *Winged Victory.* Beyond these must-sees, your best bet is to focus on whatever interests you the most—and don't despair about getting lost, for you're bound to stumble on something memorable. Pick up an excellent color-coded map at the information desk. There are slick Nintendo 3DS multimedia guides at the entrance to each wing; for €5 you get four self-guided tours and details about 250 works of art, plus a function to help you find your

DID YOU KNOW?

The magnificent Grand Palais, with its enormous glass roof, is known for its provocative and crowd-pleasing temporary art exhibits.

bearings. There are 90-minute guided tours (€9) in English daily at 11 and 2. Thematic leaflets (including some for kids) and Louvre guided tours are available from the front desk.

Bear in mind that the Louvre is much more than a museum—it represents a saga that started centuries ago, having been a fortress at the turn of the 13th century, and later a royal residence. It was not until the 16th century, under François I, that today's Louvre began to take shape, and through the years Henry IV, Louis XIII, Louis XV, Napoléon I, and Napoléon III all contributed to its construction. Napoléon Bonaparte's military campaigns at the turn of the 19th century brought a new influx of holdings, as his soldiers carried off treasures from each invaded country. During World War II the most precious artworks were hidden, while the remainder was looted. Most of the stolen pieces were recovered, though, after the liberation of Paris. No large-scale changes were made until François Mitterrand was elected president in 1981, when he kicked off the Grand Louvre project to expand and modernize the museum.

Mitterrand commissioned I.M. Pei's Pyramide, the giant glass pyramid surrounded by three smaller pyramids that opened in 1989 over the new entrance in the Cour Napoléon. In 2012, the Louvre's newest architectural wonder opened—the 30,000-square-foot **Arts of Islam wing.** Built into the Cour Visconti in the Denon wing and topped with an undulating golden roof evoking a veil blowing in the wind, the two-level galleries house one of the world's largest collections of art from all corners of the Islamic world.

The Louvre comprises three wings—the Richelieu, the Sully, and the Denon—arranged like a horseshoe, with the Pyramide nestled outside in the middle. Entering from it, head upstairs to the sculpture courtyards in the Richelieu wing, where you'll find the *Marly Horses,* four equine sculptures—two carved for Louis XIV and two for Louis XV—in Cour Marly. The ground floor and underground rooms in this wing contain 5th- to 19th-century French sculpture, and the Near East Antiquities Collection, including the *Lamassu,* carved 8th-century winged beasts. On the first floor of this wing you'll find the Royal Apartments of Napoléon III, a dozen elaborately decorated reception rooms. Continue to the second floor for the French and Northern School paintings, including Vermeer's *The Lacemaker.* The entrance to the Sully wing is the most impressive, as you can walk around the 12th-century foundations and vestiges of the original medieval moat. Belowground is also the largest display of Egyptian antiques in the world after that of the Cairo museum, featuring such artifacts as *Ramses II,* a beautifully proportioned statue from the site of Tanis. Upstairs in Salle 16 is the armless **Venus de Milo,** a 2nd-century representation of the goddess Aphrodite. She was cleaned and restored over six months in 2010, the work taking place after hours and on Tuesday, when the museum is closed. The first and second floors of the Sully Wing boast decorative arts from all over Europe, as well as 17th-century French paintings, including the *Turkish Bath* by Jean-August-Dominique Ingres. Don't miss one of the newest additions, the contemporary ceiling in Salle 32 on the first floor by American Cy Twombly, unveiled in 2010. On the first floor, period rooms with 18th-century furnishing and objets d'art were set to open in late 2013. To the south and east of the Pyramide entrance are galleries displaying early Renaissance sculpture in the Denon Wing. Don't skip the coat checks on the ground floor of the Denon or Richelieu wings—much of the museum is hot and stuffy. Walk up the marble Escalier Daru to discover the sublime **Winged Victory of Samothrace**, a statue found on a tiny Greek island that was carved in 305 BC to commemorate the naval victory of Demetrius Poliocretes over the Turks. In the paintings section of the Denon Wing, you'll find three by Leonardo da Vinci, including the most famous painting in the world: the **Mona Lisa**, located in Salle 7. Head across to Salle 75 for the *Coronation of Napoléon*, or to Salle 77 for the graphic 1819 *Raft of the Medusa*, the first work of art based on a real news event, in this case the survivors of the wreck of a French ship. ■TIP➜ To save time, avoid the main entrance at the Pyramide and head for the entrance in the underground mall, Carrousel du Louvre, which has automatic ticket machines, or to the Porte de Lions entrance (closed Friday) on the southwestern corner. Ticket-holders can come and go through the Porte Richelieu on the rue de Rivoli side. If you need a break, there are several cafés within the museum, including Café Richelieu, run by the upscale *confiseur* Angelina; or hold onto your ticket (you can reenter all day) and pop out to one of the open-air cafés in the Jardin de Tuileries. The shortest lines tend to be around 9:30 am and 1 pm. Crowds are also thinner on Wednesday and Friday nights, when the museum is open late. Remember that the Louvre is closed Tuesday. ⊠ *Palais du Louvre, Louvre/Tuileries* 🕾 *01–40–20–53–17 information* ⊕ *www.louvre. fr* 🖾 *€12; €13 for Napoléon Hall exhibitions; €16 with all temporary exhibits and same-day entry to Musée Eugène Delacroix; free 1st Sun. of month* ☉ *Mon., Thurs., and weekends 9–6; Wed. and Fri. 9–9:30; closed Tues.* Ⓜ *Palais-Royal–Musée du Louvre.*

Musée de l'Orangerie. The lines can be long to see Claude Monet's huge, meditative *Water Lilies* (*Nymphéas*), displayed in two curved galleries designed in 1914 by the master himself. But they are well worth the wait. These works are the highlight of the Orangerie Museum's small but excellent collection, which includes early-20th-century paintings by Renoir, Cézanne, and Matisse. Many hail from the private holdings of art dealer Paul Guillaume (1891–1934), including Guillaume's portrait by Modigliani entitled *Novo Pilota*, or new pilot, signaling Guillaume's status as an important presence in the arts world. Built in 1852 to shelter orange trees, the museum reopened in 2006 after a long renovation that unearthed a portion of the city's 16th-century wall (you can see remnants on the lower floor). ⊠ *Jardin des Tuileries at pl. de la Concorde, Louvre/Tuileries* 🕾 *01–44–77–80–07* ⊕ *www.musee-orangerie. fr* 🖾 *€7.50; €14 joint ticket with Musée d'Orsay* ☉ *Wed.–Mon. 9–6* Ⓜ *Concorde.*

Musée du Jeu de Paume. This Napoléon III–era building at the north entrance of the Jardin des Tuileries began life in 1861 as a place to play *jeu de paume* (or "palm game"), a forerunner of tennis. It later served as a transfer point for art looted by the Germans during World War II. Today, it's been given another lease on life as an ultramodern, white-walled showcase for excellent temporary exhibits of photography

Architect I. M. Pei's pyramid entrance reaffirms the ever-old-but-always-new vitality of the Louvre's French Baroque architecture.

featuring up-and-comers as well as icons such as Diane Arbus, Richard Avedon, Cindy Sherman, and Robert Frank. ⊠ *1 pl. de la Concorde, Louvre/Tuileries* ☎ *01–47–03–12–50* ⊕ *www.jeudepaume.org* ✉ *€8.50* ⏰ *Tues. 11–9, Wed.–Sun. 11–7; closed Mon.* Ⓜ *Concorde.*

Fodor'sChoice
★

Notre-Dame. *See highlighted listing in this chapter.*

Petit Palais, Musée des Beaux-Arts de la Ville de Paris. The Petit Palais, the city's fine art musuem, has a small, overlooked collection of excellent painting, sculpture, and objets d'art, with works by Monet, Gaughin, and Courbet, among others. Temporary exhibitions, beefed up in recent years (and often free), are particularly good, especially those dedicated to photography. The building, like the Grand Palais across the street, is a frothy concoction of marble, glass, and gilt built for the 1900 World's Fair, with huge windows overlooking the Seine. Outside, keep an eye out for two eye-catching sculptures: French World War I hero Georges Clemenceau, facing the Champs-Élysées; and Jean Cardot's resolute image of Winston Churchill, facing the Seine. ⊠ *Av. Winston Churchill, Champs-Élysées* ☎ *01–53–43–40–00* ⊕ *www.petitpalais. paris.fr* ✉ *Permanent collection free; temporary exhibit entry fees vary* ⏰ *Tues.–Sun. 10–6, Thurs. until 8 for temporary exhibits; closed Mon.* Ⓜ *Champs-Élysées–Clemenceau.*

NEED A BREAK?

Le Jardin du Petit Palais. The quiet little café hidden in the lush garden of the Petit Palais is one of this quarter's best-kept secrets. Closed Monday. ⊠ *Av. Winston Churchill, Champs-Élysées* ☎ *01–53–43–40–00* Ⓜ *Champs-Élysées-Clemenceau.*

2

Place de la Concorde. This square at the foot of Champs-Élysées was originally named after Louis XV. It later became the place de la Révolution, where crowds cheered as Louis XVI, Marie-Antoinette, and some 2,500 others lost their heads to the guillotine. Renamed Concorde in 1836, it got a new centerpiece: the 75-foot granite Obelisk of Luxor, a gift from Egypt quarried in the 8th century BC. Among the handsome 18th-century buildings facing the square is the Hôtel Crillon, which was originally built as a private home by Gabriel, the architect of Versailles's Petit Trianon. ✉ *Champs-Élysées* Ⓜ *Concorde.*

Fodor's Choice
★
Sainte-Chapelle. Built by the obsessively pious Louis IX (1226–70), this Gothic jewel is home to the oldest stained-glass windows in Paris. The chapel was constructed over three years, at phenomenal expense, to house the king's collection of relics acquired from the impoverished emperor of Constantinople. These included Christ's Crown of Thorns, fragments of the Cross, and drops of Christ's blood—though even in Louis's time these were considered of questionable authenticity. Some of the relics have survived and can be seen in the treasury of Notre-Dame, but most were lost during the Revolution.

The narrow spiral staircase by the entrance takes you to the upper chapel where the famed beauty of Sainte-Chapelle comes alive: 6,458 square feet of stained glass is delicately supported by painted stonework that seems to disappear in the colorful light streaming through the windows. Deep reds and blues dominate the background, noticeably different from later, lighter medieval styles such as those of Notre-Dame's rose windows.

The chapel is essentially an enormous magic lantern illuminating 1,130 figures from the Bible. Portions of the windows have been removed during a sweeping six-year restoration, set to finish in late 2014. (The lowest sections of the windows were restored in the mid-1800s.) Besides the dazzling glass, observe the detailed carvings on the columns and the statues of the apostles. The lower chapel is gloomy and plain, but take note of the low, vaulted ceiling decorated with fleurs-de-lis and cleverly arranged *L*s for Louis.

■**TIP**➜ Sunset is the optimal time to see the rose window; however, to avoid waiting in killer lines, plan your visit for a weekday morning, the earlier the better. Come on a sunny day to appreciate the full effect of the light filtering through all of that glorious stained glass. You can buy a joint ticket with the Conciergerie: lines are shorter if you purchase it there, though you'll still have to go through a longish metal detector line to get into Sainte-Chapelle itself. Sights aside, the chapel makes a divine setting for classical concerts; check the schedule at ⊕ *www. infoconcert.com.* ✉ *4 bd. du Palais, Ile de la Cité* ☎ *01–53–40–60–97* ⊕ *www.sainte-chapelle.monuments-nationaux.fr* ☜ *€8.50; joint ticket with Conciergerie €12.50* ☉ *Mar. 1–Oct. 31, daily 9:30–6; Nov.–Feb., daily 9–5* Ⓜ *Cité.*

WORTH NOTING

Fodor's Choice
★
Ancien Cloître Quartier. Hidden in the shadows of Notre-Dame is this evocative, often-overlooked tangle of medieval streets. Through the years lucky folk, including Ludwig Bemelmans (who created the beloved

Madeleine books) and the Aga Khan have called this area home, but back in the Middle Ages it was the domain of cathedral seminary students. One of them was the celebrated Peter Abélard (1079–1142)—philosopher, questioner of the faith, and renowned declaimer of love poems. Abélard boarded with Notre-Dame's clergyman, Fulbert, whose 17-year-old niece, Héloïse, was seduced by the compelling Abélard, 39 years her senior. She became pregnant and the vengeful clergyman had Abélard castrated; amazingly, he survived and fled to a monastery, while Héloïse took refuge in a nunnery. The poetic, passionate letters between the two cemented their fame as thwarted lovers, and their story inspired a devoted following during the romantic 19th century. They still draw admirers to the Père Lachaise Cemetery, where they're interred *ensemble*. The clergyman's house at 10 rue Chanoinesse was redone in 1849; a plaque at the back of the building at 9–11 quai aux Fleurs commemorates the lovers. ⊠ *Rue du Cloître-Notre-Dame north to quai des Fleurs, Ile de la Cité* Ⓜ *Cité.*

FAMILY	**Conciergerie.** Most of the Ile de la Cité's medieval structures fell victim to wunderkind planner Baron Haussmann's ambitious rebuilding program of the 1860s. Among the rare survivors are the jewel-like Sainte-Chapelle, a vision of shimmering stained glass, and the Conciergerie, the former prison where Marie-Antoinette and other victims of the French Revolution spent their final days.

Constructed by Philip IV in the late-13th and early-14th centuries, the Conciergerie—which takes its name from the building's concierge or keeper—was part of the original palace of the kings of France, before the royals moved into the Louvre around 1364. In 1391, it became a prison. During the French Revolution, Marie-Antoinette languished 76 days here awaiting her date with the guillotine. There is a re-creation of the doomed queen's sad little cell—plus others that are far smaller—complete with wax figures behind bars. In the chapel, stained glass, commissioned after the queen's death by her daughter, is emblazoned with the initials M. A. Outside you can see the small courtyard where women prisoners took meals and washed their clothes in the fountain (men enjoyed no similar respite). Well-done temporary exhibitions on the ground floor aim to please kids and adults alike; previous themes have included enchanted forests and Gothic castles. There are free guided tours (in French only) most days at 11 and 3. ⊠ *2 bd. du Palais, Ile de la Cité* ☎ *01–53–40–60–80* ⊕ *www.conciergerie.monuments-nationaux.fr* ⌧ *€8.50; joint ticket with Sainte-Chapelle €12.50* ⊘ *Daily 9:30–6* Ⓜ *Cité.*

Place Dauphine. The Surrealists called place Dauphine "le sexe de Paris" because of its suggestive V shape; however, its origins were much more proper. The pretty square on the western side of the Pont Neuf was built by Henry IV, who named it as a homage to his son the crown prince, or dauphin, who became Louis XIII when Henry was assassinated. ■**TIP→** Treat yourself by grabbing a table on a restaurant terrace here—the square is one of the best places in Paris to dine *en plein air.* ⊠ *Ile de la Cité* Ⓜ *Cité.*

Continued on page 63

NOTRE-DAME

Notre-Dame is the symbolic heart of Paris and, for many, of France itself. Napoléon was crowned here, and kings and queens exchanged marriage vows before its altar. There are a few things worth seeing inside the Gothic cathedral, but the real highlights are the exterior architectural details and the unforgettable view of Paris, framed by stone gargoyles, from the top of the south tower.

THE STONE GARGOYLES

Notre-Dame's gargoyles were designed by Eugène Viollet-le-Duc, the architect who oversaw the cathedral's 19th-century renovations. Technically they're chimeras, not gargoyles, as they're purely ornamental; a true "gargoyle" is a carved sculpture that functions as a waterspout.

Begun in 1163, completed in 1345, badly damaged during the Revolution, and restored by the architect Eugène Viollet-le-Duc in the 19th century, Notre-Dame may not be France's oldest or largest cathedral, but in beauty and architectural harmony it has few peers. The front entranceways seem like hands joined in prayer, the sculpted kings on the facade form a noble procession, and the west (front) rose window gleams with what seems like divine light.

The most dramatic approach to Notre-Dame is from the Rive Gauche, crossing at the Pont au Double from quai de Montebello, at the St-Michel métro or RER stop. This bridge will take you to the open square, place du Parvis, in front of the cathedral. (The more direct metro stop is Cité.)

THE WEST (FRONT) FACADE

The three front entrances are, left to right: the Portal of the Virgin, the Portal of the Last Judgment (above), and the Portal of St. Anne, the oldest of the three. Above the three front entrances are the 28 restored statues of the kings of Israel, the Galerie des Rois.

INSIDE THE CATHEDRAL

TIMELINE

1160	Notre-Dame is conceived by Bishop Maurice de Sully, the bishop of Paris.
1163	Construction begins.
1182	Choir is completed; the main altar is consecrated.
1196	Bishop de Sully dies.
c. 1200 -1245	The western facade and towers are completed.
1208	The Nave is completed.
1235 -1250	A series of chapels are added to the nave.
1250 -1270	The High Gothic–style north and south Rose windows are installed.
1296- 1330	A series of chapels are added to the apse.
1345	Construction of the original cathedral is completed.
1699 -1723	The original Gothic choir is replaced with a Baroque one.
c 1790	The church is plundered during the Revolution.
1845	Viollet-le-Duc's restoration begins, lasting 23 years.

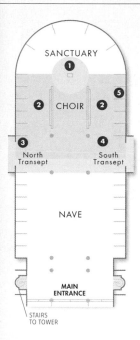

SANCTUARY

❶

❺

❷ CHOIR ❷

❸ ❹

North Transept   South Transept

NAVE

MAIN ENTRANCE

STAIRS TO TOWER

❶ **The Pietà,** behind the choir, represents the Virgin Mary mourning over the dead body of Christ.

❷ **The biblical scenes** on the north and south screens of the choir represent the life of Christ and the apparitions of Christ after the Resurrection.

❸ **The north rose window** is one of the cathedral's original stained-glass panels; at the center is an image of Mary holding a young Jesus.

❹ At the south (right) entrance to the choir, you'll glimpse the haunting 12th-century statue of **Notre-Dame de Paris,** "Our Lady of Paris," the Virgin, for whom the cathedral is named.

❺ **The treasury,** on the south side of the choir, holds a small collection of religious garments, reliquaries, and silver- and gold-plate.

MAKING THE CLIMB A separate entrance, to the left of the front facade if you're facing it, leads to the 387 stone steps of the south tower. These steps take you to the bell of Notre-Dame (as tolled by the fictional Quasimodo). Looking out from the tower, you can see how Paris—like the trunk of a tree developing new rings—has grown outward from the Ile de la Cité. To the north is Montmartre; to the west is the Arc de Triomphe, at the top of the Champs-Elysées; and to the south are the towers of St-Sulpice.

Place du Parvis

Detail of the Gallery of Kings, over the front entrance.

Notre-Dame was one of the first Gothic cathedrals in Europe and one of the first buildings to make use of **flying buttresses**—exterior supports that spread out the weight of the building and roof. At first people thought they looked like scaffolding that the builders forgot to remove. ■**TIP**➜ **The most tranquil place to appreciate the architecture of Notre-Dame is from the lovely garden behind the cathedral, Square Jean-XXIII. By night, take a boat ride on the Seine for the best view—the lights at night are magnificent.**

Place du Parvis is *kilomètre zéro*, the spot from which all distances to and from the city are officially measured. A polished brass circle set in the ground, about 20 yards from the cathedral's main entrance, marks the exact spot.

The Crypt Archéologique (entrance down the stairs in front of the cathedral) is a quick visit but very interesting, especially for kids and archaeology buffs. It gives an "under the city" view of the area, with remains from previous churches that were built on this site, scale models charting the district's development, and artifacts dating from 2,000 years ago.

☎ 01–42–34–56–10

⊕ www.notredame deparis.fr

▦ Cathedral free. Towers: €8.50. Crypt €4. Treasury €3.

⊙ Cathedral daily 7:45–6:45. Towers Apr.–June and Sept., daily 10 AM–6:30; July and Aug., weekdays 10 AM–6:30, weekends 10 AM–11 PM; Oct.–Mar., daily 10–5:30. Note: towers close early when overcrowded. Treasury Mon.–Fri. 9:30–6 PM, Sat. 9:30–6:30, Sun. 1:30–6:30. Crypt Tues.–Sun. 10–6.

SOMETHING TO PONDER

Do Notre-Dame's hunchback and its gargoyles have anything in common other than bad posture? Quasimodo was created by Victor Hugo in the novel *Notre-Dame de Paris*, published in 1831. The incredible popularity of the book made Parisians finally take notice of the cathedral's state of disrepair and spurred Viollet-le-Duc's renovations. These included the addition of the gargoyles, among other things, and resulted in the structure we see today.

■**TIP**➜ The best time to visit Notre-Dame is early in the morning, when the cathedral is at its brightest and least crowded.

■**TIP**➜ There are free guided tours in English several times a week; check website for times.

FROM THE EIFFEL TOWER TO THE ARC DE TRIOMPHE

The Eiffel Tower (or Tour Eiffel, to use the French) lords over southwest Paris, and from nearly wherever you are on this walk you can see its jutting needle. For years many Parisians felt it was an iron eyesore and called it the Giant Asparagus, a vegetable that weighed 15 million pounds and grew 1,000 feet high. But gradually the tower became part of the Parisian landscape, entering the hearts and souls of Parisians and visitors alike. Thanks to its stunning nighttime illumination, topped by four 6,000-watt projectors creating a lighthouse beacon visible for 80 km (50 miles) around, it continues to make Paris live up to its moniker *La Ville Lumière*—the City of Light. Water is the second highlight here: fountains playing beneath place du Trocadéro and boat tours along the Seine on a Bateau Mouche. Museums are the third; the area around Trocadéro is full of them. Style is the fourth, and not just because the buildings here are overwhelmingly elegant—but because this is also the center of haute couture, with the top names in fashion all congregated around avenue Montaigne, only a brief walk from the Champs-Élysées, to the north.

TOP ATTRACTIONS

Fodor's Choice
★

Arc de Triomphe. Inspired by Rome's Arch of Titus, this colossal, 164-foot triumphal arch was ordered by Napoléon—who liked to consider himself the heir to Roman emperors—to celebrate his military successes. Unfortunately, Napoléon's strategic and architectural visions were not entirely on the same plane, and the Arc de Triomphe proved something of an embarrassment. Although the emperor wanted the monument completed in time for an 1810 parade in honor of his new bride, Marie-Louise, it was still only a few feet high, and a dummy arch of painted canvas was strung up to save face. Empires come and go, but Napoléon's had been gone for more than 20 years before the Arc was finally finished in 1836. A small museum halfway up recounts its history.

The Arc de Triomphe is notable for magnificent sculptures by François Rude, including *The Departure of the Volunteers in 1792*, better known as *La Marseillaise*, to the right of the arch when viewed from the Champs-Élysées. Names of Napoléon's generals are inscribed on the stone facades—the underlined names identify the hallowed figures who fell in battle.

The traffic circle around the Arc is named for Charles de Gaulle, but it's known to Parisians as "L'Étoile," or the Star—a reference to the streets that fan out from it. Climb the stairs to the top of the arch and you can see the star effect of the 12 radiating avenues and the vista down the Champs-Élysées toward place de la Concorde and the distant Musée du Louvre.

■**TIP→** France's Unknown Soldier is buried beneath the arch, and a commemorative flame is rekindled every evening at 6:30. That's the most atmospheric time to visit, but, to beat the crowds, come early in the morning or buy your ticket online (€1.60 service fee). Be wary of the traffic circle that surrounds the arch. It's infamous for accidents—including one several years ago that involved the French transport

TOURING PARIS BY BUS

Cityrama ⊠ *4 pl. des Pyramides, 1er* ☎ *01–44–55–61–00* ⊕ *www. cityrama.info.*

Les Cars Rouges (☎ *01–53–95–39–53* ⊕ *www.carsrouges.com*) offer double-decker London-style buses with nine stops—a ticket for two consecutive days is available for €24.

Paris L'OpenTour ☎ *01–42–66–56–56* ⊕ *www.parislopentour.com.*

Paris Vision ⊠ *214 rue de Rivoli, 1er* ☎ *01–44–55–60–00* ⊕ *www. parisvision.net.*

RATP ☎ *32–46 [€0.34 per min]* ⊕ *www.ratp.com.*

minister. Use the underground passage from the northeast corner of the avenue des Champs-Élysées. ⊠ *Pl. Charles-de-Gaulle, Champs-Élysées* ☎ *01–55–37–73–77* ⊕ *arc-de-triomphe.monuments-nationaux. fr* ⌨ *€9.50, free under 18* ⊙ *Apr.–Sept., daily 10 am–11 pm; Oct.–Mar., daily 10 am–10:30 pm* Ⓜ *Métro or RER: Étoile.*

Avenue des Champs-Élysées. Marcel Proust lovingly described the genteel elegance of the storied Champs-Élysées (pronounced chahnz-*eleezay*, with an "n" sound instead of "m" and no "p") during its Belle Époque heyday, when its cobblestones resounded with the clatter of horses and carriages. Today, despite unrelenting traffic and the intrusion of chain stores and fast-food franchises, the avenue still sparkles. There's always something happening here: the stores are open late (and many are open on Sunday, a rarity in Paris), the nightclubs remain top destinations, and the cafés offer prime people-watching—though you'll pay for the privilege: after all, this is Europe's most expensive piece of real estate. Along the 2-km (1¼-mile) stretch, you can find the marquee names in French luxury, including Cartier, the perfumier Guerlain, and Louis Vuitton. Newer arrivals, like the cavernous Sephora, are fun to check out because, in the bigger-is-better spirit of the Champs, there are often events and giveaways. Car manufacturers try to out-bling each other with space-age showrooms. Old stalwarts, meanwhile, are still going strong—including the Lido cabaret and Fouquet's, whose celebrity clientele extends back to James Joyce. The avenue is also the setting for the last leg of the Tour de France bicycle race (the third or fourth Sunday in July), as well as Bastille Day (July 14) and Armistice Day (November 11) ceremonies. The Champs-Élysées, which translates as "Elysian Fields" (the resting place of the blessed in Greek mythology), began life as a cow pasture and in 1666 was transformed into a park by the royal landscape architect André Le Nôtre. Traces of its green origins are visible near Concorde, where elegant 19th-century park pavilions house the historic restaurants Ledoyen, Laurent, and Le Pavillon Élysées Lenôtre. ⊠ *Champs-Élysée* Ⓜ *Champs-Élysées–Clemenceau, Franklin-D.-Roosevelt, George V, Étoile.*

Fodor's Choice ★ **Musée Guimet.** The outstanding Musée Guimet boasts the western world's biggest collection of Asian art, thanks to the 19th-century wanderings of Lyonnaise industrialist Émile Guimet. Exhibits, enriched by the state's vast holdings, are laid out geographically in airy, light-filled rooms. Just past the entry, you can find the largest assemblage of Khmer sculpture outside Cambodia. The second floor has statuary and masks from Nepal, ritual funerary art from Tibet, and jewelry and fabrics from India. Peek into the library rotunda, where Monsieur Guimet once entertained the city's notables under the gaze of eight carytids atop ionic columns; Mata Hari danced here in 1905. The much-heralded Chinese collection, made up of 20,000-odd objects, covers seven millennia. Pick up a free English-language audio guide and brochure at the entrance. If you need a pick-me-up, stop at the Salon des Porcelaines café on the lower level for a ginger milk shake. ■**TIP→ Don't miss the Guimet's impressive Buddhist Pantheon, with two floors of Buddhas from China and Japan, and a Japanese garden. Admission is free and it's just up the street at 19 avenue d'Iéna.** ⊠ *6 pl. d'Iéna, Trocadéro/Tour Eiffel* ☎ *01–56–52–53–00* ⊕ *www.guimet.fr* ⊠ *€7.50; €9.50 with temporary exhibition* ۞ *Wed.–Mon. 10–6; closed Tues.* Ⓜ *Iéna, Boissiére.*

Fodor's Choice   **Musée Marmottan Monet.** A few years ago the underrated Marmottan
★   tacked "Monet" onto its official name—and justly so, as this is the largest collection of the artist's works anywhere. The pieces, donated by his son Michel, occupy a specially built basement gallery in an elegant 19th-century mansion, which was once the hunting lodge of the Duke de Valmy. Among them you can find such works as the *Cathédrale de Rouen* series (1892–96) and *Impression: Soleil Levant* (*Impression: Sunrise,* 1872), the painting that helped give the Impressionist movement its name. Other exhibits include letters exchanged by Impressionist painters Berthe Morisot and Mary Cassatt. Upstairs, the mansion still feels like a graciously decorated private home. Empire furnishings fill the salons overlooking the Jardin de Ranelagh on one side and the private yard on the other. There's also a captivating room of illuminated medieval manuscripts. To best understand the collection's context, buy an English-language catalog in the museum shop on your way in. ⊠ *2 rue Louis-Boilly, Passy-Auteuil* ☎ *01–44–96–50–33* ⊕ *www. marmottan.com* ⊠ *€10* ۞ *Thurs. 10–8, Wed.–Sun. 11–6* Ⓜ *La Muette.*

FAMILY   **Tour Eiffel** (*Eiffel Tower*). See highlighted listing in this chapter.
Fodor's Choice
★

WORTH NOTING

Fondation Pierre Bergé–Yves Saint Laurent. With his business partner, Pierre Bergé, the late fashion designer Yves Saint Laurent reopened his former atelier as a gallery and archive of his work in 2004. Unfortunately, YSL's private collection of dresses can be viewed only on private group tours booked in advance. What you can see here are exhibitions staged twice annually. Themes include painting, photography and, of course, fashion—such as a retrospective on couture maven Nan Kempner. Check the website to see what's on. ⊠ *3 rue Léonce Reynaud, Trocadéro/Tour Eiffel* ☎ *01–44–31–64–31* ⊕ *www.fondation-pb-ysl.net* ⊠ *€7* ۞ *Tues.–Sun. 11–6* Ⓜ *Alma-Marceau.*

Maison de Baccarat. Designer Philippe Starck brought an irreverent *Alice in Wonderland* approach to the HQ and museum of the venerable Baccarat crystal firm. Relocated to the 16e arrondissement in 2003, Starck played on the building's surrealist legacy: Cocteau, Dalí, Buñuel, and

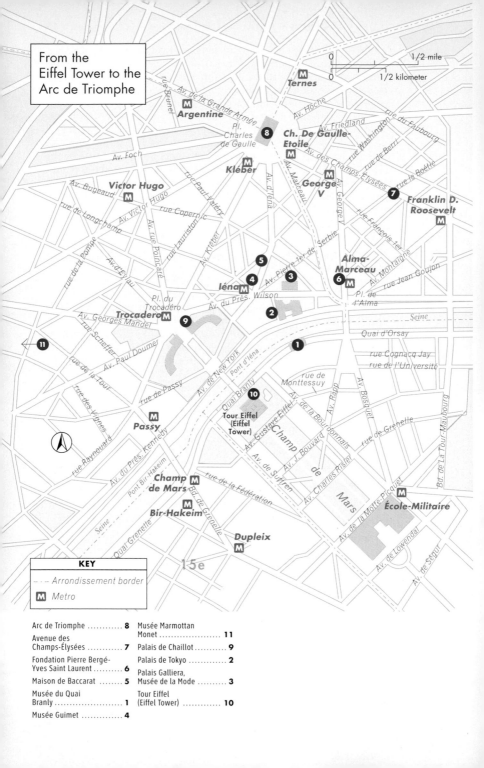

From the Eiffel Tower to the Arc de Triomphe

Man Ray were all frequent guests of the mansion's onetime owner, Countess Marie-Laure de Noailles. At the entrance, talking heads are projected onto giant crystal urns, and a lighted chandelier is submerged in an aquarium. Upstairs, the museum (which is a generous term for the splendid but rather small collection) features masterworks created by Baccarat since 1764, including soaring candlesticks made for Czar Nicholas II and the perfume flacon Dalí designed for Schiaparelli. ■**TIP➜** Set aside a few moments to enjoy the lovely little park just outside in the place des États-Unis, with a fine statue of Washington and Lafayette. ⊠ *11 pl. des États-Unis, Trocadéro/Tour Eiffel* ☎ *01–40–22–11–00* ⊕ *www.baccarat.fr* ⊡ *€5* ⊗ *Mon. and Wed.–Sat. 10–6:30* Ⓜ *Iéna.*

Musée du Quai Branly. The newest museum in Paris was built by star architect Jean Nouvel to house the state-owned collection of "non-Western" art, culled from several other venues. The exhibits mix artifacts from antiquity to the modern age, such as funeral masks from Melanesia, Siberian shaman drums, Indonesian textiles, and African statuary. A corkscrew ramp leads from the lobby to a cavernous exhibition space, which is color coded to designate sections from Asia, Africa, Oceania, and the Americas. The lighting is dim, sometimes too dim to read the information panels (which makes the €5 audio guide a good idea).

Renowned for his bold modern designs, Nouvel has said he wanted the museum to follow no rules—though many critics gave his vision a thumbs down when the museum opened in 2006. The exterior resembles a massive rust-color rectangle suspended on stilts. There are boxy shapes stuck to the facade facing the Seine, and louvered panels on the opposite side. The colors (dark reds, oranges, and yellows) are meant to evoke the tribal art within. A "living wall" comprised of some 150 species of exotic plants grows on the exterior, which is surrounded by a wild jungle garden with swampy patches—an impressive sight after dark when scores of cylindrical colored lights are illuminated. The name, strangely taken from the street address, is thought by many to be temporary until the museum is eventually rechristened in honor of its chief backer, former President Jacques Chirac. ■**TIP➜** Feel like splurging? Les Ombres restaurant on the museum's fifth floor (separate entrance) has premier views of the Tour Eiffel—and prices to match. The budget-conscious can enjoy the garden at Le Café Branly on the ground floor. ⊠ *37 quai Branly, Trocadéro/Tour Eiffel* ☎ *01–56–61–70–00* ⊕ *www.quaibranly.fr* ⊡ *€8.50; €10 with temporary exhibits* ⊗ *Tues., Wed., and Sun. 11–7; Thurs.–Sat. 11–9; closed Mon.* Ⓜ *Alma-Marceau.*

Palais de Chaillot. This honey-color Art Deco cultural center on place du Trocadéro was built in the 1930s to replace a Moorish-style building constructed for the World's Fair of 1878. The plaza-terrace is a top draw for camera-toting visitors intent on snapping the perfect shot of the Eiffel Tower. In the building to the left is the Cité de l'Architecture et du Patrimoine—an excellent architecture museum—and the Theâtre National de Chaillot, which occasionally stages plays in English. Also here is the Institut Français d'Architecture, an organization and school. The twin building to the right contains the Musée de la Marine, a

Continued on page 70

New York has the Statue of Liberty, London has Big Ben—and Paris has the Eiffel Tower. This symbol of Paris, recognized the world over, did not, however, begin life as the beloved icon it is today. Engineer Gustave Eiffel's iron creation for the 1889 World's Fair was greeted with disgust by Parisians, who dubbed it the Giant Asparagus. French author Guy de Maupassant supposedly hated the tower so much that he often ate lunch there, explaining that it was the only place in the city where he could avoid seeing it. Parisians eventually warmed to the tower, an inescapable part of the landscape that has captured the minds and hearts of generations.

Total height: 1,063 feet

- The 200 millionth visitor went to the top of the Eiffel Tower in 2002.

- To get to the first viewing platform, Gustave Eiffel originally used avant-garde

- Every 7 years the tower is repainted. The job takes 15 months and uses 60 tons of "Tour Eiffel Brown" paint in three shades—lightest on top, darkest at the bottom.

LA TOUR EIFFEL

hydraulic cable elevators designed by American Elisha Otis for two of the curved base legs of the tower. French elevators with a chain-drive system were used in the other two legs. During the 1989 renovation, all the elevators were rebuilt by the Otis company.

- An expensive way to beat the queue

is to reserve a wtable at **Le Jules Verne**, the restaurant on the 2nd level, which has a private elevator. Taken over by star chef Alain Ducasse, count on a dinner bill of €450 for 2 with wine, though there's an €85 prix-fixe menu at lunch (without wine). ⊕ *www. lejulesverne-paris.com* ☎ *01–45–55–61–44.*

- If you're in good shape, you can take the stairs to the 2nd level. If you want to go to the top you have to take the elevator.

- The tower nearly became a giant heap of scrap in 1909, when its concession expired, but its use as a radio antenna saved the day.

- The tower is most breathtaking at night, when the girders are illuminated. The light show, conceived to celebrate the turn of the millennium, was so popular that the 20,000 lights were reinstalled for permanent use in 2003. It does its electric shimmy for 5 minutes every hour on the hour (cut from 10 to save energy) until 1 am.

NEED A BITE?

58 Tour Eiffel, the restaurant on the first level, serves a good-value, self-service lunch. There is table service at dinner.

Le Café Branly, in the nearby Musée du Quai Branly (⊠ *27 Quai Branly, Trocadéro/Tour Eiffel* ☎ *01–47–53–68–01*) is a good choice for lunch or a late-afternoon snack.

The base formed by the tower's feet is 410 by 410 feet.

☎ 01–44–11–23–23

⊕ www.tour-eiffel.fr

🎫 By elevator: 1st and 2nd levels €8.20, top €13.40; By stairs: 1st and 2nd levels only, €4.50

◷ mid June through Aug., daily 9 AM–12:45 AM* (11:30 PM for summit);

Sept.–May, daily 9 AM–11 PM* (10:30 for summit); Stairs close at 6 PM in winter

*LAST TICKET SOLD

Ⓜ Bir-Hakeim, Trocadéro, Ecole Militaire; RER Champ de Mars

■**TIP**➜ Beat the crush by reserving your tickets online.

charming small museum with a nautical theme; and the Musée de l'Homme, a natural history museum closed for renovation and set to reopen in 2015. Sculptures and fountains adorn the garden leading to the Seine. ⊠ *Pl. du Trocadéro, Trocadéro/Tour Eiffel* Ⓜ *Trocadéro.*

Palais de Tokyo. The go-to address for some of the city's funkiest exhibitions, the Palais de Tokyo is a stripped-down venue that spotlights unorthodox, ambitious contemporary art. There is no permanent collection: instead, cutting-edge temporary shows are staged in a cavernous space reminiscent of a sprawling industrial loft. The programming extends to performance art, concerts, readings, and fashion shows. Night owls will appreciate the midnight closing. **■TIP➜ The museum's Tokyo Eat restaurant—serving an affordable French-Asian fusion menu—is a haunt of hip locals, especially at lunch. They like the offbeat gift shop, too.** ⊠ *13 av. du Président Wilson, Trocadéro/Tour Eiffel* ☏ *01–81–97–35–88* ⊕ *www.palaisdetokyo.com* ⊡ *€10* ☉ *Wed.–Mon. noon–midnight; closed Tues.* Ⓜ *Iéna.*

Palais Galliera, Musée de la Mode. The city's Museum of Fashion occupies a suitably fashionable mansion—the 19th-century residence of Marie Brignole-Sale, Duchess of Galliera. Following an extensive renovation (set for completion in late 2013), it is more regal than ever. Inside, temporary exhibitions focus on costume and clothing design, with previous ones spotlighting old-time glamour icons like Marlene Dietrich. The museum's collection of 100,000 dresses and accessories sometimes takes a starring role organized under themes such as the structured "high-tech" crinoline hoop styles of the Second Empire (1852–70). Details on shows (there are no permanent displays) are available at the website. **■TIP➜ Don't miss the lovely 19th-century garden that encircles the palace.** ⊠ *10 av. Pierre-1er-de-Serbie, Trocadéro/Tour Eiffel* ☏ *01–56–52–86–00* ⊕ *www.galliera.paris.fr* ⊡ *€7, admission varies* ☉ *Tues.–Sun. 10–6 during temporary exhibits only* Ⓜ *Iéna.*

THE FAUBOURG ST-HONORÉ AND LES HALLES

The impossibly posh Faubourg St-Honoré has been a fashionista destination for three centuries, as popular now as it was when royal mistresses shopped here. Just about every chic boutique has a branch here, and this is where you can find some of the city's best hotels. Once the stomping ground of kings and queens, today it's home to the French president and the American and British ambassadors. Stroll the historic passageways and arcaded streets to experience all that is elegant about Paris. Top-end boutiques, dressmakers, and perfume shops combined to make this *faubourg* (district) a symbol of luxury throughout the world. The centerpiece of the western end is ritzy place Vendome, where you'll find, yes, the Hotel Ritz. Ambitious women play a role in the history here, with rue de Castiglione named after a former denizen, Countess de Castiglione, sent to (successfully) plead the cause of Italian unity with Napoléon III. Coco Chanel founded her fashion house on rue Cambon.

As you walk east, don't miss gems such as Galerie Vivienne, the exquisitely restored 19th-century shopping arcade. Nearby is the place Colette, named after the writer Colette and home to the stately theater, the **Comédie Française,** still going strong after 400 years. Hidden just off the *place* is the Palais-Royal, a romantic garden ringed by arcades with boutiques selling everything from antique war medals to the latest frock by Stella McCartney. To the east, Les Halles has risen from its roots as the city's vermin-infested wholesale food market (closed in 1969) to become one of the city's hottest neighborhoods with expensive apartments and shops, cafés, and bars centered around rue Montorgueil, one of the city's oldest market streets. At the far end is Paris's most famous contemporary art museum, the Centre Georges Pompidou.

TOP ATTRACTIONS

FAMILY

Fodor'sChoice

★

Centre Pompidou. Love it or hate it, the Pompidou is certainly the city's most unique-looking building. Most Parisians have warmed to the industrial, Lego-like exterior that caused a scandal when it opened in 1977. Named after French president Georges Pompidou (1911–74), it was designed by then-unknowns Renzo Piano and Richard Rogers. The architects' claim to fame was putting the building's guts on the outside and color-coding them: water pipes are green, air ducts are blue, electrics are yellow, and things like elevators and escalators are red. Art from the 20th century to the present day is what you can find inside.

The Musée National d'Art Moderne (Modern Art Museum, entrance on Level 4) occupies the top two levels. Level 5 is devoted to modern art from 1905 to 1960, including major works by Matisse, Modigliani, Marcel Duchamp, and Picasso; Level 4 is dedicated to contemporary art from the '60s on, including video installations. The Galerie d'Enfants (Children's Gallery) on the mezzanine level has interactive exhibits designed to keep the kids busy. Outside, next to the museum's sloping plaza—where throngs of teenagers hang out (and where there's free Wi-Fi)—is the Atelier Brancusi. This small, airy museum contains four rooms reconstituting Brancusi's Montparnasse studios with works from all periods of his career. On the opposite side, in the place Igor-Stravinsky, is the Stravinsky fountain, which has 16 gyrating mechanical figures in primary colors, including a giant pair of ruby red lips. On the opposite side of rue Rambuteau, on the wall at the corner of rue Clairvaux and passage Brantôme, is the appealingly bizarre mechanical brass-and-steel clock, Le Défenseur de Temps.

■**TIP➜** The Pompidou's permanent collection takes up a relatively small amount of the space when you consider this massive building's other features: temporary exhibition galleries, with a special wing for design and architecture; a highly regarded free reference library (there's often a queue of university students on rue Renard waiting to get in); and the basement, which includes two cinemas, a theater, a dance space, and a small, free exhibition space. On your way up the escalator, you'll have spectacular views of Paris, ranging from the Tour Montparnasse, to the left, around to the hilltop Sacré-Coeur on the right. The trendy rooftop restaurant, Georges (☎01–44–78–47–99), is a romantic spot for dinner. Be sure to reserve a table near the window. There are public toilets on the lower level without the long lines of those on the ground floor. ⊠ *Pl. Georges-Pompidou, Beaubourg/Les Halles* ☎ *01–44–78–12–33* ⊕ *www.centrepompidou.fr* ⚲*€11; €13 dur-*

ing temporary exhibitions ☺ *Wed.–Mon. 11–9, Thurs. 11–11 during temporary exhibitions; Atelier Brancusi Wed.–Mon. 2–6* Ⓜ *Rambuteau.*

Galerie Vivienne. Considered the grande dame of Paris's 19th-century *passages couverts*—the world's first shopping malls—this graceful covered arcade evokes an age of gaslights and horse-drawn carriages. Once Parisians came to passages like this one to tred tiled floors instead of muddy streets, and to see and be seen browsing boutiques under the glass-and-iron roofs. Today, the Galerie Vivienne still attracts top-flight retailers such as Jean-Paul Gaultier (6 rue Vivienne) and the high-quality secondhand clothes seller La Marelle (No. 21), as well as shops selling accessories, housewares, and fine wine. ■**TIP**➔ The place des Victoires, a few steps away, is one of Paris's most picturesque squares. In the center is a statue of an outsized Louis XIV (1643–1715), the Sun King, who appears almost as large as his horse. ⊠ *Main entrance at 4 rue des Petits-Champs, Louvre/Tuileries* Ⓜ *Palais-Royal/Bourse.*

Les Arts Décoratifs. Sharing a wing of the Musée du Louvre, but with a separate entrance and admission charge, this arts center showcases a stellar array of decorative arts, design, fashion and graphics. Spread across nine floors, the Musée des Arts Décoratif's collection includes altarpieces from the Middle Ages and furnishings from the Italian Renaissance to the present day. There are period rooms reflecting the ages, such as the early 1820s salon of the Duchesse de Berry, who actually lived in the building, plus several rooms reproduced from designer Jeanne Lanvin's 1920s apartment. Don't miss the gilt-and–green velvet bed of the Parisian courtesan who inspired the boudoir in Émile Zola's novel *Nana.* You can hear Zola's description of it on the free English audio guide, which is highly recommended. The second-floor jewelry gallery is a must-see, and special events are often staged in the Nef (nave).

The center is also home to an exceptional collection of fashion and textiles, advertising posters, films, and related objects, which are shown in two rotating temporary exhibitions each year. Le Saut du Loup restaurant, with an outdoor terrace, is an ideal spot for lunch or afternoon tea. A joint ticket is available with the exquisite partner museum, Nissim de Camondo. ■**TIP**➔ If you're combining a visit here with the Musée du Louvre, note that the museums close on different days, so don't come on Monday or Tuesday. ⊠ *107 rue de Rivoli, Louvre/Tuileries* ☎ *01–44–55–57–50* ⊕ *www.lesartsdecoratifs.fr* ⊡ *€9.50; €13.50 with Nef temporary exhibits; €12 joint ticket with the Musée Nissim de Camondo* ☺ *Tues.–Sun. 11–6, Thurs. 11–9 during exhibits; closed Mon.* Ⓜ *Palais-Royal.*

■ NEED A BREAK? **Angélina.** Founded in 1903 and patronized by literary lights like Marcel Proust and Gertrude Stein, Angélina is famous for its *chocolat l'Africain,* ultrarich hot chocolate topped with whipped cream. ⊠ *226 rue de Rivoli, Louvre/Tuileries* ☎ *01–42–60–82–00* ⊕ *www.angelina-paris.fr* Ⓜ *Tuileries.*

Fodor's Choice ★ **Palais-Royal.** The quietest, most romantic Parisian garden is enclosed within the former home of Cardinal Richelieu (1585–1642). It's an ideal spot to while away an afternoon, cuddling with your sweetheart on a

Hemingway's Paris

There is a saying: "Everyone has two countries, his or her own—and France." For the Lost Generation after World War I, these words rang particularly true. Lured by favorable exchange rates, free-flowing alcohol, and a booming artistic scene, many American writers, composers, and painters moved to Paris in the 1920s and 1930s, Ernest Hemingway among them. He arrived in Paris with his first wife, Hadley, in December 1921 and made for the Rive Gauche—the Hôtel Jacob et d'Angleterre, to be exact (still operating at 44 rue Jacob). To celebrate their arrival the couple went to the Café de la Paix for a meal they nearly couldn't afford.

Hemingway worked as a journalist and quickly made friends with other expat writers such as Gertrude Stein and Ezra Pound. In 1922 the Hemingways moved to 74 rue du Cardinal Lemoine, a bare-bones apartment with no running water (his writing studio was around the corner, on the top floor of 39 rue Descartes). Then in early 1924 the couple and their baby son settled at 113 rue Notre-Dame des Champs. Much of *The Sun Also Rises,* Hemingway's first serious novel, was written at nearby café La Closerie des Lilas. These were the years in which he forged his writing style, paring his sentences down to the pith. As he noted in *A Moveable Feast,* "hunger was good discipline." There were some particularly hungry months when Hemingway gave up journalism and tried to publish short stories, and the family was "very poor and very happy."

They weren't happy for long. In 1926, just when *The Sun Also Rises* made him famous, Hemingway left Hadley and the next year wedded his mistress, Pauline Pfeiffer, across town at St Honoré-d'Eylau, then moved to 6 rue Férou, near the Musée du Luxembourg, whose collection of Cézanne landscapes (now in the Musée d'Orsay) he revered.

For gossip and books, and to pick up his mail, Papa would visit Shakespeare & Co., then at 12 rue de l'Odéon, owned by Sylvia Beach, who became a trusted friend. For cash and cocktails Hemingway usually headed to the upscale Rive Droite. He collected the former at the Guaranty Trust Company, at 1 rue des Italiens. He found the latter, when he was flush, at the bar of the Hôtel Crillon, or, when poor, at the Caves Mura, at 19 rue d'Antin, or Harry's Bar, still in brisk business at 5 rue Daunou. Hemingway's legendary association with the Hotel Ritz was sealed during the Liberation in 1944, when he strode in at the head of his platoon and "liberated" the joint by ordering martinis all around. Here Hemingway asked Mary Welsh to become his fourth wife, and here also, the story goes, a trunk full of notes on his first years in Paris turned up in the 1950s, giving him the raw material to write *A Moveable Feast.*

bench under the trees, soaking up the sunshine beside the fountain, or browsing the 400-year-old arcades that are now home to boutiques ranging from retro quirky (picture toy soldiers and music boxes) to modern chic (think Stella McCartney and Marc Jacobs). One of the city's oldest restaurants is here, the haute-cuisine Le Grand Véfour,

> ### ROOM WITH A VIEW
>
> Visit the arcades of the Palais-Royal to see why the French writer Colette called the view from her window "a little corner of the country" in the heart of the city.

where brass plaques recall regulars like Napoléon and Victor Hugo. Built in 1629, the *palais* became royal when Richelieu bequeathed it to Louis XIII. Other famous residents include Jean Cocteau and Colette, who wrote of her pleasurable "country" view of the *province à Paris*. Today, the garden often plays host to giant-size temporary art installations sponsored by another tenant, the Ministry of Culture. The courtyard off place Colette is outfitted with an unusual collection of short black-and-white columns created in 1986 by artist Daniel Buren. ⊠ *Pl. du Palais-Royal, Louvre/Palais-Royal* Ⓜ *Palais-Royal.*

Place Vendôme. Jules-Hardouin Mansart, an architect of Versailles Palace, designed this perfectly proportioned octagonal plaza near the Tuileries in 1702; and, to maintain a uniform appearance, he gave the surrounding *hôtels particuliers* (private mansions) identical facades. It was originally called place des Conquêtes to extoll the military conquests of Louis XIV, whose statue on horseback graced the center until Revolutionaries destroyed it in 1792. Later, Napoléon ordered his likeness erected atop a 144-foot column modestly modeled after Rome's Trajan Column. But that, too, was toppled in 1871 by painter Gustave Courbet and his band of radicals. The Third Republic raised a new column and sent Courbet the bill, though he died in exile before paying it. Chopin lived and died at No. 12, which is also where Napoléon III enjoyed trysts with his mistress; since 1902 it has been home to the high-end jeweler Chaumet. The Hotel Ritz at No. 15 and its famous Hemingway Bar closed in 2012 for a top-to-bottom renovation; reopening is set for summer 2014. ⊠ *Louvre/Tuileries* Ⓜ *Tuileries.*

WORTH NOTING

Comédie Française. Refined productions by Molière and Racine are staged regularly (though only in French) at the vintage venue where actress Sarah Bernhardt began her career. Founded in 1680 by Louis XIV, the theater finally opened its doors to the public in 1799. It nearly burned to the ground a hundred years later. The current building dates from 1900 and underwent a sweeping renovation in 2012. ⊠ *1 pl. Colette, Louvre/Tuileries* ☎ *08–25–10–16–80 [€.15 per min]* ⊕ *www. comedie-francaise.fr* Ⓜ *Palais-Royal.*

Église de la Madeleine. With its rows of uncompromising columns, this enormous neoclassical edifice in the center of the place de la Madeleine was consecrated as a church in 1842, nearly 78 years after construction began. Initially planned as a Baroque building, it was later razed and begun anew by an architect who had the Roman Pantheon in mind. Interrupted by the Revolution, the site was razed yet again when

Napoléon decided to make it into a Greek temple dedicated to the glory of his army. Those plans changed when the army was defeated and the emperor deposed. Other ideas for the building included making it into a train station, a market, and a library. Finally, Louis XVIII decided to make it a church, which it still is today. Free classical concerts are held here some Sundays. ⊠ *Pl. de la Madeleine, Faubourg* ☎ *01–44–51– 69–00* ⊕ *www.eglise-lamadeleine.com* ◷ *Daily 9:30–7* Ⓜ *Madeleine.*

St-Eustache. Built as the market neighborhood's answer to Notre-Dame, this massive church is decidedly squeezed into its surroundings. Constructed between 1532 and 1640 with foundations dating to 1200, the church mixes a Gothic exterior, complete with impressive flying buttresses, and a Renaissance interior. On the east end (rue Montmartre), Dutch master Rubens' *Pilgrims of Emmaus* (1611) hangs in a small chapel. Two chapels to the left is Keith Haring's *The Life of Christ*, a triptych in bronze and white-gold patina: it was given to the church after the artist's death in 1990, in recognition of the parish's efforts to help victims of AIDS. On the rue Montmartre side of the church, look for the small door to Saint Agnes's crypt, topped with a stone plaque noting the date, 1213, below a curled fish, an indication the patron made his fortune in fish. ⊠ *2 impasse St-Eustache, Beaubourg/ Les Halles* ⊕ *www.saint-eustache.org for concert info* ◷ *Daily 9:30–7* Ⓜ *Les Halles; RER: Châtelet Les Halles.*

THE GRANDS BOULEVARDS

In Belle Époque Paris, the Grand Boulevards were the place to see and be seen: in the cafés, at the opera, or in the ornate passages, the glass-covered arcades that were the world's first shopping malls. If you close your eyes, you can almost imagine the Grands Boulevards immortalized on canvas by the Impressionists: well-dressed Parisians strolling wide avenues dotted with shops, cafés, and horse-drawn carriages—all set against a backdrop of stately Haussmannian buildings. Today, despite the chain stores, sidewalk vendors, and fast-food joints, the Grands Boulevards remain the city's shopping epicenter, home to the most popular *grands magasins* (department stores), Galeries Lafayette and Au Printemps, near place de l'Opéra at the heart of the long chain of avenues, which change names six times.

Commerce aside, the Grands Boulevards are a cultural destination anchored by the **Opéra Garnier,** the magnificent opera house commissioned by Napoléon III. The neighborhood is also home to some of the city's best small museums, all former private collections housed in 19th-century *maisons particuliers* (mansions) that alone are worth the trip. The exquisite **Musée Jacquemart-André** plays host to an impressive collection of Italian Renaissance art, while the jewel box **Musée Nissim de Camondo** remembers one family's tragic end.

TOP ATTRACTIONS

Galeries Lafayette. The stunning Byzantine glass *coupole* (dome) of the city's most famous department store is not to be missed. Amble to the center of the main store, amid the perfumes and cosmetics, and look up. If you're not in the mood for shopping, sip a glass of champagne at the Bar à Bulles at the top of the first-floor escalator. Or have lunch at one of the restaurants, including a rooftop café in the main store (open in spring and summer). On your way down, the top floor of the main store is a good place to pick up interesting Parisian souvenirs. Next door, the excellent Lafayette Gourmet food hall, on the second floor of the men's store, has one of the city's best selections of delicacies. Try a green tea éclair from Japanese–French baker Sadaharu Aoki. ⊠ *40 bd. Haussmann, Opéra/Grands Boulevards* ☎ *01–42–82–34–56* ⊕ *www. galerieslafayette.com* ⊙ *Mon.–Wed., Fri., and Sat. 9:30–8; Thurs. 9:30–9* Ⓜ *Chaussée d'Antin, Opéra; RER: Auber.*

Fodor's Choice **Musée Cernuschi.** Wealthy Milanese banker and patriot Enrico (Henri)
★ Cernuschi fled to Paris in 1850 after the new Italian government collapsed, only to be arrested during the 1871 Paris Commune. He subsequently decided to wait out the unrest by traveling and collecting Asian art. Upon his return 18 months later, he had a special mansion built on the edge of Parc Monceau to house his treasures, notably a two-story bronze Buddha from Japan. Today, this well-appointed museum contains Paris's second-most-important collection of Asian art, after the Musée Guimet. Cernuschi had an eye not only for the bronze pieces he adored but also for Neolithic pottery (8,000 BC), *mingqi* tomb figures (300–900 AD), and an impressive array of terra-cotta figures from various dynasties. A collection highlight is *La Tigresse,* a bronze wine vessel in the shape of a roaring feline (11th century BC) purchased after Cernuschi's death. Although the museum is free, there is a charge for temporary exhibitions: previous shows have featured Japanese drawings, Iranian sculpture, and vintage photographs of Cambodia's temples. ⊠ *7 av. Velasquez, Parc Monceau* ☎ *01–53–96–21–50* ⊕ *www.paris.fr/musees* ⊠ *Free; temporary exhibitions €7* ⊙ *Tues.–Sun. 10–6* Ⓜ *Monceau.*

Fodor's Choice **Musée Jacquemart-André.** Perhaps the city's best small museum, the opu-
★ lent Musée Jacquemart-André is home to a huge collection of art and furnishings lovingly assembled in the late 19th century by banking heir Edouard André and his artist wife, Nélie Jacquemart. Their midlife marriage in 1881 raised eyebrows—he was a dashing bachelor and a Protestant, and she, no great beauty, hailed from a modest Catholic family. Still, theirs was a happy union fused by a common passion for art. For six months every year, the couple traveled, most often to Italy, where they hunted works from the Renaissance, their preferred period. Their collection also includes French painters Fragonard, Jacques-Louis David, and François Boucher, and Dutch masters Van Dyke and Rembrandt. The Belle Époque mansion itself is a major attraction. The elegant ballroom, equipped with collapsible walls operated by then-state-of-the-art hydraulics, could hold 1,000 guests. The winter garden was a wonder of its day, spilling into the *fumoir,* where the dashing André would share cigars with the *grands hommes* (important men) of the day. You can tour the separate bedrooms—his in dusty pink, hers in pale yellow. The former dining room, now an elegant café, features a ceiling by Tiepolo. Don't forget to pick up the free audio guide in English, and do inquire about the current temporary exhibition (two per year), which is usually top-notch. ■ **TIP**➔ Plan on a Sunday visit and

The Grand Foyer proves that Paris's Opéra Garnier is the most opulent theater in the world.

enjoy the popular brunch (€28) in the café from 11 to 3. Reservations are not accepted, so come early or late to avoid waiting in line. ✉ *158 bd. Haussmann, Parc Monceau* ☏ *01–45–62–11–59* ⊕ *www.musee-jacquemart-andre.com* ✉ *€11* ◷ *Daily 10–6; Mon. and Sat. until 9 during exhibitions* Ⓜ *St-Philippe-du-Roule, Miromesnil.*

Musée Nissim de Camondo. The story of the Camondo family is steeped in tragedy, and it's all recorded within the walls of this superb museum. Patriarch Moïse de Camondo, born in Istanbul to a successful banking family, built his showpiece mansion in 1911 in the style of the Petit Trianon at Versailles, and stocked it with some of the most exquisite furniture, wainscoting, and bibelots of the mid- to late 18th century. Despite his vast wealth and purported charm, his wife left him five years after their marriage. Then his son, Nissim, was killed in World War I. Upon Moïse's death in 1935, the house and its contents were left to the state as a museum named for his lost son. A few years later, daughter Irène, her husband, and two children were murdered at Auschwitz. No heirs remained and the Camondo name died out. Today, the house remains an impeccable tribute to Moïse's life, from the gleaming salons to the refined private rooms. You can even see the condolence letter written by Marcel Proust, a family friend, after Nissim's death. There are background materials and an excellent free audio guide in English. ✉ *63 rue de Monceau, Parc Monceau* ☏ *01–53–89–06–50* ⊕ *www.lesartsdecoratifs.fr* ✉ *€7; €12 joint ticket with Musée des Arts Décoratifs* ◷ *Wed.–Sun. 10–5:30* Ⓜ *Villiers or Monceau.*

Fodor's Choice
★ **Opéra Garnier.** Haunt of the Phantom of the Opera and the real-life inspiration for Edgar Degas's dancer paintings, the gorgeous Opéra

Garnier is one of two homes of the National Opera of Paris. The building, the Palais Garnier, was begun in 1860 by then-unknown architect Charles Garnier, who finished his masterwork 15 long years later, way over budget. Festooned with (real) gold leaf, colored marble, paintings, and sculpture from the top artists of the day, the opera house was about as subtle as Versailles and sparked controversy in post-Revolutionary France. The sweeping marble staircase, in particular, drew criticism from a public skeptical of its extravagance. But Garnier, determined to make a landmark that would last forever, spared no expense. The magnificent grand foyer, restored in 2004, is one of the most exquisite salons in France. In its heyday, the cream of Paris society strolled all 59 yards of the vast hall at intermission, admiring themselves in the towering mirrors. To see the opera house, buy a ticket for an unguided visit, which allows access to most parts of the building, including a peek into the auditorium. There is also a small ballet museum with a few works by Degas and the tutu worn by prima ballerina Anna Pavlova when she danced her epic Dying Swan in 1905. To get to it, pass through the unfinished entrance built for Napoléon III and his carriage (construction was abruptly halted when the emperor abdicated in 1870). On the upper level, you can see a sample of the auditorium's original classical ceiling, which was later replaced with a modern version by an octagenarian Mark Chagall. His trademark willowy figures encircling the dazzling crystal chandelier—today the world's third largest—shocked an unappreciative public upon its debut in 1964. Critics who fret that Chagall's masterpiece clashes with the fussy crimson-and-gilt decor can take some comfort in knowing that the original ceiling is preserved underneath, encased in a plastic dome.

OF OPERATIC PROPORTIONS

Over-the-top with gilt and multicolor marble both inside and out, it's no wonder the Phantom haunted the Opéra Garnier. Unable to settle on any one style, Charles Garnier, the designer, chose them all: a Renaissance-inspired detail here, a Rococo frill there, Greek shields put up at random. To best appreciate the luxury of the Second Empire style, walk around the outside of the Opéra, then pause on the steps to watch the world rush by. The building is magically illuminated on performance nights—it's worth dropping by to admire the spectacle even if you're not heading inside.

The Opéra Garnier plays host to the Paris Ballet as well as a few operas each season (most are performed at the Opéra Bastille). If you're planning to see a performance, reserve two months in advance, when tickets go on sale (€5–€180), or try your luck at the last minute at the box office. Recent renovations have unveiled a new contemporary restaurant on the premises, run by Michelin-starred chef Nicolas Le Bec. ■TIP→ To learn about the building's history, and get a taste of aristocratic life during the Second Empire, take the entertaining guided tour in English. The ticket also allows entry to the auditorium. ⊠ Pl. de l'Opéra, Opéra/ Grands Boulevards ☎ 08–92–89–90–90 ⊕ www.operadeparis.fr ☏ €9;

€12.50 for guided visit Wed. and weekends at 11:30 and 3:30 ⊗ Daily 10–5, summer until 6 Ⓜ *Opéra.*

FAMILY **Parc Monceau.** This exquisitely landscaped park began in 1778 as the Duc de Chartres's private garden. Though some of the land was sold off under the Second Empire (creating the exclusive real estate that now borders the park), the refined atmosphere and some of the fanciful faux ruins have survived. Immaculately dressed children play under the watchful eye of their nannies, while lovers cuddle on the benches. In 1797 André Garnerin, the world's first-recorded parachutist, staged a landing in the park. The rotunda—known as the Chartres Pavilion—is surely the city's grandest public restroom: it started life as a tollhouse. ⊠ *Entrances on bd. de Courcelles, av. Velasquez, av. Ruysdaël, av. van Dyck, Parc Monceau* Ⓜ *Monceau.*

WORTH NOTING

FAMILY **Chocostory: Le Musée Gourmand du Chocolat.** Considering that a daily dose of chocolate is practically obligatory in Paris, it's hard to believe that this newcomer (opened in 2010) is the city's first museum dedicated to the sweet stuff. Spread across three floors, exhibits tell the story of chocolate from the earliest traces of the "divine nectar" in Mayan and Aztec cultures, through to its introduction in Europe by the Spanish, who added milk and sugar to the spicy dark brew and launched a continental craze. There are detailed explanations in English, with many for the kids. While the production of chocolate is a major topic, there is a respectable collection of some 1,000 chocolate-related artifacts, such as terra-cotta Mayan sipping vessels (they blew into straws to create foam) and delicate chocolate pots in fine porcelain that were favored by the French royal court. There are frequent chocolate-making demonstrations, which finish with a free tasting. ⊠ *28 bd. de Bonne Nouvelle, Opéra/Grands Boulevards* ☎ *01–42–29–68–60* ⊕ *www.museeduchocolat.fr* ⊠ *€7* ⊗ *Daily 10–5* Ⓜ *Bonne-Nouvelle, Strasbourg, St-Denis.*

Musée de la Vie Romantique. A visit to the charming Museum of the Romantic Life, dedicated to novelist George Sand (1804–76), will transport you to the countryside. In a pretty 1830s mansion in a tree-lined courtyard, the small permanent collection includes drawings by Delacroix and Ingrès, among others, though Sand is the star. There are glass cases stuffed with her jewelry and snuffboxes, and even a mold of the hand of composer Frederic Chopin, one of her many lovers. The museum, about a five-minute walk from the Musée Gustave Moreau, is in a picturesque neighborhood once called New Athens, a reflection of the architectural tastes of the writers and artists who lived there. There is usually an interesting temporary exhibit. ■**TIP→** The garden café is a nice for lunch or afternoon tea (open from Easter to October). ⊠ *16 rue Chaptal, Opéra/Grands Boulevards* ☎ *01–55–31–95–67* ⊕ *www. vie-romantique.paris.fr* ⊠ *Free; €7 temporary exhibits* ⊗ *Tues.–Sun. 10–6* Ⓜ *Blanche, Pigalle, St-Georges.*

THE MARAIS AND THE BASTILLE

From swampy to swanky, Le Marais has a fascinating history that continues to evolve. Like an aging pop star, the *quartier* has remade itself many times, and today retains several identities: the city's epicenter of cool with hip boutiques, designer hotels, and art galleries galore; the hub of Paris's gay community; and, though fading, the nucleus of Jewish life. You could easily spend your entire visit to Paris in this neighborhood, there is that much to do.

Marais means "marsh" and that is exactly what this area was until the 12th century when it was converted to farmland. In 1605, Henri IV began building the place Royale (today's place des Vosges, the oldest square in Paris), which touched off a building boom, and the wealthy and fabulous moved in. Despite the odors—the area was one of the city's smelliest—it remained the chic quarter until Louis XIV moved his court to Versailles, trailed by dispirited aristocrats unhappy to decamp to the country. Here you can see the hodgepodge of narrow streets leveled by Baron Haussmann, who feared a redux of the famous *barricades* that revolutionaries threw up to thwart the monarchy. Miraculously, the Marais escaped destruction, though much of it fell victim to neglect and ruin. Thanks to restoration efforts over the past half century, the district is enjoying its latest era of greatness, and the apartments here—among the city's oldest—are also the most in demand.

To the east, the hip **Bastille**—home turf of the French Revolution—still buzzes at night, but competition has emerged from gentrifying neighborhoods farther afield, notably the **Canal St-Martin**. Once the down-and-out cousin on the city's northeastern border, the canal is now trend-spotting central, brimming with funky bars, cafés, art galleries, and boutiques.

TOP ATTRACTIONS

Fodor's Choice
★
Canal St-Martin. The once-forgotten canal has morphed into one of the city's trendiest places to wander. A good time to come is Sunday afternoon, when the quai de Valmy is closed to cars and some of the shops are open. Rent a bike at any of the many Vélib' stations, stroll along the banks, or go native and cuddle quai-side in the sunshine with someone special.

In 1802 Napoléon ordered the 4.3-km (2.7-mile) canal dug as a source of clean drinking water after cholera and other epidemics swept the city. When it finally opened 23 years later, it stretched north from the Seine at place de la Bastille to the Canal de l'Ourcq, near La Villette. Baron Haussmann later covered a 1.6-km (1-mile) stretch of it, along today's boulevard Richard Lenoir. It nearly became a highway in the 1970s, before the city's urban planners regained their senses. These days you can take a boat tour from end to end through the canal's nine locks: along the way, the bridges swing or lift open. The drawbridge with four giant pulleys at rue de Crimée, near La Villette, was a technological marvel when it opened in 1885.

In recent years gentrification has swept the once-dodgy canal, with artists taking over former industrial spaces and creating studios and galleries. The bar and restaurant scene is hipster central, and small

2

designers have arrived, fleeing expensive rents in Le Marais. To explore this evolving *quartier,* set out on foot: Start on the quai de Valmy at rue Faubourg du Temple (use the République métro stop). Here, at square Frédéric Lemaître facing north, there is a good view of one of the locks (behind you the canal disappears underground). As you head north, detour onto side streets like rue Beaurepaire, a fashionista destination with several "stock" (or surplus) shops for popular brands like Maje, some open on Sunday. The rues Lancry and Vinaigriers are lined with bars, restaurants, and small shops.

A swing bridge across the canal connects Lancry to the rue de la Grange aux Belles, where you'll find the entrance to massive Hôpital Saint-Louis, built in 1607 to accommodate plague victims and still a working hospital today. In front of you is the entrance to the chapel, which held its first Mass in July 1610, two months after the assassination of the hospital's patron, Henry IV. Stroll the grounds, flanked by the original brick-and-stone buildings with steeply sloping roofs. The peaceful courtyard garden is a neighborhood secret.

Back on quai Valmy, browse more shops near the rue des Récollets. Nearby is the Jardin Villemin, the 10e arrondissement's largest park (4.5 acres) on the former site of another hospital. The nighttime scene, especially in summer, is hopping with twentysomethings spilling out of cafés and bars and onto the canal banks. You can catch a live music show at the mostly soul Bizz'Art club-restaurant at No. 167 quai Valmy. If you've made it this far, reward yourself with a fresh taco or burrito at the tiny and authentically Mexican El Nopal taqueria at 3 rue Eugène Varlin. Farther up, just past place Stalingrad, is the Rotonde de la Villette, a lively square with restaurants and twin MK2 cinemas on either side of the canal, with a boat to ferry ticket-holders across. On the approach to Parc de la Villette there are antiques shops along the quai and a few floating restaurants and theaters. **Canauxrama** offers 2½-hour boat cruises through the locks (€16 adults). Check the website for times (⊕ *www.canauxrama.com*). Embarkation is at each end of canal: at Bassin de la Villette (*13 quai de la Loire, La Villette*) or Marina Arsenal (*50 bd. de la Bastille, Bastille*). ⊠ *Canal St-Martin* Ⓜ *Jaurès (northern end) or Bastille (southern end).*

Fodor'sChoice ★ **Cimitère du Père-Lachaise.** Bring a red rose for "the Little Sparrow" Edith Piaf when you visit the cobblestone avenues and towering trees that make this 118-acre oasis of green perhaps the world's most famous cemetery. Named for Père François de la Chaise, Louis XIV's confessor, Père-Lachaise is more than just a who's who of celebrities. The Paris Commune's final battle took place here on May 28, 1871, when 147 rebels were lined up and shot against the Mur des Fédérés (Federalists' Wall) in the southeast corner.

Aside from the sheer aesthetic beauty of the cemetery, the main attraction is what (or who, more accurately) is belowground.

Two of the biggest draws are Jim Morrison's grave (with its own guard to keep Doors fans under control) and the life-size bronze figure of French journalist Victor Noir, whose alleged fertility-enhancing power accounts for the patches rubbed smooth by hopeful hands. Other

One of the most beautiful examples of 17th-century town planning, the place des Vosges is a Parisian jewel constructed by King Henri IV.

significant grave sites include those of 12th-century French philosopher Pierre Abélard and his lover Héloïse; French writers Colette, Honoré de Balzac, and Marcel Proust; American writers Richard Wright, Gertrude Stein, and Alice B. Toklas; Irish writer Oscar Wilde; French actress Sarah Bernhardt; French composer Georges Bizet; the Greek-American opera singer Maria Callas; Franco-Polish composer Frédéric Chopin; painters of various nationalities including Georges-Pierre Seurat, Camille Pissaro, Jean Auguste Dominique Ingres, Jacques-Louis David, Eugène Delacroix, Théodore Géricault, Amedeo Clemente Modigliani, and Max Ernst; French jazz violinist Stephane Grappelli; French civic planer Baron Haussmann; the French playwright and actor Molière; and French singer Edith Piaf. ■TIP→ Pinpoint grave sites on the website before you come, but buy a map anyway outside the entrances—you'll still get lost, but that's part of the fun.

One of the best days to visit is on All Saints' Day (November 1), when Parisians bring flowers to adorn the graves of loved ones or favorite celebrities. ⊠ *Entrances on rue des Rondeaux, bd. de Ménilmontant, and rue de la Réunion, Père Lachaise* ☎ *01–55–25–82–10* ⊕ *www.pere-lachaise.com* ☉ *Daily 8–6, 5:30 in winter (opens 8:30 Sat., 9 Sun.)* Ⓜ *Gambetta, Philippe-Auguste, Père-Lachaise.*

Fodor'sChoice
★

Musée Carnavalet. If it has to do with Paris history, it's here. A fascinating hodgepodge of Parisian artifacts and art, the collection ranges from the prehistoric canoes used by Parisii tribes to the furniture of the cork-lined bedroom where Marcel Proust labored over his evocative novels. Thanks to scores of paintings, nowhere else in Paris can you get such a precise picture of the city's evolution through the ages. The museum fills two adjacent mansions, the Hôtel Le Peletier de St-Fargeau and the Hôtel Carnavalet. The latter is a Renaissance jewel that in the mid-1600s became the home of writer Madame de Sévigné. Throughout her long life, Sévigné wrote hundreds of frank and funny letters to her daughter, giving an incomparable view of both public and private life during the time of Louis XIV. The museum offers a glimpse into her world, but the collection covers far more than just the 17th century. The exhibits on the Revolution are especially interesting, with scale models of guillotines and a replica of the Bastille prison carved from one of its stones. Louis XVI's prison cell is reconstructed along with mementos of his life, even medallions containing locks of his family's hair. Other impressive interiors are reconstructed from the Middle Ages through the Rococo period and into Art Nouveau—showstoppers include the Fouquet jewelry shop and the Café de Paris's original furnishings. The sculpted garden at 36 rue des Francs Bourgeois is open from April to the end of October. ⊠ *23 rue de Sévigné, Marais* ☎ *01–44–59–58–58* ⊕ *www.carnavalet.paris.fr* ✉ *Free for permanent collection, around €7 for exhibits* ☉ *Tues.–Sun. 10–6* Ⓜ *St-Paul.*

Fodor's Choice
★

Musée Picasso. To the chagrin of Picasso fans everywhere, this immensely popular museum closed in August 2009 for a top-to-bottom overhaul. It is set to reopen at the end of 2013. (About 200 works from the permanent collection have been on the road in the United States and elsewhere during the renovation.) The $62 million face-lift will thoroughly transform the Picasso, more than quadrupling the museum's size to 75,000 square feet with new galleries and a performance space. A new 4,800-square-foot building in the back garden, dedicated to temporary exhibitions and other programs, will open when the final stage is completed in spring 2014.

The collection of more than 100,000 paintings, sculptures, drawings, and documents (much of it previously in storage for lack of space) spans Picasso's entire life's work, from the Blue Period to Surrealism, when he painted perhaps his most renowned work, the mammoth *Guernica*, which hangs in the Museo Reina Sofia in Madrid. The Paris collection does not comprise the master's most famous works, but rather "Picasso's Picassos," many of the paintings and sculptures treasured most by the artist, including his personal collection of works by friends and influences such as Matisse, Braque, Cézanne, and Rousseau. There is a detailed overview of Picasso's life and loves, with information in English. The museum opened in 1985 in the regal 17th-century Hôtel Salé as a permanent home for the collection, after much of it was given to the government by the artist's heirs to settle a hefty tax bill after the painter's death in 1973.

■**TIP→** While the museum projects its reopening for the end of 2013, delays are likely. Check the website for updates or call before you go. ⊠ *5 rue de Thorigny, Marais* ☎ *01–42–71–25–21* ⊕ *www.musee-picasso.fr* ✉ *Admission to be determined when opened* ☉ *No information until opening* Ⓜ *St-Sébastien.*

Place de la Bastille. Nothing remains of the infamous Bastille prison, destroyed more than 200 years ago, though tourists still ask bemused

Parisians where to find it. Until the late 1980s, there was little more to see here than a busy traffic circle ringing the Colonne de Juillet (July Column), a memorial to the victims of later uprisings in 1830 and 1848. The opening of the Opéra Bastille in 1989 rejuvenated the area, however, drawing art galleries, bars, and restaurants to the narrow streets, notably along rue de Lappe—once a haunt of Edith Piaf—and rue de la Roquette.

Before it became a prison, the Bastille St-Antoine was a defensive fortress with eight immense towers and a wide moat. It was built by Charles V in the late 14th century and transformed into a prison during the reign of Louis XIII (1610–43). Famous occupants included Voltaire, the Marquis de Sade, and the Man in the Iron Mask. On July 14, 1789, it was stormed by an angry mob that dramatically freed all of the remaining prisoners (there were only seven, including one lunatic), thereby launching the French Revolution. The roots of the revolt ran deep. Resentment toward Louis XVI and Marie-Antoinette had been building amid a severe financial crisis. There was a crippling bread shortage, and the free-spending monarch was blamed. When the king dismissed the popular finance minister, Jacques Necker, enraged Parisians took to the streets. They marched to Les Invalides, helping themselves to stocks of arms, then continued on to the Bastille. A few months later, what was left of the prison was razed—and 83 of its stones were carved into miniature Bastilles and sent to the provinces as a memento (you can see one of them in the Musée Carnavalet). The key to the prison was given to George Washington by Lafayette and has remained at Mount Vernon ever since. Today, nearly every major street demonstration in Paris—and there are many—passes through this square. ⊠ *Bastille* Ⓜ *Bastille.*

Place des Vosges. The oldest square in Paris and—dare we say it?—the most beautiful, the place des Vosges is one of Europe's oldest stabs at urban planning. The precise proportions offer a placid symmetry, but things weren't always so calm here. Four centuries ago this was the site of the Palais des Tournelles, home to King Henri II and Queen Catherine de Medici. The couple staged regular jousting tournaments, and during one of them, in 1559, Henry was fatally lanced in the eye. Catherine fled for the Louvre, abandoning her palace and ordering it destroyed. In 1612 it became the place Royal on the occasion of Louis XIII's engagement to Anne of Austria. Napoléon renamed it place des Vosges to honor the northeast region of Vosges, the first in the country to pony up taxes to the Revolutionary government.

At the base of the 36 redbrick-and-stone houses—9 on each side of the square—is an arcaded, covered walkway lined with art galleries, shops, and cafés. There's also an elementary school, a synagogue (whose barrel roof was designed by Gustav Eiffel), and several chic hotels. The formal, gated garden's perimeter is lined with chestnut trees; inside are a children's play area and a fountain.

Aside from hanging out in the park, people come here to see the house of the man who once lived at No. 6—Victor Hugo, the author of *Les Misérables* and *Notre-Dame de Paris* (aka *The Hunchback of Notre-Dame*).

■ TIP→ One of the best things about this park is that you're actually allowed to sit—or snooze or snack—on the grass during spring and summer. There is no better spot in the Marais for a picnic: you can pick up fixings at the nearby street market on Thursday and Saturday mornings (it's on boulevard Richard Lenoir between rues Amelot and St-Sabin). The most likely approach to the place des Vosges is from rue de Francs Bourgeois, the main shopping street. However, for a grander entrance walk along rue St-Antoine until you get to rue de Birague, which leads directly into the square. ⊠ *Off rue des Francs Bourgeois, near rue de Turenne, Marais* ☜ *Free* ☉ *Year-round* Ⓜ *Bastille or St-Paul.*

WORTH NOTING

Hôtel de Sully. This early Baroque gem, built in 1624, is one of the city's loveliest hôtels particuliers and has an equally lovely garden. Like much of the area, it fell into ruin until the 1950s, when it was rescued by the administration of French historic monuments, Centre des Monuments Nationaux, which is headquartered here. An extensive and much-delayed renovation, completed in 2012, has given the building a refreshed look. The on-site bookstore (with a 17th-century ceiling of exposed wooden beams) stocks specialized Paris guides in English. Walk through the garden past the Orangerie for a small passage to the nearby place des Vosges where Sully's best buddy, King Henri IV, would have lived had he not been assassinated in 1610. ⊠ *62 rue St-Antoine, Marais* ☏ *01–44–61–21–50 Hotel de Sully, 01–42–74–47–75 Jeu de Paume* ☉ *Tues.–Sun. 10–7 Hôtel de Sully; Tues.–Fri. noon–7, weekends 10–7 Jeu de Paume* Ⓜ *St-Paul.*

La Maison Rouge. One of the city's premier spaces for contemporary art, La Maison Rouge art foundation was established by former gallery owner Antoine de Galbert to fill a hole in the Parisian art world. Always edgy, often provocative, the foundation stages several temporary exhibitions each year in a cleverly renovated industrial space anchored by a central courtyard building that's painted bright red on the outside (hence the name). Past shows have included "*Tous Cannibales,*" themed around cannibalism, and "Memories of the Future," a death-obsessed display featuring artists from Hieronymus Bosch to Damien Hirst. Check the website to see what's on. ■ TIP→ Stop by the Rose Bakery near the entrance: it's the latest Parisian outpost of the popular English café. ⊠ *10 bd. de la Bastille, Bastille* ☏ *01–40–01–08–81* ⊕ *www. lamaisonrouge.org* ☜ *€7* ☉ *Wed.–Sun. 11–7, Thurs. 11–9* Ⓜ *Quai de la Rapée/Bastille.*

Maison de Victor Hugo. France's most famous scribe lived in this house on the northeast corner of place des Vosges between 1832 and 1848. It's now a museum dedicated to the multitalented author of *Les Misérables.* In Hugo's apartment on the second floor, you can see the tall desk, next to the short bed, where he began writing his masterwork *Les Miz* (as always, standing up). There are manuscripts and early editions of the novel on display, as well as others such as *The Hunchback of Notre Dame.* You can see illustrations of Hugo's writings by other artists, including Bayard's rendition of the impish Cosette holding her giant broom (which has graced countless *Les Miz* T-shirts). The collection includes many of Hugo's own, sometimes macabre, ink drawings (he was a fine artist) and furniture from several of his homes. Particularly impressive is the room of carved and painted Chinese-style wooden panels that Hugo designed for the house of his mistress, Juliet Drouet, on the island of Guernsey, when he was exiled there for agitating against Napoléon III. Try to spot the intertwined Vs and Js. (Hint: Look for the angel's trumpet in the left corner.) The first floor is dedicated to temporary exhibitions that often have modern ties to Hugo's work. ⊠ *6 pl. des Vosges, Marais* ☎ *01–42–72–10–16* ⊕ *www.musee-hugo. paris.fr* ▣ *Free; temporary exhibitions €7* ⊙ *Tues.–Sun. 10–6* Ⓜ *St-Paul.*

Maison Européenne de la Photographie (*Center for European Photography*). Much of the credit for the city's ascendancy as a hub of international photography goes to MEP and its director, Jean-Luc Monterosso, who also founded Paris's hugely successful Mois de la Photographie festival in November. The MEP hosts up to four simultaneous exhibitions, changing about every three months. Shows feature the work of an international crop of photographers and video artists. Works by superstar Annie Leibovitz or designer-photographer Karl Lagerfeld may overlap with a collection of self-portraits by an up-and-coming Japanese artist. MEP often stages retrospectives of the classics (by Doisneau, Cartier-Bresson, Man Ray, and others) from its vast private collection. Programs are available in English and guided tours are sometimes given in English (call ahead to find out). ⊠ *5 rue de Fourcy, Marais* ☎ *01–44–78–75–00* ⊕ *www.mep-fr.org* ▣ *€7, free Wed. after 5 pm* ⊙ *Wed.–Sun. 11–8* Ⓜ *St-Paul.*

Musée d'Art et d'Histoire du Judaïsme. This excellent museum traces the tempestuous history of French and European Jews through art and history. Opened in 1998 in the refined 17th-century Hôtel St-Aignan, exhibits have good explanatory texts in English, and the free English audio guide is a must; guided tours in English are also available on request. Highlights include 13th-century tombstones excavated in Paris; a wooden model of a destroyed Eastern European synagogue; a roomful of early paintings by Marc Chagall; and Christian Boltanski's stark, two-part tribute to Shoah (Holocaust) victims in the form of plaques on an outer wall naming the (mainly Jewish) inhabitants of the Hôtel St-Aignan in 1939, and canvas hangings with the personal data of the 13 residents who were deported and died in concentration camps. ■TIP➜ The rear-facing windows offer a view of the Jardin Anne Frank. To visit it, use the entrance on the impasse Berthaud, off rue Beaubourg, just north of rue Rambuteau. ⊠ *71 rue du Temple, Marais* ☎ *01–53–01–86–60* ⊕ *www.mahj.org* ▣ *€6.80* ⊙ *Weekdays 11–6, Sun. 10–6* Ⓜ *Rambuteau or Hôtel de Ville.*

THE ILE ST-LOUIS AND THE LATIN QUARTER

Set behind the Ile de la Cité is one of the most romantic spots in Paris, tiny Ile St-Louis. Of the two islands in the Seine—the Ile de la Cité is just to the west—the St-Louis best retains the romance and loveliness of *le Paris traditionnel.* It has remained in the heart of Parisians as it has remained in the heart of every tourist who came upon it by accident, and without warning—a tiny universe unto itself, shaded by trees, bordered by Seine-side quays, and overhung with ancient stone houses. Up until the 1800s it was reputed that some island residents never crossed the bridges to get to Paris proper—and once you discover the island's quiet charm, you may understand why. South of the Ile St-Louis on the Left Bank of the Seine is the bohemian **Quartier Latin** (Latin Quarter), the heart of student Paris for more than 800 years. The neighborhood takes its name from the fact that Latin was the common language of the students, who came from all over Europe. Today the area is full of cheap and cheerful cafés, bars, and shops, and even Roman ruins.

France's oldest university, *La Sorbonne*, was founded here in 1257 as a theology school; later it became the headquarters of the University of Paris. In 1968, the student revolution here had an explosive effect on French politics, resulting in major reforms in the education system. The aging *soixante-huitards* continue to influence French politics, as shown by the election of openly gay, Green Party member Bertrand Delanoë to the mayoralty of Paris.

TOP ATTRACTIONS

Ile St-Louis. One of the more fabled addresses in Paris, this tiny island has long harbored the rich and famous, including Chopin, Daumier, Helena Rubinstein, Chagall, and the Rothschilds. Like a tiny French village (albeit an unusually tony one) found in the heart of Paris, the island has long been prized for its "apartness": up to four decades ago, some residents never visited the "mainland." Ever since the early 17th-century, the entire isle has displayed striking architectural unity, thanks to the efforts of a group of property speculators who commissioned leading Baroque architect Louis Le Vau (1612–70) to design a series of imposing town houses, the queen of which—the Hôtel Lambert (Le Vau's masterpiece until he took he enlarged it umteen times to create Versailles)—still rides the prow of the island's east end. Other than some elegant facades and the picturesque quays along the Seine, there are no notable photo ops, but people love to visit here nevertheless, to savor the island's peace and, *bien sûr*, an ice-cream treat from famed Berthillon (located at 31 rue St-Louis-en-l'Ile). ⊠ *Pont-St-Louis, Pont-Marie, Pont de Sully* Ⓜ *Pont-Marie.*

Fodor's Choice ★ **Musée National du Moyen-Age** (*National Museum of the Middle Ages, also called the Musée Cluny*). Built on the ruins of Roman baths, the Hôtel de Cluny has been a museum since medievalist Alexandre Du Sommerard established his collection here in 1844. The ornate 15th-century mansion was created for the abbot of Cluny, leader of the mightiest monastery in France. Symbols of the abbot's power surround the building, from the crenellated walls that proclaimed his independence from the king, to the carved Burgundian grapes twining up the entrance that symbolize his valuable vineyards. The scallop shells (*coquilles St-Jacques*) covering the facade are a symbol of religious pilgrimage, another important source of income for the abbot; the well-traveled pilgrimage route to Spain once ran around the corner along the rue St-Jacques. The highlight of the museum's collection is the world-famous

Dame à la Licorne (*Lady and the Unicorn*) tapestry series, woven in the 16th century, probably in Belgium. The vermillion tapestries (Room 13) are an allegorical representation of the five senses. In each, a unicorn and a lion surround an elegant young woman against an elaborate *mille-fleur* (literally, 1,000 flowers) background. The enigmatic sixth tapestry is thought to be either a tribute to a sixth sense, perhaps intelligence, or a renouncement of the other senses. "To my only desire" is inscribed at the top. The collection also includes the original sculpted heads of the *Kings of Israel and Judah* from Notre-Dame, decapitated during the Revolution and discovered in 1977 in the basement of a French bank. The *frigidarium* (Room 9) is a stunning reminder of the city's cold-water Roman baths; the soaring space, painstakingly renovated in 2009, houses temporary exhibits. Also notable is the pocket-size chapel (Room 20) with its elaborate Gothic ceiling. Outside, in the place Paul Painlevé, is a charming medieval-style garden with flora depicted in the unicorn tapestries. ■**TIP→** The free audio guide in English is highly recommended. ⊠ *6 pl. Paul-Painlevé, Latin Quarter* 🕾 *01–53–73–78–00* ⊕ *www.musee-moyenage.fr* 🖃 *€8.50 (includes English audio guide), free 1st Sun. of month* ⊘ *Wed.–Mon. 9:15–5:45* Ⓜ *Cluny–La Sorbonne.*

WORTH NOTING

Institut du Monde Arabe. This eye-catching metal-and-glass tower by architect Jean Nouvel cleverly uses metal diaphragms in the shape of square Arabic-style screens to work like a camera lens, opening and closing to control the flow of sunlight. The vast cultural center's layout is intended to reinterpret the traditional enclosed Arab courtyard. Inside, there are various spaces—among them a museum, inaugurated in 2012, that explores the culture and religion of the 22 Arab League member nations. With the addition of elements from the Louvre's holdings and private donors, the museum's impressive collection includes Islamic art, artifacts, ceramics, and textiles, which are displayed on four floors. There is also a performance space, a sound-and-image center, a library, and a bookstore. Temporary exhibitions usually have information and an audio guide in English. ■**TIP→** Glass elevators whisk you to the ninth floor, where you can sip mint tea in the rooftop café, Le Ziryab, while feasting on one of the best views in Paris. ⊠ *1 rue des Fossés-St-Bernard, Latin Quarter* 🕾 *01–40–51–38–38* ⊕ *www.imarabe.org* 🖃 *€8* ⊘ *Tues.–Fri. 10–6, weekends 10–7, until 9:30 on Thurs.* Ⓜ *Cardinal Lemoine.*

Panthéon. Rome has St. Peter's, London has St. Paul's, and Paris has the Panthéon, whose enormous dome dominates the Left Bank. Built as the church of Ste-Geneviève, the patron saint of Paris, it was later converted to an all-star mausoleum for some of France's biggest names, including Voltaire, Zola, Dumas, Rousseau, and Hugo. Pierre and Marie Curie were reinterred here together in 1995. Begun in 1764, the building was almost complete when the French Revolution erupted. By then, architect Jacques-German Soufflot had died—supposedly from worrying that the 220-foot-high dome would collapse. He needn't have fretted: the dome is so perfect that Foucault used it in his famous pendulum test to prove the Earth rotates on its axis. A model of the pendulum still hangs from the dome and the staff offer demonstrations (there's also a

Anchoring the western end of the Ile de la Cité, the square du Vert-Galant is a great place to picnic—you can almost dangle your feet in the Seine.

video in English that explains the theory). Free guided tours run several times a day, in French only. There is information in English at the entrance and on boards in the crypt. ⊠ *Pl. du Panthéon, Latin Quarter* ☎ *01–44–32–18–00* ⊕ *pantheon.monuments-nationaux.fr/* ☑ *€8.50* ⊗ *Apr.–Sept., daily 10–6:30; Oct.–Mar., daily 10–6* Ⓜ *Cardinal Lemoine; RER: Luxembourg.*

FROM ORSAY TO ST-GERMAIN-DES-PRÉS

If you had to choose the most classically Parisien neighborhood in Paris, this would be it. St-Germain-des-Prés has it all: genteel blocks lined with upscale art galleries, storied cafés, designer boutiques, and a fine selection of museums. Cast your eyes upward after dark and you may spy a frescoed ceiling in a tony apartment. These historic streets can get quite crowded, so mind your elbows and plunge in.

This quartier is named for the oldest church in Paris, **St-Germain-des-Prés,** and it's become a prized address for Parisians and expats alike. Despite its pristine facade, though, this wasn't always silver-spoon territory. Claude Monet and Auguste Renoir shared a cramped studio at 20 rue Visconti, and the young Picasso barely eked out an existence in a room on the rue de Seine. By the 1950s St-Germain bars bopped with jazz, and the likes of Albert Camus, Jean-Paul Sartre, and Simone de Beauvoir puffed away on Gaulois while discussing the meaninglessness of existence at Café Flore. At the southern end of this district is the city's poshest park, the Jardin du Luxembourg, which is also home to the **Musée du Luxembourg.** This small museum plays host to excellent temporary exhibitions. The **Musée Delacroix,** in lovely place Furstenburg, is home to a small collection of the Romantic master's works. Not far away is the stately **Église St-Sulpice,** where you can see two impressive Delacroix frescoes.

Nearby in the 7e arrondissement, the star attraction is the Musée d'Orsay, home to a world-class collection of Impressionist paintings in a converted Belle Époque rail station on the Seine. It's famous for having some of Paris's longest lines, so a visit to d'Orsay should be planned with care. Farther along the river, the 18th-century Palais Bourbon—now home to the National Assembly—sets the tone for the 7e arrondissement. This is Edith Wharton territory, where aristocrats live in gorgeous, sprawling, apartments or maisons particuliers (*very* private town houses). Embassies—and the Hôtel Matignon, residence of the French prime minister—line the surrounding streets, overshadowed by the Hôtel des Invalides, whose gold-leaf dome climbs heavenward above the regal tomb of Napoléon. The Rodin Museum—set in a gorgeous 18th-century mansion—is only a short walk away. Less well-known is sculptor Aristide Maillol, whose impressive private collection is housed nearby in the Musée Maillol.

TOP ATTRACTIONS

Fodor's Choice
★

Carrefour de Buci. Just behind the neighborhood's namesake St-Germain church, this colorful crossroads (carrefour is French for "intersection") was once a notorious Rive Gauche landmark. During the 18th century it contained a gallows, and during the French Revolution the army used the site to enroll its first volunteers. Many royalists and priests lost their heads here during the bloody course of the Terror. There's certainly nothing sinister about the carrefour today; brightly colored flowers are for sale alongside take-out ice-cream and snack kiosks. Devotees of the superb, traditional bakery Carton (at No. 6) line up for pastries (try their *tuiles* cookies). ⊠ *St-Germain-des-Prés* Ⓜ *Mabillon.*

Fodor's Choice
★

Cour du Commerce St-André. Like an 18th-century engraving come to life, this charming street arcade is a remnant of *ancien* Paris with its enormous uneven cobblestones. Famed for its rabble-rousing inhabitants—journalist Jean-Paul Marat ran the Revolutionary newspaper *L'Ami du Peuple* at No. 8, and the agitator Georges Danton lived at No. 20—it's also home to Le Procope, Paris's oldest café. This passageway also contains a turret from the 12th-century wall of Philippe-Auguste (visible through the windows at No. 4, the chocolate shop Un Dimanche à Paris). ⊠ *Linking bd. St-Germain and rue St-André-des-Arts, St-Germain-des-Prés* Ⓜ *Odéon.*

Église St-Germain-des-Prés. Paris's oldest church was built to shelter a simple shard of wood, said to be a relic of Jesus's cross brought back from Spain in AD 542. Vikings came down the Seine and sacked the church, and Revolutionaries used it to store gunpowder. Yet the elegant building has defied history's abuses: its 11th-century Romanesque tower continues to be the central symbol of the neighborhood. The colorful 19th-century frescoes in the nave are by Hippolyte Flandrin, a pupil of the classical master Ingres. The church stages superb organ concerts and recitals. Step inside for spiritual nourishment, or pause in the square to people-watch—there's usually a street musician tucked against the church wall, out of the wind. ✉ *Pl. St-Germain-des-Prés, St-Germain-des-Prés* ☎ *01–55–42–81–10* ⊕ *www.eglise-sgp.org* ☉ *Daily 9–7* Ⓜ *St-Germain-des-Prés.*

NEED A BREAK?

Les Deux Magots, at 6 place St-Germain-des-Prés, and the neighboring **Café de Flore,** at 172 boulevard St-Germain, have been duking it out on this bustling corner in St-Germain for more than a century. Les Deux Magots, the snootier of the two, is named for the two Chinese figurines, or *magots,* inside, and has hosted the likes of Oscar Wilde, Hemingway, James Joyce, and Richard Wright. Jean-Paul Sartre and Simone du Beauvoir frequented both establishments, though they are claimed by the Flore. The two cafés remain packed, though these days you're more likely to rub shoulders with tourists than with philosophers. Still, if you're in search of that certain *je ne sais quoi* of the Rive Gauche, you can do no better than to station yourself at one of the sidewalk tables—or at a window table on a wintry day—to watch the passing parade. Stick to a croissant and an overpriced coffee or an early-evening apéritif; the food is expensive and nothing special.

Fodor's Choice
★

Hôtel des Invalides. The Baroque complex known as Les Invalides (pronounced *lehz-ahn-vah-leed*) is the eternal home of Napoléon Bonaparte (1769–1821) or, more precisely, the little dictator's remains, which lie entombed under the towering golden dome.

Louis XIV ordered the facility built in 1670 to house disabled soldiers (hence the name), and at one time 4,000 military men lived here. Today, a portion of it still serves as a veterans' residence and hospital. The Musée de l'Armée, containing an exhaustive collection of military artifacts from antique armor to weapons, is also here as is the World Wars Department, which chronicles the great wars that ravaged Europe.

If you see only a single sight, make it the Église du Dome (one of Les Invalides' two churches) at the back of the complex. Napoléon's tomb was moved here in 1840 from the island of Saint Helena, where he died in forced exile. The emperor's body is protected by a series of no fewer than six coffins—one set inside the next, sort of like a Russian nesting doll—which is then encased in a sarcophagus of red quartzite. The bombastic tribute is ringed by statues symbolizing Napoléon's campaigns of conquest. To see more Napoléoniana, check out the collection in the Musée de l'Armée featuring his trademark gray frock coat and huge bicorne hat. Look for the figurines reenacting the famous coronation scene when Napoléon crowns his empress, Josephine. (Notice the heavily rouged cheeks; Napoléon hated pale skin.) You can see a grander version of this scene hanging in the Louvre by the painter David.

The Esplanade des Invalides, the great lawns in front of the building, are favorite spots for pickup soccer, Frisbee games, sunbathing, and dog walking—despite signs asking you to stay off the grass. ■**TIP→** The best entrance to use is at the southern end, on place Vauban (avenue de Tourville). The ticket office is here, as is Napoléon's Tomb. There are automatic ticket machines at the main entrance on the place des

Invalides. ⊠ *Pl. des Invalides, Tour Eiffel* ☎ *01–44–42–38–77* ⊕ *www. invalides.org* ✍ *€9.50* ⊘ *Église du Dôme and museums Apr.–Oct., daily 10–6; Nov.–Mar., daily 10–5. Closed 1st Mon. of every month Oct– June* Ⓜ *La Tour-Maubourg/Invalides.*

FAMILY

Fodor'sChoice

★

Jardin du Luxembourg. The Luxembourg Gardens has all that is charming, unique, and befuddling about Parisian parks: cookie-cutter trees, ironed-and-pressed walkways, sculpted flower beds, and immaculate emerald lawns meant for admiring, not for lounging. The tree- and bench-lined paths are, however, a marvelous reprieve from the bustle of the two neighborhoods it borders: the Quartier Latin and St-Germain-des-Prés. Beautifully austere during the winter months, the garden grows intoxicating as spring brings blooming beds of daffodils, tulips, and hyacinths, and the circular pools teem with boats nudged along by children. The park's northern boundary is dominated by the Palais du Luxembourg and the Sénat (Senate), which is one of two chambers that make up the Parliament.

The original inspiration for the gardens came from Marie de Medici, nostalgic for the Boboli Gardens of her native Florence. She is commemorated by the Fontaine de Medicis.

Les Marionettes du Théâtre du Luxembourg is a timeless attraction, where, on weekends at 11 and 3:15 and Wednesday at 3:15 (hours may vary), you can catch classic *guignols* (marionette shows) for €4.70. The wide-eyed kids might be the real attraction—their expressions of utter surprise, despair, and glee have fascinated the likes of Henri Cartier-Bresson and François Truffaut. The park also has a merry-go-round, swings, and pony rides; the bandstand hosts free concerts on summer afternoons.

Check out the rotating photography exhibits hanging on the perimeter fence near the entrance on the boulevard St-Michel and rue Vaugirard.

■**TIP→** If the grass is en repos, a nice way of saying "stay off," feel free to move the green chairs around to create a picnic spot or people-watching perch. If you want to burn off that breakfast pain au chocolat, there's a well-maintained trail around the perimeter that is frequented by a surprising (for France) number of joggers. If you're looking for a familiar face, one of the original (miniature) casts of the Statue of Liberty was installed in the gardens in 1906. ⊠ *Bordered by bd. St-Michel and rues de Vaugirard, de Medicis, Guynemer, and Auguste-Comte, St-Germain-des-Prés* ⊕ *guignolduluxembourg.monsite-orange.fr Les Marionettes du Théâtre du Luxembourg* ✍ *Free* ⊘ *Daily 7:30–dusk (hrs may vary depending on season)* Ⓜ *Odéon; RER: B Luxembourg.*

Fodor'sChoice

★

Musée d'Orsay. Opened in 1986, this gorgeously renovated Belle Époque train station displays a world-famous collection of Impressionist and Postimpressionist paintings on three floors. To visit the exhibits in a roughly chronologic manner, start on the first floor, take the escalators to the top, and end on the second. If you came to see the biggest names here, head straight for the top floor and work your way down. English audio guides and free color-coded museum maps (both available just past the ticket booths) will help you plot your route. Note, though, that renovations will be ongoing until 2015, so expect some gallery closings.

Continued on page 99

THE SEINE

No matter how you approach Paris—historically, geographically, or emotionally—the Seine flows through its heart, dividing the City of Light into two banks, the *Rive Droite* (Right Bank) and the *Rive Gauche* (Left Bank).

The Seine has long been used as a means for transportation and commerce and although there are no longer any factories along its banks, all manner of boats still ply the water. You'll see tugboats, fire and police boats, the occasional bobbing houseboat, and many kinds of tour boats; it might sound hokey, but there's really no better introduction to the City of Light than a boat cruise, and there are several options, depending on whether you want commentary on the sights or not. Many of the city's most famous attractions can be seen from the river, and are especially spectacular at dusk, as those celebrated lights of Paris glint against the sky.

FROM ILE DES CYGNES TO THE LOUVRE

Musée d'Orsay clock

Petit Palais

Pont de l'Alma

Grand Palais

Assemblée Nationale

Pont Alexandre III

Bir Hakeim Bridge

Eiffel Tower

Ile des Cygnes

The **Zouave of the Pont de l'Alma**, sole survivor of the bridge's four original stone soldiers, is used by Parisians to judge water levels.

Whether you hop on a boat cruise or stroll the quays at your own pace, the Seine comes alive when you get off the busy streets of Paris. At the western edge of the city on the **Ile des Cygnes** (literally the Isle of Swans), a small version of the Statue of Liberty stands guard. Auguste Bartholdi designed the original statue, given as a gift from France to America in 1886, and in 1889 a group of Americans living in Paris installed this ¼ scale bronze replica—it's 37 feet, 8 inches tall.

You can get to the Ile des Cygnes via the **Bir Hakeim** bridge named for the 1942 Free French battle in Libya—whose lacy architecture horizontally echoes the nearby **Eiffel Tower**. You might recognize the view of the bridge from the movie *Last Tango in Paris.*

As you make your way downstream you can drool in envy at the houseboats docked near the bronze lamp–lined Pont Alexandre III. No other bridge over the Seine epitomizes the fin-de-siècle frivolity of the Belle Epoque: It seems as much created of cake frosting and sugar sculptures as of stone and iron, and makes quite the backdrop for fashion shoots and weddings. The elaborate decorations include Art Nouveau lamps, cherubs, nymphs, and winged horses at either end. The bridge was built, like the Grand Palais and Petit Palais nearby, for the 1900 World's Fair.

Along the banks of the Seine

Bouquinistes

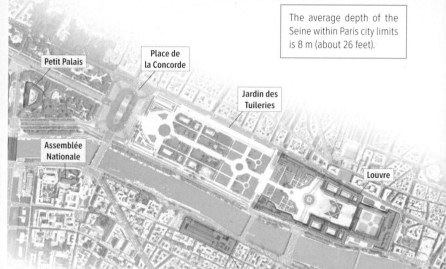

Petit Palais

Place de la Concorde

The average depth of the Seine within Paris city limits is 8 m (about 26 feet).

Jardin des Tuileries

Assemblée Nationale

Louvre

Musée d'Orsay

Past the dome of the is the 18th-century neoclassical façade of the **Assemblée Nationale**, the palace that houses the French Parliament. Across the river stands the **Place de la Concorde.** Also look for the great railway station clocks of the Musée d'Orsay that once allowed writer Anaïs Nin to coordinate her lovers' visits to her houseboat, moored below the Tuileries. The palatial **Louvre** museum, on the Right Bank, seems to go on and on as you continue up the Seine.

PERFECT PICNIC PLACES

Paris abounds with romantic spots to pause for a picnic or a bottle of wine, but the Seine has some of the best.

Try scouting out a place on the point of Ile St-Louis; at sunset you can watch the sun slip beneath receding arches of stone bridges.

The long, low quays of the Left Bank, with its public sculpture work, are perfect for an alfresco lunch.

FROM PONT DES ARTS TO JARDIN DES PLANTES

At the water's edge.

Pont des Arts
Pont Neuf
Châtelet Theatres
Hotel de Ville
Institut de France
Ile de la Cité
Conciergerie
Notre-Dame

The Institut de France

Parisians love to linger on the elegant **Pont des Arts** footbridge that streches between the palatial Louvre museum and the Institut de France. Napoléon commissioned the original cast-iron bridge with nine arches; it was rebuilt in 1984 with seven arches.

Five carved stone arches of the **Pont Neuf**—the name means "new bridge" but it actually dates from 1605 and is the oldest bridge in Paris—connect the Left Bank to the Ile de la Cité. Another seven arches connect the Ile and the Right Bank. The pale gray curving balustrades include a row of stone heads; some say they're caricatures of King Henry IV's ministers, glaring down at the river.

On the Right Bank at the end of the Ile de la Cité is the **Hôtel de Ville (City Hall)**—this area was once the main port of Paris, crowded with boats delivering everything from wood and produce to visitors and slaves.

Medieval turrets rise up from **Ile de la Cité,** part of the original royal palace; the section facing the Right Bank includes the **Conciergerie**, where Marie Antoinette was imprisoned in 1793 before her execution.

PARIS PLAGE

Paris Plage, literally Paris Beach, is Mayor Bertrand Delanoë's summer gift to Parisians and visitors. In August the roads along the Seine are closed, tons of sand are brought in and decorated with palm trees, and a slew of activities are organized, from free early-morning yoga classes to evening samba and swimming (not in the Seine, but in the fabulous Josephine Baker swimming pool). Going topless is discouraged, but hammocks, kids' playgrounds, rock-climbing, and cafés keep everyone entertained.

View of the Seine and the Pont des Arts

Paris Plage

Notre-Dame

Also on the Ile de la Cité is the cathedral of **Notre-Dame,** a stunning sight from the water. From the side it looks almost like a great boat sailing down the Seine.

As you pass the end of the island, you'll notice a small grated window: this is the evocative Deportation Memorial.

Next to the Ile de la Cite is the lovely residential **Ile St-Louis**; keep an eye out for the "proper" depth measuring stick on Ile St-Louis, near the Tour d'Argent restaurant.

Sightseeing boats turn near the public sculpture garden at the **Jardin des Plantes**, where you'll get a view of the huge national library, **Bibliothèque François Mitterrand**—the four towers look like opened books. Moored in the Seine near the bibliothèque is the Josephine Baker swimming pool with its retractable roof. Paris used to have several floating pools, including the elaborate Piscine Deligny, which was used in the Paris Olympics in 1924; it inexplicably sank in 1993.

Ile St-Louis

Jardin des Plantes

Bibliothéque Francois Mitterrand

PLANNING A BOAT TOUR ON THE SEINE

■ Most boat tours last about an hour; in the winter, even the interior of the boats can be cool, so take an extra scarf or sweater.

■ It never hurts to book ahead since schedules vary with the season and the (unpredictable) height and mood of the Seine.

■ As you float along, consider that Parisians used similar boats as a form of public transportation until the 1930s. Not really like Venice; more like the Staten Island ferry.

■ For optimal Seine enjoyment, combine a boat tour with a stroll—walk around Ile St-Louis, stroll along the Left Bank quays near the Pont Neuf, or start at the quay below the Louvre and walk to the Eiffel Tower, past the fabulous private houseboats.

WHICH BOAT IS FOR YOU?

If you want... lots of information	☎ 01–42–25–96–10 ⊕ www.bateaux-mouches.fr ⊠ €11 Ⓜ Alma-Marceau	
	The massive, double-decker **Bateaux Mouches,** literally "fly boats," offer prerecorded commentary in seven languages.	Departs from the Pont de l'Alma (Right Bank) daily April to September: every 20, 30, or 45 min., from 10:15 AM to 11 PM; daily: October through March approximately every hour from 11 AM to 9 PM.
If you want... to do your own thing	☎ 08–25–05–01–01 ⊕ www.batobus.com ⊠ €15, €18 *for 2 consecutive days*	
	The commentary-free **Batobus** boat-bus service allows you to hop on and off at any of the eight stops along the river. (Note: there's no service early January through early February.)	Departs from 8 locations: Eiffel Tower, Champs Elysées, Musée d'Orsay, Louvre, St. Germain-des-Pres, Notre-Dame, Hotel de Ville, and Jardin des Plantes.
If you want... to impress a date or client	☎ 01–44–54–14–70 ⊕ www.yachtsdeparis.fr ⊠ €198–249 *for dinner cruise* Ⓜ Bastille	
	The **Yachts de Paris** specialize in gorgeous boats—expensive, yes, but glamorous as all get-out, with surprisingly good meals.	Dinner cruises leave from Port Henri IV (near Bastille).
If you want... the Seine, with music	☎ 01–43–54–50–04 ⊕ www.calife.com ⊠ €49 *and up for dinner cruise* Ⓜ Louvre-Rivoli	
	Le Calife is the Aladdin's lamp of the Seine, moored across from the Louvre. Jazz, piano music, and evenings devoted to French song makes this a quirky and charming choice.	Departs from the Quai Malaquais, opposite the Louvre and just west of the Pont des Arts footbridge.

Ground floor: Galleries off the main alley feature early works by Manet and Cézanne in addition to pieces by masters such as Delacroix and Ingres. Later works by the likes of Toulouse-Lautrec are found in Salle 10. The Pavillon Amont has Courbet's masterpieces *L'Enterrement à Ornans* and *Un Atelier du Peintre*. His realist painting influenced the Impressionists, whose work is upstairs. Paintings by lesser-known academic artists show the prevailing artistic atmosphere of the period. More experimental visions, including Gustave Moreau's myth-laden decadence and Puvis de Chavanne's surprisingly modern lines, make the leap into Impressionism easier to understand. Hanging in Salle 14 is Édouard Manet's *Olympia*, a painting which pokes fun at the fashion for all things Greek and Roman (his nubile subject is a 19th-century courtesan, not a classical goddess). Photography and temporary exhibits are also on the ground floor.

Top floor: Impressionism gets going here, with iconic works by Degas, Pissarro, Sisley, and Renoir. Don't miss Monet's series on the cathedral at Rouen and, of course, samples of his *Water Lilies*. Other selections by these artists are housed in galleries on the ground floor.

Second floor: An exquisite collection of sculpture as well as Art Nouveau furniture and decorative objects is housed here. There are rare surviving works by Hector Guimard (designer of the swooping green Paris métro entrances), plus Lalique and Tiffany glassware. Postimpressionist galleries include work by van Gogh and Gauguin, while Neoimpressionist galleries highlight Seurat and Signac.

■ TIP➜ Lines here are among the worst in Paris. Book ahead online or buy a Museum Pass; then go directly to entrance C. Otherwise, go early. Thursday evening the museum is open until 9:45 pm and less crowded. The elegant Musée d'Orsay Restaurant once served patrons of the 1900 World's Fair; the Café du Lion offers quick fare on the ground floor by the entrance; there's also a café and a self-service cafeteria on the top floor just after the Cézanne galleries. Don't miss the views of Sacré-Coeur from the balcony—this is the Paris that inspired the Impressionists. The d'Orsay is closed Monday, unlike the Pompidou and the Louvre, which are closed Tuesday. ⊠ *1 rue de la Légion d'Honneur, St-Germain-des-Prés* ☎ *01-40-49-48-14* ⊕ *www.musee-orsay.fr* ⊠ *€12 (€9 without special exhibit); €9.50 (€6.50 without special exhibit) after 4:30 except Thurs. after 6* ☉ *Tues.–Sun. 9:30–6, Thurs. 9:30 am–9:45 pm* Ⓜ *Solférino; RER: Musée d'Orsay.*

Musée Rodin. Auguste Rodin (1840–1917) briefly made his home and studio in the Hôtel Biron, a grand 18th-century mansion that now houses a museum dedicated to his work. He died rich and famous, but many of the sculptures that earned him a place in art history were originally greeted with contempt by the general public, which was unprepared for his powerful brand of sexuality and raw physicality. During a much-needed, multi-year renovation that has closed parts of the Hôtel Biron (it's set to finish in late 2014), the museum is showcasing a pared-down, "greatest-hits" selection of Rodin's works.

Most of his best-known sculptures are in the gardens. The front garden is dominated by *The Gates of Hell* (circa 1880). Inspired by the monumental bronze doors of Italian Renaissance churches, Rodin set out to illustrate stories from Dante's *Divine Comedy.* He worked on the sculpture for more than 30 years, and it served as a "sketch pad" for many of his later works. Look carefully and you can see miniature versions of *The Kiss* (bottom right), *The Thinker* (top center), and *The Three Shades* (top center).

Inside the museum, look for *The Bronze Age,* which was inspired by the sculptures of Michelangelo: this piece was so realistic that critics accused Rodin of having cast a real body in plaster. There's also a room (condensed during renovation) of works by Camille Claudel (1864–1943), Rodin's student and longtime mistress, who was a remarkable sculptor in her own right. Her torturous relationship with Rodin eventually drove her out of his studio—and out of her mind. In 1913 she was packed off to an asylum, where she remained until her death.

■**TIP➔** For €1 you can enjoy the 7 acres of gardens. If you want to linger, the Café du Musée Rodin serves meals and snacks in the shade of the garden's linden trees. As you enter, a space on the right houses temporary exhibitions. An English audio guide (€6) is available for the permanent collection and for temporary exhibitions. Skip the line by buying a ticket online (€1.80 fee). ⊠ *79 rue de Varenne, Trocadéro/Tour Eiffel* ☎ *01–44–18–61–10* ⊕ *www.musee-rodin.fr* ✆ *€9; €1 gardens only; free 1st Sun. of month* ☉ *Tues.–Sun. 10–5:45 except Wed. until 8:45; closed Mon.* Ⓜ *Varenne.*

WORTH NOTING

Musée Delacroix. The final home of artist Eugène Delacroix (1798–1863) contains only a small collection of his sketches and drawings. But you can check out the studio he had built in the large garden at the back to work on frescoes he created for St-Sulpice Church, where they remain on display today. The museum also plays host to temporary exhibitions, such as Delacroix's experiments with photography. France's foremost Romantic painter had the good luck to live on **place Furstenberg,** one of the smallest, most romantic squares in Paris: seeing it is reason enough to come. ⊠ *6 rue Furstenberg, St-Germain-des-Prés* ☎ *01–44–41–86–50* ⊕ *www.musee-delacroix.fr* ✆ *€5 (€11 with a joint ticket to the Louvre)* Ⓜ *St-Germain-des-Prés.*

MONTMARTRE

Montmartre has become almost too charming for its own good. Yes, it feels like a village (if you can see through the crowds); yes, there are working artists here (though far fewer than there used to be); and, yes, the best view of Paris is yours for free from the top of the hill (if there's no haze). That's why on any weekend day, year-round, you can find hordes of visitors crowding these cobbled alleys, scaling the staircases that pass for streets, and queuing to see **Sacré-Coeur,** the "sculpted cloud," at the summit.

If you're lucky enough to have a little corner of Montmartre to yourself, you'll understand why locals love it so. Come on a weekday, or in the morning or later in the evening. Stroll around **place des Abbesses,** where the rustic houses and narrow streets escaped the heavy hand of urban planner Baron Haussmann. Until 1860, the area was in fact a separate village, dotted with windmills. Today, there are only two wind-mills left as well as one quaint vineyard; you cannot visit the vineyard. Always a draw for bohemians and artists, many of whom had studios at **Bateau-Lavoir** and **Musée de Montmartre,** resident painters have included Géricault, Renoir, Suzanne Valadon, Picasso, Van Gogh, and, of course, Henri Toulouse-Lautrec, whose iconic paintings of the cancan dancers at the **Moulin Rouge** are now souvenir-shop fixtures from **place du Tertre** to the Tour Eiffel. You can still see shows at the Moulin Rouge and the pocket-size cabaret **Lapin Agile**, though much of the entertainment here is on the seedier side—the area around Pigalle is the city's largest red-light district. The quartier is a favorite of filmmakers, and visitors still seek out Café des Deux Moulins (⊠ *15 rue Lepic*), the real-life café where Audrey Tautou worked in 2001's *Amélie*. Movie-biz roots run deep—the blockbuster *Moulin Rouge* took its inspiration from here.

TOP ATTRACTIONS

Moulin de la Galette. Of the 14 windmills (*moulins*) that used to sit atop this hill, only two remain. They're known collectively as Moulin de la Galette—the name being taken from the bread that the owners used to produce. The more storied of the two is Le Blute-fin. In the late 1800s there was a dance hall on the site, famously captured by Renoir (you can see the painting in the Musée d'Orsay). A face-lift recently restored the windmill to its 19th-century glory; however, it is on private land and can't be visited. Down the street is the other moulin, Le Radet. ⊠ *Le Blute-fin, corner of rue Lepic and rue Tholozé, Montmartre* Ⓜ *Abbesses.*

Place des Abbesses. This triangular square is typical of the countrified style that has made Montmartre famous. Now a hub for shopping and people-watching, the *place* is surrounded by hip boutiques, sidewalk cafés, and shabby-chic restaurants—a prime habitat for the young, neo-bohemian crowd and a sprinkling of expats. Trendy streets like rue Houdon and rue des Martyrs have attracted small designers, an inter-national beer seller, and even a cupcake shop. Some retailers remain open on Sunday afternoon. ⊠ *Intersection of rue des Abbesses and rue la Vieuville, Montmartre* Ⓜ *Abbesses.*

Fodor's Choice
★

Sacré-Coeur. It's hard to not feel as though you're climbing up to heaven when you visit Sacred Heart Basilica, the white castle in the sky, perched atop Montmartre. The French government commissioned it in 1873 to symbolize the return of self-confidence after the devastating years of the Commune and Franco-Prussian War; and architect Paul Aba-die employed elements from Romanesque and Byzantine styles when designing it—a mélange many critics dismissed as gaudy. Construction lasted until World War I, and the church was finally consecrated in 1919.

Many people come to Sacré-Coeur to admire the superlative view from the top of the 271-foot-high dome, the second-highest point in Paris after the Eiffel Tower. If you opt to skip the climb up the spiral staircase, the view from the front steps is still ample compensation for the trip.

Inside, expect another visual treat—namely the massive golden mosaic set high above the choir. Created in 1922 by Luc-Olivier Merson, *Christ*

Residents of Montmartre often talk about "going down into Paris," and after climbing the many steps to get here you'll understand why.

in Majesty depicts Christ with a golden heart and outstretched arms, surrounded by various figures, including the Virgin Mary and Joan of Arc. It remains one of the largest mosaics of its kind. Also worth noting are the seemingly endless vaulted arches in the basilica's crypt; the portico's bronze doors, decorated with biblical scenes; and the stained-glass windows, which were installed in 1922, destroyed by a bombing during World War II (there were miraculously no deaths), and later rebuilt in 1946. In the basilica's 262 foot-high campanile hangs La Savoyarde, one of the world's heaviest bells, weighing about 19 tons.

■**TIP→** The best time to visit Sacré-Coeur is early morning or early evening, and preferably not on a Sunday, when the crowds are thick. If you're coming to worship, there are daily Masses. Photographers angling for the perfect shot of the church should aim for a clear blue-sky day or arrive at dusk, when the pink sky plays nicely with the lights of the basilica. To avoid the steps, take the funicular, which costs one métro ticket each way. ⊠ *Pl. du Parvis-du-Sacré-Coeur, Montmartre* ☎ *01-53-41-89-00* ⊕ *www.sacre-coeur-montmartre.com* ✉ *Basilica free, dome €6, crypt €3, combined ticket €8* ☉ *Basilica daily 6 am–11 pm; dome and crypt Oct.–Mar., daily 9–6; Apr.–Sept., daily 9–7* Ⓜ *Anvers, plus funicular; Jules Joffrin plus Montmartrobus.*

WORTH NOTING

Bateau-Lavoir (*Wash-barge*). The birthplace of Cubism isn't open to the public, but a display in the front window details this unimposing spot's rich history. Montmartre poet Max Jacob coined the name (it means "wash barge") because the original structure here reminded him of the laundry boats that used to float in the Seine, and he joked that the

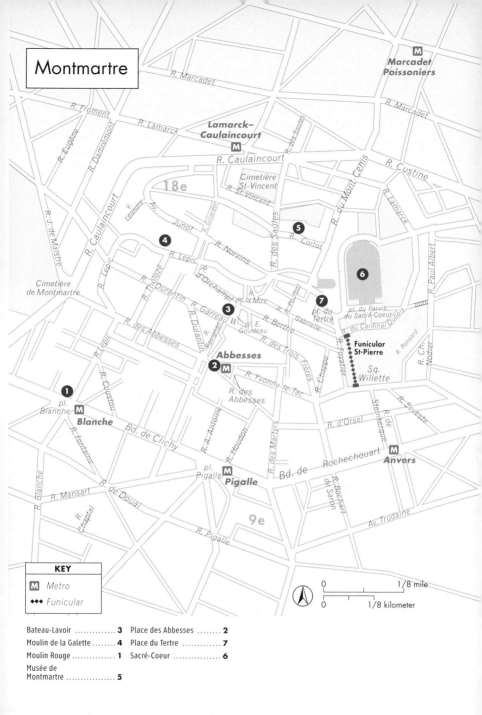

Montmartre

KEY

M *Metro*

◆◆◆ *Funicular*

0 _____ 1/8 mile

0 _____ 1/8 kilometer

warren of paint-splattered artists' studios needed a good hosing down (wishful thinking, since the building had only one water tap). It was in the Bateau-Lavoir that, early in the 20th century, Pablo Picasso, Georges Braque, and Juan Gris made their first bold stabs at Cubism, and Picasso painted the groundbreaking *Les Demoiselles d'Avignon* in 1906–07. The experimental works of the artists weren't met with open arms, even in liberal Montmartre. All but the facade was rebuilt after a fire in 1970. Like the original building, though, the current incarnation houses artists and their studios. ⊠ *13 pl. Émile-Goudeau, Montmartre* Ⓜ *Abbesses.*

Moulin Rouge. When this world-famous cabaret opened in 1889, aristocrats, professionals, and the working classes all flocked in to ogle the scandalous performers (the cancan was considerably more kinky in Toulouse-Lautrec's day, when girls kicked off their knickers). There's not much to see from the outside except for tourist buses and sex shops, but this square, called place Blanche, takes its name from the chalky haze once churned up by carts carrying plaster of Paris down from the quarries. Souvenir seekers should check out the Moulin Rouge gift shop (around the corner at 11 rue Lepic), which sells better-quality official merchandise, from jewelry to sculpture, by reputable French makers. (⇨ *See Nightlife.*) ⊠ *82 bd. de Clichy, Montmartre* ☎ *01–53–09–82–82* ⊕ *www.moulinrouge.fr* Ⓜ *Blanche.*

Musée de Montmartre. In its turn-of-the-20th-century heyday, the building—now home to Montmartre's historical museum—was a studio block for painters, writers, and cabaret artists. Foremost among them were Renoir (who painted the *Moulin de la Galette,* an archetypal scene of sun-drenched revelers, while he lived here) and Maurice Utrillo. The museum, with a lovely garden, has a charming permanent collection recapping the area's history, notably the many Toulouse-Lautrec posters and original Eric Satie scores. An ambitious renovation that will double the current museum's space is due to be completed by 2014. The museum will remain open in the meantime. ⊠ *12 rue Cortot, Montmartre* ☎ *01–49–25–89–37* ⊕ *www.museedemontmartre.fr* ⊠ *€8* ☉ *Daily 10–6* Ⓜ *Lamarck Caulaincourt.*

Place du Tertre. Artists have peddled their wares in this square for centuries. Though busloads of tourists have changed the atmosphere, if you come off-season—when the air is chilly and the streets are bare—you can almost feel what is was like when up-and-coming Picassos lived in the houses, which today are given over to souvenir shops and cafés. ⊠ *Pl. du Tertre, Montmartre* Ⓜ *Abbesses.*

WHERE TO EAT

Updated by Jennifer Ditsler-Ladonne

A new wave of culinary confidence has been running through one of the world's great food cities and spilling over both banks of the Seine. Whether cooking up *grand-mère*'s roast chicken and *riz au lait* or placing a whimsical hat of cotton candy atop wild-strawberry-and-rose ice cream, Paris chefs have been breaking free from the tyranny of tradition and following their passions.

Emblematic of this movement is the proliferation of trained bistro chefs who have opened their own restaurants. Among the newcomers to the *bistronomique* scene are David Rathgeber, who left Benoît to take over the chic Montparnasse bistro L'Assiette; Mickaël Gaignon, a veteran of Pierre Gagnaire and Le Pré Catelan who now runs the Marais bistro Le Gaigne; and Stéphane Marcouzzi, who was maître d'hôtel at Guy Savoy's Le Cap Vernet before opening L'Epigramme in St-Germain with chef Aymeric Kräml, and now L'Epicuriste, in the 15th arrondissement.

But self-expression is not the only driving force behind the current changes. A traditional high-end restaurant can be prohibitively expensive to operate. As a result, more casual bistros and cafés, which often have lower operational costs and higher profit margins, have become attractive businesses for even top chefs.

Restaurant prices are per person for a main course at dinner, including tax (5.5%) and service; note that if a restaurant offers only prix-fixe (set-price) meals, it has been given the price category that reflects the full prix-fixe price.

RESTAURANTS

In alphabetical order by neighborhood. Use the coordinate (⊕ 1:B3) at the end of each listing to locate a site on the corresponding map

1ER ARRONDISSEMENT (LOUVRE/LES HALLES/OPÉRA)

$$$ BISTRO Fodor's Choice ★

🍴 **L'Ardoise.** A minuscule storefront, decorated with enlargements of old sepia postcards of Paris, L'Ardoise is a model of the kind of contemporary bistros making waves in Paris. Chef Pierre Jay's first-rate three-course dinner menu for €36 tempts with such original dishes as mushroom and foie gras ravioli with smoked duck; farmer's pork with porcini mushrooms; and red mullet with creole sauce (you can also order à la carte, but it's less of a bargain). Just as enticing are the desserts, such as a superb *feuillantine au citron*—caramelized pastry leaves filled with lemon cream and lemon slices—and a boozy baba au rhum. With friendly waiters and a small but well-chosen wine list, L'Ardoise would be perfect if it weren't so popular (meaning noisy and crowded). [$] *Average main: €27* ✉ *28 rue du Mont Thabor, 1er, Louvre/Tuileries* ☎ *01–42–96–28–18* 🌐 *www.lardoise-paris.com* ✍ *Reservations essential* ⏲ *Closed Sun. No lunch* [M] *Concorde* ⊕ *1:D3.*

$$ MODERN FRENCH Fodor's Choice ★

🍴 **La Régalade St. Honoré.** When Bruno Doucet bought the original La Régalade from bistro-wizard Yves Camdeborde, some feared the end of an era. How wrong they were. While Doucet kept some of what made the old dining room so popular (country terrine, wine values, convivial atmosphere), he had a few tricks under his toque, creating a brilliantly successful haute-cuisine-meets-comfort-food destination with dishes like earthy morel mushrooms in a frothy cream for a starter, followed by the chef's signature succulent caramelized pork belly over tender Puy lentils, and a perfectly cooked fillet of cod, crispy on the outside and buttery within, served in a rich shrimp bouillon. For dessert, don't skip the updated take on *grand-mère*'s creamy rice pudding or the house Grand Marnier soufflé. With an excellent price-to-value ratio (€35 for the prix-fixe menu at lunch and dinner), this chic bistro and its elder

BEST BETS FOR PARIS DINING

With thousands of restaurants to choose from, how will you decide where to eat? Fodor's writers and editors have selected their favorite restaurants by price, cuisine, and experience below. You can also search by neighborhood for excellent eating experiences—peruse the following pages for spotlights on specific neighborhoods.

2

sister in the 14th have evolved into staples for Paris gastronomes. Ⓢ *Average main: €24* ✉ *123 rue Saint-Honoré, 1er, Faubourg St-Honoré* ☎ *01–42–21–92–40* ⚋ *Reservations essential* ◷ *Closed weekends, Aug., 1 wk at Christmas* Ⓜ *Louvre-Rivoli* ✛ *1:E4.*

\$\$\$\$
MODERN FRENCH

✕ **Le Grand Véfour.** Victor Hugo could stride in and still recognize this restaurant, which was in his day, as now, a contender for the title of most beautiful restaurant in Paris. Originally built in 1784, it has welcomed everyone from Napoléon to Colette to Jean Cocteau under its mirrored ceiling, and amid the early-19th-century glass paintings of goddesses and muses that create an air of restrained seduction. The rich and fashionable gather here to enjoy chef Guy Martin's unique blend of sophistication and rusticity, as seen in dishes such as frogs' legs with sorrel sauce, and oxtail *parmentier* (a kind of shepherd's pie) with truffles. There's an outstanding cheese trolley, and for dessert try the house specialty, *palet aux noisettes* (meringue cake with chocolate mousse, hazelnuts, and salted caramel ice cream). Prices are as extravagant as the decor, but there is a €98 lunch menu. Ⓢ *Average main: €120* ✉ *17 rue de Beaujolais, 1er, Louvre/Tuileries* ☎ *01–42–96–56–27* ⊕ *www.grand-vefour.com* ⚋ *Reservations essential* ◷ *Closed weekends, Aug., and Christmas holidays. No dinner Fri.* Ⓜ *Palais-Royal* ✛ *1:E3.*

\$\$\$\$
MODERN FRENCH
Fodor's Choice
★

✕ **Spring.** The private party atmosphere in this intimate, elegantly modern space may be exuberance at having finally snagged a table, but most likely it's chef Daniel Rose's inspired—often resplendent—cuisine. Though firmly rooted in technique, Rose sets himself the task of improvising two different menus each day, one for lunch and one for dinner, from whatever strikes his fancy that morning. His insistence on fresh, top-quality ingredients is evident in dishes that are both refined and deeply satisfying: you might have an updated *parmentier* with a velvety layer of deboned pig's foot topped with lemon-infused whipped potatoes or buttery venison with tart-sweet candied kumquat; for dessert, a sublime combo of whiskey-and-vanilla-infused pineapple, crunchy toasted coconut biscuits, and lime-zest-sprinkled vanilla ice cream. The 17th-century vaulted dining room is an intimate spot yet can accommodate larger groups. The €46 lunch menu provides a good introduction. Ⓢ *Average main: €45* ✉ *6 rue Bailleul, 1er, Louvre/Tuileries* ☎ *01–45–96–05–72* ⚋ *Reservations essential* ◷ *No dinner Tues.–Sat. No lunch Wed.–Fri.* Ⓜ *Louvre-Rivoli* ✛ *1:F4.*

\$\$\$\$
FRENCH FUSION
Fodor's Choice
★

✕ **Yam'Tcha.** Adeline Grattard's little bistro has become so popular that tables are snapped up several weeks ahead, which is no surprise when you learn that she worked in the kitchens of L'Astrance before spending time in Hong Kong, where she picked up many of her techniques and ingredients. Inspired by Chinese cooking, many of her dishes rely on brilliant flavor combinations and very precise cooking. A signature dish is the roasted Challans duck (a cross between wild and domestic) with Sichuan-style eggplant: two elements that create magic together. Adeline's husband Chi Wa acts as a tea sommelier, introducing diners to earthy or grassy flavors that complement the food (Yam'Tcha means "to eat small steamed dishes while sipping tea"), though alcohol is also available. It's prix fixe only. Ⓢ *Average main: €40* ✉ *4 rue Sauval, 1er, Les Halles* ☎ *01–40–26–08–07* ⚋ *Reservations essential* ◷ *Closed Sun.*

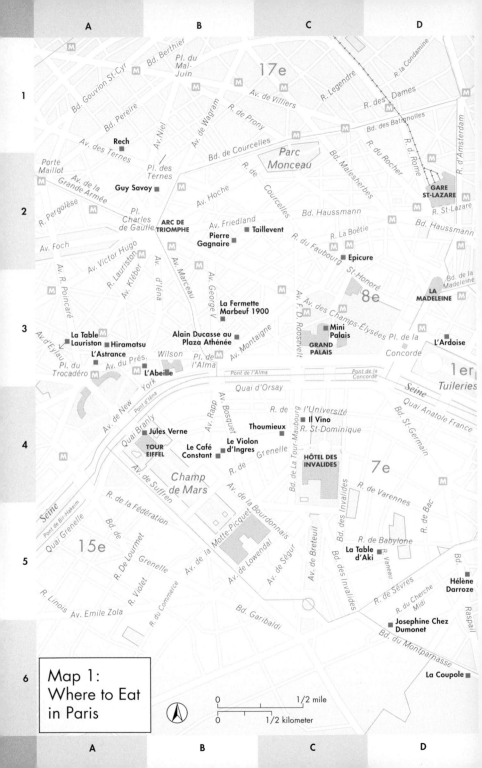

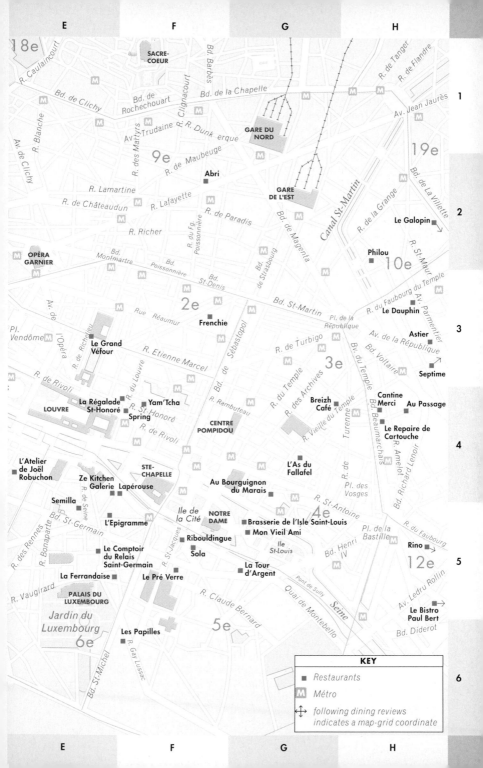

and Mon., Aug., and Christmas. No lunch Tues. [M] *Louvre-Rivoli or Les Halles* ✥ *1:F4.*

2E ARRONDISSEMENT (OPERA/GRANDS BOULEVARDS/LES HALLES)

$$ BISTRO Fodor's Choice ★

🍴 **Frenchie.** Grégory Marchand worked in New York and with Jamie Oliver in London before opening this brick-and-stone-walled bistro on a pedestrian street near rue Montorgueil, which explains the tongue-in-cheek name. Word of mouth and bloggers quickly made this one of the most packed bistros in town, with tables booked two months in advance, despite two seatings each evening. Marchand owes a large part of his success to the great-value €45 three-course menu at dinner—boldly flavored dishes such as calamari gazpacho with squash blossoms, and melt-in-the-mouth braised lamb with roasted eggplant and spinach are excellent options. Service can be, shall we say, a tad brusque, but for some that's a small price to pay for food this good. It's prix fixe only. [$] *Average main: €36* ✉ *5 rue du Nil, 2e, Les Halles* ☎ *01–40–39–96–19* 🌐 *www.frenchie-restaurant.com* ✍ *Reservations essential* ⏲ *Closed weekends, 2 wks in Aug., 10 days at Christmas. No lunch* [M] *Sentier* ✥ *1:F3.*

3E ARRONDISSEMENT (BEAUBOURG/MARAIS/RÉPUBLIQUE)

$$ BISTRO

🍴 **Au Bourguignon du Marais.** The handsome, contemporary look of this Marais bistro and wine bar is the perfect backdrop for traditional fare and excellent Burgundies served by the glass and bottle. Unusual for Paris, food is served nonstop from noon to 11 pm, and you can drop by just for a glass of wine in the afternoon. Always on the menu are Burgundian classics such as *jambon persillé* (ham in parsleyed aspic jelly), escargots, and *boeuf bourguignon* (beef stewed in red wine). More up-to-date picks include a cèpe-mushroom velouté with poached oysters, though the fancier dishes are generally less successful. The terrace is busy in warmer months. [$] *Average main: €22* ✉ *52 rue François-Miron, 3e, Marais* ☎ *01–48–87–15–40* ⏲ *Closed Sun. and Mon., 3 wks in Aug., and 2 wks in Feb.* [M] *St-Paul* ✥ *1:G4.*

$ FRENCH FAMILY Fodor's Choice ★

🍴 **Breizh Café.** Eating a crêpe in Paris might seem a bit clichéd, until you venture into this modern offshoot of a Breton crêperie. The pale-wood, almost Japanese-style decor is refreshing, but what really makes the difference are the ingredients—farmers' eggs, unpasteurized Gruyère, shiitake mushrooms, Valrhona chocolate, homemade caramel, and extraordinary butter from Breton dairy farmer Jean-Yves Bordier. You'll find all the classics among the galettes (buckwheat crêpes), but it's worth choosing something more adventurous like the *cancalaise* (traditionally smoked herring, potato, crème fraîche, and herring roe). You might also slurp a few Cancale oysters, a rarity in Paris, and try one of the 20 artisanal ciders on offer. The nonstop serving hours from noon to 11 pm can be a lifesaver if you're shopping in the Marais. Weekends are hectic, so be sure to reserve. [$] *Average main: €12* ✉ *109 rue Vieille du Temple, 3e, Marais* ☎ *01–42–72–13–77* 🌐 *www.breizhcafe.com* ✍ *Reservations essential* ⏲ *Closed Mon., Tues., and Aug.* [M] *St-Sébastien-Froissart* ✥ *1:G4.*

$ 🍴 **Cantine Merci.** Deep inside the city's latest concept store, whose proceeds go to charities for women in India and Madagascar, lurks the perfect spot for a quick and healthy lunch between bouts of shopping. The brief menu of soups, salads, risottos, and a daily hot dish is more than slightly reminiscent of another city lunch spot, Rose Bakery. Salads such as fava beans with radish and lemon wedges or melon, cherry tomato, and arugula are bright, lively, and crunchy, and you can order a freshly squeezed juice or iced tea with fresh mint to wash it all down. Delicious, homey desserts might include cherry clafoutis or raspberry and pistachio crumble. [$] *Average main: €16* ✉ *111 bd. Beaumarchais, 3e, Marais* ☎ *01–42–77–79–28* 🌐 *www.merci-merci.com* 🕒 *Closed Sun. No dinner* [M] *St-Sébastien-Froissart* ✣ *1:H4.*

MODERN FRENCH

2

4E ARRONDISSEMENT (MARAIS/ILE ST-LOUIS)

$$ 🍴 **Brasserie de l'Isle Saint-Louis.** With so much going for it, including a dream location on the tip of the Ile Saint-Louis overlooking the Seine and Notre Dame, you'd think this charming brasserie, like so many before it, would have succumbed to its own success. Yet it remains exactly what a decent neighborhood brasserie should be, with an authentic decor, efficiently friendly service, and good brassiere fare—classic leeks vinaigrette, country terrine, and a savory onion tarte à la maison for starters, followed by tender sole meuniere, classic choucroute, or buttered entrecôte. The outdoor terrace simply can't be beat. [$] *Average main: €18* ✉ *55 quai de Bourbon, 4e, Belleville* ☎ *01–43–54–02–59* 🌐 *www.labrasserie-isl.fr* ✍ *Reservations not accepted* 🕒 *Closed Wed.* [M] *Pont Marie, Maubert-Mutualité, Sully-Morland* ✣ *1:G5.*

BRASSERIE

$ 🍴 **L'As du Fallafel.** Look no further than the fantastic falafel stands on the pedestrian rue de Rosiers for some of the cheapest and tastiest meals in Paris. L'As (the Ace) is widely considered the best of the bunch, which accounts for the lunchtime line that extends down the street, despite the recent expansion of the dining room from 70 to 115 seats. A falafel sandwich costs €5 to go, €7.50 in the dining room, and comes heaped with grilled eggplant, cabbage, hummus, tahini, and hot sauce. The *shawarma* (grilled, skewered meat) sandwich, made with chicken or lamb, is also one of the finest in town. Though takeout is popular, it can be more fun (and not as messy) to eat off a plastic plate in one of the two frenzied dining rooms. Fresh lemonade is the falafel's best match. [$] *Average main: €10* ✉ *34 rue des Rosiers, 4e, Marais* ☎ *01–48–87–63–60* 🕒 *Closed Sat. No dinner Fri.* [M] *St-Paul* ✣ *1:G4.*

MIDDLE EASTERN
FAMILY

$$ 🍴 **Mon Vieil Ami.** "Modern Alsatian" might sound like an oxymoron, but once you've tasted the food here, you'll understand. The updated medieval dining room—stone walls and dark-wood tables—provides a stylish milieu for the inventive cooking orchestrated by star Alsatian chef Antoine Westermann, which showcases heirloom vegetables (such as yellow carrots and pink-and-white beets) from star producer Joël Thiébault. Pâté *en croûte* (wrapped in pastry) with a knob of foie gras is hard to resist among the starters. Among the mains, red mullet might come in a bouillabaisse sauce with sautéed baby artichokes, and the shoulder of lamb with white beans, preserved lemon, and cilantro has become a classic. This is not necessarily the place for a romantic dinner, since seating is a little tight, but the quality of the food never

MODERN FRENCH
Fodor's Choice ★

falters, and the portions are quite generous. Call during opening hours (11:30–2:30 and 7–11) to book, since they don't answer the phone the rest of the time. [$] *Average main: €23* ✉ *69 rue St-Louis-en-l'Ile, 4e, Ile St-Louis* ☎ *01–40–46–01–35* 🌐 *www.mon-vieil-ami.com* 🕒 *Closed Mon., Tues., 3 wks in Aug., and 3 wks in Jan.* [M] *Pont Marie* ✥ *1:G5.*

5E ARRONDISSEMENT (LATIN QUARTER/ST-GERMAIN)

$$$$ MODERN FRENCH 🍴 **La Tour d'Argent.** La Tour d'Argent has had a rocky time in recent years with the death of owner Claude Terrail, but chef Laurent Delarbre has found his footing, and there's no denying the splendor of the setting overlooking the Seine. If you don't want to splash out on dinner, treat yourself to the three-course lunch menu for a reduced price of €68; this entitles you to succulent slices of one of the restaurant's numbered ducks (the great duck slaughter began in 1919 and is now well past the millionth mallard, as your numbered certificate will attest). Don't be too daunted by the vast wine list—with the aid of the sommelier you can splurge a little (about €80) and perhaps taste a rare vintage Burgundy from the extraordinary cellars, which survived World War II. [$] *Average main: €95* ✉ *15–17 quai de la Tournelle, 5e, Latin Quarter* ☎ *01–43–54–23–31* 🌐 *www.latourdargent.com* ✍ *Reservations essential. Jacket and tie* 🕒 *Closed Sun., Mon., and Aug.* [M] *Cardinal Lemoine* ✥ *1:G5.*

$$ MODERN FRENCH 🍴 **Le Pré Verre.** Chef Philippe Delacourcelle knows his cassia bark from his cinnamon thanks to a long stint in Asia. He opened this lively bistro with its purple-gray walls and photos of jazz musicians to showcase his culinary style, rejuvenating archetypal French dishes with Asian and Mediterranean spices. So popular has it proved, especially with Japanese visitors, that the restaurant opened a branch in Tokyo in late 2007. His bargain prix-fixe menus (€13.90 at lunch for a main dish, glass of wine, and coffee; €30.90 for three courses at dinner) change constantly, but his trademark spiced suckling pig with crisp cabbage is always a winner, as is his rhubarb compote with gingered white-chocolate mousse. Ask for advice in selecting wine from a list that highlights small producers. [$] *Average main: €18* ✉ *8 rue Thénard, 5e, Latin Quarter* ☎ *01–43–54–59–47* 🌐 *www.lepreverre.com* ✍ *Reservations essential* 🕒 *Closed Sun. and Mon.* [M] *Maubert-Mutualité* ✥ *1:F5.*

$$ WINE BAR 🍴 **Les Papilles.** Part wineshop and épicerie, part restaurant, Les Papilles has a winning formula—pick any bottle off the well-stocked shelf and pay a €7 corkage fee to drink it with your meal; or savor one of several superb wines by the glass at your table or around the classic zinc bar. The superb no-choice menu—made with top-notch, seasonal ingredients—usually begins with a luscious *velouté*, a velvety soup served from a large tureen, and proceeds with a hearty-yet-tender meat dish alongside perfectly cooked vegetables—well worth spending a little extra time for lunch or dinner. [$] *Average main: €18* ✉ *30 rue Gay-Lussac, 5e, Latin Quarter* ☎ *01–43–25–20–79* 🌐 *www.lespapillesparis.fr* ✍ *Reservations essential* 🕒 *Closed Sun., Mon., last wk of July, and 2 wks in Aug.* [M] *Cluny–La Sorbonne* ✥ *1:F6.*

$$ BISTRO 🍴 **Ribouldingue.** Find offal off-putting? Off-cuts take pride of place on the €28 prix fixe lunch menu, €34 at dinner (there's no à la carte), but don't let that stop you from trying this bistro near the ancient St-Julien-le-Pauvre church. You can avoid odd animal bits completely, if you

must, and still have an excellent meal—opt for dishes like marinated salmon or veal rib with fingerling potatoes—or go out on a limb with the *tétine de.vache* (thin breaded and fried slices of cow's udder) and *groin de cochon* (the tip of a pig's snout). This adventurous menu is the brainchild of Nadège Varigny, daughter of a Lyonnais butcher (*quel surprise*). She runs the front of the house while chef Amélie Darvas turns out the impeccable food—veal kidney with potato gratin is a house classic, and there are always three fish dishes. Don't miss the unusual desserts, like tangy ewe's-milk ice cream. Ⓢ *Average main: €21* ✉ *10 rue St-Julien-le-Pauvre, 5e, Latin Quarter* ☎ *01–46–33–98–80* ☻ *Closed Sun., Mon., and Aug.* Ⓜ *St-Michel* ✛ *1:F5.*

$$$$
ECLECTIC
✕ **Sola.** Chef Hiroki Yoshitake was schooled in the kitchens of famed innovators Pascal Barbot of Astrance and William Ledeuil of Ze Kitchen Galerie before striking out on his own. Dishes like miso-lacquered foie gras, served with toasted *pain de mie*, or sake-glazed suckling pig—perfectly crisp on the outside and melting inside—pair traditional Japanese and French ingredients to wondrous effect. Plates are artfully arranged with a sprinkling of piquant shiso leaves or jewel-like roasted vegetables to please the eye and the palate. The three-course, €48 lunch menu—it's prix fixe only—offers a choice of fish or meat and finishes with Fukano Hirobu's stunning confections. Shoes stay on in the tranquil half-timbered dining room upstairs, but the vaulted room downstairs is totally traditional—and one of the loveliest in Paris. Ⓢ *Average main: €35* ✉ *12 rue de l'Hôtel Colbert, 5e, Latin Quarter* ☎ *01–43–29–59–04* ⊕ *restaurant-sola.com* ⚓ *Reservations essential* ☻ *Closed Sun. and Mon.* Ⓜ *Maubert Mutualié* ✛ *1:F5.*

6E ARRONDISSEMENT (ST-GERMAIN/LATIN QUARTER)

$$$$
MODERN FRENCH
✕ **Hélène Darroze.** The most celebrated female chef in Paris is now cooking at the Connaught in London, but her St-Germain dining room is an exclusive setting for her sophisticated take on southwestern French food. Darroze's intriguingly modern touch comes through in such dishes as a sublime duck foie gras confit served with an exotic-fruit chutney or a blowout of roast wild duck stuffed with foie gras and truffles. If the food, at its best, lives up to the very high prices, the service sometimes struggles to reach the same level. For a more affordable taste, try the relatively casual Salon d'Hélène downstairs, which serves a reasonable €35 seven-course tapas lunch that includes a glass of wine. Ⓢ *Average main: €85* ✉ *4 rue d'Assas, 6e, St-Germain-des-Prés* ☎ *01–42–22–00–11* ⊕ *www.helenedarroze.com* ⚓ *Reservations essential* ☻ *Closed Sun. and Mon.* Ⓜ *Sèvres-Babylone* ✛ *1:D5.*

$$$
BISTRO
✕ **Josephine Chez Dumonet.** Theater types, politicos, and locals fill the moleskin banquettes of this venerable bistro, where the frosted-glass lamps and amber walls put everyone in a good light. Unlike most bistros, Josephine caters to the indecisive, since generous half portions allow you to graze your way through the temptingly retro menu. Try the excellent boeuf bourguignon, roasted saddle of lamb with artichokes, top-notch steak tartare prepared table-side, or anything with truffles in season; game is also a specialty in fall and winter. For dessert, choose between a mille-feuille big enough to serve three and a Grand Marnier soufflé that simply refuses to sink, even with prodding. The wine list,

like the food, is outstanding if expensive. $ *Average main: €26 ✉ 117 rue du Cherche-Midi, 6e, St-Germain-des-Prés ☎ 01–45–48–52–40 ⌕ Reservations essential ⊘ Closed weekends Ⓜ Duroc ✛ 1:D6.*

$$
BISTRO

✕ **La Ferrandaise.** Portraits of cows adorn the stone walls of this bistro near the Luxembourg Gardens, hinting at the kitchen's penchant for meaty cooking (Ferrandaise is a breed of cattle). Still, there's something for every taste on the market-inspired menu, which always lists three meat and three fish mains. Dill-marinated salmon with sweet mustard sauce is a typical starter, and a thick, milk-fed veal chop might come with a squash pancake and spinach. The dining room buzzes with locals who appreciate the good-value €34 prix fixe—there is no à la carte—and the brilliant bento box–style €16 lunch menu, in which three courses are served all at once. $ *Average main: €24 ✉ 8 rue de Vaugirard, 6e, St-Germain-des-Prés ☎ 01–43–26–36–36 ⊕ www. laferrandaise.com ⊘ Closed Sun. and 3 wks in Aug. No lunch Mon. and Sat. Ⓜ Odéon, RER: Luxembourg ✛ 1:E5.*

$$$$
BISTRO

✕ **Lapérouse.** Émile Zola, George Sand, and Victor Hugo were regulars here, and the restaurant's mirrors still bear diamond scratches from the days when mistresses would double-check their jewels' value. It's hard not to fall in love with this storied 17th-century Seine-side town house with a warren of woodwork-graced salons. Christophe Guilbert's cuisine seeks a balance between traditional and modern, often drawing on Mediterranean inspirations. For a truly intimate meal, reserve one of the legendary private *salons* where anything can happen (and probably has). You can also sample the restaurant's magic at lunch, when a bargain prix-fixe menu is served for €35–€45 in both the main dining room and the private salons. $ *Average main: €45 ✉ 51 quai des Grands Augustins, 6e, Latin Quarter ☎ 01–43–26–68–04 ⊕ www. laperouse.fr ⌕ Reservations essential ⊘ Closed Sun. and Aug. No lunch Sat. Ⓜ St-Michel ✛ 1:E4.*

$$
BISTRO

✕ **Le Comptoir du Relais Saint-Germain.** Run by legendary bistro chef Yves Camdeborde, this tiny Art Deco hotel restaurant is booked up well in advance for the single dinner sitting that comprises a five-course, €65 set menu of haute-cuisine food. On weekends from noon to 10 pm and before 6 pm during the week a brasserie menu is served and reservations are not accepted, resulting in long lines and brisk, sometimes shockingly rude, service. Start with charcuterie or pâté, then choose from open-faced sandwiches like a smoked salmon–and–Comté cheese croque monsieur, gourmet salads, and a variety of hot dishes such as braised beef cheek, roast tuna, and Camdeborde's famed deboned and breaded pig's trotter. If you don't mind bus fumes, sidewalk tables make for prime people-watching in summer. Le Comptoir also runs Avant Comptoir next door; a miniscule stand-up zinc bar with hanging hams and sausages, where you can score a superb plate of charcuterie, a couple of warm dishes, and an inky glass of Morgon. Quality crêpes and sandwiches are still served from the window out front. $ *Average main: €22 ✉ 9 carrefour de l'Odéon, 6e, St-Germain-des-Prés ☎ 01– 44–27–07–50 Ⓜ Odéon ✛ 1:E5.*

$$$ BISTRO FAMILY 🍴 **L'Epigramme.** Great bistro food is not so hard to find in Paris, but only rarely does it come in a comfortable setting. At L'Epigramme, the striped orange-and-yellow chairs are softly padded, there's space between you and your neighbors, and a big glass pane lets in plenty of light from the courtyard. Chef Karine Camcian has an almost magical touch with meat: try her stuffed suckling pig with turnip choucroute, or seared slices of pink lamb with root vegetables in a glossy reduced sauce. In winter the eleborate game dish *lièvre à la royale* (hare stuffed with goose or duck liver and cooked in wine) sometimes makes an appearance. Desserts are not quite as inspired, so try to take a peek at the plates coming out of the kitchen before making your choice. [$] *Average main: €28* ✉ *9 rue de l'Eperon, 6e, St-Germain-des-Prés* ☎ *01–44–41–00–09* ✍ *Reservations essential* ⏲ *Closed Sun., Mon., 3 wks in Aug., and 1 wk at Christmas* [M] *Odéon* ⊕ *1:E5.*

$$$ BISTRO Fodor's Choice ★ 🍴 **Semilla.** The duo behind the popular neighborhood bistro Fish and the excellent La Dernière Goutte wineshop have poured their significant expertise into this laid-back new bistro in the heart of tony Saint Germain des Prés. Its sophisticated cuisine, superb wines by the bottle or glass, and total lack of pretension has quickly made Semilla the toast of the town. A lively open kitchen produces a menu of plentiful dishes either raw, roasted, baked, or steamed, with choices that will thrill both carnivores and herbivores. Velvety chestnut soup, lentil croquettes with a light curry emulsion, beet carpaccio, and the excellent marinated salmon are good choices to start, followed by roasted coquilles Saint Jacques with Jerusalem artichoke purée or venison served with celery root and quince. There are also plenty of bistro classics to choose from, like beef tartare or côte de boeuf with roasted potatoes and a fine sauce bordelaise, and it's open Sunday. [$] *Average main: €25* ✉ *54 rue de Seine, 6e, Belleville* ☎ *01–43–54–34–50* ✍ *Reservations essential* [M] *Odéon, St-Germain-des-Prés* ⊕ *1:E5.*

$$$$ MODERN FRENCH Fodor's Choice ★ 🍴 **Ze Kitchen Galerie.** William Ledeuil made his name at the popular Les Bouquinistes before opening this contemporary bistro in a loftlike space. The name might not be inspired, but the cooking shows creativity and a sense of fun: from a deliberately deconstructed menu featuring raw fish, soups, pastas, and *à la plancha* (grilled) plates, consider the roast and confit duck with a tamarind-and-sesame condiment and foie gras, or lobster with mussels, white beans, and Thai herbs. A tireless experimenter, Ledeuil buys heirloom vegetables direct from farmers and tracks down herbs and spices in Asian supermarkets. The menu changes monthly, and there are several different prix-fixe options at lunch, starting at €27. [$] *Average main: €36* ✉ *4 rue des Grands-Augustins, 6e, Latin Quarter* ☎ *01–44–32–00–32* 🌐 *www.zekitchengalerie.fr* ✍ *Reservations essential* 💳 *No credit cards* ⏲ *Closed Sun. No lunch Sat.* [M] *St-Michel* ⊕ *1:E4.*

7E ARRONDISSEMENT (TOUR EIFFEL/ TROCADÉRO/INVALIDES)

$$$$ FRENCH FUSION 🍴 **Il Vino.** It might seem audacious to present hungry diners with nothing more than a wine list, but the gamble is paying off for Enrico Bernardo at his wine-centric restaurant with a branch in Courchevel, in the French Alps. This charismatic Italian left the George V to oversee

a dining room where food plays second fiddle (in status, not quality). The hip decor—plum-color banquettes, body-hugging white chairs, a few high tables—attracts a mostly young clientele that's happy to play the game by ordering one of the blind, multicourse tasting menus. The €98 menu, with four dishes and four wines, is a good compromise that might bring you a white Mâcon with saffron risotto, crisp Malvasia with crabmeat and black radish, a full-bodied red from Puglia with Provençal-style lamb, sherrylike *vin jaune* d'Arbois with aged Comté cheese, and sweet Jurançon with berry crumble. You can also order individual wine-food combinations à la carte or pick a bottle straight from the cellar and ask for a meal to match. [$] *Average main: €40* ✉ *13 bd. de la Tour-Maubourg, 7e, Invalides* ☎ *01–44–11–72–00* 🌐 *www.ilvinobyenricobernardo.com* 🕒 *Closed Sun.* [M] *Invalides* ⊕ *1:C4.*

$$$$ MODERN FRENCH
🍴 **L'Atelier de Joël Robuchon.** Worldwide phenomenon Joël Robuchon retired from the restaurant business for several years before opening this red-and-black-lacquer space with a bento-box-meets-tapas aesthetic. High seats surround two U-shape bars, and this novel plan encourages neighbors to share recommendations and opinions. Robuchon's devoted kitchen staff whip up small plates for grazing (€19–€75) as well as full portions, which can turn out to be the better bargain. Highlights from the oft-changing menu have included an intense tomato jelly topped with avocado puree and the thin-crusted mackerel tart, although his inauthentic (but who's complaining?) take on carbonara with cream and Alsatian bacon, and the *merlan* Colbert (fried herb butter) remain signature dishes. Reservations are taken for the first sittings only at lunch and dinner. [$] *Average main: €36* ✉ *5 rue Montalembert, 7e, St-Germain-des-Prés* ☎ *01–42–22–56–56* 🌐 *joel-robuchon.net* [M] *Rue du Bac* ⊕ *1:E4.*

$$$ MODERN FRENCH
Fodor's Choice ★
🍴 **La Table d'Aki.** Did the stars align when this little spot opened? Or could it be that La Table d'Aki actually *is* the most perfect restaurant in Paris? Consider the evidence: In a lovely *quartier* near the Musée Rodin, its pale celadon walls, crisp white linen, and restrained lighting add up to a simple elegance, all the better to highlight chef Akihiro Horikoshi's thrilling cuisine centered on the sea. Amazingly Horikoshi works all alone in an open kitchen while 16 lucky diners await the next course, dishes like plump langoustine shimmering in a velvety shallot-fennel sauce, or delicate medallians of sole in a mellow red wine and leek reduction—all of such lush simplicity. In the hands of some other chef, the attempt to create these feasts alone would be an act of hubris, but chef Horikoshi is only guilty of making more unrepentant fans: some have even been known to order all four entrées or toast the chef repeatedly with their postdinner cognac, and all are practically genuflecting their way out the door. [$] *Average main: €32* ✉ *49 rue Vaneau, 7e, Invalides* ☎ *01–45–44–43–48* ✍ *Reservations essential* 🕒 *Closed Sun. and Mon.* [M] *Saint Francis-Xavier* ⊕ *1:D5.*

$ BISTRO
🍴 **Le Café Constant.** Parisians are a nostalgic bunch, which explains the popularity of this down-to-earth venue from esteemed chef Christian Constant. This is a relatively humble bistro with cream-color walls, red banquettes, and wooden tables, and you'll often see Constant himself perched at the bar at the end of lunch service. The menu reads like a

French cookbook from the 1970s—who cooks veal *cordon bleu* these days?—but with Constant overseeing the kitchen, the dishes taste even better than back in the day. There's delicious and creamy lentil soup with morsels of foie gras, and the artichoke salad comes with fresh—not bottled or frozen—hearts. A towering *vacherin* (meringue layered with ice cream) might bring this delightfully retro meal to a close. On weekdays there is a bargain lunch menu for €16 (two courses) or €23 (three courses). [$] *Average main: €16* ✉ *139 rue St-Dominique, 7e, Around the Eiffel Tower* ☎ *01–47–53–73–34* 🌐 *www.cafeconstant.com* ✍ *Reservations not accepted* [M] *Métro École Militaire, Métro or RER: Pont de l'Alma* ✥ *1:B4.*

$$$$ MODERN FRENCH 🍴 **Le Jules Verne.** Alain Ducasse doesn't set his sights low, so it was no real surprise when he took over this prestigious dining room on the second floor of the Eiffel Tower and had designer Patrick Jouin give the room a neo-futuristic look in shades of brown. Sauces and pastries are prepared in a kitchen below the Champ de Mars before being whisked up the elevator to the kitchen, which is overseen by young chef Pascal Féraud. Most accessible is the €88 lunch menu (weekdays only), which brings you à la carte dishes in slightly smaller portions. Spend more (about €175–€210 per person without drinks) and you'll be entitled to more lavish dishes such as lobster with celery root and black truffle, and fricassee of Bresse chicken with crayfish. For dessert the kitchen reinterprets French classics, as in an unsinkable pink grapefruit soufflé with grapefruit sorbet. Book months ahead or try your luck at the last minute. [$] *Average main: €75* ✉ *Tour Eiffel, south pillar, av. Gustave Eiffel, 7e, Around the Eiffel Tower* ☎ *01–45–55–61–44* 🌐 *www.lejulesverne-paris.com* ✍ *Reservations essential. Jacket and tie* [M] *Bir-Hakeim* ✥ *1:A4.*

$$$ MODERN FRENCH 🍴 **Le Violon d'Ingres.** Following in the footsteps of Joël Robuchon and Alain Senderens, Christian Constant gave up the Michelin star chase in favor of relatively accessible prices and a packed dining room (book at least a week ahead). And with Jérémie Tourdjman in charge of the kitchen here, Constant can dash among his four restaurants on this street, making sure the hordes are happy. Why wouldn't they be? The food is sophisticated and the atmosphere is lively; you can even find signature dishes like the almond-crusted sea bass with rémoulade sauce (a buttery caper sauce), alongside game and scallops (in season), and comforting desserts like *pots de crème* and chocolate tart. The food is still heavy on the butter, but with wines starting at around €25 (and a €48 lunch menu on weekdays) this is a wonderful place for a classic yet informal French meal. [$] *Average main: €34* ✉ *135 rue St-Dominique, 7e, Around the Eiffel Tower* ☎ *01–45–55–15–05* 🌐 *www.leviolondingres.com* ✍ *Reservations essential* [M] *École Militaire* ✥ *1:B4.*

$$$$ BRASSERIE 🍴 **Thoumieux.** Former Crillon chef Jean-François Piège and Thierry Costes of the fashionable brasserie clan that created Café Marly and Le Georges are behind the revival of this Old World bistro. The space has been opened up to eliminate private booths while thankfully preserving much of its vintage character with globe lights and etched mirrors. Despite its location in the sedate 7e arrondissement, this has quickly become the place to be seen, with food that's a good notch above

brasserie fare. A juicy Angus beef hamburger comes with a superfluous shower of Parmesan and ultra-skinny fries, while the more sophisticated slow-cooked salmon is accompanied by vegetables from star market gardener Joël Thiébault. For dessert, try the piping-hot churros with chocolate sauce. The new *restaurant gastronomique* upstairs is ever so chic and a good bit pricier, yet proffers an experience commensurate with the top bistros in town (€119 set menus at lunch and dinner, and a €99 three-course menu at lunch that includes two glasses of wine; closed weekends). Reservations are taken exactly six days ahead. [$] *Average main: €38* ✉ *79 rue St-Dominique, 7e, Invalides* ☎ *01–47–05–49–75* 🌐 *www.thoumieux.fr* ✍ *Reservations essential* [M] *La Tour-Maubourg* ✥ *1:C4.*

8E ARRONDISSEMENT (CHAMPS-ÉLYSÉES)

$$$$ MODERN FRENCH

🍴 **Alain Ducasse au Plaza Athénée.** The dining room at Alain Ducasse's flagship Paris restaurant gleams with 10,000 crystals, confirming that this is the flashiest place in town for a blowout meal. Clementine-color tablecloths and space-age cream-and-orange chairs with pullout plastic trays for business meetings provide an upbeat setting for the cooking of young Ducasse protégé chef Christophe Saintagne. Some dishes are subtle, whereas in others strong flavors overwhelm delicate ingredients; service is also a little inconsistent, with occasional long waits between courses. Even so, a meal here is delightfully luxe, starting with a heavenly *amuse-bouche* of perhaps langoustine with caviar and a tangy lemon cream. You can continue with a truffle-and-caviar fest, or opt for more down-to-earth dishes like lobster in spiced wine with quince or saddle of lamb with sautéed artichokes. [$] *Average main: €120* ✉ *Hôtel Plaza Athénée, 25 av. Montaigne, 8e, Champs-Élysées* ☎ *01–53–67–65–00* 🌐 *www.alain-ducasse.com* ✍ *Reservations essential. Jacket required* ⏲ *Closed weekends, 2 wks in late Dec., and mid-July–mid-Aug. No lunch Mon.–Wed.* [M] *Alma-Marceau* ✥ *1:B3.*

$$$$ MODERN FRENCH

🍴 **Epicure.** After a rapid ascent at his own new-wave bistro, which led to his renown as one of the more inventive young chefs in Paris, Eric Frechon became head chef at the restaurant for three-star Bristol hotel, the home-away-from-home for billionaires and power brokers. Frechon creates masterworks—say, farmer's pork cooked "from head to foot" with truffle-enhanced crushed potatoes—that rarely stray far from the comfort-food tastes of bistro cuisine. The €130 lunch menu makes his cooking accessible not just to the palate but to many pocketbooks. No wonder his tables are so coveted. Though the two dining rooms are impeccable—an oval oak-panel one for fall and winter and a marble-floor pavilion overlooking the courtyard garden for spring and summer—they provide few clues to help the world-weary traveler determine which city this might be. [$] *Average main: €110* ✉ *Hôtel Bristol, 112 rue du Faubourg St-Honoré, 8e, Champs-Élysées* ☎ *01–53–43–43–00* 🌐 *www.lebristolparis.com* ✍ *Reservations essential. Jacket and tie* [M] *Miromesnil* ✥ *1:C2.*

$$$ BRASSERIE

🍴 **La Fermette Marbeuf.** Graced with one of the most mesmerizing Belle Époque rooms in town—accidentally rediscovered during renovations in the 1970s—this is a favorite haunt of French celebrities, who adore the sunflowers, peacocks, and dragonflies of the Art Nouveau mosaic.

The menu rolls out updated classics: try the snails in puff pastry, beef fillet with pepper sauce, and the Grand Marnier soufflé—but ignore the limited-choice €33 prix fixe (€23.50 at lunch) unless you're on a budget: the options are a notch below what you get à la carte. Popular with tourists and businesspeople at lunch, La Fermette becomes truly animated around 9 pm. [$] *Average main: €25* ✉ *5 rue Marbeuf, 8e, Champs-Élysées* ☎ *01–53–23–08–00* 🌐 *www.fermettemarbeuf.com* [M] *Franklin-D.-Roosevelt* ✣ *1:B3.*

$$$ MODERN FRENCH

🍴 **Mini Palais.** The new Mini Palais, inside the Grand Palais, has gotten it smashingly right. With silvery ceilings, dark wood, and faux classical marble, it's among Paris's most stylish dining rooms, but the menu—designed by superchef Eric Frechon of Le Bristol and executed by protegé Stephane d'Aboville—is the real draw. The *burger de magret et foie gras,* a flavorful mélange of tender duckling breast and duck foie gras drizzled with truffled *jus* on a buttery brioche bun, underscores what's best about this place: a thoroughly modern cuisine with an old-fashioned extravagance. For a summer meal or a cocktail, the majestically pillared terrace overlooking Pont d'Alexandre III must be the most beautiful in Paris. What's more, it's open nonstop from 10 am till 2 am, an oasis in a neighborhood short on conveniences. [$] *Average main: €25* ✉ *3 av. Winston Churchill, 8e, Champs-Élysées* ☎ *01–42–56–42–42* 🌐 *www.minipalais.com* ✍ *Reservations essential* [M] *Champs-Élysées-Clemenceau* ✣ *1:C3.*

$$$$ MODERN FRENCH Fodor's Choice ★

🍴 **Pierre Gagnaire.** If you want to venture to the frontier of contemporary luxe cooking—and if money is no object—dinner here is a must. Chef Pierre Gagnaire's work is at once intellectual and poetic, often blending three or four unexpected tastes and textures in a single dish. Just taking in the menu requires concentration (ask the waiters for help), so complex are the multiline descriptions about the dishes' six or seven ingredients. The Grand Dessert, a seven-dessert marathon, will leave you breathless, though it's not as overwhelming as it sounds. The businesslike gray-and-wood dining room feels refreshingly informal, especially at lunch, but it also lacks the grandeur expected at this level. The uninspiring prix-fixe lunch (€115) and occasional ill-judged dishes (Gagnaire is a big risk taker, but also one of France's top chefs) linger as drawbacks, and prices keep shooting skyward, so Pierre Gagnaire is an experience best saved for the financial elite. [$] *Average main: €110* ✉ *6 rue de Balzac, 8e, Champs-Élysées* ☎ *01–58–36–12–50* 🌐 *www.pierre-gagnaire.com* ✍ *Reservations essential* ⏲ *Closed weekends, Aug., and at Christmas* [M] *Charles-de-Gaulle–Étoile* ✣ *1:B2.*

$$$$ MODERN FRENCH

🍴 **Taillevent.** Perhaps the most traditional—for many diners this is only high praise—of all Paris luxury restaurants, this grande dame basks in renewed freshness under brilliant chef Alain Solivérès, who draws inspiration from the Basque country, Bordeaux, and Languedoc for his daily-changing menu. Traditional dishes such as scallops *meunière* (with butter and lemon) are matched with contemporary choices like a splendid spelt risotto with truffles and frogs' legs or panfried duck liver with caramelized fruits and vegetables. One of the 19th-century paneled salons has been turned into a winter garden, and contemporary paintings adorn the walls. The service is flawless, and the exemplary

Just across the street from famed Café de Flore, the legendary Les Deux Magots was once the favorite of Hemingway, Joyce, and Sartre.

wine list is well priced. All in all, a meal here comes as close to the classic haute-cuisine experience as you can find in Paris. There's an €82 lunch menu and special wine "degustation" evenings, pairing food with exceptional wines from their legendary cave for €180. $ *Average main: €110* ✉ *15 rue Lamennais, 8e, Champs-Élysées* ☎ *01–44–95–15–01* ⊕ *www.taillevent.com* ⌒ *Reservations essential. Jacket and tie* ☽ *Closed weekends and Aug.* Ⓜ *Charles-de-Gaulle–Étoile* ✛ *1:B2.*

9E ARRONDISSEMENT (OPÉRA/PIGALLE)

$$

MODERN FRENCH

✗ **Abri.** A month after opening, this tiny storefront restaurant still has reservations at a premium, with no sign of slowing down. Its well-deserved popularity has much to do with chef Katsuaki Okiyama's fresh and imaginative food, the friendly servers, and great prices. A veteran of Taillevent and Robuchon, Okiyama works from a small open kitchen behind a zinc bar, putting forth skillfully prepared dishes, like lemon-marinated mackerel topped with micro-thin slices of beet with honey vinaigrette, succulent duck breast with vegetables au jus, or a scrumptious pumpkin soup with fragrant coffee cream. With food this good, and prices to match (€22 at lunch, €38 for a four-course dinner) be sure to reserve early. $ *Average main: €22* ✉ *92 rue du Faubourg-Poissonnière, 9e, Invalides* ☎ *01–83–97–00–00* ⌒ *Reservations essential* ☽ *Closed Sun. No lunch Tues.–Fri. or Sun.* Ⓜ *Poissonnière, Cadet* ✛ *1:F2.*

10E ARRONDISSEMENT (CANAL ST-MARTIN)

$$

BISTRO

✗ **Le Galopin.** Across from a pretty square on the border of two up-and-coming neighborhoods, this open, light-drenched spot, run by brothers Maxime and Romain Teschenko (the former a veteran of Inaki

Aizpitarte's Chateaubriand and the latter Top Chef 2010) is one of Paris's better new bistros. While the brothers adhere to a tried-and-true formula—meticulously sourced produce, natural wines, open kitchen—they've managed to make it very much their own. Dishes are small wonders of texture and flavor, like velvety Basque pork with razor-thin slices of cauliflower, briny olives, and crunchy pumpkin seeds; or crisp-moist sea bass with spring-fresh asparagus and mint. A great choice for diners eager to experience what this scene's all about in a hip, off-the-beaten-path locale. [$] *Average main: €22* ✉ *34 rue Sainte-Marthe, 10e, Belleville* ☎ *01–42–06–05–03* ✍ *Reservations essential* ⏲ *Closed Sun. and Mon.* [M] *Goncourt, Belleville, Colonel Fabien* ✥ *1:H2.*

$$ BISTRO 🍴 **Philou.** On a quiet street between Canal St-Martin and the historic Hôpital Saint-Louis, few places could be more pleasant than a sidewalk table at this most welcome addition to Paris's thriving bistro scene. On a cool day the red banquettes and Ingo Maurer chandelier cast a cozy glow, all the better to enjoy a hearty, well-priced selection of dishes, like slices of foie gras served atop crème de lentilles and sprinkled with garlicky croutons, ham clafoutis with girolle mushrooms, or a rosy beef entrecôte with roasted baby Yukon gold potatoes and mushrooms *de Paris*. In springtime, fat white asparagus is nicely paired with salty smoked haddock and spring peas. A wine list replete with well-chosen natural wines plus the reasonable €25 tasting menu at lunch and €34 at dinner make it one of more popular tables in town, so reserve ahead. [$] *Average main: €24* ✉ *12 av. Richerand, 10e, Canal St-Martin* ☎ *01–42–38–00–13* ✍ *Reservations essential* ⏲ *Closed weekends* [M] *Jacques Bonsergent* ✥ *1:H2.*

11E ARRONDISSEMENT (BASTILLE/RÉPUBLIQUE)

$$ BISTRO FAMILY 🍴 **Astier.** There are three good reasons to go to Astier: the generous cheese platter plunked on your table atop a help-yourself wicker tray, the exceptional wine cellar with bottles dating back to the 1970s, and the French bistro fare, even if portions seem to have diminished over the years. Dishes like marinated herring with warm potato salad, sausage with lentils, and baba au rhum are classics on the frequently changing set menu for €35, which includes a selection of no less than 20 cheeses. The vintage 1950s wood-panel dining room attracts plenty of locals and remains a fairly sure bet in the area, especially because it's open every day. [$] *Average main: €21* ✉ *44 rue Jean-Pierre Timbaud, 11e, République* ☎ *01–43–57–16–35* 🌐 *www.restaurant-astier.com* ✍ *Reservations essential* [M] *Parmentier* ✥ *1:H3.*

$ WINE BAR 🍴 **Au Passage.** This new-ish *bistrot à vins* has the lived-in look of a neighborhood eatery going 30 years strong, which, in fact, it was until two veterans of the raging Paris wine bar scene reinvented the place, keeping the laid-back atmosphere and adding a serious foodie menu that quickly became one of the best deals in town. For lunch (Thursday and Friday only), the two-course €18 *menu du marché* formule offers a choice of meat or fish, and at dinner the menu shifts to a blackboard selection of small €4 to €8 tapas dishes—including several house-made patés, fresh tomato or beet salad, a superb seafood carpaccio, and artisanal charcuterie and cheeses. Four or more diners can hack away at a crispy-succulent roasted lamb haunch. The excellent wine list features plenty of natural wines. It's a diverse and lively crowd of happy diners who know they've found a very good thing. [$] *Average main: €15* ✉ *1 bis, passage Saint-Sébastien, 11e, République* ☎ *01–43–55–07–52* ✍ *Reservations essential* ⏲ *Closed Sun. No lunch Sat.–Wed.* [M] *Saint Ambroise; Saint Sebastien Froissart; Richard Lenoir* ✣ *1:H4.*

$$ BISTRO Fodor's Choice ★

🍴 **Le Bistrot Paul Bert.** Faded 1930s decor: check. Boisterous crowd: check. Thick steak with real frites: check. Good value: check. The Paul Bert delivers everything you could want from a traditional Paris bistro, so it's no wonder its two dining rooms fill every night with a cosmopolitan crowd. Some are from the neighborhood, others have done their bistro research, but they've all come for the balance of ingredients that makes for a feel-good experience every time. The impressively stocked wine cellar helps, as does the cheese cart, the laid-back yet efficient staff, and hearty dishes such as monkfish with white beans and duck with pears. The reasonable prix fixe is three courses for €36, or you can order à la carte. If you're looking for an inexpensive wine, choose from the chalkboard rather than the wine list. [$] *Average main: €22* ✉ *18 rue Paul Bert, 11e, Bastille/Nation* ☎ *01–43–72–24–01* ✍ *Reservations essential* ⏲ *Closed Sun., Mon., and Aug.* [M] *Rue des Boulets* ✣ *1:H5*

$$ WINE BAR

🍴 **Le Dauphin.** Avant-garde chef Inaki Aizpatarte has struck again, transforming (with a little help from Rem Koolhaas) a dowdy little café two doors from his acclaimed Le Chateaubriand into a sleek, if chilly, all-marble watering hole for late-night cuisinistas. Honing his ever-iconoclastic take on tapas, the dishes served here—along with a thoughtful selection of natural wines—are a great way to get an idea of what all the fuss is about. Offerings like sweetly delicate crabmeat punctuated with tart marinated radish and avocado puree, or a well-prepared lemon sole drizzled with hazelnut butter highlight what this chef can do with quality ingredients. Dishes are small, well-priced, and meant to be shared to maximize exposure to the food. [$] *Average main: €20* ✉ *131 av. Parmentier, 11e, Canal St-Martin* ☎ *01–55–28–78–88* ✍ *Reservations essential* ⏲ *Closed Sun. and Mon. No lunch Sat.* [M] *Parmentier* ✣ *1:H3.*

$$ BISTRO

🍴 **Le Repaire de Cartouche.** In this split-level, dark-wood bistro between Bastille and République, chef Rodolphe Paquin applies a disciplined creativity to earthy French regional dishes. The menu changes regularly, but typical options are a salad of haricots verts topped with tender slices of squid; scallops on a bed of diced pumpkin; juicy lamb with white beans; game dishes in winter; and old-fashioned desserts like baked custard with tiny shell-shape madeleines. In keeping with cost-conscious times, there is a bargain three-course lunch menu for €18 that doesn't skimp on ingredients—expect the likes of homemade pâté to start, followed by fried red mullet or hanger steak with french fries, and chocolate tart. The wine list is very good, too, with some bargain selections from small producers. [$] *Average main: €24* ✉ *99 rue Amelot, 11e, Bastille/Nation* ☎ *01–47–00–25–86* ✍ *Reservations essential* ⏲ *Closed Sun., Mon., and Aug.* [M] *Filles du Calvaire* ✣ *1:H4.*

$$ BISTRO

🍴 **Rino.** The unanointed might walk right by this modest storefront eatery without an inkling of the gastronomic mecca within. Decor takes second place to the impressive cuisine that the welcoming Roman chef Giovani Passerini—Rino to his friends—consistently offers. Dishes like tender mackerel ravioli alongside razor-thin slices of watermelon radish, briny bottarga, and a drizzle of bitter lemon aïoli, or lightly seared monkfish with tiny samplings of sea urchin and velvety bone marrow served with a rich squid-ink sauce highlight what this restaurant is about: top-notch ingredients, original pairings, and a rare simplicity. With a reasonable four- or six-course dinner menu (€41, €58) and lunch menus of two or three courses (€23, €28)—there is no à la carte—and a small but informed wine list, what's not to love? [$] *Average main: €20* ✉ *46 rue Trousseau, 11e, Bastille/Nation* ☎ *01–48–06–95–85* 🌐 *www.rino-restaurant.com* ✍ *Reservations essential* 🕒 *Closed Sun., Mon., Aug., and 1 wk at Christmas. No lunch Tues.–Thurs.* [M] *Charonne* ✥ *1:H5.*

$$ BISTRO

🍴 **Septime.** This is the kind of bistro we'd all love in our neighborhood—good food and a convivial atmosphere where diners crane to admire each other's plates. Bertrand Grébaut, the affable young chef, can often be found chatting away with guests in the cacophonous dining room. In a neighborhood where excellent bistro fare is ridiculously plentiful—thanks to several talented young chefs who've set up shop here in the last few years—this spot stands out. Seasonal ingredients, inventive pairings, excellent natural wines, plus dishes like creamy gnochetti in an orange rind–flecked Gouda sauce sprinkled with coriander flowers; tender fillet of Landes hen in a mustard-peanut sauce, with braised endive and cabbage perfumed with lemon; fresh white asparagus with raspberries and blanched almonds, are sophisticated and satisfying. The €28 weekday lunch menu is a good place to begin. [$] *Average main: €20* ✉ *80 rue de Charonne, 11e, Bastille/Nation* ☎ *01–43–67–38–29* 🌐 *www.septime-charonne.fr* ✍ *Reservations essential* 🕒 *Closed weekends. No lunch Mon.* [M] *Ledru Rollin, Charonne* ✥ *1:H3.*

14E ARRONDISSEMENT (MONTPARNASSE)

$$ BRASSERIE FAMILY

🍴 **La Coupole.** This world-renowned cavernous spot with Art Deco murals practically defines the term *brasserie*. La Coupole might have lost its intellectual aura since it was restored by the Flo restaurant group, which has put its rather commercial stamp on many historic Paris brasseries, but it's been popular since Jean-Paul Sartre and Simone de Beauvoir were regulars, and it's still great fun. Today it attracts a mix of bourgeois families, tourists, and lone diners treating themselves to a dozen oysters. Recent additions to the classic brasserie menu are a tart of caramelized apple and panfried foie gras, beef fillet flambéed with cognac before your eyes, and profiteroles made with Valrhona chocolate. You usually can't make reservations after 8 or 8:30, so be prepared for a wait at the bar. [$] *Average main: €22* ✉ *102 bd. du Montparnasse, 14e, Montparnasse* ☎ *01–43–20–14–20* 🌐 *www.flobrasseries.com* [M] *Vavin* ✥ *1:D6.*

16E ARRONDISSEMENT (ARC DE TRIOMPHE/TOUR EIFFEL)

$$$$ FRENCH FUSION Fodor's Choice ★

🍴 **Hiramatsu.** In this Art Deco dining room near Trocadéro, Hajime Nakagawa continues his variations on the subtly Japanese-inspired French cuisine of restaurant namesake Hiroyuki Hiramatsu, who still sometimes works the kitchen. Luxury ingredients feature prominently in dishes such as thin slices of lamb with onion jam and thyme-and-truffle-spiked jus, or an unusual pot-au-feu of oysters with foie gras and black truffle. For dessert, a mille-feuille of caramelized apples comes with rosemary sorbet. Helpful sommeliers will guide you through the staggering wine list, with more than 1,000 different bottles to choose from. There's no way to get away cheaply, so save this for a special occasion, when you might be tempted to order a carte blanche menu for €115 (lunch menus at €48). $ *Average main: €50* ✉ *52 rue de Longchamp, 16e, Trocadéro* ☎ *01–56–81–08–80* ⊕ *www.hiramatsu. co.jp/fr* ⌖ *Reservations essential* ⊘ *Closed weekends, Aug., and 1 wk at Christmas* Ⓜ *Trocadéro* ✛ *1:A3.*

$$$$
MODERN FRENCH
Fodor's Choice
★

✕ **L'Abeille.** Paris Shangri-La Hotel's premier restaurant, L'Abeille refers to Napoléon's imperial emblem, the bee (the building once housed his grand-nephew), but also pays homage to Philippe Labbé, one of France's distinguished chefs. Everything, from the dove-gray decor to the sparkling silver, speaks of quiet elegance—all the better to highlight a masterful cuisine: "harlequin" of yellow, red, and white beets with a ginger-tinged yogurt and aloe vera emulsion; Breton langoustine in a cinnamon-perfumed gelée, with grapefruit pulp and a ginger- and Tahitian vanilla–infused mayonnaise; lightly caramelized scallops in an ethereal cloud of white-chocolate foam; tender fillet of wild duck with a tart-sweet apricot reduction. Desserts are subtle and surprising, like the apple Reinette, paired with fennel and candied lemon zest. For cuisine of this quality, the €210, seven-course tasting menu at dinner is not outlandish. Service is friendly, discreet, devoid of snobbery, and includes all the flourishes that make a dining experience unforgettable, from the first flute of champagne to the parting gift of—what else?—a jar of honey. $ *Average main: €100* ✉ *10 av. d'Iéna, 16e, Trocadéro* ☎ *01–53–67–19–90* ⊕ *www.shangri-la.com* ⌖ *Reservations essential* ⊘ *Closed Mon.* Ⓜ *Iéna* ✛ *1:A3.*

$$$$
MODERN FRENCH
Fodor's Choice
★

✕ **L'Astrance.** Granted, Pascal Barbot rose to fame thanks to his restaurant's amazing-value food and casual atmosphere, but after the passage of several years, Astrance has become resolutely haute, with prices to match. There's no à la carte; you can choose from a lunch menu for €70, a seasonal menu for €120, or the full tasting menu for €210 (this is what most people come for)—the latter two are available at lunch and dinner. His dishes often draw on Asian ingredients, as in grilled lamb with miso-lacquered eggplant and a palate-cleansing white sorbet spiked with chili pepper and lemongrass. Each menu also comes at a (considerably) higher price with wines to match each course. Barbot's cooking has such an ethereal quality that it's worth the considerable effort of booking a table—you should start trying at least two months in advance. $ *Average main: €120* ✉ *4 rue Beethoven, 16e, Trocadéro* ☎ *01–40–50–84–40* ⌖ *Reservations essential* ⊘ *Closed Sat.–Mon., 1 wk in May, 1 wk in early Nov., and all of Aug.* Ⓜ *Passy* ✛ *1:A3.*

$$$
BISTRO

✕ **La Table Lauriston.** Serge Barbey has developed a winning formula in his chic bistro near the Trocadéro: top-notch ingredients, simply prepared and generously served. To start, you can't go wrong with his silky foie gras *au torchon*—the liver is poached in a flavorful bouillon—or one of the seasonal salads, such as white asparagus in herb vinaigrette; his trademark dish, a gargantuan rib steak, is big enough to silence even the hungriest Texan. Given the neighborhood you might expect a businesslike setting, but the dining room feels cheerful, with vividly colored walls and velvet-upholstered chairs, and there is a 16-seat terrace. Don't miss the giant *baba au rhum*, which the waiters will douse with a choice of three rums. ⓢ *Average main: €28* ✉ *129 rue de Lauriston, Trocadéro* ☏ *01–47–27–00–07* ⊕ *www.restaurantlatablelauriston.com* ⚑ *Reservations essential* ⊘ *Closed Sun., 3 wks in Aug., and 1 wk at Christmas. No lunch Sat.* Ⓜ *Trocadéro* ✛ *1:A3.*

17E ARRONDISSEMENT (CHAMPS-ÉLYSÉES)

$$$$
MODERN FRENCH
Fodor's Choice
★

✕ **Guy Savoy.** Revamped with dark African wood, rich leather, cream-color marble, and the chef's own art collection, Guy Savoy's luxury restaurant doesn't dwell on the past. Come here for a perfectly measured haute-cuisine experience, since Savoy's several bistros have not lured him away from the kitchen. The artichoke soup with black truffles, sea bass with spices, and veal kidneys in mustard-spiked jus reveal the magnitude of his talent, and his mille-feuille is an instant classic. If the waiters see you're relishing a dish, they won't hesitate to offer second helpings. Generous half portions allow you to graze your way through the menu—unless you choose a blowout feast for set menus of €330 or €360—and reasonably priced wines are available (though beware the cost of wines by the glass). The €110 lunch special is a good way to sample some of this fine chef's inspired cooking. Best of all, the atmosphere is joyful, because Savoy knows that having fun is just as important as eating well. ⓢ *Average main: €120* ✉ *18 rue Troyon, 17e, Champs-Élysées* ☏ *01–43–80–40–61* ⊕ *www.guysavoy.com* ⚑ *Reservations essential. Jacket required* ⊘ *Closed Sun., Mon., Aug., and 1 wk at Christmas. No lunch Sat.* Ⓜ *Charles-de-Gaulle–Étoile* ✛ *1:B2.*

$$$
SEAFOOD
Fodor's Choice
★

✕ **Rech.** Having restored the historic Paris bistros Aux Lyonnais and Benoît to their former glory, star chef Alain Ducasse turned his piercing attention to this seafood brasserie founded in 1925. His wisdom lies in knowing what not to change: the original Art Deco chairs in the main floor dining room; seafood shucker Malec, who has been a fixture on this chic stretch of sidewalk since 1982; and the XL éclair (it's supersize) that's drawn in locals for decades. Original owner Auguste Rech believed in serving a limited selection of high-quality products—a principle that suits Ducasse perfectly—and legendary 60-year-old chef Jacques Maximin is now in the kitchen, turning out Med-inspired dishes such as tomato cream with crayfish and fresh almonds or Niçoise-style sea bass with thyme fritters. Save room for the whole farmer's Camembert, another Rech tradition. A great-value €32 menu is available at lunch; the dinner menu is €54. ⓢ *Average main: €32* ✉ *62 av. des Ternes, 17e, Champs-Élysées* ☏ *01–45–72–29–47* ⊕ *www.restaurant-rech.fr* ⚑ *Reservations essential* ⊘ *Closed Sun., Mon., late July–late Aug., and 1 wk at Christmas* Ⓜ *Ternes.* ✛ *1:A1.*

CAFÉS AND SALONS DE THÉ

Along with air, water, and wine (Parisians eat fewer and fewer three-course meals), the café remains one of the basic necessities of life in Paris; following is a small selection of cafés and *salons de thé* (tearooms) to whet your appetite.

A Priori Thé. American Peggy Hancock opened A Priori Thé in 1980. She—and her delicious scones and cakes—have been comforting travelers ever since. Come for lunch, afternoon tea, or weekend brunch. ✉ *35 Galerie Vivienne, Louvre/Tuileries* ☎ *01–42–97–48–75* [M] *Bourse.*

Café Charbon. This ultracool café, with a restored zinc bar, mirrored walls, and mismatched chandeliers, is a neighborhood institution. ✉ *109 rue Oberkampf, Oberkampf* ☎ *01–43–57–55–13* [M] *Parmentier.*

Café des Musées. Warm and authentic, this bustling little bistro offers a convivial slice of Parisian life—and excellent value. Here traditional French bistro fare is adapted to a modern audience, and the best choices are the old tried-and-trues: hand-cut *tartare de boeuf*; rare entrecôte served with a side of golden-crisp frites and homemade béarnaise; and the classic *parmentier* with pheasant instead of the usual ground beef. Portions are ample, but save room for dessert: old-style favorites like *diplomate aux cherises,* a rum-soaked, cherry-laden sponge cake, or the terrine de chocolate with crème Anglaise are not to be missed. Fixed menus are a bargain at €14 for lunch. À la carte at dinner. [$] *Average main: €17* ✉ *49 rue de Turenne, 3e, Marais* ☎ *01–42–72–96–17* ✍ *Reservations essential* ⏲ *Closed Aug. and 1 wk in Jan.* [M] *St-Paul.*

Ladurée. The most opulent branch of the Ladurée tea salon empire is worth the splurge for lunch. Reserve a table or grab a bite in the Art Nouveau bar in the back. Sweets are a house specialty. In addition to more than two dozen different flavors of *macaron,* it has assorted cakes and pastries, plus beautifully boxed treats: the latter make a tasty (and tasteful) gift. ✉ *75 av. des Champs-Élysées, Champs-Élysées* ☎ *01–40–75–08–75* [M] *George V.*

La Palette. The terrace of this corner café, opened in 1902, is a favorite haunt of local gallery owners and Beaux Arts students. Meals are served at lunch, while sandwiches and lighter fare are available at other times of day. Films fans may recognize it as the place where Owen Wilson's character meets Hemingway in Woody Allen's *Midnight in Paris.* ■ **TIP→ Come at sunset—or later—when the scene gets lively.** ✉ *43 rue de Seine, St-Germain-des-Prés* ☎ *01–43–26–68–15* 🌐 *www.cafelapaletteparis.com* [M] *Mabillon.*

Le Loir dans la Théière. Sink into one of the comfortable shabby armchairs at this popular tearoom, whose name translates to the Dormouse in the Teapot (from *Alice in Wonderland*). The sweet and savory tarts are stellar, but the real stars are desserts like the decadent chocolate crumble tart. ✉ *3 rue des Rosiers, Marais* ☎ *01–42–72–90–61* [M] *St-Paul.*

Mariage Frères. Mariage Frères, with its colonial *charme* and wooden counters, has 100-plus years of tea purveying behind it. Choose from more than 450 blends from 32 countries, not to mention teapots, teacups, books, and tea-flavor biscuits and candies. Both tearooms serve high tea and a light lunch, although the St. Germain location is considerably less frenzied. ✉ *30 rue du Bourg-Tibourg, 4e, Marais* 🕾 *01–42–72–28–11* Ⓜ *Hôtel de Ville.*

WHERE TO STAY

Updated by
Victoria Tang

If your Parisian fantasy involves staying in a historic hotel with the smell of fresh-baked croissants gently rousing you in the morning, here's some good news: you need not be Ritz-rich to realize it. With more than 1,450 hotels, the City of Light gives visitors stylish options in all price ranges.

In terms of location, there are more hotels on the Rive Droite (the Right Bank) offering luxury—in terms of formality—than on the Rive Gauche (the Left Bank), where the hotels are frequently smaller and richer in old-fashioned charm. The Rive Droite's 1er, 8e, and 16e arrondissements are still the most exclusive. Less expensive alternatives on the Rive Droite can be found in the fashionable Marais quarter (3e and 4e arrondissements). The hotbed of chic hotels on the Rive Gauche is the 6e arrondissement; choices get cheaper in the 5e and 7e. Some excellent budget deals can be found slightly off the beaten track in the 9e and 13e arrondissements. Wherever possible, we've located budget hotels in more expensive neighborhoods—check out the handful of budget-priced sleeps in the shadow of Notre-Dame, St-Germain-des-Prés, and the Louvre.

Although historic charm is a given, space to stretch out is not. Even budget travelers can sleep under 200-year-old wooden beams, but if you're looking for enough room to spread out multiple suitcases, better book a suite in a four-star palace hotel. Indoor spaces—from beds to elevators—may feel cramped to those not used to life on a European scale. A no-smoking law went into effect in all public spaces in January 2008. Enforcement is not always perfect, but at least now you'll have a valid complaint if your room smells like stale smoke. Amenities have also improved, with virtually every hotel now equipped with cable TV, minibars (aka refrigerators), in-room safes, and wireless Internet access (though not always free). A recent change is the increasing availability of air-conditioning, which can be saintly in August.

Alphapetical by neighborhood. Use the coordinate (✛ 2:D4) at the end of each listing to locate a site on the corresponding map.

1ER ARRONDISSEMENT (LOUVRE/LES HALLES)

$$$$
HOTEL

🎬 **Hôtel Brighton.** A few of Paris' most prestigious palace hotels face the Tuileries or place de la Concorde, and while the Brighton sits on the same prime real estate under the arcades, it offers visitors a privileged stay for a fraction of the price. **Pros:** convenient central location in a prestigious neighborhood; friendly service; breakfast buffet (free for kids under 12). **Cons:** variable quality in decor between rooms; no restaurant for lunch or dinner; no fitness center or spa. Ⓢ *Rooms from: €320* ✉ *218 rue de Rivoli, 1er, Louvre/Tuileries* 🕾 *01–47–03–61–61* 🖨 *01–42–60–41–78* ⊕ *www.paris-hotel-brighton.com* ⬳ *61 rooms* ⍾ *Breakfast* Ⓜ *Tuileries* ✛ *2:D3.*

BEST BETS FOR PARIS LODGING

Fodor's offers a selective listing of high-quality lodging experiences at every price range, from the best budget options to the most sophisticated grande-dame hotel. Below are our top recommendations by price and experience.

Fodor's Choice

Four Seasons Hôtel George V Paris, $$$$, p. 142

Hôtel Familia, $, p. 137

Hôtel Meurice, $$$$, p. 131

Hôtel Plaza Athénée, $$$$, p. 143

Shangri-La Hotel Paris, $$$$, p. 145

By Price

$

Hôtel du Champ de Mars, p. 142

Hôtel Familia, $, p. 137

Hôtel Henri IV, p. 131

Hôtel Marignan, p. 137

Hôtel Tiquetonne, p. 134

Hôtel Vivienne, p. 134

Port-Royal Hôtel, p. 138

$$

Hôtel Mama Shelter, p. 145

$$$

Hôtel Relais Saint-Sulpice, p. 140

$$$$

Four Seasons Hôtel George V Paris, p. 142

Hôtel Duc de Saint-Simon, p. 140

Hôtel Meurice, $$$$, p. 131

Hôtel Plaza Athénée, $$$$, p. 143

Hôtel Odéon Saint-Germain, p. 140

Hôtel Seven, p. 138

Shangri-La Hotel Paris, $$$$, p. 145

By Experience

MOST CHARMING

Hôtel d'Aubusson, $$$$, p. 139

HISTORIC

Hôtel de la Place des Vosges, $, p. 135

BEST DESIGN

The Five Hôtel, $$$, p. 137

Hôtel Seven, $$$$, p. 138

Le Bellechasse, $$$$, p. 142

MOST CENTRAL

Hôtel Henri IV, $, p. 131

Hôtel Meurice, $$$$, p. 131

BUSINESS TRAVEL

Four Seasons Hôtel George V Paris, $$$$, p. 142

Hôtel Mama Shelter, $$, p. 145

BEST VIEWS

Hôtel Brighton, $$$$, p. 128

Shangri-La Hotel Paris, $$$$, p. 145

MOST ROMANTIC

Hôtel Caron de Beaumarchais, $$, p. 135

Hotel Seven, $$$$, p. 138

L'Hôtel, $$$$, p. 140

WHERE SHOULD I STAY?

	NEIGHBORHOOD VIBE	PROS	CONS
St-Germain and Montparnasse (6e, 14e, 15e)	The center of café culture and the emblem of the Left Bank, the mood is leisurely, the attractions are well established, and the prices are high.	A safe, historic area with chic fashion boutiques, famous cafés and brasseries, and lovely side streets. Lively day and night.	Expensive. Noisy along the main streets. The area around the monstrous Tour Montparnasse is a soul-sucking tribute to commerce.
The Quartier Latin (5e)	The historic student quarter of the Left Bank, full of narrow, winding streets, and major parks and monuments such as the Panthéon.	Plenty of cheap eats and sleeps, discount book and music shops, and noteworthy open-air markets. Safe area for wandering walks.	Touristy. No métro stations on the hilltop around the Panthéon. Student pubs can be noisy in summer. Hotel rooms tend to be smaller.
Marais and Bastille (3e, 4e, 11e)	Cute shops, museums, and laid-back bistros line the narrow streets of the Marais, home to both the gay and Jewish communities. Farther east, ethnic eats and edgy shops.	Generally excellent shopping, sightseeing, dining, and nightlife in the super-safe Marais. Bargains aplenty at Bastille hotels. Several modern-design hotels, too.	The Marais's narrow sidewalks are always overcrowded, and rooms don't come cheap. It's noisy around the gritty boulevards of place de la Bastille and Nation.
Montmartre and northeast Paris (18e, 19e)	The hilltop district is known for winding streets leading from the racy Pigalle district to the stark-white Sacré-Coeur Basilica.	Amazing views of Paris, romantic cobblestone streets, easy access to Roissy-Charles de Gaulle airport.	Steep staircases, few métro stations, and Pigalle can be too seedy to stomach, especially late at night, when it can also be unsafe.
Champs-Élysées and western Paris (8e, 16e, 17e)	The world-famous avenue is lively 24/7 with cinemas, high-end shops, and nightclubs, all catering to the moneyed jet set.	The home to most of the city's famous palace hotels, there's no shortage of luxurious sleeps here.	The high prices of this neighborhood, along with its Times Square tendencies, repel Parisians but lure pickpockets.
Around the Tour Eiffel (7e, 15e)	The impressive Eiffel Tower and monumental Palais de Chaillot at Trocadéro straddle the Seine River.	Safe, quiet, and relatively inexpensive area of Paris with green spaces and picture-perfect views at every turn.	With few shops and restaurants, this district is very quiet at night; long distances between métro stations.
Louvre, Les Halles, Ile de la Cité (1e, 2e, 8e)	The central Parisian district around the Tuileries gardens and Louvre museum is best known for shopping and sightseeing; Les Halles is a buzzing hub of commerce and mass transit.	Convenient for getting around Paris on foot, bus, or métro. Safe, attractive district close to the Seine and shops of all types. All the major métro and RER lines are right by Les Halles.	The main drag along rue de Rivoli can be noisy with traffic during the day, and the restaurants cater mostly to tourists. Shops are tacky and fast food predominates around Les Halles.

2

$ HOTEL **Hôtel Henri IV.** This 17th-century building, which once housed King Henri IV's printing presses on the Ile de la Cité, offers few comforts or amenities, but you'll be hard-pressed to find a more central hotel for this price. **Pros:** very quiet; top rooms have balconies; basic breakfast included. **Cons:** steep stairs in poor condition and no elevator; few services or amenities; reservations by phone only. [$] *Rooms from: €78 ✉ 25 pl. Dauphine, 1er ☎ 01–43–54–44–53 🌐 www.henri4hotel.fr 🛏 15 rooms, 14 with bath 🍴 Breakfast [M] Cité, St-Michel, Pont Neuf ✥ 2:F5.*

$$$$ HOTEL **Hôtel Le Pradey.** Opened in 2011, this compact boutique hotel near the Tuileries pays homage to Parisian style, with rooms boasting themes such as Zinc and Haussmann Stone, with Michel Cluizel chocolates, Fragonard toiletries, and oil paintings of Paris. **Pros:** choice of copious breakfast buffet or quick coffee and croissant; designer touches throughout; double doors for soundproofing in suites. **Cons:** smaller rooms lack closet space; rooms vary greatly in style; nondescript entry with lackluster service results in lukewarm welcome. [$] *Rooms from: €390 ✉ 5 rue St-Roch, 1er, Louvre/Tuileries ☎ 01–42–60–31–70 🌐 www.lepradey.com 🛏 21 rooms, 7 suites 🍴 Breakfast [M] Tuileries ✥ 2:E3.*

$$ HOTEL **Hôtel Londres St-Honoré.** Across from a historic 17th century church smack-dab in the center of Paris, this no-frills inexpensive hotel is comfortable and clean. **Pros:** within walking distance of major sites; free Wi-Fi; friendly service. **Cons:** small beds with worn decor; tiny elevator that doesn't go to ground floor; extremely narrow staircase. [$] *Rooms from: €147 ✉ 13 rue St-Roch, 1er, Louvre/Tuileries ☎ 01–42–60–15–62 🌐 www.hotellondresssthonore-paris.com 🛏 24 rooms, 4 suites 🍴 Breakfast [M] Pyramides ✥ 2:E3.*

$$$$ HOTEL FAMILY Fodor's Choice ★ **Hôtel Meurice.** The first Parisian palace hotel, where most rooms have a view on the Tuileries/Louvre or Sacré-Coeur, appeals to art history aficionados: contemporary sculpture, antique furnishings, and attractive murals are spread around the rooms, corridors, and sumptuous dining areas. **Pros:** views over the Tuileries gardens; central location convenient to métro and major sites; trendy public spaces. **Cons:** popularity makes the public areas not very discreet; inconsistent front desk service at times unattentive; expensive room rates. [$] *Rooms from: €720 ✉ 228 rue de Rivoli, 1er, Louvre/Tuileries ☎ 01–44–58–10–09 📠 01–44–58–10–19 🌐 www.lemeurice.com 🛏 118 rooms, 42 suites [M] Tuileries, Concorde ✥ 2:D3.*

$$$$ HOTEL **Meliá Vendome Boutique Hotel.** Centrally located in a prestigious quarter a few minutes walk from the Tuileries gardens, place de la Concorde, Louvre, and Garnier Opera House, the Melia Vendome has handsome and spacious rooms in attractive contemporary tones to exude an understated elegance in warm woods and textural fabrics. **Pros:** oustanding location smack-dab in city center; near shops, transportation, and major sites; elegant, immaculate rooms. **Cons:** expensive breakfast; no spa or pool; in-room cooling system unreliable. [$] *Rooms from: €408 ✉ 8 rue Cambon, Around the Louvre ☎ 01–44–77–54–00 📠 01–44–77–54– 01 🌐 www.melia.com 🛏 78 rooms, 5 suites 🍴 Breakfast [M] Concorde, Madeleine ✥ 2:D3.*

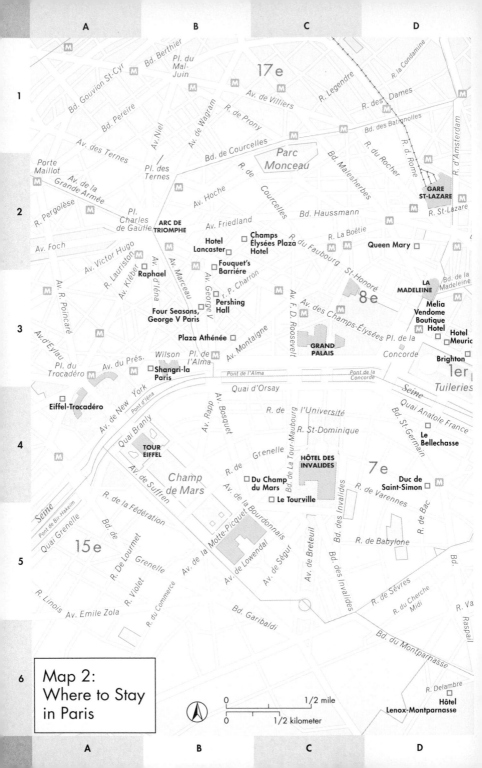

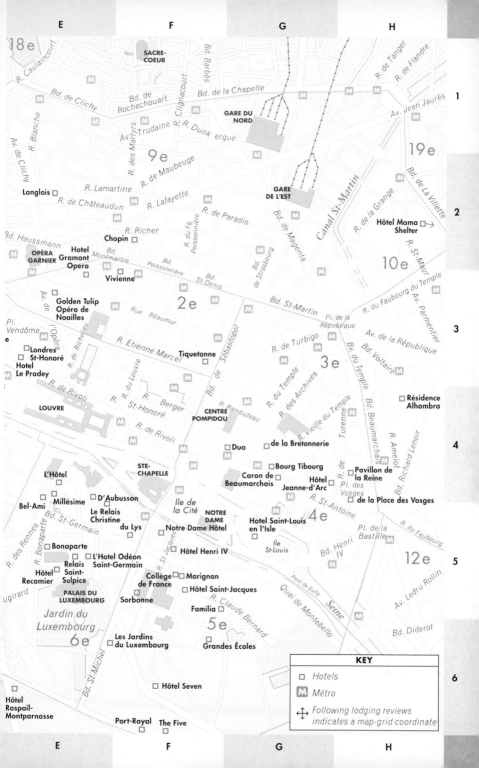

2E ARRONDISSEMENT (BOURSE/LES HALLES)

$$$ HOTEL **Golden Tulip Opera de Noailles.** With a nod to the work of postmodern designers like Putman and Starck, this stylized boutique hotel acquired by a French hotel chain conglomerate is both contemporary and cozy, and accessible to major monuments and museums. **Pros:** free Wi-Fi; a block from the airport bus; easy 15- to 20-minute walk to the Louvre and Opéra. **Cons:** small elevator; no interesting views with location in business district; some bathrooms in need of renovation. [$] *Rooms from: €255* ✉ *9 rue de Michodière, 2e, Opéra/Grands Boulevards* ☎ *01–47–42–92–90* 📠 *01–49–24–92–71* 🌐 *www.hoteldenoailles.com* 🛏 *56 rooms* 🍴 *Breakfast* [M] *Opéra* ✥ *2:E3.*

$ HOTEL **Hôtel Tiquetonne.** Just off the Montorgueil market and a short walk from Les Halles (and slightly seedy rue St-Denis), this is one of the least expensive hotels in the city center. **Pros:** dirt-cheap rooms in the center of town; in trendy shopping and nightlife area; seventh-floor views onto Sacré-Coeur. **Cons:** minimal service and no amenities; noise from the street; decor feels outdated. [$] *Rooms from: €65* ✉ *6 rue Tiquetonne, 2e, Les Halles* ☎ *01–42–36–94–58* 📠 *01–42–36–02–94* 🌐 *www.hoteltiquetonne.fr* 🛏 *45 rooms, 33 with bath* [M] *Étienne Marcel* ✥ *2:F3.*

$ HOTEL FAMILY **Hôtel Vivienne.** The hotel's central location near the Opéra Garnier and Grands Boulevards department stores make this a good bet for the price, even if the decor is a bit bipolar. **Pros:** good value for central Paris; a block from the métro station; friendly service. **Cons:** a noisy street and late-night bar across the road can make it hard to keep windows open in summer; some rooms have minimal closet space and tiny showers; eclectic interior design is a hodgepodge of aesthetic style. ■ **TIP→ All children under 10 years stay free of charge when using existing bedding. Check website for special last-minute offers.** [$] *Rooms from: €100* ✉ *40 rue Vivienne, 2e, Opéra/Grands Boulevards* ☎ *01–42–33–13–26* 📠 *01–40–41–98–19* 🌐 *www.hotel-vivienne.com* 🛏 *45 rooms, 35 with bath* 🍴 *Breakfast* [M] *Bourse, Richelieu-Drouot* ✥ *2:F3.*

3E ARRONDISSEMENT (BEAUBOURG/MARAIS)

$$$$ HOTEL **Pavillon de la Reine.** This enchanting countrylike château is hidden off the regal place des Vosges behind a stunning garden courtyard. **Pros:** Parisian historic character; proximity to place des Vosges without the noise; Carita spa treatments. **Cons:** expensive for the Marais and the size of the rooms; the nearest métro is a few blocks away; no uniform theme in interior design. [$] *Rooms from: €410* ✉ *28 pl. des Vosges, 3e, Marais* ☎ *01–40–29–19–19, 800/447–7462 in U.S.* 🌐 *www.pavillon-de-la-reine.com* 🛏 *31 rooms, 23 suites* 🍴 *Breakfast* [M] *Bastille, St-Paul* ✥ *2:H4.*

4E ARRONDISSEMENT (MARAIS/ILE ST-LOUIS)

$$$ HOTEL **Hôtel Bourg Tibourg.** Scented candles and subdued lighting announce designer-du-jour Jacques Garcia's mix of harem-like romance and Gothic contemplation. **Pros:** right in the heart of trendy Marais district; adequate rooms at moderate prices; great nightlife district. **Cons:** rooms are small, poorly lighted, and ill equipped for those with large suitcases; no hotel restaurant; lounge area small and gets easily crowded. [$] *Rooms from: €250* ✉ *19 rue Bourg Tibourg, 4e, Marais*

☎ 01–42–78–47–39 📠 01–40–29–07–00 🌐 www.hotelbourgtibourg.com 🛏 29 rooms, 1 suite 🍴 Breakfast [M] *Hôtel de Ville ⊕ 2:G4.*

$$ HOTEL 🏨 **Hôtel Caron de Beaumarchais.** For that traditional French feeling, book a room at this intimate, romantic hotel with 19 affordable rooms—the theme is the work of former next-door neighbor Pierre-Augustin Caron de Beaumarchais, supplier of military aid to American revolutionaries and playwright who penned *The Marriage of Figaro* and *The Barber of Seville*. **Pros:** cozy Parisian decor of yesteryear; breakfast in bed (served until noon); excellent location in easy walking distance to major monuments. **Cons:** small rooms with no major facilities; busy street of bars and cafés can be noisy; historic charm may feel old-fashioned and outdated for younger crowd. [$] *Rooms from: €165 ✉ 12 rue Vieille-du-Temple, 4e, Marais ☎ 01–42–72–34–12 🌐 www.carondebeaumarchais.com 🛏 19 rooms 🍴 Breakfast* [M] *Hôtel de Ville ⊕ 2:G4.*

$$$ HOTEL 🏨 **Hôtel de la Bretonnerie.** Situated in a 17th-century *hôtel particulier* (town house) on a tiny street in the Marais, this small hotel with exposed wooden beams and traditional styling is a few minutes' walk from the Centre Pompidou and numerous bars and cafés of rue Vieille du Temple. **Pros:** central location and comfortable decor at a moderate price; typical Parisian character; free Wi-Fi Internet. **Cons:** quality and size of the rooms vary greatly; no air-conditioning; rooms facing street can be noisy. **■ TIP→ Ask for rooms facing interior courtyard for a quieter sleep.** [$] *Rooms from: €179 ✉ 22 rue Ste-Croix-de-la-Bretonnerie, 4e, Marais ☎ 01–48–87–77–63 📠 01–42–77–26–78 🌐 www.bretonnerie.com 🛏 22 rooms, 7 suites 🍴 Breakfast* [M] *Hôtel de Ville ⊕ 2:G4.*

$ HOTEL 🏨 **Hôtel de la Place des Vosges.** Despite a lack of amenities and Lilliputian elevator that doesn't serve all floors, a loyal clientele swears by this small, historic hotel just off the 17th-century place des Vosges. **Pros:** excellent location near famous sites and public transportation; fans on request; historic Old World ambience. **Cons:** no air-conditioning; most rooms are very small; street-facing rooms can be noisy. [$] *Rooms from: €110 ✉ 12 rue de Birague, 4e, Marais ☎ 01–42–72–60–46 📠 01–42–72–02–64 🌐 www.hotelplacedesvosges.com 🛏 16 rooms 🍴 Breakfast* [M] *Bastille ⊕ 2:H4.*

$$$ HOTEL 🏨 **Hôtel Duo.** For this hotel in the heart of the trendy Marais district, architect Jean Philippe Nuel was commissioned to design a clean, contemporary style with bold colors and dramatic lighting; some rooms have the original 16th-century beams integrated into the decor, but the overall feel is casual urban chic. **Pros:** central location near shops and cafés; walking distance to major monuments; good amenities. **Cons:** noisy street; service not always delivered with a smile; small standard rooms and bathrooms. **■ TIP→ Ask for an upper floor room to avoid street noise.** [$] *Rooms from: €240 ✉ 11 rue du Temple, 4e, Marais ☎ 01–42–72–72–22 📠 01–42–72–03–53 🌐 www.duoparis.com 🛏 58 rooms 🍴 Breakfast* [M] *Hôtel de Ville ⊕ 2:G4.*

$ HOTEL 🏨 **Hôtel Jeanne-d'Arc.** You can get your money's worth at this hotel for its unbeatable location off the tranquil place du Marché Ste-Catherine, one of the city's lesser-known pedestrian squares. **Pros:** charming street close to major sites; good value for the Marais; lots of drinking and

Hôtel Plaza Athénée

Shangri-La Hotel Paris

dining options nearby. **Cons:** garbage trucks and late-night revelers on the square after midnight can be noisy; minimal amenities; rooms are small with dreary decor and not air-conditioned. [$] *Rooms from: €96* ✉ *3 rue de Jarente, 4e, Marais* ☎ *01–48–87–62–11* 📠 *01–48–87–37–31* 🌐 *www.hoteljeannedarc.com* 🛏 *35 rooms* [M] *St-Paul* ✣ *2:G4.*

$$$ HOTEL 🏨 **Hôtel Saint-Louis en L'Isle.** The location on the exceptionally charming Ile St-Louis is the real draw of this recently renovated hotel, which retains many of its original 17th-century stone walls and wooden beams. **Pros:** romantic location on the tiny Ile St-Louis; ancient architectural details; freshly decorated rooms. **Cons:** location makes the price high; métro stations across the bridge are not so convenient; small rooms. [$] *Rooms from: €189* ✉ *75 rue St-Louis-en-l'Ile, 4e, Ile St-Louis* ☎ *01–46–34–04–80* 📠 *01–46–34–02–13* 🌐 *www.saintlouisenlisle.com* 🛏 *20 rooms* 🍴 *Breakfast* [M] *Pont Marie* ✣ *2:G5.*

5E ARRONDISSEMENT (LATIN QUARTER)

$$$ HOTEL 🏨 **The Five Hôtel.** Small is beautiful at this original tiny design hotel on a quiet street near the Mouffetard market and Latin Quarter. **Pros:** unique stylish design; personalized welcome; quiet side street. **Cons:** most rooms are too small for excessive baggage; the nearest métro is a 15-minute walk; most rooms only have showers. [$] *Rooms from: €225* ✉ *3 rue Flatters, 5e, Latin Quarter* ☎ *01–43–31–74–21* 📠 *01–47–55–19–31* 🌐 *www.thefivehotel.com* 🛏 *24 rooms* 🍴 *Breakfast* [M] *Gobelins* ✣ *2:F6.*

$ HOTEL 🏨 **Hôtel Collège de France.** Exposed stone walls, wooden beams, and medieval artwork echo the style of the Musée Cluny, two blocks from this charming six-floor, family-run hotel. **Pros:** walking distance to major Rive Gauche sights, the islands, and restaurants; free Wi-Fi; ceiling fans. **Cons:** big difference between renovated and unrenovated rooms; no air-conditioning; thin walls between rooms. [$] *Rooms from: €110* ✉ *7 rue Thénard, 5e, Latin Quarter* ☎ *01–43–26–78–36* 🌐 *www.hotelcdf.com* 🛏 *29 rooms* 🍴 *Breakfast* [M] *Maubert-Mutualité, St-Michel–Cluny–La Sorbonne* ✣ *2:F5.*

$ HOTEL FAMILY Fodor's Choice ★ 🏨 **Hôtel Familia.** Owners Eric and Sylvie continue to update and improve this popular budget hotel without raising their prices. **Pros:** attentive, friendly service; great value; lots of character and charm. **Cons:** on a busy street; some rooms are small; noise between rooms can be loud. [$] *Rooms from: €112* ✉ *11 rue des Écoles, 5e, Latin Quarter* ☎ *01–43–54–55–27* 🌐 *www.hotel-paris-familia.com* 🛏 *30 rooms* 🍴 *Breakfast* [M] *Cardinal Lemoine* ✣ *2:F5.*

$$ HOTEL 🏨 **Hôtel Grandes Écoles.** Distributed among a trio of three-story buildings, Madame Le Floch's rooms have a distinct grandmotherly vibe with flowery wallpaper and lace bedspreads, but are downright spacious for this part of Paris. **Pros:** pretty courtyard garden; close to Latin Quarter nightlife spots; good value. **Cons:** uphill walk from the métro; some noisy rooms; few amenities. [$] *Rooms from: €150* ✉ *75 rue du Cardinal Lemoine, 5e, Latin Quarter* ☎ *01–43–26–79–23* 🌐 *www.hotel-grandes-ecoles.com* 🛏 *51 rooms* 🍴 *Breakfast* [M] *Cardinal Lemoine* ✣ *2:F6.*

$ HOTEL FAMILY 🏨 **Hôtel Marignan.** Not to be confused with the hotel of the same name near the Champs-Élysées, this Latin Quarter Marignan lies squarely between budget-basic and youth hostel (no TVs or elevator) and offers lots of communal conveniences—a fully stocked kitchen, free laundry machines, and copious tourist information. **Pros:** great value for the location; free kitchen, breakfast, and laundry facilities; free Wi-Fi. **Cons:** no elevator; room phones take only incoming calls; has a youth-hostel atmosphere. [$] *Rooms from: €115* ✉ *13 rue du Sommerard, 5e, Latin Quarter* ☎ *01–43–54–63–81* 🌐 *www.hotel-marignan.com* 🛏 *30 rooms, 12 with bath* 🍴 *Breakfast* [M] *Maubert-Mutualité* ✣ *2:F5.*

$$$$ HOTEL 🏨 **Hôtel Notre Dame.** If you love the quirky and eclectic fashions of Christian Lacroix and don't mind hauling your bags up some stairs, this unique boutique hotel overlooking Notre Dame Cathedral and Seine River is for you. **Pros:** decor by Christian Lacroix; views of Notre Dame and river; comfortable beds. **Cons:** stairs can be tricky with large bags; no minibar in rooms; some noise from busy street. ⇨ *Do not confuse with Hotel de Notre Dame on a small side street.* [$] *Rooms from: €270* ✉ *1 quai Saint-Michel, 5e, Latin Quarter* ☎ *01–43–54–20–43* 🌐 *www.hotelnotredameparis.com* 🛏 *26 rooms* 🍴 *Breakfast* [M] *St-Michel* ✣ *2:F5.*

$$ HOTEL 🏨 **Hôtel Saint Jacques.** Nearly every wall in this bargain Latin Quarter hotel is bedecked with faux-marble and trompe-l'oeil murals. **Pros:** unique Parisian decor; close to Latin Quarter sights; free Wi-Fi. **Cons:** very busy street makes it too noisy to open windows in summer; thin walls between rooms; rooms need refurbishment. [$] *Rooms from: €168* ✉ *35 rue des Écoles, 5e, Latin Quarter* ☎ *01–44–07–45–45* 🌐 *www.hotel-saintjacques.com* 🛏 *38 rooms* [M] *Maubert-Mutualité* ✣ *2:F5.*

$$$$ HOTEL 🏨 **Hotel Seven.** The "seven" refers to the level of heaven you'll find at this extraordinary boutique hotel. **Pros:** fun design elements; copious breakfast buffet; quiet location near Mouffetard market street; interesting wine bar and cocktail selection at night. **Cons:** small closet space; several blocks to closest métro; expensive room rates with few amenities. [$] *Rooms from: €340* ✉ *20 rue Berthollet, 5e, Latin Quarter* ☎ *01–43–31–47–52* 🌐 *www.sevenhotelparis.com* 🛏 *28 rooms, 7 suites* [M] *Censier-Daubentin* ✣ *2:F6.*

$$$ HOTEL 🏨 **Hotel Sorbonne.** For what French students pay to study at the Sorbonne, visitors can stay a few nights next door at this swanky design hotel. **Pros:** centrally located; fun decor; attentive service. **Cons:** tiny rooms for the price; small breakfast room; leaky plumbing. [$] *Rooms from: €240* ✉ *6 rue Victor Cousin, 5e, Latin Quarter* ☎ *01–43–54–01–52* 🌐 *www.hotelsorbonne.com* 🛏 *38 rooms* 🍴 *Breakfast* [M] *Cluny La Sorbonne* ✣ *2:F5.*

$$$ HOTEL 🏨 **Les Jardins du Luxembourg.** Blessed with a personable staff and a warm ambience, this hotel on a calm cul-de-sac a block away from the Jardin du Luxembourg is an oasis for contemplation. **Pros:** on a quiet street close to major sites and transport; sauna; hot buffet breakfast. **Cons:** extra charge to use Wi-Fi; some very small rooms; air-conditioning not very strong. [$] *Rooms from: €190* ✉ *5 impasse Royer-Collard, 5e, Latin Quarter* ☎ *01–40–46–08–88* 🌐 *www.les-jardins-du-luxembourg.com* 🛏 *26 rooms* 🍴 *Breakfast* [M] *RER: Luxembourg* ✣ *2:E6.*

$ HOTEL 🏨 **Port-Royal Hôtel.** The clean rooms and extra-helpful staff at the Port-Royal are well above average for this price range. **Pros:** excellent value for the money; attentive service; typical Parisian neighborhood close to two major markets. **Cons:** not very central; on a busy street; no air-conditioning or Wi-Fi in rooms. Ⓢ *Rooms from: €84* ⊠ *8 bd. de Port-Royal, 5e, Latin Quarter* ☎ *01–43–31–70–06* ⊕ *www.hotelportroyal. fr* ⤴ *46 rooms, 20 with bath* ⊟ *No credit cards* �𐩒 *Breakfast* Ⓜ *Les Gobelins* ✦ *2:F6.*

6E ARRONDISSEMENT (ST-GERMAIN)

$$$$
HOTEL
⛉ **Hôtel Bel-Ami.** A short stroll from the famous Café de Flore, the Bel-Ami hides its past as an 18th-century textile factory behind contemporary veneer furnishings, iMac stations, flat-screen TVs, and crisply jacketed staff. **Pros:** upscale, stylish hotel with clean rooms; central St-Germain-des-Prés location; spacious fitness center and spa. **Cons:** some guests report loud noise between rooms; some very small rooms in lower price category; not suitable for families with smaller kids. Ⓢ *Rooms from: €450* ⊠ *7–11 rue St-Benoît, 6e, St-Germain-des-Prés* ☎ *01–42–61–53–53* 🖶 *01–49–27–09–33* ⊕ *www.hotel-bel-ami.com* ⤴ *113 rooms, 2 suites* Ⓜ *St-Germain-des-Prés* ✦ *2:E4.*

$$
HOTEL
⛉ **Hôtel Bonaparte.** Services, amenities, and the *petit déjeuner* (breakfast) may be far from luxurious at this unpretentious family-run hotel, but the location in the heart of St-Germain is fabulous. **Pros:** upscale shopping neighborhood; large rooms for the Rive Gauche; air-conditioning. **Cons:** outdated decor and some tired mattresses; miniscule elevator big enough for only one person; shower-bathtubs lack curtains. Ⓢ *Rooms from: €159* ⊠ *61 rue Bonaparte, 6e, St-Germain-des-Prés* ☎ *01–43–26–97–37* 🖶 *01–43–26–97–37* ⊕ *www.hotelbonaparte.fr* ⤴ *29 rooms* �𐩒 *Breakfast* Ⓜ *St-Sulpice* ✦ *2:E5.*

$$$$
HOTEL
FAMILY
⛉ **Hôtel d'Aubusson.** The staff greets you warmly at this 17th-century town house and former literary salon in the heart of St-Germain-des-Prés. **Pros:** central location near shops and market street; live jazz on weekends; personalized welcome with free Wi-Fi. **Cons:** some of the newer rooms lack character; busy street and bar can be noisy; very touristy. Ⓢ *Rooms from: €315* ⊠ *33 rue Dauphine, 6e, St-Germain-des-Prés* ☎ *01–43–29–43–43* 🖶 *01–43–29–12–62* ⊕ *www.hoteldaubusson.com* ⤴ *49 rooms* ⟨⟩ *Breakfast* Ⓜ *Odéon* ✦ *2:E4.*

$$
HOTEL
⛉ **Hôtel du Lys.** To jump into an inexpensive Parisian fantasy, just climb the stairway to your room (there's no elevator) in this former 17th-century royal residence. **Pros:** central location on a quiet side street; historic character; free Wi-Fi. **Cons:** old-fashioned decor is decidedly outdated; perfunctory service; no air-conditioning. Ⓢ *Rooms from: €145* ⊠ *23 rue Serpente, 6e, Latin Quarter* ☎ *01–43–26–97–57* ⊕ *www. hoteldulys.com* ⤴ *22 rooms* ⟨⟩ *Breakfast* Ⓜ *St-Michel, Odéon* ✦ *2:F5.*

$$$
HOTEL
⛉ **Hôtel Millésime.** The beautiful stone archway of this 17th-century city mansion in St-Germain-des-Prés was in fact the original entrance to the Saint Germain Abbey, and on entering, you'll feel transported to the sunny south of France with its colorful interior. **Pros:** upscale shopping location close to major sites; young, friendly staff; clean rooms. **Cons:** ground-floor rooms can be noisy; smoke from courtyard when windows are open; some room furnishings and bathrooms need repair. Ⓢ *Rooms from: €250* ⊠ *15 rue Jacob, 6e, St-Germain-des-Prés* ☎ *01–44–07–97–97* 🖶 *01–46–34–55–97* ⊕ *www.millesimehotel.com* ⤴ *20 rooms, 1 suite* ⟨⟩ *Breakfast* Ⓜ *St-Germain-des-Prés* ✦ *2:E4.*

$$$$ ⊡ **Hôtel Odéon Saint-Germain.** The exposed stone walls and original
HOTEL wooden beams give this 16th-century building typical Rive Gauche
character, and designer Jacques Garcia's generous use of striped taffeta
curtains, velvet upholstery, and plush carpeting imbues the family-run
hotel with the distinct luxury of St-Germain-des-Prés. **Pros:** Occitane
toiletries; free Internet; luxuriously appointed, historic building in an
upscale shopping district near Jardin Luxembourg. **Cons:** small rooms
may feel claustrophobic and inconvenient for those with extra-large
suitcases; tiny elevator; prices high for room size and average service.
Ⓢ *Rooms from: €320* ✉ *13 rue St-Sulpice, 6e, St-Germain-des-Prés*
☎ *01–43–25–70–11* 🖷 *01–43–29–97–34* ⊕ *www.paris-hotel-odeon.*
com ⤷ *22 rooms, 5 junior suites* ⦿ *Breakfast* Ⓜ *Odéon* ✛ *2:E5.*

$$$$ ⊡ **Hôtel Recamier.** This discreet boutique hotel nestled in a quiet corner
HOTEL overlooking the Eglise St-Sulpice is perfect for those seeking a romantic
and cozy hideaway in the St-Germain-des-Près district. **Pros:** peaceful
garden courtyard; free Wi-Fi and computer station; well-appointed bathrooms. **Cons:** small closets and bathrooms; room service only until 11
pm; no fitness area, spa, or restaurant. Ⓢ *Rooms from: €260* ✉ *3 bis,*
place St-Sulpice, 6e, St-Germain-des-Prés ☎ *01–43–26–04–89* ⊕ *www.*
hotelrecamier.com ⤷ *24 rooms* ⦿ *Breakfast* Ⓜ *Mabillon* ✛ *2:E5.*

$$$ ⊡ **Hôtel Relais Saint-Sulpice.** Sandwiched between St-Sulpice and the Jar-
HOTEL din du Luxembourg, this little hotel wins for location. **Pros:** chic loca-
tion; close to two métro stations; bright breakfast room and courtyard.
Cons: smallish rooms in the lower category; noise from the street on
weekend evenings; poorly designed lighting and interior aesthetics may
be unsatisfactory to discerning clientele. Ⓢ *Rooms from: €200* ✉ *3 rue*
Garancière, 6e, St-Germain-des-Prés ☎ *01–46–33–99–00* 🖷 *01–46–*
33–00–10 ⊕ *www.relais-saint-sulpice.com* ⤷ *26 rooms* ⦿ *Breakfast*
Ⓜ *St-Germain-des-Prés, St-Sulpice* ✛ *2:E5.*

$$$$ ⊡ **L'Hôtel.** There's something just a bit naughty in the air at this eccen-
HOTEL tric and opulent boutique hotel. **Pros:** luxurious decor; elegant bar and
restaurant; walking distance to the Musée d'Orsay and Louvre. **Cons:**
some rooms are very small for the price; closest métro station is a few
blocks away; eclectic decoration seems mismatched. Ⓢ *Rooms from:*
€290 ✉ *13 rue des Beaux-Arts, 6e, St-Germain-des-Prés* ☎ *01–44–41–*
99–00 🖷 *01–43–25–64–81* ⊕ *www.l-hotel.com* ⤷ *16 rooms, 4 suites*
⦿ *Breakfast* Ⓜ *St-Germain-des-Prés* ✛ *2:E4.*

$$$$ ⊡ **Relais Christine.** On a quiet street on the Left Bank, this exquisite *hotel*
HOTEL *de charme* property dates back to the 13th century as a former abbey
of the Grands-Augustins and has an impressive stone courtyard and
interior garden. **Pros:** quiet location while still close to the Latin Quarter
action; historic character; Carita spa. **Cons:** thin walls in some rooms;
no on-site restaurant; a bit touristy. Ⓢ *Rooms from: €398* ✉ *3 rue Chris-*
tine, 6e, St-Germain-des-Prés ☎ *01–40–51–60–80, 800/525–4800 in*
U.S. ⊕ *www.relais-christine.com* ⤷ *33 rooms, 18 suites* ⦿ *Breakfast*
Ⓜ *Odéon* ✛ *2:E5.*

7E ARRONDISSEMENT (TOUR EIFFEL/INVALIDES)

$$$$ ⊡ **Hôtel Duc de Saint-Simon.** For pure French flavor, including rooms
HOTEL decorated in floral chintz, head to this intimate hotel in a hidden loca-
tion between boulevard St-Germain and rue de Bac. **Pros:** upscale

Four Seasons Hôtel George V Paris

Hôtel Meurice

neighborhood close to St-Germain-des-Prés; historic character; friendly service. **Cons:** rooms in the annex are smaller and have no elevator; small bathrooms; no room service or business facilities. $ *Rooms from: €265* ✉ *14 rue St-Simon, 7e, St-Germain-des-Prés* 🕾 *01–44–39–20–20* 🖷 *01–45–48–68–25* ⊕ *www.hotelducdesaintsimon.com* ⤵ *29 rooms, 5 suites* ❙❍❙ *Breakfast* Ⓜ *Rue du Bac* ✛ *2:D4.*

$ 🖬 **Hôtel du Champ de Mars.** With its charming homestyle feel, this afford-
HOTEL   able hotel around the corner from picturesque rue Cler welcomes guests with a vibrant Provence-inspired lobby and huge picture windows overlooking a quiet street. **Pros:** free Wi-Fi; good value in chic quarter; walking distance to Eiffel Tower, Les Invalides, and Rodin Museum. **Cons:** small rooms compared to larger hotels; no air-conditioning; inconsistent service. $ *Rooms from: €115* ✉ *7 rue du Champ de Mars, 7e, Around the Eiffel Tower* 🕾 *01–45–51–52–30* ⊕ *www.hotelduchampdemars. com* ⤵ *25 rooms* ❙❍❙ *Breakfast* Ⓜ *École Militaire* ✛ *2:B4.*

$$$$ 🖬 **Hôtel Le Tourville.** One of six boutique Parisian hotels operated by the
HOTEL   Inwood Collection, this cozy, contemporary haven near the Eiffel Tower, Champs de Mars, and Invalides is a comfortable, quiet base for exploring Paris. **Pros:** convenient location near métro; friendly service; soundproofed windows. **Cons:** standard rooms are small; air-conditioning works only during summer months; no restaurant. $ *Rooms from: €295* ✉ *16 av. de Tourville, 7e, Around the Eiffel Tower* 🕾 *01–47–05–* *62–62* 🖷 *01–47–05–43–90* ⊕ *www.hoteltourville.com* ⤵ *27 rooms, 3 suites* Ⓜ *École Militaire* ✛ *2:C4.*

$$$$ 🖬 **Le Bellechasse.** If you like eclectic modern interior design with no
HOTEL   central theme, a tiny boutique hotel right around the corner from the popular Musée d'Orsay, in St-Germain, may be a good choice for its convenient location to major sites. **Pros:** central location near top Paris museums; one-of-a-kind style with complimentary WiFi; friendly, helpful 24-hour staff. **Cons:** small rooms; street-facing rooms can be noisy; open bathrooms lack privacy. $ *Rooms from: €360* ✉ *8 rue de Bellechasse, 7e, Around the Eiffel Tower* 🕾 *01–45–50–22–31* 🖷 *01–45– 51–52–36* ⊕ *www.lebellechasse.com* ⤵ *33 rooms, 1 suite* ❙❍❙ *Breakfast* Ⓜ *Solferino* ✛ *2:D4.*

8E ARRONDISSEMENT (CHAMPS-ÉLYSÉES)

$$$$ 🖬 **Champs-Élysées Plaza Hotel and Wellness.** Discreet, contemporary ele-
HOTEL   gance sums up this graciously renovated seven-story town house steps from the hustle-and-bustle of the Champs-Élysées. **Pros:** extremely comfortable and elegant rooms; friendly, attentive service; central location. **Cons:** small spa; gym only has five machines; limited breakfast buffet $ *Rooms from: €400* ✉ *35 rue de Berri, 8e, Champs-Élysées* 🕾 *01– 53–53–20–20* 🖷 *01–53–53–20–21* ⊕ *www.champs-elysees-plaza.com* ⤵ *35 rooms and suites* ❙❍❙ *Breakfast* Ⓜ *St-Philippe-du-Roule, George V* ✛ *2:B2.*

$$$$ 🖬 **Four Seasons Hôtel George V Paris.** The George V is as poised and pol-
HOTEL   ished as the day it opened in 1928—the original plaster detailing and
FAMILY   17th-century tapestries have been restored, the bas-reliefs regilded, and
Fodor's Choice   the marble-floor mosaics rebuilt tile by tile—yet the guest rooms are
★   technologically updated with TVs integrated into bathroom mirrors and DVD/CD players. **Pros:** privileged address near couture shopping

district; courtyard dining in summer; guest-only indoor swimming pool. **Cons:** several blocks from the nearest métro; slow dial-up Internet in rooms (extra €28 for wireless connection); lacks the personal intimacy of smaller boutique hotels with service catering more to VIPs and wealthy clientele. [$] *Rooms from: €815* ✉ *31 av. George V, 8e, Champs-Élysées* ☎ *01–49–52–70–00, 800/332–3442 in U.S.* 📠 *01–49–52–70–10* 🌐 *www.fourseasons.com/paris* 🛏 *184 rooms, 60 suites* 🍴 *Breakfast* [M] *George V* ✥ *2:B3.*

$$$$ HOTEL 🏨 **Hôtel Fouquet's Barrière.** Steps away from one of the world's most famous streets, the luxury hotel adjacent to the legendary Fouquet's Brasserie at the corner of the Champs-Élysées and avenue George V is recognizable with its uniformed valets, parked sports cars, and elegant Haussmanien entryway. **Pros:** many rooms overlook the Champs-Élysées; métro very close; beautiful U Spa and fitness center. **Cons:** very expensive room and dining prices; bar can get overcrowded; many corporate group events held throughout the year can make rooms feel "soul-less." [$] *Rooms from: €730* ✉ *46 av. George V, 8e, Champs-Élysées* ☎ *01–40–69–60–00* 📠 *01–40–69–60–05* 🌐 *www.fouquets-barriere.com* 🛏 *81 rooms, 31 suites* 🍴 *Breakfast* [M] *George V* ✥ *2:B3.*

$$$$ HOTEL FAMILY 🏨 **Hôtel Lancaster.** Once a Spanish nobleman's town house, this luxurious retreat is now in French hands and it shows, from local staffing to elegant decoration. **Pros:** Sunday brunch with organic farm products; just steps away from the Champs-Élysées and five minutes from métro; excellent seasonal menus at La Table du Lancaster. **Cons:** size of rooms varies greatly; pricey room service; rooms look tired and require more refurbishment. ■ **TIP→** When weather permits, head to the outdoor terrace in the "feng shui"–inspired courtyard. An elevator goes up to wheelchair-accessible rooms on the seventh and eighth floors. [$] *Rooms from: €650* ✉ *7 rue de Berri, 8e, Champs-Élysées* ☎ *01–40–76–40–76, 877/757–2747 in U.S.* 🌐 *www.hotel-lancaster.fr* 🛏 *43 rooms, 14 suites* 🍴 *Breakfast* [M] *George V* ✥ *2:B2.*

$$$$ HOTEL FAMILY Fodor's Choice ★ 🏨 **Hôtel Plaza Athénée.** Superlative; the word sums up the overall impression of this glamorous landmark hotel on one of the most expensive avenues in Paris with luxury shops. **Pros:** Eiffel Tower views; special attention to children; Dior Institute spa. **Cons:** vast difference in style of rooms; easy to feel anonymous in such a large hotel and if not a VIP; very expensive prices. [$] *Rooms from: €995* ✉ *25 av. Montaigne, 8e, Champs-Élysées* ☎ *01–53–67–66–65, 866/732–1106 in U.S.* 🌐 *www.plaza-athenee-paris.com* 🛏 *194 rooms, 46 suites* 🍴 *Breakfast* [M] *Alma-Marceau* ✥ *2:B3.*

$$$ HOTEL 🏨 **Hôtel Queen Mary.** This cozy hotel is two blocks from place de la Madeleine and Paris's famous department stores. **Pros:** close to high-end shopping streets and department stores; air-conditioning; extra-attentive service. **Cons:** some rooms are claustrophic; those on the ground floor and facing the street can be noisy; worn furnishings and decor can feel somewhat old-fashioned. [$] *Rooms from: €219* ✉ *9 rue Greffulhe, 8e, Opéra/Grands Boulevards* ☎ *01–42–66–40–50* 📠 *01–42–66–94–92* 🌐 *www.hotelqueenmary.com* 🛏 *36 rooms, 1 suite* 🍴 *Breakfast* [M] *Madeleine, St-Lazare, Havre Caumartin* ✥ *2:D2.*

$$$$ HOTEL 🏨 **Pershing Hall.** History meets postmodern at this reliably trendy hotel-restaurant-lounge. **Pros:** prime shopping and nightlife district; excellent Sunday brunch buffet; free wireless Internet throughout hotel. **Cons:** bar noise can be heard in some rooms; expensive neighborhood; inconsistent service. [$] *Rooms from: €470* ✉ *49 rue Pierre-Charron, 8e, Champs-Élysées* ☎ *01–58–36–58–00* 📠 *01–58–36–58–01* 🌐 *www.pershinghall.com* 🛏 *20 rooms, 6 suites* 🍴 *Breakfast* [M] *George V, Franklin-D.-Roosevelt* ✥ *2:B3.*

9E ARRONDISSEMENT (OPÉRA)

$ HOTEL 🏨 **Hôtel Chopin.** A unique mainstay of the district, the Chopin recalls its 1846 birth date with a creaky-floored lobby and aged woodwork, with basic but comfortable rooms that overlook the atmospheric passage Jouffroy's quaint toy shops and bookstores. **Pros:** special location; close to major métro station; great nightlife district. **Cons:** thin walls; single rooms are very small; few amenities. [$] *Rooms from: €114* ✉ *10 bd. Montmartre, 46 passage Jouffroy, 9e, Opéra/Grands Boulevards* ☎ *01–47–70–58–10* 📠 *01–42–47–00–70* 🌐 *www.hotelchopin.fr* 🛏 *36 rooms* 🍴 *Breakfast* [M] *Grands Boulevards* ✥ *2:F2.*

$$$ HOTEL 🏨 **Hôtel Gramont Opéra.** This elegant and friendly family-owned boutique hotel near the Opéra and historic department stores has lots of little extras that make it a great value. **Pros:** good breakfast buffet with eggs to order; friendly staff; connecting rooms for families. **Cons:** singles have no desk; small bathrooms; elevator doesn't go to top-floor rooms. [$] *Rooms from: €239* ✉ *22 rue Gramont, 9e, Grands Boulevards* ☎ *01–42–96–85–90* 📠 *01–42–96–19–70* 🌐 *www.hotel-gramont-opera.com* 🛏 *22 rooms, 3 suites* 🍴 *Breakfast* ✥ *2:E3.*

$$ HOTEL 🏨 **Hôtel Langlois.** After starring in *The Truth About Charlie* (a remake of *Charade*), this darling hotel gained a reputation as one of the most atmospheric budget sleeps in the city. **Pros:** excellent views from the top floor; close to department stores and Opéra Garnier; historic decor. **Cons:** noisy street; off the beaten path; some sagging furniture and worn fabrics. ■ **TIP→ Breakfast can be served in-room at no extra cost.** [$] *Rooms from: €170* ✉ *63 rue St-Lazare, 9e, Opéra/Grands Boulevards* ☎ *01–48–74–78–24* 📠 *01–49–95–04–43* 🌐 *www.hotel-langlois.com* 🛏 *24 rooms, 3 suites* 🍴 *Breakfast* [M] *Trinité* ✥ *2:E2.*

11E ARRONDISSEMENT (BASTILLE)

$ HOTEL 🏨 **Hôtel Résidence Alhambra.** The white facade, rear garden, and flower-filled window boxes brighten this lesser-known neighborhood between the Marais and rue Oberkampf. **Pros:** popular nightlife district; friendly service; inexpensive room rates. **Cons:** small doubles with dated decor; long walk to the center of town; no air-conditioning. [$] *Rooms from: €92* ✉ *13 rue de Malte, 11e, République* ☎ *01–47–00–35–52* 🌐 *www.hotelalhambra.fr* 🛏 *58 rooms* 🍴 *Breakfast* [M] *Oberkampf* ✥ *2:H4.*

14E ARRONDISSEMENT (MONTPARNASSE)

$$$ HOTEL 🏨 **Hôtel Lenox-Montparnasse.** Right across from a local French cinema on a street lined with fish restaurants, this six-floor hotel with proximity to the Jardin du Luxembourg and extra amenities such as free Wi-Fi offers good value. **Pros:** lively district close to Montparnasse and St-Germain-des-Prés; well-stocked honesty bar; friendly multilingual

service. **Cons:** standard rooms are small; noisy street; attracts business clientele. $ *Rooms from: €250* ✉ *15 rue Delambre, 14e, Montparnasse* 🖥 *01–43–35–34–50* ⊕ *www.paris-hotel-lenox.com* ⌨ *46 rooms, 6 suites* �‖ *Breakfast* Ⓜ *Vavin* ✛ *2:D6.*

$$$

HOTEL

🖳 **Hôtel Raspail-Montparnasse.** Capturing the spirit of Montparnasse in its heyday as the art capital of the world in the 1920s and '30s, this hotel names its rooms after some of the illustrious neighborhood stars—Picasso, Chagall, and Modigliani. **Pros:** convenient to métro and bus; many markets and cafés nearby; friendly staff. **Cons:** traffic noise; some rooms small with stale cigarette smoke odor; dated interiors with worn fabrics. $ *Rooms from: €185* ✉ *203 bd. Raspail, 14e, Montparnasse* 🖥 *01–43–20–62–86* ⊕ *www.hotelraspailmontparnasse.com* ⌨ *38 rooms* �‖ *Breakfast* Ⓜ *Vavin* ✛ *2:E6.*

2

16E ARRONDISSEMENT (ARC DE TRIOMPHE/LE BOIS)

$$$$

HOTEL

🖳 **Hôtel Eiffel Trocadéro.** Be greeted with a curious blend of Second Empire and Rococo styling upon entering this "eco-friendly" hotel on a quiet corner of a small incline just off place Trocadéro. **Pros:** views of Eiffel Tower in upper-floor rooms; upscale residential district convenient to métro; organic breakfast buffet. **Cons:** no full-service restaurant; not an easy walk to center of town; basic rooms feel cramped. $ *Rooms from: €309* ✉ *35 rue Benjamin-Franklin, 16e, Around the Eiffel Tower* 🖥 *01–53–70–17–70* ⊕ *www.hoteleiffeltrocadero.com* ⌨ *16 rooms, 1 suite (under renovation)* �‖ *Breakfast* Ⓜ *Trocadéro* ✛ *2:A4.*

$$$$

HOTEL

FAMILY

🖳 **Hôtel Raphael.** This discreet palace-like hotel was built in 1925 to cater to travelers spending a season in Paris, so every space is generously sized for long, lavish stays. **Pros:** a block from the Champs-Élysées and Arc de Triomphe; rooftop garden terrace; intimate hotel bar frequented by locals. **Cons:** old-fashioned Parisian decor that can feel worn and dowdy; some soundproofing issues; neighborhood can have a majestic yet cold atmosphere. $ *Rooms from: €650* ✉ *17 av. Kléber, 16e, Champs-Élysées* 🖥 *01–53–64–32–00* 🖨 *01–53–64–32–01* ⊕ *www.raphael-hotel.com* ⌨ *53 rooms, 39 suites* �‖ *Breakfast* Ⓜ *Kléber* ✛ *2:A2.*

$$$$

HOTEL

Fodor'sChoice

★

🖳 **Shangri-La Hotel Paris.** This impressive restored 19th-century mansion overlooking the Eiffel Tower from the Right Bank was once the stately home of Prince Roland Bonaparte, grandnephew of the emperor himself. **Pros:** close to the métro and luxury shopping district; varied culinary options for all tastes; exceptional suites all equipped with complimentary wireless Internet. **Cons:** astronomically high room rates and dining; pool only open until 9 pm; some views obstructed. $ *Rooms from: €850* ✉ *10 av. Iéna, 16e, Around the Eiffel Tower* 🖥 *01–53–67–19–98* 🖨 *01–53–67–19–19* ⊕ *www.shangri-la.com* ⌨ *54 rooms, 27 suites.* Ⓜ *Iéna* ✛ *2:B3.*

20E ARRONDISSEMENT

$$

HOTEL

🖳 **Hôtel Mama Shelter.** The heir to the Club Med empire decided to do for the hotel industry what jeans did for fashion: democratize style. **Pros:** trendy design without designer prices; easy access to airport; entertainment center in each room. **Cons:** off-the-beaten track in remote part of Paris; club across the street can be noisy; extremely inconvenient and

DID YOU KNOW?

The views *of* majestic Sacré-Coeur might be as lovely as the vews *from* Sacré-Coeur, especially as the sun is setting or rising.

far from major sites and main districts. $\boxed{S}$ *Rooms from: €159* $\boxtimes$ *109 rue de Bagnolet, 20e, Bastille* ☎ *01–43–48–48–48* 🖨 *01–43–48–49– 49* ⊕ *www.mamashelter.com* 🔄 *172 rooms* $\boxed{M}$ *Gambetta* ✛ *2:H2.*

NIGHTLIFE AND THE ARTS

Updated
by Jennifer
Ditsler-Ladonne

With a heritage that includes the cancan, the Folies-Bergère, the Moulin Rouge, Mistinguett, and Josephine Baker, Paris is one city where no one has ever had to ask, "Is there any place exciting to go to tonight?" Today the city's nightlife and arts scenes are still filled with pleasures. Hear a *chansonnier* belt out Piaf, take in a *Victor/Victoria* show, catch a Molière play at the Comédie Française, or perhaps spot the latest supermodel at Johnny Depp's Mandala Ray. Detailed entertainment listings in French can be found in the weekly magazines *Pariscope* (⊕ *www. pariscope.fr*) and *L'Officiel des Spectacles* (⊕ *www.offi.fr*), available at newsstands and in bookstores; in the Wednesday entertainment insert "Figaroscope," in *Le Figaro* newspaper (⊕ *scope.lefigaro.fr/guide*); and in the weekly "A Nous Paris," distributed free in the métro. Also look for the Web zine *Paris Voice* (⊕ *www.parisvoice.com*). The website of the **Paris Tourist Office** (⊕ *www.parisinfo.com*) has theater and music listings in English.

The best place to buy tickets is at the venue itself; try to purchase in advance, as many of the more popular performances sell out. Also try your hotel or a ticket agency, such as ⊕ *www.theatreonline.com.* **FNAC** (⊕ *www.fnacspectacles.com*) sells tickets in stores and online. **Virgin Megastores** (⊕ *www.virginmega.fr*) is another supplier of tickets in stores and online. Both have locations on the Champs-Élysées and branches elsewhere.

Kiosques Théâtre. Half-price tickets for same-day theater performances are available at the Kiosques Théâtre, open Tuesday to Saturday 12:30 to 8 and Sunday 12:30 to 4. $\boxtimes$ *Across from 15 pl. de la Madeleine, Opéra/Grands Boulevards* $\boxed{M}$ *Madeleine* $\boxtimes$ *Outside Gare Montparnasse, pl. Raoul Dautry, Montparnasse* $\boxed{M}$ *Montparnasse Bienvenüe.*

THE ARTS

EARLY AND CLASSICAL MUSIC

Cité de la Musique. Cité de la Musique presents a varied program of classical, experimental, and world-music concerts in a postmodern setting. $\boxtimes$ *In Parc de La Villette, 221 av. Jean-Jaurès, 19e, La Villette* ☎ *01–44–84–44–84* ⊕ *www.citedelamusique.fr* $\boxed{M}$ *Porte de Pantin.*

IRCAM. IRCAM organizes contemporary and classical music concerts, as well as dance and other modern art performances, in its own theater and at the Centre Pompidou next door for only €14. $\boxtimes$ *1 pl. Igor-Stravinsky, 4e, Beaubourg/Les Halles* ☎ *01–44–78–48–43* ⊕ *www. ircam.fr* $\boxed{M}$ *Châtelet, Les Halles, Hôtel de Ville.*

Fodor'sChoice
★

Salle Cortot. Salle Cortot is an acoustic jewel built by Auguste Perret in 1918. At the time he promised to construct "a hall that sounds like a Stradivarious." Jazz and classical concerts are held here. ■TIP→ Free student recitals are offered at 12:30 on Tuesday and Thursday from October to April. ⊠ *78 rue Cardinet, 17e, Parc Monceau* ☎ *01–47–63–47–48* ⊕ *www.ecolenormalecortot.com* Ⓜ *Malesherbes.*

Salle Pleyel. Salle Pleyel's packed concert calendar—covering everything from jazz to Mozart—features international stars like Lionel Hampton and directors of the New York Philharmonic and the London Symphony Orchestra, plus repeat performances by the Orchestre de Paris. ⊠ *252 rue du Faubourg-St-Honoré, 8e, Concorde* ☎ *01–42–56–13–13* ⊕ *www.sallepleyel.fr* Ⓜ *Ternes.*

Théâtre des Champs-Élysées. Théâtre des Champs-Élysées was the scene of 1913's infamous Battle of the Rite of Spring, when police had to be called in after the audience ripped up seats in outrage at Stravinsky's *Le Sacre du Printemps* and Nijinsky's choreography. Today it is elegantly restored and worthy of a visit if only for the architecture (it's one of Paris's most striking examples of Art Deco). The theater also hosts first-rate opera and dance performances, along with jazz, world music, orchestral, and chamber concerts. ⊠ *15 av. Montaigne, 8e, Champs-Élysées* ☎ *01–49–52–50–50* Ⓜ *Alma-Marceau.*

Many **churches** hold classical concerts (often free). Check weekly listings and flyers posted at the churches themselves for information. The website ⊕ *www.ampconcerts.com* lists the schedule for the lovely Sainte-Chapelle and other historic churches.

DANCE

Centre National de la Danse. After being sidelined by politics and budget problems for a decade, this dance center opened in a former administrative center of the Pantin suburb of Paris. The space is dedicated to supporting professional dancers, with classes, rehearsal studios, and a multimedia dance library. A regular program of performances, expositions, and conferences is also open to the public. ⊠ *1 rue Victor Hugo, Pantin* ☎ *01–41–83–98–98* ⊕ *www.cnd.fr* Ⓜ *Hoche or RER: Pantin.*

Fodor's Choice ★ **Opéra Garnier.** Opéra Garnier—the magnificent, magical former haunt of the Phantom of the Opera, painter Edgar Degas, and any number of legendary opera stars—still hosts performances of the Opéra de Paris, along with a fuller calendar of dance performances (the theater is the official home of the Ballet de l'Opéra National de Paris). The grandest opera productions are usually mounted at the Opéra de la Bastille, whereas the Garnier now presents smaller-scale works such as Mozart's *La Clemenza di Tito* and *Così Fan Tutte.* Gorgeous and intimate though the Garnier is, its tiara-shape theater means that many seats have limited visibility, so it's best to ask specifically what the sight lines are when booking (partial view in French is *visibilité partielle.* ■TIP→ The cheaper seats are often those with partial views. Seats generally go on sale at the box office a month before any given show, earlier by phone and online; you must appear in person to buy the cheapest tickets. Last-minute discount tickets, if available, are offered 15 minutes before a performance for senior citizens and anyone under 28. The box office is open 11–6:30 daily, but you should get in line up to two hours in advance. Individual and guided tours (€9) are available; check the website for details. ⊠ *Pl. de l'Opéra, 9e, Opéra/Grands Boulevards* ☎ *08–92–89–90–90* ⊕ *www.operadeparis.fr* Ⓜ *Opéra.*

Théâtre de la Ville. Théâtre de la Ville is *the* top spot for contemporary dance. Troupes like Anne-Teresa de Keersmaeker's Rosas company are presented here. Book early; shows sell out quickly. ⊠ *2 pl. du Châtelet, 4e, Beaubourg/Les Halles* ☎ *01–42–74–22–77* Ⓜ *Châtelet.*

OPERA

Paris offers some of the best opera in the world—and thousands know it. Consequently, it's best to plan ahead if you'd like to attend a performance of the **Opéra National de Paris** at its two homes, the Opéra de la Bastille and the Opéra Garnier. Review a list of performances by checking the website ⊕ *www.opera-de-paris.fr.* For performances at either the Opéra de la Bastille or the Opéra Garnier, tickets range from €5 (for standing room at Opéra Bastille only) to €200 and generally go on sale at the box office a month before shows, earlier by phone and online. The opera season usually runs September through July (with each opera given a minirun of a week or two), and the box office is open Monday–Saturday 11–6:30. Last-minute discount tickets, when available, are offered 15 minutes before a performance for seniors and anyone under 28. The box office is open 11 to 6:30 pm daily.

Opéra Comique. Opéra Comique is a gem of an opera house whose reputation was forged by its former director, enfant terrible Jérôme Savary. As well as staging operettas, the hall hosts modern dance, classical concerts, and vocal recitals. Tickets usually range from €6 to €50 and can be purchased at the theater, by mail, online, or by phone. ⊠ *5 rue Favart, 2e, Opéra/Grands Boulevards* ☎ *08–25–01–01–23* ⊕ *www. opera-comique.com* Ⓜ *Richelieu Drouot.*

Opéra de la Bastille. Opéra de la Bastille, the mammoth ultramodern facility designed by architect Carlos Ott and built in 1989, long ago took over the role of Paris's main opera house from the Opéra Garnier (although both operate under the same Opéra de Paris umbrella). Like the building, performances tend to be on the avant-garde side—you're as likely to see a contemporary adaptation of *La Bohème* as you are to hear Kafka set to music. Tickets for Opéra de Paris productions range from €5 to €200 and generally go on sale at the box office a month before shows, earlier by phone and online. The opera season usually runs September through July, and the box office is open Monday–Saturday 11–6:30. ■TIP➔ You can buy tickets (€12) for guided tours of the opera house at the box office. Call for dates and times. ⊠ *Pl. de la Bastille, 12e, Bastille/Nation* ☎ *08–92–89–90–90, 01–40–01–19–70 Tours* ⊕ *www.operadeparis.fr* Ⓜ *Bastille.*

Théâtre du Châtelet. Also known as Théâtre Musical de Paris, this venue stages some of the finest opera productions in the city and regularly attracts international divas like Cecilia Bartoli and Anne-Sofie von Otter. It also hosts classical concerts, dance performances, classic Broadway musicals, and the occasional play. ⊠ *Pl. du Châtelet, 1er, Beaubourg/Les Halles* ☎ *01–40–28–28–40* ⊕ *www.chatelet-theatre.com* Ⓜ *Châtelet.*

THEATER

A number of theaters line the Grands Boulevards between Opéra and République, but there's no Paris equivalent of Broadway or the West End. Shows are mostly in French. English-language theater groups playing in venues throughout Paris include the **International Players** (⊕ *www. internationalplayers.co.uk*). Broadway-scale singing-and-dancing musicals are generally staged at either the Palais des Sports or the Palais des Congrès.

Fodor's Choice ★ **Comédie Française.** Comédie Française, founded in 1680, is the most hallowed institution in French theater. It specializes in splendid classical French plays by the likes of Racine, Molière, and Marivaux. ■TIP➔ Buy tickets at the box office, by telephone, or online. If the theater is sold out, the Salle Richelieu offers steeply discounted last-minute tickets an hour before the performance. ⊠ *Salle Richelieu, pl. Colette, 1er, Louvre* ☎ *08–25–10–16–80* ⊕ *www.comedie-francaise.fr/* Ⓜ *Palais-Royal–Musée du Louvre* ⊠ *Studio Théâtre, Galerie du Carrousel du Louvre, 99 rue de Rivoli, 1er, Louvre* ☎ *01–44–58–98–58* Ⓜ *Palais-Royal* ⊠ *Théâtre du Vieux Colombier, 21 rue Vieux Colombier, 6e, St-Germain-des-Prés* ☎ *01–44–39–87–00* Ⓜ *St-Sulpice.*

Théâtre des Bouffes du Nord. Théâtre des Bouffes du Nord is the wonderfully atmospheric, slightly decrepit home of English director Peter Brook, who regularly delights with his quirky experimental productions in French and, sometimes, English. ⊠ *37 bis, bd. de la Chapelle, 10e, Stalingrad/La Chapelle* ☎ *01–46–07–34–50* Ⓜ *La Chapelle.*

Théâtre du Palais-Royal. Théâtre du Palais-Royal is a sumptuous 750-seat Italian theater bedecked in gold and purple in the former residence of Cardinal Richelieu. ⊠ *38 rue Montpensier, 1er, Louvre* ☎ *01–42–97–40–00* ⊕ *www.theatrepalaisroyal.com* Ⓜ *Palais-Royal.*

Théâtre National de Chaillot. Théâtre National de Chaillot, housed in an imposing neoclassic building overlooking the Eiffel Tower, has two theaters dedicated to experimental, world and avant-garde drama, dance and music or a mix of all three. Major names in dance—like the Ballet Royal de Suède and William Forsythe's company—also visit regularly. There are programs for children, too. ⊠ *1 pl. du Trocadéro, 16e, Trocadéro/Tour Eiffel* ☎ *01–53–65–30–00* Ⓜ *Trocadéro.*

NIGHTLIFE

If you prefer clinking drinks with models and celebrities, check out the Champs-Élysées area, but be prepared to shell out *beaucoup* bucks and stare down surly bouncers. Easygoing, bohemian-chic revelers can be found in the northeastern districts like Canal St-Martin and Belleville, while students tend to pour into the Bastille, St-Germain-des-Prés, and the Quartier Latin. Grands Boulevards and rue Montorgueil, just north of Les Halles, is party central for young professionals and the fashion crowd, and the Pigalle and Montmartre areas are always hopping with plenty of theaters, cabarets, bars, and concert venues. Warmer months draw the adventurous to floating clubs and bars, moored along the Seine from Bercy to the Eiffel Tower.

The Left Bank is now home to many glittering nightclubs filled with off-duty celebs.

BARS AND CLUBS

Fodor's Choice
★ **Au Lapin Agile.** An authentic survivor from the 19th century, Au Lapin Agile considers itself the doyen of cabarets. Founded in 1860, it inhabits the same modest house that was a favorite subject of painter Maurice Utrillo. It became the home-away-from-home for Braque, Modigliani, Apollinaire, and Picasso—who once paid for a meal with one of his paintings, then promptly exited and painted another that he named after this place. There are no topless dancers; this is a genuine French cabaret with songs, poetry, and humor (in French) in a publike setting. Entry €24. ⊠ *22 rue des Saules, 18e, Montmartre* ☎ *01–46–06–85–87* ⊕ *www.au-lapin-agile.com* Ⓜ *Lamarck Caulaincourt.*

Ballroom du Beef Club. Unmarked black door, basement setting, pressed tin ceilings, atmospheric lighting—did anyone say speakeasy? All this and luscious drinks draw a sophisticated crowd that appreciates all the extra touches that make this bar a standout. ⊠ *58 rue Jean-Jacques-Rousseau, 1e, Les Halles* ☎ *09–54–37–13–65* Ⓜ *Les Halles, Palais-Royal-Musée du Louvre.*

Bar 8. Since this monolithic marble bar at the Mandarin Oriental Hotel opened its doors, it has been the "in" game in town. There's an extensive champagne menu, and the terrace was an instant hit with the Fashion Week gang. ⊠ *251 rue Saint-Honoré, 1e, Louvre/Tuileries* ☎ *01–70–98–78–88* Ⓜ *Concorde, Tuileries.*

Bar du Marché. Bar du Marché is a local legend where waiters wearing red overalls and revolutionary "Gavroche" hats serve drinks every day of the week (they demonstrate particular zeal around happy hour). With bottles of wine at about €25, it draws a quintessential Left Bank mix of expat locals, fashion-house interns, and even some professional rugby players. Sit outside on the terrace and enjoy the prime corner location. ✉ *75 rue de Seine, 6e, St-Germain/Buci* ☎ *01–43–26–55–15* Ⓜ *Mabillon, Odeon.*

Cab. Models, photographers, and stylists bypass lesser beings at the velvet rope at this popular fashion-centric club across from the Louvre. If you make it inside, you'll appreciate the chic Space Odyssey atmosphere. Depending on the night, you'll hear funk, hip-hop, electro, or house. ✉ *2 pl. du Palais-Royal, 1er, Louvre* ☎ *01–58–62–56–25* Ⓜ *Palais-Royal.*

Candelaria. If a muscled man bars your way, just whisper the magic word: cocktail. Then traverse the tiny Mexican tacqueria (the best in Paris) through an unmarked door and into a crowded, steamy room where the tang of tequila hangs in the air. You've found one of Paris's hip hideaways. ✉ *52 rue de Saintonge, 3e, Marais* ☎ *01–42–74–41–28* ⊕ *www.candelariaparis.com* Ⓜ *Filles du Calvaire.*

Closerie des Lilas. La Closerie's swank "American-style" bar lets you drink in the swirling action of the adjacent restaurant and brasserie at a piano bar adorned with plaques honoring former habitués like Man Ray, Jean-Paul Sartre, Samuel Beckett, and Ernest Hemingway, who talks of "the Lilas" in *A Moveable Feast*. ✉ *171 bd. du Montparnasse, 6e, Montparnasse* ☎ *01–40–51–34–50* Ⓜ *Montparnasse.*

Fodor'sChoice ★ **Delaville Café.** With its huge, heated sidewalk terrace, Belle Époque mosaic-tile bar, graffiti'd walls, and swishy lounge, Delaville Café boasts a funky Baroque ambience. Hot Paris DJs ignite the scene Thursday to Saturday, so arrive early on weekends if you want a seat. ✉ *34 bd. Bonne Nouvelle, 10e, Opéra/Grands Boulevards* ☎ *01–48–24–48–09* Ⓜ *Bonne Nouvelle, Grands Boulevards.*

Experimental Cocktail Club. Fashioned as a speakeasy on a tiny brick-paved street, the Experimental Cocktail Club seems like it should be lighted by gas lamps. The show is all about the *alcool*; colorful, innovative cocktails like the Lemon Drop are mixed with aplomb by friendly (and attractive) bartenders. By 11 pm it's packed with a diverse mix of locals, professionals, and fashionistas, who occasionally dress up like characters from a Toulouse-Lautrec painting on special costume nights. ✉ *37 rue Saint-Sauveur, 2e, Les Halles* ☎ *01–45–08–88–09* Ⓜ *Réamur-Sébastopol.*

Kong. Kong is glorious not only for its panoramic skyline views, but for its exquisite manga-inspired decor, the top-shelf DJs for weekend dancing, and its kooky, disco-ball-and-kid-sumo-adorned bathrooms. It was featured as a chic eatery in *Sex and the City*; need we say more? ✉ *1 rue du Pont-Neuf, 1er, Louvre* ☎ *01–40–39–09–00* Ⓜ *Pont-Neuf.*

La Perle. La Perle is a bustling, buzzy Marais masterpiece, where straights, gays, and lesbians of all types come to mingle. The crowd makes this place interesting, not the neon lights, diner-style seats, or stripped-down decor. It continues to pack in some of the city's fashion movers and shakers from midafternoon on. ✉ *78 rue Vielle-du-Temple, 3e, Marais* ☎ *01–42–72–69–93* Ⓜ *Chemin-Vert.*

Le Nouveau Casino. Le Nouveau Casino is a concert hall and club tucked behind the Café Charbon. Pop and rock concerts prevail during the week, with revelry on Friday and Saturday from midnight until dawn. Electronic, house, disco, and techno DJs are the standard. ✉ *109 rue Oberkampf, 11e, Oberkampf* ☎ *01–43–57–57–40* Ⓜ *Parmentier.*

WAGG. WAGG is tucked beneath the popular bar-resto Alcazar, in a vaulted stone cellar that was Jim Morrison's hangout back in the '70s when the Whiskey-a-Go-Go was located here. It's now a welcoming dance club with state-of-the-art sound, lighting, and guest DJs. You'll hear vintage disco, funk, groove, and salsa (the last of these on Sunday nights, with classes that start at 3:30 pm). ✉ *62 rue Mazarine, 6e, St-Germain-des-Prés* ☎ *01–55–42–22–01* Ⓜ *Odéon.*

> ## APÉRITIFS
>
> For *apéritifs* French style, try a *pastis*—anise-flavored liquor such as Pernod or Ricard that turns cloudy when water is added. Ask for *"un petit jaune, s'il vous plait."* A *pineau* is cognac and fruity grape juice. The *kir* (white wine with a dash of black-currant syrup) is a popular drink, too; a *kir royale* is made with champagne.
>
> **La Fée Verte.** Absinthe—the vivid green, once-outlawed liquor—has made a comeback around town. Try a taste at La Fée Verte in the Bastille area. The food is good here, too. ✉ *108 rue de la Roquette, 11e* ☎ *01–43–72–31–24* Ⓜ *Charonne.*

FLOOR SHOWS AND CABARET

Paris's cabarets are household names, though mostly just tourists go to them these days. Prices range from about €30 (admission plus one drink) to more than €130 (dinner plus show).

Crazy Horse. This world-renowned cabaret has honed striptease to an elegant art. Founded in 1951 and renovated in 2007, it's acclaimed for gorgeous dancers and raunchy routines characterized by lots of humor and few clothes. Burlesque artist extraordinaire and fashion show regular Dita von Teese has been known to perform here, elevating the reputation of this haunt. ✉ *12 av. George V, 8e, Champs-Élysées* ☎ *01–47–23–32–32* Ⓜ *Alma-Marceau.*

Lido. The supercalifragilisticexpialidelicious Blubell Girls (picture feathers, spangles, boas, and lots of skin) are the stars here. Lido owners claim that no show this side of Vegas rivals theirs for special effects. ✉ *116 bis, av. des Champs-Élysées, 8e, Champs-Élysées* ☎ *01–40–76–56–10* Ⓜ *George V.*

Michou. The always-decked-out-in-blue owner, Michou, presents an over-the-top show here. It features *tranformiste* men on stage in extravagant drag, performing with high camp for a radically different cabaret experience. Dinner shows are €110 and €140, or you can watch from the bar for €40, which includes a drink. ✉ *80 rue des Martyrs, 18e, Montmartre* ☎ *01–46–06–16–04* Ⓜ *Pigalle.*

Moulin Rouge. When it opened in 1889, the Moulin Rouge lured Parisians of all social stripes—including, of course, the famous Toulouse-Lautrec, who immortalized the venue and its dancers in his paintings.

Although shows are no longer quite so exotic (no elephants or donkey rides for the ladies), you will still see the incomparable French cancan. It's the highlight of what is now a classy version of a Vegas-y revue, starring 100 dancers, acrobats, ventriloquists, and contortionists, and more than 1,000 costumes. Dinner starts at 7, revues at 9 and 11 (arrive 30 minutes early). Men are expected to wear a jacket and tie. Prices range from €95 for just a revue to €200 for luxe dinner and a show. ⊠ *82 bd. de Clichy, 18e, Montmartre* ☎ *01–53–09–82–82* ⊕ *www.moulinrouge. fr* Ⓜ *Blanche.*

HOTEL BARS

Some of Paris's best hotel bars mix historic pedigrees with hushed elegance—and others go for a modern, edgy luxe. Following are some perennial favorites.

The Hemingway Bar & the Ritz Bar. Literature lovers, cocktail connoisseurs and other drink-swilling devotees drew a collective sigh when the iconic Hemingway Bar & the Ritz Bar were shuttered—along with the rest of the super-luxe Ritz—when the hotel closed for a top-to-bottom makeover in 2012. Although an opening date has not yet been set, it's expected that libations will started being poured again in late 2014 or early 2015. Watch for the big reveal: this is one of the most hotly anticipated facelifts in Paris. ⊠ *15 pl. Vendôme, 1er* ⊕ *www.ritzparis. com* Ⓜ *Opéra.*

Hôtel Costes. Hôtel Costes draws the big names, and not just during fashion week. Despite years on the scene, this place has lost none of its flair or star clientele. Expect to cross paths with anyone from Kylie Minogue to Bruce Willis, as long as you make it past the chilly greeting of the statuesque hostess. Dressing to kill is strongly advised, especially for newcomers; otherwise expect all the tables to be suddenly reserved. ⊠ *239 rue St-Honoré, 1er, Louvre* ☎ *01–42–44–50–25* Ⓜ *Tuileries.*

Hôtel Plaza Athenée. Hôtel Plaza Athenée, Paris's perfectly chic chill-out spot, has a sexy, glowing bar designed by Philippe Starck protégé Patrick Jouin. Gather here for an apéritif to stoke your energy before hitting the nearby club scene. It's party central during Paris Fashion Week. ■TIP➔ You'll find one of the most inventive cocktail lists in town here: try the acclaimed Rose Royale, with Alain Ducasse champagne and freshly crushed raspberries. ⊠ *25 av. Montaigne, 8e, Champs-Élysées* ☎ *01–53–67–66–00* ⊕ *www.plaza-athenee-paris.com* Ⓜ *Alma Marceau.*

Le Bar at George V. An ultraluxe, clubby hideaway in the Four Seasons Hotel, Le Bar at George V is perfect for star-gazing from the plush wine-red armchairs, cognac in hand. Its charm still lures the glitterati, especially during fashion weeks. Be sure to notice the hotel's signature—and stunning—flower arrangements. ⊠ *31 av. George V, 8e, Champs-Élysées* ☎ *01–49–52–70–00* Ⓜ *George V.*

L'Hôtel. L'Hôtel's hushed Baroque bar is the perfect place for a discreet rendezvous. Designed in typically jaw-dropping Jacques Garcia style, the hideaway has a photo of a louche Keanu Reeves on the wall and evokes the decadent spirit of onetime resident Oscar Wilde. ⊠ *13 rue des Beaux-Arts, 6e, St-Germain-des-Prés* ☎ *01–44–41–99–00* ⊕ *www.l-hotel.com* Ⓜ *St-Germain-des-Prés.*

2

Mama Shelter. Hip Parisians make the pilgrimage to visit the Island Bar at this hotel, the happeningest spot around. Beautiful people flock in for solid cocktails, foosball, and even an adjacent pizza bar. It's always packed, but lines will be out the door on Saturday, when DJs and other international artists perform. ✉ *109 rue de Bagnolet, 20e, Père Lachaise* ☎ *01–43–48–48–48* ⊕ *www.mamashelter.com* Ⓜ *Alexandre Dumas.*

Murano Urban Resort. This bar is Paris's epitome of space-age-bachelor-pad-hipness *du jour* with a black-stone bar, candy-color walls, and a friendly staff. It overflows nightly with beautiful Marais culture vultures and is grabbing the late-night buzz with its theme soirées. ✉ *13 bd. du Temple, 3e, République* ☎ *01–42–71–20–00* ⊕ *www.muranoresort.com* Ⓜ *Filles du Calvaire, République.*

Pershing Hall. Pershing Hall has an überstylish lounge with muted colors and minimalist lines, plus an enormous "vertical garden" in the simply stunning indoor courtyard. The chic ambience and hip lounge music make this a popular neighborhood nightspot; starting at 10 pm there's a DJ. ■**TIP➔** Try the signature Lalique cocktail—it comes in an actual Lalique crystal glass. ✉ *49 rue Pierre Charron, 8e, Champs-Élysées* ☎ *01–58–36–58–00* ⊕ *www.pershinghall.com* Ⓜ *Franklin-D.-Roosevelt.*

SHOPPING

In the most beautiful city in the world, it's no surprise to discover that the local greengrocer displays his tomatoes as artistically as Cartier does its rubies. Window-shopping is one of this city's greatest spectator sports; the French call it *lèche-vitrine*—literally, "licking the windows"—which is fitting because many of the displays look good enough to eat. Most stores, excepting department stores and flea markets, stay open until 6 or 7 pm, but many take a lunch break sometime between noon and 2 pm. Many shops traditionally close on Sunday.

THE BEST SHOPPING NEIGHBORHOODS

AVENUE MONTAIGNE

Shopping doesn't come much more chic than on avenue Montaigne, with its graceful town mansions housing some of the top names in international fashion: **Chanel, Dior, Céline, Valentino, Chloé, Jimmy Choo, Prada, Dolce & Gabbana,** and many more. Neighboring rue François 1er and avenue George V are also lined with many designer boutiques: **Versace, Fendi, Givenchy,** and **Balenciaga.** It doesn't matter, say the French, that fewer and fewer of their top couture houses are still headed by compatriots. It's the chic elegance, the classic ambience, the *je ne sais quoi,* that remain undeniably Gallic.

CHAMPS-ÉLYSÉES

Cafés and movie theaters keep the once-chic Champs-Élysées active 24 hours a day, but the invasion of exchange banks, car showrooms, and fast-food chains has lowered the tone. Four glitzy 20th-century arcade malls—**Galerie du Lido, Le Rond-Point, Le Claridge,** and **Élysées 26**—capture most of the retail action, not to mention the **Gap** and the **Disney**

Store. Some of the big luxe chain stores—also found in cities around the globe—are here: **Sephora** has reintroduced a touch of elegance, and the mothership **Louis Vuitton** (on the Champs-Élysées proper) has kept the cool factor soaring.

CANAL ST-MARTIN

One of the city's best-kept shopping secrets—for now—the Canal St-Martin draws local hipsters and in-the-know visitors looking for something different. The main drag, avenue Beaurepaire, is lined with shops like **Boutique Rehnsen** for cool jeans, **Bazar Éthic** for ecofriendly fibers, or **Liza Korn** for cute vintage-inspired clothes and accessories. Along the quai de Valmy, the funky clothing and housewares shop **Antoine & Lili,** and trendy clothier **Sandro** are open Sunday afternoon.

LEFT BANK

For an array of bedazzling boutiques with hyper-picturesque goods—antique toy theaters, books on gardening—and the most fascinating antiques stores in town, be sure to head to the area around rue Jacob, nearly lined with *antiquaires,* and the streets around superposh place Furstenberg. After decades of clustering on the Right Bank's venerable shopping avenues, the high-fashion houses have stormed the Rive Gauche. The first to arrive were **Sonia Rykiel** and **Yves St-Laurent** in the late '60s. Some of the more recent arrivals include **Christian Dior, Giorgio Armani, Catherine Malandrino, Isabel Marant,** and **Louis Vuitton.** Rue des St-Pères and rue de Grenelle are lined with designer names.

LE MARAIS

The Marais is a mixture of many moods and many influences; its lovely, impossibly narrow cobblestone streets are filled with some of the most original, small-name, nonglobal goods to be had—a true haven for the original gift—including the outposts of **Jamin Puech** and **Sentou Galerie.** Parisian "it" designers **Azzedine Alaïa** and **Vanessa Bruno** have boutiques within a few blocks of stately place des Vosges. The Marais is also one of the few neighborhoods that have a lively Sunday-afternoon (usually from 2 pm) shopping scene.

LOUVRE–PALAIS-ROYAL

The elegant and eclectic shops clustered in the 18th-century arcades of the Palais-Royal sell such items as antiques, toy soldiers, music boxes, some of the world's most exclusive vintage designer dresses at **Didier Ludot,** luxe croc gloves at **Maison Fabre,** and high-end hipness at **Stella McCartney** and **Marc Jacobs.**

OPÉRA TO LA MADELEINE

Two major department stores—**Printemps** and **Galeries Lafayette**—dominate boulevard Haussmann, behind Paris's ornate 19th-century Opéra Garnier. Place de la Madeleine tempts many with its two luxurious food stores, **Fauchon** and **Hédiard.**

PLACE DES VICTOIRES AND RUE ÉTIENNE MARCEL

The graceful, circular place des Victoires, near the Palais-Royal, is the playground of fashion icons such as **Kenzo,** while **Comme des Garçons** and **Yohji Yamamoto** line rue Étienne Marcel. In the nearby oh-so-charming

South of the Champs-Élysées you'll find the posh avenue Montaigne shopping district; to its north, the ritzy boutiques of the Faubourg St-Honoré.

Galerie Vivienne shopping arcade, **Jean-Paul Gaultier** has a shop that has been renovated by Philippe Starck, and is definitely worth a stop.

PLACE VENDÔME AND RUE DE LA PAIX

The magnificent 17th-century place Vendôme, home of the Ritz Hotel, and rue de la Paix, leading north from Vendôme, are where you can find the world's most elegant jewelers: **Cartier, Boucheron, Bulgari,** and **Van Cleef and Arpels.**

RUE ST-HONORÉ AND FAUBOURG ST-HONORÉ

A fashionable set makes its way to these chic streets to shop at the city's swankest addresses and its trendiest boutique, **Colette.** Designer names abound here, including **Hermès, Lanvin, Gucci, Prada,** and **Miu Miu,** while on nearby rue Cambon you can find the wonderfully elegant **Maria Luisa** and the **Chanel** mothership. Shopping aside, the area is also a political hub, home to the Élysée Palace and the residences of the American and British ambassadors. The Paris branches of **Sotheby's** and **Christie's** and renowned antiques galleries such as **Didier Aaron** add artistic flavor.

DEPARTMENT STORES

Au Printemps. Au Printemps is actually three major stores: the spanking new Printemps de la Maison (home furnishings) on four refurbished floors, Printemps de l'Homme (menswear—six floors of it), and the brilliant Printemps de la Mode (fashion, fashion, fashion), which has everything from cutting-edge to teeny bopper. Be sure to check out the beauty area, with the Nuxe spa, hairdressers, and seemingly every beauty product known to woman under one roof. ⊠ *64 bd. Haussmann,*

9e, Opéra/Grands Boulevards ☎ *01–42–82–50–00* ⊕ *www.printemps. com* Ⓜ *Havre Caumartin, Opéra, and RER: Auber.*

BHV. BHV, short for Bazar de l'Hôtel de Ville, houses an enormous basement hardware store that sells everything from doorknobs to cement mixers and has to be seen to be believed. The fashion offerings for men, women, and kids have been totally revamped, with many of the top labels and a fabulous, not-too-crowded lingerie department on the second floor. But BHV is most noteworthy for its huge selection of high-quality household goods, home-decor material, electronics, and office supplies. If you're looking for typically French household items (those heavy, gold-rimmed café sets, gorgeous French linen, or Savon de Marseille), this is your ticket. The extensive men's store is across the street at 36 rue de la Verrerie. ✉ *52–64 rue de Rivoli, 4e, Les Halles* ☎ *01–42–74–90–00* Ⓜ *Hôtel de Ville.*

Galeries Lafayette. Galeries Lafayette is one of those places that you wander into unawares, leaving hours later a poorer and humbler person. At the flagship store at 40 boulevard Haussmann, a Belle Époque stained-glass dome caps the world's largest perfumery. The store bulges with thousands of designers; free fashion shows are held Friday at 3 pm in the upstairs café (reservations are a must: call 01–42–82–36–40 or e-mail welcome@galerieslafayette.com). A big draw is the comestibles department, stocked with everything from herbed goat cheese to Iranian caviar. Just across the street at 35 boulevard Haussmann is Galeries Lafayette Maison. The Montparnasse branch is a pale shadow of the boulevard Haussmann behemoths. ✉ *35–40 bd. Haussmann, 9e, Opéra/ Grands Boulevards* ☎ *01–42–82–34–56* ⊕ *www.galerieslafayette.com* Ⓜ *Chaussée d'Antin, Opéra, Havre Caumartin.*

Fodor'sChoice ★ **Le Bon Marché.** Founded in 1852, Le Bon Marché has emerged as the city's chicest department store. Long a hunting ground for linens and other home items, the store got a face-lift that brought fashion to the fore. The ground floor sets out makeup, perfume, and accessories; this is where celebs duck in for essentials while everyone pretends not to recognize them. Upstairs, do laps through labels chichi (Burberry, Sonia Rykiel) and überhip (Martin Margiela, Comme des Garçons). Menswear, under the moniker Balthazar, keeps pace with designers like Saint Laurent and Paul Smith. Zip across the second floor walkway to the mode section (above the next-door *épicerie*): home to streetwise designers and edgy secondary lines, it also has a funky café. French favorites include Athé by Vanessa Bruno, Zadig & Voltaire, Manoush, Isabel Marant's Étoile line, and Madame à Paris. Best of all, this department store isn't nearly as crowded as those near the Opéra. Don't miss La Grande Épicerie next door: it's the haute couture of grocery stores. Artisanal jams, olive oils, and much more make great gifts, and the luscious pastries and fruit beg to be chosen for a snack. ✉ *24 rue de Sèvres, 7e, St-Germain-des-Prés* ☎ *01–44–39–80–00* ⊕ *www.lebonmarche.com* Ⓜ *Sèvres-Babylone.*

MARKETS

The lively atmosphere that reigns in most of Paris's open-air food markets makes them a sight worth seeing even if you don't want or need to buy anything. Every neighborhood has one, though many are open only a few days each week. Sunday morning until 1 pm is usually a good time to go. Many of the better-known markets are in areas you'd visit for sightseeing; here's a list of the top bets.

Fodor's Choice
★

Marché aux Puces St-Ouen. Also referred to as Clignancourt, this market, on Paris's northern boundary, still attracts crowds when it's open—Saturday to Monday, from 9 to 6—but its once-unbeatable prices are now a relic. The century-old labyrinth, packed with antiques dealers' booths and *brocante* stalls, sprawls for more than a square mile. Old Vuitton trunks, ormolu clocks, 1930s jet jewelry, and vintage garden furniture sit cheek by jowl. Arrive early to pick up the most worthwhile loot. Be warned—if there's one place in Paris where you need to know how to bargain, this is it! If you're arriving by métro, walk under the overpass and take the first left at rue de Rosiers to reach the center of the market. ■TIP→ Around the overpass huddle stands selling dodgy odds and ends (think designer knockoffs and questionable gadgets). These blocks are crowded and gritty; be careful with your valuables. ⊠ *18e, Montmartre* ⊕ *www.parispuces.com* Ⓜ *Porte de Clignancourt.*

Marché d'Aligre. Arguably the most locally authentic market, Marché d'Aligre is open until 1 every day except Monday. Don't miss the covered hall on place d'Aligre, where you can stop by a unique olive-oil boutique for bulk and prebottled oils from top producers. ⊠ *Rue d'Aligre, 12e, Bastille/Nation* Ⓜ *Ledru-Rollin.*

Porte de Vanves. This smaller flea market, which lies at the southern side of the city, is a hit with the fashion and design set and specializes in smaller objects—mirrors, textiles, glassware, clothing, and collectables—as well as books, posters, antique wallpapers, and postcards. With tables sprawling along both sides of the sidewalk, there's an extravagant selection, but be sure to bargain. It's open weekends only from 8 to 5, but arrive early if you want to find real deals: the good stuff goes fast, and stalls are liable to be packed up before noon. ⊠ *14e, Southern Paris* Ⓜ *Porte de Vanves.*

Rue Montorgueil. This old-fashioned market street has evolved into a chic Bobo zone; its stalls now thrive amid stylish cafés and the oldest oyster counter in Paris. ⊠ *1er, Les Halles* Ⓜ *Châtelet Les Halles.*

Rue Mouffetard. This market, near the Jardin des Plantes, reflects its multicultural neighborhood: vibrant, with a laid-back feel that still smacks of old Paris. It's best on weekends. ⊠ *5e, Latin Quarter* Ⓜ *Monge.*

SHOPPING ARCADES

Paris's 19th-century commercial arcades, called *passages* or *galeries*, are the forerunners of the modern mall. Glass roofs, decorative pillars, and mosaic floors give the passages character. The major arcades are on the Right Bank in central Paris. The loveliest of them all are:

The eye-popping atrium of the Galeries Lafayette is the subject of this entry by Elizabeth A. Millar, a Fodors. com member, to Fodor's "Show Us Your France" contest.

Galerie Véro-Dodat. Galerie Véro-Dodat was built in 1826. At what is now the Café de l'Époque, just at the gallery's entrance, the French writer Gérard de Nerval took his last drink before heading to Châtelet to hang himself. The glass-ceilinged gallery has painted medallions and copper pillars and shops selling contemporary art, instruments, and leather goods. It's best known, though, for its antiques stores. ✉ *19 rue Jean-Jacques Rousseau, 1er, Louvre/Tuileries* ☎ *01–44–71–02–48* Ⓜ *Louvre.*

Fodor's Choice ★ **Galerie Vivienne.** Galerie Vivienne, between the Bourse and the Palais-Royal, is home to a range of interesting luxury shops as well as a lovely tearoom (A Priori Thé) and a terrific wineshop (Cave Legrand). Don't leave without checking out the Jean-Paul Gaultier boutique. ✉ *4 rue des Petits-Champs, 2e, Opéra/Grands Boulevards* Ⓜ *Bourse.*

Passage des Panoramas. Passage des Panoramas, opened in 1799, is the oldest extant arcade and has become a foodie paradise, with no less than five major gourmet destinations. ✉ *11 bd. Montmartre, 2e, Grands Boulevards* Ⓜ *Opéra/Grands Boulevards.*

Passage du Grand-Cerf. Passage du Grand-Cerf has regained the interest of Parisians. La Parisette, a small boudoir-pink space at No. 1, sells fun accessories, and Marci Noum, at No. 4, riffs on street fashion. Silk bracelets, crystals, and charms can be nabbed at Eric & Lydie and Satellite. ✉ *145 rue St-Denis, 2e, Les Halles* Ⓜ *Étienne Marcel.*

Passage Jouffroy. Passage Jouffroy is full of shops selling toys, Oriental furnishings, and cinema books and posters. Pain D'épices, at No. 29, has dollhouse decor. ✉ *12 bd. Montmartre, 9e, Grands Boulevards* Ⓜ *Grands Boulevards.*

LISTINGS BY NEIGHBORHOOD

CHAMPS-ÉLYSÉES

2

WOMEN'S WEAR AND ACCESSORIES

Chanel. Chanel is helmed by Karl Lagerfeld, whose collections are steadily vibrant. The historic center is at the 31 Rue Cambon boutique around the Louvre, where Chanel once perched high up on the mirrored staircase watching audience reactions to her collection debuts. But this flagship shop is also stunning. Great investments include all of Coco's favorites: the perfectly tailored tweed suit, a lean, soigné black dress, or a quilted bag with a gold chain. ⊠ *42 av. Montaigne, 8e, Champs-Élysées* ☎ *01–47–23–74–12* Ⓜ *Franklin-D.-Roosevelt.*

Chloé. Chloé made a canny move in May 2011 when it tapped Clare Waight Keller to step up to the helm. Keller cut her teeth under Tom Ford at Gucci, but her most recent coup was to inject the century-old knitwear house, Pringle, with a much-needed dose of modernism. Keller's debut Spring 2012 was a triumph of the kind of flowing, feminine silhouettes the luxury house is known for but with a twist—a voluminous charmeuse skirt cut thigh-high; a transparent flapperesque silk dress over teeny silk shorts. ⊠ *44 av. Montaigne, 8e, Champs-Élysées* ☎ *01–47–23–00–08* Ⓜ *Franklin-D.-Roosevelt.*

Christian Dior. Christian Dior installed the flamboyant and preternaturally talented John Galliano in 1997 and embarked on a wild ride to fashion's highest pinnacle before the designer's infamous crash landing in 2011. The forward-thinking house waited more than a year before making a huge—and fortuitous—leap of faith, tapping Raf Simons (lately of Jill Sander) to man the helm in 2012. Simons's steadfast vision and clean, elegant lines have so far elated the fashion press and breathed new life into the revered house. ⊠ *30 av. Montaigne, 8e, Champs-Élysées* ☎ *01–40–73–73–73* Ⓜ *Franklin-D.-Roosevelt.*

Jean-Paul Gaultier. Jean-Paul Gaultier first made headlines by engineering that celebrated corset with the ironic iconic breasts for Madonna but now sends fashion editors into ecstasies with his sumptuous haute-couture creations. Designer Philippe Starck spun an *Alice in Wonderland* fantasy for the boutiques, with quilted cream walls and Murano mirrors. Make no mistake, though, it's all about the clothes. ⊠ *44 av. George V, 8e, Champs-Élysées* ☎ *01–44–43–00–44* Ⓜ *George V.*

UNCOMMON-SCENTS

Guerlain (⊠ *68 av. des Champs-Élysées* ☎ *01–45–62–52–57* Ⓜ *Franklin-D.-Roosevelt*) has long resided at this opulent address, a befitting home for the world-class perfumer. Still the only Paris outlet for legendary perfumes like Shalimar and L'Heure Bleue, it has added several new signature scents (Idylle, Lys Soleia), and the perfume "fountain" allows for personalized bottles in several sizes to be filled on demand. Or, for a mere €30,000, a customized scent can be blended just for you. Also here are makeup, scented candles, and a spa featuring its much-adored skin-care line.

Fodor'sChoice **Louis Vuitton.** Louis Vuitton has
★ spawned a voracious fan base from Texas to Tokyo with its mix of classic leather goods and the saucy revamped versions orchestrated by Marc Jacobs. Jacobs's collaborations, such as with Japanese artist Takashi Murakami, have become instant collectibles . . . and knockoffables. This soaring cathedral-esque paean to luxury (and consumption) is unsurpassed. ✉ *101 av. des Champs-Élysées, 8e, Champs-Élysées* ☎ *08–10–81–00–10* Ⓜ *George V.*

Petit Bateau. Petit Bateau provides a fundamental part of the classic French wardrobe from cradle to teen and beyond. The signature T-shirt—cut close to the body, with smallish shoulders—works equally well with school uniforms or vintage Chanel. High-grade cotton clothes follow designs that haven't changed in decades (think onesies and pajamas for newborns, underwear sets, and dresses with tiny straps for summer); however, lines in cotton-silk or cotton-cashmere and popular partnerships with designers like Carven and Tsumori Chisato mean there's now even more in store. Stock up: if you can find this brand back home, the prices are sure to be higher. ✉ *116 av. des Champs-Élysées, 8e, Champs-Élysées* ☎ *01–40–74–02–03* Ⓜ *George V.*

LATIN QUARTER

BOOKS

Shakespeare & Company. This sentimental Rive Gauche favorite is named after the bookstore whose American owner, Sylvia Beach, first published James Joyce's *Ulysses*. Nowadays it specializes in expat literature. Although the eccentric and beloved owner, George Whitman, passed away in 2011, his daughter Sylvia has taken up the torch. You can still count on a couple of characters lurking in the stacks, a sometimes spacey staff, the latest titles from British presses, and hidden second-hand treasures in the odd corners and crannies. Poets give readings upstairs on Monday at 8 pm; there is also music and special workshops. ✉ *37 rue de la Bûcherie, 5e, Latin Quarter* ☎ *01–43–25–40–93* Ⓜ *St-Michel.*

HOME ACCESSORIES

Le Monde Sauvage. Le Monde Sauvage is a must-visit for home accessories. Expect reversible silk bedspreads in rich colors, velvet throws, hand-quilted bed linens, silk floor cushions, colorful rugs, and the best selection of hand-embroidered curtains in silk, cotton, linen, or velvet. ✉ *11 rue de l'Odéon, 6e, Latin Quarter* ☎ *01–43–25–60–34* Ⓜ *Odéon.*

2

LES HALLES

SHOES

Christian Louboutin. These shoes carry their own red carpet with them, thanks to their trademark crimson soles. Whether tasseled, embroidered, or strappy, in Charvet silk or shiny patent leather, the heels are always perfectly balanced. No wonder they set off such legendary legs as Tina Turner's and Gwyneth Paltrow's. ⊠ *19 rue Jean-Jacques Rousseau, 1er, Les Halles* ☎ *01–42–36–53–66* Ⓜ *Palais-Royal.*

LOUVRE/TUILERIES

ACCESSORIES, COSMETICS, AND PERFUMES

Fodor'sChoice
★
Chantal Thomass. The legendary lingerie diva is back with a *Pillow Talk*–meets–Louis XIV–inspired boutique. This is French naughtiness at its best, striking the perfect balance between playful and seductive. Sheer silk negligees edged in Chantilly lace and lascivious bra-and-corset sets punctuate the signature line. ⊠ *211 rue St-Honoré, 1er, Louvre/Tuileries* ☎ *01–42–60–40–56* Ⓜ *Tuileries.*

Goyard. These colorful totes are the choice of royals, blue bloods, and the like (clients have included Sir Arthur Conan Doyle, Gregory Peck, and the Duke and Duchess of Windsor). Parisians swear by their durability and longevity; they're copious enough for a mile-long baguette, and durable enough for a magnum of champagne. What's more, they easily transition into ultrachic beach or diaper bags. ⊠ *233 rue St-Honoré, 1er, Louvre/Tuileries* ☎ *01–42–60–57–04* Ⓜ *Tuileries.*

Hermès. Hermès was established as a saddlery in 1837 and went on to create the eternally chic Kelly (named for Grace Kelly) and Birkin (named for Jane Birkin) handbags. The silk scarves are legendary for their rich colors and intricate designs, which change yearly. Other accessories are also extremely covetable: enamel bracelets, dashing silk-twill ties, and small leather goods. During semiannual sales, in January and July, prices are slashed up to 50%, and the crowds line up for blocks. ⊠ *24 rue du Faubourg St-Honoré, 8e, Louvre/Tuileries* ☎ *01–40–17–47–17* Ⓜ *Concorde.*

Maison Fabre. Until you've eased into an exquisite pair of gloves handcrafted by Fabre, you probably haven't experienced the sensation of having a second skin far superior to your own. Founded in 1924, this is one of Paris's historic *gantiers*. Styles range from classic to haute: picture elbow-length croc leather, coyote-fur mittens, and peccary driving gloves. ⊠ *128–129 Galerie de Valois, 1er, Louvre/Tuileries* ☎ *01–42–60–75–88* Ⓜ *Palais-Royal–Musée du Louvre.*

Roger Vivier. Known for decades for his Pilgrim-buckle shoes and inventive heels, Roger Vivier's name is being resurrected through the creativity of über-Parisienne Inès de la Fressange and the expertise of shoe designer Bruno Frisoni. The results are easily some of the best shoes in town: leather boots that mold to the calf perfectly, towering rhinestone-encrusted or feathered platforms for evening, and vertiginous crocodile pumps. ⊠ *29 rue du Faubourg St-Honoré, 8e, Louvre/Tuileries* ☎ *01–53–43–00–85* Ⓜ *Concorde.*

BOOKS AND STATIONERY

Librarie Galignani. Dating back to 1520s Venice, this venerable bookstore opened in Paris in 1801 and was the first to specialize in English language books. Its present location, across from the Tuileries Garden on the rue de Rivoli, opened in 1856, and the wood bookshelves, creaking floors, and hushed interior provide the perfect atmosphere for perusing Paris's best collection of contemporary and classic greats in English and French, plus a huge selection of gorgeous art books. ✉ *224 rue de Rivoli, 1e, Louvre/Tuileries* ☎ *01–42–60–76–07* ⊕ *www.galignani. com* Ⓜ *Tuileries.*

LINGERIE

Alice Cadolle. Alice Cadolle, which has been selling lingerie to Parisians since 1889, has some of the city's most sumptuous couture undergarments. Ready-to-wear bras, corsets, and sleepwear fill the rue Cambon boutique; on rue St-Honoré, Madame Cadolle offers made-to-measure service. ✉ *4 rue Cambon, 1er, Louvre/Tuileries* ☎ *01–42–60–94–22* Ⓜ *Concorde.*

WOMEN'S WEAR

Colette. This is the place for ridiculously cool fashion par excellence. So the staff barely deigns to make eye contact—who cares! There are ultramodern trinkets and trifles of all kinds: perfumes; an exclusive handful of cosmetics, including Chenot and Le Labo; and loads of superchic jewelry . . . and that's just the ground floor. The first floor has wares (clothes, shoes, and accessories) from every internationally known and unknown designer with street cred, a small library, the latest out-there CDs, and an art display space. The basement has a water bar (because that's what models eat) and a small restaurant that's good for a quick bite. ✉ *213 rue St-Honoré, 1er, Louvre/Tuileries* ☎ *01–55–35–33–90* Ⓜ *Tuileries.*

Vanessa Bruno. Vanessa Bruno stirs up a new brew of feminine dressing: some androgynous pieces (skinny pants) plus delicacy (filmy tops) with a dash of whimsy (lace insets). Separates are coveted for their sleek styling, gorgeous colors, and unerring sexiness. Wardrobe staples include perfectly proportioned cotton tops and sophisticated dresses. Athé, the diffusion line, flies off the racks, so if you see something you love, grab it. Bruno's shoes and accessories are the cherry on the cake: her ultrapopular sequin-striped totes inspired an army of knockoffs. ✉ *12 rue de Castiglione, 1er, Louvre/Tuileries* ☎ *01–42–61–44–60* Ⓜ *Pyramides.*

MARAIS

BOOKS

Comptoir de l'Image. This is where designers John Galliano, Marc Jacobs, and Emanuel Ungaro stock up on old copies of *Vogue, Harper's Bazaar,* and *The Face.* You'll also find trendy magazines like *Dutch, Purple,* and *Spoon*; designer catalogs from the past; and rare photo books. ✉ *44 rue de Sévigné, 3e, Marais* ☎ *01–42–72–03–92* Ⓜ *St-Paul.*

WOMEN'S WEAR

Azzedine Alaïa. Alaïa is one of the darlings of the fashion set, thanks to his perfectly proportioned "king of cling" dresses—and you don't have to be under 20 to look good in his garments. Tina Turner wears them well, as does every other beautiful woman with the courage and the curves. His boutique/workshop/apartment is covered with artwork by Julian Schnabel and is not the kind of place you casually wander into out of curiosity: the sales staff immediately makes you feel awkward in that distinctive Parisian way. ✉ *7 rue de Moussy, 4e, Marais* ☎ *01–42–72–19–19* Ⓜ *Hôtel de Ville.*

COS. COS, which stands for Collection of Style, is the H&M group's answer to fashion sophisticates, who flock here in droves for high-concept, minimalist design with serious attention to quality tailoring and fabrics at a reasonable price. Classic accessories and shoes look more expensive than they are. Best of all, the clothes for men, women and kids (ages two through eight) can't be found in the States—yet. ✉ *4 rue des Rosiers, 4e, Marais* ☎ *01–44–54–37–70* Ⓜ *St-Paul.*

French Trotters. The new flagship store features an understated collection of contemporary French-made classic clothes and accessories for men and women that emphasize quality fabrics, style and cut over trendiness. You'll also find a handpicked collection of exclusive collaborations with cutting-edge French brands, like sleek leather-and-suede booties by Avril Gau for FrenchTrotters, sneakers by the eco-brand Veja, and travel-savvy accessories from Bleu de Chauffe, as well as FrenchTrotters namesake label, and a limited selection of housewares for chic Parisian apartments. ✉ *128 rue Vieille du Temple, 3e, Marais* ☎ *01–44–61–00–14* ⊕ *www.frenchtrotters.fr* Ⓜ *St-Sébastien Froissart, Filles du Calvaire.*

L'Eclaireur. This boutique is Paris's touchstone for edgy, up-to-the-second styles. L'Eclaireur's knack for uncovering new talent and championing established visionaries is legendary—no surprise after 30 years in the business. Hard-to-find geniuses, like leather wizard Isaac Sellam and British prodigy Paul Harnden, cohabit with luxe labels such as Ann Demeulemeester, Haider Ackermann, and Lanvin. Women's wear is in one shop with men's around the corner. ✉ *40 rue de Sevigné, 3e, Marais* ☎ *01–48–87–10–22* Ⓜ *St-Paul.*

Vintage Clothing Paris. It's worth a detour to the Marais's outer limits to drop by Vintage Clothing Paris, where the racks read like an A-list of designer greats—Yves Saint Laurent, Hermès, Balman, Valentino, Lagerfeld, Mugler, just to name a few. Brigitte Petit's minimalist shop is the fashion insider's go-to spot for rare pieces that stand out in a crowd, like a circa 1985 Alaia suede skirt with peek-a-boo grommets and zip-up front and a jaunty Yves Saint Laurent Epoch Russe hooded cape. ✉ *10 rue de Crussol, 11e, Marais* ☎ *01–48–07–16–40* Ⓜ *Filles du Calvaire, Oberkampf.*

OPÉRA/GRANDS BOULEVARDS

GOURMET GOODIES

À la Mère de Famille. This enchanting shop is well versed in French regional specialties as well as old-fashioned bonbons, sugar candy, and more. ✉ *35 rue du Faubourg-Montmartre, 9e, Opéra/Grands Boulevards* ☎ *01–47–70–83–69* Ⓜ *Cadet.*

MENSWEAR

Charvet. Charvet is the Parisian equivalent of a Savile Row tailor. It's a conservative, aristocratic institution famed for made-to-measure shirts, exquisite ties, and accessories; for garbing John F. Kennedy, Charles de Gaulle, and the Duke of Windsor; and for its regal address. Although the exquisite silk ties, in hundreds of colors and patterns, and custom-made shirts for men are the biggest draw, refined pieces for women and girls, as well as adorable miniatures for boys, round out the collection. ✉ *28 pl. Vendôme, 1er, Opéra/Grands Boulevards* ☎ *01–42–60–30–70* Ⓜ *Opéra.*

ST-GERMAIN-DES-PRÉS

BOOKS

The scenic open-air bookstalls along the Seine sell secondhand books (mostly in French), prints, and souvenirs. Numerous French-language bookstores—specializing in a wide range of topics, including art, film, literature, and philosophy—are found in the Latin Quarter and around St-Germain-des-Prés.

EASTERN PARIS

CLOTHING

Isabel Marant. This rising design star is a honeypot of bohemian rock-star style. Her separates skim the body without constricting: layered miniskirts, loose peek-a-boo sweaters ready to slip from a shoulder, teeny-weeny hot pants, and super fox-fur jackets in lurid colors. Look for the secondary line, Étoile, for a less expensive take. ✉ *16 rue de Charonne, 11e, Bastille/Nation* ☎ *01–49–29–71–55* Ⓜ *Ledru-Rollin.*

ILE-DE-FRANCE

WELCOME TO ILE-DE-FRANCE

TOP REASONS TO GO

★ **Louis XIV's Versailles:** Famed as glorious testimony to the Sun King's megalomania, this is the world's most luxe palace and nature-tamed park.

★ **Creamy Chantilly:** Stately château, stellar art collection, fabulous forest, palatial stables . . . all within the same square mile.

★ **Van Gogh in Auvers:** The great painter spent his last, manically productive three months here—you can see where he painted, where he got drunk, where he shot himself, and where he remains.

★ **Chartres Cathedral:** A pinnacle of Gothic achievement, this 13th-century masterpiece has peerless stained glass and a hilltop silhouette visible for miles around.

★ **Monet's Water Lilies:** Come to Giverny to see his lily pond—a half-acre "Monet"—then peek around his charming home and stroll the time-warped streets to the exceptional Musée des Impressionismes.

1 **The Western Ile-de-France: Versailles to Auvers-sur-Oise.** The Ile-de-France's richest frontier for you, if you want to dig into the past, is the western half of the 60-km (35-mile) circle that rings Paris. These sylvan woods are literally full of châteaux of all descriptions, the towns are charming, and no one should miss the world's grandest palace. Haunt of Louis XIV, Madame de Pompadour, and Marie-Antoinette, Versailles is a monument to splendidly wretched excess and once home to 20,000 courtiers and servants. More spiritual concerns are embodied in Chartres Cathedral, a soaring pinnacle of Gothic architecture. Nineteen kilometers (30 miles) north are landscapes of lasting impressions: Giverny and Auvers, immortalized by Monet and Van Gogh, respectively.

GETTING ORIENTED

3

Appearing like all France in miniature, the Ile-de-France region is the heartland of the nation. The "island of France" is the poetic name for the area surrounding Paris and taking in the valleys of three rivers: the Seine, the Marne, and the Oise. Ever since the days of Julius Caesar, this has been the economic, political, and religious hub of France and, consequently, no other region boasts such a wealth of great buildings, from Chartres to Fontainebleau and Versailles. Though small, this region is so rich in treasures that a whole day of fascinating exploration may take you no more than 60 km (35 miles) from the capital.

2 The Eastern Ile-de-France: Chantilly to Fontainebleau. By traveling an eastward arc through the remainder of the Ile you can savor the icing on the cake. Begin with Chantilly, one of the most opulent châteaux in France, noted for its royal stables, art treasures, and gardens by André Le Nôtre. Northward lie medieval Senlis and the storybook castle of Pierrefonds. Heading east, Disneyland Paris is where the Mickey-smitten rejoice. Continuing south, two magnificent châteaux—Vaux-le-Vicomte and Fontainebleau—were built for some of France's most pampered monarchs and merchants.

Updated
by Jennifer
Ditsler-Ladonne

Just what is it that makes the Ile-de-France so attractive, so comfortingly familiar? Is it its proximity to the great city of Paris—or perhaps that it's so far removed?

Had there not been the world-class cultural hub of Paris nearby, would Monet have retreated to his Japanese gardens at Giverny? Or Paul Cézanne and Van Gogh to bucolic Auvers? Kings and courtiers to the game-rich forests of Rambouillet? Would Napoléon have truly settled at Malmaison and then abdicated at the palace at Fontainebleau? Would medieval castles and palaces have sprouted in the town of St-Germain-en-Laye? Would abbeys and cathedrals have sprung skyward in Chartres and Senlis?

If you had asked Louis XIV, he wouldn't have minced his words: the city of Paris—yawn—was simply *démodée*—out of fashion. In the 17th century the new power base was going to be Versailles, once a tiny village in the heart of the Ile-de-France, now the site of a gigantic château from which the Sun King's rays (Louis XIV was known as *le roi soleil*) could radiate, unfettered by rebellious rabble and European arrivistes. Of course, later heirs kept the lines open and restored the grandiose palace as the governmental hub it was meant to be—and commuted to Paris, well before the high-speed RER.

That, indeed, is the dream of most Parisians today: to have a foot in both worlds. Paris may be small as capital cities go, with slightly fewer than 2 million inhabitants, but the Ile-de-France, the region around Paris, contains more than 10 million people—a sixth of France's entire population. That's why on closer inspection the once rustic villages of the Ile-de-France reveal cosseted gardens, stylishly gentrified cottages, and extraordinary country restaurants no peasant farmer could afford to frequent.

The Ile-de-France is not really an *île* (island), of course. This green-forested buffer zone that enfolds Paris is only vaguely surrounded by the three rivers that meander through its periphery. But France's capital city seems to crown this genteel sprawl of an atoll, peppered with pretty villages, anchored by grandiose châteaux. In the end, the Ile-de-France offers a rich and varied mini sampling of everything you expect from France—cathedrals, painters' villages, lavish palaces, along with the bubblegum-pink turrets of Disneyland Paris—and all delightfully located within easy day trips from Paris.

PLANNER

WHEN TO GO

With its extensive forests, the Ile-de-France is especially beautiful in fall, particularly October. May and June are good months, too, while July through August can be sultry and crowded. On a Saturday night in summer, however, you can make a candlelight visit to Vaux-le-Vicomte.

Be aware when making your travel plans that some places are closed one or two days a week. The château of Versailles is closed Monday, and the châteaux of Chantilly and Fontainebleau are closed Tuesday. In fact, as a rule, even well-touristed towns make their *fermeture hebdomadaire* (weekly closing) on Monday or Tuesday. At these times museums, shops, and markets may be closed—call ahead if in doubt.

Disneyland Paris tends to be mobbed on summer weekends. So does Giverny (Monet's garden), which is at its best in May and June and, like Vaux-le-Vicomte, is closed November to March. During the winter months, it's always best to phone ahead to make sure your sightseeing stops are still open.

PLANNING YOUR TIME

A great advantage to exploring this region is that all its major monuments are within a half-day's drive from Paris, or less if you take the trains that run to many of the towns in this region.

The catch is that most of those rail lines connect the towns of the Ile with Paris, not, in general, with neighboring towns of the region. Thus, it may be easier to plan on "touring" the Ile in a series of side trips from Paris, rather than expecting to travel through the Ile in clockwise fashion (which, of course, can be easily done if you have a car).

This chapter is broken up into two halves. Threading the western half of the Ile, the first tour heads southwest from Paris to Versailles and Chartres, turns northwest along the Seine to Monet's Giverny, and returns to Paris after visiting Vincent van Gogh's Auvers. Exploring the eastern half of the Ile, the second tour picks up east of the Oise Valley in glamorous Chantilly, then detours north to Pierrefonds, and finishes up southward by heading to Disneyland Paris, Vaux-le-Vicomte, and Fontainebleau.

For a stimulating mix of pomp, nature, and spirituality, we suggest your three priorities should be Versailles, Giverny, and Chartres.

EXPERIENCING IMPRESSIONISM

Paris's Musée d'Orsay may have some of the most fabled Monet and Van Gogh paintings in the world, but the Ile-de-France has something (almost) better—the actual landscapes that were rendered into masterpieces by the brushes of many great Impressionist and Postimpressionist artists. At Giverny, Claude Monet's house and garden are a moving visual link to his finest daubs—its famous lily-pond garden gave rise to his legendary water-lilies series (some historians feel it was the other way around).

Nearby, villages like Vétheuil still look like three-dimensional "Monets." Here, too, is the impressive Musée des Impressionismes. In Auvers-sur-Oise, Vincent van Gogh had a final burst of creativity before ending his life; the famous wheat field where he was attacked by crows and painted his last painting is just outside town. Back then, they called him Fou-Roux (mad redhead) and derided his art. But now, more than a century after his passionate rendering of life and landscape, the townspeople here love to pay tribute to the man who helped make their village famous. André Derain lived in Chambourcy, Camille Pissarro in Pontoise, and Alfred Sisley in Moret-sur-Loing—all were inspired by the silvery sunlight that tumbles over these hills and towns.

Earlier, Rousseau, Millet, and Corot paved the way for Impressionism with their penchant for outdoor landscape painting in the village of Barbizon, still surrounded by its romantic, quietly dramatic forest. A trip to any of these towns will provide lasting impressions.

GETTING HERE AND AROUND
AIR TRAVEL
Major airports in the Ile-de-France area are Charles de Gaulle (☎ *01–48–62–22–80* ⊕ *www.adp.fr*), commonly known as Roissy, 25 km (16 miles) northeast of Paris, and Orly (☎ *01–49–75–15–15* ⊕ *www.adp. fr*), 16 km (10 miles) south. Shuttle buses link Disneyland to the airports at Roissy, 56 km (35 miles) away, and Orly, 50 km (31 miles) distant; buses take 45 minutes and run every 45 minutes from Roissy, every 60 minutes from Orly (less frequently in low season), and cost €19.

BUS TRAVEL
Although many of the major sights *in this chapter* have train lines connecting them on direct routes with Paris, the lesser towns and destinations pose more of a problem and require taking a local bus run by SNCF (☎ *36–35 [€0.34 per min]* ⊕ *www.transilien.com*) from the train station (*gare*). These include getting to Senlis from the Chantilly Gare SNCF, to Fontainebleau and Barbizon from the Avon Gare SNCF, to Vaux-le-Vicomte from the Melun Gare SNCF, or to Giverny from the Vernon Gare SNCF. Other buses travel outward from Paris's suburbs—the No. 158A bus, for instance, which goes from La Défense to St-Germain-en-Laye and Rueil-Malmaison.

CAR TRAVEL
A13 links Paris (from the Porte d'Auteuil) to Versailles. You can get to Chartres on A10 from Paris (Porte d'Orléans). For Fontainebleau take A6 from Paris (Porte d'Orléans).

For a more attractive, although slower, route through the Forest of Sénart and the northern part of the Forest of Fontainebleau, take N6 from Paris (Porte de Charenton) via Melun. A4 runs from Paris (Porte de Bercy) to Disneyland. Although a comprehensive rail network ensures that most towns in the Ile-de-France can make comfortable day trips from Paris, the only way to crisscross the region without returning to the capital is by car. There's no shortage of expressways or fast highways. However, you should be prepared for delays close to Paris, especially during the morning and evening rush hours.

TRAIN TRAVEL

Many sights can be reached by SNCF (☎ *08–91–36–20–20 [€0.23 per min]* ⊕ *www.transilien.com*) trains from Paris. The handiest of Versailles's three train stations is the one reached by the RER-C line. The main Paris stations for this train are at Austerlitz, St-Michel, Invalides, and Champ-de-Mars; the trip takes 30–40 minutes.

Both regional and main-line (Le Mans–bound) trains leave Gare Montparnasse for Chartres (50–70 mins). The former also stops at Versailles and Rambouillet.

Gare Montparnasse is also the terminal for the suburban trains that stop at Montfort-L'Amaury, a helpful train station for the northwest regions of the Ile-de-France.

Most main-line trains from Gare St-Lazare stop at Vernon (50 mins), for Monet's House at Giverny, on their way to Rouen and Le Havre.

Chantilly is on the main northbound line from Gare du Nord (the trip takes 25–40 mins).

The lovely medieval town of Senlis can be reached by bus from Chantilly. Fontainebleau—or, rather, neighboring Avon, 2 km (1½ miles) away (there is a frequent bus service)—is 45 minutes from Gare de Lyon. To reach Vaux-le-Vicomte, head first for Melun, then take a taxi or local bus (in summer there's a shuttle service). To reach Giverny, rail it to Vernon, then use the taxi or local bus. The RER-A also accesses the station for Disneyland Paris (called Marne-la-Vallée–Chessy). This leaves visitors within 100 yards of the entrance to both the theme park and Disney Village. Journey time is around 40 minutes, and trains operate every 10–30 minutes, depending on the time of day. A main-line TGV (Trains à Grande Vitesse ⊕ *www.tgv.com*) station also links Disneyland to Lille, Lyon, Brussels, and London (via Lille and the Channel Tunnel).

RESTAURANTS

The Ile-de-France's fanciest restaurants can be just as pricey as their Parisian counterparts. Close to the Channel for fresh fish, lush Normandy for beef and dairy products, and the rich agricultural regions of Picardy and the Beauce, Ile-de-France chefs have all the ingredients they could wish for, and shop for the freshest produce early each morning at the huge food market at Rungis, 18 km (10 miles) south of the capital. Traditional "local delicacies"—lamb stew, *pâté de Pantin* (pastry filled with meat), or pig's trotters—tend to be obsolete, though creamy Brie, made locally in Meaux and Coulommiers, remains queen of the cheese board.

Prices in the reviews are the average cost of a main course at dinner or, if dinner is not served, at lunch.

HOTELS

In summer, hotel rooms are at a premium, and making reservations is essential; almost all accommodations in the swankier towns—Versailles, Rambouillet, and Fontainebleau—are on the costly side. Take nothing for granted; picturesque Senlis, for instance, does not have a single hotel in its historic downtown area.

Prices in the reviews are the lowest cost of a standard double room in high season.

VISITOR INFORMATION

Special *forfait* tickets, combining travel and admission, are available for several regional tourist destinations (including Versailles, Fontaine-bleau, and Auvers-sur-Oise). Contact the Espace du Tourisme d'Ile-de-France (⊕ *www.pidf.com* ☉ *Wed.–Mon. 10–7*), under the inverted pyramid in the Carrousel du Louvre, for general information on the area. Information on Disneyland is available from the Disneyland Paris reservations office. *Local tourist offices are listed throughout by town.*

TOUR OPTIONS

Alliance Autos. has bilingual guides who give private tours of the Paris area in a luxury car or minibus for a minimum of four hours for about €80 an hour (3–8 people; call to check details and prices). ⊠ *149 rue de Charonne, Paris* ☎ *01–55–25–23–23.*

Euroscope. Take minibus excursions to Versailles (€82 half day; €145 full day) and Giverny, or a combination of Giverny/Auvers-sur-Oise, Fontainebleau/Barbizon, Vaux le Vicomte, and Rambouillet. You can also choose a combination of all four (€84 half day; €158 full day with lunch), as well as half-day tours of Chantilly and half- or full-day tours of Chartres, or a combination of Chartes/Versailles (€99–€165). ⊠ *46 rue de Provence, Paris* ☎ *01–56–03–56–81* ⊕ *www.euroscope.fr.*

Pariscityvision. This company provides guided excursions by coach to Giverny, Auvers-sur-Oise, Versailles, Vaux le Vicomte, Fontainebleau, and Barbizon, or combinations of two or three destinations (€54–€142). Some excursions are offered year-round, but most are from April through October. It also offers half- and full-day excursions by minibus (maximum eight people) to Giverny and Fontainebleau/Barbizon/Vaux le Vicomte from April through October, and to Versailles year-round (€72–€215). ⊠ *2 rue des Pyramides, Paris* ☎ *01–44–55–60–00* ⊕ *www.pariscityvision.com.*

THE WESTERN ILE-DE-FRANCE

Not only is majestic Versailles one of the most unforgettable sights in the Ile-de-France, it's also within easy reach of Paris, less than 30 minutes by either train or car (A13 expressway from Porte d'Auteuil). This is the starting point for a visit to the western half of the Ile-de-France, anchored by holy Chartres to the south and Vincent van Gogh's Auvers-sur-Oise to the north.

VERSAILLES

16 km (10 miles) west of Paris via A13.

Fodor's Choice
★

It's hard to tell which is larger at **Château de Versailles**—the world-famous château that housed Louis XIV and 20,000 of his courtiers, or the mass of tour buses and visitors standing in front of it. The grandest palace

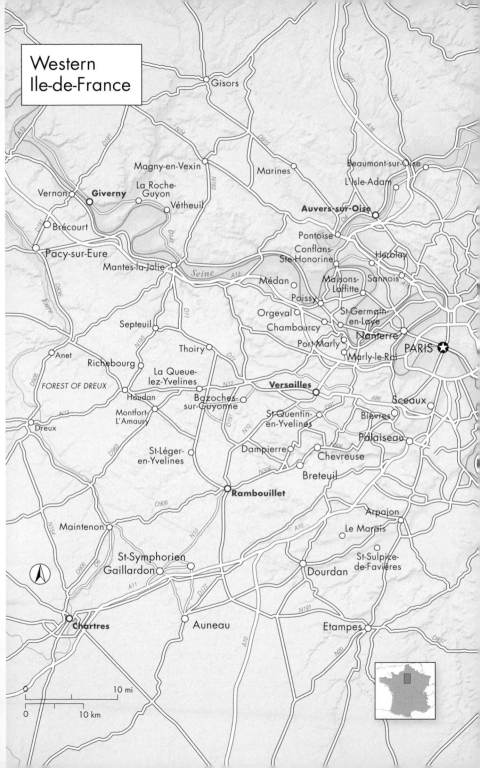

in France remains one of the marvels of the world (⇨ *Its full story is covered in the special photo feature on the château in "Gilt Trip: A Visit to Versailles")*. But this edifice was not just home to the Sun King, it was also to be the new headquarters of the French government capital (from 1682 to 1789 and again from 1871 to 1879). To accompany the palace, a new city—in fact, a new capital—had to be built from scratch. Tough-thinking town planners took no prisoners, dreaming up vast mansions and avenues broader than the Champs-Élysées.

GETTING HERE

Versailles has three train stations, all reached from different stations in Paris (journey time 25–40 mins). Versailles Rive Gauche provides the easiest access from Paris. The other two stations in Versailles are about a 10-minute walk from the château, although the municipal Bus B or a summertime shuttle service (use your métro ticket or pay a small fee in coins) can also deposit you at the front gates.

Visitor Information Versailles Tourist Office ⊠ *2 bis, av. de Paris* ☏ *01–39– 24–88–88* ⊕ *www.versailles-tourisme.com.*

EXPLORING

Musée Lambinet. Around the back of Notre-Dame, on boulevard de la Reine (note the regimented lines of trees), are the elegant Hôtel de Neyret and the Musée Lambinet, a sumptuous mansion from 1751, with collections of paintings, weapons, fans, and porcelain (including the Madame du Barry "Rose"). A tearoom, open Thursday, Saturday, and Sunday afternoons, provides an elegant way to refresh after an afternoon of sightseeing. ⊠ *54 bd. de la Reine* ☏ *01–39–50–30–32* ⊕ *www.versailles-tourisme.com* ⊠ *€4* ⊙ *Sat.–Thurs. 2–6.*

Nôtre-Dame. If you have any energy left after exploring Louis XIV's palace and park, a tour of Versailles—a textbook 18th-century town— offers a telling contrast between the majestic and the domestic. From the front gate of Versailles's palace turn left onto the rue de l'Independence-Américaine and walk over to rue Carnot past the stately Écuries de la Reine—once the queen's stables, now the regional law courts—to octagonal place Hoche. Down rue Hoche to the left is the powerful Baroque facade of Notre-Dame, built from 1684 to 1686 by Jules Hardouin-Mansart as the parish church for Louis XIV's new town.

Place du Marché-Notre-Dame. Passage de la Geôle, a cobbled alley lined with quaint antiques shops, climbs up to place du Marché-Notre-Dame, with an open-air morning market on Tuesday, Friday, and Sunday that is famed throughout the region (note the four 19th-century timber-roof halls). Fresh fruit and vegetables from the palace's own kitchen garden, *le potager du roi,* can be purchased on market days.

WHERE TO EAT

$ ✕ **Au Chapeau Gris.** This bustling wood-beam restaurant just off avenue

FRENCH de St-Cloud, overlooking elegant place Hoche, offers hearty selections of meat and fish, ranging from *bœuf Rossini* (with wild mushrooms) to salmon and scallops marinated in lime and the top-price lobster fricasséed in Sancerre. The wine list roams around the vineyards of Bordeaux and Burgundy, while desserts include pineapple tartare with hibiscus syrup, and glazed pear in pastry with hot-chocolate sauce. The prix-fixe menu makes a reasonable and satisfying lunchtime option. $ *Average main: €16* ✉ *7 rue Hoche* ☎ *01–39–50–10–81* ⊕ *www.auchapeaugris. com* ⊘ *Closed Wed. No dinner Tues. and daily late July–late Aug.*

$$$$
MODERN FRENCH
Fodor's Choice
★

✕ **Gordon Ramsay au Trianon.** Gordon Ramsay, the ebullient "bad boy de la cuisine anglaise," has already amassed a string of restaurants worldwide, including 12 British restaurants and 18 others around the world from Tokyo to Australia to L.A. to Las Vegas—all the while maintaining a consistent two stars for this establishment. Although he cut his culinary teeth in the kitchens of master chefs Guy Savoy and Joël Robuchon, this is his first eatery on French soil. The delicious results—overseen by his longstanding London number two, Simone Zanoni—are predictably conversation-worthy: raviolo of langoustines and lobster cooked in a Riesling bisque with Petrossian caviar and lime consommé; or the Périgord foie gras done "2 ways," roasted with a beetroot tart and pressed with green apple and Sauternes, are two top main dishes. Desserts are marvels, too, with chocolate meringue with vanilla ice cream, candied pear, and black currant vying for top honors with the raspberry soufflé with chocolate and tarragon ice cream. The Trianon's more casual, 60-seat Véranda restaurant is now also under Ramsay's sway, and in its black-and-white contemporary setting you can opt for Ramsay's "light, modern take" on such bistro novelties as radicchio and Parmesan risotto with chorizo oil or the fillet of sole in a parsley crust, cèpes, and sautéed artichokes. Teatime provides a delightful (and reasonable) restorative for weary château-goers, with a French take on high tea: scones, madeleines, and heavenly macaroons. $ *Average main: €150* ✉ *1 bd. de la Reine* ☎ *01–30–84–55–55* ⊕ *www.gordonramsay. com/grautrianon* ⩜ *Reservations essential. Jacket required* ⊘ *Closed Sun. and Mon. No lunch Tues.–Thurs.*

$$$
MODERN FRENCH
Fodor's Choice
★

✕ **L'Angelique.** After the stellar success of his first Michelin-starred restaurant, L'Escarbille (in Meudon), chef Régis Douysset's newest venture confirms his commitment to refined-yet-unfussy French cuisine. The dining room, in a restored 17th-century town house, is serene and comfortable, with white walls, wood-beam ceilings, dark wood paneling, and tasteful artwork—a handsome setting in which to relax into one of the best meals in town. The seasonally changing menu offers a good balance of seafood, game, and meat: a delicate perch fillet with spaghetti *de mer* (in a shellfish bouillon) or the venison shoulder with grilled turnips and a spätzle of girolle mushrooms. Desserts are not to be missed—the tart *feuilletée*, with candied peaches, cardamom, and peach sorbet, is ethereal. Having earned a Michelin star, this spot is justifiably popular, so reserve well in advance. $ *Average main: €28* ✉ *27 av. de Saint-Cloud* ☎ *01–30–84–98–85* ⊕ *www.langelique.fr* ⊘ *Closed Sun. and Mon.*

WHERE TO STAY

For expanded hotel reviews, visit Fodors.com.

$
HOTEL

▦ **Le Cheval Rouge.** This unpretentious old hotel, built in 1676, is in a corner of the town market square, close to the château and strongly recommended if you plan to explore the town on foot. **Pros:** great setting in town center; good value for Versailles. **Cons:** bland public areas;

Continued on page 187

3

GILT TRIP
A VISIT TO VERSAILLES

By Robert I.C. Fisher

Louis XIV's Hall of Mirrors

A two-century spree of indulgence in the finest bling-bling of the age by the consecutive reigns of three French kings produced two of the world's most historic artifacts: gloriously, the Palace of Versailles and, momentously, the French Revolution.

Less a monument than an entire world unto itself, Versailles is the king of palaces. The end result of 380 million francs, 36,000 laborers, and enough paintings, if laid end to end, to equal 7 miles of canvas, it was conceived as the ne plus ultra expression of monarchy by Louis XIV. As a child, the king had developed a hatred for Paris (where he had been imprisoned by a group of nobles known as the Frondeurs), so, when barely out of his teens, he cast his cantankerous royal eye in search of a new power base. Marshy, inhospitable Versailles was the stuff of his dreams. Down came dad's modest royal hunting lodge and up, up, and along went the minion-crushing, Baroque palace we see today.

Between 1661 and 1710, architects Louis Le Vau and Jules Hardouin Mansart designed everything his royal acquisitiveness could want, including a throne room devoted to Apollo, god of the sun (Louis was known as *le roi soleil*). Convinced that his might depended upon dominating French nobility, Louis XIV summoned thousands of grandees from their own far-flung châteaux to reside at his new seat of government. In doing so, however, he unwittingly triggered the downfall of the monarchy. Like an 18th-century Disneyland, Versailles kept its courtiers so richly entertained they all but forgot the murmurs of discontent brewing back home.

As Louis XV chillingly foretold, "After me, the deluge." The royal commune was therefore shocked— shocked!—by the appearance, on October 5, 1789, of a revolutionary mob from Paris ready to sack Versailles and imprison Louis XVI. So as you walk through this awesome monument to splendor and excess, give a thought to its historic companion: the French Revolution. A tour of Versailles's grand salons inextricably mixes pathos with glory.

CROWNING GLORIES:
TOP SIGHTS OF VERSAILLES

Seducing their court with their self-assured approach to 17th- and 18th-century art and decoration, a trinity of French kings made Versailles into the most vainglorious of châteaux.

Galerie des Glaces (Hall of Mirrors). Of all the rooms at Versailles, none matches the magnificence of the Galerie des Glaces (Hall of Mirrors). Begun by Mansart in 1678, this represents the acme of the Louis Quatorze (Louis-XIV) style. Measuring 240 feet long, 33 feet wide, and 40 feet high, it is ornamented with gilded candlesticks, crystal chandeliers, and a coved ceiling painted with Charles Le Brun's homage to Louis XIV's reign.

In Louis's day, the Galerie was laid with priceless carpets and filled with orange trees in silver pots. Nighttime galas were illuminated by 3,000 candles, their blaze doubled in the 17 gigantic mirrors that precisely echo the banner of windows along the west front. Lavish balls were once held here, and you can still get the full royal treatment at the Serenade Royale. This reenacts one of Louis XIV's grand soirées with dancers in period costumes. The 45-minute spectacle is held at 6:45 and 7:45 pm. (€39, €28 ages 6–18 www. chateauversailles-spectacles.fr 01–30–83–78–98).

The Grands Appartements (State Apartments). Virtual stages for ceremonies of court ritual and etiquette, Louis XIV's first-floor state salons were designed in the Baroque style on a biceps-flexing scale meant to one-up the lavish Vaux-le-Vicomte château recently built for Nicolas Fouquet, the king's finance minister.

Flanking the Hall of Mirrors and retaining most of their bombastic Italianate Baroque decoration, the Salon de la Guerre (Salon of War) and the Salon de la Paix (Salon of Peace) are ornately decorated with gilt stucco, painted ceilings, and marble sculpture. Perhaps the most extravagant is the Salon d'Apollon (Apollo Chamber), the former throne room.

Versailles from the outside

Detail of the ceiling

Hall of Mirrors

Inside the Apollo Chamber

Hall of Battles

Appartements du Roi (King's Apartments). Completed in 1701 in the Louis-XIV style, the king's state and private chambers comprise a suite of 15 rooms set in a "U" around the east facade's Marble Court. Dead center across the sprawling cobbled forecourt is Louis XIV's bedchamber—he would awake and rise (just as the sun did, from the east) attended by members of his court and the public. Holding the king's chemise when he dressed soon became a more definitive reflection of status than the possession of an entire province. Nearby is Louis XV's magnificent Cabinet Intérieur (Office of the King), shining with gold and white boiseries; in the center is the most famous piece of furniture at Versailles, Louis XV's roll-top desk, crafted by Oeben and Riesener in 1769.

Louis XIV

King's Apartments

Chambre de la Reine (Queen's Bedchamber). Probably the most opulent bedroom in the world, this was initially created for Marie Thérèse, first wife of Louis XIV, to be part of the Queen's Apartments. For Marie Antoinette, however, the entire room was glammed up with silk wall-hangings covered with Rococo motifs that reflect her love of flowers. Legend has it that the gardens directly beyond these windows were replanted daily so that the queen could enjoy a fresh assortment of blossoms each morning. The bed, decked out with white ostrich plumes *en panache*, was also redone for Louis XVI's queen. Nineteen royal children were born in this room.

VINTAGE BOURBON

Versailles was built by three great kings of the Bourbon dynasty. Louis XIV (1638–1715) began its construction in 1661. After ruling for 72 years, Louis Quatorze was succeeded by his great grandson, Louis XV (1710–74), who added the Royal Opera and the Petit Trianon to the palace. Louis XVI (1754–93) came to the throne in 1774 and was forced out of Versailles in 1789, along with Marie Antoinette, both guillotined three years later.

Queen's Bedchamber

3

IN FOCUS GILT TRIP: A VISIT TO VERSAILLES

Petits Appartements (Small Apartments). As styles of decor changed, Louis XIV's successors felt out of sync with their architectural inheritance. Louis XV exchanged the heavy red-and-gilt of Italianate Baroque for lighter, pastel-hued Rococo. On the top floor of the palace, on the right side of the central portion, are the apartments Louis XV commissioned to escape the wearisome pomp of the first-floor rooms. Here, Madame de Pompadour, mistress of Louis XV and famous patroness of the Rococo style, introduced grace notes of intimacy and refinement. In so doing, she transformed the daunting royal apartments into places to live rather than pose.

Parc de Versailles. Even Bourbon kings needed respite from Versailles's endless maze, hence the creation of one of Europe's largest parks. The sublime 250-acre grounds (☎ 01–30–83–77–88 for guided tour) is the masterpiece of André Le Nôtre, presiding genius of 17th-century classical French landscaping. Le Nôtre was famous for his "green geometries": ordered fantasies of clipped yew trees, multicolored flower beds (called *parterres*), and perspectival allées cleverly punctuated with statuary, laid out between 1661 and 1668. The spatial effect is best admired from inside the palace, views about which Le Nôtre said, "Flowers can only be walked on by the eyes."

Ultimately, at the royal command, rivers were diverted—to flow into more than 600 fountains—and entire forests were imported to ornament the park, which is centered around the mile-long Grand Canal. As for the great fountains, their operation costs a fortune in these democratic days, and so they perform only on Saturday and Sunday afternoons (⏲ 3:30–5:30) from mid-April through mid-October; admission to the park during this time is €8. The park is open daily 8 AM–8:30 PM.

LIGHTING UP THE SKY

The largest fountain at Versailles, the Bassin de Neptune, becomes a spectacle of rare grandeur during the Grandes Eaux Nocturnes, a light show to the strains of Baroque music, held Saturdays from the end of June through August at 9 pm, with fireworks at 11. Tickets are €23, €19 ages 6–18, and free for children under 6. 🌐 www.chateauversailles-spectacles.fr ☎ 01–30–83–78–98.

Dauphin's Apartments

Bassin de Neptune

Chapel and Opéra Royal: In the north wing of the château are three showpieces of the palace. The solemn white-and-gold Chapelle was completed in 1710—the king and queen attended daily mass here seated in gilt boxes. The Opéra Royal (Opera House), entirely constructed of wood painted to look like marble, was designed by Jacques-Ange Gabriel for Louis XV in 1770. Connecting the two, the 17th-century Galeries have exhibits retracing the château's history.

Opéra Royal

VERSAILLES: FIRST FLOOR, GARDENS & ADJACENT PARK

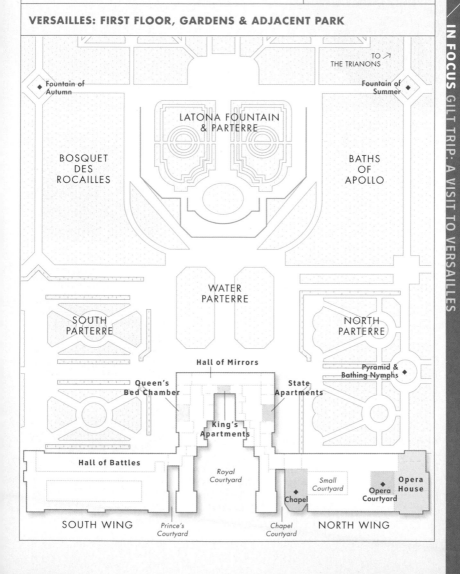

TO ↗
THE TRIANONS

Fountain of Autumn

Fountain of Summer

LATONA FOUNTAIN & PARTERRE

BOSQUET DES ROCAILLES

BATHS OF APOLLO

WATER PARTERRE

SOUTH PARTERRE

NORTH PARTERRE

Hall of Mirrors

Pyramid & Bathing Nymphs

Queen's Bed Chamber

State Apartments

King's Apartments

Hall of Battles

Royal Courtyard

Small Courtyard

Opera House

Opera Courtyard

Chapel

SOUTH WING

Prince's Courtyard

Chapel Courtyard

NORTH WING

3

IN FOCUS GILT TRIP: A VISIT TO VERSAILLES

LET THEM EAT CRÊPE:
MARIE ANTOINETTE'S ROYAL LAIR

Was Marie Antoinette a luxury-mad butterfly flitting from ball to costume ball? Or was she a misunderstood queen who suffered a loveless marriage and became a prisoner of court etiquette at Versailles? Historians now believe the answer was the latter and point to her private retreats at Versailles as proof.

R.F.D. VERSAILLES?

Here, in the northwest part of the royal park, Marie Antoinette (1755–93) created a tiny universe of her own: her comparatively dainty mansion called Petit Trianon and its adjacent "farm," the relentlessly picturesque Hameau ("hamlet"). In a life that took her from royal cradle to throne of France to guillotine, her happiest days were spent at Trianon. For here she could live a life in the "simplest" possible way; here the queen could enter a salon and the game of cards would not stop; here women could wear simple gowns of muslin without a single jewel. Toinette only wanted to be queen of Trianon, not queen of France. And considering the horrible, chamber-pot-pungent, gossip-infested corridors of Versailles, you can almost understand why.

TEEN QUEEN

From the first, Maria-Antonia (her actual name) was ostracized as an outsider, "l'Autrichienne"—the Austrian "bitch." Upon arriving in France in 1770—at a mere 14 years of age—she was married to the Dauphin, the future King Louis XVI. But shamed by her initial failure to deliver a royal heir, she grew to hate overcrowded Versailles and escaped to the Petit Trianon. Built between 1763 and 1768 by Jacques-Ange Gabriel for Madame de Pompadour, this bijou palace was a radical statement: a royal residence designed to be casual and unassuming. Toinette refashioned the Trianon's interior in the sober Neoclassical style.

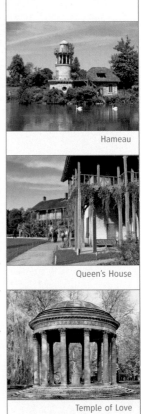

Hameau

Queen's House

Temple of Love

Petit Trianon

"THE SIMPLE LIFE"

Just beyond Petit Trianon lay the storybook Hameau, a mock-Norman village inspired by the peasant-luxe, simple-life daydreams caught by Boucher on canvas and by Rousseau in literature. With its water mill, thatched-roof houses, pigeon loft, and vegetable plots, this make-believe farm village was run by Monsieur Valy-Busard, a farmer, and his wife, who often helped the queen—outfitted as a Dresden shepherdess with a Sèvres porcelain crook—tend her flock of perfumed sheep.

As if to destroy any last link with reality, the queen built nearby a jewel-box theater (open by appointment). Here she acted in little plays, sometimes essaying the role of a servant girl. Only the immediate royal family, about seven or so friends, and her personal servants were permitted entry; disastrously, the entire official-dom of Versailles society was shut out—a move that only served to infuriate courtiers. This is how fate and destiny close the circle. For it was here at Trianon that a page sent by Monsieur de Saint-Priest found Marie-Antoinette on October 5, 1789, to tell her that Paris was marching on an already half-deserted Versailles.

Was Marie Antoinette a political traitor to France whose execution was well merited? Or was she the ultimate fashion victim? For those who feel that this tragic queen spent—and shopped—her way into a revolution, a visit to her relatively modest Petit Trianon and Hameau should prove a revelation.

Marie Antoinette

LES BEAUX TRIANONS

A mile from the château, the Grand Trianon was created by Hardouin Mansart in 1687 as a retreat for Louis XIV; it was restored in the early 19th century, with Empire-style salons. It's a memorable spot often missed by foot-weary tourists exhausted by the château, but well worth the effort. A special treat is Marie Antoinette's hideaway nearby, the Petit Trianon, presumably restored to how she left it before being forced to Paris by an angry mob of soon-to-be revolutionaries.

TAKING ON VERSAILLES (WITHOUT LOSING YOUR HEAD)

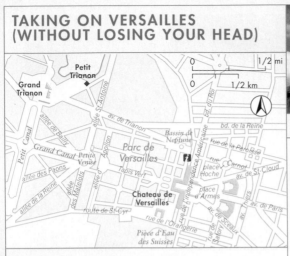

Statue of King Louis XIV

✉ Place d'Armes, Versailles

🌐 www.chateauversailles.fr

☎ 01-30-83-78-00

💶 A €25 day Passport gets you into almost all sites, with audio-guide Grand Eaux, €18 in low season (kids under 18, free).

Château only is €18. Petit and Grand Trianons (joint ticket) €10; Parc de Versailles free; Grand Eaux Musicale fountain show's €23; Serenade Royale, €39.

🕐 The château is open Apr.–Oct., Tues.–Sun. 9–6:30; Nov.–Mar., Tues.–Sun, 9–5:30. Trianons Tues.–Sun. noon–6:30, Nov.–Mar. Park open daily 8–8:30.

Ⓜ RER Line C from Paris to Versailles–Rive Gauche station (closest to the Palace) or SNCF trains from Paris's Gare St-Lazare to Versailles–Rive Droite and Gare Montparnasse to Versailles.

Train tickets are €17. The best bargain (and a line-dodging time saver) is to buy a Forfait Loisirs Château de Versailles ticket (€22) that includes round-trip transportation from Paris and entrance to the main Versailles sights. Tickets are available at SNCF transilien train stations.

TOURING THE PALACE

The army of 20,000 noblemen, servants, and sycophants who moved into Louis XIV's huge Château de Versailles is matched today by the battalion of 3 million visitors a year. You may be able to avoid the modern-day crowds if you arrive here at 9 AM and buy your ticket in advance at FNAC or SNCF or online. The main entrance is near the top of the courtyard to the right; there are different lines depending on tour, physical ability, and group status. Frequent English guided tours visit the private royal apartments. More detailed hour-long tours explore the opera house (now reopened after a spectacular renovation; book a tour or concert ticket online) or Marie Antoinette's private parlors. You can wander the grandest rooms—including the Hall of Mirrors—without a group tour. To figure out the system, pick up a brochure at the information office for details.

TOURING THE PARK

If the grandeur of the palace begins to overwhelm, the Parc de Versailles is the best place to come back down to earth. The distances of the park are vast—the Trianons themselves are more than a mile from the château—so you might want to climb aboard the train (💶€6.80 round-trip ☎01-39-54-22-00), or rent a bike from Petite-Venise (💶€6.50 per hr or €17 for 6 hrs ☎01-39-66-97-66). You can hire a rowboat on the Grand Canal (💶€15 per hr) or drive to the Trianons and canal through the Grille de la Reine (💶€5.50 per car).

some rooms need renovating. $ *Rooms from: €82* ✉ *18 rue André-Chénier* ☎ *01–39–50–03–03* ⊕ *www.chevalrougeversailles.fr* ⤳ *40 rooms* ⦿ *No meals.*

$$$$
HOTEL
⊞ **Trianon Palace Versailles, a Waldorf Astoria Hotel.** A modern-day Versailles, this deluxe hotel is in a turn-of-the-20th-century, creamy white creation of imposing size, filled with soaring rooms (including the historic Salle Clemenceau, site of the 1919 Versailles Peace Conference), palatial columns, and with a huge garden close to the château park. **Pros:** palatial glamour; wonderful setting right by château park; Gordon Ramsay. **Cons:** lack of a personal touch after recent changes of ownership. $ *Rooms from: €250* ✉ *1 bd. de la Reine* ☎ *01–30–84–50–00* ⊕ *www.placeshilton.com/trianon-palace-versailles* ⤳ *199 rooms, 23 suites* ⦿ *Breakfast.*

NIGHTLIFE AND THE ARTS

Académie du Spectacle Equestre. Directed by Bartabas, the Académie du Spectacle Equestre stages spectacular, hour-long shows on weekend afternoons of horses and their riders performing to music in the converted 17th-century Manège (riding school) at the Grandes Écuries opposite the palace. ✉ *Av. Rockefeller* ☎ *01–39–02–07–14* ⊕ *www.acadequestre.fr.*

Château de Versailles Spectacles. This organization offers opera, ballet, and other artsy options in venues like the Opéra Royal, Orangerie, and Hall of Mirrors. It's also responsible for the Château's must-see musical Fountain Show. ✉ *Versailles* ⊕ *www.chateauversailles-spectacles.fr.*

Théâtre Montansier. A well-conceived annual calendar here usually features a full program of plays. ✉ *13 rue des Réservoirs* ☎ *01–39–20–16–00* ⊕ *www.theatremontansier.com.*

SHOPPING

Aux Colonnes. A highly rated *confiserie* (candy shop), Aux Colonnes has a cornucopia of chocolates and candies. It's closed Monday. ✉ *14 rue Hoche.*

Les Délices du Palais. Everybody heads here to shop for the makings of an impromptu picnic (cold cuts, cheese, salads); it's closed Monday. ✉ *4 rue du Maréchal-Foch.*

Passage de la Geôle. Open Friday–Sunday 9–7, this is close to the town's stupendous market and houses several good antiques shops.

RAMBOUILLET

32 km (20 miles) southwest of Versailles, 42 km (26 miles) southwest of Paris.

GETTING HERE

Trains arriving and departing from the Gare de Rambouillet (place Prud'homme) connect frequently with Paris's Gare Montparnasse on a daily basis; departures for the half-hour ride are up to every 20 minutes during rush hours.

Visitor Information Rambouillet Tourist Office ✉ *1 pl. de la Libération* ☎ *01–34–83–21–21* ⊕ *www.ot-rambouillet.fr.*

EXPLORING

Haughty Rambouillet, once favored by kings and dukes, is now home to affluent gentry and, occasionally, the French president.

Château de Rambouillet. Surrounded by a magnificent 36,000-acre forest, this elegant château is a popular spot for biking and walking. Most of the château dates from the early 18th century, but the brawny **Tour François-Ier** (François I Tower), named for the king who died here in 1547, was part of the fortified castle that stood on this site in the 14th century. Highlights include the wood-panel apartments, especially the **Boudoir de la Comtesse** (Countess's Dressing Room); the marble-wall **Salle de Marbre** (Marble Hall), dating from the Renaissance; and the **Salle de Bains de Napoléon** (Napoléon's Bathroom), adorned with Pompeii-style frescoes. Compared to the muscular forecourt, the château's lakeside facade is a scene of unsuspected serenity and, as flowers spill from its balconies, cheerful informality. Guided visits in English are available on the hour (from 10–5) by reservation. ☎ *01–34–83–00–25* 🌐 *www.monuments-nationaux.fr* 🎟 *€8.50* 🕓 *Wed.–Mon. 10–noon and 2–6.*

Park du Château. An extensive park, with a lake with small islands, stretches behind the château, site of the **Laiterie de la Reine** (Queen's Dairy), built for Marie-Antoinette, who, inspired by the writings of Jean-Jacques Rousseau, came here to escape from the pressures of court life, pretending to be a simple milkmaid. It has a small marble temple and grotto and, nearby, the shell-lined Chaumière des Coquillages (Shell Pavilion). The **Bergerie Nationale** (National Sheepfold) is the site of a more serious agricultural venture: the merinos raised here, prized for the quality and yield of their wool, are descendants of sheep imported from Spain by Louis XVI in 1786. A museum alongside tells the tale and evokes shepherd life. 🎟 *Dairy and Shell Pavilion €6, Sheepfold €6* 🕓 *Weekends, Wed., and holidays 2–6.*

WHERE TO EAT

$$ BISTRO

🍴 **Auberge du Louvetier.** With a roaring fire in winter and an outdoor terrace in summer, this quaint, country-style restaurant with beamed ceilings specializes in the fruits of the sea. Traditional dishes abound, like brioche-enrobed *escargot* (snails) with Roquefort sauce, plump seafood sausage, a hearty *soup au poissons* (fish soup), or a heaping seafood platter. Although the style and service may seem a bit retro, there's an undeniable charm to this thoroughly French restaurant. [$] *Average main: €21* ✉ *19 rue de l'Etang de la Tour* ☎ *01–34–85–61–00* 🌐 *aubergedulouvetier.com* 🕓 *Closed Mon. No lunch Sat. No dinner Sun.*

$$$ MODERN FRENCH

🍴 **La Villa Marinette.** In an atmospheric 18th-century villa at the edge of the forest, husband-and-wife team Myriam and Sébastien Bourgeois welcome diners as though entertaining in their own home. Dishes like venison with celery-root mousseline, plump langoustine baked in a pistachio and lemon crust, or veal with wild mushrooms gathered in the nearby forest are prepared with herbs fresh from the kitchen garden. Tables by the fire in winter or in the spacious garden in warm weather are at a premium, and the good-value, three-course lunch menu (€29) is a big draw, so be sure to reserve. [$] *Average main: €29* ✉ *20 av. du Général de Gaulle, 3 km (2 miles) west of Rambouillet,*

Gazeran ☎ *01–34–83–19–01* ⊕ *villamarinette.fr* ⌑ *Reservations essential* ☺ *Closed Mon. and Tues. No dinner Sun.*

CHARTRES

39 km (24 miles) southwest of Rambouillet via N10 and A11, 88 km (55 miles) southwest of Paris.

If Versailles is the climax of French secular architecture, Chartres is its religious apogee. All the descriptive prose and poetry that have been lavished on this supreme cathedral can only begin to suggest the glory of its 12th- and 13th-century statuary and stained glass, somehow suffused with burning mysticism and a strange sense of the numinous. Chartres is more than a church—it's a nondenominational spiritual experience.

GETTING HERE

Both regional and main-line (Le Mans–bound) trains leave Paris's Gare Montparnasse for Chartres (50–70 mins); tickets are around €27 round-trip. Chartres's train station on place Pierre-Sémard puts you within walking distance of the cathedral.

Visitor Information Chartres Tourist Office ✉ *Pl. de la Cathédrale* ☎ *02–37–18–26–26* ⊕ *www.chartres-tourisme.com.*

EXPLORING

If you arrive in summer from Maintenon across the edge of the Beauce, the richest agrarian plain in France, you can see Chartres's spires rising up from oceans of wheat. The whole town, with its old houses and quaint streets, is worth a leisurely exploration. From rue du Pont-St-Hilaire there's an intriguing view of the rooftops below the cathedral. Ancient streets tumble down from the cathedral to the river, lined most weekends with *bouquinistes* selling old books and prints. Each year on August 15 pilgrims and tourists flock here for the Procession du Vœu de Louis XIII, a religious procession through the streets commemorating the French monarchy's vow to serve the Virgin Mary.

"Chartres en Lumieres," Chartres' festival of lights, is well worth lingering in town until dusk, when 28 of the city's most revered monuments, including the majestic Notre-Dame Cathedral, are transformed into vivid light canvases. Thematically based on the history and purpose of each specific site, the animated projections are organized into a city walk that covers a wide swath of the Old Town's cobbled streets and bridges. The spectacle is free and occurs nightly from April through September. A train tour of the illuminated city operates several times a night, from July 6 until August 25.

Fodor'sChoice
★ **Cathédrale Notre-Dame.** Worship on the site of the Cathédrale Notre-Dame, better known as Chartres Cathedral, goes back to before the Gallo-Roman period—the crypt contains a well that was the focus of druid ceremonies. In the late 9th century Charles II (known as "the Bald") presented Chartres with what was believed to be the tunic of the Virgin Mary, a precious relic that went on to attract hordes of pilgrims. The current cathedral, the sixth church on the spot, dates mainly from the 12th and 13th centuries and was erected after the previous building, dating from the 11th century, burned down in 1194.

A well-chronicled outburst of religious fervor followed the discovery that the Virgin Mary's relic had miraculously survived unsinged. Princes and paupers, barons and bourgeoisie gave their money and their labor to build the new cathedral. Ladies of the manor came to help monks and peasants on the scaffolding in a tremendous resurgence of religious faith that followed the Second Crusade. Just 25 years were needed for Chartres Cathedral to rise again, and it has remained substantially unchanged since.

The lower half of the facade survives from the earlier Romanesque church: this can be seen most clearly in the use of round arches rather than the pointed Gothic style. The **Royal Portal** is richly sculpted with scenes from the life of Christ—these sculpted figures are among the greatest created during the Middle Ages. The taller of the two spires (380 feet versus 350 feet) was built at the start of the 16th century, after its predecessor was destroyed by fire; its fanciful Flamboyant intricacy contrasts sharply with the stumpy solemnity of its Romanesque counterpart (access €3, open daily 9:30–noon and 2–4:30). The **rose window** above the main portal dates from the 13th century, and the three windows below it contain some of the finest examples of 12th-century stained-glass artistry in France.

As spiritual as Chartres is, the cathedral also had its more-earthbound uses. Look closely and you can see that the main nave floor has a subtle slant. This was built to provide drainage, as this part of the church was often used as a "hostel" by thousands of overnighting pilgrims in medieval times.

Your eyes will need time to adjust to the somber interior. The reward is seeing the gemlike richness of the stained glass, with the famous deep Chartres blue predominating. The oldest window is arguably the most beautiful: **Notre-Dame de la Belle Verrière** (Our Lady of the Lovely Window), in the south choir. The cathedral's windows are gradually being cleaned—a lengthy, painstaking process—and the contrast with those still covered in the grime of centuries is staggering. ■TIP➜ It's worth taking a pair of binoculars along with you to pick out the details. If you wish to know more about stained-glass techniques and the motifs used, visit the small exhibit in the gallery opposite the north porch. Since 2008, the cathedral has been undergoing an ambitious renovation—to the tune of a staggering €270 million (about $350 million)—that will continue through 2015. To date, two major chapels (the chapels of the Martyrs and the Apostles) have been completely restored, as have the two bays of the nave and the lower choir and the transept windows. For those who remember these dark recesses before the restoration the transformation is nothing short of miraculous, with an estimated 160,000 square feet of original plasterwork now visible and many of the sublime details for which the cathedral is famous returned to their original 13th-century glory. For even more detail, try to arrange a tour (in English) with local institution Malcolm Miller, whose knowledge of the cathedral's history is formidable. (He leads tours twice a day Monday through Saturday, April–October, once a day November–March at noon. *You can reach him at the telephone number below, or at: millerchartres@aol.com.*) The vast black-and-white labyrinth on the

DID YOU KNOW?

Chartres's beautiful Clocher Neuf ("New Bell-tower") was completed in 1134, well before the Clocher Vieux ("Old Bell-tower"), on the right, which was built between 1145 and 1165.

floor of the nave is one of the few to have survived from the Middle Ages; the faithful were expected to travel along its entire length (some 300 yards) on their knees. Guided tours of the **Crypte** start from the Maison de la Crypte opposite the south porch. You can also see a 4th-century Gallo-Roman wall and some 12th-century wall paintings. ⊠ *16 cloître Notre-Dame* ☎ *02–37–21–75–02* ⊕ *www.chartres-tourisme.com* ⊠ *Crypt €2.70, tours €7.50* ⊘ *Cathedral daily 8:30–7:30; guided tours of crypt Apr.–Oct., daily at 11, 2:15, 3:30, and 4:30; Nov.–Mar., daily at 11 and 4:15.*

STAINED GLASS IN CHARTRES

Galerie du Vitrail. *Vitrail* (stained glass) being the key to Chartres's fame, you may want to visit the Galerie du Vitrail, which specializes in the noble art. Pieces range from small plaques to entire windows, and there are books on the subject in English and French. ⊠ *17 cloître Notre-Dame* ☎ *02-37-36-10-03* ⊕ *www.galerie-du-vitrail.com.*

Musée des Beaux-Arts (*Fine Arts Museum*). Just behind the famed cathedral, the town art museum is housed in a handsome 18th-century building that once used to serve as the bishop's palace. Its varied collection includes Renaissance enamels, a portrait of Erasmus by Holbein, tapestries, armor, and some fine (mainly French) paintings from the 17th, 18th, and 19th centuries. There's also a room devoted to the forceful 20th-century landscapes of Maurice de Vlaminck, who lived in the region. ⊠ *29 cloître Notre-Dame* ☎ *02–37–90–45–80* ⊠ *€3.50; €5.50 with special exhibit* ⊘ *Wed. and Sat. 10–noon and 2–6, Sun. 2–5.*

St-Pierre. The Gothic church of St-Pierre, near the Eure River, has magnificent medieval windows from a period (circa 1300) not represented at the cathedral. The oldest stained glass here, portraying Old Testament worthies, is to the right of the choir and dates from the late 13th century. ⊠ *Rue St-Pierre.*

WHERE TO EAT

$$
FRENCH
✕ **Moulin de Ponceau.** Ask for a table with a view of the Eure River, with the cathedral looming above, at this 16th-century converted water mill. Better still, on sunny days you can eat outside, beneath a parasol on the stone terrace by the water's edge—an idyllic setting. Choose from a regularly changing menu of French stalwarts such as rabbit terrine, trout with almonds, and tarte tatin, or splurge on "la trilogie" of scallops, foie gras, and langoustine. ⓈAverage main: €21 ⊠ 21 rue de la Tannerie ☎ 02–37–35–30–05 ⊕ www.moulindeponceau.fr ⊘ Closed Mon. No dinner Sun.

WHERE TO STAY

For expanded hotel reviews, visit Fodors.com.

$$
HOTEL
🖵 **Best Western Le Grand Monarque.** On Chartres's main town square not far from the cathedral, this is a delightful option with interiors that remain seductively and warmly redolent of the 19th century—it was originally built as a coaching inn—with many guest rooms attractively outfitted with brick walls, wood antiques, lush drapes, and modern bathrooms; the best are in a separate turn-of-the-20th-century building

overlooking a garden, while the most atmospheric are tucked away in the attic. **Pros:** its old-fashioned charm still works today; the spa and fitness center offers beauty treatments and massage. **Cons:** best rooms are in an annex; uphill walk to cathedral. ⓢ *Rooms from: €135* ✉ *22 pl. des Épars* ☎ *02–37–18–15–15* ⊕ *www.bw-grand-monarque.com* ⤵ *55 rooms* ⏐○⏐ *Breakfast.*

$$$$
HOTEL
Fodor'sChoice
★

⛫ **Château d'Esclimont.** On the way south from Rambouillet to Chartres, the town of St-Symphorien is famed for one of France's most spectacular château-hotels; with pointed turrets, *pièces d'eau* (moated pools), and a checkerboard facade, the 19th-century Esclimont domaine—built by La Rochefoucaulds—is well worth seeking out if you wish to eat and sleep like an aristocrat in luxuriously furnished guest rooms (many are loftily dimensioned, others snug in corner turrets) adorned with reproduction 18th-century French pieces. **Pros:** the grand style of a country château; wonderful rural setting. **Cons:** service can be pompous; off the beaten path and not easy to find. ⓢ *Rooms from: €240* ✉ *2 rue du Château-d'Esclimont, 24 km (15 miles) northeast of Chartres via N10/D18, St-Symphorien-le-Château* ☎ *02–37–31–15–15* ⊕ *www.esclimont.com* ⤵ *48 rooms, 4 suites* ⏐○⏐ *Some meals.*

GIVERNY

70 km (44 miles) northwest of Paris.

The small village of Giverny (pronounced jee-vair-knee), just beyond the Epte River, which marks the boundary of the Ile-de-France, has become a place of pilgrimage for art lovers. It was here that Claude Monet lived for 43 years, until his death at the age of 86 in 1926. Although his house is now prized by connoisseurs of 19th-century interior decoration, it's his garden, with its Japanese-inspired water-lily pond and bridge, that remains the high point for many—a 5-acre, three-dimensional Impressionist painting you can stroll around at leisure. Most make this a day trip, although Giverny has some jewel bed-and-breakfasts, so you should consider an overnight or two.

GETTING HERE

Take a main-line train (departures every couple of hours) from Paris's Gare St-Lazare to Vernon (50 mins) on the Rouen–Le Havre line, then a taxi, bus, or bike (which you can hire at the café opposite Vernon station—head down to the river and take the cycle path once you've crossed the Seine) to Giverny, 10 km (6 miles) away. Buses, which run April through October only, meet the trains daily and whisk you away to Giverny for €6 more.

EXPLORING

Fodor'sChoice
★
Maison et Jardin Claude Monet (*Monet's House and Garden*). The Maison et Jardin Claude Monet has been lovingly restored. Monet was brought up in Normandy and, like many of the Impressionists, was captivated by the soft light of the Seine Valley. After several years in Argenteuil, just north of Paris, he moved downriver to Giverny in 1883 along with his two sons, his mistress, Alice Hoschedé (whom he later married), and her six children. By 1890 a prospering Monet was able to buy the house outright. With its pretty pink walls and green shutters, the house

An entry to Fodor's France contest, ShutterbugBill, a Fodors.com member, sent in this entrancing view of the Japanese footbridge in Monet's Garden.

has a warm feeling that may come as a welcome change after the stateliness of the French châteaux. Rooms have been restored to Monet's original designs: the kitchen with its blue tiles, the buttercup-yellow dining room, and Monet's bedroom on the second floor. The house was fully and glamorously restored only in the 1970s, thanks to the millions contributed by fans and patrons (who were often Americans). Reproductions of his works, and some of the Japanese prints he avidly collected, crowd its walls. During this era, French culture had come under the spell of Orientalism, and these framed prints were often gifts from visiting Japanese diplomats whom Monet had befriended in Paris.

Three years after buying his house and cultivating its garden—which the family called the "Clos Normand"—the prospering Monet purchased another plot of land across the lane to continue his gardening experiments, even diverting the Epte to make a pond. The resulting garden *à la japonaise* (reached through a tunnel from the "Clos"), with flowers spilling out across the paths, contains the famous "tea-garden" bridge and water-lily pond, flanked by a mighty willow and rhododendrons. Images of the bridge and the water lilies—in French, *nymphéas*—in various seasons appear in much of Monet's later work. Looking across the pond, it's easy to conjure up the grizzled, bearded painter dabbing at his canvases—capturing changes in light and pioneering a breakdown in form that was to have a major influence on 20th-century art.

The garden is a place of wonder, filled with butterflies, roosters, nearly 100,000 plants bedded every year, and more than 100,000 perennials. No matter that nearly 500,000 visitors troop through it each year; they fade into the background thanks to all the beautiful roses, purple carnations, lady's slipper, aubrieta, tulips, bearded irises, hollyhocks, poppies, daises, nasturtiums, lambs' ears, larkspur, and azaleas, to mention just a few of the blooms (note that the water lilies flower during the latter part of July and the first two weeks of August). Even so, during the height of spring, when the gardens are particularly popular, try to visit during midweek. If you want to pay your respects, Monet is buried in the family vault in Giverny's village church. ✉ *84 rue Claude Monet* ☎ *02–32–51–28–21* 🌐 *www.fondation-monet.com* 🎟 *Gardens and home €9.50* 🕒 *Apr.–Oct., daily 9:30–6.*

3

Musée des Impressionnismes. After touring the painterly grounds of Monet's house, you may wish to see some real paintings at the newly reconceived Musée des Impressionnismes (formerly the Musée Américain), farther along the road. Originally endowed by the late Chicago art patrons Daniel and Judith Terra, it featured a few works by the American Impressionists, including Willard Metcalf, Louis Ritter, Theodore Wendel, and John Leslie Breck, who flocked to Giverny to study at the hand of the master. In recent years the museum has extended its scope with an exciting array of exhibitions that explore the origins, geographical diversity, and wide-ranging influences of Impressionism, particularly in view of Giverny and the Seine Valley as essential landmarks in the history of a movement that was a major influence and transition point in 20th-century art. On-site is a restaurant and *salon de thé* (tearoom) with a fine outdoor terrace, as well as a garden "quoting" some of Monet's plant compositions. Head down the road to visit Giverny's landmark Hôtel Baudy *(see below)*, now a restaurant and once the stomping ground and watering hole of many 19th-century artists. ✉ *99 rue Claude Monet* ☎ *02–32–51–94–65* 🌐 *www.mdig.fr* 🎟 *€7* 🕒 *Apr.–Oct., daily 10–6.*

WHERE TO EAT AND STAY

For expanded hotel reviews, visit Fodors.com.

$$ BRASSERIE Fodor's Choice ★

🍴 **Hôtel Baudy.** Back in Monet's day, this pretty-in-pink villa, originally an *épicerie-buvette* (café-cum-grocer's store), was the hotel of the American painters' colony. Today, the rustic dining room and flowery patio have been overshadowed by all the hubbub at the museums down the road but be sure to detour here as this remains one of the most charming spots in the Ile-de-France, as you'll discover in the stage-set dining room (renovated to appear as in Monet's day) and the extraordinarily pretty rose garden out back, whose embowered paths lead to the adorable studio that Cézanne once used. The surroundings retain more historic charm than the simple cuisine (mainly warm and cold salads, large enough to count as a main course in their own right, or straightforward warm dishes, like an omelet or *gigot d'agneau*) or the busloads of tour groups (luckily channeled upstairs). A decent three-course prix-fixe lunch or dinner is also available. [$] *Average main: €18* ✉ *81 rue Claude-Monet* ☎ *02–32–21–10–03* 🕒 *Closed Nov.–Mar.*

$ B&B/INN

🏨 **Le Clos Fleuri.** Giverny's dire shortage of hotels is compensated by several stylish, and affordable bed-and-breakfasts in village homes, and this is among the best—the domain of the charming Danielle and Claude Fouche (Danielle speaks English thanks to years spent in Australia); within a large garden, with Giverny's picturesque church steeple looming in the background, just 600 yards from Monet's estate and a bit farther from the Musée des Impressionnismes, Le Clos beckons enticingly. **Pros:** colorful oasis in the heart of the village; gardening is in the air. **Cons:** no air-conditioning; no pets. $ *Rooms from: €95* ✉ *5 rue de la Dîme* ☎ *02–32–21–36–51* ⊕ *www.giverny-leclosfleuri.fr* ⌐? *3 rooms* ═ *No credit cards* ⊘ *Closed Oct.–Mar.* ᵢ⊙ᵢ *Breakfast.*

$$$

HOTEL

⌦ **Les Jardins d'Epicure.** Set on 7 acres of picture-perfect parkland and a 20-minute drive from Giverny, this unique hotel comprises three charming 19th-century buildings: the picturesque stables, with "Gothic" brick trim, high beamed ceilings, and the delightful Unicorn Suite; the Villa Florentine (once home to famed poet Paul Éluard), whose Chambre Marquise has no less than seven windows overlooking the park and stream; and the elegant Castel Napoléon III, with six separate guest rooms featuring period antiques and oriental rugs. **Pros:** superb setting; excellent restaurant. **Cons:** gates close at 9:30 pm, sharp. $ *Rooms from: €160* ✉ *16 Grande Rue, 15 km (9 miles) northeast of Vernon on D86* ☎ *01–34–67–75–87* ⊕ *www.lesjardinsdepicure.com* ⌐? *15 rooms, 3 suites* ⊘ *Closed Jan.*

AUVERS-SUR-OISE

74 km (46 miles) east of Giverny via D147, N14, and D4, 33 km (21 miles) northwest of Paris via N328.

Fodor's Choice

★

The tranquil Oise River valley, which runs northeast from Pontoise, retains much of the charm that attracted Camille Pissarro, Paul Cézanne, Camille Corot, Charles-François Daubigny, and Berthe Morisot to Auvers-sur-Oise in the second half of the 19th century. Despite this lofty company, it's the spirit of Vincent van Gogh that haunts every nook and cranny of this pretty riverside village, for while the great painter created many masterpieces here he also decided to end his life in a wheat field just outside the town. Today, thousands make a pilgrimage here to walk in his footsteps and pay their respects at his grave.

GETTING HERE

Getting to Auvers from Paris (Gare du Nord) invariably requires a change of train, either in Valmondois (suburban trains) or St-Ouen l'Aumone (RER-C). Journey time is 45–55 minutes. There is no connecting public transportation from the area around Vernon.

Visitor Information Auvers-sur-Oise Tourist Office ✉ *Rue de la Sansonne* ☎ *01–30–36–10–06* ⊕ *www.auvers-sur-oise.com.*

EXPLORING

Van Gogh moved to Auvers from Arles in May 1890 to be nearer his brother. Little has changed here since that summer of 1890, during the last 10 weeks of Van Gogh's life, when he painted no fewer than 70 pictures. You can find out about his haunts and other Impressionist sites in Auvers by stopping in at the tourist office at Les Colombières, a 14th-century manor house on the rue de la Sansonne (closed from 12:30 to 2 pm every day). Short hikes outside the town center—sometimes marked with yellow trail signs—will lead you to rural landscapes once beloved by Pissarro and Cézanne, including the site of one of Van Gogh's last paintings, *Wheat Fields with Crows.*

On July 27, 1890, the great painter laid his easel against a haystack, walked behind the Château d'Auvers, shot himself, then stumbled to the Auberge Ravoux, where the owner sent for the artist's brother Theo in Paris. Van Gogh died on July 29. The next day, using a hearse from neighboring Méry (because the priest of Auvers refused to provide his for a suicide victim), Van Gogh's body was borne up the hill to the village cemetery. His heartbroken brother died the following year and, in 1914, was reburied alongside Vincent in his simple ivy-covered grave.

Maison-Atelier de Daubigny. The landscape artist Charles-François Daubigny, a precursor of the Impressionists, lived in Auvers from 1861 until his death in 1878. You can visit his studio, the Maison-Atelier de Daubigny, and admire the mural and roof paintings by Daubigny and fellow artists Camille Corot and Honoré Daumier. ⊠ *61 rue Daubigny* ☎ *01–34–48–03–03* ⊕ *www.atelier-daubigny.com* ⊠ *€6* ☉ *Easter–Oct., Thurs.–Sun. 2–6.*

Maison de Van Gogh (*Van Gogh House*). Opposite the town hall, the Auberge Ravoux, the inn where Van Gogh stayed, is now the Maison de Van Gogh. The inn opened in 1876 and owes its name to Arthur Ravoux, the landlord from 1889 to 1891. He had seven lodgers in all, including the minor Dutch painter Anton Hirsching, and they paid 3.50 francs for board and lodging—cheaper than the other inns in Auvers, where 6 francs was the going rate. A dingy staircase leads up to the tiny, spartan, wood-floor attic where Van Gogh stored some of modern art's most famous pictures under his bed. A short film retraces Van Gogh's time at Auvers, and there's a well-stocked souvenir shop. Stop for a drink or for lunch in the ground-floor restaurant. ⊠ *8 rue de la Sansonne* ☎ *01–30–36–60–60* ⊕ *www.maisondevangogh.fr* ⊠ *€6* ☉ *Mar.–Nov., Wed.–Sun. 10–6.*

Maison du Dr. Gachet. A major town landmark opened to the public for the first time in 2004: the house and garden of Van Gogh's closest friend in Auvers, Dr. Paul Gachet. Documents and souvenirs at the Maison du Dr. Gachet evoke Van Gogh's stay in Auvers and Gachet's passion for the avant-garde art of his era. The good doctor was himself the subject of one of the artist's most famous portraits (and the world's second-most-expensive painting when it sold for $82 million in the late 1980s), the actual painting of which was reenacted in the 1956 biopic, *Lust for Life,* starring Kirk Douglas. Friend and patron to many of the artists who settled in and visited Auvers in the 1880s—among them Cézanne, who immortalized the doctor's house in a famous landscape—Gachet also taught them about engraving processes. The ivy covering Van Gogh's grave in the cemetery across town was provided by Gachet from the garden of this house. ⊠ *78 rue du Dr-Gachet* ☎ *01–30–36–81–27* ⊠ *Free* ☉ *Apr.–Oct., Wed.–Sun. 10:30–6:30.*

FAMILY **Voyage au Temps des Impressionnistes** (*Journey Through the Impressionist Era*). The elegant 17th-century village château (also depicted by Van Gogh), set above split-level gardens, now houses the Voyage au Temps des Impressionnistes. You'll receive a set of headphones (English available), with commentary that guides you past various tableaux illustrating life during the Impressionist years. Although there are no

Impressionist originals—500 reproductions pop up on screens interspersed between the tableaux—this is one of France's most imaginative, enjoyable, and innovative museums. Some of the special effects, including talking mirrors, computerized cabaret dancing girls, and a simulated train ride past Impressionist landscapes, are worthy of Disney. The museum's Impressionist Café restaurant has three entirely renovated dining areas: the elegant 17th-century Orangerie, the Espaces Scénographiques, and a re-creation of a 19th-century *guinguette* (café/dance hall), where more casual fare is on the menu. ✉ *Rue de Léry* ☎ *01–34–48–48–40* 🌐 *www.chateau-auvers.fr* 🎫 *€13.50* 🕒 *Apr.–Sept., Tues.–Sun. 10:30–6; Oct.–Mar., Tues.–Sun. 10:30–4:30.*

A VAN GOGH SELF-TOUR

Auvers-sur-Oise is peppered with plaques marking the spots that inspired his art. The plaques bear reproductions of his paintings, enabling you to compare his final works with the scenes as they are today. His last abode—the Auberge Ravoux—has been turned into a shrine. You can also visit the medieval village church, subject of one of Van Gogh's most famous paintings, *L'Église d'Auvers;* admire Osip Zadkine's powerful statue of Van Gogh in the village park; and visit the restored house of Dr. Gachet, Vincent's best friend.

WHERE TO EAT AND STAY

For expanded hotel reviews, visit Fodors.com.

$$$ BISTRO 🍴 **Auberge Ravoux.** For total Van Gogh immersion, have lunch—or dinner on Friday and Saturday—in the restaurant he patronized regularly more than 100 years ago, in the building where he finally expired. A three-course prix-fixe menu is available, and saddle of lamb and homemade terrine are among Loran Gattufo's specialties, but it's the genius loci that makes eating here special, with glasswork, lace curtains, and wall blandishments carefully modeled on the original designs. Table No. 5, the "*table des habitués*," is where Van Gogh used to sit. A magnificently illustrated book, *Van Gogh's Table* (published by Artisan), by culinary historian Alexandra Leaf and art historian Fred Leeman, recalls Vincent's stay at the Auberge and describes in loving detail the dishes served there at the time. [$] *Average main: €27* ✉ *52 rue Général-de-Gaulle* ☎ *01–30–36–60–63* 🌐 *maisondevangogh.fr* ✍ *Reservations essential* 🕒 *Closed Mon. and Tues. and Dec.–Feb.*

$$ HOTEL 🏨 **Hostellerie du Nord.** This sturdy white mansion, which began life as a coach house in the 17th century, is now a prim hotel, with small, white-wall bedrooms adorned with gilt-framed pictures and named after artists, including Cézanne (who stayed here in 1872) and Van Gogh—the Chambre Van Gogh, a junior suite, provides the wood-beam quaintest, if priciest, option. **Pros:** only hotel in Auvers; great location close to river, train station, and Van Gogh's house. **Cons:** bland interiors; small rooms. [$] *Rooms from: €120* ✉ *6 rue du Général de Gaulle* ☎ *01–30–36–70–74* 🌐 *www.hostelleriedunord.fr* 🛏 *8 rooms* 🍽 *Some meals.*

THE EASTERN ILE-DE-FRANCE

This area covers a broad arc, beginning northeast of Paris in Chantilly, one of the most popular day trips from the French capital. From the frozen-in-time medieval town of Senlis, we detour north to visit Pierrefonds, a fairy-tale 19th-century castle that may even outdo the one at Disneyland Paris, the very next stop on this tour heading south. The grand finale comprises three of the most spectacular châteaux in France: Vaux-le-Vicomte, Courances, and Fontainebleau.

3

CHANTILLY

37 km (23 miles) north of Paris via N16.

Celebrated for lace, cream, and the most beautiful medieval manuscript in the world—*Les Très Riches Heures du Duc de Berry*—romantic Chantilly has a host of other attractions: a faux Renaissance château with an eye-popping art collection, second only to the Louvre; splendid Baroque stables; a classy racecourse; and a 16,000-acre forest.

GETTING HERE

Chantilly can be reached on both suburban (Transilien) and main-line (to Creil and beyond) trains from Paris's Gare du Nord; the trip takes between 25 and 40 minutes and costs €8.

Visitor Information Chantilly Tourist Office ⊠ *60 av. du Maréchal-Joffre* ☎ *03-44-57-08-58* ⊕ *www.ville-chantilly.fr.*

EXPLORING

Fodor's Choice **Château de Chantilly.** Although its lavish exterior may be 19th-century
★ Renaissance pastiche, the Château de Chantilly, sitting snugly behind an artificial lake, houses the outstanding **Musée Condé,** with illuminated medieval manuscripts, tapestries, furniture, and paintings. The most famous room, the **Santuario** (sanctuary), contains two celebrated works by Italian painter Raphael (1483–1520)—the *Three Graces* and the *Orleans Virgin*—plus an exquisite ensemble of 15th-century miniatures by the most illustrious French painter of his time, Jean Fouquet (1420–81). Farther on, in the **Cabinet des Livres** (library), is the world-famous Book of Hours whose title translates as *The Very Rich Hours of the Duc de Berry.* It was illuminated by the Brothers Limbourg with magical pictures of early-15th-century life as lived by one of Burgundy's richest lords; unfortunately, due to their fragility, painted facsimiles of the celebrated calendar illuminations are on display, not the actual pages of the book. Other highlights of this unusual museum are the **Galerie de Psyché** (Psyche Gallery), with 16th-century stained glass and portrait drawings by Flemish artist Jean Clouet II; the **Chapelle,** with sculptures by Jean Goujon and Jacques Sarrazin; and the extensive collection of paintings by 19th-century French artists, headed by Jean-Auguste-Dominique Ingres. In addition, there are grand and smaller salons, all stuffed with palace furniture, family portraits, and Sèvres porcelains, making this a must for lovers of the decorative and applied arts. ☎ *03-44-27-31-80* ⊕ *www.domainedechantilly.com* ⊠ *€14 adults, €7.50 children 4–17; joint ticket with gardens* ☉ *Apr.–Oct.,*

daily 10–6; Nov.–Mar., Wed.–Mon. 10:30–5. Closed last 3 wks of Jan.

FAMILY **Grandes Écuries** (*Grand Stables*). The palatial 18th-century Grandes Écuries by the racetrack, built by Jean Aubert in 1719 to accommodate 240 horses and 500 hounds for stag and boar hunts in the forests nearby, are the grandest stables in France. With 30 breeds of horses and ponies housed in straw-lined comfort—in between dressage performances in the courtyard or beneath the majestic central dome—the stables are still in use as the home of the **Musée Vivant du Cheval** (Living Horse Museum). This fascinating museum, which reopened in June 2013 after a two-year renovation, is not just for horse lovers. The history and importance of the horse is explored through an array of artifacts, prints, paintings, textiles, sculptures, equipment, and weaponry. Visitors can enjoy the elaborate horse shows and dressage demonstrations scheduled year-round. For precise days and times check the website. ✉ *7 rue du Connétable* ☎ *03–44–27–31–80* 🌐 *www.domainedechantilly.com; www.museevivantducheval.fr* 🎟 *Horse shows €21 adults, €14 children 4–17; dressage demonstrations €11* 🕒 *Apr.–Oct., Wed.–Mon. 10–5; Jan.–Mar., Wed.–Mon. 1–5; Dec. 2–31, Wed.–Mon. 2–5.*

A DAY AT THE RACES

Since 1834 Chantilly's fabled racetrack, the Hippodrome des Princes de Condé (✉ *Rte. de la Plaine-des-Aigles* ☎ *03–44–62–44–00*) has come into its own each June with two of Europe's most prestigious events: the **Prix du Jockey-Club** (French Derby) on the first Sunday of the month, and the **Prix de Diane** for three-year-old fillies the Sunday after. On main race days, a free shuttle bus runs between Chantilly's train station and the racetrack.

Park. Le Nôtre's park is based on that familiar French royal combination of formality and romantic eccentricity, the former represented in the neatly planned parterres and a mighty, straight-banked canal, and the latter coming to the fore in the waterfall and the Hameau, a mock-Norman village that inspired Marie-Antoinette's version at Versailles. You can explore on foot or on an electric train, and, in the warmer months, take a **rowboat** for a meander down the Grand Canal. ☎ *03–44–27–31–80* 🎟 *€7 park only; €18 Chantilly Pass* 🕒 *Apr.–Oct., Wed.–Mon. 10–8; Nov.–Mar., Wed.–Mon. 10:30–6.*

WHERE TO EAT

$$ FRENCH 🍴 **La Capitainerie.** Housed in the stone-vaulted kitchens of the Château de Chantilly's legendary 17th-century chef Vorace Vatel, this quaint restaurant—which offers buffet or à la carte—has an open-hearth fireplace big enough for whole lambs or oxen to sizzle on the spit. Reflect at leisure on your cultural peregrinations over mouthfuls of grilled turbot or roast quail, and don't forget to add a good dollop of homemade crème de Chantilly to your dessert. Prix-fix menus available (€27, €31). Plunder the dessert cart at teatime or stop in for an apéro. [$] *Average main: €22* ✉ *Château de Chantilly* ☎ *03–44–57–15–89* 🕒 *Closed Tues. No dinner.*

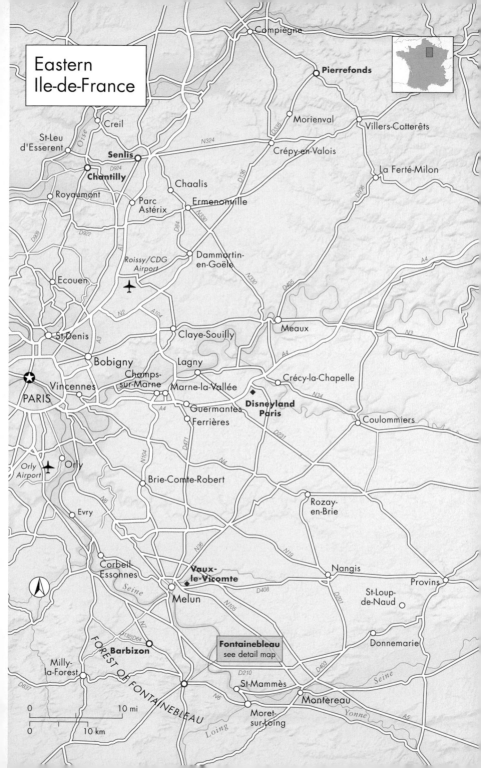

Eastern
Ile-de-France

Compiègne

Pierrefonds

Creil

Morienval

Villers-Cotterêts

St-Leu
d'Esserent

N324

Crépy-en-Valois

Senlis

La Ferté-Milon

Chantilly

Chaalis

Royaumont

Parc
Astérix

Ermenonville

Ecouen

Dammartin-
en-Goële

Roissy/CDG
Airport

N2

A104

St-Denis

Claye-Souilly

Meaux

N2

Bobigny

Lagny

Vincennes

Champs-
sur-Marne

Crécy-la-Chapelle

PARIS

Marne-la-Vallée

Guermantes

Disneyland
Paris

Coulommiers

Ferrières

Orly
Airport

Orly

Brie-Comte-Robert

Rozay-
en-Brie

Evry

Corbeil-
Essonnes

Seine

Vaux-
le-Vicomte

Nangis

Provins

St-Loup-
de-Naud

Melun

Donnemarie

Fontainebleau
see detail map

Barbizon

Milly-
la-Forest

FOREST OF FONTAINEBLEAU

St-Mammès

Monfereau

Seine

0   10 mi

0   10 km

Moret-
sur-Loing

Loing

Yonne

A5

WHERE TO STAY

For expanded hotel reviews, visit Fodors.com.

$$$ HOTEL Fodor's Choice ★ **Auberge du Jeu de Paume.** Set within the Domaine de Chantilly, the largest princely estate in France, this deluxe newcomer combines its stunning setting with Old World elegance and modern comforts—such as a spa, pool, steam room, and two restaurants—to create a luxurious country retreat (within an hour of Paris). **Pros:** proximity to all the sights; elegant country setting; luxurious amenities; lovely bar for an apéro. **Cons:** dining room could be more intimate. [$] *Rooms from: €250* ✉ *4 rue du Connétable* ☎ *03–44–65–50–00* 🌐 *www.aubergedujeudepaumechantilly.fr* 🛏 *68 rooms, 24 suites* 🍴 *All meals.*

$$$ HOTEL **Dolce Chantilly.** Surrounded by forest and its own 18-hole golf course, this luxe, sleekly modern, and meetings-friendly hotel—1½ km (1 mile) northeast of the château—has a glitzy marble-floor reception hall that is not quite matched by the guest rooms: in such a vast new building, these rooms are a bit small but they are satisfyingly functional and fit into the sleek style of the place. **Pros:** great facilities, including fitness rooms and indoor-outdoor pool; ambitious restaurant; stylish public areas. **Cons:** rooms lack character; overall the whole place can feel impersonal. [$] *Rooms from: €200* ✉ *Rte. d'Apremont, Vineuil-St-Firmin* ☎ *03–44–58–47–77* 🌐 *www.dolce-chantilly-hotel.com* 🛏 *175 rooms, 25 suites* ⏲ *Closed Christmas–New Year's* 🍴 *All meals.*

SENLIS

10 km (6 miles) east of Chantilly via D924, 45 km (28 miles) north of Paris via A1.

Senlis is an exceptionally well-preserved medieval town with a crooked maze of streets dominated by the svelte, soaring spire of its Gothic cathedral. Be sure to also inspect the moss-tile church of St-Pierre, with its stumpy crocketed spire. You can enjoy a 40-minute tour of the Vieille Ville by horse and carriage, departing from in front of the cathedral, daily April–December (€35 for up to three people).

Visitor Information Senlis Tourist Office ✉ *Pl. du Parvis Notre-Dame* ☎ *03–44–53–06–40* 🌐 *www.ville-senlis.fr.*

EXPLORING

Fodor's Choice ★ **Cathédrale Notre-Dame.** The breathtaking Cathédrale Notre-Dame, one of France's oldest and narrowest cathedrals, dates from the second half of the 12th century. The superb spire—arguably the most elegant in France—was added around 1240, and the majestic transept, with its ornate rose windows, in the 16th century. ✉ *Pl. du Parvis* 🌐 *www.notredamedeparis.fr.*

Musée d'Art et d'Archéologie. Built atop a Gallo-Roman residence, and reopened in January 2013 after a stunning four-year renovation, the town's excellent Musée d'Art et d'Archéologie displays archaeological finds ranging from Gallo-Roman votive objects unearthed in the neighboring Halatte Forest to the building's own excavated foundations (uncovered in the basement), including some macabre stone heads bathed in half light. Upstairs, paintings include works by Manet's teacher, Thomas Couture (who lived in Senlis), and the charming naïve flower paintings by Senlis's own Séraphine de Senlis. ✉ *Palais Épiscopal, pl. du Parvis Notre-Dame* ☎ *03–44–24–86–72* 🌐 *www.musees-senlis.fr/Musee-d-Art-et-d-Archeologie/historique-du-musee.html* 🎟 *€4* 🕒 *Mon., Thurs., and Fri. 10–noon and 2–6; weekends 11–1 and 2–6; Wed. 2–6.*

3

WHERE TO EAT AND STAY

For expanded hotel reviews, visit Fodors.com.

$ MODERN FRENCH 🍴 **Le Scaramouche.** This handsome and well-priced new bistro, in an enviable spot facing the cathedral, provides a pleasant setting in which to enjoy a modern take on French classics. The focus here is more on quality than quantity, yet the menu covers all the important bases: a warm casserole of escargots with parsley butter, ravioli *Dauphiné*, hand-cut steak tartare with crispy frites, buttery scallops with lentils and a garlicky mayonnaise, and an array of tempting salads and desserts. On a warm day, diners can enjoy the outdoor terrace and unparalleled views of charming Senlis. [$] *Average main: €13* ✉ *4 pl. Notre Dame* ☎ *03–44–53–01–26* 🌐 *www.le-scaramouche.fr* 🕒 *Closed Sun. and Mon.*

$ HOTEL 🏨 **L'Hostellerie de la Porte Bellon.** This old stone house with a garden, a five-minute walk from the cathedral and close to the bus station, is the closest you can get to spending a night in the historic center of Senlis. **Pros:** only hotel close to historic town center; attractive old building. **Cons:** modest facilities; some rooms need renovating. [$] *Rooms from: €85* ✉ *51 rue Bellon* ☎ *03–44–53–03–05* 🌐 *www.portebellon.fr* 🛏 *18 rooms* 🕒 *Closed 1st 2 wks of Jan.* 🍽 *Some meals.*

PIERREFONDS

38 km (24 miles) northeast of Senlis via N324, D335, and D973.

Dominating the attractive lakeside village of Pierrefonds, a former spa resort, is its immense ersatz medieval castle.

Château de Pierrefonds. Built on a huge mound in the 15th century, the Château de Pierrefonds was dismantled in 1620 then comprehensively restored and re-created to its imagined former glory in the 1860s at the behest of Emperor Napoléon III, seeking to cash in on the craze for the Middle Ages. Architect Viollet-le-Duc left a crenellated fortress with a fairy-tale silhouette, although, like the fortified town of Carcassonne, which he also restored, Pierrefonds is more a construct of what he thought it should have looked like than what it really was. A visit takes in the chapel, barracks, and the majestic keep containing the lord's bedchamber and reception hall, which is bordered by a spiral staircase—its lower and upper sections clearly reveal what is ancient and what is more recent in this former fortress. Don't miss the plaster casts of tomb sculptures from all over France in the cellars, and the **Collection Monduit**—industrially produced, larger-than-life lead decorations made by the 19th-century firm that brought the Statue of Liberty to life. Buses from Compiègne run three times daily (fewer on Sunday) from the train station. Taxis are pricey but bikes are another option—this is great bicycling countryside. ✉ *Rue Viollet-le-Duc* ☎ *03–44–42–72–72* 🎫 *€7.50* ⏲ *May–Aug., daily 9:30–6; Sept.–Apr., daily 10–1 and 2–5:30.*

WHERE TO STAY

For expanded hotel reviews, visit Fodors.com.

$ B&B/INN Fodor's Choice ★ 🏨 **Le Relais Brunehaut.** Crowned with a picturesque stepped gable, this tiny ensemble of flower-bedecked, stucco-and-stone buildings rises up from its own park, next to the village's abbey church and by the shore of a small, duck-populated river, complete with an old wooden waterwheel—this is one adorably quaint hotel; guest rooms are prettily done up in period antiques, some with Oriental rugs and chandeliers. **Pros:** bucolic setting; good restaurant; gentle rates. **Cons:** rooms are old-fashioned; management can be gruff. [$] *Rooms from: €90* ✉ *3 rue de l'Église, 5 km (3 miles) east of Pierrefonds on D85, Chelles* ☎ *03–44–42–85–05* 🌐 *www.lerelaisbrunehaut.fr* 🛏 *11 rooms* ⏲ *Closed mid-Jan.–mid-Feb.* 🍴 *Some meals.*

DISNEYLAND PARIS

68 km (40 miles) southwest of Pierrefonds via D335, D136, N330, and A4; 38 km (24 miles) east of Paris via A4.

Originally called Euro Disney, Disneyland Paris is probably not what you've traveled to France to experience. But if you have a child in tow, the promise of a day here may get you through an afternoon at Versailles or Fontainebleau. If you're a dyed-in-the-wool Disney fan, you'll want to make a beeline for the park to see how it has been molded to appeal to the tastes of Europeans (Disney's "Imagineers" call it their most lovingly detailed park). And if you've never experienced this particular form of Disney showmanship, you may want to put in an appearance if only to see what all the fuss is about.

GETTING HERE

Take the RER from central Paris (stations at Étoile, Auber, Les Halles, Gare de Lyon, and Nation) to Marne-la-Vallée–Chessy, 100 yards from the Disneyland entrance. Journey time is around 40 minutes, and trains operate every 10–30 minutes, depending on the time of day. Note that a TGV (Train à Grande Vitesse) station links Disneyland to Lille, Lyon, Brussels, and London (via Lille and the Channel Tunnel). Disneyland's hotel complex offers a shuttle-bus service to Orly and Charles de Gaulle airports for €21.

Visitor Information **Disneyland Paris reservations office** ☎ *01–60–30–60–90, 407/939–7675 in U.S.* 🌐 *www.disneylandparis.com.*

EXPLORING

FAMILY Fodor's Choice ★ **Disneyland Paris.** Disneyland Paris, a slightly downsized version of its United States counterpart, is nevertheless a spectacular sight, created with an acute attention to detail. Disney never had quite the following here as it did Stateside, so when it opened, few turned up. Today, however, the place is jammed with crowds with families from around the world reveling in the many splendors of the Disney universe.

Some of the rides can be a bit scary for little kids, but tots adore Alice's Maze, Peter Pan's Flight, and especially the whirling Mad Hatter's

The Alice in Wonderland Labyrinth delights children—and intrigues children of all ages—at Disneyland Paris.

Teacups. Also getting high marks are the afternoon parades, which feature music and introductions in five languages and huge floats swarming with all of Disney's most beloved characters—just make sure to stake your place along Main Street in advance for a good spot (check for posted times). There's a lot here, so pace yourself: kids can easily feel overwhelmed with the barrage of stimuli or frustrated by extra-long waits at the rides. (Also be aware that there are size restrictions for some rides.) The older the child, the more they will enjoy Walt Disney Studios, a cinematically driven area, where many of the newer Disney character-themed rides can be found.

Disneyland Park, as the original theme park is styled, consists of five "lands": Main Street U.S.A., Frontierland, Adventureland, Fantasyland, and Discoveryland. The central theme of each land is relentlessly echoed in every detail, from attractions to restaurant menus to souvenirs. The park is circled by a railroad, which stops three times along the perimeter. **Main Street U.S.A.** goes under the railroad and past shops and restaurants toward the main plaza; Disney parades are held here every afternoon and, during holiday periods, every evening.

Top attractions at **Frontierland** are the chilling Phantom Manor, haunted by holographic spooks, and the thrilling runaway mine train of Big Thunder Mountain, a roller coaster that plunges wildly through floods and avalanches in a setting meant to evoke Utah's Monument Valley. Whiffs of Arabia, Africa, and the Caribbean give **Adventureland** its exotic cachet; the spicy meals and snacks served here rank among the best food in the park. Don't miss the Pirates of the Caribbean, an exciting *mise-en-scène* populated by eerily humanlike, computer-driven figures, or Indiana Jones and the Temple of Doom, a breathtaking ride that re-creates some of this luckless hero's most exciting moments.

Fantasyland charms the youngest parkgoers with familiar cartoon characters from such classic Disney films as *Snow White, Pinocchio, Dumbo,* and *Peter Pan.* The focal point of Fantasyland, and indeed Disneyland Paris, is Le Château de la Belle au Bois Dormant (Sleeping Beauty's Castle), a 140-foot, bubblegum-pink structure topped with 16 blue- and gold-tipped turrets. Its design was allegedly inspired by illustrations from a medieval Book of Hours—if so, it was by way of Beverly Hills. The castle's dungeon conceals a 2-ton scaly green dragon that rumbles in its sleep and occasionally rouses to roar—an impressive feat of engineering, producing an answering chorus of shrieks from younger children. **Discoveryland** is a futuristic eye-knocker for high-tech Disney entertainment. Robots on roller skates welcome you on your way to Star Tours, a pitching, plunging, sense-confounding ride based on the *Star Wars* films. In Le Visionarium, a simulated space journey is presented by 9-Eye, a staggeringly realistic robot. One of the park's newest attractions, the Jules Verne–inspired **Space Mountain Mission 2,** pretends to catapult *exploronauts* on a rocket-boosted, comet-battered journey through the Milky Way.

Disneyland Paris is peppered with places to eat, ranging from snack bars and fast-food joints to five full-service restaurants—all with a distinguishing theme. If your child has his or her heart set on a specifically themed restaurant, say, Pirates of the Caribbean—a dark corsair's lair that looks over the ride itself—or the Auberge de Cendrillon (Cinderella's Inn), where the nasty stepmother and sisters themselves bustle through the aisles, make sure to make reservations in advance (which can be done online). In addition, Walt Disney Studios, Disney Village, and Disney Hotels have restaurants open to the public. But since these are outside the park, it's not recommended that you waste time traveling to them for lunch. Disneyland Paris has relaxed its no-alcohol policy and now serves wine and beer in the park's sit-down restaurants, as well as in the hotels and restaurants outside the park.

Walt Disney Studios opened next to the Disneyland Park in 2002. The theme park is divided into four "production zones." Beneath imposing entrance gates and a 100-foot water tower inspired by the one erected in 1939 at Disney Studios in Burbank, California, **Front Lot** contains shops, a restaurant, and a studio re-creating the atmosphere of Sunset Boulevard. In **Animation Courtyard,** Disney artists demonstrate the various phases of character animation; Animagique brings to life scenes from *Pinocchio* and *The Lion King*, while the Genie from *Aladdin* pilots Flying Carpets over Agrabah. **Production Courtyard** hosts the Walt Disney Television Studios; Cinémagique, a special-effects tribute to U.S. and European cinema; and a behind-the-scenes Studio Tram tour of location sites, movie props, studio interiors, and costuming, ending with a visit to Catastrophe Canyon in the heart of a film shoot. **Back Lot** majors in stunts. At Armageddon Special Effects you can confront a flaming meteor shower aboard the Mir space station, then complete your visit at the giant outdoor arena with a Stunt Show Spectacular involving cars, motorbikes, and Jet Skis. ☏ *01–60–30–60–90* ⊕ *www.*

disneylandparis.com ✉ €79, or €160 for 3-day Passport; includes admission to all individual attractions within Disneyland or Walt Disney Studios; tickets for Walt Disney Studios are also valid for admission to Disneyland during last 3 opening hrs of same day ☉ Disneyland mid-June–mid-Sept., daily 9 am–10 pm; mid-Sept.–Dec. 19 and Jan. 5–mid-June, weekdays 10–8, weekends 9–8; Dec. 20–Jan. 4, daily 9–8. Walt Disney Studios daily 10–6.*

WHERE TO STAY

For expanded hotel reviews, visit Fodors.com.

$$$$
HOTEL

🖼 **Sequoia Lodge.** Ranging from superluxe to still-a-pretty-penny, Disneyland Paris has 5,000 rooms in five hotels, but your best bet on all counts may be the Sequoia Lodge, just a few minutes' walk from the theme park, where the mood—a grand recreation of an American mountain lodge—is quite different from the other, glitzier big hotels here. **Pros:** package deals include admission to theme park; cozy, secluded feel; great pools. **Cons:** restaurants a bit ho-hum; many rooms do not have lake view; room rates are €400 and up (and this is considered "mid-range" in Disneyland). $ *Rooms from: €400* 🖼 *01–60–30–60–90, 407/939–7675 in U.S.* ⊕ *www.disneylandparis.com* ⦾ *All meals.*

NIGHTLIFE AND THE ARTS

Disney Village. Nocturnal entertainment outside the park centers on Disney Village, a vast pleasure mall designed by American architect Frank Gehry. Featured are American-style restaurants (crab shack, diner, deli, steak house), including **Billybob's Country Western Saloon** (☎ *01–60–45–71–00*).

Buffalo Bill's Wild West Show. Also in Disney Village, this show is a two-hour dinner extravaganza with a menu of sausage, spareribs, and chili; performances by a talented troupe of stunt riders, bronco busters, tribal dancers, and musicians; plus some 50 horses, a dozen buffalo, a bull, and an Annie Oakley–style sharpshooter, with a golden-maned "Buffalo Bill" as emcee. A re-creation of a show that dazzled Parisians 100 years ago, it's corny but great fun. ☎ *01–60–45–71–00 for reservations* ✉ *€59.90, children under 12 €46.90* ☉ *Nightly at 6:30 and 9:30.*

CHATEAU DE VAUX-LE-VICOMTE

48 km (30 miles) south of Disneyland Paris via N36, 5 km (3 miles) northeast of Melun via N36 and D215, 56 km (35 miles) southeast of Paris via A6, N104, A5, and N36.

GETTING HERE

Get to Vaux by taking the train on a 45-minute trip to Melun, then taxi (for about €20 each way) the 7 km (4 miles) to the château. From April to November, Vaux runs a special Châteaubus shuttle, which you can get at the Melun train station and costs €7 round-trip.

EXPLORING

A manifesto for French 17th-century splendor, the Château de Vaux-le-Vicomte was built between 1656 and 1661 by finance minister Nicolas Fouquet. The construction program was monstrous: entire villages were razed, 18,000 workmen called in, and architect Louis Le Vau, painter

Louis XIV was so jealous of the splendor of Vaux-le-Vicomte that he promptly went out and built Versailles.

Charles Le Brun, and landscape architect André Le Nôtre recruited at vast expense to prove that Fouquet's taste was as refined as his business acumen. The housewarming party was so lavish it had star guest Louis XIV, tetchy at the best of times, spitting jealous curses. He hurled Fouquet in the slammer and set about building Versailles to prove just who was top banana. Poor Fouquet may be gone but his home, still privately owned, has survived to astonish and delight centuries of travelers.

Fodor's Choice **Château de Vaux-le-Vicomte.** The high-roof Château de Vaux-le-Vicomte,
★ partially surrounded by a moat, is set well back from the road behind iron railings topped with sculpted heads. A cobbled avenue stretches up to the entrance, and stone steps lead to the vestibule, which seems small given the noble scale of the exterior. Charles Le Brun's captivating decoration includes the ceiling of the Chambre du Roi (Royal Bedchamber), depicting *Time Bearing Truth Heavenward*, framed by stuccowork by sculptors François Girardon and André Legendre. Along the frieze you can make out small squirrels, the Fouquet family's emblem—squirrels are known as *fouquets* in local dialect. But Le Brun's masterwork is the ceiling in the **Salon des Muses** (Hall of Muses), a brilliant allegorical composition painted in glowing, sensuous colors that some feel even surpasses his work at Versailles. On the ground floor the impressive **Grand Salon** (Great Hall), with its unusual oval form and 16 caryatid pillars symbolizing the months and seasons, has harmony and style even though the ceiling decoration was never finished.

The state salons are redolent of *le style louis quartorze*, thanks to the grand state beds, Mazarin desks, and Baroque marble busts—gathered together by the current owners of the château, the Comte et Comtesse de Vogüé—that replace the original pieces, which Louis XIV trundled off as booty to Versailles. In the basement, where cool, dim rooms were once used to store food and wine and house the château's kitchens, you can find rotating exhibits about the château's past and life-size wax figures illustrating its history, including the notorious 19th-century murder-suicide of two erstwhile owners, the Duc and Duchess de Choiseul-Praslin. The house has been featured in many Hollywood films, including *Moonraker.* Le Nôtre's carefully restored **gardens** are at their best when the fountains—which function via gravity, exactly as they did in the 17th century—are turned on (the second and final Saturday of each month from April through October, 4–6 pm). Enjoy exceptional fireworks displays here every Saturday at 10:30 pm. ☎ *01–64–14–41–90* 🌐 *www.vaux-le-vicomte.com* 🎟 *€16; candlelight château visits €19; gardens only €8* 🕓 *Mid-Mar.–Oct., daily 10–6.*

A CANDLELIGHT TOUR

Perhaps the most beautiful time to visit the château and gardens is when they are illuminated by thousands of candles during the Candlelight Evenings, held every Saturday night from 8 to midnight, from May through mid-October (also Friday in July and August). Readers complain, however, that at night the vast and grand gardens are nearly invisible and the low candlepower doesn't really do justice to the splendor of the salons.

WHERE TO EAT

$$$ MODERN FRENCH 🍴 **La Table Saint Just.** A pleasing mix of ancient and modern, this colorful, light-filled restaurant, with high-beamed ceilings and limestone walls hung with contemporary art and "candeliers," was once a farmstead on the grounds of the nearby Château de Vaux-le-Pénil. Isabelle and Fabrice Vitu's warm welcome, and Michelin-starred cuisine, are the real draws, and locals and Parisians alike appreciate the refined menu with a surprising twist on French classics and plenty of delicacies from the sea. Scallops on a bed of Puy lentils; crisp veal foot in a smoked-eel emulsion; succulent John Dory with braised salsify and truffles. Be sure to save room for a sublime caramel mousse or warm Grand Marnier soufflé, a house specialty. The four-course tasting menu (€95) is the best value; the truffle menu is a good deal more pricey. [$] *Average main: €36* ✉ *11 rue de la Libération, 6 km (4 miles) southwest of Vaux-leVicomte; 13 km (8 miles) northwest of Barbizon, Vaux-le-Pénil* ☎ *01–64–52–09–09* 🌐 *www.restaurant-latablesaintjust.com* ✍ *Reservations essential* 🕓 *Closed Sun., Mon., and holidays.*

$$$ MODERN FRENCH 🍴 **Le Pouilly.** The lofty dining room of this ancient *demeure* is everything a country manor should be: creamy stone walls, warm oak paneling, beamed ceilings, a giant central fireplace and stately balcony. In winter, hearty yet refined dishes—which have earned Le Pouilly a Michelin star—are served before a roaring fire, and in summer the garden terrace makes a lovely spot for lunch or a candlelight dinner. Chef Anthony Vallette, who hails from Normandy, has perfected the fresh, often line-caught, seafood dishes of his native St. Lô: a buttery sablé with salt-braised lobster; fleshy langoustines with butternut squash; tiny scallops in a puree of root vegetables and chestnuts. For dessert, the locally

grown glacéd peach served with a tender cookie of pistachio and raisins is perfect with a sweet Montlouis from the exceptional wine list. For the price it's also a very good deal. [$] *Average main: €35* ☒ *1 rue Fontaine Pouilly, 8 km (5 miles) northwest of Vaux-le-Vicomte, Pouilly le Fort* ☎ *01–64–09–56–64* ⊕ *www.restaurant-lepouilly.com* ⚑ *Reservations essential* ⊘ *Closed Mon. No dinner Sun.*

BARBIZON

17 km (11 miles) southwest of Vaux-le-Vicomte via Melun and D132/ D64, 52 km (33 miles) southeast of Paris.

On the western edge of the 62,000-acre Forest of Fontainebleau, the village of Barbizon retains its time-stained allure despite the intrusion of art galleries, souvenir shops, and busloads of tourists. The group of landscape painters known as the Barbizon School—Camille Corot, Jean-François Millet, Narcisse Diaz de la Peña, and Théodore Rousseau, among others—lived here from the 1830s on. They paved the way for the Impressionists by their willingness to accept nature on its own terms rather than using it as an idealized base for carefully structured compositions. Sealed to one of the famous sandstone rocks in the forest—which starts, literally, at the far end of the main street—is a bronze medallion by sculptor Henri Chapu, paying homage to Millet and Rousseau. Threading the village is a Painters Trail (marked in yellow), which ranges from main village landmarks to natural splendors such as the rocky waterfall once painted by Corot.

Visitor Information Barbizon Tourist Office ☒ *41 Grande rue* ☎ *01–60–66– 41–87* ⊕ *www.barbizon.fr.*

EXPLORING

Atelier Jean-François Millet (*Millet's Studio*). Though there are no actual Millet works, the Atelier Jean-François Millet is cluttered with photographs and mementos evoking his career. It was here that Millet painted some of his most renowned pieces, including *The Gleaners.* ☒ *27 Grande rue* ☎ *01–60–66–21–55* ⊕ *www.atelier-millet.fr* ◪ *€4* ⊙ *Nov.-Mar. open Thurs.-Mon.; Apr.-Oct. open Mon., Wed.-Sun.; July-Aug. open daily.*

Atelier Théodore Rousseau (*Rousseau's House-cum-Studio*). Annex to the Musée Départemental des Peintres de Barbizon, the Atelier Théodore Rousseau occupies a converted barn. It's crammed with personal and artistic souvenirs and also has an exhibition space for temporary shows. ☒ *55 Grande rue* ☎ *01–60–66–22–38* ◪ *€6, joint ticket with Barbizon School Museum* ⊙ *Wed.–Mon. 10–12:30 and 2–5:30.*

Musée Départemental des Peintres de Barbizon (*Barbizon School Museum*). Corot and company would often repair to the Auberge Ganne after painting to brush up on their social life; the inn is now the Musée de Peintres de Barbizon. Here you can find documents of the village as it was in the 19th century, as well as a few original works. The Barbizon artists painted on every available surface, and even now you can see some originals on the upstairs walls. Two of the ground-floor rooms have been reconstituted as they were in Ganne's time—note the trompe-l'oeil paintings on the buffet doors. There's also a video on the Barbizon School. ✉ *92 Grande rue* ☎ *01–60–66–22–27* 🎫 *€3* 🕓 *Wed.– Mon. 10–12:30 and 2–5:30. Closed Dec. 22–Jan. 1.*

WHERE TO EAT AND STAY

For expanded hotel reviews, visit Fodors.com.

$$ ✕ **Le Relais de Barbizon.** French country specialties and fish are served
FRENCH at this rustic restaurant with a big open fire and a large terrace shaded by lime and chestnut trees. The four-course weekday menu is a good value, but wine here is expensive and cannot be ordered by the *pichet* (pitcher). Reservations are essential on weekends. 💲 *Average main: €22* ✉ *2 av. Charles de Gaulle* ☎ *01–60–66–40–28* 🕓 *Closed Tues. and Wed. and part of Aug. and part of Dec.*

$ 🏨 **Les Alouettes.** This atmospheric, family-run, 19th-century inn is on 2
HOTEL acres of leafy parkland, which the better rooms—No. 9 is the largest—overlook; the interior is 1930s style, with oak beams in many rooms, and Jean-Paul Karampournis's rustic restaurant (reservations essential; no dinner Sunday, closed Monday), with its large open terrace, serves traditional French cuisine such as hare with mushrooms and lamb with eggplant. **Pros:** verdant setting; charming rustic dining room. **Cons:** bland rooms; no air-conditioning; no Internet in rooms. 💲 *Rooms from: €68* ✉ *4 rue Antoine Barye* ☎ *01–60–66–41–98* ⊕ *www.barbizon.net/ hebergement-barbizon.html* ✈ *22 rooms* 🍽 *Some meals.*

$$$$ 🏨 **Les Pléiades.** The new prestige spot in Barbizon started its days in
HOTEL 1830 as a humble village house, once home to Barbizon-school painter Charles Daubigny but, as of 2009, the much-expanded edifice has been brought sumptuously up-to-date with contemporary interiors and features. **Pros:** great location in the heart of the village; indoor-outdoor heated swimming pools to refresh after a hike in the nearby woods; impeccable service. **Cons:** contemporary interiors can be a bit austere. 💲 *Rooms from: €300* ✉ *21 Grande rue* ☎ *01–60–66–40–25* ⊕ *www. hotel-les-pleiades.com* ✈ *20 rooms* 🍽 *Some meals.*

FONTAINEBLEAU

9 km (6 miles) southeast of Barbizon via N7, 61 km (38 miles) southeast of Paris via A6 and N7.

Like Chambord, in the Loire Valley, or Compiègne, to the north, Fontainebleau was a favorite spot for royal hunting parties long before the construction of one of France's grandest residences. Although not as celebrated as Versailles, this palace is almost as spectacular.

GETTING HERE

Fontainebleau—or, rather, neighboring Avon, 2 km (1½ miles) away (there's a frequent shuttle-bus service to the château for €4.20 round-trip)—is a 45-minute train ride from Paris's Gare de Lyon; tickets are €8.65 one way.

Visitor Information Fontainebleau Tourist Office ✉ *4 rue Royale* ☎ *01–60– 74–99–99* ⊕ *www.fontainebleau-tourisme.com.*

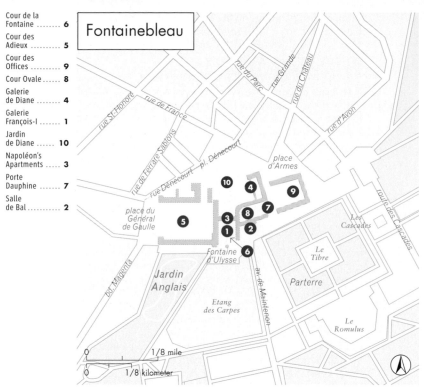

EXPLORING

Château de Fontainebleau. The château you see today dates from the 16th century, although additions were made by various royal incumbents through the next 300 years. The palace was begun under the flamboyant Renaissance king François I, the French contemporary of England's Henry VIII, who hired Italian artists Il Rosso (a pupil of Michelangelo) and Primaticcio to embellish his château. In fact, they did much more: By introducing the pagan allegories and elegant lines of Mannerism to France, they revolutionized French decorative art. Their virtuoso frescoes and stuccowork can be admired in the **Galerie François-Ier** (Francis I Gallery) and in the jewel of the interior, the 100-foot-long **Salle de Bal** (Ballroom), with its luxuriant wood paneling, completed under Henri II, François's successor, and its gleaming parquet floor that reflects the patterns on the ceiling. Like the château as a whole, the room exudes a sense of elegance and style, but on a more intimate, human scale than at Versailles—this is Renaissance, not Baroque. **Napoléon's apartments** occupied the first floor. You can see a lock of his hair, his Légion d'Honneur medal, his imperial uniform, the hat he wore on his return from Elba in 1815, and one bed in which he definitely did spend a night (almost every town in France boasts a bed in which the emperor supposedly snoozed). Joséphine's **Salon Jaune** (Yellow Room) is one of the best examples of the Empire style—the austere Neoclassical style promoted by the emperor. There's also a throne room—Napoléon spurned the one at Versailles, a palace he disliked, establishing his imperial seat in the former King's Bedchamber here—and the Queen's Boudoir, also known as the Room of the Six Maries (occupants included ill-fated Marie-Antoinette and Napoléon's second wife, Marie-Louise). The sweeping **Galerie de Diane,** built during the reign of Henri IV (1589–1610), was converted into a library in the 1860s. Other salons have 17th-century tapestries and paintings, and frescoes by members of the Fontainebleau School.

Although Louis XIV's architectural fancy was concentrated on Versailles, he commissioned Mansart to design new pavilions and had André Le Nôtre replant the gardens at Fontainebleau, where he and his court returned faithfully in fall for the hunting season. But it was Napoléon who spent lavishly to make a Versailles, as it were, out of Fontainebleau. He held Pope Pius VII here as a captive guest in 1812, signed the second church-state concordat here in 1813, and, in the cobbled **Cour des Adieux** (Farewell Courtyard), said good-bye to his Old Guard on April 20, 1814, as he began his brief exile on the Mediterranean island of Elba. The famous **Horseshoe Staircase** that dominates the Cour des Adieux, once the Cour du Cheval Blanc (White Horse Courtyard), was built by Androuet du Cerceau for Louis XIII (1610–43); it was down this staircase that Napoléon made his way slowly to take a final salute from his Vieille Garde. Another courtyard—the **Cour de la Fontaine** (Fountain Courtyard)—was commissioned by Napoléon in 1812 and adjoins the Étang des Carpes (Carp Pond). Across from the pond is the formal Parterre (flower garden) and, on the other side, the leafy Jardin Anglais (English Garden).

The **Porte Dauphine** is the most beautiful of the various gateways that connect the complex of buildings; its name commemorates the christening of the dauphin—the heir to the throne, later Louis XIII—under its archway in 1606. The gateway fronts the **Cour Ovale** (Oval Court), shaped like a flattened egg. Opposite the courtyard is the **Cour des Offices** (Kitchen Court), a large, severe square built at the same time as place des Vosges in Paris (1609). Around the corner is the informal **Jardin de Diane** (Diana's Garden), with peacocks and a statue of the hunting goddess surrounded by mournful hounds. ⊠ *Pl. du Général de Gaulle* ☎ *01–60–71–50–70* ⊕ *www.musee-chateau-fontainebleau.fr* ☑ *€11, Napoléon's Apartments €6.50 extra, €15.50 for both; gardens free* ☼ *Palace Oct.–Mar., Wed.–Mon. 9:30–5; Apr.–Sept., Wed.–Mon. 9:30–6; gardens May–Sept., daily 9–8; Oct. and Mar., daily 9–6; Nov.–Feb., daily 9–5.*

WHERE TO EAT

$$
MODERN FRENCH

✕ **Frédéric Cassel.** A must-visit for pastry and chocolate lovers alike, this master *pâtissier* excels in classic French confections without too many bells and whistles. Light-as-air and made with the best ingredients, Cassel's creations are as beautiful as they are scrumptious. The sinful *millefeuille* comes in five flavors, including sweet chestnut and Earl Gray tea, and the *Tarte Duo de Cerise* mixes tart and sweet cherries with almond cream. Chocolates are freshly made on the premises. For lunch, the tea salon is a good alternative to a full restaurant meal, with a small, inventive menu: creamy pumpkin velouté, guacamole with curried shrimp, or a more ample dish of tender *dorade* (sea bream) with potatoes and black olives. A two-course lunch menu with coffee is a good deal at €15. Great for teatime. [$] *Average main: €19* ✉ *21 rue des Sablons* ☎ *01–60–71–00–64* 🌐 *www.frederic-cassel.com* ✍ *Reservations not accepted* 🕓 *Closed Mon. and Sun. after 2 pm.*

$$$ MODERN FRENCH 🍴 **Les Prémices.** Adjoining the property of the stately 17th-century Château de Bourron, in the heart of the Forest of Fontainebleau, this lovely restaurant is well worth the short trip out of town. Bright and airy, with an open terrace in warm weather, the elegant dining room shows meticulous attention to detail—from the crisp table linens to the stylish flower arrangements—all the better to highlight chef Dominique Maes's sophisticated French fare. A starter of piquant rabbit farci, served alongside velvety tapenade and candied tomatoes, followed by a sublimely succulent hen, fattened on the salt flats of the Mont-St-Michel bay and infused with lemon thyme and white truffles, will barely leave room for the beautifully displayed local artisanal cheeses. The six-course tasting menu—with wine pairings at an extra cost—is the best deal, allowing for a well-rounded sampling of this talented chef's inventive cuisine. [$] *Average main: €32* ✉ *12 bis rue Blaise de Montesquiou, 8 km (5 miles) south of Fontainebleau via D607, Bourron-Marlotte* ☎ *01–64–78–33–00* 🌐 *www.restaurant-les-premices.com* ✍ *Reservations essential* 🕓 *Closed Mon., Tues., and Dec. 19–Jan. 5. No dinner Sun.*

WHERE TO STAY

For expanded hotel reviews, visit Fodors.com.

$$$ HOTEL 🏨 **Aigle Noir.** This may be Fontainebleau's costliest hotel, but you can't go wrong if you request one of the rooms overlooking either the garden or the palace—they have late-18th- or early-19th-century reproduction furniture, creating a Napoleonic vibe. **Pros:** period ambience; great location opposite château. **Cons:** no restaurant. [$] *Rooms from: €170* ✉ *27 pl. Napoléon Bonaparte* ☎ *01–60–74–60–00* 🌐 *www.hotelaiglenoir.com* 🛏 *53 rooms* 🍽 *Breakfast.*

$$$ HOTEL 🏨 **Londres.** Established in 1850, the Londres is a small, family-style hotel with Louis XV accents. **Pros:** château views from some rooms; airy ambience with tasteful decoration; two-minute walk to the Fontainebleau 18-hole golf course. **Cons:** no air-conditioning in some rooms; limited parking. [$] *Rooms from: €175* ✉ *1 pl. du Général de Gaulle* ☎ *01–64–22–20–21* 🌐 *www.hoteldelondres.com* 🛏 *14 rooms, 2 suites* 🕓 *Closed 1 wk in Aug. and Christmas–early Jan.* 🍽 *Breakfast.*

SPORTS AND THE OUTDOORS

Club Alpin Français. The Forest of Fontainebleau is laced with hiking trails; for more information ask for the *Guide des Sentiers* (trail guide) at the tourist office. Bikes can be rented at the Fontainebleau-Avon train station. The forest is also famed for its quirky rock formations, where many a novice alpinist first caught the climbing bug; for more information contact the Club Alpin Français. ✉ *24 av. Laumière, Paris* ☎ *01–53–72–87–00* 🌐 *www.ffcam.fr.*

THE LOIRE VALLEY

WELCOME TO THE LOIRE VALLEY

TOP REASONS TO GO

★ **Step into a fairy tale at Sleeping Beauty's castle:** Play once-upon-a-time at Ussé—gleaming white against an emerald forest backcloth, it's so beautiful it inspired Perrault's immortal tale.

★ **Witness the might of kingly Chambord:** The world's wackiest rooftop, with a forest of chimneys to match the game-rich woodlands extending in all directions, marks the Loire's grandest château.

★ **Find splendor in the grass at Villandry:** The Renaissance reblooms in these geometric gardens that have been lovingly restored to floricultural magnificence.

★ **Indulge in a bit of romance at Chenonceau:** Half bridge, half pleasure palace, this epitome of picturesque France extends across the Cher River, so why not row a boat under its arches?

★ **Revel in medieval magic at Fontevraud:** The majestic abbey is the resting place of English kings . . . and a queen.

1 From Tours to Orleans. East from Tours, strung like precious gems along the peaceful Loire, the royal and near-royal châteaux are among the most fabled sights in France. From magical Chenonceau—improbably suspended above the River Cher—to mighty Chambord, with its 440 rooms, to Amboise (where Leonardo da Vinci breathed his last), this architectural conveyor belt moves up along the southern bank to deposit you at Orléans, burnished to Old World splendor with its pedestrian-only *centre ville historique* (it was here that Joan of Arc had her most rousing successes against the English). Heading back to Tours on the northern bank, you'll discover the immense palace at Blois and some of the best hotels in the region.

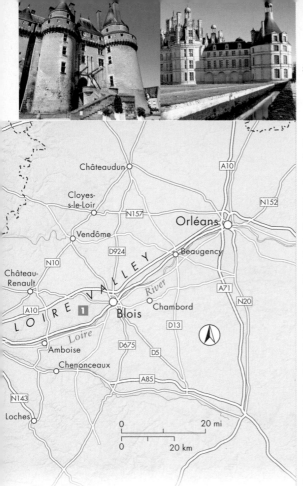

GETTING ORIENTED

The Loire Valley, which pretty much splits France in two, has been much traversed down the ages, once by Santiago pilgrims, now by Bordeaux-bound TGV trains. It retains a backwater feel that mirrors the river's sluggish, meandering waters, although trade along the river gave rise to major towns along its banks: Angers, Saumur, Blois, Orléans. Tours remains the gateway to the region, not only for its central position but because the TGV links it with Paris in little more than an hour. Angers is at the west end of the Loire Valley, and Orléans is the eastern gateway—both are also well connected with Paris by train.

2 From Villandry to Langeais. Step into a fairy tale by castle-hopping among the most beautiful châteaux in France, from Villandry's fabled gardens to Ussé, which seems to levitate over the unicorn-haunted Forest of Chinon. From the Renaissance jewel of Azay-le-Rideau, continue west to Chinon for a dip in the Middle Ages along its rue Haute St-Maurice—a pop-up illuminated manuscript. Continue time traveling at the 12th-century royal abbey of Fontevraud, resting place of Richard the Lion-Hearted and Eleanor of Aquitaine. Then fast-forward to the 15th century at the storybook castle at Saumur—looming over the Loire's choicest town—and Angers's brooding fortress.

EATING AND DRINKING WELL IN THE LOIRE VALLEY

Finesse rather than fireworks marks the gastronomy of this gentle, lovely region, known for exceptional white wines, delicate fish, and France's most bountiful fruits and vegetables.

Pike perch in beurre-blanc sauce is the Loire's most famous dish *(above)*; goat cheeses are often paired with Loire white wines *(right, top)*; tarte tatins are *delicieux (right, bottom)*.

The serene and gentle Loire imposes its placid personality throughout this fertile valley region. The weather, too, is calm and cool, ideal for creating the Loire's diverse and memorable wines, from the elegant and refined Savennières to the mildly sweet, pretty-in-pink rosés of the Anjou. No big, bold, heavily tannic wines here. The culinary repertoire evokes a sense of the good life, with a nod to the royal legacy of châteaux living over centuries past. There is more gentility than dazzle in the cuisine; many dishes are simply presented, and they couldn't be better: a perfect pike perch, called *sandre*, from the river, bathed in a silky beurre-blanc sauce; coq au vin prepared with a fruity red Sancerre; a tender fillet of beef in a Chinon red-wine-reduction sauce. It is the wines that highlight the Loire's gastronomic scene, and these alone justify a trip here, although, of course, you could make time to visit a château or two while you're in the neighborhood.

OF CABBAGES AND KINGS

The great kitchens of the royal households that set up camp throughout the Loire planned menus around the magnificent produce that thrives in this fecund region, dubbed the Garden of France. Local cooks still do. There are fat white asparagus in the spring; peas, red cherries, haricots verts, artichokes, and lettuces in the summer; followed by apples, pears, cabbages, and pumpkins in the fall.

WHITE WINES (REDS, TOO!)

The Loire region spawns not only dazzling châteaux, but also some of the best wines in France—this is an important region for white-wine lovers, thanks to great chenin blanc and sauvignon blanc grapes. Top white appellations to imbibe, starting at the eastern end of the Loire and moving west, include flinty Sancerres, slightly smoky Pouilly-Fumés, vigorous and complex Vouvrays, distinguished Savennières, sparkling Champagne-style Saumurs, and finally the light, dry Muscadets, perfect with oysters on the half shell.

In the realm of reds, try the raspberry-scented reds of Touraine, the heartier Chinons and Bourgueils, and the elegant rosés of the Anjou. For tastings, just follow the "Dégustation" signs, though it's always a good idea to call ahead.

Check out Vinci Cave in Amboise (☎ 02–47–23–41–52 ⊕ *www.vinci-cave. fr*); Domaine Huet in Vouvray (☎ *02–47–52–78–87 ⊕ www.huet-echansonne. com*); Charles Joguet in Chinon (☎ *02–47–58–55–53 ⊕ www.charlesjoguet. com*); Bouvet-Ladubay in Saumur (☎ *02–41–83–83–83 ⊕ www.bouvet-ladubay.fr*); and the Maison du Vin d'Angers (☎ *02–41–88–81–13 ⊕ www. vinsdeloire.fr*).

TARTE TATIN

This luscious "upside-down" apple tart is sometimes claimed by Normandy,

but originated, so legend has it, at the Hotel Tatin in the Loire Valley town of Beuvron-Lamotte south of Orléans.

The best tarte tatins are made with deeply caramelized apples cooked under a buttery short-crust pastry, then inverted and served while still warm.

BEURRE BLANC

Made with a shallot, wine vinegar, and fish-stock reduction, and swirled with lots of butter, this iconic white sauce originated in the western Loire about a century ago in the kitchen of an aristocrat whose chef devised this variation on the classic béarnaise sauce.

Beurre blanc is the perfect accompaniment to the Loire's delicate shad and pike.

CHÈVRE

With your glass of Pouilly Fumé, there are few things better than one of the region's tangy, herby, and assertive goat cheeses.

Among the best, appellation-controlled and farmhouse-made: the squat, pyramid-shape Pouligny-Saint-Pierre; the creamy, cylindrical Sainte-Maure de Touraine; and the piquant Crottins de Chavignol from Sancerre.

Try a warmed and gooey Crottin atop a salad for a real treat.

Updated by
Christopher
Mooney and
Jack Vermee

A fairy-tale realm par excellence, the Loire Valley is studded with storybook villages, time-burnished towns, and—*bien sûr*—the famous châteaux de la Loire. These postcard icons, like Chenonceau and Chambord, seem to be strung like a strand of pearls across a countryside so serene it could win the Nobel peace prize. With magic at every curve in the road, Cinderella's glass coach might be the optimum way to get around. If that is not available, buses and trains can beautifully ferry you to the main towns of the three Loire provinces—Anjou (to the west), Orléans (to the east), and the center ring of the show, Touraine.

But why did the Loire become so prized for its châteaux? With the wars of the 15th century fading, the Loire Valley, long known as "the garden of France," became a showplace of new and fabulous châteaux *d'agrément*, or pleasure castles. In short order, there were boxwood gardens endlessly receding toward vanishing points, moats graced with swans, parades of delicate cone-top towers, frescoes, and fancywork ceilings. The glories of the Italian Renaissance, observed by the Valois while making war on their neighbor, were brought to bear on these mega-monuments with all the elegance and proportions characteristic of antiquity.

By the time François I took charge, extravagance knew no bounds: on a 13,000-acre forest estate, hunting parties at Chambord drew A-list crowds from the far reaches of Europe—and the availability of 430 rooms made weekend entertaining a snap. Queen Claudia hired only the most recherché Italian artisans: Chambord's famous double-helix staircase may, in fact, have been Leonardo da Vinci's design (he was a frequent houseguest there when not in residence in a manor on the Amboise grounds). From massive kennels teeming with hunting hounds at Cheverny to luxurious stables at Chaumont-sur-Loire, from endless allées of pollarded lime trees at Villandry to the fairy-tale towers of Ussé—worthy of Sleeping Beauty herself—the Loire Valley became the power base and social center for the New France, allowing the monarchy to go all out in strutting its stuff.

All for good reason. In 1519 Charles V of Spain, at the age of 19, inherited the Holy Roman Empire, leaving François and his New France out in the cold. It was perhaps no coincidence that in 1519 François, in a grand stab at face-saving one-upmanship, commenced construction on his gigantic Chambord. Centuries later, even the Revolution and the efforts of latter-day socialists have not totally erased a lingering gentility in the people of the region, characterized by an air of refined assurance far removed from the shoulder-shrugging, chest-tapping French stereotypes. Here life proceeds at a pleasingly genteel pace, and—despite the delights of the 1,001 châteaux that await—you should, too.

4

PLANNER

WHEN TO GO

The best time to go to the Loire region, known as the "Garden of France," may be late spring, when the château gardens start to bloom, or in the fall when the restaurants are all serving the bounty of the local harvest and hunt. The area is greatly affected by its famous river: La Loire is the last great European river left undammed. It is at its best in May and June, when it still looks like a river but, come midsummer, the water level can drop and reveal unsightly sandbanks. The Loire Valley actually divides France in two, both geographically and climatically: north of the Loire, France has the moist, temperate climate of northern Europe; southward lies the drier climate of the Mediterranean, and it is striking how changeable the weather can be as you cross the Loire. Note that the valley can be especially hot and sultry in July and August, when the son-et-lumière shows take place and the tourist crowds arrive. During summer a few hotels and restaurants will be closed for the month of August, but the region's many castles and churches remain open, and refreshingly cool and welcoming inside. October is a good off-season option, when all is mist and mellow fruitfulness along the Loire and the mysterious pools of the Sologne, as the trees turn russet and gold. Fall is also the best time to sample regional specialties such as wild mushrooms and game. On Sunday, when most shops are closed, try to avoid the main cities—Orléans, Tours, Angers.

PLANNING YOUR TIME

More than a region in the usual sense, the Loire Valley is just that: a valley. Although most of the sites are close to the meandering river, it's a long way—225 km (140 miles)—between Orléans, on the eastern edge, and Angers away to the west. If you have 10 days or so you can visit the majority of the sites we cover. Otherwise we suggest you divide the Valley into three segments and choose the base(s) as your time and tastes dictate. To cover the eastern Loire (Chambord, Cheverny, Chaumont), base yourself in or near Blois. For the central Loire (Amboise, Chenonceaux, Villandry, Azay-le-Rideau), base yourself in or around Tours. For the western Loire (Ussé, Chinon, Fontevraud, Angers), opt for pretty Saumur. There are many other scenarios, including this interesting one posted on the Talk Forums of ⊕ *www.fodors.com*: "Angers is only about a 1.5-hour TGV ride from Paris, the train station is in the center of the city, and much is within walking distance. You might consider renting your car in Angers, if driving is your plan, and then tour the other châteaux (if you were renting a car in Paris it would save you the headache of the Paris traffic), then take the return TGV to Paris." —Randy

GETTING HERE AND AROUND
TRANSPORTATION BASICS
The regional rail line along the riverbank will get you to the main towns (Angers, Saumur, Tours, Blois, Orléans, along with 10 other towns), while some other châteaux are served by branch lines (Chenonceau, Azay, Langeais, Chinon, along with 20 or so other towns) or local bus. Occasionally, you may arrive at the rail station and need to invest in a taxi ride, if you can find one available, to get to the châteaux buried deep in the countryside.

The station staff can recommend the best regional taxi services, many of whom have advertisements at the stations. The downside of train travel is having to fit your visits within the constraints of a railroad timetable.

For some, that makes a hired car a particularly practical option. The N152, hugging the riverbank, is the region's backbone. Given the region's flattish terrain, hiring a bike may well appeal, too. There are also local bus services and coach excursions, notably from Tours.

BUS TRAVEL
Local bus services can provide a link between train stations and scenic areas off the river, making it possible to reach many villages and châteaux by bus. However, many routes are in place to service schoolchildren, meaning service is less frequent in summer and sometimes all but nonexistent on Sunday, so only consider the bus if you have no other options. Inquire at tourist offices about routes and timetables, as the bus companies rarely have any information available in English. The leading companies are Les Rapides du Val de Loire, based in Orléans; TLC, serving Chambord and Cheverny from Blois; Touraine Fil Vert and Fil Bleu, both of which serve the Touraine region, including out-of-the-way Loches; and Anjou Bus. The hardest place to reach is the magical Château d'Ussé, but there's one municipal bus line to Rigny-Ussé that connects with Chinon—when in doubt, taxi. For Fontevraud, catch buses from Saumur.

Bus Information Anjou Bus ✉ *Pl. Michel-Debré, Angers* ☎ *02–41–81–49–72* ⊕ *www.anjoubus.fr.* **Fil Bleu** ✉ *9 rue Michelet, Tours* ☎ *02–47–66–70–70* ⊕ *www.filbleu.fr.* **Les Rapides du Val de Loire** ✉ *11 av. André Marie Ampère, St Jean de Braye* ☎ *02–38–61–90–00* ⊕ *www.rvl-info.com.* **TLC (Transports du Loir-et-Cher)** ✉ *9 rue Alexandre-Vézin, Blois* ☎ *02–54–58–55–44* ⊕ *tlcinfo.net.* **Touraine Fil Vert** ✉ *Pl. du Géneral Leclerc, Tours* ☎ *02–47–05–30–49* ⊕ *www.tourainefilvert.com.*

CAR TRAVEL

The Loire Valley is an easy drive from Paris. A10 runs from Paris to Orléans—a distance of around 125 km (80 miles)—and on to Tours, with exits at Meung, Blois, and Amboise. After Tours, A10 veers south toward Poitiers and Bordeaux. A11 links Paris to Angers and Saumur via Le Mans. Slower but more scenic routes run from the Channel ports down through Normandy into the Loire region. The "easiest" way to visit the Loire châteaux is by car; N152 hugs the riverbank and is excellent for sightseeing. But note that signage can be few and far between once you get off the main road, and many a traveler has horror stories about a 15-minute trip lasting two hours ("Next time, by bus and train . . ."). You can rent a car in all the large towns in the region, or at train stations in Orléans, Blois, Tours, or Angers, or in Paris.

TRAIN TRAVEL

Train travel is quite helpful when touring the Loire Valley, as there is one line that goes up and down the river. True, you may sometimes need to avail yourself of a quick taxi ride from the station to a château door, but compared to renting a car, this adds up to little bother and expense.

As gateways to the region, Tours (70 mins, €53) and Angers (95 mins, €63) are both served by the superfast TGV (Trains à Grande Vitesse) from Paris (Gare Montparnasse); note that the main-line station in Tours is in suburban St-Pierre-des-Corps.

There are also TGV trains from Charles-de-Gaulle Airport direct to the Loire Valley to Angers (2 hrs, 30 mins; €69), and St-Pierre-des-Corps (for Tours, 1 hr, 45 mins; €59). Express trains run every two hours from Paris (Gare d'Austerlitz) to Orléans (1 hr, 10 mins; €20.30; usually you must change at nearby Les Aubrais) and Blois (1 hr, 30 mins; €27.80).

The main train line follows the Loire from Orléans to Angers (1 hr, 50 mins; €35.30); there are trains every two hours or so, stopping in Blois, Tours, and Saumur; trains stop less frequently in Onzain (for Chaumont), Amboise, and Langeais.

There are branch lines with trains from Tours to Chenonceaux (30 mins, €6.60), Azay-le-Rideau (30 mins, €5.60), and Chinon (50 mins, €9.40).

Ask the SNCF for the brochure *Les Châteaux de la Loire en Train* for more detailed information. Helpful train-schedule brochures are available at most stations.

Train Information Gare SNCF Angers ⊠ *Pl. de la Gare* ☎ *02–41–86–41–24.* **Gare SNCF Orléans** ⊠ *Av. de Paris* ☎ *02–38–79–91–64.* **Gare SNCF Tours** ⊠ *Pl. du Général Leclerc* ☎ *02–34–74–72–59.* **SNCF** ☎ *36–35 [€0.34 per min]* ⊕ *www.voyages-sncf.com.* **TGV** ⊕ *www.tgv.com.*

HOTELS

Even before the age of the railway, the Loire Valley drew vacationers from far afield, so there are hundreds of hotels of all types. At the higher end are sumptuous, stylishly converted châteaux, but even these are not as pricey as you might think. Note that most of these are in small villages, and that upscale hotels are in short supply in the major towns. At the lower end is a wide choice of gîtes, bed-and-breakfasts, and small, traditional inns in towns, usually offering terrific value for the money.

The Loire Valley is a popular destination, so make reservations well in advance—in July and August, this is essential (and we're talking weeks in advance, not days).

Beware that from November through Easter, many properties are closed.

Prices in the dining reviews are the average cost of a main course at dinner or, if dinner is not served, at lunch. Prices in the lodging reviews are the lowest cost of a standard double room in high season.

VISITOR INFORMATION

The Loire region has three area tourist offices, all of which are for written inquiries only. For Chinon and points east, contact the Comité Régional du Tourisme de la Région Centre or the Comité Départemental du Tourisme de Touraine. For Fontevraud and points west, contact the Comité Départemental du Tourisme de l'Anjou. *For specific town tourist offices, see the town entries.*

Contacts Comité Départemental du Tourisme de l'Anjou ⊠ *Pl. Kennedy, BP 32147, Angers* ☎ *02–41–23–51–51* ⊕ *www.anjou-tourisme.com*. **Comité Régional du Tourisme de la Région Centre** ⊠ *37 av. de Paris, Orléans* ⊕ *www.loirevalleytourism.com*. **Comité Départemental du Tourisme des Pays de la Loire** ⊠ *1 pl. Galarne, Nantes* ⊕ *www.enpaysdelaloire.com*. **Comité Départemental du Tourisme de Touraine** ⊠ *30 rue de la Préfecture, BP 91808, Tours Cedex* ☎ *02–47–31–47–48* ⊕ *www.tourism-touraine.fr*.

TOUR OPTIONS

Excursion bus tours of the main châteaux leave daily in summer from the main hubs like Tours, Orléans, and Saumur: tourist offices have the latest times and prices. Readers rave about Acco-Dispo van tours—usually three top châteaux are included. Its half-day trips cost €34 per person and leave from Tours or Amboise. Jet Systems makes helicopter trips over the Loire Valley on Tuesday, Thursday, and weekends from the aerodrome at Dierre, just south of Amboise; cost ranges from €75 (10 mins, flying over Chenonceau) to €299 (50 mins, from Chenonceau to Ussé) per person. Contact France Montgolfières for details of balloon trips over the Loire; prices run €185–€255 per person. Croisières de Loire offers some unique Loire River tours. Sail the Cher River on a traditional flat-bottom riverboat from the foot of Chenonceau April through October (€9).

Contacts Acco-Dispo Tours ⊠ *18 rue des Vallees, Amboise* ☎ *06–82–00–64–51* ⊕ *www.accodispo-tours.com*. **Croisières de Loire** ⊠ *Maison Eclusière de Chisseaux, Chisseaux* ☎ *02–47–23–98–64* ⊕ *www.croisieresdeloire.com*. **France Montgolfiéres** ☎ *03–80–97–38–61* ⊕ *www.franceballoons.com*. **Jet Systems** ⊠ *Aérodrome d'Amboise Dierre* ☎ *08–20–82–06–98* ⊕ *www.jet-systems.fr*.

FROM TOURS TO ORLÉANS

At Orléans, halfway along the route of the Loire—the longest river in France—the river takes a wide, westward bend, gliding languidly through low, rich country known as the Val de Loire—or Loire Valley. In this temperate region—a 225-km (140-mile) stretch between Orléans and Angers—scores of châteaux built of local *tufa* (creamy white

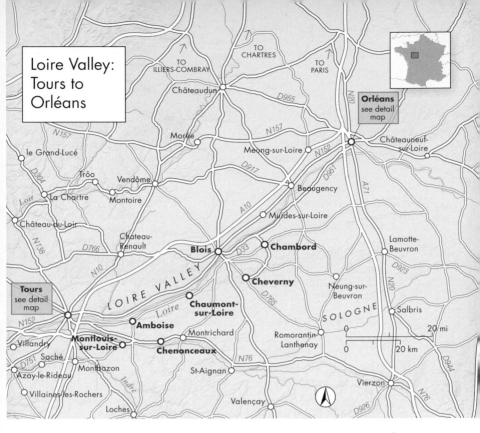

Loire Valley:
Tours to
Orléans

limestone) rise from the rocky banks of the Loire and its tributaries: the rivers Cher, Indre, Vienne, and Loir (with no *e*).

The Loire is liquid history. For centuries the river was the area's principal means of transportation and an effective barrier against invading armies. Towns arose at strategic bridgeheads, and fortresses—the earliest châteaux—appeared on towering slopes. The Loire Valley was hotly disputed by France and England during the Middle Ages; it belonged to England (under the Anjou Plantagenet family) between 1154 and 1216 and again during the Hundred Years' War (1337–1453). It was the example of Joan of Arc, the Maid of Orléans (so called after the site of one of her most stirring victories), that crystallized French efforts to expel the English.

The Loire Valley's golden age came under François I (ruled 1515–47)—flamboyant contemporary of England's Henry VIII—whose salamander emblem can be seen in many châteaux, including Chambord, the mightiest of them. Although the nation's power base shifted to Paris around 1600, aristocrats continued to erect luxurious palaces along the Loire until the end of the 18th century.

TOURS

240 km (150 miles) southwest of Paris.

Tours is the region's largest and most commercial city whose greatest asset is energy—the cobblestone streets in the pedestrian-only Vielle Ville crackle with cafés, bars, and restaurants. Students make up a quarter of the population, thanks to Tours's noted university. Although much of the city was bombed in World War II, its pretty historical district remains to allure and enchant visitors to this important gateway to the Loire Valley.

GETTING HERE

The handful of direct TGV trains from Paris (Gare Montparnasse) to Tours each day cover the 240 km (150 miles) in 70 minutes; fare is €45–€59 depending on time of day. Some trains involve a change in suburban St-Pierre-des-Corps. A cheaper, slower alternative is the twice-daily traditional (non-TGV) service from Gare d'Austerlitz that takes around two hours, 30 minutes but costs only €34.30. Tours is the Loire Valley rail hub. Trains leave every couple of hours or so for Chinon (50 mins, €9.40); Langeais (15 mins, €5.40); Amboise (20 mins, €5.40); Saumur (40 mins, €11.70); Chenonceaux (30 mins, €6.60); and Blois (30–40 mins, €10.60), in addition to other towns.

Visitor Information Tours Tourist Office ⊠ *78 rue Bernard-Palissy* 🕾 *02–47–70–37–37* ⊕ *www.ligeris.com.*

EXPLORING

Little remains of Tours's own château, but one of France's finest cathedrals more than compensates and the city serves as the transportation hub for the Loire Valley. Trains from Tours (and from its adjacent terminal at St-Pierre-de-Corps) run along the river in both directions, and regular bus services radiate from here; in addition, the city is the starting point for organized bus excursions (many with English-speaking guides). The town has mushroomed into a city of a quarter of a million inhabitants, with an ugly modern sprawl of factories, high-rise blocks, and overhead expressway junctions cluttering up the outskirts. But the timber-frame houses in "Le Vieux Tours" (Old Tours) and the attractive medieval center around place Plumereau were smartly restored after extensive damage in World War II.

TOP ATTRACTIONS

Cathédral St-Gatien. Built between 1239 and 1484, this noted cathedral, one of the greatest churches of the Loire Valley, reveals a mixture of architectural styles. The richly sculpted stonework of its majestic, soaring, two-tower facade betrays the Renaissance influence on local château-trained craftsmen. The stained glass dates from the 13th century (if you have binoculars, bring them). Also take a look at the little tomb with kneeling angels built in memory of Charles VIII and Anne of Brittany's two children; and the **Cloître de La Psalette** (Psalm Cloister, €3), on the south side of the cathedral, where the canons of St-Gatien created some of the most beautiful illuminated manuscripts in medieval Europe. ⊠ *Rue Lavoisier* 🕾 *02–47–47–05–19* ⊕ *la-psalette.monuments-nationaux.fr* 🕘 *Apr.–Sept., Mon.–Sat. 9:30–12:30 and 2–6, Sun. 2–6;*

Oct.–Mar., Wed.–Sat. 9:30–12:30
and 2–5, Sun.–Tues. 2–5.

Fodor's Choice
★ **Château de Candé.** When Edward
VIII of England abdicated his
throne in 1937 to marry the American divorcée Wallace Simpson,
the couple chose this elegant 16th-
century château (located 10 minutes south of Tours) to escape from

> **LUSCIOUS LOIRE**
>
> If the natives of Tours are known
> for one thing, it's their elegant
> French. Paris may be the capital,
> but for the Tourangeaux, Parisians
> are the ones with the accent.

international limelight and exchange their wedding vows. Open to the
public since 2000, the lovely museum offers a video and guided tour
through the rooms of the château. While decorated with period furnishings and Art Deco bathrooms, all eyes are drawn to the mementos from
the Duke and Duchess of Windsor's stay (including the famous Cecil
Beaton photographs taken on the big day) along with the haute couture
wardrobe of the fashionable lady of the house, Fern Bedaux. Befitting
the owners' flawless taste (if questionable politics, as the Bedauxs were
known fascist sympathizers), the château is a particularly pretty example of late Gothic style—the perfect setting for the Windsors' "fairy-
tale" marriage. ⊠ *37260 Monts, Monts (8 km/5 miles southwest of
Tours)* 🕾 *02–47–34–03–70* ⊕ *www.chateau-cande.fr* 🖾 *€5* ☽ *Apr.–June
and Sept., Wed.–Sun. 10:30–7; July and Aug., daily 10:30–7 (gardens
until 9).*

Fodor's Choice
★ **Place Plumereau.** North from the Basilique St-Martin to the river is **Le
Vieux Tours,** the lovely medieval quarter centered around that postcard icon, the half-timber place Plumereau. A warren of quaint streets,
wood-beam houses, and grand mansions once home to 15th-century
merchants, the Old Town has been gentrified with chic apartments
and pedestrianized streets—Tours's college students and tourists alike
love to sit at the cafés lining the place Plumereau, once the town's *car-
roi aux chapeaux* (hat market). Lining the square, Nos. 1 through 7
form a magnificent series of half-timber houses; note the wood carvings of royal moneylenders on Nos. 11 and 12. At the top of the square
a vaulted passageway leads on to a cute medieval **place St-Pierre-le-
Puellier.** Running off the place Plumereau are other streets adorned
with historic houses, notably rue Briçonnet—at No. 16 is the **Maison
de Tristan,** with a medieval staircase. ⊠ *Bordered by rues du Commerce,
Briçonnet, de la Monnaie, and du Grand-Marché.*

WORTH NOTING

Basilique St-Martin. Only two sturdy towers—the Tour Charlemagne and
the Tour de l'Horloge (Clock Tower)—remain of the great medieval
abbey built over the tomb of St. Martin, the city's 4th-century bishop
and patron saint. Most of the abbey, which once dominated the heart of
Tours, was razed during the French Revolution. Today the site is occupied by the bombastic neo-Byzantine Basilique St-Martin, which was
completed in 1924. There's a shrine to the former bishop St. Martin in
the crypt. ⊠ *Rue Descartes* ⊕ *www.basiliquesaintmartin.com.*

Musée des Beaux-Arts (*Fine Arts Museum*). In what was once the archbishop's palace (built into an ancient Roman wall), this museum features

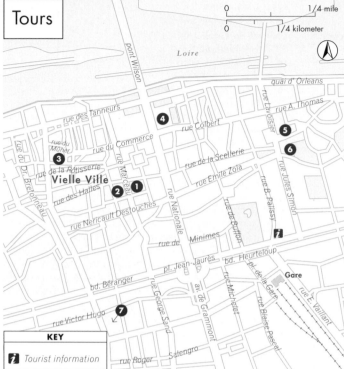

an eclectic selection of furniture, sculpture, wrought-iron work, and works by Rubens, Rembrandt, Boucher, Degas, and Calder. A favorite is Fritz the Elephant, stuffed in 1902. ⊠ *18 pl. François-Sicard* ☏ *02–47–05–68–73* ⊕ *www.mba.tours.fr* 🖭 *€4* ⊘ *Wed.–Mon. 9–12:45 and 2–6 (9–6 during special exhibitions).*

Musée du Compagnonnage (*Guild Museum*). Housed in the cloisters of the 13th-century church of St-Julien, this collection honors the *Compagnonnage*, a sort of apprenticeship-cum–trade union system. On display is virtuoso 19th-century craft work of the candidates for guild membership, some of it eccentric (an Eiffel Tower made of slate, for instance, and a château constructed of varnished noodles). ⊠ *8 rue Nationale* ☏ *02–47–21–62–20* ⊕ *www.museecompagnonnage.fr* 🖭 *Musée du Compagnonnage €5.30; multivisit card with admission to the Musées des Beaux Arts and du Compagnonnage, the Musée St-Martin, and the Centre de Création Contemporaine €8* ⊘ *Jan.–mid-June and Sept.–Dec., Wed.–Mon. 9–noon and 2–6; mid-June–Aug., daily 9–noon and 2–6.*

Musée St-Martin. Old mosaics and Romanesque sculptures from the former abbey are on display in this small museum. Housed in a restored 13th-century chapel that adjoined the abbey cloisters, the exhibits retrace the life of St. Martin, so important to the history of Tours, and the abbey's long and storied saga. Martin founded the first Benedictine abbey in France just outside Tours in the 4th century. The word "chapel" comes from the legend of Martin as a young Roman soldier who shared his cape (or "capella") with a beggar and then had a vision of Jesus. Small churches holding relics of the cape became known as chapels, and soon all small churches took the name. ✉ *3 rue Rapin* ☎ *02–47–64–48–87* 🌐 *www.tours.fr/137-musee-saint-martin.htm* 🎫 *€2* 🕒 *Mid-Mar.–mid-Nov., Wed.–Sun 10:30–1 and 2–5:30.*

WHERE TO EAT

$$ BISTRO 🍴 **Le Petit Patrimoine.** Locals in the know reserve well in advance to get a table at this tiny restaurant in Vieux Tours specializing in traditional regional cuisine. Don't miss Balzac's much-loved Rillons de Tours, a glazed pork dish, and the delicious St-Maure goat cheese. [$] *Average main: €23* ✉ *58 rue Colbert* ☎ *02–47–66–05–81* 🕒 *Closed Sun. and Mon.*

$$$ MODERN FRENCH 🍴 **L'Odéon.** Enjoy the best of traditional Loire Valley haute cuisine with modern flair in an Art Deco setting in the heart of Tours. Flavors can be surprising, such as fresh lobster with truffle sauce and walnut oil, roast beef cooked with green apples and tarragon sauce, or roasted sea bass with rhubarb and shrimp sauce. The setting is not particularly romantic, so a nice lunch (with the great lunch menu deals) is a better bet than the pricier dinner menus. [$] *Average main: €29* ✉ *10 pl. du Général Leclerc* ☎ *02–47–20–12–65* 🌐 *www.restaurant-lodeon.com* 🕒 *Closed Sun. No lunch Sat.*

WHERE TO STAY

For expanded hotel reviews, visit Fodors.com.

$$$ RESORT 🏨 **Domaine de la Tortinière.** Legend has it that this was one of Audrey Hepburn's favorites, and you can see why immediately: the storybook neo-Gothic château atop a vast, sloping lawn is complete with two fairy-tale towers, Louis Seize public salons, and soigné guest rooms—some in the two turrets, others with beamed ceilings, and some in the smartly converted stables and servants' quarters. **Pros:** gourmet restaurant overlooking the lawn; romantic setting; luxurious Louis XVI style. **Cons:** some rooms on the small side; a bit off the beaten track. [$] *Rooms from: €175* ✉ *10 rte. de Ballan-Miré, 12 km (7 miles) south of Tours, Veigné* ☎ *02–47–34–35–00* 🌐 *www.tortiniere.com* 🛏 *24 rooms, 6 suites* 🕒 *Closed mid-Dec.–Feb.* 🍽 *Some meals.*

$ HOTEL 🏨 **L'Adresse.** These guest rooms in the heart of Tours's Old Town, a block from half-timbered place Plumereau and the open-air market, have a fresh look, with a neutral color palette punctuated with touches of deep red and whitewashed wood-beam ceilings in the top-floor rooms. **Pros:** central location in Vieux Tours; flat-screen TVs and air-conditioning. **Cons:** student district can be very noisy at night; no parking. [$] *Rooms from: €85* ✉ *12 rue de la Rôtisserie* ☎ *02–47–20–85–76* 🌐 *www.hotel-ladresse.com* 🛏 *17 rooms* 🍽 *Some meals.*

$$$$ HOTEL 🏨 **Les Hautes Roches.** Far from their original role as monastic cells and even farther from the Flintstone-influenced idea of cave dwellings, these luxe-troglodyte lodgings—with their limestone walls, Louis Treize seating, rich fabrics, carved fireplaces, gas-lantern lamps, finished

Spend your first evening in the Loire Valley dining on gorgeous place Plumereau, hub of the historic district of Tours, gateway to the region.

marble steps, and riverside setting—are the epitome of quiet luxury amid the soothing elements of stone and water. **Pros:** unique troglodyte setting; river views; fabulous gourmet restaurant with terrace. **Cons:** apprentice-style service; busy road (hidden by shrubs) in front of hotel. [$] *Rooms from: €220* ✉ *86 quai de la Loire, 5 km (3 miles) east of Tours, Rochecorbon* ☎ *02–47–52–88–88* 🌐 *www.leshautesroches.com* 🛏 *15 rooms* 🕒 *Closed mid-Jan.–mid-Mar.* 🍴 *Some meals.*

$ HOTEL 🏨 **Mondial.** These contemporary rooms, decorated in neutral tones with red or floral accents, are all on the small side, but they are nicely tucked away on a small leafy square 300 yards from the Loire and a five-minute walk from historic half-timber place Plumereau. **Pros:** free Wi-Fi; good location; friendly service; good value. **Cons:** noise from downstairs nightclub Wednesday–Sunday nights until 5 am; restricted reception hours. [$] *Rooms from: €78* ✉ *3 pl. de la Résistance* ☎ *02–47–05–62–68* 🌐 *www.hotelmondialtours.com* 🛏 *19 rooms* 🍴 *No meals.*

MONTLOUIS-SUR-LOIRE

11 km (7 miles) east of Tours on south bank of the Loire.

Visitor Information Montlouis-sur-Loire Tourist Office ✉ *4 pl. Courtemanche* ☎ *02–47–45–85–10* 🌐 *www.tourisme-montlouis-loire.fr* 🕒 *Tues.–Fri. 10–12:30 and 2–5:30.*

EXPLORING

Like Vouvray—its sister town on the north side of the Loire—Montlouis is noted for its white wines. On place Courtemanche the **Cave Touristique** will help you learn all about the fine vintages produced by the wine growers of Montlouis. On the eastern side of town is one of the most alluring châteaux of the region, **La Bourdaisière.** Although open to day-trippers for guided tours, this once-royal retreat and birthplace of noted 17th-century courtesan Gabrielle d'Estrées is today the enchanted hotel-domain of Prince Louis-Albert de Broglie.

WHERE TO STAY

For expanded hotel reviews, visit Fodors.com.

$$$ HOTEL Fodor's Choice ★ **Château de la Bourdaisière.** A 15th-century, 100-carat jewel of a castle, once the favored retreat of kings François I and Henri IV, is today the luxurious country setting for the Prince de Broglie's hotel—a magnificent place that magically distills all the grace, warmth, and élan of la vie de châteaux as no other. **Pros:** exquisite setting; secluded pool; stylish salons; extensive and "eco"-style gardens. **Cons:** only offers quick and casual lunches; rooms lack air-conditioning; town is a bore. [$] *Rooms from: €170* ✉ *25 rue de la Bourdaisière* ☎ *02–47–45–16–31* 🌐 *www.chateaulabourdaisiere.com* 🛏 *17 rooms, 3 suites* 🕒 *Closed mid-Nov.–Mar.* 🍴 *Breakfast.*

AMBOISE

13 km (8 miles) northeast of Montlouis via D751, 24 km (15 miles) east of Tours.

Amboise is a major hub of the Loire and one of the most popular towns along the river, site of Leonardo da Vinci's final home, crowned with a royal château, and jammed with bustling markets and plenty of hotels and restaurants. On hot summer days, however, the plethora of tour buses turns the Renaissance town into a carbon monoxide nightmare. So why come? The main château is soaked in history (and blood), while Leonardo's very pretty Clos-Lucé mansion is a must-do on any Val de Loire itinerary.

GETTING HERE

Amboise has frequent train connections with Tours (20 mins, €5.40), Blois (20 mins, €6.80), and many other towns that lie along the main train route, which follows the banks of the river; about 10 trains a day make the Tours–Blois transit. From Amboise's station, the town is across the Loire (the island in the middle of the river is the less-than-exciting Ile d'Or); follow the signs across two bridges to the *centre ville* and place Richelieu.

Visitor Information Amboise Tourist Office ✉ *Quai du Général-de-Gaulle* ☎ *02–47–57–09–28* 🌐 *www.amboise-valdeloire.com.*

EXPLORING

Château d'Amboise. The Château d'Amboise became a royal palace in the 15th and 16th centuries. Charles VII stayed here, as did the unfortunate Charles VIII, best remembered for banging his head on a low doorway lintel (you will be shown it) and dying as a result. The gigantic **Tour des Minimes** drops down the side of the cliff, enclosing a massive circular ramp designed to lead horses and carriages up the steep hillside. François I, whose long nose appears in so many château paintings, based his court here, inviting Leonardo da Vinci as his guest. The castle was

Continued on page 237

ONCE UPON A CHÂTEAU

France's most famous châteaux range in style from medieval fortresses to Renaissance country homes, and they don't skip a beat in between. Today, travelers hop their way from the fairy-tale splendor of Ussé to the imposing dungeons at Angers to the graceful spans of Chenonceau. But to truly appreciate these spectacular structures, it helps to review their evolution from warlike stronghold to Sleeping Beauty's home.

Château de Chambord

During this time, dukes and counts began to build châteaux, from which they could watch over the king's lands and also defend themselves from each others' invasions. Spare, cold, and uninviting (that being the point), their châteaux were fancy forts. The notion of defense extended to the décor: massive high-back chairs protected the sitter from being stabbed in the back during dinner, and the *crédence* (credenza) was a table used by a noble's official taster to test for poison in the food.

These fortifications continued to come in handy during the Hundred Years' War, during which France and England quibbled over the French crown, for 116 years. When that war came to an end, in 1453, King François I went to Italy, looking for someone else to beat up on, and came back with the Renaissance (he literally brought home Leonardo da Vinci). The king promptly built a 440-room Xanadu, Chambord, in the Italianate style.

By the 15th century, under the later medieval Valois kings, the Loire was effectively functioning as the country's capital, with new châteaux springing up apace, advertising their owners' power and riches. Many were built using a chalky local stone called *tuffeau* (tufa), whose softness and whiteness made it ideal for the sculpted details which were the pride of the new architectural style. The resulting Renaissance pleasure palaces were sumptuous both inside and out—Charles Perrault found the Château de Ussé to be so peaceful and alluring it inspired him to write "Sleeping Beauty" in 1697. A few years before, Louis XIV had started building his new seat of government. It wasn't long before it was goodbye Loire Valley, hello Versailles.

Loire and château are almost synonymous. There may be châteaux in every region of France, but nowhere are they so thickly clustered as they are in the Loire Valley. There are several reasons for this. By the early Middle Ages, prosperous towns had already evolved due to being strategically sited on the Loire, and defensive fortresses—the first châteaux—were built by warlords to control certain key points along the route. And with good reason: the riches of this wildly fertile region drew many feuding lords; in the 12th century, the medieval Plantagenet kings of France and England had installed themselves here (at Chinon and Fontevraud, to be exact).

By Heather Stimmler-Hall

FROM DEFENSE TO DECORATION

13TH CENTURY

Angers

The parade of châteaux began with the medieval fortress at Angers, a brooding, muscular fort built by St. Louis to defend the gateway to the Loire against pesky English invaders. Military architecture gave birth to this château, a perfect specimen of great, massive defensiveness. Such castles were meant to look grim, advertising horrid problems for attackers—defenders shot cross-bow arrows from the slit windows—and unpleasant conditions for prisoners in the dungeons. The most important features of these fortress-châteaux were the *châtelets* (twin turrets that frame the drawbridge), the *chemin de ronde* (the machicolated passageways between towers), and the *donjon* (fortress keep).

14TH CENTURY

Saumur

When the battle cries faded and periods of peace once more beguiled the land, the château changed its appearance and the picture palaces of the Loire came into being. Elegance arrived early at Saumur, built in 1360 by Louis I of Anjou. His heir, the luxury-loving Duc de Berri, dressed up the sturdy fort with high, pointed roofs, gilded steeples, iron weather vanes, and soaring pinnacles, creating a Gothic-style castle that Walt Disney would have been proud of. Former cross-bow apertures were replaced with good-size windows, from which love-sick princesses would gaze down on chivalric tournaments, now featuring fancy cloth-of-gold trappings, and festive banquets with blaring trumpet backup became the norm.

| 1214 French king **Philippe Auguste** defeats English and German armies in Anjou. | 1270 **Death of Louis IX** (St. Louis) in Tunis during the 8th Crusade. | 1337 **Hundred Years' War** between France and England. begins. | 1360 Louis I of Anjou tranforms **Saumur** into his elegant residence. |

1300

1400

| 1228 | 1238 Constructuion of **Angers Castle.** | 1348 The **Black Death** kills one third of the French population. |

Azay-le-Rideau

16TH CENTURY

By the Renaissance—brought to France from Italy by Charles VIII at the end of the 15th century—balance, harmony, and grace were brought to the fore. Rich officials wowed the womenfolk with châteaux that were homages to the bygone days of chivalry, such as Azay-le-Rideau.

— The château may look Gothic from a distance, but its moat is actually the River Indre, and its purpose is to provide a pleasing reflection, thereby emphasizing the Italianate symmetry of this architectural bijou. Funded by the royal financier Berthelot but designed by his wife, Philippe, this was a fairy-tale castle. The turrets and machicolations were just for fun, and a grand staircase was added to showcase the ladies' sweeping skirts.

Chenonceau

16TH CENTURY

Its architecture is civilized, peaceful, and feminine, aptly so since it was constructed by three ladies. Catherine Briçonnet, a tax collector's wife, built the Gothic-style château; Diane de Poitiers, the mistress of Henri II, extended it by adding a bridge across the river

— (for easy access to her hunting grounds), before being kicked out by Henri's wife, Catherine de Medici, who tacked galleries onto the bridge in homage to the Ponte Vecchio in Florence, her home town. Although its broad facade offers a curtsey to the virtues of Baroque style, Chenonceau is actually only two rooms deep—the château had become an exquisite stage curtain and little more.

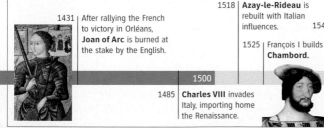

1431 | After rallying the French to victory in Orléans, **Joan of Arc** is burned at the stake by the English.

1518 | **Azay-le-Rideau** is rebuilt with Italian influences.

1525 | François I builds **Chambord.**

1547 | King Henri II gives **Chenonceau** to his mistress Diane de Poitiers.

1500

1485 | **Charles VIII** invades Italy, importing home the Renaissance.

1600

LA VIE DE CHÂTEAUX

Inside or out, the Château de la Bourdaiserie epitomizes Loire elegance.

To truly savor the châteaux of the "Valley of the Kings," you can do more than just tour them: You can sleep in them, party in them, and helicopter-ride over them.

QUEEN FOR A STAY

Here are the crème de la crème of the Loire Valley's magical châteaux-hotels:

Château de la Bordaisière, Montlouis-sur-Loire. Not far from Chenonceau, this enchanting neo-Renaissance castle is run by prince Louis-Albert de Broglie. Royal red salons, chic bedrooms, a famous tomato potager, a vast pool, and heirloom gardens are just a few of the goodies here.

Château de Colliers, Muides-sur-Loire. Close to Chambord, this *très charmant* jewel has ravishing Rococo salons and the most beautiful hotel river terrace along the Loire.

Château de Pray, Amboise. With its storybook towers, tapestried-and-chandeliered restaurant, and 19th-century style rooms, you'll be raising your glass of Veuve Clicquot to toast La Loire in no time.

AN EYE ON HIGH

Thanks to helicopter excursions, you can get a new perspective on the grand châteaux by taking to the air—appropriately so, since Leonardo da Vinci invented the contraption while residing in Amboise. Jet Systems (☎ 0820/820698 ⊕ www.jet-systems.fr) makes helicopter trips over the Loire Valley on Tuesday, Thursday, and weekends from the aerodrome at Dierre, just south of Amboise; costs range from €69 (10 minutes, flying over Chenonceau) to €289 (50 minutes, covering six châteaux) per person. For a more leisurely airborne visit, contact France Montgolfière's (☎ 02-54-32-20-48 ⊕ www.franceballoons. com) for details of their balloon trips over the Loire; prices run €195–€245.

LET THERE BE A LIGHT SHOW

In summer, several châteaux offer celebrated *son-et-lumière* (sound-and-light) extravaganzas after dark. Some are historical pageants—with huge casts of people dressed in period costume, all floodlit (the flicker of flames helps dramatize the French Revolution), and accompanied by music and commentary, sometimes in English; Amboise and Loches are the top examples. Other châteaux—including Chenonceau, Chambord, and Azay-le-Rideau—offer recorded commentary and magical effects created by slide projections (pictured), smoke-machines, and color spotlights.

also the stage for the Amboise Conspiracy, an ill-fated Protestant plot against François II; you're shown where the corpses of the conspirators dangled from the castle walls. Partly due to the fact that most interior furnishings have been lost, most halls here are haunted and forlorn. The maze of underground passages are opened to the public for guided visits (April–September). But don't miss the lovely grounds, adorned with a Flamboyant Gothic gem, the little chapel of St-Hubert with its carvings of the Virgin and Child, Charles VIII, and Anne of Brittany, and once graced by the tomb of Leonardo. Audio guides are available for €4. ☎ 02–47–57–00–98 ⊕ *www.chateau-amboise.com* ✉ €10.50 ⊙ *Mid-Nov.–Feb., daily 9–12:30 and 2–4:45; Mar. and Nov. 1–15, daily 9–5:30; Apr.–June, Sept., and Oct., daily 9–6; July and Aug., daily 9–7.*

Clos Lucé. If you want to see where "the 20th century was born"—as the curators here like to proclaim—head to the legendary Clos Lucé, about 600 yards up rue Victor-Hugo from the château. Here, in this handsome Renaissance manor, Leonardo da Vinci (1452–1519) spent the last four years of his life, tinkering away at inventions, amusing his patron, King François I, and gazing out over a garden that was planted in the most fashionable Italian manner (which was completely restored in 2008 to contain the plants and trees found in the artist's sketches, as well as a dozen full-size renderings of machines he designed). The **Halle Interactive** contains working models, built by IBM engineers using the detailed sketches in the artist's notebooks, of some of Leonardo's extraordinary inventions; by this time Leonardo had put away his paint box because of arthritis. Mechanisms on display include three-speed gearboxes, a military tank, a clockwork car, and a flying machine complete with designs for parachutes. Cloux, the house's original name, was given to Anne of Brittany by Charles VIII, who built a chapel for her that is still here. Some of the house's furnishings are authentically 16th century—indeed, thanks to the artist's presence this house was one of the first places where the Italian Renaissance made inroads in France: Leonardo's *Mona Lisa* and *Virgin of the Rocks,* both of which once graced the walls here, were bought by the king, who then moved them to the Louvre. ✉ *2 rue du Clos-Lucé* ☎ *02–47–57–00–73* ⊕ *www.vinci-closluce.com* ✉ *€13.50* ⊙ *Sept.,Oct., and Feb.–June, daily 9–7; July and Aug., daily 9–8; Nov.–Jan., daily 10–6.*

WHERE TO STAY

For expanded hotel reviews, visit Fodors.com.

$$$ **Château de Noizay.** Filled with the mystery of the past—this was **HOTEL** once the fabled redoubt of the Protestant plotters in the 1559 Amboise Conspiracy—this château is fitted out with Renaissance chimneys and salons, a parterre garden, and guest rooms so regal that you may feel like bowing or curtsying to the staff. **Pros:** historic ambience; excellent restaurant. **Cons:** some rooms have faded decor; high rates for the countryside. $ *Rooms from: €205* ✉ *Promenade de Waulsort, 8 km (5 miles) west of Tours, Noizay* ☎ *02–47–52–11–01* ⊕ *www.chateaudenoizay. com* ↩ *14 rooms* ⊙ *Closed mid-Jan.–mid-Mar.* ⊙*All meals.*

$$$ HOTEL Fodor's Choice ★ **Château de Pray.** Like a Rolls-Royce Silver Cloud, this hotel keeps purring along, decade after decade, offering many delights: a romantic, twin-tower château, a Loire River vista, tranquil guest rooms (four of the less expensive are in a charming "Pavillon Renaissance"), and an excellent restaurant. **Pros:** marvelous setting; superlative restaurant; open year-round. **Cons:** service can be haughty; no bar. [$] *Rooms from: €145* ✉ *Rue du Cèdre, 4 km (2 miles) east of Amboise, Chargé* ☎ *02–47–57–23–67* 🌐 *praycastel.online.fr* 🛏 *17 rooms, 2 suites* 🍴 *Some meals.*

HAVE THAT NIKON READY

Be sure to walk to the most distant point of Chenonceau's largest parterre garden, le Jardin de Diane de Poitiers—there you can find a tiny bridge leading to a river lookout point where you can find the most beautiful view of France's most glorious château. Sorry, no picnics allowed.

$ HOTEL **Le Blason.** Two blocks behind Château d'Amboise and a five-minute walk from the town center, this small, old hotel has welcoming, English-speaking owners, rooms of different shapes and sizes, an on-site restaurant, and, best of all, the gentlest hotel prices in town. **Pros:** quaint charm; families welcome; good-value dining menus. **Cons:** small bathrooms; traffic noise in some rooms. [$] *Rooms from: €53* ✉ *11 pl. Richelieu* ☎ *02–47–23–22–41* 🌐 *www.leblason.fr* 🛏 *26 rooms* 🕒 *Closed mid-Jan.–mid-Feb.* 🍴 *Some meals.*

$$ HOTEL **Le Manoir Les Minimes.** Picture-perfect and soigné as can be, this gorgeously stylish 18th-century *manoir* is lucky enough to preside over a Loire riverbank under the shadow of Amboise's great cliff-side château, offering a calm oasis in a busy town center. **Pros:** historic style; flawlessly elegant taste. **Cons:** overpriced breakfast; no outside food and drink allowed. [$] *Rooms from: €135* ✉ *34 quai Charles-Guinot* ☎ *02–47–30–40–40* 🌐 *www.manoirlesminimes.com* 🛏 *13 rooms, 2 suites* 🕒 *Closed mid-Nov.–mid-Mar.* 🍴 *No meals.*

$$$ B&B/INN Fodor's Choice ★ **Le Vieux Manoir.** Toile de Jouy screens, gilt-framed paintings, comfy Napoléon III covered-in-jute armchairs, timeworn armoires, and tables adorned with Shaker baskets make this extraordinary inn—run by native Californian owner Gloria—*House Beautiful* (and prolonged stay) worthy. **Pros:** real style; leafy garden; scrumptious breakfasts in glassed-in conservatoire. **Cons:** steep staircase; many "house rules." [$] *Rooms from: €162* ✉ *13 rue Rabelais* ☎ *02–47–30–41–27* 🌐 *www.le-vieux-manoir.com* 🛏 *6 rooms, 2 cottages* 🍴 *Breakfast.*

CHENONCEAUX

12 km (8 miles) southeast of Amboise via D81, 32 km (20 miles) east of Tours.

GETTING HERE

Three to five trains run daily between Tours and Chenonceaux (30 mins, €6.60), one of the main destinations on one of the extensive branch lines of the Loire rail system. The station is especially convenient, a minute walk from the front gates of the château; across the tracks is the one-road town.

Fodor's Choice **Château de Chenonceau.** Achingly beautiful, the Château de Chenon-
★ ceau has long been considered the "most romantic" of all the Loire
châteaux, thanks in part to its showpiece—a breathtaking *galerie de
bal* that spans the River Cher like a bridge. The gallery was used as an
escape point for French Resistance fighters during World War II, since
all other crossings had been bombed. Set in the village of Chenonceaux
(spelled with an *x*) on the River Cher, this was the fabled retreat for the
dames de Chenonceau, Diane de Poitiers, Catherine de' Medici, and
Mary Queen of Scots. Happily spending at least half a day wandering
through the château and grounds, you can see that this monument has
an undeniable feminine touch. During the peak summer season the only
drawback is the château's popularity: if you want to avoid a roomful
of schoolchildren, take a stroll on the grounds and come back to the
house at lunchtime.

More pleasure palace than fortress, the château was built in 1520 by
Thomas Bohier, a wealthy tax collector, for his wife, Catherine Briçonnet. When he went bankrupt, it passed to François I. Later, Henri II
gave it to his mistress, Diane de Poitiers. After his death, Henri's not-
so-understanding widow, Catherine de' Medici, expelled Diane to
nearby Chaumont and took back the château. Before this time, Diane's
five-arched bridge over the River Cher was simply meant as a grand
ceremonial entryway leading to a gigantic château, a building never
constructed. It was to Catherine, and her architect, Philibert de l'Orme,
that historians owe the audacious plan to transform the bridge itself into
the most unusual château in France. Two stories were constructed over
the river, including an enormous gallery that runs from one end of the
château to the other. This design might seem the height of originality
but, in fact, was inspired by Florence's covered Ponte Vecchio bridge,
commissioned by a Medici queen homesick for her native town.

July and August are the peak months at Chenonceau: Only then can
you escape the madding crowds by exiting at the far end of the gallery
to walk along the opposite bank (weekends only), rent a rowboat to
spend an hour just drifting in the river (where Diane used to enjoy her
morning dips), and enjoy the **Promenade Nocturne,** an evocative son
et lumière performed in the illuminated château gardens.

Before you go inside, pick up an English-language leaflet at the gate.
Then walk around to the right of the main building to see the harmonious, delicate architecture beyond the formal garden—the southern part
belonged to Diane de Poitiers, the northern was Catherine's—with the
river gliding under the arches (providing superb "air-conditioning" to
the rooms above). Inside the château are splendid ceilings, colossal fireplaces, scattered furnishings, and paintings by Rubens, del Sarto, and
Correggio. The curatorial staff have delightfully dispensed with velvet
ropes and adorned some of the rooms with bouquets designed in 17th-
century style. As you tour the salons, be sure to pay your respects to
former owner Madame Dupin, tellingly captured in Nattier's charming
portrait: Thanks to the affection she inspired among her proletarian
neighbors, the château and its treasures survived the Revolution intact
(her grave is enshrined near the northern embankment). The château's
history is illustrated with wax figures in the **Musée des Cires** (Waxwork

Museum) in one of the château's outbuildings. A cafeteria, tearoom, and the ambitious Orangerie restaurant handle the crowds' varied appetites. ☎ *02–47–23–90–07* 🌐 *www.chenonceau.com* 🎫 *Château €11; including Musée des Cires, €13; night visit of gardens €5* 🕒 *Mid-Feb.–Mar., daily 9:30–6; Apr. and May, daily 9–7; June and Sept., daily 9–7:30; July and Aug., daily 9–8; Oct., daily 9–6; mid-Nov.–mid-Feb., daily 9:30–5.*

WHERE TO STAY

For expanded hotel reviews, visit Fodors.com.

$ HOTEL 🏨 **La Roseraie.** Set around a vast pool terrace and within walking distance of the château, these delightful guest rooms designed with florals, checks, and lace are overseen by charming (and English-speaking) hosts, Laurent and Sophie Fiorito. **Pros:** wonderful welcome; free Wi-Fi; verdant setting. **Cons:** some rooms in separate block; street noise in some rooms. $ *Rooms from: €89* ✉ *7 rue du Dr-Bretonneau* ☎ *02–47–23–90–09* 🌐 *www.hotel-chenonceau.com* 🛏 *13 rooms, 2 suites* 🕒 *Closed mid-Nov.–mid-Feb.* 🍴 *Breakfast.*

$$ HOTEL Fodor's Choice ★ 🏨 **Le Bon Laboureur.** In 1882 this ivy-covered inn won Henry James's praise, and thanks to four generations of the Jeudi family, the author might be even more impressed today—this remains one of the Loire's most stylish and wonderful auberges, with guest rooms enchantingly accented in toile de Jouy fabrics and Redouté pink-and-blue pastels. **Pros:** charming decor; outstanding food. **Cons:** small bathrooms; some rooms overlook busy road. $ *Rooms from: €129* ✉ *6 rue du Dr-Bretonneau* ☎ *02–47–23–90–02* 🌐 *www.bonlaboureur.com* 🛏 *25 rooms* 🕒 *Closed mid-Nov.–mid-Dec.* 🍴 *Some meals.*

CHAUMONT-SUR-LOIRE

26 km (16 miles) northeast of Chenonceaux via D176/D62, 21 km (13 miles) southwest of Blois.

Château de Chaumont. Although a favorite of Loire connoisseurs, the 16th-century Château de Chaumont is often overlooked by visitors who are content to ride the conveyor belt of big châteaux like Chambord and Chenonceau, and it's their loss. Set on a dramatic bluff that towers over the river, Chaumont has always cast a spell—perhaps literally so. One of its fabled owners, Catherine de' Medici, occasionally came here with her court "astrologer," the notorious Ruggieri. In one of Chaumont's bell-tower rooms, the queen reputedly practiced sorcery. Whether or not Ruggieri still haunts the place (or Nostradamus, another on Catherine's guest list), there seem to be few castles as spirit-warm as this one.

Centerpiece of a gigantic park (a stiff walk up a long path from the little village of Chaumont-sur-Loire; cars and taxis can also drop you off at the top of the hill) and built by Charles II d'Amboise between 1465 and 1510, the château greets visitors with glorious, twin-tower *châtelets*—twin turrets that frame a double drawbridge. The castle became the residence of Henri II. After his death his widow Catherine de' Medici took revenge on his mistress, the fabled beauty Diane de Poitiers, and forced her to exchange Chenonceau for Chaumont. Another "refugee" was the late-18th-century writer Madame de Staël. Exiled from Paris by Napoléon, she wrote *De l'Allemagne* (*On Germany*) here, a book that helped kick-start the Romantic movement in France. In the 19th century her descendants, the Prince and Princess de Broglie, set up regal shop, as you can still see from the stone-and-brick stables, where purebred horses (and one elephant) lived like royalty in velvet-lined stalls. The couple also renovated many rooms in the glamorous neo-Gothic style of the 1870s. Today their sense of fantasy is retained in the castle's **Festival International des Jardins** (€11), held April to October in the extensive park and featuring the latest in horticultural invention, and with contemporary art installations in different rooms of the château. Chaumont is one of the more difficult locations to reach via public transportation, but you can take a five-minute cab ride from the nearest train station across the river at Onzain. ☎ *02–54–20–99–22* 🌐 *www.domaine-chaumont.fr* 🎟 *€10 (€16 for combined château-festival entrance)* 🕒 *Apr.–Sept., daily 10–6:30; Oct.–Mar., daily 10–5.*

WHERE TO STAY

For expanded hotel reviews, visit Fodors.com.

$$$$ HOTEL 🏨 **Domaine des Hauts-de-Loire.** An 18th-century, turreted, vine-covered hunting lodge is replete with a grand salon furnished with 18th-century antiques, a lovely pool, an adorable swan lake, and guest rooms that more often than not are simply beige and elegantly suave; those in the adjacent coach house can be considerably more spectacular—the best have exposed brick walls and timbered cathedral ceilings. **Pros:** kingly service; luxurious style; superb dining. **Cons:** no château architecture; pricey restaurant. [$] *Rooms from: €250* ✉ *Rte. de Herbault, across Loire from Chaumont, some 4 km (2 miles) inland, Onzain* ☎ *02–54–20–72–57* 🌐 *www.domainehautsloire.com* 🛏 *25 rooms, 11 suites* 🕒 *Closed Dec.–Feb.* 🍴 *Some meals.*

$ HOTEL 🏨 **Hostellerie du Château.** Set on a bank of the Loire directly opposite the road leading up to Chaumont's château, this quaint edifice built in the early 20th century as a hotel and soars up four stories to its half-timber eaves in a vision that charmingly conjures up the grace of earlier days, offering guest rooms with cheerfully colored walls and crisp white bed quilts. **Pros:** handy setting; good value; free Wi-Fi. **Cons:** street-facing rooms are noisy; restaurant service can be slow. [$] *Rooms from: €77* ✉ *2 rue du Mal-de-Lattre-de-Tassigny* ☎ *02–54–20–98–04* 🌐 *www.hostellerie-du-chateau.com* 🛏 *15 rooms* 🕒 *Closed mid-Nov.–mid-Mar.* 🍴 *No meals.*

CHEVERNY

24 km (15 miles) east of Chaumont, 14 km (9 miles) southeast of Blois.

Château de Cheverny. Perhaps best remembered as Capitaine Haddock's mansion in the Tintin comic books, the Château de Cheverny is also iconic for its restrained 17th-century elegance. One of the last in the area to be built, it was finished in 1634, at a time when the rich and famous had mostly stopped building in the Loire Valley. By then, the taste for quaintly shaped châteaux had given way to disciplined Classicism; so here a white, elegantly proportioned, horizontally coursed, single-block facade greets you across manicured lawns. To emphasize the strict symmetry of the plan, a ruler-straight drive leads to the front

DID YOU KNOW?

Catherine de' Medici commissioned Chenonceau's river-spanning design because, homesick for her hometown, she wanted to pay homage to Florence's covered Ponte Vecchio.

entrance. The Louis XIII interior with its stridently painted and gilded rooms, splendid furniture, and rich tapestries depicting the Labors of Hercules is one of the few still intact in the Loire region. Despite the priceless Delft vases and Persian embroideries, it feels lived in. That's because it's one of the rare Loire Valley houses still occupied by a noble family. You can visit a small Tintin exhibition called *Le Secret de Moulinsart* (admission extra) and are free to contemplate the antlers of 2,000 stags in the Trophy Room: hunting, called "venery" in the leaflets, continues vigorously here, with red coats, bugles, and all. In the château's kennels, hordes of hungry hounds lounge around dreaming of their next kill. Feeding times—*la soupe aux chiens*—are posted on a notice board (usually 5 pm in summer), and you are welcome to watch the "ceremony" (delicate sensibilities beware: the dogs line up like statues and are called, one by one, to wolf down their meal from the trainer). ☎ *02–54–79–96–29* ⊕ *www.chateau-cheverny.fr* ⊠ *€9, €13.50 with Tintin exhibition; €19.20 including Tintin exhibition and boat-and-buggy rides* ⊙ *Apr.–Sept., daily 9:15–6:15; Oct.–Mar., daily 9:45–5.*

CHAMBORD

13 km (21 miles) northeast of Chaumont-sur-Loire via D33; 19 km (12 miles) east of Blois; 45 km (28 miles) southwest of Orléans.

Fodor'sChoice The "Versailles" of the 16th century and the largest of the Loire châ-
★   teaux, the **Château de Chambord** is the kind of place William Randolph Hearst might have built if he'd had the money. Variously dubbed "megalomaniacal" and "an enormous film-set extravaganza," this is one of the most extraordinary structures in Europe, set in the middle of a royal game forest, with just a cluster of buildings—barely a village—across the road.

GETTING HERE

There is surprisingly little public transportation to famed Chambord (a state-owned château, to boot). There are no trains, but Transports du Loir-Et-Cher (⊕ *tlcinfo.net*) offers a bus route from Blois (two departures daily).

EXPLORING

FAMILY **Château de Chambord.** As you travel the gigantic, tree-shaded roadways that converge on Chambord, you first spot the château's incredible towers—19th-century novelist Henry James said they were "more like the spires of a city than the salient points of a single building"—rising above the forest. When the entire palace breaks into view, it is an unforgettable sight.

With a facade that is 420 feet long, 440 rooms and 365 chimneys, a wall 32 km (20 miles) long to enclose a 13,000-acre forest, the Château de Chambord is one of the greatest buildings in France. Under François I, building began in 1519, a job that took 12 years and required 1,800 workers. His original grandiose idea was to divert the Loire to form a moat, but someone (perhaps his adviser, Leonardo da Vinci, who some feel may have provided the inspiration behind the entire complex) persuaded him to make do with the River Cosson. François I used the château only for short stays; yet when he came, 12,000 horses were

4

required to transport his luggage, servants, and entourage. Later kings also used Chambord as an occasional retreat, and Louis XIV, the Sun King, had Molière perform here. In the 18th century Louis XV gave the château to the Maréchal de Saxe as a reward for his victory over the English and Dutch at Fontenoy (southern Belgium) in 1745. When not indulging in wine, women, and song, the marshal planted himself on the roof to oversee the exercises of his personal regiment of 1,000 cavalry. Now, after long neglect—all the original furnishings vanished during the French Revolution—Chambord belongs to the state.

There's plenty to see inside. You can wander freely through the vast rooms, filled with exhibits (including a hunting museum)—not all concerned with Chambord, but interesting nonetheless—and lots of Ancien Régime furnishings. The enormous double-helix staircase (probably envisioned by Leonardo, who had a thing about spirals) looks like a single staircase, but an entire regiment could march up one spiral while a second came down the other, and never the twain would meet. But the high point here in more ways than one is the spectacular chimneyscape—the roof terrace whose forest of Italianate towers, turrets, cupolas, gables, and chimneys has been compared to everything from the minarets of Constantinople to a bizarre chessboard. During the year there's a packed calendar of activities on tap, from 90-minute tours of the park in a 4x4 vehicle (€18) to guided tours on bike or horseback. A soaring three-story-tall hall has been fitted out to offer lunches and dinners. ☎ 02–54–50–40–00 ⊕ www.chambord.org 🎫 €11 ⊙ Apr.–Sept., daily 9–6; Oct.–Mar., daily 10–5.

WHERE TO EAT AND STAY

For expanded hotel reviews, visit Fodors.com.

$$$$
MODERN FRENCH

✕ **La Maison à Côté.** Just a five-minute drive from Chambord in a tiny village, this country inn serves traditional French haute cuisine in a cozy yet contemporary dining room with a fireplace, exposed beam ceilings, and wrought-iron entry gate. Specialties vary with the seasons, including the foie gras with apricot, pear, and lemon confit, the Challans duck filet with caramelized endives and Szechuan pepper, or the lacquered cod with carrots and Orléans mustard. Save room for the surprisingly creative desserts. There's plenty of free parking in the church parking lot across the street, and a handful of tastefully modern rooms from €98 for a double. $ *Average main: €40* ✉ *25 rte. de Chambord, Montlivault* ☎ *02–54–20–62–30* ⊕ *www.lamaisondacote.fr* ⊙ *Closed Tues. and Wed. Hotel closed Nov. 16–Dec. 3 and Dec. 28–Jan. 14.*

$$
B&B/INN
Fodor'sChoice
★

🏰 **Château de Colliers.** Small enough to consider it your own home, stuffed like a chocolate with delicious 18th-century decor, and replete with the most beautiful river terrace, this overlooked treasure proves— for a few lucky travelers—to be the most unforgettable château in the Loire. **Pros:** authentic antique furnishings; unique riverside setting. **Cons:** grounds and exterior a bit worse for wear; surrounding area fairly dull. $ *Rooms from: €145* ✉ *Rue Nationale (D951), 8 km (4 miles) northwest of Chambord, 17 km (10 miles) southwest of Blois, Muides-sur-Loire* ☎ *02–54–87–50–75* ⊕ *www.chateau-colliers.com* 🛏 *3 rooms, 2 suites* ⊚*Breakfast.*

The beautiful Château de Colliers is one of the most charming hotels along the Loire—it is so petite you'll almost think it is your own home.

$ **Grand St-Michel.** A revamped hunting lodge right out of the pages of
HOTEL   a Flaubert novel is grandly set across the lawn from Chambord's fabled
château and offers a cozy lobby, solidly bourgeois if slightly outdated
guest rooms, and a 19th-century-flavored restaurant, splendidly set with
mounted deer heads, majolica serving platters, and thick curtains. **Pros:**
wondrous location opposite Chambord; impressive, good-value restaurant; free parking. **Cons:** creeky hallways; old-fashioned decor; staff can
be rather cold. *$ Rooms from: €84 ⊠ Pl. St-Louis ☎ 02–54–20–31–31
⊕ www.saintmichel-chambord.com ⌁ 40 rooms ⊗ Closed mid-Nov.–
mid-Dec., and a few days at end of Jan. ⏉ Breakfast.*

ORLÉANS

*115 km (23 miles) northeast of Chambord; 112 km (70 miles) northeast
of Tours; 125 km (78 miles) south of Paris.*

The story of the Hundred Years' War, Joan of Arc, and the Siege of Orléans is widely known. In 1429 France had hit rock bottom. The English
and their Burgundian allies were carving up the kingdom. Besieged by
the English, Orléans was one of the last towns about to yield, when a
young Lorraine peasant girl, Joan of Arc, arrived to rally the troops and
save the kingdom. During the Wars of Religion (1562–98), much of the
cathedral was destroyed. A century ago ham-fisted town planners razed
many of the city's fine old buildings. Both German and Allied bombs
helped finish the job during World War II.

Perhaps it is no surprise that Orléans once had the biggest inferiority
complex this side of Newark, New Jersey. So the townsfolk clung to the

city's finest moment—the coming of *la pucelle d'Orléans* (the Maid of Orleans), Joan of Arc, to liberate the city from the English during the Hundred Years' War. There's little left from Joan's time, but the city is festooned with everything from her equestrian monument to a Jeanne d'Arc Dry Cleaners. Today Orléans is a thriving commercial city. Better, it has a wonderful historic Vielle Ville (Old Town) district, the creation of 10 years of sensitive urban renewal, which has succeeded in adding enormous charm, especially to the medieval streets between the Loire and the city cathedral.

GETTING HERE

Trains from Paris (Gare d'Austerlitz) leave for Orléans every hour or so; the 137-km (78-mile) trip (€20.30) takes between one hour, 5 minutes and one hour, 25 minutes with a change in suburban Les Aubrais sometimes necessary. Trains run every couple of hours from Orléans to Tours (75 mins, €19.60) via Blois (25–40 mins, €10.90). Three trains daily continue to Angers (1 hr, 50 mins; €35.30).

Visitor Information Orléans Tourist Office ⊠ *2 pl. de l'Etape* ☎ *02–38–24– 05–05* ⊕ *www.tourisme-orleans.com.*

EXPLORING

Despite the city's lackluster neighborhoods, Orléans's wide array of lodging and restaurants, and its superb transportation connections, make it a comfy and leading base for exploring the châteaux, villages, and forests nearby. Thankfully, the Vielle Ville quarter has been gorgeously restored and lends a big dollop of charm to the city with its pedestrian-only streets that are home to many sidewalk cafés and boutiques. And thanks to the tramway it's a snap getting from the train station directly to the Old Town and the banks of the Loire.

Cathédrale Ste-Croix. The Cathédrale Ste-Croix is a riot of pinnacles and gargoyles, both Gothic and pseudo-Gothic, embellished with 18th-century wedding-cake towers. After most of the cathedral was destroyed in the 16th century during the Wars of Religion, Henry IV and his successors rebuilt it. Novelist Marcel Proust (1871–1922) called it France's ugliest church, but most find it impressive. Inside are dramatic stained glass and 18th-century wood carvings, plus the modern **Chapelle de Jeanne d'Arc** (Joan of Arc Chapel), with plaques in memory of British and American war dead. ⊠ *Pl. Ste-Croix* ☉ *May–Sept., daily 9:15–6; Oct.–Apr., daily 9:15–noon and 2–6.*

Fodor'sChoice
★
Hôtel Groslot. Just across the square from the cathedral is the Hôtel Groslot, a Renaissance-era extravaganza (1549–55) bristling with caryatids, strap work, and Flemish columns. Inside are regal salons redolent of the city's history (this used to be the Town Hall), all done in the most sumptuous 19th-century Gothic Troubadour style and perhaps haunted by King François II (who died here in 1560 by the side of his bride, Mary Queen of Scots). ⊠ *Pl. de l'Étape* ☎ *02–38–79–22–30* ⊠ *Free* ☉ *June–Aug., Sun.–Fri. 9–6; Sept.–May, Sun.–Fri. 9–noon and 2–6.*

Maison de Jeanne d'Arc (*Joan of Arc House*). During the 10-day Siege of Orléans in 1429, 17-year-old Joan of Arc stayed on the site of the Maison de Jeanne d'Arc. This faithful reconstruction of the house she knew contains exhibits about her life and costumes and weapons of her time.

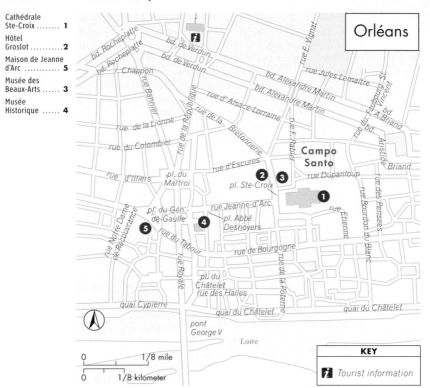

Several dioramas modeled by Lucien Harmey recount the main episodes in her life, from the audience at Chinon to the coronation at Reims, her capture at Compiègne, and her burning at the stake at Rouen. ✉ *3 pl. du Général-de-Gaulle* ☎ *02–38–68–32–63* ⊕ *www.jeannedarc.com. fr* 💶 *€4* ⏱ *Oct.–Mar., Tues.–Sun. 2–6; Apr.–Sept., Tues.–Sun. 10–6.*

Musée des Beaux-Arts (*Fine Arts Museum*). Take the elevator to the top of this five-story building across from the cathedral then make your way down to see works by such artists as Tintoretto, Velázquez, Watteau, Boucher, Rodin, and Gauguin. The museum's richest collection is its 17th-century French paintings, prints, and drawings, reputedly second only to the Louvre. ✉ *1 rue Fernand-Rabier* ☎ *02–38–79–21–55* 💶 *€4, joint ticket with History and Archaeology Museum* ⏱ *Tues.–Sun. 10–6.*

Musée Historique et Archéologique (*History and Archaeology Museum*). Housed in the **Hôtel Cabu**, a Renaissance mansion restored after World War II, the Musée Historique et Archéologique contains works of both "fine" and "popular" art connected with the town's past, including a remarkable collection of pagan bronzes of animals and dancers. These bronzes were hidden from zealous Christian missionaries in the 4th century and discovered in a sandpit near St-Benoît in 1861. An exposition is dedicated to the life of Jeanne d'Arc. ✉ *Sq. de l'Abbé-Desnoyers* ☎ *02–38–79–25–60* 💶 *€4, joint ticket with Fine Arts Museum* ⏱ *Tues.– Sat. 9:30–noon and 1:30–5:45, Sun. 2–6.*

WHERE TO EAT AND STAY

For expanded hotel reviews, visit Fodors.com.

$$$$ MODERN FRENCH 🍴 **Le Lift.** Decorated with quirky contemporary statues, this is a surprisingly modern and stylish restaurant. Using only the freshest local ingredients, chef Philippe Bardeau combines textures and flavors to create a colorfully vibrant cuisine. Large windows offer views of the leafy park across the way (and, thankfully, not of the cineplex, which sits just below the restaurant); reserve a seat on the panoramic terrace overlooking the Loire River when the weather is warm. This is an excellent choice for a night out with friends, but the noisy atmosphere doesn't lend itself to a romantic rendezvous. [$] *Average main: €33* ✉ *Pl. de la Loire* ☎ *02–38–53–63–48* 🌐 *www.restaurant-le-lift.com.*

$$ B&B/INN 🏨 **Château de Champvallins.** When you enter the gates of Jacqueline Létang's magnificent 18th-century estate, with its vast wooded grounds and guest rooms decked out in luxury, you'll immediately feel the outside world melt away. **Pros:** authentic antique furnishings; peaceful forest setting; friendly welcome. **Cons:** no restaurant; only accessible by car. [$] *Rooms from: €140* ✉ *1079 rue de Champvallins, 12 km (7 miles) southeast of Orléans, Sandillon* ☎ *02–38–41–16–53* 🌐 *www.chateaudechampvallins.com* 🛏 *5 rooms* 🍽 *Breakfast.*

$ HOTEL Fodor's Choice ★ 🏨 **L'Abeille.** Conveniently located on the main shopping street in Orléans, this charming, bright, and cozy family-run hotel—a block from the train/tram station—welcomes guests in rooms with fresh floral wall coverings, parquet flooring, and immaculate tiled bathrooms (many as large as the rooms). **Pros:** easily accessible by train; free Wi-Fi; extra-spacious rooms. **Cons:** rooms facing street can be noisy; pricey city parking. [$] *Rooms from: €79* ✉ *64 rue Alsace Lorraine* ☎ *02–38–53–54–87* 🌐 *www.hoteldelabeille.com* 🛏 *28 rooms* 🍽 *Some meals.*

$ HOTEL 🏨 **Le Rivage.** This small, white-walled hotel with restaurant views over the Loiret River is a little off the beaten track (take the N20 south from Orléans to Olivet, then turn right into avenue de Verdun and continue parallel to the River Loiret for a mile or so) but it makes a pleasant base. **Pros:** quiet setting; riverside restaurant. **Cons:** can be damp in fall and spring; tiny bathrooms; few staff speak English. [$] *Rooms from: €85* ✉ *635 rue de la Reine-Blanche, 5 km (3 miles) south of Orléans, Olivet* ☎ *02–38–66–02–93* 🌐 *www.lerivage-olivet.com* 🛏 *17 rooms* ⏰ *Closed late Dec.–mid-Jan.* 🍽 *Some meals.*

NIGHTLIFE AND THE ARTS

Fêtes de Jeanne d'Arc (*Joan of Arc Festival*). Held in early May, the Fêtes de Jeanne d'Arc celebrates the heroic Maid of Orléans with a parade, religious procession, medieval fair, and reenactments of the famous siege of Orléans. 🌐 *www.fetesjeannedarc.com.*

BLOIS

54 km (34 miles) southwest of Orléans, 58 km (36 miles) northeast of Tours.

Perched on a steep hillside overlooking the Loire, site of one of France's most historic châteaux, and birthplace of those delicious Poulain

Bike Tour Options

With its nearly flat terrain, the Loire Valley is custom-built for traveling by bike, and the recently added Loire à Vélo signposted bike trails extending 800 km (500 miles) from Orléans to the Atlantic Ocean make it even easier to cycle between each town and village. Bike rental agencies and trail maps are easily found in the towns along the route for independent exploration. For stress-free planning, local bike tour companies such as Biking France and Loire à Vélo offer turnkey self-guided vacations of two–six days for which they arrange the hotels, restaurants, itineraries, maps, baggage transfers, and bike hire for as little as €150 per day per person. They even have electric bikes for those who prefer to glide sans effort. The Anjou tourism offices in Angers and Saumur also rent out "Cyclopédia"

GPS gadgets that attach to your bike and guide you through the paths and sights of the Anjou region. The bigger towns all have bike rental agencies— one of the top agencies is Loire Vélo Nature. Though based in Bréhémont, it has more than a dozen outlets along the Loire, where you can rent bikes from €15 a day or €55 a week.

Contacts **Anjou Vélo** ☎ 08–20–15–00–49 ⊕ www.anjou-velo.com.

Biking France ⊠ 2 rue Jean Moulin, Blois ☎ 02–54–78–62–52 ⊕ www.biking-france.com.

Loire à Vélo ⊠ 37 av. de Paris, Orléans ☎ 02–38–79–95–28 ⊕ www.loire-a-velo.fr.

Loire Vélo Nature ⊠ 7 rue des Déportés, Bréhémont ☎ 06–03–89–23–14 ⊕ www.loirevelonature.com.

chocolates and gâteaux (check out the bakeries along rue Denis-Papin), the bustling big town of Blois is a convenient base, well served by train and highway.

GETTING HERE

Trains from Paris (Gare d'Austerlitz) leave for Blois every one or two hours; the 185-km (115-mile) trip (€27.80) takes between one hour, 30 minutes and one hour, 55 minutes. There are trains every two hours or so from Blois to Tours (30–40 mins, €10.60) and Orléans (25–40 mins, €10.90).

Visitor Information **Blois Tourist Office** ⊠ 23 pl. du Château ☎ 02–54–90–41–41 ⊕ www.bloispaysdechambord.com.

EXPLORING

A signposted route leads you on a walking tour of Blois's **Vieille Ville (Old Town)**—a romantic honeycomb of twisting alleys, cobblestone streets, and half-timber houses—but it's best explored with the help of a map available from the tourist office. The historic highlight is place St-Louis, where you can find the Maison des Acrobats (note the timbers carved with *jongleurs*, or jugglers), Cathédrale St-Louis, and unexpected Renaissance-era galleries and staircases lurking in tucked-away courtyards.

Château de Blois. The massive Château de Blois spans several architectural periods and is among the valley's finest. Your ticket entitles you to a guided tour—given in English when there are enough visitors who don't understand French—but you're more than welcome to roam around without a guide. Before you enter, stand in the courtyard to admire examples of four centuries of architecture. On one side stand the 13th-century hall and tower, the latter offering a stunning view of the town and countryside. The Renaissance begins to flower in the Louis XII wing (built between 1498 and 1503), through which you enter, and comes to full bloom in the François I wing (1515–24). The masterpiece here is the openwork spiral staircase, painstakingly restored. The fourth side consists of the Classical Gaston d'Orléans wing (1635–38). Upstairs in the François I wing is a series of enormous rooms with tremendous fireplaces decorated with the gilded porcupine, emblem of Louis XII, the ermine of Anne of Brittany, and, of course, François I's salamander, breathing fire and surrounded by flickering flames. Many rooms have intricate ceilings and carved, gilt paneling. In the council room the Duke of Guise was murdered by order of Henri III in 1588. Every evening mid-April through mid-September, **son-et-lumière** shows are staged (in English on Wednesday); tickets cost €7.50 (joint ticket with château €14.50). ☎ *02–54–90–33–33* 🌐 *www.chateaudeblois.fr* 🎫 *€9.50* 🕒 *Jan.–Mar., daily 9–12:30 and 1:30–5:30; Apr.–June, daily 9–6:30; July and Aug., daily 9–7; Sept., daily 9–6:30; Oct., daily 9–6; Nov. and Dec., daily 9–12:30 and 1:30–5:30.*

4

WHERE TO EAT AND STAY

For expanded hotel reviews, visit Fodors.com.

$$$$ SEAFOOD 🍴 **Au Rendez-Vous des Pêcheurs.** This friendly restaurant in an old grocery near the Loire has simple decor but impressively creative cooking. Chef Christophe Cosme was an apprentice with Burgundy's late Bernard Loiseau, and his inventive dishes range from fish and seafood specialties (try the crayfish-and-parsley flan) to succulent baby pigeon on a bed of cabbage. [$] *Average main: €35* ✉ *27 rue du Foix* ☎ *02–54–74–67–48* 🌐 *www.rendezvousdespecheurs.com* ✍ *Reservations essential* 🕒 *Closed Sun. and Mon. and 2 wks in Aug.*

$$ B&B/INN 🏨 **Le Clos Pasquier.** Time seems to have stood still at Claire and Laurent's snug 16th-century countryside manor set on the edge of the forest, an inviting place featuring heavy wooden beams, well-worn terra-cotta floor tiles, and welcoming stone fireplaces. **Pros:** luxurious bedding; historic building; direct bus to town center. **Cons:** no restaurant; not in town center. [$] *Rooms from: €115* ✉ *10–12 impasse de l'Orée du Bois* ☎ *02–54–58–84–08* 🌐 *www.leclospasquier.fr* 🛏 *2 rooms, 2 suites* 🍽 *Some meals.*

$ HOTEL 🏨 **Le Médicis.** Known far and wide for its exceptional restaurant, this smart little hotel 1 km (½ mile) from the Château de Blois has guest rooms that are comfortable, air-conditioned, and soundproof; all share a joyous color scheme but are individually decorated. **Pros:** soundproof rooms; excellent Renaissance-style dining room. **Cons:** no views; no elevator; not in town center. [$] *Rooms from: €87* ✉ *2 allée François-Ier* ☎ *02–54–43–94–04* 🌐 *www.le-medicis.com* 🛏 *8 rooms, 2 suites* 🕒 *Closed 3 wks in Jan.* 🍽 *Some meals.*

$$ B&B/INN 🏨 **16 Place Saint Louis.** Situated in the heart of Blois's Old Town across the square from the St-Louis Cathedral, this elegant bed-and-breakfast

gives guests the experience of staying in a classic haute bourgeoise home. **Pros:** convenient location in historic center; beautifully appointed, antiques-bedecked home. **Cons:** shared bathroom for the rooms; no space for large luggage. [$] *Rooms from: €90* ✉ *16 pl. Saint Louis* ☎ *02–54–74–13–61* 🌐 *www.16placesaintlouis.fr* 🛏 *2 rooms, 1 suite* 💳 *No credit cards* ⏲ *Closed 3 wks in Jan.* 🍴 *Some meals.*

FROM VILLANDRY TO LANGEAIS

To the west of Tours, breathtaking châteaux dot the Indre Valley between the regional capital and the historic town of Chinon on the River Vienne. This is the most glamorous part of the Val de Loire, and the beauty pageant begins with the fabled gardens of the Château de Villandry. Your journey then continues on to the fairy-tale châteaux of Azay-le-Rideaux, Ussé, and Montreuil-Bellay. Farther on, no one will want to miss the towns of Chinon, Saumur, Fontevraud, and Langeais, which contain sights that remain the quintessence of romantic medievalism. Along the way, you can savor such storybook delights as Saché—perhaps the Loire's prettiest village—and the historic fortress of Angers.

VILLANDRY

18 km (11 miles) west of Tours via D7, 48 km (30 miles) northwest of Loches.

Fodor's Choice ★ **Château de Villandry.** Green-thumbers get weak in the knees at the mere mention of the Château de Villandry, a grand estate near the Cher River, thanks to its painstakingly relaid 16th-century **gardens,** now the finest example of Renaissance garden design in France. These were originally planted in 1906 by Dr. Joachim Carvallo and Anne Coleman, his American wife, whose passion resulted in three terraces planted in styles that combine the French monastic garden with Italianate models depicted in historic Du Cerceau etchings. Seen from Villandry's cliff-side walkway, the garden terraces look like flowered chessboards blown up to the nth power—a breathtaking sight.

Beyond the water garden and an ornamental garden depicting symbols of chivalric love is the famous *potager,* or vegetable garden, which stretches on for bed after bed—the pumpkins here are *les pièces de résistance.* Flower lovers will rejoice in the main *jardin à la française* (French-style garden): framed by a canal, it's a vast carpet of rare and colorful blooms planted *en broderie* ("like embroidery"), set into patterns by box hedges and paths. The aromatic and medicinal garden, its plots neatly labeled in three languages, is especially appealing. Below an avenue of 1,200 precisely pruned lime trees lies an ornamental lake that is home to two swans: not a ripple is out of place. The château interior, still used by the Carvallo family, was redecorated in the mid-18th century; of particular note are the painted and gilt Moorish ceiling from Toledo and one of the finest collections of 17th-century Spanish paintings in France. Note that the quietest time to visit is usually during the two-hour French lunch break, while the most photogenic time is during the **Nuits des Mille Feux** (Nights of a Thousand Lights, held the

DID YOU KNOW?

Almost as famed as the vegetable gardens at the Château de Villandry are its gardens à la française, whose hedges are strikingly shaped into symbols of love, including hearts, fans, and daggers.

first weekend in July), when paths and pergolas are illuminated with myriad lanterns and a dance troupe offers a tableau vivant. There is a gardening weekend held in late September and a music festival in October. There is no train station at Villandry, but the Line V bus between Tours and Azay-le-Rideau stops there every Wednesday and Saturday, daily in July and August; you can also train to nearby Savonnières and taxi the rest of the 4-km (2½-mile) distance. ✉ *3 rue Principale* ☎ *02–47–50–02–09* 🌐 *www.chateauvillandry.com* 🎟 *Château and gardens €9.50, gardens only €6.50* 🕒 *Château Apr.–Oct., daily 9–6; mid-Feb., Mar., and 1st half Nov., daily 9–5. Gardens Apr.–Sept., daily 9–7; Oct.–mid-Nov., daily 9–5.*

THE VERSAILLES OF VEGETABLES

Organized in square patterns, Villandry's world-famous *potager* (vegetable garden) is seasonally ablaze with purple cabbages, bright pumpkins, and many other heirloom veggies. In total, there are nearly 150,000 plantings, with two seasonal shows presented—the spring show is a veritable "salad." The fall show comes to fruition in late September or early October and is the one with the pumpkins. Paging Cinderella.

WHERE TO STAY

For expanded hotel reviews, visit Fodors.com.

$ HOTEL 🏨 **Auberge Le Colombien.** Just a few steps away from the château, this humble yet cozy inn with country-style rooms is on the main street in the heart of Villandry village. **Pros:** on-site restaurant; free Wi-Fi; historic building. **Cons:** small windows; right on main road; few amenities. [$] *Rooms from: €78* ✉ *2 rue de la Mairie* ☎ *02–47–50–07–27* 🌐 *www.hotel-villandry.com* 🛏 *14 rooms* 🍴 *Some meals.*

AZAY-LE-RIDEAU

11 km (7 miles) south of Villandry via D39, 27 km (17 miles) southwest of Tours.

A largish town surrounding a sylvan dell on the banks of the River Indre, pleasant Azay-le-Rideau (located on the main train line between Tours and Chinon) is famed for its white-wall Renaissance pleasure palace, called "a faceted diamond set in the Indre Valley" by Honoré de Balzac.

Château d'Azay-le-Rideau. The 16th-century Château d'Azay-le-Rideau was created as a literal fairy-tale castle. When it was constructed in the Renaissance era, the nouveau-riche treasurer Gilles Berthelot decided he wanted to add tall corner turrets, a moat, and machicolations to conjure up the distant seigneurial past when knighthood was in flower and two families, the Azays and the Ridels, ruled this terrain. It was never a serious fortress—it certainly offered no protection to its builder when a financial scandal forced him to flee France shortly after the château's completion in 1529. For centuries the château passed from one private owner to another until it was finally bought by the State in 1905. Though the interior contains an interesting blend of furniture and artwork (one room is an homage to the Marquis de Biencourt who, in the early 20th century, led the way in renovating château interiors in sumptuous fashion—sadly, many of his elegant furnishings were later sold), you may wish to spend most of your time exploring the enchanting gardens, complete with a moat-like lake. Innovative **son-et-lumière** shows are held on the grounds from 10:30 pm, July and August (€10 or €14 joint ticket with château). ☎ *02–47–45–42–04* 🌐 *azay-le-rideau.monuments-nationaux.fr* 🎫 *€8.50* 🕒 *Apr.–June and Sept., daily 9:30–6; July and Aug., daily 9:30–7; Oct.–Mar., daily 10–5:15.*

WHERE TO STAY

For expanded hotel reviews, visit Fodors.com.

$ B&B/INN 🏨 **Hotel Biencourt.** Charmingly set on the pedestrian street that leads to Azay's château gates, this shuttered town house has a delightful courtyard-garden that hides an authentic, 19th-century schoolhouse, now fitted out with rooms cozily furnished in traditional country schoolhouse style (and with the stray blackboard and school desk). **Pros:** families welcome; free Wi-Fi; handicap-accessible room. **Cons:** no private parking; thin walls. [$] *Rooms from: €72* ✉ *7 rue Balzac* ☎ *02–47–45–20–75* 🌐 *www.hotelbiencourt.com* 🛏 *17 rooms* 🕒 *Closed mid-Nov.–mid-Mar.* 🍴 *No meals.*

$ HOTEL 🏨 **Le Grand Monarque.** Home to one of France's most beauteous châteaux, Azay should rightly have a hotel that befits the town jewel and this landmark—a three-minute walk from the château gates—nicely fits the bill. **Pros:** fine restaurant with large wine list; town-center setting; free Wi-Fi. **Cons:** some rooms need redecorating; distracted staff. [$] *Rooms from: €100* ✉ *3 pl. de la République* ☎ *02–47–45–40–08* 🌐 *www.legrandmonarque.com* 🛏 *22 rooms, 2 suites* 🕒 *Closed Nov.–Feb.* 🍴 *Some meals.*

THE OUTDOORS

Leprovost. Rent bikes from Leprovost to ride along the Indre; the area around Azay-le-Rideau is among the most tranquil and scenic in Touraine. ✉ *13 rue Carnot* ☎ *02–47–45–40–94.*

SACHÉ

7 km (4½ miles) east of Azay-le-Rideau via D17.

Fodor's Choice ★ A crook in the road, a Gothic church, the centuries-old Auberge du XIIe Siècle, an Alexander Calder stabile (the great American sculptor created a modern atelier nearby), and the country retreat of novelist Honoré de Balzac (1799–1850)—these few but choice elements all add up to Saché, one of the prettiest (and most undiscovered) nooks in the Val de Loire. If you're heading into the town from the east, you're first welcomed by the **Pont-de-Ruan**—a dream sequence of a flower-bedecked bridge, water mill, and lake that is so picturesque it will practically click your camera for you.

Château de Saché. In the center of town is the Château de Saché, which contains the **Musée Balzac.** If you've never read any of Balzac's "Comédie Humaine," you might find little of interest here; but if you have, and do, you can return to such novels as *Cousine Bette* and *Eugénie Grandet* with fresh enthusiasm and understanding. Much of the landscape around here, and some of the people back then, found immortality by being fictionalized in many a Balzac novel. Surrounded by 6 acres of gardens, the present château, built between the 16th and the 18th century, is more of a comfortable country house than a fortress. Born in Tours, Balzac came here—to stay with his friends, the Margonnes—during the 1830s, both to write such works as *Le Père Goriot* and to escape his creditors. The château houses substantial exhibits, ranging from photographs to original manuscripts to the coffee service Balzac used to enjoy the caffeine that helped to keep him writing up to 16 hours a day. A few period rooms impress with 19th-century charm, including a lavish emerald-green salon and the author's writing room. Be sure to study some of the corrected author proofs on display. Balzac had to pay for corrections and additions beyond a certain limit. Painfully in debt, he made emendations filling all the margins of his proofs, causing dismay to his printers. Their legitimate bills for extra payment meant that some of his books, best sellers for nearly two centuries, failed to bring him a centime. ☎ *02–47–26–86–50* 🌐 *www.musee-balzac.fr* 🎫 *€5* 🕒 *Apr.–June and Sept., daily 10–6; July and Aug., daily 10–7; Oct.–Mar., Wed.–Mon. 10–12:30 and 2–5.*

WHERE TO EAT

$$$$ FRENCH Fodor's Choice ★ 🍴 **Auberge du XIIe Siècle.** You half expect Balzac himself to come strolling in the door of this half-timber, delightfully historic auberge, so little has it changed since the 19th century. Still sporting a time-stained painted sign and its original exterior staircase, and nearly opposite the great author's country retreat, this inn retains its centuries-old dining room, now warmed by a fireplace, bouquets, and rich wood tables. Beyond this room is a modern extension—all airy glass and white walls but not exactly what you're looking for in such historic surrounds. Balzac's ample girth attested to his great love of food, and he would no doubt enjoy the sautéed lobster or the nouvelle spins on his classic *géline* chicken favorites served here today, or the *aiguillettes de canard rosées en réduction de Chinon* (slices of duck flavored in Chinon wine). Dessert is excellent, and so is the coffee, a refreshment Balzac drank incessantly (little wonder he created more than 2,000 characters). [$] *Average main: €40* ✉ *1 rue du Château* ☎ *02–47–26–88–77* ✍ *Reservations essential* 🕒 *Closed Mon. and 2 wks in Jan., 1 wk in June, 1 wk in Sept., and 1 wk in Nov. No dinner Sun., no lunch Tues.*

USSÉ-RIGNY

14 km (9 miles) west of Azay-le-Rideau via D17 and D7.

FAMILY Fodor's Choice ★ **Château d'Ussé.** The most beautiful castle in France is first glimpsed as you approach the Château d'Ussé and an astonishing array of blue-slate roofs, dormer windows, delicate towers, and Gothic turrets greets you against the flank of the Forest of Chinon. Literature describes this château, overlooking the banks of the River Indre, as the original *Sleeping Beauty* castle; Charles Perrault—author of this beloved 17th-century tale—spent time here as a guest of the Count of Saumur, and legend has it that Ussé inspired him to write the famous story. Though parts of the castle are from the 1400s, most of it was completed two centuries later.

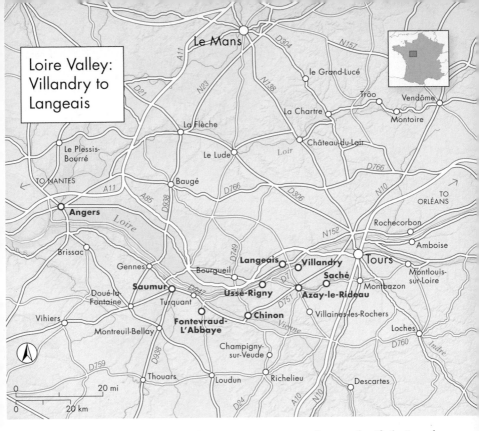

0   20 mi

0   20 km

By the 17th century, the region was so secure that one fortified wing of the castle was demolished to allow for grand vistas over the valley and the castle gardens, newly designed in the style Le Nôtre had made so fashionable at Versailles.

Only Disney could have outdone this white-tufa marvel: the château is a flamboyant mix of Gothic and Renaissance styles—romantic and built for fun, not for fighting. Its history supports this playful image: it endured no bloodbaths—no political conquests or conflicts—while a tablet in the chapel indicates that even the French Revolution passed it by. Inside, a tour leads you through several sumptuous period salons, a 19th-century French fashion exhibit, and the Salle de Roi bedchamber built for a visit by King Louis XV (the red-silk, canopied four-poster bed is the stuff of dreams). At the end of the house tour, you can go up the fun spiral staircases to the *chemin de ronde* of the lofty towers; there are pleasant views of the Indre River from the battlements, and you can also find rooms filled with waxwork effigies detailing the fable of Sleeping Beauty herself. Kids will love this.

Before you leave, visit the exquisite Gothic-becomes-Renaissance chapel in the garden, built for Charles d'Espinay and his wife in 1523–35. Note the door decorated with pleasingly sinister skull-and-crossbones carvings. Just a few steps from the chapel are two towering cedars of Lebanon—a gift from the genius-poet of Romanticism, Viscount René de Chateaubriand, to the lady of the house, the Duchess of Duras. When her famous amour died in 1848, she stopped all the clocks in the house—à la Sleeping Beauty—"so as never to hear struck the hours you will not come again." The castle then was inherited by her relations, the Comte and Comtesse de la Rochejaquelin, one of the most dashing couples of the 19th century. Today, Ussé belongs to their descendant, the Duc de Blacas, who is as soigné as his castle. If you do meet him, proffer thanks, as every night his family floodlights the entire château, a vision that is one of the Loire Valley's dreamiest sights. Long regarded as a symbol of *la vieille France,* Ussé can't be topped for fairy-tale splendor, so make this a must-do. ✉ *Rigny-Ussé* ☎ *02–47–95–54–05* 🌐 *www.chateaudusse.fr* 🎟 *€14* 🕒 *Mid-Feb.–mid-Nov., daily 10–6.*

A GARDEN NAMED L'ÉLÉGANCE

Jardins de la Chatonnière. Set 4 km (2½ miles) north of Azay-le-Rideau and tended by Madame Béatrice de Andia—one of the grandes dames of the Loire—and her staff are the Jardins de la Chatonnière, a 15-acre rose and lily garden that will make most emerald-green with envy. Framing the private, turreted Renaissance château are seven spectacular visions, each garden devoted to a theme, including L'Élégance and L'Abondance, in the extraordinary shape of a gigantic leaf. ✉ *Rte. D57, direction Lignières–Langeais* ☎ *02–47–45–40–29* 🌐 *www.lachatonniere.com* 🎟 *€8* 🕒 *Mar.–mid-Nov., daily 10–7.*

WHERE TO STAY

For expanded hotel reviews, visit Fodors.com.

$ HOTEL 🏨 **Le Clos d'Ussé.** Thank heavens for this delightful inn—the best time to see the great Château d'Ussé is in early morning light or illuminated at night, and the easiest way to do that is to overnight in the village of Rigny-Ussé here at the home of the *famille* Duchemin. **Pros:** close to château; charming restaurant. **Cons:** basic guest-room facilities; you-get-what-you-pay-for bathrooms; breakfast is extra. [$] *Rooms from: €55* ✉ *7 rue Principale, Rigny-Ussé* ☎ *02–47–95–55–47* 🌐 *www.leclosdusse.fr* 🛏 *4 rooms, 1 suite* 🕒 *Closed Nov.–mid-Feb.* 🍴 *No meals.*

CHINON

13 km (8 miles) southwest of Rigny-Ussé via D7 and D16, 44 km (28 miles) southwest of Tours.

Fodor's Choice ★ The historic town of Chinon—birthplace of author François Rabelais (1494–1553)—is dominated by the towering ruins of its medieval castle, perched high above the River Vienne. But Chinon's leading photo op is the medieval heart of town, where one of France's most time-burnished streets, the rue Haute St-Maurice, has block after block of storybook, half-timber houses. Little wonder that Jean Cocteau used Chinon's fairy-tale allure to effectively frame Josette Day when she appeared as Beauty in his 1949 film *La Belle et la Bête.*

As an overnight guest, Charles Perrault was so seduced by the secluded beauty of Château d'Ussé that he was inspired to write *Sleeping Beauty*.

GETTING HERE

SNCF trains (50 mins, €9) leave for Chinon from Tours's train station at least three times a day.

Visitor Information Chinon Tourist Office ✉ *Pl. Hofheim* ☎ *02–47–93–17–85* ⊕ *www.chinon-valdeloire.com.*

EXPLORING

Magical, medieval, and magnificent, the main road of Chinon's historic quarter, rue Haute St-Maurice is a virtual open-air museum as this street runs, spectacularly, for more than 15 blocks. Although there are some museums in town—the **Musée d'Art et d'Histoire** (Art and History Museum) in a medieval town house on rue Haute St-Maurice, the **Maison de la Rivière**, devoted to Chinon's maritime trade and set along the embankment, and the **Musée du Vin** (Wine Museum) on rue Voltaire—the medieval quarter remains the must-do, as a walk here catapults you back to the days of Rabelais.

Fortresse de Chinon. This vast fortress with walls 400 yards long dates from the time of Henry II of England, who died here in 1189, and his warring wife, Eleanor of Aquitaine, both buried at Fontevraud. Two centuries later the castle witnessed an important historic moment: Joan of Arc's recognition of the disguised dauphin, later Charles VII.

Once little more than ruins completely open to the elements, Chinon's majestic rooftop, ramparts, and towers have been carefully restored. A visitor center welcomes guests a few steps from the glass elevator that provides direct access from the center of Chinon's Old Town. Visitors can tour the **Logis Royal** (Royal Chambers), a section of which has been transformed into an interactive museum dedicated to Joan of Arc. For a fine view of the region, climb the **Tour Coudray** (Coudray Tower), where in 1307 leading members of the crusading Knights Templar were imprisoned before being taken to Paris, tried, and burned at the stake. The **Tour de l'Horloge** (Clock Tower), whose bell has sounded the hours since 1399, has a view over the ensemble of buildings, and there are sensational views from the ramparts over Chinon, the Vienne Valley, and, toward the back of the castle, the famous vineyard called Le Clos de l'Echo. A restaurant is open on the terrace from July through September. ☎ *02–47–93–13–45* 🌐 *www.forteresse-chinon.fr* 🎟 *€7.50* 🕒 *Mar., Apr., Sept., and Oct, daily 9:30–6; May–Aug., daily 9:30–7; Nov.–Feb., daily 9:30–5.*

DRINK ALWAYS AND NEVER DIE

Participants in Chinon's medieval festival, the Marché à l'Ancienne (🌐 *www.chinon.com*), are fond of quoting the presiding muse of the city, Renaissance writer François Rabelais. Held on the third Saturday of August, this free wine-tasting extravaganza has stalls, displays, and costumed locals recalling rural life of a hundred years ago. For details, contact the tourist office.

WHERE TO EAT AND STAY

For expanded hotel reviews, visit Fodors.com.

$$$ FRENCH 🍴 **Les Années Trente.** Located in the heart of medieval Chinon, at the foot of the royal fortress, this spot welcomes diners with a venerable 16th-century facade. Inside, a romantic Belle Époque atmosphere continues the historic vibe, but the food, au contraire, is prepared with a light, modern touch. Stéphane and Karine Charles's delicious dishes combine fish, game, and regional specialties that melt in your mouth without weighing you down. There are three different menus, the best of which might be the hearty Terroir, which comes perfectly paired with local wines and cheeses. [$] *Average main: €27* ✉ *78 rue Haute St Maurice* ☎ *02–47–93–37–18* 🌐 *www.lesannees30.com* ✍ *Reservations essential* 🕒 *Closed Tues. and Wed.*

$ HOTEL Fodor's Choice ★ 🏨 **Hôtel Diderot.** With its ivy-covered stone, white shutters, mansard roof, dormer windows, and Rococo spiral staircase, this hotel looks like it is on sabbatical from an 18th-century François Boucher painting. **Pros:** parking in the courtyard or in free lot nearby; cozy bar and breakfast room; accessible ground-floor rooms. **Cons:** somewhat worn decor; outdated bathrooms. [$] *Rooms from: €76* ✉ *4 rue Buffon* ☎ *02–47–93–18–87* 🌐 *www.hoteldiderot.com* 🛏 *27 rooms* 🍽 *Some meals.*

FONTEVRAUD-L'ABBAYE

20 km (12 miles) northwest of Chinon via D751.

Visitor Information Fontevraud-l'Abbaye Tourist Office ✉ *Pl. St-Michel* ☎ *02–41–51–79–45* 🌐 *www.ot-saumur.fr* 🕒 *Open May.–Sept.*

EXPLORING

A refreshing break from the worldly grandeur of châteaux, the small village of Fontevraud is crowned with the largest abbey in France, a magnificent complex of Romanesque and Renaissance buildings that were of central importance in the history of both England and France.

Fodor's Choice **Abbaye Royale de Fontevraud.**
★ Founded in 1101, the Abbaye Royale de Fontevraud (Royal Abbey) had separate churches and living quarters for nuns, monks, lepers, "repentant" female sinners, and the sick. Between 1115 and the French Revolution in 1789, a succession of 39 abbesses—among them a granddaughter of William the Conqueror—directed operations. The great 12th-century Église Abbatiale (Abbey Church) contains the tombs of Henry II of England, his wife Eleanor of Aquitaine, and their son, Richard Cœur de Lion (the Lion-Hearted). Though their bones were scattered during the Revolution, their effigies still lie *en couchant* in the middle of the echoey nave. Napoléon turned the abbey church into a prison, and so it remained until 1963, when historical restoration work—still underway, be aware of temporary closures—began. The **Salle Capitulaire** (Chapter House), adjacent to the church, with its collection of 16th-century religious wall paintings (prominent abbesses served as models), is unmistakably Renaissance; the paving stones bear the salamander emblem of François I. Next to the long refectory is the famously octagonal **Cuisine** (Kitchen), topped by 20 scaly stone chimneys led by the **Tour d'Evrault**. ⊠ *Pl. des Plantagenêts* ☎ *02–41–51–71–41* ⊕ *www.abbaye-fontevraud. com* ⊒ *€9* ⊗ *Apr.–Sept., daily 9:30–6:30; Oct.–Dec., Feb., and Mar., Tues.–Sun. 10–5:30.*

> **FAITH, HOPE, AND CLARITY**
>
> With its clean-cut lines, Fontevraud's Abbey Church is a gigantic monument of the French Romanesque, the solid style of simple geometric forms eschewing ornamentation. Home to the tombs of Eleanor of Aquitaine and Richard the Lion-Hearted, the soaring nave was intended to elevate the soul.

Allée Sainte-Catherine. After touring the Abbaye Royale, head outside the gates of the complex a block to the north to discover one of the Loire Valley's most time-burnished streets, the Allée Sainte-Catherine. Bordered by the Fontevraud park, headed by a charming medieval church, and lined with a few scattered houses (which now contain the town tourist office, a gallery that sells medieval illuminated manuscript pages, and the delightful Licorne restaurant), this street still looks like the 14th century.

Château du Petit Thouars. Try some local wines at the stunning, Renaissance-era Château du Petit Thouars, which enjoys an enchanting, fairy-tale hilltop setting just off the Vienne River (between Chinon and Fontevraud). The descendents of Aristide du Petit Thouars, a French naval officer who fought in the American Revolution, have created a small museum illustrating the adventures of their family members that visitors can tour after a *dégustation* of still and sparkling wines from their hillside vineyard. The historic château, alas, is still a private home, only to be enjoyed from the outside. ⊠ *Rte. de la Chaussee, St-Germain-sur-Vienne* ☎ *02–47–95–96–40* ⊕ *www.chateau-du-petit-thouars.com* ⊗ *Tues.–Sat. 9:30–1 and 2–5:30.*

WHERE TO EAT

$$$ FRENCH 🍴 **La Licorne.** A hanging shop sign adorned with a painted unicorn beckons you to this pretty-as-a-picture 18th-century town-house restaurant just off Fontevraud's idyllic Allée Sainte-Catherine. Past a flowery garden and table-adorned terrace, tiny salons glow with happy folks feasting on some of the best food in the region: the chef's Loire salmon, boned quail, Tripel Sec soufflé, langoustine ravioli with wild mushrooms, and lobster with fava beans make most diners purr with contentment. [$] *Average main: €30* ✉ *31 rue Robert-d'Arbrissel* ☎ *02–41–51–72–49* ✍ *Reservations essential. Jacket required* ⏲ *Closed late Dec.–mid-Jan. and Mon. and Wed. mid-Sept.–Mar. No dinner Sun.*

SAUMUR

15 km (9 miles) northwest of Fontevraud via D947, 68 km (43 miles) west of Tours.

You'll find putting up with the famous *snobisme* of the Saumurois well worth it once you get a gander at Saumur's magnificent historic center. Studded with elegant 19th-century town houses and the charming place St-Pierre, lorded over by the vast 12th-century church of St-Pierre and centerpiece of a warren of streets, cafés, and ice-cream parlors, this *centre historique* is sheer delight. Looming over it all—icon of the town and a vision right out of a fairy tale—is Saumur's mighty turreted castle high above the river. You'll be using up many of your camera's flash cards here in a jiffy.

GETTING HERE

To reach Saumur by train from Paris (Gare Montparnasse) requires a change in either Angers (2 hrs, 20 mins; €69.50) or St-Pierre-des-Corps (1 hr, 45 mins; €58.70). Regional trains link Saumur to Tours (40 mins, €11.70) and Angers (20–30 mins, €8.70) every two hours or so.

Visitor Information Saumur Tourist Office ✉ *8 bis quai Carnot* ☎ *02–41–40–20–60* 🌐 *www.ot-saumur.fr.*

EXPLORING

A gorgeous dip into the Middle Ages, Saumur is not content to rest on former glories: today it's one of the largest towns along the Loire and a key transportation hub for Anjou, the province just to the west of Touraine. Saumur is also known for its riding school and flourishing mushroom industry, which produces 100,000 tons per year. The same cool tunnels in which the mushrooms grow provide an ideal storage place for the local *mousseux* (sparkling wines); many vineyards hereabouts are open to the public for tours.

FAMILY **Cadre Noir de Saumur** (*Riding School*). The Cadre Noir de Saumur is the prestigious French National Equestrian Academy, which trains the country's future professionals, instructors, and competitors in the world of horse riding. It's unique in Europe, with 400 horses, extensive stables, five Olympic-size riding schools, and miles of specially laid tracks. Try for a morning tour, which includes a chance to admire the horses in training. The horses put on a full gala display for enthusiastic crowds during special weekends in May, July, and October, reservations are a must. ✉ *Av. de l'Ecole Nationale d'Equitation* 🕿 *02–41–53–50–60* ⊕ *www.cadrenoir.fr/visites* 🎫 *€8* ⊙ *Guided tours only, mid-Feb.– mid-Nov., Mon. 2–4, Tues.–Fri. 9:30–11 and 2–4, Sat. 9:30–11; closed during performances of Matinées.*

Château de Saumur. If you arrive in the evening, the sight of the elegant, floodlighted, white, 14th-century Château de Saumur takes your breath away. Look familiar? Probably because you've seen it in reproductions from the famous *Très Riches Heures* (Book of Hours) painted for the Duc de Berry in 1416 (now in the Musée Condé at Chantilly). Inside it's bright and cheerful, with a fairy-tale gateway and plentiful potted flowers. Owing to renovation of the castle walls,

> **THE VERY RICH HOURS**
>
> Presided over by its magnificent cliff-top castle—which has a starring role in *Les Très Riches Heures du Duc de Berry*, France's most famous illuminated book— Saumur is known as one of the ritziest towns in France. Regional government offices, wealthy wine producers, and hordes of *bon chic, bon genre* shoppers mean you can probably enjoy a blast of old-time French attitude (the waiters are even snobbier than the matrons). Little seems to have changed over the centuries: Honoré de Balzac famously wrote up the surly side of the Saumurois in *Eugénie Grandet.*

the two museums based here, the **Musée des Arts Décoratifs** (Decorative Arts Museum) and the **Musée du Cheval** (Equestrian Museum), have been closed, but the museums do exhibit on the first floor of the castle, and visitors can also access the gardens and panoramic terrace. From July through August there are temporary expositions open in certain areas of the château, as well as medieval reenactments of jousting matches during the day, and a sound-and-light show in the evening. From the cliff-side promenade beyond the parking lot there's a thrilling vista of the castle on its bluff against the river backdrop. ✉ *Esplanade du Château* 🕿 *02–41–40–24–40* ⊕ *www.chateau-saumur.com* 🎫 *€5, €9 (June–Sept.)* ⊙ *Apr.–June, Sept., and Oct., Tues.–Sun. 10–1 and 2–5:30; July and Aug., Tues.–Sun. 10–6.*

Maison du Vin (*House of Wine*). Saumur is the heart of one of the finest wine regions in France. To pay a call on some of the vineyards around the city, first stop into the Maison du Vin for the full scoop on hours and directions; you may also want to consult the website. ✉ *7 quai Carnot* 🕿 *02–41–38–45–83* ⊕ *www.vinsdeloire.fr* ⊙ *Apr.–Sept., Tues.–Sat. 9:30–1 and 2–7, Mon. 2–7; Oct.–mid-Jan. and mid-Feb.–Mar., Tues.– Fri. 10:30–12:30 and 3–6, Sat. 10:30–12:30 and 2:30–6:30. Closed mid-Jan.–mid-Feb.*

Here are some of the top vineyards of the Saumur region. If wine-tasting tours of vineyards inspire you, enterprising winemakers will arrange shipments.

Ackerman. For sparkling Saumur wine, including a rare sparkling red, try Ackerman. ✉ *13 rue Léopold-Palustre, St-Hilaire* 🕿 *02–41–53–03–21* ⊕ *www.ackerman-remypannier.com* 🎫 *€3.*

Les Caves Louis de Grenelle. Les Caves Louis de Grenelle are in the center of town, easily accessible on foot or by car (free parking). The fascinating 90-minute tour through the 15th-century quarry tunnels includes a tasting of their sparkling and still wines. ✉ *839 rue Marceau* ☎ *02–41–50–23–21* 🌐 *www.caves-de-grenelle.fr* 🎟 *€2.50* 🕓 *May–Sept., daily 9:30–6:30; Oct., Nov., and Jan.–Mar., weekdays 9:30–noon and 1:30–6; Apr. and Dec., daily 10–noon and 1:30–6.*

Veuve Amiot. Veuve Amiot is a long-established producer of Saumur wines. ✉ *21 rue Jean-Ackerman, St-Hilaire* ☎ *02–41–83–14–14* 🌐 *www.veuve-amiot.com* 🕓 *Daily 10–1 and 2–6; closed Sun. in Jan. and Feb.*

WHERE TO STAY

For expanded hotel reviews, visit Fodors.com.

$$ HOTEL 🏨 **Anne d'Anjou.** With a spectacular setting at the foot of Saumur castle, a flower-strewn courtyard, and views of the Loire from some of the guest rooms (the finest retain their original, late-18th- and early-19th-century decoration), it is an understatement to describe this elegant 18th-century hotel as "appealing." **Pros:** classic architecture; serious restaurant; free Wi-Fi. **Cons:** smallish rooms; rooms facing the river get traffic noise. [$] *Rooms from: €120* ✉ *32 quai Mayaud* ☎ *02–41–67–30–30* 🌐 *www.hotel-anneanjou.com* 🛏 *44 rooms* 🍴 *Some meals.*

$$ HOTEL Fodor's Choice ★ 🏨 **Saint-Pierre.** At the very epicenter of historic Saumur, this gorgeous little jewel is hidden beneath the medieval walls of the church of Saint-Pierre—look for the hotel's storybook entrance on one of the pedestrian *passages* that circle the vast nave—and has some of the suavest hotel rooms in the city. **Pros:** central location; sophisticated decor; generous breakfast. **Cons:** no restaurant; some rooms face busy roadway. [$] *Rooms from: €110* ✉ *Rue Haute-Saint-Pierre* ☎ *02–41–50–33–00* 🌐 *www.saintpierresaumur.com* 🛏 *14 rooms, 1 suite* 🍴 *No meals.*

ANGERS

45 km (28 miles) northwest of Saumur, 88 km (55 miles) northeast of Nantes.

The bustling city of Angers, on the banks of the Maine River, just north of the Loire, is famous for its towering castle filled with the extraordinary Apocalypse Tapestry. But it also has a fine Gothic cathedral, a selection of art galleries, and a network of pleasant, traffic-free streets around place Ste-Croix, with its half-timber houses.

GETTING HERE

TGV trains from Paris (Gare Montparnasse) leave for Angers every hour or so; the 290-km (180-mile) trip takes 95 minutes (€63). Trains run every two hours or so to Saumur (20–30 mins, €8.70) and Tours (1 hr, €18). Three regional trains daily continue to Blois (1 hr, 20 mins; €26) and Orléans (1 hr, 50 mins; €32.70).

Visitor Information Angers Tourist Office ✉ *7 pl. Kennedy* ☎ *02–41–23–50–00* 🌐 *www.angersloiretourisme.com.*

EXPLORING

Angers's principal sights lie within a compact square formed by the three main boulevards and the Maine, all accessible via the city tramway.

Carré Cointreau. To learn about the heartwarming liqueur made in Angers since 1849, head to the Carré Cointreau on the east side of the city. It has a museum and offers a guided visit of the distillery, which starts with an introductory film, moves past "cointreauversial" advertising posters, through the bottling plant and alembic room, with its gleaming copper-pot stills, and ends with a tasting. English tours are staged at 3 pm. City bus No. 7 from the Angers train station stops just outside. ⊠ *2 bd. des Bretonnières, St-Barthélémy d'Anjou* ☎ *02–41–31–50–50* ⊕ *www.cointreau.fr* 🎫 *€10* ⊘ *Tues.–Sat. 11–6 (reservations essential).*

Cathédrale St-Maurice. This 12th- and 13th-century Gothic edifice is noted for its curious Romanesque facade and original stained-glass windows; bring binoculars to appreciate both fully. The medieval Treasury is open to the public Monday through Saturday in summer (every other Saturday off-season) from 2:30 to 6. ⊠ *Pl. Monseigneur-Chappoulie.*

Château d'Angers. The banded black-and-white Château d'Angers, built by St. Louis (1228–38), glowers over the town from behind turreted moats, now laid out as gardens and overrun with flowers. As you explore the grounds, note the startling contrast between the thick defensive walls, guarded by a drawbridge and 17 massive round towers in a distinctive pattern, and the formal garden, with its delicate white-tufa chapel, erected in the 15th century. For a sweeping view of the city and surrounding countryside, climb one of the castle towers. A well-integrated modern gallery on the castle grounds contains the great **Tenture de l'Apocalypse** (Apocalypse Tapestry), woven in Paris in the 1380s for the Duke of Anjou. Measuring 16 feet high and 120 yards long, its many panels show a series of 70 horrifying and humorous scenes from the Book of Revelation. In one, mountains of fire fall from heaven while boats capsize and men struggle in the water. Another has the Beast with Seven Heads. ⊠ *2 promenade du Bout-du-Monde* ☎ *02–41–86–48–77* ⊕ *angers.monuments-nationaux.fr* 🎫 *€8.50* ⊘ *May–Aug., daily 9:30– 6:30; Sept.–Apr., daily 10–5:30.*

Musée des Beaux Arts. Set within the 15th-century Logis Barrault, the Musée des Beaux Arts (Fine Arts Museum of Angers) houses a collection of art spanning the 14th to the 21st century, as well as a section on the history of Angers through archaeological and artistic works from the Neolithic period to the present. The vast museum complex brings together the historic architecture with contemporary lighting and signage to show the collection at its best and make for a very enjoyable visitor experience. ⊠ *14 rue du Museé* ☎ *02–41–05–38–00* ⊕ *www. musees.angers.fr* 🎫 *€4* ⊘ *June–Sept., daily 10–6:30; Oct.–May, Tues.– Sun. 10–noon and 2–6 (temporary exhibitions 10–6).*

WHERE TO STAY

For expanded hotel reviews, visit Fodors.com.

$ 🖼 **Mail.** A stately lime tree stands sentinel behind wrought-iron, wisteria-framed gates outside this 17th-century mansion on a calm street between the Hôtel de Ville and the river—but inside prepare for a

HOTEL

modern surprise. **Pros:** calm; good value. **Cons:** small rooms; rooms on the top floor can get quite warm in summer; no elevator. $ *Rooms from: €75* ⊠ *8 rue des Ursules* ☎ *02–41–25–05–25* ⊕ *www.hoteldumail.fr* ➘ *26 rooms* ⦿ *No meals.*

NIGHTLIFE AND THE ARTS

Angers Tempo Rives (*Angers Summer festival*). July and August see the Angers Tempo Rives, with free concerts on the Cale de la Savatte, the riverfront overlooking the Château d'Angers. ⊠ *Cale de la Savatte* ☎ *02–41–23–50–00* ⊕ *www.temporives.fr.*

Le Tasting Room. Le Tasting Room offers all-inclusive wine tastings and tours of the Loire Valley's best wines from an insider's perspective. Based in an ancient renovated farmhouse between Angers and Saumur, the small company is run by friendly British transplants Cathy and Nigel Henton, who bring more than 25 years of their experience in the wine industry to visitors looking for a casual, fun, and informative experience. They'll pick you up at Angers train station, give you a primer on the local wines, serve a home-cooked meal, and then take you to see the neighboring vineyards, small villages, or even an barge cruise on the Loire River. They can recommend local accommodations or help plan your day trip from Paris. Prices start at €150 a person. ⊠ *37 chemin du Lavoir, Cumeray* ☎ *02–41–79–80–21* ⊕ *www.letastingroom.com.*

LANGEAIS

82 km (47 miles) east of Angers via N152.

Château de Langeais. Sometimes unjustly overlooked, the Château de Langeais—a castle in the true sense of the word—will particularly delight those who dream of lions rampant, knights in shining armor, and the chivalric days of yore. Built in the 1460s, bearing a massive portcullis and gate, and never altered, it has an interior noted for its superb collection of medieval and Renaissance furnishings—fireplaces, tapestries, chests, and beds—which would make Guinevere and Lancelot feel right at home. An hourly waxworks and video show tells the story of the secret dawn wedding of King Charles VIII with Anne of Brittany in the room where it took place in 1491. Outside, gardens nestle behind sturdy walls and battlements; kids will make a beeline for the playgrounds and tree house added in 2009. The town itself has other sites, including a Renaissance church tower, but chances are you won't want to move from the delightful outdoor cafés that face the castle entrance. Do follow the road a bit to the right (when looking at the entrance) to discover the charming historic houses grouped around a waterfall and canal. ☎ *02–47–96–72–60* ⊕ *www.chateau-de-langeais. com* ⊠ *€8.80* ⊙ *Apr.–June and Sept.–mid-Nov., daily 9:30–6:30; July and Aug., daily 9–7; mid-Nov.–Jan., daily 10–5; Feb. and Mar., daily 9:30–5:30.*

NORMANDY

WELCOME TO NORMANDY

TOP REASONS TO GO

★ **Mont-St-Michel:** The spire-top silhouette of this mighty offshore mound, dubbed the Marvel of the Occident, is one of the greatest sights in Europe. Get there at high tide, when the water races across the endless sands.

★ **Bayeux:** Come not just for the splendor of the tapestry telling how William conquered England, but also for untouched medieval buildings and the beefy, bonnet-top cathedral.

★ **Honfleur:** From France's prettiest harbor, lined with beam-fronted houses, you can head to the ravishing wooden church of Ste-Catherine.

★ **Rouen:** Sanctified by the memory of Jeanne d'Arc, hallowed by its towering Gothic cathedral (immortalized by Monet), and lined with medieval half-timber houses, Rouen makes a great gateway city to Normandy.

★ **D-Day Beaches:** From rocky Omaha to pancake-flat Utah, muse on the stirring deeds of World War II.

1 Upper Normandy. Fascinating portal city to Normandy, Rouen still contains—despite World War II's battering—such an overwhelming number of lovely churches, chapels, towers, fountains, and old cross-beam houses that many take two full days to enjoy this commercial and cultural hub. Heading some 60 km (35 miles) northwest to the Channel shore, the Côte d'Alabâtre (Alabaster Coast) beckons, named for the white cliffs that stretch north, including the spectacular rock formations often painted by Monet at Étretat. Nearby seaside Fécamp regales with its noted Benedictine palace and distillery.

5

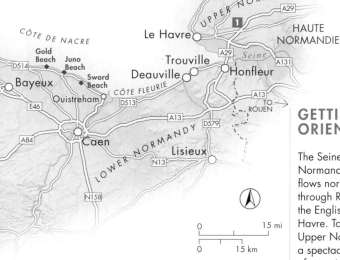

0   15 mi

0   15 km

GETTING ORIENTED

The Seine Valley divides Normandy in two as it flows northwest from Paris through Rouen and into the English Channel at Le Havre. To the north lies Upper Normandy and a spectacular coastline of towering chalk cliffs called the Côte d'Alabâtre (Alabaster Coast). West of the Seine lies Lower Normandy, full of lush meadows and lined with the sandy beaches of the Côte Fleurie, or Flower Coast. (These are the same beaches where the Allies landed on D-Day.) Far to the west, at the foot of the sparsely populated Cotentin Peninsula, the offshore Mont-St-Michel patrols one of the continent's biggest bays.

2 Honfleur to Mont-St-Michel. Basse (or Lower) Normandie begins with the sandy Côte Fleurie (Flower Coast), announced by seaside Honfleur, an artist's paradise full of half-timber houses. Just south, Rothschilds by the Rolls arrive in season at the Belle Époque seaside resorts of Trouville and Deauville—both beautiful if hard on the pocket. Modern and student-filled Caen is famed for its two gigantic abbey churches,

one begun by William the Conqueror who is immortalized in nearby Bayeux's legendary tapestry. This town makes a great base to explore the somber D-Day sites along Utah and Omaha beaches; bus tours and moving memorials make a fitting prelude for a drive across Normandy's Cotentin Peninsula to Mont-St-Michel, whose tiny island is crowned by one of the most beautiful Gothic abbeys in France.

EATING AND DRINKING WELL IN NORMANDY

The felicitous combination of dairy farms, apple orchards, and the sea inspire Normandy's crème de la crème cuisine, featuring voluptuous cream sauces, tender cheeses, lavish seafood platters, and head-spinning Calvados brandy.

As befits one of France's best regional cuisines, Normandy boasts many delightful kitchens *(above)*; fresh-this-very-hour oysters *(right, top)*; great cheeses make great desserts *(right, bottom)*.

Normandy's verdant landscape—a patchwork of pastures and orchards bordered by the sea—heralds a region of culinary delights. The apples feature in tarts, cakes, sauces, and *cidre bouché*, a sparkling cider sold in cork-top bottles. Brown-and-white cows—the famous *vaches normandes*—grazing beneath the apple blossoms each produce up to seven gallons of milk a day, destined to become golden butter, thick crème fraîche, and prized cheeses. Coastal waters from Dieppe to Granville are equally generous, yielding sole, turbot, and oysters. To fully appreciate Normandy's gastronomic wealth, stroll through a weekend market, such as the splendid Saturday morning affair in Honfleur on the place Ste-Catherine, sample a seafood platter at a boardwalk café in Deauville, or meet the omelet of your dreams at La Mère Poulard at Mont-Saint-Michel.

APPLE COUNTRY

One fragrance evokes Normandy—the pungent, earthy smell of apples awaiting the press in the autumn. Normandy is apple country, where apples with quaint varietal names, such as Windmill and Donkey Snout, are celebrated in the region's gastronomy, along the Route du Cidre, or at Vimoutier's Foire de la Pomme (Apple Festival) in October (where they vote for the Most Beautiful Apple).

CHEESE PLATTER

Camembert is king in the dairy realm of Normandy. This tangy, opulently creamy cow's-milk cheese with the star billing and worldwide reputation hails from the Auge region. The best—Véritable Camembert de Normandie—with velvety white rinds and supple, sometimes oozy interiors, are produced on small farms, such as the esteemed Moulin de Carel.

Other members of Normandy's (cheese) board are the savory, grassy Pont L'Évêque, the impressively pungent Livarot with rust-color rind, and the Pavé d'Auge, a robust cheese with a honey-hue center.

CALVADOS

There are no wines in Normandy, but the region makes its mark in the spirits world with the apple-based Calvados, a fragrant oak-aged brandy.

Like Cognac, Calvados, which is distilled from cider, gets better and more expensive with age.

Top producers, such as Dupont in Victot-Pontfol and Pierre Huet in Cambremer, sell Calvados from "Vieux," aged a minimum of three years, to "X.O." or "Napoléon," aged from 6 to 25 years.

Many producers also offer Pommeau, an aperitif blending cider with a generous dose of Calvados.

ON THE HALF SHELL

Few places in France make an oyster lover happier than Normandy's Cotentin Peninsula, where the land juts into the sea a few miles beyond the Landing Beaches.

Ports such as Blanville-sur-Mer, Granville, and particularly St-Vaast-La Hougue, are where oystermen haul in tons of plump, briny oysters distinguished by a subtle note of hazelnut.

Enjoy a dozen on the half shell at the many traditional restaurants in this region, accompanied by a saucer of shallot vinegar and brown bread.

OMELET EXTRAORDINAIRE

There is no more famous omelet in the world than the puffy, pillow-like confection offered at La Mère Poulard in Mont-Saint-Michel (☎ 02–33–89–68–68).

Whipped with a balloon whisk in a large copper bowl, then cooked in a long-handled skillet over a wood fire, the omelet is delicately browned and crusted on the outside, as soft and airy as a soufflé within.

Order the omelet with ham and cheese as a main course, or sugared and flambéed as a majestic dessert.

Updated by
Christopher
Mooney and
Jack Vermee

The maritime Garden of Eden called Normandy sprawls across France's northwestern corner in a shape roughly resembling a piece of a jigsaw puzzle. Due to its geographic position, this region is blessed with a stunning natural beauty that once inspired Maupassant and Monet. Little wonder today's sightseers pack into colorful Rouen, seaside Honfleur, and magnificent Mont-St-Michel.

Happily, it is easy to escape all those travelers. Simply lose yourself along Normandy's spectacular cliff-lined coast and in the green spaces inland, where the closest thing to a crowd is a farmer with his herd of brown-and-white cows. But whatever road you turn down, the region's time-stained history is there to enchant and fascinate.

Say the name "Normandy," and which Channel-side scenario comes to mind? Are you reminded of the dramatic silhouette of Mont-St-Michel looming above the tidal flats, its cobbles echoing with the footfalls of medieval scholars? Or do you think of iron-gray convoys massing silently at dawn, lowering tailgates to pour troops of young Allied infantrymen into the line of German machine-gun fire? At Omaha Beach you may marvel at the odds faced by the handful of soldiers who in June 1944 were able to rise above the waterfront carnage to capture the cliff-top battery, paving the way for the Allies' reconquest of Europe.

Perhaps you think of Joan of Arc—imprisoned by the English yet burned at the Rouen stake by the Church she believed in? In a modern church you may light a candle on the very spot where, in 1431, the Maiden Warrior sizzled into history at the hands of panicky politicians and time-serving clerics: a dark deed that marked a turning point in the Hundred Years' War.

The destinies of England and Normandy have been intertwined ever since William, Duke of Normandy, insisted that King Edward the Confessor had promised him the succession to the English crown. When a royal council instead anointed the Anglo-Saxon Harold Godwinsson, the irate William stormed across the Channel with 7,000 well-equipped archers, well-mounted knights, and well-paid Frankish mercenaries. They landed at Pevensey Bay on September 28, 1066, and two weeks later, conquered at Hastings.

There followed nearly 400 years of Norman sovereignty in England. For generations England and Normandie (as the French spell it) blurred, merged, and diverged. Today you can still feel the strong flow of English culture over the Channel, from the Deauville horse races frequented by high-born ladies in gloves, to silver spoons mounded high with teatime cream; from the bowfront, slope-roof shops along the harbor at Honfleur to the black-and-white row houses of Rouen, which would seem just as much at home in the setting of *David Copperfield* as they are in *Madame Bovary*.

The French divide Normandy into two: Haute-Normandie and Basse-Normandie. Upper (Haute) Normandy is delineated by the Seine as it meanders northwest from the Ile-de-France between chalky cliffs and verdant hills to Rouen—the region's cultural and commercial capital—and on to the port of Le Havre. Pebbly beaches and even more impressive chalk cliffs line the Côte d'Alabâtre (Alabaster Coast) from Le Havre to Dieppe. Lower (Basse) Normandy encompasses the sandy Côte Fleurie, stretching from the resort towns of Trouville and Deauville to the D-Day landing beaches and the Cotentin Peninsula, jutting out into the English Channel.

PLANNING

WHEN TO GO

July and August are the busiest months but also the most activity filled: Concerts are held every evening at Mont-St-Michel, and the region's most important horse races are held in Deauville, culminating with the Gold Cup Polo Championship and the Grand Prix on the last Sunday in August. June 6, the anniversary of the Allied invasion, is the most popular time to visit the D-Day beaches. If you're trying to avoid crowds, your best bet is late spring and early autumn, when it is still fairly temperate. May finds the apple trees in full bloom and miles of waving flaxseed fields spotted with tiny sky-blue flowers. Some of the biggest events of the region take place during these seasons: in Rouen, at the end of May, Joan of Arc is honored at a festival named for her; there is jazz under the apple trees in Coutances; the first week of September in Deauville is the American Film Festival.

PLANNING YOUR TIME

Normandy is a big region with lots to see. If you have 10 days or so you can do it justice. If not, you'll need to prioritize. In search of natural beauty? Head to the coastline north of Le Havre. Prefer sea and sand? Beat it to the beaches west of Trouville. Love little villages? Honfleur is one of France's most picturesque old fishing ports. Like city life? Pretty Rouen is for you. Are you a history buff? Base yourself in Caen to tour the D-Day beaches. Can't get enough of churches and cathedrals? You can go pretty much anywhere, but don't miss Bayeux, Rouen, or Mont-St-Michel. (The last is a bit isolated, so you might want to get there directly from Paris, or at the start or end of a tour of Brittany.)

GETTING HERE AND AROUND

Although this is one of the few areas of France with no high-speed rail service—perhaps because it's so close to Paris, or because it's not on a lucrative route to a neighboring country—Normandy's regional rail network is surprisingly good and most towns can be reached by train. Rouen is the hub for Upper Normandy, Caen for Lower Normandy. Unless you're driving, you'll need a bus to reach the coastal resorts like Étretat, Honfleur, and Houlgate. For Mont-St-Michel, a combination of train and bus is required. To visit the D-Day beaches, a guided minibus tour, leaving from Caen or Bayeux, is your best bet. The A13 expressway is the gateway from Paris, running northwest to Rouen and then to Caen. From here the A84 takes you almost all the way to Mont-St-Michel, and the N13 brings you to Bayeux. If you're arriving from England or northern Europe, the A16/A28 from Calais to Rouen is a scenic (and near-empty) delight.

AIR TRAVEL

Paris's Charles de Gaulle (Roissy) and Orly airports are the closest intercontinental links with the region. There are flights in summer from London to Deauville. Year-round service is offered between Jersey and Cherbourg, which sits at the northern tip of the Cotentin Peninsula, about 90 minutes' drive from Bayeux. Rouen airport has direct flights to Lyon and Montpellier. Air France flies to Caen from Paris. Ryanair flies to Dinard (in Brittany, 56 km [35 miles] west of Mont-St-Michel) from London's Stansted Airport.

Airlines and Contacts Air France ☎ *3654 within France* ⊕ *www.air-france. com.* **Ryanair** ☎ *08–92–56–21–50, 0871/246–0000 in U.K., 44–871/246–0002 from U.S.* ⊕ *www.ryanair.com.*

Airport Information Caen ☎ *02–31–71–20–10* ⊕ *www.caen-aeroport.fr.* **Cherbourg** ☎ *02–33–88–57–60* ⊕ *www.cherbourg.aeroport.fr.* **Deauville** ☎ *02–31–65–65–65* ⊕ *www.deauville.aeroport.fr.* **Rouen** ☎ *02–35–79–41–00* ⊕ *www. rouen.aeroport.fr.*

BIKE AND MOPED TRAVEL

Traveling with your bike is free on all regional trains and many national lines; be sure to ask the SNCF which ones when you're booking.

BOAT, FERRY, AND EUROTUNNEL TRAVEL

A number of ferry companies sail between the United Kingdom and ports in Normandy.

Brittany Ferries travels between Caen (Ouistreham) and Portsmouth and between Poole/Portsmouth and Cherbourg. The Dieppe-Newhaven route is covered by a daily service from Transmanche.

And don't forget the option of driving your car or motorcycle onto a Eurotunnel train at Folkestone for the 35-minute trip under the English Channel to Calais.

Boat Information Brittany Ferries ☎ *08–25–82–88–28* ⊕ *www.brittany-ferries.com.* **Eurotunnel Le Shuttle** ☎ *08–10–63–03–04 in France, 08443/353535 in U.K., 33/3–21–00–20–61 from other countries* ⊕ *www. eurotunnel.com.* **LD Lines** ☎ *08–00–65–01–00* ⊕ *www.ldlines.fr.*

BUS TRAVEL

Cars Perier runs buses from Fécamp to Le Havre, stopping in Étretat along the way. **Bus Verts du Calvados** covers the coast, connecting with Caen and Honfleur, Bayeux, and other towns. These buses depart from the train stations in Bayeux and Caen. Bus routes connect many towns, including Rouen, Dieppe, Fécamp, Étretat, Le Havre, Caen, Honfleur, Deauville, Trouville, Cabourg, and Arromanches. To get to Honfleur, take a bus from Deauville; from Rouen, train it first to Le Havre, then continue by bus to Honfleur.

For Mont-St-Michel, hook up with buses from nearby Pontorson, or from St. Malo or Rennes in adjacent Brittany. If you are traveling from Paris to the Mont, take the high-speed TGV train from Gare Montparnasse to Rennes (in high season, five departures a day), then a **Keolis** bus transfer to the Mont. Many trains depart from Paris's Gare-St-Lazare for Rouen (70 mins). Tourist offices and train stations in Normandy will have printed schedules.

Bus Information Bus Verts du Calvados ☎ *08–10–21–42–14* ⊕ *www.busverts. fr.* **Cars Perier** ☎ *02–32–84–12–60* ⊕ *www.cars-perier.fr.* **Keolis** ☎ *02–99–19– 70–70* ⊕ *www.keolis-emeraude.com.* **VTNI** ☎ *02–32–08–19–75* ⊕ *www.vtni.fr.*

CAR TRAVEL

From Paris, A13 slices its way to Rouen in 1½ hours (toll €13.70) before forking to Caen (an additional hour, toll €8.40) or Le Havre (45 mins on A131). N13 continues from Caen to Bayeux in another two hours. At Caen, the A84 forks off southwest toward Mont-St-Michel and Rennes. From Paris, scenic D915 will take you to Dieppe in about three hours. The Pont de Normandie, between Le Havre and Honfleur, effectively unites Upper and Lower Normandy.

TRAIN TRAVEL

From Paris (Gare St-Lazare), separate train lines head to Upper Normandy (Rouen and Le Havre or Dieppe) and Lower Normandy (Caen, Bayeux, and Cherbourg, via Évreux and Lisieux). There are frequent trains from Paris to Rouen (70 mins, €23); some continue to Le Havre (2 hrs, €33.50). Change in Rouen for Dieppe (2 hrs from Paris, €30.70). The trip from Paris to Deauville (2 hrs, €32) often requires a change at Lisieux. There are regular trains from Paris to Caen (1 hr, 50 mins; €35), some continuing to Bayeux (2 hrs, €38). Taking the train from Paris to Mont-St-Michel is not easy—the quickest way (2 hrs, 15 mins; €59) is to take the TGV from Gare Montparnasse to Rennes, then take the bus. There are several trains daily, but the only one that will allow you a full day on the Mont leaves at 7:04 am and arrives at 9:20 am. The other options are 9:05 (arriving 11:15 am) and 10:08 am (arriving 12:15). From Caen you can take either an early morning or an afternoon train to Pontorson (2 hrs, €27), the nearest station to the Mont; then it's another 15 minutes to the foot of the abbey by bus or taxi (buses are directly in front of the station). Unless you're content to stick to the major towns (Rouen, Dieppe, Caen, Bayeux, Cherbourg), visiting Normandy by train may prove frustrating. You can sometimes reach several smaller towns (Fécamp, Houlgate/Cabourg) on snail-paced branch lines, but the irregular intricacies of what is said to be

Europe's most complicated regional timetable will probably have driven you nuts by the time you get there. Other destinations, like Honfleur or Étretat, require train/bus journeys.

Train Information Gare SNCF Rouen ✉ *Rue Jeanne d'Arc* ☏ *36–35.* **SNCF** ☏ *36–35* ⊕ *www.ter-sncf.com.*

TOURING THE D-DAY BEACHES

One of the great events of modern history, the D-Day invasion of June 1944 was enacted on the beaches of Normandy. Omaha Beach (site of an eye-opening museum), Utah Beach, as well as many sites on the Cotentin Peninsula, and the memorials to Allied dead, all bear witness to the furious fighting that once raged in this now-peaceful corner of France. Today, as seagulls sweep over the cliffs where American rangers scrambled desperately up ropes to silence murderous German batteries, visitors now wander through the blockhouses and peer into the bomb craters, the carnage of battles that raged here thankfully now a distant, if still horrifying, memory.

Unless you have a car, the D-Day beaches are best visited on a bus tour from Bayeux. Public buses are rare, although Bus No. 75 heads to Arromanches and Bus No. 70 goes to Omaha Beach and the American cemetery (summer only). However, Bus Verts du Calvados (⊕ *www. busverts.fr*) offers a "Circuit Caen-Omaha Beach" route that connects many of the D-Day sights.

As for guided tours, Normandy Tours (☏ *02–31–92–10–70* ⊕ *www. normandy-landing-tours.com*), which carries up to eight in its minivan, leaves from Bayeux's Hotel de la Gare. The guides are walking encyclopedias of local war lore and may be flexible about points interesting to you. The half-day tours (€48) are available all year in English.

In addition, other Bayeux-based tour outfitters include D-Day Tours (☏ *02–31–51–70–52* ⊕ *www.normandy-sightseeing-tours.com*), with half-day tours (€45–€60) and full-day tours (€90). Battlebus (☏ *02–31–22–28–82* ⊕ *www.ddayhistorian.com*) has a full-day extravaganza (€90) and an excellent range of weekly and daily individual tours for groups of up to eight people (children under 12 not permitted).

HOTELS

Accommodations to suit every taste can be found throughout Normandy, from basic bed-and-breakfasts to the most luxurious hotel. Even in the resorts of Deauville and Trouville it is possible to find delightful and inexpensive little vacation spots. The region's two largest cities, Rouen and Caen, are not among France's best served when it comes to high-end hotels. To stay the night on Mont-St-Michel is a memorable experience, but be sure to reserve your room weeks in advance. Prices are ratcheted up in summer along the coast, and you will need to book ahead, especially on weekends. Many hotels are closed in winter. In the beach resorts the season runs from the end of April to October.

Prices in the dining reviews are the average cost of a main course at dinner or, if dinner is not served, at lunch. Prices in the lodging reviews are the lowest cost of a standard double room in high season.

VISITOR INFORMATION

If traveling extensively by public transportation, load up on information (Guide Regional des Transport schedules, the best taxi-for-call companies, etc.) upon arriving at the ticket counter or help desk of the bigger train and bus stations in the area, such as Rouen, Deauville, and Caen. The capital of each of Normandy's *départements* (provinces)—Caen, Évreux, Rouen, St-Lô, and Alençon—has its own central tourist office. *They and numerous other tourist offices are listed under town names below.*

BUS TOUR OPTIONS

Paris Vision (also known as Paris City Vision) runs full-day bus excursions from Paris to Mont-St-Michel for €170, meals and admissions included. This is definitely not for the faint of heart—buses leave Paris at 7 am and return around 9:45 pm. In Caen, the Mémorial organizes five-hour English-language daily minibus tours of the D-Day landing beaches; the cost is €80, including entrance fees. Normandy Sightseeing Tours runs a number of trips to the D-Day beaches and Mont-St-Michel. One of its full-day excursions to the D-Day beaches (8:30–6) costs €90.

Mémorial ⊠ *Esplanade General Eisenhower, Caen* ☎ *02–31–06–06–44* ⊕ *www.memorial.fr.*

Normandy Sightseeing Tours. Normandy Sightseeing Tours. ⊠ *618 rte. du Lavoir, Mosles* ☎ *02–31–51–70–52* ⊕ *www.normandy-sightseeing-tours.com.*

Paris Vision ⊠ *4 pl. des Pyramides, Paris* ☎ *01–44–55–61–00* ⊕ *www. pariscityrama.fr.*

UPPER NORMANDY

From Rouen to the coast—the area known as Upper Normandy—medieval castles and abbeys stand guard above rolling countryside, while resort and fishing towns line the white cliffs of the Côte d'Alabâtre (Alabaster Coast). In the 19th century, the dramatic scenery and bathing resorts along the coast attracted and inspired writers and artists like Maupassant, Monet, and Braque—and today it has the same effect on thousands of visitors.

ROUEN

32 km (20 miles) north of Louviers; 130 km (80 miles) northwest of Paris; 86 km (53 miles) east of Le Havre.

Fodor'sChoice ★ "O Rouen, art thou then to be my final abode!" was the agonized cry of Joan of Arc as the English dragged her out to be burned alive on May 30, 1431. The exact spot of the pyre is marked by a concrete-and-metal cross in front of the Église Jeanne-d'Arc, an eye-catching modern church on place du Vieux-Marché, just one of the many landmarks that make Rouen a fascinating destination. Known as the City of a Hundred Spires, Rouen is famed for its profusion of important churches.

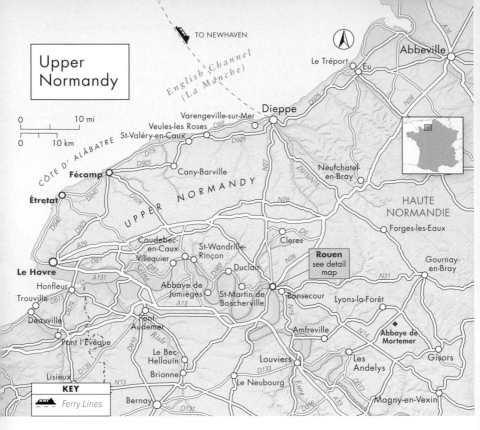

GETTING HERE

Trains from Paris (Gare St-Lazare) leave for Rouen every two hours or so (€22.80); the 135-km (85-mile) trip takes 70 minutes. Change in Rouen for Dieppe (2 hrs from Paris, €30.70). Several trains daily link Rouen to Caen (90 mins, €29.50) and Fécamp (90 mins, €14.50), sometimes requiring a change to a bus at Bréauté-Beuzeville.

Visitor Information Rouen Tourist Office ⊠ *25 pl. de la Cathédrale* ☎ *02–32– 08–32–40* ⊕ *www.rouentourisme.com.*

EXPLORING

Once the capital of the duchy of Normandy, the Seine-side city of Rouen overflows with monuments, medieval streets, and churches. Today a busy industrial port city of about a half million people, it has inspired many along the way, including Gustave Flaubert and Claude Monet, who immortalized Rouen's great cathedral in a famous series of paintings. Although much of Rouen was destroyed during World War II, a wealth of medieval half-timber houses still lines the tiny cobblestone streets of **Vieux Rouen** (Old Rouen), many of which are pedestrian-only—most famously rue du Gros-Horloge between place du Vieux-Marché and the cathedral, suitably embellished halfway along with a giant Renaissance clock. This landmark, the Gros-Horloge, is featured on 99% of the postcards sold in Rouen, so be sure to peer up at the real thing.

TOP ATTRACTIONS

Abbaye St-Ouen. Next to the imposing Neoclassical City Hall, this stupendous example of high Gothic architecture is noted for its stained-glass windows, dating from the 14th to the 16th century. They are the most spectacular grace notes of the spare interior along with the 19th-century pipe organ, among the finest in France. ⊠ *Pl. du Général-de-Gaulle, Hôtel de Ville* ☎ *02–32–08–32–40* ⊗ *Apr.–Oct., Wed.–Mon. 10–noon and 2–6; Nov.–Mar., Tues.–Thurs. and weekends 10–noon and 2–5.*

> ## MONET IN 3-D
>
> If you're familiar with the works of Impressionist artist Claude Monet, you'll immediately recognize Rouen cathedral's immense west front, rendered in an increasingly hazy fashion in his series *Cathédrales de Rouen.* Enjoy a ringside view and a coffee at the Brasserie Paul, just opposite. The facade is illuminated by a free light show, based on Monet's canvases, for an hour every evening from June through mid-September.

Cathédrale Notre-Dame. Lording it over Rouen's "Hundred Spires" this cathedral is crowned with the highest spire in France, erected in 1876, a cast-iron tour-de-force rising 490 feet above the crossing. The original 12th-century construction was replaced after a devastating fire in 1200; only the left-hand spire, the **Tour St-Romain** (St. Romanus Tower), survived the flames. Construction on the imposing 250-foot steeple on the right, known as the **Tour de Beurre** (Butter Tower), was begun in the 15th century and completed in the 17th, when a group of wealthy citizens donated large sums of money for the privilege of continuing to eat butter during Lent. Interior highlights include the 13th-century choir, with its pointed arcades; vibrant stained glass depicting the crucified Christ (restored after heavy damage during World War II); and massive stone columns topped by some intriguing carved faces. The first flight of the famous **Escalier de la Librairie** (Library Stairway), attributed to Guillaume Pontifs (also responsible for most of the 15th-century work seen in the cathedral), rises from a tiny balcony just to the left of the transept. ⊠ *Pl. de la Cathédrale, St-Maclou* ☎ *02–32–08–32–40* ⊗ *Daily 8–6.*

Gros-Horloge. The name of the pedestrian rue du Gros-Horloge, Rouen's most popular street, comes from the Gros-Horloge itself, a giant Renaissance clock. In 1527 the Rouennais had a splendid arch built especially for it, and today its golden face looks out over the street. You can see the clock's inner workings from the 15th-century belfry. Though the street is crammed with stores, a few old houses dating from the 16th century remain. Wander through the surrounding **Vieux Rouen** (Old Rouen), a warren of tiny streets lined with more than 700 half-timber houses, many artfully transformed into fashionable shops. ⊠ *Rue du Gros-Horloge, Vieux-Marché* ☐€6 ⊗ *Apr.–Oct., Tues.–Sun. 10–7; Nov.–Mar., Tues.–Sun. 2–6.*

Musée des Beaux-Arts (*Fine Arts Museum*). One of Rouen's cultural mainstays, this museum is famed for its scintillating collection of paintings

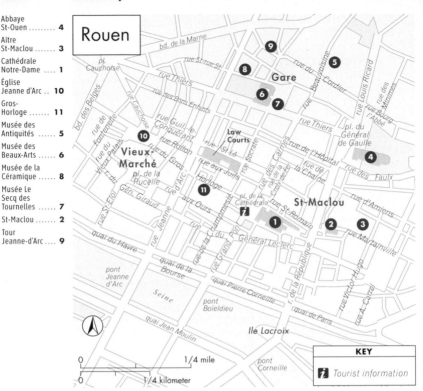

and sculptures from the 16th to the 20th century, including works by native son Géricault as well as by David, Rubens, Caravaggio, Velasquez, Poussin, Delacroix, Chassériau, Degas, and Modigliani. Most popular of all, however, is the impressive Impressionist gallery, with Monet, Renoir, and Sisley, and the Postimpressionist School of Rouen headed by Albert Lebourg and Gustave Loiseau. ⊠ *Sq. Verdrel, Gare* ☎ *02–35–71–28–40* ⊕ *www.rouen-musees.com* ⊠ *€5 (free 1st Sun. of month), €8 includes Musée Le Secq des Tournelles and Musée de la Céramique* ☉ *Wed.–Mon. 10–6.*

St-Maclou. A late-Gothic masterpiece, this church sits across rue de la République behind the cathedral and bears testimony to the wild excesses of Flamboyant architecture. Take time to examine the central and left-hand portals of the main facade, covered with little bronze lion heads and pagan engravings. Inside, note the 16th-century organ, with its Renaissance wood carving, and the fine marble columns. ⊠ *Pl. Barthélémy, St-Maclou* ☎ *02–32–08–32–40* ☉ *Weekends 10–noon and 2–6; Nov.–Feb., Sun. 10–5:30.*

Tour Jeanne-d'Arc. Sole remnant of the early-13th-century castle built by French king Philippe-Auguste, this beefy, pointed-top circular tower is a fine photo op. Inside you'll find a small exhibit of documents and models charting the history of the castle where Joan of Arc was tried and held prisoner in 1430. ⊠ *Rue Bouvreuil, Gare* ☎ *02–35–98–16–21* ⊡ *€1.50* ⊙ *Wed.–Mon. 10–12:30 and 2–6, Sun. 2–6; closed Tues.*

WORTH NOTING

Aître St-Maclou. A former ossuary (a charnel house used for the bodies of plague victims), this is a reminder of the plague that devastated Europe during the Middle Ages; these days it holds Rouen's Fine Art Academy. French composer Camille Saint-Saëns (1835–1921) is said to have been inspired by the ossuary when he was working on his *Danse Macabre.* The half-timber courtyard, where you can wander at leisure and maybe visit a picture exhibition, contains graphic carvings of skulls, bones, and gravediggers' tools. ⊠ *186 rue Martainville, St-Maclou* ⊡ *Free.*

Église Jeanne d'Arc (*Joan of Arc Church*). Dedicated to Joan of Arc, this church was built in the 1970s on the spot where she was burned to death in 1431. The aesthetic merit of its odd cement-and-wood design is debatable—the shape of the roof is supposed to evoke the flames of Joan's fire. Not all is new, however: the church showcases some remarkable 16th-century stained-glass windows taken from the former Église St-Vincent, bombed out in 1944. The adjacent **Musée Jeanne-d'Arc** relates Joan's history with waxworks and documents. ⊠ *Pl. du Vieux-Marché, Vieux-Marché* ☎ *02–32–08–32–40* ⊕ *www.jeanne-darc.com* ⊡ *Free* ⊙ *Mon.–Thurs. 10–noon, Fri.–Sun. 2–6.*

Musée de la Céramique (*Ceramics Museum*). A superb array of local pottery and European porcelain can be admired at this museum, housed in an elegant mansion near the Musée des Beaux-Arts. ⊠ *1 rue Faucon, Gare* ☎ *02–35–07–31–74* ⊡ *€3, €8 includes Musée Le Secq des Tournelles and Musée des Beaux-Arts* ⊙ *Wed.–Mon. 10–1 and 2–6.*

Musée des Antiquités. Gallo-Roman glassware and mosaics, medieval tapestries and enamels, and Moorish ceramics vie for attention at this collection, an extensive antiquities museum housed in a former monastery dating from the 17th century. There is also a display devoted to natural history, which includes some skeletons dating to prehistoric times. ⊠ *198 rue Beauvoisine, Gare* ☎ *02–35–98–55–10* ⊡ *€3* ⊙ *Tues.–Sat. 10–12:15 and 1:30–5:30, Sun. 2–6.*

Musée Le Secq des Tournelles (*Wrought-Iron Museum*). Not far from the Musée des Beaux-Arts, this museum claims to have the world's finest collection of wrought iron, with exhibits spanning the 4th through the 19th century. The displays, imaginatively housed in a converted medieval church, include the professional instruments of surgeons, barbers, carpenters, clockmakers, and gardeners. ⊠ *2 rue Jacques-Villon, Gare* ☎ *02–35–88–42–92* ⊡ *€3, €8 includes Musée des Beaux-Arts and Musée de la Céramique* ⊙ *Wed.–Mon. 10–1 and 2–6.*

WHERE TO EAT

$$
BISTRO
Fodor'sChoice
★

✕ **Gill Côté Bistro.** With two Michelin stars under his toque for his tony gastronomic restaurant Gill, chef Gilles Tournadre jumped at the chance to open a contemporary bistro on Rouen's storied place du Vieux-Marché. Sleek and modern, it specializes in updated bistro fare, which has the distinct advantage of being served up seven days a week, consisting of inspired versions of much-loved French classics, like *tête de veau* (calf's head) with sauce *gribich* (a caper, parsley, and cornichon

Hollandaise) and *andouillette* (tripe sausage), along with more contemporary dishes, like a piquant Caesar salad. Portions are ample and the small but choice menu—with a great-value fixed-price daily option—changes monthly. [$] *Average main: €22* ✉ *14 pl. du Vieux-Marché, Vieux-Marché* ☎ *02–35–89–88–72* 🕒 *Daily noon–2:30 and 7:30–10:30.*

THE MESSENGER

Before Joan of Arc was torched on Rouen's place du Vieux-Marché, she asked a friar to hold a crucifix high in the air and to shout out assurances of her salvation so that she could hear him above the roar of the fire.

$$$$ MODERN FRENCH Fodor's Choice ★

🍴 **La Couronne.** If P.T. Barnum, Florenz Ziegfeld, and Cecil B. DeMille had put together a spot distilling all the charm and glamour of Normandy, this would be it. Behind a half-timber facade gushing geraniums, the "oldest inn in France," dating from 1345, is a sometimes-ersatz extravaganza crammed with stained leaded glass, sculpted wood beams, marble Norman chimneys, leather-upholstered chairs, and damask curtains. The Salon Jeanne d'Arc is the largest room and has a wonderful wall-wide sash window and quaint paintings, but the only place to sit is the adorably cozy, wood-lined Salon des Rôtisseurs, an antiquarian's delight. The star attractions on Vincent Taillefer's menu—lobster stew with chestnut, sheeps' feet, duck in blood sauce—make few modern concessions. Dine at La Couronne and you'll be adding your name to a list that includes Sophia Loren, John Wayne, Jean-Paul Sartre, Salvador Dalí, and Princess Grace of Monaco. [$] *Average main: €35* ✉ *31 pl. du Vieux-Marché, Vieux-Marché* ☎ *02–35–71–40–90* 🌐 *www.lacouronne.com.fr.*

$$$$ FRENCH Fodor's Choice ★

🍴 **Restaurant Gill.** On the quay at the heart of Rouen's gastronomic epicenter, Rouen's only Michelin two-star restaurant goes to great lengths to make sure you feel pampered from start to finish. That's not hard to do when chef Gilles Tournadre (and his charming wife Sylvie) are in charge of things. With a reputation for culinary rigor, this native son is well versed in the splendors of the Norman woods, fields, and shore: oysters, crab, scallops, lobster, and several types of fish can be found on the menu every day, year-round, along with hare, piglet, and sweetbreads. Signature dishes include pigeon *à la Rouennaise* and succulent langoustine tails with red pepper chutney. When ordering your dinner, remember to include a request for the soufflé made with (what else?) a silky old Norman Calvados. Although the tasting menu is a bit steep, it's worth the splurge for a primer in one of France's great regional cuisines. [$] *Average main: €68* ✉ *8–9 quai de la Bourse, Vieux-Marché* ☎ *02–35–71–16–14* 🌐 *www.gill.fr* 🕒 *Closed Sun., Mon., 2 wks in Apr. and 1st 3 wks of Aug.*

WHERE TO STAY

For expanded hotel reviews, visit Fodors.com.

$ HOTEL

🏨 **Cathédrale.** There are enough half-timber walls and beams here to fill a super-luxe hotel, but the happy news is that this is a budget option—even better, this 17th-century building is found on a narrow pedestrian street just behind Rouen's cathedral. **Pros:** storybook surroundings; can't-be-beat location. **Cons:** small rooms; no car access. [$] *Rooms*

from: €79 ✉ *12 rue St-Romain, St-Maclou* ☎ *02–35–71–57–95* 🌐 *www.hotel-de-la-cathedrale.fr* *26 rooms.*

$ HOTEL 🏨 **Dieppe.** Established in 1880, the Dieppe remains up-to-date thanks to resolute management by five generations of the Guéret family—helpful, English-speaking, they welcome guests to their fine restaurant and their compact guest rooms (No. 22 is the largest), which were all handsomely renovated in 2010 and have modern color schemes, new bathrooms, and flat-screen TVs. **Pros:** personal service; convenient to train station. **Cons:** slightly corporate; street noise gets through in spite of double-glazed windows; a bit away from city center. [$] *Rooms from: €100* ✉ *Pl. Bernard-Tissot, Gare* ☎ *02–35–71–96–00* 🌐 *www.hotel-dieppe.fr* *41 rooms* 🍴 *Some meals.*

$$$$ HOTEL Fodor's Choice ★ 🏨 **Hotel de Bougtheroulde.** One of Normandy's most magnificent *hôtels particuliers* (family mansions)—a vision of Gothic glamour with soaring stone pinnacles and fairy-tale turrets—opened its doors in April 2010 to become Rouen's finest hotel. **Pros:** gorgeously Gothic; attentive staff; steps from the center of historic Rouen. **Cons:** minimalism is not for everyone. [$] *Rooms from: €250* ✉ *15 pl. de la Pucelle, Vieux-Marché* ☎ *02–35–14–50–50* 🌐 *www.hotelsparouen.com* *78 rooms* 🍴 *Some meals.*

$$ HOTEL 🏨 **Mercure Centre.** In the jumble of streets near Rouen's cathedral—a navigational challenge if you arrive by car—this modern chain hotel has small, comfortable guest rooms decorated in breezy pastels. **Pros:** functional; central; serves organic breakfasts. **Cons:** interiors lack character; hard to find. [$] *Rooms from: €134* ✉ *7 rue de la Croix-de-Fer, St-Maclou* ☎ *02–35–52–69–52* 🌐 *www.mercure.com* *125 rooms* 🍴 *Breakfast.*

$ HOTEL 🏨 **Vieux Carré.** In the heart of Old Rouen, this cute hotel has practical and comfortable rooms that, while recently refurbished, retain their taste for the exotic: lamps from Egypt, tables from Morocco, and 1940s English armoires. **Pros:** charming; central; exceptional prices. **Cons:** small rooms; hard to park. [$] *Rooms from: €68* ✉ *34 rue Ganterie, Gare* ☎ *02–35–71–67–70* 🌐 *www.hotel-vieux-carre.com* *13 rooms* 🍴 *No meals.*

NIGHTLIFE AND THE ARTS

Bar de la Crosse. Visit the popular local haunt Bar de la Crosse for an aperitif and a good chat with some (friendly?) Rouennais. ✉ *53 rue de l'Hôpital, St-Maclou* ☎ *02–35–70–16–68.*

Fête Jeanne d'Arc (*Joan of Arc Festival*). Parades, street plays, concerts, exhibitions, and a medieval market are just a few of the exciting events that mark the annual homage to Rouen's fabled martyr; it takes place on the Sunday nearest to May 30.

Théâtre des Arts. Operas, plays, and concerts are staged at the Théâtre des Arts. ✉ *7 rue du Dr-Rambert, Vieux-Marché* ☎ *02–35–98–74–78* 🌐 *www.operaderouen.com.*

FÉCAMP

Visitor Information Fécamp Tourist Office ✉ *Quai Sadi Carnot* ☎ *02–35–28–51–01* 🌐 *www.fecamptourisme.com.*

EXPLORING

Abbaye de La Trinité. The ancient cod-fishing port of Fécamp was once a major pilgrimage site. The magnificent abbey church, Abbaye de La Trinité, bears witness to Fécamp's religious past. The Benedictine abbey was founded by the Duke of Normandy in the 11th century and became the home of the monastic order of the Précieux Sang de la Trinité (Precious Blood of the Trinity—referring to Christ's blood, which supposedly arrived here in the 7th century in a reliquary from the Holy Land). ✉ *Rue Leroux.*

Palais de la Bénédictine (*Benedictine Palace*). Fécamp is also the home of Benedictine liqueur. The Palais de la Bénédictine, across from the tourist office, is a florid building dating from 1892 that mixes neo-Gothic and Renaissance styles. Watery pastiche or taste-tingling architectural cocktail? Whether you're shaken or stirred, this remains one of Normandy's most popular attractions. The interior is just as exhausting as the facade. Paintings, sculptures, ivories, advertising posters, and fake bottles of Benedictine compete for attention with a display of the ingredients used for the liqueur, and a chance to sample it. There's also a shop selling Benedictine products and souvenirs. ✉ *110 rue Alexandre-le-Grand* ☎ *02–35–10–26–10* 🌐 *www.benedictine.fr* 🎟 *€7.20, €10.20 with guide* ⏲ *July and Aug., daily 10–7; Sept.–Dec. and Feb.–June, daily 10–12:45 and 2–6.*

WHERE TO EAT AND STAY

For expanded hotel reviews, visit Fodors.com.

$$ SEAFOOD 🍴 **La Marée.** Overlooking Fécamp's lively harbor, this popular seafood restaurant makes up in conviviality what it lacks in charm. Considering the number of copious seafood *plateaux* that breeze by, it seems no one pays much attention to style anyway. For sheer volume, the dishes will please even the most insatiable gourmand, then factor in variety and freshness (most everything is caught locally) and you've got a winning combo. Gigantic langoustine, plump crabs, and the renowned Fécamp herring are standouts, along with a nice variety of warm dishes, including a sensational whole grilled sole and a hearty local specialty: salt cod poached in Normandy cream. The lunch *formule* (€18.50) is a good bargain. [$] *Average main: €18* ✉ *77 quai Bérigny* ☎ *02–35–29–39–15* 🌐 *www.fecamp-restaurant-la-maree.com* ⏲ *Closed Mon. No dinner Sun. and Thurs.*

$ SEAFOOD 🍴 **L'Escalier.** This delightfully simple little restaurant, right by the bustling, mast-peppered harbor, serves generous portions of traditional Norman cuisine with, as you might expect in the region's foremost port, fish and seafood at the top of the menu. Try the homemade fish soup or mussels in Calvados with french fries. Desserts don't always measure up to the rest of the meal—the tarte tatin has been known to be a shade limp—but the cozy ambience and great-value set menu ($) make this the perfect quayside spot for a quick, nourishing meal. [$] *Average main:*

€16 ✉ 101 quai Bérigny ☎ 02–35–28–26–79 ✍ Reservations essential ⏲ Closed Dec. and Thurs. mid-Dec.–mid Jan.

$ B&B/INN 🏨 **Auberge de la Rouge.** The Enderlins welcome you to this little inn just south of Fécamp, where you can enjoy guest rooms overlooking a pretty garden and also savor local specialties in the fine restaurant on-site. **Pros:** spacious rooms; family feel. **Cons:** away from town center; busy road outside. *[$] Rooms from: €67 ✉ 445 rte. du Havre, St-Léonard 🌐 www.auberge-rouge.com 🛏 8 rooms.*

ÉTRETAT

17 km (11 miles) southwest of Fécamp via D940, 88 km (55 miles) northwest of Rouen.

Fodor's Choice ★ Perched midway along Normandy's Alabaster Coast, Étretat might look like a spot not worth the detour. However, its end-of-the-world site on the Atlantic coast, its spectacular stone formations famously immortalized in paint by the Impressionists, and the village itself—a Fisher-Price toy village lined with houses covered with picturesque 19th-century sculpted figural carvings—all add up to one of France's most amazing, unforgettable destinations. No matter there are no museums there—the entire village could be a museum exhibit.

The plunging chalk cliffs of Étretat are so gorgeous and strange that they seem surreal at first. The crowds of camera-toting visitors, however, will bring you back to reality quickly. But if you head for the cliffs in early morning or late evening, you'll see what drew artists like Monet, Boudin, and Courbet here. Chances are you'll be just as inspired by this breathtaking natural splendor as old Claude was. For an extensive listing of the town's many hotels and restaurants, log on to 🌐 *www.seine-maritime-tourisme.com.*

GETTING HERE

Your best bet is to take the bus from either Fécamp (30 mins) or Le Havre (60 mins). There are no trains to Étretat. Occasional trains from Paris (Gare St-Lazare) are met at Bréauté-Beuzeville station, between Rouen and Le Havre, by a bus that reaches Étretat in 30 minutes. For further train information, contact SNCF (☎ *36–35*).

Visitor Information **Étretat Tourist Office** ✉ *Pl. Maurice Guillard* ☎ *02–35–27–05–21* 🌐 *www.etretat.net.*

EXPLORING

Falaises d'Étretat. This large village, with its promenade running the length of the pebble beach, is renowned for the magnificent tall rock formations that extend out into the sea. The Falaises d'Étretat are white cliffs that are as famous in France as Dover's are in England—and have been painted by many artists, Claude Monet chief among them.

A stunning white-sand beach and white-chalk rocks, such as the "Manneporte"—a limestone portal likened by author Guy de Maupassant to an elephant dipping its trunk into water—are major elements in the composition. Here Monet became a pictorial rock-climber with the help of his famous "slotted box," built with compartments for six different canvases, allowing him to switch midstream from painting to painting, as weather patterns momentarily changed. With storms and sun alternating hour by the hour, you'll quickly understand why they say, "Just wait: in Normandy we have great weather several times a day!"—yet another reason why the Impressionists, intent on capturing the ephemeral, so loved this town.

At low tide it's possible to walk through the huge archways formed by the rocks to neighboring beaches. The biggest arch is at the **Falaise d'Aval,** to the south, and for a breathtaking view of the whole bay be sure to climb the easy path up to the top. From here you can hike for miles across the Manneporte Hills, or play a round of golf on one of Europe's windiest and most scenic courses, overlooking **L'Aiguille** (The Needle), a 300-foot spike of rock jutting out of the sea just offshore. To the north towers the **Falaise d'Amont,** topped by the gloriously picturesque chapel of Notre-Dame de la Garde.

If you want to join the long list of Étretat's many fans—Offenbach and Victor Hugo favored its Château Les Aygues hotel—log on to 🌐 *www.seine-maritime-tourisme.com* to find a full list of hotels and restaurants. Étretat rocks!

5

WHERE TO EAT AND STAY

For expanded hotel reviews, visit Fodors.com.

$$ SEAFOOD 🍴 **Les Roches Blanches.** The exterior of this family-owned restaurant off the beach is a post–World War II concrete eyesore. But take a table by the window with a view of the cliffs, order the superb fresh seafood (try the tuna steak or the sea bass roasted in Calvados or champagne), and you'll be glad you came. Reservations are essential for Sunday lunch. [$] *Average main: €19* ✉ *Rue de l'Abbé-Cochet* ☎ *02–35–27–07–34* 🌐 *www.les-roches-blanches.com* ⏲ *Closed Wed. and Nov.–Feb.*

$$$$ HOTEL 🏨 **Domaine Saint Clair Le Donjon.** From the look of this charming, ivy-covered, Anglo-Norman château—complete with storybook tower, private park, and lovely sea vistas—it is easy to understand why Monet, Proust, Offenbach, and other greats accepted invitations here; built overlooking Étretat by a rich Parisian couple in 1862, the Belle Époque house has guest rooms that are spacious, comfortable, quiet, and individually furnished, with the emphasis on "individual"—vast swaths of red fabric, decorator mirrors, and antique gramophones are some flamboyant accents, while other rooms are stylish enough for *Maison Française*. **Pros:** grand architecture; gorgeous setting; outdoor swimming pool; massage relaxation center. **Cons:** pricey; strident decoration in some rooms. [$] *Rooms from: €220* ✉ *Chemin de St-Clair* ☎ *02–35–27–08–23* 🌐 *www.hoteletretat.com* 🛏 *21 rooms* 🍽 *Some meals.*

$ HOTEL 🏨 **Dormy House.** Ideally located halfway up the Étretat cliffs, this smart, modernish hotel enjoys a spectacular perch amid acres of manicured cliffside parkland—the guest rooms are simple and comfortable (refurbished in 2012, some with parquet flooring), but the real beauty is right outside your bedroom window, thanks to views of *la mer,* so wonderful they would have Debussy humming in no time. **Pros:** grand sea views; fine fish restaurant. **Cons:** small rooms; those in annex lack character. [$] *Rooms from: €100* ✉ *Rte. du Havre* ☎ *02–35–27–07–88* 🌐 *www.*

dormy-house.com 🛏 *60 rooms, 3 suites* 🕐 *Closed 1st 3 wks of Jan.* 🍴 *Breakfast.*

$ HOTEL 🏨 **Résidence.** In a picturesque 16th-century house in the heart of town, with a rather cutting-edge restaurant on the ground floor and a young, friendly, and energetic staff, this option has several strong pluses, and though the cheapest rooms are pretty basic—both the bathroom and the shower are in the hallway—the more expensive ones have in-room bathrooms, and one even has a hot tub. **Pros:** great value; eco-friendly restaurant. **Cons:** spartan facilities; unsavvy staff. [$] *Rooms from: €75* ✉ *4 bd. du Président-René-Coty* ☎ *02–35–27–02–87* 🌐 *www.hotellaresidenceetretat.com* 🛏 *15 rooms* 🍴 *Breakfast.*

SPORTS

Golf d'Étretat. Don't miss the chance to play at Golf d'Étretat, where the stupendous 6,580-yard, par-72 course drapes across the cliff tops of the Falaise d'Aval. ✉ *Rte. du Havre* ☎ *02–35–27–04–89* 🌐 *www.golfetretat.com* 🕐 *Closed Tues.*

LE HAVRE

28 km (18 miles) southwest of Étretat via D940; 88 km (55 miles) west of Rouen; 200 km (125 miles) northwest of Paris.

You might think there is little left to see in Le Havre, France's second-largest port (after Marseille), as it was bombarded 146 times during World War II. Think again. You may find the rebuilt city, with its uncompromising recourse to reinforced concrete and open spaces, bleak and uninviting; on the other hand, it is home to some of France's most spectacular modern architecture: Auguste Perret's rational planning and audacious modern structures, which have now earned the city UNESCO World Heritage status. Above all, the unforgettable **Église St-Joseph**—half rocket ship, half church—is alone worth the trip, along with such other modernist landmarks as the center-of-town "Volcanoes." Perret (d. 1954) developed a mastery of the art of reinforced concrete and this wound up lending so much élan to the rebuilding of war-devastated Le Havre.

Visitor Information Le Havre Tourist Office ✉ *186 bd. Clemenceau* ☎ *02–35–19–45–45* 🌐 *www.ville-lehavre.fr.*

EXPLORING

Fodor's Choice ★ **Église St-Joseph.** Perhaps the most eye-popping piece of 20th-century architecture anywhere, and one of the most impressive modernist churches in France, is the Église St-Joseph, built to the plans of Auguste Perret in the 1950s. The 350-foot tower powers into the sky like a fat rocket. The interior is just as thrilling. No frills here: the 270-foot octagonal lantern soars above the crossing, filled almost to the top with abstract stained glass that hurls colored light over the bare concrete walls. *Star Wars* had nothing on this! ✉ *Bd. François-Ier* ☎ *02–35–74–04–04.*

Musée d'Art Moderne André-Malraux. Bathed in the famous sea light that drew artists in their droves to Le Havre—thanks to its soaring plate-glass windows—the city's art museum is an innovative 1960s glass-and-metal structure surrounded by a moat. Two local artists who gorgeously immortalized the Normandy coast are showcased here—Raoul Dufy (1877–1953), through a remarkable collection of his brightly colored oils, watercolors, and sketches; and Eugène Boudin (1824–98), a forerunner of Impressionism, whose compelling beach scenes and landscapes tellingly evoke the Normandy sea and skyline. ✉ *2 bd. Clemenceau* ☎ *02–35–19–62–62* 🌐 *www.muma-lehavre.fr* 🎫 *€5* 🕒 *Wed.–Mon. 11–6, weekends 11–7.*

WHERE TO EAT AND STAY

For expanded hotel reviews, visit Fodors.com.

$$ SEAFOOD 🍴 **L'Orchidée.** With the port and fish market within netting distance, seafood is guaranteed to be fresh here. It's a no-frills place—the visual appeal is on your plate, in the pinks and greens of the smoked salmon and avocado sauce that accompany the chef's homemade fish terrine. Although chef Stéphane Lamotte specializes in fresh fish, notably sea bass, turbot, and sole fricassee with leaks, L'Orchidée has its share of meat dishes—the breast of duck with three-pepper sauce is usually a winner. [$] *Average main: €18* ✉ *41 rue du Général-Faidherbe* ☎ *02–76–25–38–03* 🌐 *www.restaurant-orchidee.com* 🕒 *Closed Mon. No dinner Tues. No lunch Sat.*

$$ HOTEL 🏨 **Best Western Art Hotel.** Designed by the famed architect Auguste Perret, and located by the soothing waters of the Bassin de Commerce, this hotel's light, airy rooms have contemporary furniture, and a few—like No. 63—have balconies and views of the port. **Pros:** modernist panache; functional; central. **Cons:** few rooms with balcony. [$] *Rooms from: €110* ✉ *147 rue Louis-Brindeau* ☎ *02–35–22–69–44* 🌐 *www.bestwestern.fr* 🛏 *31 rooms* 🍽 *No meals.*

HONFLEUR TO MONT-ST-MICHEL

Basse Normandy (Lower Normandy) begins to the west of the Seine Estuary, near the Belle Époque resort towns of Trouville and Deauville, extending out to the sandy Côte Fleurie (Flower Coast), stretching northwest from the D-Day landing sites past Omaha Beach and on to Utah Beach and the Cotentin Peninsula, which juts out into the English Channel. After the World War II D-Day landings, some of the fiercest fighting took place around Caen and Bayeux, as many monuments and memorials testify. Heading south, in the prosperous Pays d'Auge, dairy farms produce the region's famous cheeses. Rising to the west is the fabled Mont-St-Michel. Inland, heading back toward central France, lush green meadows and apple orchards cover the countryside starting west of the market town of Lisieux—the heart of Calvados country.

HONFLEUR

35 km (22 miles) southwest of Etretat via D940, A131, and D579, 80 km (50 miles) west of Rouen.

Fodor's Choice ★ Beloved by artists, Honfleur is the most picturesque of the Côte Fleurie's little seaside towns. Much of the city's Renaissance architecture remains intact, especially around the 17th-century Vieux Bassin harbor, which is

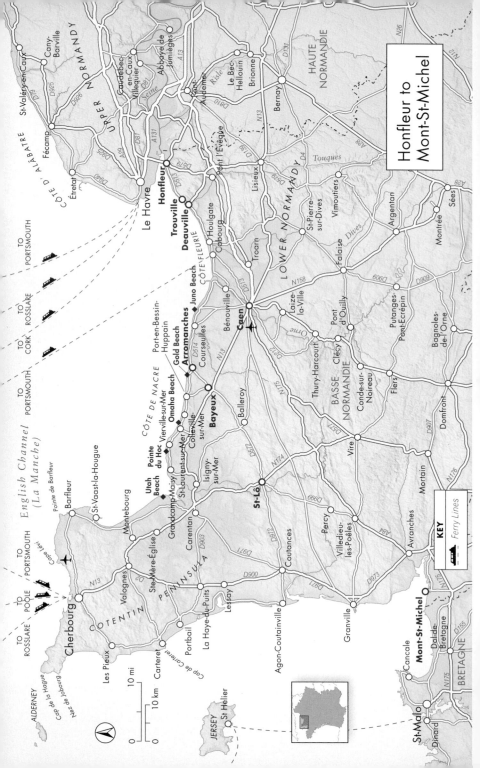

Honfleur to Mont-St-Michel

CLOSE UP

Normandy on Canvas

Long before Claude Monet created his Giverny lily pond by diverting the Epte River that marks the boundary with the Ile-de-France, artists had been scudding into Normandy for two watery reasons: the Seine and the sea. Just downstream from Vernon, where the Epte joins the Seine, Richard the Lion-Heart's ruined castle at Les Andelys, immortalized by Paul Signac and Félix Vallotton, heralds the soft-lighted, cliff-lined Seine Valley, impressionistically evoked by Albert Lebourg and Gustave Loiseau's pieces in the Arts Museum in Rouen—where Camille Corot once studied, and whose mighty cathedral Monet painted until he was pink, purple, and blue in the face.

The Seine joins the sea at Le Havre, where Monet grew up, a protégé of Eugène Boudin, often termed the precursor of Impressionism. Boudin would boat across the estuary from Honfleur, where he hobnobbed with

Gustave Courbet, Charles Daubigny, and Alfred Sisley at the Ferme St-Siméon. Le Havre in the 1860s was base camp for Monet and his pals Frédéric Bazille and Johan Barthold Jongkind to explore the rugged coast up to Dieppe, with easels opened en route beneath the cliffs of Étretat.

The railroad from Gare St-Lazare (smokily evoked by Monet) put Dieppe within easy reach of Paris. Eugène Delacroix daubed seascapes here in 1852. Auguste Renoir visited Dieppe from 1878 to 1885; Paul Gauguin and Edgar Degas clinked glasses here in 1885; Camille Pissarro painted his way from Gisors to Dieppe in the 1890s. As the nearest port to Paris, Dieppe wowed the English, too. Walter Sickert moved in from 1898 to 1905, and artists from the Camden Town Group he founded back in London often painted in Dieppe before World War I.

5

almost as supremely colorful as in the days when the great Impressionist masters often painted it. The town has become increasingly crowded since the opening of the elegant Pont de Normandie, providing a direct link with Le Havre and Upper Normandy—the world's sixth-largest cable-stayed bridge, it's supported by two concrete pylons taller than the Eiffel Tower and is designed to resist winds of 257 kph (160 mph). Honfleur remains a time-burnished place, full of half-timber houses and cobbled streets now lined with a stunning selection of stylish boutiques and shops. It was once an important departure point for maritime expeditions, including the first voyages to Canada in the 15th and 16th centuries.

GETTING HERE
To get to Honfleur, take the bus from Deauville (30 mins, €2.30); from Caen (2 hrs, €7.85; l'Express1 hr, €11.15); or from Le Havre (30 mins, €4.50). Buses run every two hours or so and are operated by **Bus Verts du Calvados** (☎ *08–10–21–42–14* ⊕ *www.busverts.fr*).

Visitor Information Honfleur Tourist Office ✉ *Quai Lepaulmier* ☎ *02–31–89–23–30* ⊕ *en.ot-honfleur.fr.*

Relentlessly picturesque Honfleur has been immortalized by many painters, most famously by J. M. W. Turner and Eugène Boudin.

EXPLORING

Looking like a 3-D Boudin painting, the heart of Honfleur is its 17th-century harbor, fronted on one side by two-story stone houses with low, sloping roofs and on the other by tall, narrow houses whose wooden facades are topped by slate roofs. Note that parking can be a problem. Your best bet is the parking lot just beyond the Vieux-Bassin (Old Harbor) on the left as you approach from the land side.

Ste-Catherine. Soak up the seafaring atmosphere by strolling around the old harbor and paying a visit to the ravishing wooden church of Ste-Catherine, which dominates a tumbling square. The church and the ramshackle belfry across the way—note the many touches of marine engineering in their architecture—were built by townspeople to show their gratitude for the departure of the English at the end of the Hundred Years' War, in 1453. ⊠ *Rue des Logettes* ☎ *02–31–89–11–83.*

WHERE TO EAT AND STAY

For expanded hotel reviews, visit Fodors.com.

$$$
MODERN FRENCH

✕ **Le Fleur de Sel.** A low-beamed 16th-century fisherman's house provides the cozy atmosphere for chef Vincent's Guyon's locally influenced cuisine, centered on the daily catch. The ambitious menu usually includes at least five different fish dishes—presented with artistic panache—along with plenty of grilled meats, like salt-marsh lamb or pigeon. For starters, the oyster ravioli with a butternut mousse and chestnut foam, draws raves; it might be followed by a delicately crusted salmon with leeks in an almond vinaigrette and fromage blanc. Three fixed-price menus ($$$–$$$$) assure a splendid meal on any budget. Be sure to save room for one of the masterful desserts or an informed cheese course. $ *Average main: €29* ✉ *17 rue Haute* ☎ *02–31–89–01–92* ⊕ *www.lafleurdesel-honfleur.com* ☾ *Closed Tues., Wed., and Jan.*

$$$$
MODERN FRENCH
Fodor's Choice
★

✗ **Sa.Qua.Na.** Chef Alexandre Bourdas earned his second Michelin star in 2010, after putting Honfleur on the gastronomic map with his first star in 2008. From the small but ravishing dining room to the impeccable presentation, his restaurant is a study in getting it right down to the smallest detail. Surprising combinations—braised cod in a lemon confit pastry with a coulis of green peas, leeks, and mushrooms; roasted pigeon breast with haricots verts, peanuts, garlic purée, and a tarragon Hollandaise—attest to Bourdas's far-flung influences: his native Aveyron, Japan (where he cooked for three years), and the regional fare he seeks out daily from local farmers and fishermen. Having also worked as a pastry chef, Bourdas creates his own desserts, like the glorious *nougatine au beurre* with strawberry sorbet, orange flower cream, and a pistachio crust. Along with two sublime tasting menus, the chef has thoughtfully provided a menu for kids under 10 that's less than half the price. *Bien sûr*, reserve well in advance. $ *Average main: €78* ✉ *22 pl. Hamelin* ☎ *02–31–89–40–80* ⊕ *www.alexandre-bourdas.com* ☾ *Closed Mon.–Wed.*

$$$$
HOTEL

⊡ **Ferme St-Siméon.** The story goes that this 19th-century manor house was the famed birthplace of Impressionism, and that its park inspired Monet and Sisley—neither of whom would have dismissed the welcoming rich mix of 19th-century elegance and down-home Norman delights inside, where rich fabrics, grand paintings, and Louis Seize chairs are married with rustic antiques, ancient beams, and half-timber walls; the result casts a deliciously cozy spell. **Pros:** famed historic charm. **Cons:** expensive; bland annex rooms. $ *Rooms from: €400* ✉ *Rue Adolphe-Marais, on D513 to Trouville* ☎ *02–31–81–78–00* ⊕ *www. fermesaintsimeon.fr* ↪ *34 rooms, 3 suites* ⦿*Some meals.*

$$
B&B/INN
Fodor's Choice
★

⊡ **La Petite Folie.** Charming simply doesn't suffice to describe this beautifully renovated 1830s town house a stone's throw from Honfleur's old port—lavished with antiques, no luxury has been spared in appointing the main house's main rooms. **Pros:** gracious welcome; a good value, with generous breakfast included and secure parking optional. **Cons:** no-children-under-10 policy. $ *Rooms from: €145* ✉ *44 rue Haute* ☎ *06–74–39–46–46* ⊕ *www.lapetitefolie-honfleur.com* ↪ *5 rooms, 5 apartments* ⦿*Breakfast.*

$$$
HOTEL

⊡ **Le Manoir des Impressionnistes.** An archetypal fin-de-siècle villa, perched on top of a small wooded hill 200 yards from the sea, this gorgeous half-timber, dormer-roof manor welcomes you with a pretty green-and-white facade in the Anglo-Norman style and guest rooms that have sweeping views; all are traditionally and tastefully furnished, and have modern marble bathrooms, and the room on the first floor has a four-poster bed and its own balcony. **Pros:** exquisitely decorated and furnished; sea views; stylish bathrooms. **Cons:** away from town center; no elevator. $ *Rooms from: €190* ✉ *Phare du Butin* ☎ *02–31–81–63–00* ⊕ *www.manoirdesimpressionnistes.eu* ↪ *10 rooms* ☾ *Closed Jan.* ⦿*Some meals.*

5

NIGHTLIFE AND THE ARTS

Fête des Marins (*Marine Festival*). The two-day Fête des Marins is held on Pentecost Sunday and Monday (50 days after Easter). On Sunday all the boats in the harbor are decked out in flags and paper roses, and a priest bestows his blessing at high tide. The next day, model boats and local children head a musical procession.

Fête du Jazz (*Jazz Festival*). There's also a five-day Fête du Jazz in August.

DEAUVILLE-TROUVILLE

16 km (10 miles) southwest of Honfleur via D513, 92 km (57 miles) west of Rouen.

Twin towns on the beach, divided only by the River Touques, Deauville and Trouville compete for the title of Most Extravagant Norman Town. In the 19th century, there were no more fashionable towns than these two, but by the 20th they were both overbuilt to such an extent that their charm was sadly diminished. Deauville, especially, has been the victim of its own success—its main avenue on the sea is now one solid wall of apartment buildings.

GETTING HERE

Trains to Deauville-Trouville (the station is between the two towns) from Gare St-Lazare in Paris (2 hrs, €27.20) often require a change at Lisieux. There are also buses to Deauville from Le Havre (1 hr, €6.85); Honfleur (30 mins, €2.30); and Caen (75 mins, €5.60). Buses run every two hours or so and are operated by **Bus Verts du Calvados** (☎ 08–10–21–42–14 ⊕ *www.busverts.fr*).

Visitor Information Deauville-Trouville Tourist Office ✉ *Pl. de la Mairie* ☎ *02–31–14–40–00* ⊕ *www.deauville.org.*

EXPLORING

Deauville and Trouville are distinctly different in character, but it's easy (and common) to shuttle between them. Trouville—whose beaches were immortalized in the 19th-century paintings of Eugène Boudin (and *Gigi*, Vincente Minnelli's 1958 Oscar-winner)—is the oldest seaside resort in France. In the days of Louis-Philippe, it was discovered by artists and the upper crust; by the end of the Second Empire it was the beach à la mode. Then the Duc de Mornay, half brother of Napoléon III, and other aristocrats who were looking for something more exclusive, built their villas along the deserted beach across the Touques (more than a few of these were built simply as love-shacks for their mistresses).

Thus was launched Deauville, a vigorous grande dame who started kicking up her heels during the Second Empire, kept swinging through the Belle Époque, and is still frequented by Rothschilds, princes, and movie stars. Few of them ever actually get in the water here, since other attractions—casino, theater, music hall, polo, galas, racecourses (some of the world's most fabled horse farms are here), marina and regattas, palaces and gardens, and extravagant shops along the rue Eugène-Colas—compete for their attention. Fashionable avenues like rue des Villas and place Morny also entice. But perhaps Deauville is known best for its **promenade des Planches**—the boardwalk extending along the seafront and lined with deck chairs, bars, striped cabanas, and an array of lovely half-timber Norman villas, elegant resort hotels, and block after block of prewar apartment houses. With its high-price hotels, designer boutiques, and one of the smartest gilt-edge casinos in Europe, Deauville is sometimes jokingly called Paris's 21st arrondissement. Trouville—a short drive or five-minute boat trip across the Touques River from its more prestigious neighbor—remains more of a family resort, harboring few pretensions.

WHERE TO EAT AND STAY

For expanded hotel reviews, visit Fodors.com.

$$$
FRENCH

✕ **L'Essentiel.** A nice change from the grand, overly formal hotel dining rooms that dominate Deauville, the relaxed atmosphere and sensational cuisine at this contemporary eatery have made it extremely popular. Chef Charles Thuillant, whose pedigree includes stints at two top Paris restaurants, focuses on a lighter, Asian-inspired cuisine, with Italian influences. Brimming with fresh, seasonal ingredients, the menu changes almost weekly. Dishes like braised cod with leek fondue, bottarga and kumquat confit; and spinach ravioli with kimchi and gambas shrimp in a carrot emulsion bring this talented chef's mastery to the forefront. A capacious terrace, a choice selection of excellent wines by the glass, and a bargain midday prix-fixe menu on weekdays make this the perfect place to linger. $ *Average main: €26* ⌂ *29–31 rue Mirabeau, Deauville* ☎ *02-31-87-22-11* ⊕ *www.lessentieldeauville.com* ☉ *Closed Mon. and Tues.*

$
HOTEL

☎ **Continental.** Vintage daguerreotypes prove that this is one of Deauville's oldest establishments (opened 1866) and its once-picturesque building—shoehorned into a triangle plot and topped with an elegant mansard roof—was painted by Eugène Boudin himself; too bad that the famed Impressionist wouldn't appreciate the modern signs that now blemish the exterior, but inside renovations still create an inviting hotel: flowering plants, comfy new chairs, and snug but tranquil guest rooms make this a good bet, especially because it's close to the train station yet within easy walking distance of the town center. **Pros:** cheap; convenient to train station. **Cons:** far from the beach; lacks character. $ *Rooms from: €90* ⌂ *1 rue Désiré-Le-Hoc, Deauville* ☎ *02-31-88-21-06* ⊕ *www.hotel-continental-deauville.com* ⟿ *42 rooms* ☉ *Closed mid-Nov.–mid-Dec.* ⦿ *No meals.*

$$$
HOTEL

☎ **81 L'Hôtel.** While this recently renovated boutique hotel pours on the gloss, the nicer original features of the 1906 mansion—parquet floors, magnificent fireplace, stained glass windows, impossibly high ceilings— remain to complement the usual postmodern touches (faux crocodile chairs, silver furniture, shrouded chandeliers, ersatz-Baroque beds) that have been added. **Pros:** catering facilities available for take-out meals; easy parking. **Cons:** a walk to the beach. $ *Rooms from: €160* ⌂ *81 av. de la République, Deauville* ☎ *02-31-14-01-50* ⊕ *www.81lhotel. com* ⟿ *20 rooms* ⦿ *Breakfast.*

$$$$
HOTEL
Fodor'sChoice
★

☎ **Normandy-Barrière.** With a facade that is a riot of pastel-green timbering, checkerboard walls, and Anglo-Norman balconies, the Normandy has been one of the town's landmarks since it opened in 1912, and crowds still pack the place, thanks to its recent face-lift by Jacques

Garcia, France's most aristo decorator; its grand salons now overflow with needlepoint sofas, fin-de-siècle chandeliers, and 19th-century armchairs. **Pros:** grand interiors; luxurious amenities; Deauville's place to be seen. **Cons:** some elements of kitschy bombast; patronizing service; can be steamy in summer. $ *Rooms from: €350* ⊠ *38 rue Jean-Mermoz, Deauville* ☏ *02–31–98–66–22, 800/223–5652 for U.S. reservations* ⊕ *www.lucienbarriere.com* ⇆ *290 rooms, 31 suites* ⏐◯⏐ *Breakfast.*

NIGHTLIFE AND THE ARTS

American Film Festival. One of the biggest cultural events on the Norman calendar is the weeklong American Film Festival, held in Deauville in early September.

Casino de Deauville. Formal attire is required at the Casino de Deauville. ⊠ *2 rue Edmond-Blanc* ☏ *02–31–98–66–00.*

Casino de Trouville. Trouville's Casino de Trouville is slightly less highbrow than Deauville's. ⊠ *Pl. du Maréchal-Foch* ☏ *02–31–87–75–00.*

Le Seven. Night owls enjoy Le Seven; it's open until 5 am. ⊠ *13 rue Albert-Fracasse, Deauville* ☏ *02–31–88–40–50.*

The Y Club. "The" place to go out dancing, according to some natives. ⊠ *14, rue Désiré Le Hoc, Deauville.*

SPORTS AND THE OUTDOORS

Club Nautique de Trouville. Sailing boats large and small can be rented from the Club Nautique de Trouville. ⊠ *Digue des Roches Noires* ☏ *02–31–88–13–59* ⊕ *www.cnth.org.*

Hippodrome de Deauville Clairefontaine. Horse races and polo can be seen most summer afternoons at the Hippodrome de Deauville Clairefontaine. ⊠ *Rte. de Clairefontaine* ☏ *02–31–14–69–00* ⊕ *www. hippodrome-deauville-clairefontaine.com.*

Hippodrome de Deauville—La Touques. Deauville becomes Europe's horse capital in August, when breeders jet in from around the world for its yearling auctions and the races at its two attractive hippodromes. Afternoon horse races are held in the heart of Deauville at the Hippodrome de Deauville—La Toques. ⊠ *Blvd. Mauger* ☏ *02–31–14–20–00.*

Poney Club. Head for the Poney Club for a wonderful horseback ride on the beach (the sunsets can be spectacular). It's open weekends and holidays, but be sure to call early to reserve a horse, or a pony for your little one. ⊠ *Rue Reynoldo-Hahn* ☏ *02–31–98–56–24.*

CAEN

54 km (35 miles) southwest of Deauville-Trouville; 28 km (17 miles) southeast of Bayeux; 120 km (75 miles) west of Rouen.

Fodor's Choice
★

With its abbeys and castle, Caen, a busy administrative city and the capital of Lower Normandy, is very different from the coastal resorts. William of Normandy ruled from Caen in the 11th century before he conquered England. Nine hundred years later, during the two-month Battle of Caen in 1944, a fire raged for 11 days, devastating much of the town. Today the city is basically modern and commercial, with a vibrant student scene. The Caen Mémorial, an impressive museum

Even in the 19th century, elegant Parisians loved to flock to Deauville to enjoy a promenade along its beautiful beach.

devoted to World War II, is considered a must-do by travelers interested in 20th-century history (many avail themselves of the excellent bus tours the museum sponsors to the D-Day beaches). But Caen's former grandeur can be seen in its extant historic monuments and along scenically restored rue Ecuyère and place St-Sauveur.

GETTING HERE

Trains from Paris (Gare St-Lazare) leave for Caen every two hours or so (€31.20); the 241-km (150-mile) trip takes less than two hours. Some trains continue to Bayeux (2 hrs, €35). Several trains daily link Caen to Rouen (90 mins, €26.70) and St-Lô (45 mins, €13.50). Bus Verts du Calvados (☎ 08–10–21–42–14 ⊕ *www.busverts.fr*) operates buses every two hours or so from the Caen train station to Le Havre (2 hrs, 30 mins, €11.20; l'Express 1 hr, 30 mins, €15.65) via Deauville (75 mins, €5.60) and Honfleur (2 hr, 45 mins, €7.95; l'Express 1 hr, €11.15).

Visitor Information Caen Tourist Office ✉ *Pl. du Canada* ☎ *02–31–27–90–30* ⊕ *www.tourisme.caen.fr.*

EXPLORING

Abbaye aux Dames (*Ladies' Abbey*). The Abbaye aux Dames was founded by William the Conqueror's wife, Matilda, in 1063. Once a hospital, the abbey—rebuilt in the 18th century—was restored in the 1980s by the Regional Council, which then promptly requisitioned it for office space; however, its elegant arcaded courtyard and ground-floor reception rooms can be admired during a free guided tour. You can also visit the squat **Église de la Trinité** (Trinity Church), a fine example of 11th-century Romanesque architecture, though its original spires were replaced by timid balustrades in the early 18th century.

Note the intricate carvings on columns and arches in the chapel; the 11th-century crypt; and, in the choir, the marble slab commemorating Queen Matilda, buried here in 1083. ⊠ *Pl. de la Reine-Mathilde* ☎ *02–31–06–98–98* ⊠ *Free* ⊙ *Tours daily at 2:30 and 4.*

Fodor'sChoice **Abbaye aux Hommes** *(Men's Abbey).* Caen's finest church, of cathedral
★ proportions, is part of the Abbaye aux Hommes, built by William the Conqueror from local Caen stone (also used for England's Canterbury Cathedral, Westminster Abbey, and the Tower of London). The abbey was begun in Romanesque style in 1066 and expanded in the 18th century; its elegant buildings are now part of City Hall and some rooms are brightened by the city's fine collection of paintings. Note the magnificent yet spare facade of the abbey church of **St-Étienne,** enhanced by two 11th-century towers topped by octagonal spires. Inside, what had been William the Conqueror's tomb was destroyed by 16th-century Huguenots during the Wars of Religion. However, the choir still stands; it was the first to be built in Norman Gothic style, and many subsequent choirs were modeled after it. To get the full historical scoop, sign up for one of the special tours. ⊠ *Pl. Louis-Guillouard* ☎ *02–31–30–42–81* ⊠ *Tours €4.50* ⊙ *Tours daily at 9:30, 11, 2:30, and 4.*

Château Ducal. Looming on a mound ahead of the church is the château—the ruins of William the Conqueror's fortress, built in 1060 and sensitively restored after the war. The castle gardens are a perfect spot for strolling, and the ramparts afford good views of the city. The citadel also contains two museums—the Musée des Beaux-Arts and the Musée de Normandie—and the medieval church of **St-Georges,** used for exhibitions.

Hôtel d'Escoville. A good place to begin exploring Caen is the Hôtel d'Escoville, a stately mansion in the city center built by wealthy merchant Nicolas Le Valois d'Escoville in the 1530s. The building was badly damaged during the war but has since been restored; the austere facade conceals an elaborate inner courtyard, reflecting the Italian influence on early Renaissance Norman architecture. The on-site city **tourist office** is an excellent resource. ⊠ *Pl. St-Pierre* ☎ *02–31–27–14–14* ⊕ *www.tourisme.caen.fr.*

Mémorial. The Mémorial, an imaginative museum erected in 1988 on the north side of the city, is a must-see if you're interested in World War II history. The stark, flat facade, with a narrow doorway symbolizing the Allies' breach in the Nazi's supposedly impregnable Atlantic Wall, opens onto an immense foyer containing a café, brasserie, shop, and British Typhoon aircraft suspended overhead. The museum itself is down a spiral ramp, lined with photos and documents charting the Nazi's rise to power in the 1930s. The idea—hardly subtle but visually effective—is to suggest a descent into the hell of war. The extensive displays range from wartime plastic jewelry to scale models of battleships, with scholarly sections on how the Nazis tracked down radios used by the French Resistance and on the development of the atomic bomb. A room commemorating the Holocaust, with flickering candles and twinkling overhead lights, sounds a jarring, somewhat tacky note. The D-Day landings are evoked by a tabletop Allies map of the theater of war and by a spectacular split-screen presentation of the D-Day invasion from both the Allied and Nazi standpoints. Softening the effect of the modern 1988 museum structure are tranquil gardens; the most recent is the British Garden, inaugurated by Prince Charles in 2004. The museum itself is fittingly located 10 minutes away from the Pegasus Bridge and 15 minutes from the D-Day beaches. ⊠ *Esplanade Dwight-D.-Eisenhower* ☏ *02–31–06–06–45* ⊕ *www.memorial-caen. fr* ⌨ *€18.50* ☯ *Mid-Feb.–Oct., daily 9–7; Nov., Dec., and late Jan.–mid-Feb., Tues.–Sun. 9:30–6.*

Musée de Normandie (*Normandy Museum*). Set in the mansion built for the castle governor, this museum is dedicated to regional arts such as ceramics and sculpture, plus some local archaeological finds. ⊠ *Entrance by château gateway* ☏ *02–31–30–47–60* ⊕ *www.musee-de-normandie.eu* ⌨ *€3.10; €5 for exhibitions* ☯ *June–Sept., daily 9:30–6; Oct.–May, Wed.–Mon. 9:30–6.*

Musée des Beaux-Arts. The Musée des Beaux-Arts, within the castle's walls, is a heavyweight among France's provincial fine-arts museums. Its old masters collection includes works by Poussin, Perugino, Rembrandt, Titian, Tintoretto, van der Weyden, and Paolo Veronese; there's also a wide range of 20th-century art. ⊠ *Entrance by château gateway* ☏ *02–31–30–47–70* ⊕ *www.mba.caen.fr* ⌨ *€3.10* ☯ *Wed.–Mon. 9:30–6.*

St-Pierre. Across the square, beneath a 240-foot spire, is the late-Gothic church of St-Pierre, a riot of ornamental stonework.

WHERE TO EAT AND STAY

For expanded hotel reviews, visit Fodors.com.

$

FRENCH

✕ **Le P'tit B.** On one of Caen's oldest streets near the castle, this typical Norman, half-timber 17th-century dining room—stone walls, beam ceilings, and large fireplace—showcases the regional cuisine of David Schiebold. The three-course prix-fixe menu is a good value, and highlights include the grilled duck, cannelloni with goat cheese, king-prawn risotto, and, to finish, red berries in flaky pastry with coconut milk. $ *Average main: €18* ⊠ *15 rue de Vaugueux* ☏ *02–31–93–50–76* ⚠ *Reservations essential.*

$

WINE BAR

✕ **Le Verre à Soi.** Smack in the city center, overlooking the river, this convivial *cave à manger* has everything necessary for a satisfying, and reasonable, dining experience. Specializing in artisanal and local charcuterie and cheeses, with an impressive selection of wines by the bottle or glass and bargain prix-fixe menus (€12–€16 at lunch; €19 dinner Friday and Saturday only), what's not to love? You may opt to stick with small plates, like a luscious fish paté or roasted Camembert, or go for a satisfying main course, like *boudin noir* served with mashed

5

potatoes, or marinated sardines, a local specialty. Friendly service and a lively clientele are an added bonus. [$] *Average main: €11* ✉ *23 quay Meslin* ☎ *02–31–83–08–77* 🌐 *www.le-verreasoi.fr* ✍ *Reservations not accepted* ⏲ *Closed Sun. and Mon.*

$$ HOTEL 🏨 **Best Western Dauphin.** Despite being in the heart of the city, this hotel, in a restored 12th-century priory, is surprisingly quiet; some of the smallish guest rooms have exposed beams, those overlooking the street are soundproof, and the ones in back look out on the courtyard. **Pros:** quiet; historic building; spa and fitness center. **Cons:** small rooms; pricey restaurant. [$] *Rooms from: €140* ✉ *29 rue Gémare* ☎ *02–31–86–22–26* 🌐 *www.le-dauphin-normandie.com* 🛏 *32 rooms, 5 suites* 🍴 *Some meals.*

$$$ HOTEL 🏨 **Hotel Ivan Vautier.** A bastion of modern luxury, this quiet, centrally located hotel is Caen's answer to stylish lodging and dining: handsome, spacious rooms are decorated in jewel and earth tones and feature sleek and sparkling bathrooms; food options include an elegant, Michelin-starred gastronomic restaurant. **Pros:** well maintained; spa; hearty breakfasts; splendid dining. **Cons:** not cheap. [$] *Rooms from: €160* ✉ *3 av. Henry Chéron* ☎ *02–31–73–32–71* 🌐 *www.ivanvautier.com* 🛏 *19 rooms* 🍴 *All meals.*

SHOPPING

Open-Air Markets (*Farmers' market*). Farmers' markets, which often include clothing and household goods, are held on Friday mornings on place St-Saveur and on Sunday mornings on place Courtonne. In May, collectors and dealers flock to Caen's bric-a-brac and **antiques fair** held at the Parc des Expositions. ☎ *02–31–27–14–14* 🌐 *www.caen-tourisme.fr.*

THE OUTDOORS

Boëdic. Take a barge trip along the canal that leads from Caen to the sea on the Boëdic; there is a daily departure at 3 pm, except on Saturday and Monday, April 1–October 15. ✉ *Quai Vendeuvre* ☎ *02–31–43–86–12* 🌐 *www.lesvedettesdenormandie.fr* 🎟 *€18, €16 one way.*

EN ROUTE

Pegasus Bridge. Early on June 6, 1944, the British 6th Airborne Division landed by glider and captured Pegasus Bridge (named for the division's emblem, showing Bellerophon astride his winged horse, Pegasus). This proved the first step toward the liberation of France from Nazi occupation. To see this symbol of the Allied invasion, from Caen take D514 north and turn right at Bénouville. The original bridge—erected in 1935—has been replaced by a similar but slightly wider bridge; but the actual original can still be seen at the adjacent **Mémorial Pegasus** visitor center (*€6.50 Feb.–Dec 15., daily*). Café Gondrée by the bridge—the first building recaptured on French soil—is still standing, still serving coffee, and houses a small museum. A 40-minute son-et-lumière show lights up the bridge and the café at nightfall between June and September. ☎ *02–31–78–19–44 Mémorial Pegasus* 🌐 *www.memorial-pegasus.org.*

ARROMANCHES-LES-BAINS

31 km (19 miles) northwest of Caen, 10 km (6 miles) northeast of Bayeux.

Musée du Débarquement. Little remains to mark the furious fighting waged hereabouts after D-Day. In the bay off Arromanches, however, some elements of the floating harbor are still visible. Head up to the terrace alongside Arromanches 360, high above the town on D65, to contemplate the seemingly insignificant hunks of concrete that form a broken offshore semicircle—and try to imagine the extraordinary technical feat involved in towing them across the Channel from England. General Eisenhower said that victory would have been impossible without this prefabricated harbor, which was nicknamed "Winston." The Musée du Débarquement, on the seafront, has models, mock-ups, and photographs depicting the creation of this technical marvel. ✉ *Pl. du 6-Juin* ☎ *02–31–22–34–31* 🌐 *www.musee-arromanches.fr* 🎟 *€7.50* 🕘 *May–Aug., daily 9–7; Sept., daily 9–6; Oct. and Mar., daily 9:30–12:30 and 1:30–5:30; Nov., Dec., and Feb., daily 10–12:30 and 1:30–5; Apr., daily 9–12:30 and 1:30–6.*

5

Arromanches 360. Arromanches 360 is a striking modern movie theater with a circular screen—actually nine curved screens synchronized to show an 18-minute film (screenings at 10 past and 40 past the hour) titled *Le Prix de la Liberté* (*The Price of Freedom*). The film, which tells the story of the D-Day landings, is a mix of archival and more recent footage from major sites and cemeteries. Evocative music and sound effects serve as dramatic substitutes for spoken commentary. Hours can vary so call ahead. ✉ *Chemin du Calvaire* ☎ *02–31–06–06–44* 🌐 *www.arromanches360.com* 🎟 *€4.90* 🕘 *Apr.–Aug., Tues.–Sun. 9:40–6:40; Sept.–Mar., Tues.–Sun. 10:10–5:40.*

WHERE TO STAY

$ HOTEL 🏨 **Le Mulberry.** This small hotel, one block back from the seafront, is run by a cheerful young couple, Sophie and Christian Le Blanc. **Pros:** sea-air location; warm welcome; breakfast included in the room rates; tasty seasonal, local home cooking and natural wines. **Cons:** rooms are small; no in-room telephones. [$] *Rooms from: €80* ✉ *6 rue Maurice-Lithare* ☎ *02–31–22–36–05* 🌐 *www.lemulberry.fr* 🛏 *9 rooms* 🕘 *Closed Jan.–mid-Feb.* 🍴 *Breakfast.*

BAYEUX

28 km (17 miles) northwest of Caen.

Bayeux, the first town to be liberated during the Battle of Normandy, was already steeped in history, as home to a Norman Gothic cathedral and the world's most celebrated piece of needlework: the Bayeux Tapestry. Bayeux's medieval backcloth makes it a popular base, especially among British travelers, for day trips to other towns in Normandy. Since Bayeux had nothing strategically useful like factories or military bases, it was never bombed by either side, leaving its beautiful cathedral and old town intact.

Visitor Information Bayeux Tourist Office ⊠ *Pointe Saint-Jean* ☎ *02–31–51–28–28* ⊕ *www.bessin-normandie.fr.*

EXPLORING

Bayeux offers both sides of the coin, old and new. The Old World mood is at its most boisterous during its Fêtes Médiévales, a market-cum-carnival held in the streets around the cathedral on the first weekend of July. A more traditional market is held every Saturday morning. But more modern sights await if you use Bayeux as a fine starting point for visits to Normandy's stirring World War II sites; there are many custom-tour guides, but Taxis du Bessin (☎ *02–31–92–92–40*) is one of the best.

Fodor's Choice ★ **Bayeux Tapestry.** Really a 225-foot-long embroidered scroll stitched in 1067, the Bayeux Tapestry, known in French as the *Tapisserie de la Reine Mathilde* (Queen Matilda's Tapestry), depicts, in 58 comic strip–type scenes, the epic story of William of Normandy's conquest of England in 1066, narrating Will's trials and victory over his cousin Harold, culminating in the Battle of Hastings on October 14, 1066. The tapestry was probably commissioned from Saxon embroiderers by the count of Kent—who was also the bishop of Bayeux—to be displayed in his newly built cathedral, the Cathédrale Notre-Dame. Despite its age, the tapestry is in remarkably good condition; the extremely detailed, often homey scenes provide an unequaled record of the clothes, weapons, ships, and lifestyles of the day. It's showcased in the **Musée de la Tapisserie** (Tapestry Museum; free audio guides let you listen to an English commentary about the tapestry). ⊠ *Centre Guillaume-le-Conquérant, 13 bis rue de Nesmond* ☎ *02–31–51–25–50* ⊕ *www.tapisserie-bayeux.fr* ⊠ *€9* ⊙ *Mid-Mar–mid-Nov., daily 9–5:45 (until 6:15 in summer); mid-Nov.–mid-Mar., daily 9:30–11:45 and 2–5:15.*

Cathédrale Notre-Dame. Bayeux's mightiest edifice, the Cathédrale Notre-Dame, is a harmonious mixture of Norman and Gothic architecture. Note the portal on the south side of the transept that depicts the assassination of English archbishop Thomas à Becket in Canterbury Cathedral in 1170, following his courageous opposition to King Henry II's attempts to control the church. ⊠ *Rue du Bienvenu* ☎ *02–31–92–01–85* ⊙ *Daily 9–noon and 2–6.*

Conservatoire de la Dentelle. Handmade lace is a specialty of Bayeux. The best place to learn about it and to buy some is the Conservatoire de la Dentelle near the cathedral, which has a good display. ⊠ *6 rue du Bienvenu* ☎ *02–31–92–73–80* ⊠ *Free* ⊙ *Mon.–Sat. 10–12:30 and 2:30–6.*

Musée Baron-Gérard. Housed in the Bishop's Palace beneath the cathedral, fronted by a majestic plane tree planted in March 1797 and known as the Tree of Liberty, the recently renovated Musée Baron-Gérard (also known as the Musée d'Art et d'Histoire de Baron Gérard or MAHB) contains a fine collection of Bayeux porcelain and lace, ceramics from Rouen, a marvelous collection of pharmaceutical jars from the 17th and 18th centuries, and 16th- to 19th-century furniture and paintings by local artists. ⊠ *1 pl. de la Liberté* ☎ *02–31–92–14–21* ⊕ *www.bessin-normandie.com* ⊠ *€7; €12 joint ticket with Bayeaux Tapestry; €15 joint ticket with Bayeaux Tapestry and Musée de la Bataille* ⊙ *Daily 10–12:30 and 2–6.*

Musée de la Bataille de Normandie (*Battle of Normandy Museum*). At the Musée de la Bataille de Normandie, exhibits trace the story of the struggle from June 7 to August 22, 1944. This modern museum near the moving British War Cemetery, sunk partly beneath the level of its surrounding lawns, contains some impressive war paraphernalia. ✉ *Bd. du Général-Fabian-Ware* ☎ *02–31–51–46–90* 🌐 *www.normandiememoire.info* 🎟 *€6* 🕒 *May–Sept., daily 9:30–5:30; Oct.–Dec., Mar., and Apr., daily 10–12:30 and 2–5.*

WHERE TO EAT

For expanded hotel reviews, visit Fodors.com.

$$$$ 🏨 **Château d'Audrieu.** Princely opulence, overstuffed chairs, wall sconces,
HOTEL antiques—this family-owned château with an elegant 18th-century facade and grand restaurant fulfills a Hollywood notion of a palatial property; guest rooms 50 and 51 have peaked ceilings with exposed-wood beams, and the enchanting restaurant (closed Monday; no lunch weekdays)—white wainscoting, crystal chandeliers, gilt accents—has an extensive wine list. **Pros:** grandiose building; magnificent gardens. **Cons:** out of the way; bland interiors in some rooms. [$] *Rooms from: €330* ✉ *13 km (8 miles) southeast of Bayeux off N13, Audrieu* ☎ *02–31–80–21–52* 🌐 *www.chateaudaudrieu.com* 🛏 *25 rooms, 4 suites* 🕒 *Closed Dec. and Jan.* 🍴 *Some meals.*

$ 🏨 **Grand Hôtel du Luxembourg.** The Luxembourg has small but adequate
HOTEL guest rooms, fully renovated with bland modern furniture but with chic color schemes (all but two face a courtyard garden), and one of the best restaurants in town. **Pros:** quiet; central; fine restaurant. **Cons:** unprepossessing lobby; some rooms are on the dark side. [$] *Rooms from: €100* ✉ *25 rue des Bouchers* ☎ *02–31–92–00–04* 🌐 *www.hotel-luxembourg-bayeux.com* 🛏 *25 rooms, 3 suites* 🍴 *Some meals.*

THE D-DAY BEACHES

History focused its sights along the coasts of Normandy at 6:30 am on June 6, 1944, as the 135,000 men and 20,000 vehicles of the Allied troops made land in their first incursion in Europe in World War II. The entire operation on this "Longest Day" was called Operation Overlord—the code name for the invasion of Normandy. Five beachheads (dubbed Utah, Omaha, Gold, Juno, and Sword) were established along the coast to either side of Arromanches. Preparations started in mid-1943, and British shipyards worked furiously through the following winter and spring building two artificial harbors (called "mulberries"), boats, and landing equipment. The British and Canadian troops that landed on Sword, Juno, and Gold on June 6, 1944, quickly pushed inland and joined with parachute regiments previously dropped behind German lines, before encountering fierce resistance at Caen, which did not fall until July 9. Today the best way to tour this region is by car. Or—since public buses from Bayeux are infrequent—opt for one of the guided bus tours leaving from Caen.

Continued on page 311

A Spire to Greatness:
MONT-ST-MICHEL

A magnetic beacon to millions
of travelers each year, this
"Wonder of the Western World"
—a 264-foot mound of rock
topped by a history-shrouded
abbey—remains the crowning
glory of medieval France.

by Jennifer Ladonne

Wrought by nature and centuries of tireless human toil, this mass of granite surmounted by the soul-lifting silhouette of the **Abbaye du Mont-St-Michel** is Normandy's most enduring image. Its fame stems not just from the majesty of its geographical situation but even more from its impressive history. Perched on the border between Normandy and Brittany, the medieval Mont (or Mount) was a political football between English conquerors and French kings for centuries. Mont-St-Michel was designed to be as much a fortress as it was a shrine, so it looks as tough as it is beautiful.

Legend has it that the Archangel Michael appeared in 709 to Aubert, Bishop of Avranches, inspiring him to build an oratory on what was then called Mont Tombe. The original church was completed in 1144, but further buildings were added in the 13th century to accommodate the hordes of pilgrims—known as *miquelots*—who flocked here even during the Hundred Years' War (1337–1453), when the region was in English hands.

Out of the French rulers' desire to protect Brittany from subjugation by the Normans (whose leader, William the Conqueror, had assumed the English throne in 1066) came the clever strategy of what we would call propaganda. Because of St. Michel's legendary role as dragon slayer and leader of the Heavenly Army, the French lords transformed him, and the Mont, into a major rallying force. During this period the abbey remained a symbol, both physical and emotional, of French independence.

By 1203, King Philippe-Auguste of France had succeeded in wresting the Mont back from the Normans and to shore up French popularity in Normandy he provided funds to restore the abbey. The resulting, greatly expanded, three-level Gothic abbey (1203–1228) became known as *La Merveille* (The Marvel).

During the French Revolution, the abbey was converted into a prison, but shortly after Victor Hugo (of *Hunchback of Notre Dame* fame) declaimed "A toad in a reliquary! When will we understand in France the sanctity of monuments?," the prison was converted into a museum in 1874 and, fittingly, Emmanuel Frémiet's great gilt statute of St. Michael was added to the spire in 1897.

Only at high tide is the Mont transformed into an island.

CLIMB EVERY MONT

Mont-St-Michel is the result of more than 500 years of construction, from 1017 to 1521, and traces the history of French medieval architecture, from earliest Romanesque to its last flowering, Flamboyant Gothic.

HOW TO TOUR THE MONT

There are two basic options for touring the abbey of Mont-St-Michel: guided tours and exploring on your own (which you can do with the aid of an excellent audioguide tour in English). Realistically, a visit to Mont-St-Michel's abbey and village needs a half a day but an entire day at least is needed if you do several of the museums, go on one of the abbey's guided tours, and fit in a walk on the surrounding expanses of sand.

General admission to the abbey includes an optional hour-long guided tour in English, offered twice a day and night in high season. A more extensive, two-hour-long guided tour in French costs an extra 4 euros. The English-language tour takes you throughout the spectacular **Église Abbatiale,** the abbey church that crowns the rock, as well as the **Merveille,** a 13th-century, three-story collection of rooms and passageways built by King Philippe-Auguste. The French tour also includes the celebrated **Escalier de Dentelle** (Lace Staircase) and other highlights. Invest in at least one tour while you are here—each of them gets you on top of or into things you can't see alone.

If you do go it alone, stop halfway up Grande-Rue at the church of St-Pierre to admire its richly carved side chapel with its dramatic statue of St. Michael slaying the dragon. The famous **Grand Degré** staircase leads to the abbey entrance, from which a wider flight of steps climbs to the **Saut Gautier Terrace** outside the sober, dignified church. After visiting the arcaded cloisters alongside, you can wander at leisure, and probably get lost, among the maze of vaulted halls.

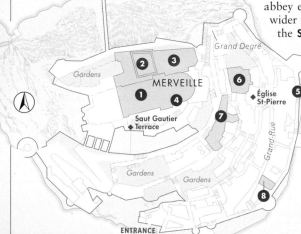

(above) Watchtower at Mont-Saint-Michel

DON'T MISS

❶ Église Abbatiale (above). Crowning the mount, the Abbey Church is in two different styles. The main nave and transepts (1020–1135) were built in the Norman Romanesque style; after the collapse of the original chancel in 1421, it was rebuilt in Flamboyant Gothic with seven Rayonnant-style chapels.

❷ La Cloitre de l'Abbatiale (above). The main cloister was the only part of the abbey complex open to "heaven"—the sky. Its southern gallery contains the lavabos (washing stands) of the monks. Look for the column capitals beautifully chiseled with flower and vine motifs.

❸ Salle des Chevaliers (above). Part of the triple-tiered "La Merveille"—the complex of state chambers, refectory, and cloister that surrounds the main church—the Knights' Hall was originally a scriptorium for copying manuscripts. It was the only heated room on the Mont.

❹ Escalier de Dentelle Set atop one of the "flying buttresses" (top right) of the main church, the famous perforated Lace Staircase is a bravura Gothic showpiece of carved stone. It leads to a parapet—adorned with stone gargoyles—390 feet above the sea.

MUSEUMS

Scattered through the Mont are four mini-museums. The most popular is the **❺ Archéoscope** (Chemin de la Ronde, 02–33–89–01–85) whose sound-and-light show, *L'Eau et La Lumiere* (Water and Light), offers the best introduction to the Mont. Some exhibits use wax figures garbed in the most elegant 15th-century–style clothes. **❻ The Logis Tiphaine** (02–33–60–23–34) is the home that Bertrand Duguesclin, a general fierce in his allegiance to the cause of French independence, built for his wife Tiphaine in 1365. **❼ The Musée Historique** (Chemin de la Ronde, 02–33–60–07–01) traces the 1,000-year history of the Mont in one of its former prisons. **❽ The Musée Maritime** (Grande Rue, 02–33–60–14–09) explores the science of the Mont's tidal bay and has a vast collection of model ships.

INFORMATION

☎ 02–33–89–80–00. ⊕ www.monum.fr; http://mont-saint-michel.monuments-nationaux.fr ✉ €9, with audioguide €13.50. Guided tour in French: €4. Museums: single ticket, €9, combined ticket €18. The abbey is open May–Aug., daily 9–7; Sept.–Apr., daily 9:30–6. The tourist office (☎ 02–33–60–14–30, ⊕ www.au-mont-saint-michel.com) is in the Corps de Garde, left of the island gates.

WHERE TO EAT AND STAY

When day-trippers depart, Mont-St-Michel becomes a completely different experience, and a stay overnight—when the island is spectacularly floodlit—is especially memorable. But if you want to save money—and perhaps your sanity—during the very crowded peak months consider staying nearby at Pontorson, Avranches, Courtils, or day-trip it from St-Malo or Rennes.

LA MÈRE POULARD €154-400

With walls plastered with photographs of illustrious guests, Mont-St-Michel's most famous hostelry can be tough to book, thanks to its historic restaurant, birthplace of Mère Poulard's legendary soufflé-like omelet. Chef Alain Grespier also offers an array of tempting Norman dishes (reservations are essential in summer). Set in adjoining houses, the hotel itself is linked by three steep and narrow stairways. Room prices start low but ratchet upward according to size; the smallest rooms are bearable for an overnight stay, not longer. You are usually requested to book two meals with the room. The hotel's location, right by the main gateway, is most convenient—just don't come expecting any views from atop the Mont.

(above) Winner of Fodor's France photo contest is this beauty by fanotravel.

$$$-$$$$ ⊠ Grande-Rue, 50116 ☎ 02-33-89-68-68 ⊕ www.merepoulard.com ⤶ 27 rooms 🛆 In-room: no a/c, refrigerator. In-hotel: restaurant, bar ⊟ AE, DC, MC, V

AUBERGE ST-PIERRE €195-260

This inn is a popular spot thanks to the fact that it's in a half-timber 15th-century building adjacent to the ramparts and has its own garden restaurant and interesting half-board rates. If you're lucky, you'll wind up in No. 16, which has a view of the bay. The hotel annex, La Croix Blanche, has another nine rooms and dining patio with awesome view.

$$-$$$ ⊠ Grande-Rue, 50170 ☎ 02-33-60-14-03 ⊕ www.auberge-saint-pierre.fr ⤶ 21 rooms 🛆 In-room: no a/c, Wi-Fi. In-hotel: restaurant, Internet terminal ⊟ AE, MC, V

FOOD WITH A VIEW

Many Mont restaurants don't have views (other than of rooms crammed with diners), so another option is to enjoy a picnic along the *promenade des remparts*, where the vistas will spice up the blandest sandwich.

LES TERRASSES POULARD   €144–270

Run by the folks who own the noted Mère Poulard hotel, this charming ensemble of buildings is clustered around a small garden in the middle of the Mount. Rooms at this hotel are some of the best—with views of the bay and rustic-style furnishings—and most spacious on the Mount, although many require you to negotiate a labyrinth of steep stairways. It's a long way to the car park.

$$–$$$ ✉ Grande-Rue, opposite parish church, 50170 ☎ 02–33–89–02–02 ⊕ www.terrasses-poulard.com ⤳ 29 rooms ⌂ In-room: no a/c, refrigerator. In-hotel: restaurant ▭ AE, DC, MC, V

MANOIR DE LA ROCHE TORIN   €110–230

Run by the Barraux family, this pretty, slate-roofed, stone-walled manor set in 4 acres of parkland is a delightful alternative to crowded Mont-St-Michel. Rooms are pleasantly old-fashioned, and the bathrooms modern. With walls of Normand stonework and its open fireplace, the main salon is lovely. In summer, apéritifs are served in the garden, with a view of Mont-St-Michel.

$$–$$$ ✉ 34 rte. de la Roche-Torin, 9 km (5 mi) from Mont-St-Michel, 50220 Courtils ☎ 02–33–70–96–55 ⊕ www.manoir-rochetorin.

com ⤳ 15 rooms ⌂ In-room: no a/c, refrigerator, Wi-Fi. In-hotel: restaurant, bar, some pets allowed (fee), Internet ▭ AE, DC, MC, V ⊘ Closed Oct.–Mar.

DU GUESCLIN   €74–89

The courtesy of the staff, the comfy and stylish guest rooms, and a choice of two restaurants make this great value hotel a most pleasant option. Downstairs try the casual brasserie for salads and sandwiches; upstairs the panoramic full-service restaurant has a wonderful view of the bay, shared by a few guest rooms.

$ ✉ Grande-Rue, 50170 ☎ 02–33–60–14–10 ⊕ www.hotelduguesclin.com ⤳ 10 rooms ⌂ In-room: no a/c. In-hotel: 2 restaurants ▭ MC, V ⊘ Closed Nov.–Mar.

NOW YOU SEE IT...

The Mont's choir was rebuilt during the 15th century and it was only then that the heaven-thrusting Gothic spire was added. To step back several centuries, place your hand to block your view of the spire and see the abbey return to its original Romanesque squatness.

TIME AND TIDE WAIT FOR NO MAN

Most visitors to the Mont see it "beached" by its sandy strands.

Mont-St-Michel can be washed by the highest tides in Europe, rising up to a crest of 45 feet at times. Dangerously unpredictable, the sea here runs out as far as nine miles before rushing back in—more than a few ill-prepared tourists over the years have drowned. Even when the tide is out, the sandy strand is treacherous because of dangerous quicksands (guided hikes over the strand are available). A 2 km (1 mi) causeway links Mont-St-Michel to the mainland.

Note that the Mont is surrounded by water only at very high tides (99% of visitors see

the island "beached" by sand). ■TIP→ To see the rare occurrence of the Mont washed by tides, plan a visit when the moon is full. Occuring only twice a month, the highest tides occur 36 to 48 hours after the full and new moons, with the most dramatic ones during the spring and fall equinoxes (around March 21 and September 23). Experts say the best time to visit is six hours after full or new moons. Time tidetables (posted on the board outside the tourist office) can be accessed on the internet at www.ot-montsaintmichel.com.

TO AND FROM

Set across from the mainland village of La Digue, Mont-St-Michel is 44 km (27 mi) south of Granville via D973, N175, and D43; 67 km (42 mi) north of Rennes 123 km (77mi) southwest of Caen; and 325 km (202 mi) west of Paris.

BY CAR Parking lots (€5) at either end of the causeway. The one just outside the Mont's main gate is reserved for hotel users, who access the lot through a pass-key issued by their hotel. The larger parking lot during very high tides is closed to the public, who can then park on the causeway or, if no room is left, in a car park on the mainland about one mile away (a shuttle bus connects the two).

BY TRAIN & BUS Taking the train from Paris to Mont-St-Michel is not easy—the quickest way (3 hrs, 45 mins, €64) is to take the high-speed TGV train from Gare Montparnasse to Rennes (in high season, five departures a day), then a SNCF (02–99–19–70—70) one-hour bus transfer to the Mont. The only train that will allow you a full day on the Mont leaves at 7 am and arrives at 10:50 am. The other options are 8 (arriving 1 pm) and 2 pm (arriving 7). From Caen you can take either an early morning or late afternoon train to Pontorson (2 hrs, €24), the nearest station to the Mont; then it is another 15 minutes to the foot of the abbey by bus or taxi.

BUS TOURS

In Caen, the Mémorial organizes five-hour English-language daily minibus tours of the D-Day landing beaches; the cost is €64 in the morning (9–2) and €80 in the afternoon (1–7), including entrance fees. Normandy Sightseeing Tours runs a number of trips to the D-Day beaches; a full-day excursion to the D-Day beaches (8:30–6) costs €90.

Mémorial ☎ 02–31–06–06–44 ⊕ *www.memorial-caen.fr.*

Normandy Sightseeing Tours ✉ 6 *rue St Jean, Bayeux* ☎ 02–31–51–70–52 ⊕ *www.normandy-sightseeing-tours.com.*

EXPLORING

Musée Airborne (*Airborne Museum*). Constructed behind the town church in 1964 in the form of an open parachute, this fascinating museum houses documents, maps, mementos, and one of the Waco CG4A gliders used to drop troops. ✉ *14 rue Eisenhower, St Mere L'Eglise* ☎ 02–33–41–41–35 ⊕ *www.musee-airborne.com* 🎫 €7 ⊙ *Apr.–Sept., daily 9–6:45; Feb., Mar., and Oct.–Dec., daily 10–5.*

Musee d'Utah Beach. In La Madeleine inspect the newly renovated, sleek, and modern **Utah Beach Landing Museum** (*Ste Marie du Mont* ☎ 02–33–71–53–35), whose exhibits include a W5 Utah scale model detailing the German defenses; it's open June–September, daily 9:30–7; April, May, and October, daily 10–6; February, March, and November, daily 10–6; closed December and January. Continue north to the **Dunes de Varreville,** set with a monument to French hero General Leclerc, who landed here. Offshore you can see the fortified **Iles St-Marcouf.** Continue to **Quinéville,** at the far end of Utah Beach, with its **museum** (*Memorial de la Liberte, rue de la Plage* ☎ 02–33–95–95–95) evoking life during the German Occupation; the museum is open March 22 through mid-November, daily 10–7. ✉ *Plage de La Madeleine, Ste Marie du Mont* ☎ 02–33–71–53–35 ⊕ *www.utah-beach.com* 🎫 €7.50.

Omaha Beach. You won't be disappointed by the rugged terrain and windswept sand of Omaha Beach,16 km (10 miles) northwest of Bayeux. Here you can find the **Monument du Débarquement** (Monument to the Normandy Landings) and the **Musée-Mémorial d'Omaha Beach,** a large shedlike structure packed with tanks, dioramas, and archival photographs that stand silent witness to "Bloody Omaha." Nearby, in Vierville-sur-Mer, is the **U.S. National Guard Monument.** Throughout June 6, Allied forces battled a hailstorm of German bullets and bombs, but by the end of the day they had taken the Omaha Beach sector, although they had suffered grievous losses. In Colleville-sur-Mer, overlooking Omaha Beach, is the hilltop **American Cemetery and Memorial,** designed by landscape architect Markley Stevenson. You can look out to sea across the landing beach from a platform on the north side of the cemetery. ✉ *Musée-Mémorial d'Omaha Beach, Les Moulins, av. de la Libération, Saint-Laurent-sur-Mer* ☎ 02–31–21–97–44 ⊕ *www.musee-memorial-omaha.com* 🎫 €6 ⊙ *Daily Feb. 15–Mar. 15, 10–12:30 and 2:30–6; Mar. 16–May 15, 9:30–6:30; May 16–Sept. 15, 9:30–7; Sept. 16–Nov. 15, 9:30–6:30. Closed mid-Nov. –mid-Feb.*

Pointe du Hoc. The most spectacular scenery along the coast is at the Pointe du Hoc, 13 km (8 miles) west of St-Laurent. Wildly undulating grassland leads past ruined blockhouses to a cliff-top observatory and a German machine-gun post whose intimidating mass of reinforced concrete merits chilly exploration. Despite Spielberg's cinematic genius, it remains hard to imagine just how Colonel Rudder and his 225 Rangers—only 90 survived—managed to scale the jagged cliffs with rope ladders and capture the German defenses in one of the most heroic and dramatic episodes of the war. A granite memorial pillar now stands on top of a concrete bunker, but the site otherwise remains as the Rangers left it—look down through the barbed wire at the jutting cliffs the troops ascended and see the huge craters left by exploded shells.

OÙ EST PRIVATE RYAN?

The American Cemetery is a moving tribute to the fallen, with its Wall of the Missing, drum-like chapel, and avenues of holly oaks trimmed to resemble open parachutes. The crisply mowed lawns are studded with 9,386 marble tombstones; this is where Stephen Spielberg's fictional hero Captain John Miller was supposed to have been buried in *Saving Private Ryan.*

Sainte-Mère Église. Head west on N13, pause in the town of **Carentan** to admire its modern marina and the mighty octagonal spire of the Église Notre-Dame, and continue northwest to Sainte-Mère Église. At 2:30 am on June 6, 1944, the 82nd Airborne Division was dropped over Ste-Mère, heralding the start of D-Day operations. After securing their position at Ste-Mère, U.S. forces pushed north, then west, cutting off the Cotentin Peninsula on June 18 and taking Cherbourg on June 26. German defenses proved fiercer farther south, and St-Lô was not liberated until July 19. Ste-Mère's symbolic importance as the first French village to be liberated from the Nazis is commemorated by the Borne 0 (Zero) outside the town hall—a large dome milestone marking the start of the Voie de la Liberté (Freedom Way), charting the Allies' progress across France. ✉ *Saint-Mère Eglise.*

Utah Beach. Head east on D67 from Ste-Mère to Utah Beach, which, being sheltered from the Atlantic winds by the Cotentin Peninsula and surveyed by lowly sand dunes rather than rocky cliffs, proved easier to attack than Omaha. Allied troops stormed the beach at dawn, and just a few hours later had managed to conquer the German defenses, heading inland to join up with the airborne troops.

WHERE TO STAY

For expanded hotel reviews, visit Fodors.com.

$ HOTEL 🏨 **Hotel du Casino.** You can't get closer to the action than this—the handsome, postwar, triangular-gabled stone hotel, run by the same family since it was built in the 1950s, looks directly onto Omaha Beach. **Pros:** calm; right by the beach. **Cons:** small bathrooms; slow service in restaurant. [$] *Rooms from: €88* ✉ *Rue de la Percée, Vierville-sur-Mer* ☎ *02–31–22–41–02* 🌐 *www.logis-de-france.fr* 🛏 *13 rooms* 🕓 *Closed mid-Nov.–mid-Mar.* 🍴 *Some meals.*

$$$$ HOTEL 🏨 **La Chenevière.** Topped by an impressive mansard roof, occupying an elegant 18th-century château mansion, and surrounded by cheerful

gardens, this is a true oasis of peace a few kilometers down the road—and yet a million miles away—from World War II sites like Omaha Beach; inland from Port-en-Bessin, the hotel allures with super-stylish guest rooms, which comprise a fetching mix of Louis Seize chairs, gilded ormolu objects, modern photographs, and very chic fabrics. **Pros:** magnificent architecture; luxurious rooms. **Cons:** three different buildings; no air-conditioning in the château. [$] *Rooms from: €300* ✉ *Les Escures, Commes* ☎ *02–31–51–25–25* 🌐 *www.lacheneviere.com* 🛏 *26 rooms, 3 suites* 🕑 *Closed Dec.–Mar.* 🍴 *Some meals.*

THE LONGEST NIGHT

Famously, one parachutist—his name was John Steele—got stuck on the church tower of Ste-Mère Église (an episode memorably re-created in the 1960 film *The Longest Day*) one evening; a dummy is strung up each summer to recall the event, and a stained-glass window inside the church honors American paratroopers.

5

ST-LÔ

78 km (49 miles) southeast of Cherbourg, 36 km (22 miles) southwest of Bayeux.

St-Lô, perched dramatically on a rocky spur above the Vire Valley, was a key communications center that suffered so badly in World War II that it became known as the "capital of ruins." The medieval **Église Notre-Dame** bears mournful witness to those dark days: its imposing, spire-top west front was never rebuilt, merely shored up with a wall of greenish stone. Reconstruction elsewhere, though, was wholesale. Some of it was spectacular, like the slender, spiral-staircase tower outside the Mairie (Town Hall); the circular theater; or the openwork belfry of the church of Ste-Croix. The town was freed by American troops, and its rebuilding was financed with U.S. support, notably from the city of Baltimore. The **Hôpital Mémorial France–États-Unis** (France–United States Memorial Hospital), designed by Paul Nelson and featuring a giant mosaic by Fernand Léger, was named to honor those links.

Visitor Information **St-Lô Tourist Office** ✉ *Plage Verte, rue de la Poterne* ☎ *02–14–29–00–17* 🌐 *www.tourisme.fr/office-de-tourisme/saint-lo.htm.*

EXPLORING

Haras National (*National Stud*). St-Lô is capital of the Manche *département* (province) and, less prosaically, likes to consider itself France's horse capital. Hundreds of breeders are based in its environs, and the Haras National was established here in 1886. ✉ *Av. du Maréchal-Juin* ☎ *02–14–29–00–17* 🌐 *www.haras-nationaux.fr* 🎟 *€5* 🕑 *Guided tours only, Apr.–June and Sept., daily 2–5; July and Aug., daily 11 and 2–5.*

Musée des Beaux-Arts. St-Lô's art museum, the Musée des Beaux-Arts, is the perfect French provincial museum. Its halls are airy, seldom busy, not too big, yet full of varied exhibits—including an unexpected masterpiece: *Gombault et Macée,* a set of nine silk-and-wool tapestries woven in Bruges around 1600 relating a tale about a shepherd couple, exquisitely showcased in a special circular room. Other highlights include brash modern tapestries by Jean Lurçat; paintings by Corot, Boudin, and Géricault; court miniatures by Daniel Saint (1778–1847); and the Art Deco pictures of Slovenian-born Jaro Hilbert (1897–1995), inspired by ancient Egypt. Photographs, models, and documents evoke St-Lô's wartime devastation. ⊠ *Centre Culturel, pl. du Champ-de-Mars* ☎ *02–33–72–52–55* ⊠ *€2.75* ⊙ *Wed.–Sun. 2–6.*

MONT-ST-MICHEL

Fodor's Choice
★

61 km (39 miles) southwest of St-Lô via D999 and N175; 123 km (77 miles) southwest of Caen; 67 km (42 miles) north of Rennes; 325 km (202 miles) west of Paris.

GETTING HERE

There are two routes to Mont-St-Michel, depending on whether you arrive from Caen or from Paris. From Caen you can take either an early-morning or an afternoon train to Pontorson (2 hrs, €27.30), the nearest station; then it's another 15 minutes to the foot of the abbey by bus or taxi. (Both leave from in front of the station.) From Paris, take the TGV from Gare Montparnasse to Rennes, then take a Keolis bus (☎ *02–99–19–70–70*). The total journey takes three hours, 20 minutes (€71). There are several early-morning choices that allow you a full day on the Mont, including options leaving at 7:04 am and arriving at 9:20 am; at 8:08 am and arriving 10:27 am; 9:08 am arriving at 11:14 am; or 10:08 am arriving just after noon.

Visitor Information Mont-St-Michel Tourist Office ⊠ *Corps de Garde, Bd. Avancée, Le Mont St Michel* ☎ *02–33–60–14–30* ⊕ *www.ot-montsaintmichel.com.*

EXPLORING

Mont-St-Michel is the third-most-visited sight in France, after the Eiffel Tower and the Louvre. This beached mass of granite, rising some 400 feet, was begun in 709 and is crowned with the "Marvel," or great monastery, that was built during the 13th century. ⇨ *For information about this spectacular sight, see "A Spire to Greatness: Mont-St-Michel."*

BRITTANY

WELCOME TO BRITTANY

TOP REASONS TO GO

★ **Waterworld:** Experience the extreme drama of the Granite Coast, with its crazy-shape outcrops, or the rippling waters of the Bay of Morbihan, snuggling in the Gulf Stream behind the angry Atlantic.

★ **The wild isle:** Venture down the untamed Quiberon Peninsula to boat across to the rugged, unspoiled beauty of Belle-Ile-en-Mer, Brittany's wildest island.

★ **Gauguin's Pont-Aven:** A *cité des artistes*, Pont-Aven and its colorful folkloric ways helped ignite the painter's interest in Tahiti.

★ **Unidentical twins:** A ferry ride across the Rance River links two delightfully contrasting towns: ancient, once pirate-ridden St-Malo and grand, genteel, Edwardian Dinard.

★ **Stone me!:** Muse upon the solemn majesty of row upon row of *anciens menhirs* at Carnac, the "French Stonehenge."

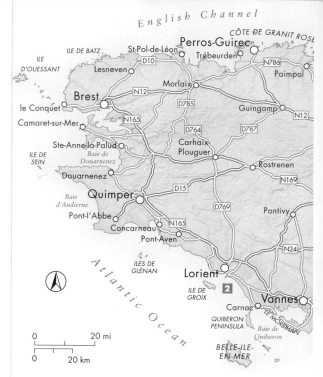

1 Northeast Brittany and the Channel Coast. The northern half of Brittany is demarcated by its 240-km (150-mile) Channel Coast, which stretches from Cancale, just west of Normandy's Mont-St-Michel, to Morlaix, and can be loosely divided into two parts: the Côte d'Emeraude (Emerald Coast), with cliffs punctuated by golden, curving beaches; and the Côte de Granit Rose (Pink Granite Coast), including the astonishing area around Trébeurden, where Brittany's granite takes amazing forms glowing an otherworldly pink. On the road heading there are the gateway city of Rennes; Vitré, a beautifully preserved historic town; the oyster mecca that is Cancale; and the great port of St-Malo, whose stone ramparts conjure up the days of the great marauding corsairs.

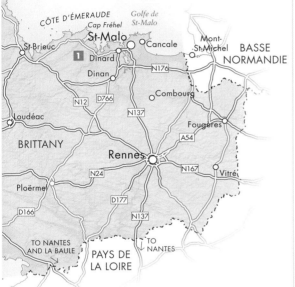

CÔTE D'ÉMERAUDE
Cap Fréhel
Golfe de
St-Malo
St-Brieuc
St-Malo
Cancale
Mont-
St-Michel
BASSE
NORMANDIE
1 Dinard
N176
Dinan
N12
D766
Combourg
Loudéac
N137
Fougères
BRITTANY
A54
Rennes
N24
N167
Vitré
Ploërmel
D177
D166
N137
TO NANTES
AND LA BAULE
TO
NANTES
PAYS DE
LA LOIRE

6

GETTING ORIENTED

Bretons like to say they are Celtic, not Gallic, and other French people sometimes feel they are in a foreign land when they visit this jagged triangle perched on the northwest tip of mainland Europe. Two sides of the triangle are defined by the sea. Brittany's northern coast faces the English Channel; its western coast defies the Atlantic Ocean. The north of Brittany tends to be wilder than the south, or Basse Bretagne, where the countryside becomes softer as it descends toward Nantes and the Loire. But wherever you go, "Côtes d'Armor"—the Land of the Sea—is never too far away.

2 The Atlantic Coast.
Bypassing the lobster-claw of Brittany's Finistère ("Land's End"), this westernmost region allures with folkloric treasures like Ste-Anne-la-Palud (famed for its *pardon* festival); Quimper, noted for its signature ceramics; and cheerful, riverside villages like Pont-Aven, which Gauguin immortalized in many sketches and paintings. Here, the 320-km (200-mile) Atlantic coast zigzags its way southeast,

with frenzied, cliff-bashing surf alternating with sprawling beaches and bustling harbors. Belle-Ile island is a jewel off the Morbihan coast, another beautiful stretch of shoreline. Enjoy its away-from-it-all atmosphere, because the bustling city of Nantes lies just to the southeast.

EATING AND DRINKING WELL IN BRITTANY

Brittany is a land of the sea. Bounded on two of its three sides by water, it's a veritable trove of fish and shellfish. These aquatic delights, not surprisingly, dominate Breton cuisine, but crêpes, lamb, and butter also play starring roles.

One taste and you'll know why Cancale oysters are so prized *(above)*; who can resist those Breton dessert crêpes? *(right, top)*; Plougastel strawberries are red as rubies *(right, bottom)*.

Maritime headliners include *coquilles St-Jacques* (scallops); langoustines, which are something between a large shrimp and a lobster; and oysters, prized for their balance of briny and sweet. Perhaps the most famous regional seafood dishes are *homard à l'armoricaine*, lobster with cream, and *cotriade*, fish soup with potatoes, onions, garlic, and butter.

Beyond the sea, the lamb that hails from the farms on the little island of Ouessant, off the coast of Brest, is well known. Called *pré-salé*, or "salt meadow," they feed on sea-salted grass, which tenderizes their meat while their hearts are still pumping. Try the regional *ragoût de mouton* and you can taste the difference. Of all its culinary treasures, however, Brittany is best known as home of the humble crêpe—a large, delicate pancake served warm with a variety of sweet or savory fillings.

CELTIC ELIXIR

Chouchen, Brittany's classic meadlike beverage made from honey, dates back to Celtic times, when it was considered an aphrodisiac and an *elixir d'immortalité.* Artisanal chouchen is often blended with luscious Breton honeys. This delicious drink is traditionally served cold as an aperitif to highlight its refreshing qualities and its soft, earthy flavor.

CRÊPES

Brittany's most illustrious contribution to French cuisine is the crêpe and its heartier sibling the *galette*. What's the difference between the two? The darker galette is made with tender buckwheat called *blé noir* or *blé sarrasin,* and has a deeper flavor best paired with savory fillings—like lobster, mushrooms, or the traditional ham and cheese. A crêpe is wafer-thin and made with a lighter batter. It is typically served with sweet fillings like strawberries and cream, apples in brandy, or chocolate. Accompanied by a glass of local cider, galettes and crêpes make an ideal light, inexpensive meal. Traditionally, crêpes are eaten from the tails toward the center point to save the most flavorful, buttery part for last.

CANCALE OYSTER

At around €8 a dozen, you simply can't do better than a plate of freshly shucked Cancale oysters and half a lemon from a seafood stand along the quay. Best enjoyed atop the breezy sea wall overlooking the Mont-St-Michel bay, the shells are simply tossed seaward after slurping the succulent insides. Cancale's oyster beds benefit from some of the world's highest tides and strongest currents, which keep the oysters oxygen- and plankton-rich, resulting in a large, firm, yet tender specimen.

PLOUGASTEL STRAWBERRY AND CAMUS DE BRETAGNE ARTICHOKE

Together, the four regions of Brittany make up France's highest-yielding farmland. Among the more prosaic crops grown here are two standouts: the large, fleshy camus artichoke and the plump Plougastel strawberry. Come spring, the markets of Brittany (and Paris, for that matter) are teeming with enthusiastic cooks just itching to get their hands on the first produce of the season. The juicy Plougastel strawberry season lasts for only a few weeks in June, while artichoke season runs into the fall.

LE BEURRE

Temperate Brittany's lush grazing lands make for exceptional milk products and, like wine, they are discussed in terms of *élévages* (maturity) and *terroir* (origin). Butter your roll at a four-star Paris restaurant and you're likely getting a taste of Brittany's finest—*le beurre Bordier*. Jacques Bordier, headquartered in St-Malo's Vieille Ville, sets the gold standard for butter, and his luscious sweet cream version is imported daily to top restaurants throughout France. Other flavors include a pungent purple- and green-flecked algae butter (best slathered on sourdough bread and eaten with oysters), and the *beurre fleur de sel de Guérande,* laced with crunchy grains of the prized gray-hued salt hand-harvested in the salt marshes of Guérande, near La Baule.

Updated by
Christopher
Mooney and
Jack Vermee

Wherever you wander in Brittany—along jagged coastal cliffs, through cobbled seaport streets, into burnished-oak cider pubs—you'll hear the primal pulse of Celtic music. Made up of bagpipes, drums, and the thin, haunting filigree of a tin whistle, these folkloric notes tell you that you are in the land of the Bretons, where Celtic bloodlines run as deep as a druid's roots into the rocky, sea-swept soil.

France's most fiercely and determinedly ethnic people, the Bretons delight in celebrating their ancient culture—circle dancing at street fairs, the women donning starched lace-bonnet *coiffes*, and the men in striped fishermen's shirts at the least sign of a regional celebration. They name their children Erwan and Edwige, carry sacred statues in ceremonial religious processions called *pardons*, pray in hobbit-scale stone churches decked with elfin, moonfaced gargoyles. And scattered over the mossy hillsides stand Stonehenge-like dolmens and menhirs (prehistoric standing stones), eerie testimony to a primordial culture that predated and has long outlived Frankish France.

Similarities in character, situation, or culture to certain islands across the Channel are by no means coincidental. Indeed, the Celts that migrated to this westernmost outcrop of the French landmass spent much of the Iron Age on the British Isles, where they introduced the indigenes to innovations like the potter's wheel, the rotary millstone, and the compass. This first influx of Continental culture to Great Britain was greeted with typically mixed feelings, and by the late 5th century AD the Saxon hordes had sent these Celtic "Brits" packing southward, to the peninsula that became Brittany. So completely did they dominate their new, Cornwall-like peninsula (appropriately named Finistère, from *finis terrae*, or "land's end") that when in 496 they allied themselves with Clovis, the king of the Franks, he felt as if he'd just claimed a little bit of England.

Needless to say, the cultural exchange flowed both ways over the Channel. From their days on the British Isles the Bretons brought a folklore that shares with England the bittersweet legend of Tristan and Iseult, and that weaves mystical tales of the Cornwall—Cornouaille—of King Arthur and Merlin. They brought a language that still renders village names unpronounceable: Aber-Wrac'h, Tronoën, Locmariaquer, Poldreuzic, Kerhornaouen. And, too, they brought a way of life with them: half-timber seaside cider bars, their blackened-oak tables softened with prim bits of lace; stone cottages fringed with clumps of hollyhock, hydrangea, and foxglove; bearded fishermen in yellow oilskins heaving the day's catch into weather-beaten boats, terns and seagulls wheeling in their wake. It's a way of life that feels deliciously exotic to the Frenchman and—like the ancient drone of the bagpipes—comfortably, delightfully, even innately familiar to the Anglo-Saxon.

PLANNING

WHEN TO GO

The tourist season is short in Brittany: late June through early September. Long, damp winters keep visitors away, and many hotels are closed until Easter. Brittany is particularly crowded in July and August, when most French people are on vacation, so why not opt for crowd-free June or September? Some say early October, with autumnal colors and crisp evenings, is even better and truly makes for an invigorating visit. But if you want to sample local folklore, late summer is the most festive time to come.

PLANNING YOUR TIME

If you have just a few days here, choose your coast: Channel or Atlantic! Cliffs and beaches, boat trips, culture and history—both shorelines offer all these and more. St-Malo makes a good base if you're Channel bound; nearby is Dinard, the elegant Belle Époque resort once favored by British aristocrats; while the lively city of Rennes is the main gateway to Brittany, 354 km (220 miles) west of Paris. Pretty Vannes is a good base for exploring the Atlantic coast. Highlights hereabouts include lively Quimper, with its fine cathedral and pottery; the painters' village of Pont-Aven, made famous by Gauguin; the prehistoric menhirs of Carnac; the rugged island of Belle-Ile-en Mer; and the picturesque Bay of Morbihan. The third side of the Brittany triangle is its verdant, unhurried hinterland. Charming—but forget it unless you're here for a month.

FESTIVALS AND PARDONS

It has been said that there are as many Breton saints as there are stones in the ground. One of the great attractions of Brittany, therefore, remains its many festivals, *pardons* (religious processions), and folklore events: Banners and saintly statues are borne in colorful parades, accompanied by hymns, and the events are often capped by a feast. In February, the great Pardon de Terre-Neuve takes place at St-Malo, and in March, Nantes celebrates with a pre-Lenten carnival procession. In mid-May there is the notable Pardon de Saint-Yves, patron saint of lawyers, at Tréguier. June is the month of St. John, honored by the ceremonial Feux de Saint-Jean at Locronan and Nantes. July sees Quimper's Celtic Festival de Cornouaille and the famed pardon in Ste-Anne-d'Auray. August

has Lorient's Festival Interceltique, Pont-Aven's Festival of the Golden Gorse, Brest's bagpipe festival, and a big pardon in Ste-Anne-la-Palud. Another pardon held in Le Folgoët during September is one of the most extraordinary, with flocks of bishops, Bretons in traditional costumes, and devout pilgrims.

GETTING HERE AND AROUND

In just over two hours the TGV train from Paris whisks you to Rennes, the region's hub. From Rennes you can continue to distant outpoints like Quimper or take a branch line to St-Malo or Dinan. You need to use buses or a car to explore the coast between Dinard and Roscoff, and the smaller towns along the Atlantic coast, like Concarneau and Pont-Aven. The A11 expressway leads from Paris to Rennes, where the N137 heads south for Nantes and the N12 divided highway continues to Brest; here it meets the N165 divided highway that heads up the coast from Nantes.

AIR TRAVEL

Aéroport de Nantes. This airport also hosts Flybe flights from Southampton.

Aéroport de Rennes. Domestic flights to and from Paris-Roissy CDG, as well as Bordeaux, Lyon, Nice, Toulouse, and Marseille land here.

Air Travel Information Aéroport de Nantes ⊠ *Southwest of the city, Bouguenais, Nantes* ☎ *02–40–84–80–00* ⊕ *www.nantes-aeroport.fr.* Aéroport de Rennes ⊠ *Southwest of city, St-Jacques de la Lande, Rennes* ☎ *02–99–29–60–00* ⊕ *www.rennes.aeroport.fr.*

BOAT TRAVEL

Brittany Ferries. This is the leading company for maritime transport to and from Brittany. ☎ *0871/244–1402 in U.K. only, 08–25–82–88–28 in France* ⊕ *www.brittany-ferries.com.*

BUS TRAVEL

Brittany is serviced by a bewildering number of companies. Although the region is nicely threaded by train lines, some towns are bus only. These include Carnac (90 mins) and Quiberon (2 hrs), on a **Keolis Atlantique** bus from Vannes; Dinard (30 mins) on a **Keolis Emeraude** bus from St-Malo; and Cancale (40 mins, €2), also from St-Malo.

As for Mont-St-Michel just across the regional boundary in Normandy, buses connect with St-Malo (1 hr, 50 mins via Dol; €11.10) and with Rennes (80 mins, €12.40). Use **Transports Caoudal** from Quimper to reach Pont-Aven.

Bus Information Cars du Kreisker ☎ *02–98–69–00–93* ⊕ *www.cars-kreisker.com.* CAT ☎ *02–96–39–21–05* ⊕ *tibus.fr.* Keolis Atlantique ☎ *02–97–47–29–64* ⊕ *www.keolis-atlantique.com.* Keolis Emeraude ☎ *02–99–19–70–70* ⊕ *www.keolis-emeraude.com.* TIV ☎ *02–99–26–11–11.* Transports Caoudal ☎ *02–98–56–82–82.* Transports Le Bayon. This company offers bus service from Auray to Quiberon (1 hr 10 mins; €2). ☎ *02–97–24–26–20.*

CAR TRAVEL

Rennes, the gateway to Brittany, is 310 km (195 miles) west of Paris. It can be reached in about three hours via Le Mans using A11 then A18 (A11 continues southwest from Le Mans to Nantes). Rennes is linked by good roads to Morlaix (E50), Quimper (N24/N165), and Vannes (N24/N166). A car is pretty much essential if you want to see out-of-the-way places.

TRAIN TRAVEL

Most towns in this region are accessible by train, though you need a car to get to some of the more secluded spots. The high-speed TGV (Train à Grande Vitesse) departs 15 times daily from Paris (Gare Montparnasse) for Rennes, making this region easily accessible. The trip takes about 2¼ hours (between €30 and €70, depending on time of departure). Some trains from Paris branch in Rennes to either Brest or Quimper (4 hrs, 45 mins from Paris; between €65 and €84, depending on time of departure), stopping in Vannes (3 hrs, 20 mins from Paris; between €56 and €69, depending on time of departure). From Rennes there are frequent regional trains via Dol-de-Bretagne to St-Malo (47–58 mins, €14.40). You can reach Dinan from Dol-de-Bretagne (25 mins, €6). Change at Auray for Quiberon (train service July and August only; otherwise, bus links; trains, 45 mins, €6; bus, 1 hr, €2).

Train Information SNCF ☎ *36–35 [€0.34 per min]* ⊕ *www.voyages-sncf.com.* **TGV** ⊕ *www.tgv.com.*

HOTELS

Outside the main cities (Rennes and Nantes), Brittany has plenty of small, appealing, family-run hotels that cater to seasonal visitors. Note that many close for one or several months between October and March. Booking ahead is strongly advised for the Easter period. In addition, this is the case during the midsummer period, when it is routine for prices to be ratcheted up by 30% to 50%. For luxury hotels Dinard, on the English Channel, and La Baule, on the Atlantic, are the area's two most expensive resorts.

Prices in the dining reviews are the average cost of a main course at dinner or, if dinner is not served, at lunch. Prices in the lodging reviews are the lowest cost of a standard double room in high season.

VISITOR INFORMATION

In addition to the Regional Tourist Boards, try the very helpful Maison de la Bretagne in Paris.

Comité Départemental du Tourisme de Finistère ⊠ *4 rue du 19 mars 1962, Quimper* ☎ *02–98–76–25–64* ⊕ *www.finisteretourisme.com.*

Comité Départemental du Tourisme de Loire-Atlantique ⊠ *11 rue du Château de l'Eraudière, Nantes* ☎ *02–51–72–95–30* ⊕ *www.ohlaloireatlantique.com.*

Comité Départemental du Tourisme des Côtes-d'Armor ⊠ *7 rue St-Benoît, St-Brieuc* ☎ *02–96–62–72–01* ⊕ *www.cotesdarmor.com.*

Maison de la Bretagne ⊠ *8 rue de l'Arrivée, Paris* ☎ *01–53–63–11–50* ⊕ *www.maison-dela-bretagne.fr.*

PARLEZ-VOUS BRETON?

Most place names in Brittany are in the Breton language; the popular term *plou* means "parish"—this is where the French got the word *plouc*, meaning "hick." Other common geographical names are *coat* (forest), *mor* (sea), *aber* or *aven* (estuary), *ster* (river), and *enez* (island). *Ty* and *ti*, like the French *chez*, mean "at the house of." While under the radar screen for the most part during the past decade, the Breton Revolutionary Army is a nationalist group committed to preserving Breton culture against French efforts to repress it. Now that everyone agrees that traditional Breton folkways are a priceless boost to tourism and cultural patrimony, this is a common goal shared by many.

NORTHEAST BRITTANY AND THE CHANNEL COAST

It's useful to know that Brittany is divided into two nearly equal parts— Upper Brittany, along the Channel coast, and Lower Brittany. The latter (called in French Basse-Bretagne or Bretagne Bretonnante) is, generally speaking, the more interesting. But the Channel coast of Upper Brittany has its share of marvels. The rolling farmland around Rennes is strewn with mighty castles, remnants of Brittany's ceaseless efforts to repel invaders during the Middle Ages and a testimony to the wealth derived from pirate and merchant ships. The beautiful Côte d'Émeraude (Emerald Coast) stretches west from Cancale to St-Brieuc, and the dramatic Côte de Granit Rose (Pink Granite Coast) extends from Paimpol to Trébeurden and the corniche Bretonne. Follow the coastal routes D786 and D34—winding, narrow roads that total less than 100 km (62 miles) but can take five hours to drive; the spectacular views that unfold en route make the journey worthwhile.

RENNES

345 km (215 miles) west of Paris; 107 km (66 miles) north of Nantes.

Packed with students during the school year—its place Ste-Anne studded with bars and cafés housed in medieval buildings with character to spare—Rennes (pronounced *wren*) is the traditional gateway to Brittany. Since the province was joined to Paris in 1532, Rennes has been the site of squabbles with the national capital, many taking place in Rennes's Palais de Justice. Long the political center of Brittany, this is the one building that survived a terrible fire in 1720 that lasted a week and destroyed half the city. The remaining cobbled streets and 15th-century half-timber houses form an interesting contrast to the classical feel of the cathedral and Jacques Gabriel's 18th-century disciplined granite buildings, broad avenues, and spacious squares. Many of the 15th- and 16th-century houses in the streets surrounding the cathedral have been converted into shops, boutiques, restaurants, and crêperies. (The cavalier manner in which the French go about running a bar out of a 500-year-old building can be disarming to New Worlders.)

GETTING HERE
The TGV Atlantique travels faster than a speeding bullet from Paris's Gare Montparnasse to Rennes (2¼ hrs, € 68), leaving every hour or so, and continuing through to Brest, while a branch line heads to St-Malo. Rennes's Gare SNCF (place de la Gare) is about a 20-minute

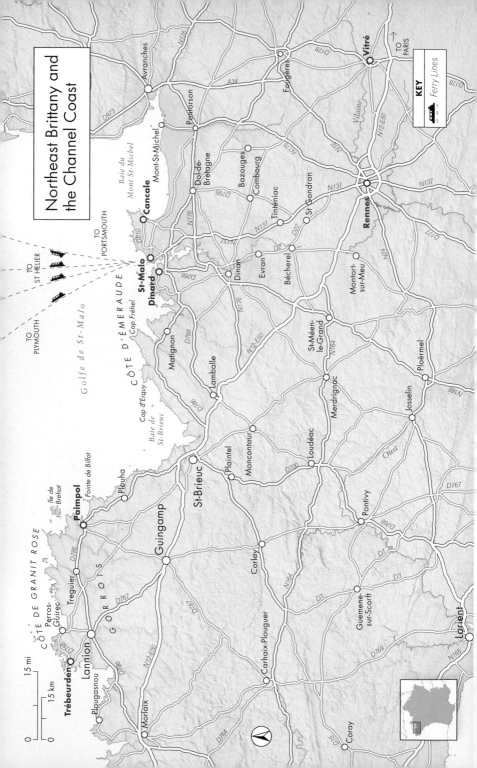

walk from the heart of the city. Trains leave for Paris (2¼ hrs), Nantes (90 mins), St-Malo (55 mins), and Bordeaux (6 hrs). The Gare Routière is next to the train station, but it's not the safest place to hang out. Buses go to Nantes (2 hrs), St-Malo (2 hrs), Dinan (1 hr), and Mont-St-Michel (85 mins). Rennes's city bus system, STAR, will deliver you to almost any destination in town. STAR also operates the two-line métro (⊕ *www.metro-rennes-metropole.fr*), which connects the major central points, links to bus routes, and offers a quick and easy route into the city from peripheral stations with parking lots. Another option for getting around in the city is the LE vélo STAR free-access bicycle rental (⊕ *www.levelostar.fr*); if you don't have a credit card with a chip, you can purchase a code (€1–€5) from the vélo STAR office at 8 rue Maréchal Joffre. There are also Flybe flights to Rennes from England (Southampton, Manchester).

Visitor Information Rennes Tourist Office ⊠ *11 rue St-Yves* ☏ *02–99–67–11–11* ⊕ *www.tourisme-rennes.com.*

EXPLORING

The capital of Brittany, Rennes is one of the liveliest cities in the region. During the school year, the town's rhythm is set by some 40,000 students. Although summer seems to happen elsewhere for most Rennais, it is still a pleasant time to wander the city's cafés and bookstores.

Cathédrale St-Pierre. A late-18th-century building in Classical style that took 57 years to construct, the Cathédrale St-Pierre looms above rue de la Monnaie at the west end of the Vieille Ville (Old Town), bordered by the Rance River. Stop in to admire its richly decorated interior and outstanding 16th-century Flemish altarpiece. ⊠ *Pl. St-Pierre* ⊕ *www. tourisme-rennes.com* ⊙ *Daily 9:30–noon and 3–6.*

The Musée de Bretagne (*Museum of Brittany*). Reopened in 2006 in a headquarters designed by superstar architect Christian de Portzamparc, the museum occupies a vast three-part space that it shares with the Rennes municipal library and Espaces des Sciences. Portzamparc's layout harmonizes nicely with the organization of the museum's extensive ethnographic and archaeological collection, which, depicts the everyday life of Bretons from prehistoric times up to the present. There's also a space devoted to the famous Dreyfus Affair; Alfred Dreyfus, an army captain who was wrongly accused of espionage and whose case was championed by Émile Zola, was tried a second time in Rennes in 1899. ⊠ *10 cours des Allies* ☏ *02–23–40–66–00* ⊕ *www.musee-bretagne.fr* 🎫 *€4 museum, €7 including exhibitions* ⊙ *Tues. noon–9, Wed.–Fri. noon–7, weekends 2–7.*

The Musée des Beaux-Arts (*Fine Arts Museum*). Containing works by Georges de La Tour, Jean-Baptiste Chardin, Camille Corot, Paul Gauguin, and Maurice Utrillo, to name a few, this museum is particularly strong on French 17th-century paintings and drawings, and has an interesting collection of works by modern French artists. ⊠ *20 quai Émile-Zola* ☏ *02–23–62–17–45* ⊕ *www.mbar.org* 🎫 *€4.65, with special exhibition €5.80* ⊙ *Wed.–Sun. 10–noon and 2–6, Tues. 10–6.*

Parc du Thabor. Make sure you stroll through this lovely park, east of the Palais des Musées. It's a large, formal French garden with regimented

One delightful lunch on a Rennes square and all your troubles will melt away.

rows of trees, shrubs, and flowers, and a notable view of the church of **Notre-Dame-en-St-Melaine.** ✉ *Pl. St-Melaine.*

The Parlement de Bretagne. Originally the palatial original home of the Breton Parliament and now of the Rennes law courts, the Parlement de Bretagne was designed in 1618 by Salomon de Brosse, architect of the Luxembourg Palace in Paris. It was the most important building in Rennes to escape the 1720 flames, but in 1994, following a massive demonstration by Breton fishermen demanding state subsidies, a disastrous fire broke out at the building, leaving it a charred shell. Fortunately, much of the artwork—though damaged—was saved by firefighters, who arrived at the scene after the building was already engulfed in flames. It was a case of the alarm that cried "fire" once too often; a faulty bell, which rang regularly for no reason, had led the man on duty to ignore the signal. Restoration has been completed. Call the tourist office (☎ *02–99–67–11–66*) to book a 90-minute guided tour (€7). ✉ *Rue Nationale* 🌐 *www.parlement-bretagne.com* 🕒 *Weekdays 8:45–noon and 1:45–5.*

WHERE TO STAY

For expanded hotel reviews, visit Fodors.com.

$ HOTEL 🏨 **Garden.** With all rooms overlooking a picturesque, stone-lined, treillage-bedecked garden, this hotel likes to welcome visitors to "silent nights"—and cheerful ones, too, thanks to the *charmant* guest rooms, which are stylishly wrought in pink and orange pastels, wicker-wood headboards, and fetching wood-trim furniture. **Pros:** pretty architecture; handy for sights. **Cons:** small rooms; difficult parking. [$] *Rooms* *from: €72* ✉ *3 rue Jean-Marie Duhamel* ☎ *02–99–65–45–06* 🌐 *www.hotel-garden.fr* 🛏 *25 rooms* 🍴 *No meals.*

$$$ HOTEL 🏨 **Le Coq-Gadby.** A 19th-century mansion with huge fireplaces and antiques sets the stage for this cozy retreat, which gets serious about pampering its guests, thanks to homey guest rooms and Julien Lemarié's cuisine—French presidents have dined here on such delicacies as langoustine *au sake* with *crème de riz*; floral accents and four-poster beds grace the best of the rooms here, while hydrotherapy facilities, a hammam (steam room), a Jacuzzi, and a sauna are temptations awaiting in the spa. **Pros:** manorial surroundings; great organic cuisine; cute shop. **Cons:** hotel rooms often booked solid; expensive. [$] *Rooms from: €200* ✉ *156 rue d'Antrain* ☎ *02–99–38–05–55* 🌐 *www.lecoq-gadby.com* 🛏 *11 rooms* 🍴 *Some meals.*

NIGHTLIFE AND THE ARTS

Top spots for nightlife options are the streets around place Ste-Anne.

L'Espace. If you feel like dancing the night away, head to L'Espace. ✉ *45 bd. de la Tour d'Auvergne* ☎ *02–99–30–21–95* 🌐 *www.discotheque-espace.fr.*

Les Tombées de la Nuit. The first week of July sees Les Tombées de la Nuit, the "Nightfalls" Festival, featuring Celtic music, dance, and theater performances staged in historic streets and churches around town. ☎ *02–99–32–56–56* 🌐 *www.lestombeesdelanuit.com.*

Les Trans Musicales. The famous annual international rock-and-roll festival, Les Trans Musicales, happens the second week of December in bars around town and at the Théâtre National de Bretagne. ☎ *02–99–31–12–10 for information* 🌐 *www.lestrans.com.*

Opéra de Rennes. Brittany's top classical music venue is the Opéra de Rennes. ✉ *Pl. de la Mairie* ☎ *02–23–62–28–28* 🌐 *www.opera-rennes.fr.*

Pym's Club. For the night owl, Pym's Club, with three dance floors, stays open all night, every night. ✉ *27 pl. du Colombier* ☎ *02–99–67–30–00* 🌐 *www.pyms.fr.*

Théâtre National de Bretagne. A range of performances are staged at the Théâtre National de Bretagne. ✉ *1 rue Saint-Hélier* ☎ *02–99–31–55–33* 🌐 *www.t-n-b.fr.*

SHOPPING

A lively **market** is held on place des Lices on Saturday morning.

CANCALE

86 km (54 miles) northwest of Rennes via N137 and D210.

Nothing says Brittany like seafood and nothing says seafood like this village, one of the most picturesque fishing villages in the region. Head here by bus from St-Malo and then make for the countless stalls or restaurants along the quay, where you can enjoy the bounty of Cancale, renowned for its offshore *bancs d'huîtres* (oyster beds). You can sample the little brutes here or have a real seafood feast at the culinary mecca not far from town, the Château Richeux.

GETTING HERE

Trains from Dinan (one connection, 50 mins, €8.40) and Rennes (50 mins, €12.90) will get you to La Gouesnière, where the twice-per-day KSMA Keolis bus (☎ *02–99–40–06–06*) will complete the trip. From St-Malo, Keolis make the 30-minute bus trip to Cancale hourly.

EXPLORING

The Musée de la Ferme Marine (*Sea Farm Museum*). Just south of town, this museum explains everything you ever wanted to know about farming oysters and has a display of 1,500 different types of shells. ✉ *L'Aurore* ☎ *02–99–89–69–99* 🌐 *www.ferme-marine.com* 🎟 *€7* 🕒 *Guided 1-hr tours in English, July–mid-Sept., daily at 2.*

WHERE TO STAY

For expanded hotel reviews, visit Fodors.com.

$$$$ HOTEL Fodor's Choice ★ 🏨 **Château Richeux.** Retired superstar-chef Olivier Roellinger and his wife Jane still preside over their family's luxurious hotel empire, which includes the beautiful, castellated, 1920s waterfront Château Richeux. **Pros:** famous cuisine; picturesque and quiet setting. **Cons:** isolated for those seeking crowds. [$] *Rooms from: €220* ✉ *Le Point du Jour, St-Méloir des Ondes* ☎ *02–99–89–64–76* 🌐 *www.maisons-de-bricourt.com* 🛏 *13 rooms* 🕒 *Closed late Jan.–mid-Mar.* 🍴 *Breakfast.*

$ B&B/INN 🏨 **Le Logis du Jerzual.** Up a storybook-perfect cobbled street lined with ancient half-timber houses, this fetching maison d'hôte dates to the 15th century and has been brought up-to-date in the best way, retaining much of its substantial character and charm. **Pros:** warm welcome; great prices; short walk into town and port. **Cons:** smallish rooms; hard to find. [$] *Rooms from: €80* ✉ *25–27 rue du Petit-fort, Dinan* ☎ *02–96–85–46–54* 🌐 *www.logis-du-jerzual.com* 🛏 *5 rooms* 🍴 *Breakfast.*

SHOPPING

Grain de Vanille. Sublime tastes of Brittany—salted butter caramels, fruity sorbets, rare honeys, and heirloom breads—are sold in upper Cancale at the Roellingers's Grain de Vanille. Tables beckon, so why not sit a spell and enjoy a cup of "Mariage" tea and—Brittany in a bite—some cinnamon-orange-flavor *malouine* cookies? ✉ *12 pl. de la Victoire* ☎ *02–23–15–12–70.*

Les Entrepôts Épices-Roellinger. Monsieur Roellinger's newest addition to his culinary empire, Les Entrepôts Épices-Roellinger, is dedicated to the exotic spices he personally searches the world to find. A treasure trove of single spices, along with his signature spice blends—such as Poudre Curry Corsaire, for mussels and shellfish; and Poudre du Vent, for squab or cream sauces—exotic peppers, *fleur de sel*, and choice vanillas. ✉ *1 rue Duguesclin* ☎ *02–23–15–13–91* 🌐 *www.maisons-de-bricourt.com.*

ST-MALO

23 km (14 miles) west of Cancale via coastal D201.

Fodor's Choice ★ Thrust out into the sea, bound to the mainland only by tenuous man-made causeways, romantic St-Malo—*le cité corsaire*, or "the pirates' city"—has built a reputation as a breeding ground for phenomenal sailors. Many were fishermen, but St-Malo's most famous sea dogs were corsairs, pirates paid by the French crown to harass the Limeys across the Channel. Robert Surcouf and Duguay-Trouin were just two of these privateers who helped make this town rich through piratical pillages. Today, the town has plenty of picturesque coastal sights.

GETTING HERE

The train station (square Jean-Coquelin) is a 15-minute walk from the walled town—walk straight up avenue Louis-Martin. More than a dozen trains daily make the 72-km (45-mile) trip from Rennes to St-Malo (55–80 mins, €15); a TGV express from Paris's Gare Montparnassse arrives several times a day in Rennes, where you can transfer. Trains also connect St-Malo to Dol-de-Bretagne (15 mins) and Dinan via Dol (65 mins), but the bus is cheaper and faster. TIV runs buses to Rennes (1¾ hrs), Dinard (40 mins), and Cancale (30 mins). CAT makes the trip to Dinan (35 mins) and Les Courriers Bretons makes the 1¼-hour journey to Mont-St-Michel in Normandy. Buses leave from the Gare Routière, immediately outside the *intra-muros* (within the walls of Old Town). You can also ferry from here to Dinan and Dinard via Emeraude Lines.

Visitor Information St-Malo Tourist Office ✉ *Esplanade St-Vincent* ☎ *08–25–13–52–00 [€0.15 per min]* ⊕ *www.saint-malo-tourisme.com.*

EXPLORING

Facing Dinard across the Rance Estuary, the stone ramparts of St-Malo have withstood the pounding of the Atlantic since the 12th century, the founding date of the town's main church, the **Cathédrale St-Vincent** (on rue St-Benoît). The ramparts were considerably enlarged and modified in the 18th century, and now extend from the castle for almost 2 km (1 mile) around the Vieille Ville—known as *intra-muros (within walls)*. The views are stupendous, especially at high tide. The town itself has proved less resistant: a weeklong fire in 1944, kindled by retreating Nazis, wiped out nearly all the old buildings. Restoration work was more painstaking than brilliant, but the narrow streets and granite houses of the Vieille Ville were satisfactorily re-created, enabling St-Malo to regain its role as a busy fishing port, seaside resort, and tourist destination. The ramparts themselves are authentic and the flames also spared houses along rue de Pelicot in the Vieille Ville. Battalions of tourists invade this quaint part of town in summer, so if you want to avoid crowds, don't come then.

Château (*Town History Museum*). At the edge of the ramparts is this 15th-century château, whose great keep and watchtowers command an impressive view of the harbor and coastline. It houses the **Musée d'Histoire de la Ville,** devoted to the great figures—from the founder of French Canada, Jacques Cartier, to Châteaubriand, "Father of Romanticism"—who have touched local history, and the **Galerie Quic-en-Grogne,** a museum in a tower, where various episodes and celebrities from St-Malo's past are recalled by way of waxworks. ✉ *Hôtel de Ville* ☎ *02–99–40–71–57* ⊕ *www.ville-st-malo.fr* 🎫 *€6* ⊙ *Apr.–Sept., daily 10–12:30 and 2–6; Oct.–Mar., Tues.–Sun. 10–noon and 2–6.*

Fort National. The "Bastille of Brittany," the Fort National, offshore and accessible by causeway at low tide only, is a massive fortress with

6

a dungeon constructed in 1689 by that military-engineering genius Sébastien de Vauban. Tours commence at the drawbridge, last 35 minutes, and have an English text available. ☎ *06–72–46–66–26* 🌐 *www.fortnational.com* 🎫 *€5* 🕒 *Mid-Apr.–Sept., Wed.–Mon. 10–1 and 2–6 (depending on tides; see website).*

Ile du Grand Bé. Five hundred yards offshore is the Ile du Grand Bé, a small island housing the somber military tomb of the great Romantic writer Viscount René de Chateaubriand, who was born in St-Malo. The islet can be reached by a causeway at low tide *only.*

St-Vincent. You can pay homage to Jacques Cartier, who set sail from St-Malo in 1535 on a voyage during which he would discover the St. Lawrence River and found Québec, at his tomb in the church of St-Vincent. His statue looks out over the town ramparts, four blocks away, along with that of swashbuckling corsair Robert Surcouf (hero of many daring 18th-century raids on the British navy), eternally wagging an angry finger over the waves at England. ✉ *Grand-Rue.*

WHERE TO EAT AND STAY

For expanded hotel reviews, visit Fodors.com.

$$$ MODERN FRENCH 🍴 **Le Saint-Placide.** This sleek, modern dining room is garnering serious accolades in a town where talent is in no short supply. Chef Luc Mobihan's impeccable cuisine, with a soft spot for local seafood, brilliantly harmonizes flavors to draw out the intrinsic qualities of the fish or meat without overpowering. Lobster and bacon risotto is both rich and light, and langoustine ravioli with basil and truffles literally melts in the mouth. With four prix-fixe menus to choose from, including the "Mélanosporum" all-truffle *formule*, diners have the pleasure of sampling a range of dishes from this talented chef. [$] *Average main: €32* ✉ *6 pl. du Poncel* ☎ *02–99–81–70–73* 🌐 *www.st-placide.com* 🕒 *Closed Mon. and Tues.*

$$$ HOTEL 🏨 **Beaufort.** A gracious welcome and infinite sea views greet you at this beachfront hotel, handsomely accented with a terra-cotta facade and stylish mansard roof. **Pros:** lovely facade, few minutes' ride to the *intra-muros* Old Town and walking distance from good restaurants and shops. **Cons:** rooms are on the small side and not all face the water. [$] *Rooms from: €180* ✉ *25 Chaussée du Sillon* ☎ *02–99–40–99–99* 🌐 *www.hotel-beaufort.com* 🛏 *22 rooms* 🍽 *Breakfast.*

$ HOTEL 🏨 **Elizabeth.** Done up with impressive style and Breton antiques, this 17th-century town house, built into the ancient city walls and near the Porte St-Louise, is a little gem of sophistication in touristy St-Malo. **Pros:** central; good value. **Cons:** hard to park; big difference between bland rooms and stylish suites. [$] *Rooms from: €97* ✉ *2 rue des Cordiers* ☎ *02–99–56–24–98* 🌐 *www.saintmalo-hotel-elizabeth.com* 🛏 *17 rooms* 🍽 *Breakfast.*

NIGHTLIFE AND THE ARTS

Bar de l'Univers. If you ever wanted to enjoy sipping a drink in a pirate's-lair setting, this is your chance. ✉ *12 pl. Chateaubriand* ☎ *02–99–40–89–52* 🌐 *www.hotel-univers-saintmalo.com.*

Festival de Musique Sacrée. July and August bring a monthlong religious music festival, the Festival de Musique Sacrée. ☎ *06–08–31–99–93* ⊕ *www.festivaldemusiquesacree-stmalo.com.*

Fête du Clos Poulet. Bastille Day (July 14) sees the Fête du Clos Poulet, a town festival with traditional dancing. ☎ *08–25–13–52–00 St-Malo tourism office* ⊕ *www.saint-malo-tourisme.com.*

La Belle Époque. A popular hangout for all ages, this rages until the wee hours. ✉ *11 rue de Dinan* ☎ *02–99–40–82–23* ⊕ *www.bar-labelleepoque.com.*

Théâtre Chateaubriand. In summer, performances are held at the Théâtre Chateaubriand. ✉ *6 rue du Grout-de-St-Georges* ☎ *02–99–40–98–05.*

SHOPPING

Join other browsers at the bustling outdoor **market** is held in the streets of Old St-Malo every Tuesday and Friday.

DINARD

13 km (8 miles) west of St-Malo via Rance Bridge.

Fodor's Choice
★

The most elegant resort town on this stretch of the Brittany coast, Dinard enjoys a picture-book perch on the Rance Estuary opposite the walled town of St-Malo. Toward the end of the 19th century, the English aristocracy was lured here in droves as sea air became a fashionable "cure." As a result, what started out as a small fishing port soon became a seaside mecca of lavish Belle Époque villas (more than 400 still dot the town and shoreline), grand hotels, and a bustling casino.

GETTING HERE

No trains head here, so you have to train it to St-Malo, then transfer to a bus (frequent departures, €2.10) for the 15-minute ride to Dinard. From April to September a ferryboat links the two towns (10 mins, €7). Buses arrive here from Rennes and other towns in Brittany.

Visitor Information Dinard Tourist Office ✉ *2 bd. Féart* ☎ *02–99–46–94–12* ⊕ *www.ot-dinard.com.*

EXPLORING

While a number of modern establishments punctuate the landscape, Dinard still retains something of an Edwardian tone. To make the most of Dinard's beauty, head down to the pointe de la Vicomté, at the town's southern tip, where the cliffs offer panoramic views across the Baie du Prieuré and Rance Estuary, or stroll along the narrow promenade.

Promenade Clair de Lune. The promenade Clair de Lune hugs the seacoast on its way toward the English Channel and passes in front of the small jetty used by boats crossing to St-Malo. In Dinard, the road weaves along the shore and is adorned with luxuriant palm trees and mimosa blooms, which, from July to the end of September, are illuminated at dusk with spotlights; strollers are serenaded with recorded music. The promenade really hits its stride as it rounds the **pointe du Moulinet** and heads toward the sandy **plage du Prieuré,** named after a priory that once stood here. River meets sea in a foaming mass of rock-pounding surf: use caution as you walk along the slippery path to the calm shelter of the **plage de l'Écluse,** an inviting sandy beach bordered by the casino and numerous stylish hotels. The coastal path picks up on the west side of plage de l'Écluse, ringing the pointe de la Malouine and the pointe des Étêtés before arriving at the **plage de St-Énogat.**

WHERE TO EAT AND STAY

For expanded hotel reviews, visit Fodors.com.

$$$ MODERN FRENCH 🍴 **Didier Méril.** Nudging right up to the beach in Dinard's historic center, this chic restaurant serves up gourmet fare along with breathtaking sea views. Chef Méril takes his inspiration from the local bounty: fresh-from-the-sea dishes, such as salty-sweet Cancale oysters, *fricassée de* langoustines, and *Trilogie de poisson* with lobster coulis vie with Breton specialties, like terrine *paysanne au sanglier* (wild boar), on four fixed-price menus. An impressive pages-long wine list, with 450 wines from every region imaginable, satisfies the most discerning wine connoisseur. In warm weather, the seaside terrace is a fine place to enjoy a frosty glass of champagne or an *apéro,* if so inclined. For lodging, six stylish rooms come with some endearing quirks. For example, the top floor's room No. 6 offers spectacular ocean vistas from the bed or the bathtub, as it's smack in the center of the room. [$] *Average main: €30* ✉ *1 pl. du Général de Gaulle* ☎ *02–99–46–95–74* 🌐 *www.restaurant-didier-meril.com.*

$ B&B/INN 🏨 **Manoir de Rigourdaine.** Between Dinard and St-Malo on the beautiful Rance estuary, Patrick Van Valenberg's renovated country estate provides exceptional comfort inside and great views out, courtesy of its promontory perch. **Pros:** wonderful view; great ambiance; friendly service; above-average breakfast. **Cons:** some rooms are on the smallish side. [$] *Rooms from: €97* ✉ *Rigourdaine, Plouër-sur-Rance* ☎ *02–96–86–89–96* 🌐 *www.hotel-rigourdaine.fr* 🛏 *19 rooms* 🕒 *Closed Nov.–Mar.* 🍽 *Breakfast.*

$$$ HOTEL 🏨 **Villa Reine-Hortense.** All the Napoléon-III glamour of 19th-century-resort France is yours when you stay at this *folie*—a villa built by the Russian Prince Vlassov in homage to his "queen," Hortense de Beauharnais (daughter of Napoléon's beloved Joséphine and mother to Emperor Napoléon III). **Pros:** high-style paradise; intimate; quirky. **Cons:** a bit "de trop." [$] *Rooms from: €162* ✉ *19 rue de la Malouine* ☎ *02–99–46–54–31* 🌐 *www.villa-reine-hortense.com* 🛏 *8 rooms* 🕒 *Closed Oct.–Mar.* 🍽 *All meals.*

NIGHTLIFE

Casino. The main nightlife activity in town is at the casino. ✉ *4 bd. du Président-Wilson* ☎ *02–99–16–30–30.*

Clair de Lune. During July and August, stretches of the Clair de Lune promenade become a nighttime son-et-lumière wonderland, thanks to spotlights and recorded music.

SPORTS AND THE OUTDOORS

Wishbone Club. For windsurfing, wander over to the Wishbone Club. ✉ *Plage de l'Écluse* ☎ *02–99–88–15–20* 🌐 *www.wishbone-club-dinard.com.*

A Belle Époque beauty, Dinard adds a big dollop of 19th-century elegance to the natural splendor of the Breton coast.

PAIMPOL

92 km (57 miles) west of Cap Fréhel via D786, 45 km (28 miles) north-west of St-Brieuc.

Paimpol is one of the liveliest fishing ports in the area and a good base for exploring this part of the coast. The town is a maze of narrow streets lined with shops, restaurants, and souvenir boutiques. The harbor, where fishermen used to unload their catch from far-off seas, is its main focal point; today most fish are caught in the Channel. From the sharp cliffs you can see the coast's famous pink-granite rocks. For centuries, but now no longer, Breton fishermen sailed to Newfoundland each spring to harvest cod—a long and perilous journey. The **Fête des Terres-Neuvas** is a celebration of the traditional return from Newfoundland of the Breton fishing fleets; it's held on the third Sunday in July. From Paimpol, trains go to Guingamp, and CAT buses go to St-Brieuc; both towns are on the Paris–Brest TGV line.

GETTING HERE

Six trains per day leave Rennes for Paimpol, via Guingamp (2 hrs, 10 mins; €22), while the Tibus lines (☎ *08–10–22–22–22*) connect Paimpol with Guingamp, Saint-Brieuc, St.-Malo, Dinan, and Dinard for a one-way price of €2.

WHERE TO STAY

For expanded hotel reviews, visit Fodors.com.

$ 🛏 **Le K'Loys.** Built in the late 19th century for a prominent ship owner,
HOTEL   this picturesque stone house nestles right up to Paimpol's main quay, with a view over a yacht- and sailboat-stocked marina that is shared by

most of the 17 rooms—if you're lucky enough to nab No. 6, breakfast can be enjoyed on your own flower-bedecked balcony, or if you prefer to catch some moonbeams, the Capitaine room offers a glass ceiling and splendid views from the bed.**Pros:** free parking; easy walk to the beach and the Old Town. **Cons:** some rooms lack a view. [$] *Rooms from: €105* ✉ *21 quai Morand* ☎ *02–96–20–40–01* 🌐 *www.k-loys.com* 🛏 *17 rooms* 🍴 *Breakfast.*

TRÉBEURDEN

46 km (27 miles) west of Paimpol via D786 and D65, 9 km (6 miles) northwest of Lannion.

Fodor's Choice ★ Trébeurden is just one of the scenic highlights of the Côtes d'Armor, the long stretch of Brittany's northern coast, loosely divided into two parts, the Côte d'Emeraude (Emerald Coast) and the peaceful Côte de Granit Rose (Pink Granite Coast). A small, pleasant fishing village that is now a summer resort town, it makes a good base for exploring the rosy-hue cliffs of the corniche Bretonne, starting with the rocky point at nearby Le Castel.

GETTING HERE

To get to Trébeurden or Perros-Guirec you must first take the train to Plouraret-Trégor, which is found on the main Paris-Brest train line. From there, take the train to Lannion, a town 12 km (7 miles) inland. From Lanion, CAT runs several buses a day to Trébeurden, along with five buses a day to Perros-Guirec, with stops at Trestraou beach and neighboring Ploumanac'h (35 mins).

Visitor Information Trébeurden Tourist Office ✉ *Pl. de Crec'h hery* ☎ *02–96–23–51–64* 🌐 *www.tourisme-trebeurden.com.*

EXPLORING

Trébeurden is near the center of the most picturesque stretches of the Breton coastline. Take a look at the profile of dramatic rocks off the coast near Trégastel and Perros-Guirec and use your imagination to see La Tête de Mort (Death's Head), La Tortoise, Le Sentinel, and Le Chapeau de Wellington (Wellington's Hat). The coastal scene changes with the sunlight and the sweep and retreat of the tide, whose caprices can strand fishing boats among islands that were, only hours before, hidden beneath the sea.

Sentier des Douaniers. The famous seaside footpath, the Sentier des Douaniers, starts up at the west end of the Trestraou beach in the resort town of **Perros-Guirec,** 3 km (2 miles) east of Trébeurden; from there this beautifully manicured, fence-lined, and gorgeously scenic path provides a two-hour walk eastward, through fern forests, past cliffs and pink granite boulders to the pretty beach at Ploumanac'h. If you keep your eye out, you might even spot one of the mythical, 900-year-old Korrigans—native sprites with pointed ears, beards, and hooves, who come out at night from seaside grottoes to dance around fires. From Perros-Guirec you can take a boat trip out to the Sept Iles, a group of seven islets that are bird sanctuaries. On a hillside perch above **Ploumanac'h** is the village of La Clarté, home to the little Chapelle

Notre Dame de la Clarté (place de la Chapelle), built of local pink granite and decorated with 14 stations of the cross painted by the master of the Pont-Aven school, Maurice Denis. During the **Pardon of la Clarté** (August 15), a bishop preaches an outdoor Mass for the Virgin Mary, village girls wear Trégor costumes, and the statue of the Virgin Mary wears a gold crown (she wears a fake one for the rest of the year). On Ploumanac'h's pleasant beach, plage de la Bastille, you'll find the Oratoire de St-Guirec, a rose-granite chapel lodged in the sand with other rocks; facing the beach is the neo-medieval, 19th-century **Château de Costaeres,** where Henryk Sienkiewicz wrote *Quo Vadis*. Unfortunately, the magical castle-by-the-sea—whose image graces many postcards of the region—was partly destroyed by a fire and remains private property. 🌐 *www.perros-guirec.com.*

WHERE TO STAY

For expanded hotel reviews, visit Fodors.com.

$$$$ HOTEL 🏨 **Manoir de Lan Kerellec.** The beauty of the Breton coastline is embraced by this Relais & Châteaux hotel, where guest rooms are far more than just comfortable; long and cruise-liner-low, this renovated 19th-century Breton manor house has now been outfitted with dramatic windows—plate-glass, round, panoramic—so as to frame stirring vistas of the endless sea and the cliffs of the Côte de Granit Rose (all rooms have sea views and some have terraces). **Pros:** great views; comfy rooms. **Cons:** pricey; restaurant only serves lunch from Thursday to Sunday. [$] *Rooms from: €287* ✉ *11 allée Centrale* ☎ *02–96–15–00–00* 🌐 *www.lankerellec.com* 🛏 *19 rooms* ⏲ *Closed mid-Nov.–mid-Mar.* 🍴 *Some meals.*

THE ATLANTIC COAST

What Brittany offers in the way of the sea handsomely makes up for its shortage of mountain peaks and passes. Its hundreds of miles of sawtooth coastline reveal the Atlantic Ocean in its every mood and form—from the peaceful cove where waders poke about hunting seashells to the treacherous bay whose waters swirl over quicksand in unpredictable crosscurrents; from the majestic serenity of the breakers rolling across La Baule's miles of golden-sand beaches to the savage fury of the gigantic waves that fling their force against jagged rocks 340 dizzy feet below the cliffs of pointe du Raz.

Consisting of the territory lying west of Saint-Brieuc to the Atlantic coast a short distance east of Vannes, Lower Brittany contains in abundance all things Breton, including many of the pardons and other colorful religious ceremonies that take place hereabouts. As for bright lights, Rennes, the student-fueled mind of Brittany, gives way to poets and painters, bringing a refreshing breeze to the historical heaviness of the region. On the Atlantic coast, Nantes—part of Brittany until regional boundaries were redrawn in the 1940s, placing it in the Pays de la Loire—is an industrial port that pumps the economy of the region and provides a bracing swig of daily life. Head inland to find a landscape studded with bent trees and craggy rocks that look like they've been bewitched by Merlin in a bad mood.

6

STE-ANNE-LA-PALUD

136 km (82 miles) southwest of Frébeurden via D767 and D787.

Fodor's Choice ★ One of the great attractions of the Brittany calendar is the celebration of a religious festival known as a village pardon, replete with banners, saintly statues, a parade, bishops in attendance, women in folk costume, a feast, and hundreds of attendees. The seaside village of Ste-Anne-la-Palud has one of the finest and most authentic age-old pardons in Brittany, held on the last Sunday in August.

Another celebrated pardon is held in early September some 40 km (25 miles) north of Ste-Anne. Pilgrims come from afar to Le Folgoët, 24 km (15 miles) northeast of Brest, to attend the town's ceremonial procession. Many also drink from the Fontaine de Salaün, a fountain behind the church, whose water comes from a spring beneath the altar. The splendid church, known as the Basilique, has a sturdy north tower that serves as a beacon for miles around and, inside, a rare, intricately carved granite rood screen separating the choir and nave.

GETTING HERE

More than a dozen trains daily journey from Vannes to Quimper (80 mins, €20.10). From there, a bus to Plonévez-Porzay and the beach of Ste-Anne-la-Palud will set you back €2.

WHERE TO STAY

For expanded hotel reviews, visit Fodors.com.

$$$$ HOTEL 🏨 **Hôtel de la Plage.** Nestled in a cove on a quiet strip of sandy beach on the Bay of Douarnenez, this mansion, with its sturdy round tower, is a remote retreat perfect for long, restorative walks; some of the comfortably furnished guest rooms face the water, as does the glass-front restaurant, where reservations are essential. **Pros:** Relais & Châteaux taste; waterfront setting; top-rank restaurant; spa facilities. **Cons:** very expensive; rather formal. [$] *Rooms from: €276* ☎ *02–98–92–50–12* 🌐 *www.plage.com* 🛏 *24 rooms, 4 suites* 🕒 *Closed Nov.–Mar.* 🍴 *Some meals.*

DOUARNENEZ

14 km (8 miles) south of Ste-Anne-la-Palud.

Douarnenez is a quaint old fishing town of quayside paths and zigzagging narrow streets. Boats come in from the Atlantic to unload their catches of mackerel, sardines, and tuna. Just offshore is the Ile Tristan, accessible on foot at low tide (guided tours only, organized by the tourist office, €6), and across the Port-Rhu channel is Tréboul, a seaside resort town favored by French families.

GETTING HERE

From Quimper, a 25-minute ride (€2) on a CAT bus (☎ *08–10–81–00–29*) deposits you in Douarnenez. CAT also serves the region around Douarnenez with buses coming from Brest and Plonévez-Porzay, home to the beach of Ste-Anne-la-Palud.

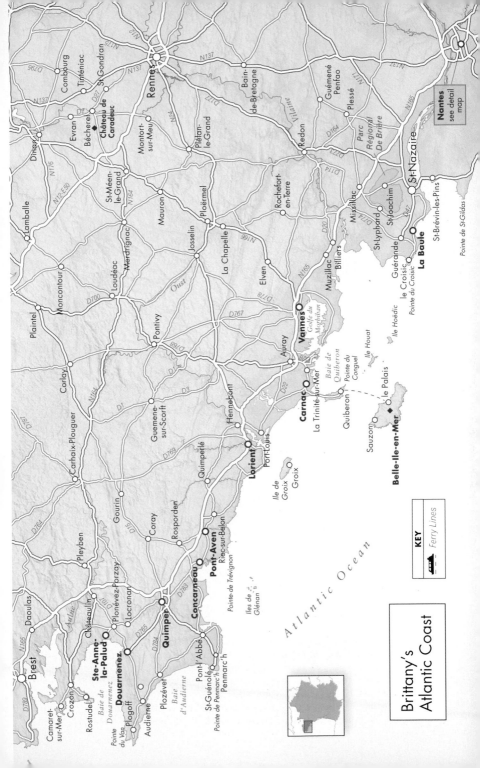

Brittany's Atlantic Coast

KEY

⌐═ Ferry Lines

EXPLORING

FAMILY **Port-Musée** (*Port Museum*). One of the three town harbors is fitted out with a unique Port-Musée, which was extensively renovated in 2006. Along the wharves you can visit the workshops of boatbuilders, sailmakers, and other old-time craftspeople, then go aboard the historic trawlers, lobster boats, Thames barges, and a former lightship anchored alongside. On the first weekend in May you can sail on an antique fishing boat. ✉ *Pl. de l'Enfer* ☎ *02–98–92–65–20* 🌐 *www.port-musee.org* 🎫 *€7.50* 🕒 *July and Aug., daily 10–7; Apr.–June, Sept., and Oct., Tues.–Sun. 10–12:30 and 2–6; Feb. and Mar., Tues.–Sun. 10–12:30 and 2–6 (quai museum only)* 🕒 *Closed Nov.–Jan.*

WHERE TO STAY

For expanded hotel reviews, visit Fodors.com.

$ HOTEL 🏨 **Manoir de Moëllien.** Surrounded by extensive forested grounds, this textbook 17th-century granite Breton manor house, landmarked by a sturdy tower and filled with precious antiques, makes an enviable choice—another plus is the fine restaurant (open to residents only), famous for its local seafood dishes. **Pros:** charming setting; historic atmosphere. **Cons:** out of the way; restaurant service can be offhand. [$] *Rooms from: €96* ✉ *12 km (7 miles) northeast of Douarnenez, Plonévez-Porzay* ☎ *02–98–92–50–40* 🛏 *18 rooms* 🕒 *Closed mid-Nov.–Mar.* 🍴 *All meals.*

$$ HOTEL 🏨 **Ty Mad.** Courtesy of a recent renovation, this landmark hotel—frequented by artists and writers such as Picasso and Breton native Max Jacob in the 1920s—has been completely refitted with cool, light, modern furnishings that blend perfectly with its cove and beach setting. **Pros:** delightful seaside setting; stylish modern interior. **Cons:** rooms are small and modestly equipped. [$] *Rooms from: €130* ✉ *Plage St-Jean, Treboul* ☎ *02–98–74–00–53* 🌐 *www.hoteltymad.com* 🛏 *15 rooms* 🕒 *Closed mid-Nov.–mid-Mar.* 🍴 *Some meals.*

QUIMPER

22 km (14 miles) southeast of Douarnenez via D765.

A traditional crowd-puller, the twisting streets and tottering medieval houses of Quimper (pronounced cam-*pair*) supply rich postcard material, but lovers of decorative arts head here because this is the home of Quimperware, one of the more famous variants of French hand-painted earthenware pottery. The techniques were brought to Quimper by Normands in the 17th century, but the Quimpérois customized them by painting typical local Breton scenes on the pottery. Today they remain some of the most prized French collectibles and gifts.

GETTING HERE

The direct TGV travels 560 km (350 miles) from Paris's Gare Montparnasse five times per day to reach Quimper's train station, on the avenue de la Gare, in four hours, 30 minutes (€79). Five direct trains each day make the 75-minute trip from Quimper to Brest (€17.20) and three make the two-hour, 30-minute trip to Nantes (€36.60). Buses from the Gare Routière on place Louis-Armand make infrequent connections to such destinations as Concarneau and Pont-Aven.

Visitor Information Quimper Tourist Office ✉ *Pl. de la Résistance* ☎ *02–98–53–04–05* ⊕ *www.quimper-tourisme.com.*

EXPLORING

Quimper's lively commercial town began life as the ancient capital of the Cornouaille province, founded, it's said, by King Gradlon 1,500 years ago. It owes its strange name to its site at the confluence (*kemper* in Breton) of the Odet and Steir rivers. Stroll along the banks of the Odet and through the **Vieille Ville**, with its cathedral, then walk along the lively shopping street, rue Kéréon, and down narrow medieval rue du Guéodet (note the house with caryatids), rue St-Mathieu, and rue du Sallé. Have your camera handy.

Cathédrale St-Corentin. The Cathédrale St-Corentin is a masterpiece of Gothic architecture and the second-largest cathedral in Brittany (after Dol-de-Bretagne's). Legendary King Gradlon is represented on horseback just below the base of the spires, harmonious mid-19th-century additions to the medieval ensemble. The church interior remains very much in use by fervent Quimperois, giving the candlelit vaults a meditative air. The 15th-century stained glass is luminous. Behind the cathedral is the stately **Jardin de l'Évêché** (Bishop's Garden). ✉ *Pl. St-Corentin.*

6

Musée de la Faïence (*Earthenware Museum*). In the mid-18th century Quimper sprang to nationwide attention as a pottery manufacturing center, when it began producing second-rate imitations of Rouen faïence, or ceramics with blue motifs. Today's more colorful designs, based on floral arrangements and marine fauna, are still often hand-painted. To understand Quimper's pottery past with the help of more than 500 examples of "style Quimper," take one of the guided tours at the Musée de la Faïence. ✉ *14 rue Jean-Baptiste-Bousquet* ☎ *02–98–90–12–72* ⊕ *www.musee-faience-quimper.com* ⊡ *€4* ☉ *Mid-Apr.–Sept., Mon.–Sat. 10–6.*

Musée Départemental Breton (*Brittany Regional Museum*). Local furniture, ceramics, and folklore top the bill at the Musée Départemental Breton. ✉ *1 rue du Roi-Gradlon* ☎ *02–98–95–21–60* ⊕ *www.museedepartementalbreton.fr* ⊡ *€4 (free weekends Oct.–May)* ☉ *June–Sept., daily 9–6; Jan.–May and Oct.–Dec., Tues.–Sat. 9–12:30 and 1:30–5, Sun. 2–5.*

Musée des Beaux-Arts (*Fine Arts Museum*). More than 400 works by such masters as Rubens, Corot, and Picasso mingle with pretty landscapes from the local Gauguin-inspired Pont-Aven school in the Musée des Beaux-Arts, next to the cathedral. Of particular note is a fascinating series of paintings depicting traditional life in Breton villages. ✉ *40 pl. St-Corentin* ☎ *02–98–95–45–20* ⊕ *www.mbaq.fr* ⊡ *€5* ☉ *July and Aug., daily 10–7; Apr.–June, Sept., and Oct., Wed.–Mon. 9:30–noon and 2–6; Nov.–Mar., Wed.–Sat. and Mon. 9:30–noon and 2–5:30, Sun. 2–5:30.*

WHERE TO EAT AND STAY

For expanded hotel reviews, visit Fodors.com.

$$$

MODERN FRENCH

✕ **L'Ambroisie.** This cozy little restaurant has soft-yellow walls, huge contemporary paintings, and different settings at every table. Chef Gilbert Guyon's traditional yet nouvelle menu is seasonal; local products

Quimper hosts many parades but the largest is reserved for the nine-day Celtic extravaganza known as the Festival de Cornouaille.

are chosen by hand or come from the restaurant's garden. Try the buckwheat *galette* crêpe stuffed with egg and salmon; the fresh cod, mullet, or sole; the spiced fillet of turbot with stuffed artichokes; the sautéed crawfish with buckwheat; or the pigeon roasted in apple liqueur with whipped potatoes and mushrooms. The homemade desserts, like the omelet *norvégienne* with warm chocolate and nougat ice cream in meringue, are delicious. Weekday menus are a bargain. $ *Average main:* €28 ⊠ *49 rue Élie-Fréron* ☏ *02–98–95–00–02* ⊕ *www.ambroisie-quimper.com* ⚄ *Reservations essential* ☉ *Closed Mon. No dinner Sun.*

$ ✕ **Le Comptoir des Tapas.** The owners of this compact *épicerie* and tapas
WINE BAR bar in Quimper's old covered market had the novel approach of pairing delicacies from Spain and Brittany. An auspicious match, it turns out, as small plates of artisanal cured meats, like Iberico and chorizo, served *à la planche* with bread and spicy olive oil, pair nicely with local specialties like a velvety langoustine flan. Other plates highlight both cuisines—crispy beignets of fried John Dory or octopus served steaming hot, tiny marinated sardines from Spain or Brittany. With Spanish or French regional wines by the glass for as little as €3—and small plates starting at €4—it's a great opportunity to experiment with pairings. Ah, but this is the point, *non*? $ *Average main:* €12 ⊠ *Halles Saint-François* ☏ *02–98–98–00–81* ⚄ *Reservations not accepted* ☉ *Closed Sun. and Mon.*

$$ ▦ **Les Sables Blancs.** One of the fine-white-sand beaches that distinguish
HOTEL the Morbihan coast serves as the perfect backdrop and motif for this spare, modern hotel, strongly reminiscent of a cruise ship. **Pros:** miles of paths on the cliffs overlooking the sea make for lovely walks; open year-round. **Cons:** the relentless crashing of waves can stir light sleepers.

ⓈＲooms from: €122 ✉ 45 rue des Sables Blancs, 20 km (12 miles) from Quimper, Concarneau ☎ 02–98–50–10–12 ⊕ www.hotel-les-sables-blancs.com ⤵ 16 rooms, 4 suites ✦ No meals.

SHOPPING

Faïencerie d'Art Breton. Faïence and a wide selection of hand-painted pottery can be purchased at the Faïencerie d'Art Breton. ✉ 16 bis, rue du Parc ☎ 02–98–95–34–13 ⊕ www.bretagne-faience.com.

Rue du Parc. The streets around the cathedral, especially rue du Parc, are full of shops selling woolen goods (notably thick marine sweaters). Keep an eye out for such typical Breton products as woven and embroidered cloth, woolen goods, brass and wood objects, puppets, dolls, and locally designed jewelry. When it comes to distinctive Breton folk costumes, Quimper is the best place to look.

CONCARNEAU

22 km (14 miles) southeast of Quimper via D783.

Concarneau may be an industrial town known for its sardine packaging but its 17th-century Vaubau-designed Ville Close has to be one of the most picturesque sites in Brittany.

GETTING HERE

No trains arrive in Concarneau, so you'll have to come by car or bus. Buses run almost every hour until 7 pm from Quimper (45 mins, €2) and Pont-Aven (30 mins).

Visitor Information Concarneau Tourist Office ✉ Quai d'Aiguillon ☎ 02–98–97–01–44 ⊕ www.tourismeconcarneau.fr.

EXPLORING

Fodor'sChoice ★ **Château de Keriolet.** Eight kilometers (5 miles) away from Concarneau is the village of Beuzec-Conq, home to the Château de Keriolet. Walt Disney would have loved this fairy-tale, neo-Gothic extravaganza dating from the 19th century. Replete with gargoyles, storybook towers, and Flamboyant Gothic-style windows, this showpiece was constructed by the Comtesse de Chauveau, born Zenaide Narishkine Youssoupov, an imperial Russian princess who was niece to Czar Nicholas II (and related to Prince Youssoupov, famed assassin of Rasputin). Hour-long tours guide you through the Arms Room, folkloric kitchen, and other grand salons. ✉ Beuzec-Conq ☎ 02–98–97–36–50 ⊕ www.chateaudekeriolet.com ⛭ €5.50 ⊗ June–Sept., Sun.–Fri. 10:30–1 and 2–6, Sat. 10:30–1.

Fodor'sChoice ★ **Ville Close.** Sitting in the middle of Concarneau's harbor, topped by a cupola-clock tower, and entered by way of a quaint drawbridge, the fortress-islet of the Ville Close is a particularly photogenic relic of medieval days. Its fortifications were further strengthened by the English under John de Montfort during the War of Succession (1341–64). Three hundred years later Sébastien de Vauban remodeled the ramparts into what you see today: a kilometer (half mile) long, with splendid views across the two harbors on either side. The Fête des Filets Bleus (Blue Net Festival), a weeklong folk celebration in which Bretons in costume swirl and dance to the wail of bagpipes, is held here during the second half of August. It is also home to the Musée de la Pêche (Maritime Museum). ✉ *Ramparts* 🎫 *€4.50 (museum)* ⏱ *Daily, July and Aug., 10–7; Apr.– June and Sept., 10–6; Feb., Mar., Oct., and Nov., 10–12:30 and 2–6.*

PONT-AVEN

37 km (23 miles) east of Quimper via D783.

Fodor's Choice ★ Long beloved by artists, this lovely village sits astride the Aven River as it descends from the Montagnes Noires to the sea, turning the town's mills along the way (there were once 14; now just a handful remain). Surrounded by one of Brittany's most beautiful stretches of countryside, Pont-Aven is a former artists' colony where, most famously, Paul Gauguin lived before he headed off to the South Seas.

GETTING HERE

There are no direct trains, so take the rails to nearby Quimperlé and transfer to a bus (25 mins, €2). Buses make the 20-km (12-mile) run from Quimper (1¼ hrs) and Concarneau (30 mins) several times a day. The last buses leave early in the evening, and service is limited on Sunday.

Visitor Information Pont-Aven Tourist Office ✉ *5 pl. de l'Hôtel de Ville* ☎ *02–98–06–04–70* ⊕ *www.pontaven.com.*

EXPLORING

Wanting to break with traditional Western culture and values, in 1888 lawyer-turned-painter Paul Gauguin headed to Brittany, a destination almost as foreign to Parisians as Tahiti. Economy was another lure: the Paris stock market had just crashed and, with it, Gauguin's livelihood, so cheap lodgings were also at the top of his list. Shortly after settling in to Pont-Aven, Gauguin took to wearing Breton sweaters, berets, and wooden clogs; in his art he began to leave dewy, sunlit Impressionism behind for a stronger, more linear style. The town museum captures some of the history of the Pont-Aven School, whose adherents painted Breton landscapes in a bold yet dreamy style called Syntheticism.

One glance at the **Bois d'Amour** forest, just to the north of town (from the tourist office, go left and walk along the river for five minutes), will make you realize why artists continue to come here. Past some meadows, just outside the Bois d'Amour woods, you can find Gauguin's inspiration for his famous painting *The Yellow Christ*—a wooden crucifix inside the secluded **Chapelle de Trémalo** (usually open, per private owners, from 9 to 7). While in Brittany, Gauguin painted many of his earliest masterpieces, now given pride of place in great museums around the world.

Gauguin and the Pont-Aven School

Surrounded by some of Brittany's most beautiful countryside, Pont-Aven was a natural to become a "cité des artistes" in the heady days of Impressionism and Postimpressionism. It was actually the introduction of the railroad in the 19th century that put travel to Brittany in vogue, and it was here that Gauguin and other like-minded artists founded the noted Pont-Aven School. Inspired by the vibrant colors and lovely vistas to be found here, they created *Synthétisme,* a painting style characterized by broad patches of pure color and strong symbolism, in revolt against the dominant Impressionist school back in Paris. Gauguin arrived in the summer of 1886, happy to find a place "where you can live on nothing" (Paris's stock market had crashed and cost Gauguin his job). At Madame Gloanec's boardinghouse, he welcomed a circle of painters to join him in his artistic quest for monumental simplicity and striking color.

Today Pont-Aven seems content to rest on its laurels. Although it's labeled a "city of artists," the galleries that line its streets display paintings that lack the unifying theme and common creative energy of the earlier works of art. The first Pont-Aven painters were American students who came here in the 1850s. Though Gauguin is not surprisingly absent (his paintings now go for millions), except for a few of his early zincographs, the exhibit *Hommage à Gauguin* is an interesting sketch of his turbulent life. Also on view in the museum are works by other near-great Pont-Aven artists: Maurice Denis, Émile Bernard, Émile Jordan, and Emmanuel Sérusier.

Biscuiterie Traou Mad. Those with a sweet tooth can fill up on the buttery Traou Mad cookies at the Biscuiterie Traou Mad; they're baked with local wheat from the last working windmill in Pont-Aven. ⌂ *10 pl. Gauguin* ☎ *02–98–06–01–94* ⊕ *www.traoumad.fr.*

Moulin du Grand Poulguin. Head to the Moulin du Grand Poulguin, a delightful setting in which to eat a crêpe or pizza on a terrace directly beside the flowing waters of the Aven River, in view of the footbridge. ⌂ *2 quai Théodore Botrel* ☎ *02–98–06–02–67* ⊕ *www.moulin-pontaven.com.*

Place de l'Hôtel-de-Ville. The creperies and pizzerias that surround **place de l'Hôtel-de-Ville** cater to hungry visitors, including those just emerging from the tourist office at No. 5; note the office's helpful list of *chambres d'hôte* accommodations offered by the residents in town. ☎ *02–98–06–04–70* ⊕ *www.pontaven.com.*

After exploring the village, cool off (in summer) with a boat trip down the estuary.

WHERE TO EAT AND STAY

For expanded hotel reviews, visit Fodors.com.

$$$$
MODERN FRENCH
✕ **La Taupinière.** In this roadside inn with an attractive garden, chef Guy Guilloux's open kitchen—with the large hearth he uses to grill langoustine, crab and fish—turns out Breton ham specialties and other local delicacies, such as galette crêpes stuffed with spider crab. Indulge without guilt on the light homemade rhubarb and strawberry compote.

$ *Average main: €60* ✉ *Croissant St-André, 3 km (2 miles) west on Concarneau road* ☎ *02–98–06–03–12* 🌐 *www.la-taupiniere.fr* ✍ *Reservations essential* ⏲ *Closed Mon. and Tues., and mid-Sept.–mid-Oct.*

$$$ HOTEL Fodor's Choice ★ 🏨 **Domaine de Kerbastic.** This beautiful gated estate—a hotel only since 2008—served as the country getaway for generations of Princesses de Polignacs and their eminent friends, including Stravinsky, Colette, and Proust. **Pros:** everything done with exquisite taste; enormous marble bathrooms; stirring historic vibe. **Cons:** somewhat off the beaten path; you can't stay forever. $ *Rooms from: €185* ✉ *Rte. de Locmaria, 28 km (17 miles) southeast of Pont-Aven, off major rte. E60, Guidel* ☎ *02–97–65–98–01* 🌐 *www.domaine-de-kerbastic.com* 🛏 *15 deluxe rooms* ⏲ *Closed Jan.–mid-Feb.* 🍴 *Some meals.*

$ HOTEL 🏨 **La Chaumière Roz-Aven.** Partly built into a rock face on a bank of the Aven, this efficiently run hotel is a perfect blend of antique and modern—offering simple, clean rooms with 18th- and 19th-century-style touches. **Pros:** families welcome; rooms tastefully modernized. **Cons:** small rooms; rooms in annex lack character. $ *Rooms from: €75* ✉ *11 quai Théodore-Botrel* ☎ *02–98–06–13–06* 🌐 *www.hotelpontaven.com* 🛏 *14 rooms* ⏲ *Closed Jan. and Feb.* 🍴 *No meals.*

$ HOTEL Fodor's Choice ★ 🏨 **Le Moulin de Rosmadec.** You'll want to set up your easel in a second once you spot this pretty-as-a-picture, 15th-century stone water mill, set at the end of a quiet street and in the middle of the rushing, rocky Aven River. **Pros:** great setting; great value. **Cons:** attic rooms can be stuffy in midsummer. $ *Rooms from: €98* ✉ *Venelle de Rosmadec* ☎ *02–98–06–00–22* 🌐 *www.moulinderosmadec.com* 🛏 *4 rooms* ⏲ *Closed mid-Feb.–mid-Mar.* 🍴 *Some meals.*

BELLE-ILE-EN-MER

45 mins by boat from Quiberon, 78 km (52 miles) southeast of Pont-Aven.

Fodor's Choice ★ At 18 km (11 miles) long, Belle-Ile is the largest of Brittany's islands. It also lives up to its name: it is indeed beautiful, and less commercialized than its mainland harbor town, Quiberon. Monet created several famous paintings here, and you may also be tempted to set up an easel and canvas.

GETTING HERE

Take the 45-minute ferry trip (hourly July and August, €34 round-trip) to Belle-Ile's Le Palais from Quiberon's Gare Maritime, which can be reached in one hour by bus from Auray train station (on the Quimper–Vannes line) that runs several times daily in summer (€2).

Visitor Information Belle-Ile-en-Mer Tourist Office ✉ *Le Palais, Quai Bonnelle* ☎ *02–97–31–81–93* 🌐 *www.belle-ile.com.*

EXPLORING

Because of the cost and inconvenience of reserving car berths on the ferry, cross over to Belle-Ile as a pedestrian and rent a car—or, if you don't mind the hilly terrain, a bicycle. The mainland departure point is at Quiberon, a spa town with pearl-like beaches on the eastern side of the 16-km- (10-mile) long Presqu'île de Quiberon (Quiberon Peninsula), a stretch of coastal cliffs and beaches whose dramatic western coast, the Côte Sauvage (Wild Coast), is a mix of crevices and coves lashed by the sea. The ferry lands on Belle-Ile at **Le Palais,** crushed beneath a monumental Vauban citadel built in the 1680s.

Grand Phare (*Great Lighthouse*). Built in 1835, the Grand Phare at Port Goulphar rises 275 feet above sea level and has one of the most powerful beacons in Europe, visible from 120 km (75 miles) across the Atlantic. If the keeper is available and you are feeling well rested, you may be able to climb to the top.

Grotte de l'Apothicairerie. Continue on to the Grotte de l'Apothicairerie, which derives its name from the local cormorants' nests, said to resemble apothecary bottles.

Sauzon. From Le Palais head northwest to Sauzon, the prettiest fishing harbor on the island; from here you can see across to the Quiberon Peninsula and the Gulf of Morbihan.

WHERE TO STAY
For expanded hotel reviews, visit Fodors.com.

$$$ 🏨 **Castel Clara.** Perched on a cliff overlooking the surf and the narrow
RESORT Anse de Goulphar Bay, this '70s-era hotel was François Mitterrand's address when he vacationed on Belle-Ile and it still retains its presidential glamour, with its renowned spa, saltwater pool, and spectacular views. **Pros:** great facilities; spectacular setting. **Cons:** impersonal service; hard to get to. 💲 *Rooms from: €215* ✉ *Port-Goulphar, Bangor* ☎ *02–97–31–84–21* ⊕ *www.castel-clara.com* ⤴ *59 rooms, 4 suites* ☾ *Closed mid-Nov.–mid-Dec.* ❑ *Some meals.*

NIGHTLIFE AND THE ARTS
Lyrique-en-Mer. Every year, from mid-July to mid-August, Belle-Ile hosts Lyrique-en-Mer, an ambitious little festival whose heart is opera (the festival was founded by the American bass baritone, Richard Cowan) but which offers up a generous lyric menu of sacred music concerts, gospel, jazz, even the occasional sea chantey and Broadway musical number. Operas and concerts are performed by rising talents from around the world at various romantic locations around the island. ☎ *02–97–31–59–59* ⊕ *www.belle-ile.org.*

THE OUTDOORS
Roue Libre. The ideal way to get around to the island's 90 spectacular beaches is by bike. The best place to rent two-wheelers (and cars—this is also the island's Avis outlet) is at Roue Libre in Le Palais. ✉ *Rue du Pont Orgo, Le Palais* ☎ *02–97–31–49–81* ⊕ *www.belle-ile-evasion.com.*

CARNAC

19 km (12 miles) northeast of Quiberon via D768/D781.

Fodor's Choice At the north end of Quiberon Bay, Carnac is known for its expansive
★ beaches and its ancient stone monuments.

GETTING HERE
Trains from Vannes to Auray, followed by a bus to Carnac, are packaged together by SNCF (from 1 hr to 2 hrs, 15 mins, depending on time of day; €8). A bus from Quiberon on the peninsula, again through SNCF, travels to Carnac six times daily (35 mins, €3.70).

One of France's prettiest islands, Belle-Ile-en-Mer casts an especially potent spell at sunset.

Visitor Information Carnac Tourist Office ⊠ *74 av. des Druides* ☎ *02–97–52–13–52* ⊕ *www.ot-carnac.fr.*

EXPLORING

Menhirs. Dating from around 4500 BC, Carnac's menhirs remain as mysterious in origin as their English contemporaries, Stonehenge, although religious beliefs and astronomy were doubtless an influence. The 2,395 megalithic monuments that make up the three *alignements*—Kermario, Kerlescan, and Ménec—form the largest megalithic site in the world, and are positioned with astounding astronomical accuracy in semicircles and parallel lines over about a kilometer (half mile). The site, just north of the town, is fenced off for protection, and you can examine the menhirs up close only from October through March; in summer you must join a guided tour (some tours are in English [€6]). ⊕ *www.carnac.monuments-nationaux.fr.*

   Maison des Mégalithes. This visitor center explains the menhirs' history and significance, and offers an excellent selection of interesting books in all languages, DVDs, and regional gifts. ⊠ *Alignements du Ménec* ☎ *02–97–52–29–81* ⊙ *Sept.–Apr., daily 10–5; May and June, daily 9–6; July and Aug., daily 9:30–7:30.*

Tumulus de St-Michel. Carnac also has smaller-scale dolmen ensembles and three *tumuli* (mounds or barrows), including the 390-foot-long, 38-foot-high Tumulus de St-Michel, topped by a small chapel with views of the rock-strewn countryside.

WHERE TO STAY

For expanded hotel reviews, visit Fodors.com.

$$$$ HOTEL Fodor's Choice ★ **Château de Locguénolé.** Overlooking a sweeping 250-acre estate, this 19th-century mansion offers a grand refuge, with 22 guest rooms adorned with damask wallpapers, elegant antiques, marble fireplaces, and plenty of crystal and porcelain, along with stunning views over water and lush gardens. **Pros:** peace and quiet reign; large bathrooms are all in marble. **Cons:** out of the way (but well worth the detour). [$] *Rooms from: €240* ✉ *Rte. de Port-Louis, 25 km (16 miles) south of Carnac, direction Hennebont, Kervignac* ☎ *02–97–76–76–76* 🌐 *www.chateau-de-locguenole.com* 🛏 *18 rooms, 4 suites* 🍴 *All meals.*

6

VANNES

35 km (20 miles) east of Carnac via D768, 108 km (67 miles) southwest of Rennes.

Scene of the declaration of unity between France and Brittany in 1532, historic Vannes is one of the few towns in Brittany to have been spared damage during World War II. Though it draws visitors in droves to its wonderful Vielle Ville (Old Town), Vannes remains relatively untainted.

GETTING HERE

Direct TGVs from Paris (Gare Montparnasse) leave for Vannes eight times daily (3 hrs, 10 mins; €65). Six trains daily (some with a change at Redon) link Vannes to Nantes (1 hr, 20 mins; €22) and trains run every half hour or so between Vannes and Quimper (1 hr, 10 mins; €20.10). The two most useful bus companies are Cariane Atlantique and Transports Le Bayon, with frequent buses to Quiberon and Nantes (3 hrs).

Visitor Information Vannes Tourist Office ✉ *Quai Tabarly* ☎ *02–97–47–24–34* 🌐 *www.tourisme-vannes.com.*

EXPLORING

The true appeal of Vannes is walking through the winding pedestrian streets, shopping at the lively outdoor market, or sipping coffee outside near the sedate harbor. Be sure to saunter through the promenade de la Garenne, a colorful park, and admire the magnificent gardens nestled beneath the adjacent ramparts. Many of the prettiest sights are concentrated in the Old Town, hemmed in by rue Thiers on the west and ramparts and gates to the east and south. The ramparts crumble prettily under ivy blankets and each gateway has a character all its own. Also visit the medieval washhouses and the cathedral; browse in the antiques shops in the pedestrian streets around pretty place Henri-IV; check out the Cohue, the medieval market hall now used as an exhibition center; and take a boat trip around the scenic Golfe du Morbihan.

Cathédrale St-Pierre. A panoply of medieval art, St-Pierre boasts a 1537 Renaissance chapel, a Flamboyant Gothic transept portal, and a treasury. ✉ *Pl. de la Cathédrale* ☎ *02–97–42–40–55* ⏲ *Treasury July and Aug., Mon.–Sat. 10:30–6; June and Sept., Mon.–Sat. 1:30–5:30.*

WHERE TO EAT AND STAY

For expanded hotel reviews, visit Fodors.com.

$$$
MODERN FRENCH

✕ **Le Roscanvec.** Nestled on a pedestrian street in the charming old city, this modern gastronomic restaurant dispenses with stuffiness in favor of a relaxed, contemporary approach to food. What it doesn't dispense with is seriousness in the kitchen. Chef Thierry Seychelles seeks out top-quality ingredients from a wealth of local suppliers for his seasonal and meticulously presented cuisine. Start with oysters from the nearby Bay of Pénerf, cocotte of asparagus with lime hollandaise, tender foie gras–stuffed ravioli, smoked local eel with lemon confit in a parsley reduction, followed up by monkfish served with French caviar (depending on market availability and the chef's mood, of course). His take on the traditional Kouign Aman pastry is made with apples and served warm with salty caramel ice cream. Three-course lunch or dinner prix-fixe menus (€25–€66) are the way to go. $ *Average main: €32* ⊠ *17 rue des Halles* ☎ *02–97–47–15–96* ⊕ *www.roscanvec.com* ⌘ *Reservations essential* ☉ *Closed Mon. and last wk of June–1st wk of July. No dinner Sun. No lunch Tues. Sept.–June.*

$$$$
RESORT
Fodor's Choice
★

⌂ **Domaine de Rochevilaine.** At the tip of the magical Pen Lan peninsula, this enchanting and luxurious collection of 15th- and 16th-century Breton stone buildings resembles a tiny village; one, however, that is surrounded by terraced gardens, has a spectacular spa, and offers grand vistas of the Baie de Vilaine (Vilaine Bay). **Pros:** stylish interiors; ocean views; superb spa facilities. **Cons:** the staff seems to favor French guests; tons of steps from one house to another. $ *Rooms from: €322* ⊠ *Pointe de Pen-Lan, 30 km (19 miles) southeast of Vannes, Billiers* ☎ *02–97–41–61–61* ⊕ *www.domainerochevilaine.com* ⇝ *35 rooms, 3 suites* ⎮⊙⎮ *All meals.*

$
HOTEL

⌂ **Kyriad.** In an old, but thoroughly modernized building, this hotel attracts a varied foreign clientele, drawn by the homey guest rooms—clean, bright, and simple, with check-pattern quilts and warm yellow walls—and the friendly and efficient staff. **Pros:** tastefully modernized; fine restaurant. **Cons:** some rooms on the small side; some a bit noisy. $ *Rooms from: €82* ⊠ *8 pl. de la Libération* ☎ *02–97–63–27–36* ⊕ *www.kyriad-vannes.fr* ⇝ *33 rooms* ⎮⊙⎮ *Breakfast.*

LORIENT

50 km (30 miles) west of Vannes via N165, 36 km (22 miles) southeast of Pont-Aven via D24.

Founded by Colbert in 1666 as a base for the spice-seeking vessels of France's East India Company (Compagnie des Indes) bound for the Orient (thus the name "L'orient"), France's most exotically named town was smashed into semi-oblivion during World War II. A handful of Art Deco mansions survived, and you may want to visit the brazen concrete church of Notre-Dame-de-Victoire for its modern frescoes and stained glass. The town is at its liveliest during the Celtic Festival in August. Lorient is a major fishing port, as you'll deduce from all the activity along the mile-long quay and from the eye-slapping choice at the Halles de Merville fish market. It's also France's leading Atlantic submarine

Brittany's version of Stonehenge, this stone menhir at Carnac is just one of the area's impressive megalithic sights.

base. The giant concrete Base de Sous-Marins Keroman, built by the Nazis during World War II, claims to be the world's largest 20th-century fort—with a capacity of more than 30 submarines—and its 27-foot-thick roof withstood intensive Allied bombing virtually intact.

GETTING HERE

Direct TGVs from Paris (Gare Montparnasse) leave for Lorient five times per day (3 hrs, 45 mins; €66). Trains run frequently from Nantes (2 hrs, 20 mins; €26), Vannes (40 mins, €10), and Quimper (40 mins, €10). For trips by bus or boat to any of the surrounding towns, CTRL (the Compagnie des Transports de la Région Lorientaise ☎ 02–97–37–85–86 ⊕ www.ctrl.fr) will serve all your needs.

Visitor Information Lorient Tourist Office ✉ *Quai de Rohan, Lorient* ☎ *02–97–84–78–00* ⊕ *www.lorient-tourisme.fr.* **Port de Keroman**. Call ahead to the port to book a guided tour (90 mins) of the submarine base. ☎ *02–97–84–78–00.*

EXPLORING

Base de Sous-Marins Keroman. Built by the Nazis during World War II, this submarine base is the world's largest 20th-century fort. Thirty submarines could be comfortably housed in the squat concrete bunker—and its 27-foot-thick roof withstood intensive Allied bombing virtually intact. Open year-round; call ahead to be part of a 90-minute tour. ✉ *Port de Keroman, Lorient* ☎ *02–97–84–78–00* ⊕ *www.lorient-tourisme.fr* 🎫 *€6.*

Beaches. There's a good beach, **Larmor-Plage**, 5 km (3 miles) south of Lorient. Or you could take a ferry to the rocky **Ile de Groix**, or cross the bay to **Port-Louis,** a harbor renowned for tuna fishing and its 17th-century fort and ramparts. ✉ *Lorient.*

Festival Interceltique. Held in the first half of August, this festival is a jamboree of Celtic culture—music, drama, poetry, dance—with fellow Celts pouring into Lorient from all over western Europe (Cornwall, Wales, Ireland, Scotland, and Galicia) to celebrate. ✉ *Lorient* ☎ *02–97–21–24–29* 🌐 *www.festival-interceltique.com.*

LA BAULE

72 km (45 miles) southeast of Vannes via N165 and D774.

Star of the Côtes-d'Armor coast and gifted with a breathtaking 5-km (3-mile) beach, La Baule is a popular resort town that can make you pay dearly for your coastal frolics. Though it once rivaled Biarritz, today tackiness has replaced sophistication, but you still can't beat that sandy beach, or the lovely, miles-long seafront promenade lined with hotels. Like Dinard, La Baule is a 19th-century creation, founded in 1879 to make the most of the excellent sandy beaches that extend around the broad, sheltered bay between Pornichet and Le Pouliguen. A pine forest, planted in 1840, keeps the shifting local sand dunes firmly at bay. All in all, this can offer an idyllic stay for those who will enjoy a day on the beach, an afternoon at the shops on avenue du Général-de-Gaulle and avenue Louis-Lajarrige, and an evening at the casino.

WHERE TO EAT AND STAY

For expanded hotel reviews, visit Fodors.com.

$ FRENCH 🍴 **La Ferme du Grand Clos.** At this lively restaurant in an old farmhouse, 200 yards from the sea, you should understand the difference between *crêpe* and *galette* to order correctly, since the menus showcase both in all their forms (try the *galette* with scallops and leeks). Or you can opt for the simple, straightforward menu featuring food the owner Christophe Mercy likes to call *la cuisine de grand-mère* (grandma's cooking). Come early for a table; it's a very friendly and popular place. [$] *Average main: €11* ✉ *52 av. du Lattre-de-Tassigny* ☎ *02–40–60–03–30* 🌐 *www.lafermedugrandclos.com* 🕒 *Closed Mon., Mon–Wed. from Oct.–Apr., and mid-Nov.–mid-Dec.*

$ HOTEL 🏨 **Concorde.** Complete with some rooms flaunting sea views and Louis Treize-style antiques, this bright-blue-shuttered, white-walled establishment numbers among the least expensive good hotels in pricey La Baule. **Pros:** close to beach; good value. **Cons:** no restaurant; lengthy annual closure. [$] *Rooms from: €98* ✉ *1 bis, av. de la Concorde* ☎ *02–40–60–23–09* 🌐 *www.hotel-la-concorde.com* 🛏 *47 rooms* 🕒 *Closed Oct.–Mar.*

$$ HOTEL 🏨 **Hôtel de la Plage.** One of the few hotels on the beach in St-Marc-sur-Mer, southeast of La Baule, this comfortable lodging was the celebrated setting for Jacques Tati's classic comedy *Mr. Hulot's Holiday.* **Pros:** silver-screen claim to fame; beachside setting. **Cons:** old-fashioned; overrun by French families in midsummer. [$] *Rooms from: €139* ✉ *37 rue du Commandant-Charcot, 10 km (6 miles) southeast of La Baule, St-Marc-sur-Mer* ☎ *02–40–91–99–01* 🌐 *www.hotel-delaplage.fr* 🛏 *30 rooms* 🍽 *All meals.*

NIGHTLIFE

Casino. Occasionally you see high stakes on the tables at La Baule's casino. ⊠ *24 Esplanade Lucien Barrière* ☎ *02–40–11–48–28.*

NANTES

72 km (45 miles) east of La Baule via N171 and N165, 108 km (67 miles) south of Rennes.

The writer Stendhal remarked of 19th-century Nantes, "I hadn't taken twenty steps before I recognized a great city." Since then, the river that flowed around the upper-crust Ile Feydeau neighborhood has been filled in and replaced with a rushing torrent of traffic on the major highways that now cut through the heart of town. Still, Nantes is more than the sum of its traffic jams, and even the bureaucratic severance of the city from Brittany—it's now the capital of the Pays de la Loire region—has not robbed it of its historic Breton character. Stay a spell to discover its many charms.

GETTING HERE

TGV trains leave Paris's Gare Montparnasse for Nantes every hour, covering the 387 km (240 miles) in just two hours, 15 minutes (€62). Trains make the two-hour, 30-minute run up the coast from Nantes to Quimper (€36.60) 10 times per day, some direct and some stopping at Rennes (1 hr, 40 mins; €24.90) or Vannes (1 hr, 25 mins; €22.20). The train station in Nantes, at 27 boulevard Stalingrad, is across the street from the Jardin des Plantes and a 10-minute walk from the Vieille Ville. A number of companies also run buses to Rennes (2 hrs), as well as other nearby towns.

Visitor Information Nantes Tourist Office ⊠ *9 rue des États* ☎ *08–92–46–40–44* ⊕ *www.nantes-tourisme.com.*

EXPLORING

Nantes's 15th-century château is still in relatively good shape, despite having lost an entire tower during a gunpowder explosion in 1800. The 15th-century cathedral floats heavenward as well, and its white stones, immense height, and airy interior make it one of France's best. Across the broad boulevard, cours des 50-Otages, is the 19th-century city. The unlucky Ile Feydeau, surrounded and bisected by highways, still preserves the tottering 18th-century mansions built with wealth from Nantes's huge transatlantic slave trade. The Loire River flows along the southern edge of the Vieille Ville, and Nantes is officially part of the Loire region, although historically it belonged to Brittany—and still does in the psyche of many of its residents. In town you can see many references to Anne de Bretagne, the last independent ruler of Brittany, who married the region away to King Charles VIII of France in 1491. Bretons have never quite recovered from the shock. Note that one of the city's more splendid collections, the Musée Thomas-Dobrée, is closed for renovation until 2015.

Cathédrale St-Pierre–St-Paul. One of France's last Gothic cathedrals, this was begun in 1434, well after most other medieval cathedrals had been completed. The facade is ponderous and austere, in contrast to the light,

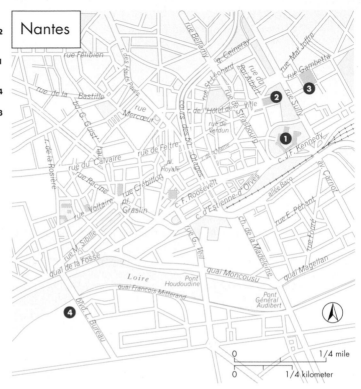

Nantes

wide, limestone interior, whose vaults rise higher (120 feet) than those of Notre-Dame in Paris. ✉ *Pl. St-Pierre* ☎ *02–40–47–84–64* ✆ *Free* ☼ *Crypt Sept.–Easter, weekends 3–6; Easter–July 14, Sat. 10–12:30 and 3–6; July 15–Aug., Tues.–Fri. and Sun. 3–6, Sat. 10–12:30 and 3–6.*

Château des Ducs de Bretagne. Built by the dukes of Brittany, who had no doubt that Nantes belonged in their domain, this château is a massive, well-preserved 15th-century fortress with a moat. François II, the duke responsible for building most of it, led a hedonistic life here, surrounded by ministers, chamberlains, and an army of servants. Numerous monarchs later stayed in the castle, where in 1598 Henri IV signed the famous Edict of Nantes advocating religious tolerance. The castle reopened in 2007 after extensive renovations. ✉ *4 pl. Marc-Elder* ☎ *02–51–17–49–48* ⊕ *www.chateau-nantes.fr* ✆ *€5* ☼ *Tues.–Sun. 10–6; July–Aug., daily 10–7.*

Fodor'sChoice
★ **Grand Eléphant et Galerie de les Machines de l'Ille.** Had Jules Verne (a son of Nantes) and Leonardo da Vinci somehow got together when they were both in a particularly whimsical frame of mind, they may well have instigated this unique and engaging workshop-gallery. Their spirit certainly lives in the imaginative, artistic, and mechanically brilliant creations that are built and displayed here. The Grand Eléphant gets most attention—hardly surprising, since the 50-ton giant, just short of

40 feet high, regularly "ambles" along the quay carrying 49 passengers. Inside the gallery are more works in many shapes and sizes—some of them interactive—and you can view work in progress (weekdays) on the workshop's latest projects; the recently completed *Carrousel des Mondes Marins* (Marine World carousel) is the newest eye-popping addition, located just outside the gallery on the banks of the Loire. ✉ *Les Chantiers, bd. Léon Bureau, Ile de Nantes* ☎ *08–10–12–12–25, 332–51–17–49–89 from outside France* 🌐 *www.lesmachines-nantes.fr* 🎟 *€8; elephant ride €8; carousel €8* ⏲ *July and Aug., daily 10–7; Sept.–early Jan. and mid-Feb.–June, hrs vary (see website).*

Musée des Beaux-Arts (*Museum of Fine Arts*). Designed by Clément-Marie Josso, this noted museum was opened in 1900. Inside, skylights cast their glow over a fine array of paintings, extending from the Renaissance period onward, including works by Jacopo Tintoretto, Georges de La Tour, Jean-Auguste-Dominique Ingres, and Gustave Courbet. To go from the sublime to the ridiculous, look for the famous late-19th-century painting of a gorilla running amok with a maiden. The main *palais* is closed for renovations, but the *Chapelle de l'Oratoire* will host exhibitions for the time being. ✉ *10 rue Georges-Clemenceau* ☎ *02–51–17–45–00* 🌐 *www.museedesbeauxarts.nantes.fr* 🎟 *€2* ⏲ *Wed.–Mon., 10–6, Thurs. until 8.*

6

WHERE TO EAT AND STAY

For expanded hotel reviews, visit Fodors.com.

$ BRASSERIE 🍴 **La Cigale.** Palm trees, gleaming woodwork, colorful enamel tiles, and painted ceilings have led to the official recognition of La Cigale brasserie (built in 1895) as a *monument historique.* You can savor its Belle Époque blandishments without spending a fortune—the prix-fixe lunch menus are a good value. But the banks of fresh oysters and well-stacked dessert cart may tempt you to order à la carte. Best of all, it's open every day from early morning till after midnight, a rare convenience in France. [$] *Average main: €18* ✉ *4 pl. Graslin* ☎ *02–51–84–94–94* 🌐 *www.lacigale.com* ✍ *Reservations essential.*

$$$ FRENCH 🍴 **L'Embellie.** Sweet and simple, this spot lures diners with its modern, inventive attitude and friendly service. New chef Patrice Bierg has brought renewed vigor to the "creative regional" cuisine that has been a staple of this bright and elegant venue. The menu is dependent on Bierg's daily trips to markets, so don't hesitate to try any of the fresh fish specials, such as the scallops with turnips, fennel, and chives in a Muscadet, orange, and vermouth bath, or other delights, such as the roasted and deboned, locally raised pigeon in a simple au jus sauce. A delicious lemon tart with yuzu meringue makes for a fitting and exotic finale. [$] *Average main: €25* ✉ *14 rue Armand-Brossard* ☎ *02–40–48–20–02* 🌐 *www.restaurantlembellie.com* ⏲ *Closed Aug. No dinner Sun.*

$$ BISTRO 🍴 **Les Chants d'Avril.** It may not be the fanciest restaurant in Nantes, but it's where the locals go for "bistronomic" food and good, well-priced wines. Cozy and welcoming, the murals, dark-wood paneling, and leather banquettes give the look and feel of a traditional bistrot, but the attention to market-driven ingredients and interesting wines puts it in league with the modern *bistrôt à vins*. Labels aside, dishes like the excellent homemade foie gras or *boudin noir*, baked Scottish salmon

with black sesame and parsley root rémoulade, or crab gazpacho speak for themselves. The luscious caramel clafoutis for dessert is a must. Although dinner is served on Thursday and Friday, it's best for lunch, when the superb three-course menu (€22) is extremely good value. [$] *Average main: €19* ✉ *2 rue Laënnec* ☎ *02–40–89–34–76* 🌐 *www.leschantsdavril.fr* ⏲ *Closed weekends. No dinner Mon.–Wed.*

$ HOTEL 🏨 **La Pérouse.** Bare parquet floors, plain off-white walls, simple high-tech lighting, and minimal contemporary furnishings by celebrated modernist designers all helped earn La Pérouse the accolade of Europe's Design Hotel of the Year in 1995—shortly after this big white cube of a hotel opened its doors. **Pros:** stylish interiors; friendly staff; organic breakfasts. **Cons:** hard to park; no restaurant; noisy bar. [$] *Rooms from: €105* ✉ *3 allée Dusquesne* ☎ *02–40–89–75–00* 🌐 *www.hotel-laperouse.fr* 🛏 *46 rooms* 🍴 *Breakfast.*

NIGHTLIFE AND THE ARTS

Le Lieu Unique. Le Lieu Unique is the "in" place to go for an impressive selection of cutting-edge cultural and leisure events, including music, dance, art exhibitions, and creative "happenings." The contemporary space includes a bar, restaurant, boutique, and, yes, a hammam, too. ✉ *Quai Ferdinand-Favre* ☎ *02–40–12–14–34* 🌐 *www.lelieuunique.com.*

Théâtre Graslin. Nantes's principal concert hall also does double duty as its grand opera house. ✉ *1 rue Molière* ☎ *02–40–69–77–18.*

Univers. The informal Univers has live jazz concerts every other week. ✉ *16 rue Jean-Jacques-Rousseau* ☎ *02–40–73–49–55.*

THE OUTDOORS

FAMILY **Bateaux Nantais.** You can take a 100-minute cruise along the pretty Erdre River, past a string of gardens and châteaux, on the Bateaux Nantais. There are also four-course lunch and dinner cruises that last about 2½ hours (€56–€89). ✉ *Quai de la Motte Rouge* ☎ *02–40–14–51–14* 🌐 *www.bateaux-nantais.fr* 🎟 *€12* ⏲ *June–Aug., daily at 3:30 and 5:30, Sun. and holidays at 10:30, 3:30, and 5:30; May and Sept., daily at 3:30; Mar., Apr., Oct., and Nov., Sun. and holidays at 3:30.*

SHOPPING

The commercial quarter of Nantes stretches from place Royale to place Graslin. Various antiques shops can be found on rue Voltaire.

Devineau. The Devineau family has been selling wax fruit and vegetables at Devineau since 1803, as well as handmade candles and wildflower honey. ✉ *4 rue Belle Image* ☎ *02–40–47–19–59.*

Gautier-Debotté. For chocolate, head to Gautier-Debotté; try the local Muscadet grapes macerated in the local Muscadet wine and enrobed in chocolate. ✉ *9 rue de la Fosse* ☎ *02–40–48–23–19* 🌐 *www.debotte.fr.*

CHAMPAGNE COUNTRY

WELCOME TO CHAMPAGNE COUNTRY

TOP REASONS TO GO

★ **Drink Champagne— what else!:** Sample some bubbly, see the vineyards, and visit the cavernous chalk cellars where bottles are stored by the million.

★ **Bask in Gothic glory:** No fewer than 10 Gothic cathedrals dot the region— don't miss the biggest (Amiens) or the tallest (neighboring Beauvais).

★ **Look up in Laon:** With its cathedral towers patrolling the hilly horizon, the **"Crowned Mountain"** has a site whose grandeur rivals Mont-St-Michel.

★ **Drink now, pray later in Reims:** Beyond being a center for Champagne production, regal Reims is also home to France's great coronation cathedral.

★ **Exercise your options:** Hiking on one of Champagne's fabulous, forested *sentiers de Grandes Randonnées* can be an intoxicating outdoor activity.

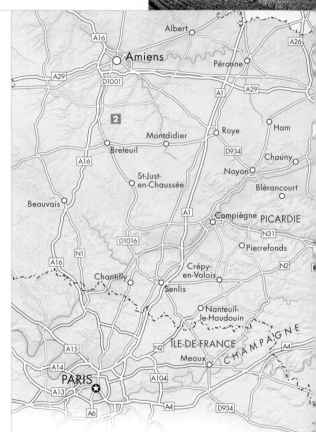

1 Champagne. The local obsession with Champagne is especially evident in Reims, the region's hub, which is home to the great Champagne houses and site of one of the most historically important cathedrals in France. Once you've paid tribute to the 34 VIPs who have been crowned here and toured some Champagne cellars to bone up on the backstory behind this noble beverage, you can head south. Smack-dab in the middle of the 280 square km (108 square miles) that make up the entire Champagne-producing area, Épernay lives and dies for the bubbly brew. Continue on the Route du Champagne to other wine villages.

2 **The Cathedral Cities.**
To the west of Champagne lies a region where the popping of Champagne corks is only a distant murmur, and not just because Reims is 160 km (100 miles) away. For here you'll find some of the most gargantuan Gothic hulks of architectural harmony—namely the cathedrals of Beauvais, Amiens, Laon, and Soissons. Beauvais is positively dizzying from within (it features the highest choir in France, and you nearly keel over craning your neck back to see it); Amiens, the largest church in the land, is fantastically ornate in places; while Laon is notable for its majestic towers, and Soissons shows Gothic at its most restrained.

GETTING ORIENTED

As you head toward Reims, the landscape loosens and undulates, and the hills tantalize with vineyards that—thanks to *la méthode champenoise*—produce the world's antidote to gloom. Each year, millions of bottles of bubbly mature in hundreds of kilometers of chalk tunnels carved under the streets of Reims and Épernay, both of which fight for the title "The Champagne City." Long before a drink put it on the map, though, this area of northern France was marked by great architecture, and it contains many of France's greatest medieval cathedrals.

7

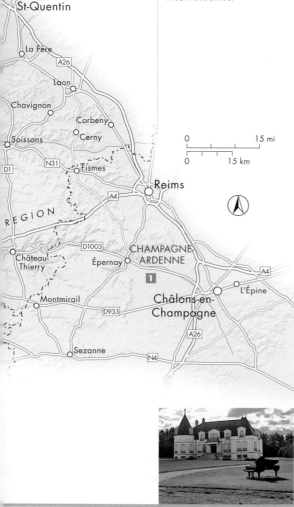

St-Quentin

La Fère

A26

Laon

Chavignon

Corbeny

Soissons   Cerny

D1   N31   Fismes

REGION

Reims

A4

0 ____ 15 mi
0 ____ 15 km

Château-Thierry   D1003   CHAMPAGNE ARDENNE

Épernay

Montmirail   D933

1

L'Épine

A4

Châlons-en-Champagne

A26

Sezanne   N4

Updated by
Lyn Parry

Few drinks in the world have such a pull on the imagination as Champagne, yet surprisingly few tourists visit the pretty vineyards south of Reims. Perhaps it's because the Champagne region is seen as a bit of a backwater, halfway between Paris and Luxembourg. The arrival of the TGV line serving eastern France and Germany has helped to change this perception.

Champagne, a place-name that has become a universal synonym for joy and festivity, actually began as a word of humble meaning. Like *campagna*, its Italian counterpart, it's derived from the Latin *campus*, or "open field." In French *campus* became *champ*, with the old language extending this to *champaign*, for "battlefield," and *champaine*, for "district of plains." The gentle vine-covered slopes of the hillsides rising from vast chalky plains here have been the center of Champagne production for more than two centuries, stocking the cellars of its many conquerors (Napoléon, Czar Nicholas I, the Duke of Wellington) as well as those of contemporary case-toting bubblyphiles.

Meanwhile, great cathedrals testify to the wealth this region enjoyed thanks to its prime location between Paris and northern Europe. The flying buttresses and heaven-seeking spires of these sanctuaries remind us that medieval stoneworkers sought to raise radically new Gothic arches to improbable heights, running for cover if their ambitious efforts failed. Most have stood the test of time, though you might want to hover near the exits at Beauvais, the tallest cathedral in France—its height still makes some engineers nervous.

The region's crossroads status also exacted a heavy toll, and it paid heavily for its role as a battleground for the bickering British, German, and French. From pre-Roman times to the armistice of 1945, some of Europe's costliest wars were fought on northern French soil. World War I and World War II were especially unkind: epic cemeteries cover the plains of Picardy, and you can still see bullet-pocked buildings in Amiens. These days, happily, the vineyards of Champagne attract tourists interested in less sobering events.

PLANNER

WHEN TO GO

Of course, the optimal time to visit vineyards is around the fall harvest, when the weather is usually at its best. Summer also has its advantages. Compared to many other regions of France, Champagne remains relatively uncrowded in July and August; and the coolness of the chalk cellars makes it a pleasure to tour the Champagne houses then (note that many close after the busy winter holidays for the first few months of the year, as do some of the smaller hotels and restaurants). Spring is generally unpredictable weather-wise, but on the dry and sunny days it can idyllic. Whatever you plan to do, be sure to come between May and October; the ubiquitous vineyards are a dismal, leafless sight the rest of the year.

MAKING THE MOST OF YOUR TIME

Threading the triangle between Reims, Épernay, and Château-Thierry are the famous **Routes Touristique de Champagne** (Champagne Roads), which divvy up the region into four fabulous itineraries. These follow the main four côtes of the Champagne vineyards. Northwest of Reims (use the Tinqueux exit) is the Massif de Saint-Thierry—a vineyard-rich region once hallowed by kings. Heading south of Reims to Épernay, veer west along the Vallée de la Marne through the Hauteurs d'Épernay, traveling west on the right bank of the river and east on the left. To the east of Épernay lies the most beautiful stretch of Champagne Country: the Montagne de Reims. To the south of Épernay is the Côte de Blancs, the "cradle of Chardonnay." More than 80 producers of Champagne are scattered along these roads, and you can guarantee a better reception if you call the ones you'd like to visit in advance.

The two main centers to the Champagne Wine Road are Reims and Épernay, which are about 64 km (40 miles) apart if you work your way through the wine villages that dot the slopes of the Montagne de Reims. Start in Reims, with its host of major Champagne houses, then go south on N51 and east on D26 through pretty Rilly-la-Montagne, Mailly-Champagne, and Verzy, where you can visit local producers Étienne and Anne-Laure Lefevre at 30 rue de Villers (☎ *03–26–97–96–99* ⊕ *www. champagne-etienne-lefevre.com*). Continue south to Ambonnay, then track back west to Bouzy, Ay, and Hautvillers—where Dom Pérignon is buried in the village church—before crossing the Marne River to Épernay, whose main street is home to several producers.

From Épernay, spear south along the Côte de Blanc to Vertus, 19 km (12 miles) away, where Pierre and Sophie Larmandier will sell and tell you all about their organic bio-Champagne at 19 avenue du General-de-Gaulle (☎ *03–26–52–13–24* ⊕ *www.larmandier.fr*). If you're heading back to Paris, take D1 from Épernay west along the banks of the Marne to Château-Thierry 50 km (30 miles) away. The steep-climbing vineyards hugging the river are the most scenic in Champagne. For maps of the four Routes Touristique de Champagne, stop at the Marne Regional Tourist Office in Châlons-en-Champagne or the tourist offices in Reims or Épernay.

GETTING HERE AND AROUND

As always in France, intercity buses are less frequent than trains, and much slower.

Happily, there are trains to all the towns and cities mentioned in this chapter.

The natural hub remains Reims—especially now that it's just 45 minutes from Paris by TGV. Reims is linked to Laon by the A26 expressway, and to Châlons-en-Champagne by the A4 expressway arriving from Paris. The west, Amiens and Beauvais, are connected by the A16. Épernay, south of Reims, can be reached from Reims by the twisting wine road or quicker N51. Only Soissons, 32 km (20 miles) southwest of Laon, is a bit off the beaten track.

AIR TRAVEL

If you're coming from the United States or most other locales, count on arriving at Paris's Charles de Gaulle or Orly airport. Charles de Gaulle offers easy access to the northbound A16 and A1 for Beauvais and Amiens, and the eastbound A4 for Reims. If coming from within the European Union, consider the direct flights into Beauvais.

BUS TRAVEL

As train travel is so much more efficient and dependable, we don't recommend relying on bus service outside Paris. There are more than a dozen different bus operators in the Champagne and Picardy regions, but since few of them have websites, reliable schedules, or any personnel who speak English, it's best to contact the local tourism office if you're looking into bus options. In Picardy the main bus hub is at the Gare Routière in Amiens, next to the train station. In the Champagne region, the main hub is Châlons-en-Champagne, with routes from Reims to Troyes, Épernay to Châlons, and Reims to Laon. In Reims, municipal buses depart from the train station.

CAR TRAVEL

The A4 heads east from Paris to Reims; allow 90 minutes to two hours, depending on traffic. The A16 leads from L'Isle-Adam, north of Paris, up to Beauvais and Amiens.

If you're arriving by car via the Channel Tunnel, you'll disembark at Coquelles, near Calais, and join A16 not far from its junction with A26, which heads to Reims (2 hrs, 30 mins).

TRAIN TRAVEL

It's easy to get to major towns in the region by train. Most sites can be reached by regular service, except for the Champagne vineyards, which require a car. There are frequent daily trains from Paris (Gare du Nord) to Beauvais, Amiens, and Laon, which take up to two leisurely hours to travel 140 km (87 miles). The super-express TGV service covers the 170 km (105 miles) from Paris (Gare de l'Est) to Reims in 45 minutes. Cross-country services connect Reims to Épernay (20 mins), Châlons (40 mins), Amiens (2 hrs, 30 mins), and Laon (35 mins).

Train Information Gare SNCF Reims ⊠ *Bd. Joffre* ☎ *36–35 SCNF [€0.34 per min], 08–91–67–10–08 TER Regional, [€0.22 per min].* **SNCF** ☎ *36–35 [€0.34 per min]* ⊕ *www.voyages-sncf.com.* **TGV** ⊕ *www.tgv.com.*

RESTAURANTS

This region is less dependent on tourism than many in France, and most restaurants are open year-round. However, in the largest cities, Reims and Amiens, many do close for two to three weeks in July and August.

Smoked ham, pigs' feet, gingerbread, and Champagne-based mustard are specialties of the Reims area, along with sautéed chicken, kidneys, stuffed trout, pike, and snails.

One particularly hearty dish is *potée champenoise,* consisting of smoked ham, bacon, sausage, and cabbage. Rabbit (often cooked with prunes) is common, while boar and venison are specialties in fall and winter, when vegetable soups are high on the menu.

In Picardy, the popular *ficelle picarde* is a pancake stuffed with cheese, mushrooms, and ham.

Apart from Champagne, try drinking the region's *hydromel* (mead, made from honey) and Ratafia, a sweet aperitif made from grape juice and brandy.

Prices in the reviews are the average cost of a main course at dinner or, if dinner is not served, at lunch.

HOTELS

The Champagne Region has a mix of old, rambling hotels, often simple rather than pretentious. In addition, there are a handful of stylish hostelries catering to those with more discerning tastes, including a large contingent of staffers who work in the Champagne industry. *Be warned, though, that few of the destinations mentioned in this chapter have much in the way of upscale choice.* Many of the region's most characterful establishments are in the countryside and require a car to reach.

Prices in the reviews are the lowest cost of a standard double room in high season.

VISITOR INFORMATION

If traveling extensively by public transportation, be sure to load up on information ("Guide Régional des Transports" schedules, the best taxi-for-call companies, etc.) upon arriving at the ticket counter or help desk of the bigger train and bus stations in the area, such as Reims and Amiens. In addition to the main tourist offices in these two cities, other smaller towns have their own tourist bureaus, *which are listed in this chapter under the town names.*

Marne Regional Tourist Office. The Marne Regional Tourist Office is a mine of information about the Champagne region. ⊠ *13 bis, rue Carnot, Châlons-en-Champagne* ☎ *03–26–68–37–52* ⊕ *www.tourisme-en-champagne.com.*

Two main websites for the region (⊕ *www.tourisme-champagne-ardenne.com, www.picardietourisme.com*) are packed with data and suggestions for Champagne-bound travelers.

7

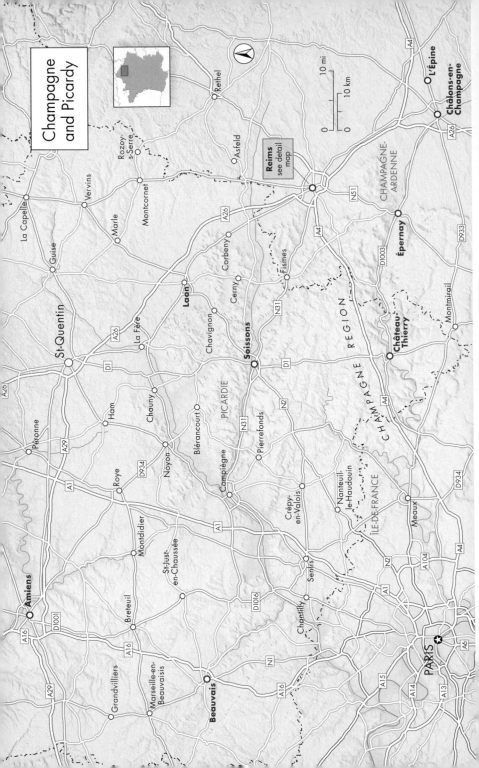

Champagne and Picardy

Amiens Tourist Office ✉ *40 pl. Notre Dame, Amiens* ☎ *03–22–71–60–50* ⊕ *www.amiens-tourisme.com.*

Reims Tourist Office ✉ *2 rue Guillaume-de-Machault, Reims* ☎ *08–21– 61–01–60 [€0.11 per min]* ⊕ *www.reims-tourisme.com.*

CHAMPAGNE

An uplifting landscape tumbles about Reims and Épernay, perhaps because its inhabitants treat themselves to a regular infusion of the local, world-prized elixir. But unlike the great vineyards of Bordeaux and Burgundy, there are few country châteaux to go with the fabled names of this region—Mumm, Taittinger, Pommery, and Veuve-Clicquot. Most of the glory is to be found in *caves* (wine cellars), not to mention the fascinating guided tours offered by the most famous producers.

Despite its glamorous image as the home of Champagne, the region in fact has a laid-back rustic charm where "life in the fast lane" refers strictly to the Paris-bound A4 expressway. On the map, Champagne encompasses Reims and the surrounding vineyards and chalky plains. The province starts just beyond Château-Thierry, 96 km (60 miles) northeast of Paris, and continues along the towering Marne Valley to Épernay. Cheerful villages line the Routes Touristique de Champagne (Champagne Road; *for details, see our chapter Planner section*), which twines north to Reims, the largest city in Champagne. To the southeast the grapes of Champagne flourish on the steep slopes of the Marne Valley and the Montagne de Reims, really more of a mighty hill than a mountain. For a handy web source covering many of the great Champagne houses in the region, log on to ⊕ *www.maisons-champagne.com.*

REIMS

161 km (100 miles) northeast of Paris.

Behind a facade of austerity, Champagne's largest city remains one of France's richest tourist sites, thanks especially to the fact that it sparkles with some of the biggest names in Champagne production. This thriving industry has conferred wealth and sometimes an arrogant reserve on the region's inhabitants. The maze of Champagne cellars constitutes a leading attraction here. Several of these producers organize visits to their cellars, combining video presentations with guided tours of their cavernous, hewn-chalk underground warehouses. ⇨ *See the special "Champagne Uncorked" photo feature for details about visiting Taittinger, Mumm, and other fabled Champagne houses.*

GETTING HERE

The TGV (⊕ *www.tgv.com*) express train covers the 170 km (105 miles) from Paris (Gare de l'Est) to Reims in 45 minutes. Trains depart from Paris 13 times daily and cost €29–€56. Several SNCF trains daily connect Reims to Épernay (20–30 mins, €6.40), and there is regular daily train service from Châlons-en-Champagne (40 mins, €10.50). There are two direct trains each day from Amiens to Reims (2 hrs, 30 mins; €25.20). STDM Trans-Champagne (☎ *03–26–65–17–07* ⊕ *www.stdmarne.fr*)

runs three daily buses to Reims from Châlons-en-Champagne (line 140; 50 mins, €10.50).

Visitor Information Reims Tourist Office ⌧ *2 rue Guillaume-de-Machault* ☎ *08–21–61–01–60 [€0.11 per min]* ⊕ *www.reims-tourisme.com* ⌧ *Parvis de la Gare* ☎ *08–21–61–01–60.*

EXPLORING

Although many of Reims's historic buildings were flattened in World War I and replaced by drab, modern architecture, those that do remain are of royal magnitude. Top of the list goes to the city's magnificent cathedral, in which the kings of France were crowned until 1825, while the Musée des Beaux-Arts has a stellar collection of paintings, and Le Vergeur Museum is home to a complete edition of Dürer prints. The new tramway, opened in 2011, makes it even easier to get around the compact town and its many sites from the train station.

Tourist office. For a complete list of Champagne cellars, head to the tourist office near the cathedral. ⌧ *2 rue Guillaume-de-Machault* ☎ *08–21–61–01–60 [€0.11 per min]* ⊕ *www.reims-tourisme.com.*

A useful website that can help with planning Champagne cellar visits throughout the region is: ⊕ *www.tourisme-en-champagne.com.*

TOP ATTRACTIONS

Basilique St-Rémi. This 11th-century Romanesque-Gothic basilica honors the 5th-century saint who gave his name to the city and baptized Clovis (the first king of France) in 498. The interior seems to stretch into the endless distance, an impression created by its relative murk and lowness. The airy four-story Gothic choir contains some fine original 12th-century stained glass. The Abbaye Royale, alongside the basilica, was formerly the keeper of the holy vial used at the coronations of the kings of France. Today it houses an interesting museum which highlights the history of the abbey, the Gallo-Roman history of the town, and the regional military history. ⌧ *Pl. Chandoine Ladame* ☎ *03–26–85–06–69* ⊕ *stremi-reims.cef.fr/* ⌧ *Museum, €4* ◷ *Daily 8–7; museum weekdays 2–6:30, weekends 2–7.*

Fodor's Choice ★   **Cathédrale Notre-Dame de Reims.** Recently restored for its 800th birthday, this magnificent Gothic cathedral provided the setting for the coronations of French kings. The great historical saga began with Clovis, king of the Franks, who was baptized in an early structure on this site in the 6th century; Joan of Arc led her recalcitrant Dauphin here to be crowned King Charles VII; Charles X's coronation, in 1825, was the last. The east-end windows have stained glass by Marc Chagall and Imi Knoebel. Admire the vista toward the west end, with an interplay of narrow pointed arches. The glory of Reims's cathedral is its facade: it's so skillfully proportioned that initially you have little idea of its monumental size. Above the north (left) door hovers the *Laughing Angel*, a delightful statue whose famous smile threatens to melt into an acid-rain scowl now that pollution has succeeded war as the ravager of the building's fabric. With the exception of the 15th-century towers, most of the original building went up in the 100 years after 1211. You can climb to the top of the towers, and peek inside the breathtaking timber-and-concrete roof (reconstructed in the 1920s with Rockefeller money) for

Tally up the 34 kings who were crowned at Notre-Dame de Reims, one of the largest and greatest of French cathedrals.

€7.50. A stroll around the outside reinforces the impression of harmony, discipline, and decorative richness. The east end presents an idyllic sight across well-tended lawns. ✉ *Pl. du Cardinal-Luçon* ☎ *03–26–47–81–79* ⊕ *www.cathedrale-reims.monuments-nationaux.fr* ⊙ *Cathedral daily 7:30–7:30. Towers mid-Mar.–early May, Sept., and Oct., Sat. at 10, 11, 2, 3, and 4, Sun. at 2, 3, and 4; early May–Aug., Tues.– Sat. every ½ hr 10–11:30 and 2–5:30, Sun. 2–5.*

Musée des Beaux-Arts (*Museum of Fine Arts*). Two blocks southwest of Reims's massive cathedral, this noted museum has an outstanding collection of paintings, which includes no fewer than 27 Corots, as well as Jacques-Louis David's unforgettable *Death of Marat* (the portrait shows the revolutionary polemicist Jean-Paul Marat stabbed to death in his bath, a deed done by Charlotte Corday, in 1793). Unfortunately, the museum is only open for temporary exhibitions at the moment, and the main collection is already packed away in preparation for a major move. In 2017, the museum is set to open in new premises, designed by David Chipperfield, near Les Halles du Boulingrin on the rue de Mars. ✉ *8 rue Chanzy* ☎ *03–26–35–36–00* ⊕ *www.ville-reims.fr* 🖂 *€4* ⊙ *Wed.–Mon. 10–noon and 2–6.*

WORTH NOTING

Hôtel Le Vergeur Museum. One of the best examples of late medieval and early Renaissance architecture in Reims was built during the 13th century. Originally overlooking the historic linen and wheat market in the center of town, this noble town house changed hands between aristocrats and Champagne traders before being acquired in 1910 by Hugues Kraft—a man whose sole passion was preserving the city's

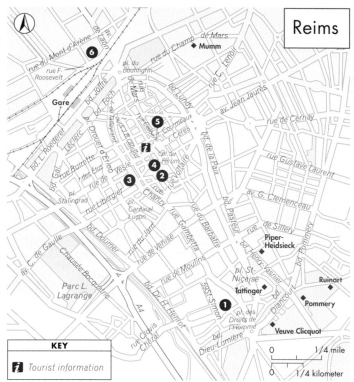

historic buildings. It was completely restored after the WWI bombings and today houses an impressive collection of historical prints, paintings, and furnishings from the region, as well as an original, complete series of 15th-century Albert Dürer prints of the "Apocalypse" and "Large Passion." There are guided tours of the collection Tuesday through Sunday in summer, from 10 to 6. ✉ *36 pl. du Forum* ☎ *03–26–47–20–75* ⊕ *www.museelevergeur.fr* ☞*€5* ⊙ *Sept.–May, Tues.–Sun. 2–6; June–Aug., daily 10–noon and 2–6.*

Musée de la Reddition (*Museum of the Surrender*). Also known as the Salle du 8-Mai-1945 or the "little red schoolhouse," this museum is a well-preserved map-covered room used by General Eisenhower as Allied headquarters at the end of World War II. It was here that General Alfred Jodl signed the German surrender at 2:41 am on May 7, 1945. Fighting officially ceased at midnight the next day. The museum also presents a collection of local photos, documents, uniforms, and artifacts recounting the fighting, occupation, and liberation of Reims. Guided tours begin with a short film in English and French. ✉ *12 rue Franklin-Roosevelt* ☎ *03–26–47–84–19* ☞*€4* ⊙ *Wed.–Mon. 10–noon and 2–6.*

Palais du Tau. Formerly the Archbishop's Palace (alongside the cathedral), this UNESCO World Heritage List museum now houses an impressive display of tapestries and coronation robes of 32 French kings, as well as several statues rescued from the cathedral facade. The second-floor views of the cathedral are terrific. ✉ *2 pl. du Cardinal-Luçon* ☎ *03–26–47–81–79* 🌐 *www.palais-tau.monuments-nationaux.fr* 🎟 *€7.50* 🕒 *May–Aug., Tues.–Sun. 9:30–6:30; Sept.–Apr., Tues.–Sun. 9:30–12:30 and 2–5:30.*

WHERE TO EAT

$$$ BRASSERIE 🍴 **Brasserie Flo.** This authentic brasserie, part of the Flo chain, has polished wood floors, Art Nouveau glass windows, and mirrored walls. The food is sophisticated and dependable, the service sleek. Signature dishes like panfried escalope of foie gras served with gingerbread and caramelized mango, or roast monkfish with cèpe mushrooms and chateaubriand are just some of the delicious choices. There are also good fixed-price menus, which change on a weekly basis. The terrace is an added bonus in the summer. [$] *Average main: €25* ✉ *96 pl. Drouet d'Erlon* ☎ *03–26–91–40–50.*

$$ BISTRO 🍴 **Café du Palais.** Walls at this 1930s eatery are crammed with gilt-edged mirrors, golden cherubs, old posters, and paintings, while crystal chandeliers hang from the ceiling which itself is topped by a magnificent Art Deco glass roof signed by Jacques Simon. Authentic bistro-style food adorns the plates, with daily specials including dishes such as quail breast or poached salmon in a creamy leek sauce. Desserts are regional favorites (like ice cream with the famous *biscuits roses de Reims*), and the selection of Champagnes is extensive—there's a good choice of red Coteaux Champenois wines, too. The café is a few minutes by foot from the cathedral and popular among locals, so it's best to reserve a table in advance. ■ **TIP→ Request one inside as the terrace now looks out over a new tramline.** [$] *Average main: €23* ✉ *14 pl. Myron T-Herrick* ☎ *03–26–47–52–54* 🌐 *www.cafedupalais.fr* 🕒 *Closed Sun. and Mon.*

$$ SEAFOOD 🍴 **Le Bocal.** Freshness is guaranteed at this tiny treasure, hidden at the back of a fishmonger's shop across from the old food court (les Halles du Boulingrin). Everything is just off the boat, but most of the dozen lucky diners automatically go with the catch of the day. Tempting as that is, no one should pass up the divine cooked oysters in season. Tables in the bright, contemporary room are in demand, so it's best to reserve ahead. [$] *Average main: €20* ✉ *27 rue de Mars* ☎ *03–26–47–02–51* 🕒 *Closed Sun. and Mon. No lunch Wed.*

$$$$ MODERN FRENCH 🍴 **Le Millénaire.** Appearances deceive at this traditional town house just off place Royale, a few feet from the cathedral. Inside, it has an updated art deco feel with plush eggplant-color carpets and sleek, chic chairs. Chef Laurent Laplaige, seconded by Frédéric Dupont, finds an outlet for his decorative artistry in colorful food presented on elegant white plates; stunning specialties range from roast lobster with wild mushrooms and panfried scallops served with a creamy walnut-speckled pumpkin soup, to seared pigeon breast in a spicy sauce. Dessert dazzlers include apricots with caramel glacé. [$] *Average main: €50* ✉ *4 rue Bertin* ☎ *03–26–08–26–62* 🌐 *www.lemillenaire.com* 🕒 *Closed Sun. No lunch Sat.*

WHERE TO STAY

For expanded hotel reviews, visit Fodors.com.

$$$$ HOTEL 🏨 **Château Les Crayères.** In a grand park with towering trees planted by Champagne legend Madame Pommery, this celebrated hotel remains the showplace of Reims—a stylish, late-19th-century château featuring guest rooms bedecked with antiques, boiseries, and couture fabrics, plus the finest Champenoise restaurant of them all, Le Parc. **Pros:** hotel and two restaurants in same luxurious setting; innovative food and Champagne pairings; glorious salons are gilt trimmed and bouquet laden. **Cons:** only one set menu in Le Parc; outside the center of town. [$] *Rooms from: €395* ✉ *64 bd. Henry-Vasnier* ☎ *03–26–82–80–80* 🌐 *www.lescrayeres.com* 🛏 *16 rooms, 4 suites.*

$ HOTEL 🏨 **Hôtel Azur.** At this comfortable, friendly spot on a residential street in the center of Reims, rooms are simply furnished and decorated in cheerful primary colors with modern white tile bathrooms. **Pros:** free Wi-Fi; near train station and 10-minute walk to cathedral; secure parking. **Cons:** few rooms have bathtubs; limited reception hours. [$] *Rooms from: €86* ✉ *9 rue des Ecrevées* ☎ *03–26–47–43–39* 🌐 *www.hotel-azur-reims.com* 🛏 *18 rooms.*

$$ HOTEL 🏨 **La Paix.** An antidote to historical overload, this contemporary eight-story Best Western–branded property, 10 minutes on foot from the cathedral, has modern furnishings, dramatic artworks, plus an up-to-date color palette (think mustard, aubergine, pomegranate, and cocoa). **Pros:** central location; stylish hotel bar; free Wi-Fi. **Cons:** often hosts corporate groups. [$] *Rooms from: €170* ✉ *9 rue Buirette* ☎ *03–26–40–04–08* 🌐 *www.bestwestern-lapaix-reims.com* 🛏 *164 rooms, 1 suite.*

L'ÉPINE

56 km (35 miles) southeast of Reims via A4/D933, 7 km (4½ miles) east of Châlons via D933.

The tiny village of L'Épine is dominated by its church, the twin-tower Flamboyant Gothic **Basilique de Notre-Dame de l'Épine.** The church's facade is a magnificent creation of intricate patterns and spires, and the interior exudes elegance and restraint.

WHERE TO STAY

For expanded hotel reviews, visit Fodors.com.

$$ B&B/INN 🏨 **Aux Armes de Champagne.** Guest rooms at this former coaching inn are furnished with traditional reproductions, wall hangings, and thick carpets, but the standout is the restaurant, with its renowned Champagne list and imaginative cuisine. **Pros:** garden; friendly service; free Wi-Fi. **Cons:** out-of-the-way location. [$] *Rooms from: €110* ✉ *31 av. du Luxembourg* ☎ *03–26–69–30–30* 🌐 *www.aux-armes-de-champagne.com* 🛏 *19 rooms, 2 suites* ⏲ *Closed mid-Oct.–Apr.* 🍴 *Breakfast.*

CHÂLONS-EN-CHAMPAGNE

7 km (4½ miles) west of L'Épine via D933, 34 km (21 miles) southeast of Épernay via D1003.

Several major churches bear eloquent testimony to Châlons's medieval importance. It is also one of the few towns in Champagne that has good bus and train service.

GETTING HERE

Trains from Paris (Gare de l'Est) leave for Châlons every 2 hours or so (€26.40); the 174-km (108-mile) trip takes around 1 hour, 30 minutes. There's also limited TGV service from Paris: one train in the afternoon, one in the evening (1 hr, €41.50). There are four direct trains a day from Reims to Châlons-en-Champagne (58 km/36 miles; 45 mins, €10.50). STDM Trans-Champagne (☎ *03–26–65–17–07* 🌐 *www.stdmarne.fr*) runs regular buses from Reims to Châlons-en-Champagne (50 mins, €10.50) and several buses each day from Épernay (1 hr, €6.60).

EXPLORING

Cathédrale St-Étienne. The 13th-century Cathédrale St-Étienne is a harmonious structure with large nave windows and tidy flying buttresses; the exterior effect is marred only by the bulky 17th-century Baroque west front. ✉ *Rue de la Marne* 🕐 *July and Aug., Tues.–Sat. 10–noon and 2–6, Sun. 2:30–6; Oct.–Apr., weekends 2–4.30.*

Notre-Dame-en-Vaux. With its twin spires, Romanesque nave, and early Gothic choir and vaults, the church of Notre-Dame-en-Vaux is one of the most imposing in Champagne. The small **museum** beside the excavated cloister contains outstanding medieval statuary. ✉ *Rue Nicolas-Durand* ☎ *03–26–69–99–61* 🎟 *€3.50, free under 18* 🕐 *Apr.–Sept., Wed.–Mon. 10–noon and 2–6; Oct.–Mar., Wed.–Fri. 10–noon and 2–5, weekends 10–noon and 2–6.*

7

WHERE TO STAY

For expanded hotel reviews, visit Fodors.com.

$$$ HOTEL 🏨 **Hôtel d'Angleterre.** Guests at this stylish spot in central Châlons can enjoy well-appointed rooms (think modern furniture, marble bathrooms, and either wooden floors or plush carpets) along with outstanding dining options. **Pros:** finely modernized rooms; inventive cuisine. **Cons:** the hotel and restaurants are all closed Sunday; dinner service ends early. [$] *Rooms from: €150* ✉ *19 pl. Monseigneur-Tissier* ☎ *03–26–68–21–51* 🌐 *www.hotel-dangleterre.fr* 🛏 *25 rooms* 🕐 *Closed late July–mid-Aug., late Dec.–early Jan., and Sun.*

ÉPERNAY

28 km (18 miles) south of Reims via N51; 35 km (24 miles) west of Châlons-en-Champagne via D1003; 50 km (31 miles) east of Château-Thierry via D1003.

Although Reims loudly proclaims itself to be the last word in Champagne production, Épernay—set on the south bank of the Marne—is really the center of the bubbly drink's spirit. It was here in 1741 that the

Continued on page 378

Champagne Uncorked

Dom Pierre Pérignon was the first to discover the secret of Champagne's production by combining the still wines of the region and storing the beverage in bottles. Today, the world's most famous sparkling wine comes from the very same vineyards, along the towering Marne Valley between Épernay and Château-Thierry and on the slopes of the Montagne de Reims between Épernay and Reims.

When you take a Champagne tasting tour, you won't be at the vineyards—it's all done inside the various houses, miles away from where the grapes are grown. Champagne firms—Veuve-Clicquot, Mumm, Pommery, Taittinger, and others—give travelers tours of their chalky, mazelike *caves* (cellars). The quality of the tours is inconsistent, ranging from hilarious to despairingly tedious, though a glass of Champagne at the end makes even the most mediocre worth it (some would say). On the tours, you'll discover that Champagne is not made so differently from the way the Dom did it three centuries ago.

By Heather Stimmler-Hall

A view along the Routes du Champagne; for details on the Champagne Roads see this chapter's Planner section.

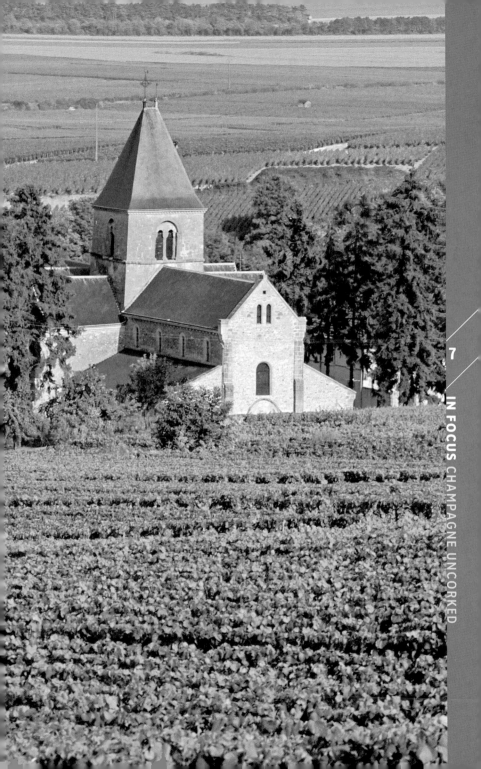

BUBBLY BASICS

ALL ABOUT GRAPES

Three types of grape are used to make Champagne: pinot noir, chardonnay, and pinot meunier. The two pinots, which account for 75% of production, are black grapes with white juice. Rosé Champagne is made either by leaving pinot noir juice in contact with the grape skins just long enough to turn it pink, or by mixing local red wine with Champagne prior to bottling. Blanc de Blancs is Champagne made exclusively from white grapes. Blanc de Noirs is made exclusively from black grapes.

HOW SWEET IT IS

The amount of residual sugar determines the category—ranging from Demi-Sec (literally half-dry, actually sweet) with 33–55 grams of residual sugar per liter, to Extra-Brut (very dry) at less than 6 grams of residual sugar per liter. Classifications in between include Sec at 17 to 35 grams, Extra Dry at 12–20 grams, and Brut, under 15 grams.

VINTAGE VS. NONVINTAGE

Vintage Champagne is named for a specific year, on the premise that the grapes harvested in that year were of extraordinary quality to produce a Champagne by themselves without being blended with wine from other years. Cuvées de Prestige are the finest and most expensive Champagnes that a firm has to offer.

LABEL KNOW-HOW

Along with specific descriptors—such as Blanc de Blancs, Blanc de Noirs, Vintage, etc.—the label carries the following information:

❶ The Champagne appellation
❷ The brand or name of the producer

❸ The level of alcohol volume. Champagne is permitted to vary between 10 and 13%. The amount of sugar (dosage) added results in the styles of Brut, Extra Brut, and Demi-Sec.

THE MERRY WIDOW & THE STARSTRUCK MONK

MADAME CLICQUOT (1777–1866)

WHY THE NICKNAME? Born Nicole-Barbe Ponsardin and married into the Clicquot family, Madame Clicquot was widowed just seven years after she married François Clicquot (in French, *veuve* means widow).

I'M A HOTSHOT BECAUSE ...: After her husband's death, she took over the firm and was one of France's earliest female entrepreneurs and the smartest marketer of the Napoléonic era. During her 60 years in control of the firm, business soared.

GREATEST CONTRIBUTION: She invented the *table de remuage*—the slanted rack used for "riddling," a method for capturing and releasing sediment that collects in the wine—a process that is still used today.

BRAGGING RIGHTS: She persuaded Czar Alexander I to toast Napoléon's demise with Champagne rather than vodka, and other royal courts were soon in bubbly pursuit.

DOM PIERRE PÉRIGNON (1638–1715)

WHY THE NICKNAME? When Dom Pierre first tasted his creation, he is quoted as saying that he was drinking stars.

I'M A HOTSHOT BECAUSE ...: He discovered Champagne when he was about 30 years old while he was the cellarmaster at the Abbey of Hautvillers, just north of Épernay.

GREATEST CONTRIBUTION: He blended wines from different vats and vineyards (now a common practice but then a novelty), reintroduced corks—forgotten since Roman times—and used thicker glass bottles to prevent them from exploding during fermentation.

BRAGGING RIGHTS: Who else can claim the title Father of Champagne?

"Brother, come quickly! I'm drinking stars!"

—Dom Pierre Pérignon

WHAT YOU'LL PAY

Champagne relentlessly markets itself as a luxury product—the sippable equivalent of perfume and haute couture—so it's no surprise that two of the top Champagne brands, Krug and Dom Pérignon, are owned by a luxury goods conglomerate (Louis Vuitton-Moët Hennessy). Sure, at small local producers, or in giant French hypermarkets, you can find a bottle of nonvintage bubbly for $15. But it's more likely to be nearer $40 and, if you fancy something special—say a bottle of vintage Dom Perignon Rose—be prepared to fork out $350. One of the priciest Blanc de Noirs is Bollinger's Vieilles Vignes—tagged at around $400. At the very top of the line is Krug's single-vineyard Clos du Mesnil, with the stellar 1995 vintage retailing at around $750. Just 12,624 bottles were ever produced of this golden elixir.

TOURING THE CELLARS

Experiencing the underground *crayères* is a must for any visit to Champagne. Many firms welcome visitors; for some you need to book in advance (by phone or via Web sites). All tours end with a tasting or three. Don't forget a jacket or sweater—it's chilly down there.

REIMS

CLOSEST TO CITY CENTER

Mumm. Not the most spectacular cellars but a practical option if you have little time: You can walk it from the cathedral and the train station. Mumm was confiscated by the French state in World War I because it had always remained in German ownership. Visit starts with 10-minute film and ends with choice of three dégustations: the €20 option includes a rosé and a vintage grand cru.

✉ 29 rue du Champ-de-Mars ☎ 03-26-49-59-69 ⊕ www.ghmumm.com 🎫 €13, €20 🕐 Mar.–Oct., daily, 9–6 PM; Nov.–Feb., Mon.–Sat., 9–noon, 2–6.

FANCIEST ARCHITECTURE

Pommery. This turreted wedding-cake extravaganza on the city outskirts, was designed by Jeanne-Alexandrine Pommery (1819–90), another formidable Champagne widow. The 11 miles of cellars (about a hundred feet underground) are reached by a grandiose 116-step staircase. Visit the Art Nouveau Villa Demoiselle across the street (owned by Pommery).

✉ 5 pl. du General-Gouraud ☎ 03-26-61-62-55 ⊕ www.vrankenpommery.fr 🎫 €12 🕐 Apr.–Oct., daily 10–6; Nov.–Mar., daily 10–5.

MOST EXPENSIVE VISIT

Ruinart. Founded back in 1729, just a year after Louis XV's decision to allow wine to be transported by bottle (previously it could only be moved by cask) effectively kick-started the Champagne industry. Four of its huge, church-sized 24 chalk galleries are listed historic monuments. This is the costliest visit on offer—and, if you shell out €35, you can taste a vintage champagne.

✉ 4 rue des Crayères ☎ 03–26–77–51–21 ⊕ www.ruinart.com 💶 €35 ⊙ Open by appointment May–Dec, Tues.–Fri.

BEST FOR HISTORY BUFFS

Taittinger. Cavernous chalk cellars, first used by monks for wine storage, house 15 million bottles and partly occupy the crypt of the 13th century abbey that used to stand on the spot. You can see a model of the abbey and its elegant church, both demolished at the Revolution.

✉ 9 pl. St-Nicaise ☎ 03–26–85–84–33 ⊕ www.tattinger.com 💶 €16 ⊙ By appointment only: Mid-Mar.–mid-Nov., daily 9:30–1 & 2–5:30; mid-Nov.–mid-Mar. weekdays only.

ÉPERNAY

BEST MUSEUM

Castellane. Above the cellars there's a museum with an intriguing display of old tools, bottles, labels and posters. There's also the chance to see the bottling and labeling plant, and climb to the top of a 200-foot tower for a great view over Épernay and the surrounding Marne vineyards.

✉ 57 rue de Verdun ☎ 03–26–51–19–11 ⊕ www.castellane.com 💶 €10 (incl. museum) ⊙ Mar.–Dec., daily 10–noon and 2–6; Jan. and Feb. closed.

"Cellar-brate" with a guided tour.

BEST HIGH-TECH VISIT

Mercier. Ride an electric train and admire the giant 200,000-bottle oak barrel it took 24 oxen three weeks to cart to the Exposition Universelle in Paris in 1889. An elevator down to (and up from) the cellars is a welcome plus.

✉ 75 av. de Champagne ☎ 03–26–51–22–22 ⊕ www.champagnemercier.fr 💶 €11–€19 ⊙ Mid-Mar.–mid-Nov., daily 9:30–11 and 2–4; closed mid-Nov.–mid-Mar.

LONGEST CELLAR WALK

Moët & Chandon. Foreign royalty, from Czar Alexander I to Queen Elizabeth II, have visited this most prestigious of all Champagne houses, founded by Charles Moët in 1743. The chalk-cellar galleries run for a mind-blowing 17 miles. The visit includes a glass of Brut Imperial; for €29.50 you can also taste a couple of vintages.

✉ 18 av. de Champagne ☎ 03–26–51–20–20 ⊕ www.moet.com 💶 €16.50–29.50 ⊙ Mid-Nov.–Dec., Feb.–Mar. Mon.–Fri. 9:30–11:30 and 2:30–4:30; Apr.–mid-Nov., daily 9:30–11:30 and 2:30–4:30.

7

IN FOCUS CHAMPAGNE UNCORKED

Hiking Champagne: Lift Your Spirits!

There's nothing like getting out into Mother Nature to send the spirits soaring and, as it turns out, the region of Champagne is custom-made for easy and scenic hiking.

Just south of Reims rises the Montagne de Reims, a vast forested plateau on whose slopes grow the Pinot Noir and Pinot Meunier grapes used to make Champagne.

Several *sentiers de Grandes Randonnées* (long hiking trails; also known as GRs) run across the top of the plateau, burrowing through dense forest and looping around the edges.

For example, the GR141 and the GR14 form a loop more than 50 km (30 miles) long around the plateau's eastern half, passing by several train stations en route.

You can access some of these hiking trails from the Rilly-la-Montagne, Avenay, and Ay stops on the Reims-Épernay rail line.

If you're a serious hiker, make for the Ardennes region, which lies just to the northeast of Champagne.

first full-blown Champagne house, Moët (now Moët et Chandon), took the lifetime passion of Dom Pérignon and turned it into an industry.

GETTING HERE

Trains from Paris (Gare de l'Est) leave for Épernay every hour or so (€22.50); the 145-km (90-mile) trip takes around 1 hour, 15 minutes. Several trains daily link Épernay to Reims (32 km/20 miles; 30 mins, €6.40) and Châlons (24 km/15 miles; 15 mins, €6.30). STDM Trans-Champagne runs several buses each day to Épernay from Châlons (1 hr, €6.60).

Visitor Information Épernay Tourist Office ⊠ *7 ave. Champagne* ☎ *03–26–53–33–00* ⊕ *www.ot-epernay.fr.*

EXPLORING

Unfortunately, no relation exists between the fabulous wealth of Épernay's illustrious wine houses and the drab, dreary appearance of the town as a whole. Most Champagne firms—Moët et Chandon (⊠ *20 av. de Champagne*); Mercier (⊠ *70 av. de Champagne*); and De Castellane (⊠ *57 rue de Verdun*)—are spaced out along the long, straight avenue de Champagne, and although their names may provoke sighs of wonder, their facades are either functional or overly dressy. ⇨ *The attractions are underground—see "Champagne Uncorked" for details on guided tours.*

Hautvillers. To understand how the region's still wine became sparkling Champagne, head across the Marne to Hautvillers. Here Dom Pérignon (1638–1715)—a blind monk who was reputedly blessed with exceptional taste buds and a heightened sense of smell—invented Champagne as everyone knows it by using corks for stoppers and blending wines from different vineyards. Legend has it that upon his first sip he cried out, "Come quickly, I am drinking the stars." Dom Pérignon's simple tomb, in a damp, dreary Benedictine abbey church (now owned by Moët et Chandon), is a forlorn memorial to the man behind one of the world's most exalted libations.

WHERE TO EAT AND STAY

For expanded hotel reviews, visit Fodors.com.

$$ FRENCH 🍴 **La Cave à Champagne.** This convivial little restaurant in the center of Épernay serves authentic regional dishes with a refined twist at reasonable prices. Chef Bernard Ocio executes a perfect marriage of flavors by highlighting the local wines; classics include homemade foie gras cooked in *ratafia de champagne*, chicken braised in a red Bouzy sauce, cod accompanied by a Chardonnay sauce, and the quintessential *potée à la champenoise*. There are also more rustic choices for the daring, such as snails in parsley butter and *tête de veau*. The desserts hold no surprises, so expect to see old favorites like pear poached in red wine and crème brûlée. Reservations are essential on weekends. [$] *Average main: €22* ✉ *16 rue Gambetta* ☎ *03–26–55–50–70* 🌐 *www.la-cave-a-champagne.com* 🕓 *Closed Wed. No dinner Tues.*

$$$ HOTEL 🏨 **La Briqueterie.** Épernay is short on good hotels, so it's worth driving south to Vinay and booking into this luxurious manor, which has spacious accommodations, wonderful gardens, an indoor pool, plus a well-equipped spa. **Pros:** pool has garden view; spa includes sauna and hamam facilities. **Cons:** rooms can be small; corporate feel (frequent business seminars). [$] *Rooms from: €210* ✉ *4 rte. de Sézanne, 6 km (4 miles) south of Épernay, Vinay* ☎ *03–26–59–99–99* 🌐 *www.labriqueterie.fr* 🛏 *36 rooms, 4 suites* 🕓 *Closed late Dec.*

7

CHÂTEAU-THIERRY

37 km (23 miles) east of Épernay via D1003.

Built along the Marne River beneath the ruins of a hilltop castle that dates from the time of Joan of Arc, and within sight of the American **Belleau Wood** War Cemetery (open daily 9–5), commemorating the 2,300 American soldiers slain here in 1918, Château-Thierry is best known as the birthplace of the French fabulist Jean de La Fontaine (1621–95).

Musée Jean de La Fontaine. Recently restored, the 16th-century mansion where La Fontaine was born and lived until 1676 is now a museum, furnished in the style of the 17th century. It contains La Fontaine's bust, portrait, and baptism certificate, plus editions of his fables magnificently illustrated by Jean-Baptiste Oudry (1755) and Gustave Doré (1868). ✉ *12 rue Jean-de-La-Fontaine, Château-Thierry* ☎ *03–23–69–05–60* 🌐 *www.musee-jean-de-la-fontaine.fr* 🎫 *€3.65* 🕓 *Tues.–Sun. 9:30–noon and 2–5:30.*

EXCURSION: THE CATHEDRAL CITIES

Champagne's eastern neighbor, the province of Picardy, located to the northeast of the region, is traversed by the Aisne and Oise rivers, and remains home to some of France's greatest cathedrals. The hundreds of kilometers of chalk tunnels throughout northern France, some dug by the ancient Romans as quarries, may serve as the damp and moldy berth for millions of bottles of Champagne, but they also gave up tons of blocks to create other treasures of the region: the magical and magnificent Gothic cathedrals.

Rumor has it that even the air is 30-proof in Champagne—discover whether this is true or not on the many hiking trails in the region.

Here, in the wake of regal Reims, we visit four more of the most superlative: Amiens, the largest; Beauvais, the tallest; Laon, with the most towers and fantastic hilltop setting; and Soissons, beloved by Rodin. Add in those at St-Omer, St-Quentin, and Châlons-en-Champagne, along with the bijou churches in rue, St-Riquier, and L'Épine (⇨ *above*), and aficionados of medieval architecture may wish to explore the region more extensively, to follow the development of Gothic architecture from its debut at Noyon to its flamboyant finale at Abbeville, where, according to the 19th-century English essayist John Ruskin, Gothic "lay down and died."

LAON

66 km (41 miles) north of Château-Thierry via D1/N2, 52 km (32 miles) northwest of Reims.

Thanks to its awe-inducing hilltop site and the forest of towers sprouting from its ancient cathedral, lofty Laon basks in the title of the "Crowned Mountain." The medieval ramparts, virtually undisturbed by passing traffic, provide a ready-made itinerary for a tour of old Laon. Panoramic views, sturdy gateways, and intriguing glimpses of the cathedral lurk around every bend. There's even a funicular, which makes frequent trips (except on Sunday in winter) up and down the hillside between the station and the Vieille Ville (Old Town).

GETTING HERE

There are regular direct trains from Paris (Gare du Nord) to Laon (145 km/90 miles; 1 hour, 40 mins; €22.30). Trains departing nearly every hour also link Reims to Laon (40 mins, €9.70), and 10 run daily from Amiens (104 km/65 miles; 1 hr, 45 mins; €17.60).

Visitor Information Laon Tourist Office ⊠ *Pl. du Parvis* ☏ *03-23-20-28-62* ⊕ *www.tourisme-paysdelaon.com.*

EXPLORING

Fodor'sChoice **Cathédrale Notre-Dame.** The Cathédrale Notre-Dame, constructed between
★ 1150 and 1230, is a superb example of early Gothic. The light interior
gives the impression of order and immense length, and the first flourishing
of Gothic architecture is reflected in the harmony of the four-tier nave:
from the bottom up, observe the wide arcades, the double windows of
the tribune, the squat windows of the triforium, and, finally, the upper
windows of the clerestory. The majestic towers can be explored during
guided visits that leave from the tourist office, housed in a 12th-century
hospital on the cathedral square. Medieval stained glass includes the rose
window dedicated to the liberal arts in the left transept, and the windows
in the flat east end, an unusual feature for France although common in
England. ⊠ *Pl. du Parvis* ☒ *Guided tours €5, audio guide €4* ☉ *Daily
8:30–6:30. Guided tours July and Aug., daily at 2:30 and 4; June and
Sept.–Dec., Fri.–Sun. at 2:30 and 4.*

Musée d'Art et d'Archéologie. The Musée d'Art et d'Archéologie has
some fine work by the celebrated local-born Le Nain brothers, Antoine,
Louis, and Mathieu, active in the 17th century, as well as a collection
of Mediterranean archaeological finds from the Bronze Age through the
Gallo-Roman era second in importance only to that at the Louvre. The
Chapelle des Templiers in the garden—a small, octagonal 12th-century
chapel topped by a shallow dome—houses fragments of the cathedral's
gable and the chilling effigy of Guillaume de Harcigny, doctor to the
insane king Charles VI. ⊠ *32 rue Georges-Ermant* ☏ *03-23-22-87-00*
⊕ *www.ville-laon.fr* ☒ *€3.90* ☉ *June–Sept., Tues.–Sun. 11–6; Oct.–May,
Tues.–Sun. 2–6.*

WHERE TO STAY

For expanded hotel reviews, visit Fodors.com.

$ **⌕ Bannière de France.** In business since 1685, this ancient hostelry is five
HOTEL minutes from the cathedral and welcomes visitors with its cozy accommodations and venerable dining room. **Pros:** comfy rooms; traditional
French cuisine; free Wi-Fi. **Cons:** some rooms need modernizing; short
on parking space. ⟦$⟧ *Rooms from: €86* ⊠ *11 rue Franklin-Roosevelt*
☏ *03-23-23-21-44* ⊕ *www.hoteldelabannieredefrance.com* ⬐ *18
rooms* ☉ *Closed mid-Dec.–mid-Jan and 2 wks end of July.*

SOISSONS

38 km (22 miles) southwest of Laon.

Visitor Information Soissons Tourist Office ⊠ *16 pl. Fernand-Marquigny*
☏ *03-23-53-17-37* ⊕ *www.tourisme-soissons.fr.*

EXPLORING

Although much damaged in World War I, Soissons commands attention
for its two huge churches, one intact, one in ruins.

Cathédrale Saint-Gervais Saint-Protais. The Gothic Cathédrale Saint-
Gervais Saint-Protais was appreciated by Rodin, who famously declared

that "there are no hours in this cathedral, but rather eternity." The interior, with its pure lines and restrained ornamentation, creates a more harmonious impression than the asymmetrical, one-tower facade. The most remarkable feature, however, is the rounded two-story transept, an element more frequently found in the German Rhineland than in France. Rubens's *Adoration of the Shepherds* hangs on the other side of the transept. ✉ *Pl. Fernand-Marquigny* ⊙ *Daily 9:30–noon and 2:30–5:30.*

Musée de Soissons. Partly housed in the medieval abbey of St-Léger, the town museum has a varied collection of local archaeological finds and paintings, with fine 19th-century works by Gustave Courbet and Eugène Boudin. ✉ *2 rue de la Congrégation* ☎ *03–23–55–94–73* ⊕ *www.museesoissons.org* ⬛ *Free* ⊙ *Apr.–Sept., weekdays 9–noon and 2–6, weekends 2–7; Oct.–Mar., weekdays 9–noon and 2–5, weekends 2–6.*

St-Jean-des-Vignes. The twin-spire facade, arcaded cloister, and airy refectory, constructed from the 14th to the 16th century, are all that is left of the hilltop abbey church of St-Jean-des-Vignes, which was largely dismantled just after the Revolution. Its fallen stones were used to restore the Cathédrale Saint-Gervais Saint-Potrais and neighboring homes. The abbey church remains the most impressive sight in Soissons, the hollow of what was once its rose window peering out over the town like the eye of some giant Cyclops. ✉ *Cours St-Jean-des-Vignes* ⊕ *www. musee-soissons.org* ⬛ *Free* ⊙ *Daily 8–6.*

WHERE TO STAY

For expanded hotel reviews, visit Fodors.com.

$$$$ ⬛ **Château de Courcelles.** Loaded with charm, this refined château by
HOTEL the Vesles River has a Louis XIV facade, and the classic exterior somehow harmonizes nicely with the sweeping brass main staircase attributed to Jean Cocteau. **Pros:** verdant setting; historic decor; welcomes families. **Cons:** accommodations vary in size and grandeur; no elevator. $ *Rooms from: €240* ✉ *8 rue du Château, 20 km (12 miles) east of Soissons via N31, Courcelles-sur-Vesles* ☎ *03–23–74–13–53* ⊕ *www. chateaucourcelles.com* ↪ *12 rooms, 6 suites* ⦿ *Some meals.*

AMIENS

112 km (70 miles) northwest of Soissons via N31/D935, 58 km (36 miles) north of Beauvais via A16.

Although Amiens showcases some pretty brazen postwar reconstruction, epitomized by Auguste Perret's 340-foot Tour Perret (a soaring concrete stump by the train station), the city is well worth exploring. It has lovely Art Deco buildings in its traffic-free center, as well as elegant, older stone structures like the 18th-century Beffroi (Belfry) and neoclassical prefecture. Crowning the city is its great Gothic cathedral, which has survived the ages intact. Nearby is the waterfront quarter of St-Leu—with its small, colorful houses—rivaling the squares of Arras and streets of old Lille as the cutest city district north of Paris.

DID YOU KNOW?

Lift your eyes to discover why Amiens—the largest church in France—is also the country's most architecturally success-ful cathedral.

GETTING HERE

Trains from Paris (Gare du Nord) leave for Amiens every hour or so (€21.10); the 129-km (80-mile) trip takes 1 hour, 10 minutes. There are two direct trains each day from Reims to Amiens (2 hrs, 30 mins; €25.20); and 10 trains daily connect Laon to Amiens (1 hr, 45 mins; €17.60). Buses run by the CAB'ARO line (☎ 03–44–48–08–47 ⊕ www.cabaro.info) run between Beauvais and Amiens (line 30E) six times daily (81 km/50 miles; 1 hr, 20 mins; €13).

Visitor Information Amiens Tourist Office ⊠ 40 pl. Notre-Dame ☎ 03–22–71–60–50 ⊕ www.amiens-tourisme.com.

EXPLORING

Fodor's Choice
★

Cathédrale Notre-Dame d'Amiens. By far the largest church in France, the Cathédrale Notre-Dame d'Amiens could enclose Paris's Notre-Dame twice. It may lack the stained glass of Chartres or the sculpture of Reims, but for architectural harmony, engineering proficiency, and sheer size, it's without peer. The soaring, asymmetrical facade has a notable Flamboyant Gothic rose window, and is brought to life on summer evenings when a sophisticated 45-minute light show re-creates its original color scheme. Inside, there's no stylistic disunity to mar the perspective, creating an overwhelming sensation of pure space. Construction took place between 1220 and 1264, a remarkably short period in cathedral-building spans. One of the highlights of a visit here is hidden from the eye, at least until you lift up some of the 110 choir-stall seats and admire the humorous, skillful misericord seat carvings executed between 1508 and 1518. ⊠ Pl. Notre-Dame ☎ 03–22–92–03–32 cathedral, 03–22–80–03–41 tours ⊕ cathedrale-amiens.monuments-nationaux.fr ☞ Free; guided tours €5.50 ⊗ Wed.–Mon. 8:30–6:15 (closed Sun. mornings; Oct.–Mar. closes at 5:15).

Hortillonnages. The Hortillonnages, on the east side of town, are commercial water gardens—covering more than 700 acres—where vegetables have been cultivated since Roman times. Every Saturday the products grown here are sold at the water market in the Saint Leu district. There's a 45-minute boat tour of these aquatic jewels. ⊠ Boats leave from 54 bd. de Beauvillé ☎ 03–22–92–12–18 ☞ €5.90 ⊗ Apr.–Oct., daily 1:30–5.

Maison Jules-Verne. Jules Verne (1828–1905) lived in Amiens for the last 35 years of his life, and his former home contains some 15,000 documents about his life as well as original furniture and a reconstruction of the writing studio where he created his science-fiction classics. ⊠ 2 rue Charles-Dubois ☎ 03–22–45–45–75 ☞ €7 ⊗ Mid-Apr.–mid-Oct., Mon. and Wed.–Fri. 10–12:30 and 2–6:30, Tues. 2–6:30, weekends 11–6:30; mid-Oct.–mid-Apr., Mon. and Wed.–Fri. 10–12:30 and 2–6, weekends 2–6.

Musée de Picardie. Behind an opulent columned facade, the Musée de Picardie, built 1855–67, looks like a pompous offering from the Second Empire. Initial impressions are hardly challenged by the grand staircase lined with monumental frescoes by local-born Puvis de Chavannes, or the central hall hung with huge canvases, like Gérôme's 1855 *Siècle d'Auguste* and Maignon's 1892 *Mort de Carpeaux*. One step beyond, though, and you're in a rotunda painted top to bottom in modern minimalist fashion by Sol LeWitt. The basement is filled with subtly lighted archaeological finds and Egyptian artifacts beneath masterly brick vaulting. The ground floor houses the 18th- and 19th-century paintings of artists such as Fragonard and Boucher. Note that there are major renovations underway, so parts of the museum may be closed to the public until 2016. ✉ *48 rue de la République* ☎ *03–22–97–14–00* 🌐 *www.amiens.fr/musees* 🎟 *€5* 🕒 *Tues., Fri., and Sat. 10–noon and 2–6; Wed. 10–6; Thurs. 10–noon and 2–9; Sun. 2–7.*

WHERE TO EAT

$$$ MODERN FRENCH

🍴 **Les Marissons.** This picturesque waterside restaurant occupies an elegantly transformed boatbuilding shed in the scenic St-Leu section of Amiens. Chef Guillaume Grain offers creative takes on foie gras and regional ingredients—crayfish, eel from Haute-Somme, Amiens duck, and lamb raised at the Baie de Somme among them. In season there is a special Picardie truffle menu. The specialties are homemade Amiens duck pâté and Artic char with a watercress sauce. To avoid pricey dining à la carte, order from the prix-fixe menus. [$] *Average main: €32* ✉ *Pont de la Dodone, 68 rue des Marissons* ☎ *03–22–92–96–66* 🌐 *www.les-marissons.fr* 🕒 *Closed Sun. and 3 wks in May. No lunch Wed. or Sat.*

THE ARTS

Théâtre de Marionnettes. The Théâtre de Marionnettes presents a rare glimpse of the traditional Picardy marionettes, known locally as Chés Cabotans d'Amiens. Shows—performed in French, with plot synopses printed in English—are usually held on Sunday afternoons at 3, September through mid-July, and Tuesday to Sunday at 6, from mid-July through August. ✉ *31 rue Edouard-David* ☎ *03–22–22–30–90* 🌐 *www.ches-cabotans-damiens.com* 🎟 *€5–€10.*

7

BEAUVAIS

56 km (35 miles) south of Amiens via A16, 96 km (60 miles) west of Soissons.

Beauvais and its neighbor Amiens have been rivals since the 13th century, when they locked horns over who could build the bigger cathedral. Beauvais lost—gloriously.

GETTING HERE

Trains from Paris (Gare du Nord) leave for Beauvais every hour (€14.90), with the 80-km (50-mile) trip taking around 1 hour, 15 minutes. Buses operated by the CAB'ARO line (☎ *03–44–48–08–47* 🌐 *www.cabaro.info*) run between Amiens and Beauvais six times daily (80 km/50 miles; 1 hr, 20 mins; €13). The Beauvais airport bus (municipal line No. 12) stops in the town center and train station daily (20 mins; €4.50 for 48-hour ticket).

Visitor Information **Beauvais Tourist Office** ✉ *1 rue Beauregard* ☎ *03–44–15–30–30* 🌐 *www.beauvaistourisme.fr.*

EXPLORING

Fodor's Choice ★

Cathédrale St-Pierre. Soaring above the town center is the tallest cathedral in France: the Cathédrale St-Pierre. You may have an attack of vertigo just gazing up at its vaults, 153 feet above the ground. Despite its grandeur, the cathedral has a shaky past. The choir collapsed in 1284, shortly after completion, and was rebuilt with extra pillars. This engineering fiasco, paid for by the riches of Beauvais's wool industry, proved so costly that the transept was not attempted until the 16th century. It was worth the wait: an outstanding example of Flamboyant Gothic, with ornate rose windows flanked by pinnacles and turrets. However, a megalomaniacal 450-foot spire erected at the same time came crashing down after just four years, and Beauvais's dream of having the largest church in Christendom vanished forever. Now the cathedral is starting to lean, and cracks have appeared in the choir vaults because of shifting water levels in the soil. No such problems bedevil the **Basse Oeuvre** (Lower Edifice; closed to the public), which juts out impertinently where the nave should have been. It has been there for 1,000 years. Fittingly donated to the cathedral by the canon Étienne Musique, the oldest surviving **chiming clock** in the world—a 1302 model with a 15th-century painted wooden face and most of its original clockwork—is built into the wall of the cathedral. Perhaps Auguste Vérité drew his inspiration from this humbler timepiece when, in 1868, he made a gift to his hometown of the gilded, temple-like **astrological clock** (displays at 10:40, 11:40, 2:40, 3:40, and 4:40; English audio guide available), which features animated religious figurines representing the Last Judgment. ✉ *Rue St-Pierre* 🌐 *www.cathedrale-beauvais.fr* 🕒 *May and Oct., daily 9–12:30 and 2–6:30; June–Sept. daily 9–6.30; Nov.–Apr., daily 9–12:30 and 2–5:30.*

Musée Départemental de l'Oise (*Regional Museum*). One of the few remaining testaments to Beauvais's glorious past, the old Bishop's Palace is now the Musée Départemental de l'Oise. Don't miss Thomas Couture's epic canvas of the French Revolution, the 14th-century frescoes of instrument-playing sirens on a section of the palace's vaults, or the 1st-century brass *Guerrier Gaulois* (Gallic Warrior). ✉ *1 rue du Musée* ☎ *03–44–11–43–83* 🌐 *www.cg60.fr* 🎟 *Free* 🕒 *Wed.–Mon. 10–noon and 2–6.*

WHERE TO EAT AND STAY

For expanded hotel reviews, visit Fodors.com.

$ BISTRO 🍴 **L'Ecume du Jour.** Half community-run café, half art gallery (and fair-trade products boutique), this spot near the train station has a friendly, bohemian vibe and is a great place to stop for a cool drink or a simple meal. After enjoying your *repas* on the pretty mosaic tiled tables, head past the outdoor patio to the covered barn for the ever-changing art exhibitions. [$] *Average main: €12* ✉ *5 rue du Faubourg St-Jacques* ☎ *03–44–02–07–37* 🌐 *www.ecumedujour.org* 💳 *No credit cards* 🕒 *Closed Sun. and Mon.*

$$ HOTEL 🏨 **Chenal Hotel.** There are few hotels in central Beauvais and this four-square street-corner establishment is perhaps the most convenient of them, being close to the train station, a 10-minute walk from the cathedral, and served by a shuttle bus from the Beauvais airport. **Pros:** free Wi-Fi; convenient location. **Cons:** small rooms; lacks charm. [$] *Rooms from: €109* ✉ *63 bd. Général-de-Gaulle* ☎ *03–44–06–04–60* 🌐 *www.chenalhotel.fr* 🛏 *29 rooms.*

ALSACE-LORRAINE

WELCOME TO ALSACE-LORRAINE

TOP REASONS TO GO

★ **Follow the wine road:** Ribeauvillé and Riquewihr, a pair of medieval villages filled with "Hansel and Gretel" houses and bottle-laden cellars, are at the heart of the Alsatian wine route.

★ **Be enchanted by Colmar:** After two world wars Colmar rebuilt itself—today the mazelike cobblestone streets and Petite Venise waterways of its Vieille Ville are as atmospheric as ever.

★ **Get an architectural eyeful in Nancy:** Classic 18th-century elegance and fanciful Art Nouveau innovation meet reminders of the medieval past in this city.

★ **Pay tribute to Joan of Arc:** If you're a fan of Jeanne d'Arc, you've come to the right place; she was born right here in Domrémy-la-Pucelle.

★ **Discover the charms of Strasbourg, capital of Alsace:** The symbolic capital of Europe is a cosmopolitan French city rivaled only by Paris in its medieval allure, history, and haute cuisine.

1 Nancy. When Stanislas Leszczynski, ex-king of Poland, succeeded in marrying his daughter to Louis XV, he paid homage to the monarch by transforming Nancy into another Versailles, embellishing it with elegant showstoppers like place Stanislas. Elsewhere in the city, you can sate your appetite for the best Art Nouveau at the Musée École de Nancy and the Villa Majorelle—after all, the style originated here.

2 Lorraine. In long-neglected Lorraine, many make the pilgrimage to Joan of Arc Country. The faithful, feisty teen, who went on to become one of France's patron saints, was born in Domrémy in the early 1400s; and nearby spots like Vaucouleurs featured prominently in her short but inspiring life story. If you listen carefully, you might hear the church bells in which Joan discerned voices challenging her to save France.

3 Strasbourg. An appealing combination of medieval alleys, international think tanks, and the European Parliament, Strasbourg is best loved for the villagelike atmosphere of La Petite France, the looming presence of the Cathédrale de Notre-Dame, the rich museums, and the pints of beer sloshing around in the *winstubs* (wine-bistros, pronounced Veen-shtoob).

4 **Alsace.** Tinged with a German flavor, Alsace is a never-ending procession of colorful towns and villages, many fitted out with spires, gabled houses, and storks' nests in chimney pots. Here you can find the Route du Vin, the famous Alsatian Wine Road, with its vineyards of Riesling and Gewurztraminer. This conveniently heads south to Colmar, where the half-timber yellow-and pink buildings of the *centre ville* seem cut out of a child's coloring book. The town's main treasure is Grünewald's unforgettable 16th-century Issenheim Altarpiece.

GETTING ORIENTED

Bordered by Germany, Alsace-Lorraine has often changed hands between the two countries in the past 350 years. This back-and-forth has left a mark—you'll find that Germanic half-timber houses sometimes clash with a very French café scene. Art also pays homage to both nations, as you can see in the museums of Strasbourg, Alsace's hub. Westward lies Lorraine, birthplace of Joan of Arc (and the famous quiche). Due west of Strasbourg on the other side of the Vosges Mountains, the main city of Nancy entices with Art Nouveau and grand 18th-century architecture.

LUXEMBOURG
Luxembourg
A31
Thionville
Saarbrücken
GERMANY
Metz
A4
Bitche
D674
D955
LORRAINE
2
A4
ALSACE
4
Hagenau
N4
Saverne
A35
N4
Strasbourg **3**
A5
Lunéville
N59
D1420
D1083
N57
St Dié
A35
Route de Vin
Épinal
Ribeauvillé
Sélestat
Rhine River
GERMANY
Riquewihr
Colmar
Freiburg
N57
VOSGES
D1083
Rhine
N66
A35
FRANCHE COMTE
A36
Mulhouse
Basel
SWITZERLAND

0   20 mi
0   20 km

8

EATING AND DRINKING WELL IN ALSACE-LORRAINE

Bountiful is the watchword in this region where lush vineyards flourish, vintage winstubs serve heaping platters of *choucroute garnie* (sauerkraut, meat, and potatoes), and restaurants boast more Michelin stars than anywhere else in France.

Quiches on parade in Obernai in a photo submitted by Klondike for Fodor's France contest *(above)*; luxurious fois gras *(right, top)*; the best of the würsts *(right, bottom)*.

A visit to the proud region of Alsace promises sensory overload: gorgeous vistas, antique walled towns, satisfying meals—from farm-style to richly gastronomic—and, of course, superb wines. The predominantly white varietals, such as Riesling and Pinot Gris, complement the rich and varied old-school cooking. It's not for nouvelle-style or fusion dishes that you come to Alsace: tradition is king here, and copious is an understatement. Rustic regional fare includes hearty stews, custardy quiches, sauerkraut platters, and the thin-crusted onion tarts known as *flammekueche*. Also to be savored are some of the best restaurants in France—among them the noble, romantic L'Auberge de L'Ill in Illhausern, where a salmon mousse with a Riesling reduction might catch your fancy.

FOLLOW THE WINES

Alsace is one of France's most important but least-known wine-producing regions, where vintners designate wines by varietals, not by town or château. Look for distinctive whites, like full-bodied Pinot Gris, fruity Sylvaner, citrusy Riesling, and spicy Gewurztraminer. In reds, Pinot Noir stands alone.

KOUGELHOPF

This tall, fluted, crown-shape cake, dusted with sugar and studded with raisins and almonds, beckons invitingly from every pastry-shop window in the region. You won't resist. The delicately sweet, yeast-based dough is kneaded and proofed, baked in a Bundt-style mold, and traditionally served, sometimes sprinkled with kirsch, at Sunday breakfast. Locals say it's even better on the second day, when it achieves a perfect, slightly dry texture.

CHOUCROUTE GARNIE

Daunting in size, a heaping platter of choucroute garnie, laden with fermented sauerkraut, smoked bacon, ham, pork shoulder, sausages, and potatoes, is the signature dish of the region. The best places serving it, usually winstubs such as the atmospheric Zum Pfifferhüs in Ribeauvillé, are worth a detour. You've never had sauerkraut like this, tender and delicate, dotted with juniper berries and often cooked with a splash of Riesling or Sylvaner white wine. Complement your choucroute with the region's own sweet white mustard.

MUNSTER CHEESE

This round, semisoft cow's-milk cheese with the orange rind, distinctive nutty aroma, and pungent flavor is Alsace's only claim to cheese fame, but it's a standout. The cheese, which is aged from five weeks to three months, originated in the Vosges valley town of Munster, just west of Colmar, and the best—farm produced—come from this area. Sample it with fresh cherries or pears, thin-sliced rye bread, and a glass of Gewurztraminer.

FOIE GRAS

The production sure ain't pretty, but the product is sublime—satiny, opulent goose foie gras. Many gastronomes believe that Alsace produces the best in the world. The meltingly tender, fattened livers of plump Alsatian geese are prepared in a number of luscious ways: wrapped in a towel and gently poached—the classic *à la torchon* method; panfried and served on a slice of toasted gingerbread; wrapped in puff pastry and baked; or pressed into terrines and pâtés.

BAECKEOFFE

You can't get much heartier or homier than this baked casserole of pork, lamb, and beef marinated in white wine and slow-cooked in a terra-cotta pot with potatoes, onions, garlic, and herbs. The name—pronounced "bake-eh oafeh"—means "baker's oven" in the Germanic Alsatian dialect. It was so named because this was a dish traditionally assembled at home, then carried to the local baker to cook in his hot ovens. It's soul-warming fare for a chilly evening.

8

Updated by
Lyn Parry

Only the Rhine separates Germany from Alsace-Lorraine, a region that often looks German and even sounds German. But its heart—just to prove how deceptive appearances can be—is passionately French. One has only to remember that Strasbourg was the birthplace of the Marseillaise national anthem to appreciate why Alsace and Lorraine remain among the most intensely French of all France's provinces.

No matter how forcefully the French tout its Frenchness, though, Alsace's German roots do run deep, as one look at its storybook medieval architecture reveals. Gabled, half-timber houses, ornate wells and fountains, oriels (upstairs bay windows), storks' nests, and carved-wood balustrades—all calling to mind the Brothers Grimm—will satisfy a visitor's deepest craving for Old World Germanic atmosphere. Strasbourg, perhaps France's most fascinating city outside Paris, offers this and urban sophistication as well.

Lorraine, on the other hand, has suffered a decline in its northern industry and the miseries of its small farmers have left much of it tarnished and neglected—or, as others might say, kept it unspoiled. Yet Lorraine's rich caches of verdure, its rolling countryside dotted with *mirabelle* (plum) orchards and crumbling-stucco villages, abbeys, fortresses, and historic cities, such as Art Nouveau–ed Nancy, offer a truly French view of life in the north. Its borders flank Belgium, Luxembourg, and Germany's mellow Mosel (Moselle in French). Home of Baccarat and St-Louis crystal (thanks to limitless supplies of firewood from the Vosges Forest), the birthplace of Gregorian chant, Art Nouveau, and Joan of Arc, Lorraine-the-underdog has much of its own to contribute.

The question remains: Who put the hyphen in Alsace-Lorraine? Alsace's strip of vine-covered hills squeezed between the Rhine and the Vosges Mountains started out being called Prima Germania by the Romans, and belonged to the fiercely Germanic Holy Roman Empire for more than 700 years. West of the Vosges, Lorraine served under French and Burgundian lords as well as the Holy Roman Empire, coming into its own under the powerful and influential dukes of Lorraine in the Middle Ages and Renaissance. Stanislas, the duke of Lorraine who transformed Nancy into a cosmopolitan Paris of the East, was Louis XV's father-in-law. Thus Lorraine's culture evolved as decidedly less German than its neighbor to the southeast.

But then, in the late 19th century, Kaiser Wilhelm sliced off the Moselle chunk of Lorraine and sutured it, à la Dr. Frankenstein, to Alsace, claiming the unfortunate graft as German turf—a concession after France's 1871 surrender in the Franco-Prussian War. At that point the region was systematically Teutonized—architecturally, linguistically, culinarily ("Ve haff our own vays of cookink sauerkraut!")—and the next two generations grew up culturally torn. Until 1918, that is, when France undid its defeat and reclaimed its turf. Until 1940, when Hitler snatched it back and reinstated German textbooks in the primary schools. Until 1945, when France once again triumphantly raised the *bleu-blanc-rouge* over Strasbourg. Today, the regions remain both officially and proudly French.

PLANNER

WHEN TO GO

Alsace is blessed with four distinct seasons and one of the lowest rainfalls in all of France—so anytime at all is the right time to visit. Snow in winter adds magic to the Christmas markets; spring brings forth the scent of burgeoning grape flowers as the world turns green with life; summer can be warm, which rhymes with swarm; autumn is nature's symphony of color—the leaves of tree and vine become a riot of golden yellows and oranges, as the bountiful grapes are harvested.

PLANNING YOUR TIME

If an overall experience is what you're after, setting up headquarters in Strasbourg or Colmar will give you the best access to the greatest number of sites, either by public transport or car, while also residing in one. If wine tasting and vineyards are your priority, setting up in either Riquewihr or Ribeauvillé will put you at the heart of the action. Remember that many of the region's towns and villages stage summer festivals—among them the spectacular pagan-inspired burning of the three pine trees in Thann (late June), the Flower Carnival in Sélestat (mid-August), and the wine fair in Colmar (first half of August). And although Lorraine is a lusterless place in winter, Strasbourg pays tribute to the Germanic tradition with a Christmas fair.

GETTING HERE AND AROUND

Alsace is a small region and fairly well interconnected with bus and train routes, making it possible to travel extensively by public transportation. Be sure to stock up on information (schedules, the best taxi-for-call companies, etc.) upon arriving at the ticket counter or help desk of the bigger train and bus stations in the area, such as Nancy, Strasbourg, and Colmar. In Alsace, trains are the way to go. In Lorraine you may need to take short bus jaunts to the smaller towns. If you're relying on trains, download the handy widgets from the TER website at ⊕ *www. ter-sncf.com*. A useful up-to-date website with details on buses and

DID YOU KNOW?

As this fountain on place Stanislas proves, the city of Nancy is a spectacular showcase of the 18th-century Rococo style.

trams is ⊕ *www.vialsace.eu.* Unfortunately, schedules change rather frequently in Alsace-Lorraine.

AIR TRAVEL

International flights connect with Entzheim, near Strasbourg. The airport shuttle bus Navette Routière leaves the city center every 15 minutes weekdays, and every half hour on the weekends from place de la Gare.

Aéroport International Strasbourg ⊠ *Rte. de Strasbourg, 15 km (9½ miles) southwest of city, Entzheim* ☎ *03–88–64–67–67* ⊕ *www.strasbourg. aeroport.fr.*

BUS TRAVEL

The two main bus companies are **Les Rapides de Lorraine,** based in Metz, and **Compagnie des Transports Strasbourgeois,** based in Strasbourg. Nancy, Strasbourg, and Colmar all have civic transit systems, too.

Compagnie des Transports Strasbourgeois (*CTS*). ⊠ *Strasbourg* ☎ *03–88–77–70–70* ⊕ *www.cts-strasbourg.fr.*

Les Rapides de Lorraine ⊠ *Metz* ☎ *03–87–63–65–65, 03–87–75–26–62 Agence Ted and TIM for ticket information and tariffs* ⊕ *www. rapidesdelorraine.fr.*

CAR TRAVEL

A4 heads east from Paris to Strasbourg, via Verdun, Metz, and Saverne. It's met by A26, descending from the English Channel, at Reims. A31 links Metz to Nancy, continuing south to Burgundy and Lyon. N83/A35 connects Strasbourg, Colmar, and Mulhouse. A36 continues to Belfort and Besançon. A4, linking Paris to Strasbourg, passes through Lorraine via Metz, linking Lorraine and Alsace. Picturesque secondary roads lead from Nancy and Toul through Joan of Arc country. Several scenic roads climb switchbacks over forested mountain passes through the Vosges, connecting Lorraine to Alsace. A quicker alternative is the tunnel *under* the Vosges at Ste-Marie-aux-Mines, linking Sélestat to Lunéville. Alsace's Route du Vin, winding from Marlenheim, in the north, all the way south to Thann, is the ultimate in scenic driving.

TRAIN TRAVEL

Sixteen TGV trains per day leave Paris (Gare de l'Est) for the 140-minute, 490-km (304-mile) journey to Strasbourg. Nancy is only 90 minutes away on one of the 10 direct TGVs, and from there you can connect to Toul and Épinal. Four daily direct TGVs will get you from Paris to Colmar in just under three hours; several local trains also run each day between Strasbourg and Colmar (40 mins), stopping in Sélestat (bus link to Ribeauvillé). There's a snail's-pace daily service as well from Strasbourg to Obernai, Barr, and Dambach-la-Ville. But you'll need a car to visit smaller villages.

Train Information Gare SNCF Colmar ⊠ *9 pl. de la Gare, Colmar* ☎ *36–35.* **Gare SNCF Nancy** ⊠ *3 pl. Thiers, Nancy* ☎ *36–35.* **Gare SNCF Strasbourg** ⊠ *20 pl. de la Gare, Strasbourg* ☎ *36–35.* **SNCF** ☎ *36–35 [€0.34 per min]* ⊕ *www.voyages-sncf.com.* **TGV** ⊕ *www.tgv.com.*

8

RESTAURANTS

Strasbourg and Nancy may be two of France's more expensive cities, but you wouldn't know it judging by all the down-to-earth eating spots with down-to-earth prices—most notably winstubs, which are cozier and more wine-oriented than the usual French brasserie. In Strasbourg and Nancy, as well as the villages along Alsace's wine road, you'll need to arrive early (soon after noon for lunch, before 8 for dinner) to be sure of a restaurant table in July and August. Out-of-season is a different matter throughout.

Prices in the reviews are the average cost of a main course at dinner or, if dinner is not served, at lunch.

HOTELS

Alsace-Lorraine is well served in terms of accommodations. From the picturesque village inns of the Route du Vin and the "Fermes Auberges" of the Vosges to four-star palaces or international-style hotels in the main cities of Nancy and Strasbourg, the range is vast. Since much of Alsace is in the "countryside" there's also a range of *gîtes*, self-catering cottages or houses that provide a base for longer stays (⊕ *www.gites-de-france.com*).

Prices in the reviews are the lowest cost of a standard double room in high season.

VISITOR INFORMATION

The Alsace-Lorraine region has three main area tourist offices, all of which can be contacted by telephone, mail, or email. For the Alsace area, contact the Comité Régional du Tourisme d'Alsace. For Lorraine, contact the Comité Régional du Tourisme de Lorraine. For the city of Strasbourg and its environs, contact the Office de Tourisme de Strasbourg et Sa Region. *For specific town tourist offices, see the town entries in this chapter.*

Contacts Comité Régional du Tourisme d'Alsace ⊠ *20A rue Berthe Molly, Colmar* ☎ *03–89–24–73–50* ⊕ *www.tourisme-alsace.com.* **Comité Régional du Tourisme de Lorraine** ⊠ *Abbaye des Prémontrés, Pont-à-Mousson* ☎ *03–83–80–01–80* ⊕ *www.tourisme-lorraine.fr.* **Office de Tourisme de Strasbourg et Sa Région** ⊠ *17 pl. de la Cathédrale, Strasbourg* ☎ *03–88–52–28–28* ⊕ *www.otstrasbourg.fr.*

NANCY

For architectural variety, few French cities match Nancy, which is in the heart of Lorraine, 300 km (190 miles) east of Paris. Medieval ornamentation, 18th-century grandeur, and Belle Époque fluidity rub shoulders in the town center, where the bustle of commerce mingles with stately elegance. Its majesty derives from a long history as domain to the powerful dukes of Lorraine, whose double-barred crosses figure prominently on local statues and buildings. Never having fallen under the rule of the Holy Roman Empire or the Germans, this Lorraine city retains an eminently Gallic charm.

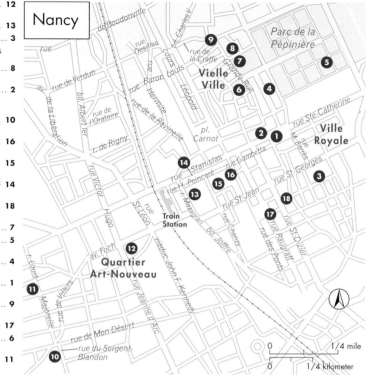

GETTING HERE AND AROUND

STAN bus service. Nancy's central core is manageable on foot, but STAN—the civic public transit system—has buses and trams to help you navigate the greater Nancy area. ☎ *03–83–30–08–08* ⊕ *www.reseau-stan.com.*

TED bus service. The 54 lines of the TED bus service cover the entire département, leaving from place de la République, for a €2.50 flat rate. ☎ *08–20–20–54–54 [€0.09 per min]* ⊕ *www.ted.cg54.fr.*

TGV Est European. The jewel in Lorraine's tourism crown, Nancy, has benefited greatly from the introduction of the record-breaking TGV Est European service. Ten direct TGVs daily (one leaving almost every hour from 7:13 am to 8:13 pm) depart Paris's Gare de l'Est, arriving here about 90 minutes later. Four others (8:40 am, 10:40 am, 1:58 pm, and 8:40 pm) take over an hour longer; three involve a change in Metz and one in Bar Le Duc. One-way fares vary from €30 to €71 depending on the train type, time of day, and how far in advance you book. ⊕ *www.tgv.com/en.*

Train station. Nancy's train station, a 15-minute walk down rue Stanislas from the town center, is open 5:30 am to 11:30 pm (6:30 am to 11:30 pm Sunday and holidays). Eleven direct trains to Strasbourg (€24.20) leave from Nancy each day at intervals varying from 45 minutes to two hours, and roughly every 10 minutes a train leaves for Metz (€10.40). There are daily TER services running approximately every 15 minutes to Luneville (€6.80). ⊠ *3 pl. Thiers.*

Visitor Information Nancy Tourist Office ⊠ *14 pl. Stanislas* ☎ *03–83–35–22– 41* ⊕ *www.nancy-tourisme.fr.*

EXPLORING

Nancy's French character is most evident in its harmoniously constructed squares and buildings, which, as vestiges of the 18th century, have the quiet refinement associated with the best in French architecture. Ironically, it was a Pole, and not a Frenchman, who was responsible for much of what is beautiful in Nancy. Stanislas Leszczynski, ex-king of Poland and father of Maria Leszczynska (who married Louis XV of France) was given the Duchy of Lorraine by his royal son-in-law on the understanding that on his death it would revert to France. Stanislas installed himself in Nancy and devoted himself to the glorious embellishment of the city. Today place Stanislas remains one of the loveliest and most perfectly proportioned squares in the world, with place de la Carrière—reached through Stanislas's Arc de Triomphe—with its elegant, homogeneous 18th-century houses, its close rival for this honor.

THE HISTORIC CENTER

Concentrated northeast of the train station, this neighborhood—rich in architectural treasures as well as museums—includes classical place Stanislas and the shuttered, medieval Vieille Ville.

TOP ATTRACTIONS

Cathédrale. This vast, frigid edifice was built in the 1740s in a ponderous Baroque style, eased in part by the florid ironwork of Jean Lamour. The most notable interior feature is a murky 19th-century fresco in the dome. The **Trésor** (Treasury) contains minute 10th-century splendors carved of ivory and gold but is only open to the public on rare occasions. ⊠ *Rue St-Georges, Ville Neuve.*

Musée des Arts et Traditions Populaires (*Museum of Folk Arts and Traditions*). Just up the street from the Palais Ducal, this quirky, appealing museum is housed in the **Couvent des Cordeliers** (Convent of the Franciscans, who were known as Cordeliers until the Revolution). Displays re-create how local people lived in preindustrial times, using a series of evocative rural interiors. Craftsmen's tools, colorful crockery, somber stone fireplaces, and dark waxed-oak furniture accent the tableaulike settings. The dukes of Lorraine are buried in the crypt of the adjoining **Église des Cordeliers**, a Flamboyant Gothic church; the *gisant* (reclining statue) of Philippa de Gueldra, second wife of René II, is executed in limestone in flowing detail and is a moving example of Renaissance portraiture. The octagonal Ducal Chapel was begun in 1607 in the Renaissance style, modeled on the Medici Chapel in Florence. ⊠ *64 Grande-Rue, Vieille Ville* ☎ *03–83–32–18–74* ⊕ *www.1nancy.fr* ⊠ *€3.50, €5.50 joint ticket with Palais Ducal (Musée Lorrain)* ☉ *Tues.– Sun. 10–12:30 and 2–6.*

CLOSE UP

Nancy 1900

History has a curious way of having similar events take place at the same time in different places. The creation of the Art Nouveau movement is one such event. Simultaneously emerging from Pre-Raphaelite, High Victorian, and the Arts and Crafts movement in England, it was also a synthesis of the Jugenstil (Youth style) movement in Germany; the Skonvirke movement in Denmark; the Mloda Polska (Young Poland) movement in Poland; Secessionism in Vienna, exemplified by the paintings of Gustav Klimt; and Modernism in Spain, centered around Gaudi's outlandish architectural achievements in Barcelona. Its fluid, undulating, organic forms drawn from the natural world (picture seaweed, grasses, flowers, birds, and insects) also drew inspiration from Symbolism, Japanese woodcuts, and assorted other sources.

was a major advance on the bourgeois bad taste for mass-produced pieces of dubious quality that imitated styles of the past.

One of its founding centers was Nancy, which at the time was drawing the wealthy French bourgeoisie of Alsace, recently invaded by Germany, who refused to become German. Proud of their opulence, they had sublime houses built that were entirely furnished—from simple vases and wrought-iron beds to bathtubs in the shape of lily pads—in the pure Art Nouveau style.

Emile Gallé (1846–1904), the driving force behind Nancy's Art Nouveau movement, called on his fellow artists to follow examples in nature (as opposed to the Greek or Roman models then in favor) and aim for innovation. Working primarily in glass and inventing new, patented techniques, Gallé brought luxury craftsmanship to a whole range of everyday products, thus reestablishing the link between the ordinary and the exceptional. This

Everywhere stylized flowers suddenly became the preferred motif. The tree and its leaves, and plants with their flowers, were modified, folded, and curled to the artist's demand. Among the main Art Nouveau emblems figure the lily, the iris, morning glory, bracken fern, poppies, peacocks, birds that feed on flowers, ivy, dragonflies, butterflies, and anything that evokes the immense poetry of the seasons. It reveals a world that is as fragile as it is precious.

By giving an artistic quality to manufactured objects, Gallé and the other creators of the École de Nancy accomplished a dream that had been growing since the romantic generation of Victorian England of making an alliance between art and industry. As a meeting point for the hopes and interests of artists, intellectuals, industrials, and merchants, the École de Nancy was a thoroughly global phenomenon. From Chicago to Turin, Munich to Brussels, and on to London, the industries of Nancy went on to conquer the world.

8

Musée des Beaux-Arts (*Fine Arts Museum*). In a splendid building that now spills over into a spectacular modern wing, a broad and varied collection of art treasures lives up to the noble white facade designed by Emmanuel Héré. The showpiece is Rubens's massive *Transfiguration*, and among the most striking works are the freeze-the-moment realist tableaux painted by native son Émile Friant at the turn of the 20th century. A sizable collection of Lipschitz sculptures includes portrait busts of Gertrude Stein, Jean Cocteau, and Coco Chanel. You'll also find 19th- and 20th-century paintings by Monet, Manet, Utrillo, and Modigliani; a Caravaggio *Annunciation* and a wealth of other old masters from the Italian, Dutch, Flemish, and French schools; and impressive glassworks by Nancy native Antonin Daum. Audio guides (1€) in English are available at reception. ⊠ *3 pl. Stanislas, Ville Royale* 🖀 *03–83–85–30–72* ⊕ *mban.nancy.fr/* ⊡ *€6* ⊙ *Wed.–Mon. 10–6.*

Palais Ducal (*Ducal Palace*). This palace, built in the 13th century, completely restored at the end of the 15th century and again after a fire at the end of the 19th century, is now occupied by the **Musée Lorrain** (Lorraine History Museum). At the main entrance (80 yards down the street from a stunning Flamboyant Renaissance portal), a spiral stone staircase leads up to the palace's most impressive room, the **Galerie des Cerfs** (Stags Gallery). Exhibits here (including pictures, armor, and books) recapture the Renaissance mood of the 16th century—one of elegance and merrymaking, with an undercurrent of stern morality: an elaborate series of huge tapestries, *La Condemnation du Banquet* (Condemnation of the Banquet), expounds on the evils of drunkenness and gluttony. Exhibits showcase Stanislas and his court, including his oft-portrayed dwarf; a section on Nancy in the revolutionary era; and works of Lorraine native sons, including a collection of Jacques Callot engravings and a handful of works by Georges de La Tour. ⊠ *64 Grande-Rue, Vieille Ville* 🖀 *03–83–32–18–74* ⊕ *www1.nancy.fr* ⊡ *€4, €5.50 joint ticket with Musée des Arts et Traditions Populaires* ⊙ *Tues.– Sun. 10–12:30 and 2–6.*

Place Stanislas. With its severe, gleaming-white Classical facades given a touch of Rococo jollity by fanciful wrought gilt-iron railings, this perfectly proportioned square may remind you of Versailles. It is named for Stanislas Leszczynski, twice dethroned as king of Poland but offered the Duchy of Lorraine by Louis XV (his son-in-law) in 1736. Stanislas left a legacy of spectacular buildings, undertaken between 1751 and 1760 by architect Emmanuel Héré and ironwork genius Jean Lamour. The sculpture of Stanislas dominating the square went up in the 1830s. Framing the exit, and marking the divide between the Vieille Ville and the Ville Neuve (New Town), is the **Arc de Triomphe,** erected in the 1750s to honor Louis XV. The facade trumpets the gods of war and peace; Louis's portrait is here. ⊠ *Ville Royale.*

WORTH NOTING

FAMILY **La Pépinière.** This picturesque, landscaped city park has labeled ancient trees, a rose garden, playgrounds, a carousel, and a small zoo. ⊠ *Entrance off pl. de la Carrière, Vieille Ville.*

Place de la Carrière. Lined with pollarded trees and handsome 18th-century mansions (another successful collaboration between King Stanislas and Emmanuel Héré), this UNESCO World Heritage Site's elegant rectangle leads from place Stanislas to the colonnaded facade of the **Palais du Gouvernement** (Government Palace), former home of the governors of Lorraine. ✉ *Vieille Ville.*

Porte de la Craffe. A fairy-tale vision out of the late Middle Ages, this 14th- and 15th-century gate is all that remains of Nancy's medieval fortifications. With its twin turrets looming at one end of the Grande-Rue, the arch served as a prison through the Revolution. Above the main portal is the Lorraine Cross, comprising a thistle and cross. ✉ *Vieille Ville.*

> **EVERYONE LOVES A LAMOUR**
>
> A fitting showpiece of the southern flank of the square is the 18th-century Hôtel de Ville, Nancy's Town Hall, where the handiwork of Jean Lamour can be seen to stunning effect on the wrought-iron handrail of the *grand escalier* (grand staircase) leading off the lobby. You can get a closer view when the building is open to the public (July and August, see the tourist office for exact dates); mounting the staircase to the Grands Salons lets you survey the full beauty of place Stanislas.

St-Epvre. A 275-foot spire towers over this splendid neo-Gothic church, completed in 1451 and rebuilt in the 1860s. Most of the 2,800 square yards of stained glass were created by the Geyling workshop in Vienna; the chandeliers were made in Liège, Belgium; many carvings are the work of Margraff of Munich; the heaviest of the eight bells was cast in Budapest; and the organ, though manufactured by Merklin of Paris, was inaugurated in 1869 by Austrian composer Anton Bruckner. ✉ *Pl. St-Epvre, Vieille Ville* ☉ *Daily 10–6.*

ART NOUVEAU NANCY

Fodor's Choice ★ Think *Art Nouveau*, and many will conjure up the rich salons of Paris's Maxim's restaurant, the lavender-hue Prague posters of Alphonse Mucha, or the stained-glass dragonflies and opalescent vases that, to this day, remain the darlings of such collectors as Barbra Streisand. All of that beauty was born, to a great extent, in 19th-century Nancy. Inspired and coordinated by the glass master Émile Gallé, the local movement was formalized in 1901 as L'École de Nancy—from here, it spread like wildfire through Europe, from Naples to Monte-Carlo to Prague. The ensuing flourish encompassed the floral *pâte de verre* (literally, "glass dough") works of Gallé and Antonin Daum; the Tiffany-esque stained-glass windows of Jacques Gruber; the fluidity of Louis Majorelle's furniture designs; and the sinuous architecture of Lucien Weissenburger, Émile André, and Eugène Vallin. Thanks to these artists, Nancy's downtown architecture gives the impression of a living garden suspended above the sidewalks. ⇨ *For more on Art Nouveau's birthplace, see our Close-Up box in this chapter, "Nancy 1900."*

TOP ATTRACTIONS

Fodor's Choice **Musée de l'École de Nancy** (*School of Nancy Museum*). The only museum
★ in France devoted to Art Nouveau is housed in an airy turn-of-the-last-century garden–town house built by Eugène Corbin, an early patron of the School of Nancy. Re-created rooms show off original works of art by local Art Nouveau glassmakers Emile Gallé, Antonin and Auguste Daume, Amairac Walter, and other artisans. Allow yourself to immerse in the fanciful, highly stylized, curlicue style that crept into interiors and exteriors throughout Nancy in the early 20th century, then became a sensation around the world. ⊠ *36 rue du Sergent-Blandan, Quartier Art-Nouveau* ☎ *03–83–40–14–86* ⊕ *www.ecole-de-nancy.com* ⊠ *€6* ⊙ *Wed.–Sun. 10–6.*

Villa Majorelle. In this villa, built in 1902 by Paris architect Henri Sauvage for Art Nouveau furniture designer Louis Majorelle, sinuous metal supports seem to sneak up on the unsuspecting balcony like swaying cobras. The two grand windows are by Jacques Gruber: one lights the staircase (visible from the street) and the other is set in the dining room on the south side of the villa (peek around from the garden side). ⊠ *1 rue Louis-Majorelle, Quartier Art-Nouveau.*

WORTH NOTING

Avenue Foch. This busy boulevard lined with mansions was laid out for Nancy's affluent 19th- and early 20th-century middle class. At No. 69, built in 1902 by Émile André, the occasional pinnacle suggests Gothic influence; André designed the neighboring No. 71 two years later. No. 41, built by Paul Charbonnier in 1905, bears ironwork by Louis Majorelle. ⊠ *Quartier Art-Nouveau.*

No. 2 rue Bénit. This elaborately worked metal exoskeleton, the first in Nancy (1901), exudes functional beauty. The floral decoration reminds you of the building's past as a seed supply store. Windows were worked by Jacques Gruber; the building was designed by Henry-Barthélemy Gutton, while Victor Schertzer conceived the metal frame. ⊠ *Quartier Art-Nouveau.*

No. 9 rue Chanzy. Designed by architect Émile André, this lovely structure—now a bank—can be visited during business hours. You can still see the cabinetry of Louis Majorelle, the decor of Paul Charbonnier, and the stained-glass windows of Jacques Gruber. ⊠ *Quartier Art-Nouveau.*

No. 40 rue Henri-Poincaré. The Lorraine thistle (a civic emblem) and brewing hops weave through this undulating exterior, designed by architects Émile Toussaint and Louis Marchal. Victor Schertzer conceived this metal structure in 1908, after the success of No. 2 rue Bénit. Gruber's windows are enhanced by the curving metalwork of Louis Majorelle. ⊠ *Quartier Art-Nouveau.*

Nos. 42–44 rue St-Dizier. Furniture maker Eugène Vallin and architect Georges Biet left their mark on this graceful 1903 bank. ⊠ *Quartier Art-Nouveau* ⊙ *Weekdays 9–5:30.*

Rue Raugraff. Once there were two stores here—Vaxelaire and Pignot, both built in 1901. The facade is the last vestige of the work of Émile André and Eugène Vallin. ⊠ *13 rue Raugraff, Quartier Art-Nouveau.*

Place Stanislas—the crown jewel of the city—is a huge public square enclosed by gold-and-black gates and gorgeous neoclassical buildings.

8

WHERE TO EAT AND STAY

For expanded hotel reviews, visit Fodors.com.

$$$ BRASSERIE 🍴 **Brasserie l'Excelsior.** Above all, you'll want to eat in this 1911 restaurant, part of the dependable Flo group, for its sensational Art Nouveau stained glass, mosaics, Daum lamps, and sinuous Majorelle furniture. But the food is stylish, too, with succulent choices ranging from seared duck fois gras with a cep mushroom pancake to grilled lobster flambé (in whiskey, no less)—and don't miss out on regional desserts like *kouglof* (a distinctively shaped Alsatian cake) with Mirabelle plums. The waiters are attentive and exude Parisian chic. [$] *Average main: €27* ✉ *50 rue Henri-Poincaré, Quartier Art-Nouveau* ☎ *03–83–35–24–57* 🌐 *www.brasserie-excelsior.com.*

$$$$ FRENCH 🍴 **Le Capu.** Barely a stone's throw from place Stanislas, this stylish landmark, with its chic new decor and name (it was formerly called the Capucin Gourmand), puts its best foot forward under chef Hervé Fourrière. The menu includes revisited favorites, such as lamb cooked in a salt crust, along with more adventurous choices like slow-cooked venison steak (in season) served with a licorice-infused sauce and chestnut-flour gnocchi. Desserts are also noteworthy, with daring combinations like apple and truffle served with a beetroot sorbet, plus a rotating selection of desserts du jour. A buffet brunch is served Sunday between 11 and 4, and cooking lessons are held Saturday at lunchtime. The choice of Toul wines is extensive. [$] *Average main: €38* ✉ *31 rue Gambetta, Ville Royale* ☎ *03–83–35–26–98* 🌐 *www.lecapu.com* ✍ *Reservations essential* 🕒 *No lunch Sat.*

$ BISTRO 🍴 **Le P'tit Cuny.** If you were inspired by the rustic exhibits at the Musée des Arts et Traditions Populaires, cross the street and sink your teeth into authentic Lorraine cuisine in the form of mouthwatering choucroutes, *tête de veau* (calf's head), or foie gras-stuffed pig's trotter. Tables inside are tight, creating a bustling, canteen-like atmosphere, and the quality of the service seems to vary with the weather, but the hearty food is irreproachable. [$] *Average main: €17* ✉ *97 Grande-Rue, Vieille Ville* ☎ *03–83–32–85–94* 🌐 *www.lepetitcuny.fr.*

$$ HOTEL 🏨 **Grand Hôtel de la Reine.** Every bit as grand as place Stanislas, on which it stands, this magnificent 18th-century building is officially classified as a historic monument with an interior that is just as regal: guest rooms are decorated in Louis XV style (the most luxurious overlook the square). **Pros:** sumptuous location; Old World atmosphere. **Cons:** rooms get street noise; indifferent staff. [$] *Rooms from: €107* ✉ *2 pl. Stanislas, Ville Royale* ☎ *03–83–35–03–01* 🌐 *www.hoteldelareine.com* 🛏 *41 rooms, 2 suites.*

$ HOTEL 🏨 **Hôtel de Guise.** Deep in the shuttered Vieille Ville, this quiet, convivial hotel occupies an 18th-century nobleman's mansion with a magnificent stone-floor entry, a delightful walled garden, and guest rooms furnished with period pieces and charmingly incongruous floral patterns. **Pros:** tidy rooms; central location; helpful staff. **Cons:** no air-conditioning; overheated, stuffy rooms. [$] *Rooms from: €97* ✉ *18 rue de Guise, Vieille Ville* ☎ *03–83–32–24–68* 🌐 *www.hoteldeguise.com* 🛏 *46 rooms, 4 suites.*

NIGHTLIFE AND THE ARTS

Nancy has a rich cultural life that includes ballet, opera, and a highly renowned symphony orchestra.

Ballet de Lorraine. The Ballet de Lorraine was created in 1978 to assume the mission of a national ballet; performances are staged in the Opéra de Nancy in the place Stanislas. ☎ *03–83–85–69–01* 🌐 *www.ballet-de-lorraine.eu.*

Le Chat Noir. Le Chat Noir is a hit with a thirtysomething crowd, who enjoy retro-themed dance parties. ✉ *63 rue Jeanne-d'Arc, Ville Neuve* ☎ *03–83–28–49–29* 🌐 *www.lechatnoir.fr.*

Opéra National de Lorraine. The Opéra National de Lorraine is the fifth-ranked national regional opera of France, with a repertoire ranging from ancient to contemporary music. ☎ *03–83–85–30–60* 🌐 *www.opera-national-lorraine.fr.*

Orchestre Symphonique et Lyrique. The Orchestre Symphonique et Lyrique organizes concerts from fall through spring. ☎ *03–83–85–30–60* 🌐 *www.opera-national-lorraine.fr.*

SHOPPING

Daum Boutique. Daum Boutique sells deluxe crystal and examples of the city's traditional Art Nouveau *pâte de verre*, in which crushed glass is mixed with a binding material to form a decorative surface. ✉ *14 pl. Stanislas, Vieille Ville* ☎ *03–83–32–21–65* 🌐 *www.daum.fr.*

Librairie Ancienne Dornier. Librairie Ancienne Dornier, near the Musée des Arts et Traditions Populaires, is an excellent bookstore that sells engravings as well as old and new books devoted to local history. ✉ *74 Grande-Rue, Vieille Ville* ☎ *03–83–36–50–62.*

LORRAINE: JOAN OF ARC COUNTRY

Lorraine is the land of Joan of Arc, one of France's patron saints and an iconic figure worldwide. Following D64, which winds between Contrexéville and Void, puts you on her home turf; almost unchanged since the Middle Ages, it's a landscape that Joan would probably find familiar today. Certainly the names of some local communities will be familiar to her fans. Domrémy was the place where she was born in 1411 or 1412; Neufchâteau, then a fortified town guarding the region, was where a teenage Joan and her fellow villagers sought refuge from the menacing English armies; and Vaucouleurs was where she went in 1428 to enlist the aid of the governor and prepare for a mission that would take her onward to the king—and her destiny.

VAUCOULEURS

73 km (41 miles) southwest of Nancy on N4 and D964.

Above the modest main street in the market town of Vaucouleurs, you can see ruins of Robert de Baudricourt's medieval castle and the Porte de France. The barefoot Maid of Orléans spent several months here, arriving on May 13, 1428 to ask Governor de Baudricourt for help. After wheedling an audience at the castle, she convinced him of the necessity of her mission, learning to ride and to wield a sword. Won over finally by her conviction and by popular sentiment, de Baudricourt offered to give her an escort to seek out the king. On February 23, 1429, clad in page's garb and with her hair cut short, Jeanne d'Arc rode out through the Porte de France, en route to Orléans. A train route runs to Vaucouleurs from Toul and Nancy.

WHERE TO STAY

For expanded hotel reviews, visit Fodors.com.

$$ B&B/INN 🏨 **Hostellerie de l'Isle en Bray.** A night in the fine Renaissance-style Château de Montbra—where grand public salons are crammed with antiques and spacious guest rooms are graced with period furniture elegantly offset by modern fabrics—is ideal for anyone indulging in Joan-of-Arc-related medieval musings. **Pros:** romantic and secluded; timeless charm and luxury; marvelous museum atmosphere; gentle prices. **Cons:** car indispensable. [$] *Rooms from: €130* ✉ *3 rue des Erables, 10 km (6 miles) south of Vaucouleurs on the D964, Montbras* ☎ *03–29–90–86–36* 🌐 *www.chateau-montbras.com* 🛏 *5 rooms, 2 suites* 🍴 *Breakfast.*

DOMRÉMY-LA-PUCELLE

19 km (12 miles) south of Vaucouleurs on D964.

Joan of Arc was born in a cottage here in either 1411 or 1412. You can see her birthplace, as well as the church where she was baptized,

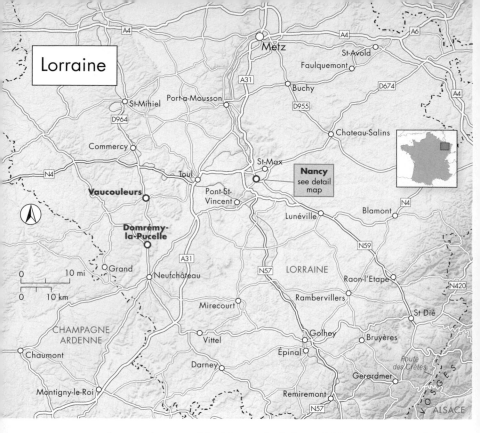

the actual statue of St. Marguerite before which she prayed, and the hillside where she tended sheep and first heard voices telling her to take up arms and save France from the English.

In the nearby forest of Bois-Chenu, perhaps an ancient sacred wood, Jeanne d'Arc gathered flowers. Near the village of Coussy, she danced with other children at country fairs attended by Pierre de Bourlémont, the local seigneur, and his wife Beatrice—the Château of Bourlémont may still be seen. Associated with Coussey and Brixey are Saints Mihiel and Catherine, who, with the Archangel Saint-Michael, appeared before Joan. In the Chapel of Notre-Dame at Bermont, where Joan vowed to save France, are the statues that existed in her time.

GETTING HERE

From Nancy, 15 trains connect with Toul (€6.80); change for Neuf-château, 39 km (24 miles) southwest of Nancy, for the twice-daily bus connection to Domrémy-la-Pucelle (€2.50), 10 km (6 miles) to the north of Neufchâteau, on the Vaucouleurs line.

EXPLORING

Basilique du Bois-Chenu (*Bois-Chenu Basilica*). The ornate late-19th-century Basilique du Bois-Chenu, high up the hillside above Domrémy, boasts enormous painted and mosaic panels expounding on Joan's legend in glowing Pre-Raphaelite tones. Outside lurk serene panoramic views over the emerald, gently rolling Meuse Valley. ☉ *Daily 7:30–7.*

Fodor's Choice **Maison Natale de Jeanne d'Arc** (*Joan of Arc's Birthplace*). The humble ★ stone-and-stucco Maison Natale de Jeanne d'Arc—an irregular, slope-roof, two-story cottage—has been preserved with style and reverence. The modern museum alongside, the **Centre Johannique,** shows a film (French only), while mannequins in period costume present Joan of Arc's amazing story. After she heard mystical voices, Joan walked 19 km (12 miles) to Vaucouleurs. Dressed and mounted like a man, she led her forces to lift the siege of Orléans, defeated the English, and escorted the unseated Charles VII to Reims, to be crowned king of France. Military missions after Orléans failed—including an attempt to retake Paris— and she was captured at Compiègne. The English turned her over to the Church, which sent her to be tried by the Inquisition for witchcraft and heresy. She was convicted and burned at the stake in Rouen. One of the latest theories is that Jeanne d'Arc was no mere "peasant" but was distantly connected to France's royal family—a controversial proposal that many historians discount. ⊠ *2 rue de la Basilique* ☎ *03–29–06– 95–86* ⊠ *€3* ☉ *Oct.–mid-Dec., late Jan.–Mar., Wed.–Mon. 10–1 and 2–5; Apr.–Sept., Wed.–Mon. (daily July and Aug.) 10–1 and 2–6:30. Closed mid-Dec.–early Jan.*

STRASBOURG

Although situated in the heart of Alsace 490 km (304 miles) east of Paris, and drawing appealingly on Alsatian *gemütlichkeit* (coziness), the city of Strasbourg is a cosmopolitan French cultural center and the symbolic if unofficial capital of Europe. The Romans knew Strasbourg as Argentoratum before it came to be known as Strateburgum, or City of (Cross) Roads. After centuries as part of the Germanic Holy Roman Empire, it was united with France in 1681, but retained independence regarding legislation, education, and religion under the honorific title Free Royal City.

Against an irresistible backdrop of old half-timber houses, waterways, and the colossal single spire of its red-sandstone cathedral, which seems to insist imperiously that you pay homage to its majestic beauty, Strasbourg is a symbolic city, embodying Franco-German reconciliation and the wider idea of a united Europe. You'll discover an incongruously sophisticated mix of museums, charming neighborhoods like La Petite France, elite schools (including that notorious hothouse for blooming politicos, the École Nationale d'Administration, or National Administration School), international think tanks, and the European Parliament. The *Strasbourgeoisie* have a lot to be proud of.

GETTING HERE AND AROUND

With the TGV Est Européen (⊕ *www.tgv.com*), Strasbourg is two hours, 20 minutes away from Paris on any one of the daily 16 direct TGV trains, with one-way fares ranging from €33 to €89. In addition to the extra-regional links to Nancy, Metz, Saarbrucken, Lyon, and Geneva, Strasbourg's train station (⊠ *20 pl. de la Gare*) is at the heart of the

8

A finalist by M. J. Glauber in Fodor's France contest, this stunning photo captures the Gothic grace of Strasbourg's cathedral in all its glory.

regional TER train system and has direct trains at least every 30–60 minutes to Colmar (€11.70) and Sélestat (€8.30), where you can change for bus services to Ribeauvillé (€2.50) and Rosheim/Molsheim (for Dambach la Ville and Obernai, €4.40). Call the "on-demand" service (☎ 08–00–10–09–48) in Sélestat to arrange transport to Orschwiller (a short walk to Haut-Koenigsbourg) for €1.20. Buses head out to Obernai and Wangenbourg from the Gare Routière (☎ 03–88–43–23–43) in place des Halles. Strasbourg's main train station is across the river from the city center, three-quarters of a mile from the cathedral, in the far west corner of the city.

Strasbourg has an extensive tram and bus network; most of the efficient lines of Companie des Transports Strasbourgeois (☎ 03–88–77–70–70 ⊕ *www.cts-strasbourg.fr*) leave from the train station at 20 place de la Gare, travel down rue du Vieux Marché aux Vins, and part ways at place de la République. Tickets can also be used on Strasbourg's sleek tram that travels from the train station to place de l'Homme and out to the burbs.

Visitor Information Strasbourg Tourist Office There's also a city tourist office at the train station and another at the Parc de l'Etoile. ⊠ *17 pl. de la Cathédrale* ☎ *03–88–52–28–28* ⊕ *www.otstrasbourg.fr* ⊠ *Gare SNCF* ☎ *03–88–32–51–49.* ⊠ *Parc de l'Etoile, Strasbourg.*

EXPLORING

The city center is effectively an island within two arms of the River Ill; most major sites are found here, but the northern districts also contain some fine buildings erected over the past 100 years, culminating in the Palais de l'Europe. You can buy a three-day city pass for €14 per adult, and €7 per child, which includes one free entrance plus one reduced-rate ticket to the museums, free admission to the astronomical clock, and a boat trip on the canal.

Note to drivers: The configuration of downtown streets makes it difficult to approach the center via the autoroute exit marked Strasbourg Centre. Instead, hold out for the exit marked place de l'étoile and follow signs to Cathédrale/Centre Ville. At place du Corbeau, veer left across the Ill, and go straight to the place Gutenberg parking garage, a block from the cathedral.

THE HISTORIC HEART

This central area, from the cathedral to picturesque Petite France, concentrates the best of Old Strasbourg, with its twisting backstreets, flower-lined courts, tempting shops, and inviting winstubs.

TOP ATTRACTIONS

FAMILY **Cathédrale Notre-Dame.** Dark pink, ornately carved Vosges sandstone masonry covers the facade of this most novel and Germanic of French cathedrals, a triumph of Gothic art begun in 1176. Not content with the outlines of the walls themselves, medieval builders lacily encased them with slender stone shafts. The off-center **spire,** finished in 1439, looks absurdly fragile as it tapers skyward some 466 feet; you can climb 330 steps to the base of the spire to take in sweeping views of the city, the Vosges Mountains, and the Black Forest.

The interior presents a stark contrast to the facade: it's older (mostly finished by 1275), and the nave's broad windows emphasize the horizontal rather than the vertical. Note Hans Hammer's ornately sculpted pulpit (1484–86) and the richly painted 14th- to 15th-century organ loft that rises from pillar to ceiling. The left side of the nave is flanked with richly colored Gothic windows honoring the early leaders of the Holy Roman Empire—Otto I and II, and Heinrich I and II. The **choir** is not ablaze with stained glass but framed by chunky Romanesque masonry. The elaborate 16th-century **Chapelle St-Laurent,** to the left of the choir, merits a visit; turn to the right to admire the **Pilier des Anges** (Angels' Pillar), an intricate column dating from 1230.

Just beyond the pillar, the Renaissance machinery of the 16th-century **Horloge Astronomique** whirs into action daily at 12:30 pm (but the line starts at the south door at 11:45 am): macabre clockwork figures enact the story of Christ's Passion. One of the highlights: when the apostles walk past, a likeness of Christ as a rooster crows three times. ⊠ *Pl. de la Cathédrale* ⊕ *www.cathedrale-strasbourg.fr* ⊒ *Clock €2, spire platform €5* ⊙ *Cathedral daily 7–11:20 and 12:35–7.*

Musée Alsacien (*Alsatian Museum*). In this labyrinthine half-timber home, with layers of carved balconies sagging over a cobbled inner courtyard, local interiors have been faithfully reconstituted. The diverse activities of blacksmiths, clog makers, saddlers, and makers of artificial flowers are explained with the help of old-time craftsmen's tools and equipment. ⊠ *23 quai St-Nicolas* ☎ *03–88–52–50–01* ⊕ *www.musees-strasbourg.org* ⊒ *€6* ⊙ *Mon. and Wed.–Fri. noon–6, weekends 10–6.*

Strasbourg

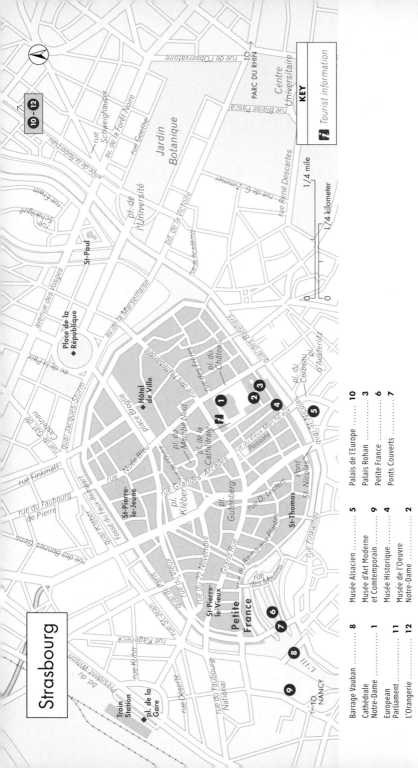

KEY

🛈 *Tourist information*

0   1/4 mile

0   1/4 kilometer

Musée d'Art Moderne et Contemporain (*Modern and Contemporary Art Museum*). A magnificent sculpture of a building (designed by contemporary architect Adrien Fainsilber) that sometimes dwarfs its contents, this spectacular museum frames a relatively thin collection of new, esoteric, and unsung 20th-century art. Downstairs, a permanent collection of Impressionists and Modernists up to 1950 is heavily padded with local heroes but happily fleshed out with some striking furniture; all are juxtaposed for contrasting and comparing, with little to no chronological flow. Upstairs, harsh, spare works must strive to live up to their setting; few contemporary masters are featured. Drawings, watercolors, and paintings by Gustave Doré, a native of Alsace, are enshrined in a separate room. ⊠ *1 pl. Hans-Jean Arp* ☎ *03–88–23–31–31* ⊕ *www. musees-strasbourg.eu* ⊠ *€7* ☉ *Tues.–Sun.10–6.*

> **STRASBOURG STEP-BY-STEP**
>
> Audio-guide walking tours of Strasbourg's Vielle Ville and other sights, offered in five languages, are available through the tourist office for €6.80 per headset (plus €100 deposit). If you want to give your weary feet a break, try the Strasbourg minitrain tour (☎ *03–88–77–70–03* ⊠ *€5.50*); it leaves from place du Château, by the cathedral.

Musée de l'Oeuvre Notre-Dame (*Cathedral Museum*). There's more to this museum than the usual assembly of dilapidated statues rescued from the cathedral before they fell off (you'll find *those* rotting in the Barrage Vauban). Sacred sculptures stand in churchlike settings, and secular exhibits are enhanced by the building's fine old architecture. Subjects include a wealth of Flemish and Upper Rhine paintings, stained glass, gold objects, and massive, heavily carved furniture. ⊠ *3 pl. du Château* ☎ *03–88–52–50–00* ⊕ *www.musees-strasbourg.eu* ⊠ *€6* ☉ *Tues.–Fri. noon–6, weekends 10–6.*

Palais Rohan (*Rohan Palace*). The exterior of this massive neoclassical palace (1732–42) by architect Robert de Cotte may be austere, but there's plenty of glamour inside. Decorator Robert le Lorrain's magnificent ground-floor rooms include the great **Salon d'Assemblée** (Assembly Room) and the book- and tapestry-lined **Bibliothèque des Cardinaux** (Cardinals' Library). The library leads to a series of less august rooms that house the **Musée des Arts Décoratifs** (Decorative Arts Museum) and its elaborate display of ceramics. This is a comprehensive presentation of works by Hannong, a porcelain manufacturer active in Strasbourg from 1721 to 1782; dinner services by other local kilns reveal the influence of Chinese porcelain. The **Musée des Beaux-Arts** (Fine Arts Museum), also in the château, includes masterworks of European painting from Giotto and Memling to El Greco, Rubens, and Goya. Downstairs, the **Musée Archéologique** (Archaeology Museum) displays regional finds, including gorgeous Merovingian treasures. ⊠ *2 pl. du Château* ☎ *03–88–52–50–00* ⊕ *www.musees-strasbourg.eu* ⊠ *€6 each museum* ☉ *Mon. and Wed.–Fri. noon–6, weekends 10–6.*

Fodor's Choice
★ **Petite France.** With gingerbread half-timber houses that seem to lean precariously over the canals of the Ill, plus old-fashioned shops, and inviting little restaurants, "Little France" is the most magical neighborhood

8

Strasbourg is studded with medieval buildings that look airlifted in from Germany and stunningly ornament the city's squares.

in Strasbourg. The district, just southwest of the center, is historically Alsatian in style and filled with Renaissance buildings that have survived plenty of wars. Wander up and down the tiny streets that connect rue du Bain-aux-Plantes and rue des Dentelles to Grand-Rue, and stroll the waterfront promenade.

WORTH NOTING

Barrage Vauban (*Vauban Dam*). Just beyond the Ponts Couverts is the grass-roofed Vauban Dam, built by its namesake in 1682. Climb to the top for wide-angle views of the Ponts Couverts and, on the other side, the Museum of Modern Art. Then meander through its echoing galleries, where magnificent cathedral statuary lies scattered among pigeon droppings. ⊠ *Ponts Couverts* 🎫 *Free* ☉ *Daily 9–7:30.*

Musée Historique (*Local History Museum*). This museum, in a step-gabled slaughterhouse dating from 1588, contains a collection of maps, armor, arms, bells, uniforms, traditional dress, printing paraphernalia, and two huge relief models of Strasbourg. Note that the museum is being renovated to include exhibits covering the history of Strasbourg: some sections of it may be closed to the public until work is completed. ⊠ *3 pl. de la Grande-Boucherie* ☎ *03–88–52–50–00* ⊕ *www.musees-strasbourg.eu* 🎫 *€5* ☉ *July–Sept., daily 10–6; Oct.–June, Tues.–Fri. noon–6, weekends 10–6.*

Ponts Couverts (*Covered Bridges*). These three bridges, distinguished by their four stone towers, were once covered with wooden shelters. Part of the 14th-century ramparts that framed Old Strasbourg, they span the Ill as it branches into four fingerlike canals.

BEYOND THE ILL

If you've seen the center and have time to strike out in new directions, head across the Ill to view an architectural landmark unrelated to Strasbourg's famous medieval past: the Palais de l'Europe.

EXPLORING

European Parliament. This sleek building testifies to the growing importance of the governing body of the European Union, which used to make do with rental offices in the Palais de l'Europe. Eurocrats continue to commute between Brussels, Luxembourg, and Strasbourg, hauling their staff and files with them. One week per month, visitors can slip into the hemicycle and witness the tribune in debate, complete with simultaneous translation. Note: You must obtain a written appointment beforehand and provide a *pièce d'identité* (ID) before entering. ⌂ *Behind Palais de l'Europe* ☎ *03–88–17–40–01* ⊕ *www.europarl.europa.eu* ⊠ *Free* ☉ *Call or write ahead for appointment.*

L'Orangerie. Like a private backyard for the Eurocrats in the Palais de l'Europe, this delightful park is laden with flowers and punctuated by noble copper beeches. It contains a lake and, close by, a small reserve of rare birds, including flamingos and noisy local storks. ⌂ *Av. de l'Europe.*

Palais de l'Europe. Designed by Paris architect Henri Bernard in 1977, this continental landmark is headquarters to the Council of Europe, founded in 1949 and independent of the European Union. A guided tour introduces you to the intricacies of its workings and may allow you to eavesdrop on a session. Arrange your tour by telephone in advance (a minimum of 15 people must sign up before a tour will be conducted); appointments are fixed according to language demands and usually take place in the afternoon. Note: You must provide ID before entering. ⌂ *Av. de l'Europe* ☎ *03–88–41–20–29 for appointment* ✉ *visites@coe. int* ⊠ *Free* ☉ *Guided tours by appointment weekdays.*

Place de la République. The spacious layout and ponderous architecture of this monumental *cirque* (circle) have nothing in common with the Vieille Ville except for the local red sandstone. A different hand was at work here—that of occupying Germans, who erected the former Ministry (1902), the Academy of Music (1882–92), and the Palais du Rhin (1883–88). The handsome neo-Gothic church of **St-Paul** and the pseudo-Renaissance **Palais de l'Université** (University Palace), constructed between 1875 and 1885, also bear the German stamp. Heavy turn-of-the-20th-century houses, some reflecting the whimsical curves

STRASBOURG BY WATER

Fluvial Strasbourg. Strasbourg is a big town, but the center is easily explored on foot, or, more romantically, by boat. Fluvial Strasbourg works with the company Batorama to organize 70-minute boat tours along the Ill four times a day in winter and up to every half hour starting at 10:30 from April through October (there are also nocturnal tours until 10 pm May–September). Boats leave from behind the Palais Rohan; the cost is €9.20. ☎ *03–88–84–13–13* ⊕ *www.batorama.fr.*

8

of the Art Nouveau style, frame **Allée de la Robertsau,** a tree-lined boulevard that would not look out of place in Berlin.

WHERE TO EAT

$ FRENCH
🍴 **Chez Yvonne.** Just around the corner from the cathedral is an eatery that is almost as exalted. Behind red-checked curtains you can find artists, tourists, lovers, and heads of state sitting elbow-to-elbow in this classic winstub, founded in 1873. All come to savor steaming platters of local specialties: watch for pike-perch on choucroute, braised ham hocks, and quails stuffed with foie gras. Warm Alsatian fabrics dress tables and lamps, the china is regional, the photos historic—all making for chic, not kitsch. [$] *Average main: €16* ✉ *10 rue du Sanglier* ☎ *03–88–32–84–15* 🌐 *www.chez-yvonne.net* ✍ *Reservations essential* 🕒 *Daily noon–2:15 and 6–midnight.*

$$$$ MODERN FRENCH
Fodor's Choice ★
🍴 **Le Buerehiesel.** This lovely farmhouse, reconstructed in the Orangerie park, warrants a pilgrimage if you're willing to pay for the finest cooking in Alsace. Chef Eric Westermann focuses on the freshest of local-terroir specialties, supplemented by the best seafood from Brittany. The seasonal desserts are a standout. Two small salons are cozy, but most tables are set in a modern annex that is mostly glass and steel. In any event, plump European *parlementaires* come on foot; others might come on their knees. [$] *Average main: €37* ✉ *4 parc de l'Orangerie* ☎ *03–88–45–56–65* 🌐 *www.buerehiesel.fr* ✍ *Reservations essential* 🕒 *Closed Sun. and Mon., 2 wks in Jan.,and 2 wks in Aug.*

$$ GERMAN
🍴 **Maison des Tanneurs.** This half-timber 16th-century landmark (one of oldest riverside buildings in Petite France) is draped with geranium-filled flower pots and perennially popular. Come for generous and delicious proportions of choucroute garnie, as well as other regional favorites such as goose foie gras, trout with almonds, and coq au Riesling. [$] *Average main: €22* ✉ *42 rue Bain aux Plantes* ☎ *03–88–32–79–70* 🌐 *www.maison-des-tanneurs.com* 🕒 *Closed Sun. and Mon. and 3 wks in early Jan.*

$$ FRENCH
🍴 **Maison Kammerzell.** This restaurant occupies what must be the most familiar house in Strasbourg—a richly carved, half-timber 15th-century building adorned with sumptuous allegorical frescoes by the aptly nicknamed Léo Schnug. Fight your way through the crowds on the terrace and ground floor to one of the atmospheric rooms above, with their gleaming wooden furniture, stained-glass windows, and unrivaled views of the cathedral. Foie gras and choucroute are best bets, though you may want to try the chef's pet discovery, choucroute with freshwater fish. [$] *Average main: €22* ✉ *16 pl. de la Cathédrale* ☎ *03–88–32–42–14* 🌐 *www.maison-kammerzell.com.*

$ BISTRO
🍴 **Zum Strissel.** This rustic winstub near the cathedral has been in business since the 16th century. The charming decor provides a perfect backdrop for traditional Alsace fare such as baeckoffe and choucroute served with pike perch. To wash it down, you can choose from an extensive list of Alsace wines. Try for a room upstairs to admire the stained-glass windows with their tales depicting life in the vines, or opt for the outdoor terrace, which spills out over the square. [$] *Average main: €17* ✉ *5 pl. de la Grande-Boucherie* ☎ *03–88–32–14–73* 🌐 *www.strissel.fr.*

WHERE TO STAY

For expanded hotel reviews, visit Fodors.com.

$$
HOTEL
☷ **Hôtel Cour du Corbeau.** Opened as an inn in 1580 and magnificently restored to its half-timber former glory, the "courtyard of the crow" retains its Middle Ages facade while the interiors are another thing completely: luxe design, crystal chandeliers, period furniture, and colorful fabrics are the essence of modern style, sumptuousness, and comfort. **Pros:** dazzling and luxurious; great location a short walk from the cathedral. **Cons:** tea salon, but no restaurant. Ⓢ*Rooms from: €139* ⊠*6–8 rue des Couples* ☏*03–90–00–26–26* ⊕*www.cour-corbeau.com* ↝*38 rooms, 19 suites.*

$
HOTEL
☷ **Hôtel Gutenberg.** In a recently renovated 250-year-old mansion just off place Gutenberg, this budget-priced urban hotel has colorful, modernized rooms with charming highlights from the past. **Pros:** excellent value; Old World style with modern conveniences and design touches; picturesque location only a few blocks from the cathedral. **Cons:** some street noise; elevator doesn't reach the top floor. Ⓢ*Rooms from: €80* ⊠*31 rue des Serruriers* ☏*03–88–32–17–15* ⊕*www.hotel-gutenberg. com* ↝*42 rooms* ⓄⓁ*Breakfast.*

$$$
HOTEL
☷ **Régent-Petite France.** Surrounded by canals in the heart of the quaint La Petite France quarter, this centuries-old former ice factory—replete with noble pediment and mansard roofs—has been transformed into a boldly modern luxury hotel, where Philippe Starck–inspired sculptural room furnishings contrast sharply with the half-timber houses and roaring river viewed from nearly every window. **Pros:** beautiful rooms; ideal location; great service; no skimping on the amenities—the beds and the bathrooms are divine. **Cons:** disappointing breakfast; restaurant closed Sunday and Monday. Ⓢ*Rooms from: €160* ⊠*5 rue des Moulins* ☏*03–88–76–43–43* ⊕*www.regent-petite-france.com* ↝*55 rooms, 17 suites* ⓄⓁ*Some meals.*

NIGHTLIFE AND THE ARTS

Festival Musica (*Contemporary Music Festival*). The annual Festival Musica is held in September and October. ⊠*Cité de la Musique et de la Danse, 1 pl. Dauphine* ☏*03–88–23–46–46* ⊕*www.festival-musica.org.*

Jazzdor *(Jazz Festival).* Jazzdor is an international jazz festival that is held annually in November at venues both in and around Strasbourg. ⊠*25 rue des Frères, Strasbourg* ☏*03–88–36–30–48* ⊕*www.jazzdor. com.*

La Laiterie. The Vieille Ville neighborhood east of the cathedral, along rue des Frères, is the nightlife hangout for university students and twentysomethings; among a clutch of heavily frequented bars is La Laiterie, a multiplex concert hall showcasing art, workshops, and music ranging from electronic to post-rock and reggae. ⊠*13 rue Hohwald* ☏*03–88–23–72–37* ⊕*www.laiterie.artefact.org.*

Opéra National du Rhin. The Opéra National du Rhin has a sizable repertoire. ⊠*19 pl. Broglie* ☏*03–88–75–48–40* ⊕*www.operanationaldurhin.eu.*

8

Orchestre Philharmonique. Classical concerts are staged by the Orchestre Philharmonique. ⊠ *Palais des Congrès* ☎ *03–69–06–37–00* ⊕ *www. philharmonique-strasbourg.com.*

SHOPPING

The lively city center is full of boutiques, including chocolate shops and delicatessens selling locally made foie gras. Look for warm paisley linens and rustic homespun fabrics, Alsatian pottery, and local wines. Forming the city's commercial heart are **rue des Hallebardes**, next to the cathedral; **rue des Grandes Arcades**, with its shopping mall; and **place Kléber**. An **antiques market** takes place behind the cathedral on rue du Vieil-Hôpital, rue des Bouchers, and place de la Grande Boucherie every Wednesday and Saturday morning.

ALSACE

The Rhine River forms the eastern boundary of both Alsace and France. But the best of Alsace is not found along the Rhine's industrial waterfront. Instead it's in the Ill Valley at the base of the Vosges, southwest of cosmopolitan Strasbourg. Northwest is the beginning of the **Route du Vin,** the great Alsace Wine Road, which winds its way south through the Vosges foothills, fruitful vineyards, and medieval villages. Signs for the road help you keep your bearings on the twisting way south, and you'll find limitless opportunities to stop at wineries and sample the local wares. The Wine Road stretches 170 km (105 miles) between Thann and Marienheim, and is easily accessible from Strasbourg or Colmar. Many of the towns and villages have designated "vineyard trails" winding between towns (a bicycle will help you cover a lot of territory). Riquewihr and Ribeauvillé—accessible by bus from Colmar and Sélestat rail stations—are connected by an especially picturesque route. Along the way, stop at any "Dégustation" sign for a tasting and pick up brochures on the Alsace Wine Road at any tourist office.

OBERNAI

30 km (19 miles) southwest of Strasbourg via A35/N422.

Many visitors begin their saunter down the Route du Vin at Obernai, a thriving, colorful Renaissance market town named for the patron saint of Alsace. Head to the central town enclosed by the ramparts to find some particularly Nikon-friendly sites, including a medieval belfry, Renaissance well, and late-19th-century church.

GETTING HERE

Strasbourg's train station (⊠ *20 pl. de la Gare*) is at the heart of the regional TER train system and has trains via Sélestat (€8.30) every 30 minutes to Colmar (€11.70)—the city at the southern end of Alsace's Route du Vin. At Sélestat you can catch another TER to Rosheim (€5.90) or Molsheim (€11.10), or go directly from Strasbourg to Obernai (€5.90), Rosheim (€4.90), or Molsheim (€.10). Strasbourg also has

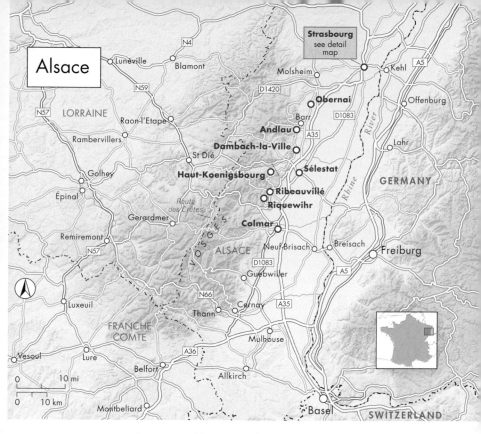

<figure>

Alsace

N4
N59
N57 LORRAINE
N57

Lunéville
Blamont
Molsheim
Kehl
A5
Strasbourg
see detail
map
Offenburg
D1420
Obernai
Raon-l'Etape
Barr
D1083
Rambervillers
Andlau
A35
Lahr
St Dié
Dambach-la-Ville
Golbey
Haut-Koenigsbourg
Sélestat
GERMANY
Épinal
Route
des Crêtes
Ribeauvillé
Riquewihr
Gerardmer
Colmar
Remiremont
ALSACE
Neuf-Brisach
Breisach
Freiburg
N57
D1083
Guebwiller
A5
N66
Luxeuil
Thann
Cernay
A35
FRANCHE
COMTE
Mulhouse
A36
Vesoul
Lure
Belfort
Allkirch
Montbeliard
Basel
SWITZERLAND

VOSGES
Rhine River

0   10 mi
0   10 km

</figure>

an extensive tram and bus network that includes buses to Obernai from its Gare Routière in place des Halles.

Visitor Information Obernai Tourist Office ✉ *Pl. du Beffroi* ☎ *03-88-95-64-13* ⊕ *www.obernai.fr.*

EXPLORING

Kapelturm Beffroi (*Chapel Tower Belfry*). Place du Marché, in the heart of town, is dominated by the stout, square 13th-century Kapelturm Beffroi, topped by a pointed steeple flanked at each corner by frilly openwork turrets added in 1597.

Puits à Six-Seaux (*Well of Six Buckets*). An elaborate Renaissance well near the belfry, the Puits à Six-Seaux was constructed in 1579; its name recalls the six buckets suspended from its metal chains.

St-Pierre–St-Paul. The twin spires of the parish church of St-Pierre–St-Paul compete with the belfry for skyline preeminence. They date, like the rest of the church, from the 1860s, although the 1504 Holy Sepulchre altarpiece in the north transept is a survivor from the previous church. Other points of interest include the flower-bedecked **place de l'Étoile** and the **Hôtel de Ville,** which is open to visitors during *Les Journées du Patrimoine.*

WHERE TO STAY

For expanded hotel reviews, visit Fodors.com.

$ B&B/INN Fodor's Choice ★ **L'Ami Fritz.** Set several miles west of Obernai, this reader-recommended, 18th-century, white-shuttered, flower-bedecked stone house treats visitors to fine meals and accommodates overnight guests in impeccable rooms done up in toile de Jouy and homespun checks (opt for one in the main hotel, not the adjacent annex). **Pros:** beautiful location; friendly staff; combines style, rustic warmth, and three generations of family tradition. **Cons:** a car is needed to reach property; uneven service. [$] *Rooms from: €93* ✉ *8 rue des Châteaux, 5 km (3 miles) west of Obernai, Ottrott-le-Haut* ☎ *03–88–95–80–81* 🌐 *www.amifritz.com* 🛏 *19 rooms, 3 suites* ⏲ *Closed 2nd wk of July and 2 wks mid-Jan.* 🍴 *Some meals.*

SHOPPING

Dietrich. Dietrich has a varied selection of Beauvillé linens, locally hand-blown Alsatian wineglasses, and Obernai-pattern china. ✉ *74 rue du Général-Gouraud* ☎ *03–88–95–57–58* 🌐 *www.dietrich-obernai.fr.*

ANDLAU

3 km (2 miles) southwest of Barr on rte. du Vin.

Abbaye d'Andlau. Built in the 12th century, the Abbaye d'Andlau has the richest ensemble of Romanesque sculpture in Alsace. Sculpted vines wind their way around the doorway as a reminder of wine's time-honored importance to the local economy. A statue of a female bear, the abbey mascot—bears used to roam local forests and were bred at the abbey until the 16th century—can be seen in the north transept. Legend has it that Queen Richarde, spurned by her husband, Charles the Fat, founded the abbey in AD 887 when an angel enjoined her to construct a church on a site to be shown to her by a female bear.

WHERE TO STAY

For expanded hotel reviews, visit Fodors.com.

$ HOTEL **Arnold.** Like Itterswiller—the cute wine village it overlooks—this yellow-wall, half-timber hillside hotel exudes charm, from the wood-beam lobby with its wrought-iron staircase right through to the "country deluxe" guest rooms with views across the nearby vineyards. **Pros:** all-around excellence; good half-board meal plan. **Cons:** no air-conditioning; inconsistent service. [$] *Rooms from: €96* ✉ *98 rte. des Vins, 3 km (2 miles) south of Andlau on D253, Itterswiller* ☎ *03–88–85–50–58* 🌐 *www.hotel-arnold.com* 🛏 *29 rooms* 🍴 *Some meals.*

DAMBACH-LA-VILLE

8 km (5 miles) southeast of Andlau via Itterswiller.

GETTING HERE

From Colmar it's a 30-minute TER train trip (€6.10) to Dambach-la Ville. From Strasbourg you can get there directly (€8.50), or via Sélestat (€9.40), in under an hour. ✉ *20 pl. de la Gare.*

A Tippler's Guide to Alsace

Threading south along the eastern foothills of the Vosges from Marienheim to Thann, the Alsatian Wine Road is home to delicious wines and beautiful vineyards. The 170-km (105-mile) Route du Vin passes through small towns, and footpaths interspersed throughout the region afford the opportunity to wander through the vineyards.

Buses from Colmar head out to the surrounding towns of Riquewihr, St-Hippolyte, Ribeauvillé, and Eguisheim; pick up brochures on the Wine Route from Colmar's tourist office. Although the route is hilly, bicycling is a great way to take in the countryside and avoid the parking hassle in the towns along this heavily traveled route.

Wine is an object of veneration in Alsace, and anyone traveling along the Route du Vin will want to become part of the cult. Just because Alsatian vintners use German grapes, don't expect their wines to taste like their counterparts across the Rhine.

German vintners aim for sweetness, creating wines that are best appreciated as an aperitif. Alsatian vintners, on the other hand, eschew sweetness in favor of strength, and their wines go wonderfully with knockdown, drag-out meals.

The main wines you need to know about are Gewurztraminer, Riesling, Muscat, Pinot Gris, and Sylvaner, all whites. The only red wine produced in the region is the light and delicious Pinot Noir. Gewurztraminer, which in Germany is an ultrasweet dessert wine, has a much cleaner, drier taste in Alsace, despite its fragrant bouquet. It's best served with the richest of Alsace dishes, such as goose.

Riesling is the premier wine of Alsace, balancing a hard structure with certain fruity roundness. With a grapy bouquet and clean finish, dry Muscat does best as an aperitif. Pinot Gris, also called "Tokay," is probably the most full-bodied of Alsatian wines.

Sylvaner falls below those grapes in general acclaim, tending to be lighter and a bit dull. You can discover many of these wines as you drive along the Route du Vin.

EXPLORING

One of the prettiest villages along the Alsace Wine Road, Dambach-la-Ville is a fortified medieval town protected by ramparts and three powerful 13th-century gateways. It's particularly rich in half-timber, high-roof houses from the 17th and 18th centuries, clustered mainly around **place du Marché** (Market Square). Also on the square is the 16th-century **Hôtel de Ville**. As you walk the charming streets, notice the wrought-iron signs and rooftop oriels.

WHERE TO STAY

For expanded hotel reviews, visit Fodors.com.

$

B&B/INN

🖼 **Le Vignoble.** Set in a beautifully restored 18th-century barn next to the village church, this unpretentious hotel offers real, rustic Alsatian charm and quiet, comfy guest rooms, with functional dark-wood furnishings and, in the best, balconies overlooking the street. **Pros:** wine-route location; warm Alsatian welcome. **Cons:** no air-conditioning; no

Alsace's Wine Road passes a parade of "Hansel and Gretel" villages, each more picturesque than the last.

restaurant; some rooms are on the small side. $ *Rooms from: €72* ✉ *1 rue de l'Eglise* ☎ *03–88–92–43–75* ⊕ *www.hotel-vignoble-alsace.fr* ⤳ *7 rooms* ☾ *Closed Jan.–mid-Feb.*

SÉLESTAT

9 km (5½ miles) southeast of Dambach via D210 and N422, 47 km (29 miles) southwest of Strasbourg.

Sélestat, midway between Strasbourg and Colmar, is a lively, historic town with a Romanesque church and a library of medieval manuscripts (plus, it's important to note, a railway station with trains to and from Strasbourg). Head directly to the Vieille Ville and explore the quarter on foot.

GETTING HERE

From Strasbourg, there are three TER trains every hour to Sélestat (€8.30). ✉ *1 pl. de la Gare.*

Visitor Information Sélestat Tourist Office ✉ *10 bd. Leclerc* ☎ *03–88–58–87–20* ⊕ *www.selestat-tourisme.com.*

EXPLORING

Bibliothèque Humaniste (*Humanist Library*). Among the precious medieval and Renaissance manuscripts on display at the Bibliothèque Humaniste, founded in 1452 and installed in the former Halle aux Blés, are a 7th-century lectionary and a 12th-century Book of Miracles. There's also a town register from 1521, with the first-ever recorded reference to a Christmas tree! ✉ *1 rue de la Bibliothèque* ☎ *03–88–58–07–20* ⊕ *www.bh-selestat.fr* 🎟 *€4.20* ☾ *Sept.–June, Mon. and Wed.–Fri.*

9–noon and 2–6, Sat. 9–noon; July and Aug., Mon. and Wed.–Fri. 9–noon and 2–6, Sat. 9–noon and 2–5, Sun. 2–5.

St-Foy. The church of St-Foy dates from between 1155 and 1190; its Romanesque facade remains largely intact (the spires were added in the 19th century), as does the 140-foot octagonal tower over the crossing.

> **FLOWER POWERED**
>
> The colorful Corso Fleuri Flower Carnival takes place on the second Saturday in August, when Sélestat decks itself—and the floats in its vivid parade—with a magnificent display of dahlias.

Sadly, the interior was mangled over the centuries, chiefly by the Jesuits, whose most inspired legacy is the Baroque pulpit of 1733 depicting the life of St. Francis Xavier. Note the Romanesque bas-relief next to the baptistery, originally the lid of a sarcophagus. ⊠ *Pl. du Marché-Vert.*

HAUT-KOENIGSBOURG

11 km (7 miles) west of Sélestat via D159.

One of the most popular spots in Alsace is the romantic, crag-top castle of Haut-Koenigsbourg, originally built as a fortress in the 12th century.

FAMILY
Fodor's Choice
★
Château du Haut-Koenigsbourg. The ruins of the Château du Haut-Koenigsbourg were presented by the town of Sélestat to German emperor Wilhelm II in 1901. The château looked just as a kaiser thought one should, and he restored it with some diligence and no lack of imagination—squaring the main tower's original circle, for instance. The site, panorama, drawbridge, and amply furnished imperial chambers may lack authenticity, but they are undeniably dramatic. There is a shuttle bus from the Selestat train station to the château every day from June to September and on weekends from March to December. ⊠ *Orschwiller* ☎ *03–88–82–50–60* ⊕ *www.haut-koenigsbourg.fr* ⊠ *€8; free 1st Sun. of the month, Nov.–Mar.* ☉ *Nov.–Feb., daily 9:30–noon and 1–4:30; Mar. and Oct., daily 9:30–5; Apr., May, and Sept., daily 9:15–5:15; June–Aug., daily 9:15–6.*

RIBEAUVILLÉ

13 km (8 miles) south of Haut-Koenigsbourg via St-Hippolyte, 16 km (10 miles) southwest of Sélestat.

Fodor's Choice
★
The beautiful half-timber town of Ribeauvillé, surrounded by rolling vineyards and three imposing châteaux, produces some of the best wines in Alsace. (The Trimbach family has made Riesling and superb Gewurztraminer here since 1626.) The town's narrow main street, crowded with winstubs, pottery shops, bakeries, and wine sellers, is bisected by the 13th-century **Tour des Bouchers,** a clock-belfry completed (gargoyles and all) in the 15th century.

GETTING HERE

From Strasbourg's train station there trains every 30 minutes to Colmar (€11.70) via Sélestat (€8.30), where you can change for bus services to Ribeauvillé (€2.50).

Visitor Information Ribeauvillé Tourist Office ✉ *1 Grand-Rue* ☎ *03–89–73–23–23* 🌐 *www.ribeauville-riquewihr.com.*

EXPLORING

Storks' nests crown several towers in Ribeauvillé, while streets are adorned with quaint shop signs, fairy-tale turrets, and tour guides herding the crowds with directions in French and German. Head for the place de la Marie and its Hôtel de Ville to see a famous collection of silver-gilt 16th-century tankards and chalices.

Place de la Marie is a great place to perch every first Sunday in September, when the town hosts a grand parade to celebrate the Fête des Ménétriers (Festival of the Minstrels), a day when at least one fountain here spouts free Riesling. Headlined by medieval musicians, the party begins midafternoon, and the best street seats go for €8 each. Contact the tourist office early for information.

WHERE TO EAT AND STAY

For expanded hotel reviews, visit Fodors.com.

$$$$ MODERN FRENCH Fodor's Choice ★

🍴 **L'Auberge de L'Ill.** England's late Queen Mother, Marlene Dietrich, and Montserrat Caballé are just a few of the famous who have feasted at this culinary temple, where chef Marc Haeberlin marries Alsatian cuisine with Asian nuances (there's a second Auberge de l'Ill in Japan). The results are impressive: salmon soufflé, saddle of Aveyron lamb, and showstoppers like *le homard Prince Vladimir,* lobster with shallots braised in Champagne and crème fraîche. Germanic-Alsatian flair is particularly apparent in such dishes as the truffled baeckeoffe, a casserole-terrine of lamb and pork with leeks. The kitchen's touch is incredibly light, so you'll have room left to try master desserts like Mirabelle plums poached in Sauternes with a frothy bergamot sauce. [$] *Average main: €80* ✉ *2 rue de Collonges au Mont d'Or, 10 km (6 miles) east of Ribeauvillé, Illhaeusern* ☎ *03–89–71–89–00* 🌐 *www.auberge-de-l-ill.com* ⏲ *Closed Mon. and Tues. and mid-Feb.–mid-Mar.*

$$ GERMAN

🍴 **Zum Pfifferhüs.** This is a true-blue winstub, with yellowed murals, glowing lighting, and great local wines available by the glass. The cooking is pure Alsace, with German-scale portions of choucroute, ham hock, and fruit tarts. Book ahead. [$] *Average main: €24* ✉ *14 Grand-Rue* ☎ *03–89–73–62–28* ✍ *Reservations essential* ⏲ *Closed Thurs. Nov.–July, Wed. year-round, mid-Feb.–mid-Mar., and 1st 2 wks in July.*

$ HOTEL

🏨 **Hôtel de la Tour.** Guest rooms at this erstwhile family winery in the center of Ribeauvillé, with an ornate Renaissance fountain outside its front door, are modern, surprisingly spacious and well positioned for experiencing the atmospheric town by night; those on the top floor have exposed timbers and wonderful views of ramshackle rooftops. **Pros:** family run; good amenities, including a sauna and Jacuzzi. **Cons:** no air-conditioning; little English spoken. [$] *Rooms from: €74* ✉ *1 rue de la Mairie* ☎ *03–89–73–72–73* 🌐 *www.hotel-la-tour.com* 🛏 *31 rooms* ⏲ *Closed Jan.–early Mar.*

$$$$ B&B/INN

🏨 **Hôtel des Berges.** If you want to enjoy the pleasant surroundings of the celebrated L'Auberge de L'Ill restaurant *(⇨ see restaurant review above),* with its terraced riverside lawns, book a night in the luxury annex. **Pros:** romantic and opulent; close to excellent restaurant. **Cons:**

pricey, but special "youth" rates available to those under 35. $ *Rooms from: €300 ⊠ 4 rue de Collonges au Mont d'Or, 10 km (6 miles) east of Ribeauvillé, Illhaeusern ☎ 03–89–71–87–87 ⊕ www.hoteldesberges.fr ⬎ 7 rooms, 6 suites ⊙ Closed Mon. and Tues. and Feb.*

$$$

B&B/INN

Seigneurs de Ribeaupierre. On the edge of Ribeauvillé's old quarter, this gracious half-timber, 18th-century inn offers a warm regional welcome—exposed timbers, sumptuous fabrics, and slick bathrooms await upstairs, while a fire crackling downstairs greets you on your way to the generous breakfast. **Pros:** tasteful and cozy; central location; gracious hosts. **Cons:** stuffy in summer (no air-conditioning). $ *Rooms from: €150 ⊠ 11 rue du Château ☎ 03–89–73–70–31 ⊕ www.ribeaupierre. com ⬎ 3 rooms, 2 suites ⊙ Closed Jan.–early Mar.* ❍*Breakfast.*

RIQUEWIHR

Fodor's Choice
★

5 km (3 miles) south of Ribeauvillé.

With its unique once-upon-a-timeliness, Riquewihr is the Wine Route's pièce de résistance and a living museum of old Alsace's quaint architecture. Its steep main street, ramparts, and winding back alleys have scarcely changed since the 16th century, and could easily serve as a film set. Merchants cater to the sizable influx of tourists with a plethora of kitschy souvenir shops; bypass them and instead peep into courtyards with massive wine presses, study the ornately decorated houses, stand in the narrow old courtyard that was once the Jewish quarter, or climb up a narrow wooden stair to the ramparts. You would also do well to settle into a winstub to sample some of Riquewihr's famous wines. Just strolling at will down the heavenly romantic streets will reward your eye with bright blue, half-timber houses, storybook gables, and storks'-nest towers. The facades of certain houses dating from the late Gothic period take pride of place, including the Maison Kiener (1574), the Maison Priess (1686), and the Maison Liebrich (1535), but the Tower of Thieves and the Postal Museum, ensconced in the château of the duke of Württemberg, are also fascinating.

WHERE TO EAT AND STAY

For expanded hotel reviews, visit Fodors.com.

$

FRENCH

✕**Au Tire-Bouchon.** "The Corkscrew," with its sky-blue walls and red-and-white-checkered tablecloths, is the best winstub in town in which to feast on Alsatian varieties of choucroute garnie, including some rare delights like the *verte* ("green," flavored with parsley) and the "Choucroute Royale." There are also some adventurous innovations on the menu, which changes seasonally, and a fine selection of muscats and in-house fruit brandies. With communal tables and friendly service, this is heartily recommended for that guaranteed touch of authenticity. If booked up, try the nearby Auberge du Schoenebourg. $ *Average main: €17 ⊠ 29 rue du Général-de-Gaulle ☎ 03–89–47–91–61 ⊕ www. riquewihr-zimmer.com ⊙ Closed mid-Jan.–early Feb., 1st wk in Mar., and Mon. No dinner Sun. No lunch Wed.*

$

HOTEL

Hôtel de la Couronne. Like an illustration out of the Brothers Grimm, this hotel is set in a 16th-century house with central tower,

8

DID YOU KNOW?

Colmar may be mostly modern, but it has an enchanting Old Town—head to the Lauch River to find La Petite Venise, a gorgeous district crammed with camera-ready buildings.

steep mansard roof, country shutters, and rusticated stone trim; inside, several guest rooms have grand timber beams and folkloric wall stencils, making this a truly charming base for touring a truly charming town. **Pros:** good location; outdoor dining in summer, Old World charm. **Cons:** no elevator; service can be inconsistent. [$] *Rooms from: €60* ✉ *5 rue de la Couronne* ☎ *03-89-49-03-03* 🌐 *www.hoteldelacouronne.com* 🛏 *41 rooms* 🍴 *Some meals.*

COLMAR TOURS

Les Circuits d'Alsace. For Colmar and its enchanting environs, take a highly recommended van tour with Les Circuits d'Alsace. Castles, villages, and vineyards make for an exhilarating itinerary. ✉ *8 pl. de la Gare* ☎ *03-89-41-90-88* 🌐 *www.alsace-travel.com.*

COLMAR

13 km (8 miles) southeast of Riquewihr via D3/D10, 71 km (44 miles) southwest of Strasbourg.

Forget that much of Colmar's architecture is modern (because of the destruction wrought by World Wars I and II): its Vieille Ville heart—an atmospheric maze of narrow streets lined with candy-color, half-timber Renaissance houses hanging over cobblestone lanes in a disarmingly ramshackle way—out-charms Strasbourg.

GETTING HERE

The four daily direct TGV high-speed trips from Paris's Gare de l'Est to Colmar (€65), taking two hours, 50 minutes, are perfectly complemented by 12 semi-direct, TGV/TER combos from the same station. They all require a change at either Strasbourg or Mulhouse but barely 10 minutes, in most cases, is added to the trip. More than a dozen daily trains will take you from Colmar to Sélestat (€4.70), and nine daily buses (the last at 7:10 pm) make the 45-minute trip to Ribeauvillé (€4.10). The LK Groupe (🌐 *www.l-k.fr*) has regular bus service from the Gare SNCF to towns throughout the region. Colmar's train station on rue de la Gare is in the far southwestern corner of town; from here, walk 15 minutes down avenue de la République for the tourist office, or take municipal TRACE buses (☎ *03-89-20-80-80* 🌐 *www.trace-colmar.fr*).

Visitor Information Colmar Tourist Office ✉ *4 rue Unterlinden* ☎ *03-89-20-68-92* 🌐 *www.ot-colmar.fr.*

EXPLORING

Église des Dominicains (*Dominican Church*). The Église des Dominicains houses the Flemish-influenced *Madonna of the Rosebush* (1473), by Martin Schongauer (1445–91), the most celebrated painting by the noted 15th-century German artist. Stolen from St-Martin's in 1972 and later recovered, the work has almost certainly been reduced in size from its original state but retains enormous impact. The grace and intensity of the Virgin match that of the Christ Child; yet her slender fingers dent the child's soft flesh (and his fingers entwine her curls) with immediate intimacy. Schongauer's text for her crown is: *Me carpes genito tuo o santissima virgo* ("Choose me also for your child, O holiest Virgin").

✉ *Pl. des Dominicains* 🎬 *03–89–24–46–57* 🎫*€1.30* ⊙ *Mid-Mar.– Dec., daily 10–1 and 3–6.*

La Petite Venise (*Little Venice*). To find Colmar at its most charming, wander along the calm canals that wind through La Petite Venise, an area of bright Alsatian houses with colorful shutters and window boxes that's south of the center of town. Here, amid half-timber houses bedecked with flowers and weep-

ing willow trees that shed their tears into the eddies of the Lauch River, you have the sense of being in a tiny village.

Elsewhere, the Vieille Ville streets fan out from the beefy towered church of **St-Martin**. Each shop-lined backstreet winds its way to the 15th-century customs house, the **Ancienne Douane,** and the square and canals that surround it.

Maison aux Arcades (*Arcades House*). Up the street from the Ancienne Douane on the Grand-Rue, the Maison aux Arcades was built in 1609 in High Renaissance style with a series of arched porches (arcades) anchored by two octagonal towers.

Maison Pfister. The Maison Pfister, built in 1537, is the most striking of Colmar's many old dwellings. Note the decorative frescoes and medallions, carved balcony, and ground-floor arcades. ✉ *11 rue Mercière.*

Musée Bartholdi (*Bartholdi Museum*). The Musée Bartholdi is the birthplace of Frédéric-Auguste Bartholdi (1834–1904), the sculptor who designed the Statue of Liberty. Exhibits of Bartholdi's works claim the ground floor; a reconstruction of the artist's Paris apartment and furniture are upstairs; and, in adjoining rooms, the creation of Lady Liberty is explored. ✉ *30 rue des Marchands* 🎬 *03–89–41–90–60* ⊕ *www. musee-bartholdi.com* 🎫*€5* ⊙ *Mar.–Dec., Wed.–Mon. 10–noon and 2–6.*

Fodor's Choice ★ **Musée d'Unterlinden.** The cultural highlight of Colmar is the Musée d'Unterlinden, once a medieval Dominican convent and hotbed of Rhenish mysticism. Its star attraction is one of the greatest altarpieces of the 16th century, the *Retable d'Issenheim* (1512–16), by Matthias Grünewald, which is majestically displayed in the convent's Gothic chapel. Originally painted for the convent at Issenheim, 22 km (14 miles) south of Colmar, the multi-panel work is either the last gasp of medievalism or a breathtaking preview of modernism and all its neuroses. Framed with two-sided wings that unfold to reveal the Crucifixion and Incarnation, the masterpiece includes depictions of the Annunciation, the Resurrection, and scenes from the life of St. Anthony, including a Temptation involving monsters that even outdo those of Hieronymous Bosch. Replete with raw realism (note the chamber pots, boil-covered bellies, and dirty linen), Grünewald's altarpiece was believed to have miraculous healing powers over ergotism: widespread in the Middle Ages, this malady was produced by the ingestion of fungus-ridden grains and caused its victims—many of whom were being nursed at

8

the Issenheim convent—to experience delusional, nearly hallucinogenic fantasies. Other treasures can be found around the enchanting 13th-century cloister, including arms and armor. Upstairs are fine regional furnishings and a collection of Rhine Valley paintings from the Renaissance, including Martin Schongauer's opulent 1470 altarpiece painted for Jean d'Orlier. There is a collection of contemporary and modern art as well; however, it will be closed to the public until an ongoing renovation project is completed in mid-2014. ✉ *1 rue Unterlinden* ☎ *03–89–20–15–50* 🌐 *www.musee-unterlinden.com* 🎫 *€8* 🕓 *May–Oct., daily 9–6; Nov.–Apr., Wed.–Mon. 9–noon and 2–5.*

WHERE TO EAT AND STAY

For expanded hotel reviews, visit Fodors.com.

$ FRENCH 🍴 **Au Koïfhus.** Not to be confused with the shabby little Koïfhus winstub on rue des Marchands, this popular landmark (the name means "customhouse") serves huge portions of regional standards, plus changing specialties: crayfish and grapefruit salad, coq au vin with spaetzle, and choucroute "Colmarienne" with six different meats. Appreciative tourists and canny locals contribute to the lively atmosphere. If you can cut a swath through this enthusiastic horde, choose between the big, open dining room, glowing with wood and warm fabric, and a shaded table on the broad, lovely square. [$] *Average main: €15* ✉ *2 pl. de l'Ancienne-Douane* ☎ *03–89–23–04–90* 🌐 *www.restaurant-koifhus-colmar.fr.*

$$ FRENCH 🍴 **Chez Hansi.** Named after the Norman Rockwell–like illustrator whose clog-wearing folk children adorn most of the souvenirs of Alsace, this hyper-traditional beamed tavern serves excellent down-home classics such as quiche Lorraine, choucroute, and pot-au-feu. Offerings are prepared and presented with a sophisticated touch, despite the friendly waitresses' folksy dirndls, and prices are surprisingly reasonable, given the quality of the food and the eatery's location in the Vielle Ville. [$] *Average main: €18* ✉ *23 rue des Marchands* ☎ *03–89–41–37–84* 🕓 *Closed Wed. and Thurs. and Jan.*

$$$$ FRENCH 🍴 **Le Rendez-vous de Chasse.** The stellar cuisine of Julien Binz is as refined, elegant, and chic as the decor of this opulent Renaissance mansion. It's well worth the wrangle to secure a table here, where some of the region's finest dishes are prepared with aplomb. An extensive cellar perfectly accents dishes like foie gras served with a truffle *gelée*, and lamb cooked in a nori (red seaweed) crust. [$] *Average main: €40* ✉ *7 pl. de la Gare* ☎ *03–89–41–10–10* ✍ *Reservations essential.*

$$ B&B/INN Fodor's Choice ★ 🏨 **Le Maréchal.** Built in 1565 in the fortified walls that encircle the Vieille Ville, this romantic, riverside inn is made up of a series of Renaissance houses lavished with glossy rafters, rich brocades, four-poster beds, Jacuzzis, and other extravagant details; a vivid color scheme—scarlet, sapphire, candy pink—further enhances the Vermeer-like atmosphere (for the full experience, request the Wagner or Bach rooms). **Pros:** pretty location; good food; amiable staff. **Cons:** some rooms are small and unimpressive; parking is difficult to find. [$] *Rooms from: €127* ✉ *4 pl. des Six-Montagnes-Noires* ☎ *03–89–41–60–32* 🌐 *www.hotel-le-marechal.com* 🛏 *30 rooms* 🍽 *Some meals*

BURGUNDY

WELCOME TO BURGUNDY

TOP REASONS TO GO

★ **Sip your way through Burgundy vineyards:** They are among the world's best, so take the time to stroll through Clos de Vougeot and really get a feel for the "terroir."

★ **Discover Dijon:** One of France's prettiest cities, with colorful banners and polished storefronts along narrow medieval streets, Dijon is perpetually being dolled up for a street fair.

★ **Relish the Romanesque:** Burgundy is home to a knee-weakening concentration of Romanesque churches, and Vézelay's Basilique has the region's greatest 12th-century sculptures.

★ **Get your viticultural and cultural fix in Beaune:** The "Capital of Caves" is famed for its wine caves and its 15th-century Flemish-style hospices.

★ **Be inspired by Cluny, "Light of the World":** Erstwhile center of a vast Christian empire and today a ruin, the sheer volume of this Romanesque abbey still impresses.

1 Northwest Burgundy. The northern part of Burgundy came under the sway of the medieval Paris-based Capetian kings, and the mighty Gothic cathedrals they built are still much in evidence, notably St-Étienne at Sens. Thirty-two kilometers (20 miles) to the east is Troyes, its charming half-timber houses adding to the appeal of a town overlooked by most air-conditioned bus tours. Southeast lies Auxerre, beloved for its steep, crooked streets and magnificent churches; the wine village of Chablis; and two great Renaissance châteaux, Tanlay and Ancy-le-Franc. Closer to Dijon are the great Cistercian abbey at Fontenay and the noted Romanesque basilica at Vézelay, with a delightful hilltop setting.

2 Dijon. Burgundy's only real city, Dijon became the capital of the duchy of Burgundy in the 11th century, and acquired most of its important architecture and art treasures during the 14th and 15th centuries under four Burgundian dukes. The churches, the ducal palace, and one of the finest art museums in France are evidence of their patronage. Other treasures are culinary, including the world's best *bœuf bourguignon*.

3 **Wine Country.** South of Dijon, follow the Côte d'Or, one of the most famous wine routes, south as it heads past the great wine villages of Clos de Vougeot and Nuits-St-Georges to Beaune, the heart of Burgundy's wine region. At the Hospices take in the great Rogier van der Weyden *Last Judgment* and the intimate cour d'honneur, the perfect postcard setting. Continuing south you'll find Autun, with renowned Roman ruins, and the Romanesque landmark of Cluny, once the largest Christian church until Rome's St. Peter's was built.

GETTING ORIENTED

Burgundy, on the main route from Paris to both the Riviera and Switzerland/Italy, has always had an excellent fast train service, with Dijon serving as the region's Grand Central Station. This lively city makes the best hub, enabling travelers to discover Burgundy's many spokes, perhaps with the help of local bus stations (which often conveniently hook up with train stations).

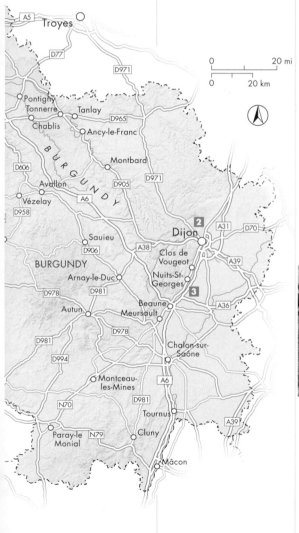

EATING AND DRINKING WELL IN BURGUNDY

In a land where glorious wines define both lifestyle and cuisine, you'll find savory, soul-warming dishes, from garlicky escargots to coq au vin, both of which pair beautifully with the local vintages.

Bœuf bourguignon is the ne plus ultra of Burgundian cuisine (*above*); wake up those taste buds with a Kir (*right, top*); escargots are regional delights (*right, bottom*).

While Burgundy's glittering wine trade imparts a sophisticated image to the region, Burgundy itself is basically prosperous farm country. Traditional cuisine here reflects the area's farm-centric soul, with lots of slow-cooked, wine-laced dishes. Distinctive farm-produced cheeses, such as the magnificent, odiferous Époisses, and the mild Cîteaux, made by Trappist monks, cap meals with rustic flourish. During a day of wine tasting in the Côte d'Or, dine at a traditional bistro to savor the *jambon persillé*, chunks of ham enrobed in a parsleyed aspic jelly, or a rich bœuf bourguignon. In summer, be sure to spend a morning at one of the region's bountiful weekend markets—maybe Saulieu on Saturday mornings. Afterward, enjoy a Charolais steak *à la moutarde* at a local café and raise a glass to the good life.

SOME LIKE IT HOT

Visit the 18th-century Maille mustard emporium at 32 rue de la Liberté to savor Dijon's world-famous mustards. Produced from stone-ground dried black or brown seeds macerated in *verjus* (the juice of unripe white grapes), these mustards accompany many dishes and heat up *lapin à la moutarde*, rabbit in mustard sauce. There is coarse-grained *à l'ancienne* or the classic, creamy, much hotter variety.

ESCARGOTS

Burgundy's plump snails, which grow wild in the vineyards, star on menus throughout the region. The signature preparation is *à la Bourguignonne*—simmered in white wine, stuffed with a garlicky parsley-shallot butter, and baked until bubbling. The delicacy is served in portions of six or eight on ceramic escargot dishes called *escargotières*, accompanied by tongs and a little fork.

Those immune to the true snail's charms may succumb to the luscious imposters made of solid chocolate and available at local candy shops and pâtisseries.

ÉPOISSES CHEESE

The greatest of Burgundian cheeses, the rich, earthy, cow's-milk Époisses is not for the faint of heart.

This assertive—yes, even odorous—cheese with the russet-hue rind develops its character from a daily scrubbing with marc-de-Bourgogne brandy as it ripens, a process that inhibits mold but encourages the growth of a particular bacteria necessary for the development of its creamy interior and distinctive flavor.

Go to the modest village of Époisses and buy your cheese from top producer Robert Berthaut. Caveat: transport in a tightly sealed container.

BŒUF À LA BOURGUIGNONNE

Burgundy is the birthplace of this beloved beef stew, aka bœuf bourguignonne, and no place on Earth makes it better.

A bottle or two of hearty red wine cooked down in the sauce is one secret to its success; the other is the region's prime Charolais beef.

The beef is braised with wine, onions, bacon, and mushrooms, turning tender as the sauce reduces and intensifies.

Other wine-soaked specialties here include coq au vin and *œufs en meurette*—eggs poached in red wine.

KIR

This rosy and refreshing aperitif, combining an inexpensive white wine called *aligoté* with a dose of crème de cassis (black-currant liqueur), was dubbed a "Kir" during World War II when the Resistance hero and mayor of Dijon, Canon Félix Kir, began promoting the drink to boost local sales of cassis liqueur.

Traditionally made, the Kir has four to five parts dry white wine to one part crème de cassis. In the Kir's aristocratic cousin, the Kir Royale, Champagne replaces the wine.

9

Updated by
Lyn Parry

Producing a rarefied concentration of what many consider the world's greatest wines and harboring a sigh-worthy collection of magnificent Romanesque abbeys, Burgundy hardly needs to be beautiful—but it is. Its green-hedgerowed countryside, medieval villages, and stellar vineyards deserve to be rolled on the palate and savored. Like glasses filled with Clos de Vougeot, the sights here—from the stately city of Dijon to the medieval sanctuaries of Sens, Auxerre, Vézelay, and Cluny—invite us to tarry and partake of their mellow splendor.

Although you may often fall under the influence of extraordinary wine during a sojourn in Burgundy—called *Bourgogne* by the French—the beauty surrounding you will be no boozy illusion. Passed over by revolutions, left unscarred by world wars, and relatively inaccessible thanks to circuitous country roads, the region still reflects the lovely pastoral prosperity it enjoyed under the Capetian kings. Those were the glory days, when self-sufficient Burgundy held its own against the creeping spread of France and the mighty Holy Roman Empire. This grand period was characterized by the expanding role of the dukes of Bourgogne. Consider these Capetians, history-book celebrities all: there was Philippe le Hardi (the Bold), with his power-brokered marriage to Marguerite of Flanders. There was Jean sans Peur (the Fearless), who murdered Louis d'Orléans in a cloak-and-dagger affair in 1407 and was in turn murdered, in 1419. And then there was Philippe le Bon (the Good), who threw in with the English against Joan of Arc.

Yet the Capetians couldn't hold a candle to the great Abbaye de Cluny: founded in 910, it grew to such overweening ecclesiastical power that it dominated the European Church on a papal scale for some four centuries. It was Urban II himself who dubbed it "*la Lumière du Monde*" ("the Light of the World"). But the stark geometry of

Burgundy's Cistercian abbeys, such as Clairvaux and Cîteaux, stands in silent rebuke to Cluny's excess. The basilicas at Autun and Vézelay remain today in all their noble simplicity, yet manifest some of the finest Romanesque sculpture ever created; the tympanum at Autun rejects all time frames in its visionary daring.

It's almost unfair to the rest of France that all this history, all this art, all this natural beauty comes with delicious refreshments. As if to live up to the extraordinary quality of its Chablis, its Chassagne-Montrachet, its Nuits-St-Georges, its Gevrey-Chambertin, Burgundy flaunts some of the best plain food in the world. Once you taste a licensed and diploma'd *poulet de Bresse* (Bresse chicken) embellished by the poetry of one perfect glass of Burgundian Pinot Noir, you won't be surprised to see that food and drink entries will take up as much space in your travel diary as the sights you see.

PLANNER

WHEN TO GO
Whenever it's gray and cloudy in Paris, chances are the sun is shining in Burgundy. Situated in the heart of France, Burgundy has warm, dry summers. The climate in spring and fall isn't quite as idyllic, with a mixture of sun and scattered showers. The winter months vary from year to year, and although snow is not common, freezing temperatures mean the bare vines and trees are covered with a soft white hue. Layers of clothing are always advisable, so you're ready for cooler mornings and hotter afternoons. Waterproof outer layers are wise on longer day trips if the weather forecast is changeable. May in Burgundy is lovely, as are September and October, when the sun is still warm on the shimmering golden trees, and the grapes, now ready for harvesting, are scenting the air with anticipation. This is when the vines are colorful and the *caves* (cellars) are open for business. Many festivals also take place around this time.

PLANNING YOUR TIME
France's prime preoccupations with food and wine are nowhere better celebrated than in Burgundy. Though it might sound glib, the best way to experience the region is to stay for as long as possible because there is so much to see and do here. If you want to go bike riding, the obvious place to set up is Beaune. If, on the other hand, you're an amateur medieval art historian or are interested in the lesser-known wines of Irancy, Chitry, and Tonnerre, base yourself at Auxerre or Vézelay in northern Burgundy. This will allow you to focus on these pursuits while also visiting vineyards, the cathedral of Sens, and (on a northward detour) the elegant, delightful town of Troyes. If you prefer the conveniences of modern cities but also want a taste of medieval Burgundy, then Dijon offers you the best of both worlds. Burgundy's capital has all the charm of another era and all the functionality of a major metropolis. It's the gateway to the Côte d'Or, as well as the perfect place to set off for exploring the back roads of Burgundy.

GETTING HERE AND AROUND

Burgundy, whose northern perimeter begins 75 km (50 miles) from Paris, is one of the largest regions in France. It's sliced in half by the north–south A6, so it's generally quicker to move in this direction than from west to east or vice versa. But a vast network of secondary roads makes travel from city to city or even village to village both practical and picturesque.

BUS TRAVEL

Local bus services are extensive; where the biggest private companies, **Les Rapides de Bourgogne** and **TRANSCO**, do not venture, the national SNCF routes often do. TRANSCO's No. 44 bus travels through the Côte d'Or wine region, connecting Dijon to Beaune (1 hr) via Vougeot (40 mins) and Nuits-St-Georges (47 mins), all trips costing €1.50. The buses of Les Rapides de Bourgogne connect Auxerre to Chablis (20 mins), Pontigny (20 mins), and Sens (90 mins), all trips costing €2.50. The No. 7 bus from Chalon-sur-Saône's train station takes you over to Cluny.

It's hard to reach Vézelay: the best bet may be to train it to nearby Sermizelles, then catch the bus, which runs twice daily. To get to Avallon and Saulieu, take a train to Montbard, a TGV station stop, and then get a bus to either town. Always inquire at the local tourist office for timetables and ask your hotel concierge for information.

Bus Information Les Rapides de Bourgogne ✉ *3 rue des Fontenottes, Auxerre* ☎ *03–86–94–95–00* ⊕ *www.rapidesdebourgogne.com.* **TRANSCO** ✉ *Gare Routière, 15 Cour de la Gare, Dijon* ☎ *03–80–11–29–29 toll-free from landline* ⊕ *www.mobigo-bourgogne.com/.*

CAR TRAVEL

Although bus lines do service smaller towns, traveling through Burgundy by car allows you to explore its meandering country roads at leisure. A6 is the main route through the region; it heads southeast from Paris through Burgundy, past Sens, Auxerre, Chablis, Saulieu, and Beaune, continuing on to Lyon and the south. A38 links A6 to Dijon, 290 km (180 miles) from Paris; the trip takes around three hours. A31 heads down from Dijon to Beaune, a distance of 45 km (27 miles). D974 is the slower, more scenic route of the two, but if it's scenery you want, D122 is the Route des Grands Crus, which reads like a wine list as it meanders through every wine village. The uncluttered A5 links Paris to Troyes, where the A31 segues south to Dijon.

TRAIN TRAVEL

The TGV zips from Paris (Gare de Lyon) to Dijon (1hr, 30 mins; €42–€62) up to 15 times a day, and to Mâcon (1 hr, 30 mins; €57–€77) six times a day. Some TGVs stop at Le Creusot, between Chalon and Autun, 90 minutes from Paris—from here, you can hop on a bus for a 45-minute ride to Autun.

There's also TGV service direct from Roissy Airport to Dijon (1 hr, 40 mins). Beaune is well serviced by trains arriving from Dijon, Lyon, and Paris. Sens is on a main-line route from Paris (60 mins). The region has two local train routes: one linking Sens, Dijon, Beaune, Chalon, Tournus, and Mâcon and the other connecting Auxerre, Saulieu, and

9

Autun. If you want to get to smaller towns or to vineyards, use bus routes or a car.

Train Information SNCF ☎ *36–35 [€0.34 per min]* ⊕ *www.voyages-sncf.com.* **TGV** ☎ *36–35 [€0.34 per min]* ⊕ *www.tgv.com.*

RESTAURANTS

For many French people, mention of Burgundy's capital, Dijon, conjures up images of round, rosy, merry men enjoying large suppers of *bœuf à la Bourguignonne* and red wine. And admittedly, chances are that in any decent restaurant you can find at least one Dijonnais true to the stereotype.

Dijon ranks with Lyon as the gastronomic capital of France, and Burgundy's hearty traditions help explain why. It all began in the early 15th century when Jean, Duc de Berry, arrived here, built a string of castles, and proceeded to make food, wine, and art top priorities for his courtiers. Today, Parisian gourmands consider a three-hour drive a small price to pay for the cuisine of Burgundy's best restaurants, such as L'Espérance in Vézelay, Le Pré aux Clercs and Stéphane Derbord in Dijon, and Relais Bernard Loiseau in Saulieu.

These days, Dijon is not quite the wine–mustard capital of the world it used to be, but the happy fact remains that mustard finds its way into many regional specialties, including the sauce that usually accompanies *andouillette*, a fabled sausage made with pork chitterlings (intestine). Other sausages—notably the *rosette du Morvan* and others served with a potato puree—are great favorites. Game, freshwater trout, coq au vin, *poulet au Meursault* (chicken in white wine sauce), snails, and, of course, *bœuf à la Bourguignonne* (incidentally, this dish is only called *bœuf bourguignon* when you are *not* in Burgundy) also number among the region's specialties.

The queen of chickens is the *poulet de Bresse,* which hails from east of the Côte d'Or and can be as pricey as a bottle of fine wine. Ham is a big item, especially around Easter, when garlicky *jambon persillé*— ham boiled with pig's trotters and served cold in jellied white wine and parsley—often tops the menu. Also look for *saupiquet des Amognes*—a Morvan delight of hot braised ham served with a spicy cream sauce. As for desserts, *pain d'épices* (gingerbread) is the dessert staple of the region. And, like every other part of France, Burgundy has its own cheeses. The Abbaye de Cîteaux, birthplace of Cistercian monasticism, has produced its mild cheese for centuries. Chaource and hearty Époisses also melt in your mouth—as do Bleu de Bresse and Meursault.

Prices in the reviews are the average cost of a main course at dinner or, if dinner is not served, at lunch.

HOTELS

This is perhaps one of the best-served regions of France in terms of lodging, and the vast range includes everything from simple *gîtes d'étape* (bed-and-breakfasts) to four-star châteaux. But Burgundy is often overrun with tourists, especially in summer, so finding accommodations can be a problem. It's wise to make advance reservations—particularly if you're bound for wine country (from Dijon to Beaune).

Prices in the reviews are the lowest cost of a standard double room in high season.

VISITOR INFORMATION

Comité Régional du Tourisme de Bourgogne ⊠ *5 av. Garibaldi, Dijon* ☎ *03–80–28–02–80* ⊕ *www.burgundy-tourism.com.*

Dijon Tourist Office ⊠ *11 rue des Forges, Dijon* ☎ *08–92–70–05–58 [€0.34 per min]* ⊕ *www.visitdijon.com.*

Local tourist offices are listed under their respective towns in this chapter.

NORTHWEST BURGUNDY

If you're arriving in Burgundy from Paris by car, we suggest you grand-tour it from Sens to Autun. In northern Burgundy, the accents are thinner than around Dijon, and sunflowers cover the countryside instead of vineyards. Near Auxerre, many small, unheard-of villages boast a château or a once-famous abbey; they happily see few tourists, partly because public transportation is more than a bit spotty. Highlights of northern Burgundy include Sens's great medieval cathedral, historic Troyes, Auxerre's Flamboyant Gothic cathedral, the great Romanesque sculptures of the basilica at Vézelay, and the cathedral at Autun. Outside these major centers of northwest Burgundy, countryside villages are largely preserved in a rural landscape that seems to have remained the same for centuries. If you're driving down from Paris, we suggest you take the A6 into Burgundy (or alternatively the A5 direct to Troyes) before making a scenic clockwise loop around the Parc du Morvan, an imposing nature reserve—and the closest mountain range to Paris—dense with lush forests and laced with an extensive network of lakes and rivers.

9

SENS

112 km (70 miles) southeast of Paris on D606.

Sens may be world famous for its spectacular cathedral but it also has a reputation as a very pretty town. It enjoys a "four-leaf" ranking as a *ville fleurie*, or floral city. This finds full botanical expression in the excellently manicured city parks (the Moulin à Tan and the square Jean-Cousin) and municipal greenhouses, as well as during the Fête de la Saint-Fiacre, named after the patron saint of gardeners. For the latter, on the second Sunday in September, everything and everyone are festooned with flowers as entertainment fills the streets. But anytime during the year, the great **Cathédrale St-Étienne** makes a trip here worthwhile.

GETTING HERE

It makes sense for Sens to be your first stop in Burgundy, because it's only 90 minutes by car from Paris on the D606, a fast road that hugs the pretty Yonne Valley south of Fontainebleau. Training in and out of Sens is a breeze as it's on a major route with 27 direct TER trains (€18.80) leaving the Paris Gare de Bercy train station on weekdays and 23 on weekends. TER trains from Paris Gare de Bercy can take

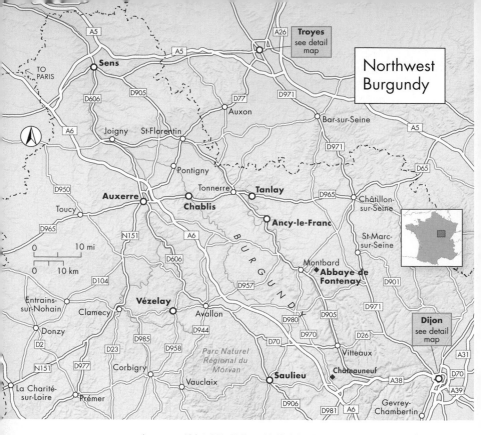

you to Auxerre (€26.90), Dijon (€42.80), Beaune (€54.30), and many points between. Avallon (€33) can be reached directly three times a day, leaving Paris at 8:38 am, 12:38 pm, and 4:31 pm. The regional Trans-Yonne bus network, in conjunction with Les Rapides de Bourgogne (☎ 03–86–64–83–91 ⊕ *www.rapidesdebourgogne.com*), runs a noon link from the SNCF station in Sens to Auxerre on Wednesday and on demand on Saturday (☎ *0800–303–309 for information and mandatory reservation with TransYonne*).

Visitor Information Sens Tourist Office ⊠ *Pl. Jean-Jaurès* ☎ *03–86–65–19–49* ⊕ *www.office-de-tourisme-sens.com.*

EXPLORING

Fodor's Choice ★ **Cathédrale St-Étienne.** Historically linked more with Paris than with Burgundy, Sens was for centuries the ecclesiastical center of France and is still dominated by its Cathédrale St-Étienne, once the French sanctuary for Thomas à Becket and a model for England's Canterbury Cathedral. You can see the cathedral's 240-foot south tower from miles away. As you draw near, the pompous 19th-century buildings lining the town's narrow main street—notably the meringue-like Hôtel de Ville—can give you a false impression: the streets leading off it near the cathedral (notably rue Abelard and rue Jean-Cousin) are full of half-timber medieval houses. On Monday the cathedral square is crowded with merchants' stalls, and the beautiful late-19th-century market hall—a distant cousin of Baltard's former iron-and-glass Halles in Paris—throbs with people buying meat and produce. A smaller market is held on Friday morning.

Begun around 1140, the cathedral once had two towers; one was topped in 1532 by an elegant though somewhat incongruous Renaissance campanile that contains two monster bells; the other collapsed in the 19th century. Note the trefoil arches decorating the exterior of the remaining tower. The gallery, with statues of former archbishops of Sens, is a 19th-century addition, but the statue of St. Stephen, between the doors of the central portal, is thought to date from late in the 12th century. The vast, harmonious interior is justly renowned for its stained-glass windows; the oldest (circa 1200) are in the north transept and include the stories of the Good Samaritan and the Prodigal Son; those in the south transept were manufactured in 1500 in Troyes and include a much-admired *Tree of Jesse.* Stained-glass windows in the north of the chancel retrace the story of Thomas à Becket: Becket fled to Sens from England to escape the wrath of Henry II before returning to his cathedral in Canterbury, where he was murdered in 1170. Below the window (which shows him embarking on his journey in a boat, and also at the moment of his death) is a medieval statue of an archbishop said to have come from the site of Becket's home in Sens. Years of restoration work have permitted the display of Becket's *aube* (vestment) in the annex to the Palais Synodal. ⊠ *Pl. de la République* ☏ *03–86–65–06–57* ☉ *Daily 8–6 (until 7 in summer).*

Palais Synodal (*Synodal Palace*). The roof of the 13th-century Palais Synodal, alongside Sens's cathedral, is notable for its yellow, green, and red diamond-tile motif—incongruously added in the mid-19th century by monument restorer Viollet-le-Duc. Six grand windows and the vaulted Synodal Hall are outstanding architectural features; the building now functions as an exhibition space. Annexed to the Palais is an ensemble of Renaissance buildings with a courtyard offering a fine view of the cathedral's Flamboyant Gothic south transept, constructed by master stonemason Martin Chambiges at the start of the 16th century (rose windows were his specialty, as you can appreciate here). Inside is a museum with archaeological finds from the Gallo-Roman period. The cathedral treasury, now on the museum's second floor, is one of the richest in France, comparable to that of Conques. It contains a collection of miters, ivories, the shrouds of St. Sivard and St. Loup, and sumptuous reliquaries. But the star of the collection is Thomas à Becket's restored brown-and-silver-edged linen robe. His chasuble, stole, and sandals are too fragile to display. ⊠ *Pl. de la République* ☏ *03–86–64–46–22, 03–86–83–88–90 museum info* ⊠ *€4.20* ☉ *June and Sept., Wed.–Mon. 10–noon and 2–6; July and Aug., Wed.–Mon. 10–6; Oct.–May, Wed. and weekends 10–noon and 2–6, Mon., Thurs., and Fri. 2–6.*

WHERE TO EAT AND STAY

For expanded hotel reviews, visit Fodors.com.

$$$
MODERN FRENCH
✗**Clos des Jacobins.** At this popular restaurant in the center of town, done in shades of chocolate and taupe, the balance between elegant and casual finds expression in the wide choice of dishes on offer. The upscale

Home to a famous cathedral, Sens also has many streets leading to atmospheric half-timber houses.

à la carte menu is replete with exceptional fish specialties, while La Tradition menu, served only during the week, includes a *terrine de la mer tiède et sa crème de Chablis* (warm seafood terrine with a Chablis cream sauce) and *joues de porc aux abricots secs s et sa petite semoule* (pig cheeks with dried apricots and savory semolina). $ *Average main: €25* ✉ *49 Grande-Rue* ☎ *03–86–95–29–70* ⊕ *www.restaurantlesjacobins. com* ⚑ *Reservations essential* ⊗ *Closed Wed. No dinner Sun. or Tues.*

$
HOTEL
⌂ **Paris & Poste.** At this inn, which began life as a canon's house in 1776, guest rooms are clean, spacious, and well equipped—plus most open onto a patio (No. 42 is especially nice). **Pros:** unbeatable value; central location; great food. **Cons:** rooms get some early-morning street noise. $ *Rooms from: €95* ✉ *97 rue de la République* ☎ *03–86–65– 17–43* 🖷 *03–86–64–48–45* ⊕ *www.hotel-paris-poste.com* ⚑ *30 rooms* ¶⊙ *Some meals.*

TROYES

64 km (40 miles) east of Sens, 150 km (95 miles) southeast of Paris.

The inhabitants of Troyes would be dismayed if you mistook them for Burgundians. Troyes is the historic capital of the counts of Champagne but is, as the crow—if not this book—flies, some 80 km (50 miles) south of the heart of Champagne province, so we retain it here, closer to Burgundy's treasures. Troyes was also the home of the late-12th-century writer Chrétien (or Chrestien) de Troyes who, in seeking to please his patrons, Count Henry the Liberal and Marie de Champagne, penned the first Arthurian legends. Few, if any, other French town centers contain so much to see. In the Vauluisant and St-Jean districts, a web of enchanting pedestrian streets with timber-frame houses, magnificent churches, fine museums, and a wide choice of restaurants makes the Old Town—Vieux Troyes—especially appealing.

GETTING HERE

With the first train at 6:42 am, and then around one every hour until 10:12 pm, you can get to Troyes in about 90 minutes from Paris Gare de l'Est for the princely sum of €25.90 or less. Sens to Troyes is a little harder, with trains at 10:34 am, 2:34 pm, 3:34 pm, and 6:34 pm, which involve changing in Laroche Migennes or Saint Florentin Vergigny. The journey takes almost three hours and costs €18.90.

Visitor Information Troyes Tourist Office ✉ *16 bd. Carnot ✛ next to SNCF station* ☎ *03–25–82–62–70* 🖷 *03–25–73–06–81* ⊕ *www.tourisme-troyes.com* ✉ *Rue Mignard* ☎ *03–25–73–36–88* ⊙ *May–Oct.*

EXPLORING

Troyes is divided by the quai Dampierre, a broad, busy thoroughfare. On one side is the quiet cathedral quarter, on the other the more upbeat commercial part. Keep your eyes peeled for the delightful architectural accents that make Troyes unique: *essentes*, geometric chestnut tiles that keep out humidity and are fire resistant; and sculpted *poteaux* (in Troyes they are called *montjoies*), carvings at the joint of corner structural beams. There's a lovely one of Adam and Eve next door to the Comtes de Champagne hotel. Along with its neighbors Provins and Bar-sur-Aube, Troyes was one of Champagne's major fair towns in the Middle Ages. The wool trade gave way to cotton in the 18th century when Troyes became the heartland of hosiery; today Troyes draws millions of shoppers from all over Europe, who come to scour for bargains at its outlet clothing stores.

Tourist Office. The dynamic tourist office has information and sells €12 passes in the form of coupons that admit you to the town's major museums with a couple of glasses of champagne or prunelle, a local *eau de vie*, thrown in. It also offers three theme-based state-of-the-art GPS audio guides (€4). *See the tourism website for further information on all the museums listed below.* ✉ *16 bd. Carnot* ☎ *03–25–82–62–70* ⊕ *www.tourisme-troyes.com.*

TOP ATTRACTIONS

Basilique St-Urbain. Started in 1261 and eventually consecrated in 1389 by Pope Urban IV (a native son), St-Urbain is one of the most remarkable churches in France, a perfect culmination of the Gothic quest to replace stone walls with stained glass. Its narrow porch frames a 13th-century *Last Judgment* tympanum, whose highly worked elements include a frieze of the dead rising out of their coffins (witness the grimacing skeleton) and an enormous crayfish (a testament to the local river culture). Inside, a chapel on the south side houses the *Vièrge au Raisin* (*Virgin with Grapes*), clutching Jesus with one hand and a bunch of champagne grapes in the other. ✉ *Pl. Vernie* ☎ *03–25–73–37–13* 🎫 *Free* ⊙ *May–Sept., Mon.–Sat. 10–12:30 and 2–7, Sun. 2–7; Oct.–Apr., Mon.–Sat. 9:30–12:30 and 2–5, Sun. 2–5.*

Cathédrale St-Pierre St-Paul. Noted monument of Flamboyant Gothic—a style regarded as the last gasp of the Middle Ages—this remarkable

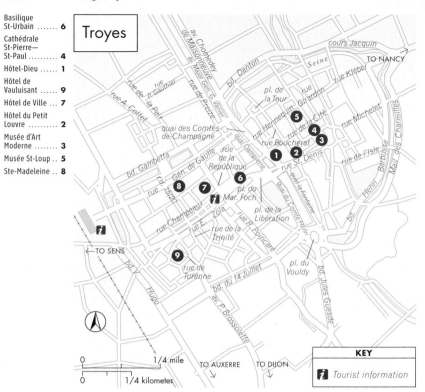

cathedral dominates the heart of Troyes; note the incomplete single-tower west front, the small Renaissance campaniles on top of the tower, and the artistry of Martin Chambiges, who worked on Troyes's facade (with its characteristic large rose window and flamboyant flames) around the same time as he did the transept of Sens. At night the floodlighted features burst into dramatic relief. The cathedral's vast five-aisle interior, refreshingly light thanks to large windows and the near-whiteness of the local stone, dates mainly from the 13th century. It has fine examples of 13th-century stained glass in the choir, such as the *Tree of Jesse* (a popular regional theme), and richly colored 16th-century glass in the nave and west front rose window. ⊠ *Pl. St-Pierre* ☎ *03–25–76–98–18* ✆ *Free* ☉ *May–Sept., Mon.–Sat. 10–1 and 2–7; Oct.–Apr., Mon.–Sat. 9–noon and 1–5, Sun. 2–5.*

Musée d'Art Moderne (*Modern Art Museum*). Housed in the 16th- to 17th-century bishop's palace, this museum's magnificent interior features a wreath-and-cornucopia carved oak fireplace, ceilings with carved wood beams, and a Renaissance staircase. The jewel of the museum is the Lévy Collection (one of the finest provincial collections in France), which includes Art Deco glassware, tribal art, and an important group of Fauve paintings by André Derain and others. ⊠ *Palais Épiscopal, pl. St-Pierre* ☎ *03–25–76–26–80* ✆ *€5* ☉ *May–Sept., Tues.–Fri. 10–1* *and 2–7, weekends 11–7; Oct.–Apr., Tues.–Fri. 10–noon and 2–5, weekends 11–6.*

Musée St-Loup. The former 18th-century abbey of St-Loup to the side of the cathedral now houses this arts and antiquities museum, which has a superlative collection of old-master paintings. Works from the 15th to the 19th century include paintings by Peter Paul Rubens, Anthony Van Dyck, Antoine Watteau, François Boucher, and Jacques-Louis David. Other exhibits are devoted to natural history, with impressive collections of birds and meteorites; local archaeological finds, especially gold-mounted 5th-century jewelry and a Gallo-Roman bronze statue of Apollo; and medieval statuary and gargoyles. ⊠ *1 rue Chrestien-de-Troyes* ☎ *03–25–76–21–68* 🖼 *€4* ☉ *May–Sept., Mon. and Wed.–Fri. 10–1 and 2–7, weekends 11–7; Oct.–Apr., Mon. and Wed.–Fri. 10–noon and 2–5, weekends 11–6.*

A TOWN MADE FOR WALKERS

The tourist literature is quick to tell you that Troyes's Old Town resembles a Champagne cork: the Seine flows around what would be the top half and the train station is at the bottom. Though large for a cork, Troyes is small for a town. Everything is accessible by foot—although you can hop a TCAT bus (⊕ *www.tcat.fr*) to get around if you wish.

Ste-Madeleine. The oldest church in Troyes, Ste-Madeleine is best known for its elaborate triple-arch stone rood screen separating the nave and the choir. Only six other such screens still remain in France—most were dismantled during the French Revolution. This filigreed Flamboyant Gothic beauty was carved with panache by Jean Gailde between 1508 and 1517. The superbly tranquil Garden of the Innocents, newly established on the ancient "children's graveyard," symbolizes medieval spirituality. ⊠ *Rue de la Madeleine* ☎ *03–25–73–82–90* 🖼 *Free* ☉ *May–Sept., Mon.–Sat. 10–12:30 and 2–7, Sun. 2–7; Oct.–Apr., Mon.–Sat. 9:30–12:30 and 2–5, Sun. 2–5.*

WORTH NOTING

FAMILY **Hôtel de Vauluisant.** This charmingly turreted 16th- to 17th-century mansion contains two museums: the **Musée d'Art Champenois** (Regional Art Museum) and the **Musée de la Bonneterie** (Textile-Hosiery Museum). The former traces the development of Troyes and southern Champagne, with a particularly rich selection of religious sculptures and paintings of the late-Gothic era; the latter outlines the history and manufacturing procedures of the town's 18th- to 19th-century textile industry. ⊠ *4 rue de Vauluisant* ☎ *03–25–43–43–20* 🖼 *Joint ticket for both museums €3* ☉ *May–Sept., Wed. 2–7, Thurs. and Fri. 10–1 and 2–7, weekends 11–1 and 2–7; Oct.–Apr., Wed. and Thurs. 2–5, Fri.–Sun. 10–noon and 2–5.*

Hôtel de Ville (*Town Hall*). Place du Maréchal-Foch, the main square of Troyes, is flanked by cafés, shops, and this delightful town hall. The central facade has black marble columns and a niche with a helmeted Minerva, which replaced a statue of Louis XIV that was destroyed during the French Revolution. In summer the square is filled with people from morning to night. ⊠ *Pl. du Maréchal-Foch.*

9

Hôtel-Dieu (*Hospital*). Across the Bassin de la Préfecture, an arm of the Seine, is this historic hospital, fronted by superb 18th-century wrought-iron gates topped with the blue-and-gold fleurs-de-lis emblems of the French monarchy. Around the corner is the entrance to the **Apothicairerie de l'Hôtel-Dieu,** a former medical laboratory, the only part of the Hôtel-Dieu open to visitors. Inside, time has been suspended: floral-painted boxes and ceramic jars containing medicinal plants line the antique shelves. ✉ *Quai des Comtes de Champagne* ☎ *03–25–80–98–97* 🎟 *€2* 🕒 *May–Sept., Wed. 2–7, Thurs. and Fri. 10–1 and 2–7, weekends 11–1 and 2–7; Oct.–Apr., Wed. and Thurs. 2–5, Fri.–Sun. 10–noon and 2–5.*

Hôtel du Petit Louvre. This former coaching inn is a handsome example of 16th-century architecture. ✉ *Pl. du Préau.*

WHERE TO EAT AND STAY

For expanded hotel reviews, visit Fodors.com.

$$ BRASSERIE 🍴 **Le Bistroquet.** Everything here is authentic, from the splendid Belle Époque decor to the rustic homemade cuisine. The two- and three-course dinner menus offer a choice of brasserie classics, including homemade pâté, homemade blood sausage brochettes, and a crack at the infamous, local delicacy: a homemade AAAAA andouillette sausage—the acronym stands for Association Amicale des Amateurs d'Andouillette Authentique (Amicable Association of Lovers of Authentic Andouillette), a very select designation. Although andouillette (made with pork intestines) is an acquired taste, it's one well worth acquiring, and is made especially well here. Desserts are equally imposing, including the all-you-can-eat chocolate mousse. [$] *Average main: €18* ✉ *10 rue Louis Ulbach* ☎ *03–25–73–65–65* 🌐 *www.bistroquet-troyes.fr* 🕒 *No dinner Sun. Closed Sun. end of July–mid Sept.*

$ HOTEL 🏨 **Comtes de Champagne.** In Vieux Troyes's topsy-turvy 16th-century former mint, this bargain find has a quaint inner courtyard and pleasant, refurbished rooms with iron bedsteads. **Pros:** good value; old-fashioned charm; central location. **Cons:** bathrooms are a bit spartan and small; no air-conditioning. [$] *Rooms from: €70* ✉ *54–56 rue de la Monnaie* ☎ *03–25–73–11–70* 🌐 *www.comtesdechampagne.com* 🛏 *29 rooms, 6 suites.*

$$$ HOTEL Fodor's Choice ★ 🏨 **Le Champ des Oiseaux.** Tin chandeliers, Nantes silk and calico hangings, antique scrollwork panels, and other traditional luxe touches make lodgings in this trio of vine-clad pink-and-yellow 15th- and 16th-century houses especially alluring. **Pros:** quiet, comfortable rooms; friendly service; kid friendly. **Cons:** breakfast and parking cost extra. [$] *Rooms from: €189* ✉ *20 rue Linard-Gonthier* ☎ *03–25–80–58–50* 📠 *03–25–80–98–34* 🌐 *www.champdesoiseaux.com* 🛏 *9 rooms, 3 suites* 🍽 *Breakfast.*

$ HOTEL 🏨 **Relais St-Jean.** In this half-timber hotel, in the pedestrian zone near the church of St-Jean, good-size rooms are refreshingly done in a sleek modern style, with white-and-pastel-color walls that contrast tastefully with sophisticated, multihued furnishings. **Pros:** good-size rooms; friendly service; interesting bar. **Cons:** rooms sometimes feel overheated and some get street noise; breakfast is extra. [$] *Rooms from: €95* ✉ *51 rue Paillot-de-Montabert* ☎ *03–25–73–89–90* 🌐 *www.relais-st-jean.com* 🛏 *24 rooms.*

AUXERRE

21 km (13 miles) southwest of Pontigny, 58 km (36 miles) southeast of Sens.

Fodor'sChoice
★

Auxerre is a beautifully evocative town with three imposing and elegant churches perched above the Yonne River. Its steep, undulating streets are full of photogenic, half-timber houses in every imaginable style and shape. Yet this harmonious, architecturally interesting town is underappreciated, perhaps because of its location, midway between Paris and Dijon.

GETTING HERE

Auxerre is quite easily reached by rail from Gare Paris-Bercy: seven direct trains (€26.90) depart daily, leaving roughly every two hours from 6:13 am to 8:38 pm. Five trains a day put Sermizelles-Vézelay (€8) less than one hour away, and from there you can connect to Vézelay proper by taxi (☎ *03–86–32–31–88*) during the week or by bus any day. Twelve daily trains link Auxerre to Montbard (€17.30), mostly via Laroche-Migennes, with Dijon at the end of the line (€7.20). The TransYonne bus network (Les Rapides de Bourgogne) links Auxerre to Sens, Avallon, and Tonnerre with a daily service. Chablis can be reached daily at 11:45 am, 4:15 pm (both on request only ☎ *0800–303–309*), and 5:55 pm by bus from the SNCF station.

If you're driving, Auxerre is served by several major arteries, including the A6 autoroute (Autoroute of the Sun) and the N6 (National 6).

Visitor Information Auxerre Tourist Office ✉ *1 quai de la République* ☎ *03–86–52–06–19* ⊕ *www.ot-auxerre.fr.*

EXPLORING

Fanning out from Auxerre's main square, **place des Cordeliers** (just up from the cathedral), are a number of venerable, crooked streets lined with half-timber and stone houses. The best way to see them is to start from the riverside on the quai de la République, where you can find the tourist office (and pick up a handy local map); then continue along the quai de la Marine. The medieval arcaded gallery of the **Ancien Evêché** (Old Bishop's Palace), now an administrative building, is just visible on the hillside beside the tourist office. At **9 rue de la Marine** (which leads off one of several riverside squares) are the two oldest houses in Auxerre, dating from the end of the 14th century. Continue up the hill to rue de l'Yonne, which leads into the **rue Cochois.** Here, at No. 23, is the higgledy-piggledy home and shop of a *maître verrier* (lead-glass maker). Closer to the center of town, the most beautiful of Auxerre's many *poteaux* (the carved tops of wooden corner posts) can be seen at **8 rue Joubert.** The building dates from the late 15th century, and its Gothic tracery windows, acorns, and oak leaves are an open-air masterpiece.

Abbaye de St-Germain. North of place des Cordeliers is the former Abbaye de St-Germain, which stands parallel to the cathedral some 300 yards away. The church's earliest aboveground section is the 12th-century Romanesque bell tower, but the extensive underground crypt was inaugurated by Charles the Bald in 859 and contains its original Carolingian frescoes and Ionic capitals. It's the only monument of its

9

kind in Europe—a labyrinth retaining the plan of the long-gone church built above it—and was a place of pilgrimage until Huguenots burned the remains of its namesake, a Gallo-Roman governor and bishop of Auxerre, in the 16th century. ✉ *Pl. St-Germain* ☎ *03–86–18–02–90* 🎟 *€6 crypt* 🕐 *May–Sept., Wed.–Mon. 9:45–6:45; Oct.–Apr., Wed.–Mon. 10–noon and 2–5. Closed Tues.*

> **A MAP IS A MUST**
>
> Get a map from the tourist office because Auxerre's layout is confusing. The main part of the Old Town is west of the Yonne River and *ripples* out from place des Cordeliers.

Cathédrale St-Étienne. The town's dominant feature is the ascending line of three magnificent churches—St-Pierre, St-Étienne, and St-Germain—with the Cathédrale St-Étienne, in the middle, rising majestically above the squat houses around it. The 13th-century choir, the oldest part of the edifice, contains its original stained glass, dominated by brilliant reds and blues. Beneath the choir, the frescoed 11th-century Romanesque crypt keeps company with the treasury, which has a panoply of medieval enamels, manuscripts, and miniatures plus a rare depiction of Christ on horseback. A 75-minute son-et-lumière show focusing on Roman Gaul is presented every evening from June to September. ✉ *Pl. St-Étienne* ☎ *03–86–52–23–29* ⊕ *www.cathedrale-auxerre.com* 🎟 *Crypt €3, treasury €1.90* 🕐 *Easter–Nov., Mon.–Sat. 7:30–6, Sun. 2–5; Dec.–Easter, Mon.–Sat. 10–5.*

WHERE TO EAT AND STAY

For expanded hotel reviews, visit Fodors.com.

$$$$

MODERN FRENCH

✕ **Le Jardin Gourmand.** This restaurant in a former manor house has a pretty garden (*jardin*) where you can dine on summer evenings as well as an organic vegetable garden producing fresh herbs, gorgeous greens, and other foods that wind up on the table. The interior, accented by subtle-yellow panels and polished wooden floors, is congenial and elegant, while the menu, which changes eight times a year, shows both flair and invention, drawing inspiration from the finest, seasonal ingredients and an excellent cellar. The staff is discreet and friendly. $ *Average main: €38* ✉ *56 bd. Vauban* ☎ *03–86–51–53–52* ⊕ *www.lejardingourmand. com* 🕐 *Closed Mon. and Tues., 1 wk in Mar., and mid-June–July 1. No dinner Sun.*

$

B&B/INN

🏠 **Château de Ribourdin.** Retired farmer Claude Brodard began building his *chambres d'hôte* (bed-and-breakfast) in an old stable, bucolically enshrined just south of Auxerre, almost 20 years ago, and the cozy, comfortable, reasonably priced rooms overlook his fields. **Pros:** tasteful rooms; beautiful location; great breakfast; swimming pool. **Cons:** can feel a little isolated; no credit cards. $ *Rooms from: €88* ✉ *8 rte. de Ribourdin, 8 km (5 miles) southwest of Auxerre on D1, Chevannes* ☎ *03–86–41–23–16* ⊕ *www.chateauderibourdin.com* ⇨ *5 rooms* ▭ *No credit cards* ⊙ *Breakfast.*

$

HOTEL

🏠 **Normandie.** This rather grand, vine-covered 19th-century mansion close to the center of Auxerre, just a short walk from the cathedral, provides unpretentious guest rooms, as well as a terrace that is a nice place to relax after a long day of sightseeing. **Pros:** tidy rooms with nice

Presided over by the Cathédrale St-Etienne, Auxerre is a medieval beauty filled with historic churches.

bathrooms; helpful staff; games room and gym. **Cons:** not in town center. [$] *Rooms from: €88* ✉ *41 bd. Vauban* ☎ *03–86–52–57–80* 🌐 *www.hotelnormandie.fr* 🛏 *47 rooms.*

CHABLIS

16 km (10 miles) east of Auxerre.

EXPLORING

The pretty village of Chablis nestles amid the towering vineyards that produce its famous white wine on the banks of the River Serein and is protected, perhaps from an ill wind, by the massive, round, turreted towers of the Porte Noël gateway. Although in America Chablis has become a generic name for cheap white wine, it's not so in France: here it's a bone-dry, slightly acacia-tasting wine of tremendous character, with the premier cru and grand cru wines standing head to head with the best French whites. Prices in the local shops tend to be inflated, so your best bet is to buy directly from a vineyard; keep in mind that most are closed Sunday. Check out 🌐 *www.chablis.fr* for more information on Chablis and the region's vineyards.

Chablis Tourist Office. The town's tourist office can provide information on nearby cellars where you can take tours, taste wine, and learn all you need to know about the region's illustrious wine tradition. The Bureau Interprofessionnel des Vins de Bourgogne's website (🌐 *www.vins-bourgogne.fr*) is another helpful resource—it's a veritable portal to everything wine related in Burgundy. ✉ *Rue du Maréchal de Lattre de Tassigny* ☎ *03–86–42–80–80* 🌐 *www.chablis.net* 🕒 *June–Sept., daily*

10–12:30 and 1:30–7; Oct.–Easter, Mon.–Sat. 10–12:30 and 1:30–6; Easter–May, daily 10–12:30 and 1:30–6.

WHERE TO STAY

For expanded hotel reviews, visit Fodors.com.

$ HOTEL **Hostellerie des Clos.** The comfortable rooms at this moderately priced inn are simply, yet smartly, decorated, but most people come for chef Michel Vignaud's cooking, which is some of the best in the region. **Pros:** newer rooms are large and well appointed; stellar food; great location. **Cons:** older rooms are a bit small; hot in summer and only a few higher-grade rooms have air-conditioning. [$] *Rooms from: €90* ✉ *18 rue Jules-Rathier* ☎ *03–86–42–10–63* 🌐 *www.hostellerie-des-clos.fr* 🛏 *26 rooms, 10 suites* 🍴 *Some meals.*

TANLAY

26 km (16 miles) east of Chablis.

Fodor's Choice ★ **Château de Tanlay.** Unlike most aristocrats who heeded the royal summons to live at Versailles and fled the countryside, the Marquis and Marquise de Tanlay opted to live here among their village retainers. As a result, the Château de Tanlay, built around 1550, never fell into neglect and is a masterpiece of French early Baroque. Spectacularly adorned with rusticated obelisks, pagoda-like towers, the finest in French Classicist ornamentation, and a "grand canal," the château is centered around a typical cour d'honneur. Inside, the Hall of Caesars vestibule, framed by wrought-iron railings, leads to a wood-panel salon and dining room filled with period furniture. A graceful staircase climbs to the second floor, which has the showstopper: a gigantic gallery frescoed in Italianate trompe l'oeil. A small room in the tower above was used as a secret meeting place by Huguenot Protestants during the 1562–98 Wars of Religion; note the cupola with its fresco of scantily clad 16th-century religious personalities. ☎ *03–86–75–70–61* 🌐 *www.chateaudetanlay.fr* 🎟 *Gardens €3, guided tours €9* ⏲ *Gardens Apr.–Oct., Wed.–Mon. 10–12:30 and 2:15–6; chateau by guided tour Wed.–Mon. at 10, 11:30, 2:15, 3:15, 4:15, and 5:15.*

ANCY-LE-FRANC

14 km (9 miles) southeast of Tanlay.

It may be strange to find a textbook example of the Italian Renaissance in Ancy-le-Franc, but in mid-16th-century France the court had taken up this import as the latest rage. So, quick to follow the fashion and gain kingly favor, the Comte de Tonnerre decided to create a family seat using all the artists François I (1515–47) had summoned from Italy to his court at Fontainebleau.

Fodor's Choice ★ **Château d'Ancy-le-Franc.** Built from Sebastiano Serlio's designs, with interior blandishments by Primaticcio, the Château d'Ancy-le-Franc is an important example of Italianism, less for its plain, heavy exterior than for its sumptuous rooms and apartments, many with carved or painted walls and ceilings and original furnishings. Niccolò dell'Abate and other court artists created the magnificent Chambre des Arts (Art Gallery) and other rooms filled with murals depicting the signs of the zodiac, the Battle of Pharsala, and the motif of Diana in Her Bath (much favored by Diane de Poitiers, sister of the Comtesse de Tonnerre). Such grandeur won the approval of no less than the Sun King, Louis XIV, who once stayed in the Salon Bleu (Blue Room). ⊠ *18 pl. Clermont-Tonnerre* ☎ *03–86–75–14–63* ⊕ *www.chateau-ancy.com* ⊠ *Château €9, château and park €13.* ☉ *Apr.–mid-Nov., tours Tues.–Sun. at 10:30, 11:30, 2, 3, 4, and 5. Closed Mon.; Oct.–mid-Nov., no tour at 5.*

ABBAYE DE FONTENAY

32 km (20 miles) southeast of Ancy-le-Franc.

Fodor's Choice
★

Abbaye de Fontenay. The best preserved of the Cistercian abbeys, the Abbaye de Fontenay was founded in 1118 by St. Bernard. The same Cistercian criteria applied to Fontenay as to Pontigny: no-frills architecture and an isolated site—the spot was especially remote, for it had been decreed that these monasteries could not be established anywhere near "cities, feudal manors, or villages." The monks were required to live a completely self-sufficient existence, with no contact whatsoever with the outside world. By the end of the 12th century the buildings were finished, and the abbey's community grew to some 300 monks. Under the protection of Pope Gregory IX and Hughes IV, duke of Burgundy, the monastery soon controlled huge land holdings, vineyards, and timberlands. It prospered until the 16th century, when religious wars and administrative mayhem hastened its decline. Dissolved during the French Revolution, the abbey was used as a paper factory until 1906. Fortunately, the historic buildings emerged unscathed. The abbey is surrounded by extensive, immaculately tended gardens dotted with the fountains that gave it its name. The church's solemn interior is lightened by windows in the facade and by a double row of three narrow windows, representing the Trinity, in the choir. A staircase in the south transept leads to the wooden-roof dormitory (spare a thought for the bleary-eyed monks, obliged to stagger down for services in the dead of night). The chapter house, flanked by a majestic arcade, and the scriptorium, where monks worked on their manuscripts, leads off from the adjoining cloisters. ⊠ *6 km (3 miles) from Montbard TGV station, Marmagne* ☎ *03–80–92–15–00* ⊕ *www.abbayedefontenay.com* ⊠ *€8.50* ☉ *Apr.–mid-Nov., daily 10–6; mid-Nov.–Mar., daily 10–noon and 2–5.*

VÉZELAY

48 km (30 miles) west of Abbaye de Fontenay.

In the 11th and 12th centuries one of the most important places of pilgrimage in the Christian world, hilltop Vézelay is today a picturesque, somewhat isolated, village. Its one main street, rue St-Étienne, climbs steeply and stirringly to the summit and its medieval basilica, world-famous for its Romanesque sculpture. In summer you have to leave your car at the bottom and walk up. Off-season you can drive up and look for parking in the square.

Visitor Information Vézelay Tourist Office ☒ *Rue St-Étienne* ☎ *03–86–33–23–69* ⊕ *www.vezelaytourisme.com* ☼ *Daily 10–1 and 2–6 (July and-Aug., weekdays10–7). Closed Thurs. Oct.–May, Sun. Nov.–Mar.*

EXPLORING

It's easy to ignore this tiny village, but don't: in addition to the artistic treasures of **Basilique Ste-Madeleine,** Vézelay has an array of other Romanesque-era delights. Hiding below its narrow *ruelles* (small streets) are several medieval cellars that once sheltered pilgrims and are now opened to visitors by homeowners in summer. Sections of several houses have arches and columns dating from the 12th and 13th centuries: don't miss the hostelry across from the tourist office and, next to it, the house where Louis VII, Eleanor of Aquitaine, and the king's religious supremo Abbé Suger, stayed when they came to hear St. Bernard preach the Second Crusade in 1146.

Fodor's Choice **Basilique Ste-Madeleine.** In the 11th and 12th centuries the celebrated
★ Basilique Ste-Madeleine was one of the focal points of Christendom. Pilgrims poured in to see the relics of St. Mary Magdalene (in the crypt) before setting off on the great trek to the shrine of St. James at Santiago de Compostela, in northwest Spain. Several pivotal church declarations of the Middle Ages were made from here, including St. Bernard's preaching of the Second Crusade (which attracted a huge French following) and Thomas à Becket's excommunication of English king Henry II. By the mid-13th century the authenticity of St. Mary's relics was in doubt; others had been discovered in Provence. The basilica's decline continued until the French Revolution, when the basilica and adjoining monastery buildings were sold by the state. Only the basilica, cloister, and dormitory escaped demolition, and were falling into ruin when ace restorer Viollet-le-Duc, sent by his mentor Prosper Merimée, rode to the rescue in 1840 (he also restored the cathedrals of Laon and Amiens and Paris's Notre-Dame).

Today the UNESCO-listed basilica has recaptured much of its glory and is considered to be one of France's most prestigious Romanesque showcases. The exterior tympanum was redone by Viollet-le-Duc (have a look at the eroded original as you exit the cloister), but the narthex (circa 1150) is a Romanesque masterpiece. Note the interwoven zodiac signs and depictions of seasonal crafts along its rim, similar to those at both Troyes and Autun. The pilgrims' route around the building is indicated by the majestic flowers, which metamorphose into full-blown blooms, over the left-hand entrance on the right; an annual procession is still held on July 22. The basilica's exterior is best seen from the leafy terrace to the right of the facade. Opposite, a vast, verdant panorama encompasses vines, lush valleys, and rolling hills. In the foreground is the Flamboyant Gothic spire of St-Père-sous-Vézelay, a tiny village 3 km (2 miles) away that is the site of ⇨ *L'Espérance, Marc Meneau's famed restaurant.* ☒ *Pl. de la Basilique* ☎ *03–86–33–39–50* ⊕ *www.vezelaytourisme.com* ⛨ *Free, €3.60 for guided tour (phone for reservations)* ☼ *Tues.–Fri. 9–11 and 2:30; Sat. 9–11 and 3–4; Sun. 9:30 and 2:30–4.*

Continued on page 458

GRAPE EXPECTATIONS
A BURGUNDY WINE PRIMER

From the steely brilliance of Premier Cru Chablis in the north to the refined Pouilly-Fuissés in the south, Burgundy—Bourgogne to the French—is where you can sample deep-colored reds and full-flavored whites as you amble from one fabled vineyard to another along the **Route des Grands Crus**.

An oenophile's nirvana, Burgundy is accorded almost religious reverence, and with good reason: its famous chardonnays and pinot noirs, and the "second-tier" gamays and aligotés, were perfected in the Middle Ages by the great monasteries of the region.

The specific character of a Burgundy wine is often dependent on the individual grower or négociant's style. There are hundreds of vintners and merchants in this region, many of them producing top wines from surprisingly small parcels of land.

Get to know the *appellation controllée*, or AOC, wine classification system. In Burgundy, it specifies vineyard, region, and quality. The most expensive, top-tiered wines are called *monopole* and *grand cru*, followed by *premier cru*, *village*, and generic *Bourgogne*. Although there are 100 different AOC wines in the area, the thicket of labels and names is navigable once you learn how to read the road signs; and the payoff is tremendous, with palate-pleasing choices for all budgets.

By Christopher Mooney

GEOGRAPHY + CLIMATE = *TERROIR*

Soil, weather conditions, grapes, and savoir-faire are the basic building blocks of all great wines, but this is particularly true in Burgundy, where grapes of the same variety, grown a few feet apart, might have different names and personalities, as well as tremendously varying prices.

CHABLIS

Chablis' famous chardonnays are produced along both banks of the Serein River. The four appellations, in ascending order of excellence, are Petit Chablis AOP, Chablis AOP, Chablis Premier Cru AOP, and Chablis Grand Cru AOP. Flinty and slightly acidic, with citrus, pineapple, and green apple flavors and aromas, they age well (except the Petit Chablis, which is best drunk young) and are typically less intense than other burgundy whites, due to their colder northern climate.

CÔTE D'OR

The 30-mile long Côte d'Or contains two of the world's most gorgeous and distinguished wine regions: **Côte de Nuits** and **Côte de Beaune.**

The northern area, the **Côte de Nuits**, is sometimes called the "Champs-Elysées of Burgundy" as it is the site of Burgundy's top-rated grand cru wines. These Burgundian pinot noirs are ruby colored with red fruit and spice flavors. They tend to be richly textured with a full body. The wines develop savory, gamey notes with age, and are perfect matches for hearty Burgundian beef and game dishes. The best wines come from the grand cru appelations of Gevrey-Chambertin, Vougeot, Vosne-Romanée, and Nuits-St-Georges.

The **Côte de Beaune,** just to the south, is known for making the world's best dry whites, made from from chardonnay. These wines are green-gold in color and aromatically complex. They typically have a buttery texture and are medium- to full-bodied. Search out wines from the appelations of Aloxe-Corton, Beaune, and Pommard, then head south for the storied Montrachets, which are the most expensive chardonnay wines in the world. Renowned reds are also made here, though are lighter and less concentrated than their counterparts from the Côte de Nuits.

CÔTE CHALONNAISE

Farther south is the Côte Chalonnaise. Although not as famous, it produces chardonnays almost as rich as its northern neighbors. Pinot noirs with *villages* appellations Rully, Givry, and Mercurey are well-structured, with body, bouquet, and a distinction very similar to Côte de Beaune reds. Montagny and Rully whites are dry, light, well balanced, and fruity—much ends up in sparkling Crémant de Bourgogne. Bourgogne Aligoté de Bouzeron are worth a stop, too. Named after its grape, it is the fresh and lively white wine traditionally mixed with Crème de Cassis to make a Kir, but is just as delicious on its own.

CÔTE MÂCONNAISE

Next is the Côte Mâconnaise, the largest of the four Côtes, which brings its own quality dry whites to the market, particularly the distinctive and refined Saint Vérans, Virés and the more famous Pouilly-Fuissés. With lightly oaked aromas of toast and hazelnuts, these are three of France's best wines for seafood. Macon *villages* light and fruity reds are drinkable but hardly worth a detour. The best are found between Hurigny and Viré and, like the whites, should be drunk young while they still have their freshness.

LABEL KNOW—HOW

❶ The name and address of the proprietor.
❷ This wine was produced in the Montrachet region
❸ Number of bottles made
❹ Bottle number 1,201 and Vintage
❺ 'Made and bottled on the estate'—a great signifier of quality

FOR THE VINE INSPIRED

If you're going to spend a fortune on a bottle of Romanée-Conti and want to know how to savor it, sign up for one of the wine classes offered by Beaune's Ecole des Vins de Bourgogne, sponsored by the Bureau Interprofessionel des Vins de Bourgogne (✉ B.I.V.B.; 6 rue du 16éme Chasseur, 21200, Beaune ☎ 03–80–26–35–10 ⊕ www.bivb.com, www.ecoledesvins-bourgogne.com). They offer several choices, ranging from a two-hour intro to a full weekend jammed with trips to vineyards and cellars in Mâcon and Chablis.

TOURING AND TASTING

Route des Grands Crus

Cote de Nuits, Burgundy

There are a countless number of vineyards here, but these are a few of our favorites. Vineyards accept drop-ins but it's best to reserve by phone or e-mail. General tastings are almost always free, but buying a bottle is in good form. By-appointment tour prices vary with number of attendees and wines tasted. If you're not up for a drive you can taste many of these wines in town cellars or local restaurants.

Antonin Rodet

Makers of fine wines since 1875, Antonin Rodet's delivers a complete range of high quality but reasonably priced Burgundies. Six house-labeled wines can be tasted. Rodet has acquired a number of château wineries all over the region, but a visit to Château de Rully (Hautes Côtes de Beaune) or Domaine des Perdrix (Côte de Nuits), is an unforgettable experience. ☎ 03–85–98–12–12 ✉ rodet@rodet.com ⊕ www.rodet.com

Bouchard Père et Fils Château de Beaune

Bouchard is one of the major domaines and négociants in Beaune. Its unparalleled legacy of 50,000 bottles from the Côte de Beaune and Côte de Nuits appellations includes a unique collection of rare vintages dating back to the 19th century. The museum and 15th-century cellar is accessible year round (8–12:30, 2:30–6:30 (5:30 in winter) but the personalized tour and extensive tasting is by appointment only. ☎ 03–80–24–80–24 ✉ contact@bouchard-pereetfils.com ⊕ www.bouchardpereetfils.com

Château De Chorey Les Beaune

This magnificent 17th-century château, with 13th-century moat and towers, has been in the Germain family for five generations. The wines are frequently found in cellars of France's top restaurants and though drop-in tastings are possible, a stay in one of the chambres d'hôtes, combined with the cellar visit and comprehensive tasting (3 reds and 3 whites) of the estate's wines, is a rare and exceptional experience. The château is open from Easter to end of October, up to 16 people can be accommodated overall in the luxurious five bedrooms (€185–€220) overlooking the vineyard, park or tower. English is spoken and pets are welcome. ☎ 03–80–22–06–05 ✉ Contact@Chateau-De-Chorey-Les-Beaune.fr ⊕ www.chateau-de-chor ey-les-beaune.fr

■ **TIP →** Late summer is the most popular time to visit—which is reason enough to avoid it. Visit in spring, or the fall, just before the October harvests. Harvest time is exciting, but with everyone out in the fields, you're less likely to find anyone in the cellars to open a bottle for you to sample—unless you pitch in and help bring in the crop.

Château de Meursault
This elegant well-visited château has been producing a miraculous Meursault since the 7th century. Walk up the recently opened Allée des Maronniers, through the vines to the château's *cour d'honneur*. Cellars dating from the 14th and 16th centuries and an art gallery are included in tour. As well as a tasting of five wines, 9:30–12; 2:30–6, €18 per person. English is spoken. ☎ *03–80–26–22–75* ✎ *www.meursault.com*

Château de Santenay
This majestic 9th–16th century castle is also the former residence (1302–1404) of Philippe le Hardi, son of the king of France. The estate has a total of 237 acres of vines, one of the largest in Burgundy. The château is open year round, seven days a week, a visit to the gardens and surrounding park culminates in a wine-tasting with bottles available for purchase. The award-wining Saint-Aubin 'En Vesvau', matured and aged in wooden casks, is a must-try as is the Château Philippe le Hardi AOP Aloxe-Corton "Les Brunettes et Planchots". The tour and wine tasting is €6 per person. English is spoken. ☎ *03–80–20–61–87* ✎ *contact@chateau-de-santenay.com* ⊕ *www.chateau-de-santenay.com* Open Apr.–Oct. closed Wednesdays.

The 74-km (50-mi) **Route des Grands Crus**, which meanders through every wine town, is known as D122. Less scenic is A31 from Dijon to Beaune and D974.

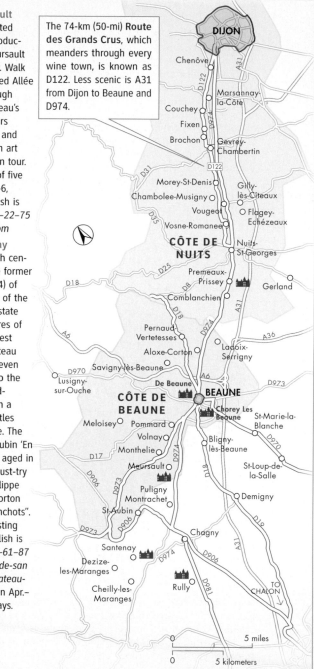

WHERE TO EAT AND STAY

For expanded hotel reviews, visit Fodors.com.

$$$
FRENCH
✕ **Le Bougainville.** One of the few affordable restaurants in this well-heeled town occupies an old house with a fireplace in the dining room and the requisite Burgundian color scheme of brown, yellow, and ocher. Philippe Guillemard presides in the kitchen, turning out such regional favorites as hare stew, crayfish, escargot ragout in Chardonnay sauce, and venison with chestnuts. He has also devised a vegetarian menu—a rarity in Burgundy—with such deeply satisfying dishes as oven-baked vegetables served with a saffron and ratatouille coulis. $ *Average main:* €30 ⊠ *26 rue St-Étienne* ☎ *03–86–33–27–57* ⚠ *Reservations essential* ⊘ *Closed Mon.–Wed. and mid-Nov.–mid-Feb.*

$$$
HOTEL
Fodor's Choice
★
⊞ **L'Espérance.** Chef Marc Meneau heads one of the greatest kitchens in Burgundy, serving fillet of venison with a wine and cacao sauce, cod fillet turbot with a sea urchin–based sauce, and other creations next to a stream and in a large, statue-filled garden, and his luckiest diners lodge onsite in charming guest quarters. **Pros:** spectacular restaurant; bucolic setting. **Cons:** uneven service; some rooms are uninspiring. $ *Rooms from:* €150 ⊠ *St-Père-en-Vézelay* ☎ *03–86–33–39–10* ⊕ *www.marcmeneau-esperance.com* ↴ *17 rooms, 8 suites* ⊘ *Closed mid-Jan.–early Mar.* ⦿ *Some meals.*

$$
B&B/INN
⊞ **Manoir de Val en Sel.** Five classically decorated, color-coded rooms, all with private entrances and en suite bathrooms, are set in a picturesque 18th-century country residence and surround a spectacular walled flower garden that's hailed as one of the world's finest. **Pros:** gardens are a fragrant haven of calm; comfortable, spacious rooms. **Cons:** car essential; breakfast is extra; no credit cards. $ *Rooms from:* €100 ⊠ *1 chemin de la Fontaine, St-Père-sous-Vézelay, 2 km (1 mile) east of Vézelay* ☎ *03–86–33–26–95* ⊕ *valensel.vezelay.free.fr* ↴ *3 rooms, 2 suites* ▬ *No credit cards* ⊘ *Closed mid-Nov.–Mar.* ⦿ *Breakfast.*

SAULIEU

48 km (30 miles) southeast of Vézelay.

Saulieu's reputation belies its size: it's renowned for good food (Rabelais, that roly-poly 16th-century man of letters, extolled its gargantuan hospitality) and Christmas trees (a staggering million are packed and sent off from the area each year).

Basilique St-Andoche. The town's Basilique St-Andoche, one of Burgundy's finest Romanesque churches, is almost as old as that in Vézelay, though less imposing and much restored. Note the impressive Romanesque nave with 12th-century carved capitals. ⊠ *4 rue Savot* ⊘ *Nov.–Apr., Tues.–Sat. 9–noon and 2–4:30; May–Oct., Tues.–Sat. 9–noon and 2–6:30, Sun. 2–6:30.*

Musée François-Pompon. The Musée François-Pompon, adjoining the basilica, is partly devoted to the work of animal-bronze sculptor Pompon (1855–1933), whose smooth, stylized creations seem contemporary but predate World War II. The museum also contains Gallo-Roman funeral stones, sacred art, and a room highlighting local gastronomic lore. ⊠ *3 pl. docteur Roclore* ☎ *03–80–64–19–51* ▰ *€3* ⊘ *Apr.–Sept., Mon. 10–12:30,*

Wed.–Sat. 10–12:30 and 2–6, Sun. 10:30–noon and 2:30–5; Oct.–Dec. and Mar., Mon. 10–12:30, Wed.–Sat. 10–12:30 and 2–5:30, Sun. 10:30–noon and 2:30–5.

WHERE TO STAY
For expanded hotel reviews, visit Fodors.com.

$$
HOTEL

🖼 **Chez Camille.** Small, quiet, and friendly sum up this hotel in a 16th-century house with an exterior so ordinary you might easily pass it by. **Pros:** good value; traditional decor and food. **Cons:** restaurant and hotel could both use a bit of refreshing. $ *Rooms from: €86 ⊠ 1 pl. Édouard-Herriot, on N6 between Saulieu and Beaune, Arnay-le-Duc ☎ 03–80–90–01–38 ⊕ www.chez-camille.fr ⇆ 11 rooms ⦿ Some meals.*

$$$
ALL-INCLUSIVE
Fodor's Choice
★

🖼 **Relais Bernard Loiseau.** At Relais Bernard Loiseau, lovely lodgings combine exposed beams and glass panels with cheerful furnishings. **Pros:** first-class facilities include a spa and pool; stellar food. **Cons:** service in hotel and restaurant can be uneven; restaurant prices are stratospheric. $ *Rooms from: €195 ⊠ 2 rue d'Argentine, off N6 ☎ 03–80–90–53–53 🖨 03–80–64–08–92 ⊕ www.bernard-loiseau.com ⇆ 23 rooms, 9 suites ⦿ Closed late Jan. and Feb. and Tues. and Wed. ⦿ Multiple meal plans.*

DIJON

38 km (23 miles) northeast of Châteauneuf, 315 km (195 miles) southeast of Paris.

You may never have been to Dijon but you've certainly tasted it. Many of the gastronomic specialties that originated here are known worldwide. They include snails (many now imported from the Czech Republic), mustard (although the handmade variety is becoming a lost art), and Cassis (a black-currant liqueur often mixed with white wine—preferably Burgundy Aligoté—to make Kir, the popular aperitif). The city itself is a feast for the eyes, with charming streets, chic shops, and an impressive array of medieval art. It has magnificent half-timber houses and *hôtels particuliers*, some rivaling those in Paris. There's also a striking trio of central churches, built one following the other for three distinct parishes—St-Bénigne, its facade distinguished by Gothic galleries; St-Philibert, Dijon's only Romanesque church (with Merovingian vestiges); and St-Jean, an asymmetrical building now used as a theater. Dijon scores as high artistically as it does gastronomically.

GETTING HERE AND AROUND
As the administrative capital of Burgundy, Dijon has most everything a city should, including fast train service. Between 11 and 15 TGV trains leave Paris daily (€49–€62), so getting to Dijon by train is perhaps the most efficient way of arriving on Burgundy's doorstep. Once here, the extensive TER network (Express Regional Transport) can take you almost anywhere within the region, with frequent connections to Sens (€29.90), Nevers (€31.40), Beaune (€7.40), and Auxerre

(€27.20). There are also two sleek new tram lines that link the suburbs to Dijon's city center (⊕ *www. diviabusettram.fr*). Right next to the Dijon Ville train station is the Gare Routière from which the regional TRANSCO (☎ *03–80–11–29–29* ⊕ *www.cotedor.fr*) bus company operates 32 regular shared school/public bus routes that crisscross the Côte d'Or. For wine lovers the No. 44 (Dijon–Beaune) represents the logical choice, with an itinerary that reads like an oenologist's wish list. The 12:25 pm will get you to the cellar(s) of your choice in time for an early afternoon tasting. Price is based on the number of sections traveled, and at €1.50 per, the trip to Beaune will cost you €3.

> **THE ORIGINAL GREY POUPON**
>
> Dijon's legendary Maille mustard shop at 32 rue de la Liberté (⊕ *www.maille.com*), established in 1777, still sells Grey Poupon in painted ceramic pots at outrageous prices, along with a huge selection of oils, vinegars, and spices.

Visitor Information Dijon Tourist Office ✉ *11 rue des Forges* ☎ *08–92–70– 05–58 [€0.34 per min]* ⊕ *www.visitdijon.com.*

EXPLORING

Dijon, the age-old capital of Burgundy, is also the erstwhile wine–mustard center of the world, the site of an important university, and a repository of impressive art and architecture. On top of that, it has a tourist-friendly scale: indeed many travelers feel it is the perfect French community, possessing the charm of a village as well as the sophistication and liveliness you'd expect of a capital.

Dijon was a major player in the history of the region. Throughout the Middle Ages Burgundy was a duchy that led a separate existence from the rest of France, culminating in the rule of the four "Grand Dukes of the West" between 1364 and 1477—Philippe le Hardi (the Bold), Jean Sans Peur (the Fearless), Philippe le Bon (the Good), and the unfortunate Charles le Téméraire (the Foolhardy, whose defeat by French king Louis XI at Nancy spelled the end of Burgundian independence). A number of monuments date from this period, including the Palais des Ducs (Ducal Palace), now largely converted into an art museum. Luckily, Dijon's fame and fortune outlasted the dukes, and it flourished under French rule from the 17th century on. It has remained the largest city in Burgundy—and the only one with more than 150,000 inhabitants; moreover, its location, on the major European north–south trade route and within striking distance of the Swiss and German borders, has helped maintain its economic importance. Dijon continues to be a thriving cultural center as well. *Just a selection of its museums are mentioned below.*

THE HISTORIC CENTER

EXPLORING

TOP ATTRACTIONS

Cathédrale St-Bénigne. The chief glory of this comparatively austere cathedral is its atmospheric 11th-century crypt, in which a forest of pillars are surmounted by a rotunda. ✉ *Rue du Dr. Maret* ⊕ *www.*

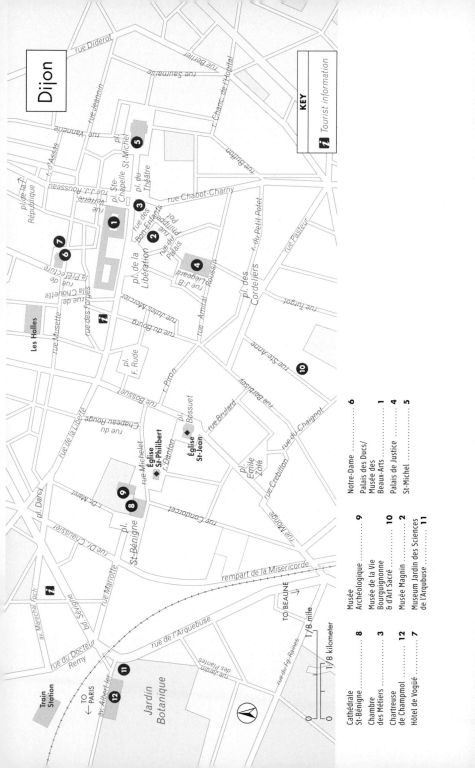

Dijon

rue Diderot

rue Berbier

rue de l'Hôpital

rue Saumaise

rue Jeannin

rue Vannerie

rue d'Assas

pl. Ste-Chapelle St-Michel

pl. du Théâtre

rue Chabot-Charny

pl. de la République

rue J.-J. Rousseau

rue Verrerie

rue Bon-Enfants

rue du Palais

pl. de la Libération

rue J.-B. Liégeard

rue de la Préfecture

rue de la Chouette

rue des Forges

rue Musette

rue des Jules Mercier

Les Halles

rue du Bourg

pl. F. Rude

r. Piron

rue Bossuet

rue de la Liberté

rue du Chapeau Rouge

rue Michelet

pl. Bossuet

r. Danton

Église St-Philibert

Église St-Jean

rue Brûlard

pl. Émile Zola

rue Crébillon

rue du Chaignot

rue Ste-Anne

rue Turbot

pl. des Cordeliers

r.-du-Petit-Potet

rue Pasteur

rue Buffon

rue Amiral Roussin

pl. St-Bénigne

pl. du Mart

rue du Dr. Maret

pl. Darcy

rue Dr. Chaussier

rue Condorcet

rue Monge

rempart de la Miséricorde

TO BEAUNE →

av. Maréchal Foch

bd. de Sévigné

rue Marrotte

rue du Docteur Remy

← TO PARIS

av. Albert Ier

rue de l'Arquebuse

rue du Fg.-Raines

rue du Jardin des Plantes

Jardin Botanique

Train Station

Cathédrale St-Bénigne **8**	Notre-Dame **6**
Chambre des Métiers **3**	Palais des Ducs/ Musée des Beaux-Arts **1**
Chartreuse de Champmol **12**	Palais de Justice **4**
Hôtel de Vogüé **7**	St-Michel **5**
Musée Archéologique **9**	
Musée de la Vie Bourguignonne ð d'Art Sacré **10**	
Musée Magnin **2**	
Museum Jardin des Sciences de l'Arquebuse **11**	

0 1/8 mile

0 1/8 kilometer

cathedrale-dijon.fr ✉ *Crypt 2€* ☉ *Crypt weekdays 10–6 (5 in winter), Sat. 10–4, Sun. 2–6 (5 in winter).*

Chartreuse de Champmol. All that remains of this former charterhouse—a half-hour walk from Dijon's center and now surrounded by a psychiatric hospital—are the exuberant 15th-century church porch and the *Puits de Moïse* (*Well of Moses*), one of the greatest examples of late-medieval sculpture. The well was designed by Flemish master Claus Sluter, who also created several other masterpieces during the late 14th and early 15th centuries, including one of the tombs of the dukes of Burgundy. If you closely study Sluter's six large sculptures, you will discover the Middle Ages becoming the Renaissance right before your eyes. Representing Moses and five other prophets, they are set on a hexagonal base in the center of a basin and remain the most compellingly realistic figures ever crafted by a medieval sculptor. ✉ *Centre Hospitalier Spécialisé de la Chartreuse, Av. Albert 1er* ✉ *€3.50 Well of Moses* ☉ *Jan.–Mar., Nov., and Dec., daily 9–12:30 and 1:30–5; Apr.–Oct., daily 9–12:30 and 1:30–6.*

Hôtel de Vogüé. This stately 17th-century Renaissance mansion has a characteristic red, yellow, and green Burgundian tile roof—a tradition whose disputed origins lie either with the Crusades and the adoption of Arabic tiles or with Philip the Bold's wife, Marguerite of Flanders. ✉ *8 rue de la Chouette.*

Musée de la Vie Bourguignonne et d'Art Sacré (*Museum of Burgundian Traditions and Religious Art*). Housed in the former Cistercian convent, one museum contains religious art and sculpture; the other has crafts and artifacts from Burgundy, including old storefronts saved from the streets of Dijon that have been reconstituted, in Hollywood movie-making style, to form an imaginary street. ✉ *17 rue Ste-Anne* ☎ *03–80–48–80–90* ✉ *Free* ☉ *May–Sept., Wed.–Mon. 9–12:30 and 1:30–6; Oct.–Apr., Wed.–Mon. 9–noon and 2–6. Closed Tues.*

Musée Magnin. In a 17th-century mansion, this museum showcases a private collection of original furnishings and paintings from the 16th to the 19th century. ✉ *4 rue des Bons-Enfants* ☎ *03–80–67–11–10* ⊕ *www.musee-magnin.fr* ✉ *€3.50 (free 1st Sun. of month)* ☉ *Tues.–Sun. 10–noon and 2–6.*

Notre-Dame. One of the city's oldest churches, Notre-Dame stands out with spindlelike towers, delicate arches gracing its facade, and 13th-century stained glass. Note the windows in the north transept tracing the lives of five saints, as well as the 11th-century Byzantine linden wood Black Virgin. Local tradition has it that stroking the small owl sculpted on the outside wall of the adjoining chapel with your left hand grants you a wish. ✉ *Rue de la Préfecture.*

Fodor's Choice
★ **Palais des Ducs** (*Ducal Palace*). The elegant, classical exterior of this former palace can best be admired from the half-moon place de la Libération and the cour d'honneur. The **kitchens** (circa 1450), with their six huge fireplaces and (for their time) state-of-the-art aeration funnel in the ceiling, catch the eye, as does the 15th-century **Salle des Gardes** (Guard Room), with its richly carved and colored tombs and late-14th-century altarpieces. The palace now houses one of France's

major art museums, the **Musée des Beaux-Arts** (Fine Arts Museum). The magnificent tombs sculpted for dukes Philip the Bold and his son John the Fearless (note their dramatically moving mourners, hidden in shrouds) are just two highlights of a rich collection of medieval objects and Renaissance furniture gathered here as testimony to Marguerite of Flanders (Philip the Bold's wife). She brought to Burgundy not only her dowry, namely the rich province of Flanders, but also a host of distinguished artists—including Rogier van der Weyden, Jan van Eyck, and Claus Sluter. Their artistic legacy can be seen here, as well as at several of Burgundy's other museums and monuments. Among the paintings are works by Italian old masters and French 19th-century artists, such as Théodore Géricault and Gustave Courbet, plus their Impressionist successors, notably Édouard Manet and Claude Monet. Already a top stop, the museum will be even more impressive in 2014 when a new wing opens. ⊠ *Cours de Flore* 🖀 *03–80–74–52–70* ⊕ *mba.dijon.fr* 🖾 *Free* ☉ *May–Oct., Wed.–Mon. 9:30–6; Nov.–Apr., Wed.–Mon. 10–5.*

WORTH NOTING

Chambre des Métiers. This mansion with Gallo-Roman stelae incorporated into the walls (a remaining section of Dijon's 5th-century "Castrum" wall) was built in the 19th century. ⊠ *Rue Philippe-Pot.*

Musée Archéologique (*Antiquities Museum*). This museum, in the former abbey buildings of the church of St-Bénigne, outlines the history of the region through archaeological finds. ⊠ *5 rue Dr. Maret* 🖀 *03–80–48–83–70* 🖾 *Free* ☉ *Mid-May–Sept., Wed.–Mon. 9–12:30 and 1:30–6; Oct.–mid May, Wed.–Sun. 9–12:30 and 1:30–6.*

Museum Jardin des Sciences de l'Arquebuse (*Natural History Museum*). This natural history museum is part of the impressive botanical garden, **Jardin de l'Arquebuse,** showcasing local and exotic plant life and a pleasant place to stroll amid the wide variety of trees and tropical flowers. ⊠ *1 av. Albert 1er* 🖀 *03–80–48–82–00 museum* 🖾 *Free* ☉ *Museum: Mon. and Wed.–Fri. 9–12:30 and 2–6, weekends 2–6; garden: daily 7:30–7 (until 10 in summer).*

Palais de Justice. The meeting place for the old regional Parliament of Burgundy serves as a reminder that Louis XI incorporated the province into France in the late 15th century. ⊠ *Rue du Palais.*

St-Michel. This church, with its chunky Renaissance facade, fast-forwards 300 years from Notre-Dame. ⊠ *Pl. St-Michel.*

WHERE TO EAT

As a culinary capital of France, Dijon has many superb restaurants, with three areas popular for casual dining: place Darcy (a square catering to all tastes and budgets), place Émile-Zola, and the old market (Les Halles), along rue Bannelier.

$
BISTRO
✕ **Le Bistrot des Halles.** Under new ownership, this eatery facing Les Halles marketplace has tossed the traditional French decor but still caters to savvy locals, who are now tempted by trendy bistro dishes such as braised pork with lentils topped with an extra drizzle of balsamic vinegar. Pull up a seat on the sidewalk or dine inside, where glass-topped wine casks serve as tables. A good choice of wines by the glass and pret-

Making an entrance: Palais des Ducs white-on-white exterior projects a regal elegance over the Cours de Flore.

tily presented desserts are added bonuses. $ *Average main: €17* ⊠ *10 rue Bannelier* ☎ *03–80–35–45–07* ☉ *Closed Sun. and Mon.*

$$$$
FRENCH

✕ **Le Pré aux Clercs.** This bright, beautiful Napoléon III-style restaurant is the perfect showcase for chef Jean-Pierre Billoux's golden touch, which can turn the lowliest farmyard chicken into a palate-plucking pièce de résistance—the roast *volaille* (chicken) de Bresse with perfect truffle puree is a case in point. Most house specialties are inventive, like the panfried sole enhanced by a light pomegranate sauce, or, to finish, a hazelnut Dacquoise with pecan ice cream. The welcome is always convivial, and the wine list features the region's best—though not necessarily best-known—winemakers. The lunch menu (including wine) is a startling introduction to modern Burgundian cuisine. $ *Average main: €40* ⊠ *13 pl. de la Libération* ☎ *03–80–38–05–05* ⊕ *www. jeanpierrebilloux.com* ☽ *Reservations essential* ☉ *Closed Mon. No dinner Sun.*

$$$
MODERN FRENCH

✕ **Les Oenophiles.** A collection of superbly restored 17th-century buildings belonging to the Burgundian Company of Wine Tasters forms the backdrop to this pleasant restaurant. It's lavishly furnished but also quaint (candles sparkle in the evening) and the food is good, too. Vincent Bourdon juggles creativity and tradition to conjure sumptuous culinary surprises, including a confit of lamb with chickpea mousse, and audacious deserts such as his concoction of just-cooked vanilla cake served with mascarpone cream and fruit salad seasoned with ginger. An excellent four-course menu is available for lunch or dinner. $ *Average main: €28* ⊠ *18 rue Ste-Anne* ☎ *03–80–30–73–52* ⊕ *www.restaurant-lesoenophiles.com* ☽ *Reservations essential* ☉ *Closed Sun.*

$$$$ ✕ **Stéphane Derbord.** The talented Derbord, this city's rising gastronomic
FRENCH star, ensures that dinner in his eponymous restaurant is an elegantly
refined affair. Tempting prix-fixe menus range from a three-course lunch
to a 12-dish dining extravaganza and might include starters like duck
foie gras with beetroot tempura and quince puree, followed by trout-
and-crayfish stuffed cannelloni, and, to cap things off, an apple crumble
served with a yuzu-laced yogurt sorbet. $ *Average main: €40* ⊠ *10
pl. Wilson* ☎ *03–80–67–74–64* ⊕ *www.restaurantstephanederbord.fr*
🗋 *Reservations essential* 🕙 *Closed Sun. and Mon., early Jan., last wk.
in Feb., and 1st 2 wks. in Aug.*

WHERE TO STAY
For expanded hotel reviews, visit Fodors.com.

$$$ 🗔 **Hostellerie du Chapeau Rouge.** Colorful, well-appointed rooms display
HOTEL charm and designer chic, and the pleasant surroundings are comple-
mented by the restaurant, which is renowned for classic cuisine laced
with inventive counterpoints. **Pros:** celebrated cuisine; central loca-
tion. **Cons:** Breakfast is extra; staff can be gruff. $ *Rooms from: €120*
⊠ *5 rue Michelet* ☎ *03–80–50–88–88* ⊕ *www.chapeau-rouge.fr* 🛌 *28
rooms, 1 suite.*

$$$$ 🗔 **La Cloche.** At this luxurious, 19th-century grand hotel, ask for one
HOTEL of the large, plush guest rooms overlooking the tiny, tranquil back gar-
den and its reflecting pool. **Pros:** very comfortable beds; attentive staff;
imposing entry hall and smart bar. **Cons:** bad soundproofing; ostenta-
tious lobby; breakfast is extra. $ *Rooms from: €215* ⊠ *14 pl. Darcy*
☎ *03–80–30–12–32* ⊕ *www.hotel-lacloche.com* 🛌 *53 rooms, 15 suites.*

$ 🗔 **Le Jacquemart.** In an 18th-century building in Old Dijon surrounded
HOTEL by antiques shops, a steep staircase leads up to high-ceilinged guest
rooms of variable comfort, decorated with rustic furniture. **Pros:** cheer-
ful; good value; nice bathrooms. **Cons:** far from the train station; no
elevator or air-conditioning; breakfast is extra; some rooms do not
have private bathrooms; might be too basic for some. $ *Rooms from:
€60* ⊠ *32 rue Verrerie* ☎ *03–80–60–09–60* ⊕ *www.hotel-lejacquemart.
fr* 🛌 *33 rooms.*

NIGHTLIFE AND THE ARTS

Bar Messire. Bar Messire attracts an older crowd. ⊠ *3 rue Jules-Mercier*
☎ *03–80–30–16–40* ⊕ *www.bar-lemessire.com.*

Bell-Ringing Festival. During the Bell-Ringing Festival, in July, St-Bénigne's
bells chime and chime. .

Eden Bar. Eden Bar caters to a broad clientele and features live sports
coverage. ⊠ *12 rue des Perrieres* ☎ *03–80–41–48–64* ⊕ *www.eden-bar-
dijon.fr.*

Festival International de Musiques et Danses Populaires (*Fêtes de la Vigne*).
Every two years at the end of August Dijon puts on the Festival Interna-
tional de Musiques et Danses Populaires. The next festival takes place
in 2014. ⊕ *www.fetesdelavigne.fr.*

9

Flea Market—La Grande Brocante (*Puces dijonnaises*). In the first week of September, Dijon holds a picturesque flea market in the Parc des Expositions de Dijon. .

International Gastronomy Fair. Dijon plays host to the International Gastronomy Fair the first two weeks in November. Each year a different country is invited to show off its produce and cuisine. .

Le Chat Noir. Le Chat Noir is a popular disco and draws a huge crowd of dedicated groovers. Styles are eclectic and prices are reasonable: €9 for a glass of champagne, €7 for a beer. ⊠ *20 av. Garibaldi* ☎ *03–80– 73–39–57* ⊕ *dijon.lechatnoir.fr* ⊠ *€6–€12 (includes drink).*

WINE COUNTRY

Burgundy has given its name to one of the world's great wines. Although many people will allow a preference for Bordeaux, others for Alsace, Loire, or Rhône wines, some of the leading French gourmets insist that the precious red nectars of Burgundy have no rivals, and treat them with reverence. So, for some travelers a trip to Burgundy's Wine Country takes on the feel of a spiritual pilgrimage. East of the mountainous Parc du Morvan, the low hills and woodland gradually open up, and vineyards, clothing the contour of the land in orderly beauty, appear on all sides. Their steeply banked hills stand in contrast to the region's characteristic gentle slopes. Burgundy's most famous vineyards run south from Dijon through Beaune to Mâcon along what has become known as the Côte d'Or. You can go from vineyard to vineyard tasting the various samples—both the powerfully tannic young reds and the mellower older ones. Purists will remind you that you're not supposed to actually drink what is offered but rather take a sip, then spit it into the little buckets discreetly provided. But who wants to be a purist?

While the "d'Or" in Côte d'Or doesn't mean "gold" (it's an abbreviation of orient, or east), the area does represent a golden opportunity for wine lovers as it branches out over the countryside in four great vineyard-*côtes* (slopes or hillsides). The northernmost, the Côte de Nuits, sometimes called the "Champs-Élysées of Burgundy," is the land of the unparalleled grand-cru reds from the Pinot Noir grape. The Côte de Beaune, just to the south, is known for both full-bodied reds and some of the best dry whites in the world. Even farther south is the Côte Chalonnaise. Although not as famous, it produces bottle after bottle of Chardonnay almost as rich as its northern neighbors. Finally, the Côte Mâconnaise, the largest of the four, brings its own quality whites to the market. There are hundreds of vintners in this region, many of them producing top wines from surprisingly small parcels of land. To connect these dots, consult the regional tourist offices for full information about noted wine routes *and be sure to see our special photo-feature, "Grape Expectations," in this chapter.* The 74-km (50-mile) Route des Grands Crus ranges from Dijon to Beaune and Santenay. You can extend this route southward by the Route Touristique des Grands Vins, which travels some 98 km (60 miles) in and around Chalon-sur-Saône. Coming from the north, you can tour the areas around Auxerre and Chablis on the Route des Vignobles de l'Yonne *(covered above)*. Wherever you go in this killer countryside, you'll find that small towns with big wine names draw many travelers to their cellars.

CLOS DE VOUGEOT

16 km (10 miles) south of Dijon.

The reason to come to Vougeot is to see its *grange viticole* (wine-making barn) surrounded by its famous vineyard—a symbolic spot for all Burgundy aficionados.

EXPLORING

Abbaye de Cîteaux. The austere Cistercian order was founded at this abbey near Clos de Vougeot at St-Nicolas-lès-Cîteaux in 1098 by Robert de Molesmes, and the complex has housed monks ever since. Destroyed and rebuilt over the centuries, it is, understandably, a mix of styles and epochs: 13th-century cloisters, a 16th-century library, and a large, imposing 18th-century main building form an eclectic ensemble. From D996, follow signs pointing the way along a short country road that breaks off from the road to Château de Gilly, a four-star hotel. Call ahead for a guided tour. ⊠ *Off D996, Vougeot* ☎ *03–80–61–32–58* ⊕ *www.citeaux-abbaye.com* ✉ *€7.50 guided tour* ☉ *July and Aug., Tues.–Sat. 9:45–6:30, Sun. noon–6:30; May, June, and Sept., Wed.–Sat. 9:45–12:45 and 2:15–6, Sun. noon–6; see website for tour times.*

Fodor's Choice ★ **Château du Clos de Vougeot.** The Château du Clos de Vougeot was constructed in the 12th century by Cistercian monks from neighboring Cîteaux—who were in need of wine for Mass and also wanted to make a diplomatic offering—and completed during the Renaissance. It's best known as the seat of Burgundy's elite company of wine lovers, the Confrérie des Chevaliers du Tastevin, who gather here in November at the start of an annual three-day festival, Les Trois Glorieuses. You can admire the château's cellars, where ceremonies are held, and ogle the huge 13th-century grape presses, marvels of medieval engineering. There are regular photo exhibitions and concerts and an accompanied, 45-minute tour in English on request. ☎ *03–80–62–86–09* ⊕ *www. closdevougeot.fr* ✉ *€5* ☉ *Apr.–Sept., daily 9–6:30; Oct.–Mar., daily 9–11:30 and 2–5:30 (closes at 5 on Sat.).*

WHERE TO STAY

For expanded hotel reviews, visit Fodors.com.

$$$
HOTEL
Château de Gilly. Considered by some to be an obligatory stop on their tour of Burgundy's vineyards, this château retains glorious vestiges of bygone days: painted ceilings, a gigantic vaulted crypt-cellar (now the dining room), suits of armor, and (some) guest rooms with magnificent beamed ceilings and lovely views. **Pros:** beautiful location; friendly staff. **Cons:** pricey; heavily touristed; least expensive rooms

9

WORD OF MOUTH

"Rent a car and drive along the Côte de Nuits towns that sound like the wine list at a fine restaurant. And in October the vineyard leaves are in their autumn colors."

—smueller

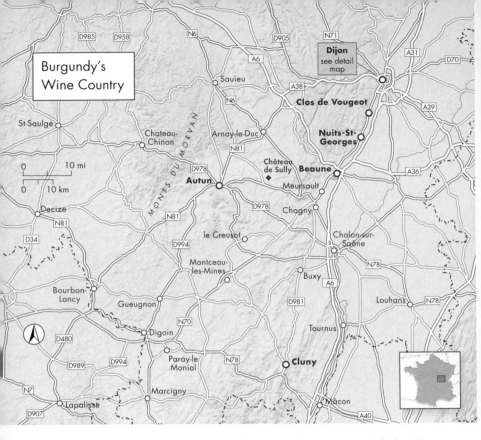

Burgundy's
Wine Country

0   10 mi
0   10 km

have standard furnishings. 💲 *Rooms from: €170* ✉ *Gilly-lès-Cîteaux, Vougeot* ☎ *03–80–62–89–98* ⊕ *www.grandesetapes.fr* ↗ *37 rooms, 11 suites* ❍ *Some meals.*

NUITS-ST-GEORGES

21 km (13 miles) south of Dijon, 5 km (3 miles) south of Clos de Vougeot.

Wine has been made in Nuits-St-Georges since Roman times; its "dry, tonic, and generous qualities" were recommended to Louis XIV for medicinal use. But this is also the heart of currant country, where crops yield the wonderfully delicious ingredient known as cassis (the signature flavor in the famous Kir cocktail).

Cassissium. The Cassissium, in a sparkling glass-and-steel building, explores the world of cassis using films, interactive displays, and a 90-minute guided tour of Védrenne's liqueur production. A cassis tasting is the final stop. ✉ *8 passage Montgolfier* ☎ *03–80–62–49–70* ⊕ *www.cassissium.com* 💲 *€8* ⊙ *Apr.–mid-Nov., daily 10–1 and 2–7; mid-Nov.–Mar., Tues.–Sat. 10:30–1 and 2–5:30 (last tour begins 1 hr, 45 mins before closing).*

WHERE TO EAT AND STAY

For expanded hotel reviews, visit Fodors.com.

$ FRENCH 🍴 **Au Bois de Charmois.** About 3 km (2 miles) out of Nuits-St-Georges, on the way toward Meuilley, this fabulous little inn serves local fare at tasty prices. A lunch menu available on weekdays includes wine and coffee. Dinner menus include six garlicky snails, followed by coq au vin or entrecôte enlivened with a tongue-tantalizing Époisses sauce, cheese, and dessert. It's especially pleasant to sit in the courtyard under the ancient trees, though on chilly, gray days the small dining room is full of good cheer. [$] *Average main: €16* ✉ *8 rte. de la Serrée* ☎ *03–80–61–04–79* 🌐 *www.auboisdecharmois.com* ✍ *Reservations essential* 🕒 *Closed Wed. No dinner Tues. and Sun.*

$$ BISTRO 🍴 **La Toute Petite Auberge.** Vosne-Romanée, the greatest wine village on the côte, also entices with one of the most charming restaurants in Burgundy. The menu changes four times a year and is replete with succulent local dishes (picture a generous mound of frogs legs, farm-reared capon, andouillette from Chablis, coq au vin, and crème brûlée). Everything is excellent and prices are more than reasonable. As you would expect, the wine list is top-notch. [$] *Average main: €21* ✉ *On the R. D. 974, 2 km (1 mile) north of Nuits-St-Georges, Vosne-Romanée* ☎ *03–80–61–02–03* 🌐 *www.latoutepetiteauberge.fr* ✍ *Reservations essential* 🕒 *Closed Wed. No dinner Tues.*

$ HOTEL 🏨 **Château de la Berchère.** Originally a medieval fortification and a battlefield during the Franco-Prussian wars, this majestic château offers elegant rooms that are simply but tastefully furnished—though some, especially No. 29, with its massive four-poster bed and marble fireplace, are in a much grander vein.**Pros:** good value; steeped in French history. **Cons:** no air-conditioning; no restaurant; bathrooms are basic, but some are equipped with sauna and whirlpool. [$] *Rooms from: €70* ✉ *4 km (2½ miles) west of Nuits-St-Georges, Boncourt-le-Bois* ☎ *03–80–61–01–40* 🌐 *www.hotelchateauberchere.com* 🛏 *22 rooms* 🕒 *Closed Dec.–Feb.*

$ B&B/INN 🏨 **Domaine Comtesse Michel de Loisy.** People who are serious about their wine flock here to stay in the eclectic guest rooms—memorably tempered with old-fashioned charm and furnished with fine antiques, tapestries, chintz-covered walls, and Oriental carpets. **Pros:** cultured hostess; large, comfortable rooms. **Cons:** no elevator; no air-conditioning in some rooms. [$] *Rooms from: €94* ✉ *28 rue du Général-de-Gaulle, rte. de Beaune* ☎ *03–80–61–02–72* 🌐 *www.domaine-de-loisy.com* 🛏 *3 rooms, 2 suites* 🕒 *Closed late Dec.–early Jan.* 🍽 *Breakfast.*

BEAUNE

19 km (12 miles) south of Nuits-St-Georges; 40 km (25 miles) south of Dijon; 315 km (197 miles) southeast of Paris.

Fodor's Choice ★ Beaune is sometimes considered the wine capital of Burgundy, because it is at the heart of the region's vineyards, with the Côte de Nuits to the north and the Côte de Beaune to the south. In late November, Les Trois Glorieuses, a three-day wine auction and fête at the Hospices de Beaune, pulls in connoisseurs and the curious from France and abroad. Despite the hordes, Beaune remains one of France's most attractive provincial towns, teeming with art aboveground and wine barrels down below.

GETTING HERE

The wine capital of Burgundy is also one of the most visited towns in the region. Though there are only two direct TGV trains leaving Paris's Gare de Lyon daily (at 6:53 am and 4:53 pm), there are 22 trains in all, with changes at Dijon. Travel times vary from two hours, 13 minutes to four hours, depending on transfers; and the fares range from the flat rate of €46.30 with the slower TER to €86.80 on the TGV. Beaune is 20 minutes from Dijon (€7.40) and gets plenty of train traffic from the through lines to Lyon (€29.30) and Nevers (€31.40). For those heading farther north, trains to Auxerre (€31.30), via Laroche Migennes, and a direct service to Sens (€34) are available. Beaune also benefits from the broad regional TRANSCO bus network and buses, which depart from the SNCF station, run to Dijon via Nuits-St-Georges (60 mins on the No. 44 wine-lovers line), and to Saulieu (weekdays at 6 pm) with the No. 72.

Visitor Information Beaune Tourist Office. ⊠ *Porte Marie de Bourgogne, 6 bd. Perpreuil* ☎ *03–80–26–21–30* ⊕ *www.ot-beaune.fr* ⊠ *Pl. de la Halle.*

EXPLORING

Collégiale Notre-Dame. A series of tapestries relating the life of the Virgin hangs in Beaune's main church, the 12th-century Romanesque Collégiale Notre-Dame. They are on public display from Easter to mid-November. ⊠ *Pl. du General Leclerc, just off av. de la République* ☎ *03–80–24–77–95* ☎ *Free; guided tour available for tapestries, €3* ☉ *Oct.–May., Mon.–Sat. 9:30–12:30 and 2–5, Sun. 1–5; June–Sept., Mon.–Sat. 9:30–12:30 and 2–7, Sun. 1–7.*

Hospices de Beaune (*Hôtel-Dieu*). The star attraction of Beaune is its famed Hospices de Beaune (better known to some as the Hôtel-Dieu), one of the icons of Burgundy, with a spectacular tile roof and Flemish architecture—the same glowing colors and intricate patterns are seen throughout the region. It was founded in 1443 as a hospital to provide free care for men who had fought in the Hundred Years' War. The interior looks medieval but was repainted by 19th-century restorer Viollet-le-Duc and centers on the **grand salle,** more than 160 feet long, with the original furniture, a great wooden roof, and the super-picturesque **cour d'honneur.** The Hospices carried on its medical activities until 1971—its nurses still wearing their habit-like uniforms—and the hospital's history is retraced in the museum, whose wide-ranging collections contain some weird medical instruments from the 15th century. You can also see a collection of tapestries that belonged to the repentant founder of the Hospices, ducal chancellor Nicolas Rolin, who hoped charity would relieve him of his sins—one of which was collecting wives. Outstanding are both the tapestry he had made for Madame Rolin III, with its repeated motif of "my only star," and one relating the legend of St. Eloi and his miraculous restoration of a horse's leg.

But the showstopper at the Hôtel-Dieu is Rogier van der Weyden's stirring, gigantic 15th-century masterpiece *The Last Judgment*, commissioned for the hospital by Rolin. The intense colors and mind-tripping

Showing off its colorfully patterned roof tiles, medieval courtyard, and Rogier van der Weyden altarpiece, the Hôtel-Dieu is Beaune's most eye-popping edifice.

imagery were meant to scare the illiterate patients into religious submission. Notice the touch of misogyny; more women are going to hell than to heaven, while Christ, the judge, remains completely unmoved. Note that the Hospices own around 150 acres of the region's finest vineyards, much of it classified as Grand and Premier Cru. ⊠ *Pl. de la Halle, rue de l'Hôtel-Dieu, across from tourist office* ☎ *03–80–24–45–00* ⊕ *www. hospices-de-beaune.com* ⊠ *€7* ⊘ *Late Mar.–late Nov., daily 9–6:30; late Nov.–late Mar., daily 9–11:30 and 2–5:30.*

Marché aux Vins (*Wine Market*). To many, the liquid highlight of a Burgundian vacation is a visit to the Marché aux Vins, where, in flickering candlelight and armed with your own *tastevin* (which you get to keep as a souvenir), you can sample a tongue-tingling, mind-spinning array of regional wines in the atmospheric setting of barrel-strewn cellars and vaulted passages. The selection runs from young Beaujolais to famous old Burgundies, and there's no limit on how much you drink and no need to reserve. Other Beaune tasting houses include Cordelier on the rue de l'Hôtel-Dieu and the Caves Patriarche on the rue du Collège. ⊠ *2 rue Nicolas-Rolin* ☎ *03–80–25–08–20* ⊕ *www.marcheauxvins.com* ⊠ *€9* ⊘ *Sept.–June, daily 9:30–11:30 and 2–5:30; July and Aug., daily 9:30–5:30.*

WHERE TO EAT

$$$
FRENCH ✕ **L'Écusson.** Don't be put off by its unprepossessing exterior: this is a comfortable, friendly, oak-beamed restaurant with good-value prix-fixe menus. Chef-owner Thomas Campagnon's sure-footed culinary mastery is evident in dishes like duck foie gras cooked two ways or fillet of beef Charolais in a rich Pinot Noir sauce with red onions and cèpe

Wine tastings abound in and around Beaune—check in with the tourist office to get a full list of vineyards and wine caves.

mushrooms. $ *Average main: €36* ⊠ *2 rue du Lieutenant-Dupuis* ☎ *03–80–24–03–82* ⊕ *www.ecusson.fr* ⌕ *Reservations essential* ☉ *Closed Wed., Sun., and Feb.*

$$ ✕ **Le P'tit Paradis.** It's well worth squeezing into this tiny corner of paradise to experience the generous and modern bistro fare of Beaune's most capable culinary couple. Rabbit terrine with hazelnut oil and Charolais beef with an Époisses cream sauce grace a menu fit for a stint with the angels. Excellent value menus are offered. $ *Average main: €20* ⊠ *2 rue du Paradis* ☎ *03–80–24–91–00* ⊕ *www.restaurantleptitparadis.fr* ⌕ *Reservations essential* ☉ *Closed Sun., Mon., Aug., Dec., and Jan.*

FRENCH
Fodor's Choice
★

$$$$ ✕ **Loiseau des Vignes.** Where else would you expect one of Burgundy's leading culinary establishments to open a wine bar? A massive range of 70 wines, all available by the glass, is the perfect accompaniment to a selection of Bernard Loiseau's famous regional dishes (along with some old-fashioned essentials). Lunch and dinner menus include such delights as *œufs meurette Bernard Loiseau* (poached eggs in red-wine sauce) and pigeon breast accompanied by a delicate black-currant sauce. Indulge in the wine-tasting menu and sample five of Burgundy's best, or go by the glass. $ *Average main: €60* ⊠ *31 rue Maufoux* ☎ *03–80–24–12–06* ⊕ *www.bernard-loiseau.com* ⌕ *Reservations essential* ☉ *Closed Sun., Mon., and Feb.*

FRENCH FUSION

WHERE TO STAY
For expanded hotel reviews, visit Fodors.com.

$$$ 🏨 **Château de Chorey.** Complete with storybook tower, mansard roofs, and elegant white shutters, the *authentique* château at this family winery really lets you soak up the flavor of the vineyards. **Pros:** lovely

B&B/INN

example of domestic Burgundian architecture; well-appointed bathrooms; attractive furnishings. **Cons:** no restaurant; not inexpensive; beds are on the small side. [$] *Rooms from: €175* ✉ *2 rue Jacques-Germain, 3 km (almost 2 miles) north of Beaune, Chorey-les-Beaune* ☎ *03–80–22–06–05* 🌐 *www.chateau-de-chorey-les-beaune.fr* 🛏 *3 rooms, 2 suites* ⏲ *Closed Nov.–Easter* 🍴 *Breakfast.*

$$$ B&B/INN 🏨 **Hostellerie de Levernois.** This idyllic Relais & Châteaux property—a gracious country manor, smartly run by Jean-Louis and Susanne Botigliero—enchants on many levels, from its unique fleur-de-lys topiary to its superb restaurant to its wood-beam cathedral guest rooms. **Pros:** lovely, spacious rooms; personable staff; great food. **Cons:** pricey; no elevator; main restaurant closed Sunday and Wednesday for dinner. [$] *Rooms from: €185* ✉ *Rue du Golf, 3 km (2 miles) east of Beaune, Levernois* ☎ *03–80–24–73–58* 🌐 *www.levernois.com* 🛏 *20 rooms, 6 suites* ⏲ *Closed Feb.–mid-Mar.* 🍴 *Some meals.*

$$ HOTEL 🏨 **Hôtel Central.** This well-run establishment 100 yards from the Hospices de Beaune lives up to its name and offers good, clean guest rooms at a gentle price. **Pros:** central location; comfortable rooms. **Cons:** not all rooms have private baths; street-facing rooms can be noisy; breakfast is extra. [$] *Rooms from: €89* ✉ *2 rue Victor-Millot* ☎ *03–80–24–77–24* 🌐 *www.hotelcentral-beaune.com* 🛏 *20 rooms, 10 with bath* ⏲ *Closed Jan.*

$$$ HOTEL Fodor's Choice ★ 🏨 **Hôtel Le Cep.** This stylish ensemble of buildings spanning the 14th to the 16th century oozes history from every arcade of its Renaissance courtyard, and, even better, all guest rooms—named for different Burgundy wines—have been luxuriously modernized and decorated with crystal chandeliers and individual panache; some have wood beams, others canopied or four-poster beds. **Pros:** luxurious rooms; historical location; friendly staff. **Cons:** thin walls; pricey breakfast. [$] *Rooms from: €174* ✉ *27 rue Jean François Maufoux* ☎ *03–80–22–35–48* 🌐 *www.hotel-cep-beaune.com* 🛏 *40 rooms, 18 suites, 6 apartments.*

$$$$ HOTEL 🏨 **La Cueillette.** Sitting pretty in the middle of manicured rows of Meursault vines, the Château de Citeaux provides a stately setting for this hotel and spa. **Pros:** excellent spa; gastronomic restaurant. **Cons:** few rooms have bathtubs. [$] *Rooms from: €220* ✉ *Rue de Cîteaux, 9 km (5½ miles) southwest of Beaune, Meursault* ☎ *03–80–20–62–80* 🌐 *www.lacueillette.com* 🛏 *17 rooms, 2 suites* 🍴 *Some meals.*

THE ARTS

Beaune Tourist Office. For festival information, contact Beaune's Office de Tourisme. ✉ *6 bd. Perpreuil* ☎ *03–80–26–21–30* 🌐 *www.ot-beaune.fr.*

International Festival of Baroque Opera. In July Beaune celebrates its annual, monthlong International Festival of Baroque Opera, which draws big stars of the music world. It's possible to reserve online. 🌐 *www.festivalbeaune.com.*

Internatonal Thriller Film Festival. Beaune plays host to the Internatonal Thriller Film Festival at the end of March and early April. ☎ *03–80–26–21–30 tourist office* 🌐 *www.beaunefestivalpolicier.com.*

Les Trois Glorieuses. On the third weekend in November Beaune holds its famous wine festival—Les Trois Glorieuses. It starts with a public tasting on Saturday, continues with an auction on Sunday, and closes with a tipsy lunch for the wine elite at Château de Meursault on Monday.

CHÂTEAU DE SULLY

Château de Sully. "The Fontainebleau of Burgundy" was how Madame de Sévigné described this turreted Renaissance château, proclaiming the inner court, whose Italianate design was inspired by Sebastiano Serlio, as the latest in chic. The building is magnificent, landmarked by four lantern-top corner towers that loom over a romantic moat filled with the waters of the River Drée. Originally constructed by the de Rabutin family and once owned by Gaspard de Saulx-Tavannes—an instigator of the St. Bartholomew's Day Massacre, August 24, 1572, in which mobs attacked Huguenots in and around Paris—the château was partly reconstructed in elegant Régence style in the 18th century. Maurice de MacMahon, the Irish-origin president of France from 1873 to 1879, was born here in 1808. ⊠ *35 km (19 miles) west of Beaune* ☎ *03–85–82–09–86* ⊕ *www.chateaudesully.com* ⊿ *€3.95 (gardens only), €8.20 for guided tour* ⊙ *Apr.–June and Sept.–Nov., daily 10–6; July and Aug., daily 10–7. Closes 1 hr earlier on Sat.*

AUTUN

48 km (30 miles) west of Beaune.

Fodor's Choice ★ One of the most richly endowed *villes d'art* in Burgundy, Autun is a great draw for fans of both Gallo-Roman and Romanesque art. It is unfortunate that people don't often think of Autun when creating their Burgundian itineraries. Once the second city of Burgundy, it has a host of visual delights from its ancient Roman theater to its medieval cathedral to its Musée Rolin, one of the region's best museums.

Visitor Information Autun Tourist Office ⊠ *13 rue Général Demetz* ☎ *03–85–86–80–38* ⊕ *www.autun-tourisme.com.*

EXPLORING

Major roads and railways bypass Autun, enabling its ancient remains, medieval streets, and magnificent cathedral to be admired amid calm and serenity. Autun's name derives from Augustodonum—city of Augustus—and it was Augustus Caesar who called it "the sister and rival of Rome itself." You can still see traces of the Roman occupation, dating from an era when Autun was much larger and more important than it is now, in its well-preserved archways (Porte St-André and Porte d'Arroux) and Théâtre Romain (once the largest arena in Gaul). Parts of the Roman walls surrounding the town also remain and give a fair indication of its size in those days. The significance of the curious Pierre de Couhard, a pyramid-like Roman construction, baffles archaeologists. Logically enough, this Roman outpost became a center for the new 11th-century style based on Roman precedent, the Romanesque, and its greatest sculptor, Gislebertus, left his precocious mark on the town cathedral. Several centuries later, Napoléon and his brother Joseph studied here at the military academy.

The basilica of the Abbaye de Cluny, built between 1088 and 1130, was the world's largest church before St. Peter's in Rome took the title.

Cathédrale St-Lazare. Autun's principal monument is the Cathédrale St-Lazare, a Gothic cathedral in Classical clothing. It was built between 1120 and 1146 to house the relics of St. Lazarus; the main tower, spire, and upper reaches of the chancel were added in the late 15th century. Lazarus's tricolor tomb was dismantled in 1766 by canons: vestiges of exquisite workmanship can be seen in the neighboring Musée Rolin. The same canons also did their best to transform the Romanesque-Gothic cathedral into a Classical temple, adding pilasters and other ornaments willy-nilly. Fortunately, the lacy Flamboyant Gothic organ tribune and some of the best Romanesque stonework, including the inspired nave capitals and the tympanum above the main door, emerged unscathed. Jean-Auguste-Dominique Ingres's painting *The Martyrdom of St. Symphorien* has been relegated to the dingy north aisle of the nave, partly masked by the organ. The *Last Judgment* carved in stone above the main door was plastered over in the 18th century, which preserved not only the stylized Christ and elongated apostles but also the inscription "Gislebertus hoc fecit" (Gislebertus did this). Christ's head, which had disappeared, was found by a local canon shortly after World War II. Make sure to visit the cathedral's **Salle Capitulaire,** which houses Gislebertus's original capitals, distinguished by their relief carvings. ■**TIP➔** The cathedral provides a stunning setting for **Musique en Morvan,** a festival of choral music in late July. ⊠ *Pl. St-Louis* ☎ *03–85–52–12–37* ⊕ *www.art-roman.net/autun/autun.htm* 🖂 *Salle Capitulaire.*

Musée Rolin. Built by Chancellor Nicolas Rolin, an important Burgundian administrator and famous art patron (he's immortalized in one of the Louvre's greatest paintings, Jan van Eyck's *Madonna and the*

Chancellor Rolin), this museum across from the cathedral is noteworthy for its early Flemish paintings and sculpture. Among them is the magisterial *Nativity* painted by the Maître de Moulins in the 15th century, but the collection's star is a Gislebertus masterpiece, the *Temptation of Eve,* which originally topped one of the side doors of the cathedral. Try to imagine the missing elements of the scene: Adam on the left and the devil on the right. ✉ *5 rue des Bancs* ☎ *03–85–52–09–76* 🎟 *€5.15* 🕒 *Apr.–Sept., Wed.–Mon. 9:30–noon and 1:30–6; Oct.–mid-Dec. and Mar., Mon., and Wed.–Sat. 10–noon and 2–5, Sun. 2:30–5.*

FAMILY **Théâtre Romain.** The Théâtre Romain, at the edge of town on the road to Chalon-sur-Saône, is a historic spot for lunch. Pick up the makings for a picnic in town and eat it on the stepped seats, where as many as 15,000 Gallo-Roman spectators perched two millennia ago. In August a themed performance—the only one of its kind—is put on by locals wearing period costumes. The peak of a Gallo-Roman pyramid can be seen in the foreground. Elsewhere on the outskirts of town are the remains of an ancient Roman Temple of Janus.

WHERE TO STAY

For expanded hotel reviews, visit Fodors.com.

$ B&B/INN 🏨 **Hostellerie du Vieux Moulin.** This converted mill sits in a tree-lined garden complete with pond and exudes a rustic Burgundian charm, while the spacious guest rooms—some with views of the river, others looking out over the countryside—are cozy and clean. **Pros:** calm surroundings; good restaurant. **Cons:** 15-minute walk from town center; no elevator; breakfast is extra. [$] *Rooms from: €75* ✉ *Porte d'Arroux, rte. de Saulieu* ☎ *03–85–52–10–90* 🛏 *16 rooms* 🕒 *Closed Dec.–Feb.* 🍴 *Some meals.*

$$ HOTEL Fodor's Choice ★ 🏨 **Les Ursulines.** Placed above the Roman ramparts of the old city, this gorgeous 17th-century convent has been transformed into a delightful hotel, complete with spacious guest rooms, an antiques-adorned restaurant, and a splendid, geometric, French-style garden. **Pros:** historical setting; quiet yet central location; fine views from some rooms. **Cons:** hodgepodge decor. [$] *Rooms from: €108* ✉ *14 rue de Rivault* ☎ *03–85–86–58–58* 🌐 *www.hotelursulines.fr* 🛏 *38 rooms, 5 suites* 🍴 *Some meals.*

CLUNY

77 km (46 miles) southeast of Autun.

The village of Cluny is legendary for its medieval abbey, once the center of a vast Christian empire. Although most of the complex was destroyed in the French Revolution, one soaring transept of this church remains standing, today one of the most magnificent sights of Romanesque architecture.

GETTING HERE

Getting to Cluny is fairly easy as there are two TGV trains leaving Paris's Gare de Lyon daily (9:49 am and 5:49 pm), although they both require a 30-minute bus liaison from Mâcon. There are also regular, daily TGV and TER trains that can take you directly to Chalon-sur-Saône

(€48.40–€83.90). TRANSDEV (Les Rapides de Saône et Loire ⊕ *www.r-s-l.fr*) has regular buses that link Cluny to Chalon-sur-Saône, where you can connect to Mâcon, Autun, and Le Creusot TGV railway stations. Driving to Cluny is a delight, as the surrounding countryside of the Mâconnais is among the most beautiful of France, with rolling fields and picturesque villages reminding one of why it is so easy to fall in love with France.

> ### CIRCLING THE WAGONS À LA FRANÇAISE
>
> On Friday and Saturday nights from late July to early August, time rewinds in Autun as its ancient Roman theater brings the Celtic and Gallo-Roman periods to life in a Busby Berkeley–esque extravaganza featuring Celtic fairies, Roman gladiators, and chariot races. Log on to ⊕ *www.autun-tourisme.com* for all the details.

Visitor Information Cluny Tourist Office ✉ *6 rue Mercière* ☎ *03–85–59–05–34* ⊕ *www.cluny-tourisme.com.*

EXPLORING

Fodor'sChoice
★
Ancienne Abbaye. Founded in the 10th century, the Ancienne Abbaye was the largest church in Europe until the 16th century, when Michelangelo built St. Peter's in Rome. Art historians have written themselves into knots tracing the fundamental influence of its architecture in the development of early Gothic style. Cluny's medieval abbots were as powerful as popes; in 1098 Pope Urban II (himself a Cluniac) assured the head of his old abbey that Cluny was the "light of the world." That assertion, of dubious religious validity, has not stood the test of time—after the Revolution the abbey was sold as national property and much of it used as a stone quarry. Today Cluny stands in ruins, a reminder of the vanity of human grandeur. The ruins, however, suggest the size and gorgeous super-romantic glory of the abbey at its zenith, and piecing it back together in your mind is part of the attraction.

In order to get a clear sense of what you're looking at, start at the **Porte d'Honneur,** the entrance to the abbey from the village, whose classical architecture is reflected in the pilasters and Corinthian columns of the **Clocher de l'Eau-Bénite** (a majestic bell tower), crowning the only remaining part of the abbey church, the south transept. Between the two is the reconstructed monumental staircase, which led to the portal of the abbey church, and the excavated column bases of the vast narthex. The entire nave is gone. On one side of the transept is a national horse-breeding center (*haras*) founded in 1806 by Napoléon and constructed with materials from the destroyed abbey; on the other is an elegant pavilion built as new monks' lodgings in the 18th century. The gardens in front of it once contained an ancient lime tree (destroyed by a 1982 storm) named after Abélard, the controversial philosopher who sought shelter here in 1142. Off to the right is the 13th-century *farinier* (flour store), with its fine oak-and-chestnut roof and collection of exquisite Romanesque capitals from the vanished choir. The **Musée d'Art et d'Archéologie,** in the Palais Jean de Bourbon, contains Europe's foremost Romanesque lapidary museum. Vestiges of both the abbey and the village constructed around it are conserved here, as well as part of

9

the Bibliothèque des Moines (Monks' Library). ⊠ *Pl. de l'abbaye* 🕾 *03–85–59–15–93 Abbaye, 03–85–59–89–99 Palais de Bourbon* ⊕ *www. monuments-nationaux.fr* 🖃 *€9.50 one ticket for both sites valid for 2 days* ⊙ *Jan.–Mar. and Oct.–Dec., daily 9:30–5; Apr.–June and Sept., daily 9:30–6; July and Aug., daily 9:30–7.*

Hôtel des Monnaies (*Abbey Mint*). The village of Cluny was built to serve the abbey's more practical needs, and several fine Romanesque houses around the rue d'Avril and the rue de la République—including the so-called Hôtel des Monnaies—are prime examples of the period's different architectural styles. ⊠ *6 rue d'Avril* 🕾 *03–85–59–05–56.*

Tour des Fromages. Parts of the town ramparts, the much-restored 11th-century defensive Tour des Fromages (now home to the tourist office) and several noteworthy medieval churches also remain. ⊠ *6 rue Mercière* 🕾 *03–85–59–05–34 tourist office* 🖃 *€2* ⊙ *Jan.–Mar. and Oct.–Dec., Mon.–Sat. 10–12:30 and 2:30–5; May, June, and Sept., daily 9:30–12:30 and 2:30–6:30; July and Aug., daily 9:30–6:30; Apr., Mon.–Sat. 9:30–12:30 and 2:30–6:30.*

WHERE TO STAY

For expanded hotel reviews, visit Fodors.com.

$$
HOTEL

🏠 **Hôtel de Bourgogne.** Time-burnished if not time-stained, this old-fashioned hotel was built in 1817, where parts of the abbey once stood. **Pros:** historic setting; good value; helpful staff; service comes with a no-holds-barred smile. **Cons:** no elevator; breakfast is extra but copious. 💲 *Rooms from: €133* ⊠ *Pl. de l'Abbaye* 🕾 *03–85–59–00–58* ⊕ *www. hotel-cluny.com* ⤵ *13 rooms, 3 suites* ⊙ *Closed Dec. and Jan., and Tues. and Wed. in Feb.* ⎹⦿⎸ *Some meals.*

THE ARTS

Grandes Heures de Cluny. The ruined abbey of Cluny forms the backdrop of the Grandes Heures de Cluny, a classical music festival held late July to mid-August. Free Burgundy wine-tastings are offered after concerts. ⊠ *Hotel des Monnaies, 6 rue d'Avril* 🕾 *03–85–59–25–66 for details.*

LYON AND
THE ALPS

10

Visit Fodors.com for advice, updates, and bookings

WELCOME TO LYON AND THE ALPS

TOP REASONS TO GO

★ **Vieux Lyon:** Lyon's Old Town *traboules*, or passageways, and 16th-century courtyards reveal a hidden trove of Renaissance architecture.

★ **Le Beaujolais Nouveau est arrivé!:** The third Thursday of November is a party like no other in France, when celebrations in honor of the new Beaujolais wine go around the clock.

★ **Mont Blanc:** Whether you brave the vertiginous slopes at Chamonix or enjoy the gentler skiing of Megève, you'll be singing "Ain't No Mountain High Enough" once you see Mont Blanc, France's tallest peak.

★ **Grenoble's market day:** Sunday morning offers a chance to walk miles through half a dozen different markets selling everything from herbs to haberdashery.

★ **Epic epicureanism:** There is no possible way to cite Lyon-Rhône Alps without mentioning Paul Bocuse, Mathieu Viannay, and all the other resident superstar chefs.

1 Lyon. This city is most famous for the Vieux Lyon district, with its Renaissance *traboules* (passageways), and the bustling Presqu'île, a peninsula between the two rivers. Lyon's historic industrial power has generated ample cultural resources and the energy to create first-rate music, cinema, theater, opera, dance, and cuisine.

2 Beaujolais. Follow the Saône River north from Lyon to the area around Villefranche and you will find the vineyards of Beaujolais, a moving pilgrimage for any wine lover. Diminutive villages with poetic names such as St-Amour, Fleurie, and Juliénas are surrounded by rolling hillsides bristling with grapevines. To the east lies Bourg-en-Bresse, famed for its church and its chickens.

GETTING ORIENTED

Lyon is France's natural hub, where the rivers Rhône and Saône meet and the mountainous wilderness of the Massif Central leans toward the lofty Alps. Lyon is a magnet for the surrounding region, including the vineyards of Beaujolais. South of Lyon is the quaint Rhône Valley. Along the southeastern border of France rises a mighty barrier of mountains that provides some of the most spectacular scenery in Europe: the French Alps, soaring to their climax in Western Europe's highest peak, Mont Blanc.

4 Grenoble and the Alps. Grenoble, in the Dauphiné, is the gateway to the Alps at the nexus of rivers and highways connecting Marseille, Valence, Lyon, Geneva, and Turin. Literati will love its Stendahl sites and art-filled musée. To the east, rustic towns announce the Alps, none more idyllic than Annecy, thanks to its blue lake, covered lanes, and quiet canals. The region's natural Alpine splendors are showcased at Chamonix and Megève, ski resorts that buzz with life from December to April.

3 The Rhône Valley. Like predestined lovers, the masculine Rhône joins the feminine Saône to form a fluvial force rolling south to the Mediterranean. Their bounty includes hundreds of steep vineyards and small-town winemakers tempting you with samples. The ancient Roman ruins of Vienne and the Romanesque relics of Valence reflect the Rhône's importance as an early trade route.

10

Updated
by Jennifer
Ditsler-Ladonne

Lyon and the Alps are as alike as chocolate and broccoli. Lyon is fast, congested, and saturated with culture (and smog). In the bustling city—often called the gateway to the Alps—it's hard to believe that those pristine peaks are only an hour's train ride away. Likewise, when you're in a small Alpine village you could almost forget France has any large cities at all, because everything you imagined about the Alps—soaring snowcaps, jagged ridges, refreshing lakes— is true. Culturally, Lyon and the Alps could well be on different continents but geographically they make for a great vacation combo.

Cheek by jowl, they share a patch of earth sculpted by the noble Rhône as it courses down from Switzerland, flowing out of Lake Geneva. And this soil, or as the French call it, the *terroir,* provides many tasty treasures, beginning with the region's saucy Beaujolais wines. Glinting purple against red-checked linens in a Lyonnais *bouchon* (tavern), pink-cheeked Beaujolais vintages flatter every item listed on those famous blackboard menus: a fat *boudin noir* bursting from its casing, a tangle of country greens in tangy mustard vinaigrette, or a taste of crackling roast chicken.

If you are what you eat, then Lyon itself is real and hearty, as straightforward and unabashedly simple as a *poulet de Bresse.* Yet the refinements of superlative opera, theater, and classical music also happily thrive in Lyon's gently patinated urban milieu, one strangely reminiscent of 1930s Paris—lace curtains in painted-over storefronts, elegant bourgeois town houses, deep-shaded parks, and low-slung bridges lacing back and forth over the broad, lazy Saône and Rhône rivers.

When you've had your fill of this, pack a picnic of victuals to tide you over and head for the hills—the Alps, to be exact. Here is a land of green-velvet slopes and icy mists, ranging from the modern urban hub of Grenoble and the crystalline lake of Annecy to the state-of-the-art ski resorts of Chamonix and Megève. Let your grand finale be Mont Blanc: at 15,700 feet, it's Western Europe's highest peak.

PLANNER

WHEN TO GO

Lyon and the Rhône-Alpes are so diverse in altitude and climate that the weather will depend mostly on where you are, when you're there, and which way the wind blows. Freezing gales have been known to turn Lyon's late September dance festival into a winter carnival, with icy blasts from the Massif Central sweeping down the Saône. As a rule, however, Lyon may be rainy and misty, but not especially cold. Conversely, Grenoble and the Alps can be bitter at any time of year, especially from December to April. The Beaujolais wine region is generally temperate, though a recent Nouveau Beaujolais fest (held on the third Thursday in November) froze vines and revelers alike. South of Lyon along the Rhône the sun beats down on the vineyards in full summer, but the winds howl in winter.

PLANNING YOUR TIME

Lyon, with its ample range of architecture, food, and culture, deserves several days—two at the very least. The wine country of the Beaujolais up the River Saône is another two-day visit, unless a drive-through directly to Bourg-en-Bresse is all that time constraints will allow. Medieval Pérouges is another good day's browse, with time left over for a late afternoon and evening drive into the Alps to Annecy, where the Vieille Ville (Old Town) is an eyeful by day or night. It's also worth making time for visits to Talloires and other pretty towns around the lake.

The mountain resort of Megève is a place to either settle in for a few days or blow through on your way to Chambéry. Grenoble offers opportunities for perusing masterpieces in its superb museum or following the novelist Stendhal's footsteps through the old quarter. From Grenoble it's a quick transfer, via the autoroute, to Valence to admire the cathedral and art museum. If you're headed back to Lyon from here, stop at Vienne for its Roman sites.

HOW TO TALK WINE

The Beaujolais region has hundreds of village wine *caves* (cellars). Opt for those with signs that state "Dégustation, vente en direct" (sold directly from the property) or "Vente au détail" (sold by the bottle). Also look for the town's co-op *caveau*, where you can pay a few euros to taste all the wine you want. *À votre santé* (to your health).

GETTING HERE AND AROUND

Lyon is best explored on foot, with the occasional tramway or subway connection to get you across town in a hurry. Boat tours around the Presqu'île open up another perspective on this riverside metropolis, while bike rentals can also be handy. Consider taking advantage of the Lyon City Card, a one-, two-, or three-day pass (€18, €27, and €36 respectively) to museums, with discounts at boutiques, restaurants, and cultural events. Lyon is an important rail hub with three major stations.

10

Trains from the Gare de la Part-Dieu connect easily with Villefranche-sur-Saône in the middle of the Beaujolais country, while the Gare de Perrache serves points south such as Valence and Vienne.

The main train stations in this chapter are in Lyon, Annecy, and Grenoble, but most small towns along the way have them, too, or, more accurately, a building with a few wooden seats alongside the tracks. So one of the best ways to explore the Alps is to keep your eye out for a stop that looks interesting and hop off.

If you can swing it, a car is probably the best way to get around the Beaujolais wine country and the rest of Rhône-Alpes, although bus routes, if infrequent, do usually extend to the far reaches of these regions.

AIR TRAVEL

The region's international gateway airport is Aéroport-Lyon-Saint-Exupéry (☎ *08–26–80–08–26 from within France, 33–426–007–007 from abroad*), 26 km (16 miles) east of Lyon, in Satolas. There are domestic airports at Grenoble, Valence, Annecy, Chambéry, and Aix-les-Bains.

BUS TRAVEL

Buses from Lyon and Grenoble thoroughly and efficiently serve the region's smaller towns. Many ski centers, such as Chamonix, have shuttle buses connecting them with surrounding villages. Grenoble's Gare Routière (✉ *11 pl. de la Gare* ☎ *04–76–87–90–31* ⊕ *www.transisere.fr*) is the place to catch buses to Annecy (1 hr, 40 mins; €12.90). As for Alpine villages, regional buses head out from the main train stations at Annecy, Chambéry, Megève, and Grenoble.

CAR TRAVEL

Regional roads are fast and well maintained, though smaller mountainous routes can be difficult to navigate and high passes may be closed in winter. A6 speeds south from Paris to Lyon—a distance of 463 km (287 miles). The Tunnel de Fourvière, which cuts through Lyon, is a classic hazard, and at peak times you may sit idling for hours. Lyon is 313 km (194 miles) north of Marseille on A7.

To make the 105-km (63-mile) trip southeast to Grenoble from Lyon, take A43 to A48. Coming from the south, take A7 to Valence and then swing east on A49 to A48 to Grenoble. From Grenoble to Megève and Chamonix through Annecy take A41–E712 to Annecy (direction Geneva), and then A40 (direction Montblanc-Chamonix). Turn off A40 at Sallanches for the 17-km (10½-mile) drive on the N212 to Megève.

TRAIN TRAVEL

High-speed TGV trains (☎ *36–35 [€0.34 per min]* ⊕ *www.tgv.com*) leave Paris's Gare de Lyon hourly and arrive in Lyon just two hours later. There are also six TGVs daily between Paris's Charles de Gaulle Airport and Lyon. Two in-town train stations and a third at the airport (Lyon-Saint-Exupéry) make the city a major transportation hub. The Gare de la Part-Dieu (✉ *Bd. Vivier-Merle*) is used for the TGV routes and links Lyon with many other cities, including Bordeaux, Montpellier and Marseilles, along with Grenoble. On the other side of town, the *centre-ville* station at Gare de Perrache (✉ *Cours de Verdun, pl. Carnot* ☎ *04–72–56–95–30)* is the more crowded option and serves all the sights of the centre ville—many trains stop at both stations. The TGV station at Aéroport-Lyon-Saint-Exupéry serves Avignon, Arles, Valence, Annecy, Aix-les-Bains, and Chambéry, as well as Paris. The TGV also has a less frequent service to Grenoble, where you can connect to local SNCF trains (☎36–35 [€0.34 per min] ⊕ www.sncf.com) headed for villages in the Alps. For the Beaujolais Wine Country, most people travel to Villefranche-sur-Saône's station on the place de la Gare; trains run to smaller towns from here.

RESTAURANTS

The food you'll find in the Rhône-Alps region is some of France's best—after all, this is considered the birthplace of the country's traditional cuisine, while also being the engine room of tomorrow's latest trends and gourmet styles. *(For the full scoop, see our special feature in this chapter, "Lyon: France's Culinary Cauldron.")* In Lyon's countless *bouchons* (taverns or eating houses), you'll find everything from *gras double* (tripe) to *boudin noir* (black sausage) to *paillasson* (fried hashed potatoes). If it's a light or vegetarian meal you're after, you'll be hard-pressed to find one here.

Prices in the reviews are the average cost of a main course at dinner or, if dinner is not served, at lunch.

HOTELS

Hotels, inns, *gîtes d'étapes* (hikers' way stations), and *chambres d'hôte* (bed-and-breakfasts) run the gamut from grande luxe to spartanly rustic in this multifaceted region embracing ultraurban chic in Lyon as well as ski huts in the Alps. Lyon accommodations range from guest rooms with panoramic views high in the hilltop Croix Rousse district to chic hotels in Vieux Lyon. The Alps, of course, are well furnished with top hotels, especially in Grenoble and the time-honored ski resorts such as Chamonix and Megève. Many hotels expect you to have at least your evening meal there, especially in summer; in winter they up the ante and hope travelers will take all three meals.

Prices in the reviews are the lowest cost of a standard double room in high season.

VISITOR INFORMATION

Comité Régional du Tourisme Rhône-Alps ⊠ *78 rte. de Paris, Charbonnières-les-Bains* ☎ *04–72–59–21–59* ⊕ *www.rhonealpes-tourisme.com.*

L'Office du Tourisme. The Office du Tourisme deals with the Isère *département* and the area around Grenoble. ⊠ *14 rue de la République, Grenoble* ☎ *04–76–42–41–41* ⊕ *www.grenoble-tourisme.com.*

Local tourist offices are listed under their respective towns in this chapter.

TOUR OPTIONS

BOAT TOURS

LyonCityBoat. LyonCityBoat arranges daily boat trips—with or without a meal—from Lyon's quai des Célestins along the Saône and Rhône rivers. ⊠ *13 bis, quai Rambaud, Lyon* ☎ *04–78–42–96–81* ⊕ *www. lyoncityboat.com.*

10

BUS TOURS

Philibert. Philibert runs bus tours of the region from April to October starting in Lyon. ⊠ *24 av. Barthélemy-Thimonnier, Caluire-et-Cuire* ☎ *04–72–23–10–56.*

WALKING TOURS

Lyon tourist office. The Lyon tourist office organizes walking tours of the city in English. ⊠ *Pl. Bellecour, Lyon* ☎ *04–72–77–69–69* ⊕ *www. lyon-france.com.*

LYON

The city's setting at the confluence of the Saône and the Rhône is a spectacular riverine landscape overlooked from the heights to the west by the imposing Notre-Dame de Fourvière church and from the north by the hilltop neighborhood of La Croix Rousse. Meanwhile, La Confluence Project at the southern tip of the Presqu'île (the land between the Saône and the Rhône) has reclaimed from the rivers nearly a square mile of center-city real estate that has become a neighborhood of parks, shops, restaurants, and cultural sites. Another attraction is Lyon's extraordinary dining scene—the city has more good restaurants per square mile than any other European city except Paris.

GETTING HERE AND AROUND

To get between the Aéroport-Lyon-Saint-Exupéry and the city center take the Rhone Express (☎ *08–26–00–17–18* ⊕ *www.rhonexpress.fr* €*15*), a tramway that makes the 30-minute trip every quarter hour between 6 am and 9 pm (every half hour 5 am–6 am and 9 pm–12:40 am), with various stops along the way—including the Lyon Part-Dieu train station. If you're coming by train, Lyon has three major stations so is easily reached by rail. To get here by car, take A6 south from Paris for 463 km (287 miles). The city's squeaky-clean and efficient subway gets you from one end of town to the other in 5 to 10 minutes. Four métro lines and three tramway lines crisscross the city. A single ticket costs €1.60 and a 10-ticket book is €14.30. Both two-hour and evening passes cost €2.60. A day "Liberté" pass for bus and métro is €5 (available from bus drivers and the automated machines in the métro).

Visitor Information Lyon Tourist Information ⊠ *Pl. Bellecour* ☎ *04–72–77–69–69* ⊕ *www.lyon-france.com* ⊠ *Av. Adolphe Max, near cathedral*

EXPLORING

Lyon and Marseille both claim to be France's "second city." In terms of size and industrial importance, Marseille probably deserves that title. But for tourist appeal, gastronomy, and culture Lyon is the clear winner. It has its share of historic buildings and quaint *traboules*, the passageways under and through town houses dating from the Renaissance (in Vieux Lyon) and the 19th century (in La Croix Rousse). Originally designed as dry, high-speed shortcuts for silk weavers delivering their wares, these passageways were used by the French Resistance during World War II to elude German street patrols.

Lyon's development owes much to its riverside site halfway between Paris and the Mediterranean, and within striking distance of Switzerland,

Italy, and the Alps. Lyonnais are proud that their city has been important for more than 2,000 years. Under the Romans, who called it Lugdunum (meaning "hill or fortress of Lug," the supreme deity of Celtic mythology), it became the second-largest city in their empire and was named the capital of Gaul around 43 BC. The remains of the Roman theater and the Odéon, the Gallo-Roman music hall, are among the most spectacular Roman ruins in the world.

In the middle of the city is the Presqu'île (literally, "almost an island"), a fingerlike peninsula between the rivers where modern Lyon throbs with shops, restaurants, museums, theaters, and a postmodern Jean Nouvel–designed opera house. West of the Saône is Vieux Lyon (Old Lyon), with its peaceful Renaissance charm; above it is the old Roman district of Fourvière. To the north is the hilltop Croix Rousse District, where Lyon's silk weavers once operated their looms in lofts designed as workshop dwellings, while across the Rhône to the east are a mix of older residential areas, the famous Halles de Lyon market, and the ultramodern Part-Dieu business district with its landmark *gratte-ciel* (skyscraper) beyond.

VIEUX LYON AND FOURVIÈRE

Vieux Lyon—one of the richest groups of urban Renaissance dwellings in Europe—has narrow cobblestone streets, 15th- and 16th-century mansions, small museums, and a divine cathedral. When Lyon became an important silk-weaving town in the 15th century, Italian merchants and bankers built dozens of Renaissance-style town houses. Officially cataloged as national monuments, the courtyards and passageways are open to the public during the morning. The excellent Renaissance Quarter map of the traboules and courtyards of Vieux Lyon, available at the tourist office and in most hotel lobbies, offers the city's most gratifying exploring. Above Vieux Lyon, in hilly Fourvière, are the remains of two Roman theaters and the Basilique de Notre-Dame, visible from all over the city.

EXPLORING
TOP ATTRACTIONS
Basilique de Notre-Dame-de-Fourvière. The rather pompous late-19th-century basilica, at the top of the *ficelle* (funicular railway), is—for better or worse—the symbol of Lyon. Its mock-Byzantine architecture and hilltop site make it a close relative of Paris's Sacré-Coeur. Both were built to underline the might of the Roman Catholic Church after the Prussian defeat of France in 1870 gave rise to the birth of the anticlerical Third Republic. The excessive gilt, marble, and mosaics in the interior underscore the Church's wealth, although they masked its lack of political clout at that time. One of the few places in Lyon where you can't see the basilica is the adjacent terrace, whose panorama reveals the city—with the cathedral of St-Jean in the foreground and the glass towers of the reconstructed Part-Dieu business complex glistening behind. For a more sweeping view still, climb the 287 steps to the basilica observatory. ⊠ *8 pl. de Fourvière, Fourvière* ☎ *04–78–25–13–01* ⊕ *www.fourviere.*

10

org ✉ *Observatory* €6 ⊙ *Observatory Easter–Oct., daily 10–noon and 2–6; Nov.–Easter, weekends 2–6. Basilica daily 8–noon and 2–6.*

Cathédrale St-Jean. Solid and determined—having withstood the sieges of time, revolution, and war—the cathedral's stumpy facade is stuck almost bashfully onto the nave. Although the mishmash inside has its moments—the fabulous 13th-century stained-glass windows in the choir and the varied window tracery and vaulting in the side chapels—the interior lacks drama and harmony. Still, it's an architectural history lesson. The cathedral dates from the 12th century, and the chancel is Romanesque, but construction on the whole continued over three centuries. The 14th-century astronomical clock, in the north transept, is a marvel of technology very much worth seeing. It chimes a hymn to St. John on the hour at noon, 2, 3, and 4 as a screeching rooster and other automatons enact the Annunciation. To the right of the Cathédrale St-Jean stands the 12th-century **Manécanterie** (choir school). ✉ *70 rue St-Jean, Vieux Lyon* ☎ *04–78–92–82–29* ⊕ *www.cathedrale-lyon.cef. fr* ⊙ *Weekdays 8:15–7:45, Sat. 8:15–7, Sun. 8–7.*

Hôtel Bullioud. This superb Renaissance mansion, close to the Hôtel Paterin, is noted for its courtyard, with an ingenious gallery built in 1536 by Philibert Delorme, one of France's earliest and most accomplished exponents of classical architecture. Delorme also worked on several spectacular châteaux in central France, including those at Fontainebleau and Chenonceaux. ✉ *8 rue Juiverie, off pl. St-Paul, Vieux Lyon* ✉ *Free* ⊙ *Daily 10–noon and 2–6.*

Maison du Crible. This 17th-century mansion is one of Lyon's oldest. In the courtyard you can glimpse a charming garden and the original Tour Rose—an elegant pink tower. In those days, the higher the tower, the greater the prestige. This one was owned by a tax collector. *Plus ça change, plus c'est la même chose* (the more things change, the more it's the same thing). ✉ *16 rue du Bœuf, off pl. du Petit-Collège, Vieux Lyon* ✉ *Free* ⊙ *Daily 10–noon and 2–6.*

FAMILY   **Musées Gadagne** (*Lyon Historical Museum and Puppet Museum*). These two museums are housed in the city's largest ensemble of Renaissance buildings, the Hôtel de Gadagne, built between the 14th and 16th century. The **Musée d'Histoire de Lyon** traces the city's history from its pre-Roman days onward, displaying sculpture, furniture, pottery, paintings, and engravings. The **Musée des Marionnettes du Monde** focuses on the history of puppets, beginning with Guignol and Madelon—Lyon's Punch and Judy—created by Laurent Mourguet in 1795. After extensive restoration and reform, the museum reopened in 2009 with doubled exhibition space distributed over 39 rooms, two workshops, an auditorium, a documentation center, two hanging gardens, a café, and a museum shop. ✉ *1 pl. du Petit-Collège, Vieux Lyon* ☎ *04–78–42–03–61* ⊕ *www.gadagne.musees.lyon.fr* ✉ *€6 one museum, €8 for both museums* ⊙ *Wed.–Sun. 11–6:30.*

Musée Gallo-Romain de Fourvière (*Gallo-Roman Museum*). Since 1933, systematic excavations have unearthed vestiges of Lyon's opulent Roman precursor. The statues, mosaics, vases, coins, and tombstones are excellently displayed in this partially subterranean museum next to

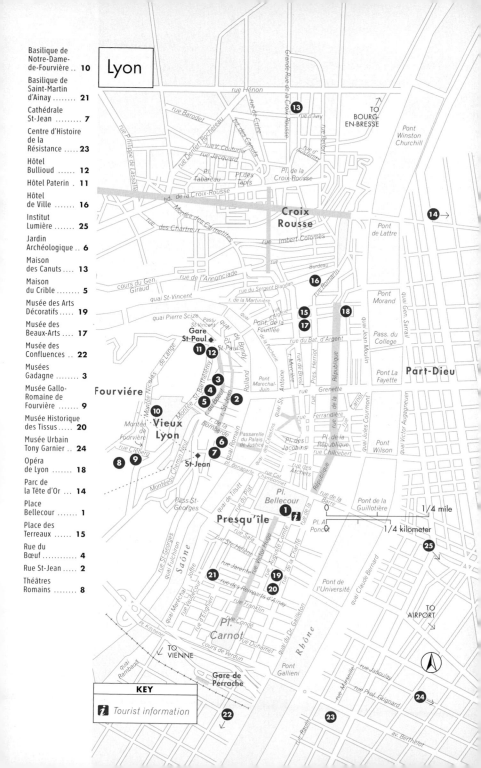

Lyon

KEY

🛈 *Tourist information*

Lyon's economic and cultural success has always owed much to its location at the confluence of the Saône and the Rhône.

the Roman theaters. The large, bronze Table Claudienne is inscribed with part of Emperor Claudius's address to the Roman Senate in AD 48, conferring senatorial rights on the Roman citizens of Gaul. ⊠ *17 rue Clébert, Fourvière* ☎ *04–72–38–81–90* ⊕ *www.musees-gallo-romains. com* ☞ *€4 (€7 during temporary exhibits)* ⊗ *Tues.–Sun. 10–6.*

Place Bellecour. Shady, imposing place Bellecour is one of the largest squares in France, and is Lyon's fashionable center, midway between the Saône and the Rhône. Classical facades erected along its narrower sides in 1800 lend architectural interest. The large, bronze equestrian statue of Louis XIV, installed in 1828, is the work of local sculptor Jean Lemot. On the south side of the square is the **tourist office** (☎ *04–72–77–69–69*). ⊠ *Presqu'île.*

Fodor's Choice **Rue du Bœuf.** Like the parallel rue St-Jean, rue du Bœuf has traboules, ★ courtyards, spiral staircases, towers, and facades. The traboule at No. 31 hooks through and out onto rue de la Bombarde. No. 36 has a notable courtyard. At No. 19 is the standout Maison de l'Outarde d'Or, so named for the great bustard, a gooselike game bird, depicted in the coat of arms over the door. The late-15th-century house and courtyard inside have spiral staircases in the towers, which were built as symbols of wealth and power. The Hotel Tour Rose at No. 22 has, indeed, a beautiful *tour rose* (pink tower) in the inner courtyard. At the corner of place Neuve St-Jean and rue du Bœuf is the famous sign portraying the bull for which rue du Bœuf is named, the work of the Renaissance Italy–trained French sculptor Jean de Bologne. No. 18 contains Antic Wine, the emporium of English-speaking Georges Dos Santos, "the flying sommelier," who has a wealth of information (throw away this book and just ask Georges). No. 20 conceals one of the rare open-shaft spiral staircases allowing for a view all the way up the core. At No. 16 is the Maison du Crible, and No. 14 has another splendid patio. ⊠ *Vieux Lyon.*

Fodor's Choice ★ **Rue St-Jean.** Once Vieux Lyon's major thoroughfare, this street leads north from place St-Jean to place du Change, where money changers operated during medieval trade fairs. The elegant houses along it were built for illustrious Lyonnais bankers and Italian silk merchants during the French Renaissance. The traboule at No. 54 leads all the way through to rue du Bœuf (No. 27). Beautiful Renaissance courtyards can be visited at No. 50, No. 52, and No. 42. At No. 27 rue St-Jean, an especially beautiful traboule winds through to No. 6 rue des Trois Maries. No. 28 has a pretty courtyard; No. 24, the Maison Laurencin, has another; Maison Le Viste at No. 21 has a splendid facade. The courtyard at No. 18 merits a close look. The houses at No. 5 place du Gouvernement and No. 7 and No. 1 rue St-Jean also have arresting facades. ⊠ *Vieux Lyon.*

Théâtres Romains (*Roman Theaters*). Two ruined, semicircular, Roman-built theaters are tucked into the hillside, just down from the summit of Fourvière. The **Grand Théâtre,** the oldest Roman theater in France, was built in 15 BC to seat 10,000. The smaller **Odéon,** with its geometric flooring, was designed for music and poetry performances. Lyon International Arts Festival performances are held here each September. ⊠ *Colline Fourvière, Fourvière* ▣ *Free* ☉ *Daily 9–dusk.*

WORTH NOTING

Hôtel Paterin. This is a paradigmatic example of the Renaissance mansions of Vieux Lyon. ⊠ *4 rue Juiverie, off pl. St-Paul, Vieux Lyon.*

Jardin Archéologique (*Archaeological Garden*). Inside this garden are the excavated ruins of two churches that succeeded one another. The foundations of the churches were unearthed during a time when apartment buildings—constructed here after churches had been destroyed during the Revolution—were being demolished. One arch still remains and forms part of the ornamentation in the garden. ⊠ *Entrance on rue de la Bombarde, Vieux Lyon.*

10

PRESQU'ÎLE AND THE CROIX ROUSSE DISTRICT

Presqu'île, the peninsula flanked by the Saône and the Rhône, is Lyon's modern center, with fashionable shops, a trove of restaurants and museums, and squares graced by fountains and 19th-century buildings. This is the core of Lyon, and you'll be tempted to explore the entire stretch, from the southern point of the peninsula at La Confluence, up past the Gare de Perrache train station to place Bellecour, and all the way up to place des Terreaux.

The hillside and hilltop district north of place des Terreaux—the Croix Rousse—has the Jardin des Plantes on the west and the Rhône on the east. It once resounded to the clanking of looms churning out the exquisite silks and other cloth that made Lyon famous. By the 19th century more than 30,000 *canuts* (weavers) worked on looms on the upper floors of the houses. So tightly packed were the buildings that the only way to transport fabrics was through the traboules, which had the additional advantage of protecting the fine cloth in poor weather.

EXPLORING
TOP ATTRACTIONS

Hôtel de Ville (*Town Hall*). Architects Jules Hardouin-Mansart and Robert de Cotte redesigned the very impressive facade of the Town Hall after a 1674 fire. The rest of the building dates from the early 17th century. ⊠ *Pl. des Terreaux, Presqu'île.*

Institut Lumière. On the site where the Lumière brothers, Auguste and Louis, invented cinematography in their family home, this museum has daily showings of early film classics and contemporary movies as well as a permanent exhibit about the Lumières. Researchers may access the archives, which contain numerous films, books, periodicals, photo files, posters, and more. ⊠ *25 rue du premier Filme, Part-Dieu* ☎ *04–78–78–18–95* ⊕ *www.institut-lumiere.org* ✑ *€7.20* ☯ *Tues.–Sun. 10–6:30.*

Musée des Beaux-Arts (*Fine Arts Museum*). In the elegant 17th-century Palais St-Pierre, formerly a Benedictine abbey, this museum houses one of France's largest art collections after that of the Louvre. Byzantine ivories, Etruscan statues, Egyptian artifacts, and top-notch sculptures (most notably Rodin's *Walker*) are all on display; however, paintings remain the highlight. Amid old master, Impressionist, and modern paintings are works by the tight-knit Lyon School, characterized by exquisitely rendered flowers and overbearing religious sentimentality. Note Louis Janmot's *Poem of the Soul,* immaculately painted visions that are by turns heavenly, hellish, and downright spooky. A recent legacy has endowed the museum with a new trove of treasures including works by Manet, Monet, Degas, Bacon, Braque, and Picasso. ⊠ *Palais St-Pierre, 20 pl. des Terreaux, Presqu'île* ☎ *04–72–10–17–40* ⊕ *www.mba-lyon.fr* ✑ *€7 permanent collection only; €9 for temporary exhibit; €12 for both* ☯ *Wed.–Mon. 10–6.*

Musée des Confluences (*Confluence Museum*). This innovative new glass-and-titanium museum—an architectural extravaganza designed by the Austrian firm Coop Himmelblau—proposes a sweeping three-part overview of scientific knowledge and social science. Scheduled to be fully open in 2014 (tours and temporary exhibits are offered in the interim), the museum's initial section will tackle big questions, like "where do we come from?" or "what are we doing?" A second section will be dedicated to topics such as evolution and biodiversity; while a third examines the roles of cooperation, competition, and the creative process in society. ⊠ *Centre d'Information, 86 quai Perrache, Presqu'île* ☎ *04–78–37–30–00* ⊕ *www.museedesconfluences.fr* ✑ *Free* ☯ *Tues.–Sat. 1–6, Sun. 10–noon and 1–6.*

Musée Historique des Tissus (*Textile Arts Museum*). A sister museum to the Arts Décoratifs, this one is dedicated to the woven-arts industries that were so crucial to Lyon's fame and fortune. Highlights include Asian tapestries from as early as the 4th century, Turkish and Persian carpets from the 16th to the 18th century, and 18th-century Lyon silks, so lovingly depicted in many portraits of the time and still the stars of many costume exhibits mounted throughout the world today. ⊠ *34 rue de la Charité, Presqu'île* ☎ *04–78–38–42–00* ⊕ *www.musee-des-tissus.com* ✉ *€10 joint ticket with nearby Musée des Arts Décoratifs* ⊙ *Tues.–Sun. 10–5:30.*

Musée Urbain Tony Garnier (*Tony Garnier Urban Museum*). Built between 1920 and 1933, this project (also known as the Cité de la Création), was France's first attempt at low-income housing. Tenants have tried over the years to bring some art and cheerfulness to their environment: 22 giant murals depicting the work of Tony Garnier, the turn-of-the-20th-century Lyon architect, were painted on the walls. Artists from around the world, with the support of UNESCO, have added their vision to the creation of the ideal housing project. ⊠ *4 rue des Serpollières, Quartier des États-Unis* ⊕ *Take the métro to Monplaisir-Lumière, then walk 10 mins south along rue Antoine* ☎ *04–78–75–16–75* ⊕ *www. museeurbaintonygarnier.com* ✉ *€8* ⊙ *Tues.–Sat. 2–6.*

Opéra de Lyon. The barrel-vaulted Lyon Opera, a reincarnation of a moribund 1831 building, was designed by star French architect Jean Nouvel and built in the early 1990s. It incorporates a columned exterior, soaring glass vaulting, neoclassical public spaces, an all-black interior down to and including the bathrooms and toilets, and the latest back-stage magic. High above, looking out between the heroic statues lined up along the parapet, is a small but excellent restaurant, Les Muses de l'Opéra. ⊠ *1 pl. de la Comédie, Presqu'île* ☎ *08–26–30–53–25* ⊕ *www. opera-lyon.com.*

Place des Terreaux. The four majestic horses rearing up from a monumental 19th-century fountain in the middle of this large square are an allegory of the River Saône by Frédéric-Auguste Bartholdi, who sculpted New York Harbor's Statue of Liberty. The 69 fountains embedded in the wide expanse of the square are illuminated by fiber-optic technology at night. The notable buildings on either side are the Hôtel de Ville and the Musée des Beaux-Arts. ⊠ *Presqu'île.*

10

WORTH NOTING

Basilique de Saint-Martin d'Ainay. This fortified church dates back to a 10th-century Benedictine abbey and a 9th-century sanctuary before that. The millenary energy field is palpable around the hulking structure, especially near the rear of the apse where the stained-glass windows glow richly in the twilight. In 1844 it became one of the first buildings in France to be classified a national monument; its interior murals and frescoes, though, are disappointingly plain and austere compared to the quirky, rough exterior. ⊠ *Pl. de l'Abbaye d'Ainay, Presqu'île* ☎ *04–78–72–10–03* ✉ *Free* ⊙ *Daily 9–1 and 4–7.*

Centre d'Histoire de la Résistance et de la Déportation (*Museum of the History of the Resistance and the Deportation*). During World War II, especially after 1942, Lyon played an important role in the Resistance movement against the German occupation of France. Newly renovated displays include equipment, such as radios and printing presses, photographs, and exhibits re-creating the clandestine lives and heroic exploits of Resistance fighters. ✉ *14 av. Berthelot, Part-Dieu* ✥ *Métro: Jean Macé; tramway T2: Centre Berthelot* ☎ *04–78–72–23–11* 🌐 *www.chrd.lyon.fr* 🎫 *€4, €7 guided tour (requires reservation); prices subject to change* ⏲ *Currently closed for renovation, due to reopen fall 2012. Usual hours: Wed.–Fri. 9–5:30, weekends 9:30–6.*

FAMILY **Maison des Canuts** (*Silk Weavers' Museum*). Despite the industrialization of silk and textile production, old-time Jacquard looms are still in action at this historic house in the Croix Rousse. The weavers are happy to show children how to operate a miniature loom. ✉ *10–12 rue d'Ivry, La Croix Rousse* ☎ *04–78–28–62–04* 🌐 *www.maisondescanuts.com* 🎫 *€6.50* ⏲ *Mon.–Sat. 10–6; guided tours by appointment at 11 and 3:30.*

Musée des Arts Décoratifs (*Decorative Arts Museum*). Housed in an 18th-century mansion, the museum has fine collections of silverware, furniture, objets d'art, porcelain, and tapestries. ✉ *34 rue de la Charité, Presqu'île* ☎ *04–78–38–42–00* 🌐 *www.musee-des-tissus.com* 🎫 *€10 joint ticket with Musée Historique des Tissus (€8 after 4 pm)* ⏲ *Tues.–Sun. 10–5:30.*

FAMILY **Parc de la Tête d'Or** (*Golden Head Park*). On the bank of the Rhône, this 300-acre park comes complete with a lake, pony rides, and a small zoo. It's ideal for an afternoon's outing with children. ✉ *Pl. du Général-Leclerc, quai Charles-de-Gaulle, Cité Internationale* ✥ *Metro: Masséna* 🎫 *Free* ⏲ *Daily dawn–dusk.*

WHERE TO EAT

$$$ MODERN FRENCH 🍴 **Au 14 Février.** Cupid's arrows don't quite account for the rapturous reviews garnered by Tsuyoshi Arai in his tiny chocolate box of a restaurant. The young chef trained in French kitchens for over a decade, honing his natural genius before striking out on his own in 2009. A Michelin star later, the persnickety Lyonnais have fallen hard, waiting weeks to savor dishes that combine Japanese subtlety with rigorous French technique—like poached foie gras and creamy parsnip purée with caramelized carrot sauce, scallops rolled in sole and smoky bacon, verbena-infused lobster consommé with caviar, and salmon tartare in a gingery court bouillon with zucchini mousse. The quirky atmosphere (*hello* mirrored ceilings!) and excellent-value menu only add to its allure. [$] *Average main: €32* ✉ *6 rue Mourguet, 5e, Vieux Lyon, Lyon* ☎ *04–78–92–91–39* 🌐 *www.au14fevrier.com* ✍ *Reservations essential* ⏲ *Closed Sun. and Mon. No lunch Sat.*

$$$$ FRENCH 🍴 **Auberge de l'Île.** If you're taking a pretty one-hour walk up the River Saône's right bank and down the other, this enchanted eatery on lush, leafy Île Barbe is the perfect place to refuel. Whether outside on the terrace or inside the graceful former 17th-century monastery refectory, it serves smart, contemporary cuisine based on fresh market products prepared with originality. Chef Jean-Christophe Ansanay-Alex

Continued on page 500

LYON: FRANCE'S CULINARY CAULDRON

Rue Saint-Jean

No other city in France teases the taste buds like Lyon, birthplace of traditional French cuisine. Home to both the workingman's *bouchons* and many celebrity chefs, the capital of the Rhône-Alpes region has become the engine room for France's modern cooking canon.

Lyon owes much of its success as a gastronomic center to its auspicious location at the crossroads of several regional cuisines—the hearty cooking traditions and smoked meats of the mountainous east; the Massif Central cattle farms and Auvergne's lambs to the west; the tomato- and olive oil-kissed Mediterranean dishes to the south; and the excellent butters and cheeses of the north. Not to mention the Rhône-Alpes' own natural riches—fish from local lakes and rivers, apricots and cherries from hillside orchards, and dairy and pork products from valley farms.

Restaurants here offer a compelling juxtaposition between simple workingman's fare and sophisticated *haute* cuisine. Casual restaurants called *bouchons* offer classic everyday dishes like *gratinée lyonnaise* (onion soup) and *boudin noir* (pork blood) sausages. At the other end of the spectrum, über-chef Paul Bocuse—the original master of Nouvelle Cuisine—serves elevated preparations like black-truffle soup encased in pastry. And a coterie of creative young chefs like Anthony Bonnet have emerged, making it hard to go wrong in this food-focused city.

By George Semler

THE ORIGINAL CELEBRITY CHEF: PAUL BOCUSE

Born: February 11, 1926, in Collonges-au-Mont d'Or, outside Lyon, France

Personality Profile: Perfectionist, polygamous, public relations genius

Trademark: Towering white toque

Favorite pastime: *L'Amour*—with a happy 60-year marriage, and mistresses of 50 and 35 years duration, Monsieur is a busy man in the kitchen and *d'ailleurs*

Claim to Fame: Leader of the Nouvelle Cuisine movement

Bocuse at his Best: Based since 1960 at L'Auberge du Pont de Collonges restaurant outside Lyon in Collonges-au-Mont d'Or, he also owns four brasseries in town—Le Nord, L'Est, L'Ouest, and Le Sud

Best-Known Dish: *Soupe aux truffes noires VGE* (black-truffle soup in pastry, named for former French president Valéry Giscard d'Estaing)

Quote: "Food and sex have much in common. We consummate a union, devour a lover with our eyes, hunger for one another."

For forty years, Paul Bocuse has reigned as Lyon's culinary lion. Not only did he daringly remake French cooking in one of its most tradition-bound centers, he also ascended to become one of the first great male chefs in a city long famous for its *cuisine des femmes*, or women's cuisine.

As an apprentice under legendary Fernand Point at La Pyramide in Vienne, just south of Lyon, Bocuse moved away from the richness of *la grande cuisine* and introduced a lighter, fresher way of cooking that emphasized natural sauces, barely cooked baby vegetables, the parsimonious use of sauces and dressings, and artful yet simple presentation. This new style of cooking came to be known as Nouvelle Cuisine.

By the early 1970s, Bocuse had become the leading ambassador for Nouvelle Cuisine. He often traveled the world as a Nouvelle evangelist while his 60-cook staff back home cooked under his eagled-eyed wife.

These days, Bocuse's once-revolutionary cooking style has matured into the country's *cuisine classique*. "It's not nouvelle cuisine anymore," he has said, "it's now *ancienne* cuisine." But because Bocuse's touch remains so sublime, foodies from around the world still make culinary pilgrimages to L'Auberge du Pont de Collonges to experience the birthplace of modern French cooking.

Bocuse at L'Auberge du Pont de Collonges

THE NEW GUARD: MARKET-DRIVEN CREATIVITY

(far left) chef Nicolas Le Bec, (left) caviar-topped potato with sour cream, (above) sea urchin with coconut cream The bistro-like Le Comptoir de la Rue Le Bec (14 rue Grôlée, 04-78-42-15-35).

A Michelin road map of the region's top dining establishments reveals a Rhône-Alpes galaxy totaling more than 60 stars, a full third of which are grouped around the city of Lyon. A new generation of chefs is shaking up Lyon's culinary scene, developing a cooking style that is even lighter and more inventive than Nouvelle Cuisine. Some of the most important players are young talents like Anthony Bonnet, Tsuyoshi Arai, Jean-Christophe Ansanay-Alex, Christian Têtedoie, and Mathieu Viannay.

ANTHONY BONNET

Having earned his first Michelin star in 2012, weeks before his 29th birthday, this exemplary young chef with a deep knowledge of the local terroir has what it takes to shine in Lyon's most elegant luxury hotel. (⌧ *ELes Loges, 6 rue du Boeuf,* ☏ *04–72–77–44–44* ⊕ *www.courdesloges.com*)

TSUYOSHI ARAI

A Japanese aesthetic combined with expert French technique has led to a stunning success (⌧ *EAu 14 Février,* *6 rue Mourguet,* ☏ *04–78–92–91–39* ⊕ *www.au14fevrier.com*) at this tiny gem of a restaurant in Vieux Lyon.

JEAN-CHRISTOPHE ANSANAY-ALEX

For a quick escape from the city, walk up the Saône and over the bridge to **Auberge de l'Ile** (⌧ *L'Ile Barbe, Collonges au Mont-D'Or* ☏ *04–78–83–99–49* ⊕ *www.aubergedelile.com*), located in a 17th-century monastery, where Ansanay-Alex cooks up modern French fare.

CHRISTIAN TÊTEDOIE

Overlooking Lyon from the Fourvière hillside, restaurant **Christian Têtedoie** (⌧ *Montée du Chemin Neug, Fourvière* ☏ *04–78–29–40–10* ⊕ *www.tetedoie.com*) is a multispace operation with an outdoor terrace, private dining rooms, and a bottom-floor wine bar.

MATHIEU VIANNAY

At the formal **La Mère Brazier** (⌧ *12 rue Royal, Presqu'île* ☏ *04–78–23–17–20*), Mathieu Viannay is celebrated for his creative signature dishes, such as pâté en croûte of Bresse chicken and foie gras with black cherry jam.

THE BOUCHON TRADITION

Lyon's iconic bouchons are casual bistro-like restaurants with modest décor along the lines of tiled walls, wooden benches, and zinc counters. In the late 19th-century, these informal eateries dished out hearty fare for working-class customers like pony express riders, stagecoach drivers, silk workers, and field laborers.

The term bouchon originated as a description for the bundles of straw that hung over the entrance of early bouchons, indicating the availability of food and drink for horses as well as humans. These friendly, family-run taverns were customarily run by female chefs, serving cuisine that relied heavily on humble pork and beef cuts, such as stomachs, brains, trotters, ears, cheeks, and livers.

Today many restaurants call themselves bouchons that would not fit the traditional definition. For the real thing, look for a little plaque at the door showing Gnafron, a drunken marionette with red nose and wine glass in hand. He sig-

(top) Bouchons on Rue Merciere, (bottom) Ives Rivoiron, owner of Café des Fédérations

nifies that the establishment is part of the official bouchon association. Bouchons are still a frugal dining choice: in many establishments, $25 will buy an appetizer, main course, salad, and dessert or cheese plate.

Lyon's best bouchons are located around Place des Terreaux and include **Chez Hugon** (✉ *12 rue Pizay, Presqu'île* ☎ *04–78–28–10–94* ⊙ *closed weekends*) and **Café des Fédérations** (✉ *8 rue du Major-Martin, Presqu'île* ☎ *04–78–28–26–00* ⊙ *closed weekends*) to the west toward the River Saône.

CLASSIC LYONNAIS FARE

At bouchons around the city, look for these traditional dishes:

Andouillette à la lyonnaise tripe sausages stuffed with veal and traditionally served with fried onions

Bavette skirt steak with shallots

Blanquette de veau veal stewed in cream, egg yolks, onions, and mushrooms

Boudin blanc sausage made from pork, onion, and eggs, without the blood

Boudin noir pork-blood sausage

Bresse chicken à la lyonnaise poached and stuffed chicken with truffles

Bugnes beignets of fried pork fat

Cervelas Lyonnais brioche filled with smoked sausage, truffles, and pistachio nuts

Frisée aux lardons curly leafed salad with bacon and eggs

Galette lyonnaise mashed potatoes with onions, browned in the oven and served in a gratin dish

Gâteau de foies blonds de volaille chicken liver mousse

Lyon's famous blue-footed chickens, poulet de Bresse

Gras double breaded, fried tripe with onions and butter

Gratinée lyonnaise onion soup topped with bread and cheese

Paillasson fried hashed potatoes

Pot-au-feu vegetable and meat stew, a winter favorite

Pots de Lyon wine flagons, heavy-bottomed bottles originally conceived to satirize government attempts to limit silk workers' wine consumption in favor of increased labor productivity

Poularde demi-deuil chicken with black truffles sliced thinly under the skin

Quenelle de brochet velvety dumplings made from pike fish, flour, butter, and eggs, served with béchamel sauce

Rosette a garlicky pork sausage

Sabodet pig's-head sausage

Saucissons chauds slices of warm sausage with potatoes drizzled with oil and vinegar

Saucisson en brioche sausage encased in brioche

Tablier de sapeur breaded, fried tripe

Boudin noir sausages, the dark links at right, are just one of the area's famed pork products

is famous for his oral daily menu performance (listen for game in fall or winter), and the wine list is strong in local Condrieu and Côte-Rotie selections. Ordering a prix-fixe lunch menu (Tuesday to Friday; $$$$) will help you avoid a major economic hemorrhage. $ *Average main: €50* ⊠ *L'Ile Barbe, Collonges au Mont-D'Or* ☎ *04–78–83–99–49* ⊕ *www.aubergedelile.com* ⚓ *Reservations essential* ⊘ *Closed Mon. No dinner Sun. and Aug. 1–24.*

$$ ╳ **Brasserie Georges.** This inexpen-
FRENCH sive brasserie at the south end of rue de la Charité next to the Perrache train station is one of the city's largest and oldest, founded in 1836 but now housed in a palatial 1925 Art Deco building. Meals range from hearty veal stew or sauerkraut and sausage to more refined fare. Cooking is less than creative—stick with the great standards, such as *saucisson brioché* (sausage in brioche stuffed with truffled foie gras)—and, like the vast room setting, service is a bit impersonal. Nevertheless, the deco style is as delicious as it comes. $ *Average main: €22* ⊠ *30 cours Verdun, Perrache* ☎ *04–72–56–54–54* ⊕ *www.brasseriegeorges.com.*

$ ╳ **Café 203.** This happening spot near the opera is always teeming with
FRENCH young people and artists. Named for the Peugeot 203 parked in front of the terrace, the café-restaurant-chill-out is open daily from dawn to after midnight (but no Sunday breakfast). Its delicious Italianate cuisine is fresh, fast, original, and inexpensive. For a quick pre- or post-opera meal, this is the place. $ *Average main: €12* ⊠ *9 rue du Garet, Presqu'île* ☎ *04–78–28–66–65.*

$$ ╳ **Café des Fédérations.** For 80 years this sawdust-strewn café with
FRENCH homey red-check tablecloths has reigned as one of the city's leading bouchons; however, it may have overextended its stay by trading on past glory—some readers report a desultory hand in the kitchen, and native Lyonnais seem to head elsewhere since the legendary Raymond Fulchiron's recent retirement. Still, for a taste of classic Lyon gastronomy in a historic setting, the deftly prepared local classics like *boudin blanc* (white-meat sausage), *boudin noir* (black sausage), or *andouillettes* (veal and pork tripe sausage) are hard to beat. $ *Average main: €16* ⊠ *8 rue du Major-Martin, Presqu'île* ☎ *04–78–28–26–00* ⊕ *www.lesfedeslyon. com* ⊘ *Closed Sun. and July 23–Aug. 23.*

$$ ╳ **Chez Hugon.** This typical bouchon-tavern with the de rigueur red-
FRENCH check tablecloths is behind the Musée des Beaux-Arts and is one of the city's top-rated insider spots. Practically a club, it's crowded with regulars, who trade quips with the owner while Madame prepares the best *tablier de sapeur* (tripe marinated in wine and fried in bread crumbs) in town. Whether you order the hunks of homemade pâté, the stewed chicken in wine vinegar sauce, or the plate of *ris de veau* (sweetbreads), your dinner will add up to good, inexpensive food and plenty of it.

Lyon's place des Terreaux is a true spectacle, thanks to 69 Daniel Buren fountains and Bartholdi's centerpiece watery marvel.

[$] *Average main: €18* ⊠ *12 rue Pizay, Presqu'île* ☎ *04–78–28–10–94* ⊕ *www.bouchonlyonnais.fr* ☉ *Closed weekends and Aug.*

$$$$

MODERN FRENCH

✕ **Christian Têtedoie.** Star chef Christian Têtedoie opened his newer, albeit no less eponymous, eatery on Fourvière hill. The multilevel restaurant is a rambling contemporary design fest and "restaurant gastronomique" with room for 90 diners and immense bay windows with staggering panoramas over the city. The upstairs T-Bar is a lounge and bar area, while Le Phosphore, downstairs, is a wine-tasting area serving light cuisine. A copious €38 lunch menu will sustain you for the rest of the day. [$] *Average main: €42* ⊠ *Chemin Neuf, 1, rue de l'Antiquaille, Fourvière* ☎ *04–78–29–40–10* ⊕ *www.tetedoie.com* ⚶ *Reservations essential* ☉ *Closed Sun.*

$$

FRENCH

Fodor's Choice

★

✕ **Comptoir Abel.** About 400 years old, this charming house is one of Lyon's most frequently filmed and photographed taverns. Simple wooden tables in wood-panel dining rooms, quirky art on every wall, heavy-bottom *pot lyonnais* wine bottles—every detail is obviously pampered and lovingly produced. The *salade lyonnaise* (green salad with homemade croutons and sautéed bacon, topped with a poached egg) or the *rognons madère* (kidneys in a Madeira sauce) are standouts. [$] *Average main: €24* ⊠ *25 rue Guynemer, Presqu'île* ☎ *04–78–37–46–18* ⊕ *www.cafecomptoirabel.com* ☉ *No dinner Sun.*

$

FRENCH

✕ **Jura.** Founded in 1864, the rows of tables, the 1934 mosaic-tile floor, and the absence of anything pretty gives this place the feel of a men's club. The *gateau de foies de volaille aux raviolis* (chicken liver ravioli) is a masterpiece. The game and steak dishes are robust, as is the *cassoulet des escargots* (stew of beans, mutton, and snails). For dessert, stick with the terrific cheese selection. $ Average main: €16 ⊠ 25 rue Tupin, Presqu'île ☎ 04–78–42–20–57 ⊕ www.lejura.cartesurtables.com ⊘ Closed weekends May–Sept., Sun. and Mon. Sept.–Apr.

$
FRENCH
Fodor'sChoice
★

× **La Famille.** True to the name of this low-key, low-cost bistro high on the Croix-Rousse hillside, family photographs adorn the walls, while the simple cuisine tends toward traditional recipes and authentic Lyon fare. From the *poulet fermier* (farm, or free range, chicken) to the grilled trout, the daily chalkboard announces the market specialties that Chef Gilles Mozziconacci has managed to cobble together on his early morning marketing tour through Les Halles de Lyon. In summer, opt for a table on the terrace. $ Average main: €17 ⊠ 18 rue Duviard, Croix Rousse ☎ 04–72–98–83–90 ⊕ www.la-famille-croix-rousse.fr ⌕ Reservations essential ⊘ Closed Sun. and Mon.

$$
FRENCH

× **La Mâchonnerie.** The verb *mâchonner* (to bite, gnaw, or chew) derives from the morning snack of Lyon's iconic silk weavers and has come to mean the typical food of the Lyon region. This respected bistro, which specializes in it, is found under the *ficelle,* or "string," as the funicular up to the Fourvière hill is called. Try the *pot au feu* (meat and vegetable stew) or the *blanquette de veau* (veal stewed in white sauce). $ Average main: €18 ⊠ 36 rue Tramassac, Vieux Lyon ☎ 04–78–42–24–62 ⊕ www.lamachonnerie.com ⊘ Closed Sun. No lunch weekdays.

$$$$
FRENCH
Fodor'sChoice
★

× **La Mère Brazier.** The house of Eugénie Brazier is a legendary location in Lyon—and even more so now that Mathieu Viannay, one of the top representatives of this city's contemporary cuisine scene, has honored one of the founding forces behind the city's culinary fame by opening a restaurant in her old space. A former winner of the coveted Meilleur Ouvrier de France (top chef) prize, Viannay continues to experiment with taste, textures, and ingredients in this carefully restored restaurant built into a traditional house. He describes the menu as "mixed" between completely modern cuisine and "Mère Brazier recipes revisited" such as the *poularde de Bresse demi-deuil* (Bresse poultry in "half mourning," that is, with black truffles under the breast skin). $ Average main: €55 ⊠ 12 rue Royale, Presqu'île ☎ 04–78–23–17–20 ⊕ www. lamerebrazier.fr ⌕ Reservations essential ⊘ Closed weekends and 1st 2 wks in Aug.

$
MODERN FRENCH

× **L'Ame Soeur.** Just behind the Palais de Justice, this little neo-bistrot (think comfortable everyday vibe but contemporary design) has a €20 prix-fixe "formule" that is nothing short of superb in terms of both value and quality. Artisanal terrine of free-range duck, *rillettes de maquereau en salade de chou chinois* (mackerel fillets in Chinese cabbage salad), or fillet of rockfish with peppers are just some of the interesting morsels at this innovative, affordable address. $ Average main: €13 ⊠ 209 rue Duguesclin, Vieux Lyon ☎ 04–78–42–47–78 ⌕ Reservations essential ⊘ Closed weekends. No dinner Mon. and Tues.

$$
MODERN FRENCH

× **La Table de Suzanne.** Arnaud and Carine Leclercq racked up impressive successes from Zurich to Dubai before opening this 65-seat restaurant where good value and good cooking meet. The lunchtime three-course menu (€22) and the menu-carte (€46) both offer fine classic-contemporary French cuisine. The *soupe mousseuse de châtaignes et crème fermière* (soup-mousse of chestnuts and farmhouse cream) has a Corsican flavor, while the *tartine de canard séché* (crispy duck pie), steamed fish with sea algy, and jumbo shrimp tempura are all excellent. $ *Average main: €27* ⊠ *39 rue Auguste Comte, Presqu'île* ☎ *04–78–37–49–83* ⊕ *www.latabledesuzanne.com* ⌦ *Reservations essential* ⊘ *Closed Sun. and Mon.*

$$ ✕ **Le Garet.** From *quenelles* (fish dumplings) to the house favorite, FRENCH *andouillettes* (tripe sausage), this is the perfect primer course in bouchon
Fodor's Choice fare, celebrated in a cozy and joyful atmosphere that is, perhaps even
★ more than the food itself, what makes Lyon's version of the French bistro so irresistible. The *salade lyonnaise* (frisée lettuce, pork lardons, croutons, and a poached egg, with a Dijon vinaigrette) is an institution at this famous dining room near the Hôtel de Ville, while the roast veal chop and ratatouille provide a welcome break from the standard porcine bouchon lineup. $ *Average main: €20* ⊠ *7 rue Garet, Presqu'île* ☎ *04–78–28–16–94* ⌦ *Reservations essential* ⊘ *Closed weekends Feb. 15–Mar. 10, and July 24–Aug. 24.*

$$ ✕ **Le Nord.** Should you want to sample cooking by Paul Bocuse–trained-
FRENCH and-supervised chefs and still keep some change in your pocket, four Bocuse bistros are distributed around Lyon's cardinal points. Le Nord specializes in Eastern cuisine, with specialties including dishes cooked over coals and excellent fish and seafood. The setting is classical turn-of-the-20th-century brasserie, with wooden benches, paneled walls, and good views of the action on the street. $ *Average main: €23* ⊠ *18 rue Neuve, Presqu'île* ☎ *04–72–10–69–69* ⊕ *www.nordsudbrasseries.com.*

Le Sud. For cooking from around the Mediterranean amid bright sun-drenched colors, Le Sud is the Bocusian homage to southern Europe. $ *Average main: €23* ⊠ *11 pl. Antonin-Poncet, Presqu'île* ☎ *04–72–77–80–00* ⊕ *www.nordsudbrasseries.com.*

L'Est. The rollicking L'Est—another of Lyon's Paul Bocuse brasseries—is set in the old 19th-century Brotteaux train station and cooks up a travel theme, thanks to a menu that includes dishes from all over the planet and a setting flavored with railroad memorabilia, paraphernalia, and a soupçon of nostalgia. $ *Average main: €23* ⊠ *Gare des Brotteaux, 14 pl. Jules Ferry, Les Brotteaux* ☎ *04–37–24–25–26* ⊕ *www. nordsudbrasseries.com.*

L'Ouest. L'Ouest exults in a postmodern wood-and-steel design, a fitting setting for Bocuse's maritime culinary adventures in the islands of the Atlantic, Caribbean, and the South Seas. $ *Average main: €23* ⊠ *1 quai du Commerce, Villefranche* ☎ *04–37–64–64–64* ⊕ *www. nordsudbrasseries.com.*

$$ ✕ **Le Palegrié.** A shining example of the *bistronomie* movement that's
BISTRO sweeping France, chef Guillaume Monjuré's sophisticated, fastidiously sourced cuisine is earning accolades from all quarters. Modest wooden tables and a spare decor belie a rich fare that is rooted firmly in the bistro lexicon, yet imaginatively, if not thrillingly updated. Dishes like risotto perfumed with saffron and anise or mackerel with quinoa and fennel attest to this up-and-coming chef's imagination and flair. The excellent-value three-course lunch menu (€22.50) is the perfect introduction to his ambitious cuisine. $ *Average main: €18* ⊠ *8 rue Palais-Grillet, 2e, Presqu'île* ☎ *04–78–92–94–84.*

10

$$$$
FRENCH

✗ **Les Loges.** This lovely dining room, lavishly appointed with mahogany chairs, modern art, and a giant medieval hearth, serves a range of culinary delights that deliciously represent the New Lyon cooking. Chef Anthony Bonnet's *poitrine de veau* (breast of veal) with asparagus and essence of almonds, or his superb foie gras *poèlé au coing* (sautéed duck or goose liver with quince) are two specialties to look for, though the menu is in constant flux according to markets and seasons. $ *Average main: €39 ⊠ 6 rue du Bœuf, Vieux Lyon ☎ 04–72–77–44–44 ⊕ www. courdesloges.com ☯ Closed Aug. 4–26. No dinner weekends.*

$$
FRENCH

✗ **Les Lyonnais.** Decorated with photographs of local celebrities, this popular bistro is particularly animated. The simple food—chicken simmered for hours in wine, meat stews, and grilled fish—is served on bare wood tables. A blackboard announces plats du jour, which are usually less expensive than items on the printed menu. Try the *caille aux petits legumes* (quail with baby vegetables) for a change from heavier bouchon fare such as the quenelle or *bugnes* (beignets of fried pork fat). $ *Average main: €20 ⊠ 1 rue Tramassac, Vieux Lyon ☎ 04–78–37–64–82 ⊕ www.restaurantlyonnais.com ☯ Closed Aug. and 1st wk in Jan.*

$$$
FRENCH

✗ **Les Muses de l'Opéra.** High up under the glass vault of the Opéra de Lyon, this small restaurant looks out past the backs of sculptures of the eight Muses over the Hôtel de Ville. The quality and variety of the creative contemporary cuisine make it hard to decide between the choices offered, but the salmon in butter sauce with watercress mousse is always a winner. $ *Average main: €28 ⊠ Opéra de Lyon, 7th fl., pl. Comédie, Presqu'île ☎ 04–72–00–45–58 ⚱ Reservations essential ☯ Closed Sun.*

$$
FRENCH

✗ **L'Étage.** Hidden over place des Terreaux, this semisecret upstairs dining room in a former silk-weaving loft prepares some of Lyon's finest and most daring new cuisine. A place at the window (admittedly hard to come by), overlooking the facade of the Beaux Arts academy across the square, is a moment to remember—especially during the December 8 Festival of Lights. $ *Average main: €22 ⊠ 4 pl. des Terreaux, 3rd fl., Presqu'île ☎ 04–78–28–19–59 ⚱ Reservations essential ☯ Closed Sun., Mon., and July 19–Aug. 21.*

$$
FRENCH

✗ **Le Vivarais.** Robert Duffard's simple, tidy restaurant is an outstanding culinary value. Don't expect napkins folded into flower shapes—the excitement is on your plate, with dishes like *lièvre royale* (hare rolled and stuffed with foie gras and a hint of truffles). $ *Average main: €22 ⊠ 1 pl. du Dr-Gailleton, Presqu'île ☎ 04–78–37–85–15 ⊕ www. restaurant-le-vivarais.com ⚱ Reservations essential ☯ Closed Sun. and July 24–Aug. 22.*

$$$
FRENCH

✗ **M Restaurant.** When Matthieu Viannay moved to his new restaurant La Mère Brazier, his former gastronomical sanctuary in the upper Brotteaux district east of the Rhône became a creative but relaxed and non-wallet-busting bistro under the direction of former Léon de Lyon chef Julien Gautier. Market cuisine, new good-value wines, plus sleek contemporary design and cuisine are the rules of thumb at this popular place on a well-known culinary corner. $ *Average main: €20 ⊠ 47 av. Foch, Les Brotteaux ☎ 04–78–89–55–19 ⊕ www.mrestaurant.fr ⚱ Reservations essential ☯ Closed weekends and Aug.*

$$$$ FRENCH Fodor's Choice ★ 🍴 **Paul Bocuse.** Parisians hop the TGV to Lyon, then transfer to a train bound for suburban Collonges-au-Mont-d'Or, simply to dine at this culinary shrine. Whether Bocuse—who kick-started the "new" French cooking back in the 1970s and became a superstar in the process—is here or not, the legendary black-truffle soup in pastry crust he created in 1975 to honor President Giscard d'Estaing will be. So will the frogs'-leg soup with watercress; the green bean–and-artichoke salad with foie gras; and the Bresse wood-pigeon "tripled," consisting of a drumstick in puff pastry with young cabbage, breast roasted and glazed in cognac, plus an aromatic dark pâté of the innards. For a mere €240 per person, the Menu Grand Tradition Classique includes the *volaille de Bresse truffée en vessie "Mère Fillioux"* (Bresse hen cooked in a pig bladder with truffles), which comes to the table looking something like a basketball—the bladder is removed and discarded revealing a poached chicken within. Like the desserts, the grand dining room is done in traditional style. Call ahead if you want to find out whether Bocuse will be cooking, and be sure to book far in advance. ⇨ *For more on Bocuse, see "Lyon: France's Culinary Cauldron" in this chapter.* [$] *Average main: €60* ✉ *40 quai de la plage, 10 km (6 miles) north of city center, Collongues au Mont d'Or* ☎ *04–72–42–90–90* 🌐 *www.bocuse.fr* ✍ *Reservations essential. Jacket required.*

WHERE TO STAY

For expanded hotel reviews, visit Fodors.com.

$$$$ HOTEL 🏨 **Boscolo Grand Hôtel.** Erté prints try hard to set a stylish tone in the guest rooms, the Rhône is just across the street, and tour groups are kept happy and content at this stylish Belle Époque hotel off place de la République. **Pros:** central location on the Rhône side of Presqu'île, good for shopping and exploring; adequately appointed and comfortable. **Cons:** a little impersonal; not an intimate hideaway. [$] *Rooms from: €390* ✉ *11 rue Grôlée, Presqu'île* ☎ *04–72–40–45–45* 🌐 *www.boscolohotels.com* 🛏 *140 rooms* 🍽 *No meals.*

$$ HOTEL Fodor's Choice ★ 🏨 **Collège.** A faithful reproduction of the owner's schoolboy days in Vieux Lyon, this charmingly nostalgic theme hotel ("taking us back to our dreams," as the owner puts it) offers public spaces decorated as antique classrooms, complete with polished wooden desks with inkwells and geography maps; the breakfast room is a study hall while rooms range from simple "undergraduate" quarters to "postgraduate" suites. **Pros:** in the heart of Vieux Lyon at a reasonable price; schoolboy theme pervasive (oddly libidinous) and funny. **Cons:** spartan interiors; rooms a bit short on space. [$] *Rooms from: €145* ✉ *5 pl. St-Paul, Vieux Lyon* ☎ *04–72–10–05–05* 🌐 *www.college-hotel.com* 🛏 *39 rooms* 🍽 *Breakfast.*

$ HOTEL 🏨 **Dock Ouest.** The newest feather in Paul Bocuse's voluminous cap, Dock Ouest aims for a young, sophisticated crowd. **Pros:** one of the best values in town; many nearby conveniences; underground parking. **Cons:** outside city center. [$] *Rooms from: €70* ✉ *39 rue des Docks, 9e, Saint-Rambert* ☎ *04–78–22–34–34* 🌐 *www.dockouest.com* 🛏 *42 rooms, 4 suites* 🍽 *Breakfast.*

10

$$ ⊞ Hôtel des Artistes. Sitting on an elegant square opposite the Théâtre des
HOTEL   Célestins, this intimate hotel has a sense of traditional theatrical chic—
√   logically enough because it has long been popular among stage and
screen artists (many of whose photographs adorn the lobby walls). **Pros:**
central location for Presqu'île; pretty view over square. **Cons:** slightly
cluttered spaces; a few clicks behind cutting-edge technology. $ *Rooms
from: €129* ⊠ *8 rue Gaspard-André, Presqu'île* ☎ *04–78–42–04–88*
⊕ *www.hotel-des-artistes.fr* ⟿ *45 rooms* ⏚ *No meals.*

$ ⊞ Hôtel du Théâtre. Location, simple but clean rooms, and reasonable
HOTEL   prices—along with a friendly and enthusiastic owner—make this a rec-
ommendable address; the guest rooms not only have theatrical views
overlooking place des Célestins, some also have bathrooms with tubs
(some have showers only). **Pros:** sense of being at the center of the
action; wallet friendly. **Cons:** small to tiny spaces in and around the
hotel; street-side rooms can be noisy at night. $ *Rooms from: €85* ⊠ *10
rue de Savoie, Presqu'île* ☎ *04–78–42–33–32* ⊕ *www.hotel-du-theatre.
fr* ⟿ *24 rooms* ⏚ *Breakfast.*

$$$$ ⊞ La Cour des Loges. King Juan Carlos of Spain, Celine Dion, and the
HOTEL   Rolling Stones have all graced this spectacular hotel which began life
Fodor's Choice as a Jesuit convent but whose glowing fireplaces, Florentine crystal
★   chandeliers, Baroque credenzas, and guest rooms swathed in Vene-
tian red and antique Lyon silks now make monastic austerity a very
distant memory. **Pros:** top Vieux Lyon location; cheerful, patient ser-
vice; extraordinary restaurant. **Cons:** hard on the budget. $ *Rooms
from: €375* ⊠ *6 rue du Bœuf, Vieux Lyon* ☎ *04–72–77–44–44* ⊕ *www.
courdesloges.com* ⟿ *57 rooms, 4 suites.*

$$$$ ⊞ La Tour Rose. An education in traditional Lyonnnais silks and velvets,
HOTEL   this textile-swathed Vieux Lyon classic—in a Renaissance-period con-
vent with an impressive Florentine-style courtyard—is also surrounded
by some of the city's prettiest traboules; most eyes are drawn upward
to study the cylindrical rose-washed tower that looms over all, while
the glass-roof restaurant—a former chapel—offers views of the hanging
garden overhead. **Pros:** gorgeous interiors; lovely patio; architectural
high notes, like the tower. **Cons:** not the best price-to-value quotient;
cramped spaces in rooms and public areas; so much drapery and textiles:
claustrophobes beware! $ *Rooms from: €250* ⊠ *22 rue du Bœuf, Vieux
Lyon* ☎ *04–78–92–69–10* ⊕ *www.latourrose.fr* ⟿ *11 rooms, 8 suites.*

$$$ ⊞ Phénix Hôtel. This little hotel overlooking the River Saône in Vieux
HOTEL   Lyon is a winning combination of location, charming staff, tastefully
Fodor's Choice decorated rooms, and moderate prices, and its modern style is grace-
★   fully juxtaposed with its 16th-century ceiling beams and Renaissance
facade—some rooms have fireplaces, and the smallish but cozy upper-
floor rooms are charmingly built into the eaves and rooftop dormers.
Pros: walking distance (45 minutes up the Saône) from Île Barbe and
Bocuse; convenient to but not in the middle of Vieux Lyon. **Cons:** interior rooms on the air shaft can be noisy; a long walk to the middle of the
Presqu'île. $ *Rooms from: €175* ⊠ *7 quai Bondy, Vieux Lyon* ☎ *04–78–
28–24–24* ⊕ *www.hotel-le-phenix.fr* ⟿ *36 rooms* ⏚ *Breakfast.*

$$$$ ⊞ Villa Florentine. High above the Vieille Ville, near the Roman theaters
HOTEL   and the basilica, this pristine hotel was once a 17th-century convent;

glowing in its ocher-yellow exterior, it has vaulted ceilings, lovely terraces, and marvelous views, seen to best advantage from the Terrasses de Lyon restaurant—an extravaganza, complete with glassed-in winter garden and tomato-red salons, this excellent eatery offers an exciting nouvelle menu. **Pros:** panoramic location above the Saône; good access to Vieux Lyon, Fourvière, and Roman Lyon. **Cons:** a hot climb up to the hotel in summer; tricky automobile access around upper Vieux Lyon; somewhat removed from the action. $ *Rooms from: €340* ⊠ *25–27 montée St-Barthélémy, Fourvière* ☎ *04–78–28–24–24* ⊕ *www. villaflorentine.com* ⟿ *20 rooms, 8 suites.*

NIGHTLIFE AND THE ARTS

Lyon is the region's liveliest arts center; check the weekly *Lyon-Poche,* published on Wednesday and sold at newsstands, for cultural events and goings-on at the dozens of discos, bars, and clubs.

Bar de la Tour Rose. Romantics rendezvous at the Bar de la Tour Rose. ⊠ *22 rue du Bœuf, Vieux Lyon* ☎ *04–78–92–69–12* ⊕ *www.latourrose. fr* ⊘ *Closed Sun. and Mon.*

Bar La Chapelle. Multiple bars, a terrace, and lively dance spaces await at gay-friendly Bar La Chapelle. ⊠ *Impasse de Choulans, Vieux Lyon* ☎ *04–78–37–23–95.*

Biennale d'Art Contemporain (*Contemporary Art Biennial*). The Biennale d'Art Contemporain is held in odd-number years during the second half of September. ☎ *04–78–30–50–66* ⊕ *www.biennaledelyon.com.*

Biennale de la Danse (*Dance Biennial*). Early fall sees the unforgettable Biennale de la Danse, which takes place in even-number years. ⊕ *www. biennaledeladanse.com.*

Bouchon aux Vin. Bouchon aux Vin is a wine bar with 30-plus vintages. ⊠ *64 rue Mercière, Presqu'île* ☎ *04–78–42–88–90.*

Café Cuba. Café Cuba provides interesting tapas, cocktails, and Havana cigars until the early hours, near the Jean Nouvel opera house. ⊠ *19 pl. Tolozan, Presqu'île* ☎ *04–78–28–35–77.*

Café Sevilla. Café Sevilla is salsa central on the Pentes de la Croix Rousse hillside. ⊠ *7 rue Ste-Catherine, Presqu'île* ☎ *04–78–30–12–98.*

Café-Théâtre de L'Accessoire. Café-Théâtre de L'Accessoire is a leading café-theater where you can eat and drink while watching a review. ⊠ *26 rue de l'Annonciade, Presqu'île* ☎ *04–78–27–84–84* ⊕ *www.accessoire-cafe-theatre.com.*

Espace Gerson. The café-theater Espace Gerson presents revues and assorted one-man shows. ⊠ *1 pl. Gerson, Vieux Lyon* ☎ *04–78–27–96–99* ⊕ *www.espacegerson.com.*

Festival Bach. October brings the Festival Bach. ☎ *04–78–72–75–31.*

Festival du Vieux Lyon. The Festival du Vieux Lyon is a music festival in November and December. ☎ *04–78–42–39–04.*

Fête des Lumières. On December 8—the Fête de La Immaculée Conception (Feast of the Immaculate Conception)—startling lighting creations transform the city into a fantasy for the ever-more-creative Fête des Lumières, Lyon's Festival of Lights. ⊕ *www.fetedeslumieres.lyon.fr.*

Foire aux Tupiniers. September is the time for the Foire aux Tupiniers, a pottery fair. ☎ *04–78–37–00–68* ⊕ *www.tupiniers.com.*

Hot Club. Live jazz has been played in the stone-vault basement of Hot Club since 1948, so they are obviously getting it right. ✉ *26 rue Lanterne, Presqu'île* ☎ *04–78–39–54–74* ⊕ *www.hotclubdelyon.org.*

La Cave des Voyageurs. La Cave des Voyageurs, just below the St-Paul train station, is a cozy place to try some carefully selected wines. ✉ *7 pl. St-Paul–St-Barthélémy, Vieux Lyon* ☎ *04–78–28–92–28* ⊕ *lacavedesvoyageurs.free.fr.*

Le Boudoir. Le Boudoir is a popular saloon in the old Brotteaux train station, with a DJ on Wednesday and Saturday and live music events. ✉ *13 pl. Jules Ferry, Les Brotteaux* ☎ *04–72–74–04–41* ⊕ *www.leboudoir.fr.*

Le Complexe du Rire. Le Complexe du Rire, also known as the Minette Theatre, is a lively satirical café-theater above place des Terreaux. ✉ *7 rue des Capucins, Presqu'île* ☎ *04–78–27–23–59* ⊕ *www. complexedurire.com.*

Le First Revolution. In the old Les Brotteaux train station, Le First Revolution is a popular macro-disco with capacity for 600 subversives. It shares the venue with the upscale Aperiklub. ✉ *13–14 pl. Jules Ferry, Les Brotteaux* ☎ *04–37–24–19–46* ⊕ *www.aperiklub-first.com.*

Le Loft. For a student vibe and bachelor/bachelorette send-offs have a look at Le Loft. ✉ *7 rue Renan, La Guillotière* ☎ *04–78–43–35–42* ⊕ *www.loftclub.fr.*

Le Marché Gare. Live music from salsa to hip-hop rules at Le Marché Gare. ✉ *34 rue Casimir Périer, Presqu'île* ☎ *04–72–77–50–25* ⊕ *www. marchegare.fr.*

Opéra de Lyon. Center stage for Lyon's amazing arts scene, the Opéra de Lyon presents plays, concerts, ballets, and opera from October to June. ✉ *1 pl. de la Comédie, Presqu'île* ☎ *04–72–00–45–45* ⊕ *www. opera-lyon.org.*

Salle Molière. Lyon's Société de Musique de Chambre performs at Salle Molière. ✉ *18 quai Bondy, Vieux Lyon* ☎ *04–78–28–03–11, 04–78–38–09–09 for tickets* ⊕ *www.musiquedechambre-lyon.org.*

Smoking Dog. For the hottest English pub in Lyon, the Smoking Dog is the place to head. ✉ *16 rue Lainerie, Vieux Lyon* ☎ *04–78–37–25–90* ⊕ *www.smoking-dog.com.*

SHOPPING

Lyon remains France's silk-and-textile capital, and all big-name designers have shops here. The 19th-century **passage de l'Argue** (between rue du Président Édouard-Herriot and rue de la République in the center of town) is lined with traditional shops. The **Carré d'Or** district has more than 70 luxury ones between place Bellecour and Cordeliers. **Passage Thiaffait**, on the Croix Rousse hillside, is home to the Creators' Village, with young designers offering original one-of-a-kind creations. For arts and crafts there are several places you will find irresistible.

À Ma Vigne. A wineshop with an excellent selection is À Ma Vigne. ✉ *18 rue Vaubecour, Presqu'île* ☎ *04–78–37–05–29* ⊕ *amavigne.free.fr.*

Lyon's Biennale de la Dance

Lyon is thrown into perpetual motion for nearly three weeks every other September (in even-number years). Brainchild of local choreographer Guy Darmet, each *biennale* celebrates a different theme and each adds up to a dance blowout. In addition to the 100-plus performances scheduled in the city's finest venues—such as the Jean Nouvel opera house, the Maison de la Danse, and the cookie box–like Théâtre des Célestins—popular highlights include the tumultuous 4,500-dancer street parade that roars down the left bank of the Rhône on the festival's first Sunday, and the three Saturday-night dance galas held in the graceful Brotteaux train station, the Halle Tony Garnier, or the place des Terreaux. Collective dance classes for thousands and spontaneous outbursts of tango, salsa, or nearly any other genre of rhythmic movement, pop up all over town, while newspaper front pages feature little else. For details: ⊕ *www.biennaledeladanse.com.*

Antic Wine. For great wines, tasting sessions, and up-to-the-minute information on food and restaurants, don't miss the (prize-winning and English-speaking) "flying sommelier," Georges Dos Santos at Antic Wine. ✉ *18 rue du Bœuf, Vieux Lyon* ☎ *04–78–37–08–96* ⊕ *www.anticwine.com.*

Bernachon. For chocolates, head to Bernachon; some say it's the best *chocolaterie* in France. ✉ *42 cours Franklin-Roosevelt, Les Brotteaux* ☎ *04–78–24–37–98* ⊕ *www.bernachon.com.*

Bouillet. Bouillet, with a stunning selection of artisanal chocolate, is paradise for chocoholics. It also has stores at 14 rue des Archers and 3 rue d'Austerlitz. ✉ *15 pl. de la Croix Rousse, Croix Rousse* ☎ *04–78–28–90–89* ⊕ *www.chocolatier-bouillet.com.*

Captiva. Captiva is the boutique of a young designer who works mainly in silk and specializes in wedding dresses. ✉ *8 rue de la Charité, Perrache* ☎ *04–78–37–96–15.*

Cha Yuan. For fragrances, photos, furniture, philosophy, and comprehensive Oriental tea culture, Cha Yuan is the best boutique in Lyon, with more than 300 varieties of tea on sale from all over the world. ✉ *7–9 rue des Remparts d'Ainay, Presqu'ile* ☎ *04–78–41–04–60* ⊕ *www.cha-yuan.com.*

Cité des Antiquaires. Cité des Antiquaires in the eastern Villeurbanne suburb amasses more than 100 antiques dealers Thursday through Sunday. ✉ *117 bd. Stalingrad, Vieux Lyon* ☎ *04–72–69–00–00* ⊕ *www.cite-antiquaires,fr.*

Clémentine. Lyonnais designer Clémentine is good for well-cut, tailored clothing. ✉ *18 rue Émile-Zola, Presqu'île* ☎ *08–99–23–08–47.*

Diogène. Diogène smells of old leather and ancient paper and sells rare and antique books. ✉ *29 rue St-Jean, Vieux Lyon* ☎ *04–78–42–29–41* ⊕ *www.librairiediogene.fr.*

Food markets. Food markets are held daily, except Monday, on boulevard de la Croix-Rousse, at Les Halles on cours Lafayette, on quai Victor Auganeur, and on quai St-Antoine.

Galeries Lafayette. France's major department stores are well represented in Lyon. Galeries Lafayette has always brought Parisian flair to its outlying branches. ✉ *In Part-Dieu Shopping Center, rue du Dr-Bouchut, Part-Dieu* ☎ *04–72–61–44–44* ⊕ *www.galerieslafayette.com.* ✉ *200 bd. Pinel, Villeurbanne* ☎ *04–78–77–82–12.*

Georges Rech. Georges Rech displays top European fashions for women. ✉ *59 rue du Président-Herriot, Part-Dieu* ☎ *04–78–37–82–90* ⊕ *www. georges-rech.fr.*

La Cave d'à Côté. La Cave d'à Côté specializes in Côte du Rhône wines. ✉ *5 rue Pleney, Presqu'île* ☎ *04–78–28–31–46* ⊕ *www.cave-vin-lyon. com.*

La Maison des Canuts. Lyon's important silk-making past (and present) are brought vividly to life through tours of the silk manufacture in Lyon's old silk *quartier* (€6.50). The boutique is replete with fine examples to wear or take home with you. ✉ *10–12 rue d'Ivry, La Croix Rousse* ☎ *04–78–28–62–04* ⊕ *www.maisondescanuts.com* ☉ *Closed Sun.*

L'Atelier de Soierie. To see how silk prints are made and take home a piece of Lyon visit L'Atelier de Soierie. ✉ *33 rue Romarin, Presqu'île* ☎ *04–72–07–97–83* ⊕ *www.atelierdesoierie.com.*

Les Halles. For culinary variety, do like superstar chef Paul Bocuse and shop at the market stalls of Les Halles de Lyon. ✉ *102 cours Lafayette, Part-Dieu* ☎ *04–78–62–39–33.*

Les Puces du Canal (*Flea Market*). A Marché aux Puces (flea market) takes place here on Thursday and Saturday mornings 7–noon and on Sunday 7–2. ✉ *1 rue du Canal, Villeurbanne* ✢ *Take Bus 37.*

Marché des Artisans (*Crafts Market*). Held on Sunday morning is another Marché des Artisans. ✉ *Quai Fulchiron, Vieux Lyon.*

Marché des Artistes (*Artists' Market*). For new art, try the Marché des Artistes every Sunday morning from 7 to 1. ✉ *Quai Romain-Rolland, Vieux Lyon.*

Nicolas Fafiotte. Nicolas Fafiotte specializes in wedding dresses and high-end evening wear, but you need an appointment to visit the boutique. ✉ *8 rue du Plat, Presqu'île* ☎ *04–72–41–84–79.*

Part-Dieu Shopping Center. Lyon's biggest shopping mall is the Part-Dieu Shopping Center, where there are 250 shops and 14 movie theaters. ✉ *Rue du Dr-Bouchut, Part-Dieu* ☎ *04–72–60–60–62* ⊕ *www. centrecommercial-partdieu.com.*

Pignol. Pignol's offerings of pastries, meats, and sandwich makings are so good that it has expanded to become a mini-chain, with other stores at 8 place Bellecour, 48 rue Vendôme, and 42 rue de la République. ✉ *17 rue Émile-Zola, Presqu'île* ☎ *04–78–92–43–92* ⊕ *www.pignol.fr.*

Place du Change. Look for Lyonnais puppets on place du Change.

10

Printemps. Printemps is the Lyon outpost of the big Paris store. ⊠ *42 rue de la République, Presqu'île* ☎ *04–72–41–29–29* ⊕ *www.printemps. com.*

Reynon. Reynon is *the* place for charcuterie. ⊠ *13 rue des Archers, Presqu'île* ☎ *04–78–37–39–08* ⊕ *www.reynonlyon.com.*

Rue Auguste-Comte. For antiques, wander down rue Auguste-Comte. ⊠ *From pl. Bellecour to Perrache.*

secondhand books. For secondhand books try the market along quai de la Pêcherie near place Bellecour, held every weekend 10–6.

Voisin. For the famous chocolate *coussins* (pillows), check out Voisin— their confections have become so popular that there are now eight shops in Lyon, including one at 11 place Bellecour, right next to the main tourist office. ⊠ *28 rue de la République, Presqu'île* ☎ *04–78–42–46–24* ⊕ *www.chocolat-voisin.com.*

BEAUJOLAIS

North of Lyon along the Saône, the vineyards of Beaujolais are a thrill for any oenophile. In the area around Villefranche, small villages— perhaps comprising a church, a bar, and a boulangerie—pop up here and there out of the rolling vine-covered hillsides. The region's best wines are all labeled "Grands Crus," a more complex version of the otherwise light, fruity Beaujolais. Although these get better with age, many Beaujolais wines are drunk nearly fresh off the vine; every third Thursday in November marks the arrival of the Beaujolais Nouveau, a bacchanalian festival that also showcases regional cuisine. North of La Dombes region and east of the Beaujolais wine villages is Bourg-en-Bresse, famous for its marvelous church and a breed of poultry that impassions gourmands; it makes a good base after Lyon. South toward the Rhône, the great river of southern France, is the well-preserved medieval village of Pérouges.

BEAUJOLAIS ROUTE DU VIN

Fodor's Choice
★

16 km (10 miles) north of Villefranche-sur-Saône, 49 km (30 miles) north of Lyon.

GETTING HERE AND AROUND

Autocars du Rhône. Autocars du Rhône (lines 161 and 164) connects Lyon with Villefranche-sur-Saône with multiple connections to surrounding towns.

SNCF. For the Beaujolais wine country, most people take the train to the station on the place de la Gare in Villefranche-sur-Saône, 31 km (19 miles) north of Lyon, where trains to smaller towns are available. SNCF trains link Lyon Part-Dieu with Villefranche-sur-Saône (26 mins, €8.05). ☎ *36–35* ⊕ *www.sncf.fr.*

Visitor Information Beaujolais Tourist Office ⊠ *96 rue de la Sous-Préfecture, Villefranche* ☎ *04–74–07–27–40* ⊕ *www.villefranche-beaujolais.fr.*

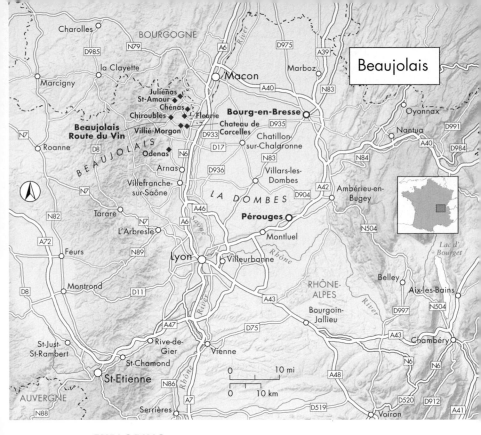

EXPLORING

Not all Beaujolais wine is promoted as *vin nouveau (new wine)*, despite the highly successful marketing campaign that has made Beaujolais Nouveau synonymous with French wine. Wine classed as "Beaujolais Villages" is higher in alcohol and produced from a clearly defined region northwest of Villefranche. Beaujolais is made from one single variety of grape, the *gamay noir à jus blanc*. However, there are 12 different appellations: Beaujolais, Beaujolais Villages, Brouilly, Chénas, Chiroubles, Côte de Brouilly, Fleurie, Juliénas, Morgon, Moulin à Vent, Régnié, and St-Amour. The Beaujolais Route du Vin (Wine Road), a narrow strip 23 km (14 miles) long, is home to nine of these deluxe Beaujolais wines, also known as *grands crus*.

Château de Corcelles. At Monternot, east of Villié-Morgon, you can find the 15th-century Château de Corcelles, noted for its Renaissance galleries, canopied courtyard well, and medieval carvings in its chapel. The guardroom is now an atmospheric tasting cellar. ⊠ *3 km (2 miles) east of Villié-Morgon via D9* ☎ *04–74–66–00–24* ⊕ *www.chateaudecorcelles. fr* ☉ *Mon.–Sat. 10–noon and 2:30–6:30.*

Chénas. Well-known Chénas is favored for its two *crus*: the robust, velvety, and expensive Moulin à Vent and the fruity and underestimated Chénas. ⊠ *Chénas.*

Chiroubles. From Villié-Morgon D68 wiggles north through several more wine villages, including Chiroubles, where a rare, light wine that's best drunk young is produced. ✉ *Chiroubles.*

Fleurie. The wines from Fleurie, "Queen of Beaujolais," are elegant, fruity, and flowery. ✉ *Fleurie.*

Juliénas. The wines of Juliénas are sturdy and a deep color; sample them in the cellar of the town church (closed Tuesday and lunchtime), amid bacchanalian surroundings. ✉ *Juliénas.*

Odenas. In the southernmost and largest *vignoble* (vineyard) of the Beaujolais crus is Odenas, producing Brouilly, a soft, fruity wine best consumed young. In the vineyard's center is towering Mont Brouilly, a hill whose vines produce a tougher, firmer wine classified as Côte de Brouilly. ✉ *Odenas.*

St-Amour. St-Amour, west of Juliénas, produces light but firm reds and a limited quantity of whites. ✉ *St-Amour.*

Villié-Morgon. From Odenas take D68 via St-Lager to Villié-Morgon, in the heart of the Morgon vineyard; robust wines that age well are produced here. ✉ *Villié-Morgon.*

WHERE TO EAT AND STAY

For expanded hotel reviews, visit Fodors.com.

$$ FRENCH
🍴 **Juliénas.** This simple little restaurant delivers what other, pricier restaurants in town don't, won't, or can't: bistro fare that does honor to traditional Beaujolais cookery. All the all-stars are here: *andouillette* (tripe sausage), hot sausage, pork with tarragon, and, for dessert, a luscious *île flottante* ("floating island" meringue). The prix-fixe menu—served at lunch (€25) or dinner (€36)—is one of the region's best deals. [$] *Average main: €31* ✉ *236 rue d'Anse, Ville-sur-Saône* ☎ *04–74–09–16–55* 🌐 *www.restaurant-lejulienas.com* 🕑 *Closed Sun. No lunch Sat.*

$$$$ HOTEL Fodor's Choice ★
🏨 **Château de Bagnols.** A destination in itself, Lady Hamlyn's dazzlingly elegant (and very pricey) castle-hotel is one of the glories of the Beaujolais, as anyone can tell with one glance at the interior. **Pros:** grandly elegant; panoramic views; nonpareil dining in the massive Salle des Gardes. **Cons:** a little like living in a museum; hyper-expensive. [$] *Rooms from: €560* ✉ *15 km (9 miles) southwest of Villefranche on D38 to Tarare, Bagnols* ☎ *04–74–71–40–00* 🌐 *www.chateaudebagnols.fr* 🛏 *16 rooms, 5 apartments* 🕑 *Closed Jan.–Mar.*

BOURG-EN-BRESSE

30 km (18 miles) east of St-Amour on N79, 81 km (49 miles) northeast of Lyon.

GETTING HERE

Baladain. Baladain connects Lyon-Saint-Exupéry airport with Bourg-en-Bresse four times daily (1 hr, 20 mins; €26). ☎ *04–74–45–19–29* 🌐 *www.baladain.fr.*

SNCF. SNCF trains link Lyon Perrache station with Bourg-en-Bresse (1 hr, 22 mins; €12.35). ☎ *36–35* 🌐 *www.sncf.fr.*

For a true Beaujolais blowout book a stay at Lady Hamlyn's Château de Bagnols, where even Louis XIV would feel right at home.

Visitor Information Bourg-en-Bresse Tourist Office ✉ *6 av. Alsace Lorraine* ☎ *04–74–22–49–40* ⊕ *www.bourg-en-bresse.org.*

EXPLORING

Cheerful, flower-festooned Bourg-en-Bresse is esteemed among gastronomes for its chickens— the striking-looking *poulet de Bresse*, with plump white bodies, bright blue feet, and red combs (adding up to France's *tricolore*, or national colors). The town's southeasternmost district, Brou, is its most interesting and the site of a singular church. This is a good place to stay before or after a trip along the Beaujolais Wine Road.

Église de Brou. A marvel of the Flamboyant Gothic style, the Église de Brou is no longer in religious use. The church was built between 1513 and 1532 by Margaret of Austria in memory of her husband, Philibert le Beau, Duke of Savoy, and their finely sculpted tombs highlight the rich interior. Outside, a massive restoration of the roof has brought it back to its 16th-century state, with the same gorgeous, multicolor, intricate patterns found throughout Burgundy. The museum in the nearby **cloister** stands out for its paintings: 16th- and 17th-century Flemish and Dutch artists keep company with 17th- and 18th-century French and Italian masters, 19th-century artists of the Lyon School, Gustave Doré, and contemporary local painters. Note that on Saturday evenings from mid-July to mid-September, the **A la Folie . . . pas du Tout music festival** takes the theme "love and death," with musical events ranging from classical to jazz (no extra charge with ticket). ✉ *63 bd. de Brou* ☎ *04–74–22–83–83* 🎟 *€7.50* ⊙ *Apr.–Sept., daily 9–12:30 and 2–6:30; Oct.–Mar., daily 9–noon and 2–5.*

WHERE TO EAT AND STAY

For expanded hotel reviews, visit Fodors.com.

$$$$ FRENCH Fodor's Choice ★ 🍴 **Georges Blanc.** In the village of Vonnas, a simple 19th-century inn with 30 rooms full of antique country furniture doubles as one of the greatest gastronomic addresses in all of Gaul. *Poulet de Bresse*, truffles, and lobster are just some of the divine dishes featured on the legendary menu created by three-star chef Monsieur Blanc, whose culinary DNA extends back to innkeepers from the French Revolution. He made his mark in the 1980s with a series of cookbooks, notably *The Natural Cuisine of Georges Blanc*. Today, he serves his traditional-yet-nouvelle delights in a vast dining room, renovated—overly so, some might say—in a stately manner, replete with Louis Treize-style chairs, fireplace, and floral tapestries. Wine connoisseurs will go weak at the knees at the cellar here, overflowing with 130,000 bottles. The guest rooms range from (relatively) simple to luxurious. It's worth the trip from Bourg-en-Bresse, but be sure you bring a well-padded wallet. ■ **TIP→ A block south you can repair to Blanc's cheaper, more casual restaurant, L'Ancienne Auberge, most delightfully set in a 1900s Fabrique de Limonade (soda-water plant) and now festooned with antique bicycles and daguerreotypes.** [$] *Average main: €85* ✉ *Pl. du Marché, 23 km (14 miles) from Bourg-en-Bresse, Vonnas* ☎ *04–74–50–90–90* 🌐 *www.georgesblanc.com* ✍ *Reservations essential* ⏲ *Closed Mon., Tues., and Jan. No lunch Wed. and Thurs.*

$$$$ FRENCH 🍴 **L'Auberge Bressane.** Overlooking the Brou church, the modern, polished dining room and chef Jean-Pierre Vullin's cuisine are a good combination. Frogs' legs and Bresse chicken with wild morel–cream sauce are specialties; also try the *quenelles de brochet* (poached-fish dumplings). Jean-Pierre wanders through the dining room ready for a chat while his staff provides excellent service. Don't miss the house aperitif, a champagne cocktail with fresh strawberry purée. The wine list has 300 vintages. [$] *Average main: €34* ✉ *166 bd. de Brou* ☎ *04–74–22–22–68* 🌐 *www.aubergebressane.fr* ✍ *Reservations essential* ⏲ *Closed Tues. except holidays.*

$ HOTEL 🏨 **Hôtel de France.** This centrally located and impeccably renovated hotel offers comfortable rooms equipped with the full range of modern amenities, along with an adjoining restaurant, Chez Blanc, that has been glamorously taken over by Georges Blanc—as expected, it is rising to the top of local gastronomical charts. **Pros:** convenient location for exploring the town; good combination of traditional shell with contemporary infrastructure and equipment; close to Georges Blanc cuisine. **Cons:** in the midst of the hustle and bustle of a provincial town. [$] *Rooms from: €105* ✉ *19 pl. Bernard* ☎ *04–74–23–30–24* 🌐 *www.grand-hoteldefrance.com* 🛏 *42 rooms, 2 suites* 🍽 *No meals.*

PÉROUGES

21 km (13 miles) southeast of Villars-les-Dombes, 36 km (22 miles) northeast of Lyon.

Wonderfully preserved (though a little too precious), hilltop Pérouges, with its medieval houses and narrow cobbled streets surrounded by ramparts, is only 200 yards across. Hand-weavers first brought it prosperity; but the Industrial Revolution meant their downfall, and by the late 19th century the population had dwindled from 1,500 to 12. Now the government has restored the most interesting houses, and a potter, bookbinder, cabinetmaker, and weaver have given the town a new lease on life. A number of restaurants make Pérouges a good lunch stop.

Encircling the town is **rue des Rondes,** a road offering fine countryside views that (on clear days) extend to the Alps. Park your car by the main gateway, **Porte d'En-Haut,** alongside the 15th-century fortress-church. Rue du Prince, the town's main street, leads to the **Maison des Princes de Savoie** (Palace of the Princes of Savoie), the erstwhile home of the influential Savoie family that once controlled the eastern part of France. **Place de la Halle,** a pretty square with great charm, around the corner from the Maison des Princes de Savoie, is the site of a lime tree planted in 1792.

Musée du Vieux Pérouges (*Old Pérouges Museum*). The Musée du Vieux Pérouges, to one side of the place de la Halle, contains local artifacts and a reconstructed weaver's workshop. The medieval **garden** is noted for its array of rare medicinal plants. ⊠ *Pl. du Tilleul* 🕾 *04–74–61–00–88* 🎫 *€4* ⏱ *May–Sept., daily 10–noon and 2–6.*

WHERE TO STAY

For expanded hotel reviews, visit Fodors.com.

$$$$
HOTEL
🛏 **Hostellerie du Vieux Pérouges.** If you want a sense of stepping back into medieval France, tarry a while at "The Old Man of Pérouges," a gorgeous complex of four ancient stone residences set around an extraordinary corbeled, 14th-century timber-frame house that's now home to the inn's famous restaurant—regional delights are served up on pewter plates by waitresses in folk costumes, recipes handed down from the days of Charles VII inspire the cook, and everybody partakes of the famous *galette pérugienne à la crème* (the "pancake of Pérouges") dessert. **Pros:** age-old aura; graceful manor house surroundings; cheerful service. **Cons:** *sans* air-conditioning it can be hot during the *canicule* (literally the "dog days" of summer); some bathrooms lack modern showers. 🛈 *Rooms from: €265* ⊠ *Pl. du Tilleul* 🕾 *04–74–61–00–88* ⊕ *www.hostelleriedeperouges.com* 🛏 *13 rooms, 2 suites.*

10

THE RHÔNE VALLEY

At Lyon, the Rhône, joined by the Saône, truly comes into its own, plummeting south in search of the Mediterranean. The river's progress is often spectacular, as steep vineyards conjure up vistas that are more readily associated with the river's Germanic cousin, the Rhine. All along the way, small-town vintners invite you to sample their wines. Early Roman towns like Vienne and Valence reflect the Rhône's importance as a trading route. To the west is the rugged, rustic Ardèche *département*, where time seems to have slowed to a standstill.

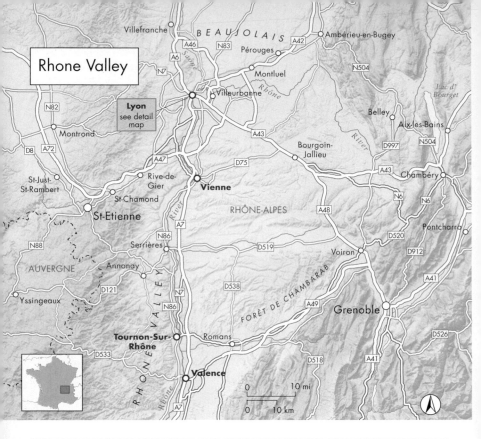

Rhone Valley

VIENNE

27 km (17 miles) south of Lyon via A7.

Fodor'sChoice
★
If you do nothing but head up to this town's famed Roman Theater and look out over the red-tile roofs of the Rhône Valley, you'll be happy you made the 20-minute trip to Vienne from Lyon. Vienne is a historian's dream, and every street seems to take you to yet another ancient church, another austere Roman ruin, or another postcard-perfect view of crumbling walls and sloped roofs.

GETTING HERE
SNCF trains. SNCF trains link Lyon Perrache or Lyon Part-Dieu stations with Vienne (18–32 mins, €7.40). From Lyon-Saint-Exupéry, the best connection to Vienne is to take the shuttle to Lyon Part-Dieu and the train to Vienne. ☎ 36–35 ⊕ *www.sncf.fr.*

Visitor Information Vienne Tourist Office ⊠ *Cours Brillier* ☎ *04–74–53–80–30* ⊕ *www.vienne-tourisme.com.*

EXPLORING
One of Roman Gaul's most important towns, Vienne retains considerable historic charm despite being a major road and train junction. It saw its second renaissance during the Middle Ages when it became a

major religious and cultural center under its count-archbishops. Today, the tourist office anchors cours Brillier in the leafy shadow of the Jardin Public (Public Garden). The €6 Billet Intermusée admits you to all local monuments and museums within a 48-hour period. Even better, the €4.60 Billet-Pass admits you to three museums and the Théâtre Roman. Both are available at the tourist office or at the first site that you visit.

Cité Gallo-Romaine de St-Romain-en-Gal (*Gallo-Roman City*). Across the Rhône from the town center is the excavated Cité Gallo-Romaine, covering several acres. Here you can find villas, houses, workshops, public baths, and roads, all built by the Romans. ⊠ *Rte. Départementale 502, Saint-Romain-en-Gal* ☎ *04–74–53–74–01* ⊕ *www.musees-galloromains.com* ⊠ *€4; €6 includes Théâtre Romain and St-André-le-Bas museums* ☉ *Tues.–Sun. 9–6.*

Roman gateway. The last vestige of the city's sizable Roman baths is a Roman gateway decorated with delicate friezes. ⊠ *Rue Chantelouve.*

St-André-le-Bas. Rue des Orfèvres (off rue de la Charité) is lined with Renaissance facades and distinguished by the church of St-André-le-Bas, once part of a powerful abbey, with finely sculpted—and recently restored—12th-century capitals (made of Roman stone) and the 17th-century wood statue of St. Andrew. It's best to see the cloisters during the music festival held here and at the cathedral from June through August. ⊠ *Pl. du jeu de Paume* ☎ *04–74–85–18–49* ⊠ *€2.30; €6, includes Cité Gallo-Romaine and Théâtre Romain museums. Free 1st Sun. of month* ☉ *Apr.–Oct., Tues.–Sun. 9:30–1 and 2–6; Nov.–Mar., Tues.–Fri. 9:30–12:30 and 2–5, weekends 1:30–5:30.*

St-Maurice. Although religious wars deprived the cathedral of St-Maurice of many of its statues, much original decoration is intact; the portals on the 15th-century facade are carved with Old Testament scenes. The cathedral was built between the 12th and 16th century, with later additions, such as the splendid 18th-century mausoleum to the right of the altar. A frieze of the zodiac adorns the entrance to the vaulted passage that once led to the cloisters but now opens onto place St-Paul. ☎ *04–74–53–41–41* ☉ *Daily 10–6.*

St-Pierre. On quai Jean-Jaurès, beside the Rhône, is the church of St-Pierre. Note the rectangular 12th-century Romanesque bell tower with its arcaded tiers. The lower church walls date from the 6th century, and there is a collection of Gallo-Roman architectural fragments on display. ⊠ *Quai Jean-Jaurès.*

Temple d'Auguste et de Livie (*Temple of Augustus and Livia*). The remains of the Temple d'Auguste et de Livie, accessible via place St-Paul and rue Clémentine, probably date in part from Vienne's earliest Roman settlements (1st century BC). The Corinthian columns were walled in during the 11th century, when the temple was used as a church; in 1833 Prosper Mérimée intervened to have the temple restored. ⊠ *Pl.du Palais.*

Fodor's Choice ★ **Théâtre Romain** (*Roman Theater*). The Théâtre Romain is one of the largest in Gaul (143 yards across). It held 13,000 spectators and is only slightly smaller than Rome's Theater of Marcellus. Rubble buried Vienne's theater until 1922; excavation has uncovered 46 rows of seats, some marble flooring, and the frieze on the stage. Concerts take place

10

One of the most important towns of Roman Gaul, Vienne is a historian's fantasyland famed for its ancient theater.

here in summer. ✉ *7 rue du Cirque* ☎ *04–74–85–39–23* 🎟 *€2.30; €6, includes Cité Gallo-Romaine and St-André-le-Bas museums* ⏲ *Apr.–Aug., daily 9–1 and 2–6; Sept. and Oct., Tues.–Sun. 9:30–1 and 2–6; Nov.–Mar., Tues.–Fri. 9:30–12:30 and 2–5, weekends 1:30–5:30.*

WHERE TO EAT

$$$$ FRENCH Fodor's Choice ★ 🍴 **La Pyramide.** Back when your grandmother's grandmother was making the grand tour, La Pyramide was *le must.* Fernand Point had perfected haute cuisine for a generation and became the first superstar chef, teaching a regiment of students—Bocuse, Chapel, and the brothers Troisgros among them—who went on to streamline and glamorize French dining the world over. Many decades later, La Pyramide has dropped its museum status and now offers contemporary classics by acclaimed Chef Patrick Henriroux, accompanied by a peerless selection of wines featuring local stars from the nearby Côte Rôtie and Condrieu vineyards. Both classical and avant-garde dishes triumph here, from *crème soufflée de crabe au croquant d'artichaut* (creamy crab soufflé with crunchy artichoke) to the *veau de lait aux légumes de la vallée* (suckling veal with vegetables from the Drôme Valley). For those who wish to sleep off the feast, there are graceful guest rooms at hand, but the mysterious Relais & Chateaux fatigue syndrome may have had a cooling effect on this previously exciting establishment. [$] *Average main: €62* ✉ *14 bd. Fernand-Point* ☎ *04–74–53–01–96* 🌐 *www.lapyramide.com* ⏲ *Closed Tues., Wed., Feb. 17–Mar. 22, and Aug. 12–22.*

$$$ FRENCH 🍴 **Le Bec Fin.** With its understatedly elegant dining room and an inexpensive weekday menu (€24 at lunch), this unpretentious enclave opposite the cathedral is a good choice for lunch or dinner. Red meat, seafood,

and both fresh- and saltwater fish are well prepared here. Try the turbot cooked with saffron. $\boxed{S}$ *Average main: €25* $\boxtimes$ *7 pl. St-Maurice* ☎ *04–74–85–76–72* ⌀ *Reservations essential* ☉ *Closed Mon. and Dec. 24–Jan. 12. No dinner Sun. or Wed.*

TOURNON-SUR-RHÔNE

36 km (20 miles) south of Serrières, 59 km (37 miles) south of Vienne.

EXPLORING

Château. Tournon is on the Rhône at the foot of granite hills. Its hefty Château, dating from the 15th and 16th centuries, is the chief attraction. The castle's twin terraces have wonderful views of the Vieille Ville, the river, and—towering above Tain-l'Hermitage across the Rhône—the steep vineyards that produce Hermitage wine, one of the region's most refined, and costly, reds. In the château is a museum of local history, the **Musée Rhodanien** (or du Rhône). $\boxtimes$ *Pl. Auguste-Faure* ☎ *04–75–08–10–23* ⌑ *€6* ☉ *June–Aug., Wed.–Mon. 10–noon and 2–6; Apr., May, Sept., and Oct., Wed.–Mon. 2–6.*

WHERE TO STAY

For expanded hotel reviews, visit Fodors.com.

$$$$
HOTEL
⌑ **Michel Chabran.** Michel Chabran's traditional Drôme-style stone-and-wood design has taken a strikingly modern turn, replete with floral displays, airy picture windows over the garden, and guest rooms displaying contemporary Danish touches—even better, the hotel's restaurant is famed for its truffle menu (available December–March), though no one will complain about other delights, such as the foie gras millefeuille with artichokes or lamb from Rémuzat. **Pros:** bright and cheerful; friendly service. **Cons:** close to main road; touristy; steep staircase; very expensive (€55) breakfast. $\boxed{S}$ *Rooms from: €175* $\boxtimes$ *29 av. du 45e Parallèle, on left (east) bank of Rhône, 10 km (6 miles) south of Tournon via N7 and 7 km (4½ miles) north of Valence, Pont de l'Isère* ☎ *04–75–84–60–09* ⊕ *www.michelchabran.fr* ⤴ *11 rooms.*

VALENCE

10

17 km (11 miles) south of Tournon; 92 km (57 miles) west of Grenoble; 127 km (79 miles) north of Avignon.

GETTING HERE

SNCF trains. SNCF trains link Lyon Part-Dieu station with Valence (1 hr, 12 mins; €19.50). The high-speed TGV also connects Lyon Part-Dieu to Valence (39 mins, €16.10) with six or seven trains daily. Lyon Perrache connects with Valence on the local train (1 hr, 12 mins; €17.75). From Lyon-Saint-Exupéry airport, the best connection to Valence is by shuttle to Lyon Part-Dieu station and train to Valence. ☎ *36–35* ⊕ *www.sncf.fr.*

Visitor Information Valence Tourist Office $\boxtimes$ *Parvis de la Gare* ☎ *08–92–70–70–99* ⊕ *www.tourisme-valence.com.*

EXPLORING

Valence, the Drôme département's capital, has plenty of dreary industrial-district streets—with one that is home to the world-famous Pic hotel and restaurant.

St-Apollinaire. Follow some steep-curbed alleyways, called *côtes,* from the banks of the Rhône into the Vieille Ville to discover, at its center, the imposing cathedral of St-Apollinaire. Although begun in the 12th century in the Romanesque style, it's not as old as it looks: parts of it were rebuilt in the 17th century, with the belfry rebuilt in the 19th. ✉ *Pl. des Ormeaux.*

WHERE TO STAY

For expanded hotel reviews, visit Fodors.com.

$$$$ HOTEL Fodor's Choice ★ 🏨 **Pic.** Celebrated as a culinary landmark for decades, the Maison Pic is also a feast for the eyes, with vaulted white salons, deep maroon-velvet sofas, 18th-century billiard tables, gigantic Provençal armoires, lovely gardens, and an inviting swimming pool. **Pros:** renowned chef; ravishing decor; sports and leisure activities from golf to flying. **Cons:** Valence is industrial and tedious, and this street is among the worst. [$] *Rooms from: €335* ✉ *285 av. Victor Hugo* ☎ *04–75–44–15–32* 🌐 *www.pic-valence.com* 🛏 *12 rooms, 3 apartments.*

GRENOBLE AND THE ALPS

This is double-treat vacationland: in winter some of the world's best skiing is found in the Alps; in summer chic spas, shimmering lakes, and hilltop trails offer additional delights. The Savoie and Haute-Savoie départements occupy the most impressive territory; Grenoble, in the Dauphiné (so named for the dolphin in the coat of arms of an early noble family), is the gateway to the Alps and the area's only city, occupying the nexus of highways from Marseille, Valence, Lyon, Geneva, and Turin.

This is the region where Stendhal, the groundbreaking 19th-century novelist, was born and where the great 18th-century philosopher Jean-Jacques Rousseau lived out his old age. So, in addition to natural splendors, the traveler should also expect worldly pleasures: eye-knockingly charming Annecy, set with arcaded lanes and quiet canals in the old quarter around the lovely 16th-century Palais de l'Isle, and old-master treasures on view at Grenoble's Musée are just some of the civilized enjoyments to be discovered here.

As for *le skiing,* the season for most French resorts runs from December 15 to April 15. By late December resorts above 3,000 feet usually have sufficient snow. January is apt to be the coldest—and therefore the least popular—month; in Chamonix and Megève, this is the time to find hotel bargains. At the high-altitude resorts the skiing season lasts until May. In summer the lake resorts, as well as the regions favored by hikers and climbers, come into their own.

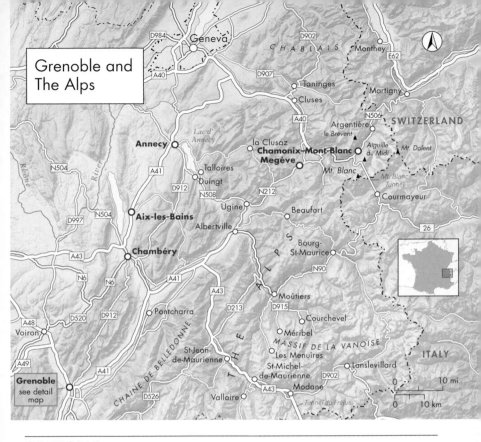

GRENOBLE

104 km (65 miles) southeast of Lyon, 86 km (52 miles) northeast of Valence.

Capital of the Dauphiné (Lower Alps) region, Grenoble sits at the confluence of the Isère and Drac rivers and lies within three *massifs* (mountain ranges): La Chartreuse, Le Vercors, and Belledonne. This cosmopolitan city's skyscrapers seem intimidating by homey French standards. But along with Grenoble's nuclear research plant, they bear witness to the fierce local desire to move ahead with the times, and it's not surprising to find one of France's most noted universities here. Grenoble's main claim to fame is as the birthplace of the great French novelist Henri Beyle (1783–1842), better known as Stendhal, author of *The Red and the Black* and *The Charterhouse of Parma*. The native Grenoblois, known for their down-home friendliness, are delighted—and generally surprised—if you know of him.

GETTING HERE

Paris's Gare de Lyon dispatches more than a dozen trains daily (either direct or via Lyon Part-Dieu) to Grenoble (3 hrs, 10 mins; €82 or 3 hrs, 50 mins; €96 via Lyon). Six TGV trains daily connect Lyon-Saint-Exupéry airport with Grenoble (1 hr, 33 mins; €23). Faure buses

10

(☎ *04–76–88–08–80* ⊕ *www.faurevercors.fr*) also connect Lyon-Saint-Exupéry with Grenoble every hour on the half hour (1 hr, 5 mins; €23). Altibus (☎ *08–20–32–03–68* ⊕ *www.altibus.com*) connects Grenoble with 60 ski stations and towns throughout the Alps.

Grenoble's layout is maddening: your only hope lies in the big, illuminated maps posted throughout town or the free map from the tourist office. Use the mountains for orientation: the sheer Vercors plateau is behind the train station; the Chartreux, topped by the Bastille and *téléphérique* (cable car), are on the other side of the Isère River; and the distant peaks of the Belledonne are behind the park. TAG (☎ *08–20–48–60–00* ⊕ *www.tag.fr*) runs 21 local bus and tram routes, many starting at place Victor Hugo.

Visitor Information Grenoble Tourist Office ✉ *14 rue de la République* ☎ *04-76-42-41-41* ⊕ *www.grenoble-tourisme.com* ✉ *Train station* ☎ *04-76-54-34-36* ⊕ *www.grenoble-tourisme.com.*

EXPLORING

Grenoble's cultural sights are tucked within a setting of considerable natural beauty. The heart of the city forms a crescent around a bend of the Isère, with the train station at the western end and the university all the way at the eastern tip. As it fans out from the river toward the south, the crescent seems to develop a more modern flavor. The hub of the city is **place Victor Hugo,** with its flowers, fountains, and cafés, though most sights and nightlife are near the Isère in place St-André, place de Gordes, and place Notre-Dame; avenue Alsace-Lorraine, a major pedestrian street lined with modern shops, cuts right through it.

For a tour of Grenoble's oldest and most attractive streets, wander the area between place aux Herbes and the **Halles Ste-Claire,** the splendid glass-and-steel-covered market in place Ste-Claire, several blocks southeast. Facing the market's spouting fish fountain, at the end of the street is the Baroque Lyçee Stendhal entryway. A tour of Grenoble's **four Sunday markets** begins at L'Estacade food and flea market around the intersection of avenue Jean Jaurès and the train tracks, followed by Les Halles, place aux Herbes, and place St-André.

Cathédrale Notre-Dame. Despite its 12th-century exterior, the 19th-century interior of the Cathédrale Notre-Dame is somewhat bland. But don't miss the adjoining bishop's house, now a museum on the history of Grenoble; the main treasure is a noted 4th-century baptistery. ✉ *Pl. Notre-Dame* 🎫 *Free* ⊙ *Museum Wed.–Mon. 10–noon and 2–5.*

FAMILY **La Bastille.** Near the center curve of the River Isère is a **téléphérique** (cable car), starting at quai St-Stéphane-Jay, which whisks you over the River Isère and up to the hilltop and its **Fort de la Bastille,** where there are splendid views and a good restaurant. Walk back down via the footpath through the Jardin Dauphinoise. ✉ *Quai Stéphane Jay* ☎ *04–76–44–89–65* ⊕ *www.bastille-grenoble.fr* 🎫 *€7.15 round-trip* ⊙ *May–Sept., daily; Oct.–Apr., Tues.–Sun. Hrs vary, so call or check website.*

Musée Archéologique St-Laurent. The church of St-Laurent, near the Musée Dauphinois, has a hauntingly ancient 6th-century crypt—one of the country's oldest Christian monuments—supported by a row of

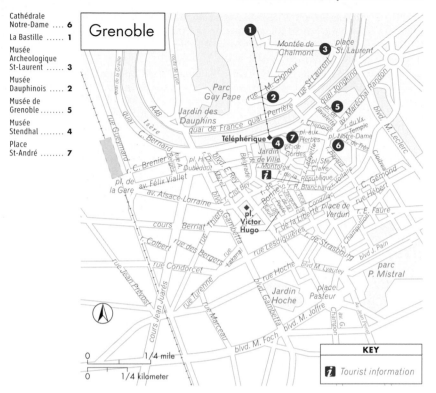

formidable marble pillars. A tour of the church traces the emergence of Christianity in the Dauphiné. ✉ *2 pl. St-Laurent* ☎ *04–76–44–78–68* ⊕ *www.musee-archeologique-grenoble.fr* 🎟 *Free* ☉ *Wed.–Mon. 8–noon and 2–6.*

Musée Dauphinois. On the north side of the River Isère is rue Maurice-Gignoux, lined with gardens, cafés, mansions, and a 17th-century convent that contains the Musée Dauphinois, featuring the history of mountaineering and skiing. The Premiers Alpins section explores the evolution of the Alps and its inhabitants. The museum restaurant is one of Grenoble's best. ✉ *30 rue Maurice-Gignoux* ☎ *04–76–85–19–01* ⊕ *www.musee-dauphinois.fr* 🎟 *Free* ☉ *Nov.–Apr., Wed.–Mon. 10–6; May–Oct., Wed.–Mon. 10–7.*

Musée de Grenoble. Place de Lavalette—on the south side of the river, where most of Grenoble is concentrated—is where you'll find the Musée de Grenoble, formerly the Musée de Peinture et de Sculpture. Founded in 1796 and since enlarged, it's one of France's oldest museums and was the first to concentrate on modern art (Picasso donated his *Femme Lisant* in 1921); an addition incorporates the medieval Tour de l'Isle (Island Tower), a Grenoble landmark. The collection includes 4,000 paintings and 5,500 drawings, among them works by Impressionists such as Renoir and Monet, and 20th-century masters like Matisse,

Signac, Derain, Vlaminck, Magritte, Ernst, Miró, and Dubuffet. Artists from the Italian Renaissance and Flemish School are also represented. ⊠ *5 pl. de Lavalette* ☎ *04–76–63–44–44* ⊕ *www.museedegrenoble.fr* ⌧ *€5* ⊘ *Wed.–Mon. 10–6:30.*

Le Magazin-CNAC (Centre National d'Art Contemporain). Contemporary art enthusiasts should also check out the Centre National d'Art Contemporain. Behind the train station in an out-of-the-way district, it is noted for its distinctive warehouse museum and avant-garde collection. ⊠ *155 cours Berriat* ☎ *04–76–21–95–84* ⊕ *www.magasin-cnac. org* ⌧ *€3.50* ⊘ *Tues.–Sun. 2–7.*

Fodor's Choice ★ **Musée Stendhal.** This newly opened museum, established in Stendhal's grandfather's house, is a fascinating testament to the eminent author, and one of three local landmarks where the his legacy can be explored—the others being his birthplace and the Bibleotèque Municipale, which houses his manuscripts. The full "Stendhal Itinerary," offered by the Grenoble Chamber of Commerce (in English), recaps all the major sites associated with him. ⊠ *20 Grande Rue* ☎ *04–76–86–52–08* ⊕ *www. bm-grenoble.fr/596-stendhal.htm* ⌧ *€5 with audio guide* ⊘ *Tues., Wed., and Fri. 2–6; Sat. 10–noon and 2–6; last Sun. of the month 10–noon and 2–6.*

Place St-André. Place St-André is a medieval square, now filled with umbrella-shaded tables and graced with the **Palais de Justice** on one side and the **Église St-André** on the other.

WHERE TO EAT AND STAY
For expanded hotel reviews, visit Fodors.com.

$ ✕ **Café de la Table Ronde.** The second-oldest café in France, junior only
FRENCH   to the Procope in Paris, this was a favorite haunt of Henri Beyle (aka Stendhal) as well as the spot where Choderlos de Laclos sought inspiration for (or perhaps a rest from) his 1784 *Liaisons Dangereuses.* Traditionally known for gatherings of *les mordus* (literally, "the bitten," or passionate ones), the café still hosts poetry readings and concerts and serves dinner until nearly midnight. Ⓢ *Average main: €16* ⊠ *7 pl. St-André* ☎ *04–76–44–78–68.*

$$$ ✕ **L'Auberge Napoléon.** Frédéric Caby's culinary haven in a meticulously
FRENCH   restored town house—once inhabited by Napoléon Bonaparte himself—is where Chef Agnès Chotin, one of France's top *cuisinières* (female chefs), puts together the best table in Grenoble. She specializes in dishes unique to the region, ranging from *daube de sanglier en aumònière croustillante* (wild boar stewed in port wine with lemon crust) to *crème de potiron* (cream of squash soup); and proposes a foie-gras menu that is nearly as wicked and wonderful as her regional *cru* chocolate dessert. Ⓢ *Average main: €32* ⊠ *7 rue Montorge* ☎ *04–76–87–53–64* ⊕ *www. auberge-napoleon.fr* ⊘ *Closed Sun., Jan. 5–12, May 1–10, and Aug. 10–25. No lunch.*

$$$ ⛺ **Chavant.** It's worth the drive to this ivy-covered mansion-hotel, where
HOTEL   elegant, spacious guest rooms overlook the meadows and forests that
Fodor's Choice ★   lie beyond the lush garden and pool; it's also home to a celebrated restaurant, where your rewards include a wonderfully wicked and wholly delicious lobster smothered in black truffles, or—once the watchful eye

of the delightful Danièle Chavant sizes you up—perhaps the unforgettable *civet de biche en robe d'automne* (venison with apples, potatoes, and turnips in a daube sauce). **Pros:** lovely village with pretty views and walks; classic cuisine and outstanding wine cellar; tasteful rooms; lovely grounds. **Cons:** not handy to the cultural attractions of Grenoble's old town; tricky driving directions from Grenoble. S *Rooms from: €165* ⊠ *Rue Bresson, 8 km (5 miles) south of Grenoble via D269, Bresson* ✛ *Leave Grenoble on av. J. Perrot to av. J. Jaurès, which becomes rte. D269* ☎ *04–76–25–25–38* ⊕ *www.chavanthotel.com* ⌦ *5 rooms, 2 suites* ☾ *Closed Aug. 9–17 and Dec. 20–28.*

$
HOTEL
⊞ **Europe.** This modest hotel, the town's oldest, is in a handy, central location at the edge of old Grenoble on a corner of place Grenette; rooms are adequate, staff is helpful, and it's an easy walk from the river, the Jardin de Ville, and the city museums—once you're ensconced here, you're set to explore the town. **Pros:** location at Grenoble's nerve center; good value; the feel of old Grenoble. **Cons:** very small rooms; minimal comforts, such as tiny towels. S *Rooms from: €84* ⊠ *22 pl. Grenette* ☎ *04–76–46–16–94* ⊕ *www.hoteleurope.fr* ⌦ *45 rooms* ❄ *No meals.*

$$$
HOTEL
⊞ **Park Hôtel Grenoble.** Grenoble's finest hotel, with spacious corner rooms overlooking the leafy Parc Paul Mistral, is a sleek, smoothly run establishment that attends to guests with skill, good cheer, and the fabulous Le Louis 10 restaurant, where seasoned chef Jerôme Lebeau now in command. **Pros:** highly professional service; fine dining; first-rate in-room comforts and equipment. **Cons:** a good hike from old Grenoble; characterless modern building. S *Rooms from: €210* ⊠ *10 pl. Paul Mistral* ☎ *04–76–85–81–23* ⊕ *www.park-hotel-grenoble.fr* ⌦ *50 rooms, 10 suites* ❄ *No meals.*

NIGHTLIFE AND THE ARTS

Look for the monthly *Grenoble-Spectacles* for a list of events around town.

Barberousse. Barberousse, near place Notre-Dame, is an always-popping, pirate ship–like rum mill. ⊠ *3 rue Bayard* ☎ *04–76–51–14–53* ⊕ *www.barberousse.com.*

La Soupe aux Choux. La Soupe aux Choux is the prime spot for jazz in Grenoble. ⊠ *7 rte. de Lyon* ☎ *04–76–87–05–67* ⊕ *www.jazzalasoupe.fr.*

Fodor'sChoice
★
Les Détours de Babel. The late winter Grenoble jazz festival, Cinq Jours de Jazz (Five Days of Jazz), fused with 38th Rugissants (38th Ragers) in 2010 and produced an expanded music festival with contemporary music from around the world. The first three weeks of April is prime time for 50 or more concerts of exceptional originality and cultural breadth. ⊕ *www.detoursdebabel.fr.*

Session Internationale de Grenoble-Isère. In summer, classical music characterizes the Session Internationale de Grenoble-Isère.

10

Starting at quai St-Stéphane-Jay, Grenoble's téléphérique (cable car) help visitors cross the Isère and ascend to the Fort de la Bastille.

CHAMBÉRY

44 km (27 miles) northeast of Voiron, 40 km (25 miles) north of St-Pierre-de-Chartreuse.

Visitor Information Chambéry Tourist Office ⊠ *24 bd. de la Colonne* ☎ *04–79–33–42–47* ⊕ *www.chambery-tourisme.com.*

EXPLORING

As for centuries—when it was the crossroads for merchants from Germany, Italy, and the Middle East—elegant old Chambéry remains the region's shopping hub. Townspeople congregate for coffee and people-watching on pedestrians-only **place St-Léger.**

Château des Ducs de Savoie. Chambéry's premier sight is the mammoth, 14th-century Château des Ducs de Savoie, which features one of Europe's largest carillons. Its Gothic **Ste-Chapelle** has good stained glass and houses a replica of the Turin Shroud. Elsewhere, the city entices with a Vieille Ville festooned with historic houses—from medieval to Premier Empire—a Musée des Beaux-Arts, and the Fountain of the Elephants. ⊠ *24 bd. de la Colonne* ☎ *04–79–33–42–47* 🖼 *€6* ☉ *Guided tours of town and part of Château (check with tourist office).*

WHERE TO STAY

For expanded hotel reviews, visit Fodors.com.

$$$ 🖼 **Château de Candie.** If you wish to experience *la vie Savoyarde* in **HOTEL** all its pastel-hue, François Boucher glory, head to this towering 14th-century manor on a hill east of Chambéry, where guest rooms range from sweet peasant-luxe to blowout magnificent (the chandeliered nuptial chamber, for one, has a canopied red-velvet bed); owner Didier Lhostis, an avid antiques collector, spent four years renovating and rooms feature an array of delights, including antique panels of boiserie, honey-gold beams, carved armoires, and glorious regional fabrics. **Pros:** glorious views over the neighboring Chartreuse monastery and village; authentic, interesting antiques abound; warm, personal service from host. **Cons:** not right in town, so a car required; won't appeal to minimalists. $ *Rooms from: €210* ⊠ *Rue du Bois de Candie, 6 km (4 miles) east of Chambéry, Chambéry-le-Vieux* ☎ *04–79–96–63–00* ⊕ *www.chateaudecandie.com* ⤳ *23 rooms, 5 suites* ⊚*No meals.*

AIX-LES-BAINS

14 km (9 miles) north of Chambéry, 106 km (65 miles) east of Lyon.

Visitor Information Aix-les-Bains Tourist Office ⊠ *Pl. Maurice Mollard* ☎ *04–79–88–68–00* ⊕ *www.aixlesbains.com.*

EXPLORING

The family resort and spa town of Aix-les-Bains takes advantage of its position on the eastern side of **Lac du Bourget,** the largest natural freshwater lake in France, with a fashionable lakeshore esplanade.

Although the lake is icy cold, you can sail, fish, play golf and tennis, or picnic on the 25 acres of parkland at the water's edge (try to avoid it on weekends, when it gets really crowded). The main town of Aix is 3 km (2 miles) inland from the lake itself. Its sole reason for being is its thermal waters.

Many small hotels line the streets, and streams of the weary take to the baths each day; in the evening, for a change of pace, they play the slot machines at the casino or attend tea dances.

Musée Archéologique (*Archaeology Museum*). The Roman Temple of Diana (2nd to 3rd century AD) now houses the Musée Archéologique; enter via the tourist office on place Maurice Mollard. ⊠ *Pl. Maurice Mollard* ☎ *04–79–61–06–57* ⊘ *May–Sept., daily 9–12:30 and 3–6:30; Oct.–Apr., Mon.–Sat. 8:30–12:30 and 2–6.*

Thermes Nationaux (*National Thermal Baths*). The ruins of the original Roman baths are underneath the present Thermes Nationaux, built in 1934. ⊠ *Pl. Maurice Mollard* ⊘ *Guided tours only Apr.–Oct., Mon.–Sat. at 3; Nov.–Mar., Wed. at 3.*

ANNECY

33 km (20 miles) north of Aix-les-Bains; 137 km (85 miles) east of Lyon; 43 km (27 miles) southwest of Geneva.

Fodor'sChoice ★ Sparkling Annecy is on crystal clear **Lac d'Annecy,** surrounded by snow-tipped peaks. Though the canals, flower-decked bridges, and cobbled pedestrian streets are filled with shoppers and tourists on market days—Tuesday and Friday—the town is still tranquil.

Does it seem to you that the River Thiou flows backward, that is, out of the lake? You're right: it drains the lake, feeding the town's canals. Most of the Vieille Ville (Old Town) is now a pedestrian zone lined with

10

half-timber houses. Here is where the best restaurants are, so you'll probably be back in the evening.

GETTING HERE

Crolard. Crolard connects Lyon-Saint-Exupéry airport with Annecy (2 hrs, €34) and the main winter sport stations in the Alps year-round. Tickets must be purchased online or at the airport or bus station. ☎ 04–50–51–08–51 ⊕ www.voyages-crolard.com.

There's a direct TGV train connection from Lyon-Saint-Exupéry airport to Annecy (1 hr, 47 mins; €27.30). TGV connects Paris's Gare de Lyon to Annecy (3 hrs, 42 mins; €72.80). Annecy Haute-Savoie Airport (⊕ www.annecy.aeroport.fr) receives flights from other French and some European destinations.

Visitor Information Annecy Tourist Office ✉ Centre Bonlieu, 1 rue Jean-Jaurès ☎ 04–50–45–00–33 ⊕ www.lac-annecy.com.

EXPLORING

Annecy is one big photo op. Its flower-filled canals, medieval castles, stunning lake (one of the few in the Alps where you can swim without turning blue), and spectacular mountain backdrop all make it a winner in the region's beauty contest.

The funky, asymmetrical, added-on, squished-in buildings of its Vieille Ville and the sheer limestone cliffs and jagged peaks of its mountain setting are impossibly picturesque. No matter that the paddleboat vendors try to outcharm each other for your business, you'll be tempted to stay here and dawdle awhile.

Château de Duingt. Just after Veyrier-du-Lac, keep your eyes open for the privately owned medieval Château de Duingt.

Fodor'sChoice
★
Château de Menthon-Saint-Bernard. Continue around the eastern shore to get to the magnificent Château de Menthon-Saint-Bernard. The exterior is the stuff of fairy tales (so much so that Walt Disney modeled Sleeping Beauty's castle on it); the interior is even better. The castle's medieval rooms—many adorned with tapestries, Romanesque frescoes, Netherlandish sideboards, and heraldic motifs—have been lovingly restored by the owner, who can trace his ancestry directly back to Saint Bernard himself. All in all, this is one of the loveliest dips into the Middle Ages you can make in all of Europe. You can get a good view of the castle by turning onto the Thones road out of Veyrier. ☎ 04–50–60–12–05 ⊕ www.chateau-de-menthon.com ≋€8 (€9 for costumed visits on weekends and holidays) ⏱ July and Aug., daily noon–6; May, June, and Sept., Fri., weekends, and holidays 2–6; Oct.–Apr., Thurs. and weekends 2–4:30.

Fodor'sChoice
★
Musée-Château d'Annecy. Crowning the city is one of France's most gorgeous castles, the medieval Musée-Château d'Annecy. High on a hill opposite the Palais and bristling with stolid towers, the complex is landmarked by the Tour Perrière, which dominates the lake, and the Tour St-Paul, Tour St-Pierre, and Tour de la Reine (the oldest, dating from the 12th century), which overlook the town. All provide storybook views over the town and countryside. Dwellings of several eras line the castle courtyard, one of which contains a small museum on Annecy

history and how it was shaped by the Nemeurs and Savoie dynasties. ✉ *Pl. du Château* ☎ *04–50–33–87–31* 🌐 *www.musees.agglo-annecy.fr* 🎟 *€5.20, with Palais de l'Ile €7* ⏰ *June–Sept., daily 10:30–6; Oct.–May, Wed.–Mon. 10–noon and 2–5.*

Palais de l'Isle (*Island Palace*). Meander through the Vieille Ville, starting on the small island in the River Thiou, at the 12th-century Palais de l'Isle, once site of law courts and a prison, now a landmark. Like a stone ship, the small islet perches in midstream, surrounded by cobblestone quays, and is easily one of France's most photographed sites. ✉ *3 passage de l'Ile* ☎ *04–50–33–87–30.*

WORD OF MOUTH

"Annecy has such a wonderful feel to it. The beauty of the place just takes your breath away, yet it is so welcoming and relaxing, and small enough to be absolutely charming. The town is made for strolling around—the beautiful old buildings we expected, but the gardens and flowers everywhere were an unexpected pleasure. Like walking around in a Disney movie."

—AJ Kersten

Talloires. A drive around Lake Annecy—or at least along its eastern shore, which is the most attractive—is a must; set aside a half day for the 40-km (25-mile) trip. Pretty Talloires, on the eastern side, has many charming hotels and restaurants.

WHERE TO EAT AND STAY

For expanded hotel reviews, visit Fodors.com.

$$ FRENCH 🍴 **L'Étage.** This small second-floor restaurant serves inexpensive local fare—from cheese and beef fondue to grilled freshwater fish from Lake Annecy, and raclette made from the local Reblochon cheese. Minimal furnishings and plain wooden tables give it a rather austere look, but the lively crowd makes up for it with large doses of true bonhomie. [$] *Average main: €22* ✉ *13 rue du Pâquier, 2nd fl.* ☎ *04–50–51–03–28* 🌐 *www.letageannecy.fr.*

$$ HOTEL Fodor's Choice ★ 🏨 **Hôtel du Palais de l'Isle.** Steps away from the lake, in the heart of Old Annecy, this delightful small hotel directly overlooks one of the most enchanting corners of town (if not Europe). **Pros:** contemporary Starck interiors in a vintage building; Annecy's most historic location. **Cons:** all but the largest, most expensive rooms are somewhat cramped; overpriced breakfast; difficult to access by car. [$] *Rooms from: €155* ✉ *13 rue Perrière* ☎ *04–50–45–86–87* 🌐 *www.hoteldupalaisdelisle.com* 🛏 *33 rooms* 🍽 *No meals.*

$$$$ HOTEL 🏨 **L'Impérial Palace.** Across the lake from the town center, Annecy's leading hotel has spacious, high-ceiling guest rooms in subdued contemporary colors behind its Belle Époque exterior, and the best rooms face the public gardens on the lake; if you have one of those rooms, waking up to breakfast on the terrace is a great way to start the day. **Pros:** beautiful location; splendid rooms; superior cuisine in La Voile. **Cons:** sluggish to haughty service; overpriced; lacks warmth. [$] *Rooms from: €390* ✉ *Allée de l'Impérial* ☎ *04–50–09–30–00* 🌐 *www.hotel-imperial-palace.com* 🛏 *91 rooms, 8 suites.*

Just one of the scenic delights of Annecy, the photogenic Palais de l'Isle (Island Palace).

CHAMONIX–MONT BLANC

94 km (58 miles) east of Annecy, 83 km (51 miles) southeast of Geneva.

Chamonix is the oldest and biggest of the French winter-sports resort towns and was the site of the first Winter Olympics, held in 1924. As a ski resort, however, it has its limitations. The ski areas are spread out, none is very large, and the lower slopes often suffer from poor snow conditions.

On the other hand, some runs are extremely memorable, such as the 20-km (12-mile) one through the **Vallée Blanche** or the off-trail area of **Les Grands Montets.** And the situation is getting better: many lifts have been added, improving access to the slopes as well as shortening lift lines. In summer it's a great place for hiking, climbing, and enjoying dazzling views. If you're heading to Italy via the Mont Blanc Tunnel, Chamonix will be your gateway.

GETTING HERE

Alpybus. Alpybus transfers passengers from Geneva to Chamonix (1 hr, 10 mins; €26 in groups of one to three). ☎ *00–41/(0) –22–7–232–984 (CH), 00–44/(0) –1509–213696 (UK)* ⊕ *www.alpybus.com.*

Crolard. Crolard connects Lyon-Saint-Exupéry airport with Annecy (2 hrs, €34) and the main winter sport stations in the Alps year-round. Tickets must be purchased online or at the airport or bus station. ☎ *04–50–51–08–51* ⊕ *www.voyages-crolard.com.*

The direct TGV train from Lyon-Saint-Exupéry airport (⊕ *www.sncf. fr*) to Annecy takes one hour, 47 minutes (€27.30). TGVservice also connects Paris's Gare de Lyon to Annecy (3 hrs, 42 mins; €74.30). The required train ride from St-Gervais-Les-Bains to Chamonix is in itself an incredible trip, up the steepest railway in Europe. You'll feel your body doing strange things to adjust to the pressure change.

Visitor Information Chamonix Tourist Office ✉ *85 pl. du Triangle de l'Amitié* ☎ *04–50–53–00–24* ⊕ *www.chamonix.com.*

EXPLORING

Aiguille du Midi. Nowadays the valley's complex transportation infra-structure takes people up to peaks like the Aiguille du Midi and past freeway-size glaciers like La Mer de Glace via *téléphériques* (cable cars), *télécabines* (gondolas), *télésièges* (chairlifts), and narrow-gauge rail-roads. Aiguille du Midi is a 12,619-foot granite peak topped with a needle-like observation tower, terrace, and restaurants. The world's highest cable car soars 12,000 feet up, almost to the top (an elevator completes the journey to the summit), providing positively staggering views of 15,700-foot **Mont Blanc,** Europe's loftiest peak. Be prepared for a lengthy wait, both going up and coming down—and wear warm clothing. ✉ *35 pl. de la Mer de Glace, Chamonix-Mont-Blanc* ☎ *33/04–51–53—22–75* ⊕ *www.compagniedumontblanc.fr* 🚠 *Cable car: €50 round-trip from Chamonix, €150 family pass, €3 extra for elevator to summit; Télécabine Panoramic Mont-Blanc: €78, includes Plan de l'Aiguille, Aiguille du Midi, and Pointe Helbronner* ☉ *May–Sept., daily 8–4:45; Oct.–Apr., daily 8–3:45.*

Mer de Glace. Literally, the "sea of ice," the Mer de Glace glacier can be seen up close from the Train du Montenvers, a cogwheel moun-tain train that leaves from behind the SNCF train station. At the top end of the track you can mount yet another transportation device—a mini-*téléphérique* (cable car) that suspends you over the glacier for five minutes and venture into the *grotte de glace* (ice cave). The hike back down is an easy two-hour ramble. ⊕ *www.compagniedumontblanc.fr* 🚠 *€27.40 one-way (family package €82.50)* ☉ *Téléphérique and ice cave may be closed for periods during spring and fall.*

Musée Alpin. Chamonix was little more than a quiet mountain village until a group of Englishmen "discovered" the spot in 1741 and sang its praises far and wide. The town became forever tied to mountain-eering when Horace de Saussure offered a reward for the first Mont Blanc ascent in 1760. Learn who took home the prize at the town's Musée Alpin, which documents the history of mountaineering; exhibits include handmade skis, early sleds, boots, skates, Alpine furniture, and geological curios and mementos from every area of Alpine climbing lore. ✉ *89 av. Michel Groz* ☎ *04–50–53–25–93* 🚠 *€5* ☉ *June 10–Oct. 18 and Dec 24–May 18.*

WHERE TO STAY

For expanded hotel reviews, visit Fodors.com.

$$$$ ⊡ **Hameau Albert 1er.** At Chamonix's most desirable hotel, guest rooms
HOTEL are furnished with elegant reproductions, and most have balconies, with many (such as No. 33) offering unsurpassed views of Mont Blanc; choose between rooms in the original building or Alpine lodge–style

10

accommodations—with touches of contemporary rustic elegance—in the complex known as le Hameau. **Pros:** dazzling panoramas; superb cuisine; polished and cheerful service. **Cons:** hard to get a reservation in season; the actual location is less than pristine. [$] *Rooms from: €235* ✉ *119 impasse du Montenvers* ☎ *04–50–53–05–09* 🌐 *www.hameaualbert.fr* 🛏 *21 rooms, 3 chalets, 12 rooms in farmhouse* ⏲ *Closed 2 wks in May, 3 wks in Nov.* 🍴 *All meals.*

$$ HOTEL 🏨 **L'Auberge Croix-Blanche.** If you want to enjoy top value and simultaneously savor a historic Alpine vibe, head to the heart of Chamonix and this small, ancient inn, founded in 1793; although lodgings here may be modest and tidy, they offer good views—there's nothing quite like lying in your tub and looking out the window at Mont Blanc. **Pros:** top value for Chamonix; the L'M café terrace is iconic. **Cons:** overall comfort is basic at best; charm and tradition at the expense of functionality and luxury. [$] *Rooms from: €140* ✉ *87 rue Vallot* ☎ *04–50–53–00–11* 🌐 *www.bestmontblanc.com* 🛏 *31 rooms, 4 suites* ⏲ *Closed May 2–June 11* 🍴 *No meals.*

NIGHTLIFE

Chamonix après-ski begins at the saloons in the center of town: the Chamouny, the Brasserie du Rond Point, or, in spring, the outdoor tables. Argentière's L'Office is an Anglo refuge, while Francophones head for the Savoie. Le Jeckyll, next to the Hotel Des Aiglons, is a hardcore party headquarters, along with Cantina and Le Pub, although Wild Wallabies Bar may be the wildest of all.

Casino. The Casino has a bar, a restaurant, roulette, and blackjack. Entrance to the casino is gratis with a passport or driver's license. ✉ *Pl. de Saussure* ☎ *04–50–53–07–65.*

Chambre Neuf. Fabled landmark Chambre Neuf is once again hot. ✉ *272 av. Michel Croz* ☎ *04–50–55–89–81.*

MEGÈVE

35 km (22 miles) west of Chamonix, 69 km (43 miles) southeast of Geneva.

GETTING HERE

Driving is by far the best way to get to Megève. From Grenoble to Megève the journey takes about 2½ hours whether via Annecy or Albertville. The Annecy route is safer, but the Albertville route through the Gorges d'Árly is (appropriately) gorgeous. SNCF rail connections (🌐 *www.sncf.fr*) from Annecy to Megéve (1 hr, 31 mins; €17.10) are routed to Sallanches, 12 km (8 miles) away. Shuttle buses connect Sallanches and Megève (18 mins, €5.80).

Visitor Information Megève Tourist Office ✉ *Rue Monseigneur Conseil* ☎ *04–50–21–27–28* 🌐 *www.megeve.com.*

EXPLORING

The smartest of the Mont Blanc stations, idyllic Alpine Megève is not only a major ski resort but also a chic winter watering hole that draws royalty, celebrities, and fat wallets from all over the world (many will

Even at the bottom of one of its ski runs, you'll feel on top of the world in stunning Chamonix.

fondly recall Cary Grant bumping into Audrey Hepburn here in the opening scenes of the 1963 thriller *Charade*).

Because the slopes are comparatively easy, beginners and skiers of only modest ability will find Megève more to their liking than Chamonix: Megève, conveniently, also has one of France's largest ski schools. In summer the town is a popular spot for golfing and hiking.

WHERE TO EAT AND STAY
For expanded hotel reviews, visit Fodors.com.

$$$$
FRENCH
Fodor's Choice
★

✕ **Flocons de Sel.** Emmanuel Renaut's three-star Flocons de Sel (flakes of salt), located in Leutaz, brings new meaning to the world of haute cuisine—and, even with the drive out of town, it's an excellent Megève dining option. The nine-course tasting menu is very expensive; however, it offers priceless taste experiences based on simple but carefully selected ingredients—freshwater crayfish, scallops en croute with Maldon sea salt, and roast wood pigeon are just a few of the creatively prepared specialties. The dining room is rustic-simple, allowing the food to take center stage. Surrounded by a series of chalets and much natural splendor, the restaurant now includes six rooms (from €460) for crawl-away convenience. $ *Average main: €55* ⊠ *1775 rte. du Leutaz, 4 km (2½ miles) southwest of Megève, Leutaz* ☎ *04–50–21–49–99* ⊕ *www.floconsdesel. com* ⌂ *Reservations essential* ⊗ *Closed Tues.,Wed., May, and Nov.*

$$
FRENCH

✕ **Le Chamois.** A cozy mid-Megève fondue specialist, Le Chamois offers plenty of Haute Savoyarde authenticity at this rustic restaurant just a few steps from the bottom of the gondola lift up to the ski slopes. A wild mushroom fondue with a Côtes du Rhône Vaqueyras and a flaming herb-and-wild mint Starfu (the house after-dinner digestif especially designed to penetrate congealing cheese) is guaranteed to be restorative after a day of skiing all over the rolling slopes of Côte 2000. $ *Average main: €24* ⊠ *20 rue Monseignor Conseil* ☎ *04–50–91–39–97* ⚎ *Reservations essential.*

$$$$
HOTEL
⊡ **Hôtel Mont-Blanc.** Wood predominates, as does artwork collected from all over Europe, in this hotel in the heart of Megève's pedestrian-only zone; each wood-paneled guest room has a different theme, from Austrian to English to Haute Savoie, while half have small balconies overlooking the courtyard—an ideal spot for summer breakfasts and evening cocktails. **Pros:** walking distance from the gondolas up to the ski lifts; shares the clubby feel of the chic part of Megève town. **Cons:** in the thick of the crowds in high season; erratic service and upkeep. $ *Rooms from: €340* ⊠ *Pl. de l'Église* ☎ *04–50–21–20–02* ⊕ *www.hotelmontblanc.com* ⌁ *40 rooms* ☾ *Closed May 1–June 10* ⦿ *No meals.*

$$
B&B/INN
⊡ **Les Cîmes.** This tiny, reasonably priced hotel, run by an English couple, offers small, neat rooms and a pleasant little restaurant where simple food is served, such as roast lamb or grilled fish. **Pros:** friendly and comfortable; young and gregarious clientele; central location. **Cons:** cramped spaces; on a busy central street. $ *Rooms from: €80* ⊠ *341 av. Charles Feige* ☎ *04–50–21–11–13* ⊕ *www.hotellescimes.info* ⌁ *8 rooms* ⦿ *Breakfast.*

$$$$
HOTEL
⊡ **Les Fermes de Marie.** By reassembling a number of Alpine chalets and hay houses brought down from the mountains and decorating rooms with old Savoie furniture (including shepherds' tables, sculptured chests, and credenzas), Jocelyne and Jean-Louis Sibuet have created a luxury hotel with a delightfully rustic feel for both winter and summer getaways. **Pros:** ultra-comfortable quarters in authentic Alpine chalets; beautiful taste down to smallest detail; top Megève cuisine. **Cons:** somewhat isolated within the town; shuttle or car necessary to reach ski lifts. $ *Rooms from: €375* ⊠ *Chemin de Riante Colline* ☎ *04–50–93–03–10* ⊕ *www.fermesdemarie.com* ⌁ *61 rooms, 7 suites, 3 duplex apartments* ☾ *Closed late Apr.–late June and mid-Sept.–mid-Dec.* ⦿ *Some meals.*

NIGHTLIFE

Fodor's Choice
★
Jazz Club des Cinc Rues. Hot both figuratively and literally (be sure to have a T-shirt to strip down to), this popular music bar near the Plaza de l'Église packs in the après-ski party animals as soon as the sun is over the yardarm, which can be as early as 4 or 5 pm in December. ⊠ *19 rue Comte de Capre* ☎ *04–50–91–35–17.*

PROVENCE

WELCOME TO PROVENCE

TOP REASONS TO GO

★ **See Vincent van Gogh's Arles:** Ever since the fiery Dutchman immortalized Arles in all its chromatic drama, this town has had a starring role in museums around the world.

★ **Experience unplugged Provence:** The marshy landscapes of the Camargue will swamp you with their strange beauty, white horses, pink flamingoes, and black bulls.

★ **Get hip-deep in lavender:** Tour the Lavender Route from the Abbaye de Sénanque (near Gordes) to a wide, blue-purple swath that ranges across the Drôme and the Vaucluse.

★ **Go fishing for Marseille's best bouillabaisse:** The version at Chez Fonfon will make your taste buds stand up and sing "La Marseillaise."

★ **Tour Cézanne Country:** Views of Mont Ste-Victoire, rising near the artist's hometown of Aix-en-Provence, may inspire you to pick up a brush.

1 Arles and the Camargue. Still haunted by the genius of Van Gogh, Arles remains fiercely Provençal and is famed for its folklore events. A bus ride away and bracketed by the towns of Aigues-Mortes and Stes-Maries-de-la-Mer, the vast Camargue nature park is one of France's most remarkable terrains, complete with cowboys, horseback rides, and exclusive *mas* (converted farmhouse) hotels.

2 Avignon and the Vaucluse. This area is the heart of Provençal delights. Presided over by its medieval Palais des Papes, Avignon is an ideal gateway for exploring the nearby Roman ruins of Orange. About 16 km (10 miles) east of Avignon is the Sorgue Valley, where everybody goes "flea"-ing in the famous antiques market at L'Isle-sur-la-Sorgue. Just east are the Luberon's hilltop villages (made chic by Peter Mayle), such as picture-perfect Gordes. South lies Roussillon, set like a ruby in its red cliffs.

3 Aix-en-Provence and the Mediterranean Coast. For one day, join all those fashionable folk for whom café-squatting, people-watching, and boutique-shopping are a way of life in Aix-en-Provence. Enjoy the elegant 18th-century streets, then channel the spirit of Cézanne by visiting his studio and nearby Mont Ste-Victoire, one of his favorite subjects. Head south to become a Calanques castaway before diving into Marseille, which ranks among France's most vibrant and colorful cities.

Remoulins

Nîmes
D999

Beaucaire
Tarascon
A9   A54

LANGUEDOC
ROUSSILLON

Arles
D979   D570   1
Aigues-Mortes

THE CAMARGUE
Etang de Vaccarès

BOUCHES-DU-RHÔNE

Stes-Maries-
de-la-Mer

11

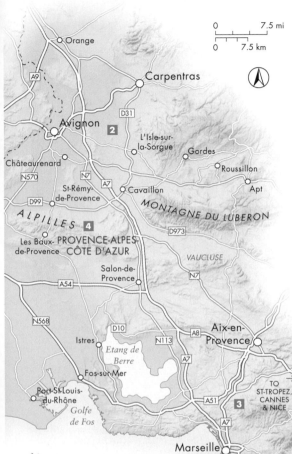

0   7.5 mi

0   7.5 km

Orange

Carpentras

A9

D31

Avignon **2**

L'Isle-sur-
la-Sorgue

Gordes

Châteaurenard

Roussillon

N570

N7

St-Rémy-
de-Provence

A7

Cavaillon

Apt

D99

MONTAGNE DU LUBERON

ALPILLES **4**

D973

Les Baux-
de-Provence

PROVENCE-ALPES-
CÔTE D'AZUR

VAUCLUSE

Salon-de-
Provence

N7

A54

N568

D10

N113

A8

Aix-en-
Provence

Istres

Etang de
Berre

A7

Fos-sur-Mer

TO
ST-TROPEZ,
CANNES
& NICE

Port-St-Louis-
du-Rhône

A51

3

Golfe
de Fos

A7

A52

Marseille

A50

_M e d i t e r r a n e a n   S e a_

Cassis

Les Calanques

GETTING ORIENTED

What many visitors remember best about Provence is the light. The sunlight here is vibrant and alive, bathing the vineyards, olive groves, and fields full of lavender and sunflowers with an intensity that captivated Cézanne and Van Gogh. Bordering the Mediterranean and flanked by the Alps and the Rhône River, Provence attracts hordes of visitors. Fortunately, many of them are siphoned off to the resorts along the Riviera, which is part of Provence but whose jet-set image doesn't fit in with the tranquil charm of the rest of the region.

The Alpilles. These spiky mountains guard treasures like Les Baux-de-Provence—be bewitched by its _ville morte_ (dead town) and its luxurious L'Oustau de la Baumanière inn. Nearby is ritzy St-Rémy-de-Provence, Van Gogh's famous retreat.

PROVENCE'S MARKETS

Provence is market heaven. There are all kinds—food, collectibles, antiques, clothing—and there is a (often famous) street market in every town. If you don't buy something, you're missing out on a truly Provençal experience.

Among the most prized gifts are Provençal *santon* figurines (*above*); less overhead means cheap prices (*right, top*); gourmet goodies for sale (*right, bottom*).

There are plenty of châteaux, museums, and Roman ruins to tour in Provence. And yet there always seem to be even more rows of sheltered booths, more tents draped with pink-and-yellow Souleiado fabric, more jumbles of handwoven baskets. Fight a brief inner battle, but most travelers know that they will yield yet again to the delight of puttering through a village market. Markets are a daily occurrence here, passed from village to town—Sunday is for Isle-sur-la-Sorgue, Wednesday for St-Rémy, Saturday for Arles. The market is a deeply ingrained part of Provençal life, and each one reflects something organic and intrinsic to the town itself. Remember that you'll want to pick the wheat from the chaff, giving wide clearance to products such as bubble-gum-scented olive-oil soaps, pottery mugs with good-luck cicadas, sunflower coasters, and Day-Glo versions of Van Goghs.

FEATS OF CLAY

Many prize the miniature figures called *santons*, or "little saints." When the French Revolution cracked down on Christmas reenactments, a crafty Marseillais decided to sculpt tiny terra-cotta figures that soon upstaged their human counterparts. These figurines are now sold year-round. In crèches that resemble Provençal villages more than Bethlehem, look for tiny lavender-cutters, goat herders, and folk dancers.

ARLES AND THE CAMARGUE

Every Saturday morning along the boulevard des Lices (which joins boulevard Clemenceau) Arles hosts one of the best textile markets in the area. Here you'll find the famous *boutis* (quilted cotton throws), textured fabrics, and an endless array of brightly dyed and embroidered tablecloths, children's clothes, and Arlesian costumes. On the first Wednesday of every month, boulevard Emile Combes converts into an antiques market—all the more interesting since wares are mostly regional.

AVIGNON AND THE VAUCLUSE

Avignon has a great mix of French chains and youthful clothing shops. Every Wednesday morning, St-Rémy-de-Provence hosts one of the most popular markets in France. The place de la Republic and the narrow town streets overflow with fresh produce, olives, tapenade by the vat, and a variety of other delicacies. In the Vaucluse area, you can find anything made from lavender (⇨ *see our photo feature, "Blue Gold: the Lavender Route"*), including soaps, oils, creams, perfumes, and little sachets filled with dried lavender to keep your clothes—and your suitcase—fresh.

MARSEILLE

The main shopping drag lies between La Canebière and the Préfecture, but Marseille offers up a large selection of

quirky shops, urban youth boutiques, and brand-name stores all over the city.

There are more than a dozen street markets, the most renowned of which is the fish market in the port.

Probably the most famous item sold, however, is the Savon de Marseille (Marseille soap).

It can be bought all over the city but some of the prettiest cubed and scented blocks are found at La Compagnie de Provence (⊠ *1 rue Caisserie* ☎ *04–91–56–20–94*).

AIX-EN-PROVENCE

Aix has some delightful street markets. Unlike the more traditional markets, the one in Aix is more focused on food: you'll find rare delicacies side by side with spicy dried sausages, vats of olives and oils from the Pays d'Aix (Aix region), or bags of orange-spice boat-shape *navettes* (cookies).

The food market takes place every day in place Richelème, and just up the street in place Verdun is a very good collectibles market Tuesday, Thursday, and Saturday mornings.

Aix is also a very modern shopping mecca with high-end stores that rival those on any of the other, more famous retail strips in France.

Updated by
Nancy Heslin

As you approach Provence there's a magical moment when you finally leave the north behind: cypresses and red-tile roofs appear; you hear the screech of cicadas and breathe the scent of wild thyme and lavender. Along the highway, oleanders bloom against a backdrop of austere, sun-filled landscapes, the very same that inspired the Postimpressionists. Yes, you have entered Provence, a totally enchanting place where café-sitting, people-watching, and boutique shopping are a way of life.

Ever since Peter Mayle abandoned the London fog and described with sensual relish a life of unbuttoned collars and espadrilles in his bestselling *A Year in Provence*, the world has beaten a path here. Now Parisians are heard in the local marketplaces passing the word on the best free-range rabbit and the lowest price on a five-bedroom *mas* (a traditional Provençal farmhouse). This *bon-chic-bon-genre* city crowd languishes stylishly at Provence's country inns and restaurants. Ask them, and they'll agree: when Princess Caroline of Monaco moved to St-Rémy, Provence became the new Côte d'Azur.

But chichi Provence hasn't eclipsed idyllic Provence, and it's still possible to melt into a Monday-morning market crowd, where blue-aproned *paysannes* scoop fistfuls of mesclun into willow baskets, matron-connoisseurs paw through bins containing the first Cavaillon asparagus, and a knot of *pépés* in workers' blues takes a pétanque break.

Relax, join them—and plan to stick around awhile. There are plenty of sights to see: great Roman ruins; the pristine Romanesque abbeys of Senanque and de Montmajour; weathered mas; the monolithic Papal Palace in old Avignon; the narrow streets in Arles immortalized on canvas by Van Gogh. Check out all these treasures but remember that highlights of any trip here are those hours spent dawdling at a sidewalk café, wandering aimlessly down narrow cobbled alleyways, and, after a three-hour lunch, taking a quick snooze in the cool shade of a

500-year-old olive tree. Allow yourself time to feel the rhythm of modern Provençal life, to listen to the pulsing *breet* of the insects, smell the *parfum* of a tiny country path, and feel the night air on your skin.

PLANNER

WHEN TO GO

Spring and fall are the best months to experience the dazzling light, rugged rocky countryside, and fruited vineyards of Provence. Though the lavender fields show peak color in July, summertime here is beastly hot; worse, it's always crowded on the beaches and connecting roads. Winter has some nice days, when the locals are able to enjoy their cafés and their town squares tourist-free—but it's often wet, and the razor-sharp mistral wind can cut to the bone. Be prepared for four distinct seasons: there's a summer, a fall, a winter, and a spring, and it's best to find out what the temperature is before you disembark. Surprisingly enough, it does rain (and has even snowed) for about four weeks out of the year. It can get chilly at night, too, so it's wise to bring warm clothing for those evening strolls through the lavender fields; in winter, it can be fleece-jacket-mitts-and-scarf cold.

PLANNING YOUR TIME

The rugged, unpredictable charm of Provence catches the imagination and requires long, thoughtful savoring—like a fine wine over a delicious meal. Come here in any season except November or January, when most of the hotels close and all of Provence seems to be on holiday. The area's best in late spring, summer, or early fall, when the temperature rises and you can eat outdoors after sunset. The best place to start your trip is in Avignon. It's on a fast train link from Paris, but even if you arrive in record time, it's at exactly this moment that you need to slow down. As you step off the train and are confronted with all that magnificent architecture and art, breathe deeply. Provence is about lazy afternoons and spending "just one more day," and Avignon is a good place to have a practice run: it's cosmopolitan enough to keep the most energetic visitor occupied, while old and wise enough to teach the value of time.

GETTING HERE AND AROUND

Public transport is well organized in Provence, with most towns accessible by train or bus. It's best to plan on combining the two—often smaller Provençal communities won't have their own train station, but rather a local bus connection to one in the nearest town over. The high-speed TGV *Méditerranée* line ushered in a new era in Trains à Grande Vitesse travel in France; the route means that you can get from Paris's Gare de Lyon to Avignon (first class, one-way tickets €66–€158) in 2 hours and 40 minutes, with a mere 3-hour trip to Nîmes, Aix-en-Provence, and Marseille. You can even whisk yourself away to Provence directly on arrival at Paris's Charles de Gaulle airport. Driving is also a good option, although for the first-time visitor negotiating the highways in Provence can be a scary experience. They're fast . . . regardless of the speed limit. Off the highway, however, on the national roads, or the district roads, driving can be the best and most relaxing way to get around.

AIR TRAVEL

Marseille has one of the largest airports in France, the Aéroport de Marseille Provence in Marignane (☎ 04–42–14–14–14 ⊕ www.marseille. aeroport.fr), about 20 km (12 miles) northwest of the city center. Regular flights come in daily from Paris and London. In summer Delta Airlines flies direct from New York to Nice (about 200 km [118 miles] from Marseille and about 150 km [93 miles] from Toulon). The 25-minute airport shuttle buses to Marseille center leave daily every 20 minutes 5:10 am–9:50 am and 6:30 pm–12:10 am, and every 15 minutes 10:10 am–6:10 pm (€8). Shuttles to Aix leave every half hour 5:30 am–11:30 pm, with two late shuttles leaving at 11:40 pm and 12:15 am (€7.60).

BUS TRAVEL

Aix-en-Provence: One block west of La Rotonde, the station on rue Lapierre (✉ Av. de l'Europe ☎ 08–91–02–40–25) is crowded with many bus companies. Destinations include Marseille (30 mins, every 10 mins, €5.20 ⊕ www.lepilote.com), Arles (1½ hrs, 6:15 am–6:55 pm most days except Sun., €9.70 ⊕ www.lepilote.com), and Avignon (1 hr, 15 mins; 7 am–6:45 pm every day except Sun., €17.40 ⊕ www.lepilote.com).

Arles: Arles is one of the largest hubs, serviced out of the *Gare Routière* (bus station) on avenue Paulin-Talabot, opposite the train station. You can travel from Arles to such stops as Nîmes (1 hr, 3 daily, €1.50 ⊕ www.edgard-transport.fr) and Avignon (1 hr, 5 mins; 8 daily, €6.30 ⊕ www.info-ler.fr). Several buses daily head out to Aix-en-Provence and the Marseille A bus (☎ 08–11–88–01–13 ⊕ www.lepilote.com) also goes to the Camargue's Stes-Maries-de-la-Mer (50 mins, daily although schedule varies throughout the year, €2.70) and Pont de Gau. The bus to Cavaillon (€4.30) stops at St-Rémy-de-Provence, with daily service except on Sunday. Daily in July and August and on weekends in June and September, there's a bus (€2.20) to Les Baux-des-Provence (☎ 04–32–76–00–40 ⊕ www.sudest-mobilites.fr).

Avignon: The bus station is right by the rail station on boulevard St-Roch (✉ 58 bd. St-Roch ☎ 04–90–82–07–35); lines connect to nearby towns. St-Rémy-de-Provence is 45 minutes from Avignon by bus.

Les Baux: Buses connect with St-Rémy-de-Provence or Arles but only during July and August, with weekend service in June and September (☎ 04–32–76–00–40 ⊕ www.sudest-mobilites.fr).

Luberon villages: A number of bus companies feature routes with (infrequent) buses. You can get to Gordes on the Cavaillon-Roussillon bus. It runs twice a day in summer, morning and night, and costs €2. Voyages Arnaud has routes that include L'Isle-sur-la-Sorgue and Bonnieux (⊕ www.vaucluse.fr).

Marseille: The station on rue Honnorat (☎ 04–91–08–16–40) is next to the St-Charles train station and offers myriad connections to cities and small towns.

Nîmes: The bus station (✉ Rue Ste-Félicité) connects with Montpellier, Pont du Gard, and many other places.

Stes-Maries-de-la-Mer: There is little or no public transportation within the Camargue region, but Stes-Maries-de-la-Mer is served by bus from Arles (50 mins, €2.70).

11

St-Rémy-de-Provence: The bus station on place de la République is connected by frequent buses to and from Avignon (45 mins, €3.30). A website that provides in-depth info on bus travel in the region is ⊕ *www.beyond.fr*.

CAR TRAVEL

A6–A7 (a toll road) from Paris, known as the Autoroute du Soleil—the Highway of the Sun—takes you straight to Provence, where it divides at Orange, 659 km (412 miles) from Paris; the trip can be done in a fast six or so hours. After route A7 divides at Orange, A9 heads west to Nîmes (723 km [448 miles] from Paris) and continues into the Pyrénées and across the Spanish border. Route A7 continues southeast from Orange to Marseille, on the coast (1,100 km [680 miles] from Paris), while A8 goes to Aix-en-Provence (with a spur to Toulon) and then to the Côte d'Azur and Italy.

TRAIN TRAVEL

Aix-en-Provence: The station (✉ *Pl. Victor Hugo*) is a five-minute walk from place du Général-de-Gaulle and offers many connections, including Marseille (40 mins, 12–40 trains daily, €7.40), Nice (3 hrs, 40 mins; up to 15 trains daily, €39.60), and Cannes (3 hrs, 10 mins; up to 15 trains daily, €33.10), along with other destinations. Note that the TGV station for Aix (which now has free Wi-Fi) is about 13 km (8 miles) west of the city—a shuttle bus connects it with the town station.

Arles: Two TGV trains from Paris arrive daily; from the Gare Centrale station (✉ *Av. Paulin Talabot*) you can connect to Nîmes (25 mins, €8.20), Marseille (1 hr, €14.60), Avignon Centre (20 mins, €7.10), and Aix-en-Provence (2 hrs with connection, €20).

Avignon: The Gare Avignon TGV station is a few miles southwest of the city in the district of Courtine (a shuttle bus connects with the train station in town); other trains (and a few TGVs) use the Gare Avignon Centre station at 42 boulevard St-Roch, where you can find trains to Orange (22 mins, €5.90) and Arles (20 mins, €7.10), as well as L'Isle-sur-la-Sorgue, Nîmes, Marseille, and Aix-en-Provence.

Marseille: The station on esplanade St-Charles (✉ *Sq. Narvik* ☎ *04–91–08–16–40*), serving all regions of France, is at the northern end of the city center, a 20-minute walk from the Vieille Ville. Marseille has train routes to Aix-en-Provence (40 mins, 12–40 trains daily, €7.40), Avignon (1 hr, 50 mins; almost hourly, €19.80), Nîmes (1 hr, 40 mins; €20.70), Arles (1 hr, €14.60), and Orange (1½ hrs, €23.50). Once in Marseille, you can link up with the coastal train route, which connects all the resort towns lining the coast eastward to Monaco and Menton, along with trains to Cassis, Bandol, and Toulon.

Nîmes: Eleven TGV trains daily make the three-hour trip from Paris; frequent trains connect with Avignon Centre (30 mins, €9.20) and Arles (25 mins, €8.20), along with Montpellier and Marseille; to reach the Vieille Ville from the station, walk north on avenue Feuchères.

■**TIP→** For up-to-the minute departure and arrival times at any train station in France, plus practical information about the gare, including address and shopping facilities (all in English), see ⊕ www.gares-en-mouvement.com.

Contacts SNCF ☎ *36–35 [€0.34 per min]* ⊕ *www.voyages-sncf.com.*
TGV ☎ *36–35 [€0.34 per min]* ⊕ *www.tgv.com.*

RESTAURANTS

You'll eat late in the south, rarely before 1 for lunch, usually after 9 for dinner. In summer, shops and museums may shut down, after their morning hours, from noon until 3 or even 4 pm, as much to accommodate lazy lunches as for the crowds taking sun on the beach. But a late lunch works nicely with a late breakfast—and that's another southern luxury. As morning here is the coolest part of the day and the light is at its sweetest, hotels and cafés of every class take pains to make breakfast memorable and whenever possible serve it outdoors. Complete with tables in the garden with sunny-print cloths and a nosegay of flowers, accompanied by birdsong, it's one of the three loveliest meals of the day.

Prices in the reviews are the average cost of a main course at dinner or, if dinner is not served, at lunch.

HOTELS

Accommodations in Provence range from luxurious villas to elegantly converted mas to modest city-center hotels. Reservations are essential for much of the year. Provence is more about charming bed-and-breakfasts and lovely expensive hideaways than big hotels, so space is at a premium—especially in summer. Book as far in advance as possible for high season (return guests often reserve next year's stay at the end of the current year's visit); even in low season, you should call ahead because many hotels close for the winter. Assume that all hotel rooms have TV, telephones, and private bath, unless otherwise noted.

Prices in the reviews are the lowest cost of a standard double room in high season.

VISITOR INFORMATION

Arles, St-Rémy, and Environs Comité Départemental du Tourisme des Bouches-du-Rhône ✉ *13 rue de Brignoles, Marseille* ☎ *04–91–13–84–13* ⊕ *www.visitprovence.com.*

Avignon to the Luberon Comité Départemental de Tourisme en Vaucluse ✉ *12 rue Collège de la Croix, Avignon* ☎ *04–90–80–47–00* ⊕ *www.provenceguide.com.*

Marseille to Nice and Environs Comité Regional du Tourisme de Provence-Alpes-Côte d'Azur ✉ *61 La Canebière, Marseille* ☎ *04–91–56–47–00* ⊕ *www.tourismepaca.fr.*

A helpful Web resource for all the villages of Provence is ⊕ *www.provencebeyond.com/villages.*

TOUR OPTIONS

Private Guides: Bus tours through the Camargue are offered by **Provence Organisation** (✉ *28 bis rue Joseph Vernet* ☎ *04–90–27–10–53* ⊕ *www.agence-po.com*) and tailored specifically to your needs.

Taxis: T.R.A.N. (☎ *04–66–29–40–11* ⊕ *www.taxinimes.fr*) can take you round-trip from Nîmes to the Pont du Gard (ask the driver to wait while you explore for 30 minutes).

Walking Tours: The tourist offices in Arles, Nîmes, Avignon, Aix-en-Provence, and Marseille all organize a full calendar of walking tours (mostly in summer only).

ARLES AND THE CAMARGUE

Sitting on the banks of the Rhône River, with a Vieille Ville where time seems to have stood still since 1888—the year Vincent van Gogh immortalized the city in his paintings—Arles remains both a vibrant example of Provençal culture and the gateway to the Camargue, a wild and marshy region that extends south to the Mediterranean. Arles, in fact, once outshone Marseille as the major port of the area before sea gave way to sand. Today it competes with nearby Nîmes for the title of "Rome of France," thanks to its magnificent Roman theater and Arènes (amphitheater). Just west and south of these landmarks, the Camargue is a vast watery plain formed by the sprawling Rhône delta and extending over 800 square km (300 square miles)—its landscape remains one of the most extraordinary in France.

ARLES

36 km (22 miles) southwest of Avignon; 31 km (19 miles) east of Nîmes; 92 km (57 miles) northwest of Marseille; 720 km (430 miles) south of Paris.

If you were obliged to choose just one city to visit in Provence, lovely little Arles would give Avignon and Aix a run for their money. It's too chic to become museumlike, yet has a wealth of classical antiquities and Romanesque stonework, quarried-stone edifices and shuttered town houses, plus graceful, shady Vieille Ville streets and squares. Throughout the year, Arles hosts pageants, parades, festivals, and assorted arts events. Its panoply of restaurants and small hotels also makes it the ideal headquarters for forays into the Alpilles and the Camargue.

GETTING HERE

If you're arriving by plane, note that Arles is roughly 20 km (12 miles) from the Nîmes-Arles-Camargue airport (☎ *04–66–70–49–49*). The easiest way from the landing strip to Arles is by taxi (about €75). Commerical buses run between Nîmes and Arles three times daily (No. C30, €1.50 ⊕ *www.edgard-transport.fr*) and four times daily between Arles and Stes-Maries-de-la-Mer (€2.70 ⊕ *www.lepilote.com*). The TGV navette (€6.30 ☎ *08–21–20–22–03*) also runs eight buses daily from Avignon to Arles, and SNCF (☎ *08–00–11–40–23* ⊕ *www.ter-sncf.com*) runs numerous trains daily between Marseille and Arles.

Visitor Information Arles Tourist Office ✉ *Esplanade Charles de Gaulle, bd. des Lices* ☎ *04–90–18–41–20* ⊕ *www.arlestourisme.com.*

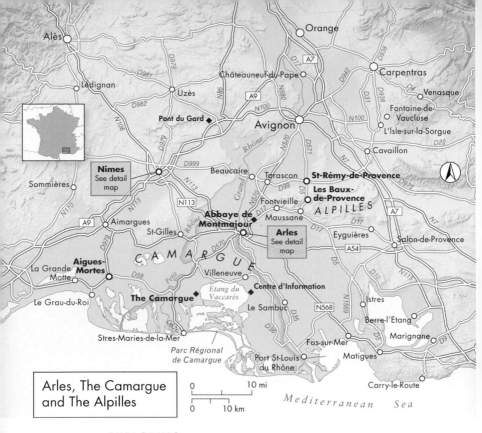

Arles, The Camargue and The Alpilles

| 0 | 10 mi |
| 0 | 10 km |

Mediterranean Sea

EXPLORING

A Greek colony since the 6th century BC, little Arles took a giant step forward when Julius Caesar defeated Marseille in the 1st century BC. The emperor-to-be designated Arles a Roman colony and lavished funds and engineering know-how on it. The settlement became an international crossroads by sea and land and a market to the world, with goods from Africa, Arabia, and the Far East. The emperor Constantine himself moved to Arles and brought Christianity with him.

The remains of this golden age are reason enough to visit Arles, yet its character nowadays is as gracious and low-key as it once was cutting-edge. Seated in the shade of the plane trees on place du Forum or strolling the rampart walkway along the sparkling Rhône, you can see what enchanted Gauguin and drove Van Gogh to creative madness.

If you plan on doing a lot of sightseeing in Arles, buy a *Passeport Avantage* ticket for €13.50. Good for the length of your stay, it covers the entry fee to the Musée de l'Arles et de la Provence Antiques and most of the other museums and monuments.

TOP ATTRACTIONS

Arènes (*Arena*). Rivaled only by the even better-preserved version in Nîmes, the arena dominating old Arles was built in the 1st century AD to seat 21,000 people, with large tunnels through which wild beasts were forced to run into the center. Before being plundered in the Middle Ages, the structure had three stories of 60 arcades each; the four medieval towers are testimony to a transformation from classical sports arena to feudal fortification. Complete restoration began in 1825, and today the arena holds nearly as many people as it once did. It's primarily a venue for the traditional spectacle of the *corridas* (bullfights), which take place annually during the *féria pascale*, or Easter festival. The less bloodthirsty local variant *Course Carmarguaise* (in which the bull is not killed) also takes place here. Festivities start with the Gardian festival on May 1, when the Queen of Arles is crowned, and culminate in early July with the award of the Cocarde d'Or (Golden Rosette) to the most successful toreador. Tickets are usually available, but for the more popular fights, it is advisable to book ahead. ✉ *24 bis, Rond Point des Arènes* ☎ *04–90–18–41–20, 08–91–70–03–70 Courses Carmarguaise* ⊕ *www.arlestourisme.com* ✉ *€6.50* ⊘ *May–Sept., daily 9–7; Oct., daily 9–6; Nov.–Feb., daily 10–5; Mar. and Apr., daily 9–6.*

Église St-Trophime. Classed as a world treasure by UNESCO, this extraordinary Romanesque church alone would justify a visit to Arles. The transepts date from the 11th century and the nave from the 12th; the church's austere symmetry and ancient artworks (including a stunning Roman-style 4th-century sarcophagus) are fascinating. But it's the church's superbly preserved Romanesque sculpture on the 12th-century **portal**—the recently renovated entry facade—that earns international respect. Particularly remarkable is the frieze of the Last Judgment, with souls being dragged off to Hell in chains or, on the contrary, being lovingly delivered into the hands of the saints. Christ is flanked by his chroniclers, the evangelists: the eagle (John), the bull (Luke), the angel (Matthew), and the lion (Mark). ✉ *Pl. de la République* ⊕ *www.arlestourisme.com* ✉ *Free* ⊘ *Closed to the public noon–2 pm.*

Fodor's Choice **Espace Van Gogh.** A strikingly resonant site, this was the hospital to
★ which the tortured artist repaired after cutting off his earlobe. Its courtyard has been impeccably restored and landscaped to match one of Van Gogh's paintings. The cloistered grounds have become something of a shrine for visitors, and there are photo plaques comparing the renovation to some of the master's paintings, including *Le Jardin de la Maison de Santé.* The exhibition hall is open for temporary exhibitions; the garden is always on view. Also check out shows of contemporary art inspired by the artist at the Fondation Vincent Van Gogh, which reopens in 2014, at 5 place Honoré Clair. ✉ *Pl. Dr. Félix Rey* ☎ *04–90–18–41–20* ⊕ *www.arlestourisme.com* ✉ *Free.*

**OFF THE
BEATEN
PATH**

Les Alyscamps. Though the romantically melancholic Roman cemetery lies 1 km (½ mile) southeast of the Vieille Ville, it's worth the hike—certainly Van Gogh thought so, as several of his famous canvases prove. This long necropolis amassed the remains of the dead from antiquity to the Middle Ages. Greek, Roman, and Christian tombs line the shady road that was once the main entry to Arles, the Aurelian Way. Next to the ruins rise the Romanesque tower and ruined church of St. Honorat, where (legend has it) St. Trophimus fell to his knees when God spoke to him. ✉ *Allée des Sarcophages* ☎ *04–90–49–36–74* ⊕ *www. arlestourisme.com* ✉ *€3.50* ⊘ *May–Sept., daily 9–7; Oct., daily 9–noon*

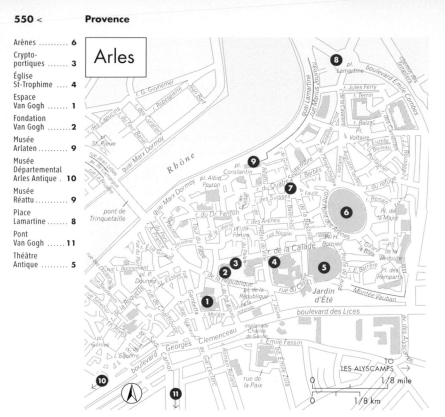

and 2–6; Nov.–Feb., daily 10–noon and 2–5; Mar. and Apr., daily 9–noon and 2–6.

Musée Départemental Arles Antiques (*Museum of Ancient Arles*). Though it's a hike from the center, this state-of-the-art museum is a good place to set the tone and context for your exploration of Arles. You can learn all about Arles in its Roman heyday, from the development of its monuments to details of daily life. The bold, modern triangular structure (designed by Henri Ciriani) lies on the site of an enormous Roman *cirque* (chariot-racing stadium), and the permanent collection includes jewelry, mosaics, town plans, and carved 4th-century sarcophagi. The quantity of these treasures gives an idea of the extent of Arles's importance. Seven superb floor mosaics can be viewed from an elevated platform, and you exit via a hall packed tight with magnificently detailed paleo-Christian sarcophagi. As you leave you will see the belt of St-Césaire, the last bishop of Arles, who died in AD 542 when the countryside was overwhelmed by the Franks and the Roman era met its end. Ask for the English-language guidebook. ⊠ *Av. de la 1ère Division Française Libre, Presqu'île du Cirque Romain* ☎ *04–13–31–51–03* ⊕ *www.arles-antique. cg13.fr* ⊒ *€6, free 1st Sun. of the month* ☉ *Wed.–Mon. 10–6.*

Musée Réattu. Three rooms of this museum, housed in a Knights of Malta priory dating to the 15th century, are dedicated to local painter Jacques

Réattu. But the standouts are works by Dufy, Gauguin, and 57 drawings done by Picasso in 1971—including one delightfully tongue-in-cheek depiction of noted muse and writer Lee Miller in full Arles dress. They were donated to Arles by Picasso himself, to thank the town for amusing him with bullfights. ⊠ *10 rue Grand Prieuré* ☎ *04–90–49–37–58* ⊕ *www.museereattu.arles.fr* ✉ *€7* ☉ *Nov.–June, Tues.–Sun. 10–12:30 and 2–6:30; July–Sept., Tues.–Sun. 10–7.*

Museon Arlaten (*Museum of Arles*). After six years of renovation, this fascinating museum is scheduled to reopen 2014 (check website for updates). When it does, the quirky collection will plunge you right into post-Roman Arles. Created by the father of the Provençal revival, turn-of-the-20th-century poet Frédéric Mistral, it enshrines a seemingly bottomless collection of regional treasures ranging from 18th-century furniture and ceramics to a mixed-bag collection of toothache-prevention cures. There are spindled-oak bread boxes (mounted high on the wall like bird cages); bizarre traditional talismans (a ring fashioned from the third nail of a horseshoe to ward off hemorrhoids); the signature Arlésienne costumes, with their pretty shoulder scarves crossed at the waist; dolls and miniatures; an entire Camargue gardian hut, with reconstructed interior; and dioramas with mannequins—tiny tableaux of Provençal life. Following Mistral's wishes, women in full Arlésienne costume oversee the labyrinth of lovely 16th-century halls. ⊠ *29–31 rue de la République* ☎ *04–90–93–58–11* ⊕ *www.museonarlaten.fr* ☉ *Closed until 2014 (old hrs: Apr., May, and Sept., Tues.–Sun. 9:30–noon and 2–5:30; June–Aug., daily 9:30–12:30 and 2–6; Oct.–Mar., Tues.–Sun. 9:30–12:30 and 2–6:30).*

WORTH NOTING

Cryptoportiques. Entering through City Hall, you can gain access to these ancient underground passages at the entrance of a 17th-century Jesuit college. Dating from 30 BC to 20 BC, the horseshoe of vaults and pillars buttressed the ancient forum from below ground. Used as a refuge for Resistance members in World War II, the galleries still have a rather ominous atmosphere. Yet openings let in natural daylight, and artworks of considerable merit have been unearthed here, adding to the mystery of the site's original function. ⊠ *Rue Balze, pl. de la République, City Hall* ☎ *04–90–18–41–20* ⊕ *www.arlestourisme.com* ✉ *€3.50* ☉ *May–Sept., daily 9–noon and 2–7; Oct., daily 9–noon and 2–6; Nov.–Feb., daily 10–noon and 2–5; Mar. and Apr., daily 9–noon and 2–6.*

Fondation Van Gogh. After being temporarily housed at 30 rue de la République, the Fondation Van Gogh will reopen in 2014 at a new location on place Honoré Clair. The foundation showcases artists—such as painter Francis Bacon and photographer Robert Doisneau—who have been inspired by the Post-Impressionist master. ⊠ *Hôtel Léautaud de Donines, 5 pl. Honoré Clair* ☎ *04–90–49–94–04* ⊕ *www. fondation-vincentvangogh-arles.org* ✉ *Not set at press time* ☉ *Tues.–Sat. 10–12:30 and 2–5.*

Place Lamartine. Stand on the site of Van Gogh's residence in Arles—the now-famous Maison Jaune (Yellow House), destroyed by bombs in 1944. The artist may have set up his easel on the quais du Rhône,

In the Footsteps of Van Gogh

It was the light that lured Vincent van Gogh to Arles. For a man raised under the gray skies of the Netherlands and the gaslight pall of Paris, Provence's clean, clear sun was a revelation. In his last years he turned his frenzied efforts toward capturing the "...golden tones of every hue: green gold, yellow gold, pink gold, bronze or copper colored gold, and even from the yellow of lemons to the matte, lusterless yellow of threshed grain."

Arles, however, was not drawn to Van Gogh. Though it exerts every effort today to make up for this misjudgment, Arles treated the artist very badly during the time he passed here near the end of his life—a time when his creativity, productivity, and madness all reached a climax.

Van Gogh began working in Arles in 1888 with an intensity and tempestuousness that first drew, then drove away, his companion Paul Gauguin, with whom he had dreamed of founding an artists' colony. Astonishingly productive—he applied a pigment-loaded palette knife to some 200 canvases in that year alone—he nonetheless lived in intense isolation, counting his sous, and writing his visions in lengthy letters to his long-suffering, infinitely patient brother Theo. Often drinking heavily, Vincent alienated his neighbors, driving them to distraction and ultimately goading them to action. The people of Arles circulated a petition to have him evicted just a year after he arrived, a shock that left him more and more at a loss to cope with life and led to his eventual self-commitment in an asylum in nearby St-Rémy.

The houses he lived in are no longer standing, though many of his subjects remain as he saw them (or are restored to a similar condition). Happily, the city has provided helpful markers and a numbered itinerary to guide you between landmarks. You can stand on the place Lamartine, where his famous Maison Jaune stood until it was destroyed by World War II bombs. Starry Night may have been painted from the quai du Rhône just off place Lamartine, though another was completed at St-Rémy.

The Café La Nuit on place Forum is an exact match for the terrace platform, scattered with tables and bathed in gaslight under the stars, from the painting Terrace de café le Soir; Gauguin and Van Gogh used to drink here. Both the Arènes and Les Alyscamps were featured in paintings, and the hospital where he broke down and cut off his earlobe is now a kind of shrine, its garden reconstructed exactly as it figured in Le Jardin de l'Hôtel-Dieu. (As for that infamous ear—actually, just the left lobe—historians theorize Van Gogh wielded the knife in a kind of desperate homage to Gauguin, whom he had come to idolize, by following the fashion in Provençal bullrings for a matador to present his lady love with an ear from a dispatched bull.)

The drawbridge in Le pont de Langlois aux Lavandières has been reconstructed outside town, at Port-de-Bouc, 3 km (2 miles) south on D35.

About 25 km (16 miles) away is St-Rémy-de-Provence, where Van Gogh retreated to the asylum St-Paul-de-Mausolée. Here he spent hours in silence, painting the cloisters and nearby orchards, vineyards, and star-spangled crystalline skies—the stuff of inspiration.

Van Gogh immortalized the courtyard of this former hospital—now the Espace Van Gogh, a center devoted to his works—in several masterpieces.

just off place Lamartine, to capture the view that he transformed into his legendary *Starry Night*. Eight other sites are included on the city's "Promenade Vincent van Gogh" (⊕ *www.arlestourisme.com*), linking sight to canvas, including the place du Forum; the Trinquetaille bridge; rue Mireille; the Summer Garden on the boulevard des Lices; and the road along the Arles à Bouc canal. A map (*le Circuit Van Gogh*) can be purchased for €1 at the tourist office.

Pont Van Gogh (*Langlois Bridge*). Van Gogh immortalized many everyday objects and captured views still seen today, but his famous painting of this bridge—on the southern outskirts of Arles, about 4 km (2½ miles) from the old city—seems to touch a particular chord among locals. Bombed in World War II, the bridge has been restored to its former glory. ⊠ *Rte. de Port St-Louis.*

Théâtre Antique (*Ancient Theater*). Directly up rue de la Calade from place de la République, you'll find these ruins of a theater built by the Romans under Augustus in the 1st century BC. It's here that the noted Venus of Arles statue, now in the Louvre, was dug up and identified. The theater was once an entertainment venue that held 20,000 people, and is now a pleasant, park-like retreat. None of the amphitheater's stage walls and only one row of arches remain; the fine local stone was used to build early Christian churches. Only a few vestiges of the original stone benches are left, along with the two great Corinthian columns. Today the ruins are a stage for the Festival d'Arles, in July and August, and site of Les Recontres d'Arles (Photography Festival) from early July to mid-September. ⊠ *Rue de la Calade* ☎ 04–90–49–59–05

🌐 *www.tourisme.ville-arles.fr* 🎫 *€6.50* ⏲ *May–Sept., daily 9–7; Oct., daily 9–6; Nov.–Feb., daily 10–5; Mar. and Apr., daily 9–6.*

WHERE TO EAT

$ TAPAS

🍴 **Bodeguita.** This popular institution near place du Forum is known for excellent tapas at more than reasonable prices. Embrace the bullfighter within and try a range of morsels: spicy stuffed dumplings, roasted Camembert with chorizo bread, or sliced chicken Catalonia-style. Grilled bull steak with creamed garlic sauce and a few other entrées are also available. The warm reception by chef Anthony is matched by the vivid yet simple interior. [$] *Average main: €20* ✉ *49 rue des Arenes* ☎ *04–90–96–68–59* 🌐 *www.bodeguita-arles.fr* ⏲ *Closed Nov.–Apr. No lunch Sun.–Thurs.*

$$$$ FRENCH Fodor's Choice ★

🍴 **La Chassagnette.** Reputedly the original registered "organic" restaurant in Provence, this sophisticated yet down-home comfortable spot—located 12 km (7½ miles) south of Arles—is fetchingly designed and has a dining area that extends outdoors, where large family-style picnic tables await under a wooden-slate canopy overlooking the extensive gardens. Using ingredients that are grown right on the property, innovative master chef Armand Arnal (who has been awarded a Michelin star) serves prix-fixe menus that are a refreshing, though not inexpensive, mix of modern and classic French-country cuisine—you can expect to pay €85–€125 per person. The à la carte options are equally admirable and much more affordable: picture a fillet of wild sole with roasted asparagus and bottarga for €35. Environmentally conscious oenophiles can wash it all down with a glass of eco-certified wine. [$] *Average main: €36* ✉ *Rte. du Sambuc, D36* ☎ *04–90–97–26–96* 🌐 *www.chassagnette.fr* ✍ *Reservations essential* ⏲ *Closed Feb.; May–Oct., closed Tues. and Wed.; Nov.–Apr., closed Mon.–Wed.*

$ FRENCH

🍴 **La Gueule du Loup.** You reach your table through the kitchen, bustling with chopping, sizzling, and wafting scents, which is a nice introduction to what awaits. The cooking is serious—Provençal specialties such as *rouget* (red mullet) with pureed potatoes, *caillette d'agneau* (lamb baked in herbs), and crème brûlée with anise; and the four set menus, priced from €15 to €33, will surely appeal to all appetites. Jazz music and vintage magic posters bring the old Arles stone-and-beam interior up to date for a memorably pleasant experience. [$] *Average main: €17* ✉ *39 rue des Arènes* ☎ *04–90–96–96–69* ✍ *Reservations essential* ⏲ *Closed mid-Jan.–mid-Feb.; Apr.–Sept., no lunch Sun. and Mon.; Oct.–Mar., closed Sun. and Mon.*

$$$$ FRENCH

🍴 **L'Atelier de Jean-Luc Rabanel.** Jean-Luc Rabanel is the culinary success story of the region, famous for fresh garden-inspired cuisine that he features in a stylish restaurant–cum–cooking school, the only organic eatery in France to merit two Michelin stars. A super chic Japanese-style reception area, which includes the five elements—water, fire, earth, air and, vegetation—ensures that "guests will come into harmony with their cuisine." The seven-dish tapas-style lunch (€55) is a treat not to be missed. Those keeping to a budget should try **A Côté** (☎ *04–90–47–61–13* 🌐 *www.bistro-acote.com*), a few doors down, where you can more affordably experience the genius of this super-chef by sampling a tasty selection of upmarket tapas and regional wines. [$] *Average main:*

€100 ✉ 7 rue des Carmes ☎ 04–90–91–07–69 🌐 www.rabanel.com ✍ Reservations essential ⏲ Closed Mon. and Tues.

$ FRENCH 🍴 **Le 16.** Plates here might be considered simple by gastronomic aficionados—tender grilled steak, perfectly seasoned fresh fish, or copious salads—but this charmingly decorated restaurant has kept warm the essential ingredient: taste, and at a reasonable price. There is a lovely, shaded back garden patio with a grape vine trellis creeping up the wrought-iron structure, and the inside dining room is small and cozy. The icing on the cake? The desserts are *fantastique.* [$] *Average main: €15 ✉ 16 rue du Docteur-Fanton ☎ 04–90–93–77–36 🌐 www.le16restaurant.com ✍ Reservations essential ⏲ Closed Sun. and 2 wks in June and Nov.*

$$$$ MODERN FRENCH 🍴 **Le Cilantro.** With so many typical and rather ho-hum Provençal menus around, it's refreshing to find the modern, innovative cooking dished up by star chef Jerome Laurent, who has brought Arles gastronomy into the 21st century with this Michelin-starred gem. Menus, changing with the seasons, include the catch of the day with white asparagus in Bellota bacon and rack of lamb roasted with black garlic nougat. Reserve in advance and save room for dessert. [$] *Average main: €38 ✉ 31 rue Porte de Laure ☎ 04–90–18–25–05 🌐 www.restaurantcilantro.com ✍ Reservations essential ⏲ Closed Sun. and Mon., and last wk of Feb. No dinner Sat.*

WHERE TO STAY

For expanded hotel reviews, visit Fodors.com.

$$$ HOTEL Fodor's Choice ★ 🏨 **Grand Hotel Nord-Pinus.** A richly atmospheric stage-set for literati (or literary poseurs), decor-magazine shoots, and people who prize ambience, this scruffy-chic landmark is not for everyone—but if Picasso once felt at home here, perhaps you may, too. **Pros:** unique atmosphere transports you to a less complicated time, when bullfighting was not part of the political arena and people still dressed for dinner; free mineral water in rooms. **Cons:** rooms at front of hotel can be noisy, especially in summer. [$] *Rooms from: €180 ✉ Pl. du Forum ☎ 04–90–93–44–44 🌐 www.nord-pinus.com 🛏 25 rooms, 1 apartment ⏲ Closed 2 to 3 months, dates vary, between Nov. and Feb. 🍽 No meals.*

$ HOTEL 🏨 **Hotel l'Arlatan.** At this Provençal-style mansion, the elegant salon and fireplace are only a prelude to the inviting rooms with exposed beams, stone walls, and original tile work—further enhanced with soft lighting and large, cozy beds. **Pros:** warm welcome; three elevators. **Cons:** some rooms are small and a bit sparse; tricky to find when arriving by car. [$] *Rooms from: €85 ✉ 26 rue du Sauvage ☎ 04–90–93–56–66 🌐 www.hotel-arlatan.fr 🛏 46 rooms ⏲ Closed Nov. 15–Mar. 15. 🍽 No meals.*

$$$$ HOTEL Fodor's Choice ★ 🏨 **L'Hôtel Particulier.** Once owned by the Baron of Chartrouse, this extraordinary 18th-century *hôtel particulier* (mansion) is delightfully intimate and decorated in sophisticated yet charming style, with gold-framed mirrors, white-brocade chairs, marble writing desks, artfully hung curtains, and hand-painted wallpaper. **Pros:** quiet and secluded but only a short walk to town; combines historical ambience with modern high-tech conveniences. **Cons:** a 50% nonrefundable deposit is required when booking; the pool is small, which can be difficult in summer when every guest wants to be in the water; optional breakfast steep

One of the centers of Provençal folklore, Arles is host to a bevy of parades featuring locals dressed in regional costumes.

(€23). [$] *Rooms from: €309* ✉ *4 rue de la Monnaie* ☎ *04–90–52–51–40* 🌐 *www.hotel-particulier.com* 🛏 *18 rooms* 🍴 *No meals.*

$ HOTEL 🏨 **Muette.** This Old Town option has 12th-century exposed stone walls, a 15th-century spiral staircase, and weathered wood, plus Provençal prints and fresh sunflowers in every room to add just the right homey touch. **Pros:** excellent value; enthusiastic welcome; generous buffet breakfast (extra). **Cons:** some rooms can be very noisy, especially in the summer; parking can be tricky. [$] *Rooms from: €74* ✉ *15 rue des Suisses* ☎ *04–90–96–15–39* 🌐 *www.hotel-muette.com* 🛏 *18 rooms* 🕒 *Closed 2 wks in Feb.* 🍴 *No meals.*

NIGHTLIFE AND THE ARTS

To find out what's happening in and around Arles (even as far away as Nîmes and Avignon), check the free monthly *Le César* (🌐 *www.cesar.fr*), which lists films, plays, cabarets, and music events. It's distributed at the tourist office and in bars, clubs, and cinemas.

In high season the cafés stay lively until the wee hours; in winter the streets empty out by 11.

Brasserie Nord-Pinus. For many locals, the place to tipple is at the hip bar in the Hôtel Nord-Pinus. ✉ *Pl. du Forum.*

Le Cargo de Nuit. Le Cargo de Nuit is the main venue for live jazz, reggae, and rock, with a dance floor next to the stage. A meal allows you reduced entry to see the show. ✉ *7 av. Sadi-Carnot* ☎ *04–90–49–55–99* 🌐 *www.cargodenuit.com.*

Passage du Méjan. Passage du Méjan is a large arts complex with its own publishing house, arts cinema, restaurant, and hamam. ✉ *Pl. Nina*

Berberova ☎ *04–90–49–09–12, 04–90–96–10–32 hamam, 04–90–49–56–78 concerts, theater* ⊕ *www.actes-sud.fr.*

THE CAMARGUE

19 km (12 miles) east of Aigues-Mortes, 15 km (9 miles) south of Arles.

Fodor's Choice ★ Stretching to the horizon for about 800 square km (309 square miles), the vast alluvial delta of the Rhône known as the Camargue is an austere, flat marshland, scoured by the mistral and swarmed over by mosquitoes. Between the endless flow of sediment from the Rhône and the erosive force of the sea, its shape is constantly changing. Even the Provençal poet Frédéric Mistral described it in bleak terms: "*Ni arbre, ni ombre, ni âme*" ("Neither tree, nor shade, nor a soul"). Yet its harsh landscape harbors a concentration of exotic wildlife unique in Europe, and its isolation has given birth to an ascetic and ancient way of life that transcends national stereotypes. People find the Camargue intriguing, birds find it irresistible. The protected marshes lure some 400 species, including more than 160 in migration.

Visitor Information Camargue Tourist Office ⊠ *1 pl. Frédéric Mistral, Saint-Gilles* ☎ *04-66-87-33-75* ⊕ *www.ot-saint-gilles.fr.*

EXPLORING

The strange region that is the Camargue is worth discovering slowly, either on foot or on horseback—especially as its wildest reaches are inaccessible by car. Either way, you'll quickly discover that the Camargue is truly one of a kind.

Parc Ornithologique du Pont de Gau (*Pont du Gau Ornithological Park*). The easiest place to view birdlife is the Parc Ornithologique du Pont de Gau. On some 150 acres of marsh and salt lands, birds are welcomed and protected (but in no way confined); injured birds are treated and kept in large pens, to be released if and when able to survive. A series of boardwalks (including a short, child-friendly inner loop) snakes over the wetlands, the longest leading to an observation blind, where a half hour of silence, binoculars in hand, can reveal unsuspected satisfactions. ⊠ *Rte. d'Arles, Saintes Maries de la Mer* ☎ *04-90-97-82-62* ⊕ *www.parcornithologique.com* 💳 *€7.50* ☉ *Apr.–Sept., daily 9–sunset; Oct.–Mar., daily 10–sunset.*

Parc Regional de Camargue. As you drive the scarce roads that barely crisscross the Camargue, you are usually within the boundaries of the Parc Regional de Camargue. Unlike state and national parks in the United States, this area is privately owned and utilized following regulations imposed by the French government. The principal owners are the *manadiers* (the Camargue equivalent of small-scale ranchers) and their *gardians* (a kind of open-range cowboy), who graze wide-horn bulls and dappled-white horses. When not participating in a bloodless bullfight (mounted players try to hook a red ribbon from its horns), a bull may well end up in the wine-rich regional stew called *gardianne de taureau*. Riding through the marshlands in leather pants and wide-rim black hats and wielding long prongs to prod their cattle, the gardians themselves are as fascinating as the wildlife. Their homes—tiny and whitewashed—dot the countryside. **■ TIP→ In these parts, it's a good idea to slather on the mosquito repellent.** ☎ *04–90–97–10–82* 🌐 *www.parc-camargue.fr.*

WHERE TO EAT AND STAY

For expanded hotel reviews, visit Fodors.com.

$$$$ HOTEL 🏨 **Le Mas de Peint.** Sitting on roughly 1,250 acres of Camargue ranch land, this exquisite 17th-century farmhouse may just offer the ultimate *mas* experience. **Pros:** isolated setting makes for a perfect escape—romantic or otherwise; reception is warm; no detail is missed in service or style. **Cons:** make sure you confirm room has a shower; unheated pool is a tad chilly even in September; not much to do once sun goes down. [$] *Rooms from: €260* ✉ *Le Sambuc, 20 km (12 miles) south of Arles* ☎ *04–90–97–20–62* 🌐 *www.masdepeint.com* 🛏 *8 rooms, 5 suites* 🕓 *Closed mid-Nov.–end of Mar.; open for 2 wks at Christmas* 🍴 *Breakfast.*

AIGUES-MORTES

41 km (25 miles) south of Nîmes, 48 km (30 miles) southwest of Arles.

Visitor Information Aigues-Mortes Tourist Office ✉ *Pl. St. Louis* ☎ *04–66–53–73–00* 🌐 *www.ot-aiguesmortes.fr.*

EXPLORING

Like a tiny illumination in a medieval manuscript, Aigues-Mortes is a precise and perfect miniature fortress-town contained within symmetrical crenellated walls, its streets laid out in geometric grids. Now awash in a flat wasteland of sand, salt, and monotonous marsh, it was once a major port town from which no less than St-Louis himself (Louis IX) set sail in the 13th century to conquer Jerusalem. In 1248 some 35,000 zealous men launched 1,500 ships toward Cyprus, engaging the infidel on his own turf and suffering swift defeat; Louis was briefly taken prisoner. A second launching in 1270 led to more crushing loss, and Louis succumbed to the plague.

Fortress-port. Louis's state-of-the-art fortress-port is astonishingly well preserved. The stout walls now contain a small Provençal village filled with tourists, but the visit is more than justified by the impressive scale of the original structure. ✉ *Pl. Anatole France, Porte de la Gardette* ☎ *04–66–53–61–55* 🎟 *€7.50* 🕓 *May–Aug., daily 10–7; Sept.–Apr., daily 10–1 and 2–5:30.*

Place St-Louis. Place St-Louis, where a 19th-century statue of the father of the fleur-de-lis reigns under shady pollards, has a mellow village feel and is a welcome retreat from the clutter of souvenir shops on surrounding lanes. The pretty, bare-bones **Église Notre-Dame des Sablons,** on one corner of the square, has a timeless air (the church dates from the 13th century, but the stained glass is modern), and the spectacular Chapelle des Pénitents Blancs and Chapelle des Pénitents Gris are Baroque-era marvels. ☎ *04–66–53–73–00* 🎟 *Free.*

WHERE TO EAT AND STAY

For expanded hotel reviews, visit Fodors.com.

$$$$
FRENCH ✕ **Chez Bob.** In a smoky, isolated stone farmhouse filled with old posters, you'll taste Camargue cooking at its rustic best. There's only the daily menu, which can include anything from *anchoïade* (crudités with hard-cooked egg—still in the shell—and anchovy vinaigrette), homemade duck pâté thick with peppercorns, and often the pièce de résistance: a thick, sizzling slab of bull steak grilled in the roaring fireplace. Sprinkle on hand-skimmed sea salt and dig in, while listening to the migrating birds pass by. Sunday at lunch, professional musicians to add to the already authentic ambience. Ⓢ *Average main: €43* ⊠ *Mas Petite Antonelle, rte. du Sambuc, Villeneuve* ☎ *04–90–97–00–29* ⊕ *www.restaurantbob.fr* ⚮ *Reservations essential* ⊗ *Closed Mon., and Tues. No dinner Sun.*

$$
B&B/INN ⊺ **Les Arcades.** Long a success as an upscale seafood restaurant, this beautifully preserved 16th-century house also has large, airy guest accommodations, some with tall windows overlooking a green courtyard. **Pros:** rooms overlook lovely courtyard; free parking card provided at check-in. **Cons:** restaurant may be closed unannounced; not much English spoken at hotel. Ⓢ *Rooms from: €104* ⊠ *23 bd. Gambetta* ☎ *04–66–53–81–13* ⊕ *www.les-arcades.fr* ⤳ *9 rooms* ⧖ *No meals.*

NÎMES

35 km (20 miles) north of Aigues-Mortes; 43 km (26 miles) south of Avignon; 121 km (74 miles) west of Marseille.

With one of the best-preserved Roman amphitheaters in the world and a near-perfect Roman temple, Nîmes beats out Arles for the title of "French City Best Able to Cash In on the Roman Empire's Former Glory." Although the ancient ruins always take center stage, keep in mind that this town also has other allurements, including refurbished medieval streets and a calendar rich in cultural events.

GETTING HERE AND AROUND

On the Paris–Avignon–Montpellier rail line, Nîmes has a direct, three-hour TGV link with Paris. From the Nîmes bus station (just behind the train station) you can travel to Arles (1 hr, 3 daily, €1.50 ⊕ *www.edgard-transport.fr*) or take the E51 bus to Avignon (1½ hrs, 3 daily, €1.50 ⊕ *www.edgard-transport.fr*). The B21 bus (direction Pont-St-Esprit) stops at Remoulins for the Pont du Gard (35 mins, €1.50, ☎ *08–10–33–42–73*). Note that although all sites in Nîmes are within walking distance, La Citadine Ecusson bus (Tango ☎ *08–20–22–30–30*) does a good loop from the station, passing many of the principal attractions along the way. It runs every 8 minutes (every 30 on Sunday); and five tickets cost €1.80, so you can hop on and off.

Visitor Information Nîmes Tourist Office ⊠ *6 rue Auguste* ☎ *04-66-58-38-00* ⊕ *www.nimes-tourisme.com.*

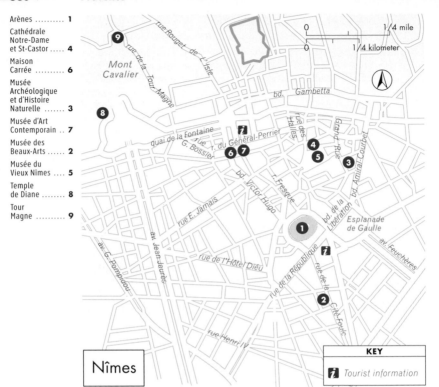

Nîmes

KEY

i *Tourist information*

EXPLORING

If you've come to the south seeking Roman treasures, you need look no further than Nîmes (pronounced *neem*): the Arènes and Maison Carrée are among continental Europe's best-preserved antiquities. But if you've come in search of a more modern mythology—of lazy, graceful Provence—give Nîmes a pass. It's a feisty, run-down rat race of a town, with jalopies and Vespas roaring irreverently around the ancient temple. Its medieval Vieille Ville lacks the grace of those in Arles or St-Rémy. Yet its rumpled and rebellious ways trace directly back to its Roman incarnation, when its population swelled with newly victorious soldiers flaunting arrogant behavior after their conquest of Egypt in 31 BC.

Already anchoring a fiefdom of pre-Roman *oppida* (elevated fortresses) before ceding to the empire in the 1st century BC, this ancient city grew to formidable proportions under the Pax Romana. Its next golden age bloomed under the Protestants, who established an anti-Catholic stronghold here and wreaked havoc on iconic architectural treasures—not to mention the papist minority. Their massacre of some 200 Catholic citizens in 1567 is remembered as the Michelade; many of those murdered were priests sheltered in the *évêché* (bishop's house), now the Museum of Old Nîmes.

TOP ATTRACTIONS

Fodor'sChoice
★

Arènes. The best-preserved Roman amphitheater in the world is a miniature of the Colosseum in Rome (note the small carvings of Romulus and Remus—the wrestling gladiators—on the exterior and the intricate bulls' heads etched into the stone over the entrance on the north side). More than 435 feet long and 330 feet wide, it had a seating capacity of 24,000 in its day. Bloody gladiator battles, criminals being thrown to animals, and theatrical wild-boar chases drew crowds to its bleachers—and the vomitoria beneath them. Nowadays the corrida (bullfight) transforms the arena (and all of Nîmes) into a sangria-flushed homage to Spain. Concerts are held here year-round, thanks to a high-tech glass-and-steel structure that covers the arena for winter use. ⊠ *Bd. des Arènes* ☎ *04–66–21–82–56, 04–66–02–80–80 feria box office* ⊕ *www. arenes-nimes.com* ✉ *€8.50; €11 joint ticket woth Tour Magne and Maison Carrée* ⊗ *Mar. and Oct., daily 9–6; Apr., May, and Sept., daily 9–6:30; June, daily 9–7; July and Aug., daily 9–8; Nov.–Feb., daily 9:30–5.*

Maison Carrée (*Square House*). Lovely and forlorn in the middle of a busy downtown square, this exquisitely preserved temple strikes a timeless balance between symmetry and whimsy, purity of line and richness of decor. Modeled on the Temple to Apollo in Rome, adorned with magnificent marble columns and elegant pediment, the Maison Carrée remains one of the most noble surviving structures of ancient Roman civilization anywhere. Built around 5 BC and dedicated to Caius Caesar and his grandson Lucius, the temple has survived subsequent use as a medieval meeting hall, an Augustine church, a storehouse for Revolutionary archives, and a horse shed. Temporary art and photo exhibitions are held here, and among a permanent display of photos and drawings of ongoing archaeological work is a splendid ancient Roman fresco of Cassandra (being dragged by her hair by a hunter) that was discovered in 1992 and carefully restored. There's even a fun 3-D projection of the heroes of Nîmes. ⊠ *Pl. de la Maison Carrée* ☎ *04–66–21–82–56* ⊕ *www.arenes-nimes.com* ✉ *€4.80; joint ticket with Tour Magne and Arénes €11* ⊗ *June, daily 10–7; July and Aug., daily 10–8; Apr., May, and Sept., daily 10–6:30; Mar. and Oct., daily 10–6; Nov.–Feb., daily 10–1 and 2–4:30.*

Musée Archéologique et d'Histoire Naturelle (*Museum of Archaeology and Natural History*). This old Jesuit college houses a wonderful collection of local archaeological finds, including sarcophagi, beautiful pieces of Roman glass, statues, busts, friezes, tools, coins, and pottery. Among the highlights is a rare pre-Roman statue called *The Warrior of Grezan* and the Marbacum Torso, which was dug up at the foot of the Tour Magne. ⊠ *13 bd. Amiral Courbet* ☎ *04–66–76–74–80* ⊕ *www.nimes. fr* ✉ *Free* ⊗ *Tues.–Sun. 10–6.*

Temple de Diane (*Temple of Diana*). This shattered Roman ruin dates from the 2nd century BC. The temple's function is unknown, though it's thought to have been part of a larger Roman complex that is still unexcavated. In the Middle Ages Benedictine nuns occupied the building before it was converted into a church. Destruction came during the Wars of Religion. ⊠ *Jardins de la Fontaine.*

Tour Magne (*Magne Tower*). At the far end of the Jardins de la Fontaine, you'll find the remains of a tower the emperor Augustus had built on Gallic foundations; it was probably used as a lookout post. Despite losing 30 feet in height over the course of time, the tower still provides fine views of Nîmes for anyone energetic enough to climb the 140 steps. ⊠ *Jardins de la Fontaine, pl. Guillaume-Apollinaire* ☎ *04–66–21–82–56* 🖰 *€3; joint ticket with Arènes and Maison Carrée €11* ⊙ *Nov.–Feb., daily 9:30–1 and 2–4:30; Mar. and Oct., daily 9:30–1 and 2–6; Apr., May, and Sept., daily 9:30–6:30; June, daily 9–7; July and Aug., daily 9–8.*

WORTH NOTING

Cathédrale Notre-Dame et St-Castor (*Nîmes Cathedral*). Destroyed and rebuilt in several stages, Nîmes Cathedral was damaged by Protestants during the 16th-century Wars of Religion but still shows traces of its original construction in 1096. A remarkably preserved Romanesque frieze portrays Adam and Eve cowering in shame, the gory slaughter of Abel, and a flood-wearied Noah. Inside, look for the 4th-century sarcophagus (third chapel on the right) and a magnificent 17th-century chapel in the apse. ⊠ *Pl. aux Herbes* ☎ *04–66–67–27–72* ⊙ *Weekdays 8:30–6; Sat. 8:30–noon and 2–6.*

Musée d'Art Contemporain (*Contemporary Art Museum*). Musée d'Art Contemporain is inside the Carré d'Art, along with a vast library and media center, le Bibliotheque Carré d'Art. The gallery is in an atrium filled with glass staircases and houses art from 1960 onward by artists such as Yves Arman, Martial Raysse, and Bertrand Lavier, as well as temporary exhibitions. The chic café on the top floor serves good coffee and has great views—stop here before heading off to the public library section, which has a fine collection of old manuscripts. ⊠ *Pl. de la Maison Carrée* ☎ *04–66–76–35–70* ⊕ *www.nimes.fr* 🖰 *€5* ⊙ *Tues.– Sun. 10–6.*

Musée des Beaux-Arts. The centerpiece of this early-20th-century building, stunningly refurbished by architect Jean-Michel Wilmotte, is a vast ancient mosaic depicting a marriage ceremony that provides intriguing insights into the lifestyle of Roman aristocrats. Also in the varied collection are seven paintings devoted to Cleopatra by 18th-century Nîmes-born painter Natoire Italian, plus some fine Flemish, Dutch, and French works (notably Rubens's *Portrait of a Monk* and Giambono's *The Mystic Marriage of St. Catherine*). ⊠ *Pl. de la Maison Carrée* ☎ *04–66–67–38–21* ⊕ *www.nimes.fr.*

Musée du Vieux Nîmes (*Museum of Old Nîmes*). Housed in the 17th-century bishop's palace opposite the cathedral, this museum shows off garments embroidered in the exotic and vibrant style for which Nîmes was once famous. Look for the 14th-century jacket made of blue serge de Nîmes—the famous fabric (now simply called denim) from which Levi-Strauss first fashioned blue jeans. ⊠ *Pl. aux Herbes, pl. aux Herbes* ☎ *04–66–76–73–70* ⊕ *www.nimes.fr* 🖰 *Free* ⊙ *Tues.–Sun. 10–6.*

An entry in Fodor's France contest, this photo by Mike Tumchewics, a Fodors.com member, captures Nîmes bathed in Provence's extraordinary light.

WHERE TO EAT

$$$$ FRENCH 🍴 **Alexandre.** Chef Michel Kayser adds a personal touch to local specialties at this *à la mode* modern restaurant. The menu changes according to the season and the chef's creative whimsy. Golden zuchinni flowers with frothy truffle mousseline followed by a rich bull steak, roasted in its own juice and served with pan-roasted potatoes, may not leave room for dessert. Decor is elegantly spare, with stone walls, and large bay windows; but the gardens are extensive, and apricots and peaches plucked from the overhanging branches will often appear on your plate, magically transformed into some delicious creation. Two Michelin stars indeed! [$] *Average main: €54* ✉ *2 rue Xavier Tronc, rte. de l'Aeroport* ☎ *04–66–70–08–99* 🌐 *www.michelkayser.com* ✍ *Reservations essential* 🕓 *Closed Sun. dinner, Mon. and Tues. from Sept.–June, and Sun. and Mon. in July and Aug. Closed 2 wks end of Feb. and Aug.*

$$$ FRENCH 🍴 **Le Jardin d'Hadrien.** This chic enclave, with its quarried white stone, ancient plank-and-beam ceiling, and open fireplace, would be a culinary haven even without its lovely hidden garden, a shady retreat for summer meals. Chef Christophe Adlin changes menus monthly to bring the freshest seasonal combinations to your palate, so you might be treated to fresh cod and zucchini flowers filled with *brandade* (the creamy, light paste of salt cod and olive oil) or, in winter, sautéed veal and crayfish with saffron potatoes. Two prix-fixe menus served year-round—gourmand and saveur—change every other month. [$] *Average main: €31* ✉ *11 rue Enclos Rey* ☎ *04–66–21–86–65* 🌐 *www.lejardindhadrien.fr* ✍ *Reservations essential* 🕓 *No lunch Mon.–Thurs., no dinner Sun.*

$$$ BISTRO 🍴 **Le Patio Littré.** Le Patio has maintained the bistro flavor of its former incarnation (Marché sur la Table), and the locals have remained devoted. Chef Julien Labonne Barrera, who clearly learned a trick or two during his four years at the three-star Michelin L'Arpège in Paris, uses only the freshest local and organic ingredients to create edible exaltations. Alongside the Mediterranean catch of the day and Camargue bull, you'll find vegetarian selections. **■TIP→ You can't beat the €19 lunch menu.** [$] *Average main: €30* ✉ *10 rue Littré* ☎ *04–66–67–22–50* 🌐 *www.patiolittre.fr* 🕓 *Closed Mon. and Tues.*

$ BAKERY 🍴 **Patisserie Courtois.** Although officially a bakery, you can also fill up on *croque-monsieurs*, quiches, salads, pasta, and steak in this little spot that's open from 8 am to 7:30 pm (until midnight in July and August). The location—at the market, next to the fountain—is convenient; and the reasonably priced food is simple but delicious. If you're in a hurry, best to get a *patisserie* to go as ordering a homemade dish off the menu may take a while. When time isn't an issue, prepare to linger over the mouthwatering *gateaux maison.* [$] *Average main: €11* ✉ *8 pl. Marché* ☎ *04–66–67–20–09* 🕓 *Closed Wed. No dinner Sept.–June.*

WHERE TO STAY

For expanded hotel reviews, visit Fodors.com.

$ HOTEL 🏨 **Hotel des Tuileries.** English owners Andrew and Caryn offer tastefully quaint, clean, and spacious rooms that are a welcome retreat from the clamor of Nîmes but are right near restaurants and the sights. **Pros:** excellent value; helpful service; accommodating check-in/check-out times. **Cons:** Wi-Fi signal can be weak in some parts of the hotel. [$] *Rooms from: €80* ✉ *22 rue Roussy* ☎ *04–66–21–31–15* 🌐 *www.hoteldestuileries.com* 🛏 *11 rooms* 🍽 *No meals.*

$$$ HOTEL 🏨 **Hotel Imperator.** Character-filled decor and a flavorful restaurant make this gracious old hotel near the Jardins de la Fontaine a local institution, and handsome woods and rich fabrics ensure guest rooms live up to the reputation. **Pros:** richly atmospheric; staff speak enough English; good deals online. **Cons:** some rooms can be small and a little noisy, especially in summer; grandeur is said to be fading. [$] *Rooms from: €210* ✉ *15 rue Gaston Boissier, quai de la Fontaine* ☎ *04–66–21–90–30* 🌐 *www.hotel-imperator.com* 🛏 *60 rooms* 🍽 *Breakfast.*

THE ALPILLES

The low mountain range called the Alpilles (pronounced ahl-*pee*-yuh) forms a rough-hewn, rocky landscape that rises into nearly barren limestone hills, the surrounding fields silvered with ranks of twisted olive trees and alleys of gnarled *amandiers* (almond trees). There are superb antiquities in St-Rémy and feudal ruins in Les Baux.

ABBAYE DE MONTMAJOUR

35 km (20 miles) southeast of Nîmes, 5 km (3 miles) northeast of Arles.

Abbaye de Montmajour. This magnificent Romanesque abbey looming over the marshlands north of Arles stands in partial ruin. Begun in the 12th century by a handful of Benedictine monks, the abbey grew according to an ambitious plan of church, crypt, and cloister and, under the management of corrupt lay monks in the 17th century, became more sumptuous. When the Church ejected those monks, they sacked the place, and what remained was eventually sold off as scrap. A 19th-century medieval revival spurred a partial restoration, but portions are still in ruins. What remains is a spare and beautiful piece of Romanesque architecture. The cloister rivals that of St-Trophime in Arles for its balance, elegance, and air of mystical peace. Van Gogh, drawn to its isolation, came often to the abbey to paint and reflect. The interior, renovated by contemporary architect Rudy Ricciotti, is used for temporary art exhibitions, and the Chapelle St Croix is open for visits—but you need to ask for the keys. ⊠ *On D17 northeast of Arles, rte. De Fontvielle, direction Fontvieille* ☎ *04–90–54–64–17* ⊕ *www.montmajour. monuments-nationaux.fr* ⊠ *€7* ⊙ *Apr.–June, daily 9:30–6; July–Sept., daily 10–6:30; Oct.–Mar., daily 10–5.*

LES BAUX-DE-PROVENCE

17 km (10 miles) west of Montmajour; 18 km (11 miles) northeast of Arles; 29 km (18 miles) south of Avignon.

When you first search the craggy hilltops for signs of Les Baux-de-Provence (pronounced lay-*bo-duh-pro-vance*), you may not quite be able to distinguish between bedrock and building, so naturally does the ragged skyline of towers and crenellations blend into the sawtooth jags of stone. This tiny château-village ranks as one of the most visited tourist sites in France, with natural scenery and medieval buildings of astonishing beauty. From this intimidating vantage point, the lords of Les Baux ruled over one of the largest fiefdoms in the south throughout the 11th and 12th centuries. In the 19th century Les Baux found new purpose: the mineral bauxite, valued as an alloy in aluminum production, was discovered in its hills and named for its source. A profitable industry sprang up that lasted into the 20th century before fading into history.

Today Les Baux offers two famous faces to the world: its beautifully preserved medieval village and the ghostly ruins of its fortress, once referred to as the *ville morte* (dead town). In the village, lovely 12th-century stone houses, even their window frames still intact, shelter the shops, cafés, and galleries that line the steep cobbled streets. At the edge of the village is a cliff that offers up a stunning view over the Val d'Enfer (Hell's Valley), said to have inspired Dante's Inferno.

Visitor Information Les Baux-de-Provence Tourist Office ⊠ *Maison du Roy* ☎ *04–90–54–34–39* ⊕ *www.lesbauxdeprovence.com.*

EXPLORING

Carrières de Lumières. The Carrières de Lumières is a vast old bauxite quarry in the Val d'Enfer, with 66-foot-high stone walls that makes a dramatic setting for a multimedia show in which thousands of images are projected onto the walls. Exhibitions change periodically, but recent showings have showcased the life and work of Vincent van Gogh. ⊠ *Petite rte. de Mailliane, D27* ☎ *04–90–54–47–37* ⊠ *€9.50; €14.50* *joint ticket with Château des Baux* 🕑 *Apr.–Sept., daily 9:30–7:30; Oct.–Mar., daily 10–6.*

FAMILY **Château des Baux.** High above the Val d'Enfer, the 17-acre cliff-top sprawl of ruins is contained under the umbrella name the Château des Baux. At the entry, the Tour du Brau contains the **Musée d'Histoire des Baux,** a small collection of relics and models which shelters a permanent music-and-slide show called *Van Gogh, Gauguin, Cézanne au Pays de l'Olivier,* featuring artworks depicting olive orchards in their infinite variety. From April through September there are fascinating medieval exhibitions: people dressed up in authentic costumes, displays of medieval crafts, and even a few jousting tournaments with handsome knights carrying fluttering silk tokens of their beloved ladies. The exit gives access to the wide and varied grounds, where the tiny **Chapelle St-Blaise** and towers mingle with skeletal ruins. ✉ *Rue du Trencat* ☎ *04–90–54–55–56* 🌐 *chateau-baux-provence.com* 🎟 *€9.50 with audio guide; €14.50 joint ticket with Carrières de Lumières* 🕑 *Mar.–May, daily 9:15–7:15; June–Aug., daily 9–8:15; Sept.–Nov., daily 9:30–6; Dec.–Feb., daily 10–5.*

WHERE TO STAY

For expanded hotel reviews, visit Fodors.com.

$ B&B/INN 🏨 **La Reine Jeanne.** Churchill and Jacques Brel, Sartre and de Beauvoir (who had separate rooms but a shared balcony—and what a balcony) were all happy guests at this modest but majestically placed inn nicely situated to provide rugged views of the château up the street. **Pros:** views are lovely; a *chambre familiale* sleeps four. **Cons:** some rooms are tiny; only two rooms have small balconies. [$] *Rooms from: €60* ✉ *Grande Rue* ☎ *04–90–54–32–06* 🌐 *www.la-reinejeanne.com* 🛏 *7 rooms* 🕑 *Closed Jan.* 🍴 *Breakfast.*

$$$$ HOTEL Fodor's Choice ★ 🏨 **L'Oustau de la Baumanière.** Spread over three historic buildings just outside the village of Les Baux, guest rooms at this fabled hotel are the last word in Provençal chic—breezy, private, and beautifully furnished with antiques yet done with a contemporary flair. **Pros:** low-key in style and flair with lots of ammenities; one of the greatest restaurant in Provence. **Cons:** so low-key, with some rooms bordering on generic, you wonder if it is worth it; can be hit and miss with service. [$] *Rooms from: €370* ✉ *Val d'Enfer* ☎ *04–90–54–33–07* 🌐 *www.oustaudebaumaniere.com* 🛏 *17 rooms, 13 suites* 🕑 *Hotel and restaurant closed Jan. and Feb.; restaurant closed Wed. and Thurs. in Mar., and Oct.–mid-Dec.* 🍴 *Some meals.*

ST-RÉMY-DE-PROVENCE

8 km (5 miles) north of Les Baux; 24 km (15 miles) northeast of Arles; 19 km (12 miles) south of Avignon.

Fodor's Choice ★ There are other towns as pretty as St-Rémy-de-Provence, and others in more dramatic or picturesque settings. Ruins can be found throughout the south, and so can authentic village life. Yet something felicitous has happened in this market town in the heart of the Alpilles—a steady infusion of style, of art, of imagination—all brought by people with a respect for local traditions and a love of Provençal ways. As many of them have been gossip-column names or off-duty celebs, it is easy to understand why this pretty town has earned its nickname, the Hamptons of Provence.

GETTING HERE AND AROUND

For such a popular town, St-Rémy has surprisingly few public transportation links. Buses run by Cartreize (☎ *08–10–00–13–26* ⊕ *www. lepilote.com*) provide service between Avignon and St-Rémy via Chateaurenard (No. 57, daily, €3.30) or Arles-Cavaillon via St-Rémy (No. 54, daily except Sunday, €4.30). Service to Les Baux runs daily, but only during July and August, with weekend service in June and September (No. 59, €2.20).

Local trains stop at Tarascon (⊕ *www.voyages-sncf.com*), and from here you can take a Cartrieze bus to St-Rémy (20 mins, €2.20). As with Les Baux-de-Provence, the easiest way to get to St-Rémy is by car. Take the A7 until you reach exit 25, then the D99 between Tarascon and Cavaillon, direction St-Rémy on the D5.

Visitor Information St-Rémy-de-Provence Tourist Office ⊠ *Pl. Jean Jaurès* ☎ *04–90–92–05–22* ⊕ *www.saintremy-de-provence.com.*

EXPLORING

St-Rémy, more than anywhere, allows you to meditate quietly on antiquity, browse pungent markets with basket in hand, peer down the very row of plane trees you remember from a Van Gogh painting, and also enjoy urbane galleries, cosmopolitan shops, and specialty food boutiques. An abundance of chic choices in restaurants, mas, and even châteaux awaits you; the almond and olive groves conceal dozens of stone-and-terra-cotta *gîtes* (furnished houses for vacation rentals), many with pools. In short, St-Rémy has been gentrified through and through.

First established by an indigenous Celtic-Ligurian people who worshipped the god Glan, the village Glanum was adopted by the Greeks of Marseille in the 2nd and 3rd centuries BC. Under the Pax Romana there developed a veritable city, with temples and forum, luxurious villas, and baths. The Romans (and Glanum) eventually fell, but a village grew up next to their ruins, taking its name from their protectorate, the Abbey St-Remi, which was based in Reims. St-Rémy de Provence grew to be an important market town, and wealthy families built fine mansions in its center—among them the de Sade family (whose black-sheep relation held forth in the Luberon at Lacoste). Another famous native son was the eccentric doctor, scholar, and astrologer Michel Nostradamus (1503–66), who is credited by some as having predicted much of the modern age. Perhaps the best known of St-Rémy's residents, though, was the ill-fated Vincent van Gogh. Shipped unceremoniously out of Arles at the height of his madness (and creativity), he committed himself to the asylum St-Paul-de-Mausolée.

A visit to St-Rémy should start from the outskirts inward. To visit Glanum you must park in a dusty roadside lot on D5 south of town (toward Les Baux).

The Pass Culture et Patrimoine gives you reduced rates to historical sites and museums after you pay for your first entry. Available on-site or from the tourist office, it's free and valid for up to 15 days.

Les Antiques. Two of the most miraculously preserved classical monuments in France are simply called Les Antiques. Dating from 30 BC, the **Mausolée** (mausoleum), a wedding-cake stack of arches and columns, lacks nothing but a finial on top, and is dedicated to a Julian, probably Caesar Augustus. A few yards away stands another marvel: the **Arc Triomphal,** dating from AD 20.

Glanum. Across the street from Les Antiques and set back from D5, a slick visitor center prepares you for entry into the ancient village of Glanum, with scale models of the site in its various heydays. A good map and an English brochure guide you stone by stone through the maze of foundations, walls, towers, and columns that spread across a broad field; helpfully, Greek sites are noted by numbers, Roman ones by letters. ✉ *Rte. des Baux de Provence, off the D5, direction Les Baux* ☎ *04–90–92–35–07* ⊕ *www.glanum.monuments-nationaux.fr* ✆ *€7.50* ⊙ *Apr.–Aug., daily 10–6:30; Sept., Tues.–Sun. 10–6:30; Oct.–Mar., Tues.–Sun. 10–5.*

St-Paul-de-Mausolée. You can cut across the fields from Glanum to St-Paul-de-Mausolée, the isolated asylum where Van Gogh spent the last year of his life (1889–90). Enter quietly: the hospital shelters psychiatric patients to this day, all of them women. You're free to walk up the beautifully manicured garden path to the church and its jewel-box Romanesque **cloister,** where the artist found womblike peace. ☎ *04–90–92–77–00* ✆ *€4* ⊙ *Apr.–Sept., daily 9:30–6:45; Oct., Nov., and Mar., daily 10:15–5. Closed Jan. and Feb.*

Vieille Ville. Within St-Rémy's fast-moving traffic loop, a labyrinth of narrow streets leads you away from the action and into the slow-moving inner sanctum of the Vieille Ville. Here trendy, high-end shops mingle pleasantly with local life, and the buildings, if gentrified, blend in unobtrusively.

WHERE TO EAT AND STAY

For expanded hotel reviews, visit Fodors.com.

$$
BISTRO

✕ **Bistrot Découverte.** Claude and Dana Douard were happy to collaborate with some of the greatest chefs of our time before getting away from the big-city lights to open this boutique-bistro hot spot in the center of St-Rémy. With a seamless transition under new mangament, the wine selection remains magnificent, as does the tour through their cave, and the simple food based on top-notch local ingredients. Try the braised veal in wild-lemon sauce served on fresh tagliatelle pasta or made-to-order beef tartare. $ *Average main: €22* ✉ *19 bd. Victor Hugo* ☎ *04–90–92–34–49* ⊕ *www.bistrotdecouverte.com* ⌂ *Reservations essential* ⊙ *Closed Mon. and Oct.–mid-Mar. No dinner Sun. and Thurs.*

DID YOU KNOW?

St-Rémy-de-Provence has more than its share of chic shops and restaurants; nevertheless, the town has succeeded in remaining true to its Provençal roots.

$$ FRENCH 🍴 **La Gousse d'Ail.** This intimate, family-run bistro lives up to its name (the Garlic Clove), serving robust, highly flavored southern dishes in hearty portions. Try the house specialties: grilled bull steak with creamed garlic or the foie gras. The set menu is excellent value at only €18. [$] *Average main: €18* ✉ *6 bd. Marceau* ☎ *04–90–92–16–87* 🌐 *www.la-goussedail.com* ⏲ *Closed Thurs. and Jan. No lunch Fri. No dinner Sun. in winter.*

$$$$ FRENCH 🍴 **La Maison Jaune.** This 18th-century retreat with a Michelin star in the Vieille Ville draws crowds of summer people to its pretty roof terrace, with accents of sober stone and lively contemporary furniture both indoors and out. The look reflects the cuisine: with vivid flavors and a cool, contained touch, chef François Perraud prepares fresh Mediterranean sea bream, bouillabaisse, grilled lamb from Provence, and other specialties on his seasonally changing menus. [$] *Average main: €38* ✉ *15 rue Carnot* ☎ *04–90–92–56–14* 🌐 *www.lamaisonjaune.info* ✍ *Reservations essential* ⏲ *Closed Sun. and Mon. andNov.–Feb. No lunch Sun. and Mon. in July and Aug.*

$$$$ B&B/INN Fodor's Choice ★ 🏨 **Chez Bru.** Belgian chef Wout Bru has gained a reputation (and Michelin stars) for his understated, subtly balanced cuisine; his wife Suzy has earned kudos for her equally savvy sense of style; and together they have created a tranquil haven of deluxe comfort. **Pros:** an elegant stay in the country; excellent sommelier. **Cons:** some visitors have found the reception a little cool; restaurant a short distance away from inn. [$] *Rooms from: €300* ✉ *Rte. D'Orgon, 4 km (2½ miles) from Eygalières, which is 10 km (6 miles) southeast of St-Rémy on D99 then D24, Eygalières* ☎ *04–90–90–60–34* 🌐 *www.chezbru.com* 🛏 *7 rooms, 2 suites* ⏲ *Closed mid-Nov.–Mar.* 🍽 *Breakfast.*

$$ HOTEL 🏨 **Mas des Carassins.** A textbook example of a Provençal *mas*, this rambling 19th-century farmhouse—replete with stonework walls and wrought-iron canopy beds—has an impressive amount of style. **Pros:** service-friendly atmosphere makes for a stress-free stay; breakfast (included) is good and substantial; short walk to town. **Cons:** each room is unique so inquire when booking. [$] *Rooms from: €170* ✉ *1 chemin Gaulois* ☎ *04–90–92–15–48* 🌐 *www.masdescarassins.com* 🛏 *22 rooms* ⏲ *Closed Dec.–Mar. except for 2 wks at Christmas* 🍽 *Breakfast.*

SHOPPING

Every Wednesday morning St-Rémy hosts one of the most popular **markets** in Provence, during which place de la République and narrow Vieille Ville streets overflow with fresh produce and herbs, as well as fabrics and *brocantes* (antiques). With all the summer people, it's little wonder that food shops and *traiteurs* (take-out caterers) do the biggest business in St-Rémy. Olive oils are sold like fine old wines, and the breads heaped in boulangerie windows are as knobby and rough-hewn as they should be. The best food shops are concentrated in the Vieille Ville.

Chocolaterie Joel Durand. At Chocolaterie Joel Durand the sweet treats are numbered to indicate the various flavors, from rose petal to Camargue saffron. ✉ *3 bd. Victor Hugo* ☎ *04–90–92–38–25* 🌐 *www.chocolat-durand.com.*

La Cave aux Fromages. Local goat cheeses are displayed like jewels and wrapped like delicate pastries at La Cave aux Fromages. ✉ *1 Pl Joseph-Hilaire* ☎ *04–90–92–32–45.*

AVIGNON AND THE VAUCLUSE

Anchored by the magnificent papal stronghold of Avignon, the Vaucluse spreads luxuriantly east of the Rhône. Its famous vineyards—Gigondas, Vacqueyras, Beaumes-de-Venise—seduce connoisseurs, and its Roman ruins in Orange and Vaison-la-Romaine draw scholars and arts lovers. Arid lowlands with orchards of olives, apricots, and almonds give way to a rich and wild mountain terrain around the formidable Mont Ventoux and flow into the primeval Luberon, made a household name by Peter Mayle. The hill villages around the Luberon—Gordes, Roussillon, Oppède, Bonnieux—are as lovely as any you'll find in the south of France.

AVIGNON

83 km (51 miles) northwest of Aix-en-Provence; 98 km (59 miles) northwest of Marseille; 229 km (140 miles) south of Lyon.

Avignon is anything but a museum; it surges with modern ideas and energy and thrives within its ramparts as it did in the heyday of the popes—and, like those radical church lords, it's sensual, cultivated, and cosmopolitan, with a taste for worldly pleasures. Avignon remained papal property until 1791, and elegant mansions bear witness to the town's 18th-century prosperity. From its famous Palais des Papes (Papal Palace), where seven exiled popes camped between 1309 and 1377 after fleeing from the corruption and civil strife of Rome, to the long, low bridge of childhood-song fame stretching over the river, you can beam yourself briefly into 14th-century Avignon, so complete is the context, so evocative the setting.

GETTING HERE AND AROUND

The main bus station is on boulevard St-Roch (☎ *04–90–82–07–35*), next to the train station. Buses run between Avignon and Arles (1 hr, 5 mins; €6.30 ⊕ *www.info-ler.fr*), Nîmes (1½ hrs, €1.50 ⊕ *www. edgard-transport.fr*), and, farther afield, to Orange, Isle-sur-la-Sorgue, Marseille, Nice, and Cannes. You can take the A15 to Pont du Gard from here, too (45 mins, €1.50 ⊕ *www.edgard-transport.fr*). There are a few different bus agencies: try Lignes Express Régionales (☎ *08–21–20–22–03*), Voyages Arnaud (☎ *04–90–38–15–58*), or visit the helpful Vaucluse government website (⊕ *www.vaucluse.fr*). Town buses and services connecting the Centre Ville station with the TGV station (several times an hour) are run by TCRA (☎ *04–32–74–18–32* ⊕ *www.tcra. fr*). Avignon is at the junction of the Paris–Marseille and Paris–Montpellier rail lines. The Gare Centre Ville has frequent links to Arles, Nîmes, Orange, Toulon, and Carcassonne. Taxi Radio Avignonnais (✉ *Porte de la République, Tourelle Est* ☎ *04–90–82–20–20*) provides an easy way to get around town. If you're coming by car, take advantage of Avignon's 4,000-plus free parking places.

Visitor Information **Avignon Tourist Office** ✉ *41 cours Jean-Jaurès* ☎ *04–32–74–32–74* ⊕ *www.avignon-tourisme.com.*

EXPLORING

Everything worth seeing (except the St. Bénézet Bridge) is confined within the medieval city walls. Most sights cluster around place du Palais, with signs pointing the way. This is the Avignon of the visitors. To see Avignonnais leading their daily lives, however, turn off these tourist paths and get lost among the city's cobblestone streets. Note that the free Avignon-Villeneuve PASSion (available at the tourist office) gives 10% to 50% reductions on most museums and sites after you buy your first ticket at regular price. ■**TIP**➔ Live like a local and pedal away on one of Vélopop's 200 city bikes; there are 17 practically located stations across Avignon and rental is only €1 (⊕ www.velopop.fr). La Baladine, an electric, nonpolluting vehicle that travels along the pedestrian and shopping streets, is another green option (⊕ www.tcra.fr). The fare is €0.50; just stick out your hand if you want it to stop and pick you up.

TOP ATTRACTIONS

Musée Calvet. Worth a visit for the beauty and balance of its architecture alone, this fine old museum contains a rich collection of antiquities and classically inspired works. Acquisitions include Neoclassical and Romantic pieces and are almost entirely French, including works by Manet, Daumier, and David. There's also a good modern section, with works by Bonnard, Duffy, and Camille Claudet (note Claudet's piece depicting her brother Paul, who incarcerated her in an insane asylum when her relationship with Rodin caused too much scandalous talk). The main building itself is a Palladian-style jewel in pale Gard stone dating from the 1740s; the garden is so lovely that it may distract you from the art. ✉ *65 rue Joseph-Vernet* ☎ *04–90–86–33–84* ⊕ *www. musee-calvet.org* ⌑ *€6* ⊙ *Wed.–Mon. 10–1 and 2–6.*

Palais des Papes. This colossal palace creates a disconcertingly fortress-like impression, underlined by the austerity of its interior. Most of the original furnishings were returned to Rome with the papacy; others were lost during the French Revolution. Some imagination is required to picture the palace's medieval splendor, awash with color and with worldly clerics enjoying what the 14th-century Italian poet Petrarch called "licentious banquets." On close inspection, two different styles of building emerge at the palace: the severe **Palais Vieux** (Old Palace), built between 1334 and 1342 by Pope Benedict XII, a member of the Cistercian order, which frowned on frivolity, and the more decorative **Palais Nouveau** (New Palace), built in the following decade by the artsy, lavish-living Pope Clement VI. The Great Court, entryway to the complex, links the two.

The main rooms of the Palais Vieux are the **Consistory** (Council Hall), decorated with some excellent 14th-century frescoes by Simone Martini; the **Chapelle St-Jean,** with original frescoes by Matteo Giovanetti; the **Grand Tinel,** or Salle des Festins (Feast Hall), with a majestic vaulted roof and a series of 18th-century Gobelin tapestries; the **Chapelle St-Martial,** with more Giovanetti frescoes; and the **Chambre du Cerf,** with a richly decorated ceiling, murals featuring a stag hunt, and a delightful

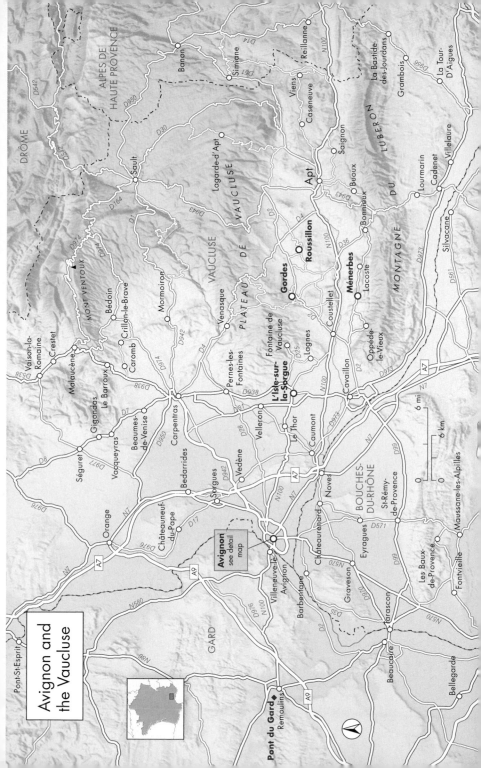

Avignon and
the Vaucluse

view of Avignon. The principal attractions of the Palais Nouveau are the **Grande Audience,** a magnificent two-nave hall on the ground floor, and, upstairs, the **Chapelle Clémentine,** where the college of cardinals once gathered to elect the new pope. ✉ *Pl. du Palais, 6 rue Pente Rapide* ☎ *04–90–27–50–00* ⊕ *www.palais-des-papes.com* ☐ *€12.50, includes PDA audio guide; €13, includes tour of Pont St-Bénézet* ☉ *Mar., daily 9–6:30; Apr.–June, Sept., and Oct., daily 9–7; July, daily 9–8; Aug., daily 9–8:30; Nov.–Feb., daily 9:30–5:45.*

Pont St-Bénézet (*St. Bénézet Bridge*). This bridge is the subject of the famous children's song: "*Sur le pont d'Avignon on y danse, on y danse . . .*" ("On the bridge of Avignon one dances, one dances . . ."). Unlike London Bridge, which fell down in another nursery ditty, Pont St-Bénézet still stretches its arches across the river, but only partway: half was washed away in the 17th century. Its first stones allegedly laid with the miraculous strength granted St-Bénézet in the 12th century, it once reached all the way to Villeneuve. ✉ *Port du Rochre* ⊕ *www. palais-des-papes.com* ☐ *€4.50 includes new tactile PDA audio guide; €13 includes entry to Palais des Papes* ☉ *Mar., daily 9–6:30; Apr.–June, Sept., and Oct., daily 9–7; July, daily 9–8; Aug., daily 9–8:30; Nov.–Feb., daily 9:30–5:45.*

Fodor's Choice
★

Rocher des Doms (*Rock of the Domes*). Set on bluff above town, this lush hilltop garden has grand Mediterranean pines, a man-made lake (complete with camera-ready swans), plus glorious views of the palace, the rooftops of Old Avignon, the Pont St-Bénézet, and formidable Villeneuve across the Rhône. On the horizon loom Mont Ventoux, the Luberon, and Les Alpilles. The garden has lots of history as well: Often called the "cradle of Avignon," its rocky grottoes were among the first human habitations in the area. ✉ *Montée du Moulin off pl. du Palais* ☎ *04–32–74–32–74* ⊕ *www.avignon-tourisme.com* ☉ *Dec. and Jan., daily 7–5:30; Feb. and Nov., daily 7:30–6; Mar., daily 7:30–7; Apr., May, and Sept., daily 7:30–8; June–Aug., daily 7:30–9; Oct., daily 7:30-6:30.*

WORTH NOTING

Cathédrale Notre-Dame-des-Doms. Built in a pure Provençal Romanesque style in the 12th century, this cathedral was soon dwarfed by the extravagant palace that rose beside it. The 14th century saw the addition of a cupola, which promptly collapsed. As rebuilt in 1425, the cathedral is a marvel of stacked arches with a strong Byzantine flavor and is topped with a gargantuan Virgin Mary lantern—a 19th-century afterthought—whose glow can be seen for miles around. ✉ *Pl. du Palais* ☎ *04–90–86–81–01* ☉ *Daily 8–6.*

Musée Lapidaire. Housed in a pretty little Jesuit chapel on the main shopping street, this collection of sculpture and stonework is primarily from Gallo-Roman times but also includes Greek and Etruscan works. There are several interesting inscribed slabs, a selection of *shabtis* (small statues buried with the dead to help them get to the afterlife), and a notable depiction of *Tarasque of Noves,* the man-eating monster immortalized by Alphonse Daudet. Sadly, most items are haphazardly labeled and insouciantly scattered throughout the chapel, itself slightly crumbling

Beautiful town squares form the hub of Avignon's historic heart, as seen in this view from the roof of the famed Palais des Papes.

yet awash with light. ✉ *27 rue de la République* ☎ *04–90–85–75–38* 🌐 *www.musee-lapidaire.org* 🎟 €2 🕒 *Tues.–Sun. 10–1 and 2–6.*

Petit Palais. The residence of bishops and cardinals before Pope Benedict built his majestic palace houses a large collection of old-master paintings. The majority are Italian works from the early-Renaissance schools of Siena, Florence, and Venice—styles with which the Avignon popes would have been familiar. Later works include Sandro Botticelli's *Virgin and Child*, and Venetian paintings by Vittore Carpaccio and Giovanni Bellini. ✉ *Pl. du Palais* ☎ *04–90–86–44–58* 🌐 *www.petit-palais.org* 🎟 €6 🕒 *Wed.–Mon. 10–1 and 2–6.*

WHERE TO EAT

$$$$ FRENCH Fodor's Choice ★

🍴 **Christian Étienne.** Stellar period decor in a renovated 12th-century mansion makes for an impressive backdrop to innovative and delicious cuisine. Try the pan-roasted medaillon of veal with dried porcini blinis and thinly sliced mushrooms with chervil, or splurge for the whole lobster sautéed in olive oil, muscat grapes, and beurre blanc with verjuice. The seasonal truffle menu may be too rich for some (€150), but a €35 lunch menu offers nice balance for budget-conscious travelers. [$] *Average main: €75* ✉ *10 rue de Mons* ☎ *04–90–86–16–50* 🌐 *www.christian-etienne.fr* ✍ *Reservations essential* 🕒 *Closed Sun., Mon., and 2 wks in Nov.*

$$ FRENCH Fodor's Choice ★

🍴 **La Fourchette.** The food here is some of the best in town, as the bevy of locals clamoring to get in proves. It all smells so good that you may be tempted to rip one of the decorative forks off the wall and attack your neighbor's plate. Service is prompt and friendly and you can dig in to heaping portions of escalope of salmon, chicken cilantro à l'orange, or

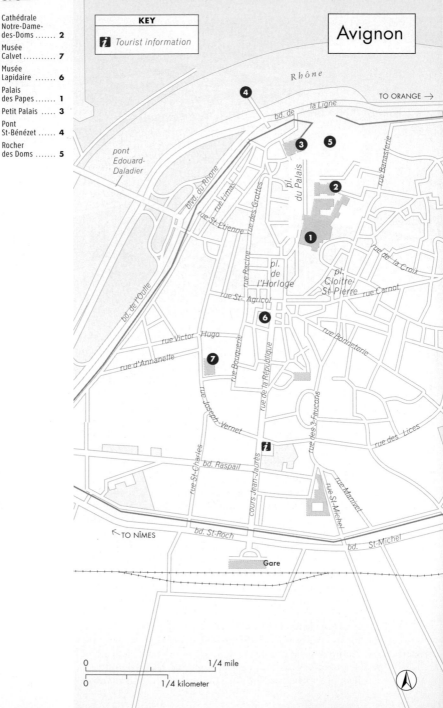

what is likely the best Provençal daube (served with macaroni gratin) in France. [$] *Average main: €20* ✉ *17 rue Racine* ☎ *04–90–85–20–93* 🌐 *www.lafourchetteavignon.fr* ✍ *Reservations essential* ⏲ *Closed Sat., Sun., and 1st 3 wks in Aug.*

$$ BISTRO 🍴 **Le 26.** The Piedoie, as this place was formerly known, built a die-hard following of locals by providing excellent cuisine at fair prices. New chef-owner Joël Laurent and his wife Laurence have kept the crowds coming with set menus that include a starter, main dish, and dessert, with four choices for each course (they change every two months to reflect what the markets are selling). If you like to try a little of this and a little of that, the *gourmande* lunch menu (only €15) serves all four starters—and for an extra euro, they'll add in dessert. If you are traveling *avec enfants*, a children's menu is available as well. [$] *Average main: €22* ✉ *26 rue des Trois Faucons* ☎ *04–90–86–51–53* 🌐 *www.le26avignon.fr* ✍ *Reservations essential* ⏲ *Closed Mon. No dinner Wed. No lunch Sat.*

$$ FRENCH 🍴 **Le 46.** Stylishly decorated in a hip, retro-bistro style with urbane shades of gray (look for the Philippe Starck chairs), this Avignon favorite entices with down-home yet sophisticated fare prepared by the talented Antoine Tamekloe. Picture grilled John Dory with artichoke hearts, parchment-wrapped mullet with eggplant, peppers, and tomatoes, or breast of duck served with oven-roasted apples; for a sweet finish, try the caramelized apples in tender pastry. [$] *Average main: €23* ✉ *46 rue de la Balance* ☎ *04–90–85–24–83* ✍ *Reservations essential* ⏲ *Closed Sun. Nov.–Apr.*

$ FRENCH 🍴 **Maison Nani.** Crowded inside and out with trendy young professionals, this pretty lunch spot serves stylish home cooking in generous portions. Choose from heaping salads sizzling with fresh meat, enormous kebabs, and a creative quiche du jour. It's just off rue de la République. [$] *Average main: €13* ✉ *29 rue Théodore Aubanel* ☎ *04–90–82–60–90* 💳 *No credit cards* ⏲ *Closed Sun. No dinner Mon.–Thurs.*

$ BISTRO 🍴 **Restaurant Manutention.** Occupying the former army-supply depot behind Palais des Papes—note the carefully preserved industrial decay—an urban-chic entertainment complex combines an international cinema, a bar, and this popular bistro. Long known as Le Grand Café, it had a midlife crisis in 2013 and renamed itself Restaurant Manutention. Gigantic 18th-century mirrors and dance-festival posters hang against crumbling plaster and brick, and votive candles half-light the raw metal framework—an inspiring environment for passionate talks over Mediterranean fare, such as sautéed beef or giant shrimps. [$] *Average main: €15* ✉ *La Manutention, cours Maria Casares* ☎ *04–90–86–86–77.*

WHERE TO STAY

For expanded hotel reviews, visit Fodors.com.

$$$$ HOTEL Fodor's Choice ★ 🏨 **Hôtel de la Mirande.** A designer's dream of a hotel, this *petit palais* permits you to step into 18th-century Avignon, thanks to painted coffered ceilings, sumptuous antiques, extraordinary handmade wall coverings, and other superb *grand siècle* touches (those rough sisal mats on the floors were the height of chic back in the Baroque era). **Pros:** spectacular setting of the hotel; free bottled water from minibar during your stay. **Cons:** rooms can be a little stuffy; breakfast is expensive.

Ⓢ*Rooms from: €425* ✉ *Pl. de la Mirande* ☎ *04–90–14–20–20* ⊕ *www. la-mirande.fr* ⤳ *25 rooms, 1 suite, 1 apt* ¶©¶ *No meals.*

$$$
HOTEL
꙰ **Hôtel d'Europe.** This classic vine-covered 16th-century home once hosted Victor Hugo, Napoléon Bonaparte, and Emperor Maximilian. Regally discreet, it is notable for its walled, tree-shaded courtyard and an interior filled with Aubusson tapestries, porcelains, and Provençal antiques; guest rooms are mostly emperor-size, and two suites overlook the Papal Palace. **Pros:** authentic historical setting close to everything; perfect as a secluded romantic hideaway. **Cons:** least expensive rooms are small; high season can make for some noisy evenings. Ⓢ*Rooms from: €194* ✉ *12 pl. Crillon* ☎ *04–90–14–76–76* ⊕ *www.heurope.com* ⤳ *39 rooms, 5 suites* ¶©¶ *Breakfast.*

$
HOTEL
꙰ **Hotel du Palais des Papes.** With chic ironwork furniture, rich fabrics, and exposed stone and beams, this hotel just off the place du Palais fulfills fantasies of life in a medieval city. **Pros:** richly atmospheric setting is a perfectly inexpensive way to make the most out of the city; rooms are large and airy and some have city views. **Cons:** rooms with no air-conditioning can be stuffy in summertime; rooms facing the street can be a little noisy. Ⓢ*Rooms from: €98* ✉ *3 pl. du Palais des Papes* ☎ *04–90–86–04–13* ⊕ *www.hotel-avignon.com* ⤳ *26 rooms, 2 suites* ¶©¶ *Breakfast.*

NIGHTLIFE AND THE ARTS

AJMI (*Association Pour le Jazz et la Musique Improvisée*). At AJMI, in La Manutention, you can hear live jazz acts of some renown. ✉ *4 rue Escaliers Ste-Anne* ☎ *04–90–86–08–61* ⊕ *www.jazzalajmi.com.*

Extramuros. Just in front of the Ramparts, this chic lounge bar is the place to relax over a glass a wine at one of the weekly jazz or blues nights. ✉ *44 bd. Saint Michel* ☎ *04–32–70–00–20* ⊕ *www.extramuros-avignon.fr.*

Festival d'Avignon (*Festival d'Avignon*). Held annually over three weeks in July, the Festival d'Avignon has brought the best of world theater to this ancient city since 1947. Avignon's version of fringe, the OFF Festival (⊕ *www.avignonleoff.com*), is staged at the same time. The two combined host around 1,000 performances, with the main venue being the Palais des Papes. ■TIP→ Tickets go on sale around June and sell out quickly. ☎ *04–90–27–66–50 tickets and information* ⊕ *www. festival-avignon.com.*

Le Palais Royal. Le Palais Royal music hall, steps aways from the Palais des Papes, presents a dinner cabaret show. Call to reserve. ✉ *10 bis, rue Peyrollerie, behind palace* ☎ *04–90–14–02–54* ⊕ *lepalaisroyalavignon.com.*

Red Zone. Avignon's trendy twenty- and thirty-somethings dance at the Red Zone, from 9 pm to 3 am every night. ✉ *25 rue Carnot* ☎ *04–90–27–02–44* ⊕ *www.redzonebar.com.*

SHOPPING

Avignon has a cosmopolitan mix of French chains, hip clothing shops (it's a college town), and a few choice boutiques. The pedestrian area has a stretch of stores along rue du Vieux Sextier, rue des Fourbisseurs,

Straddling the Gardon River, and built during the rule of Emperor Claudius, the Pont du Gard was an aqueduct to bring waters to nearby Nîmes.

and **rue des Marchands,** where you'll find Hermès at the corner of place de l'Horlage. But **rue de la République** is the main shopping artery.

PONT DU GARD

22 km (13 miles) southwest of Avignon; 37 km (23 miles) southwest of Orange; 48 km (30 miles) north of Arles.

Fodor's Choice

★

No other architectural sight in Provence rivals the Pont du Gard, a mighty, three-tier aqueduct nearly midway between Nîmes and Avignon. Erected 2,000 years ago as part of a 48-km (30-mile) canal supplying water to the Roman settlement of Nîmes, the structure is astonishingly well preserved. In the early morning the site offers an amazing blend of natural and classical beauty—the rhythmic repetition of arches resonates with strength, bearing testimony to an engineering concept relatively new in the 1st century AD, when it was built under Emperor Claudius. Later in the day, even off-season, crowds intrude upon the serenity.

You can approach the aqueduct from either side of the Gardon River. If you choose the south side (Rive Droite), the walk to the *pont* (bridge) is shorter and the views arguably better. Note there have been reports of break-ins in the parking area, so get a spot close to the booth. Although access to the spectacular walkway along the top of the aqueduct is now off-limits, the sight of the bridge is still a breathtaking experience. ⊠ *Concession Pont-du-Gard* ☎ *08–20–90–33–30* ⊕ *www.pontdugard.fr* ⊠ *€18, for up to 5 people including parking* ☉ *Mar.–*

May and Oct., daily 9–6; June and Sept., daily 9–7; July and Aug., daily 9–8; Nov.–Feb., daily 9–5.

Espaces Culturels. At the Espaces Culturels, a museum and themed cinema detail the history of the aqueduct; in addition, there is a hands-on children's area and an interactive exhibition about life in Roman times that covers topics such as archaeology, nature, and water. ✉ *Pont du Gard* ☎ *04–66–37–50–99* 🎟 *Included with entry to Pont du Gard* 🕒 *Mar.–May and Oct., daily 9–6; June and Sept., daily 9–7; July and Aug., daily 9–8; Nov.–Feb., daily 9–5.*

WHERE TO EAT

$$$ FRENCH 🍴 **La Sommellerie.** This inspired regional restaurant serves local ingredients in deliciously inventive ways. Arguably the best in the area, it's often full with locals and tourists alike (book ahead). There are some extremely comfortable rooms available in which to sleep off all that great wine, too. [$] *Average main: €26* ✉ *2268 rte. de Roquemaure, 4 km (10 miles) down D17, Châteauneuf-du-Pape* ☎ *04–90–83–50–00* 🌐 *www.la-sommellerie.fr* ✍ *Reservations essential* 🕒 *No dinner Sun. and Mon. Oct.–Apr.*

L'ISLE-SUR-LA-SORGUE

Fodor's Choice ★ *26 km (16 miles) east of Avignon, 41 km (25 miles) southeast of Orange.*

GETTING HERE

The No. 6 Voyages-Roux bus from the Avignon train station stops at place Robert Vasse in Isle-sur-la-Sorgue (40 mins, €2). You can also take a train from Avignon (€4.70).

Visitor Information L'Isle-sur-la-Sorgue Tourist Office ✉ *Pl. de la Liberté* ☎ *04–90–38–04–78* 🌐 *www.oti-delasorgue.fr.*

EXPLORING

Crisscrossed with lazy canals and alive with moss-covered waterwheels that once drove its silk, wool, and paper mills, this old valley town retains a gentle appeal—except on Sunday, when it transforms itself into a Marrakech of marketeers, its streets crammed with antiques and brocante markets. There are also street musicians, food stands groaning under mounds of rustic breads, vats of tapenade, and cloth-lined baskets of spices, plus miles of café tables offering ringside seats to the spectacle. On a nonmarket day life returns to its mellow pace, with plenty of antiques dealers open year-round, as well as fabric and interior-design shops, bookstores, and food stores for you to explore.

Collégiale Notre-Dame-des-Anges. L'Isle's 17th-century church, the Collégiale Notre-Dame-des-Anges, is extravagantly decorated with gilt, faux marble, and sentimental frescoes. The double-colonnade facade commands the center of the Vieille Ville. Visiting hours change frequently, so check with the tourist office.

WHERE TO STAY

For expanded hotel reviews, visit Fodors.com.

$ B&B/INN 🏨 **La Gueulardière.** After a Sunday glut of antiquing along the canals, you can dine and sleep just up the street in a hotel full of collectible finds, from the school posters in the restaurant to the oak armoires and brass beds that furnish the simple lodgings. **Pros:** ideal location makes this a perfect place for antiques hunters to stay; rooms are bright and cheerful. **Cons:** some rooms are noisy; can be stuffy and hot in summer. *[$] Rooms from: €59 ✉ 1 cours René Char ☎ 04–90–38–10–52 🌐 www.gueulardiere.com 🛏 5 rooms 🕒 Closed mid-Dec.–mid-Jan. Restaurant closed Mon. dinner and Tues. during winter 🍴 No meals.*

$$ B&B/INN Fodor's Choice ★ **La Prévôté.** Five beautifully decorated and freshly painted rooms, each styled with exquisite taste in soft colors and Provence chic, offer an ideal respite after a long day of antiques shopping. **Pros:** price includes breakfast; top dining; antiques-bedecked decor. **Cons:** a little tricky to find; parking may be difficult. *[$] Rooms from: €160 ✉ 4 bis, rue Jean Jacques Rousseau ☎ 04–90–38–57–29 🌐 www.la-prevote.fr ✍ Reservations essential 🛏 5 rooms 🕒 Closed Feb. and Nov. 🍴 Breakfast.*

SHOPPING

Hôtel Dongler. A major group of *antiquaires* is found at Hôtel Dongler. It's open Friday–Monday and holidays 10–7. *✉ 15 esplanade Robert Vasse ☎ 04–90–38–63–63 🌐 www.hoteldongierantiquites.fr.*

Le Quai de la Gare. A tempting selection of brocante is on view at Le Quai de la Gare Friday from 2 to 7, and Saturday through Monday (plus holidays) from 10 to 7. *✉ 4 av. Julien Guigue ☎ 04–90–20–73–42 🌐 www.antiquites-quai-de-la-gare.com.*

L'Isle-sur-la-Sorgue Sunday morning flea market. The famous L'Isle-sur-la-Sorgue Sunday morning flea market runs from the place Gambetta up the length of avenue des Quatre Otages. Vendors start packing up around 1 pm.

Passage du Pont. Of the dozens of antiques shops in L'Isle, one conglomerate concentrates some 40 dealers under the same roof: passage du Pont (formerly L'Isle aux Brocantes); it's open Friday afternoons and all day the rest of the week. *✉ 7 av. des Quatre Otages ☎ 04–90–20–69–93.*

Village des Antiquaires de la Gare. One of the most popular antiques shopping grounds is Village des Antiquaires de la Gare, open Saturday through Monday, and holidays, from 10 to 7. *✉ 2 bis, av. de l'Égalité ☎ 04–90–38–04–57 🌐 www.levillagedesantiquairesdelagare.com.*

Xavier Nicod. Higher-end antiques are in plentiful supply at the twin shops of Xavier Nicod et Gérard Nicod. *✉ 9 av. des Quatre Otages ☎ 06–07–85–54–59 🌐 www.xaviernicod.com.*

GORDES

35 km (22 miles) east of Avignon.

Fodor's Choice ★ Gordes was once merely an unspoiled hilltop village; it's now a famous unspoiled hilltop village surrounded by luxury vacation homes, modern hotels, restaurants, and B&Bs. No matter: the ancient stone village still rises above the valley in painterly hues of honey gold, and its cobbled streets—lined with boutiques, galleries, and real-estate offices—still wind steep and narrow to its Renaissance château, making this certainly one of the most beautiful towns in Provence.

GETTING HERE

A single bus stops at the place du Château in Gordes, and that's the one on the Cavaillon-Roussillon route. It runs twice a day, morning and night, and costs €2. Otherwise you'll need a car or take a taxi: to Avignon it's about €85. Another cost-friendly alternative is to take the bus from Avignon to Coustellet (€2) and then take a taxi for the short trip to Gordes (about €5).

Visitor Information Gordes Tourist Office ✉ *Le Chateau* ☎ *04–90–72–02–75* ⊕ *www.gordes-village.com.*

EXPLORING

Fodor'sChoice
★
Abbaye de Sénanque. If you've fantasized about Provence's famed lavender fields, head to the wild valley some 4 km (2½ miles) north of Gordes (via D177), where this photogenic 12th-century Romanesque abbey seemingly floats above a redolent sea of lavender (in full bloom late June to August; ⇨ *for more information, see the special photo feature, "Blue Gold—The Lavender Route," in this chapter*). Begun in 1150 and completed at the dawn of the 13th century, the **church** and adjoining **cloister** are without decoration, but still touch the soul with their chaste beauty. In this orbit, the gray-stone buildings seem to have special resonance—ancient, organic, with a bit of the *borie* about them. Next door, the enormous vaulted **dormitory** contains an exhibition on Abbaye de Sénanque's construction, and the **refectory** shelters a display on the history of Cistercian abbeys. ☎ *04–90–72–05–72* ⊕ *www.senanque.fr* 🖃 *€7 (with or without guide)* ⊘ *Guided tours (in French) only; see website for hrs and reserve in advance* ⊘ *Without guided tours (silence must be respected): Feb.–Nov. 11, daily 9:45–11; Nov. 12–Jan. 31, daily 2:30-5.*

Château de Gordes. The only way you can get into this château is by paying to see a collection of photo paintings by pop artist Pol Mara, who lived in Gordes. It's worth the price of admission, though, just to look at the fabulously decorated stone fireplace, created in 1541. Unfortunately, opening hours change constantly (afternoon visits are your best bet). ☎ *04–90–72–02–75* 🖃 *€4* ⊘ *No set hrs.*

Village des Bories. Just outside Gordes, on a lane heading north from D2, you'll see signs leading to the Village des Bories. The bizarre and fascinating little stone hovels called *bories* are found throughout this region of Provence, and here they are concentrated some 20 strong in an ancient community. Their origins are provocatively vague: built as shepherds' shelters with tight-fitting, mortarless stone in a hive-like form, they may date to the Celts, the Ligurians, even the Iron Age—and were inhabited or used for sheep through the 18th century. A photo exhibition shows other structures, similar to bories, in countries around the world. ☎ *04–90–72–03–48* ⊕ *www.gordes-village.com* 🖃 *€6* ⊘ *Daily 9–dusk.*

WHERE TO EAT AND STAY

For expanded hotel reviews, visit Fodors.com.

$$
FRENCH
✕ **Les Cuisines du Château.** This tiny but deluxe bistro across from the château has daily *aioli,* a smorgasbord of fresh cod and lightly steamed vegetables crowned with the garlic mayonnaise. Evenings are reserved

Continued on page 591

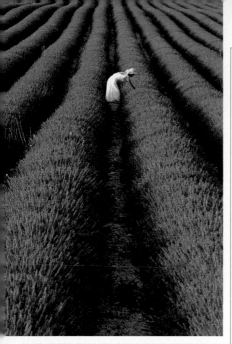

Van Gogh may have made the sunflower into the icon of Provence, but it is another flower —one that is unprepossessing, fragrant, and tiny—that draws thousands of travelers every year to Provence. They come to journey the famous "Route de la Lavande" (the Lavender Route), a wide blue-purple swath that connects over 2,000 producers across the south of France.

BLUE GOLD: THE LAVENDER ROUTE

Once described as the "soul of Haute-Provence," lavender has colored Provence's plains since the days of the ancient Romans. Today it brings prosperity, as consumers are madly buying hundreds of beauty products that use lavender essence. Nostrils flared, they are following this route every summer. To help sate their lavender lust, the following pages present a detail-rich tour of the Lavender Route.

By Nancy Heslin

TOURING THE LAVENDER ROUTE

Gordes

❶ Have your Nikon ready for the beautifully preserved Cistercian simplicity of the **Abbaye Notre-Dame de Sénanque**, a perfect foil for the famous waving fields of purple around it.

❷ No shrinking violet, the hilltop village of **Gordes** is famous for its luxe hotels, restaurants, and lavender-stocked shops.

❸ Get a fascinating A to Z tour—from harvesting to distilling to production—at the **Musée de la Lavande** near Coustellet.

❹ If you want to have a peak lavender experience—literally—detour 18 km (10 mi) to the northwest and take a spectacular day's drive up the winding road to the **summit of Mont Ventoux** (follow signs from Sault to see the lavender-filled valleys below).

❺ Even if you miss the biggest blow-out of the year, the Fête de la Lavande in **Sault** (usually on August 15), take in the charming *vieille ville* boutiques or the fabulous lavender fields that surround the hillside town.

❻ The awe-inspiring lavender fields around **Forcalquier** are one step away from perfection, and the Monday morning market is a treasure trove of local products.

❼ **Distillerie "Le Coulets"** on the outskirts of Apt has been a lavender farm for generations and offers free tours and products for sale at its boutique.

❽ You've bought the famous lavender products of L'Occitane everywhere, so how can you resist a tour of their **Manosque** factory?

Provence is threaded by the "Routes de la Lavande" (the Lavender Routes), a wide blue-purple swath that connects over 2,000 producers across the Drôme, the plateau du Vaucluse, and the Alpes-de-Haute-Provence, but our itinerary is lined with some of the prettiest sights—and smells—of the region. Whether you're shopping for artisanal bottles of the stuff (as with wine, the finest lavender carries its own Appellation d'Origine Contrôlée), spending a session at a lavender spa, or simply wearing hip-deep purple as you walk the

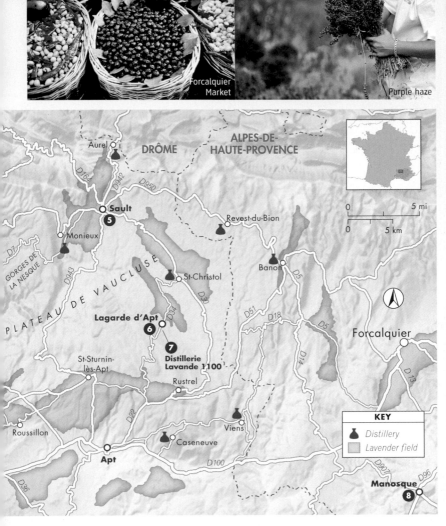

Forcalquier Market

Purple haze

KEY

🏺 Distillery

☐ Lavender field

fields, the most essential aspect on this trip is savoring a magical world of blue, one we usually only encounter on picture postcards.

To join the lavender-happy crowds, you have to go in season, which runs from June to early September. Like Holland's May tulips, the lavender of Haute-Provence is in its true glory only once a year: the last two weeks of July, when the harvesting begins—but fields bloom throughout the summer months for the most part. Below, we wind through

the most generous patches of lavender. Drive the colorful gambit southeastward (Coustellet, Gordes, Sault, Forcalquier, and Manosque), which will give you good visiting (and shopping) time in a number of the villages that are *fou de la lavande* (crazy for lavender). And for the complete scoop on the hundreds of sights to see in lavender land, contact **Les Routes de la Lavande** through the association La Grande Traversée des Alpes in Grenoble (☎ *04–58–00–11–66* ⊕ *www. grandetraversee-alpes.com*).

Abbaye Notre-Dame de Sénanque

DAY 1

SÉNANQUE
A Picture-Perfect Abbey

An invisible Master of Ceremonies for the Lavender Route would surely send you first to the greatest spot for lavender worship in the world: the 12th-century Cistercian **Abbaye Notre-Dame de Sénanque**, which in July and August seems to float above a sea of lavender, a setting immortalized in a thousand travel posters. Happily, you'll find it via the D177 only 4 km (2½ mi) north of Gordes, among the most beautiful of Provence's celebrated perched villages. An architecture student's dream of neat cubes, cylinders, and pyramids, its pure Romanesque form alone is worth contemplating in any context.

But in this arid, rocky setting the gray stone building seems to have special resonance— ancient, organic, with a bit of the borie about it. Along with the abbeys of Le Thornet and Silvacane, this is one of the trio of "Three Sisters" built by the Cistercian order in this area. Sénanque's **church** is a model of symmetry and balance. Begun in 1150, it has no decoration but still touches the soul with its chaste beauty.

The adjoining **cloister,** from the 12th century, is almost as pure in design. Next door, the enormous vaulted dormitory and the refectory shelter a display on the history of Cistercian abbeys. The few remaining monks here now preside over a cultural center that presents concerts and exhibitions. The bookshop is one of the best in Provence, with a huge collection of Provençaliana (a decent selection in English). ☎ *04–90–72–05–72* ⊕ *www.abbayede sena nanque.com, www.senanque.fr* ⌚ *€7* ☾ *Guided tours of the abbey in French only by reservation (you can visit on your own in silence). Bookshop open Feb.–Nov. 13, Mon.–Sat. 10–6, Sun. 2–6; Nov. 14–mid-Jan., Mon.–Sat. 2–6. Closed 2nd and 3rd week in January.*

THE ESSENCE OF THE MATTER

Provence and lavender go hand in hand— but why? The flower is native to the Mediterranean, and grows so well because the pH balance in the soil is naturally perfect for it (pH 6–8). But lavender was really put on the map here when ancient Romans arrived to colonize Provence and used the flower to disinfect their baths and perfume their laundry (the word comes from Latin *lavare,* "to wash"). From a small grass-roots industry, lavender proliferated over the centuries until the first professional distillery opened in Provence in the 1880s to supply oils for southern French apothecaries. After World War I, production boomed to meet the demand of the perfumers of Grasse (the perfume center of the world). Once described as the "soul of Haute-Provence," lavender is now farmed in England, India, and the States, but the harvest in the South of France is still one of the world's largest.

After spending the morning getting acquainted with the little purple flower at Sénanque, drive south along the D2 (or D177) back to **Gordes**, through a dry, rocky region mixed with deep valleys and far-reaching plains.

Wild lavender is already omnipresent, growing in large tracts as you reach the entrance of the small, unspoiled hilltop village, making for a patchwork landscape as finely drawn as a medieval illumination. A cluster of houses rises above the valley in painterly hues of honey gold, with cobbled streets winding up to the village's picturesque Renaissance château, making it one of the most beautiful towns in Provence.

Gordes has a great selection of hotels, restaurants, and B&Bs to choose from (see our listings under Gordes). Spend the early afternoon among tasteful shops that sell lovely Provençal crafts and produce, much of it lavender-based, and then after lunch, head out to Coustellet.

COUSTELLET
A Great Lavender Museum
Set 2 mi south of Gordes, Coustellet is noted for its **Musée de la Lavande** (take the D2 southeast to the outskirts of Coustellet). Owned by one of the original lavender families, who have cultivated and distilled the flower here for

ON THE CALENDAR

If you plan to be at the Musée de la Lavande between July 1 and August 25 you can watch animations of workers swathing lavender with a copper scythe. A few visitors may be invited to participate, but you can no longer make your own distillation in the museum's lab.

over five generations, this museum lies on the outskirts of more than 80 acres of prime lavender-cultivated land.

Not only can you visit the well-organized and interesting museum (note the impressive collection of scythes and distilling apparatus), you can buy up a storm in the boutique, which offers a great selection of lavender-based products at very reasonable prices. ☎ *04–90–76–91–23* ⊕ *www.museedelalavande.com* 🎟 *€6.40* ☼ *May–Sept., daily 9–7; Oct.–Dec. and Feb.–Mar., daily 9–12:15 and 2–6. Closed Jan.*

There are four main species. True lavender (*Lavandula angustifolia*) produces the most subtle essential oil and is often used by perfume makers and laboratories. Spike lavender (*Lavandula latifolia*) has wide leaves and long floral stems with several flower spikes. Hybrid lavender (*lavandin*) is obtained from pollination of true lavender and spike lavender, making a hybrid that forms a highly developed large round cluster. French lavender (*Lavendula stoechas*) is wild lavender that grows throughout the region and is collected for the perfume industry. True lavender thrives in the chalky soils and hot, dry climate of higher altitudes of Provence. It was picked systematically until the end of the 19th century and used for most lavender-based products. But as the demand for this remarkable flower grew, so did the need for a larger production base. By the beginning of the 20th century, the demand for the flower was so great that producers planted fields of lavender at lower altitudes, creating the need for a tougher, more resistant plant: the hybrid *lavandin*.

In many towns, Provence's lavender harvest is celebrated with charming folkloric festivals.

DAY 2

LAGARDE D'APT
A Top Distillerie
On the second day of your lavender adventure, begin by enjoying the winding drive 25 km (15 mi) east to the town of **Apt**. Aside from its Provençal market, busy with all the finest food products of the Luberon and Haute Provence, Apt itself is unremarkable (even actively ugly from a distance) but is a perfect place from which to organize your visits to the lavender fields of Caseneuve, Viens, and Lagarde d'Apt.

Caseneuve (east exit from Apt onto the D900 and then northwest on the D35) and Viens (16 km/10 mi east from Apt on the D209) are small but charming places to stop for a quick bite along the magnificent drive through the rows upon rows of lavender, but if you have to choose between the three, go to the minuscule village of Lagarde d'Apt (12 km/7 mi east from Apt on the D209).

Or for a closer look, take the D22 (direction Rustrel) a few kilometres outside of Apt to **Distillerie "Les Coulets."** From mid-July to mid-August, you can take a free tour of the distillery, visit the farm and browse the gift shop. ⊠ *Hameau Les Coulets* ☎ *04–90–74–07–55* ⊙ *July and Aug. 9–noon and 1:30–6.*

SAULT
The Biggest Festival
To enjoy a festive overnight, continue northwest from Lagarde d'Apt to the village of **Sault**, 15 km (9 mi) to the northeast. Beautifully perched on a rocky outcrop overlooking the valley that bears its name, Sault is one of the key stops along the Lavender Route.

There are any number of individual distilleries, producers, and fields to visit— to make the most of your visit, ask the Office du Tourisme (☎ *04–90–64–01–21* ⊕ *www.saultenprovence.com*) for a list of events. Aim to be in Sault for the not-to-be-missed **Fête de la Lavande** (⊠ *along the D950 at the Hippodrome le Defends* ⊕ *www.saultenprovence. com*), a day-long festival entirely dedicated to lavender, the best in the region, and usually held around August 15.

Village folk dress in traditional Provençal garb and parade on bicycles, horses leap over barrels of fragrant bundles of hay, and local producers display their wares at the market—all of which culminates in a communal Provençal dinner (€25) served with lavender-based products.

DAY 3

FORCALQUIER
The Liveliest Market
On your third day, the drive from Sault over 53 km (33 mi) east to Forcalquier is truly spectacular.

As you approach the village in late July, you will see endless fields of *Lavandula vera* (true wild lavender) broken only by charming stone farmhouses or discreet distilleries.

The epicenter of Haute-Provence's lavender cultivation, **Forcalquier** boasts a lively Monday morning market with a large emphasis on lavender-based products, and it is a great departure point for walks, bike rides, horse rides, or drives into the lavender world that surrounds the town.

In the 12th century, Forcalquier was known as the capital city of Haute-Provence and was called the *Cité des Quatre Reines* (City of the Four Queens) because the four daughters (Eleanor of Aquitaine among them) of the ruler of this region, Raimond Béranger V, all married royals.

Relics of this former glory can be glimpsed in the Vieille Ville of Forcalquier, notably its Cathédrale Notre-Dame and the Couvent des Cordeliers.

However, everyone heads here to marvel at the lavender fields outside town. Contact Forcalquier's Office du Tourisme (⊠ *13 pl. Bourguet* ☎ *04–92–75–*

MAKING SCENTS

BLOOMING
Lavender fields begin blooming in late June, depending on the area and the weather, with fields reaching their peak within the first two weeks of July. The last two weeks in July are considered the best time to catch the fields in all their glory.

HARVESTING
Lavender is harvested from July to early September, when the hot summer sun brings the essence up into the flower. Harvesting is becoming more and more automated; make an effort to visit some of the older fields with narrow rows—these are still picked by hand. Lavender is then dried for two to three days before being transported to the distillery.

DISTILLING
Distillation is done in a steam alembic, with the dry lavender steamed in a double boiler. Essential oils are extracted from the lavender by water vapor, which is then passed through the cooling coils of a retort.

10–02 ⊕ *www.forcalquier.com*) for information on the lavender calendar, then get saddled up on a bicycle for a trip into the countryside at the town's Moulin de Sarret.

Plan on enjoying a fine meal (reserve way in advance) at the town's most historic establishment, the **Restaurant des Deux Lions** (✉ *1 chemin des Hybourgues* ☎ *04–92–75–25–30*).

MANOSQUE
Love That L'Occitane

Fifteen mi (25 km) south of Forcalquier is Manosque, home to the **L'Occitane** factory.

You can get a glimpse of what the Luberon was like before it became so hip—Manosque is certainly not a tourist epicenter—but a trip here is worth it for a visit to the phenomenally successful cosmetics and skin care company that is now the town's main employer.

Once you make a reservation through the Manosque Tourist Office (✉ *Pl. du Docteur Joubert* ☎ *04–92–72–16–00* ⊕ *www.manosque-tourisme.com*) you can take a 75-minute tour Monday through Friday of the production site, view a documentary film, then rush into the shop where you can stock up on L'Occitane products for very reasonable prices. In the summer season, you need to book your tour a few weeks in advance by phone or email with the Tourist Office.

From Manosque you can head back to Apt and the Grand Luberon area or turn south about 52 km (30 mi) to Aix-en-Provence. ✉ *Z. I. St-Maurice* ☎ *04–92–70–19–00* ⊕ *www.loccitane. com* ☉ *Mon.–Sat. 10–7.*

BRINGING IT HOME

Yes, you've already walked in the pungent-sweet fields, breathing in the ephemeral scent that is uniquely a part of Provence. Visually, there is nothing like the waving fields rising up in a haze of bees. But now it's time to shop! Here are some top places to head to stop and smell the lavender element in local wines, honey, vinegar, soaps, and creams. A fine place to start is a few kilometers northeast of Sault at the **Aroma'Plantes** distillerie on Route du Mont Ventoux (⊕ www. distillerie-aromaplantes.com ☎ 04–90–64–04–02). Take a free guided visit and walk through the lavender fields before buying up all the inventory available in the shop.

In Gordes and Sault there are lovely Provençal markets that have a wide range of lavender-based products, from honey to vinegar to creams. A great selection of the finest essential oils is available at **Distillerie du Vallon** (✉ Rte. des Michouilles, Sault ☎ 04–90–64–14–83). **L'Occitane** (✉ Z.I. St-Maurice, Manosque ☎ 04–92–70–19–00) is the mother store. In nearby Volx you can hit the **Maison aux Huiles Essentiels** (✉ Z.I. La Carretière, Volx ☎ 04–92–78–46–77) for aromatherapy in all its glory.

SCENT-SATIONAL

for intimate, formal indoor meals à la carte—roast Luberon lamb, beef with truffle sauce, and the like. The '30s-style bistro tables and architectural lines are a relief from Gordes's ubiquitous rustic-chic, and there is a revolving array of paintings by local artists, many of which are for sale. There are only 26 seats, so book well in advance. $ *Average main: €20* ✉ *Pl. du Château* ☎ *04–90–72–01–31* ✍ *Reservations essential* ⏲ *Closed Wed., Nov.–mid-Dec., and mid-Jan.–Easter. No dinner Tues., Sept.–May and mid-Jan.–mid-Mar.*

$$$$ HOTEL 🏨 **La Bastide de Gordes.** Spectacularly perched on Gordes's hilltop, the smartly renovated 16th-century Bastide houses traditional and comfortable guest rooms, with a few *haut-Provençal* accents, and a superb restaurant with an impressive 800 labels in the wine cellar. **Pros:** views are unmatched in the area; wine cellar is an enthusiast's dream. **Cons:** dress code has become increasingly select; service can be correspondingly pretentious. $ *Rooms from: €395* ✉ *Le Village* ☎ *04–90–72–12–12* 🌐 *www.bastide-de-gordes.com* 🛏 *33 rooms, 6 suites* ⏲ *Closed Jan. and Feb.* 🍴 *Breakfast.*

$ HOTEL 🏨 **La Ferme de la Huppe.** This 17th-century stone farmhouse just outside Gordes has several sweet touches, including a courtyard and rooms furnished with secondhand finds. **Pros:** warm familial welcome makes you feel right at home; food is a delight. **Cons:** service can be slow on busy nights; wine list is small. $ *Rooms from: €105* ✉ *Les Pourquiers, 3 km (2 miles) east of Gordes, R.D. 156* ☎ *04–90–72–12–25* 🌐 *www.lafermedelahuppe.com* 🛏 *10 rooms* ⏲ *Closed Nov.–Mar 15.* 🍴 *Multiple meal plans.*

$$ B&B/INN 🏨 **Le Mas des Romarins.** At this intimate hilltop inn on the outskirts of Gordes, Oriental rugs, antique furniture, and a pool all add to your contentment. **Pros:** views are lovely; nights are so quiet you can hear the buzzing of insects in the fields; five-minute walk to village. **Cons:** can be difficult to find; some rooms are small. $ *Rooms from: €139* ✉ *Rte. de Sénanque* ☎ *04–90–72–12–13* 🌐 *www.masromarins.com* 🛏 *13 rooms* ⏲ *Closed mid-Nov.–mid-Dec., Jan., and Feb.* 🍴 *Breakfast.*

ROUSSILLON

10 km (6 miles) east of Gordes, 45 km (28 miles) east of Avignon.

Fodor's Choice ★ In shades of deep rose and russet, this quintessential cluster of hilltop houses blends into the red-ocher cliffs from which its stone was quarried. The ensemble of buildings and jagged, hand-cut slopes is equally dramatic, and views from the top look out over a landscape of artfully eroded bluffs that Georgia O'Keeffe would have loved. Roussillon is definitely one of the finalists in Provence's beauty contest.

GETTING HERE

The Cavaillon-Roussillon bus runs twice a day, morning and night, and costs €2. The only other way to arrive in Roussillon is by car from the D4.

Visitor Information Roussillon Tourist Office ✉ *Pl. de la Poste* ☎ *04–90–05–60–25* 🌐 *www.roussillon-provence.com.*

CLOSE UP

Treasure Hunting

On a Sunday morning in the middle of the high season, l'Isle sur la Sorgue is assuredly the busiest place in France. Idle tourists fill the cafés, the squares buzz with eager conversations, and the more serious market strollers adjust reading glasses and study notebooks crammed with hastily jotted remarks. All this anticipation is for good reason: this is the antiques mecca of the region.

Dealers began settling here in the 1960s and slowly acquired a reputation; these days there are an estimated 300 concentrated in picturesque booths along the main streets. Merchandise ranges from high-quality antiques and garden statuary to quirky collectibles, while the buyers could be big-name designers or first-time visitors with more money than sense. Beware, the dealers know how to sniff out the unprepared and the unwary: do not hesitate to bargain. There are also architectural salvage specialists offering old zinc bars, bistro fittings, and hotel reception booths. Should you succumb, there are transport firms to ship your chosen items around the world.

EXPLORING

Unlike neighboring hill villages, Roussillon offers little of real historic significance; the pleasure of a visit lies in the richly varied colors that change with the light of day, and in the views of the contrasting countryside, where dense-shadowed greenery sets off the red stone with Cézanne-esque severity. There are pleasant *placettes* (tiny squares) to linger in nonetheless, and a Renaissance fortress tower crowned with a clock in the 19th century; just past it, you can take in expansive panoramas of forest and ocher cliffs. Unfortunately, the village can get overcrowded with tourists in summer—the best time to visit is in spring or early fall.

Sentier des Ocres (*Ocher Trail*). The Sentier des Ocres starts out from the town cemetery and allows you to wend your way through a magical, multicolor palette *de pierres* (of rocks) replete with eroded red cliffs and chestnut groves; the circuit takes about 45 minutes. €2.50, €7 joint ticket with Usine Mathieu Roussillon ☉ July and Aug., daily 9–7:30; Sept. and May, daily 9:30–6:30; Oct., daily 10–5:30; Nov. 1–15, daily 10–4:30; Nov. 16–Dec. and Feb. 14–27, daily 11–3:30; Feb. 28–Mar., daily 10–5; Apr., daily 9:30–5:30; June, daily 9–6:30.

Usine Mathieu de Roussillon (*Roussillon's Mathieu Ocher Works*). The area's famous vein of natural ocher, which spreads some 25 km (16 miles) along the foot of the Vaucluse plateau, has been mined for centuries, beginning with the ancient Romans, who used it for their pottery. You can visit the old Usine Mathieu de Roussillon to learn more about ocher's extraction and its modern uses. ⊠ On D104 southeast of town ☎ 04–90–05–66–69 ⊕ www.okhra.com €6, €7 joint ticket with Sentier des Ochres ☉ Feb.–June and Sept.–Nov., daily 9–1 and 2–6; Dec. and Jan., Wed.–Sun. 9–1 and 2–6; July and Aug., daily 9–7.

Uniting natural and man-made beauty, ocher quarried from the surrounding painted-desert cliffs is applied directly to many roofs and facades in Roussillon.

MÉNERBES

30 km (19 miles) southeast of Avignon.

Famous as the former home base of *A Year in Provence* author Peter Mayle (he has since moved on to another spot in the Luberon), the town of Ménerbes clings to a long, thin hilltop, looming over the surrounding forests like a great stone ship. At its prow juts the **Castellet**, a 15th-century fortress. At its stern looms the 13th-century **Citadelle**. These redoubtable fortifications served the Protestants well during the 16th-century Wars of Religion—until the Catholics wore them down with a 15-month siege. Artists Picasso, Nicholas de Stael, and Dora Maar all lived here at one time, attracted by the remarkable views and eccentric character of the town.

Fodor's Choice **Festival Lacoste.** Seven kilomerers (4 miles) east of Ménerbes is the eagle's-nest village of Lacoste, presided over by the once-magnificent Château de Sade, erstwhile retreat of the notorious Marquis de Sade (1740–1814). For some years, Paris couturier Pierre Cardin has been restoring the castle wall by wall, and under his generous patronage the Festival Lacoste takes place here throughout the months of July and August. A lyric, musical, and theatrical extravaganza, events (and their dates) change yearly, ranging from outdoor poetry recitals to ballet to colorful operettas. ⊠ *Carrières du Château, Lacoste* ☎ *04–90–75–93–12* ⊕ *www.festivaldelacoste.com* 🖾 *€20–€140.*

Musée du Tire-Bouchon (*Corkscrew museum*). Don't miss the quirky Musée du Tire-Bouchon, which has an enormous selection of corkscrews on display and interesting historical detail on various wine-related subjects. ✉ *Domaine de la Citadelle, rte de Cavaillon* ☎ *04–90–72–41–58* 🌐 *www.domaine-citadelle.com* 🎟 *€4* ⏲ *Apr.–Oct., daily 9–noon and 2–7; Nov.–Mar., Mon.–Sat. 9–noon and 2–7.*

> **WORD OF MOUTH**
>
> "[Aix-en-Provence] is rather light on sights, but very long on atmosphere. I really enjoyed Cézanne's studio. I find myself smiling now when I encounter one of his still lifes in a museum and think, I have seen *that* table, *that* towel, *that* vase—since all of these items are on display in his studio here."
>
> —artsnletters

Place de l'Horloge (*Clock Square*). A campanile tops the Hôtel de Ville on pretty place de l'Horloge, where you can admire the delicate stonework on the arched portal and mullioned windows of a Renaissance house. Just past the tower on the right is an overlook taking in views toward Gordes, Roussillon, and Mont Ventoux.

WHERE TO STAY

For expanded hotel reviews, visit Fodors.com.

$$ B&B/INN 🏨 **Hostellerie Le Roy Soleil.** In the imposing shadow of the Luberon, this luxurious 17th-century country inn has pulled out all stops on comfort and decor: witness the marble and granite bathrooms, wrought-iron beds, and coordinated Provençal fabrics. **Pros:** softer-than-clouds beds are marvelous; attractive online rates. **Cons:** some say service can be hit and miss; food sometimes rather ordinary for such a seductive setting. [$] *Rooms from: €110* ✉ *Rte. des Beaumettes* ☎ *04–90–72–25–61* 🌐 *www.roy-soleil.com* 🛏 *10 rooms, 9 suites, 3 apartments* ⏲ *Restaurant closed mid-Nov.–Mar.* 🍴 *Breakfast.*

AIX-EN-PROVENCE AND THE MEDITERRANEAN COAST

The southeastern part of this area of Provence, on the edge of the Côte d'Azur, is dominated by two major towns: Aix-en-Provence, considered the main hub of Provence and the most cultural community in the region; and Marseille, a vibrant port city that combines seediness with fashion and metropolitan feistiness with classical grace. For a breathtaking experience of the dramatic contrast between the azure Mediterranean Sea and the rocky, olive tree–filled hills, take a trip along the coast east of Marseille and make an excursion to the Iles d'Hyères.

AIX-EN-PROVENCE

82 km (51 miles) southeast of Avignon; 176 km (109 miles) west of Nice; 759 km (474 miles) south of Paris.

Fodor's Choice ★ Gracious, posh, cultivated, and made all the more cosmopolitan by the presence of some 45,000 international university students, the lovely old town of Aix (pronounced *ex*) was once the capital of Provence. The vestiges of its erstwhile power—fine art, noble architecture, and graceful urban design—remain beautifully preserved today. That and its thriving market, enviable café life, and world-class music festival make Aix vie with Arles and Avignon as one of the towns in Provence that shouldn't be missed.

GETTING HERE

The Aix TGV station is 13 km (8 miles) west of the city and is served by regular shuttle buses. The old Aix station is on the slow Marseille–Sisteron line, with trains arriving roughly every hour from Marseille St-Charles. The center of Aix is best explored on foot, but a municipal bus service covers the entire town and the outlying suburbs. Most buses leave from La Rotonde in front of the tourism office (☎ *04–42–16–11–61* ⊕ *www.aixenprovencetourism.com*), where you can also buy tickets (€1) and grab a bus route map.

Visitor Information Aix-en-Provence Tourist Office ⊠ *Les allées provençales, 300 av. Giuseppe Verdi, B.P. 160* ☎ *04–42–16–11–61* ⊕ *www. aixenprovencetourism.com.*

EXPLORING

The museums and churches in Aix are overshadowed by the city itself, with its beautiful fountains, elegant hôtels particuliers, and time-burnished streets. Aix's centre ville is a maze of narrow roadways and it is difficult to keep your sense of direction. Happily, the main drag, the tree-lined and gorgeous cours Mirabeau, neatly divides old Aix in half, with the Quartier Ancien's narrow medieval streets to the north and the 18th-century houses and fancy restaurants of the Quartier Mazarin to the south. At the very center, and always photo-ready, are place Richelme and place de l'Hôtel de Ville, the main squares. You can't go wrong either ending up or beginning with them.

Romans were first drawn here by mild thermal baths, naming the town Aquae Sextiae (Waters of Sextius) in honor of the consul who founded a camp near the source in 123 BC. Just 20 years later some 200,000 Germanic invaders besieged Aix, but the great Roman general Marius pinned them against the mountain known ever since as Ste-Victoire. Marius remains a popular local first name to this day. Under the wise and generous guidance of *Roi* (King) René in the 15th century, Aix became a center of Renaissance arts and letters. At the height of its political, judicial, and ecclesiastic power in the 17th and 18th centuries, Aix profited from a surge of private building, each grand hôtel particulier vying to outdo its neighbor. Its signature *cours* (courtyards) and *places* (squares), punctuated by grand fountains and intriguing passageways, date from this time.

It was into this exalting elegance that artist Paul Cézanne (1839–1906) was born, though he drew much of his inspiration from the raw countryside around the city and often painted Ste-Victoire. A schoolmate of Cézanne's made equal inroads: the journalist and novelist Émile Zola (1840–1902) attended the Collège Bourbon with Cézanne and described their friendship as well as Aix itself in several of his works. You can still sense something of the ambience that nurtured these two geniuses in the streets of modern Aix.

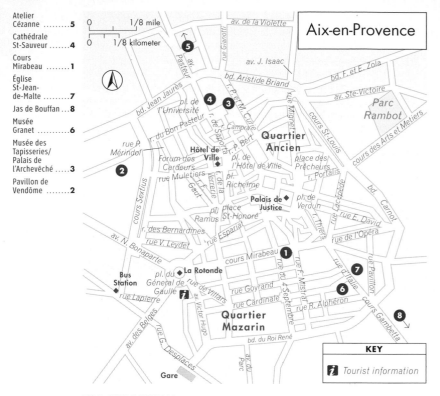

TOP ATTRACTIONS

Atelier Cézanne (*Cézanne's Studio*). Just north of the Vieille Ville loop you'll find Cézanne's studio. After the death of his mother forced the sale of the painter's beloved country retreat, Jas de Bouffan, he had this atelier built and some of his finest works, including *Les Grandes Baigneuses* (*The Large Bathers*), were created in the upstairs workspace. But what is most striking is the collection of simple objects that once featured prominently in his portraits and still lifes—redingote, bowler hat, ginger jar—all displayed as if awaiting his return. The atelier is behind an obscure garden gate on the left as you climb the avenue Paul-Cézanne. After-dark shows that take place in July and August include movie screenings in the garden. ✉ *9 av. Paul-Cézanne* ☎ *04–42–21–06–53* ⊕ *www.atelier-cezanne.com* 🖾 *€5.50* ⊗ *Apr.–June and Sept., daily 10–noon and 2–6; July and Aug., daily 10–6; Oct.–Mar., daily 10–noon and 2–5. Closed Sun. Dec.–Feb.*

Cathédrale St-Sauveur. Many eras of architectural history are clearly delineated and preserved here. The cathedral has a double nave—Romanesque and Gothic side by side—and a Merovingian (5th-century) **baptistery,** its colonnade mostly recovered from Roman temples built to honor pagan deities. The deep bath on the floor is a remnant of total-immersion baptism. Shutters hide the ornate 16th-century carvings on the **portals,** opened by a guide on request. The guide can also lead you into the tranquil Romanesque **cloister** next door, with carved pillars and slender columns.

The extraordinary 15th-century *Triptyque du Buisson Ardent* (*Mary and the Burning Bush*) was painted by Nicolas Froment in the heat of inspiration following his travels in Italy and Flanders and depicts the generous art patrons King René and Queen Jeanne kneeling on either side of the Virgin, who is poised above a burning bush. To avoid light damage, it's only opened for viewing on Tuesday from 3 to 4. ⊠ *Pl. des Martyrs de la Résistance* ☎ *04–42–23–45–65* ⊕ *www.cathedrale-aix. net* ⊙ *Daily 8–noon and 2–6.*

Cours Mirabeau. Shaded by a double row of tall plane trees, the cours Mirabeau is one of the most beautiful avenues anywhere, designed so its width and length would be in perfect porportion with the height of the dignified 18th-century hôtels particuliers lining it. You can view this lovely assemblage from one of the dozen or so cafés that spill onto the pavement.

Fodor'sChoice ★ **Musée Granet.** Once the École de Dessin (Art School) that granted Cézanne a second-place prize in 1856, the former priory of the Église St-Jean-de-Malte now showcases eight of Cézanne's paintings, as well as a nice collection of his watercolors and drawings. Also hanging in the galleries are works by Bonnard, Picasso, Klee, Rubens, David, and Giacometti. ⊠ *Pl. St-Jean-de-Malte* ☎ *04–42–52–88–32* ⊕ *www. museegranet-aixenprovence.fr* ⊠ *€4* ⊙ *June–Sept., Tues.–Sun. 10–7; Oct.–May, Tues.–Sun. noon–6.*

Fodor'sChoice ★ **Pavillon de Vendôme.** This extravagant Baroque villa was built in 1665 as a country house for the Duke of Vendome; its position just outside the city's inner circle allowed the duke to commute discreetly from his official home on the cours Mirabeau to this retreat, where his mistress, La Belle du Canet, was comfortably installed. The villa was expanded and heightened in the 18th century to draw attention to the classical orders—Ionic, Doric, and Corinthian—on parade in the row of neo-Grecian columns. Inside the cool, broad chambers you can find a collection of Provençal furniture and artwork. Note the curious two giant Atlantes that hold up the interior balcony. ⊠ *32 rue Celony* ☎ *04– 42–91–88–75* ⊠ *€3.30* ⊙ *Oct. 15–Apr. 15, Wed.–Mon. 1:30–5; Apr. 16–Oct. 14, Wed.–Mon. 10–6. Closed Jan.*

WORTH NOTING

Église St-Jean-de-Malte. This 12th-century church served as a chapel of the Knights of Malta, a medieval order of friars devoted to hospital care. The church was Aix's first attempt at the Gothic style, and it was here that the counts of Provence were buried throughout the 18th century; their tombs (in the upper left) were attacked during the Revolution and have been only partially repaired. ⊠ *Intersection of rue Cardinale and rue d'Italie.*

Jas de Bouffan. Cézanne's father bought this lovely estate, whose name translates as "the sheepfold," in 1859 to celebrate his rise from hatmaker to banker. The budding artist lived here until 1899 and painted his first images of Mont Ste-Victoire—the founding seeds of 20th-century art—from the grounds. Today the salons are empty but the estate is full of the artist's spirit, especially the Allée des Marronniers out front. The Jas is a mile south of the center of town and can only be visited on tour by booking a minibus seat through the central tourist office, either in person or online. ✉ *80 rte. de Valcros* ☎ *04–42–16–10–91* 🌐 *www.aixenprovencetourism.com* 🎟 *€5.50* 🕓 *Reserved tours in English vary. Contact office tourism.*

NEED A BREAK?

Orienthé. For an excellent cup of flavored tea (there are more than 60 choices), wander into Orienthé any afternoon. Comfy pillows, low tables, and lively student patronage make this place pleasantly casual, and the Middle Eastern desserts are delicious. ✉ ***5 rue Félibre Gaut*** 🌐 ***www.orienthe-aix.com.***

Musée des Tapisseries. Housed in the 17th-century **Palais de l'Archevêché** (Archbishop's Palace), this museum showcases a sumptuous collection of tapestries that once decorated the bishops' quarters. There are 17 magnificent hangings from Beauvais and a series on the life of Don Quixote from Compiègne. Temporary exhibitions offer looks at contemporary textile art. The main opera productions of the Festival International d'Art Lyrique take place in the broad courtyard. ✉ *28 pl. des Martyrs de la Resistance* ☎ *04–42–23–09–91* 🎟 *€3.30* 🕓 *Oct. 16–Apr. 15, Wed.–Mon. 1:30–5; Apr. 16–Oct. 15, Wed.–Mon. 10–12:20 and 1:30–6. Closed Jan.*

WHERE TO EAT

$$$ FRENCH 🍴 **Brasserie Les Deux Garçons.** As you revel in the exquisite gold-ivory *style Consulate* decor, which dates from the restaurant's founding in 1792, it's not hard to picture the greats—Churchill, Sartre, Picasso, Delon, Belmondo, and Cocteau among them—enjoying a drink under these mirrors. The food is not memorable, but 365 days a year you can savor the linen-decked sidewalk tables that look out to the cours Mirabeau. [$] *Average main: €25* ✉ *53 cours Mirabeau* ☎ *04–42–26–00–51* 🌐 *www.les2garcons.fr.*

$$ FRENCH 🍴 **Café La Chimère.** Although the decor in this artists' hangout is a bit overdone, there's a sense of playful whimsy in the vertically arranged concoctions of fresh, local ingredients garnished with shaved fennel, spun sugar, or drizzled sauces. The prices are reasonable, the atmosphere is lively, there's an honorable wine selection, and—even better—a new Champagne bar—making this an altogether fun place to spend an evening. [$] *Average main: €20* ✉ *15 rue Brueys* ☎ *04–42–38–30–00* 🌐 *www.lachimerecafe.com* 🕓 *No lunch.*

$$$ FRENCH 🍴 **Coté Cour.** Filled with trendy insiders and fashion-conscious Aixois who want to devour Chef Ronan Kernan's creations, this très chic restaurant has floor-to-ceiling windows that give almost every table a view of the plant-filled courtyard. Delicious smells waft out from the kitchen as diners await specialties likes artichokes stuffed with foie gras over lentils and herring caviar, or slowly cooked beef with potatoes in hazelnut oil and wild mushroom gravy. [$] *Average main: €27* ✉ *19 cours Mirabeau* ☎ *04–42–93–12–51* 🌐 *www.restaurantcotecour.fr* ✍ *Reservations essential* 🕓 *Closed Sun. Oct.–Apr.*

$$ MODERN FRENCH 🍴 **La Rotonde.** Trendy, young, and cool, this hotter-than-hot spot is the place to hit before heading out for a night on the town. The trappings are Baroque, the service is fun, and the food is very good. Chef Cedric Bonamy comes up with easy-to-eat, fresh, and inexpensive cuisine while the house DJ plays soft Buddha Bar–style music in the background—a combination that is a sure recipe for a convivial evening. Try the veal and mushroom cannelloni, or the risotto with giant shrimps and saffron. And don't forget the moist almond cake *fiancier* with chocolate sauce and pistachio ice cream—it is exactly the right way to finish off the meal. [$] *Average main: €18* ✉ *2 pl. Jeanne D'Arc* ☎ *04–42–91–61–70* 🌐 *www.larotonde-aix.com.*

$$$$ FRENCH 🍴 **Le Clos de la Violette.** Whether you dine under the chestnut trees or in the airy, pastel dining room, you can experience the cuisine of one of the south's top chefs, Jean-Marc Banzo. For more than 25 years he has been spinning tradition into gold, from roasted lamb with thyme ravioli and gnocchi with fresh goat cheese to grilled sea bass with chard lasagna and shellfish. The restaurant isn't far from the Atelier Cézanne, outside the Vieille Ville ring. Some feel that the service can be erratic, but the welcome is warm. [$] *Average main: €55* ✉ *10 av. de la Violette* ☎ *04–42–23–30–71* 🌐 *www.closdelaviolette.fr* ✍ *Reservations essential. Jacket required* 🕒 *Closed Sun. and Mon.*

$$$ FRENCH 🍴 **Le Formal.** Named after Chef Jean Luc le Formal, this intimate white, stone-wall cellar room is anything but stuffy. Signature dishes include an artichoke, truffle, and tuna sashimi sandwich and classic grilled beef tenderloin with pan-seared foie gras; these, and other wonderful creations, are available à la carte or on several well-priced set menus. [$] *Average main: €25* ✉ *32 rue Espariat* ☎ *04–42–27–08–31* 🌐 *www.restaurant-leformal.fr* ✍ *Reservations essential* 🕒 *Closed Sun. and Mon. No lunch Sat.*

$$$ MEDITERRANEAN 🍴 **O Zen Le Passage.** This is an edgy, urban brasserie that serves as a wildly popular setting for good food. In a sleekly converted former candy factory in the center of town, the complex also has a cooking workshop, plus a small wine store and épicerie arranged around a sunny atrium. A New York vibe runs from the Andy Warhol reproductions in the main dining room to the young chefs who create casual mod-Med meals, such as roasted beef fillet with mashed sweet potatoes. [$] *Average main: €29* ✉ *10 rue Villars* ☎ *04–42–37–09–00* 🌐 *www.le-passage.fr* ✍ *Reservations essential.*

WHERE TO STAY

For expanded hotel reviews, visit Fodors.com.

$ HOTEL 🏨 **Grand Hotel Nègre-Coste.** This 18th-century town house lives up to its prominent cours Mirabeau position with lavish ground-floor salons, Provençal decor, and large windows. **Pros:** a perfect location for visiting Aix; the welcome is warm; affordable. **Cons:** rooms, especially those near the elevator, can be noisy; some rooms are quite small; not a lot of sockets for recharging phones, iPads etc. [$] *Rooms from: €96* ✉ *33 cours Mirabeau* ☎ *04–42–27–74–22* 🌐 *www.hotelnegrecoste.com* 🛏 *36 rooms, 1 suite* 🍴 *Breakfast.*

Crammed with elegant shops, chic cafés, and 18th-century houses, Aix-en-Provence is one of France's most charming towns.

$$$$ HOTEL Fodor's Choice ★ **Le Pigonnet.** Cézanne painted Ste-Victoire from what is now the large flower-filled terrace of this enchanting abode, and you can easily imagine former guests Princess Caroline, Iggy Pop, and Clint Eastwood swanning their way through the magnificent, pool-adorned, topiary-accented garden or relaxing in the spacious, light-filled guest rooms, each a marvel of decoration—and renovated in 2013. **Pros:** unique garden setting in the center of Aix; welcome is friendly; rooms all have large French windows. **Cons:** reception area has been called stuffy and old-fashioned; some of the antiques are a little threadbare; breakfast is extra (€25). [$] *Rooms from: €360* ✉ *5 av. du Pigonnet* ☎ *04–42–59–02–90* 🌐 *www.hotelpigonnet.com* 🛏 *41 rooms, 3 suites* 🍴 *No meals.*

$ HOTEL **Quatre Dauphins.** A noble hôtel particulier in the quiet, soigné, and chic Mazarin quarter offers modest but impeccable lodging, with pretty, comfortable little rooms that have been spruced up with *boutis* (Provençal quilts), Les Olivades fabrics, quarry tiles, jute carpets, and hand-painted furniture. **Pros:** ideal center-of-town location; friendly staff; rooms with showers are cheaper than ones with a bath. **Cons:** rooms are small; in summer it is impossible to get a room; breakfast is extra. [$] *Rooms from: €85* ✉ *54 rue Roux-Alphéran* ☎ *04–42–38–16–39* 🌐 *www.lesquatredauphins.fr* 🛏 *13 rooms* 🍴 *No meals.*

$$$$ HOTEL **Villa Gallici.** Hued in the lavenders, blues, ochers, and oranges of Aix, rooms here swim in the most gorgeous Souleiado and Rubelli fabrics: this all conjures up the swank Provence that used to be colonized by Parisian barons and ducs in the 19th century, far from the usual Provençal farmhouse idyll. **Pros:** rich fabrics and decor create a harmonious look; beautiful environment. **Cons:** no elevator, some showers are

hand held; breakfast is extra. $ *Rooms from: €390* ⊠ *Av. de la Violette* ☎ *04–42–23–29–23* ⊕ *www.villagallici.com* ➹ *16 rooms, 6 suites* ⊘ *Closed Jan.* ❍ *No meals.*

NIGHTLIFE AND THE ARTS

To find out what's going on in town, pick up a copy of the events calendar *L'Agenda cuturel* (formerly *Le Mois à Aix*) at the tourist office.

Casino Aix en Provence. In between bouts at the roulette tables and slot machines of the Casino Aix en Provence, you can grab a bite at one of five restaurants or take in a floor show. ⊠ *21 av. de l'Europe* ☎ *04–42–59–69–00* ⊕ *www.casinoaix.com.*

Festival d'Aix en Provence (*International Festival of Lyric Art*). Every July during the Festival d'Aix en Provence—also known as the International Festival of Lyric Art—you can see world-class opera productions in the spectacular courtyard of the Palais de l'Archevêché. ☎ *04–42–17–34–00 for information, 08–20–92–29–23 for tickets [€0.12 per min]* ⊕ *www.festival-aix.com.*

Le Scat Club. Le Scat Club is the place for live soul, funk, reggae, rock, blues, and jazz. ⊠ *11 rue de la Verrerie* ☎ *04–42–23–00–23.*

SHOPPING

Aix is a market town, and a sophisticated **food and produce market** sets up every morning on place Richelme; just up the street, on place Verdun, a good high-end *brocante* market opens on Tuesday, Thursday, and Saturday mornings. A famous Aixois delicacy is *calissons,* a blend of almond paste and glazed melon in almond shapes.

Bechard. The most picturesque shop specializing in calissons is the venerable bakery Bechard. ⊠ *12 cours Mirabeau.*

Leonard Parli. Leonard Parli, near the train station, also offers a lovely selection of calissons. ⊠ *35 av. Victor Hugo* ⊕ *www.leonard-parli.com.*

In addition to its old-style markets and jewel-box candy shops, Aix is a modern shopping town—perhaps the best in Provence. The winding streets of the Vieille Ville above cours Mirabeau—centered on **rue Clemenceau, rue Marius Reinaud, rue Espariat, rue Aude,** and **rue Maréchal Foch**—have a head-turning parade of goods.

MARSEILLE

31 km (19 miles) south of Aix-en-Provence; 188 km (117 miles) west of Nice; 772 km (483 miles) south of Paris.

Marseille is sometimes given a wide berth by travelers, but that's their loss. After all, it is vibrant enough to have been named 2013's European City of Culture (⊕ *marseillecityofculture.eu*). Some 400 events were staged to celebrate that honor; and the legacy of 2013 will live on, thanks to a slew of new or renewed cultural attractions. Ten primary ones were inaugurated, either in formerly abandoned buildings (like the old tobacco factory) or purpose-built ones—most notably the glitzy, glassy National Museum of the Civilizations of Europe and the Mediterranean, otherwise known as MuCEM.

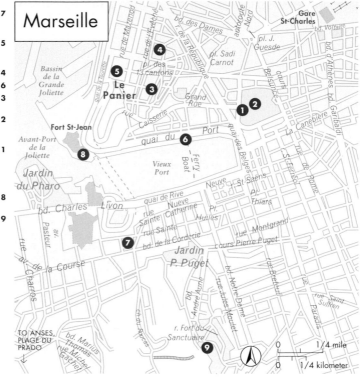

Moreover, the port area (Marseille is France's leading cruise port, attracting some 700,000 passengers per year) has become a pedestrian zone and benefited from a multimillion-dollar face-lift, which includes a seaside shopping center with 160 restaurants and shops. Even without such enhancements, Marseille's Cubist jumbles of white stone rising up over the waterfront, bathed in light of blinding clarity and crowned by larger-than-life neo-Byzantine churches, could still dazzle—and literally, too, as the city sees 300 days of sunlight a year.

Neighborhoods here teem with multiethnic life, souklike African markets reek deliciously of spices and coffees, and the labyrinthine Vieille Ville is painted in broad strokes of saffron, cinnamon, and robin's-egg blue. Feisty and fond of broad gestures, Marseille is a dynamic city, as cosmopolitan now as when the Phoenicians first founded it, and with all the exoticism of the international shipping center it has been for 2,600 years. Vital to the Crusades in the Middle Ages and crucial to Louis XIV as a military port, Marseille flourished as France's market to the world—and still does today.

GETTING HERE

The main rail station—Gare St-Charles, on the TGV line—has frequent trains to and from Paris, Nice, and Italy, as well as Arles. Note that inside the station, SOS Voyageurs (☎ *04–91–62–12–80* ⊕ *www.*

sosvoyageurs.org ☉ *Mon.–Sat. 9–7*) helps with children, senior citizens, and lost luggage. Next to the train station is the bus station (✆ *04–91–08–16–40*): Cartrieze (✆ *08–10–00–13–26* ⊕ *www.lepilote.com*) controls bus routes to and from the Bouches du Rhone; Lignes Express Régionales—the LER—(✆ *08–21–20–22–03* ⊕ *www.info-ler.fr*) operates coaches between Marseille and Nice via Aix-en-Provence. Marseille has a good local bus, tram, and métro system (⊕ *www.rtm.fr*). Most of the lines service the suburbs, but several stop in the city center (including Gare St-Charles, Colbert, Vieux Port, and Notre-Dame); tickets are €1.50 for trips up to an hour or €5 for day passes.

Visitor Information Marseille Tourist Office ✉ *11 la Canebière* ✆ *08–26–50–05–00 [€0.15 per min]* ⊕ *www.marseille-tourisme.com.*

EXPLORING

The heart of Marseille is clustered around the Vieux Port—immortalized in all its briny charm in the 1961 Leslie Caron film version of *Fanny*. The hills to the south of the port are crowned with megamonuments, such as Notre-Dame-de-la-Garde and Fort St-Jean. To the north lies the ramshackle hilltop Vieille Ville known as Le Panier. East of the port you can find the North African neighborhood and, to its left, the famous thoroughfare called La Canebière. South of the city, the clifftop waterfront highway leads to obscure and colorful ports and coves.

If you plan on visiting many of the museums in Marseille, buy a City-Pass for €22 (2 days €29) at the tourism office. It covers the entry fee into all the museums and monuments in Marseille, plus transport, a ride on the *petit train*, and a free, guided tour of the city.

TOP ATTRACTIONS

Abbaye St-Victor. Founded in the 4th century by St-Cassien, who sailed into Marseille full of fresh ideas on monasticism that he acquired in Palestine and Egypt, this church grew to formidable proportions. With a Romanesque design, the structure would be as much at home in the Middle East as its founder was. The **crypt**, St-Cassien's original, is buried under the medieval church, and in the evocative nooks and crannies you can find the 5th-century sarcophagus that allegedly holds the martyr's remains. Upstairs, a reliquary contains what's left of St. Victor, who was ground to death between millstones, probably by Romans. There's also a passage into tiny **catacombs** where early Christians worshipped St-Lazarus and Mary Magdalene, said to have washed ashore at Stes-Maries-de-la-Mer. ✉ *3 rue de l'Abbaye, Rive Neuve* ✆ *04–96–11–22–60* ⊕ *www.saintvictor.net* ⊠ *Crypt €2* ☉ *Daily 9–7.*

Centre de la Vieille Charité (*Center of the Old Charity*). At the top of the Panier district you'll find this superb ensemble of 17th- and 18th-century architecture designed as a hospice for the homeless by Marseillais artist-architects Pierre and Jean Puget. Even if you don't enter the museums, walk around the inner court, studying the retreating perspective of triple arcades and admiring the Baroque chapel with its novel egg-peaked dome. Of the complex's two museums, the larger is the **Musée d'Archéologie Méditerranéenne** (Museum of Mediterranean Archaeology), with a sizable collection of pottery and statuary from classical Mediterranean civilization, elementally labeled (for example, "pot"). There's also a display on the mysterious Celt-like Ligurians who first peopled the coast, cryptically presented with emphasis on the digs instead of the finds themselves. The best of the lot is the evocatively mounted Egyptian collection—the second-largest in France after the Louvre's. There are mummies, hieroglyphs, and gorgeous sarcophagi in a tomblike setting. Upstairs, the **Musée d'Arts Africains, Océaniens, et Amérindiens** (Museum of African, Oceanic, and American Indian Art) creates a theatrical foil for the works' intrinsic drama: the spectacular masks and sculptures are mounted along a pure black wall, lighted indirectly, with labels across the aisle. ⊠ *2 rue de la Charité, Le Panier* ☎ *04–91–14–58–80* 💶 *€5 per museum* ☉ *Jan–May., Tues.–Sun. 11–6; June–Sept., Tues.–Sun. 10–6.*

OFF THE BEATEN PATH

Château d'If. In the 16th century, François I recognized the strategic advantage of an island fortress surveying the mouth of Marseille's vast harbor and built this imposing edifice. Its effect as a deterrent was so successful that the fortress never saw combat, and was eventually converted into a prison. It was here that Alexandre Dumas locked up his most famous character, the Count of Monte Cristo. Though the count was fictional, the hole through which Dumas had him escape is real enough, on display in the cells. On the other hand, the real-life Man in the Iron Mask, whose cell is also erroneously on display, was not imprisoned here. The IF Frioul Express boat ride (from the quai des Belges, €10; for information call ☎ *04–96–11–03–50*) and the views from the broad terrace are worth the trip. ☎ *08–26–50–05–00* ⊕ *if.monuments-nationaux.fr/en* 💶 *€5* ☉ *Apr.–mid-May., daily 9:30–4:45; mid-May–mid-Sept., daily 9:30–6:10; mid-Sept.–Mar., Tues–Sun., 9:30–4:45.*

Fodor's Choice ★

Ferry Boat. This Marseille treasure departs from the quai below the Hôtel de Ville. For a pittance (although technically free, it is appropriate to tip the crew) you can file onto this little wooden barge and chug across the Vieux Port. ⊠ *Pl. des Huiles on quai de Rive Neuve side and Hôtel de Ville on quai du Port, Vieux Port* 💶 *Free.*

Le Panier. This is the old heart of Marseille, a maze of high-shuttered houses looming over narrow cobbled streets, *montées* (stone stairways), and tiny squares. Long decayed and neglected, the quarter is the principal focus of the city's efforts at urban renewal. Wander this neighborhood at will, making sure to stroll along rue du Panier, the montée des Accoules, rue du Petit-Puits, and rue des Muettes.

Musée d'Histoire de Marseille (*Marseille Museum of History*). A modern and open space, this museum illuminates Marseille's history with a treasure of archaeological finds and miniature models of the city as it appeared in various stages of history. Best by far is the presentation of Marseille's Classical halcyon days. There's a recovered wreck of a Roman cargo boat, its 3rd-century wood amazingly preserved, and the hull of a Greek boat dating from the 4th century BC. The model of the Greek city should be authentic—it's based on the eyewitness description of Aristotle. The museum reopened after a €21-million renovation in the summer of 2013. ⊠ *9 rue Henri Barbrusse* ☎ *04–91–90–42–22* ⊕ *musee-histoire-de-marseille.marseille.fr* 💶 *€5 joint ticket with Jardin des Vestiges* ☉ *June–Sept., Mon.–Sat. noon–7; Oct.–May., Tues.–Sun. 10–5.*

The heart of Marseille is its Vieux Port (Old Port), with its small boats and port-side cafés, while the city's soul is hilltop Notre-Dame-de-la-Garde.

WORTH NOTING

Cathédrale de la Nouvelle Major. This gargantuan, neo-Byzantine 19th-century fantasy was built under Napoléon III—but not before he'd ordered the partial destruction of the lovely 11th-century original, once a perfect example of the Provençal Romanesque style. You can view the flashy decor (think marble and rich red porphyry inlay) in the newer of the two churches; the medieval one is being restored. ⊠ *Pl. de la Major, Le Panier.*

Le Port Antique. This garden behind the Musée d'Histoire de Marseille stands on the site of the city's classical waterfront and includes remains of the Greek fortifications and loading docks. Newly restored in 2013, it was discovered in 1967 when roadwork was being done next to the Bourse (Stock Exchange). ⊠ *Centre Bourse, Vieux Port* ☎ *04–91–90–42–22* 🎫 *€5 joint ticket with Marseille Museum of History* ☽ *Mon.–Sat. noon–7.*

Musée National des Civilisations de L'Europe et de la Mediterranée. After a lengthy renovation, the National Museum of the Civilizations of Europe and the Mediterranean (MuCEM) opened its doors to great fanfare in the summer of 2013. Made up of three sites designed by Rudy Ricciotti, MuCEM is all about new perspectives on Mediterranean cultures. Themes like "the invention of gods, "the treasures of the spice route," the citizens' banquet," or "the curiosity cabinet" are explored in a permanent exhibition at the J4 (yes, it's a building). Through that building, you can access the 12th-century Fort St-Jean, built by Louis XIV with the guns pointing *toward* the city, in order to keep the feisty, rebellious Marseillais under his thumb. If you're not the queasy type, take a suspended footbridge over the sea; it provides spectacular photo-ops and never-been-seen panoramas; on the other side, you can visit a new Mediterranean garden and a folk-art collection. A third building—the Center for Conservation and Resources, near the St-Charles train station—establishes the museum's backstory. ✉ *Quai du Port, Vieux Port* ☎ *04–96–13–80–90* 🌐 *www.mucem.org* 🎟 *Not set at press time* 🕓 *Not set at press time.*

Notre-Dame-de-la-Garde. Towering above the city and visible for miles around, this overscaled neo-Byzantine monument was erected in 1853 by Napoléon III. The interior is a Technicolor bonanza of red-and-beige stripes and glittering mosaics, and the gargantuan *Madonna and Child* on the steeple (almost 30 feet high) is covered in real gold leaf. While the panoply of ex-votos, mostly thanking the Virgin for deathbed interventions and shipwreck survivals, is a remarkable sight, most impressive are the views of the seaside city at your feet. ✉ *Off bd. André Aune* ✥ *On foot, climb up cours Pierre Puget, cross Jardin Pierre Puget, cross bridge to rue Vauvenargues, and hike up to pl. Edon. Or catch Bus 60 from cours Jean-Ballard* ☎ *04–91–13–40–80* 🕓 *May–Sept., daily 7 am–8 pm; Oct.–Apr., daily 7–7.*

WHERE TO EAT

$ PIZZA 🍴 **Au Petit Naples.** With huge portions, a convivial atmosphere, and a small, busy beachfront location, this restaurant is jammed with locals and savvy tourists from every walk of life. Some connoisseurs say that the pizza here is even better than at Marseille's noted Étienne. [$] *Average main: €15* ✉ *14 plage de l'Estaque, L'Estaque* ☎ *04–91–46–05–11* 💳 *No credit cards* 🕓 *No lunch Sat.*

$$$$ SEAFOOD 🍴 **Chez Fonfon.** Tucked into the filmlike tiny fishing port Vallon des Auffes, this Marseillais landmark has one of the loveliest settings in greater Marseille. Once presided over by cult chef "Fonfon," it used to be a favorite movie-star hangout. A variety of fresh seafood, impeccably grilled, steamed, or roasted in salt crust are served in two pretty dining rooms with picture windows overlooking the fishing boats that supply your dinner. Try classic bouillabaisse served with all the bells and whistles—broth, hot-chili rouille, and flamboyant table-side filleting. [$] *Average main: €50* ✉ *140 rue du Vallon des Auffes* ☎ *04–91–52–14–38* 🌐 *www.chez-fonfon.com* ✍ *Reservations essential* 🕓 *Closed Sun. and Mon. in winter and 1st 3 wks in Jan. No lunch Sun. and Mon. in summer.*

$$ PIZZA 🍴 **Étienne.** A historic Le Panier hole-in-the-wall, this small pizzeria is filled with politicos and young professionals who enjoy the personality of chef Stéphane Cassero, who was once famous for announcing the price of the meal only after he'd had the chance to look you over. Remarkably little has changed over the years, except now there is a posted menu (with prices). Brace yourself for an epic meal, starting with a large anchovy pizza from the wood-burning oven, then fried squid, eggplant gratin, and a slab of rare grilled beef, all served with a background of laughter, rich patois, and abuse from the chef. [$] *Average main: €20* ✉ *43 rue de la Lorette, Le Panier* 💳 *No credit cards.*

$$$ FRENCH 🍴 **Les Arcenaulx.** At this book-lined, red-wall haven in the stylish book-and-boutique complex of a renovated arsenal, you can have a

sophisticated regional lunch and read while you're waiting. If you've had your fill of fish, indulge in the grilled fillet of beef with fried artichokes with sweet onion. The terrace (on the Italian-scale cours d'Estienne d'Orves) is as pleasant as the interior. [$] *Average main: €25* ✉ *25 cours d'Estienne d'Orves, Vieux Port* ☎ *04–91–59–80–30* 🌐 *www.les-arcenaulx.com* 🕒 *Closed Sun.*

$$$$ SEAFOOD ✕ **Une Table au Sud.** Lionel Lévy left this gorgeously situated eatery with its panoramic views of the Old Port in the capable hands of Ludovic Turac—a candidate on TV's *Top Chef 2011*. A Mediterranean menu, with a Michelin-star rating, changes every two months depending on what's in season. A standard is the creamy, fishy Milkshake de Bouille-Abaisse, a one-of-a-kind gourmand delight. [$] *Average main: €39* ✉ *2 quai du Port, Vieux Port* ☎ *04–91–90–63–53* 🌐 *www.unetableausud.com* ✍ *Reservations essential* 🕒 *Closed Mon. No dinner Sun.*

WHERE TO STAY

For expanded hotel reviews, visit Fodors.com.

$$ HOTEL 🏨 **Alizé.** On the Vieux Port, with front rooms taking in postcard views, this straightforward lodging has been modernized to include tight double-pane windows, slick modular baths, and a laminate-and-all-weather carpeted look. **Pros:** ideal location on the waterfront gives access to shops and sights; friendly service. **Cons:** somewhat generic room decor; Wi-Fi signal may be weak in some rooms; breakfast is extra. [$] *Rooms from: €109* ✉ *35 quai des Belges, Vieux Port* ☎ *04–91–33–66–97* 🌐 *www.alize-hotel.com* 🛏 *39 rooms* 🍴 *No meals.*

$$$ HOTEL 🏨 **Grand Hotel Beauvau Vieux Port.** Genuine Old World charm is on tap at this historic hotel overlooking the Vieux Port, perhaps not surprisingly since it was once favored by Chopin and George Sand. **Pros:** filled with charm from years past; a landmark with modern amenities; wheelchair accessible; excellent location. **Cons:** some rooms are a bit dark; breakfast is extra. [$] *Rooms from: €165* ✉ *4 rue Beauvau, Vieux Port* ☎ *04–91–54–91–00, 800/637–2873 for U.S. reservations* 🌐 *www.grandhotelbeauvaumarseille.com* 🛏 *71 rooms, 2 suites* 🍴 *No meals.*

$$$$ HOTEL 🏨 **Le Petit Nice Passédat.** On a rocky promontory overlooking the sea, this fantasy villa was bought from a countess in 1917 and converted to a sleek hotel-restaurant; happily, the Passédat family has been getting it right ever since, especially in the famous restaurant. **Pros:** a memorable (if expensive) hotel experience; breathtaking views; good service. **Cons:** pool is small though lovely. [$] *Rooms from: €290* ✉ *Anse de la Maldormé, corniche J.-F.-Kennedy, Endoume* ☎ *04–91–59–25–92* 🌐 *www.petitnice-passedat.com* 🛏 *13 rooms, 3 suites* 🕒 *Closed Sun. and Mon. Nov–Apr. Restaurant closed Sun. and Mon.* 🍴 *Breakfast.*

$ HOTEL 🏨 **Mama Shelter Marseille.** Opened since spring 2012, this is the second boutique hotel brought to you from the Club Med people, the Trigano family. **Pros:** 27-inch iMac in every room (ask for a keyboard at reception) and free Wi-Fi; free movies on demand. **Cons:** corner rooms may have even smaller bathrooms; room cancellation 48 hours before noon France time or you could be charged one night; parking is pricey. [$] *Rooms from: €89* ✉ *64 rue de la Loubière, Notre-Dame-du-Mont, Marseille* ☎ *33/04–84–35–20– 00* 🌐 *www.mamashelter.com/en/marseille* 🛏 *123 rooms.*

NIGHTLIFE AND THE ARTS

With a population of more than 860,000, Marseille is a big city by French standards, with all the nightlife that entails. Arm yourself with the monthly *In Situ*, a free guide to music, theater, and galleries, or *Sortir*, a weekly about film, art, and concerts in southern Provence. They're both in French.

Abbaye St-Victor. Classical music concerts are given in the Abbaye St-Victor. ⊠ *3 rue de l'Abbaye* ☎ *04–91–05–84–48 for information* ⊕ *saintvictor.chez.com.*

Le Trolleybus. Le Trolleybus is the most popular disco in town, with a young, *branché* (hip) crowd. ⊠ *24 quai de Rive Neuve, Bompard* ☎ *04–91–54–30–45* ⊕ *www.letrolley.com.*

Opéra Municipal de Marseille. Operas and orchestral concerts are held at the Opéra Municipal. ⊠ *2 rue Molière, Vieux Port* ☎ *04–91–55–11–10* ⊕ *opera.marseille.fr.*

Red Lion. The Red Lion is a mecca for English-speakers, who pour onto the sidewalk, pints in hand, pub-style. There's live music, DJs on the weekend, and a lounge for the diehard rugby and football fans who can't go without watching a match. ⊠ *231 av. Pierre Mendès France, Vieux Port* ☎ *04–91–25–17–17* ⊕ *www.pub-redlion.com.*

SHOPPING

Savon de Marseille (Marseille soap) is a household standard in France, often sold as a satisfyingly crude and hefty block in odorless olive-oil green. But its chichi offspring are dainty pastel guest soaps in almond, lemon, vanilla, and other scents.

Four des Navettes. The famous bakery Four des Navettes, up the street from Notre-Dame-de-la-Garde, makes orange-spice, shuttle-shape *navettes*. These cookies are modeled on the little boat which, it is said, carried Lazarus and the "Three Marys" (Mary Magdalene, Mary Salome, and Mary Jacobe) to the nearby shore. ⊠ *136 rue Sainte, Garde Hill* ☎ *04–91–33–32–12* ⊕ *www.fourdesnavettes.com.*

CASSIS

30 km (19 miles) southeast of Marseille, 42 km (26 miles) west of Toulon.

Fodor's Choice
★   Surrounded by vineyards and monumental cliffs, guarded by the ruins of a medieval castle, and nestled around a picture-perfect fishing port, Cassis is the prettiest coastal town in Provence. Way back in the 19th century, famed author Colette raved about this town. Today, many visitors do the same.

Visitor Information Cassis Tourist Office ⊠ *Quai des Moulins* ☎ *08–92–25–98–92* ⊕ *www.ot-cassis.com.*

EXPLORING

Stylish without being too recherché, Cassis is where pleasure-boaters come to spend the night, restock their galleys at the market, replenish their nautical duds in the boutiques, and relax with a bottle of cassis and a platter of sea urchins in one of the numerous waterfront cafés.

From Cassis be sure to take an excursion boat to the Calanques, the rocky finger-coves washed by emerald and blue waters.

Pastel houses set at Cubist angles frame the port, and the mild rash of parking-garage architecture that scars its outer neighborhoods doesn't spoil the general effect—one of pure and unadulterated charm. The **Château de Cassis** has loomed over the harbor since the invasions of the Saracens in the 7th century, evolving over time into a walled enclosure crowned with stout watchtowers. It's private property today and best viewed from a port-side café.

From Cassis, head east out of town and cut sharply right up the **route des Crêtes.** This road takes you along a magnificent crest over the water and up to the very top of **Cap Canaille.** Venture out on the vertiginous trails to the edge, where the whole coast stretches below.

Les Calanques. You can't visit Cassis without touring the calanques, the fjord-like finger bays that probe the rocky coastline. Either take a sightseeing cruise or hike across the cliff tops, clambering down the steep sides to these barely accessible retreats. Or you can combine the two, going in by boat and hiking back; make arrangements at the port. The calanque closest to Cassis is the least attractive: **Port Miou** was a stone quarry until 1982, when the calanques became protected sites. Now it's an active leisure and fishing port. **Calanque Port Pin** is prettier, with wind-twisted pines growing at angles from the white-rock cliffs. But it's the third calanque that's the showstopper: the **Calanque En Vau** is a castaway's dream, with a tiny beach at its root and jagged cliffs looming overhead. The series of massive cliffs and calanques stretches all the way to Marseille.

Icard Maritime. Note that boats make round-trips several times a day to the Calanques de Cassis from Marseille's quai de la Fraternité

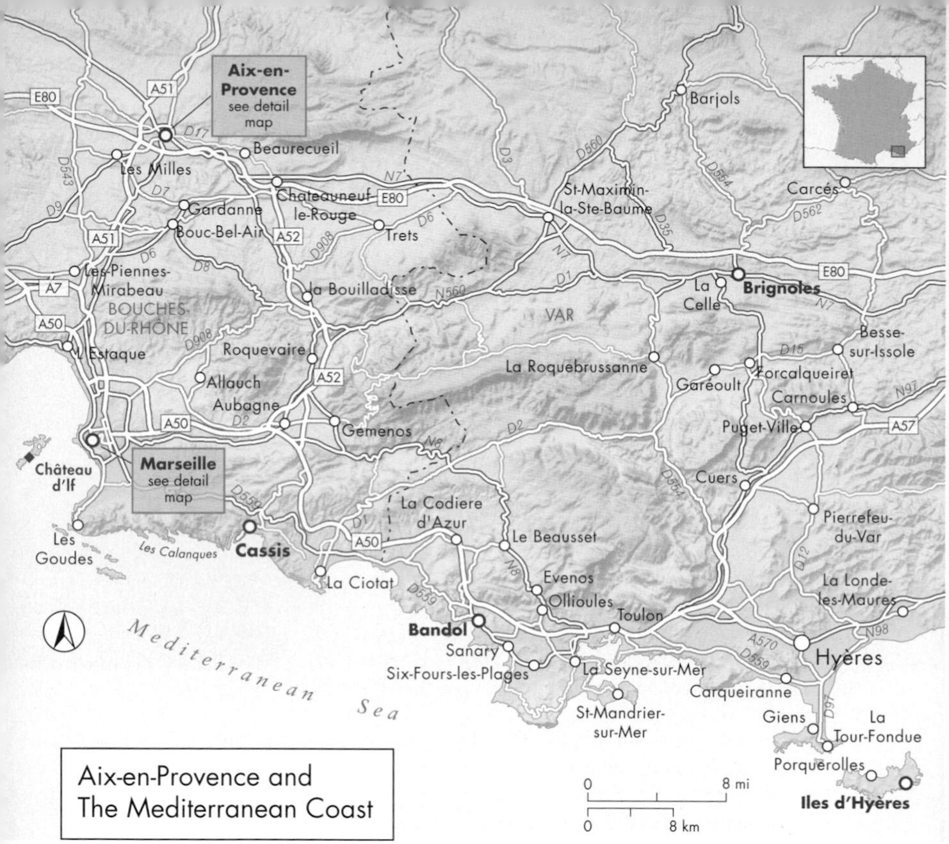

Aix-en-Provence and The Mediterranean Coast

(quai des Belges). Tours are organized by various firms, including Icard Maritime, with a three-hour round-trip costing around €26. ✉ *1 quai Marcel Pagnol, Marseille* 🌐 *visite-des-calanques.com.*

WHERE TO EAT AND STAY

For expanded hotel reviews, visit Fodors.com.

$$$ SEAFOOD 🍴 **Nino.** This is the best of the many restaurants lining the harbor, with top-notch Provençal food and wine, plus a spectacular terrace view. The owners, Claudie and Bruno, are extremely hospitable as long as you stick to the menu (don't ask for sauce on the side!) and are as passionate about seafood as they are. The sardines in *escabeche* are textbook perfect, as are the grilled fish and the bouillabaisse. If you wish to linger, two suites and one guest room are beautifully decorated and feature views of the sea. [$] *Average main: €25* ✉ *1 quai Barthélémy* ☎ *04–42–01–74–32* 🌐 *www.nino-cassis.com* ✍ *Reservations essential* ⏲ *Closed Mon. and Nov.–Feb. No dinner Sun. off-season.*

$$$ HOTEL 🏨 **Les Roches Blanches.** First built as a private home in 1887, this cliff-side villa takes in smashing views of the port and the Cap Canaille, both from the best rooms and from the panoramic dining hall. **Pros:** sweeping vistas are captivating; service is quick and friendly; 75% of rooms have balconies. **Cons:** can be hard to find; breakfast is expensive. [$] *Rooms from: €180* ✉ *Rte. des Calanques* ☎ *04–42–01–09–30*

⊕ www.roches-blanches-cassis.com ⇨ 19 rooms, 5 suites ⊙ Closed Nov.–Mar. ⏹ Some meals.

SPORTS AND THE OUTDOORS

To go on a **boat ride** to Les Calanques, arrive at the port around 9:30 and look for a vessel that's loading passengers. Round-trips should include visits to at least three calanques and average €18. To **hike** the calanques, gauge your skills: the GR98 (marked with red-and-white bands) is the most scenic, but requires scrambling to get down the sheer walls of En Vau. The alternative is to follow the green markers and approach En Vau from behind. If you're ambitious, you can hike the length of the GR98 between Marseille and Cassis, following the coastline.

BANDOL

25 km (16 miles) southeast of Cassis, 15 km (9 miles) west of Toulon.

Although its name means wine to most of the world, Bandol is also a popular and highly developed seaside resort town. It has seafood snack shacks, generic brasseries, a harbor packed with yachts, and a waterfront promenade. Yet the east end of town conceals lovely old villas framed in mimosas, bougainvillea, and pine. And a port-side stroll up the palm-lined allée Jean-Moulin feels downright Côte d'Azur. But be warned: the sheer concentration of high-summer crowds cannot be exaggerated. If you're not a beach lover, pick up an itinerary from the tourist office and visit a few Bandol vineyards just outside town.

BRIGNOLES

86 km (47 miles) northwest of Bandol, 70 km (39 miles) north of Toulon.

This rambling backcountry hill town, crowned with a medieval château, is the market center for the wines of the Var—it's also the crossroads of an up-and-coming region. With a Ducasse restaurant now in the area, real estate has rocketed, and le tout Paris whispers that this little corner of nowheresville is *the* next Luberon. The region's main point of interest is the **Abbaye de La Celle**, a 12th-century Benedictine abbey that served as a convent until the 17th century. There's a refectory and a ruined cloister; the simple Romanesque chapel still serves as the parish church.

ILES D'HYÈRES

32 km (20 miles) off coast south of Hyères. To get to islands, follow narrow Giens Peninsula to La Tour-Fondue, at its tip. Boats (leaving every half hr in summer, every 60 or 90 mins rest of year, for €17.30 round-trip) make a 20-min beeline to Porquerolles. For Port-Cros and Levant, depart from Port d'Hyères at Hyères-Plages (⊕ www.tlv-tvm. com).

Off the southeastern point of France's star and spanning some 32 km (20 miles), this archipelago could be a set for a pirate movie; in fact, it has been featured in several, thanks to a soothing microclimate and a wild, rocky coastline dotted with palms. And not only film pirates have made their appearances: in the 16th century the islands were seeded with convicts to work the land. They soon ran amok and used their adopted base to ambush ships heading into Toulon. A more honest population claims the islands today, which are made up of three main areas. **Port-Cros** is a national park, with both its surface and underwater environs protected. **Levant** has been taken over, for the most part, by nudists.

Porquerolles is the largest and best of the lot—and a popular escape from the modern world. Off-season, it's a castaway delight of pine forests, sandy beaches, and vertiginous cliffs above rocky coastline. Inland, its preserved pine forests and orchards of olives and figs are crisscrossed with dirt roads to be explored on foot or on bikes; except for the occasional jeep or work truck, the island is car-free. In high season (April to October), day-trippers pour off the ferries and surge to the beaches. For information on the islands, contact the tourism office of Hyères.

WHERE TO STAY

For expanded hotel reviews, visit Fodors.com.

$$$$ B&B/INN 🏨 **Les Glycines.** In soft shades of yellow-ocher and sky-blue, this sleekly modernized little bastide has an idyllic enclosed courtyard, as well as some lovely guest rooms with views over a jungle of mimosa and eucalyptus. **Pros:** quiet and simply elegant; set just back from the port in the village center. **Cons:** some rooms are small; beds can be creaky. [$] *Rooms from: €338* ✉ *Pl. d'Armes, Ile de Porquerolles* ☎ *04–94–58–30–36* 🌐 *www.auberge-glycines.com* 🛏 *8 rooms, 3 suites* 🍴 *Some meals.*

$$$$ HOTEL 🏨 **Mas du Langoustier.** A fabled forgetaway, the Langoustier comes with a lobster-orange building, pink bougainvillea, a choice of California-modern- or old-Provençal-style guest rooms, and a secluded location at the westernmost point of the Ile de Porquerolles. **Pros:** a bastion of taste; can "upgrade" to dinner at L'Olivier; beach nearby and pool on-site. **Cons:** a hike to get here; no rooms have a sea view. [$] *Rooms from: €450* ✉ *Pointe du Langoustier, 3 km (2 miles) from the harbor, Ile de Porquerolles* ☎ *04–94–58–30–09* 🌐 *www.langoustier.com* 🛏 *44 rooms, 5 apartments* 🕒 *Closed Oct.–Apr. Restaurant L'Olivier: No dinner Sun.; closed Mon. Sept.–June* 🍴 *Some meals.*

THE FRENCH
RIVIERA

WELCOME TO THE FRENCH RIVIERA

TOP REASONS TO GO

★ **Mingle with Picasso and company:** Because artists have long loved the Côte d'Azur, it's blessed with superb art museums, including the Fondation Maeght in St-Paul and the Musée Picasso in Antibes.

★ **Soak up the scene in St-Tropez:** Brave the world's most outlandish fishing port in high summer, but don't forget the sunglasses and suntan lotion.

★ **Step into the toy kingdom of Monaco:** On your foray into one of the world's most expensive addresses, you'll encounter tropical gardens, Belle Époque grace notes, casinos, and skyscrapers.

★ **Take in the views from Èze:** An island in the sky, Èze has some of the most breathtaking views this side of a NASA space capsule.

★ **Get a sense of the Old Riviera in Nice:** With its bonbon-color palaces, blue Baie des Anges, time-stained Old Town, and Musée Matisse, this is one of France's most colorful and fabled cities.

1 St-Tropez to Antibes. Put on the map by Brigitte Bardot, St-Tropez remains one of France's ritziest vacation spots, small and laid-back. Conspicuous consumption characterizes the celluloid city of Cannes when its May film fest turns it into Oscar-goes-to-the-Mediterranean, but the Louis Vuitton set enjoys this city year-round. For the utmost in Riviera charm, head up the coast to Antibes: once Picasso's home, it has a harbor and an Old Town so dreamy you'll be reaching for your paintbrush.

ITALY

Menton

Vence
St-Paul-de-Vence
Villefranche-sur-Mer
Èze
Monte-Carlo
MONACO
St-Jean-Cap-Ferrat
Nice
Cagnes-sur-Mer

Baie des Anges

EASTERN CÔTE d'AZUR

Antibes

Cap d'Antibes

Cannes

N202
N7
A8
A8
N7

0   7.5 mi

0   7.5 km

12

GETTING ORIENTED

The French Riviera can supply visitors with everything their hearts desire—and the purse can stand. Home to sophisticated resorts beloved by billionaires, remote hill villages colonized by artists, Mediterranean beaches, and magnificent views, the Côte d'Azur (to use the French name) stretches from Marseille to Menton. Thrust out like two gigantic arms, divided by the Valley of the Var at Nice, the peaks of the Alpes-Maritimes throw their massive protection, east and west, the length of the favored coast all the way from St-Tropez to the Italian frontier.

2 The Hill Towns. High in the hills overlooking Nice are the medieval walled villages of St-Paul-de-Vence and Vence, invaded by waves of artists in the 20th century. Today, you can hardly turn around without bumping into a Calder mobile, and top sights include the famous inn La Colombe d'Or, Matisse's sublime Chapelle du Rosaire, and the Fondation Maeght—probably the best museum this side of the Louvre.

3 Nice. Walking along the seaside promenade des Anglais is one of the iconic Riviera experiences. Add in top-notch museums, a charming old quarter, scads of ethnic restaurants, and a world-class Carnival, and Nice is one of France's most rewarding cities.

4 The Eastern Côte d'Azur. The 24-karat sun shines most brightly on the glamorous ports of Villefranche-sur-Mer and St-Jean-Cap-Ferrat. If you want to kiss the sky, head up to the charming, mountaintop village of Èze. To the east of glittering Monaco—looking more like Manhattan every day—lies Menton, an enchanting Italianate resort where winters are so mild that lemon trees bloom in January.

Updated by
Nancy Heslin

You may build castles in Spain or picture yourself on a South Sea island, but when it comes to serious speculation about how to spend that first $10 million and slip easily into the life of the idle rich, most people head for the French Riviera.

This is where the azure waters and indigo sky begin, where balustraded white villas edge the blue horizon, the evening air is perfumed with jasmine, and parasol pines are silhouetted against sunsets of ripe apricot. As emblematic as the sheet-music cover for a Jazz Age tune, the French Riviera seems to epitomize happiness, a state of being the world pursues with a vengeance.

But the Jazz Age dream confronts modern reality: on the hills that undulate along the blue water, every cliff bristles with cubes of hot-pink cement and balconies of ironwork, each skewed to catch a glimpse of the sea and the sun. Like a rosy rash, these crawl and spread, outnumbering the trees and blocking each other's views. But the Côte d'Azur (or Azure Coast) has always been exceedingly popular, starting with the ancient Greeks, who were drawn eastward from Marseille to market their goods to the natives. From the 18th-century English aristocrats who claimed the coast as one vast spa, to the 19th-century Russian nobles who transformed Nice into a tropical St. Petersburg, to the 20th-century American tycoons who cast themselves as romantic sheiks, the beckoning coast became a blank slate for their whims. Like the modern vacationers who followed, they all left their mark—villas, shrines, Moroccan-fantasy castles—temples all to the sensual pleasures of the sun and the sultry sea breezes. Artists, too, made the French Riviera their own, as museumgoers who have studied the sunny legacy of Picasso, Renoir, Matisse, and Chagall will attest.

Today's admirers can take this all in, along with the Riviera's textbook points of interest: animated St-Tropez; the Belle Époque aura of Cannes; the towns made famous by Picasso—Antibes, Vallauris, Mougins; the urban charms of Nice; and a number of spots where the per-capita population of billionaires must be among the highest on the planet: Cap d'Antibes, Villefranche-sur-Mer, and Monaco. The latter, once a Belle Époque fairyland, now has enough skyscrapers to earn it the nickname of the Hong Kong of the Riviera. The ghosts of Grace Kelly and Cary Grant must have long since gone elsewhere.

But with just a little luck and a bus ride or two, you can find towns and villages far from the madding crowd, especially if you head to the low-lying mountains known as the *arriére-pays* (backcountry). Here, medieval stone villages cap rocky hills and play out scenes of Provençal life, with games of boules and slowly savored drinks of pastis (the anise-and-licorice-flavor spirit). Some of them—Èze, St-Paul, Vence—may have become virtual Provençal theme parks but even so you'll probably find a gorgeous and deserted Riviera alleyway hidden in one of their cobblestone mazes.

12

PLANNER

WHEN TO GO

Unless you enjoy jacked-up prices, traffic jams, and sardine-style beach crowds, avoid the coast like the plague in July and August. Many of the better restaurants simply shut down to avoid the coconut-oil crowd, and the Estérel—the rocky hillside that overlooks the Mediterranean—is closed to hikers during this flash-fire season. Cannes books up early for the film festival in May, so aim for another month (April, June, September, or October). Between Cannes and Menton, the Côte d'Azur's gentle microclimate usually provides moderate winters; it's protected by the Estérel from the mistral wind that razors through places like Fréjus and St-Raphaël.

Sexy south of France may be reputed for many steamy things, but it's not at all humid. It is, in fact, hot and dry for most of the year. Over the past 10 years high-season temperatures have gone up to 105°F, while spring and fall still see highs of 68°F. Summer wear usually boils down to a bikini and light wrap. Rainfall between March and October cools things off. Although the area is famous for having more than 340 days of sunshine per year, locals will say winter (November–early March) is cold, rainy, and miserable; in recent years, official snow days—complete with surging sea waves and road closures—have even hit parts of the coast at the end of January. This is a sign that Nice's Carnaval is around the corner.

PLANNING YOUR TIME

If you're settling into one town and making day trips, it's best to divide your time by visiting west and then east of Nice. Parallel roads along the corniches allow for access into towns with different personalities. The A8 main *autoroute* (keep spare change at the ready, as there's a toll to use different parts of this road—€2.90 between Cannes and Nice, for example) makes zipping up and down from Monaco to Fréjus-St-Raphaël a breeze. The coastal train is equally efficient.

Visit different resort towns, but make sure you tear yourself away from the coastal *plages* (beaches) to visit the perched villages that the region is famed for. Venture farther north to reach these villages, east or west, either by the route Napoléon (RN98), the D995, or on the corniche roads, and plan on at least one overnight.

RIVIERA FESTIVALS

Every month of the year there's a festival somewhere on the Riviera, catering to all manner of tastes and pastimes. The queen of all festivals is, of course, the International Film Festival in Cannes, where all the stars of today and yesterday play for 10 jam-packed days in May, but there's every other type of festival imaginable, too. To give you a small taste: in May there's the Monaco Grand Prix; in June there's the Advertising festival in Cannes; in July, the lavender festivals as well as both the Nice and Juan-les-Pins Jazz festivals; in August, the fireworks festivals; in February, the Fête du Citron (Citrus festival) in Menton, and Carnival in Nice. Check with the local tourism office to see what's happening during your stay. Tickets can be bought at local tourist offices, FNAC branches (⊕ *www.fnac.com*), or through agencies like France Billet (☎ *08–92–69–26–94* ⊕ *www.francebillet.com*) or Ticketnet (☎ *08–92–39–01–00* ⊕ *www.ticketnet.fr*).

GETTING HERE AND AROUND

The less budget-conscious can consider zipping around by helicopter (there are heliports in Monaco, Nice, Cannes, St-Tropez, and some of the hill towns) or by speedboat (providing service to all resort towns), but affordable transport along the Riviera translates to the train, the bus, or a rental car. Trains access major coastal areas, and most of the *gares* (train stations) are in town centers. Note that only a handful of hill towns have train stations, and St-Tropez is not on the train route. The bus network between towns is fantastic, and a helpful website ⊕ *www.ceparou06.fr* allows you to calculate your route anywhere in the Alpes-Maritime region. Renting a car is a good option, and the network of roads here is well marked and divided nicely into slow and very curvy (Bord de Mer Coast Road), faster and curvy (route National 98), and fast and almost straight (Autoroute A8). Make sure you leave extra time if you're driving or taking the bus, as traffic is always heavy.

AIR TRAVEL

Nice is the main point of entry into the French Riviera. It's home to the second-largest airport in France, which sits on a peninsula between Antibes and Nice. The Aéroport Nice-Côte d'Azur is 7 km (4 miles) south of the city, or a good hour's walk from the landmark Hôtel Negresco.

Contact Aéroport Nice-Côte d'Azur ☎ *08–20–42–33–33* ⊕ *www.nice. aeroport.fr*.

BOAT TRAVEL

Considering the congestion on the road to St-Tropez, the best way to get to that resort is to take the train to St-Raphaël, then hop on one of the two to four boats (April–November) that leave daily from Gare Maritime de St-Raphaël on rue Pierre-Aublé. The ride takes an hour (€14, cash only ☎ *04–94–95–17–46*). Les Bateaux Verts (✉ *Quai L.-Condroyer, Ste-Maxime* ☎ *04–94–49–83–39* ⊕ *www.bateauxverts. com*) has shuttle boats (April–October) that make the trip between St-Tropez and Ste-Maxime in 15 minutes (€7.30). Navette Bateau also offers shuttles (€6.50 ☎ *06–22–77–24–00* ⊕ *www.navette-bateau.com*). Once in St-Tropez, do the one-hour boat tour organized by Bateau

Brigantin of the Baie des Cannebiers (nicknamed "Millionaires Bay") to see some celebrity villas. Boats depart from quai Suffren in the port (☎ 06–07–09–21–27 ⊕ *www.lebrigantin.com*).

BUS TRAVEL

Note that the quickest way to get around by public transportation is the great coastal train line that connects the main cities and many villages from Cannes to Menton, but if you want to explore more remote villages, you can take a bus out of Cannes, Nice, Antibes, or Menton. Lignes d'Azur's Bus No. 100—which normally departs every 15 minutes, Monday to Saturday (every 30 minutes on Sunday) between 6 am and 8 pm—makes stops from Nice place Garibaldi to Menton via Monaco; the fare is just €1 one way. For the villages on the Moyenne corniche, take Bus No. 112, which departs from Nice Vauban six times a day (no Sunday service). Lignes d'Azur also runs buses to 24 different communes in the Alpes-Maritimes, again for the bargain price of €1 one way (an exception is the express Nice airport Bus 99 or 98, which costs €6). Ski enthusiasts, furthermore, can take advantage of the line's new "100% Snow Bus," with daily departures in season from Nice to Isola 2000, Valberg, and Auron; tickets are only €8 when purchased online.

You can catch a bus from the Antibes bus station at 1 place Guynemer, connecting with Biot (25 mins) and to Vallauris (30 mins). The new Envibus line, which originates in Antibes, covers Antibes and Biot before heading into the hills. Going west to Cannes or east to Nice, jump on the No. 200 bus (€1.50) at the Briand stop behind place de Gaulle (but note that each direction has a bus stop on a different street due to one-way traffic). Cagnes-sur-Mer is one of the coastal towns served by train, but you can easily connect with nearby St-Paul-de-Vence and Vence using Bus No. 400, with departures every 35 to 45 minutes from Cagnes Ville's bus stop in square Bourdet. From St-Tropez's Gare Routière, on avenue du Général de Gaulle, buses operated by VarLib travel to and from St-Raphaël (1½ hrs, €2), the town with the nearest railway station, with stops along the way in Port Grimaud and Fréjus (1 hr, €2). In high season, traffic can lead to two-plus-hour bus rides, so if you arrive in St-Raphaël, it may be best to hop on the shuttle boats that connect the two ports.

In Monaco, Compagnie des Autobus de Monaco (CAM) runs five bus lines with service throughout the principality. You can purchase the €2 ticket or €5 all-day pass from the driver or at the main station (where the fare costs slightly less) on 3 avenue du President J. F. Kennedy. CAM's *bateau* (boat) bus (€2) crosses the port 8 am–8 pm and connects with its bus line.

Nice bus stations are spread across the city, in: Vaubun (north and regional buses to Marseille, Aix); Gare SNCF; place Blanqui (airport bus); Station J. C. Bermond (main hub); Cathédrale Vieille Ville; Alberti/Gioffredo and Albert 1er. ■**TIP→** You'll find a comprehensive listing of all bus routes at ⊕ www.cg06.fr. Click on Servir-les-habitants>Deplacements>Transport collectifs>Lignes et horaires.

Contacts **Compagnie des Autobus de Monaco** ☎ *377/97–70–22–22* ⊕ *www. cam.mc*. **Envibus**. Antibes, Juans-les-Pins, Biot, Valbonne, Saint-Paul, and

Gordon. ☎ *04-89-87-72-00* ⊕ *www.envibus.fr*. **Lignes d'Azur**. Urban routes in Nice and the Côte d'Azur including Beaulieu, Eze, Nice, Vence, Villefranche etc., and the Nice tram. ☎ *08-10-06-10-06* ⊕ *www.lignesdazur.com*.
VarLib. Included in the 248 routes between Var municipalities are Toulon, Draguignan, Fréjus-St-Raphaël, and St-Tropez, with links to smaller villages between. ☎ *08-10-00-61-77* ⊕ *www.varlib.fr*.

CAR TRAVEL

The best way to explore the secondary sights in this region is by car. A car also allows you the freedom to zip along A8 between the coastal resorts and to enjoy the views from the three corniches that trace the shoreline from Nice to the Italian border. N98, which connects to coastal resorts in between, can be slow, though scenic. A8 parallels the coast from above St-Tropez to Nice to the resorts on the Grand corniche; N98 follows the coast more closely. From Paris the main southbound artery is A6/A7, known as the Autoroute du Soleil; it passes through Provence and joins the eastbound A8 at Aix-en-Provence. ■**TIP→** The website ⊕ **www.prix-carburants.gouv.fr** compares gas prices across the country to help you find the cheapest stations where you can fill up.

TRAIN TRAVEL

Nice is the rail crossroads for trains arriving from Paris and other northern cities and from Italy, too. To get from Paris to Nice (with stops along the coast), you can take the TGV (☎ *36-35 [€0.34 per min]* ⊕ *www.tgv.com*), though it only maintains high speeds to Valence. Night trains arrive at Nice in the morning from Paris.

You can easily move along the coast between Cannes, Nice, and Ventimiglia by train on the slick double-decker Côte d'Azur line, a dramatic and highly tourist-pleasing branch of the SNCF (☎ *36-35 [€0.34 per min]* ⊕ *www.sncf.com*) that offers panoramic views as it rolls from one famous resort to the next, with more than two dozen trains running a day. This line is also called Marseille–Vintimille (Ventimiglia, in Italy) heading east to Italy and Vintimille–Marseille in the west direction. Some main stops on this line are: Antibes, Cannes, Menton, and Monaco; other stops include Villefranche-sur-Mer, Beaulieu, Cap-Martin, St-Jean-Cap-Ferrat, and Èze-sur-Mer. However, to reach St-Paul, Vence, Peillon, and other backcountry villages, you must take a bus or car.

For the western parts of the French Riviera, catch trains at Fréjus's main station on rue Martin-Bidoure and St-Raphaël's Gare de St-Raphaël on rue Waldeck-Rousseau, where the rail route begins its scenic crawl along the coast. St-Raphaël is the main hub on the line between Menton and Marseille (it's about 1 hr, 40 mins from the latter by rail, with hourly trains costing €27). The resort port of Mandelieu-La Napoule is on the main rail line between St-Raphaël and Cannes. There's no rail access to St-Tropez; St-Raphaël and Fréjus are the nearest stops. ■**TIP→** "Tarifs prem" are the cheapest train fares available from SNCF on a limited number of TGV tickets purchased 90 days before travel date, but there is no exchange. "Loisir" fares are flexible and offer peace of mind for the spontaneous traveler.

Contacts **SNCF** ☏ *36–35 [€0.34 per min]* ⊕ *www.sncf.com*. **TGV** ☏ *36–35 [€0.34 per min]* ⊕ *www.tgv.com*.

RESTAURANTS

Even in tiny villages some haute-cuisine places can be as dressy as those in Monaco, if not more so, but in general, restaurants on the Côte d'Azur are quite relaxed. At lunchtime, a T-shirt and shorts are just fine in all but the fanciest places; bathing suits, however, should be kept for the beach. Nighttime wear is casual, too—but be aware that for after-dinner drinks, many clubs and discos draw the line at running shoes. Food plays a crucial role in the south of France, and some of the best restaurants aren't so easy to access; make sure to include taxi money in your budget to get to some of the more remote restaurants, or plan on renting a car. Try to come in truffle, lavender, or olive season.

Prices in the reviews are the average cost of a main course at dinner or, if dinner is not served, at lunch.

HOTELS

It's up in the hills above the coast that you'll find the charm you expect from France, both in sophisticated hotels with gastronomic restaurants and in friendly mom-and-pop auberges (inns); the farther north you drive, the lower the prices. Of course, certain areas of the Riviera book up faster than others, but all hit overload from June to September. It's essential to book in advance; up to half a year for the summer season is not unheard of, and is, in fact, much appreciated. Festivals and good weather will also affect your chances. If you arrive without a reservation, try the tourist information centers, which can usually be of help.

Prices in the reviews are the lowest cost of a standard double room in high season.

VISITOR INFORMATION

Regional tourist offices prefer written queries only. *Local tourist offices for major towns are listed under the towns covered in this chapter.* For information on travel around St-Tropez, write to the Tourisme du Var. For Marseille to Cannes over to Menton, write to the Comité Regional du Tourisme de Provence-Alpes-Côte d'Azur.

Contacts **Comité Regional du Tourisme de Provence-Alpes-Côte d'Azur** ⊠ *61 La Canabière, Marseille* ☏ *04–91–56–47–00* ⊕ *www.tourismepaca.fr*. **Tourisme du Var (L'Agence de Développement Touristique)** ⊠ *1 bd. de Strasbourg, BP 5147, Toulon* ☏ *04–94–18–59–60* ⊕ *www.visitvar.fr*.

TOUR OPTIONS

Bus Tours: Santa Azur (⊠ *11 av. Jean-Médecin* ☏ *04–97–03–60–00*) orga-nizes all-day bus excursions to sights near Nice, including Monaco, Cannes, and nearby hill towns, either leaving from its offices or from several stops along the promenade des Anglais, mainly in front of the big hotels. Also in Nice, Phocéens Voyages (⊠ *4 pl. Masséna* ☏ *04–93–13–18–20*) organizes some excellent bus explorations of the region.

Bike Tours: For a fun, active way to discover the region, consider a guided bike tour. Departing from Hi Beach, near the Hôtel Negresco on the promenade in Nice, the female-run Cycle Côte d'Azur (⊕ *www.*

cyclecotedazur.com) gives tours on two wheels for all ages, all levels. Beginners can take three rides for €30; more experienced riders can make a day trip to a medieval village for €45 (plus bike rental, in some cases). It's an exceptional way to see the *pays-arrière*—backcountry—in the hills behind Nice, and the temperatures are pleasantly cooler in the summer months.

Personalized Tours: From jet-skiing to helicopter lessons, wine tasting to whale-watching, Mira Guchan-Mclean is the one to hook you up. As your Friend in France (⊕ *www.friend-in-france.com*), Mira could quickly become your BFF by taking you on some rather exceptional adventures including "Meet Friendly Locals" and "Family Friendly" activities. Half- and full-day tours in the region and to Provence are also possible.

THE WESTERN FRENCH RIVIERA

Flanked at each end by subtropical capes and crowned by the red-rock Estérel, this stretch of the coast has a variety of waterfront landmarks. St-Tropez first blazed into fame when it was discovered by painters like Paul Signac and writers like Colette, and since then it has never looked back. It remains one of the most animated stretches of territory on the French Riviera, getting flooded at high season with people who like to roost at waterfront cafés to take in the passing parade. St-Tropez vies with Cannes for name recognition and glamour, but the more modest resorts—Ste-Maxime, Fréjus, and St-Raphaël—offer a more affordable Riviera experience. Historic Antibes and jazzy Juan-les-Pins straddle the subtropical peninsula of Cap d'Antibes.

ST-TROPEZ

35 km (22 miles) southwest of Fréjus, 66 km (41 miles) northeast of Toulon.

At first glance, St-Tropez really doesn't look all that lovely: there's a moderately pretty port full of bobbing boats, a picturesque Vieille Ville (Old Town) in candied-almond hues, sandy beaches, and old-fashioned squares with plane trees and *pétanque* (lawn bowling) players. So what made St-Tropez a household name? In two words: Brigitte Bardot. When this *pulpeuse* (voluptuous) teenager showed up in St-Tropez on the arm of the late Roger Vadim in 1956 to film *And God Created Woman*, the world snapped to attention. Neither the gentle descriptions of writer Guy de Maupassant (1850–93) nor the watercolor tones of Impressionist Paul Signac (1863–1935), nor even the stream of painters who followed him (including Matisse and Bonnard), could focus the world's attention on this seaside hamlet as could this one luscious female, in head scarf, Ray-Bans, and capri pants. With the film world following in her steps, St-Tropez became the hot spot it—to some extent—remains.

GETTING HERE

You can only get to St-Trop by car, bus, or boat (from nearby ports like St-Raphaël). If you decide to drive, take the N98 coast road (the longest route but also the prettiest, with great picnic stops along the way).

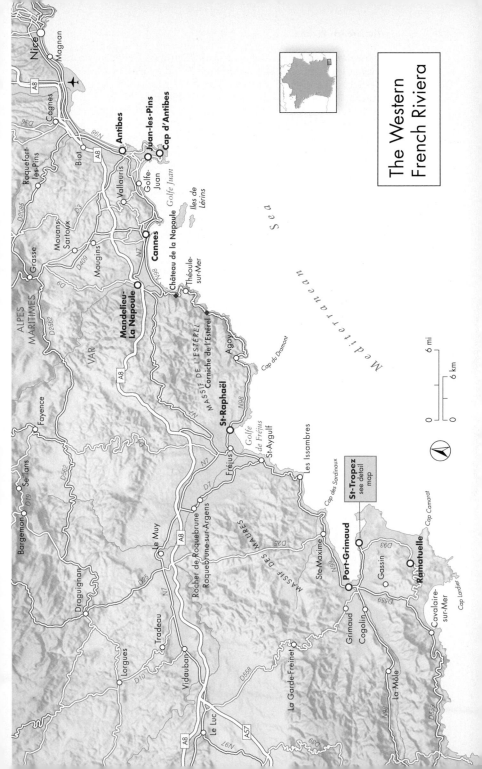

The Western French Riviera

Note that the Parking du Port parking lot (opposite the bus station on avenue du Général de Gaulle) and the Parc des Lices (beneath the place des Lices) in the center of town charge a staggering €5 an hour in peak season. A train-bus connection can be made from Nice; the train runs to St-Raphaël, where you can catch the No. 7601 VarLib bus (☏ 08–10–00–61–77 ⊕ www.varlib.fr) for the 90-minute trip onward to St-Tropez (€2). The other option is to take a boat from the Nice harbor with Trans Côte d'Azur (☏ 04–92–00–42–30 ⊕ www.trans-cote-azur.com), which has daily trips from June to September and costs around €61 round-trip. Within St-Tropez, three free shuttle routes (including one that deposits you near plage de Pampelonne) run year-round from place des Lices.

Visitor Information St-Tropez Tourist Office ✉ Quai Jean-Jaurès, BP 183 ☏ 04-94-97-45-21 ⊕ www.ot-saint-tropez.com.

EXPLORING

Anything associated with the distant past seems almost absurd in St-Tropez. Still, the place has a history that predates the invention of the string bikini, and people have been finding reasons to come here since AD 68, when a Roman soldier from Pisa named Torpes was beheaded for professing his Christian faith in front of Emperor Nero, transforming this spot into a place of pilgrimage.

Since then people have come for the sun, the sea, and, more recently, the celebrities. The latter—ever since St-Tropez became "hot" again, there have been Elton, Barbra, and Oprah sightings—stay hidden in villas, so the people you'll see are mere mortals, lots of them, many intent on displaying the best, and often the most, of their youth, beauty, and wealth.

Get up early (before the 11 am breakfast rush at Le Gorille Café and other port-side spots lining quai Suffern and quai Jean-Jaurès) and wander the narrow medieval backstreets and waterfront by yourself—the rest of the town will still be sleeping off the Night Before. At this hour, you can experience what the artists found to love: the soft light, warm pastels, and the scent of the sea wafting in from the waterfront. Later, when you're tired, you can sit under a colored awning at a cute café and watch the spectacle that is St-Trop (*trop* in French means "too much") saunter by.

Start your St-Trop tour at the *nouveau bassin* (new harbor) for private pleasure boats. There's a large parking lot and the bus station here. With the sea on your left, walk around to the Vieux Port (old harbor), enjoying the life of the quays and the views around the bay as you go. Then head over to plage de Pampelonne's Club 55 on boulevard Patch: what used to be the original canteen during the filming of *And God Created Women* is now a legendary lunch location. (☏ 04–94–55–55–55 ☞ *Reservations essential*).

Citadelle. Head up rue de la Citadelle to these 16th-century ramparts, which stand in a lovely hilltop park offering a fantastic view of the town and the sea. Amid today's bikini-clad sun worshippers it's hard to imagine St-Tropez as a military outpost, but inside the Citadelle's donjon the new *Musée de l'histoire maritime tropézienne* proves otherwise. ✉ *Rue de la Citadelle* ☎ *04–94–97–59–43* 🎫 *Citadelle €2.50* ⊙ *Oct.–Mar., daily 10–12:30 and 1:30–5:30; Apr.–Sept., daily 10–6:30.*

Musée de l'Annonciade (*Annunciation Museum*). The legacy of the artists who loved St-Tropez has been lovingly preserved in this extraordinary museum, housed in a 14th-century chapel just inland from the southwest corner of the Vieux Port. Cutting-edge temporary exhibitions keep visitors on their toes while works stretching from Pointillists to Fauves to Cubists line the walls. Signac, Matisse, Signard, Braque, Dufy, Vuillard, and Rouault are all here, and their work traces the evolution of painting from Impressionism to Expressionism. The museum also hosts temporary exhibitions every summer, from local talent to up-and-coming international artists. ✉ *Quai de l'Épi/pl. Georges Grammont* ☎ *04–94–17–84–10* 🎫 *€6* ⊙ *Jan.–Oct. and Dec., Wed.–Mon. 10–noon and 2–6.*

Place des Lices. Enjoy a time-out in the the social center of the Old Town, also called the place Carnot, just off the Montée G.-Ringrave as you descend from the Citadelle. A symmetrical forest of plane trees provides shade to rows of cafés and restaurants, skateboarders, children, and grandfatherly pétanque players. The square becomes a moveable feast (for both eyes and palate) on market days—Tuesday and Saturday—while at night a café seat is as hotly contested as a quayside seat during the day. Just as Deborah Kerr and David Niven once did in *Bonjour Tristesse,* watch the boule players under the glow of hundreds of electric bulbs. Heading back to the Vieux Port area, take in the boutiques lining rues Sibilli, Clemenceau, or Gambetta to help accessorize your evening look—you never know when that photographer from *Elle* will be snapping away at the trendoisie.

Quartier de la Ponche. This Old Town maze of backstreets and ramparts is daubed in shades of gold, pink, ocher, and sky-blue. Trellised jasmine and wrought-iron birdcages hang from the shuttered windows, and many of the tiny streets dead-end at the sea. Here you can find the **Port des Pécheurs** (Fishermen's Port), on whose beach Bardot did a star-turn in *And God Created Woman.* Twisting, narrow streets, designed to break the impact of the mistral, open to tiny squares with fountains. The main drag here, rue de la Ponche, leads into place l'Hôtel de Ville, landmarked by a **mairie** (town hall) marked out in typical Tropezienne hues of pink and green.

Vieux Port. Bordered by quai de l'Épi, quai Bouchard, quai Peri, quai Suffren, and quai Jean-Jaurès, Vieux Port is a place for strolling and looking over the shoulders of artists painting their versions of the view on easels set up along the water's edge. Meanwhile, folding director's chairs at the famous port-side cafés Le Gorille (named for its late, exceptionally hirsute manager), Café de Paris, and Sénéquier's are well placed for observing the cast of St-Tropez's living theater play out its colorful roles.

WHERE TO EAT

$$$$ ✗ **Au Caprice des Deux.** After overdosing on the high-octane people—

FRENCH and prices—that pepper the popular spots of St-Trop, it is a wonderful surprise to come across this charmingly authentic restaurant in a picturesque village house tucked behind the port. Filled with happy,

St-Tropez

relaxed regulars, the menu features tasty French delicacies such as spicy beef salad, egg cocotte with truffles, crab cannelloni with shrimp sauce, and grilled scallops with truffle risotto. The extensive dessert menu —which includes choices like *moelleux au chocolat* and *crème caramel façon grand-mère*—will make things difficult, but you can take your time deciding on the charming terrace. $ *Average main: €35* ⊠ *40 rue Portail Neuf* ☎ *04–94–97–76–78* ⊕ *www.aucapricedesdeux.com* ⊘ *Closed Jan.–mid-Feb.; closed Sun.–Wed. in Nov., Dec., Feb., and Mar. No lunch.*

$$$ ✕ **La Table du Marché.** This charming bistro, tearoom, and boutique from
BISTRO   celebrity chef Christophe Leroy offers up a mouthwatering spread of regional specialties in a surprisingly casual atmosphere. The service is warm, and the homey fare includes mac-and-cheese made chic with lobster, tomato *pistou* tart, and whipped potatoes with truffles. Lunchtime visitors can dive into a nicely balanced set menu or choose from a selection of goods seductively on display. $ *Average main: €35* ⊠ *21 bis rue Allard* ☎ *04–94–97–91–91* ⊕ *www.christophe-leroy.com* ⊘ *Closed Nov.–end Mar.*

$$ ✕ **Le Café.** The busy terrace here often doubles as a stadium for differ-
BISTRO   ent factions cheering on favorite local pétanque players in the place des Lices. You, too, can play: just borrow some boules from the friendly bar staff, and get your pastis bottle at the ready—you'll need it to properly

appreciate the full pétanque experience. Hilarious "beginner" pétanque soirees are on tap Saturday nights in spring and summer. The food is as good as the setting (try the Provençal beef stew or traditional fish soup), and there's a well-priced lunch menu. Open daily from 8 am to 3 am, Le Café is always busy, so reservations are strongly recommended. $ *Average main: €22* ⊠ *5 pl. des Lices* ☏ *04–94–97–44–69* ⊕ *www.lecafe.fr.*

$$$ ✕ **Le Girelier.** Fish, fish, and more fish—sea bass, salmon, sole, sardines,
SEAFOOD monkfish, lobster, crayfish: They're painted on the walls, sizzle on the grill, fill the boats that pull into the Old Port, and find their way into the hands of chefs David Didelot and Laurent Simon, who've earned two Michelin *fourchettes*. A buffed and bronzed clientele enjoy the casual sea-shanty atmosphere and highly visible Vieux Port terrace tables. Grilling (with a little thyme and perhaps a whisper of olive oil and garlic) is the order of the day here, with most fish sold by weight (beware the check), but this is also a stronghold for bouillabaisse. There's beef on the menu, too. The set menu is one of the best bargains in town. $ *Average main: €34* ⊠ *Quai Jean-Jaurès* ☏ *04–94–97–03–87* ⊕ *www. legirelier.fr* ☉ *Closed Nov.–mid-Mar.*

WHERE TO STAY
For expanded hotel reviews, visit Fodors.com.

$$$$ ⌂ **Café Hotel Ermitage.** Surrounded by mimosas and lemon trees atop the
HOTEL rocky hills of St-Tropez, this secluded hotel with its arty 1950s decor guarantees unobstructed vistas. **Pros:** Khiel's beauty products in rooms; only two minutes from place des Lices. **Cons:** rooms facing the street can be noisy; "S" rooms are indeed small. $ *Rooms from: €320* ⊠ *Av. Paul-Signac* ☏ *04–94–81–08–10* ⊕ *www.ermitagehotel.fr* ⌁ *24 rooms* ☉ *Closed Jan. and Feb.*

$$$ ⌂ **Hôtel B. Lodge.** All the small, delicately contemporary rooms of this
HOTEL four-story charmer overlook the Citadelle's green park, some from tiny balconies. **Pros:** good deal for location; rooms without air-conditioning are cheaper. **Cons:** with only two available parking spots, street parking is a sticky proposition; small rooms. $ *Rooms from: €180* ⊠ *23 rue de l'Aïoli* ☏ *04–94–97–06–57* ⊕ *www.hotel-b-lodge.com* ⌁ *13 rooms, 2 suites* ☉ *Closed 3 wks from mid-Jan.* ⦿ *Breakfast.*

$$$$ ⌂ **La Bastide de St Tropez.** Clean lines, tasteful decor, elegant colors, a
HOTEL private terrace or garden—and in some cases a Jacuzzi—for each room add to the allure of this luxe hotel. **Pros:** free shuttle from May to September into the town center; warm welcome. **Cons:** a bit far from the heart of the action; can be rather noisy (for quiet, ask for a room on the top floor). $ *Rooms from: €660* ⊠ *Rte. des Carles* ☏ *04–94–55–82–55* ⊕ *www.bastide-saint-tropez.com* ⌁ *26 rooms* ☉ *Closed Jan.–mid-Feb.* ⦿ *Some meals.*

$ ⌂ **La Belle Isnarde.** The Robert family has been greeting guests at this
HOTEL villa, just minutes from place des Lices, since 1965. **Pros:** lots of free parking; cheap rates for St-Tropez. **Cons:** a three-minute taxi to town costs €20; zero amenities; beds on the soft side. $ *Rooms from: €100* ⊠ *Début rte. de la plage Tahiti, B.P. 39* ☏ *04–94–97–13–64* ⌁ *11 rooms* ▭ *No credit cards* ☉ *Closed Oct. 15–Easter.*

$$$$ ⌂ **Le Byblos.** At this toy Mediterranean village grouped around court-
HOTEL yards landscaped with palms, olive trees, and lavender, guest rooms

Problems in paradise? St-Tropez may be a beaut but it is outrageously priced, has hard-to-get-to beaches, and doesn't have much public transportation.

are *à la provençale* but ultra-modern in comfort. **Pros:** exquisite service, service, service; one of the world's best massages is to be had at the Byblos Spa. **Cons:** glitz wears thins; some rooms are small for the price. $ *Rooms from: €825* ⊠ *Av. Paul-Signac* ☎ *04–94–56–68–00* ⊕ *www.byblos.com* ➳ *41 rooms, 50 suites* ⊗ *Closed end of Oct.–Easter* ⏍ *Some meals.*

$$
HOTEL
Fodor's Choice
★

⚏ **Lou Cagnard.** Set inside a lovely garden courtyard, this pretty little villa hotel is owned by an enthusiastic young couple, who have fixed it up room by room; recent renovations include satellite TV and Wi-Fi (at no extra charge) in each. **Pros:** fantastic value for your money (try room No. 17); walking distance to everything. **Cons:** a few of the older rooms share a bathroom. $ *Rooms from: €108* ⊠ *18 av. Paul-Roussel* ☎ *04–94–97–04–24* ⊕ *www.hotel-lou-cagnard.com* ➳ *19 rooms* ⊗ *Closed Nov.–Jan.*

NIGHTLIFE AND THE ARTS

Château de la Moutte. Every July and August, classical music concerts are given in the gardens of the Château de la Moutte. For ticket information, inquire at the tourist office. ⊠ *Chemin de la Moutte* ☎ *04–94–96–96–94 information* ⊕ *www.lesnuitsduchateaudelamoutte.com* ⊠ *€45.*

Les Caves du Roy. Costing the devil and often jammed to the scuppers, Les Caves du Roy, a disco in the Byblos Hotel, is *the* place to see and be seen; it's filled with svelte model types and their wealthy, silver-haired fans. When you hear the theme from *Star Wars*, take note that someone other than yourself has just spent €35,000 on a Methuselah of Champagne. Virtually impossible to get into unless you book long in advance, there's a horrific door policy during high season; don't worry, it's *not* you. ✉ *Av. Paul-Signac* ☎ *04–94–97–16–02.*

VIP Room. The VIP Room draws flashy, gilded youths with deep pockets—although more and more question the "VIP" in the club's name. You can only dance the night away from Easter to October. ✉ *Residence du Nouveau Port* ☎ *01–58–36–46–00* ⊕ *st-tropez.viproom.fr.*

SHOPPING

Designer boutiques may be spreading like wild mushrooms all over St-Tropez, but the main fashionista strutting platform is along **rue Gambetta** or **rue Allard.** For those who balk at spending a small fortune on the latest strappy sandal, **rue Sibilli,** behind the quai Suffren, is lined with all kinds of trendy, more affordable boutiques. The **place des Lices** overflows with produce, regional foods, clothing, and *brocantes* (collectibles) on Tuesday and Saturday mornings. Don't miss the picturesque little fish market that fills up **place aux Herbes** every morning.

■**TIP→** La Grande Braderie (St-Tropez's end-of-season sale) takes place the last weekend in October, from Friday to Monday, 9 to 9. Be prepared to fight the crowds for bargains on clothing you couldn't have afforded in May (and maybe still can't!).

RAMATUELLE

12 km (7 miles) southwest of St-Tropez.

Plage de Pamplonne. Not far from town, this famous, highly commercialized beach has a 5-km (3-mile) sweep of sand and is home to some 50 beachside restaurants—including the classic Club 55. After lingering over lunch there, head to über-stylish Nikki Beach and rent a bed poolside for a digestive nap. Don't worry, you won't oversleep—the DJ turns up the volume at 5 pm announcing that's it's time for champagne showers (at €250 a pop). The No. 7703 bus runs from the St. Tropez bus station to the plage's boulevard Patch (€2). ✉ *Plage de Pamplonne, 6 km (3.5 miles) from St-Tropez via D93* ☎ *04–94–55–55–55* ⊕ *www. leclub55.com.*

PORT-GRIMAUD

7 km (4½ miles) west of St-Tropez.

Although much of the coast has been targeted with new construction of extraordinary ugliness, this modern architect's version of a Provençal fishing village works. A true operetta set begun in 1966, the village has grown gracefully over the years, and offers hope for the pink-concrete-scarred coastal landscape. It's worth parking and wandering up the village's Venice-like canals to admire its Old Mediterranean canal-tile roofs and pastel facades, already patinated with age. Even the church, though resolutely modern, feels Romanesque. There is, however, one modern touch some might appreciate: small electric tour boats (get them at place du Marché) that carry you for a small charge from bar to shop to restaurant throughout the complex of pretty squares and bridges.

ST-RAPHAËL

38 km (24 miles) northeast of St-Tropez, 41 km (25½ miles) southwest of Cannes.

Right next door to Fréjus, with almost no division between, St-Raphaël is a sprawling resort town with a busy downtown anchored by a casino. It's also a major sailing center, has three golf courses nearby, and draws the weary and indulgent to its seawater-based thalassotherapy spas. St-Raphaël serves as a major rail crossroads, the closest stop to St-Tropez.

GETTING HERE

St-Raphaël is the western terminus of SNCF's regional TER line that runs along the Riviera. To get to towns farther west, you have to take a bus from just behind the St-Raphaël-Valescure train station (✉ *Pl. de la Gare*); various companies connect with Cannes, Fréjus, and St-Tropez. Popular ferries leave from St-Raphaël's Vieux Port for St-Tropez, the Iles-de-Lérins, and the Calanques de l'Esterel.

Visitor Information St-Raphaël Tourist Office ✉ *Quai Albert 1er, BP 210* ☎ *04–94–19–52–52* 🌐 *www.saint-raphael.com.*

EXPLORING

Vieille Ville (*Old Town*). St-Raphaël's Vieille Ville is a tiny enclave of charm crowned by the 12th-century **Église St-Pierre-des-Templiers,** a miniature-scale Romanesque church, and the intimate little **Musée Archéologique Marin** (Marine Archaeology Museum), both located on rue des Templiers.

St-Raphaël's port has a rich history: Napoléon landed here on his triumphant return from Egypt in 1799; it was also from here in 1814 that he cast off for Elba in disgrace. F. Scott Fitzgerald and his wife Zelda had a hideaway here, reportedly throwing some very wild parties; Dumas, Maupassant, and Berlioz also settled in for a time.

WHERE TO EAT AND STAY

For expanded hotel reviews, visit Fodors.com.

$ BRASSERIE 🍴 **La Brasserie.** Philippe Troncy is one of St. Raphael's most respected chefs, and his menus change according to the season, with market-fresh produce and simple recipes made nouveau with original twists. It will be hard to chose from the varied pasta, fish and meat dishes, but the sinfully smooth fois gras or delightful *bourride raphaëlois* (fish stew) are always good bets. The garden terrace is a shady oasis filled with magnolia and lemon trees, perfect for digesting the dark chocolate cake with bourbon and vanilla ice cream. [$] *Average main: €18* ✉ *6 av. Valescure* ☎ *04–94–95–25–00* 🌐 *www.labrasserietg.fr* ✍ *Reservations essential* 🕒 *Closed Sun. and 1st 3 wks of Jan.*

$ B&B/INN 🏨 **Le Thimothée.** This attractive 19th-century villa offers comfortable, well-priced rooms (the two on the top floor have poster-perfect sea views) as well as a lovely garden, where grand palms and pines shade the walk leading to a pretty little swimming pool. **Pros:** familial atmosphere and gentle hospitality; clean rooms and modern bathrooms. **Cons:** beach and waterfront cafés are a 20-minute walk away. [$] *Rooms from: €80* ✉ *375 bd. Christian-Lafon* ☎ *04–94–40–49–49* 🌐 *www.thimothee.com* 🛏 *12 rooms* 🕒 *Closed mid.-Dec.–1st wk in Feb.* 🍽 *Some meals.*

12

Corniche de l'Estérel. The corniche de l'Estérel (N98, the road along the dramatic coast) clings to sheer rocks faces plunging down to the waves, tiny calanques, and little coves dotted with sunbathers. Try to leave early in the morning, as tempers tend to fray when the route gets congested with afternoon traffic. ✉ *St-Raphaël.*

Massif de l'Estérel. The rugged Massif de l'Estérel, between St-Raphaël and Cannes, is a hiker's dream. Made up of rust-red volcanic rocks (porphyry) carved by the sea into dreamlike shapes, the harsh landscape is softened by patches of lavender, scrub pine, and gorse. By car, take N7, the mountain route to the north, and lose yourself in the desert landscape far from the sea. ■**TIP➜** A helpful website for walkers eager to trek the area is ⊕ www.visitvar.fr. ✉ *St-Raphaël.*

MANDELIEU–LA NAPOULE

32 km (20 miles) northeast of St-Raphaël, 8 km (5 miles) southwest of Cannes.

La Napoule is the small, old-fashioned port village, Mandelieu the big-fish resort town that devoured it. You can visit Mandelieu for a golf-and-sailing retreat—the town is replete with many sporting facilities and hosts a bevy of sporting events, including sailing regattas, windsurfing contests, and golf championships (there are two major golf courses in Mandelieu right in the center of town overlooking the water). By the sea, a yacht-crammed harbor sits under the shadow of some high-rise resort hotels. La Napoule, on the other hand, offers the requisite quaintness, ideal for a port-side stroll, casual meal, beach siesta, or visit to its peculiar castle. Mandelieu-La Napoule's train and bus stations offer frequent connections between Cannes and St-Raphaël.

Château de la Napoule. Set on Pointe des Pendus (Hanged Man's Point), the Château de la Napoule looms over the sea and the port and is a spectacularly bizarre hybrid of Romanesque, Gothic, Moroccan, and Hollywood cooked up by the eccentric American sculptor Henry Clews (1876–1937). Working with his architect-wife, Clews transformed the 14th-century bastion into something that suited his personal expectations and then filled the place with his own fantastical sculptures. The couple reside in their tombs in the tower crypt, its windows left slightly ajar to permit their souls to escape and allow them to "return at eventide as sprites and dance upon the windowsill." Today the château's foundation hosts visiting writers and artists, who set to work surrounded by Clews's gargoyle-ish sculptures. ✉ *Av. Henry Clews* ☎ *04-93-49-95-05* ⊕ *www.chateau-lanapoule.com* 💶 *€6, gardens only €3.50* ⊙ *Feb.7–Nov 7., daily 10–6, guided visits at 11:30, 2:30, 3:30, and 4:30; Nov 8.–Feb 6., weekdays 2–5, guided visits at 2:30 and 3:30; weekends 10–5, guided visits at 11:30, 2:30, and 3:30.*

WHERE TO EAT

$$$
SEAFOOD

✕ **Le Boucanier.** Wraparound plate-glass views of the marina and château make this low-ceilinged room a waterfront favorite. For 30-plus years locals have gathered here for mountains of oysters and whole fish, grilled simply and served with a drizzle of fruity olive oil, a pinch of rock salt, or a brief flambé in pastis. If you're not fish fan but want to experience the scenery, you'll also find pasta, pizzas, and steak on the menu. $ *Average main: €30* ⊠ *273 av. Henry Clews, Port de La Napoule* ☎ *04–93–49–80–51* ⊕ *www.boucanier.fr* ⊘ *Closed Dec.*

$$$$ ✕ **L'Oasis.** A culinary landmark with two Michelin stars, this Gothic
MODERN FRENCH   villa by the sea is home to Stéphane Raimbault—a master of Provençal cuisine who creates unexpected flavor collisions (think medallions of roasted blue lobster in a risotto of spaghetti *à la Puttanesca* or hazelnut venison with a pepper sauce and blueberries). A meal is accented with attentive service plus lots of extras in between courses; and few can quibble with the beauty of the famous garden terrace shadowed by gorgeous palm trees. The €98 menu shouldn't be dismissed. Le Bistro, upstairs, has earned a Michelin BIB designation for "good food at moderate prices" and offers excellent set menus Tuesday to Saturday for both lunch and dinner. Did we mention the cigar collection? $ *Average main: €80* ⊠ *Rue J. H. Carle* ☎ *04–93–49–95–52* ⊕ *www.oasis-raimbault.com* ⚐ *Reservations essential* ⊘ *Closed Sun. and Mon. and mid-Dec.–mid-Jan.*

SPORTS

Golf Club de Cannes-Mandelieu. The Golf Club de Cannes-Mandelieu is one of the most beautiful in the south of France; it's bliss to play on English turf under Mediterranean pines with mimosa blooming here and there. The club has two courses—one with 18 holes (par 71) and one with 9 (par 33). Green fees are nearly 40% less if you tee off after 4 pm. ⊠ *Rte. du Golf* ☎ *04–92–97–32–00* ⊕ *www.golfoldcourse.com.*

CANNES

6 km (4 miles) east of Mandelieu-La Napoule; 73 km (45 miles) northeast of St-Tropez; 33 km (20 miles) southwest of Nice.

A tasteful and expensive breeding ground for the upscale, Cannes is a sybaritic heaven for those who believe that life is short and sin has something to do with the absence of a tan. Backed by gentle hills and flanked to the southwest by the Estérel, warmed by dependable sun but kept bearable in summer by the cool Mediterranean breeze, Cannes is pampered with the luxurious climate that has made it one of the most popular and glamorous resorts in Europe. The cynosure of sun worshippers since the 1860s, Cannes reputation has been further enhanced by the modern success of its film festival.

GETTING HERE

Cannes has one central train station, the *Gare SNCF* (⊠ *Rue Jean Jaurès* ⊕ *www.voyages-sncf.com*), and it's under massive renovation until summer 2014, so be prepared when you see the surrounding building in a state of disarray. All major trains pass through here—check out the SNCF website for times and prices—but many of the trains run the St-Raphaël–Ventimiglia route. You can also take the TGV directly from Paris (5 hrs). Cannes's main bus station, on place de l'Hôtel-de-Ville by the port, serves all coastal destinations. Bus Azur (☎ *08–25–82–55–99* ⊕ www.silteplait.info) will take you to Mandelieu-La Napoule and Le Cannet for a fare of €1.50. Lignes d'Azur (☎ *08–00–06–01–06* ⊕ *www.lignesdazur.com*) runs most of the routes out of the bus station on place

Bernard Cornut Gentille, including Mougins (20 mins, €1.50), Grasse (45 mins, €1.50), and Vallauris (30 mins, €1.50). Bus No. 200 to Nice (2 hrs, €1.50) goes along the coast road, stopping in all villages along the way including Antibes. From the Gare SNCF, Lignes d'Azur goes to Grasse every 20 minutes Monday–Saturday and every hour Sunday, via Mougins for €1.50. To get to the Nice airport, the No. 210 Airport Express goes every 30 minutes starting at 6 am via the autoroute with a travel time of 45 minutes (⊕ *www.rca.tm.fr*). The last airport bus leaves Cannes at 7 pm and leaves the airport's T1 for Cannes at 8 pm. For the big spender, Cannes also has a heliport, with a free shuttle to the center of town: Heli Air Monaco helicopters (⊕ *www.heliairmonaco. com*) leave from the airport in Nice—the ride takes about six minutes to Cannes and costs around €100, depending on the season.

Visitor Information Cannes Tourist Office ⊠ *1 bd, de la Croisette* ☎ *04–92– 99–84–22* ⊕ *www.cannes-destination.fr.*

EXPLORING

With the democratization of modern travel, Cannes has become a tour-ist and convention town; there are now 20 compact Twingos for every Rolls-Royce. It didn't start life that way for, up to 1834, the bay served as nothing more than a fishing port. But when an English aristocrat, Lord Brougham, fell in love with the site that year during an emergency stopover with a sick daughter, he had a home built and returned every winter for a sun cure—a ritual quickly picked up by his peers. Today, glamour—and the perception of glamour—is self-perpetuating, and as long as Cannes enjoys its ravishing climate and setting, it will maintain its incomparable panache. If you're a culture lover of art of the non-celluloid type, however, you should look elsewhere—there is only one museum here, devoted to history. Still, as his lordship instantly under-stood, this is a great place to pass the winter.

La Croisette. Head to this famous waterfront promenade—which runs for 1.6 km (1 mile) from its western terminus by the Palais des Festi-vals—and allow the *esprit de Cannes* to take over. La Croisette is pre-cisely the sort of place for which the verb *flâner* (to dawdle, saunter) was invented, so stroll among the palm trees and flowers and crowds of poseurs (fur coats in tropical weather, cell phones on Rollerblades, and sunglasses at night). Continue east past the broad expanse of pri-vate beaches, glamorous shops, and luxurious hotels (among them the wedding-cake Carlton, famed for its see-and-be-seen terrace-level bras-serie). The beaches along here are almost all private, though open for a fee—each is marked with from one to four little life buoys, rating its quality and cost.

Le Suquet. Climb up rue St-Antoine into the picturesque Vieille Ville neighborhood known as Le Suquet, on the site of the original Roman *castrum*. Shops proffer Provençal goods, and the atmospheric cafés provide a place to catch your breath; the pretty pastel shutters, Gothic stonework, and narrow passageways are lovely distractions.

Malmaison. If you need a culture fix, check out the modern art and pho-tography exhibitions (admission prices vary) held at the Malmaison, a 19th-century mansion that was once part of the Grand Hotel. ⊠ *47 bd.*

La Croisette, La Croisette ☎ *04–97–06–44–90* 🎟 *€3.50* ⏲ *Oct.–Apr., Tues.–Sun. 10–1 and 2–6; July and Aug., daily 11–8 (Fri. to 9); Sept., daily 11–7.*

Musée de la Castre. The hill is topped by an 11th-century château, housing the Musée de la Castre, with its mismatched collection of weaponry, ethnic artifacts, and ceramics amassed by a 19th-century aristocrat. The imposing four-sided **Tour du Suquet** (Suquet Tower) was built in 1385 as a lookout against Saracen-led invasions. ✉ *Pl. de la Castre, Le Suquet* ☎ *04–93–38–55–26* 🎟 *€6* ⏲ *Oct.–Mar., Tues.–Sun. 10–1 and 2–5; Apr.–June and Sept., Tues.–Sun. 10–1 and 2–6; July and Aug., daily 10–7 (Wed. until 8).*

Palais des Festivals. Pick up a map at the tourist office in the Palais des Festivals, the scene of the famous Festival International du Film, otherwise known as the Cannes Film Festival. As you leave the information center, follow the Palais to your right to see the red-carpeted stairs that movie A-listers ascend every year. Set into the surrounding pavement, the **Allée des Étoiles** (Stars' Walk) enshrines some 400 autographed hand imprints—including those of Depardieu, Streep, and Stallone. ✉ *La Croisette* 🌐 *www.palaisdesfestivals.com.*

NEED A BREAK?

Le 72 Croisette. Head down the Croisette and fight for a spot at Le 72 Croisette, the most feistily French of all the Croisette bars. It offers great ringside seats for watching the rich and famous enter the Martinez hotel next door, and it's open nearly 24 hours a day from May to September (7 am to 4 am) with long hours during the rest of the year as well. ✉ ***71 La Croisette*** ☎ ***04–93–94–18–30.***

Rue d'Antibes. Two blocks behind La Croisette lies rue d'Antibes, Cannes's high-end shopping street. At its western end is **rue Meynadier,** packed tight with trendy clothing boutiques and fine food shops. Not far away is the covered **Marché Forville,** the scene of the animated morning food market. **Rue Houche,** behind rue d'Antibes and down from Galleries Lafayette, has lots of boutiques and cafés; Volupté makes a fabulously creamy cappucinno and Chez Bruno is the stop for chocolate.

WHERE TO EAT

$$$$ SEAFOOD

🍴 **Astoux et Cie Brun.** This beacon to all fish lovers since 1953 is deserving of its reputation for impeccably fresh *fruits de mer.* Well-trained staff negotiate cramped quarters to lay down heaping seafood platters, shrimp casseroles, and piles of oysters shucked to order. Open 365 days a year, Astoux is noisy, cheerful, and always busy, so arrive early (noon for lunch, 6 pm for dinner) to get a table and avoid the line—they do not accept reservations. [$] *Average main: €35* ✉ *27 rue Felix Faure, La Croisette* ☎ *04–93–39–21–87* 🌐 *www.astouxbrun.com* ✍ *Reservations not accepted.*

$$$$ FRENCH

🍴 **L'Affable.** When Chef Battaglia decided to set up shop in Cannes, gastronomes were delighted—and the chef does not disappoint. The curried lobster is fantastic, the lamb rack succulent, and the risotto impossibly creamy. Jammed daily since its opening, reservations are essential. Note that dinner service is a fixed price with lots of tempting

CARLTON

choices. $ *Average main: €42* ✉ *5 rue Lafontaine, La Croisette* ☎ *04–93–68–02–09* ⊕ *www.restaurant-laffable.fr* ⚓ *Reservations essential* ⊗ *Closed Sun. and Aug. No lunch Sat.*

$ ✕ **La Pizza.** Sprawling up over two floors in front of the old port—and

PIZZA open 365 days a year, from noon till midnight—this bustling restaurant serves steaks, fish, and salads, but most folks come for gloriously good, right-out-of-the-wood-fire-oven pizza in huge portions. Two sister eateries (La Pizza and Le Quebec) are located in Nice. $ *Average main: €13* ✉ *3 quai St-Pierre* ☎ *04–93–39–22–56* ⊕ *www.crescere.fr.*

$ ✕ **La Sousta.** There are some restaurants you just don't want to share

BISTRO for fear of never being able to get a table. One of them is La Sousta, neatly tucked away from the touristy side of the Croisette in Cannes's old quarter, Le Suquet. The selective Provençal menu is scribbled on the blackboard, yet the kitchen is very willing to adapt orders—something almost unheard of in France. Whatever is market fresh is what you'll find on your plate. You may have to fight some locals for a seat, but just say "merci" and all will be forgiven. $ *Average main: €13* ✉ *11 rue du Pré, Le Suquet* ☎ *04–93–39–19–18* ⊗ *No dinner Sun.–Thurs. Oct.–Film Festival.*

$$$$ ✕ **La Villa Archange.** You wouldn't expect to find a restaurant with two

FRENCH Michelin stars set in such a residential background, 10 minutes by car from La Croisette. But Bruno Oger, ex-chef at the Villa des Lys, promises you a rather unforgettable evening in this très cozy spot surrounded by centennial trees and gardens. Yes, it's pricey. Now that's out of the way, concentrate on the menus—which features dishes like veal shank cooked for 24 hours and served with truffle mashed potatoes, or Breton lobster and roasted squid served with chard ravioli. His creations have dazzled Tilda Swinton and Diane Kruger; and, frankly, a restaurant with its own app for the *plat du jour* in real time is surely in a league of its own. $ *Average main: €95* ✉ *15 bis rue Notre Dame des Anges, Le Cannet* ☎ *04–92–18–18–28* ⊕ *bruno-oger.com* ⊗ *Closed Sun. and Mon. No lunch Tues.–Thurs.*

$$ ✕ **Pastis.** With its sleek milk-bar decor and reasonable prices, this busy

FRENCH hot spot is a must in Cannes. Just off the Croisette, the service is remarkably friendly and the food good. There are nice American touches—grilled-chicken Caesar salad, ribs with home-cut fries, pizza—that can make for a comfortable day off from your gourmet voyage through Provençal cuisine. Reservations are recommended, especially with all the conventions at the nearby Palais. $ *Average main: €20* ✉ *28 rue Commandant André, La Croisette* ☎ *04–92–98–95–40* ⊕ *www.pastis-cannes.com* ⊗ *Closed Jan–mid.-Feb. No lunch Sun.*

WHERE TO STAY
For expanded hotel reviews, visit Fodors.com.

$$$$ ⛱ **Carlton InterContinental.** This deliciously pompous Neoclassical option

HOTEL enjoys a prime beachfront position—La Croisette seems to radiate symmetrically from its figurehead waterfront site—and 10 deluxe suites on the top floor, each with unsurpassed sea views, as well as snazzy seafront rooms add to the cachet. **Pros:** with the best location in Cannes, this iconic hotel has all the cliché and style that the rich and famous look for; service is remarkably unpretentious. **Cons:** Wi-Fi is free in public spaces but costly for in-room use; some bathrooms are tiny; rooms at the back compensate for the lack of a sea view with cheery Provençal prints but avoid those looking out over the back parking/delivery area (very noisy early in the morning). $ *Rooms from: €670* ⊠ *58 bd. de la Croisette, La Croisette* ☎ *04–93–06–40–06* ⊕ *www.intercontinental. com* ⤳ *304 rooms, 39 suites* ⦿*Breakfast.*

$$$$
HOTEL
⊤ **Five Hotel.** Housed in the town's old post office, steps from the Palais de Festival, Five has a stylish decor reminiscent of voyages to the Far East: red fabrics blend with exquisite dark wood furniture against all white linens and bathroom fixtures. **Pros:** excellent service, food, and location; iPad rentals available. **Cons:** minibar very expensive; who needs a scale in the bathroom when on holiday in France? $ *Rooms from: €450* ⊠ *1 rue Notre Dame* ☎ *04–63–36–05–05* ⊕ *www.five-hotel-cannes.com* ⤳ *30 rooms, 15 suites* ⊘ *Closed 3 wks in Feb.* ⦿ *Some meals.*

$
HOTEL
⊤ **Hotel Colette.** Facing the train station, this four-star boutique hotel is incredibly affordable—not just for Cannes, but for any luxurious lodging near the beach. **Pros:** close to the Palais de Festival; interior courtyard; L'Occitane toiletries provided. **Cons:** walls may be a little thin but no street noise; local parking could be expensive. $ *Rooms from: €67* ⊠ *5 pl. de la Gare* ☎ *04–93–39–01–17* ⊕ *www.hotelcolette. com* ⤳ *45 rooms.*

$$$
HOTEL
⊤ **Le Cavendish Boutique Hotel.** Lovingly restored by friendly owners Christine and Guy Welter, the giddily opulent former residence of Lord Cavendish is a true delight, playing up both contemporary decor and 19th-century elegance. **Pros:** genuine welcome is a refreshing change from the notoriously frosty reception at other Cannes palace hotels; bar has complimentary drinks and snacks for guests each evening from 6 to 9. **Cons:** even though rooms all have double-pane windows, the hotel is on the busiest street in Cannes, which means an inevitable amount of noise. $ *Rooms from: €195* ⊠ *11 bd. Carnot* ☎ *04–97–06–26–00* ⊕ *www.cavendish-cannes.com* ⤳ *34 rooms* ⊘ *Closed mid-Dec–mid-Mar.* ⦿ *Breakfast.*

$$$
HOTEL
⊤ **Molière.** Nearly all rooms at this plush, intimate, and low-key retreat a short stroll from the Croisette overlook the vast front garden and are done in cool shades of peach and indigo with white-waxed oak furnishings. **Pros:** low price for excellent service; one room with three single beds is good for families; some rooms have balconies. **Cons:** nights can be noisy as high season; breakfast is extra but is served in the garden most of the year. $ *Rooms from: €160* ⊠ *5 rue Molière, La Croisette* ☎ *04–93–38–16–16* ⊕ *www.hotel-moliere.com* ⤳ *24 rooms* ⊘ *Closed late Nov.–late Dec.* ⦿ *Breakfast.*

NIGHTLIFE AND THE ARTS

International Film Festival. The Riviera's cultural calendar is splashy and star-studded, and never more so than during the International Film Festival in May. The film screenings are not open to the public, so unless you have a pass, your stargazing will be on the streets or in restaurants (though if you hang around the back exits of the big hotels around 7 pm, you may bump into a few celebs *en route* to the red carpet). Don't despair. *Cinéma de la Plage* shows Cannes Classics and Out of

Competition films free at Macé beach at 8:30 pm. Now that's really watching movies with the stars. ⊕ *www.palaisdesfestivals.com.*

Le Baoli. The biggest player to date in the Cannes nightlife scene is Le Baoli, where the likes of Leonardo DiCaprio and Lindsay Lohan have been known to stop by; it's usually packed until dawn even outside of festival time. Open daily from mid-April through to October, but only Friday and Saturday during winter. ⊠ *Port Canto, La Croisette* 🕾 *04–93–43–03–43* ⊕ *www.lebaoli.com.*

Palais de Festival Performing Arts. The Palais de Festival offers a varied menu of performing arts and events, with contemporary, classical, and world music concerts alongside operas, ballets and dance troupes, providing a little dose of culture to the glam that is Cannes. The ticket office is located inside the Visitor's Bureau, to the right of the Palais's stairs. ⊠ *La Croisette* 🕾 *04–92–98–62–77 tickets* ⊕ *www.palaisdesfestivals. com.*

As befits a glamorous seaside resort, Cannes has two casinos.

Casino Barrière. The famous Casino Barrière on La Croisette—open 10 am to 3 am— is said to draw more crowds to its slot machines than any other casino in France. ⊠ *In Palais des Festivals, La Croisette* 🕾 *04–92– 98–78–00* ⊕ *www.lucienbarriere.com.*

Palm Beach Casino Club. The Palm Beach Casino Club, with slot machines and (during the festival season) a disco, manages to retain an exclusive atmosphere even though you can show up in jeans. ⊠ *Pl. Franklin-Roosevelt, Point de la Croisette, La Croisette* 🕾 *04–97–06–36–90* ⊕ *www.casinolepalmbeach.com.*

THE OUTDOORS

Most of the beaches along La Croisette are owned by hotels and restaurants, and they rent out chaise longues, mats, and umbrellas to the public and hotel guests (who also have to pay). Public beaches are between the color-coordinated private beach umbrellas and offer simple open showers and basic toilets. ■**TIP**➔ Plage Macé, near the Palais, sets up a beach library from mid-June to August, 10 am to 6 pm. For a €10 deposit readers can sign out books for up to two days; English publications are available.

Sailboats can be rented at either port or at some of the beachfront hotels.

JUAN-LES-PINS

5 km (3 miles) southwest of Antibes.

If Antibes is the elderly, historic parent, then Juan-les-Pins is the jazzy, younger-sister resort town that, with Antibes, bracelets the wrist of the Cap d'Antibes. The scene along Juan's waterfront is something to behold, with thousands of international sun seekers flowing up and down the promenade or lying flank to flank on its endless stretch of sand. Yes, the **plage de Juan-les-Pins** is made up of sand, not pebbles, and ranks among the Riviera's best (rent a beach chair from the nearby hotel concessions, the best of which is Les Belles Rives). Along with these white-powder wonders, Juan is famous for the quality—some pundits say quantity—of its nightlife. There are numerous nightclubs where you can do everything but sleep, ranging from casinos to discos to strip clubs. If all this sounds like too much hard work, wait for July's jazz festival—one of Europe's most prestigious—or simply repair to Les Belles Rives; if you're lucky enough to be a guest, you'll understand why F. Scott Fitzgerald set his *Tender Is the Night* in "Juantibes," as the place retains the golden glamour of the Riviera of yore and is surrounded by the last remnants of the pine forests that gave Juan its name. Elsewhere, Juan-les-Pins suffers from a plastic feel and you might get more out of Antibes.

WHERE TO STAY

For expanded hotel reviews, visit Fodors.com.

$ HOTEL **Hotel des Mimosas.** Situated in an enclosed hilltop garden studded with tall palms, mimosas, and tropical greenery, this is the sort of place where only the quiet buzzing of cicadas interrupts silent nights. **Pros:** nice garden and grounds; easy walk to train station. **Cons:** some rooms are small; breakfast extra (€10). [$] *Rooms from: €99* ✉ *Rue Pauline* ☎ *04–93–61–04–16* 🌐 *www.hotelmimosas.com* *34 rooms* ⏲ *Closed Oct.–Apr.* 🍴 *No meals.*

$$$$ HOTEL **Les Belles Rives.** Lovingly restored to 1930s glamour, this fabled landmark proves that what's old is new again, as France's stylish young set make this endearingly *neoclassique* place with lovely Art Deco accommodations one of their latest favorites. **Pros:** views are quite spectacular; lots of water sports. **Cons:** gastronomic restaurant is pricey; some rooms are on the small side. [$] *Rooms from: €350* ✉ *33 bd. Baudoin* ☎ *04–93–61–02–79* 🌐 *www.bellesrives.com* *43 rooms* ⏲ *Closed Jan. and Feb.* 🍴 *Breakfast.*

NIGHTLIFE AND THE ARTS

Eden Casino. The glassed-in complex of the Eden Casino houses a panoramic restaurant, bars, and a casino. ✉ *17 bd. Baudoin* ☎ *04–92–93–71–71* 🌐 *www.casinojuanlespins.com.*

Festival International Jazz à Juan. Every July the world-renowned Jazz à Juan festival stages a stellar lineup in a romantic venue under ancient pines. This 50-plus-year-old festival hosted the European debut performances of such stars as Meels Dah-*vees* (Miles Davis) and Ray Charles. ☎ *04–97–23–11–10* 🌐 *www.jazzajuan.com.*

Le Village. By far the most popular club in the town—and rumored to be the favorite haunt of Noel Gallagher—is Le Village. ✉ *Pl. de la Nouvelle Orléans, 1 bd. de la Pinède* ☎ *04–92–93–90–00* ⏲ *Closed Sun.–Thurs. Oct.–June.*

CAP D'ANTIBES

2 km (1 mile) south of Antibes.

This extravagantly beautiful peninsula, protected from the concrete plague infecting the mainland coast, has been carved up into luxurious estates shaded by thick, tall pines. Since the 19th century the wild greenery and isolation have drawn a glittering guest list of aristocrats, artists, literati, and the merely fabulously wealthy: Guy de Maupassant,

Along with its time-burnished alleys and cul-de-sacs, Antibes is packed with little squares that offer the perfect chance to chill out and to get to know the locals.

Anatole France, Claude Monet, the Duke and Duchess of Windsor, the Greek shipping tycoon Stavros Niarchos, and the cream of the Lost Generation, including Ernest Hemingway, Gertrude Stein, and Scott and Zelda Fitzgerald. Now the most publicized focal point is the Hotel Eden Roc, rendezvous and weekend getaway of film stars. The Cap is about 8 km (5 miles) long, so don't consider it a gentle stroll from downtown Antibes. Happily, the No. 2 municipal bus (☎ 04-89-87-72-00 ⊕ www.envibus.fr ≊ €1.50) often connects the two.

EXPLORING

Jardin Thuret (*Thuret Garden*). To fully experience the Riviera's heady hothouse exoticism, visit the glorious Jardin Thuret, established by botanist Gustave Thuret in 1856 as a testing ground for subtropical plants and trees. Thuret was responsible for the introduction of the palm tree, forever changing the profile of the French Riviera. On his death the property was left to the Ministry of Agriculture, which continues to dabble in the introduction of exotic species. The Jardin is in the middle of the Cap; from the Port Gallice, head up chemin du Croûton, turn right on the boulevard du Cap, then right again on chemin Raymond. ⊠ *90 chemin Raymond* ☎ 04-97-21-25-00 ⊕ www7.sophia. inra.fr/jardin_thuret ≊ Free ☺ Winter, weekdays 8:30–5:30; summer, weekdays 8–6.

Fodor's Choice ★ **Le Sentier du Littoral** (*Sentier Tirepoil*). Bordering the Cap's zillion-dollar hotels and over-the-top estates runs one of the most spectacular footpaths in the world: the Sentier du Littoral (aka Sentier Tirepoil), which stretches about 5 km (3 miles) along the outermost tip of the peninsula. It begins gently enough at the pretty plage de la Garoupe (where Cole

Porter and Gerard Murphy used to hang out), with a paved walk-way and dazzling views over the Baie de la Garoupe and the faraway Alps. Round the far end of the cap, however, and the paved promenade soon gives way to a boulder-studded pathway that picks its way along 50-foot cliffs, dizzying switchbacks, and thundering breakers (*Attention Mort*—"Beware: Death"—read the signs, reminding you this path can be very dangerous in stormy weather). On sunny days, with exhilarating winds and spectacular breakers, you'll have company, although for most stretches all signs of civilization completely disappear—except for a yacht or two. The walk is long, and takes about two hours to complete, but it may prove to be two of the more unforgettable hours of your trip (especially if you tackle it at sunset). ■**TIP**➜ To get back to la Garoupe, at the end of the walk look for chemin des Douaniers and follow it until you reach boulevardKennedy. After you pass the Château de la Croë and Villa Eilenroc, take a right to avenue de la Tour Gandolphe and then to André Sella back to the carpark. Or, take the No. 2 bus from Les Contrabandiers stop.

Phare de la Garoupe (*Garoupe Lighthouse*). You can sample a little of what draws famous people to this part of the world by walking up the chemin de Calvaire from the plage de la Salis in Antibes—about 1 km (½ mile)—and taking in the extraordinary views from the hill surmounted by the old lighthouse, the Phare de la Garoupe. Next to the lighthouse, the 16th-century double chapel of **Notre-Dame-de-la-Garoupe** contains ex-votos and statues of the Virgin, all in memory and for the protection of sailors. ☎ *04–93–67–36–01* ⊗ *Chapel, Mon. and Fri. 2:30–5:30; Mass at 11:30.*

Fodor'sChoice **Villa Eilenroc.** The Sentier du Litterol passes below (but unfortunately
★ does not access) the Villa Eilenroc, designed by Charles Garnier, who created the Paris Opéra—which should give you some idea of its style. It commands the tip of the peninsula from a grand and glamorous garden. On Wednesday from September to June, visitors are allowed to wander through the reception salons, which retain the Louis Seize-Trianon feel of the noble facade. The Winter Salon still has its 1,001 Nights ceiling mural painted by Jean Dunand, the famed Art Deco designer; display cases are filled with memorabilia donated by Caroline Groult-Flaubert (Antibes resident and goddaughter of the great author); and the boudoir has boiseries from the Marquis de Sévigné's Paris mansion. As you leave, be sure to detour to La Rosaerie, the rose garden of the estate—in the distance you can spot the white portico of the Château de la Crôe, another legendary villa (now reputedly owned by a syndicate of Russian billionaires). Whether or not the Eilenroc is haunted by Helene Beaumont, the rich singer who built it, or King Leopold II of Belgium, King Farouk of Egypt, Aristotle Onassis, or Greta Garbo—who all rented here—only you will be able to tell. ⊠ *At peninsula's tip* ☎ *04–93–67–74–33* ⊕ *www.antibesjuanlespins.com* ⊠ *Free Oct.–Mar.; €2 Apr.–Sept.* ⊗ *Oct.–Mar., Wed. and Sat. 1–4; Apr.–June, Wed. and Sat. 10–5; July–Sept., Wed. and weekends 3–7.*

WHERE TO EAT AND STAY

For expanded hotel reviews, visit Fodors.com.

$$$$
SEAFOOD

✕ **Restaurant de Bacon.** Since 1948, under the careful watch of the Sordello brothers, this has been *the* spot for seafood on the French Riviera. The catch of the day may be minced in lemon ceviche, floating in a top-of-the-line bouillabaisse, or simply grilled with fennel, crisped with hillside herbs. The warm welcome, discreet service, sunny dining room, and dreamy terrace over the Baie des Anges, with views of the Antibes ramparts, justify extravagance, and a Michelin star. Many of the à la carte fish dishes are pricey, but not-too-extravagant fixed menus are available. $ *Average main: €80* ⊠ *Bd. de Bacon* ☎ *04–93–61–50–02* ⊕ *www.restaurantdebacon.com* ⚲ *Reservations essential* ۞ *Closed Mon. and Nov.–Feb. No lunch Tues.*

$$$$
HOTEL

⊤ **Hôtel du Cap–Eden Roc.** In demand by celebrities from De Niro to Madonna, this extravagantly expensive hotel looking out on 22 acres of immaculate tropical gardens bordered by rocky shoreline has long catered to the world's fantasy of a subtropical idyll on the French Riviera. **Pros:** no other hotel in southern France has the same reputation or style; specially designed children's programs; mosquito spray in each room. **Cons:** if you're not a celebrity, tip big to keep the staff interested; don't even try to book a room during the Cannes Film Festival in early May; there *are* prettier hotels on the coast. $ *Rooms from: €550* ⊠ *Bd. J.F. Kennedy* ☎ *04–93–61–39–01* ⊕ *www.edenroc-hotel.fr* ⤳ *118 rooms, 7 suites* ۞ *Closed mid-Oct.–Apr.* �(O) *Breakfast.*

$$
HOTEL

⊤ **Hôtel La Garoupe Gardiole.** Cool, simple, and accessible to non–movie stars, this hotel offers a chance to sleep on the hallowed Cap d'Antibes peninsula and bike or walk to the pretty Garoupe beach. **Pros:** affordable luxury on the Cap; rooms are large; service is correct. **Cons:** short walk to the beach; limited choices for restaurants within an easy distance. $ *Rooms from: €135* ⊠ *60–74 chemin de la Garoupe* ☎ *04–92–93–33–33* ⊕ *www.hotel-lagaroupe-gardiole.com* ⤳ *40 rooms* ۞ *Closed Nov.–Mar.* ⟨O⟩ *No meals.*

ANTIBES

11 km (7 miles) east of Cannes, 15 km (9 miles) southeast of Nice.

Fodor's Choice
★

No wonder Picasso once called this home—Antibes (pronounced Awn-*teeb*) is a stunner. With broad stone ramparts scalloping in and out over the waves and backed by blunt medieval towers and a skew of tile roofs, Antibes remains one of the most enchantingly romantic old towns on the Mediterranean coast.

GETTING HERE

Antibes has one central train station, the *Gare SNCF* (⊠ *Pl. Pierre-Semard* ⊕ *www.sncf.com*), which is at the far end of town but still within walking distance of the Vieille Ville and only a block or so from the beach. Local trains (TER) are frequent, coming from Nice (30 mins, €4.40), Juan-les-Pins, Biot, Cannes (10 mins, €2.80), and almost all other coastal towns. High-speed TGVs also depart from Antibes (Paris is a little more than five hrs away on this service). Bus service, available at Antibes's Gare Routière (bus station) (⊠ *1 pl. Guynemer*) is supplied by Envibus (☎ *04–89–87–72–00* ⊕ *www.envibus.fr*). Lignes d'Azur's (☎ *08–10–06–10–06* ⊕ *www.lignesdazur.com*) No. 200 bus between Cannes and Nice stops in Antibes and runs every 15 to 20 minutes (1 hr, €1.50).

Visitor Information Antibes Tourist Office ⊠ *11 pl. du Gén. de Gaulle* ☎ *04–97–23–11–11* ⊕ *www.antibesjuanlespins.com.*

EXPLORING

As gateway to the Cap d'Antibes, Antibes's Port Vauban harbor has some of the largest yachts in the world tied up at its berths—their millionaire owners won't find a more dramatic spot to anchor, with the tableau of the snowy Alps looming in the distance and the formidable medieval block towers of the Fort Carré guarding entry to the port. Stroll promenade Amiral-de-Grasse along the crest of Vauban's seawalls, and you can understand why the views inspired Picasso to paint on a panoramic scale. Yet a few steps inland you can enter a souklike maze of old streets that are relentlessly picturesque and joyously beautiful—some say this district is perhaps the most enchanting along the entire Riviera coast, while others are turned off by the heavy presence of English speakers. Think about stopping off at the tourist office to buy a *billet combiné* (combined ticket) for €10, which gives prepaid access to all museums over a period of seven days.

To visit Old Antibes, pass through the **Porte Marine,** an arched gateway in the rampart wall. Follow rue Aubernon to **cours Masséna,** where the little sheltered market sells lemons, olives, and hand-stuffed sausages, and the vendors take breaks in the shoe-box cafés flanking one side. Along the way, wander back alleys, check out the shops, and relax at one of the dawdle-and-dine cafés. Perhaps the most beguiling street in all Antibes is rue St-Esprit, located just a block or two from the Musée Picasso (if you head past the Eglise de l'Immaculée-Conception). Continue farther on to discover other magical cul-de-sacs.

Fodor'sChoice
★
Commune Libre du Safranier (*Free Commune of Safranier*). A few blocks south of the Château Grimaldi is the Commune Libre du Safranier, a magical little neighborhood with a character (and mayor) all its own. Here, not far off the seaside promenade and focused around the place du Safranier, tiny houses hang heavy with flowers and vines, and neighbors carry on conversations from window to window across the stone-stepped rue du Bas-Castelet. It's said that place du Safranier was once a tiny fishing port; now it's the scene of festivals.

Eglise de l'Immaculée-Conception. From cours Masséna head up to the Eglise de l'Immaculée-Conception, which served as the region's cathedral until the bishopric was transferred to Grasse in 1244. The church's 18th-century facade, a marvelously Latin mix of classical symmetry and fantasy, has been restored in stunning shades of ocher and cream. Its stout medieval watchtower was built in the 11th century with stones "mined" from Roman structures. Inside is a Baroque altarpiece painted by the Niçois artist Louis Bréa in 1515. ⊠ *Rue St-Esprit.*

FAMILY **Marineland.** At "Le Must on the Côte d'Azur," more than a million visitors per year delight in dolphins, sea lions, killer whales, and polar bears—there's even a 98-foot tunnel cutting through a shark-filled aquarium. This huge family amusement park also offers water shows and other main attractions: the Far West, Aquasplash, and Adventure Golf. Kids can spend a ton of energy and parents a ton of cash, but it's worth the compromise for the less kid-friendly sightseeing parts of your trip. ■ **TIP→ Book tickets online for reduced prices.** ✉ *RN7* ☎ *08–92–30–06–06* 🌐 *www.marineland.fr* 🎟 *Marineland €38 adult; €30 ages 3–12 (other attractions extra)* ⏲ *Closed Jan.–mid-Feb.*

Musée d'Archéologie (*History and Archaeology Museum*). The bastion St-André, a squat Vauban fortress, contains the recently renovated Musée d'Archéologie. Its collection focuses on Antibes's classical history, displaying amphorae and sculptures found in local digs or salvaged from shipwrecks in the harbor, including a collection of ceremics from Greece, Eturia, and Magna Gracia. ✉ *Bastion Saint-Andre* ☎ *04–93–95–85–98* 🎟 *€3* ⏲ *Tues.–Sun. 10–noon and 2–5.*

Musée Picasso. Next door to the cathedral, the famed Musée Picasso rises high over the water in its stunning home, the medieval Château Grimaldi. Famed as rulers of Monaco, the Grimaldi family lived here until the Revolution; this fine old castle, however, was little more than a monument until its curator offered use of its chambers to Picasso in 1946, when that extraordinary genius was enjoying a period of intense creative energy. The result was a bounty of exhilarating paintings, ceramics, and lithographs inspired by the sea and by Greek mythology—all very Mediterranean. The château, which became the **Musée Picasso** in 1966, houses some 245 works by the artist, as well as pieces by Miró, Calder, and Léger; the first floor displays more than 100 paintings of Russian-born artist Nicholas de Staël. Even those who are not great Picasso fans should enjoy his vast paintings on wood, canvas, paper, and walls, alive with nymphs, fauns, and centaurs. ✉ *Château Grimaldi, pl. Mariejol* ☎ *04–92–90–54–20* 🌐 *www.antibes-juanlespins.com* 🎟 *€6* ⏲ *Tues.–Sun. 10–noon and 2–6.*

WHERE TO EAT

$$$ FRENCH Fodor's Choice ★

🍴 **La Taverne du Safranier.** At this bastion of local cuisine, sit on the lively terrace jammed with locals and dig in to mountains of sardine fritters, *petit farcis* (stuffed vegetables), or a mini-bouillabaisse that is not mini at all. The servers know everybody, and friendly banter wafts over the crowds; don't be surprised if they treat you like a long-lost friend—including taking liberal license to tease. Reserve well in advance. [$] *Average main: €26* ✉ *1 pl. du Safranier* ☎ *04–93–34–80–50* 🌐 *www.taverne-du-safranier.fr* ⏲ *Closed mid-Nov.–Dec.*

$ FRENCH

🍴 **Le Brûlot.** This bistro, set one street back from the market, has remained one of the most popular in Antibes for more than 20 years. Burly chef Christian Blancheri hoists anything from pigs to apple pies in and out of his roaring wood oven, and it's all delicious. Watch for the duck and crispy chips, sardines *à l'escabèche* (in a tangy sweet-sour marinade), sizzling lamb chops, and grilled fresh fish. [$] *Average main: €20* ✉ *3 rue Frédéric Isnard* ☎ *04–93–34–17–76* 🌐 *www.brulot.fr* ⏲ *Closed Sun. No lunch Mon.–Wed.*

Vauban's Fort Carré and the seawalls he designed guard Antibes's harbor, home to some of the most envy-inducing yachts in the world.

NIGHTLIFE

La Siesta. Open Friday and Saturday from June to September, La Siesta is an enormous summertime entertainment center with seven dance floors and the largest beach *piste* in France. A casino—complete with bar, restaurant, slot machines, and roulette tables—is open daily throughout year. ⊠ *Rte. du Bord de Mer* 📞 *04–93–33–31–31* ⊕ *www.joa-casino.com.*

THE OUTDOORS

Antibes and Juan together claim 25 km (15½ miles) of coastline and 48 **beaches.** In Antibes you can choose between small sandy inlets—such as **La Gravette,** below the port; the central **plage du Ponteil; plage de la Salis,** toward the Cap; rocky escarpments around the Vieille Ville; or the vast stretch of sand above the Fort Carré.

THE HILL TOWNS

The hills that back the French Riviera are often called the *arrière-pays,* or backcountry. This particular wedge of backcountry—behind the coast between Cannes and Antibes—has a character all its own: deeply, unselfconsciously Provençal, with undulating fields of lavender watched over by villages perched on golden stone. Many of these villages look as if they do not belong to the last century—but they do, since they played the muse to some of modern art's most famous exemplars, notably Pablo Picasso and Henri Matisse. A highlight here is the Maeght Foundation in St-Paul de Vence (also home to the incomparable inn, La Colombe d'Or), one of France's leading museums of modern art. The town's neighbor, Vence, has the Chapelle du Rosaire, entirely designed

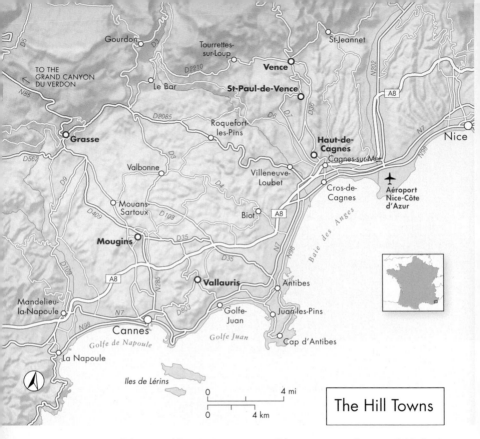

The Hill Towns

and decorated by Matisse. It's possible to get a small taste of this back-country on a day trip out of Cannes or Antibes; even if you're vacationing on the coast, you may want to settle in for a night or two, for this is when the scent of the boutiques' strawberry potpourri is washed away by the natural perfume of bougainvillea and jasmine wafting from terra-cotta jars. ■ TIP➔ One of the best local Provençal markets is held on Friday morning in the delightful 16th-century Valbonne village, about 7 km (4 miles) north of Mougins. There are no museums in this English-friendly spot, but you'll find endless restaurants and cafés around the place des Arcades for post-shopping hunger. There's plenty of free parking if you're driving; otherwise take a €1.50 bus from Nice (No. 230), Cannes (No. 630), or Antibes (No. 10).

VALLAURIS

6 km (4 miles) northeast of Cannes, 6 km (4 miles) northwest of Antibes.

In the low hills over the coast, dominated by a blocky Renaissance château, this ancient village was ravaged by waves of the plague in the 14th century, then rebuilt in the 16th century by 70 Genoese families imported to repopulate the abandoned site. They brought with them a taste for Roman planning—hence the grid format in the Old Town—but, more important in the long run, a knack for pottery making as well. Their skills and the fine clay of Vallauris proved to be a marriage made in heaven, and the village thrived as a pottery center for hundreds of years.

Musée National Picasso. In the 1940s Picasso settled here in a simple stone house, creating pottery art from the malleable soil with a single-minded passion. But he returned to painting in 1952 to create one of his masterworks in the château's Romanesque chapel, the vast multi-panel oil-on-wood composition called *La Guerre et la Paix* (*War and Peace*). The chapel is part of the Musée National Picasso today, where several of Picasso's ceramic pieces are displayed. ⊠ *Pl. de la Libération* ☎ *04–93–64–71–83* ⊕ *www.musee-picasso-vallauris.fr* ⚄ *€3.25* ⊗ *June 16–30 and Sept. 1–15, Wed.–Mon. 10–12:15 and 2–6; Sept. 16–June 15, Wed.–Mon. 10–12:15 and 2–5; July and Aug., Wed.–Mon. 10–7.*

MOUGINS

6 km (4 miles) northwest of Valluris; 8 km (5 miles) north of Cannes; 11 km (7 miles) northwest of Antibes.

Passing through Mougins, a popular summerhouse community convenient to Cannes and Nice and famously home to a group of excellent restaurants, you may perceive little more than suburban sprawl. But in 1961 Picasso found much to admire and settled into a *mas* (farmhouse) that verily became a pilgrimage spot for artists and art lovers; he died here in 1973.

Notre-Dame-de-Vie. You can find Picasso's final home and see why, of all spots in the world, he chose this one, by following D35 2 km (1 mile) south of Mougins to the ancient ecclesiastical site of Notre-Dame-de-Vie. This was the hermitage, or monastic retreat, of the Abbey of Lérins, and its 13th-century bell tower and arcaded chapel form a pretty ensemble. Approached through an allée of ancient cypresses, the former priory house Picasso shared with his wife, Jacqueline, overlooks the broad bowl of the countryside (now blighted with modern construction). Unfortunately, his residence is closed to the public. Elsewhere in the village is the small municipal **Espace Culturel & Musée Maurice Gottlob**, set in the 17th-century St-Bernardin Chapel at place du Commandant Lamy. Also of note: the **Musée d'Art Classique de Mougins**, which opened at 32 rue Commandeur in 2011 and was nominated as European Museum of the Year in 2013. It houses 600 artworks "highlighting the dialogue between the old and the new," as well as the world's largest private collection of antique weapons. The **Musée de la Photographie** near Porte Sarrazine permanently displays André Villers's portraits of his good friends—Picasso and Dali, among them. ⊠ *Chemin de la Chapelle.*

WHERE TO EAT AND STAY

For expanded hotel reviews, visit Fodors.com.

$$$$

FRENCH

✕ **Le Bistrot de Mougins.** A 15th-century stable with high, curved brick ceilings, rustic chairs, and flowered tablecloths, offers a real picnic-in-the-country feel. Simple, Provençal-style dishes are hard to beat: escargots in butter and herbs, steak with a green peppercorn sauce, or sea bass grilled with fennel are top choices. Reservations are recommended in the summer months but suggested year-round for terrace seating. $ Average main: €55 ⊠ Pl. du Village ☎ 04–93–75–78–34 ⊕ lebistrotdemougins.com ⊘ Closed Wed. and Jan. and Feb.

$$$$
HOTEL

⚟ **Le Mas Candille.** Nestled in a huge private park, this 19th-century mas (farmhouse) has been cleverly transformed into an ultraluxurious hotel—antique wallpapers, "reissued" vintage furniture, and many other high-gloss touches make the place Elle Decor–worthy, if not really authentic to the locale. **Pros:** award-winning service; beautiful views; decadent spa. **Cons:** hard to find. $ Rooms from: €455 ⊠ Bd. Clément-Rebuffel ☎ 04–92–28–43–43 ⊕ www.lemascandille.com ⇗ 39 rooms, 7 suites ⊘ Closed 4 wks in Jan.–Feb. ⎁ Breakfast.

GRASSE

10 km (6 miles) northwest of Mougins; 17 km (10½ miles) north of Cannes; 22 km (14 miles) northwest of Antibes; 42 km (26 miles) west of Nice.

High on a plateau over the coast, this busy, modern town is usually given a wide berth by anyone who isn't interested in its prime tourist industry, the making of perfume. But its unusual art museum features works of the 18th-century artist Fragonard, while the famed perfume museum and the picturesque backstreets of its very Mediterranean Vieille Ville round out a pleasant day trip from the coast. You can't visit the laboratories where the great blends of Chanel, Dior, and Guerlain are produced, but to accommodate the crowds of tourists who come here wanting to know more, Grasse has three functioning perfume factories that create simple blends and demonstrate production techniques for free. The No. 500 bus from Nice has daily service to Grasse for €1.50.

■ **TIP→** If sniffing scents isn't your thing, why not get in a round of golf at the reopened and decently priced Claux Amic golf club (⊕ www. claux-amic.com) on route des 3 Ponts in Grasse? The view down the 3rd will knock even the best players of their stroke.

Fragonard. Fragonard operates in a factory built in 1782 and is open to the public daily. ⊠ 20 bd. Fragonard ☎ 04–93–36–44–65 ⊕ www. fragonard.com ⊡ Free ⊘ Apr.–Sept., daily 10–7; Oct.–Mar., Wed.–Sun. 11–6. Closed 3 wks in Nov.

Galimard. Galimard traces its pedigree back to 1747, and the factory is open to visitors. ■ **TIP→** For €45 you can create and name your own perfume in a two-hour workshop at Galimard's Studio des Fragrances around the corner at 5 route de Pegomas. ⊠ 73 rte. de Cannes ☎ 04–93–09–20–00 ⊕ www.galimard.com ⊡ Free ⊘ Daily 9–6.

Molinard. Molinard was established in 1849 and offers an extensive factory tour. ⊠ 60 bd. Victor Hugo ☎ 04–92–42–33–28 ⊕ www.molinard. com ⊡ Free ⊘ Daily 9:30–1 and 2–6 (open to 7 and nonstop in July and Aug.; closed Sun. Oct.–Mar.).

Musée d'Art et d'Histoire de Provence (Museum of the Art and History of Provence). The Musée d'Art et d'Histoire de Provence, just down from the Fragonard perfumery, has a large collection of faïence from

Continued on page 654

CUISINE OF THE SUN by Rosa Jackson

Don't be surprised if colors and flavors seem more intense in Provence. It could be the hot, dry climate, which concentrates the essence of fruit and vegetables, or the sun beaming down on market tables overflowing with produce. Or maybe you're seeing the world anew through rosé-tinted wine glasses. Whatever the reason, here's how to savor Provence's *incroyable* flavors and culinary favorites.

Provence's rustic cuisine, based on local tomatoes, garlic, olive oil, anchovies, olives, and native wild herbs—including basil, lavender, mint, rosemary, thyme, and sage—has more in common with other Mediterranean cuisines than it does with most regional French fare. Everywhere you'll find sun-ripened fruit dripping with nectar and vegetables so flavor-packed that meat may seem like a mere accessory.

The natural bounty of the region is ample, united by climate—brilliant sunshine and fierce winds—and divided by dramatically changing landscapes. In the Vaucluse, scorched plains give way to lush, orchard-lined hills and gently sloped vineyards. The wild Calanques of Marseille, source of spiky sea urchins, ease into the tranquil waters of St-Tropez, home to gleaming bream and sea bass. Provence's pantry is overflowing with culinary treasures.

Simple preparations, like grilled vegetables with crusty bread, are best enjoyed with the region's famous rosé wine

RUSTIC FARE: NATURE AS MUSE AND MASTER

As you bite into a honey-ripe Cavaillon melon or a fennel-perfumed sea bass fillet, you might think that nature has always been kind to Provence. Not so.

On the wind-battered coast of Marseille, fishermen salvaged the boniest rock fish to create a restorative soup—bouillabaisse—that would become legendary worldwide.

In the sun-blasted mountains north of Nice, impoverished farmers developed a repertoire of dishes found nowhere

(top left) Provence's markets have bountiful produce, (top right) *soupe au pistou*, a version of minestrone

else in France, using hardy Swiss chard, chickpea flour, and salt cod.

Olive oil, the very symbol of Provençal food, is only now overcoming a 1950s frost that entirely wiped out France's olive groves. Even the tomato has a relatively short history here, having been introduced in the 1820s and at first used only in cooked dishes.

The best Provençal chefs remain fiercely proud of the dishes that define their region or their village, even while injecting their own identities and ideas into the food. Thanks to its ports, Provence has always been open to outside influences, yet the wealth of readily available ingredients prevents chefs from straying too far from their roots—when the local basil is so headily perfumed, why use lemongrass?

If menus at first seem repetitive, go beyond the words (tapenade, ratatouille, pistou) to notice how each chef interprets the dish: this is not a land of printed recipes but of spontaneity inspired by the seasons and the markets. Don't expect perfect food every time, but seek out those who love what they do enough to make *la cuisine de soleil* dazzle.

A FESTIVAL OF FOOD

Les Étolies de Mougins (⊕ www. lesetoilesdemougins.com; €5-€15) transforms the medieval village of Mougins into a vast "open air theater of gastronomy", according to organizers. Launched in 2006 as a tribute to Roger Vergé—the mastermind who put this community on the worldwide gourmet map—this yearly festival welcomes hundreds of the greatest chefs from around the globe who share their passion for cooking with equally enthusiastic audiences. Over three days in September, demonstrations, workshops, and professional sommeliers or amateur chef competitions will dazzle spectators. And yes, there are glorious tastings as far as the stomach can stretch. Park in one of the recognized lots around Mougins and use the free navette that shuttles festival-goers to the village.

TASTEMAKERS AND THEIR RESTAURANTS

While Provence is best-known for its rustic fare, the region also has a sophisticated side. It was here—outside of Cannes—that the founding father of French haute cuisine, **Auguste Escoffier** (1846–1935), was born and raised. His former villa has been transformed into a culinary museum, **Musee Escoffier de l'Art Culinare** (✉ *3 rue Auguste Escoffier, Villenueve-Loubet Village* ☎ *04–93–20–80–51*), displaying Escoffier's kitchen and collection of cookware, along with artwork and reproductions of his famous feasts.

These days, upscale culinary creations are best experienced at the "new Mediterranean" restaurants of the region's star chefs. Former Moulin de Mougins Michelin-starred super chef **Alain Llorca** has found the perfect setting for his Spanish-influenced style at his **Alain Llorca Restaurant-Hotel** (✉ *350 rte. de Saint Paul, La Colle sur Loup* ☎ *04–93–32–02–93*). At this hillside property, Llorca loves to do upscale riffs on earthy dishes, such as gazpacho with lobster or steak flavored with Iberian ham. For a taste of Llorca's style of cooking in a less formal atmosphere, try the newly opened **Café Llorca Monaco** (✉ *10 Ave. Princesse Grace, Monaco,* ☎ *00–377–99–99–29–29*).

Everyone from antique dealers to fashionable hipsters feel at home at **Le Jardin**

Chef Alain Llorca is known for his fanciful presentations

du Quai (✉ *91 av. Julien Guigne, L'Isle-sur-la-Sorgue* ☎ *04–90–20–14–98*), where jovial young chef **Daniel Hébet** runs the restaurant like an open house. In summer, regulars linger on the garden patio, while in winter the high-ceiling bistro-style dining room exudes the same welcoming vibe. Shrugging off the constraints of haute cuisine with a no-choice set menu at lunch and dinner, Hébet makes creative presentations like an open-faced tart filled with baby fava beans, cherry tomatoes, and chorizo-stuffed baby squid.

At **Restaurant Christian Etienne** (✉ *10 rue de Mons, Avignon* ☎ *04–90–86–16–50*), the summer tomato menu has become a much-anticipated annual tradition, where each year chef Etienne celebrates the versatility of this vegetable with a tasting extravaganza that might include tartare of three tomato varieties with olive oil from the Bleu Argent mill in Provence, foie gras with Roma tomato petals, and tomato macaroon with lime sorbet. Etienne is one of the long-established masters of Provençal cooking, and if his cooking sometimes makes generous use of butter (rather than the area's renowned olive oil), his customers aren't complaining.

Dining on the terrace of Le Jardin du Quai

PROVENCE'S TOP REGIONAL DISHES

Ratatouille   Fougasse

AÏOLI

The name for a deliciously pungent mayonnaise made with generous helpings of garlic, *aïoli* is a popular accompaniment for fish, meat, and vegetable dishes. The mayonnaise version shares its name with "grand aïoli," a recipe featuring salt cod, potatoes, hard-boiled eggs, and vegetables. Both types of aïoli pop up all over Provence, but they seems most beloved in Marseille. In keeping with Catholic practice, some restaurants serve grand aïoli only on Fridays. And it's a good sign if they ask you to place your order at least a day in advance. A grand aïoli is also a traditional component of the Niçois Christmas feast.

BOUILLABAISSE

Originally a humble fisherman's soup made with the part of the catch that nobody else wanted, bouillabaisse—the famous fish stew—consists of four or five kinds of fish: the villainous-looking *rascasse* (red scorpion fish), *grondin* (sea robin), *baudroie* (monkfish), *congre* (conger eel), and *rouget* (mullet). The fish are simmered in a stock of onions, tomatoes, garlic, olive oil, and saffron,

which gives the dish its golden color. When presented properly, the broth is served first, with croutons and *rouille*, a creamy garlic sauce that you spoon in to suit your taste. The fish comes separately, and the ritual is to place pieces into the soup to enjoy after slurping up some of the broth.

BOURRIDE

This poached fish dish owes its anise kick to pastis and its garlic punch to aïoli. The name comes from the Provençal bourrido, which translates less poetically as "boiled." Monkfish—known as baudroie in Provence and lotte in the rest of France—is a must, but chefs occasionally dress up their bourride with other species and shellfish.

DAUBE DE BOEUF

To distinguish their prized beef stew from *boeuf bourguignon*, Provençal chefs make a point of not marinating the meat, instead cooking it very slowly in tannic red wine that is often flavored with orange zest. In the Camargue, daube is made with the local taureau (bull's meat), while the Avignon variation uses lamb.

Bourride

Bouillabaisse

FOUGASSE

The Provençal answer to Italian focaccia, this soft flatbread is distinguished by holes that give it the appearance of a lacy leaf. It can be made savory—flavored with olives, anchovy, bacon, cheese, or anything else the baker has on hand—or sweet, enriched with olive oil and dusted with icing sugar. When in Menton, don't miss the sugary *fougasse mentonnaise*.

LES PETITS FARCIS

The Niçois specialty called *les petits farcis* are prepared with tiny summer vegetables (usually zucchini, tomatoes, peppers, and onions) that are traditionally stuffed with veal or leftover *daube* (beef stew). Like so many Niçois dishes, they make great picnic food.

RATATOUILLE

At its best, *ratatouille* is a glorious thing—a riot of eggplant, zucchini, bell peppers, and onions, each sautéed separately in olive oil and then gently combined with sweet summer tomatoes. A well-made ratatouille, to which a pinch of saffron has been added to heighten its flavor, is also delicious served chilled.

SOUPE AU PISTOU

The Provençal answer to pesto, *pistou* consists of the simplest ingredients—garlic, olive oil, fresh basil, and Parmesan—ideally pounded together by hand in a stone mortar with an olive-wood pestle. Most traditionally it delivers a potent kick to *soupe au pistou*, a kind of French minestrone made with green beans, white beans, potatoes, and zucchini.

SOCCA

You'll find *socca* vendors from Nice to Menton, but this chickpea pancake cooked on a giant iron platter in a wood-fired oven is really a Niçois phenomenon, born of sheer poverty at a time when wheat flour was scarce. After cooking, it is sliced into finger-lickin' portions with an oyster knife. Enjoy it with a glass of chilled rosé.

TIAN DE LÉGUMES

A *tian* is both a beautiful earthenware dish and one of many vegetable gratins that might be cooked in it. This thrifty dish makes a complete meal of seasonal vegetables, eggs, and a little cheese.

the region, including works from the famous pottery towns of Moustiers, Biot, and Vallauris. ✉ *2 rue Mirabeau* ☎ *04–93–36–80–20* 🖰 *Free* 🕙 *Apr–Sept., daily 10–7; Oct.–Mar., Wed.–Sun. 10–noon and 2–6. Closed 3 wks in Nov.*

Musée Fragonard. The Musée Fragonard headlines the work of Grasse's own Jean-Honoré Fragonard (1732–1806), one of the great French "chocolate-box" artists of his day. The lovely villa contains a collection of Fragonard's drawings, engravings, and paintings; also on display are works by his son Alexandre-Evariste and his grandson, Théophile. ✉ *23 bd. Fragonard* ☎ *04–93–36–93–10* 🖰 *Free* 🕙 *Apr.–Sept., daily 10–7; Oct.–Mar., Wed.–Sun. 11–6. Closed 3 wks in Nov.*

Musée International de la Parfumerie (*International Museum of Perfume*). The Musée International de la Parfumerie is one of the more sleekly spectacular museums along the coast. Housed in a soaring structure of steel, glass, and teak, the museum traces the 3,000-year history of perfume making; highlights include a fascinating collection of 4,000 antique perfume bottles. In the rooftop greenhouse you can breathe in the heady smells of different herbs and flowers, while the expert and amusing guide crushes delicate petals under your nose to better release the scents. ✉ *2 bd. du Jeu de Ballon* ☎ *04–97–05–58–00* 🖰 *€3* 🕙 *May–Sept., daily 10–7 (Sat. to 9); Oct.–Apr., Wed.–Sun. 11–6. Closed 3 wks in Nov.*

Vieille Ville (*Old Town*). Go down the steps to rue Mirabeau and lose yourself in the dense labyrinth of the Vieille Ville, where steep, narrow streets are thrown into shadow by shuttered houses five and six stories tall.

WHERE TO EAT AND STAY

For expanded hotel reviews, visit Fodors.com.

$$ ✕ **Le Gazan.** A local institution, this cozy and crowded restaurant serves
FRENCH consistently good food. Champagne tones and fresh flowers enliven the surroundings, while the cuisine remains traditional French. Try the succulent house specialties: lobster stew or tender lamb tajine. Ⓢ *Average main: €20* ✉ *3 rue Gazan* ☎ *04–93–36–22–88* 🕙 *No dinner Oct.–May.*

$ ✕ **Les Trois Garçons.** This easygoing corner bistro, just off place aux Aires,
FRENCH is one of the oldest in Grasse and serves up inventive home cooking under a vaulted ceiling decorated with stenciled grapevines. Choose from an ambitious and varied Mediterranean menu of à la carte specialties—including calf's head and hearty homemade fois gras—or opt for a three-course set menu. You'll be pleased with the excellent service and quality for your euro, with the added bonus of public parking across the street (a blessing in Grasse). Ⓢ *Average main: €16* ✉ *10 pl. de la Foux* ☎ *04–93–60–15–49* 🕙 *Closed Sun.*

$$$$ 🏠 **La Bastide Saint-Antoine.** This ocher mansion, once the home of an
B&B/INN industrialist who hosted Kennedys and the Rolling Stones, is now the domain of celebrated chef Jacques Chibois, who welcomes you with old stone walls, shaded walkways, an enormous pool, and guest rooms that glossily mix Louis Seize, Provençal, and high-tech delights. **Pros:** a bastion of culinary excellence; perks like iPod docks, 1,000 TV channels, and coffee/organic tea in each room. **Cons:** rooms are a touch too

Provençal for some tastes; breakfast not included. [$] *Rooms from: €335* ✉ *48 av. Henri-Dunant* ☎ *04–93–70–94–94* 🌐 *www.jacques-chibois.com* 🛏 *9 rooms, 7 suites* 🍴 *No meals.*

VENCE

20 km (12 miles) east of Grasse; 4 km (2½ miles) north of St-Paul; 22 km (14 miles) northwest of Nice.

La Vieille Ville, the historic part of Vence, is encased behind stone walls inside a thriving modern market town and dates from the 15th century. Though crowded with boutiques and souvenir shops, the Old Town is conscious of its history—plaques guide you through historic squares and *portes* (gates).

GETTING HERE

No trains run to Vence or St-Paul-de-Vence. The No. 400 and No. 94 buses operated by Lignes d'Azur (☎ *08–10–06–10–06* 🌐 *www.lignesdazur.com*) frequently make the hour-long run to and from Nice for €1.50 a ticket; frequent buses also connect Vence and St-Paul-de-Vence with Cagnes-sur-Mer's train station, a little less than 10 km (6 miles) from Vence. A free *navette* (shuttle) follows a route from the bus station through Vence and runs every 15 minutes from Tuesday to Saturday, 9–1 and 3–7, connecting with buses to Nice and elsewhere on the coast. Inquire at the bus station about taxi service—but don't be surprised to have a Mercedes pull up and find your female chauffeur garbed in a pink Chanel suit!

Visitor Information Vence Tourist Office ✉ *8 pl. du Grand Jardin* ☎ *04–93–58–06–38* 🌐 *www.vence.fr/tourism.*

EXPLORING

Leave your car on place du Grand Jardin and head to the Vieille Ville gate, passing place du Frêne, with its ancient ash tree planted in the 16th century, and then through the Portail du Peyra to the place du Peyra, enlivened with fountains. Ahead lies the former cathedral on place Clemenceau, adjacent to the ocher-color Hôtel de Ville (town hall). A flea market is held on the place du Grand Jardin on Wednesday, and there's also a Provençal market Tuesday in the Vieille Ville and Friday in both spots; backstreets and alleys hereabouts have been colonized by crafts stores and "art galleries."

Cathédrale de la Nativité de la Vierge (*Cathedral of the Birth of the Virgin, on place Godeau*). In the center of the Vieille Ville, the Cathédrale de la Nativité de la Vierge was built on the Romans' military drilling field in the 11th and 12th centuries and is a hybrid of Romanesque and Baroque styles. The cathedral has been expanded and altered many times over the centuries. Note the rostrum added in 1499—its choir stalls are carved with particularly vibrant and amusing scenes of daily life in the Middle Ages. In the baptistery is a ceramic mosaic of Moses in the bulrushes by Chagall.

Fodor's Choice ★ **Chapelle du Rosaire** (*Chapel of the Rosary*). On the outskirts of "new" Vence, toward St-Jeannet is the Chapelle du Rosaire, better known to the world-at-large as the Matisse Chapel. The artist decorated it with beguiling simplicity and clarity between 1947 and 1951 as his gift to nuns who had nursed him through illness. It reflects the reductivist style of the era: walls, floor, and ceiling are gleaming white, and the small stained-glass windows are cool greens and blues. "Despite its imperfections I think it is my masterpiece . . . the result of a lifetime devoted to the search for truth," wrote Matisse, who designed and dedicated the chapel when he was in his eighties and nearly blind. ✉ *466 av. Henri-Matisse* ☎ *04–93–58–03–26* 🎫 *€5* 🕒 *Tues. and Thurs. 10–11:30 and 2–5:30; Mon., Wed., and Sat. 2–5:30; Sun. Mass at 10. Closed mid-Nov.–Dec.*

WHERE TO EAT AND STAY

For expanded hotel reviews, visit Fodors.com.

$$$ FRENCH 🍴 **La Farigoule.** A long, beamed dining room that opens onto a shady terrace casts a convivial spell and provides the setting for some sophisticated Provençal cooking. Watch for the five-cheese ravioli in cream sauce, rack of herb-crusted lamb, wild boar stew with polenta delicately flavoured with truffle oil, and the apple tart with vanilla-caramel ice cream. Only fixed-menus are served, and they change with the seasons. Reservations are recommended. [$] *Average main: €30* ✉ *15 rue Henri Isnard* ☎ *04–93–58–01–27* 🌐 *www.lafarigoule-vence.fr* 🕒 *Closed Mon. and Tues. Oct.–Apr. and Tues. May–Sept.*

$$$$ FRENCH 🍴 **Les Bacchanales.** Star chef Christophe Dufau's weekly changing menu puts an inventive spin on traditional local ingredients; the sea bass served with white cabbage, green onion, thyme, coriander, and mullet caviar is a must when it's available. Meals are served in a sun-filled, beautifully decorated garden villa, a mere 10 minutes by foot from Vence. In summer, the terrace is an idyllic place to linger over a three-, four-, five-, or seven-course set menu. [$] *Average main: €58* ✉ *247 av. de Provence* ☎ *04–93–24–19–19* 🌐 *www.lesbacchanales.com* ✍ *Reservations essential* 🕒 *Closed Tues., Wed., and mid-Jan. for 3 wks.*

$$$$ HOTEL 🏨 **Château du Domaine St. Martin.** Occupying the site of an ancient Knights Templar fortress and set amid acres of greenery designed by Jean Mus, this hilltop domain welcomes you with light, airy public salons and luxurious guest quarters that include two- and three-bedroom villas accented with beautiful antiques. **Pros:** stunning views; helicopter pad; famous guests often stay (Brad Pitt and Angelina Jolie, among others), so servers are used to discreet excellence. **Cons:** restaurant decor has been labeled fussy and old-fashioned; some renovations may seem a bit too sleek. [$] *Rooms from: €585* ✉ *Av. des Templiers* ☎ *04–93–58–02–02* 🌐 *www.chateau-st-martin.com* 🛏 *40 suites, 6 villas* 🕒 *Closed Nov.–Mar.* 🍽 *Breakfast*

$ B&B/INN 🏨 **L'Auberge des Seigneurs et du Lion d'Or.** Dating to the 17th century and the only hotel set within Vence's old walls, this inn has an ambience *à la François Premier*. **Pros:** lovely family atmosphere; nice touches, such as fresh flowers or fruit in the rooms. **Cons:** rooms can be noisy, especially those facing street; the smell of cooking can waft up into the rooms. [$] *Rooms from: €90* ✉ *Pl. du Frêne* ☎ *04–93–58–04–24* 🌐 *www.auberge-seigneurs.com* 🛏 *6 rooms* 🕒 *Closed mid-Dec.–mid-Jan.* 🍽 *Some meals.*

ST-PAUL-DE-VENCE

4 km (2½ miles) south of Vence, 18 km (11 miles) northwest of Nice.

Fodor'sChoice
★ The famous medieval village of St-Paul-de-Vence can be seen from the coast, standing out like its companion, Vence, against the skyline. In the Middle Ages St-Paul was basically a city-state, and it controlled its own political destiny for centuries. But by the early 20th century St-Paul had faded to oblivion, overshadowed by the growth of Vence and Cagnes—until it was rediscovered in the 1920s when a few penniless artists began paying for their drinks at the local auberge with paintings. Those artists turned out to be Signac, Modigliani, and Bonnard, who met at the Auberge de la Colombe d'Or, now a sumptuous inn, where the walls are still covered with their ink sketches and daubs. Today art of a sort still dominates in the myriad tourist traps that take your eyes off the beauty of St-Paul's old stone houses and its rampart views. The most commercially developed of Provence's hilltop villages, St-Paul is nonetheless a magical place when the tourist crowds thin. Artists are still drawn to St-Paul's light, its pure air, its wraparound views, and its honey-color stone walls, soothingly cool on a hot Provençal afternoon. Film stars continue to love its lazy yet genteel ways, lingering on the garden-bower terrace of the Colombe d'Or and challenging the locals to a game of pétanque under the shade of the plane trees. Even so, you have to work hard to find the timeless aura of St-Paul; arrive early in the day to get a jump on the cars and tour buses, which can clog the main D36 departmental road here by noon, or plan on a stay-over. Either way, do consider a luncheon or dinner beneath the Picassos at the Colombe d'Or (reserve in advance), even if the menu prices seem almost as fabulous as the collection. And note, if you're using an in-car GPS, type in St Paul without "de Vence," and then the street name. If you're coming from Nice, you're best off taking the €1.50 Lignes d'Azur No. 400 Nice-Vence bus (☎ *08–10–06–10–06* ⊕ *www.lignesdazur.com*), which takes an hour to get to St-Paul-de-Vence.

Visitor Information St-Paul-de-Vence Tourist Office ⊠ *2 rue Grande* ☎ *04–93–32–86–95* ⊕ *www.saint-pauldevence.com.*

EXPLORING

Fondation Maeght. Many people come to St-Paul just to visit the Fondation Maeght, founded in 1964 by art dealer Aimé Maeght high above the medieval town. It's not just a small modern art museum but also an extraordinary marriage of the arc-and-plane architecture of Josep Sert; the looming sculptures of Miró, Moore, and Giacometti; the mural mosaics of Chagall; and the humbling hilltop setting, complete with pines, vines, and flowing planes of water. On display is an intriguing and ever-varying parade—one of the most important in Europe—of works by modern masters, including Chagall's wise and funny late-life masterpiece *La Vie* (*Life*). On the extensive grounds, fountains and impressive vistas help to beguile even those who aren't into modern art. ⊠ *623 Chem. des Gardettes* ☎ *04–93–32–81–63* ⊕ *www.fondation-maeght.com* ☎ *€15* ⊙ *Oct.–June., daily 10–6; July–Sept., daily 10–7.*

Our vote for France's most beautiful *village perché*, Haut-de-Cagnes is an enchanting place filled with tiny piazzas, winding alleys, and staircase streets.

WHERE TO STAY

For expanded hotel reviews, visit Fodors.com.

$ B&B/INN **Hostellerie les Remparts.** With original stone walls, coved ceilings, and a perfect location in the center of the Vieille Ville, this small medieval hotel is an uncut gem, even if it's in need of a little polishing. **Pros:** affordable, friendly and loaded with charm; rooms are airy and big; ideal location; most expensive room is €130, breakfast included. **Cons:** in summer prepare to book at least two months in advance; village shuts down at night. [$] *Rooms from: €105* ✉ *72 rue Grande* ☎ *04–93–24–10–47* 🌐 *www.hostellerielesremparts.com* ➡ *9 rooms* 🍴 *Breakfast.*

$$$$ B&B/INN Fodor's Choice ★ **La Colombe d'Or.** Often called the most beautiful inn in France, "the golden dove" occupies a rose-stone Renaissance mansion just outside the walls of St-Paul and is so perfect overall that some contend you haven't really been to the French Riviera until you've stayed or dined here. **Pros:** where else can you have an aperitif under a real Picasso? Where else can you wander in the garden, glass of wine in hand, and stare at a real Rodin? **Cons:** some rooms in the adjoining villa have blocked views; menu often outshone by the art. [$] *Rooms from: €310* ✉ *Pl. Général-de-Gaulle* ☎ *04–93–32–80–02* 🌐 *www.la-colombe-dor.com* ➡ *13 rooms, 12 suites* ⏲ *Closed Nov.–mid Jan. except for 1 wk at Christmas* 🍴 *Breakfast.*

HAUT-DE-CAGNES

6 km (4 miles) south of St-Paul-de-Vence; 21 km (13 miles) northeast of Cannes; 10 km (6 miles) north of Antibes; 14 km (9 miles) west of Nice.

12

Although from N7 you may be tempted to give wide berth to **Cagnes-sur-Mer**—with its congested sprawl of freeway overpasses, beachfront pizzerias, and train station—don't. Just follow the brown signs inland touting "Bourg Médiéval" and head up into one of the most beautiful *villages perchés* (perched villages) along the Riviera: Haut-de-Cagnes. Alice, of Wonderland fame, would adore this steeply cobbled Old Town, honeycombed as it is with tiny little piazzas, return-to-your-starting-point-twice alleys, and winding streets that abruptly change to stairways. This town is so pretty you'll wish you could paint, not photograph, it!

GETTING HERE

Cagnes-sur-Mer is the station stop on the main Marseilles–Ventimiglia coastal train line. More than two dozen trains pull into the station at avenue de la Gare in the commercial sector called Cagnes-Ville. Sample trips: from Nice (15 mins, €2.80), from Cannes (25 mins, €4.40). A free *navette* (shuttle), No. 44, connects place du Général-de-Gaulle in the center of Cagnes-Ville (turn right out of train station and walk about nine blocks) to Haut-de-Cagnes every 25 minutes Monday to Sunday 7 am–10:30 pm (6:30 am–12:30 am, June to September). Another free navette (No. 45) runs in the summer along the sea in Cagnes-sur-mer from Parc de Cros to the Parc de l'Hippodrome. Lignes d'Azur's No. 200 Nice–Cannes, No. 400 Nice–Vence, and No. 500 Nice–Grasse buses (all €1.50) stop at square Bourdet in Cagnes-sur-Mer, from where you can also take the navette to Hautes-de-Cagnes.

Visitor Information Haut-de-Cagnes Tourist Office ⊠ *Antenne du Haut-Cagnes, pl. du Dr Maurel, Haut-de-Cagnes* 🕾 *04–92–02–85–05* ⊕ *www.cagnes-tourisme.com.*

EXPLORING

Anyone would find it a pleasure to wander the old byways of Haut-de-Cagnes, some with cobbled steps, others passing under vaulted arches draped with bougainvillea. Many of the pretty residences are dollhouse size (especially the hobbit houses on rue Passebon) and most date from the 14th and 15th centuries. There's nary a shop, so the commercial horrors of Mougins or St-Paul-de-Vence are left far behind. It's little wonder the rich and literate—Soutine, Modigliani, and Simone de Beauvoir, among them—have long kept Haut-de-Cagnes a secret hideaway. Or almost: enough cars now arrive that a garage (Parking du Planastel) has been excavated out of the hillside.

Château-musée Grimaldi. Haut-de-Cagnes's steep-cobbled Vieille Ville is crowned by the fat, crenellated Château Grimaldi, built in 1310 by the Grimaldis (who now rule over Monaco) and reinforced over the centuries. You are welcomed inside the château by a grand Renaissance courtyard, off which are vaulted medieval chambers, adorned with, among other things, a vast Renaissance fireplace, a splendid 17th-century trompe-l'oeil fresco of the fall of Phaëthon from his sun-chariot, and three small specialized collections: the history of the olive, memorabilia of the cabaret star Suzy Solidor, and a collection of modern Mediterranean artists, including Cocteau and Dufy. Across the château's plaza, take some time to explore the grand **Chapelle Notre-Dame-de-la-Protection,** nearly hidden inside some medieval buildings—the Italianate bell tower gives it away. The chapel is open to the public on weekends during the same hours as the Château-musée. ⊠ *Pl. Grimaldi* ☏ *04–92–02–47–30* ▱ *€4; €6 joint ticket with Musée Renoir* ☉ *Oct.– May, Wed.–Mon. 10–noon and 2–5; June–Sept., Wed.–Mon. 10–noon and 2–6.*

Musée Renoir. After staying up and down the coast, Auguste Renoir (1841–1919) settled into a house in Les Collettes, just east of the Vieille Ville, which is now the Musée Renoir. He passed the last 12 years of his life here, painting the landscape around him, working in bronze, and rolling his wheelchair through the luxuriant garden tiered with roses, citrus groves, and some of the most spectacular olive trees along the coast. You can view this sweet and melancholic villa as it has been preserved by Renoir's children, and admire 11 of his last paintings. Although up a steep hill, Les Collettes is walkable from place du Général-du-Gaulle in central Cagnes-Ville. ⊠ *Chemindes Collettes* ☏ *04–93–20–61–07* ▱ *€4; €6 joint ticket with Château-musée Grimaldi* ☉ *Oct.–May, Wed.–Mon. 10–noon and 2–5; June–Sept., Wed.–Mon. 10–noon and 2–6.*

NICE

These days Nice strikes an engaging balance between historic Provençal grace, port-town exotica, urban energy, whimsy, and high culture. You could easily spend your entire vacation here, attuned to Nice's quirks, its rhythms, its very multicultural population, and its Mediterranean tides. The high point of the year falls in mid-February, when the city hosts one of the most spectacular Carnival celebrations in France—it ranks among the world's top three (⊕ *www.nicecarnaval.com*). As the fifth-largest city in France, this distended urban tangle is sometimes avoided, but that decision is one to be rued: Nice's 10 km-long (6 mile-long) waterfront, paralleled by the famous promenade des Anglais and lined by grand hotels, is one of the noblest and most gorgeous in France. Vieux Nice is capped by a dramatic hilltop château, below which the slopes plunge almost into the sea and at whose base a bewitching warren of ancient Mediterranean streets unfolds.

It was in this old quarter that the Greeks established a market-port in the 4th century BC and named it Nikaia. After falling to the Saracen invasions, Nice regained power and developed into an important port in the early Middle Ages. In 1388, under Louis d'Anjou, Nice, along with the hill towns behind, effectively seceded from the county of Provence and allied itself with Savoie as the Comté de Nice (Nice County). It was a relationship that lasted some 500 years, and added rich Italian flavor to the city's culture, architecture, and dialect. June 2010 marked the 150th anniversary of the County of Nice joining France, which included the inauguration of Bernar Venet's "nine movements" sculpture at the quai des États-Unis. Most residents agree it is eight movements too many.

Nice, of course, continues to evolve. The popular mayor Christian Estrosi—who is also president of France's first metropolis, Metropole Nice Côte d'Azur, created in 2010 with 46 communes—has introduced initiatives that have resulted in two recent honors. On the national front, Nice has earned the "Family Plus" label (think of the airport with its free strollers, play areas, and child-friendly restaurants); moreover, it has earned a "Gay Comfort" label from the International Gay and Lesbian Travel Association. (English brochures for Family Friendly Nice and Gay Friendly Nice can be downloaded at ⊕ *en.nicetourisme.com*). Estrosi's most ambitious project, however, is to make Nice "the Green City of the Mediterranean," and he's pulling out all the stops—witness the Green Corridor, a 30-acre park in the middle of town. The redevelopment of Nice's port is another enhancement, making it easier for amblers who want to take in the area's Genoese architecture or peruse the antiques at the Puces de Nice along quai Papacino.

■**TIP→** From the port, you can take the No. 14 bus to the 16th-century Fort du Mont-Ablan, which was just opened to the public and has exceptional views of Bordighera and St-Jean-Cap-Ferrat all the way over to Antibes.

GETTING HERE

From the airport (☎ *08–20–42–33–33* ⊕ *www.nice.aeroport.fr*), you have several options to get into Nice or beyond. The No. 98 bus (€4) stops along the promenade and the port (get off at the J.C. Bermond stop for connections to buses up and down the Riviera); the No. 99 (€4) goes to the train station with a few stops in between. The No. 23 (€1.50) stops at Terminal 1 and also goes to the train station; there are free shuttles between Terminal 1 and Terminal 2. All these buses are operated by Lignes d'Azur (☎ *08–10–06–10–06* ⊕ *www.lignesdazur. com*). The other option from the airport is a taxi (☎ *04–93–13–78–78*), costing €25 at least (for approximate fares, look under "Directions" on ⊕ *en.nice.aeroport.fr*). Nice taxis have a reputation for overcharging, so always ask for a receipt (*un reçu—"ray-sue"*). If you're using Nice as a base for exploring and want to rent a vehicle, consider Greenrent (⊕ *www.greenrent.fr*), at the corner of rue de France and rue Meyerbeer: a first in France, it rents electric or hybrid cars at prices similar to traditional rentals.

Visitor Information Nice Tourist Office ⊠ *5 promenade des Anglais* ☎ *08–92–70–74–07* ⊕ *www.nicetourism.com.*

VIEUX NICE

EXPLORING

Framed by the "château"—really a rocky promontory—and cours Saleya, Nice's Vieille Ville is the city's strongest drawing point and the best place to capture historic atmosphere. Its main core leading to the famous market has been converted into a very attractive pedestrian zone, while the grid of narrow streets, darkened by houses five and six

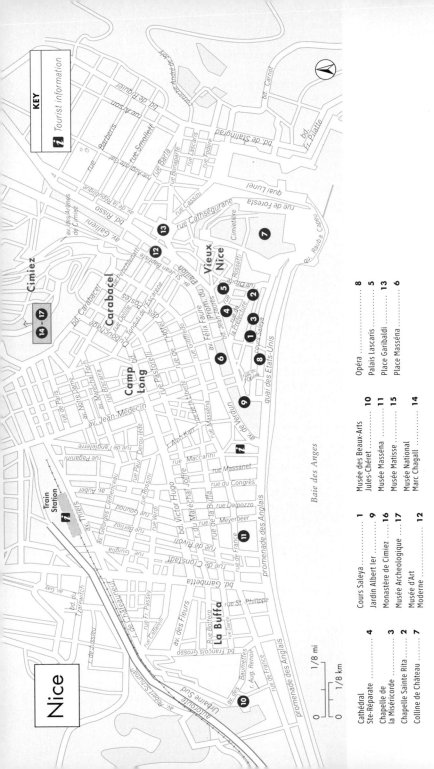

stories high with bright splashes of laundry fluttering overhead and jewel-box Baroque churches on every other corner, creates a magic that seems utterly removed from the French Riviera fast lane.

TOP ATTRACTIONS

Chapelle de la Miséricorde. A superbly balanced *pièce-montée* (wedding cake) of half-domes and cupolas, this chapel is decorated within an inch of its life with frescoes, faux marble, gilt, and crystal chandeliers. A magnificent altarpiece by Renaissance painter Ludivico Brea crowns the ensemble. ⊠ *Cours Saleya, Vieux Nice.*

Colline de Château (*Château Hill*). This hilltop park, accessible by elevator from the east end of the promenade des Anglais or by steps from place Garibaldi, commands the site of a once-massive medieval stronghold of which only a few ruins remain. From here take in extraordinary views of the Baie des Anges, the length of the promenade des Anglais, and the red-ocher roofs of the Vieille Ville. ⊙ *Daily 7–7.*

Cours Saleya. This long pedestrian thoroughfare—half street, half square—is the nerve center of Old Nice, the heart of the Vieille Ville, and the stage-set for the daily dramas of marketplace and café life. Framed with 18th-century houses and shaded by plane trees, the narrow square bursts into a fireworks-show of color Tuesday through Sunday, when flower-market vendors roll armloads of mimosas, irises, roses, and orange blossoms into *cornets* (paper cones) and thrust them into the arms of shoppers. Cafés and restaurants, all more or less touristy, fill outdoor tables with onlookers who bask in the sun. At the far-east end, antiques and *brocantes* (collectibles) draw avid junk-hounds every Monday morning. At this end you can also find place Charles Félix. From 1921 to 1938, Matisse lived in the imposing yellow stone building at Number 1, and you don't really need to visit the local museum that bears his name to understand this great artist: simply stand in the doorway of his former home and study the place de l'Ancien Senat 10 feet away—the scene is a golden Matisse pumped up to the nth power.

NEED A BREAK?

Fennocchio. Choose from a fantastic array of colorful sorbets, gelati, and ice creams—more than 100 flavors in all—and settle in to do some serious people-watching at one of the patio tables overlooking the fountain at Fennocchio. ⊠ *2 pl. Rossetti, Vieux Nice* ☎ *04–93–80–72–52* ⊕ *www.fenocchio. fr* ⊙ *Closed Dec.–Feb.*

Palais Lascaris. The aristocratic Lascaris Palace was built in 1648 for Jean-Baptiste Lascaris-Vintimille, *marechal* to the duke of Savoy. The magnificent vaulted staircase, with its massive stone balustrade and niches filled with classical gods, is surpassed in grandeur only by the Flemish tapestries (after Rubens) and the extraordinary trompe-l'oeil fresco depicting the fall of Phaëthon. With a little luck, you'll be in time for one of the many classical concerts performed here. ⊠ *15 rue Droite, Vieux Nice* ☎ *04–93–62–72–40* ⊠ *Free; €5 guided tour, including Vieille Ville* ⊙ *Wed.–Mon. 10–6.*

12

WORTH NOTING

Cathédrale Ste-Réparate. An ensemble of columns, cupolas, and symmetrical ornaments dominates the Vieille Ville, flanked by its own 18th-century bell tower and capped by its glossy ceramic-tile dome. The cathedral's interior, restored to a bright palette of ocher, golds, and rusts, has elaborate plasterwork and decorative frescoes on every surface. Note that it's usually closed between noon and 2 pm. ⊠ *3 pl. Rossetti, Vieux Nice* ⊕ *cathedrale-nice.com.*

Chapelle Sainte Rita (*Église de l'Annonciation*). This 17th-century Carmelite chapel, officially known as the Église de l'Annonciation, is a classic example of pure Niçoise Baroque, from its sculpted door to its extravagant marble work and the florid symmetry of its arches and cupolas. ⊠ *1 rue de la Poissonerie, Vieux Nice* ⊕ *www.sainte-rita.net.*

Musée d'Art Moderne. The assertive contemporary architecture of the Modern Art Museum makes a bold statement regarding Nice's presence in the modern world. The collection inside focuses intently and thoroughly on works from the late 1950s onward, but pride of place is given to sculptor Nikki de Saint Phalle's recent donation of more than 170 exceptional pieces. The rooftop terrace, sprinkled with minimalist sculptures, has stunning views over the city. Guided tours are offered by reservation Wednesday at 3 pm. ⊠ *Promenade des Arts, Vieux Nice* ☎ *04–97–13–42–01* ⊕ *www.mamac-nice.org* ⌨ *Free; guided tours €5* ☉ *Tues.–Sun. 10–6.*

Place Garibaldi. Encircled by grand vaulted arcades stuccoed in rich yellow, the broad pentagon of this square could have been airlifted out of Turin. In the center, the shrine-like fountain sculpture of Garibaldi seems to be surveying you as you stroll under the arcades and lounge in the surrounding cafés. An antiques market takes over the square on Saturday mornings.

ALONG THE PROMENADE DES ANGLAIS

Nice takes on a completely different character west of cours Saleya, with broad city blocks, vast Neoclassical hotels and apartment houses, and a series of inviting parks dense with palm trees, greenery, and splashing fountains. From the Jardin Albert Ier, once the delta of the Paillon River, the famous promenade des Anglais (which is seeking recognition as a UNESCO World Heritage Site) stretches the length of the city's waterfront. The original promenade was the brainchild of Lewis Way, an English minister in the then-growing community of British refugees drawn to Nice's climate. Nowadays it's a wide multilane boulevard thick with traffic—in fact, it's the last gasp of the N98 coastal highway. Beside it runs its charming parallel, a wide, sun-washed pedestrian walkway with intermittent steps leading down to the smooth-rock beach. A daily parade of *promeneurs*, rollerbladers, joggers, and sun baskers strolls its broad pavement, looking out over the hypnotic blue expanse of the sea. Take note of the green-painted bike path that shares parts of the promenade. The sea can be mesmerizing, so be sure not to veer over into the path of oncoming bell-ringing cyclists. Only in the wee hours is it possible to enjoy the waterfront stroll as the cream of

Like the Rio of France, Nice is lined with a gigantic crescent beach, whose prime spot, the promenade des Anglais, is home to many palace-hotels.

Nice's international society once did, when there were nothing more than hoofbeats to compete with the roar of the waves.

EXPLORING

Jardin Albert Ier (*Albert I Garden*). Along the promenade des Anglais, this luxurious garden stands over the delta of the River Paillon, underground since 1882. Every kind of flower and palm tree grows here, thrown into exotic relief by night illumination. Home base for many city festivals and sporting events, the jardin is also now the starting point for Nice's Green Corridor—a 30-acre park running right through the city, from here up to the Museum of Modern Art.

Musée des Beaux-Arts Jules-Chéret (*Jules-Chéret Fine Arts Museum*). Originally built for a member of Nice's Old Russian community, the Princess Kotschoubey, this Italianate mansion is a Belle Époque wedding cake, replete with one of the grandest staircases on the coast. After the *richissime* American James Thompson took over and the last glittering ball was held here, the villa was bought by the municipality as a museum in the 1920s. Unfortunately, much of the period decor was sold; but in its place are paintings by Degas, Boudin, Monet, Sisley, Dufy, and Jules Chéret, whose posters of winking *damselles* distill all the *joie* of the Belle Époque. From the Negresco Hotel area the museum is about a 15-minute walk up a gentle hill. ✉ *33 av. des Baumettes, Centre Ville* ☎ *04-92-15-28-28* ⊕ *www.musee-beaux-arts-nice.org* ✆ *Free; guided tours €5 (reservations required)* ☉ *Tues.–Sun. 10–6.*

Musée Masséna (*Masséna Palace*). This spectacular Belle Époque villa houses the **Musée d'Art et d'Histoire** (Museum of Art and History), where familiar paintings from French, Italian, and Dutch masters line the walls. A visit to the palace gardens set with towering palm trees, a marble bust of the handsome General Masséna, and backdropped by the ornate trim of the Hôtel Negresco, is a delight; this is one of Nice's most imposing oases. ⊠ *Entrance at, 65 rue de France, Centre Ville* ☎ *04–93–91–19–10* ⊠ *Free* ◷ *Wed.–Mon. 10–6.*

Opéra. A half block west of the cours Saleya stands a flamboyant Italian-style theater designed by Charles Garnier, architect of the Paris Opéra. It's home today to the Opéra de Nice, with a permanent chorus, orchestra, and ballet corps. The season runs from mid-November to mid-June, and tickets cost anywhere from €8 to €85. ⊠ *4 rue St-François-de-Paule, Vieux Nice* ☎ *04–92–17–40–00* ⊕ *www.opera-nice.org.*

Place Masséna. As cours Saleya is the heart of the Vieille Ville, so this impressive and broad square is the heart of the entire city. It's framed by early 17th-century, Italian-style arcaded buildings, their facades stuccoed in rich red ocher. On the west flank sits the city's Belle Époque icon, the Hôtel Negresco. This enticing space hosts an event at least once a month.

CIMIEZ

Once the site of the powerful Roman settlement Cemenelum, the hilltop neighborhood of Cimiez—4 km (2½ miles) north of cours Saleya—is Nice's most luxurious quarter (use Bus No. 15 from place Masséna or avenue Jean-Médecin to visit its sights).

EXPLORING

Monastère de Cimiez. This fully functioning monastery is worth the pilgrimage. You can find a lovely **garden,** replanted along the lines of the original 16th-century layout; the **Musée Franciscain,** a didactic museum tracing the history of the Franciscan order; and a 15th-century **church** containing three works of remarkable power and elegance by Bréa. ⊠ *Pl. du Monastère, Cimiez* ☎ *04–93–81–00–04* ⊠ *Free* ◷ *Church Thurs.–Tues. 9–6 , Sun. 2:30–8:30; museum Mon.–Sat. 10–noon and 3–6.*

Musée Archéologique (*Archaeology Museum*). This museum, next to the Musée Matisse, has a dense collection of objects extracted from digs around the Roman city of Cemenelum, which flourished from the 1st to the 5th century. Among the fascinating ruins are an amphitheater, frigidarium, gymnasium, baths, and sewage trenches, some dating back to the 3rd century. ■TIP➜ It's best to avoid midday visits on warm days. ⊠ *160 av. des Arènes-de-Cimiez, Cimiez* ☎ *04–93–81–59–57* ⊕ *www. musee-archeologique-nice.org* ⊠ *Free; €5 guided tour* ◷ *Wed.–Mon. 10–6.*

Fodor'sChoice ★ **Musée Matisse.** In the '60s the city of Nice bought this lovely, light-bathed 17th-century villa, surrounded by the ruins of Roman civilization, and restored it to house a large collection of Henri Matisse's works. Matisse settled along Nice's waterfront in 1917, seeking a sun cure after a bout with pneumonia, and remained here until his death in 1954. During his years on the French Riviera, Matisse maintained intense friendships and artistic liaisons with Renoir, who lived in Cagnes, and with Picasso, who lived in Mougins and Antibes. He eventually moved up to the rarefied isolation of Cimiez and took an apartment in the Hôtel Regina (now an apartment building, just across from the museum), where he lived out the rest of his life. Matisse walked often in the parklands around the Roman remains and was buried in an olive grove outside the Cimiez cemetery. The collection of artworks includes several pieces the artist donated to the city before his death; the rest were donated by his family. In every medium and context—paintings, gouache cutouts, engravings, and book illustrations—the collection represents the evolution of his art, from Cézanne-like still lifes to exuberant dancing paper dolls. Even the furniture and accessories speak of Matisse, from the Chinese vases to the bold-printed fabrics with which he surrounded himself. A series of black-and-white photographs captures the artist at work, surrounded by personal—and telling—details. ✉ *164 av. des Arènes-de-Cimiez, Cimiez* ☎ *04–93–81–08–08* 🌐 *www.musee-matisse-nice.org* 🎫 *Free* 🕒 *Wed.–Mon. 10–6.*

Musée National Marc Chagall (*Marc Chagall Museum of Biblical Themes*). Having just celebrated its 40th anniversary last year, this museum has one of the finest permanent collections of Chagall's (1887–1985) late works. Superbly displayed, 17 vast canvases depict biblical themes, each in emphatic, joyous colors. Chamber music and classical concert series also take place here, though admission fees may apply. ✉ *Av. du Dr-Ménard, head up av. Thiers, then take left onto av. Malausséna, cross railway tracks, and take first right up av. de l'Olivetto, Cimiez* ☎ *04–93–53–87–20* 🌐 *www.musee-chagall.fr* 🎫 *€7.50–€9.50 (under-26 free)* 🕒 *Wed.–Mon. 10-6.*

WHERE TO EAT

$ ITALIAN 🍴 **Attimi.** Specializing in salads, pizzas, and pastas—prepared on the spot from local produce—this place offers a refreshing, light alternative to all those heavy French dishes. But Attimi is as hot as the lasagna Bolognese it serves, so you'll need to reserve or eat early. A seat on the terrace next the fountain at the end of place Masséna lets you dine with a side order of people-watching. [$] *Average main: €14* ✉ *10 pl. Masséna* ☎ *04–93–62–00–22* 🌐 *www.attimi.fr* ✍ *Reservations essential.*

$ BISTRO 🍴 **Bistrot de l'École de Nice.** You might walk past this unassuming building, facing a Laundromat, without figuring out it's a place to eat. But the restaurant deserves a double-take. At this art-and-gastronomy fusion, chef Kei collaborates with a Franco-Japanese DJ and *artiste* devoted to promoting Niçois arts and culture internationally. The result is a relaxed and very affordable bistrot (note that second t) serving two-, three-, and four-course menus. How can you really choose between gnocchi carbonara with black truffles and lobster risotto with pastis? [$] *Average main: €18* ✉ *15 rue de la Buffa, New Town* ☎ *04–93–81–39–30* 🌐 *www.lecoledenice.com* 🕒 *Closed Sun. No lunch Sat.*

$ FRENCH 🍴 **Chez René Socca.** This back-alley landmark is the most popular dive in town for *socca*, the chickpea-pancake snack food unique to Nice. Rustic olive-wood tables line the street, and curt waiters splash down your drink order. Then you get in line, choose your plate, and carry it steaming to the table yourself. It's off place Garibaldi on the edge of the Vieille Ville, across from the old Gare Routière (bus station).

$ *Average main: €4* ✉ *2 rue Miralheti, Vieux Nice* ☎ *04–93–92–05–73* 🚫 *No credit cards* ⊙ *Closed Mon. and Jan.*

$ ✕ **Co-t-Café.** This brightly colored local café, a block from both the
CAFÉ Hôtel Negresco and the promenade, has the best coffee in Nice; expect creamy lattés, iced coffees, and cappuccinos, plus teas and smoothies, in all sizes, to stay or to go. Sandwiches and wraps, excellently priced and made fresh each morning, are perfect for the beach. A Champagne brunch for two is also on the menu. $ *Average main: €8* ✉ *11 rue Meyerbeer, Promenade Nice* ☎ *04–93–16–09–84* ⊙ *Closed Dec.–Feb.*

$$ ✕ **Don Camillo Creations.** The once-fading Don Camillo has shed its staid,
FRENCH old maid–ish decor, introduced a swanky, modern look, and added a wine bar. The food, always good, is now even better with just a touch more inspiration; chef Jean-David Colom reinvents Niçois classiques that are as tasty as they are affordable. Try the roast lobster and cauliflower stuffed with lobster claws and caviar. $ *Average main: €22* ✉ *5 rue des Ponchettes, Vieux Nice* ☎ *04–93–85–67–95* ⊕ *www. doncamillo-creations.fr* ⊙ *Closed Sun. and Mon.*

$$$ ✕ **Grand Café de Turin.** Whether you squeeze onto a banquette in the
SEAFOOD dark, low-ceiling bar or win a coveted table under the arcaded porticoes on place Garibaldi, this is *the* place to go for shellfish in Nice: sea snails, clams, plump *fines de claires* and salty *bleues* oysters, plus urchins by the dozen. It's packed noon and night (and has been since it opened in 1908), so don't be too put off by the sometimes brusque reception of the waiters. ■ TIP→ You may want to take a sweater as there's always a breeze. $ *Average main: €30* ✉ *5 pl. Garibaldi, Vieux Nice* ☎ *04–93–62–29–52* ⊕ *www.cafedeturin.fr.*

$ ✕ **La Mérenda.** The back-to-bistro boom climaxed here when Dominique
FRENCH Le Stanc retired his crown at the Negresco to take over this tiny, unpretentious temple of Provençal cuisine. Now he and his wife work in the miniature open kitchen, creating the ultimate versions of stuffed sardines, pistou, and slow-simmered *daubes* (beef stews). To reserve entry to the inner sanctum for one of the two lunch or dinner sittings, you must stop by in person (there's no telephone and it's cash only). $ *Average main: €16* ✉ *4 rue Raoul Bosio, Vieux Nice* ⊕ *www.lamerenda.net* 🚫 *No credit cards* ⊙ *Closed weekends and 1st 2 wks in Aug.*

$$$ ✕ **Terres de Truffes.** Celebrity chef Bruno Clément opened this stylish
FRENCH bistrot-deli in an effort to bring the exquisite but expensive taste of truffles to the masses. He succeeded. Truffles come with everything, from caramelized truffle ice cream to truffle-infused baked Brie, and even the most budget-conscious can afford to indulge. Even so, how many truffles can one person consume? $ *Average main: €30* ✉ *11 rue St-Francois-de-Paule, Vieux Nice* ☎ *04–93–62–07–68* ⊕ *www. terresdetruffes.com* ⊙ *Closed. Sun. and Mon.*

WHERE TO STAY

For expanded hotel reviews, visit Fodors.com.

$$$$ 🏨 **Boscolo Hotel Exedra Nizza.** One step inside the lobby of this Belle
HOTEL Époque extravaganza and you've blasted off into the nether regions of
Fodor's Choice the 21st century—think the white-on-white, Rococo-ed rooms at the
★ end of Kubrick's *2001: A Space Odyssey*—and arrived at a place that raises the hotel experience to brand new heights. **Pros:** infinite chic;

infinite taste; infinite service; very attractive online packages. **Cons:** the building is a 1910 beauty, but don't look for Old World Nice inside; some rooms are on the small side. Ⓢ *Rooms from: €250* ✉ *12 bd. Victor Hugo, New Town* ☎ *04–93–16–75–70* ⊕ *www.boscolohotels.com* ↪ *105 rooms, 8 suites* ⍝ *Breakfast.*

$ ⍟ **Hotel Felix Beach.** This hotel sits a block from the beach on popular rue
HOTEL Masséna—and, if you choose one of the four rooms that feature a tiny balcony, you'll have a ringside seat over the pedestrian thoroughfare. **Pros:** prime location of hotel makes perfect touring sense; owners are so nice that you feel right at home. **Cons:** rooms can be noisy, especially those facing the street; some rooms are very basic. Ⓢ *Rooms from: €85* ✉ *41 rue Masséna, Pl. Masséna* ☎ *04–93–88–67–73* ⊕ *www.hotel-felix.com* ↪ *14 rooms* ⍝ *Breakfast.*

$$$$ ⍟ **Hôtel Negresco.** This white-stucco slice of old-fashioned Riviera
HOTEL extravagance has hosted everyone from the Beatles to the Burtons and
Fodor's Choice remains the icon of Nice today, accommodating well-heeled guests in
★ elegant, uniquely decorated guest rooms replete with swagged drapes and fine antiques (plus a few unfortunate "with-it" touches like those plastic-glitter bathtubs). **Pros:** for those interested in the past, this elegant hotel is a must; food at the famous Chantecler is *formidable*. **Cons:** breakfast is expensive (€30). Ⓢ *Rooms from: €225* ✉ *37 promenade des Anglais* ☎ *04–93–16–64–00* ⊕ *www.hotel-negresco-nice.com* ↪ *96 rooms, 21 suites* ⍝ *No meals.*

$$ ⍟ **Windsor.** This is a memorably eccentric hotel—most of its white-on-
HOTEL white rooms either have frescoes of mythological themes or are works of artists' whimsy—but the real draw at this otherworldly place is its astonishing city-center garden, a tropical oasis of lemon, magnolia, and palm trees. **Pros:** private pool and garden in heart of city; enthusiastic welcome; you can print your boarding pass for free in lobby. **Cons:** decor is not for everyone (look online before booking!); street rooms can be noisy; Ultra-Violet elevator is cool the first time, annoying by the end of the week. Ⓢ *Rooms from: €128* ✉ *11 rue Dalpozzo* ☎ *04–93–88–59–35* ⊕ *www.hotelwindsornice.com* ↪ *57 rooms* ⍝ *Some meals.*

NIGHTLIFE AND THE ARTS

Acropolis. Classical music, ballet performances and traditional French pop concerts take place at Nice's convention center, the Acropolis. ✉ *Palais des Congrès, esplanade John F. Kennedy, Centre Ville* ☎ *04–93–92–83–00* ⊕ *www.nice-acropolis.com.*

Bar Le Relais. If you're all dressed up and have just won big, invest in a drink in the intimate walnut-and-velour Bar Le Relais, in the iconic Hôtel Negresco. It's worth the price just to get a peak at the washrooms (just don't trip over the owner's lounging cat Carmen). Live music plays nightly from 7:30 pm on. ✉ *37 promenade des Anglais, Promenade* ☎ *04–93–16–64–00* ⊕ *www.hotel-negresco-nice.com.*

Casino du Palais de la Méditerranée. In the 1920s, the swanky Palais de la Méditerranée drew performers like Charlie Chaplin and Edith Piaf; however, the establishment lost its glory and was demolished in 1990, save for the facade we see today. Reopened with hotel service in 2004, the contemporary version has 200 slot machines, plus roulette,

No wonder Matisse lived on the top floor of the golden yellow building seen here at the end of the cours Saleya—this marketplace is one of France's most colorful.

blackjack, and Texas hold 'em poker tables. Theme-night Thursdays include a buffet and live entertainment (€25–€40). The casino is open weekdays from 10 am to 3 am and until 4 on the weekends. ✉ *15 promenade des Anglais, Promenade* ☎ *04–92–14–68–00 show reservations* ⊕ *www.casinomediterranee.com.*

Casino Ruhl. The Casino Ruhl is still gleaming neon-bright, but it's not as sophisticated as in days gone by. You can enjoy a Las Vegas–style show and try your luck in the gaming rooms (passport required for entry). ✉ *1 promenade des Anglais, Promenade* ☎ *04–97–03–12–22* ⊕ *www. lucienbarriere.com* 🖃 *Free* ☺ *Daily 9 am–4 am.*

Glam. The hottest gay club in Nice, Glam has the best dance music in town and is open to all clubbers in the know. The only criteria: be cool. ✉ *6 rue Eugène Emmanuel, Port Nice* ☎ *06–60–55–26–61* ⊕ *www. leglam.org.*

High Club. Nice was a sleepy city until High came around. Open from 11:45 pm until 6 am Friday, Saturday, and every other Sunday, tables here come with a bottle: €120 for four people, €400 for a VIP magnum (four or five people) on top of the cover charge at door (up to €20). ✉ *45 promenade des Anglais, Port Nice* ☎ *06–16–95–75–87* ⊕ *www. highclub.fr.*

Nice Jazz Festival. Over four days in July, the Nice Jazz Festival draws performers from around the world. ☎ *08–92–68–36–22* ⊕ *www. nicejazzfestival.fr.*

Opéra de Nice. The season at the Opéra de Nice runs from September to June. ✉ *4 rue St-François-de-Paule, Vieux Nice* ☎ *04–92–17–40–40* ⊕ *www.opera-nice.org.*

Seven Blue Bar. Don't forget your camera when you head up to this panoramic bar on the seventh floor of the Clarion Grand Hôtel Aston. The scenes of old Nice and the new "Coulée Verte" (Green Corridor) across to the airport are spectacular. In the summer season, the bar moves to the rooftop, where there's a pool (for guests) and 360-degree views of Nice. The best part is that drinks are more than reasonably priced. ✉ *12 av. Felix Faure, Centre Ville* ☎ *04–92–17–53–00* ⊕ *www. hotel-aston.com.*

THE OUTDOORS

Nice's **beaches** extend all along the Baie des Anges, backed full length by the promenade des Anglais. Public stretches alternate with posh private beaches that have restaurants—and bar service, mattresses and parasols, waterskiing, parasailing, windsurfing, and jet-skiing. The general public can access the private beaches; mattresses cost on average €20 per, and you're expected to buy any food or drink from the restaurant that controls the beach. ■**TIP**➔ There have been more frequent jellyfish sightings (méduse) along the coast in recent years. A helpful website which shows alerts is ⊕ www.medazur.obs-vlfr.fr/previsions-d-echouage. It's smart to keep antihistamines handy, and remember to clean a sting with sea water—fresh water will make it worse.

Beau Rivage. One of the handiest and biggest private beaches is the Beau Rivage, across from the Opéra and next to the Jardin Albert Ier. The €19 daily rental fee for a lounger is a good investment (book the night before) as it allows access to the toilets and the shade of a parasol. The beach restaurant is excellent, but you can bring your own beach bag of goodies. ✉ *24 rue Saint François de Paule* ☎ *04–92–47–82–82* ⊕ *www. plagenicebeaurivage.com* ☉ *Closed Nov.–Mar.*

Florida Beach. One of the new private beaches making a splash on the Prom, Florida is très hip and has an excellent restaurant and bar service. ✉ *71 promenade des Anglais* ☎ *04–93–44–72–86* ☉ *Closed Nov.–Mar.*

Hi Beach. Just west of the Negresco's Neptune plage (with its not-so-friendly service), Hi Beach is a tad more pricy than its sister strands—you'll pay €22 for a mattress or €14 for chips and guacamole, for example. But there's free Wi-Fi and three dedicated zones: Hi Energy, Hi Relax and, for the kids, Hi Play. There's a beach bar and tons of food (including sushi), too, along with Hi Body if you need a massage to help you relax after relaxing. ✉ *47 promenade des Anglais, Promenade* ☎ *04–97–14–00–83* ⊕ *www.hi-beach.net.*

SHOPPING

Alziari. Olive oil by the gallon in the famous blue-and-yellow cans with old-fashioned labels is sold at tiny Alziari. ✉ *14 rue St-François-de-Paule, Vieux Nice* ⊕ *www.alziari.com.fr* ☉ *Mon.–Sat. 8:30–12:30 and 2:15–7.*

antiques and brocante market. The antiques and brocante market, by the old port, is held Tuesday through Sunday. ✉ *Pl. Robilante, Vieux Nice.*

Confiserie Florian du Vieux Nice. A good source for crystallized fruit (a Nice specialty) is the Confiserie Florian du Vieux Nice, open every day except Christmas, on the west side of the port. ⊠ *14 quai Papacino, Vieux Nice* ⊕ *www.confiserieflorian.com.*

flower market. You can find all kinds of plants, fruits, and vegetables at the flower market, Tuesday through Sunday. On Monday an antiques market fills the space. ⊠ *Cours Saleya, Vieux Nice.*

Henri Auer. The venerable Henri Auer has sold crystallized fruit since 1820. It's open Tuesday through Saturday 9-6. ⊠ *7 rue St-François de Paule, Vieux Nice* ⊕ *www.maison-auer.com.*

La Chapellerie. For every sort of hat imaginable, from the basic beret to huge creations with many a flower and ostrich plume, check out La Chapellerie at their cours Saleya boutique (there are two other shops in Nice). ⊠ *36 cours Saleya, Vieux Nice* ⊕ *www.chapellerie.com.*

Mademoiselle. You have to hand it to the French, they even do second-hand fashion right. Steps away from the Hôtel Negresco, Mademoiselle has quickly become a must-stop shop in Nice: Chanel, Dior, Louis Vuitton, Hermès . . . you name it, the gang's all here, at least in vintage terms. You'll find lots of luxury brand clothes, shoes, bags, and belts to rummage through—all of it excellently priced and gorgeously displayed. Open every day, don't be surprised to walk by at 10 pm on a summer's evening to find owners Jeremy and Sephora sipping champagne with clients. ⊠ *41 rue de France, New Town.*

THE EASTERN FRENCH RIVIERA

With the mistral-proof Alps and Pre-Alps playing bodyguard against inland winds, this stretch of the Riviera is the most renowned and glamorous stretch of coastline in Europe. Here, coddled by mild Mediterranean breezes, waterfront resorts—Villefranche and Menton—draw energy from the thriving city of Nice, while jutting tropical peninsulas—Cap Ferrat, Cap Martin—frame the tiny principality of Monaco. Here the corniche highways snake above sparkling waters, their pink-and-white villas turning faces toward the sun. Cliffs bristle with palm trees and parasol pines, and a riot of mimosa, bougainvillea, jasmine, and even cactus blooms in the hothouse climate. Crowded with sunseekers and billionaires, the Riviera still reveals quiet corners with heart-stopping views of sea, sun, and mountains—all within one memorable frame.

The lay of the land east of Nice is nearly vertical, as the coastline is one great cliff, terraced by three parallel highways—the **Basse corniche**, the **Moyenne corniche**, and the **Grande corniche**—that wind along its graduated crests. The lowest (*basse*) is the slowest, following the coast and crawling through the main streets of resorts—including downtown Monte Carlo, Cap-Martin, Beaulieu, and Villefranche-sur-Mer. The highest (*grande*) is the fastest, but its panoramic views are blocked by villas, and there are few safe overlooks. The middle (*moyenne*) runs from Nice to Menton and offers views down over the shoreline and villages—plus it passes through a few picturesque towns, most notably Èze.

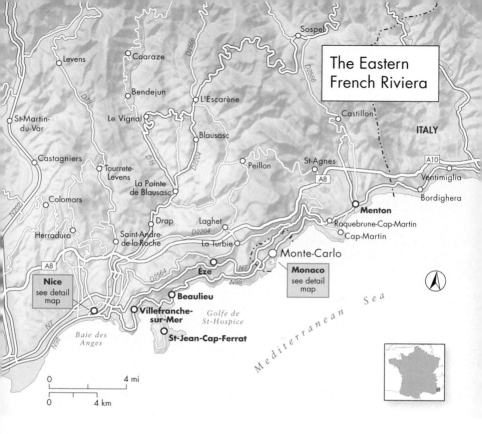

VILLEFRANCHE-SUR-MER

10 km (6 miles) east of Nice.

Fodor's Choice Nestled discreetly along the deep scoop of harbor between Nice and Cap
★ Ferrat, this pretty watercolor of a fishing port seems surreal, flanked as
it is by the big city of Nice and the assertive wealth of Monaco. Famed
for its big harbor, Villefranche is pretty and pleasant, a somewhat overbuilt stage set of brightly colored houses.

GETTING HERE

Villefranche is a major stop on the Marseilles–Ventimiglia coastal train
route, with more than 40 arrivals every day from Nice (7 mins, €1.70).
Buses connect with Nice and Monaco via Lignes d'Azur's No. 100 (Nos.
80, 81, and 84 also connect Villefranche and Nice). ■TIP→ When you
get off the No. 100, there's an excellent bakery on the corner in front
of the garden—it's best to have a little sustenance before tackling all
those stairs (a few feet to the right) that lead down to the sea.

Visitor Information Villefranche-sur-Mer Tourist Office ⊠ *Jardin Francois
Binon* ☎ 04–93–01–73–68 ⊕ www.villefranche-sur-mer.fr.

EXPLORING

Whether it's just the force of gravity, or the fact that it remains picturesque, the harbor here relentlessly draws visitors down Villefranche's hillsides to the main waterfront. Here, genuine fishermen actually skim up to its docks in weathered-blue *barques*. They occasionally bid welcome to travelers who amble along the streets of the Vieille Ville, which tilt downhill just as they did in the 13th century. Some of the prettiest spots in town are around place de la Paix, rue du Poilu, and place du Conseil, which overlooks the water. The deep harbor, in the caldera of a volcano, was once preferred by the likes of Onassis and Niarchos and royals on their yachts (today, unfortunately, these are usually replaced by warships, from the nearby naval base). The character of Villefranche was subtly shaped by the artists and authors who gathered at the Hôtel Welcome—Diaghilev and Stravinsky, taking a break from the Ballet Russe in Monaco; Somerset Maugham and Evelyn Waugh; and, above all, Jean Cocteau, who came here to recover from the excesses of Paris life. Guided tours of the village (sometimes in English) depart every Friday morning at 10 from the tourist office (€5). Just remember to wear flat shoes—there are lots of cobblestone streets and slope-y climbs here.

Chapelle St-Pierre. So enamored was Jean Cocteau of this painterly fishing port that he decorated the 14th-century Chapelle St-Pierre with images from the life of St. Peter and dedicated it to the village's fishermen. ✉ *Quai Courbet* ☎ *04–93–76–90–70* 🎟 *€2.50* 🕓 *Spring and summer, Tues.–Sun. 10–noon and 3–7; fall and winter.–Apr., Tues.–Sun. 10–noon and 2–6.*

Citadelle St-Elme. Open year-round, the stalwart 16th-century Citadelle St-Elme, restored to perfect condition, anchors the harbor with its broad, sloping stone walls. Beyond its drawbridge lie the city's administrative offices and a group of minor gallery-museums, with a scattering of works by Picasso and Miró. Whether or not you stop into these private collections of local art (all free of charge), you're welcome to stroll around the inner grounds and circle the imposing exterior. ✉ *Harbor* 🎟 *Free* 🕓 *Museums: June–Sept., Tues.–Sat. 10–noon and 3–6:30, Sun. 3–6:30; Oct.–May, Tues.–Sat. 10–noon and 2–5:30, Sun. 2–5:30.*

Rue Obscure. Running parallel to the waterfront, the extraordinary 13th-century rue Obscure (literally, "Dark Street") is entirely covered by vaulted arcades; it sheltered the people of Villefranche when the Germans fired their parting shots—an artillery bombardment—near the end of World War II.

WHERE TO EAT AND STAY

For expanded hotel reviews, visit Fodors.com.

$$$ FRENCH 🍴 **La Grignotière.** Tucked down a narrow side street, just a few steps away from the marketplace (and from the heat of the sun), this small, friendly eatery offers up generous portions of top-quality, inexpensive dishes. The homemade lasagna is excellent, as is the spaghetti pistou. [$] *Average main: €25* ✉ *3 rue du Poilu* ☎ *04–93–76–79–83* 🕓 *Closed Tues. No lunch Mon.–Sat.*

$$$ FRENCH 🍴 **La Mayssa.** Perched high on the port building's large rooftop terrace, this is the place to see and be seen. It offers spectacular views of the bay

and Cap Ferrat, along with a nice selection of cosmopolitan à la carte dishes, such as seared beef tenderloin with mushroom sauce or sole cooked in dill butter sauce with vegetable tagliatelle. [$] *Average main: €26* ✉ *Pl. Wilson* ☎ *04–93–01–75–08* 🌐 *www.lemayssa.fr* 🕒 *Closed Tues. No dinner Sun. and Mon.*

12

$$$$ HOTEL **Hôtel Welcome.** Somerset Maugham holed up in one of the tiny crow's-nest rooms at the top, Jean Cocteau lived here while writing *Orphée*, and Elizabeth Taylor and Richard Burton used to tie one on in the bar (now nicely renovated), at this waterfront landmark—which remains a comfortable and noteworthy retreat. **Pros:** artistic heritage makes for a nostalgic trip into the Roaring Twenties, with photos of stars who've spent the night here adorning the walls; service is excellent; accommodating staff; credit card payments in American dollars. **Cons:** decor, especially on the top floor, is distinctly nautical in flavor; some rooms are oddly shaped—narrow and long—so feel smaller. [$] *Rooms from: €198* ✉ *3 quai Amiral Courbet* ☎ *04–93–76–27–62* 🌐 *www.welcomehotel.com* 🛏 *35 rooms, 3 suites* 🕒 *Closed 5 wks from mid-Nov.* 🍴 *Breakfast.*

BEAULIEU

4 km (2½ miles) east of Villefranche, 14 km (9 miles) east of Nice.

With its back pressed hard against the cliffs of the corniche and sheltered between the peninsulas of Cap Ferrat and Cap Roux, this once-grand resort basks in a tropical microclimate that earned its central neighborhood the name *Petite Afrique*. The town was the pet of 19th-century society, and its grand hotels welcomed Empress Eugénie, the Prince of Wales, and Russian nobility. Beaulieu is still a posh address, but if you're a picky atmosphere-hunter, you may find the town center too built-up with apartment buildings.

GETTING HERE

With frequent arrivals and departures, Beaulieu is a main stop on the Marseille–Ventimiglia coastal train line. From Beaulieu hourly No. 81 buses (€1.50) connect with neighboring St-Jean-Cap-Ferrat.

Visitor Information Beaulieu Tourist Office ✉ *Pl. Georges Clemenceau* ☎ *04–93–01–02–21* 🌐 *www.beaulieusurmer.fr.*

EXPLORING

Fodor's Choice ★ **Villa Kerylos.** One manifestation of Beaulieu's Belle Époque excess is the eye-knocking Villa Kerylos, a 1902 mansion built in the style of classical Greece (to be exact, of the villas that existed on the island of Delos in the 2nd century BC). It was the dream house of amateur archaeologist Théodore Reinach, who hailed from a wealthy German family, helped the French in their excavations at Delphi, and became an authority on ancient Greek music. He commissioned an Italian architect from Nice, Emmanuel Pontremoli, to surround him with Grecian delights: cool Carrara marble, rare fruitwoods, and a dining salon where guests reclined to eat *à la grecque*. Don't miss this—it's one of the most unusual houses in the south of France. Not far from away is the **promenade Maurice Rouvier,** an enchanting coastal path that leads to St-Jean-Cap-Ferrat. ■ **TIP→ A combination ticket allows you to also** visit Villa Ephrussi del Rothschild in nearby St-Jean-Cap-Ferrat in the same week. ✉ *Rue Gustave-Eiffel* ☎ *04–93–01–01–44* ⊕ *www.villa-kerylos.com* 🖅 *€9.50; €18 for both villas* ☉ *Mid-Feb.–June, Sept., and Oct., daily 10–6; July and Aug., daily 10–7; Nov.–mid-Feb., weekdays 2–6, weekends 10–6.*

ST-JEAN-CAP-FERRAT

2 km (1 mile) south of Beaulieu on D25.

This luxuriously sited pleasure port moors the peninsula of Cap Ferrat; from the port-side walkways and crescent of beach you can look over the sparkling blue harbor to the graceful green bulk of the corniches. Yachts purr in and out of port, and their passengers scuttle into cafés for take-out drinks to enjoy on their private decks. Unfortunately, Cap Ferrat is a vast peninsula and hides its secrets—except for the Villa Ephrussi, most estates are well hidden behind iron gates and towering hedges.

Coastline promenade. While Cap Ferrat's villas are sequestered for the most part in the depths of tropical gardens, you can nonetheless walk its entire coastline promenade if you strike out from the port; from the restaurant Capitaine Cook, cut right up avenue des Fossés, turn right on avenue Vignon, and follow the chemin de la Carrière. The 11-km (7-mile) walk passes through rich tropical flora and, on the west side, follows white cliffs buffeted by waves. When you've traced the full outline of the peninsula, veer up the chemin du Roy past the fabulous gardens of the **Villa des Cèdres,** owned by King Leopold II of Belgium at the turn of the last century. The king owned several opulent estates along the French Riviera, undoubtedly paid for by his enslavement of the Belgian Congo. Past the gardens, you can reach the **plage de Passable,** from which you cut back across the peninsula's wrist. A shorter loop takes you from town out to the **Pointe de St-Hospice,** much of the walk shaded by wind-twisted pines. From the port, climb avenue Jean Mermoz to place Paloma and follow the path closest to the waterfront. At the point are an 18th-century prison tower, a 19th-century chapel, and unobstructed views of Cap Martin. ∎**TIP➔** You can arrange a visit to the Villa des Cèdres by calling Mr. Marteau at ☎ 04–93–77–00–16. .

Villa Ephrussi de Rothschild. Between the port and the mainland, the floridly beautiful Villa Ephrussi de Rothschild bears witness to the wealth and worldly flair of the baroness who had it built. Constructed in 1905 in neo-Venetian style (its flamingo-pink facade was thought not to be in the best of taste by the local gentry), the house was baptized "Ile-de-France" in homage to the Baroness Bétrice de Rothschild's favorite ocean liner. In keeping with that theme, her staff used to wear sailing costumes and her ship travel kit is on view in her bedroom. Precious artworks, tapestries, and furniture adorn the salons—in typical Rothschildian fashion, each is given over to a different 18th-century "époque." Upstairs are the private apartments of Madame la Baronne, which can only be seen on a guided tour offered around noon. The grounds are landscaped with no fewer than seven gardens and topped off with a Temple of Diana. Be sure to allow yourself time to wander here, as this is one of the few places on the coast where you'll be allowed to experience the lavish pleasures characteristic of the Belle Époque Côte d'Azur. Tea and light lunches, served in a glassed-in porch overlooking the grounds and spectacular coastline, encourage you to linger. ■ TIP➜ A combination ticket allows you to also visit Villa Kerylos in nearby Beaulieu in the same week. ⊠ *Av. Ephrussi* ☎ *04–93–01–33–09* ⊕ *www.villa-ephrussi.com* 🖳 *€12; €19 for both villas* ⊗ *Mid-Feb–June, Sept., and Oct., daily 10–6; July and Aug., daily 10–7; Nov.–mid-Feb., weekdays 2–6, weekends 10–6.*

WHERE TO EAT AND STAY

For expanded hotel reviews, visit Fodors.com.

$$$ ✕ **Le Sloop.** This sleek port-side restaurant caters to the yachting crowd
SEAFOOD and sailors who cruise into dock for lunch. The focus is fish, of course: *soupe de poisson* (fish soup), *St-Pierre* (John Dory) steamed with asparagus, roasted whole sea bass. Outdoor tables surround a tiny "garden" of potted palms. Chef Alain Therlicocq has manned the kitchen for 28 years and his five-course fixed menu, including a fish and meat dish, is one of the best values on the coast. Reservations are necessary in the summer, but if you arrive without, ask with a smile for a table and Alain's wife, Regine, will find you *une p'tite place.* $ *Average main: €25* ⊠ *Port de St Jean Cap Ferrat* ☎ *04–93–01–48–63* ⊕ *www. restaurantsloop.com* ⊗ *Closed Tues. dinner and Wed. and Sun. mid-Sept.–June and mid-Nov.–Dec 20. No lunch Wed. July–mid-Sept.*

$$$ 🏨 **Brise Marine.** With a glowing Provençal-yellow facade, bright blue
HOTEL shutters, balustraded sea terrace, and pretty pastel guest rooms, Brise Marine fulfills most desires for that perfect, picturesque Cap Ferrat hotel. **Pros:** nighttime quiet broken only by gently breaking waves; excellent value for location; close walking distance to beach. **Cons:** some rooms are small; only five available parking spots (paid) and they must be reserved in advance. $ *Rooms from: €172* ⊠ *58 av. Jean Mermoz* ☎ *04–93–76–04–36* ⊕ *www.hotel-brisemarine.com* 🛏 *16 rooms* ⊗ *Closed Nov.–Feb.* ⦿ *No meals.*

$$$$ 🏨 **Grand Hôtel du Cap-Ferrat.** Just this side of paradise, this extrava-
HOTEL gantly expensive hotel has always been the exclusive playground for Hollywood's elite; now, after a grand refurbishment, it is *the* new standard for discreet Cap-Ferrat moneyed luxury. **Pros:** epitome of wealth and luxury; every detail is well thought out and promptly attended to; legendary hotel swim instructor Pierre Gruneberg has taught Picasso to Sinatra to Robin Williams. **Cons:** forget it if you're on a budget. $ *Rooms from: €690* ⊠ *71 bd. du Charles du Gaulle* ☎ *04–93–76–50–50* ⊕ *www.ghcf.fr* 🛏 *49 rooms, 24 suites (8 with private pools)* ⊗ *Le Cap and Club Dauphin restaurants closed Oct.–Mar.*

ÈZE

2 km (1 mile) east of Beaulieu; 12 km (7 miles) east of Nice; 7 km (4½ miles) west of Monte Carlo.

Fodor's Choice Towering above the coast and crowned with ramparts and the ruins
★ of a medieval château, preposterously beautiful Èze (pronounced *ehz*) is the most accessible of all the perched villages—this means crowds,

many of whom head here to shop in the boutique-lined staircase-streets. (Happily the shops are largely quite stylish, and there's a nice preponderance of bric-a-brac and vintage fabric dealers.) But most travelers come here to drink in the views, for no one can deny that this is the most spectacularly sited of all coastal promontories. It's no wonder U2's Bono and the Edge have beach houses here.

GETTING HERE

Èze Village is the famous hilltop destination, but Èze extends down to the coastal beach and the township of Èze-sur-Mer. To get to the hilltop village from the train station, take bus No. 83 run by Lignes d'Azur (☎ 08–10–06–10–06 ⊕ *www.lignesdazur.com*). The trip, with its 1,001 switchbacks up the steep mountainside, takes 20 minutes; buses run hourly year-round.

From the Nice Station Ségurane (⊠ *Rue Catherine Ségurine*) you can catch the No. 100, which will take you directly to Èze-bord-de-Mer along the lower corniche; or the No. 112 from Nice Vauban station, which goes from Nice to Col de Villefranche and stops at Èze Village. All buses cost €1.50. By car, you should arrive using the Moyenne corniche, which deposits you near the gateway to Èze Village.

Visitor Information Èze Tourist Office ⊠ *Pl. du Général de Gaulle* ☎ 04–93–41–26–00 ⊕ *www.eze-riviera.com.*

EXPLORING

If you can manage to shake the crowds and duck off to a quiet overlook, the village of Èze commands splendid views up and down the coast. It's one of the draws that once lured distinguished visitors (including Georges Sand, Friedrich Nietzsche, and lots of crowned heads), as well as noteworthy residents —among them Consuelo Vanderbilt, who traded in Blenheim Palace for a custom-built house here when she was tired of being duchess of Marlborough.

Jardin Exotique (*Tropical Garden*). From the crest-top Jardin Exotique, full of rare succulents, you can pan your videocam all the way around the hills and waterfront. But if you want a prayer of a chance at enjoying the magnificence of Eze's arched passages, stone alleyways, and ancient fountains, come at dawn or after sunset—or (if you have the means) stay the night and spend the midday elsewhere. The church of **Notre-Dame,** consecrated in 1772, glitters inside with Baroque altarpieces. Èze's tourist office, on place du Général-de-Gaulle, can direct you to the numerous footpaths—the most famous being the **Sentier Friedrich Nietzsche**—that thread Èze with the coast's three corniche highways. ⊠ *Moyenne corniche* ☑ *May–Oct., €6; Nov.–Apr., €4* ☉ *Nov.–Jan., daily 9–4:30; Feb. and Mar., daily 9–5; Apr. and May, daily 9–6; June and Sept., daily 9–7; July and Aug., daily 9–7:30; Oct., daily 9–5:30.*

WHERE TO EAT AND STAY

For expanded hotel reviews, visit Fodors.com.

$$$$ ✕ **Cap Estel.** For over 50 years celebs have holidayed and dined at Cap
FRENCH Estel along Eze's *bord de mer*. On a private 2-hectare peninsula with all-encompassing views of the Med, it's no wonder. And now that chef Patrick Raingeard, whose produce comes directly from the hotel's garden,

The "eagle's-nest" village of the Riviera, Èze perches 1,300 feet above the sea and travelers never fail to marvel at the dramatic setting.

has added a 2013 Michelin Star to his table, food in France can't get any better than this. Start with the asparagus salad with creamed cauliflower and wild truffles (€35), followed by the Charolais beef fillet *à la Parillada* in a "Los Lobos" red wine sauce served with a potato and truffle cake (€39), and finish it all off with a banana soufflé. Vegetarian options also available. $ *Average main: €42* ⊠ *1312, av. Raymond-Poincaré, Charbonnières-les-Bains* 🕾 *33/04–93–76–29–29* ⊕ *www.capestel.com* 🍴 *Reservations essential* ⊘ *Closed Jan. and Feb.*

$$$$ ✕ **Troubadour.** Amid the clutter and clatter of the nearby coast, Trou-
FRENCH badour is a wonderful find (and has been for more than 30 years!). Comfortably relaxed, this old family house proffers pleasant service and excellent dishes like roasted scallops with chicken broth and squab with citrus zest and beef broth. $ *Average main: €39* ⊠ *4 rue du Brec* 🕾 *04–93–41–19–03* ⊘ *Closed Sun. and Mon. mid-Nov.–mid-Dec.*

$$$$ 🛏 **Château de la Chèvre d'Or.** The "Château of the Golden Goat" is actu-
HOTEL ally an entire stretch of the village, streets and all, bordered by gardens
Fodor's Choice that hang from the mountainside in nearly Babylonian style. **Pros:** unique
★ setting; fabulous infinity pool; faultless service (although can be cool at times). **Cons:** one-night deposit required for all bookings; no elevator. $ *Rooms from: €380* ⊠ *Rue du Barri* 🕾 *04–92–10–66–66* ⊕ *www.chevredor.com* 🛏 *30 rooms, 7 suites* ⊘ *Closed Dec.–Feb.* 🍽 *No meals.*

$$ 🛏 **La Bastide aux Camelias.** There are only four bedrooms and one suite
B&B/INN in this lovely B&B, each individually decorated with softly draped fabrics and polished antiques. **Pros:** heartwarming welcome is genuine; breakfast is scrumptious; perfect place to get away from it all. **Cons:** walking distance from the village is significant; you need a car (free parking) to tour the coast from here. $ *Rooms from: €140* ⊠ *Rte.*

de l'Adret ☎ *04–93–41–13–68* ⊕ *www.bastideauxcamelias.com* ➲ *4 rooms, 1 suite* ¶◯ *Breakfast.*

MENTON

14 km (9 miles) east of Èze, 9 km (5½ miles) east of Monaco.

Fodor's Choice
★

Menton, the most Mediterranean of the French resort towns, rubs shoulders with the Italian border and owes its balmy climate to the protective curve of the Ligurian shore. Its picturesque harbor skyline seems to beg artists to immortalize it, while its Cubist skew of terracotta roofs and yellow-ocher houses, Baroque arabesques capping the church facades, and ceramic tiles glistening on their steeples all evoke the villages of the Italian coast. Also worth a visit are the many exotic gardens set in the hills around the town.

GETTING HERE
Lignes d'Azur (☎ *08–10–06–10–06* ⊕ *www.lignesdazur.com*) runs a regular daily bus service from Menton's main bus station (✉ *Gare Routière, av. de Sospel* ☎ *04–93–35–93–60*). This route (bus No. 100) runs along the scenic Basse corniche to the Nice Ségurane bus station at rue Catherine Ségurane (turn right at the Café Turin at place Garibaldi), making stops at all the little villages along the way; tickets cost €1.50, and the journey takes just over an hour. Menton is serviced by regular trains on the Nice–Ventimiglia line (⊕ *www.voyages-sncf.com*); the trip from Nice takes 35 minutes and costs €5. The Menton Gare SNCF train station is within walking distance of the sea and the center of town.

Visitor Information Menton Tourist Office ✉ *8 av. Boyer, Palais de l'Europe* ☎ *04-92-41-76-76* ⊕ *www.tourisme-menton.fr.*

EXPLORING
Set several miles to the east of Monaco (which we leapfrog over here; *see our entry on Monaco below*), Menton is the least pretentious of the French Riviera resorts and all the more alluring for its modesty.

Basilique St-Michel. The majestic, Baroque Basilique St-Michel dominates the skyline of Menton with its bell tower. Beyond the beautifully proportioned facade—a 19th-century addition—the richly frescoed nave and chapels contain several works by Genovese artists plus a splendid 17th-century organ. Keep in mind that volunteers man the doors here, so you may have to wait for the church to open. ✉ *Parvis St-Michel* ⊙ *Weekdays 10–noon and 2–5.*

Chapelle de l'Immaculée-Conception. Just above the main church, the smaller Chapelle de l'Immaculée-Conception answers St-Michel's grand gesture with its own pure Baroque beauty, dating from 1687. During summer months you can slip in to see the graceful trompe l'oeil over the altar and the ornate gilt lanterns early penitents carried in processions.

Hôtel de Ville. The 19th-century Italianate Hôtel de Ville conceals another Cocteau treasure: he decorated the **Salle des Mariages** (Marriage Room), in which civil marriages take place, with vibrant allegorical scenes. ✉ *17 av. de la République* 🗒 *€1.50* ⊙ *Weekdays 8:30–12:30 and 1:30–5.*

CLOSE UP

Menton's Magnificent Gardens

The French Riviera is renowned for its grand villas and even grander gardens built by Victorian dukes, Spanish exiles, Belgian royals, and American blue bloods. Although its hothouse crescent blooms everywhere with palm and lemon trees and jungle flowers, nowhere does it bloom so extravagantly as in Menton, famous for its temperate climes and 24-karat sun.

Menton attracted a great share of wealthy hobbyists during the 1920s and 1930s, including Major Lawrence Johnston, a gentleman gardener best known for his Cotswolds wonderland, Hidcote Manor. Fair-haired and blue-eyed, this gentle American wound up buying a choice estate in the village of Gorbio—one of the loveliest of all perched seaside villages, 10 km (6 miles) west of Menton—and spent two decades making the **Serre de la Madone** a horticultural masterpiece. He brought back exotica from his many trips to South Africa, Mexico, and China, planting them in a series of terraces, accented by little pools, vistas, and stone steps. Although most of his creeping plumbago, pink

belladonna, and night-flowering cacti are now gone, his garden has been reopened by the municipality (it's best to visit during its summer glory). Car facilities are very limited but the garden can also be reached from Menton via bus No. 7 (get off at Serre de la Madone).

Back in Menton, green-thumbers will also want to visit the town's Jardin Botanique, the **Val Rahmeh Botanical Garden** (✉ *Av. St-Jacques* ☎ *04–93–35–86–72* ⏾ *Closed Tues.* 🎟 *€6*). Planted by Maybud Campbell in the 1910s and much prized by connoisseurs, it's bursting with rare ornamentals and subtropical plants, and adorned with water-lily pools and fountains.

The tourist office can also give you directions to other gardens around Menton, including the Fontana Rosa, the Villa Maria Serena, and the Villa Les Colombières.

✉ *Serre de la Madone: 74 rte. de Gorbio* ☎ *04–93–57–73–90* ⊕ *www. serredelamadone.com* 🎟 *€8 for Serre* ⏾ *Apr.–Oct., Tues.–Sun. 10-6; Dec.– Mar., Tues.–Sun. 10-5.*

Marché Couvert (*Covered Market*). Between the lively pedestrian rue St-Michel and the waterfront, the marvelous Marché Couvert sums up Menton style with its Belle Époque facade decorated in jewel-tone ceramics. It's equally appealing inside, with merchants daily selling chewy bread, mountain cheeses, oils, fruit, and Italian delicacies in Caravaggesque disarray.

Musée Jean Cocteau. On the waterfront opposite the market, a squat medieval bastion crowned with four tiny watchtowers houses the extraordinary Musée Jean Cocteau, France's memorial to the epony-mous artist-poet-filmmaker (1889–1963). Cocteau spotted the fortress, built in 1636 to defend the port, as the perfect site for a group of his works. While the museum has nearly 1,800 *oeuvres graphic*, about 990 are original Cocteaus, a donation from the late California businessman and Holocaust survivor Severin Wunderman's personal collection. ✉ *2 quai Monléon, Vieux Port* ☎ *04–93–57–72–30* ⊕ *museecocteaumenton.*

fr 🎟 *€6; €8 with temporary exhibition* 🕒 *July and Aug., Wed., Thurs., and Sat.–Mon. 10–6, Fri. 10–10; Sept.–June, Wed.–Mon. 10–6.*

Palais Carnolès (*Carnolès Palace*). At the far west end of town stands the 18th-century Palais Carnolès in vast gardens luxuriant with orange, lemon, and grapefruit trees. This was once the summer retreat of the princes of Monaco; nowadays it contains a sizable collection of European paintings from the Renaissance to the present day, plus some interesting temporary exhibits. ✉ *3 av. de la Madone* ☎ *04–93–35–49–71* 🎟 *Free* 🕒 *Wed.–Mon. 10–noon and 2–6; July and Aug., Wed.–Mon. 10–noon and 3–7.*

Rue St-Michel. Two blocks below the square, rue St-Michel serves as the main commercial artery of the Vieille Ville, lined with shops, cafés, and orange trees.

WHERE TO STAY

For expanded hotel reviews, visit Fodors.com.

$ HOTEL 🏨 **Aiglon.** Sweep down the curving stone stairs to the terrazzo mosaic lobby of this truly lovely 1880 garden villa; tarry a while in the grand salon, a confection of 19th-century elegance that wouldn't shame some of the nobler houses in Paris; and settle into one of the soft-edged, comfortable, and romantic guest rooms. **Pros:** romantic air is highly contagious; hidden spots, like love seats in archways, abound. **Cons:** some rooms are small, with an almost cramped feel to them; bathrooms are tiny. [$] *Rooms from: €110* ✉ *7 av. de la Madone* ☎ *04–93–57–55–55* 🌐 *www.hotelaiglon.net* 🛏 *28 rooms, 1 apartments* 🕒 *Closed 3rd wk in Nov.–mid-Dec.* 🍴 *Breakfast.*

FESTIVALS

Festival de Musique (*Chamber Music Festival*). Over the first two weeks of August, the Festival de Musique classical concerts take place at four locations around town, including the stone-paved plaza outside the church of St-Michel. ☎ *04–92–41–76–95* 🌐 *www.musique-menton.fr.*

Fête du Citron (*Lemon Festival*). The Fête du Citron, running from the end of February through the first week of March, is a full-blown lemon love-in: citrus floats and sculptures, all made of real fruit, glide through town, and musicians are on hand with entertainment. Think of it as France's answer to the Rose Bowl Parade. ☎ *04–92–41–76–95* 🌐 *www.fete-du-citron.com.*

MONACO

7 km (4½ miles) east of Èze, 21 km (13 miles) east of Nice.

It's the tax system, not the gambling (actually, the latter helps pay for the former), that has made Monaco one of the most sought-after addresses in the world. The principality bristles with gleaming glass-and-concrete corncob towers 20, 30, even 49 stories high, and vast apartment complexes, their terraces, landscaped like miniature gardens, jutting over the sea. You now have to look hard to find the Belle Époque grace of yesteryear. But if you repair to the town's great 1864 landmark Hôtel de Paris—still a veritable crossroads of the buffed and befurred

Euro-gentry—or enjoy a *grande bouffe* at the famous Louis XV restaurant, or attend the Opéra, or visit the ballrooms of the Casino (avert your eyes from the flashy gambling machines), you may still be able to conjure up Monaco's elegant past and the much-missed spirit of Princess Grace.

12

GETTING HERE
From Terminal 1 at the Nice airport, there's a direct bus service operated by Rapides Côte d'Azur (☎ *08–00–06–01–06* ⊕ *www.rca.tm.fr*); the No. 110 takes 45 minutes and costs €18. RCA also has a 50-minute express bus (No. 100X) connecting with Nice's Vauban bus station; tickets cost €4. The No. 100 Lignes d'Azur bus (☎ *08–00–06–10–06* ⊕ *www.lignesdazur.com*) costs €1.50, and leaves from the Ségurane bus station in Nice at place Garibaldi, arriving about an hour later. From Nice's train station (✉ *Gare SNCF, av. Thiers* ⊕ *www.sncf.com*), Monaco is serviced by regular trains along the Cannes–Ventimiglia line; Monaco's train station is on avenue Prince Pierre. From Nice the journey costs €3.70 one way and takes 20 minutes.

Visitor Information Monaco Tourist Office ✉ *2a bd. des Moulins, Monte Carlo* ☎ *377/92–16–61–16* ⊕ *www.visitmonaco.com.*

EXPLORING
It's positively feudal, the idea that an ancient dynasty of aristocrats could still hold fast to its patch of coastline—the last scrap of a once-vast domain. But that's just what the Grimaldi family did, clinging to a few acres of glory and maintaining their own license plates, their own telephone area code (377—don't forget to dial this when calling Monaco from France or other countries), and their own highly forgiving tax system. Today the Principality of Monaco covers just 499 acres and would fit comfortably inside New York's Central Park or a family farm in Iowa, while its 7,634 pampered citizens would fill only a small fraction of the seats in Yankee Stadium. The harbor district, known as **La Condamine,** connects the new quarter, officially known as **Monte Carlo,** with the Vieille Ville, officially known as **Monaco-Ville** (or Le Rocher). Have no fear that you'll need to climb countless steps to get to the latter, as there are plenty of elevators and escalators ascending the steep cliffs.

Prince Rainier III, the family patriarch who famously wed Grace Kelly and brought Hollywood glamour to his toy kingdom, passed away in 2005; his son, the eminently responsible Prince Albert, took over as head of the family and principality. Now a married man himself, Albert wed South African Charlene Whitstock (a former Olympic swimmer) in 2011.

TOP ATTRACTIONS
Casino. Place du Casino is the center of Monte Carlo and a must-see, even if you don't bet a sou. Into the gold-leaf splendor of the Casino, the hopeful traipse from tour buses to tempt fate beneath the gilt-edge Rococo ceiling (but do remember the fate of Sarah Bernhardt, who lost her last 100,000 francs here). Jacket and tie are required in the back rooms, which open at 3 pm. Bring your passport (under-18s not admitted). Note that there are special admission fees to get into any of the period gaming rooms. For €10 (less than playing the slots) you

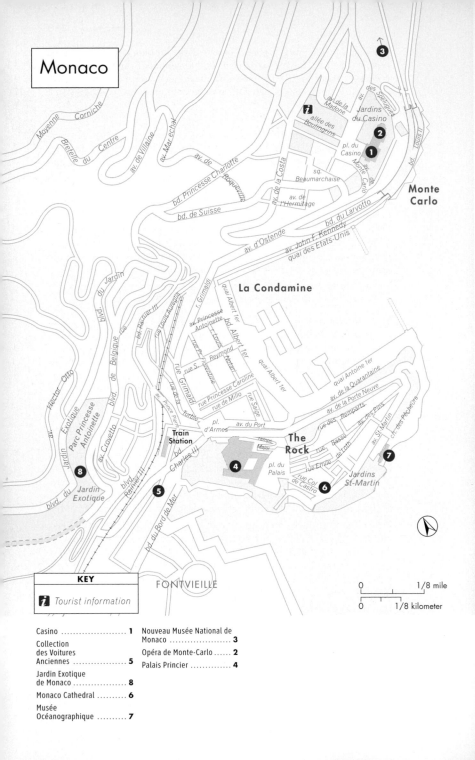

12

can also visit the Casino daily from 9 am to 12:30 am with access to all rooms. ⊠ *Pl. du Casino* ☎ *377/98–06–20–12* ⊕ *www.sbm.mc* ⊘ *Daily 2 pm–4 am.*

WORD OF MOUTH

"In Monaco, definitely see the changing of the guard, take the palace tour, and visit the cathedral during the day. But the casino is much more interesting at night. I enjoyed Monaco as two separate excursions—one time at night, and one time in the morning on a different day." —robertino

Fodor's Choice ★ **Jardin Exotique de Monaco** (*Monaco Exotic Garden*). Carved out of the rock face and one of Monte Carlo's most stunning escapes, the gardens are studded with thousands of succulents and cacti, all set along promenades and belvederes over the sea. There are rare plants from Mexico and Africa, and the hillside plot, threaded with bridges and grottoes and studded with faux boulders (actually hollow sculptures), can't be beat for coastal splendor. Prince Albert I established the gardens in the late 19th century. Also on the grounds, or actually under them, are the **Grottes de l'Observatoire**—spectacular grottoes and caves a-drip with stalagmites and spotlighted with fairy lights. The largest cavern is called "La Grande Salle" and looks like a Romanesque rock cathedral. Traces of Cro-Magnon civilization have been found here, so the grottoes now bear the official name of the **Musée d'Anthropologie.** ⊠ *62 bd. du Jardin Exotique* ☎ *377/93–15–29–80* ⊕ *www.jardin-exotique.mc* ⊠*€7* ⊘ *Mid-May–mid-Sept., daily 9–7; mid-Sept.–mid-May, daily 9–6.*

FAMILY **Musée Océanographique** (*Oceanography Museum*). Perched dramatically on a cliff, this museum is a splendid Edwardian structure, built by Prince Albert I to house specimens collected on amateur explorations. Jacques Cousteau (1910–97) led the missions from 1957 to 1988. The main floor displays skeletons and taxidermy of enormous sea creatures; early submarines and diving gear dating from the Middle Ages; and a few interactive science displays. The main draw is the famous **aquarium,** a vast complex of backlighted tanks containing countless species of fish, crab, and eel. ⊠ *Av. St-Martin* ☎ *377/93–15–36–00* ⊕ *www.oceano.mc* ⊠*€14* ⊘ *July and Aug., daily 9:30–8:30; Apr.–June and Sept., daily 9:30–7; Oct.–Mar., daily 10–6.*

Nouveau Musée National de Monaco. Here you'll find a beguiling assortment of 18th- and 19th-century dolls and automatons. The museum is housed in Villa Sauber, within a rose garden, in the Larvotto Beach complex—which is artfully created with imported sand. To get here, take the elevator down from place des Moulins. The Villa Paloma (next door to the Jardin Exotique), recently restored with fabulous stained-glass windows, is also part of NMNM and hosts temporary exhibits. ⊠ *Villa Sauber, 17 av. Princesse Grace* ☎ *377/98–98–91–26* ⊕ *www. nmnm.mc* ⊠*€6* ⊘ *June–Sept., daily 11–7; Oct.–May, daily 10–6.*

Opéra de Monte-Carlo. This grand theater was designed by Charles Garnier, who also built the Paris Opéra, and is graced with an 18-ton gilt-bronze chandelier and extravagant frescoes. Sarah Bernhardt inaugurated the main auditorium, the Salle Garnier, in 1879. ⊠ *Pl. du Casino* ☎ *377/98–06–28–00* ⊕ *www.opera.mc*

A golden ghetto for the rich, Monaco has a Belle Époque opulence epitomized by its Opéra de Monte-Carlo, designed in 1879 by Garnier.

Palais Princier. The famous Rock, crowned by the palace where the royal family resides, stands west of Monte Carlo. An audio guide leading you through this sumptuous chunk of history, first built in the 13th century and expanded and enhanced over the centuries, reveals an extravagance of 16th- and 17th-century frescoes, as well as tapestries, gilt furniture, and paintings on a grand scale. Note that the **Relève de la Garde** (Changing of the Guard) is held outside the front entrance of the palace most days at 11:55 am. Les Grands Appartements are open to the public from late March through October, and you can buy a joint ticket with the Musée Océanographique. ⊠ *Pl. du Palais* ☎ *377/93–25–18–31* ⊕ *www.palais.mc* ⊠ *€8 (includes audio guide); €19 joint ticket with Oceanography Museum* ⊗ *Mar. 29–Oct., daily 10–6.*

WORTH NOTING

FAMILY **Collection des Voitures Anciennes** (*Collection of Vintage Cars*). In the impressive Collection des Voitures Anciennes, an assemblage of Prince Rainier's vintage cars, you'll find everything from a De Dion Bouton to a Lamborghini Countach. Also on the Terrasses de Fontvieille is the **Jardin Animalier** (Animal Garden), a mini-zoo housing the Grimaldi family's animal collection—an astonishing array of wild beasts that includes monkeys and exotic birds. ⊠ *Terrasses de Fontvieille* ☎ *377/92–05–28–56, 377/93–25–18–31* ⊠ *€6 Voitures; €5 Animalier* ⊗ *Museum: daily 10–6. Garden: Oct.–Feb., daily 10–noon and 2–5; Mar.–May, daily 10–noon and 2–6; June–Sept., daily 9–noon and 2–7.*

Monaco Cathedral. Follow the crowds down the last remaining streets of medieval Monaco to the 19th-century Cathédrale de l'Immaculée-Conception, which contains the tomb of Princess Grace as well as a magnificent altarpiece, painted in 1500 by Louis Bréa. It's best to call ahead to check on opening hours; they tend to vary, although you can usually visit daily until 6 pm. ✉ *Av. St-Martin* ☎ *377/93-30-87-70* 🌐 *www.cathedrale.mc.*

WHERE TO EAT

$$$ BRASSERIE

🍴 **Café de Paris.** The landmark Belle Époque "La Brasserie 1900"—better known as Café de Paris—offers the usual classics (shellfish, steak tartare, matchstick frites, and fish boned table-side). Supercilious, super-pro waiters fawn gracefully over titled preeners, jet-setters, and tourists alike. Open daily from 8 am, there's good hot food until 2 am. [$] *Average main: €34* ✉ *Pl. du Casino* ☎ *377/98-06-76-23* 🌐 *www.casinocafedeparis.com.*

$$ MODERN FRENCH

🍴 **Explorers Pub.** This gastropub "devoted to adventurers" has stone walls lined with photos of intrepid folks (including Prince Albert II), plus a year-round terrace perfect for sampling roast pig or lamb shank. Wash your meal down with one of the 150 well-priced beers. Premium spirits, world wines, and Café de Monaco freshly roasted on-site, are also available. For your late-night munchies, the pub serves food until 5:30 am on Friday and Saturday in summer. [$] *Average main: €25* ✉ *Port of Monaco* ☎ *377/97-98-70-70* 🌐 *www.explorers-pub.com.*

$$$$ FRENCH

🍴 **La Trattoria.** For those wanting to try Alain Ducasse cuisine without having to pay Louis XV prices, this concept—Tuscan spirit and recipes meets Riviera colors and generosity—is a treat. Dinner only is served, and on offer are such dishes as French bean salad, cured ham prosciutto with Parmesan, and summer truffle risotto. The sea views are gorgeous for those seated on the terrace, and the up-to-the-minute service is actually laid back enough for you to relax. [$] *Average main: €40* ✉ *Le Sporting—Monte Carlo, av. Princesse Grace* ☎ *377/98-06-71-71* 🌐 *www.alain-ducasse.com* 🕒 *Closed Oct.-mid-May. No lunch.*

$$$$ FRENCH
Fodor's Choice ★

🍴 **Le Louis XV.** Louis Quinze to the initiated, this extravagantly showy restaurant stuns with neo-Baroque details, yet it manages to be upstaged by its product: the superb cuisine of Alain Ducasse, one of the world's most respected chefs. He leaves the Louis XV kitchen, for the most part, in the more-than-capable hands of Chef Franck Cerutti, who draws much of his inspiration from the cours Saleya market in Nice. Glamorous iced lobster with chestnuts and Alba white truffles slum happily with stockfish (stewed salt cod) and tripe. The decor is magnificent—a surfeit of gilt, mirrors, and chandeliers—and the waitstaff seignorial as they proffer a footstool for madame's handbag. In Ducasse fashion, the Baroque clock on the wall is stopped just before 12. Cinderella should have no fears. If your wallet is a chubby one, this is a must. The 400,000 bottles in the wine cellar should offer you enough of a choice. [$] *Average main: €100* ✉ *Hôtel de Paris, pl. du Casino* ☎ *377/98-06-88-64* 🌐 *www.alain-ducasse.com* ✍ *Reservations essential. Jacket required* 🕒 *Closed Nov., 3 wks mid-Feb., and Tues. and Wed. (but open Wed. dinner mid-June–Aug.).*

WHERE TO STAY

For expanded hotel reviews, visit Fodors.com.

$$$$ HOTEL **Hôtel Metropole.** From the moment you walk through the colossal neo-Roman arch, down the cypress-studded lane, and into the cozy Jacques Garcia–designed lounge, you're swept away into a cosseted world where Rothschild Renaissance meets contemporary style. **Pros:** magical setting is further enhanced by the decor and food; environmentally conscious. **Cons:** level of service can be depend on what you look like and how much you tip. [$] *Rooms from: €600* ✉ *4 av. de la Madonne* ☎ *377/93–15–15–15* 🌐 *www.metropole.com* 🛏 *69 rooms, 64 suites* 🍴 *Breakfast.*

$$$ HOTEL **Hotel Miramar.** Next to the port, but at a fraction of the price of other port hotels, this little spot is one of the few real bargains in Monaco. **Pros:** good rates for Monaco—especially since breakfast is included. **Cons:** some rooms are a little small and dated; no parking but you get a discount with parking garage (ask for clear tunnel access directions). [$] *Rooms from: €195* ✉ *1 av. President J-F Kennedy, La Condamine* ☎ *377/93–30–86–48* 🌐 *www.miramarmonaco.com* 🛏 *11 rooms* 🍴 *Breakfast.*

NIGHTLIFE AND THE ARTS

There's no need to go to bed before dawn in Monte Carlo when you can go to the **casinos** *(⇨ See Exploring above).*

Opéra de Monte-Carlo. Opera, ballet, and classical music can be enjoyed year-round at the magnificently sumptuous Salle Garnier auditorium of the Opéra de Monte-Carlo. This is the main venue of the Opéra de Monte-Carlo and the Orchestre Philharmonique de Monte-Carlo, both worthy of the magnificent hall. ✉ *Pl. du Casino* ☎ *337/98–06–28–28* 🌐 *www.opera.mc.*

SPORTS

Grand Prix de Monaco. When the tennis stops, the auto racing begins: the Grand Prix de Monaco takes place the last Sunday of the Cannes Film Festival in May. ☎ *377/93–15–26–00 for information* 🌐 *www.grand-prix-monaco.com.*

Monte-Carlo Rolex Masters Tennis. Held at the beautiful Monte-Carlo Country Club, the Monte-Carlo Rolex Masters Tennis series is held during mid-April every year. ✉ *155 Sentier des Tennis, Roquebrune-* ☎ *377/97–98–70–00* 🌐 *www.monte-carlorolexmasters.com.*

CORSICA

WELCOME TO CORSICA

TOP REASONS TO GO

★ **Island Hiking:** From a stroll in the countryside to an overnight hike in the mountains, Corsica offers more than 100 peaks and scenic trails, including the famous 201-km (125-mile) "GR20" trek across the island.

★ **Water Adventures:** The warm and crystal waters here are ideal for snorkeling, diving, boating, and windsurfing.

★ **Rich Cuisine:** Blending French specialties with Italian cuisine, Corsica tempts the palate with the rich flavors of honey, chestnuts, wine, and Brin d'Amour cheese.

★ **Coastal Drives:** These curvy mountain roads, skirted by turquoise waters, are not to be missed.

★ **Cultural Exploration:** Dotting the island are chapels, towers, and more than 350 villages framed by fields of grazing goats and sheep. Corsica's cultural treasures, preserved through centuries of tradition, find expression in the island's art, music, food, and festivals.

1 Corse du Sud. Southern Corsica prides itself on its picturesque coastline, ancient hilltop villages, fortified cities, prehistoric sites, and breathtaking natural wonders. The regional capital of Ajaccio, Napoléon's birthplace, remains the island's modern commercial hub. Famous for its dramatic white limestone cliff-top setting, historic Bonaficio is the stunning backdrop to the postcard-perfect marine reserve surrounding the Lavezzi Islands—a UNESCO World Heritage Site.

2 Haute Corse. The natural savage beauty that defines northern Corsica begins in the lush promontory of Cap Corse with its mountain ridges running down the peninsula's center to traditional fishing villages and picturesque harbors. The north is also renowned as an important wine-producing region where some of the finest vineyards benefit from the area's fertile soil and perfect temperatures.

GETTING ORIENTED

The northern half of the island (Haute Corse) is generally wilder than the southern half (Corse du Sud), which is hotter and more barren. Southern Corsica's archaeological sites at the Col de Bavella and its majestic Laricio pine forest, and the ancient towns of Bonifacio all rank indisputably among the island's finest treasures. One of the prettiest drives is the tour around the northward-pointing finger of Cap Corse. Don't hesitate to drive into the interior highlands, the true Corsica; if you spend too much time at sea level you'll be missing the remote villages and dramatic heights for which the island is famous.

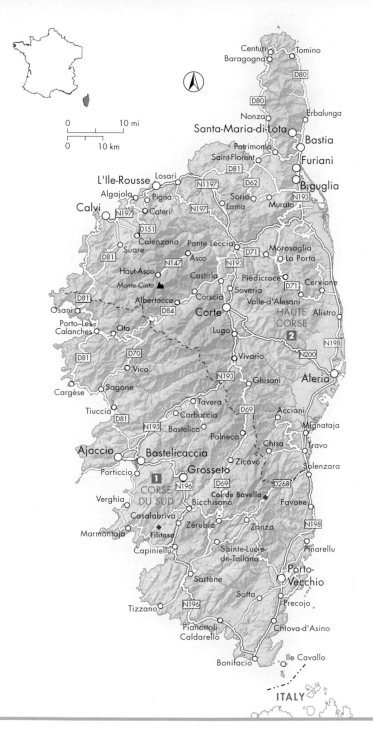

13

Centuri
Baragogna
Tomino

D80

D80

Nonza
Erbalunga

Santa-Maria-di-Lota
Bastia

Patrimonio
Furiani

Saint-Florent
D81

Losari
D62
Biguglia

L'Ile-Rousse
N1197
N193

Algajola
Pigna
Sorio
Murato

Calvi
Cateri
Lama

N197
N197

D151

Calenzana
Ponte Leccia
Morosaglia

Suare
Asco
La Porta

D81
N147

Haut-Asco
Castirla
D71

Monte Cinto ▲
Piedicroce
Cervione

Albertacce
Corscia
Soveria
D71

Osani
D84
Valle-d'Alesani
HAUTE

Corte
CORSE
Alistro

Porto–Les
Lugo
2

Calanches
Ota
N198

D81
D70
Vivario
N200

Vico

Cargèse
Sagone
Ghisoni
Aleria

Tiuccia
Tavera

D81
Carbuccia
D69
Acciani

N193
Bastelica
Mignataja

Palneca
Chisa
Travo

Ajaccio
Bastelicaccia
Zicavo
Solenzara

Porticcio
Grosseto

1
N196
D69
Col de Bavella
D268

CORSE
Bicchisano
Favone

Verghia
DU SUD

Casalabriva
Zérubia
Zanza
N198

Marmontaja
Filitosa

Capiniellu
Sainte-Lucie-
Pinarellu
de-Tallano

Sartène
Porto-
Vecchio

Softa

Tizzano
Precojo

N196

Pianottoli-
Chiova-d'Asino
Caldarello

Bonifacio
Ile Cavallo

ITALY

Updated by
Victoria Tang

"The best way to know Corsica," according to Napoléon, "is to be born there." Not everyone has had his luck, so chances are you'll be arriving on the overnight ferry from Marseille or flying in from Paris or Rome to discover "the Isle of Beauty." This vertical chalky granite world of its own, rising in the Mediterranean between Provence and Tuscany, remains France's very own Wild West: a powerful natural setting and, literally, a breath of fresh air.

Corsica's strategic location 168 km (105 miles) south of Monaco and 81 km (50 miles) west of Italy made Corsica a prize hotly contested by a succession of Mediterranean powers, notably Genoa, Pisa, and France. Their vestiges remain: the city-state of Genoa ruled Corsica for more than 200 years, leaving impressive citadels, churches, bridges, and nearly 100 medieval watchtowers around the island's coastline. The Italian influence is also apparent in village architecture and in the Corsican language: a combination of Italian, Tuscan dialect, and Latin.

Corsica gives an impression of immensity, seeming far larger than its 215-km (133-mile) length and 81-km (50-mile) width, partly because its rugged, mountainous terrain makes for very slow traveling and partly because the landscape and the culture vary greatly from one microregion to another. Much of the terrain of Corsica that is not wooded or cultivated is covered with a dense thicket of undergrowth, which along with chestnut trees makes up the maquis, a variety of wild and aromatic plants including lavender, myrtle, and heather that gave Corsica one of its sobriquets, "the perfumed isle." The maquis, famous for harboring fugitives, became the term used for the French Resistance movement during World War II.

In the end you'll find Corsica composed of equal parts vendetta, witchcraft, dream hunters, and shepherds improvising the rough and haunting chestnuts, free-range livestock, sweet liqueurs, full-bodied wines, and powerful cheeses. Lest we forget the lemon-pepper fragrance of the ubiquitous maquis, an aroma like no other, described by Dorothy

Carrington in her *Granite Island* as "akin to incense" and the only fitting perfume for Balzac's "back of beyond."

PLANNER

WHEN TO GO

The best time to visit Corsica is fall or spring, when the weather is cool. Most Corsican culinary specialties are at their best between October and June. Try to avoid July and August, when mostly French and Italian vacationers fill hotels, crowd beaches, and jam roads. Prices soar and the Corsican temperament is at its most volatile. In winter the island has the best weather in France, but a majority of the hotels and restaurants are closed.

General Travel Advisory: In recent years, there has been a spate of bombings and fatal shootings in Corsica. Organized crime feuds plague the serene landscape, and recent attacks of government offices, restaurants, supermarkets, discos, and private villas have earned Corsica the highest homicide rate per capita in France and Western Europe. Tourists have not been direct targets; however, travelers should be vigilant when driving and touring, especially solo.

GETTING HERE AND AROUND

AIR TRAVEL

Air France has daily service connecting Paris and Lyon with Ajaccio and Bastia. Air Corsica (formerly Compagnie Corse Méditérranée) connects Ajaccio and Bastia to Nice and Marseille with several flights a day. Delta connects with Air France for flights from the United States to Corsica from May to October.

AIRPORTS Corsica has four major airports: Ajaccio, Bastia, and Figari. The airports at Ajaccio and Bastia run regular shuttle-bus services to and from town. Taxis are also available in front of the terminals. Expect to pay around €25 to €30 to go from Campo dell'Oro to Ajaccio; €37 from Poretta Airport to Bastia. At Figari a bus during summer months meets all incoming flights and will take passengers as far as Bonifacio and Porto-Vecchio for about €9.

Contacts Bastia–Poretta (*BIA*). ✉ *Aéroport International de Bastia-Poretta, Luciana* ☎ *04–95–55–96–96* ⊕ *www.bastia.aeroport.fr.* **Figari–Sud Corse** (*FSC*). ✉ *BP 20, Figari* ☎ *04–95–71–10–10* ⊕ *www.aeroport.fr.* **Ajaccio–Campo dell'Oro** (*AJA*). ✉ *Campo Dell'Oro* ☎ *04–95–23–56–56* ⊕ *www.2a.cci.fr/ Aeroport_Napoleon_Bonaparte_Ajaccio.html.* **Calvi-Ste Catherine** (*CLY*). ✉ *Rue du Nouveau Port, 6.5 km (4 miles) southeast of Calvi, Bastia* ☎ *04–95–65–88–88* ⊕ *www.calvi.aeroport.fr.*

BOAT AND FERRY TRAVEL

Regular car ferries run from Marseille, Nice, and Toulon to Ajaccio, Bastia, and Propriano. These crossings take from 5 to 10 hours, with sleeping cabins available. The high-speed ferry from Nice to Bastia takes about three hours. Package deals, which include making the crossing with a car, an onboard cabin, and a hotel in Corsica, are available from SNCM, the Société Nationale Maritime Corse-Méditérranée.

Contacts SNCM ⊠ *12 rue Godot-de-Mauroy, Paris* ☎ *01–49–24–24–61* ⊕ *www.sncm.fr* ⊙ *Apr. 1–July 31, weekdays 9–6, at. 9–noon; Aug. 1–Mar. 31, weekdays 9–5:30* ⊠ *27 rue Mazenod, Marseille* ☎ *04–91–56–33–90* ⊙ *Weekdays 9–12:30 and 1:30–6, Sat. 8:30–12:30* ⊠ *3 pl. Masséna, Nice* ☎ *04–93–62–63–07* ⊙ *Weekdays 9–6, Sat. 9–noon* ⊠ *49 av. de l'Infanterie-de-Marine, Toulon* ☎ *04–94–16–66–62* ⊙ *Weekdays . 9–noon and 2–5:45, Sat. 9:15–12:15* ⊠ *Quai L'Herminier, B.P. 242, Ajaccio* ☎ *04–95–29–66–65* ⊙ *Weekdays 9–noon and 2–6* ⊠ *Nouveau Port, BP 57, Bastia* ☎ *04–95–54–66–58* ⊙ *Weekdays 7:30–7 pm, Sat. 8–noon.*

CAR TRAVEL

Though driving is undoubtedly the best way to explore the island's scenic stretches, note that winding, mountainous roads, uneven surfaces, and microclimates with fog or precipitation can actually double or triple your expected travel time. The Michelin 1/200,000 map No. 90 is essential. Be prepared for spelling anomalies, many of which are Corsican, not French. **Drive defensively:** you'll find that others on the road tend to move at terrifying speeds unrelenting even at curves. **Drive during the day:** night driving, especially in the mountains, is not recommended since many areas are poorly lighted or void of any illumination. Signage is extremely difficult to see.

TRAIN TRAVEL

The main line of Corsica's simple rail network runs from Ajaccio, in the west, to Corte, in the central valley, then divides at Ponte Leccia. From here one line continues to L'Ile Rousse and Calvi, in the north, and the other to Bastia, in the northeast. Another service runs four times daily between Ajaccio and Bastia. Telephone numbers for local train stations are listed here by town.

Contacts SNCF Ajaccio ⊠ *Pl. de la Gare, Ajaccio* ☎ *04–95–23–11–03, 08–99–54–60–18 reservations in France* ⊕ *www.ter-sncf.com.* **SNCF Bastia** ⊠ *Pl. de la Gare, sq. du Maréchal Leclerc, Bastia* ☎ *04–95–32–80–61, 08–99–54–60–18 reservations in France.*

RESTAURANTS

While entire geopolitical campaigns have been waged over warm-water harborage, this mountain in the Mediterranean has traditionally fled to its highest crags and crannies for defensive reasons, taking its best cooking along with it. The Corsican maquis grows some of Europe's wildest flora and fauna, ranging from free-range pigs to woodcock and pigeon. Chestnuts are a Corsican staple not to miss, whether in pastries, *pulenta,* or beer, while cheeses, especially the characteristic *brocciu* fresh cheese, are omnipresent upland delicacies. Dorothy Carrington accurately described Corsican cuisine as "winter cuisine," better between October and May, when game like sanglier (wild boar) as well as brocciu are well represented on all menus.

Prices in the restaurant reviews are the average cost of a main course at dinner or, if dinner is not served, at lunch; taxes and service charges are generally included.

HOTELS

The amount of construction around Porto-Vecchio in the 1950s was so burdensome to Corsicans that, with some extra unwanted encourage-ment from separatist bombers, they resolved to avoid excessive, tourist-driven development. Instead, *fermes-auberges* (farmhouse-inns) have had a healthy dose of restoration, and tastefully designed hotels are still being built. During the peak season (from July to mid-September) prices are significantly higher, and some hotels insist that breakfast and dinner be included as part of the price. The best seaside hotels are priced only marginally lower than on the Riviera, but lodgings in the interior villages remain substantially cheaper. Off-season, good prices can be found all over. Assume all rooms have air-conditioning, TV, telephones, and private bath unless otherwise noted.

Prices in the hotel reviews are the lowest cost of a standard double room in high season, excluding taxes, service charges, and meal plans (except at all-inclusives). Prices for rentals are the lowest per-night cost for a one-bedroom unit in high season.

VISITOR INFORMATION

The Agence du Tourisme de la Corse can provide practical and in-depth information about the whole island. The Parc Naturel Régional de la Corse, Corsica's wildlife and natural-resource management authority, controlling well over a third of the island, can provide trail maps, book-lets, and a wide variety of information.

Contacts Agence du Tourisme de la Corse. Plan your visit and research activ-ities, sites, and local culture for the island's nine regions. ✉ *17 bd. Roi-Jérôme, Ajaccio* ☎ *04-95-51-77-77* ⊕ *www.visit-corsica.com/* ⊙ *Mon.–Thur. 8–noon and 2–5:30, Fri. 8–noon and 2–5. Closed weekends.* **Parc Naturel Régional de la Corse.** Consult the park website for information and 3-D images on hiking, trek-king, ski trails, and camping throughout the GR20 mountain range. ✉ *Office de Pole Touristique, La Citadelle, Corte* ☎ *04–95–50–59–04* ⊕ *www.parc-corse.org.*

TOURS OPTIONS

BOAT TOURS

Most of Corsica's spectacular scenery is best viewed from the water. Colombo Line and Promenades en Mer, in Calvi, organize whole-day glass-bottom boat tours. Promenades en Mer, in Ajaccio, organizes twice-daily trips (at 9 and 2) to the Iles Sanguinaires.

Contacts Colombo Line Cruises. Colombo's scenic touring boats and catama-rans access hard-to-reach coves and protected areas on the rugged coastline. ✉ *Quai Landry, Calvi* ☎ *04-95-65-32-10 or 04-95-65-03-40* ⊕ *www.colombo-line.com.* **NAVE VA Promenades en Mer** ✉ *Port de l'Amirauté, quai Napoléon, Aja-ccio* ☎ *04–95–51–31–31 reservations* ⊕ *www.naveva.com* ✉ *Port de Plaisance, Propriano* ☎ *04–95–76–35–27* ⊕ *www.promenade-en-mer-a-propriano.com.*

SPMB Promenades en Mer. Discover marine flora and fauna with a one-hour glass-bottom boat cruise that tours the famous nature reserve of Iles Lavezzi and Cavallo via the extreme southern Pointe de St. Antoine. Departures every 30 minutes from Bonifacio. Children under eight are free. Free parking. ✉ *Port de Bonifacio, Bonifacio* ☎ *04–95–10–97–50* ⊕ *www.spmbonifacio.com* 🎫 *€17.50–€35.*

BUS TOURS

Ollandini arranges whole- and half-day bus tours of the island, leaving from Ajaccio.

Contacts Les Autocars Ollandini. Founded in 1890 and specializing in tourism since 1933, the Ollandini group operates travel agencies, car rental, bus, and autocar excursions. ⊠ *1 rue Paul Colonna d'Istria, Ajaccio* ☎ *04–95–23–92–00, 04–95–23–92–91 group reservations* ⊕ *www. groupencorse.com.*

CORSE DU SUD

Corse du Sud includes the French administrative capital of Ajaccio, the more mountainous zones, and the fortressed towns of Bonifacio and Porto-Vecchio. A beautiful combination of natural beauty and ancient history, the region is known as Napoléon's birthplace and visited for its exceptional sandy beaches, dramatic promontories, and stunning coves. Forest fires and the resulting flooding scarred much of the southern part of the island in the mid-1990s; since then, the irrepressible maquis has rebounded.

AJACCIO

40 mins by plane, 5–10 hrs by ferry from Marseille, Nice, or Toulon.

Considered Corsica's primary commercial and cultural hub, the largest city and regional capital of Ajaccio is situated on the west coast of the island, approximately 644 km (400 miles) southeast of Marseille, France. Founded in 1492, vestiges of ancient Corsica in this ville impériale revolve around the city's most famous son, Napoléon Bonaparte, whose family home—now the national museum Maison Bonaparte—pays tribute to the emperor's historical influence. Indeed, Napoléon takes center stage in this lively city of approximately 64,000 inhabitants, from the exceptional Palais Fesch/ Musée des Beaux Arts to eponymous street names and statues sprinkled around the town's accessible squares, gardens, and courtyards. Festivities crescendo in mid-August with a colorful three-day celebration to honor Napoléon's birth. Remnants from what was originally a 12th-century Genoese colony are still visible around the Old Town near the imposing citadel and watchtower. Perfect for exploring, the luminous seaside city surrounded by snow-capped mountains and pretty beaches offers numerous sites, eateries, side streets, and a popular harbor, where sailboats and fishing vessels moor in the picturesque Tino Rossi port lined with well-established restaurants and cafés serving fresh local fare.

GETTING HERE

Flights into Aéroport d'Ajaccio-Campo dell'Oro arrive regularly. To travel the short 5-km (3-mile) distance into the city center, take a shuttle bus to the main Gare Routière station that operates Monday to Saturday (except on bank holidays; €4.50). Alternatively, a taxi (€15) or car will take approximately 15–20 minutes. Ferries from Nice, Toulon, and Marseilles in France connect directly to Ajaccio and operate up to eight times daily. The average ferry crossing time is six hours.

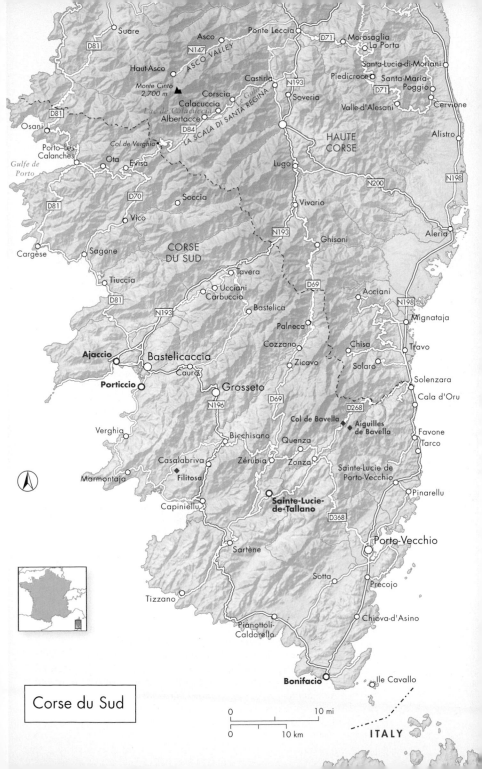

Corse du Sud

EXPLORING

Cathédrale Notre Dame de L'Assomption. The 16th-century Baroque cathedral where Napoléon was baptized is at the end of rue St-Charles. The interior is covered with trompe-l'oeil frescoes, and the high altar, from a church in Lucca, Italy, was donated by Napoléon's sister Eliza after he made her princess of Tuscany. Eugène Delacroix's *The Triumph of Religion* hangs above the Virgin of the Sacred Heart marble altar from the 17th century. ⊠ *Rue F.-Conti* 🕾 *04–95–21–41–14* ⊕ *www.ajaccio-tourisme.com/* 🎫 *Free* ⊙ *Daily 9–11 am.*

Chapelle Impériale. Located on the south wing of the Palais Fesch, the neo-Renaissance-style Imperial Chapel was built in 1857 by Napoléon's nephew, Napoléon III, to accommodate the tombs of the Bonaparte family (Napoléon Bonaparte himself is buried in the Hôtel des Invalides in Paris). The Coptic crucifix over the altar was taken from Egypt during the general's 1798 campaign. Renovated in 2012, the somber chapel officially classified as a historic monument is constructed from the white calcified stone of St. Florent and worth a visit to view its neoclassical cupola and ecclesiastical iconography. ⊠ *50–52 rue Cardinal Fesch* 🕾 *04–95–21–48–17* ⊕ *www.ajaccio.fr/La-Chapelle-Imperiale_a353.html* 🎫 *€1.50; children under 15 free* ⊙ *Tues.–Sat. 10–12:30 and 3–7.*

Eglise St-Jean Baptiste. Wander narrow streets lined with Ajaccio's oldest houses built around 1492, when the city was founded. At the intersection of rue du Roi-de-Rome and rue Saint Charles, you can visit the *confrérie*, or religious brotherhood, of St. Jean Baptiste. On June 24, the patron saint is honored with a solemn Mass conducted by the city's bishop and a Corsican music concert. Follow the ancestral religious procession from the chapel to the Old Town and place Charles de Gaulle, where the celebration ends with traditional fire lighting in the evening. ⊠ *Rue du Roi-de-Rome* 🕾 *04–95–22–27– 38* ⊕ *www.ajaccio.fr/Confreries-et-pelerinages_a21.html.*

Fodor's Choice
★

Maison Bonaparte (*Bonaparte House*). One of four national historic museums dedicated to Napoléon, the multilevel house where the emperor was born on August 15, 1769 contains memorabilia and paintings of the extended Bonaparte family. History aficionados can tour bedrooms, dining rooms, and salons where Charles and Letitzia Bonaparte raised their eight children. Period furnishings and antiques in Corsican and Empire styles are scattered about and pay tribute to the family's bourgeoisie upbringing. Head downstairs below the Gallery to see the cellars and granite oil pressing mill acquired by Napoléon III in 1860, which depict the importance of rural industry for the Bonapartes' income. Visit the trapdoor room and find the ground opening located next to the door through which Napoléon allegedly escaped in 1799. The building itself changed hands multiple times through Bonaparte heirs until 1923, when it was donated to the state of France by Prince Victor, elder son of Prince Jérôme Napoleon. ⊠ *Rue St-Charles* 🕾 *04– 95–21–43–89* ⊕ *www.musee-maisonbonaparte.fr* 🎫 *€7 (Apr.–Oct.), €6 (low season), under-26 free* ⊙ *Oct.–Mar., Tues.–Sun. 10–noon and 2–4:45; Apr.–Sept., Tues.–Sun. 10:30–12:30 and 1:15–6* ⊙ *Last admission 30 mins prior to closing.*

The birth of an empire: Napoléon's birthplace and childhood home are on display in Ajaccio.

FAMILY **Marché Central (food market).** For an authentic view of daily Corsican life, tour this wonderful open-air food market brimming with gastronomic delights. There is an array of local cheeses, charcuterie, breads, pastries, olives, condiments, and aromatic meats for sale. Taste samples of chorizo, nougat, liqueur, honeys, and oils from friendly food stalls managed by original producers and farmers. Everything from artisanal candy to fresh-from-the-field vegetables and fruits, spices, and traditional indulgences like chestnut-infused beignets can be savored in an atmosphere guaranteed to be lively and local. Bring your euros—cash is the preferred method of payment. ⊠ *Sq. César Campinchi, bd. du Roi Jérôme* ⊕ *www.ajaccio-tourisme.com* ⊗ *Tues.–Sun. 8–1; hrs may vary due to weather.*

FAMILY **Musée des Beaux Arts-Palais Fesch.** Adjacent to the Chapelle Impérial, this
Fodor's Choice internationally recognized museum houses one of the most important
★ collections from the Napoleonic era; it's undoubtedly one of the most significant displays in France of ancient Italian masterpieces spanning the 14th to 20th century. The massive treasure trove of *objets d'art*, sculptures, and paintings is impressive on scale alone—there are nearly 18,000 items, including nearly 16,000 awe-inspiring works from Italian painters. Seek out the dramatic realism of Neapolitan Baroque artists Giordano and Giaquinto; view Renaissance masters Botticelli, Titian, Veronese, and Fra Bartolomeo—all part of an astounding inventory that belonged to Napoléon's uncle, Cardinal Fesch, archbishop of Lyon and art lover, following the French Revolution. Thanks to his nephew's military conquests, the cardinal was able to amass (steal, some would say) many celebrated old master paintings, the most famous of which

are now in Paris's Louvre. The museum's beautiful vaulted corridors, recently renovated for nearly €7 million, also showcase 700 paintings, portraits, still lifes, and sculptures from the First and Second Empire from the French school. Don't miss the new gallery with engravings and drawings depicting historic Corsica. The building itself, constructed by the cardinal as the Institute of Arts and Sciences, dates back to 1837. ✉ *50–52 rue Cardinal Fesch* ☎ *04–95–21–48–17* 🌐 *www.musee-fesch.com* 🎫 *€8* 🕒 *Oct.–Apr., Mon., Wed., and Sat. 10–5; Thurs., Fri., and 3rd Sun. of each month noon–5; May–Sept., Mon., Wed., and Sat. 10:30–6; Thurs., Fri., and Sun. noon–6* 🕒 *Closed Tues.*

WHERE TO EAT

$$ FRENCH 🍴 **20123.** Tables are full at this very popular Ajaccio establishment known for its traditional homemade cuisine, fresh daily catches, and, in season, game specials such as *civet de sanglier* (wild boar stew) served in a bubbling earthenware casserole of cheese-infused polenta. The rustic interior invites with a "starry sky" in a mock French village, antique lanterns, music, and stone fountain where guests pour their own water into ceramic jugs. In keeping with the familial style of service and food presentation, cutting boards with fresh-baked loaves of wheat bread are provided to start your copious meal. Three-course fixed menus are offered in two seatings at 7:30 and 9:30, and include an exquisite cheese platter with homemade fig confiture. [$] *Average main: €35* ✉ *2 rue Roi-de-Rome* ☎ *04–95–21–50–05* 🌐 *www.20123.fr* 🕒 *Closed Mon. and Jan. 15–Feb. 15. No lunch June 15–Sept. 15.*

$$$ SEAFOOD FAMILY 🍴 **Le Week End.** Head 10 minutes north of downtown Ajaccio to this family-owned eatery where white rattan furniture and blue tablecloths are overshadowed by a spectacular ocean view and fine seafood menu. Here you'll find everything from marinated octopus and tuna spring rolls to grilled *sar* (red sea bream) and rockfish soup. Family-run since 1956, this restaurant flourishes by secret recipes handed down from generations. History can still be found in the fireplace lounge, where velvet chairs and family paintings date back to 1920. [$] *Average main: €60* ✉ *Rte. des Iles Sanguinaires* ☎ *04–95–52–1–39* 🌐 *www.leweekend-plage.com* 🕒 *Closed Mon. and Tues. Oct.–Mar.*

WHERE TO STAY

$$$ HOTEL FAMILY 🏨 **La Dolce Vita.** Spread out over whitewashed terraces at the edge of the Golfe d'Ajaccio, this Best Western hotel-restaurant is Italianate in design with contemporary details. **Pros:** splendid sea views; good amenities with modern bathrooms. **Cons:** rocky beach; pricey rooms; chain hotel ambience and decor [$] *Rooms from: €320* ✉ *Rte. des Iles Sanguinaires, 8 km (5 miles) from center of town* ☎ *04–95–52–42–42* 🌐 *www.hotel-dolcevita.com* 🛏 *32 rooms* 🕒 *Closed Nov. 1–Mar. 31* 🍽 *No meals.*

$$ B&B/INN 🏨 **Palazzu u Domu.** Steps away from the house in which Napoléon was born, this property once served as the ancestral residence of Duke Charles-Andre Pozzo di Borgo of the notable Ajaccio family. **Pros:** comfortable beds; central location; outdoor terrace. **Cons:** unreliable Internet access; inconsistent service; no pool [$] *Rooms from: €129* ✉ *17 rue Bonaparte* ☎ *04–95–50–00–20* 🌐 *www.palazzu-domu.com* 🛏 *45 rooms, 1 suite* 🍽 *Breakfast.*

SPORTS AND THE OUTDOORS

BICYCLING

BMS. Near the water's edge, BMS rents bicycles year-round. ⊠ *Quai de la Citadelle, Port de Plaisance, Tino Rossi* ☎ *04–95–21–33–75.*

JET SKIING

Cappai Jet. Spend a fun nautical day at plage du Neptune where you can rent a Jet Ski for €70 for half an hour, €120 for an hour, or €210 for two hours. For a cheaper alternative, stand-up paddle boards are available for €10/hour. ⊠ *Rte. des Sanguinaires, lage du Neptune* ☎ *06–21–33–92–84* ⊕ *www. cappai-jet.com.*

WATER SPORTS

A L'Eau Plongée. One of the most experienced dive centers is found in the city's capital, where lessons are available for all levels. Book exploration dives for individuals and groups. Enjoy a nautical day trip with a picnic led by knowledgeable Corsicans. ⊠ *Port Charles Ornano* ☎ *06–09–60–14–09* ⊕ *www.aleauplongee.com.*

SHOPPING

Art'Insula. A large selection of fabrics, leather, and knives crafted by local artisans is available here. Find beautiful jewelry, pottery, and Corsican "batik" to take home as souvenirs. For the gourmand, select an assortment of confitures, honeys, vinegars, and liqueurs. ⊠ *57 rue Fesch* ☎ *04–95–50–54–67* ⊕ *www.artisula.com.*

Casa Napoléon. Belonging to Charles Antona, a native Corsican producer of fine gastronomic goods for more than 30 years, Casa Napoléon is the well-stocked boutique selling organic jams, terrines, traditional dishes, olives oils, wine, sweets, and other delicacies straight from his Campestra factory and plantations. A second store is in Porticcio's Espace Commercial La Viva. ⊠ *3 rue Fesch* ☎ *04–95–21–47–88* ⊕ *www.charlesantona.com.*

Librairie la Marge. Much more than just a bookstore specializing in books about Corsica, this is a hub of Corsican literature, associated with the Ministry of Culture and Communication since 1977, where you can also buy music and attend poetry readings. ⊠ *4 rue Emmanuelle-Arène* ☎ *04–95–51–23–67* ⊙ *Mon.–Sat. 9–7:30.*

U Stazzu. Look for the big red awning and stone façade of this excellent source for high-quality Corsican charcuterie, cheese, and wine. The award-winning shop offers some of the best hams and saucisson on the island, including the waist-busting Coppa and Lonzu. Ask for tasting samples before purchasing. ⊠ *1 rue Bonaparte* ☎ *04–95–51–10–80* ⊕ *www.ustazzu.com.*

PORTICCIO

17 km (11 miles) south of Ajaccio on N196.

Between the sea and mountain, this upscale resort town a short scenic drive from the capital benefits from unforgettable views and a palette of nautical activities perfect for the clear, calm waters of the Ajaccio Gulf. It's an oasis, dotted with a number of luxury resorts, notable for its beaches, verdant countryside, and ancient Tower of Capitello.

GETTING HERE

Boat shuttles between Ajaccio and Porticcio are available throughout the summer season with companies like **Découvertes Naturelle** (one way €5, round-trip €8). Buses leave Ajaccio's Gare Routière and stop at Porticcio Mare e Monti Sud and Mare a Mare Centre (€3; winter/summer timetables). The 19-km (11-mile) drive by taxi (€28) or car takes approximately 20–30 minutes from the airport and 30–40 minutes from downtown Ajaccio.

WHERE TO STAY

$$$$ HOTEL FAMILY Fodor's Choice ★ **Le Maquis.** Ranking as one of the island's finest *hôtels de charme,* this graceful ivy-covered Genoese-style retreat rambles down through terraced gardens to a private beach overlooking the Golfe d'Ajaccio. **Pros:** excellent restaurant; exceptional service; indoor pool. **Cons:** loud plane noise with airport proximity; no gym or spa; outdoor pool (freshwater) not heated. [$] *Rooms from: €450* ✉ *D55* ☎ *04–95–25–05–55* 🌐 *www.lemaquis.com* *19 rooms, 6 apartments* ⏲ *Closed Jan.–Mar.* 🍴 *No meals.*

STE-LUCIE-DE-TALLANO

85 km (53 miles) southeast of Porticcio.

Fodor's Choice ★ The pretty little village of Ste-Lucie-de-Tallano is in the heart of Mérimée country, the setting for *Colomba,* the tale of a beautiful young Corsican woman caught in an Andromaque-like web of love, honor, vendetta, and death. Driving up the Rizzanese Valley, the Spin'a Cavallu (Horse's Back) Bridge, one of the oldest and loveliest Genoese bridges on the island, is the first important sight. The St-François convent and the church of Ste-Lucie are the main religious buildings in town.

GETTING HERE

The dangerous descents on winding roads are best driven by day. If renting a car, follow D69 for 6 km (3 miles). Take a right onto the D268 and drive another 13 km (8 miles). Bus lines connecting Ajaccio and Bavella make a stop in Ste-Lucie-de-Tallano (€11.50; seasonal timetables) between the villages of Sartène and Levie.

BONIFACIO

70 km (43 miles) south of Ste-Luice-de-Tallano.

Fodor's Choice ★ The ancient fortress town of Bonifacio occupies a spectacular cliff-top aerie above a harbor carved from limestone cliffs. It's 13 km (8 miles) from Sardinia, and the local speech is heavily influenced by the accent and idiom of that nearby Italian island. Established in the 12th century as Genoa's first Corsican stronghold, Bonifacio remained Genoese through centuries of battles and sieges. As you wander the narrow streets of the **Haute Ville** (Upper Village), inside the walls of the citadel, think of Homer's *Odyssey.* It's here, in the harbor, that scholars place the catastrophic encounter (Chapter X) between Ulysses's fleet and the Laestrygonians, who hurled lethal boulders down from the cliffs.

GETTING HERE

Bonifacio is approximately 20 km (12 miles) south of Figari airport (Figari-Sud Corse), with transfer options by car, taxi (€45), or intermittent seasonal shuttle bus (€10). There is no train service in the extreme southern region of Corsica. In summer months, expect congested streets in and around Bonifacio, delaying journey times. The main entrance road is guaranteed to be jammed with dense crowds of tourists.

Saremar (☎ 04–95–73–00–96) and **Moby Lines** (☎ 04–95–73–00–29) operate ferries from Sardinia (Santa Teresa di Gallura) to Bonifacio, with three or four daily crossings each. One-way tickets cost approximately €20.

13

EXPLORING

Bastion de l'Étendard (*Bastion of the Standard*). From place d'Armes at the city gate, enter the 13th-century bastion de l'Étendard, where you can still see the system of weights and levers used to pull up the drawbridge. The former garrison, the last remaining part of the original fortress, now houses life-size dioramas of Bonifacio's history which describes the bombardment of the bastion in the 16th-century Franco-Turkish war. A visit gives you access to the memorial and Vestiges garden. Climb the steep steps and be rewarded with an incredible panoramic view of the white-chalk cliffs and stunning coastline. ✉ *Av. Charles de Gaulle* 🎫 *€2.50* ⏱ *Mid-June–mid-Sept., weekdays 9–8, weekends 10–7.*

FAMILY **Dragon Grottoes.** From Bonifacio hop on a number of boats that can bring you to see the blue Dragon Grottos, a spectacular geological site. Comprehensive tours typically venture to Venus's Bath (the trip takes one hour on boats that set out every 15 minutes during July and August), sea caves at Sdragonatto and St-Angoine, and the Lavezzi Islands. ✉ *Boats leave from Bonifacio marina* ⊕ *www.bonifacio.fr.*

Eglise Sainte Marie Majeure. The oldest structure in the city, the 12th-century church with buttresses attaching it to surrounding houses is located in the center of the citadel's maze of cobblestone streets. Inside the Pisan-Genoese church, look for the Renaissance baptismal font, carved in bas-relief, and the 3rd-century white-marble Roman sarcophagus. Walk around the back to see the loggia built above a huge cistern that stored water for use in times of siege, as did the circular stone silos seen throughout the town. The 14th-century bell tower rises 82 feet. Relics of the patron Saint Bonifacio reside in the central altar. ✉ *Rue du Saint Sacrement* ☎ *04–95–73–11–88* ⊕ *www.bonifacio.fr.*

WHERE TO EAT

$$$ ✕ **Kissing Pigs.** For traditional Corsican meat, cheese, and wine, head to
BISTRO this cozy charcuterie and grill where aged salamis hang from the rafters.
FAMILY Adding rustic authenticity are stone walls, terra-cotta tile flooring, and illuminated inlets holding books, bottles, and baskets. Start with the selection of farmers' cheese served with chestnut bread, fig jam, dried fruit, and purple grapes. The summer menu features gourmet salads like La Basse Cour (duck, bacon, and apples on a bed of greens) and open-faced sandwiches like the Pertusato *tartine* (foie gras with muscat-marinated macerated figs). Organic pork is the specialty here since it comes directly from the owner's pig farm. Save room for the homemade

ice cream that comes in flavors of fig, myrte, and chestnut. Right near the busy marina, the local eatery has not changed its winning formula since opening in 2008 and remains a popular tourist magnet for lunch, dinner, and Sunday brunch. [$] *Average main: €30* ✉ *5 quai Banda del Ferro* ☎ *04–95–73–56–09* ✍ *Reservations essential.*

WHERE TO STAY

$$$$ HOTEL Fodor's Choice ★ 🏨 **Grand Hotel de Cala Rossa.** Hidden within a gated community, this secluded hotel has an extraordinary garden fringed by a white-sand beach. **Pros:** Bulgari bath products; excellent amenities; superb restaurant. **Cons:** extremely expensive; dress code enforced in common areas; small rooms. [$] *Rooms from: €530* ✉ *Rte. de Cala Rossa, Porto Vecchio* ☎ *04–95–71–61–51* 🌐 *www.hotel-calarossa.com* 🛏 *42 rooms* 🕒 *Closed Jan.–Mar.* 🍴 *Multiple meal plans.*

SPORTS AND THE OUTDOORS

KITE BOARDING

Corsica Kiteboarding. This well-known *école de kite* offers lessons and equipment rental for beginners to advanced levels. Experienced trainers choose the best and safest spots according to weather conditions, including the long beaches of Balistra and Piantarella. ✉ *Chemin de Finocchio* ☎ *06–75–01–50–04* 🌐 *www.corsica-kiteboarding.com.*

WATER SPORTS

Club Atoll. This PADI-endorsed club offers a variety of water sports for beginners or advanced, with equipment rental and training. ✉ *Rte. de Porto-Vecchio, Cavallo Morto* ☎ *04–95–73–02–83.*

COL DE BAVELLA

29 km (18 miles) southwest of Ste-Lucie-de-Tallano.

Fodor's Choice ★ The granite peaks known as the **Aiguilles de Bavella** (Needles of Bavella) tower some 6,562 feet overhead as you reach the Col de Bavella (Bavella Pass). Hiking trails are well marked. The narrow but mostly well-paved roadway over the pass will take you back to the coast along the Solenzara River.

GETTING HERE

Access Col de Bavella from Porto Vecchio. Reserve a local minibus or rent a car. The succession of curvy roads and dangerously steep descents require heightened attention and lower speeds. Driving during the daytime is highly recommended. From Sartène, follow D69 and D268 via Ste-Lucie-de-Tallano and Foce Di Furnu for 45 km (27 miles). From Porto Vecchio, take D368 for 38 km (23 miles) passing Bocca d'Illarata and Zonza. Continue on D268 passing Foce Di Furnu for another 10 km (6 miles) until you reach Col de Bavella.

HAUTE CORSE

Haute Corse (Upper Corsica) is the northeastern end of the island and is, indeed, higher in mean altitude than Corse du Sud, topped by the 8,876-foot Monte Cinto. Most Corsica enthusiasts agree that Haute Corse is the island's finest trove of highland forests, remote villages, hidden cultural gems, vineyards, beaches, and alpine lakes and streams. In the center of Haute Corse is the city of Corte, Corsica's historic heart. To the east is the forested region of La Castagniccia, named for its *châtaigniers* (chestnut trees), one of Corsica's treasures, especially in the fall, when fallen leaves and chestnuts blanket the ground. The forest's tiny roadways go through villages with stunning Baroque churches and houses still roofed in traditional blue-gray slate. To the northwest is Calvi, Corsica's Riviera-like beach resort, while farther north the island's finger pointing to the continent is Cap Corse, with the port city of Bastia, Corsica's largest and most Italianate city, at its base.

13

CORTE

83 km (51 miles) northeast of Ajaccio.

Fodor's Choice

★

Set amid spectacular cliffs and gorges at the confluence of the Tavignano, Restonica, and Orta rivers, Corte is the spiritual heart and soul of Corsica. Capital of Pasquale Paoli's government from 1755 to 1769, it was also where Paoli established the Corsican University in 1765. Closed by the victorious French in 1769, the university, always a symbol of Corsican identity, was reopened in 1981. To reach the upper town and the 15th-century château overlooking the rivers, walk up the cobblestone ramp from place Pasquale-Paoli. Stop in lovely place Gaffori at one of the cafés or restaurants. Note the bullet-pocked house where the Corsican hero Gian Pietro Gaffori and his wife, Faustina, held off the Genoese in 1750.

GETTING HERE

Public transport is quite poor in Corsica, so to access stunning views of interior Corsica, your best bet is to rent a car or hire a driver or local minibus. The shortest distance to Corte is from Bastia. Count on at least an hour to negotiate the 68-km (42-mile) drive. From Ajaccio, a distance of 80 km (49 miles) will take at least 90 minutes.

The Corsican train called the trinighellu is infrequent and slow, and the journey from Ajaccio to Corte takes about one hour and 40 minutes; from Bastia, it's 90 minutes. A main bus line connects Bastia to Corte (90 minutes).

EXPLORING

Belvédère. For an unforgettable view of the river junction and the Genoese bridge below and the citadel's tiny watchtower above, walk left along the citadel wall to the Belvédère. ⊕ *www.corte-tourisme.com.*

FAMILY **Citadelle.** One of six island fortifications of its kind, the Citadelle, a Vauban-style fortress (1769–78), is built around the original 15th-century bastion at the highest point of the cliff, with the river below. In 1769, after the defeat of Ponte Novu, Corsica came under French rule. Count de Vaux, who held Corte, undertook the construction of the citadel's second reconstruction to strengthen the defense system of the city. Trapezoidal in shape and large in size, it's bordered by scarps 26–45 feet high. The building contains the **Musée de la Corse** (Corsica Museum), dedicated to the island's history and ethnography. ⊠ *Musée régional d'Anthropologie, La Citadelle* ☎ *04–95–45–25–45* ⊕ *www.*

musee-corse.com ⬚ *€5* ☉ *Nov.–Apr., Tues.–Sat. 10–7; May–Oct., daily 10–8.*

FAMILY
Fodor's Choice
★
Gorges de la Restonica (*Restonica Gorges*). Put on your hiking boots. The Gorges de la Restonica make a spectacular day tour. At the top of the Restonica Valley, leave your car in the parking area at the end of the road. A two-hour climb will take you to Lac de Mélo, a trout-filled mountain lake 6,528 feet above sea level sourcing the gorges. Another hour up is the usually snow-bordered Lac de Capitello. Information on trails is available from the tourist office or the Parc Naturel Régional. Light meals are served in the stone shepherds' huts at the Bergeries de Grotelle. Visitors should be advised of falling rocks in the rugged region. ⬚ *Access by D623* ⊕ *www.parc-corse.org.*

13

WHERE TO EAT

$$
MODERN FRENCH
Fodor's Choice
★
✕ **Le 24.** Stone archways, rock walls and dim lighting give this chic restaurant a cavernous feel. The chalkboard menu, brought to each table, features shrimp tempura, seafood pasta, and sautéed dorado. Grilled to perfection is the filet mignon, topped with foie gras and served with a baked potato and artichoke. Portions are large and the presentation is extraordinary. Order a signature seasonal dish. And definitely try one of the decadent desserts like the chocolate soufflé or homemade sorbet. $ *Average main: €50* ⬚ *24 cours Paoli* ☎ *04–95–46–02–90* ⊕ *www. visit-corsica.com* ☉ *Closed Sun. Oct.–Mar.*

WHERE TO STAY

$$
B&B/INN
⊡ **Hôtel Dominique Colonna.** This modern hotel with surprising designer features across from the **Auberge de la Restonica** has sliding doors leading directly out to breakfast nooks by the stream. **Pros:** incredible breakfast; spacious rooms; gracious staff. **Cons:** hard mattresses; no sun umbrellas or shade at the pool; far from coast $ *Rooms from: €190* ⬚ *Vallée de la Restonica* ☎ *04–95–45–25–65* ⊕ *www. dominique-colonna.com* ⬏ *29 rooms and suites* ☉ *Closed Nov. 5– Mar. 14* ⦶ *Some meals.*

LA SCALA DI SANTA REGINA

20 km (12 miles) northwest of Corte.

Fodor's Choice
★
La Scala di Santa Regina (Stairway of the Holy Queen) is one of Corsica's most spectacular roads, and one of the most difficult to navigate, especially in winter. The route follows the twisty path of the Golo River, which has carved its way through layers of red granite, forming dramatic gorges and waterfalls. Be prepared to stop for herds of animals crossing the road. Follow the road to the **Col de Verghio** (Verghio Pass) for superb views of Tafunatu, the legendary perforated mountain, and Monte Cinto. On the way up you'll pass through the **Valdo Niello Forest,** Corsica's most important woodlands, filled with pines and beeches. The col is considered the border between Haute Corse and Corse du Sud. As you descend from the Verghio Pass through the **Forêt d'Aitone** (Aitone Forest), note how well manicured it is—the pigs, goats, and sheep running rampant through the tall Laricio pines keep it this way. As you pass the village of Evisa, with its orange roofs, look across the

La Scala di Santa Regina loops through arresting—and rocky—terrain.

impressive **Gorges de Spelunca** (Spelunca Gorge) to see the hill village of Ota. A small road on the right will take you across the gorge, where there's an ancient Genoese-built bridge.

GETTING HERE
By car, depart from Ponte-Leccia, following the N193 for 7 km (4 miles). Take a right onto D84, crossing Francardo. Continue about 13 km (8 miles) until you reach La Scala di Santa Regina.

PIGNA

71 km (44 miles) from La Scala di Santa Regina.

Fodor'sChoice
★
The village of Pigna is dedicated to bringing back traditional Corsican music and crafts. Here you can listen to folk songs in cafés, visit workshops, and buy handmade musical instruments. The Casa Musicale, a concert hall, auberge, and restaurant, is the center of it all. During the first half of July, the Casa Musicale hosts a Festivoce (song festival) of international vocalists and a cappella groups.

GETTING HERE
Follow the N197 towards Lumio, where you take a right onto D71. Cross Lavatoggio and Cateri, where you take a left onto D151. At Aregno, take a right to continue onto D151 until you enter Pigna.

WHERE TO STAY

$

B&B/INN
Casa Musicale. This enchanting locale has traditional home-style cuisine and music of all kinds—often authentic Corsican polyphonic chanting—and a commanding panorama of La Balagne towards Calvi. **Pros:** beautiful rooms overlooking Algajola Bay; unique concept; relaxed

bohemian ambience. **Cons:** tiny rooms; thin walls; sparse, uninspiring decor. [$] *Rooms from: €85* ✉ *Fondu Di U Paese* ☎ *04–95–61–77– 31* 🌐 *www.casa-musicale.org* 🛏 *7 rooms* 🕒 *Closed Jan. 5–Mar. 5. No dinner Sun. and Mon. except July 14–Aug. 30* 🍴 *No meals.*

SHOPPING

Casa di l'Artigiani. The Casa di l'Artigiani, created in 1995 to showcase local artisans, is the perfect place to find handmade crafts, from traditional forged Corsican knives, leather, musical instruments, and hand-knit sweaters to locally produced culinary treasures such as olive oils, jam, honey, and *canistrelli* biscuits. ✉ *Rte. des Artisans* ☎ *04–95–61–77–29* 🌐 *www.balagne-corsica.com.*

13

BASTIA

170 km (105 miles) north of Bonifacio, 153 km (95 miles) northeast of Ajaccio.

Notably more Italianate than the "Continental" French capital at Ajaccio, Bastia is, along with Corte, quintessentially Corsican. Despite sprawling suburbs, the Baroque coastal resort town has a historic center that retains the timeless, salty flavor of an ancient Mediterranean port, so approaching and departing by sea are particularly dramatic while rounding the Cap Corse peninsula. With its four churches, an ethnographical museum, many picturesque corners, and a number of fine dining options overlooking the comings and goings of boats to the tune of foghorn blasts, Bastia has a full bouquet of sights to savor. Its name is derived from the word "bastion," in reference to the fortress the Genoese built here in the 14th century as a stronghold against rebellious islanders and potential invaders. Today the city, with a population hovering around 45,000, is Corsica's business center and second-largest town after Ajaccio. The **Terra Vecchia** (Old Town) is best explored on foot. Start at the wide, palm-filled **place St-Nicolas,** bordered on one side by docked ships looming large in the port and on the other by two blocks of popular cafés along boulevard Général-de-Gaulle.

GETTING HERE

You can reach Bastia by air or sea. Flights arrive regularly from main cities in Europe at the Aéroport de Bastia-Poretta situated in Lucciana, southeast of the city. From here, Autobus Bastiais shuttle bus lines run from 6:30 am to 10 pm (depending on season) to downtown in 40 minutes for €8. Expect to pay €30–€35 for a taxi between the airport and city center.

Ferries cross from France (Nice, Toulon, Marseilles) and Italy (Livorno, Genova, Verde Ligure). The average crossing time is around five hours.

Train services link Bastia to Ajaccio and Calvi. The station is only a short distance from Bastia's ferry port, on Rond-point Maréchal Leclerc.

EXPLORING

FAMILY **Cathédrale Ste-Marie.** A network of cobbled alleyways rambles across the citadel to the 15th-century Cathédrale Ste-Marie, one of the town's prettiest churches. Inside, classic Baroque style abounds in an explosion of gilt decoration. The 18th-century silver statue of the Assumption is

A microcosm of mountains, beaches, fishing ports, wilderness, Corsica is the purest strain of proto-Mediterranean culture.

paraded at the head of a religious procession every August 15. Numerous works of art from the 18th and 19th centuries, forged metalwork, sculptures, and statues that were generous gifts from the bishops of Mariana, residents of the cathedral from 1600 to 1622, are showcased. ⊠ *Rue Notre-Dame* ⊕ *www.bastia-tourisme.com.*

Chapelle Sainte Croix (*Chapel of the Holy Cross*). The sumptuous Rococo style of the Chapelle Ste-Croix, behind the cathedral, makes it look more like a theater than a church. The chapel owes its name to a blackened oak crucifix, dubbed "Christ of the Miracles," discovered by fishermen at sea in 1428 and venerated to this day by Bastia's fishing community. The most ancient church in the town, this chapel has officially been classified as a historic monument since 1931. ⊠ *4 rue de l'Evêché.*

Église de la Conception (*Church of the Conception*). From place St. Nicolas head south on boulevard Général de Gaulle, which becomes rue Napoléon, for two blocks to the 16th-century Église de la Conception, occupying a cobblestoned square as originally built. Step inside the Baroque portal to admire the church's ornate 18th-century interior, requiring a bright day to see much detail as interior lighting is quite dim. The walls are covered with wood carvings, gold, marble, and velvet fabric; the ceiling is painted with vibrant frescoes. Check out the altar's interpretation of the Assumption of Murillo, whose original version sits in Madrid's El Prado Museum. ⊠ *Rue Napoléon* ⊕ *www.bastia-tourisme.com.*

Palais des Nobles Douzes. The vaulted, colonnaded galleries of the Palais des Nobles Douzes (situated next to the Palais des Gouverneurs Genois, or Genoese Governors' Palace) houses the **Musée d'Ethnographie Corse**

(Corsican Ethnographic Museum). Don't miss the *Casablanca,* a French submarine used by the Resistance with swastikas on the turret representing downed Nazi aircraft. The building itself has been undergoing modifications since the 18th century, when it used as the meeting place for rural commune leaders. Today, it's function is less political as the working office for delegates representing the region's cultural heritage. ✉ *Pl. du Donjon* ☎ *04–95–31–09–12* 🌐 *www.musee-bastia.com* 🕓 *July–Sept. 17, Tues.–Sun. 10–7:30; Apr.–June and Sept. 18–Oct., Tues.–Sun. 10–6; Nov.–Mar., Tues.–Sat. 9–noon and 2–5:30* 🕓 *Closed Mon., Dec. 25, and 31.*

13

Place du Marché. Place du Marché, the central market square near the town hall, buzzes with activity every morning (8 am–1 pm) except Monday. The warren of narrow streets that make up the old fishermen's quarter begins at the far side of the square. ✉ *Pl. du Marché* 🌐 *www.bastia-tourisme.com.*

FAMILY **Terra Nova** (*New Town*). Stroll around Terra Nova, a maze of newer streets and houses at the base of the 15th-century fortress. Opposite to the old district of Terra Vecchia, the more modern quarter of the city is worth a promenade to see the Governor's Palace, Saint Croix church, and Sainte Marie cathedral. Climb the Escalier Romieu steps beside the leafy Jardins Romieu for a sweeping view of the Italian islands of Capraia, Elba, and Montecristo. 🌐 *www.bastia-tourisme.com.*

WHERE TO EAT

$$ SEAFOOD 🍴 **A Scaletta.** Just across the Saint Baptiste church, enjoy the view of the Vieux Port from a pretty balcony as you choose from a range of fish and seafood specials at this popular spot with friendly, homestyle service. Three-course menus (€18–€29) may include beignets de fromage (fried cheese), ravioli in tomato sauce, or sautéed sardines with eggplant. (Lavezzi, next door, has the same view, fine cuisine, and higher prices.) Expect traditional Corsican fare made from fresh local ingredients. [$] *Average main: €30* ✉ *4 rue St-Jean* ☎ *04–95–32–28–70* ✍ *Reservations essential* 🕓 *Closed Sun.*

$$$$ BISTRO 🍴 **La Citadelle.** This rustic and intimate spot, built in an ancient oil press, has been updated in recent years and is near the Governor's Palace on the heights of the Terra Nova. Serving trendy cuisine in nouvelle Corsican style, the restaurant has views of the Bastia port and offers three-course menus (€35–€48) that feature veal, lobster, and fresh fish. Dishes are elegantly prepared and presented; especially popular are the swordfish garnished with wild mint and roasted eggplant, caramelized suckling pig, and sea-bass fillet draped in panzetta. [$] *Average main: €60* ✉ *5 rue du Dragon* ☎ *04–95–31–44–70* 🕓 *Closed Sun. and Mon. Nov.–Dec. No lunch Sat.*

WHERE TO STAY

$ HOTEL 🏨 **Hotel Posta Vecchia.** Located at the end of a quiet promenade near the water's quai, the asset of this old-fashioned hotel, a former post office, is its convenience to place St-Nicolas, Citadelle, and port. **Pros:** central location; clean rooms; friendly staff. **Cons:** tiny bathrooms with no amenities and accordion folding doors in shower; overpriced breakfast; noisy rooms on boulevard side. [$] *Rooms from: €65* ✉ *Quai des*

Martyrs-de-la-Libération, 8 rue Posta Vecchia ☎ *04–95–32–32–38* ⊕ *www.hotel-postavecchia.com* ⌁ *50 rooms* ⊘ *Closed Dec. 25–Jan. 15* ⏐◎⏐ *Breakfast.*

SPORTS AND THE OUTDOORS

FISHING

Objectif Nature. Objectif Nature organizes outings geared for nature and sports lovers. Groups and individuals can canyon, hike, horseback ride, parasail, fish, dive, mountain-bike, or kayak for an hour, day, or longer holiday. Rental equipment and experienced guides are available. ⊠ *3 rue ND de Lourdes* ☎ *04–95–32–54–34, 06–12–02–32–02 cell* ⊕ *www. objectif-nature-corse.com.*

SHOPPING

Cap Corse Mattei. The most legendary Corsican distillery founded in 1917, Cap Corse Mattei sells the Mattei family's special grape-based Cap Corse liqueur in its iconic labeled bottles. A range of derivative products make perfect souvenirs, including aromatic honeys, jams, chutneys, and oils. ⊠ *15 bd. Général de Gaulle* ☎ *04–95–32–44–38.*

Casa di l'Artigiani. Casa di l'Artigiani has a wide selection of artisanal crafts, including ceramics, woodwork, engravings, leather goods, jewelry, stringed instruments, and embroidered fabrics. Cash is the preferred method of payment. ⊠ *Rte. des Artisans, 8 km (5 miles) from Di L'Isula Rossa* ☎ *04–95–61–75–55* ⊕ *www.routedesartisans.org* ⊘ *Closed Sun. Apr.–June 30.*

Marché traditionnel. In front of the town hall, meander through myriad stalls selling everything from local cheeses to charcuterie, oils, and other fine Corsican gastronomic products every Saturday and Sunday. On weekday mornings, locally produced myrtle liqueur is sold. On Sunday mornings, head to the Marché aux Puces (flea market) on place Saint Nicolas to find knickknacks and antiques at bargain-basement prices. The same spot has the Marché du Blanc et du Textile every second Friday morning where you can find beautifully handcrafted fabrics and embroidery. ⊠ *Pl. de l'Hotel de Ville behind St-Jean-Baptiste* ⊕ *www. bastia-tourisme.com.*

THE MIDI-PYRÉNÉES AND LANGUEDOC-ROUSSILLON

WELCOME TO THE MIDI-PYRÉNÉES AND LANGUEDOC-ROUSSILLON

TOP REASONS TO GO

★ **Matisse madness:** Captivating Collioure, the main town of the Vermilion Coast, was where Matisse and Derain went crazy with color and created the Fauvist art movement in the early 20th century.

★ **Fairy-tale Carcassonne:** Complete with towers, turrets, and battlements, Carcassonne's forti-fied upper town is a UNESCO World Heritage Site that feels like a medieval theme park.

★ **Tumultuous Toulouse:** With rosy roofs and red-brick mansions, the "Pink City" is a place where high culture is an evening at an outdoor café.

★ **Albi's Toulouse-Lautrec:** Presided over by the fortresslike Cathédrale Ste-Cécile, Albi hon-ors its most famous native son, Toulouse-Lautrec, with the largest museum of his works.

★ **Abbey in the sky:** At an altitude of nearly 3,600 feet, the picture-postcard medieval Abbaye St-Martin du Canigou enjoys a perch that (literally) takes your breath away.

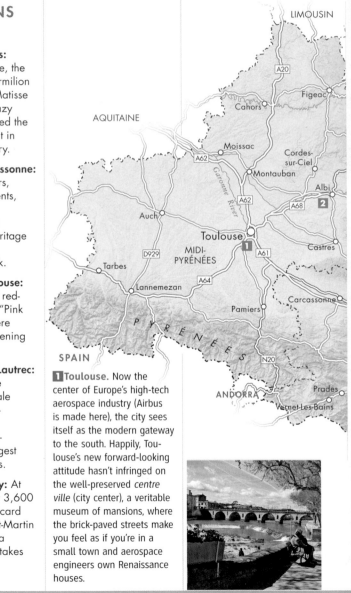

1 Toulouse. Now the center of Europe's high-tech aerospace industry (Airbus is made here), the city sees itself as the modern gateway to the south. Happily, Tou-louse's new forward-looking attitude hasn't infringed on the well-preserved *centre ville* (city center), a veritable museum of mansions, where the brick-paved streets make you feel as if you're in a small town and aerospace engineers own Renaissance houses.

2 **Albi.** Some 75 km (47 miles) northeast of Toulouse, Albi sits on the Tarn River and was once a major center of the Cathars, a medieval Christian sect; the huge Cathédrale Ste-Cécile was a symbol of the Roman Catholic Church's victory over these heretics. Art lovers make a pilgrimage to the famed Musée Toulouse-Lautrec.

GETTING ORIENTED

Spend some time in the Midi-Pyrénées, the country's largest region, and the term "the south of France" takes on new meaning. This western half of France's south is less glamorous (and much less expensive) than the Riviera and Provence but has an array of must-sees, beginning with lively Toulouse. East lies Languedoc, a province of contrasts—of rolling sun-baked plains around Carcassonne, of stone-and-shrub-covered hills spiked with ruins of ancient civilizations. Stretching south along the Mediterranean is the southernmost province of Roussillon, home to that artists' paradise, the Vermilion Coast.

14

RHÔNE-ALPES

A75

Mende

0   30 mi

0   30 km

Rodez

N88

Millau

Alès

D999   A75

LANGUEDOC-ROUSSILLON

3

Mazamet

Nîmes

A9   Avignon

A7

A54

Montpellier

A75   A9

PROVENCE-ALPES-CÔTE D'AZUR

Béziers

A61

Narbonne

Golfe du Lion

VERMILION COAST

Salses

A9

D117

N116   Perpignan

Ceret   Collioure

SPAIN

3 **Languedoc-Roussillon.** Studded with vineyards and ghosts of famed artists, Languedoc is a vast province that ranges from Carcassonne in the Black Mountains eastward to aristocratic Montpellier on the Mediterranean. Included in the region are famous sights like Carcassonne's La Cité—the largest medieval town extant—and *le littoral Languedocien* (the Languedoc coast), where France's "second Riviera" draws both artists and sun worshippers to Collioure and other towns along the Côte Vermeille (Vermilion Coast).

Updated by
Avery Sumner

Like the most celebrated dish of this area, cassoulet, the southwestern region of France is made up of diverse ingredients. Just as it would be a gross oversimplification to refer to cassoulet merely as a mixture of baked beans, southwestern France is much more than just Toulouse, the peaks of the Pyrénées, and the fairy-tale ramparts of Carcassonne.

For here you'll also find, like so many raisins sweetening up a spicy stew, the pretty seaside town of Collioure, the famed Côte Vermeille (where Matisse, Picasso, and Braque first vacationed to paint), and Albi, a hilltop town that honors its hometown hero, Toulouse-Lautrec, with a great museum. But in most cases, every traveler heading to this area begins with the regional gateway: "La Ville Rose," so-called for Toulouse's redbrick buildings.

Big enough to be France's fourth-largest city and yet with the look and vibe of a gorgeous small town, Toulouse is all that more famous regional capitals would like to have remained, or to become. The cultural hub of this corner of France, the city has a vibrancy that derives from its large student population and lively music scene, plus a rich heritage of sculpture and architectural gems. Snaking along the banks of the Garonne as it meanders north and west from the Catalan Pyrénées on its way to the Atlantic, romantic Toulouse has a Spanish sensuality unique in all of Gaul. The city began as the ancient capital of the province called Languedoc, so christened when it became royal property in 1270, langue d'oc meaning the country where *oc*—instead of the *oil* or *oui* of northeastern France—meant "yes."

If you head out in any direction from Toulouse you'll enjoy a feast for the eyes. Albi, with its Toulouse-Lautrec legacy, is a star attraction, while Céret is the gateway to a fabled "open-air museum" prized by artists and poets, the Côte Vermeille. The Vermilion Coast is centered around Collioure, the lovely fishing village where Matisse, Derain, and the Fauvists—the "wild beasts" of the early-20th-century art world—threw out the pretty pastel rule book, drawing inspiration instead from the savage tones found in Mother Nature hereabouts. When you see picturesque Collioure's stunning Mediterranean setting, you can understand why Matisse went color-mad. Sheer heaven for painters, the town's magic did not go unnoticed, and it soon drew vacationers by the boatload, who quickly discovered that everything around here seems to be asking to be immortalized on canvas: the Mediterranean, smooth and opalescent at dawn; villagers dancing Sardanas to the music of the raucous and ancient woodwind *flavioles* and *tenores*; and the flood of golden light so peculiar to the Mediterranean.

PLANNER

WHEN TO GO

14

You can expect pleasantly warm weather as early as April and as late as October, but be prepared for rainstorms and/or heat waves at almost any time. The weather is especially unpredictable in the Pyrénées: a few passing clouds can rapidly turn into a full-blown storm. Needless to say, during July and August towns high on tourist lists—like Albi, Carcassonne, and Collioure—are packed, so perhaps opt for April and May, which are delightful months on the Côte Vermeille and also the time when the Pyrénéan flowers are at their best. June and September (grape-picking season, or *vendange*) are equally good for the inland areas. As October draws near, the chilly winds of winter begin to blow and frenzied mushroom hunters ferret amid the chestnut and pine trees.

No matter the season, there's plenty here to occupy those who love the outdoors, whether it be hiking the Grandes Randonnées (GRs), scaling lofty peaks, or skiing sun-dappled snowfields.

PLANNING YOUR TIME

Getting to know this vast region would take several weeks, or even years. But it's possible to sample all of its finest offerings in nine days, if that's all the time you have. Begin by practicing your "Olé's" in Spanish-soul Toulouse; after two days and two nights in this vibrant city, veer west to the Gers département to spend Day 3 in Albi and take a virtual art class with Toulouse-Lautrec at the famous museum here devoted to his masterworks. On Day 4, continue some 112 km (70 miles) south to once-upon-a-timefied Carcassonne to introduce your kids to the Puss-in-Boots fantasy of this castellated wonder. After a night filled with medieval history and glamour, travel southeast on Day 5 to the Vermilion Coast. It's time to pack your crayons for a trip to Matisse Country and head to the Roussillon's coastal town of Collioure to channel the spirits of the famous Fauve painters. Spend all of Day 6 here. Then on Day 7, drive north past Perpignan, the historic hub city of the Roussillon, and head to marvelous Montpellier. After your seventh night, enjoy Day 8 by touring this city's fascinating Vieille Ville (Old Town), steeped in culture, history, and young blood (a famous university is based here). Add on a Day 9 to chill out before returning to reality.

GETTING HERE AND AROUND

AIR TRAVEL

All international flights for Toulouse arrive at Blagnac Airport, 8 km (5 miles) northwest of the city. The airport shuttle (⊕ *www.tisseo.fr*) runs every 20 minutes between 5:30 am and 12:15 pm from the airport to the bus-train station in Toulouse (fare €5).

From the Toulouse bus station to the airport, buses leave every 20 minutes 5 am–9:20 pm.

Air Information **Airport Carcassonne-Salvaza** ☎ *04–68–71–96–46*. **Airport International, Perpignan** ☎ *04–68–52–60–70*. **Airport Montpellier-Méditerranée** ☎ *04–67–20–85–00*. **Blagnac Airport** ☎ *08–25–38–00–00, 33/170–46–74–74 from outside France.*

CARRIERS In addition, be sure to check out Ryanair, easyJet, and Flybe, who offer surprisingly cheap flights from the United Kingdom to Perpignan, Montpellier, Carcassonne, Beziers, or Toulouse—often as low as €30 one way.

Airlines and Contacts **Air France** ☎ *800/992–3932 in U.S.* ⊕ *www.airfrance. com.* **easyJet** ☎ *08–20–42–03–15* ⊕ *www.easyjet.com.* **Flybe** ☎ *44/0871–700–2000 in U.K.* ⊕ *www.flybe.com.* **Ryanair** ☎ *08–92–78–02–10* ⊕ *www.ryanair. com.*

BUS TRAVEL

Many bus companies thread through the Midi-Pyrénées countryside (in addition to SNCF buses, you'll find Tisseo, Véolia, and Salt Autocars, among others). Toulouse's bus routes run to and from Albi (1½ hrs, €13) and Carcassonne (2 hrs, €12); Albi connects with Cordes-sur-Ciel (summer only; other times take a train to Cordes-Vindrac, 5 km [3 miles] away) and with Montauban; while Montpellier connects with Narbonne. Courriers Catalans and Cars Capeille buses to the Côte Vermeille, Collioure, Céret, and Prades depart from Perpignan. Also from Perpignan the Conseil General (⊕ *www.cg66.fr*) operates an extensive network of buses for €1 linking almost all towns and villages in the entire département. All destinations on the train line from Perpignan to Villefranche are also just €1. The train to Carcassonne is scenic and romantic, although buses (cheaper and faster) go there as well.

Bus Information **Gare Routière Carcassonne** ✉ *Bd. de Varsovie, Ville Basse, Carcassonne.* **Gare Routière Montpellier** ✉ *Rue Grand St. Jean, Montpellier.* **Gare Routière Perpignan** ✉ *Bd. Saint Assicle, Perpignan* ☎ *04–68–35–29–02.* **Gare Routière Toulouse** ✉ *68 bd. Pierre Sémard, Toulouse* ☎ *05–61–61–67–67.*

CAR TRAVEL

The fastest route from Paris to Toulouse, 677 km (406 miles) south, is via Limoges on A20, then A62; the journey time is about six hours. If you choose to head south over the Pyrénées to Barcelona, the Tunnel du Puymorens saves half an hour of switchbacks between Hospitalet and Porta; but in good weather—and with time to spare—the drive over the Puymorens Pass is spectacular. Plan on taking three hours between Toulouse and Font-Romeu and another three to Barcelona. The fastest route from Toulouse to Barcelona is the under-three-hour, 391-km (235-mile) drive via Carcassonne and Perpignan on A61 and A9, which becomes AP7 at Le Perthus. A62/A61 slices through the region on its way through Carcassonne to the coast at Narbonne, where A9 heads south to Perpignan. At Toulouse, where A62 becomes A61, various highways fan out in all directions: N124 to Auch; A64 to St-Gaudens, Tarbes, and Pau; A62/A20 to Montauban and Cahors; N20 south to Foix and the Ariège Valley; A68 to Albi and Rodez. A9 (La Languedocienne) is the main highway artery that connects Montpellier with Beziers to the south and Nîmes to the north.

TRAIN TRAVEL

Most trains for the southwest leave from Paris's Gare d'Austerlitz, with direct services to Toulouse and Montauban. Carcassonne connects with either Toulouse or Montpellier.

There are 15 daily departures from Paris to Narbonne and 13 to Perpignan. Most of these trips take between 6 and 7 hours, but if you get the TGV (Trains à Grande Vitesse) from the Gare de Lyon you can be in Narbonne in 4½ hours. Note that at least 10 high-speed TGVs per day leave Paris (Gare Montparnasse and Gare Austerlitz) for Toulouse; the journey time is more than five hours. A TGV line also serves Montpellier 18 times a day (departing from Paris's Gare de Lyon). The regional French rail network (TER) in the southwest provides regular service to many towns, though not all. Within the Midi-Pyrénées region, Toulouse is the biggest hub, with a major line linking Carcassonne (1 hr, €15), Béziers, Narbonne (1½ hrs, €21; change here for Perpignan), and Montpellier (2 hrs, €32); trains link up with Albi (1 hr, €15), too. Toulouse trains also connect with Biarritz (5 hrs, €45), Pau (3 hrs, €30), and Bordeaux (3 hrs, €35). Montpellier connects with Carcassonne (2 hr, €23), Perpignan (2 hrs, €25), Narbonne, and other towns. From Perpignan, take one of the dozen or so daily trains to Collioure (20 mins, €6).

Train Information Gare SNCF Carcassonne ✉ *1 av. Marechal Joffre, Carcassonne* ☎ *08–92–35–35–35, 36–35.* **Gare SNCF Montpellier** ✉ *Rue Jules Ferry, Montpellier* ☎ *36–35.* **Gare SNCF Perpignan** ✉ *Av. du Général de Gaulle, Perpignan* ☎ *36–35.* **SNCF** ☎ *36–35 [€0.34 per min]* ⊕ *www.voyages-sncf.com.* **SNCF Toulouse-Matabiau** ✉ *64 bd. Pierre Semard, Toulouse* ☎ *05–61–10–17–10, 36–35.* **TGV** ⊕ *www.tgv.com.*

RESTAURANTS

As a rule, the closer you get to the Mediterranean coast, the later you dine and the more you pay for your seafood platter and that bottle of iced rosé. The farther you travel from the coast, the higher the altitude, the more rustic the setting, and the more reasonable the prices will be. During the scorching summer months in sleepy mountain villages, lunches are light, interminable, and *bien arrosé* (with lots of wine). Here you can also find that small personal restaurant where the chickens roasting on spits above the open fire have first names and the cheese comes from the hippie couple down the road who arrived here in the '60s and love their mountains, their goats, and the universe in general.

Prices in the reviews are the average cost of a main course at dinner or, if dinner is not served, at lunch.

HOTELS

Hotels range from Mediterranean modern to medieval baronial to Pyrenean chalet, and most are small and cozy rather than luxurious and sophisticated. Toulouse has the usual range of big-city hotels, for which you need to make reservations well in advance if you plan to visit in spring or fall. Look for *gîtes d'étape* (hikers' way stations) and *chambres d'hôtes* (bed-and-breakfasts), which offer excellent value, a chance to meet local and international travelers, and, perhaps, to sample life on a farm, as well as the delights of *cuisine du terroir* (country cooking). As for off-season—if there is such a thing, since chic Parisians often arrive in November in their SUVs with a hunger for the authentic—call ahead and double-check when hotels close for their annual hibernation. This usually starts sometime in winter, either before, or right after, the Christmas holidays.

Prices in the reviews are the lowest cost of a standard double room in high season.

VISITOR INFORMATION

The regional tourist office for the Midi-Pyrénées is the Comité Régional du Tourisme. For Pyrénées-Orientales information, contact the Comité Départemental de Tourisme du Pyrénées-Orientales. For Languedoc-Roussillon contact the Comité Régional du Tourisme du Languedoc-Roussillon.

Contacts Comité Départemental de Tourisme du Pyrénées-Orientales ✉ *16 av. Des Palmiers, Perpignan* ☎ *04–68–51–52–53* ⊕ *www.cdt-66.com.* **Comité Régional du Tourisme (CRT).** ✉ *15 rue Rivals, Toulouse* ☎ *05–61–13–55–55* ⊕ *www.tourisme-midi-pyrenees.com.* **Comité Régional du Tourisme du Languedoc-Roussillon** ✉ *954 av. Jean Mermoz, Montpellier* ☎ *04–67–20–02–20* ⊕ *www.sunfrance.com.*

Handy websites for this region are ⊕ *www.audetourisme.com* and ⊕ *www.tourisme-tarn.com.*

TOULOUSE: LA VILLE ROSE

The ebullient city of Toulouse is the capital of the Midi-Pyrénées and the fourth-largest city in France. Just 100 km (60 miles) from the border with Spain, Toulouse is in many ways closer in flavor to southern European Spanish than to northern European French. Weathered redbrick buildings line sidewalks, giving the city its nickname, "La Ville Rose" (the Pink City). Downtown, the sidewalks and restaurants pulse late into the night with tourists, workers, college students, and technicians from the giant Airbus aerospace complex headquartered outside the city.

Despite Toulouse's bustling, high-tech attitude, its well-preserved *centre ville*—the brick-paved streets between the Garonne River and the Canal du Midi—retains the feel of a small town, where food, Beaujolais nouveau, and the latest rugby victory are the primary concerns. So be prepared to savor the Mediterranean pace, southern friendliness, and youthful spirit of the city. Toulouse was founded in the 4th century BC and quickly became an important part of Roman Gaul. In turn, it was made into a Visigothic and Carolingian capital before becoming a separate county in 843. Ruling from this Pyrénéan hub, the counts of Toulouse held sovereignty over nearly all of the Languedoc and maintained a brilliant court known for its fine troubadours and literature. In the early 13th century, Toulouse was attacked and plundered by troops representing an alliance between the northern French nobility and the papacy, ostensibly to wipe out the Albigensian heresy (Catharism), but more realistically as an expansionist move against the power of Occitania, the French southwest. The counts toppled, but Toulouse experienced a cultural and economic rebirth thanks to the *woad* (blue dye) trade, and, consequently, wealthy merchants' homes constitute a major portion of Toulouse's architectural heritage.

GETTING AROUND

For the most part, Toulouse's hotels, restaurants, and sights are within walking distance of one another. The main square of the *centre ville* is place du Capitole, a good 15-minute walk from the train station but only a few blocks away from the city's other focal points—place Wilson, place Esquirol, and the Basilique St-Sernin. Within Toulouse, the public transit system (⊕ *www.tisseo.fr*) includes a two-line métro (subway), which conveniently connects the Gare Matabiau with place du Capitole and place Esquirol, as well as a tram with one line and an efficient bus network.

14

Toulouse, at the intersection of the Garonne and the Canal du Midi, midway between the Massif Central and the Pyrénées, became an important nexus between Aquitania, Languedoc, and the Roussillon. Today, Toulouse is France's second-largest university town after Paris and the center of France's aerospace industry.

GETTING HERE

If you take the train to Toulouse you arrive at its Gare Matabiau (☎ *08–0031–31–31 or SNCF 36–35*), which is right beside the Toulouse Gare Routière (bus station), on boulevard Pierré-Sémard. The Gare Routière (☎ *05–61–61–67–67*) is also the terminal for the airport shuttle, which departs every 20 minutes from Blagnac Airport (☎ *08–25–38–00–00*). If you want the TGV (⊕ *www.tgv.com*), there are at least 10 trains a day from Paris, from €75 a trip.

Visitor Information Toulouse Tourist Office ⊠ *Donjon du Capitole* ☎ *08–92–18–01–80* ⊕ *www.toulouse-tourisme.com.*

OLD TOULOUSE

The area between the boulevards and the Garonne forms the historic nucleus of Toulouse. Originally part of Roman Gaul and later the capital for the Visigoths and then the Carolingians, Toulouse was one of the artistic and literary centers of Europe by AD 1000. Although defeated by the lords of northern France in the 13th century, Toulouse quickly reemerged as a cultural and commercial power and has remained so ever since. Religious and civil structures bear witness to this illustrious past, even as the city's booming student life mirrors a dynamic present. This is the heart of Toulouse, with place du Capitole at its center. The huge garage beneath place du Capitole is a good place to park, and offers easy walking distance to all the major sites. If you leave your car in another garage, you can take the subway that runs north–south to central Toulouse for €1.60.

EXPLORING
TOP ATTRACTIONS

Fodor's Choice **Basilique St-Sernin.** Toulouse's most famous landmark and the world's ★ largest Romanesque church once belonged to a Benedictine abbey, built in the 11th century to house pilgrims on their way to Santiago de Compostela in Spain. Inside, the aesthetic high point is the magnificent central apse, begun in 1080, glittering with gilded ceiling frescoes, which date from the 19th century. When illuminated at night, St-Sernin's five-tier octagonal tower glows red against the sky. Not all the tiers are the same: the first three, with their rounded windows, are Romanesque; the upper two, with pointed Gothic windows, were added around 1300. The ancient crypt contains the relics and reliquaries of 128 saints, but the most famous item on view is a thorn that legend says is from the Crown of Thorns. ✉ *Pl. Saint-Sernin* ☎ *05–61–21–80–45* ⛪ *Basilica free; crypt €2* ⏲ *Oct.–May, Mon.–Sat. 8:30–6, Sun. 8:30–7:30; June –Sept., Mon.–Sat. 8:30–7, Sun. 8:30–7:30.*

Capitole/Hôtel de Ville (*Capitol/Town Hall*). The 18th-century Capitole is home to the Hôtel de Ville and the city's highly regarded opera company; the reception rooms are open to the public when not in use for official functions or weddings. Halfway up the **Grand Escalier** (Grand Staircase) hangs a large painting of the *Jeux Floraux*, the "floral games" organized by a literary society created in 1324 to promote the local Occitanian language, Langue d'Oc. The festival continues to this day: poets give public readings here each May, and the best are awarded silver- and gold-plated violets, one of the emblems of Toulouse. At the top of the stairs is the **Salle Gervaise,** a hall adorned with a series of paintings inspired by the themes of love and marriage. The mural at the far end of the room portrays the Isle of Cythères, where Venus received her lovers, alluding to a French euphemism for getting married: *embarquer pour Cythères* (to embark for Cythères). More giant paintings in the **Salle Henri-Martin,** named for the artist (1860–1943), show the passing seasons set against the eternal Garonne. Look for Jean Jaurès (1859–1914), one of France's greatest socialist martyrs, in *Les Rêveurs* (*The Dreamers*); he's wearing a boater-style hat and a beige coat. At the far left end of the elegant **Salle des Illustres** (Hall of the Illustrious) is a large painting of a fortress under siege, portraying the women of Toulouse slaying Simon de Montfort, leader of the Albigensian crusade against the Cathars, during the siege of Toulouse in 1218. ✉ *Pl. du Capitole* ☎ *05–61–22–34–12* ⛪ *Free* ⏲ *Weekdays 8:30–7, weekends 10–7.*

Église des Jacobins. An extraordinary structure built in the 1230s for the Dominicans (renamed Jacobins in 1216 for their Parisian base in rue St-Jacques), the church is dominated by a single row of seven columns running the length of the nave. The easternmost column (on the far right) is one of the finest examples of palm-tree vaulting ever erected, the much-celebrated *Palmier des Jacobins,* a major masterpiece of

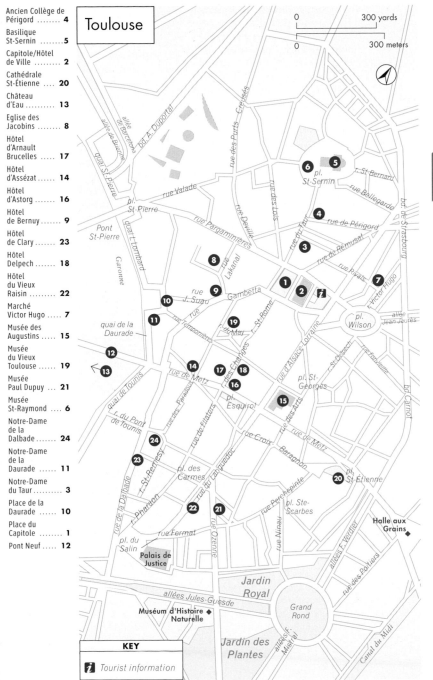

14

Toulouse

KEY

i *Tourist information*

Gothic art. Fanning out overhead, its 22 ribs support the entire apse. The original refectory site is used for temporary art exhibitions. The cloister is one of the city's aesthetic and acoustical gems, and in summer hosts piano and early music concerts. ✉ *Rue Lakanal s/n* ☎ *05–61–22–21–92* 🔗 *Church free; cloister €3* ⊙ *Daily 9–7.*

Hôtel d'Assézat. Built in 1555 by Toulouse's top Renaissance architect, Nicolas Bachelier, this mansion, considered the city's most elegant, has arcades and ornately carved doorways. It's now home to the **Fondation Bemberg,** an exceptional collection of paintings ranging from Tiepolo to Toulouse-Lautrec, Monet, and Bonnard. ✉ *Pl. Assézat* ☎ *05–61–12–06–89* 🔗 *€6* ⊙ *Tues.–Sun. 10–12:30 and 1:30–6, Thurs. 10–12:30 and 1:30–9.*

TOURING TOULOUSE

Toulouse Tourist Office. The Toulouse Tourist Office has information about local walking and cycling tours. If you're particularly interested in the latter, it's worth noting that Toulouse has been working to make streets more bicycle friendly, and you can now rent bikes at conveniently placed Vélô Toulouse stations. Stop at La Maison du Vélo de Toulouse by the train station to learn more about *cyclotourisme* in and around the city. ✉ *Donjon du Capitole* ☎ *08-92-18-01-80* 🌐 *www.toulouse-tourisme.com.*

Hôtel de Bernuy. Now part of a school, this mansion, around the corner from the Église des Jacobins, was built for Jean de Bernuy in the 16th century, the period when Toulouse was at its most prosperous. De Bernuy made his fortune exporting woad, the dark-blue dye that brought unprecedented wealth to the city; his success is reflected in the use of stone (a costly material in this region of brick) and by the octagonal stair tower. You may wander freely around the courtyard or take a tour organized by the tourist office. ✉ *Rue Gambetta* ⊙ *Weekdays 8–6:30.*

Musée des Augustins (*Augustinian Museum*). Occupying a former Augustinian convent, this museum displays one of Europe's richest collections of Romanesque sculpture and religious paintings in the sacristy, chapter house, and cloisters. Built in Mediterranean-Gothic style and created around the same time as the Louvre, the medieval architectural complex is vast, and, like the Louvre, holds many treasures from Napoléon's conquests. ✉ *21 rue de Metz* ☎ *05–61–22–21–82* 🔗 *Museum €3* ⊙ *Thurs.–Tues. 10–6, Wed. 10–9* ⊙ *Closed Christmas wk.*

Musée du Vieux Toulouse (*Museum of Old Toulouse*). This museum is worthwhile for the building itself as much as for its collection of Toulouse memorabilia, paintings, sculptures, and documents. Be sure to note the ground-floor fireplace and wooden ceiling. ✉ *7 rue du May* ☎ *05–62–27–11–50* 🔗 *€2.50* ⊙ *May–Oct., Mon.–Sat. 2–6.*

Musée St-Raymond. The city's archaeological museum, next to the Basilica of St-Sernin, has an extensive collection of imperial Roman busts, as well as ancient coins, vases, and jewelry. It's second only to the Louvre in the richness of its sculptures and Gallo-Roman vestiges. ✉ *Pl. St-Sernin* ☎ *05–61–22–31–44* 🔗 *€3* ⊙ *Oct.–May, daily 10–6; June–Sept., daily 10–7.*

Place de la Daurade. On the Garonne, this is one of Toulouse's nicest squares. A stop at the Café des Artistes is almost obligatory. The corner of the quay offers a romantic view of the Garonne, the Hôtel Dieu across the river, and the Pont Neuf.

Place du Capitole. Lined with shops and cafés, this vast, open square in the city center is a good spot to get your bearings, soak up some sun, or peruse the outdoor markets held here weekly. A parking garage is conveniently underneath.

WORTH NOTING

Ancien Collège de Périgord (*Old Périgord College*). The wooden gallery-like structure on the street side of the courtyard is the oldest remnant of a 14th-century residential college. ⊠ *56–58 rue du Taur.*

Château d'Eau. This 19th-century water tower at the far end of the Pont Neuf, once used to store water and build water pressure, is now used for photography exhibits. It was built in 1822, the same year Nicéphore Nièpce created the first permanent photographic images. ⊠ *1 pl. Laganne* ☎ *05–61–77–09–40* ⊠ *€2.50* ⊘ *Tues.–Sun. 1–7.*

Hôtel d'Arnault Brucelles. One of the tallest and best of Toulouse's 49 towers can be found at this 16th-century mansion. ⊠ *19 rue des Changes.*

Hôtel d'Astorg et St-Germain. This 16th-century mansion is notable for its lovely Romanesque wooden stairways and galleries and for its top-floor *mirande*, a wooden balcony. ⊠ *16 rue des Changes.*

Hôtel Delpech. Look for the 17th-century biblical inscriptions carved in Latin in the stone under the windows. ⊠ *20 rue des Changes.*

Marché Victor Hugo (*Victor Hugo Market*). This hangarlike indoor market is always a refreshing stop. Consider eating lunch at one of the seven upstairs restaurants. **Chez Attila**, just to the left at the top of the stairs, is among the best. ⊠ *Pl. Victor Hugo* ☎ *05–61–22–76–92* ⊕ *www.marchevictorhugo.fr* ⊘ *Tues.–Sun. sunrise–1.*

Notre-Dame de la Daurade. Overlooking the Garonne is this 18th-century church. The name *Daurade* comes from *doré* (gilt), referring to the golden reflection given off by mosaics decorating the 5th-century temple to the Virgin Mary that once stood on this site. ⊠ *1 pl. de la Daurade* ☎ *05–61–21–38–32* ⊘ *Daily 8:30–7.*

Notre-Dame du Taur. Built on the spot where St. Saturnin (or Sernin), the martyred bishop of Toulouse, was dragged to his death in AD 250 by a rampaging bull, this church is famous for its *cloche-mur*, or wall tower. The wall looks like an extension of the facade and has inspired many similar versions throughout the region. ⊠ *Rue du Taur* ☎ *05–61–21–80–45* ⊘ *Mon.–Sat. 2–7, Sun. 9–1; July and Aug. closed Sun.*

Pont Neuf (*New Bridge*). Despite its name, the graceful span of the Pont Neuf opened to traffic in 1632. The remains of the old bridge—one arch and the lighter-color outline on the brick wall of the **Hôtel-Dieu** (hospital)—are visible across the river. The 16th-century hospital was used for pilgrims on their way to Santiago de Compostela. Just over the bridge, on a clear day in winter, the snowcapped peaks of the Pyrénées are often visible in the distance, said to be a sign of imminent rain.

14

SOUTH OF RUE DE METZ

South of rue de Metz you'll discover the Cathédral St-Étienne, the antiques district along rue Perchepinte, and town houses and palaces on rue Ninau, rue Ozenne, and rue de la Dalbade—all among the top sights in Toulouse.

EXPLORING

Cathédrale St-Étienne. The cathedral was erected in stages between the 13th and the 17th century, though the nave and choir languished unfinished because of a lack of funds. A fine collection of 16th- and 17th-century tapestries traces the life of St. Stephen. In front of the cathedral is the city's oldest fountain, dating from the 16th century. ✉ *Pl. St-Étienne* ☎ *05–61–52–03–82* 🕒 *Mon.–Sat. 8–7, Sun. 9–7.*

Hôtel de Clary. This mansion—one of the finest on the street—is known as the Hôtel de Pierre because of its unusually solid *pierre* (stone) construction, which was considered a sign of great wealth at the time. The ornately sculpted facade was designed by Nicolas Bachelier in the 16th century. ✉ *25 rue de la Dalbade.*

Hôtel du Vieux Raisin. Officially the Hôtel Beringuier Maynier, this building was dubbed the Vieux Raisin (Old Grape) after the early name of the street and even earlier inn. Built in the 15th and 16th centuries, the mansion has an octagonal tower, male and female figures on the facade, and allegorical sculptures of the three stages of life—infancy, maturity, and old age—over the windows to the left. ✉ *36 rue de Languedoc.*

Musée Paul Dupuy. This museum, dedicated to medieval applied arts, is housed in the Hôtel Pierre Besson, a 17th-century mansion. ✉ *13 rue de la Pleau* ☎ *05–61–14–65–50* 🎫 *€3* 🕒 *Oct.–May, Wed.–Mon. 10–5; June–Sept., Wed.–Mon. 10–6.*

Notre-Dame de la Dalbade. Originally Sancta Maria de Ecclesia Alba, in Langue d'Oc (Ste-Marie de l'Église Blanche, in French, or St. Mary of the White Church—*alba* meaning "white"), the name of the church evolved into "de Albata" and later "Dalbade." Ironically, one of its outstanding features today is the colorful 19th-century ceramic tympanum over the Renaissance door. ✉ *Pl. de la Dalbade* ☎ *05–61–52–68–90.*

WHERE TO EAT

$$ BISTRO 🍴 **Bistrot de l'Étoile.** Don't let the dismal exterior put you off, as it conceals a convivial and delightfully retro 1960s pub. With a great choice of dishes on the blackboard menu (including excellent grilled meats cooked on the fire in the center of the restaurant), fresh ingredients, smiling staff, and fast service, this restaurant is well worth traipsing around the backstreets. The homemade desserts are great, too, especially the tiramisu. [$] *Average main: €23* ✉ *6 rue de l'Étoile* ☎ *05–61–63–13–43* 🌐 *www.bistrotdeletoile.fr* ✍ *Reservations essential* 🕒 *Closed weekends, 3 wks in Aug., and Dec. 24–Jan. 1.*

$$ BRASSERIE 🍴 **Brasserie Flo "Les Beaux Arts.".** Overlooking the Pont Neuf, this elegant brasserie is idyllic at sunset, as artists Ingres and Matisse—who were regulars—knew all too well; watch the colors change over the Garonne from a quayside window or a sidewalk table while enjoying a seafood

Seat of the municipal government, the place du Capitole is an elegant square often transformed into an open market.

platter that includes six varieties of oysters. The house white wine, a local St-Lannes from the nearby Gers region, is fresh and fruity yet dry, and the service is impeccable. It's open late, too (a rarity in France), which is perfect if you want to eat out after a show or a movie. $ *Average main: €24* ✉ *1 quai de la Daurade* ☎ *05–61–21–12–12* ⊕ *www. brasserielesbeauxarts.com.*

$$$ ✕ **Chez Emile.** With a great location and lovely summer terrace, this
FRENCH is the place to savor such regional specialties as cassoulet—the locals love it, which speaks volumes here in the heart of cassoulet country. $ *Average main: €28* ✉ *13 pl. St-Georges* ☎ *05–61–21–05–56* ⊕ *www. restaurant-emile.com* ⊙ *Closed Sun. and Mon. in winter and 2 wks around Christmas. No lunch Mon. in summer.*

$$$$ ✕ **Jardins de l'Opéra.** Stéphane Tournié's elegant restaurant next to the
FRENCH Grand Hôtel de l'Opéra is a perennial favorite, with intimate rooms and a covered terrace around a little pond making for undeniable charm, though some will find the grand flourishes—glass ceilings and mammoth chandeliers—a little too, well, operatic, and might prefer the adjacent brasserie, Grand Café de l'Opéra. The food is gastronomical local fare, with seductive nouvelle or Gascon touches that incorporate three different *recettes* (dishes) on each plate, albeit three different fish, or three different fowl. $ *Average main: €33* ✉ *1 pl. du Capitole* ☎ *05– 61–23–07–76* ⊕ *www.lesjardinsdelopera.com* ⊜ *Reservations essential* ⊙ *Closed Sun. and Mon. and 1 wk in Jan.*

$$ ✕ **Le Bon Vivre.** This bustling bistro, brightened with Jean Vier–designed
FRENCH striped Basque tablecloths, fills up at lunch and dinner every day. Quick, unpretentious, and always good, the house specialties include such dishes as cod, cassoulet, and wild boar in season (September–March).

■TIP→ If you forgot to book, ask if you can wait for a table with a drink at the bistro's recently added salon next door. $ *Average main: €20* ⊠ *15 bis pl. Wilson* ☎ *05–61–23–07–17* ⊕ *www.lebonvivre.com.*

$$ ✕ **L'Empereur de Huê.** This sleek-lined contemporary space, open for dinner only, produces traditional Vietnamese cuisine at attractive prices. Soup dumplings and pea shoots are always excellent here, as are the duck-based dishes. Annual closure varies year to year, so it's best to call first in the off-season. $ *Average main: €22* ⊠ *17 rue Couteliers* ☎ *05–61–53–55–72* ⊕ *www.empereurdehue.com* ☾ *Closed Tues. No lunch.*

VIETNAMESE

$ ✕ **Les curieux gâteaux de Tata Bidule.** If you need a pick-me-up, head to this retro, gourmet, cupcake-and-coffee shop with Wi-Fi and a choice of inside or street-side tables. The homage to pastel pastries is run by three crafty women who claim their traveling great-aunt discovered the Anglo-Saxon cupcake after her circus act won her an invitation to tea with Queen Elizabeth. Try the violette, black tea, and royal icing cupcake or the chocolate and hot red pepper with your espresso. Hot chocolate and fresh-squeezed seasonal juices are also available. Though old-school in style, this shop is *au courant* in that it uses no additives or preservatives and has gluten-free options. Best news: it's open on Sunday. $ *Average main: €5* ⊠ *14 rue Tempónières* ⊕ *www.tatabidule.com.*

BAKERY

$$$$ ✕ **Michel Sarran.** The post-nouvelle haven for what is arguably Toulouse's finest dining departs radically from traditional stick-to-your-ribs southwest-France cuisine in favor of Mediterranean formulas suited to the rhythms and reasons of modern living. The air of the place is contemporary sophistication expertly blended with warmth; and delicacies like foie gras soup with Belon oysters or wild salmon in green curry sauce exemplify Michel Sarran's light but flavorful cuisine. Just don't count on a Saturday night *fête* here, as the restaurant is closed weekends—the obvious mark of a sought-after chef who is free to choose his own hours. $ *Average main: €50* ⊠ *21 bd. A. Duportal* ☎ *05–61–12–32–33* ⊕ *www.michel-sarran.com* ⚖ *Reservations essential* ☾ *Closed weekends and Aug. No lunch Wed.*

MODERN FRENCH
Fodor's Choice
★

WHERE TO STAY

For expanded hotel reviews, visit Fodors.com.

$$$$ 🛏 **Grand Hôtel de l'Opéra.** Little wonder the likes of Deneuve, Pavarotti, and Aznavour favored this downtown doyen, for its keynote grandeur is obvious the moment you step into the lobby, complete with soaring columns, Second Empire bergères, and sofas of blue tasseled velvet. **Pros:** ideally situated on main square; within five minutes of the train station. **Cons:** splendor and a certain reserved professionalism rank higher than intimacy $ *Rooms from: €230* ⊠ *1 pl. du Capitole* ☎ *05–61–21–82–66* ⊕ *www.grand-hotel-opera.com* ⇝ *44 rooms, 6 suites.*

HOTEL

$ 🛏 **Grand Hôtel d'Orléans.** While in a slightly sketchy neighborhood, this picturesque former stagecoach relay station—built in 1867—still retains a certain 19th-century charm and is home to a good restaurant. **Pros:** fine restaurant; close to train and bus stations. **Cons:** surrounding neighborhood is a little dicey. $ *Rooms from: €75* ⊠ *72 rue*

HOTEL

EATING WELL

Dining in France's Southwest is a rougher, heartier, and more rustic version of classic Mediterranean cooking—the peppers are sliced thick, the garlic and olive oil used with a heavier hand, the herbs crushed and served au naturel.

Expect *cuisine de marché* (market-based cooking), savory seasonal dishes based on the culinary trinity of the south—garlic, onion, and tomato—straight from the village market. Languedoc is known for powerful and strongly seasoned cooking.

Garlic and goose fat are generously used in traditional recipes. Be sure to try some of the renowned foie gras (goose or duck liver) and *confit de canard* (preserved duck). The most

famous regional dish is cassoulet, a succulent white-bean stew with *confit d'oie* (preserved goose), duck, lamb, or a mixture of all three.

Keep your eyes open for festive *cargolades*—Catalan for huge communal barbecues starting off with thousands of buttery-garlic snails roasted on open grills and eaten with your fingers, followed by cured bacon and lamb cutlets and vats (and vats) of local wine. In the Roussillon and along the Mediterranean coast from Collioure up through Perpignan to Narbonne, the prevalent Catalan cuisine features olive-oil-based cooking and sauces such as the classic *aioli* (crushed and emulsified garlic and olive oil). When you're on the coast, it's fish, of course, often cooked over a wood fire.

14

Bayard, near Matabiau train station ☎ *05–61–62–98–47* ⊕ *www. grand-hotel-orleans.fr* ↰ *56 rooms.*

$ · **Hôtel Albert I.** The building may seem undistinguished and the recep-
HOTEL tion hall is no Versailles, but the guest rooms are cheerful and spacious (especially the older ones with giant fireplaces) and this is a good value considering the location. **Pros:** champagne location, Orangina budget. **Cons:** parking lot is difficult to find. $ *Rooms from: €65* ✉ *8 rue Rivals* ☎ *05–61–21–17–91* ⊕ *www.hotel-albert1.com* ↰ *47 rooms.*

$$$ · **Hôtel Garonne.** In the thick of the most Toulousain part of town, next
HOTEL to the Pont Neuf and the former fish market (although somewhat far
Fodor'sChoice from the city center), this is a small but hyper-stylish spot with new-
★ world services—like gourmet take-out ordered for you and delivered to your room on request. **Pros:** hip design wherein the modern style actually works really well; Bobo neighborhood with eclectic shops and restaurants nearby. **Cons:** a hike to the city center; the lobby and rooms feel a bit small. $ *Rooms from: €180* ✉ *22 descente de la Halle aux Poissons* ☎ *05–34–31–94–80* ⊕ *www.hotelgaronne.net* ↰ *11 rooms, 3 suites.*

$ · **Hôtel Royal Wilson.** With a quiet city-center location across from the
HOTEL Théâtre National, this two-star hotel—one of the best deals in Tou-
louse—attracts theater professionals, business travelers, and garden-variety tourists. **Pros:** super location central to all; breakfast service in room for no extra charge. **Cons:** some bathrooms don't have wall-mounted shower heads; though unobtrusive, some color schemes might not appeal (think pink). $ *Rooms from: €59* ✉ *6 rue Labéda* ⊕ *www. hotelroyalwilson-toulouse.com* ↰ *27 rooms.*

NIGHTLIFE AND THE ARTS

For a schedule of events, contact the city tourist office. If you want to stay up late—as many do in Toulouse—grab a copy of the free chronicle *Clutch* found in any hotel lobby. Toulouse is jammed with small, independent concert halls and theaters, most of them covered in this minimag. As for cultural highlights, so many opera singers perform at the **Théâtre du Capitole** and the **Halle aux Grains** that the city is known as the *capitale du bel canto*. The opera season lasts from October until late May, with occasional summer presentations as well. A wide variety of dance companies perform in Toulouse: the **Ballet du Capitole** stages classical ballets; **Ballet-Théâtre Joseph Russillo** and **Compagnie Jean-Marc Matos** put on modern-dance performances. The **Centre National Chorégraphique de Toulouse**, in the St-Cyprien quarter, welcomes international companies each year.

Bar Basque. Bar Basque is one of the many good watering holes around place St-Pierre. ⊠ *7 pl. St-Pierre* ☎ *05–61–21–55–64.*

Chez Ton Ton. Chez Ton Ton, with a somewhat raucous crowd, is a very popular place St-Pierre dive. ⊠ *14 pl. St-Pierre* ☎ *05–61–21–89–54.*

Halle Aux Grains. The most exciting music venue in Toulouse is the auditorium-in-the-round Halle Aux Grains. ⊠ *Pl. Dupuy* ☎ *05–61–63–13–13* ⊕ *www.onct.mairie-toulouse.fr.*

La Bonita. Brazilian guitarists perform at La Bonita, a festive *restaurant musical.* ⊠ *112 Grand-rue St-Michel* ☎ *05–62–26–36–45* ⊕ *www.labonita.fr.*

Le Bistro Étienne. Le Bistro Étienne, near the Cathedral of St-Étienne, is a hot spot for the third-Thursday-in-November Beaujolais Nouveau blowout. ⊠ *5 rue Riguepels* ☎ *09–61–28–36–41.*

Le Mandala. Be sure to stop by Le Mandala for a bit of the bubbly and some of the best jazz in town. ⊠ *23 rue des Aminodiers* ☎ *05–61–21–10–05* ⊕ *www.lemandala.com.*

Le Purple. Le Purple is a hot multispace disco. ⊠ *2 rue Castellane* ☎ *09–67–16–04–67* ⊕ *www.purepurple.fr.*

Les Terrasses de Saint-Rome. If you're looking for a pretty terrace for lunch or a late dinner (until 10:30), head to Les Terrasses de Saint-Rome. ⊠ *39 rue St-Rome* ☎ *05–62–27–06–06* ⊕ *www.lesterrassesdesaintrome.com.*

L'Opera Bouffe. L'Opera Bouffe is always a lively spot for music, dance, and food. ⊠ *5 rue Labeda* ☎ *05–62–30–89–49.*

Melting Pot. Melting Pot lives up to its title, with young people from around the world crowding the bar and dance floor. ⊠ *26 bd. de Strasbourg* ☎ *05–61–62–82–98.*

Père Louis. Begin your night on the town at Père Louis, an old-fashioned winery (and restaurant), with barrels used as tables. ⊠ *45 rue des Tourneurs* ☎ *05–61–21–33–45.*

SHOPPING

Toulouse is a chic design center for clothing and artifacts of all kinds. **Rue St-Rome, rue Croix Baragnon, rue des Changes,** and **rue d'Alsace-Lorraine** are all good shopping streets.

ALBI AND THE GERS

Along the banks of the Tarn to the northeast of Toulouse, Albi rivals Toulouse in rose colors. West from Albi, along the river, the land opens up to the rural Gers *département*, home of the heady brandy, Armagnac, and heart of the former dukedom of Gascony. Studded with châteaux— from simple medieval fortresses to ambitious classical residences—and with tiny, isolated village jewels like Cordes-sur-Ciel, the Gers is an easy place to fall in love with, or in.

14

ALBI

75 km (47 miles) northeast of Toulouse.

Toulouse-Lautrec's native Albi is a busy, beautifully preserved provincial market town. In its heyday Albi was a major center for the Cathars, members of a dualistic and ascetic religious movement critical of the hierarchical and worldly ways of the Catholic Church.

GETTING HERE

About 18 trains daily (1 hr, €15) run between Toulouse and Albi's main station on place Stalingrad (in a somewhat isolated part of town). In summer months, you can catch infrequent buses to adjoining towns, including Cordes-sur-Ciel (1 hr) from the bus station on place Jean Jaurès.

Visitor Information Albi Tourist Office ✉ *Pl. Ste-Cecile* ☏ *05–63–36–36–00* ⊕ *www.albi-tourisme.com.*

EXPLORING

Fodor's Choice **Cathédrale Ste-Cécile.** One of the most unusual and dazzling churches in
★ France, the huge Cathédrale Ste-Cécile, with its intimidating cliff-like walls, resembles a cross between a castle and an ocean liner. It was constructed as a symbol of the Church's return to power after the 13th-century crusade that wiped out the Cathars. The interior is an astonishingly ornate contrast to the massive austerity of the outer walls. Maestro Donnelli and a team of 16th-century Italian artists (most of the Emilian school) covered every possible surface with religious scenes and brightly colored patterns—it remains the largest group of Italian Renaissance paintings in

MY WAY OR THE HIGHWAY

Beneath Ste-Cécile's organ is an impressive 15th-century mural depicting punishments for the seven deadly sins in the Last Judgment. The scenes of torture and hellfire give an indication of how the Vatican kept its Christian subjects in line during the crusade against the Cathars and subsequent Inquisition trials.

a French church. On the west wall you can find one of the most splendid organs in the world, built in 1734 and outfitted with 3,500 pipes, which loom over a celebrated fresco of the Last Judgment. ⊠ *Pl. Ste-Cécile* ☎ *05–63–43–23–43* ⊙ *June–Sept., daily 9–6:30; Oct.–May, daily 9–noon and 2–6.*

Cloître St-Salvi. From the central square and parking area in front of the Palais de la Berbie, walk to the 11th- to 15th-century college and Cloître de St-Salvy. ⊠ *Rue Maries* ⊙ *Daily 7–8.*

Maison du Vieil Albi (*Old Albi House*). Next, take a look at Albi's finest restored traditional house, the Maison du Vieil Albi. ⊠ *Corner of rue de la Croix-Blanche and Puech-Bérenguer.*

Maison Natale de Toulouse-Lautrec. If you're a real fan of Toulouse-Lautrec, you might view his birthplace, the Maison Natale de Toulouse-Lautrec, although there are no visits to the house, the Hôtel du Bosc, which remains a private residence. ⊠ *14 rue Henri de Toulouse-Lautrec.*

Fodor's Choice
★

Musée Toulouse-Lautrec. In a garden designed by the famed André Le Nôtre, creator of the "green geometries" at Versailles, the landmark **Palais de la Berbie** (Berbie Palace), between the cathedral and the Pont Vieux (Old Bridge), is the setting for this exceptional museum. Built in 1265 as a residence for Albi's archbishops, the fortresslike structure was transformed in 1922 into a museum to honor Albi's most famous son, Belle Époque painter Henri de Toulouse-Lautrec (1864–1901). Toulouse-Lautrec left Albi for Paris in 1882 and soon became famous for his colorful, tumultuous evocations of the lifestyle of bohemian glamour found in and around Montmartre. Son of a wealthy and aristocratic family (Lautrec is a village not far from Toulouse), the young Henri suffered from a genetic bone deficiency and broke both legs as a child, which stunted his growth. But it was the artist's fascination with the decadent side of life that led him to an early grave at the age of 37. A 10-year renovation of the museum was completed in 2004, with vast new infrastructure and loan exhibition rooms excavated beneath the building. Upstairs, the collection of artworks—more than a thousand, representing the world's largest Toulouse-Lautrec corpus—has been deftly organized into theme rooms, including galleries devoted to some of his greatest portraits and scenes from Paris's *maisons closées* (brothels), with paintings stylishly hung amid the palace's brick ogival arches. There are other masterworks here, including paintings by Georges de la Tour and Francesco Guardi. ⊠ *Palais de la Berbie, off pl. Ste-Cécile* ☎ *05–63–49–48–70* ⊕ *www.musee-toulouse-lautrec.com* ⊠ *€8, gardens free* ⊙ *June 21–Sept. 30, daily 9–6; Oct.–Dec, Wed.–Mon. 10–noon and 2–5:30; Jan., Wed.–Mon. 10–noon and 2–5; Feb. and Mar., Wed.–Mon. 10–noon and 2–5:30; Apr. and May, daily 10–noon and 2–6; June 1–20, daily 9–noon and 2–6.*

Place du Vigan. Rue de l'Hôtel de Ville, two streets west of the Maison Natale, leads past the Mairie (City Hall), with its hanging globes of flowers, to Albi's main square, place du Vigan. Take a break in one of the two main cafés, Le Pontie or Le Vigan.

Albi honors native son Toulouse-Lautrec with a museum crammed with his masterpieces, including *Salon in the Rue des Moulins.*

WHERE TO EAT AND STAY

For expanded hotel reviews, visit Fodors.com.

$ FRENCH 🍴 **Le Jardin des Quatre Saisons.** A good-value menu and superb fish dishes are the reasons for this restaurant's excellent reputation. Chef-owner Georges Bermond's house specialties—which change seasonally—include *pot au feu* (stew) of the sea and *suprême de sandre* (a freshwater fish cooked in wine). Though the traditional setting could use some spunk, the warm service and *correcte* (fair) bill make up for any old-fashioned ambience. [$] *Average main: €18* ✉ *5 rue de la Pompe* ☎ *05–63–60–77–76* 🌐 *www.lejardindesquatresaisons.fr* ⏲ *Closed Mon. No dinner Sun.*

$$ HOTEL 🏨 **Hostellerie St-Antoine.** Founded in 1734, this eminently comfortable hotel in the center of town is one of the oldest in France and has been run by the same family for five generations (note the Toulouse-Lautrec sketches given to the owner's great-grandfather, a friend of the painter). **Pros:** slightly off the beaten path in a quiet area; friendly staff. **Cons:** breakfast is very expensive; overall, doesn't quite live up to its four-star rating. [$] *Rooms from: €147* ✉ *17 rue St-Antoine* ☎ *05–63–54–04–04* 🌐 *www.hotel-saint-antoine-albi.com* 🛏 *41 rooms, 3 suites* ⏲ *Closed 2 wks in Dec.*

$ HOTEL 🏨 **Hôtel Chiffre.** A former stagecoach inn, this centrally located town house has fairly lackluster rooms and a hearty restaurant all overlooking a cozy garden. **Pros:** restaurant is good and a great value. **Cons:** foyer and rooms are sparsely decorated; some beds need to be replaced. [$] *Rooms from: €76* ✉ *50 rue Séré-de-Rivières* ☎ *05–63–48–58–48* 🌐 *www.hotelchiffre.com* 🛏 *38 rooms* ⏲ *Closed mid-Dec.–mid-Jan.*

SHOPPING

Around **place Ste-Cécile** are numerous clothing, book, music, and antiques shops.

Alby Foie Gras. The finest foie gras in town is found at Alby Foie Gras. ⊠ *29 rue Mariès* ☎ *05–63–38–21–33.*

Flea and antiques market. A Saturday-morning flea and antiques market is held in the Halle du Castelviel. ⊠ *Pl. du Castelviel.*

L'Artisan Chocolatier. L'Artisan Chocolatier is deservedly famous. ⊠ *4 rue Dr-Camboulives, on pl. du Vigan* ☎ *05–63–54–07–12.*

Produce markets. Albi has many produce markets: one takes place Tuesday to Sunday in the market halls near the cathedral; another is held on Saturday morning on place Ste-Julien.

CORDES-SUR-CIEL

25 km (15 miles) northwest of Albi, 80 km (50 miles) northeast of Toulouse.

Fodor'sChoice A must-stop for many travelers, the picture-book hilltop village of
★ Cordes-sur-Ciel, built in 1222 by Count Raymond VII of Toulouse, is one of the most impressively preserved bastides in France.

GETTING HERE

In July and August, a bus runs the 25 km (16 miles) from Albi's bus station on place Jean Jaurès to the bottom of Cordes twice daily. At other times of the year, you'll have to take the train to Cordes-Vindrac, where it's frequently served from Toulouse (1¼ hrs) and Albi (1 hr). There's also a year-round bus from Albi to Cordes-Vindrac; from Cordes-Vindrac, it's 3 km (2 miles) to Cordes by bike, taxi, or foot. Note that traffic is banned in the upper town in summer and parking nearby is virtually impossible.

EXPLORING

When mists steal up from the Cérou Valley and enshroud the hillside, Cordes-sur-Ciel appears to hover in midair, hence the name—sur-ciel means "in the sky/heaven." Named in honor of Andalusian Cordoba, it was built as a redoubt after the Occitan wars waged against the region's Cathars; its conical hill is riddled with caves once used as granaries during times of siege. When peace arrived in the 15th century, the town thrived as a center for leather and fabric makers and many rich residents built pink-sandstone Gothic-style houses, a sizable number of which still line the main street, Grande-rue Haute (also called rue Droite). Today, many are occupied by painters, sculptors, weavers, leatherworkers, and even creators of illuminated manuscripts, whose ateliers and stores lure the summer crowds. The annual blowout is the Fêtes Médiévales du Grand Fauconnier (⊕ *www.grandfauconnier.com*); named after the town's most historic abode, it's a three-day festival held around mid-July, replete with an artisanal fair and costumed Bal Médiéval. The village's 14th-century St-Michel church and the venerable covered market, supported by 24 octagonal stone pillars, are also noteworthy, as is the nearby well, which is more than 300 feet deep. The small Musée Charles-Portail has relics from the town's medieval

CLOSE UP

Crusading Cathars

Scorched by the southern heat, the dusty ruins high atop cliffs in southern Languedoc were once the refuges of the Cathars, the notoriously ascetic religious group persecuted out of existence by the Catholic Church in the 12th and 13th centuries. The Cathars inhabited an area ranging from present-day Germany all the way to the Atlantic Ocean. Adherents to this dualistic doctrine of material abnegation and spiritual revelation abstained from fleshly pleasures in all forms, forgoing procreation and the consumption of animal products. In some cases, they even committed suicide by starvation; diminishing the amount of flesh in the world was the ultimate way to foil the forces of evil. However, not thrilled by a religion that did not "go forth and multiply" (and that saw no need to pay taxes to the Church), Pope Innocent III launched the Albigensian Crusade (Albi was one of the major Cathar strongholds), and Pope Gregory IX rounded up the stragglers during a period of inquisition starting in 1233.

All these forces had been given scandalously free rein by the French court, which allowed dukes and counts from northern France to build *bastides* (fortified medieval towns built along a strict grid plan) through the area to entrap the peasantry.

The counts were more than happy to oblige the pope with a little hounding, an inquisition or two, and some burnings at the stake. Entire towns were judged to be guilty of heresy and inhabitants by the dozens were thrown to their deaths from high town walls. The persecuted "pure" soon took refuge in the Pyrénées Mountains, where they survived for 100 years. Now all that remains of this unhappy sect are their former hideouts, with tour groups visiting the vacant stone staircases and roofless chapels of haunted places like Peyrepertuse and Quéribus. For more information, log on to ⊕ *www.cathar. info* or go hiking with medievalist Ingrid Sparbier (⊕ *www.guide-sudfrance.com*).

14

past; closer to the Haut de la Cité is the two-room Musée de la Sucre (Sugar), which showcases the works of noted chef Yves Thuriès.

WHERE TO STAY

For expanded hotel reviews, visit Fodors.com.

$ ⊞ **L'Hostellerie du Vieux Cordes.** One of famed chocolatier Yves Thuriès's
HOTEL   lovely Cordes hotels, this 13th-century house, built around a spectacular courtyard dotted with tiny tables and shaded by a magnificent 300-year-old wisteria, has stylishly decorated guest rooms and a fine on-site eatery. **Pros:** some rooms have views of the valley (book well in advance). **Cons:** cramped Room 4 should be avoided; uphill hike to the hotel from parking area. $ *Rooms from: €68* ⊠ *Rue St-Michel* ☎ *05–63–53–79–20* ⊕ *www.vieuxcordes.fr* ⇆ *19 rooms* ☉ *Closed Jan.–mid-Feb.*

LANGUEDOC-ROUSSILLON

One of the most diverse backdrops in France, Languedoc-Roussillon skirts the Mediterranean coast southward toward Spain where the Pyrénées plunge dramatically into the sea. The southern half of the region, Roussillon was long dominated by Spanish Catalonia's House of Aragon—which explains why the area is also known as French Catalonia. Historically rooted in agricultural pursuits, Roussillon's varied landscape allows for citrus and cherry trees, while the snowcapped Pic du Canigó towers over palm trees in the valley. Olive groves and vineyards thrive on arid hillsides inland and earthy cheeses come from herds in the bordering high mountains. Beaches stretch down the coast to Cerbère at the Spanish border. Immortalized by Matisse and Picasso, this strip is known as the Côte Vermeille and attracts droves of European sun worshippers (plus aspiring painters) to its craggy shoreline. Heading northward, Languedoc begins around the ancient Roman capitol of Narbonne and extends to the region's hub, the elegant city of Montpellier. The Canal du Midi flows through the vineyard-laden region to Le Littoral Languedocien (the Languedoc Coast), famous for fresh Bouzigues oysters and resident flamingos. Life in Languedoc-Roussillon is distinctly relaxed and casual, so you'll probably be taking afternoon siestas before you know it.

CARCASSONNE

88 km (55 miles) southeast of Toulouse, 105 km (65 miles) south of Albi.

Fodor's Choice Poised atop a hill overlooking lush green countryside and the Aude
★ River, Carcassonne is a spectacular medieval town that looks lifted from the pages of a storybook—literally, perhaps, as its circle of towers and battlements (comprising the longest city walls in Europe) is said to be the setting for Charles Perrault's classic tale *Puss in Boots*. With its turrets and castellated walls, it appeals to children and those with a penchant for the Middle Ages.

GETTING HERE

The shuttle to Salvaza Airport from the train station (beside the Canal du Midi on avenue du Maréchal Joffre) also links you up with La Cité and place Gambetta. Ryanair (⊕ *www.ryanair.com*) has daily flights to and from Stansted and Dublin. Due to the high volume of visitors, many trains arrive at Carcassone's station—16 trains from Narbonne and 15 from Toulouse alone. Cars Teissier (☎ *04–68–25–85–45*) will bus you to all the same places as the trains, and at times a lot faster, too.

Visitor Information Carcassonne Tourist Office ⊠ *28 rue de Verdun* ☎ *04–68–10–24–30* ⊕ *www.carcassonne-tourisme.com*.

EXPLORING

The town is divided by the river into two parts—La Cité, the fortified upper town, and the lower, newer city (the *ville basse*), known simply as Carcassonne. Unless you are staying at a hotel in the upper town, you are not allowed to enter it with your vehicle; you must park

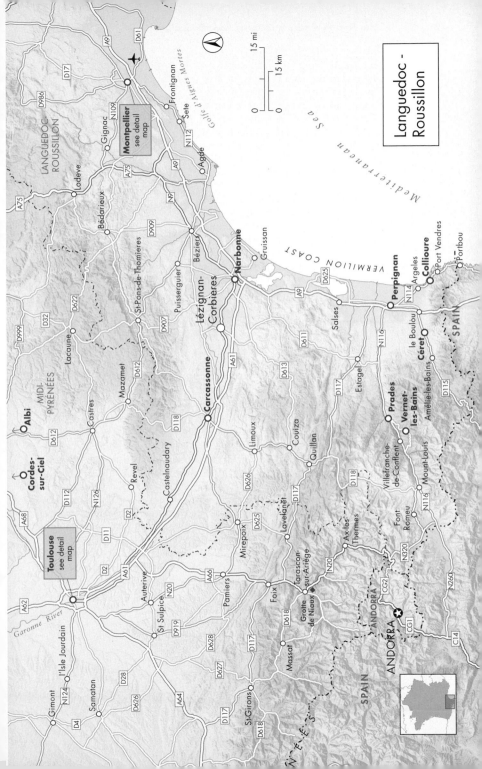

in the lot (fee by the hour) across the road from the drawbridge. Be aware that the train station is in the lower town, which means a cab ride, a ride on the *navette* shuttle bus, or a 30-minute walk up to La Cité. Plan on spending at least a couple of hours exploring the walls and peering over the battlements across sun-drenched plains toward the distant Pyrénées. Once inside the walls of the upper town, a florid carousel announces that 21st-century tourism is about to take over. The streets are lined with souvenir shops, crafts bou-

tiques, restaurants, and tiny "museums" (a Cathars Museum, a Hat Museum), all out to make a buck and rarely worth that. Staying overnight within the ancient walls lets you savor the timeless atmosphere after the daytime hordes are gone.

As for the town history, legend has it that Charlemagne once besieged the settlement in the early 9th century, only to be outdone by one Dame Carcas, a clever woman who boldly fed the last of the city's wheat to a pig in full view of the conqueror. Charlemagne, thinking this indicated endless food supplies, promptly decamped, and the exuberant townsfolk named their city after her. During the 13th century, Louis IX (Saint Louis) and his son Philip the Fair strengthened Carcassonne's fortifications—so much so that the town came to be considered inviolable by marauding armies and was duly nicknamed "the virgin of Languedoc."

A town that can never be taken in battle is often abandoned, however, and for centuries thereafter Carcassonne remained under a Sleeping Beauty spell. It was only awakened during the 19th-century craze for chivalry and the Gothic style, when, in 1835, the historic-monument inspector (and poet) Prosper Mérimée arrived. He was so appalled by the dilapidated state of the walls that he commissioned the architect, painter, and historian Viollet-le-Duc (who found his greatest fame restoring Paris's Notre-Dame) to undertake repairs. Today the 1844 renovation is considered almost as much a work of art as the medieval town itself. No matter if the town is more Viollet than authentic; it still remains one of the most romantic sights in France.

Château Comtal. The 12th-century château is the last inner bastion of Carcassonne. It has a drawbridge and a museum, the **Musée Lapidaire,** where medieval stone sculptures unearthed in the area are on display. ▦ *04–68–11–70–70* ▧ *€8* ◷ *Apr.–Sept., daily 10–6:30; Oct.–Mar., daily 9:30–5.*

Musée des Beaux-Arts (*Fine Arts Museum*). The real draw in the *ville basse* (lower town), built between the Aude and the Canal du Midi, this museum houses a nice collection of porcelain, 17th- and 18th-century Flemish paintings, and works by local artists—including some stirring battle scenes by Jacques Gamelin (1738–1803). ✉ *1 rue de Verdun, Ville Basse* ☎ *04–68–77–73–70* 🎫 *Free* 🕓 *Mid-Sept.–mid-June, Tues.–Sat. 10–noon and 2–6; mid-June–mid-Sept., daily 10–6.*

WHERE TO EAT AND STAY

For expanded hotel reviews, visit Fodors.com.

$$
MODERN FRENCH

✗ **Bloc G.** Just outside the upper city walls, this all-white urbanesque restaurant and wine bar, run by three food-and-design-savvy sisters, offers a reality check after the touristic, turreted streets of La Cité. The blackboard menu highlights experimental touches to classic dishes (like sautéed foie gras in a Thai broth) and helps attract a sophisticated, casual clientele. If returning to the crowds leaves you feeling claustrophobic, consider one of the five loft-style guest rooms in the upstairs inn—each with enough space for a full-on yoga practice. ■ **TIP➜ Also ask about sister Delphine's B&B not far away.** $ *Average main: €18* ✉ *112 rue Barbacane* ☎ *04–68–47–58–20* ⊕ *www.bloc-g.com* 🕓 *Closed Sun. and Mon. in winter.*

$$$$
MODERN FRENCH

✗ **Le Puits du Tresor.** At the foot of the famous Cathar castles of Lastours, in an old textile factory above the Orbiel River, this Michelin-starred treat comes as something of a surprise. Headed by the talented Jean-Marc Boyer, the restaurant serves inventive and artistic "néo-classique" meals inspired by the seasons and based on local ingredients. ■ **TIP➜ Strapped for cash? You can always eat at Boyer's Auberge du Diable au Thym, right next door, for a fraction of the price.** $ *Average main: €45* ✉ *Rte. des Châteaux, Lastours, 12 km (8 miles) north of Carcassonne* ☎ *04–68–77–50–24* ⊕ *www.lepuitsdutresor.fr* 🕓 *Closed Mon. and Tues.,Jan. 3–Jan. 18, and Feb. 28–Mar. 3. No dinner Sun.*

$
FRENCH

✗ **Sire de Cabaret.** Nestled beneath the château of Roquefère, an unspoiled *village fleuri* in the Cabardés region of the Montagne Noire, this regional favorite dishes up amazing steaks *à la Languedocienne.* Cooked over chestnut-wood fires, they're accompanied by mushrooms picked from nearby mountains by the genial chef Patrick Malea and served by his wife, Carmen (and a famously droll waiter, Jean-Pierre). The charcuterie *fait maison* (homemade sausages, pâtés, rillettes, and cured meats) is also recommended, but this place is worth visiting as much for its rustic charm as for its great food. In warm weather, ask for a table on the terrace amid hills cloaked with green oaks and chestnut trees. They also have a lovely B&B cottage next door, but make sure to reserve well in advance as it is nearly always booked. $ *Average main: €15* ✉ *Roquefère, 25 km (11 miles) north of Carcassonne* ☎ *04–68–26–31–89* ⊕ *www.auberge-siredecabaret.fr* 🕓 *Closed Jan.–Feb. 10 and Wed. Sept.–June. No dinner Mon. and Tues.*

$
B&B/INN

▦ **Château La Villatade.** Ensconced in this sprawling wine estate, far from Carcassonne's madding crowd, you can enjoy La Villatade's exceptional reds (notably the special "Rituel") and gentle prices while drinking in amazing views of Montagne Noire from one of the many terraces. **Pros:** real French living off the beaten tourist track; vineyard on-site. **Cons:** somewhat isolated—a car is essential. $ *Rooms from: €95* ✉ *15 km (10 miles) north of Carcassonne, Salleles* ☎ *04–68–77–57–51* ⊕ *www.villatade.com* ⇱ *2 rooms, 1 villa, 1 cottage.*

14

An entry to Fodor's "Show Us Your France" contest, this view of Carcassonne's ramparts was sent in by seeyourworld, a Fodors.com member.

$$$$ HOTEL 🏨 **Domaine d'Auriac.** Minutes away from Carcassonne, this elegant 19th-century manor house has one of the best Languedoc restaurants around and the entire building oozes grace and charm—the largest of the bedrooms have views over a magnificent park and vineyards (room prices vary according to size and view). **Pros:** excellent 18-hole golf course; personalized service; delightful interiors. **Cons:** a few miles from Carcassonne's center. [$] *Rooms from: €270* ✉ *Rte. de St-Hilaire, 4 km (2½ miles) southwest of Carcassonne* ☎ *04–68–25–72–22* 🌐 *www.domaine-d-auriac.com* 🛏 *19 rooms, 5 suites* 🕒 *Closed Jan., 1st wk of Feb., and 2nd wk of Nov.*

$$$$ HOTEL 🏨 **Hôtel de la Cité.** Enjoying the finest location within the walls of the old city, this ivy-covered former Episcopal palace provides a high level of creature comfort, which the ascetic Cathars would most definitely have deprived themselves of. **Pros:** no better location in the old city. **Cons:** must coordinate parking behind the city walls in advance; pool is small. [$] *Rooms from: €299* ✉ *Pl. August-Pierre Pont, La Cité* ☎ *04–68–71–98–71* 🌐 *www.hoteldelacite.com* 🛏 *47 rooms, 14 suites.*

$ HOTEL 🏨 **Hôtel Montségur.** With its central lower-city location, this hotel isn't only convenient—it also has special touches that belie the sweet prices here. **Pros:** Faugras family has been in the hotel business for over a century, so they know how to take care of their guests. **Cons:** central location is a big plus, but it also lends itself to street noise. [$] *Rooms from: €97* ✉ *1 av. Bunau Varilla* ☎ *04–68–25–31–41* 🌐 *www.hotelmontsegur.com* 🛏 *18 rooms* 🕒 *Closed Dec. 22–Feb. 1* 🍴 *Breakfast.*

THE ARTS

Pôle Culturel. Carcassonne hosts a major arts festival in July, with dance, theater, classical music, and jazz—for details, contact the town's Pôle Culturel. ☎ *04–68–77–74–67* ⊕ *www.festivaldecarcassonne.fr.*

PERPIGNAN

118 km (71 miles) southeast of Carcassonne, 27 km (17 miles) northwest of Collioure.

GETTING HERE

Ryanair (⊕ *www.ryanair.com*) has a daily flight from London and Brussels to Perpignan. The airport has shuttles from the train station (⊠ *At end of av. du Général de Gaulle*) an hour before each takeoff. If you're coming from Paris by rail, the TGV (⊕ *www.tgv.com*) takes about six hours and costs about €95. Plenty of trains connect Perpignan with Narbonne, some 64 km (40 miles) north, as well as many other communities on the coast. Bus links are also available from the bus station on boulevard St. Assicle, next to the TGV station.

Visitor Information Perpignan Tourist Office ⊠ *Pl. Armand Lanoux* ☎ *04-68-66-30-30* ⊕ *www.perpignantourisme.com.*

EXPLORING

Although Perpignan is big, you need stray no farther than the few squares of the centre ville grouped near the quays of the Basse River; this is the place to be for evening concerts and casual tapas sessions—you might even succumb to the "cosmological ecstasy" Dalí said he experienced here. In medieval times Perpignan was the second city of Catalonia (after Barcelona), before falling to Louis XIV's French army in 1659.

Castillet. Perpignan's town center is sweet and alluring, lined with blooming rosemary bushes and landmarked by a medieval monument, the 14th-century Castillet, with its tall, crenellated twin towers. Originally this hulking brick building was the main gate to the city; later it was used as a prison. Now the **Casa Pairal,** a museum devoted to Catalan art and traditions, is housed here. ⊠ *Pl. de Verdun* ☎ *04–68–35–42–05* 🎟 *€4* ☉ *Oct.–Apr., Tues.–Sun. 11–5; May–Sept., daily 10–6.*

Cathédrale St-Jean. Note the frilly wrought-iron campanile and dramatic medieval crucifix on the Cathédrale St-Jean. ⊠ *Pl. Gambetta.*

Palais des Rois de Majorque (*Kings of Majorca Palace*). The Spanish influence is evident in Perpignan's leading monument, the fortified Palais des Rois de Majorque, begun in the 13th century by Jacques II of Majorca. Highlights here are the majestic **Cour d'Honneur** (Courtyard of Honor), the two-tier Flamboyant Gothic chapel of **Ste-Croix Marie-Madelene,** and the **Grande Salle** (Great Hall), with its monumental fireplaces. ⊠ *Rue des Archers* ☎ *04–68–34–64–93* 🎟 *€4* ☉ *Oct.–May, daily 9–5; June–Sept., daily 10–6.*

Petite Rue des Fabriques d'En Nabot. To see some interesting medieval buildings, walk along the Petite rue des Fabriques d'En Nabot—near Le Castillet—and to the adjacent place de la Loge, the town's nerve center.

Promenade des Plantanes. Across boulevard Wilson from Le Castillet, this is a cheerful place to stroll among flowers, plane trees, and fountains.

ORGANIC OLIVE OIL OBSESSION

Historically, Roussillon was France's leader in olive oil production—that is, until the crippling winter of 1956 persuaded growers to abandon their trees for more lucrative crops. But the biblical fruit regained popularity with the Mediterranean diet buzz of the 1980s, once again making olive oil a profitable endeavor. Today, high-quality, aromatic, organic ones are the most sought after. Visit Domaine Les Fonts, about 14 km (8½ miles) west of Perpignan, for a detailed tasting and olive-grove tour with passionate producers Carmen and Didier Lamirand (☎ *04–68–92–82–05* 🌐 *www.olivesbiolesfonts.fr*).

WHERE TO EAT AND STAY

For expanded hotel reviews, visit Fodors.com.

$ FRENCH 🍴 **Crêperie du Théâtre.** Walk past the pubs and bars on this narrow alley for the best crêperie in Perpignan. Owned by a young couple from Brittany, it prepares authentic buckwheat crêpes with a modern twist and relies heavily on organic ingredients. Top picks include a galette stuffed with endive, smoked duck, pine nuts, cheese, and a honey-cream sauce, which can be gobbled down in the colorful, casual dining room. Two outside tables are good for enjoying coffee and a dessert crêpe. ■ **TIP→ Gluten-free travelers will be pleased to know buckwheat is not a wheat—bon appetit.** [$] *Average main: €8* ✉ *12 rue du Théâtre* ☎ *04–68–34–29–06* 🌐 *www.creperie-du-theatre.fr* 🕒 *Closed Sun., Mon., and 10 days in Jan.*

$$$$ INTERNATIONAL 🍴 **Garriane.** Foodies like Garriane's direct approach to eating and drinking well. Here a plain-Jane decor and a dim neighborhood spectacularly contrast with immaculate plates presented by the Aussi-bred chef (who incidentally shook up Perpignan's sleepy food scene with a strictly seasonal menu emphasizing local produce boldly prepared for an exotic outcome). Wine is the only choice you'll need make; after that the nine-course *degustation* (€35) begins, with dishes like citrusy wild partridge and butternut squash mousse promptly appearing one after the other, ending with three separate desserts (picture chocolate gazpacho garnished with ultrafresh peppery olive oil). ■ **TIP→ For a quick rendition, book a table at lunch for half the price and half the time.** [$] *Average main: €35* ✉ *15 rue Valette* ☎ *04–68–67–07–44* 🕒 *Closed Sun. and Mon. No lunch Sat.*

$ BISTRO 🍴 **Le France.** Occupying a 15th-century former stock market with exposed beams and arcades, this café-restaurant in the center of Perpignan is perfect for a light meal or a glass of iced champagne under the umbrellas as you watch the world go by. Try appetizers such as scallop salad or foie gras with green beans and raisins. Grilled duck breast with apples and big plates of tapas are also served. Although the menu isn't particularly original, all-day nonstop service and a large array of choices make the place popular. [$] *Average main: €15* ✉ *1 pl. de la Loge* ☎ *04–68–51–61–71.*

$$ ╳ **Les Antiquaires.** With traditional Roussillon specialties served in a
FRENCH rustic setting in a corner of old Perpignan, this friendly spot is known
for unpretentious yet refined cuisine and lives up to its name as a refuge
for things antique. Duck à l'orange, a house favorite, has, by popular
demand, been on the menu here for decades. Foie gras in a Banyuls
(wine vinegar) sauce is another staple. But let's be clear, this is an old-
school Catalan option, so trend seekers may want to consider eating
elsewhere. $ *Average main: €20* ✉ *Pl. Joseph Després* ☎ *04–68–34–
06–58* ⊘ *Closed Mon., last wk in June, 1st 2 wks in July, and last 2
wks in Jan. No dinner Sun.*

$ ╳ **Les Indigènes.** You'll find a well-rounded crowd at this wine and tapas
WINE BAR bar where Rousillon's top *vignerons* often mingle. Owned by two musi-
cians with lots of friends, its walls are lined with bottles and long oak
tables are filled with locals who spill out into the alley. If you've had
one too many a drawn-out French meal, this is the place to enjoy fla-
vorful salads and small bites (like pesto and mozzarella *entre pains*)
washed down with an excellent glass *du sud*. But don't count on this
address in August because the bar's closed when everyone's at the beach.
■**TIP**➔ Order wine by the bottle and pay the cellar rate plus corking
fee—by the glass can get expensive. $ *Average main: €12* ✉ *26 rue de
la Cloche d'Or* ☎ *04–68–35–65–02* ⊘ *Closed 1st wk in Jan. and several
wks in summer. No lunch.*

$$ ☷ **Château la Tour Apollinaire.** This Belle Époque château-turned-post-
B&B/INN modern B&B was once the mayor's residence surrounded by sprawl-
ing vineyards. **Pros:** great location; lovely grounds with pool and
gardens. **Cons:** rooms have private en suite bathrooms but share kitchens and common areas; laminate flooring in places. $ *Rooms from:
€120* ✉ *5 rue Guillaume Apollinaire* ☎ *04–68–92–43–02* ⊕ *www.
latourapollinaire.com* ⤵ *13 rooms.*

$$$ ☷ **La Villa Duflot.** In a large park filled with olive and cypress trees, this
HOTEL hotel-restaurant complex prepares some of the best meals in one of the
calmest, prettiest settings just outside the city center. **Pros:** restaurant is
a local favorite; trees screen the property from the road. **Cons:** located
in the commercial zone on the outskirts of town; hotel gets traffic noise.
$ *Rooms from: €165* ✉ *Rond Point Albert Donnezan* ☎ *04–68–56–
67–67* ⊕ *www.villa-duflot.com* ⤵ *23 rooms, 1 suite.*

SHOPPING

Rue des Marchands, near Le Castillet, is thick with chic shops.

Maison Quinta. This is a multilevel Catalan design shop with the attic
housing a studio where custom orders are cut out of the famous brightly
colored Catalan fabric. ✉ *3 rue Grande des Fabriques* ⊕ *www.maison-
quinta.com.*

Sant Vicens Crafts Center. Excellent local ceramics can be found at the
picturesque Sant Vicens Crafts Center. ✉ *Rue Sant Vicens, off D22 east
of town center* ⊕ *www.santvicens.fr.*

14

PRADES

45 km (27 miles) west of Perpignan.

ESSENTIALS

Visitor Information Prades Tourist Office ✉ *10 pl. de la Republique* ☎ *04–68–05–41–02* 🌐 *www.prades-tourisme.fr.*

EXPLORING

Once home to world-renowned Catalan cellist Pablo Casals, the market town of Prades is famous for its annual summer music festival, the **Festival Pablo Casals** (🌐 *www.prades-festival-casals.com*), from late July to mid-August.

Abbaye de St-Michel de Cuxa. One of the gems of the Pyrénées, the medieval abbey's sturdy, crenellated bell tower is visible from afar. If the remains of the cloisters here seem familiar, it may be because you have seen the missing pieces in New York City's Cloisters Museum. The town's music festival, founded by cellist Pablo Casals in 1950, is primarily held in the 10th-century pre-Romanesque church—the biggest in France—a superb aesthetic and acoustical venue. The six-voice Gregorian vespers service held (somewhat sporadically; call to confirm) at 7 pm in the monastery next door is hauntingly simple and medieval in tone and texture. ✉ *3 km (2 miles) south of Prades and Codalet on D27* ☎ *04–68–96–15–35* 🌐 *www.prades-festival-casals.com* 🎟 *€5* 🕒 *May–Sept., daily 9:30–11:50 and 2–6; Oct.–Apr., daily 9:30–11:50 and 2–5.*

WHERE TO EAT AND STAY

$$ MODERN FRENCH

🍴 **El Taller.** Run by four entrepreneurial friends in the small village of Taurinya (just down the road from the famous Abbaye de St-Michel de Cuxa), this hip bistro serves fine locally sourced fare. Like the food, the setting is modern and stylish: its sleek glass-walled building and steel-framed terrace were constructed by the village specifically to house this *Bistrot de Pays* (a government-subsidized network of village restaurants promoting commerce in rural areas). The contemporary air of the place, complete with art exhibits, concerts, and theater nights, makes El Taller a popular out-of-the-way gathering place for locals and travelers. [$] *Average main: €24* ✉ *5 km (3 miles) south of Prades, Taurinya* ☎ *04–68–05–63–35* 🕒 *Closed Wed. and Jan. 9–22.*

$ B&B/INN

🏨 **Castell Rose.** Original hardwood floors, conservatively fine interiors, and a well-educated adolescent greeting you at the door make a night at Castell Rose like staying with a modern-day French bourgeois family. **Pros:** warm and welcoming hosts; beautiful view of Mount Canigou. **Cons:** interiors might be too traditional for some tastes. [$] *Rooms from: €110* ✉ *Chemin de la Litera* ☎ *04–68–96–07–57, 06–32–68–72–26 cell phone* 🌐 *www.castellrose-prades.com* 🛏 *5 rooms, 3 apartments, 1 villa* 🍽 *Breakfast.*

$ B&B/INN

🏨 **Maison 225.** Don't let the bland street-front facade of this late 1800s town house turn you away—inside, the renovated interior blends stately original attributes with clean, contemporary edges, and natural light spills in from the quiet gardens and terrace that give front-seat views of snowcapped Mount Canigou; though all four rooms are spacious, combining modern style and nice antique details, the upstairs Terrace

THE LITTLE TRAIN THAT COULD

To fully understand the diverse geography of this region, a detour inland is almost essential. If you think the snowcapped mountains are beautiful from your beach towel, imagine how the blue-green Mediterranean looks from those mountain heights. One way to see the spectacular panorama is by riding le Petit Train Jaune, aka the Little Yellow Train, over France's highest track. Built to link the region's mountain villages with the towns on the coastal plane, this life-size toy train makes the 63-km (40-mile), three-hour climb from the fortified village of Villefranche to La Tour de Carole about five times a day, passing through 19 tunnels and crossing two viaducts en route. For information about hours and prices, check with the Vernet-les-Bains Tourist Office (☎ *04-68-05-55-35*) or the SNCF website (🌐 *www.ter-sncf.com*).

Suite stands out with its glassed-in Florida room. **Pros:** locally respected hosts can call on contacts and point you in the right direction in the area; now has a pool. **Cons:** if you like contemplative mornings, you may find it hard sharing breakfast around the one dining room table. [$] *Rooms from: €70* ✉ *225 av. du General de Gaulle* ☎ *04–68–05–52–79, 06–42–91–79–21 cell phone* 🌐 *www.225prades.com* 🛏 *4 rooms* 🍴 *Breakfast.*

VERNET-LES-BAINS

12 km (7 miles) southwest of Prades, 55 km (34 miles) west of Perpignan.

ESSENTIALS

Visitor Information Vernet-les-Bains Tourist Office ✉ *2 rue de la Chapelle* ☎ *04-68-05-55-35* 🌐 *www.vernet-les-bains.fr.*

EXPLORING

A long-established spa town dwarfed by imposing Mont Canigou, Vernet-les-Bains's waters were so famed that many celebs, including English writer Rudyard Kipling, came to take the cure.

Fodor's Choice ★ **Abbaye St-Martin du Canigou.** Visitors, tackling a steep, half-hour climb from the parking area, come to make a pilgrimage—esthetic or spiritual—to this celebrated medieval abbey. It's one of the most photographed in Europe thanks to its sky-kissing location atop a triangular promontory at an altitude of nearly 3,600 feet. St-Martin du Canigou's breathtaking mountain setting was due, in part, to an effort to escape the threat of marauding Saracens from the Middle East. Constructed in 1009 by Count Guifré of Cerdagne, then damaged by an earthquake in 1428 and abandoned in 1783, the abbey was diligently (perhaps too diligently) restored by the Bishop of Perpignan early in the 20th century. The oldest parts are the cloisters and the two churches, of which the lower church, dedicated to Notre-Dame-sous-Terre, is the most ancient. Rising above is a stocky, fortified bell tower. Although the hours vary, Masses are sung daily; call ahead to confirm. Easter Mass here is especially joyous and moving. ✉ *Casteil, 2 km (1 mile)* *south of Vernet-les-Bains* ☎ *04–68–05–50–03* 🌐 *stmartinducanigou.org* 🎫 *€5* 🕘 *Oct.–Dec. and Feb.–May, tours Tues.–Sat. at 10, 11, 2, 3, aqnd 4, Sun. and holidays at 10, 12:30, 2, 3, and 4; June–Sept., tours Mon.–Sat. at 10, 11, noon, 2, 3, 4, and 5, Sun. and holidays at 10, 12:30, 2, 3, 4, and 5.*

CÉRET

68 km (41 miles) southeast of Prades; 35 km (21 miles) west of Collioure; 31 km (19 miles) southwest of Perpignan.

Visitor Information Céret Tourist Office ✉ *1 av. Georges Clemenceau* ☎ *04–68–87–00–53* 🌐 *www.ot-ceret.fr.*

EXPLORING

The "Barbizon of Cubism," Céret achieved immortality when leading artists found this small Catalan town irresistible at the beginning of the 20th century. Here in this medieval enclave set on the banks of the Tech River, Picasso and Gris developed a vigorous new way of visualizing that would result in the fragmented forms of Cubism, a thousand years removed from the Romanesque sculptures of the Roussillon chapels and cloisters. The town famously grows the first and finest crop of cherries in France.

Fodor's Choice ★ **Musée d'Art Moderne** (*Modern Art Museum*). Some of the town landscapes captured in paintings by Picasso, Gris, Dufy, Braque, Chagall, Masson, and others are on view in the fine collection of the Musée d'Art Moderne. ✉ *8 bd. Maréchal-Joffre* ☎ *04–68–87–27–76* 🌐 *www.musee-ceret.com* 🎫 *€8* 🕘 *July–mid-Sept., daily 10–7; early May–June and mid- to end Sept., daily 10–6; Oct.–early May, Wed.–Mon 10–6.*

Vieux Céret (*Old Céret*). The heart of town is, not surprisingly, the place Picasso and, as a town that's proud of its Catalan heritage, it often hosts sardana dances and *castellers* (human towers) troops. Be sure to stroll through the rest of pretty Vieux Céret, with its **place de la Fontaine des Neuf Jets** (Nine Fountains Square) where scenes were shot for the 2008 French film *J'ai oublie de te dire* starring Omar Sharif. Include a visit to the church, wander out to the lovely fortified **Porte de France** gateway, then head toward the single-arched medieval **Pont du Diable** (the Devil's Bridge), said to have been built by the devil himself in one single night.

WHERE TO STAY

For expanded hotel reviews, visit Fodors.com.

$$$$ B&B/INN Fodor's Choice ★ 🏨 **Can Rigall.** Poised at the end of a long, winding drive, this restored farmstead–turned–elite eco-hotel draws nature lovers and hedonists alike with inspiring vistas and modern design infused with regional history. **Pros:** that view, worth the steep road and steep prices; locally sourced organic meals. **Cons:** very remote, so a car is absolutely essential (along with nerves of steel to cross a very narrow bridge en route). [$] *Rooms from: €260* ✉ *29 km (18 miles) west of Céret, Arles-sur-Tech* ☎ *06–04–14–65–51* 🌐 *www.canrigall.com* 🛏 *8 rooms, 3 suites* 🕘 *Closed Dec.–Mar.*

$$ HOTEL 🏨 **La Terrasse au Soleil.** Although guest rooms here don't quite live up to the high prices, this hostelry—set high above Céret—has terrific terrace

As color-splashed as a Matisse or Braque painting, Collioure's harbor once inspired those masters and continues to seduce today's artists.

views of Mont Canigou and its verdant valley. **Pros:** outdoor pool, onsite spa with Turkish bath perfumed by organic essential oils. **Cons:** not in town center; somewhat flat ambiance. $ *Rooms from: €165* ✉ *Rte. de Fontfrede* ☎ *04–68–87–01–94* ⊕ *www.terrasse-au-soleil.com* ↳ *37 rooms, 2 suites* ☉ *Closed Dec. 15–Feb. 15.*

$ 🍴 **Les Arcades.** This comfortable spot in mid-Céret looks and feels
HOTEL   exactly the way an inn ensconced in the heart of a provincial French town should, and having both the world-class collection of paintings of the Musée d'Art Moderne and the top-rated Restaurant del Bisbe just next door further elevates it as a desirable place to stay. **Pros:** family-run business with great customer service; superior art in the public areas. **Cons:** some rooms are small, so check them out first. $ *Rooms from: €59* ✉ *1 pl. Picasso* ☎ *04–68–87–12–30* ⊕ *www.hotel-arcades-ceret. com* ↳ *30 rooms.*

COLLIOURE

35 km (21 miles) east of Céret, 27 km (17 miles) southeast of Perpignan.

Fodor's Choice   The fishing village where famed painters Henri Matisse, André Der-
★   ain, and the Fauvists committed chromatic mayhem in the early 20th century, Collioure is still the jewel of the Vermilion Coast. A town of espadrille merchants, anchovy packers, and lateen-rigged fishing boats in the shadow of a 13th-century Château Royal, it is now as much a magnet for travelers (beware the crowds in July and August) as it once was and remains a lure for artists.

Matisse Country

The little coastal village of Collioure continues to play muse to the entire Côte Vermeille—after all, it gave rise to the name of the Vermilion Coast, because the great painter Henri Matisse daringly painted Collioure's yellow-sand beach using a bright red terra-cotta hue. For such artistic daredevilry, he was branded a "fauve." Considered, along with Picasso, to be one of the most influential artists of the modern period, Matisse (1869–1954) and fellow painter André Derain (1880–1954) discovered Fauvism *en vacances* in Collioure in 1905.

Holed up here during that summer, the friends were seduced by its pink and mauve houses, ocher rooftops, and the dramatic combination of sea, sun, and hills. Back then, further touches of color were added by the red and green fishing boats. With nature's outré palette at hand, Matisse was inspired to passionate hues and a brash distortion of form.

At summer's end, Matisse made the trip to Paris to show his Collioure works at the Salon d'Automne, the season's biggest art event. Because the canvases of Matisse, Derain, and their kindred spirits were so shocking, they were made to hang their paintings in a back room (No. 7, which became known as "the cage"). The public jeered the works, saying they were primitive, coarse, and extreme. But before long, their *sucess de scandale* quickly won them new adherents, including the painters Rouault, Van Dongen, Braque, and Dufy. Fauvism became the rage from 1905 to 1908; by 1909 Matisse was famous all around the world.

Today Matisse's masterpieces grace the walls of the greatest museums in the world. In a sense, Collioure has something better: a host of virtual Matisses, 3-D Derains, and pop-up Dufys. Realizing this, the mayor decided to create the Chemin du Fauvisme (Fauvist Way) more than a decade ago, erecting 20 reproductions of Matisse's and Derain's works on the very spots where they were painted.

Matisse could return today and find things little changed: the Château Royal still perches over the harbor, the Fort Saint-Elme still makes a striking perspectival point on its hilltop, and the plage Boramar still looks like a 3-acre "Matisse."

Pick up the Chemin's trail at the town's Espace Fauve by going to quai de l'Amiraute (📠 04–68–98–07–16) or check out its history at ⊕ *www.collioure.com.*

GETTING HERE

Collioure has about a dozen trains that make the trip to and from Perpignan (20 mins away). The train station is at the end of avenue Aristide Maillol (☎ *04–68–82–05–89*). But the subsidized bus network that gets you anywhere in the département for €1 is the most economical, and thus popular, mode of transportation. Buses leave year-round from the parking lots at place du 8 Mai and place Jean Jaurès. For specific times, see ⊕ *www.voyages-sncf.com* and *www.cg66.fr.*

Visitor Information Collioure Tourist Office ⊠ *Pl. du 18-Juin* ☎ *04–68–82–15–47* ⊕ *www.collioure.com.*

EXPLORING

14

Today Collioure—composed of narrow, cobbled streets and pretty houses—is a living museum, as you can discover by walking the Chemin du Fauvisme (Fauvist Way), a pedestrian trail winding through town with 20 points where you can compare reproductions of noted Fauvist canvases with the actual scenes that were depicted in them. The information center, behind the plage Boramar, has an excellent map. View-finder picture frames let you see how delightfully little of what the artists once admired has changed in the ensuing century. To the north, the rocky Îlot St-Vincent juts out into the sea, a modern lighthouse at its tip, and inland the Albères mountain range rises to connect the Pyrénées with the Mediterranean. The town harbor is a painting unto itself, framed by a 13th-century castle and a 17th-century church fortified with a tower.

Matisse set up shop here in the summer of 1905 and was soon inspired by the colors of the town's terra-cotta roofs (⇨ see *"Matisse Country" above*). André Derain, Henri Martin, and Georges Braque—who were dubbed Fauves for their "savage" (*fauve* means "wild beast") approach to color and form—quickly followed. Detour to the streets behind the Vieux Port to find former fishermen's stores now occupied by smart boutiques and restaurants.

To discover tomorrow's Matisses and Derains, head to the streets behind the place du 18-Juin and to the old quarter of Le Mouré, beneath Fort Miradou—the studios here are filled with contemporary artists at work. Today the most prized locales in town are the café-terraces overlooking the main beach and the fashionable rue Camille Pelletan by the harbor, where you can feast on Collioure's tender, practically boneless anchovies and the fine Banyuls and Collioure AOC wines coming from the impeccably cultivated vineyards surrounding the town. Although nearby villages are apparently only rich in quaintness, Collioure is surprisingly prosperous, thanks to the cultivation of *primeurs*, early ripening fruit and vegetables, shipped to the markets of northern France.

Château Royal. A slender jetty divides the Boramar Beach, beneath Notre-Dame-des-Anges, from the small landing area at the foot of the Château Royal, a 13th-century castle, once the summer residence of the kings of Majorca (from 1276 to 1344), and remodeled by Vauban 500 years later. ☎ *04–68–82–06–43* ⌧ *€4* ☉ *June and Sept., daily 10–6; Oct.–May, daily 9–5; July and Aug., daily 10–7.*

Musée d'Art Moderne Fonds Péské. No Matissses hold pride of place at the town's Musée d'Art Moderne Fonds Péské, but the collection of 180 works deftly sums up the influence the painter had on this *cité des peintures* (city of artists). Works by Cocteau, Valtat, and others are impressively housed in a picturesque, ivy-shrouded villa on a beautiful hillside site. ⊠ *Rte. de Porte-Vendres* ☏ *04–68–82–10–19* 🎫 *€2* ⊙ *July and Aug., daily 10–noon and 2–6; Sept.–June, Wed.–Mon. 10–noon and 2–6.*

Notre-Dame-des-Anges. At the end of boulevard du Boramar is the 17th-century church of Notre-Dame-des-Anges. It has exuberantly carved, gilded Churrigueresque altarpieces by celebrated Catalan master Joseph Sunyer and a pink-dome bell tower that doubled as the original lighthouse. ⊠ *Pl. de l'Église.*

WHERE TO EAT AND STAY

For expanded hotel reviews, visit Fodors.com.

$$ ✕**Le 5eme Péché.** On one of Collioure's quieter cobblestoned streets
FRENCH FUSION you'll find Le 5eme Péché, where the clean-lined decor seems in synch with simple, artful dishes like tempura shrimp with chestnut cream and apple crisps. Iijima Masashi, the young Japanese chef who dared open this tiny French-fusion bistro, is more than just tolerated among local traditional French gourmets—he's celebrated. With only 18 seats and an open kitchen plan, you'll feel like you know him personally by the time dinner is done. ■TIP➔ The limited menu may not please finicky eaters. Ⓢ *Average main: €22* ⊠ *18 rue de la Fraternité* ☏ *04–68–98–09–76* ⊕ *www.le5peche.com.*

$ 🏨**Les Templiers.** Matisse, Maillol, Dalí, Picasso, and Dufy used to hang
HOTEL out here, and today owner Jojo Pous (son of the driving force behind
Fodor's Choice Collioure's art colony) is proud to show off the 2,500-plus original
★ works hanging from every nook and cranny of this celebrated inn and restaurant—one of the most glorious sights in Languedoc-Roussillon and now universally considered the "soul" of Collioure. **Pros:** in the center of town, close to a bus stop and an easy walk from the train station. **Cons:** no access for cars (on a pedestrian alley); noisy during the hustle and bustle of August. Ⓢ *Rooms from: €70* ⊠ *12 quai de l'Amirauté* ☏ *04–68–98–31–10* ⊕ *www.hotel-templiers.com* ⤳ *47 rooms, 1 suite* ⊙ *Closed Jan. and last wk of Nov.*

$$$ 🏨**Relais des Trois Mas.** With a perfect perch overlooking the harbor from
HOTEL the cliffs south of town, this hotel enjoys vistas that are priceless—the main reason why the rooms here are very pricey. **Pros:** breathtaking views of Collioure. **Cons:** some standard rooms are very small; accommodations are basic for the price; no lobby, sitting area, or bar. Ⓢ *Rooms from: €170* ⊠ *Rte. de Port-Vendres* ☏ *04–68–82–05–07* ⊕ *www. relaisdes3mas.com* ⤳ *19 rooms, 4 suites* ⊙ *Closed Nov. 15–Feb. 4.*

NARBONNE

61 km (38 miles) north of Perpignan; 60 km (37 miles) east of Carcassonne; 94 km (58 miles) south of Montpellier.

In Roman times, bustling, industrial Narbonne was the second-largest town in Gaul (after Lyon) and an important port, though today little remains of its Roman past, except an impressive underground warehouse (*horreum* in Latin) once used to store the wines and goods shipped through its harbor. Until the sea receded during the Middle Ages, Narbonne prospered.

GETTING HERE

Narbonne is an important rail junction for the region. The train station is on boulevard Frédéric Mistral, north of the city center and adjacent to the Gare Routière (bus station) on avenue Carnot. Via train, it takes nearly an hour to get here from Perpignan and Montpellier, and 1½ hours from Toulouse. There are plenty of connections from Perpignan (about 20 per day), as well as many other communities along the coast. If you're taking the TGV (🌐 *www.tgv.com*) from Paris, the trip will last about 4½ hours and cost about €105 one way.

Visitor Information Narbonne Tourist Office ✉ *31 rue Jean Juares* ☎ *04–68–65–15–60* 🌐 *www.narbonne-tourisme.com.*

EXPLORING

Cathédrale St-Just-et-St-Pasteur. The town's former wealth is evinced by the 14th-century Cathédrale St-Just-et-St-Pasteur—its vaulting rises 133 feet from the floor, making it the tallest cathedral in southern France. Only Beauvais and Amiens (both in Picardy) are taller, and, as at Beauvais, the nave at Narbonne was never built. The "Creation" tapestry is the cathedral's finest treasure. ✉ *Rue Armand-Gauthier.*

Palais des Archevêques (*Archbishops' Palace*). Richly sculpted cloisters link the cathedral to the former Palais des Archevêques, now home to museums of archaeology, art, and history. Note the late-13th-century keep, the Donjon Gilles-Aycelin; climb the 180 steps to the top for a view over the town and surrounding region. ✉ *Pl. de l'Hôtel de Ville* ☎ *04–68–90–30–65* 🎟 *€4, €9 includes admission to 7 town sites* 🕒 *Apr.–July 14, Wed.–Mon. 10–noon and 2–5; July 15–Oct., daily 10–1 and 2:30–6; Nov.–Mar., Wed.–Mon. 2–5.*

WHERE TO STAY

For expanded hotel reviews, visit Fodors.com.

$$ HOTEL 🏨 **Château L'Hospitalet.** A stay at this sprawling family-owned wine estate, located between Narbonne's city center and its beaches, is like a course in the art of Mediterranean living complete with surrounding vineyards, sea breezes, an immense wine-tasting cellar, organic kitchen garden, and resident artist studios. **Pros:** a good sampling of wine, art, and lifestyle. **Cons:** guest rooms lack character. [$] *Rooms from: €120* ✉ *Rte. de Narbonne plage* ☎ *04–68–45–28–50* 🌐 *www.chateau-lhospitalet.com* 🛏 *38 rooms* 🕒 *Closed 3 wks in Jan.*

MONTPELLIER

140 km (87 miles) northeast of Perpignan, 42 km (26 miles) southwest of Nîmes.

Vibrant Montpellier (pronounced monh-pell-*yay*), capital of the Languedoc-Roussillon region, has been a center of commerce and learning since the Middle Ages, when it was a crossroads for pilgrims on their way to Santiago de Compostela, in Spain, and an active shipping center trading in spices from the East. With its cargo of exotic luxuries,

TOURING MONTPELLIER

Montpellier Tourist Office. In addition to publishing mapped itineraries, the Montpellier Tourist Office provides guided walking tours of the city's neighborhoods and monuments. These go daily in summer and on Wednesday, Saturday, and Sunday during the school year (roughly, September–June). English-speaking tours are offered on Saturday, otherwise an English language audio guide is available. All leave from the place de la Comédie, and spaces can be booked online. ⊠ 30 allée Jean de Lattre de Tassigny, esplanade Comédie ☎ 04-67-60-60-60 ⊕ www.ot-montpellier.fr ⊠ €7.50 guided tour.

Tourist train. A small tourist train with broadcast commentary leaves from the place de la Comedie daily at 11, noon, 2, 3, and 4 (extra runs are added in high season). ☎ 04-67-66-24-38 information ⊠ €7 ⊙ Closed Nov. 15–Jan.

it also imported Renaissance learning, and its university—founded in the 13th century—has nurtured a steady influx of ideas through the centuries. Though the port silted up by the 16th century, Montpellier never became a backwater, and as a center of commerce and conferences it keeps its focus on the future.

GETTING HERE

Easyjet, Ryanair, and Air France fly out of the Airport Montpellier-Méditerranée (☎ 04-67-20-85-00), to the southeast of Montpellier. Shuttles (€2.40) leave the bus station about every hour for the airport from rue Grand St-Jean (⊕ www.montpellier.aeroport.fr). The TGV takes three hours, 30 minutes from Paris, and tickets cost about €85; there are also direct trains as far afield as Avignon, Nice, and Marseille. If you're trying to get to the sea, hail bus No. 131 (which passes every half hour for Palavas).

Visitor Information Montpellier Tourist Office ⊠ 30 allée Jean de Lattre de Tassigny, esplanade Comédie ☎ 04-67-60-60-60 ⊕ www.ot-montpellier.fr.

EXPLORING

An imaginative urban planning program has streamlined Montpellier's 17th-century Vieille Ville, and monumental perspectives dwarf passersby on its promenade du Peyrou. An even more utopian venture in urban planning is the Antigone district, a vast, harmonious 100-acre complex designed in 1984 by Barcelona architect Ricardo Bofill. A student population of some 75,000 keeps things lively—especially on the place de la Comédie, the city's nerve center. Happily, the Vielle Ville is a pedestrian paradise, and you can travel around the entire city on an excellent bus and tram system.

TOP ATTRACTIONS

Arc de Triomphe. Looming majestically over the peripheral highway that loops around the city center, this enormous arch is the centerpiece of the Peyrou. Designed by d'Aviler in 1689, it was finished by Giral in 1776. Together, the noble scale of these harmonious stone constructions and the sweeping perspectives they frame make for an inspiring

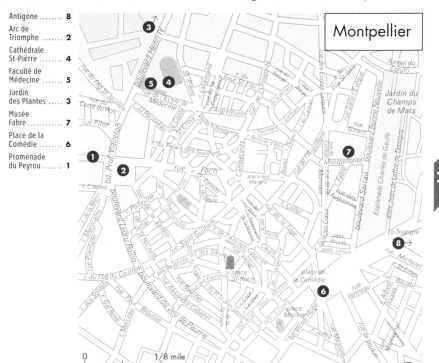

Montpellier

14

stroll through this upscale stretch of town. At the end of the park is the historic **Château d'Eau,** a Corinthian temple and the terminal for **les Arceaux,** an 18th-century aqueduct; on a clear day the view from here is spectacular, taking in the Cévennes Mountains, the sea, and an ocean of red-tile roofs (it's worth coming back at night to see the entire promenade illuminated).

Musée Fabre. From crowd-packed place de la Comédie, boulevard Sarrail leads north past the shady esplanade Charles de Gaulle to this rich, renowned art museum. Renovated in 2006, it is a mixed bag of architectural styles (a 17th-century *hôtel,* a vast Victorian wing with superb natural light, and a remnant of a Baroque Jesuit college). The collection inside is surprisingly big, thanks to the museum's namesake, a Montpellier native. François-Xavier Fabre, a student of the great 18th-century French artist David, established roots in Italy and acquired a formidable collection of masterworks—which he then donated to his hometown, supervising the development of this fine museum. Among his gifts were the *Mariage Mystique de Sainte Catherine,* by Veronese, and Poussin's coquettish *Venus et Adonis.* Later contributions include a superb group of 17th-century Flemish works (Rubens, Steen), a collection of 19th-century French canvases (Géricault, Delacroix, Corot, Millet) that inspired Gauguin and Van Gogh, and a growing group of

Both the Three Graces fountain and the Opéra Comédie theater anchor the place de la Comédie, the social and cultural hub of Montpellier.

20th-century acquisitions that buttress a legacy of paintings by early Impressionist Frédéric Bazille. ✉ *39 bd. Bonne Nouvelle* ☎ *04–67–14–83–00* ⊕ *museefabre.montpellier-agglo.com* ✆ *€8* ⊗ *Tues.–Sun. 10–6.*

Place de la Comédie. The number of bistros and brasseries increases as you leave the Vieille Ville to cross place des Martyrs, and if you veer right down rue de la Loge, you emerge onto the festive gathering spot known as place de la Comédie. Anchored by the Neoclassical 19th-century **Opéra-Comédie**, this broad square is a beehive of leisurely activity, a cross between Barcelona's Ramblas and a Roman *passeggiata* (afternoon stroll, en masse). Eateries and entertainment venues draw crowds, but the real pleasure is getting here and seeing who came before, wearing what, and with whom.

Promenade du Peyrou. Montpellier's grandest avenue, the promenade was built at the end of the 17th century and dedicated to Louis XIV.

WORTH NOTING

Antigone. At the far-east end of the city loop, Montpellier seems to transform itself into a futuristic city, all in one smooth, low-slung postmodern style. This is the Antigone district, the result of city planners' efforts (and local industries' commitment) to pull Montpellier up out of its economic doldrums. It worked. This ideal neighborhood, designed by the Catalan architect Ricardo Bofill, covers 100-plus acres with plazas, esplanades, shops, restaurants, and low-income housing constructed out of stone-color, pre-stressed concrete.

Hôtel de Region. Be sure to visit place du Nombre d'Or—symmetrically composed of curves—and the long vista that stretches down a mall of cypress trees to the glass-fronted Hôtel de Region. ✉ *Rue de Pompegnane.*

Cathédrale St-Pierre. After taking in the broad vistas of the promenade de Peyrou, cross over into the Vieille Ville and wander its maze of narrow streets full of pretty shops and intimate restaurants. At the northern edge of the Vieille Ville, visit this imposing cathedral, its fantastical and unique 14th-century entry porch alone worth the detour: two cone-top towers—some five stories high—flank the main portal and support a groin-vaulted shelter. The interior, despite 18th-century reconstruction, maintains the formal simplicity of its 14th-century origins. ✉ *Pl. St-Pierre.*

GETTING AROUND

Montpellier's historic *centre ville,* with its labyrinth of stone paths and alleys leading from courtyard to courtyard, is well suited to walkers. Hotels, restaurants, and sights can all accessed on foot from place de la Comédie, but the city also has a comprehensive tramway and bus system, TAM (☎ *04-67-22-87-87* 🌐 *www.montpellier-agglo.com/tam*). The Gare Routière bus and tram stations are by the train terminal on rue Jules Ferry. Cycling is another popular way to get around, and rental bikes are readily available.

14

Faculté de Médecine. Peek into this noble institution on rue de l'École de Médecine, next door to Cathédrale St-Pierre. Founded in the 13th century and infused with generations of international learning (especially Arab and Jewish scholarship), it is one of France's most respected medical schools.

Jardin des Plantes. Boulevard Henri IV runs north from the promenade du Peyrou to France's oldest botanical garden, which was planted on order of Henri IV in 1593. An exceptional range of plants, flowers, and trees grows here. ✉ *Bd. Henri IV* ☎ *04–34–43–36–20* 🌐 *www.univ-montp1.fr/patrimoine/jardin_des_plantes* 🎫 *Free* 🕒 *Tues.–Sun., noon–8; noon–6 in winter.*

WHERE TO EAT

$$ FRENCH
🍴 **Le Chat Perché.** People flock here for the warm bistro ambience, the terrace overlooking the square below, the carefully selected regional wines, and the traditional dishes served with flair. The cuisine varies with the seasons, the markets, and the humor of the chef, but *everything* is homemade and reasonably priced. [$] *Average main: €18* ✉ *10 rue college Duvergier, l. de la Chapelle Neuve* ☎ *04–67–60–88–59* ✍ *Reservations essential* 🕒 *Closed Sun. No lunch.*

$$$$ MODERN FRENCH Fodor's Choice ★
🍴 **Le Jardin des Sens.** Blink and look again: twins Laurent and Jacques Pourcel, trained under separate masters, combine forces here to achieve a quiet, almost cerebral cuisine based on southern French traditions. At every turn are happy surprises, including foie gras crisps, dried-fruit risotto, and lamb sweetbreads with prawns. The interior is minimal stylish, with steel beams and tables on three tiers. Truth is, the restaurant is in a rather *delabré* working-class neighborhood, and from the outside looks like an anonymous warehouse incongruous with its Michelin-starred reputation. **■ TIP→ A modest lunch menu lets you indulge at a lower cost.** [$] *Average main: €50* ✉ *11 av. St-Lazare*

☎ *04–99–58–38–38* ⊕ *www.jardindessens.com* ⊙ *Closed Sun. and 1st wk in Jan. No lunch Mon. and Wed.*

$$$
FRENCH
✕ **Le Petit Jardin.** On a quiet Vieille Ville backstreet, this simple restaurant lives up to its name: you dine looking over (or seated in) a lovely, deep-shaded garden with views of the cathedral. A simple omelet with pepper sauce, fresh foie gras in a rhubarb sauce, or turbot in a honey and balsamic vinegar sauce mirrors the welcome, which is warm and unpretentious. ■ **TIP→** For a lighter version, ask for a bar table where a pared-down menu is available. Ⓢ *Average main: €32* ⊠ *20 rue Jean-Jacques-Rousseau* ☎ *04–67–60–78–78* ⊙ *Oct.–May, closed Mon. and no dinner Sun.*

$
MEDITERRANEAN
✕ **Le Petit Mickey.** Since 1885 this eatery—the oldest in the city, known historically as Casimir—has been feeding locals fine Mediterranean fare such as bull stew and fish of the day *à la plancha* (grilled with olive oil, garlic, and herbs) at great prices. You might have to endure the crowds and a sometimes irascible owner, but when the copious traditional plates hit the table you'll quickly forget the wait at lunchtime. Ⓢ *Average main: €15* ⊠ *15 rue du Petit Jean* ☎ *04–67–60–60–41* ⊙ *Closed Sun. and Aug. No dinner Tues.*

WHERE TO STAY

For expanded hotel reviews, visit Fodors.com.

$$$
B&B/INN
Fodor's**Choice**
★
📍 **Baudon de Mauny.** The finest rooms in Montpellier (and quite possibly the whole region) can be found at this chic guesthouse on one of the historic district's nicest streets. **Pros:** architectural success; extra-spacious rooms; flawless service. **Cons:** no on-site parking; only eight rooms. Ⓢ *Rooms from: €180* ⊠ *1 rue de la Carbonnerie* ☎ *04–67–02–21–77* ⊕ *www.baudondemauny.com* ⌁ *8 rooms.*

$$
HOTEL
📍 **Le Guilhem.** On the same quiet backstreet as the restaurant Le Petit Jardin, this jewel of a *hôtel de charme* is actually a series of 16th-century houses rebuilt from ruins, replete with an extraordinary old garden. **Pros:** location close to Cathedrale St-Pierre, Jardin des Plantes, and the promenade du Peyrou. **Cons:** it's a long walk from the place de la Comédie. Ⓢ *Rooms from: €119* ⊠ *18 rue Jean-Jacques-Rousseau* ☎ *04–67–52–90–90* ⊕ *www.leguilhem.com* ⌁ *35 rooms.*

NIGHTLIFE AND THE ARTS

Orchestre National de Montpellier. The Orchestre National de Montpellier is a young and energetic group of some reputation, performing regularly in the Salle Molière as well as the Opéra Berlioz in the Corum conference complex. ⊕ *www.opera-orchestre-montpellier.fr.*

Salle Molière-Opéra de Montpellier. Opera and orchestral concerts are performed in the very imposing Salle Molière-Opéra de Montpellier. ⊠ *11 bd. Victor Hugo* ☎ *04–67–60–19–99* ⊕ *www.opera-montpellier.com.*

THE BASQUE COUNTRY, GASCONY, AND HAUTES-PYRÉNÉES

WELCOME TO THE BASQUE COUNTRY, GASCONY, AND HAUTES-PYRÉNÉES

TOP REASONS TO GO

★ **Catch a wave in Biarritz:** Today Biarritz is Europe's surf capital, a far cry from its start as the favorite watering place of Empress Eugénie, but, face it, this is one party everyone is invited to.

★ **Be charmed by Basque chic:** The camera-ready villages of Ainhoa, Sare, and St-Jean-de-Luz show off quirky, color-ful, and asymmetrical Basque architecture.

★ **Indulge yourself in Michel Guérard's Les Prés d' Eugénie:** The co-father (with Paul Bocuse) of nou-velle cuisine still creates glorious meals in tucked-away Eugénie-les-Bains.

★ **Gasp at gorgeous Gavarnie:** Victor Hugo called the 1,400-foot-high waterfall here "the greatest architect's greatest work."

★ **Take in the view from pretty Pau:** With a panoramic view of the Pyrénées, Pau is the historic capital of Béarn—and regal monuments recall its royal past as the birth-place of King Henri IV.

1 The Atlantic Pyrénées. From the first important height at 2,969-foot La Rhune, towering over the edge of the Atlantic, the Basque Pyrénées rise east-ward through picturesque valleys and villages to the Iparla Ridge above Bidarrai and the range's first major peak at the 6,617-foot Orhi. The hills cosset cozy vil-lages like Sare and Ainhoa. Colorful architecture and flower-festooned balconies help preserve St-Jean-Pied-de-Port's charm. Gateway to the Pyrénées, Pau is the most culturally vibrant city in Gascony, with elegant *hôtels particuliers* and a royal château.

2 Hautes-Pyrénées. The Hautes-Pyrénées include the most spectacular natural wonders in the cordillera. Although mountains soar in this region, making travel difficult, the area has always attracted cultural luminar-ies including Victor Hugo, Montaigne, and Rossini, who came to marvel at the Cirque de Gavarnie, a natu-ral mountain amphitheater. Millions of others venture here to the healing holy waters of Lourdes.

3 The Basque Coast.
Fine-sand beaches in tawny yellows and red, brightly painted fishing boats, and vibrant villages keep your eyes busy with their competing palettes on the lush Basque Coast, where world-class chefs make the most of local produce. Bayonne as the graceful French provincial city, Biarritz as the imperial beach domain, and St-Jean-de-Luz as the colorful fishing port all play their parts to perfection along this southwestern coastline backed by the soft green pastures of the Basque hills.

GETTING ORIENTED

The most southwestern corner of France's sprawling "Southwest," the rolling hills of the French Basque provinces stretch from the Atlantic beaches of glittering Biarritz to the first Pyrenean heights: the hills and highlands of Gascony around the city of Pau. These are mere stepping-stones compared to the peaks of the Hautes-Pyrénées, which lie to the east and sit in the center of the towering barrier historically separating the Iberian Peninsula from continental Europe.

15

0   10 mi
0   10 km

Updated
by Avery
Sumner

Several years back, a mayor in the province of Soule welcomed a group of travelers with the following announcements: the Basque Country is the most beautiful place in the world; the Basque people are very likely direct descendants of Adam and Eve via the lost city of Atlantis; his own ancestors fought in the Crusades; and Christopher Columbus was almost certainly a Basque. There, in brief, was a composite picture of the pride, dignity, and humor of the Basques.

And if Columbus was not a Basque (a claim very much in doubt), at least historians know that whalers from the regional village of St-Jean-de-Luz sailed as far as America in their three-mast ships, and that Juan Sebastián Elkano, from the Spanish Basque village of Getaria, commanded the completion of Magellan's voyage around the world after Magellan's 1521 death in the Philippines. The distinctive culture—from berets and pelota matches to Basque cooking—of this little "country" has cast its spell over the corners of the Earth.

The most popular gateway to the entire region is Biarritz, the "king" of France's Atlantic coast resorts, whose refinements once attracted the crowned heads of Europe. It was Empress Eugénie who gave Biarritz its coming-out party, transforming it, in the era of Napoléon III, from a simple bourgeois town into an international glitterati favorite. Today, after a round of sightseeing, you can still enjoy the Second Empire trimmings from a perch at the roulette table in the town's casino. Then work on your suntan at Biarritz's famous beach or, a few miles away, really bask under the Basque sun at the picturesque port of St-Jean-de-Luz. As for the entire Pays Basque (Basque Country), it's happily compact: the ocher sands along the Bay of Biscay are less than an hour from the emerald hills of St-Jean-Pied-de-Port in the Basque Pyrénées.

Heading eastward toward the towering peaks of the central Pyrenean cordillera lies the Béarn region, with its splendid capital city of Pau, while northward lies a must-detour for lovers of the good life: Eugénie-les-Bains, where you can savor every morsel of a Michel Guérard feast at one (or all!) of his magnificently stylish restaurants and hotels. East through the Aubisque Pass, at the Béarn's eastern limit, is the heart of the Hautes-Pyrénées, where the mountains of Vignemale and Balaïtous compete with the Cirque de Gavarnie, the world's most spectacular natural amphitheater, centered around a 1,400-foot waterfall. Whether you finish up with a vertiginous Pyrenean hike or choose to pay your respects to the religious shrine at Lourdes, this region will lift your spirits.

PLANNER

WHEN TO GO

The Basque Country is known for its wet climate, but when the skies clear the hillsides are so green and the air so clean that the weather gods are immediately forgiven. Late fall and winter are generally rainier than early autumn or late spring. The Pyrenean heights such as Brèche de Roland and Gavarnie, on the other hand, may only be approached safely in midsummer. Treacherous ice and snow plaques can be present even in mid-June, and summer blizzards remain a risk. Climate change may be shrinking glaciers and extending the safety period in the high Pyrénées, but freak conditions—the reverse side of the same coin—may be creating even more unpredictable and dangerous weather patterns. Beach weather is from May through September, and sometimes lasts until mid-October's *été de la Saint-Martin* (Indian summer). Skiing conditions are reliable from December through March and, on occasion, into April.

PLANNING YOUR TIME

Traveling west to east, with the sun behind you as the shadows lengthen, is the best way to approach this part of the Pyrénées. Bayonne is the natural starting point, at the mouth of the Atlantic Pyrenean watershed, with the Basque Museum as an instructive primer for the culture of the villages you are about to go through. Biarritz and St-Jean-de-Luz offer opportunities for beach time and glamour. The picturesque villages of Sare and Ainhoa guide you into the mountains and valleys, threaded by rivers flowing into the Nive. St-Jean-Pied-de-Port is a Pyrenean hub from which Eugénie-les-Bains, Sauveterre de Béarn, and Navarrenx are short detours before continuing east to Pau, the Hautes-Pyrénées, and their crowning glory, Gavarnie.

Wherever you head, take your time: this region's proximity to Spain comes to life in its architecture, in the expressive Midi accent, which turns the word *demain* (tomorrow) into "demaing," and the slow-paced lifestyle.

GETTING HERE AND AROUND

A car is best for getting around the Basque Coast and the Pyrénées. Train and bus connections will get you from Bayonne to Biarritz and Hendaye and up to St-Jean-Pied-de-Port easily. Unfortunately, less pivotal destinations will entail much waiting and loss of valuable time. The mountain roads are good, albeit slow—60 kph–70 kph (37 mph–43 mph) on average. But the A64 highway from Bayonne to Pau is fast and has spectacular views of the Pyrénées. For walking the hills or long-distance hikes across the GR10 or the Haute Randonnée Pyrénéenne along the crest of the cordillera, bus and trains such as the SNCF Bayonne to St-Jean-Pied-de-Port connection are the first step. They will then drop you off and pick you up at trailheads such as the one at Bidarrai's Pont d'Enfer. Bus lines from St-Jean-Pied-de-Port will take you east to Larrau, Mauléon, and Pau. From Pau there are SNCF connections up into the Pyrénées, with subsequent SNCF buses to points such as Gavarnie.

BUS TRAVEL

Various private bus concerns—**Chronoplus** (serving the Bayonne–Anglet–Biarritz metropolitan areas; ☎ *05–59–59 –04–61* ⊕ *www. chronoplus.eu*), **ATCRB** (up and down the coast and inland to many Basque towns, such as Bayonne, Biarritz, St-Jean-de-Luz, and Bidart), and **R.D.T.L** (the departmental transportation system for Landes)—service the region. Where they don't go, the trusty **SNCF** national bus lines occasionally do (☎ *36–35 [€0.34 per min]* ⊕ *www.voyages-sncf. com*). Other bus companies also wind through the area. **T.P.R. Buses**, for instance, head from Pau to Lourdes (1 hr, 15 mins; €6; six times a day). From Lourdes, SNCF-run TER buses go to Cauterets and to Luz-St-Sauveur. The direct Maligne bus leaves twice daily from Lourdes for the 55-km (33-mile), one hour and 40 minute (€3) trip up to Gavarnie. **Le Basque Bondissant** (The Bouncing Basque) buses leave from the train station in St-Jean-de-Luz and go to upland villages such as Sare and Hasparren. Buses to Ainhoa leave from Bayonne at noon and 6 pm for the 55-km (33-mile), 55 minute (€3) run up to one of France's prettiest villages. Beware of peak-hour traffic on roads in summer, which can mean both delays and fewer seats on buses. Check in with the local tourist office for schedules or ask your hotel concierge for the best advice.

Bus Information ATCRB ☎ *09–70–80–90–74*. **Le Basque Bondissant** ✉ *St-Jean-de-Luz* ☎ *05–59–26–25–87* ⊕ *www.basque-bondissant.com*. **R.D.T.L. Buses** ✉ *Pl. Pereire, Bayonne* ☎ *05–59–55–17–59* ⊕ *www.rdtl.fr*. **T.P.R Buses** ✉ *Lons* ☎ *05–59–27–45–98* ⊕ *www.transports-palois-reunis-lons.fr*.

CAR TRAVEL

A64 connects Pau and Bayonne in less than an hour, and A63 runs up and down the Atlantic coast. N134-E7 connects Bordeaux, Pau, Oloron-Ste-Marie, and Spain via the Col de Somport and Jaca. The D918 from Saint-Jean-de-Luz through Cambo and along the Nive River to St-Jean-Pied-de-Port is a pretty drive, continuing on (as D933, D918, D919, and N134-E7) through the Béarn country to Oloron-Ste-Marie and Pau. Roads are occasionally slow and tortuous in the more mountainous areas, but valley and riverside roads are generally quite smooth and fast. D132, which goes between Arette and Pierre-St-Martin, can be snowed in between mid-November and mid-May. This can also be the case for N134 through the Vallée d'Aspe and the Col de Somport into Spain.

TRAIN TRAVEL

High-speed TGV trains link Paris to Bayonne (4 hrs, 30 mins) and Biarritz (5 hrs, 15 mins). Biarritz's La Négresse station has trains connecting with Bayonne, Bordeaux, St-Jean-de-Luz, and many other places.

Bayonne and Toulouse are connected by local SNCF trains via Pau, Tarbes, and Lourdes. From Bayonne, trains connect with many destinations, including St-Jean-de-Luz, St-Jean-Pied-de-Port, Toulouse, Bordeaux, and Pau. Local trains also go from Bayonne into the Atlantic Pyrénées, a slow but picturesque trip. A local train runs along the Nive from Bayonne to St-Jean-Pied-de-Port. Hendaye is connected to Bayonne and to San Sebastián via the famous *topo* (mole) train, so called for the number of tunnels it passes through.

Train Information Gare Ville Bayonne ⊠ *Quartier St-Esprit, Bayonne* ☎ *36–35* ⊕ *www.gares-en-mouvement.com.* **Gare Ville Biarritz La Négresse** ⊠ *18 allée Moura, Biarritz* ☎ *36–35* ⊕ *www.gares-en-mouvement.com.* **SNCF** ☎ *36–35 [€0.34 per min]* ⊕ *www.voyages-sncf.com.* **TGV** ⊕ *www.tgv.com.*

RESTAURANTS

Dining in the regions of the Basque Country is invariably a feast, whether it's seafood, local lamb, or the famous migratory *palombes* (wood pigeons). Dishes to keep in mind include *ttoro* (hake stew), *pipérade* (tomatoes and green peppers cooked in olive oil, and often scrambled eggs), *bakalao al pil-pil* (cod cooked in oil "al pil-pil"—the bubbling sound the fish makes as it creates its own sauce), *marmitako* (tuna and potato stew), and *zikiro* (roast lamb). Home of the eponymous *sauce béarnaise,* Béarn is also famous for its *garbure,* a thick vegetable soup with *confit de canard* (preserved duck) and *fèves* (broad beans).

Civets (stews) made with *isard* (wild goat) or wild boar are other specialties. La Bigorre and the Hautes-Pyrénées are equally dedicated to garbure, though they may call their version *soupe paysanne bigourdane* (Bigorran peasant soup) to distinguish it from that of their neighbors. The Basque Coast's traditional fresh seafood is unsurpassable every day of the week except Monday, the fleet having stayed in port on Sunday. The inland Basque Country and upland Béarn are famous for game in fall and winter and lamb in spring. In the Hautes-Pyrénées, the higher altitude makes power dining attractive and thick bean soups and wild-boar stews come into their own.

Prices in the reviews are the average cost of a main course at dinner or, if dinner is not served, at lunch.

HOTELS

From palatial beachside splendor in Biarritz to simple mountain auberges in the Basque country to Pyrenean refuges in the Hautes-Pyrénées, the gamut of lodging in southwest France is conveniently broad. Be sure to book summertime lodging on the Basque Coast well in advance, particularly for August. In the Hautes-Pyrénées, only Gavarnie during its third-week-of-July music festival presents a potential booking problem.

Prices in the reviews are the lowest cost of a standard double room in high season.

VISITOR INFORMATION

The Atlantic and Hautes Pyrénées region has three main tourist offices. For Biarritz and France's Big Sur in the southwest corner of the country, contact the Comité Régional du Tourisme d'Aquitaine. For Pau and

15

the Basque and Béarnaise Pyrénées, contact the Comité Départemental du Tourisme de Béarn Pays Basque (Délégation Béarn) in Pau. For Gavarnie and the Hautes Pyrénées contact the Hautes Pyrénées Tourist Office in Tarbes. ⇨ *For specific town tourist offices, see the town entries in this chapter.*

Contacts **Comité Départemental du Tourisme de Béarn Pays Basque** ✉ *Délégation Béarn, 22 ter, rue J.J. de Monaix, Pau* ☎ *05–59–30–01–30* ⊕ *www. tourisme64.com.* **Comité Régional du Tourisme d'Aquitaine** ✉ *4/5 pl. Jean Jaurès, Bordeaux–Cedex* ☎ *05–56–01–70–00* ⊕ *www.tourisme-aquitaine.fr.* **Hautes Pyrénées Tourisme** ✉ *11 rue Gaston Manent, BP 9502, Tarbes Cedex 9* ☎ *05–62–56–70–65* ⊕ *www.tourism-hautes-pyrenees.com.*

TOUR OPTIONS

In Biarritz, Passion Côte Basque organizes tours of Bayonne, Biarritz, the Basque Coast, and the Basque Pyrénées. The Bayonne tourist office gives guided tours of the city. La Guild du Tourisme des Pyrénées-Atlantiques offers information on and organizes tours of the Basque Country and the Pyrénées. Guides Culturels Pyrénéens, in Tarbes, arranges many tours, including explorations themed around subjects such as cave painting, art and architecture, Basque sports, hiking, and horseback riding.

Contacts **Bayonne tourist office** ☎ *08–20–42–64–64.* **Guides Culturels Pyrénéens** ☎ *05–62–44–15–44* ⊕ *www.guides-culturels-pyreneens.com.* **La Guild du Tourisme des Pyrénées-Atlantiques** ☎ *05–59–46–37–05.* **Passion Côte Basque** ✉ *33 rue de Madrid, Biarritz* ☎ *05–59–24–36–05* ⊕ *www.passioncote-basque.com.*

THE BASQUE COAST

La Côte Basque—a world unto itself with its own language, sports, and folklore—occupies France's southwest corner along the Spanish border. Inland, the area is laced with rivers: the Bidasoa River border with Spain marks the southern edge of the region, and the Adour River, on its northern edge, separates the Basque Country from the neighboring Les Landes. The Nive River flows through the heart of the verdant Basque littoral to join the Adour at Bayonne, and the smaller Nivelle River flows into the Bay of Biscay at St-Jean-de-Luz. Bayonne, Biarritz, and St-Jean-de-Luz are the main towns along the coast, all less than 40 km (25 miles) from the first peak of the Pyrénées.

BAYONNE

48 km (30 miles) southwest of Dax; 184 km (114 miles) south of Bordeaux; 295 km (183 miles) west of Toulouse.

At the confluence of the Adour and Nive rivers, Bayonne—France's most indelibly Basque city—was a Roman fort, or *castrum*, in the 4th century and for 300 years (1151–1451) a British colony. The city gave its name to the bayonet blade (from the French *baïonnette*), invented here in the 17th century, but today's Bayonne is more famous for its

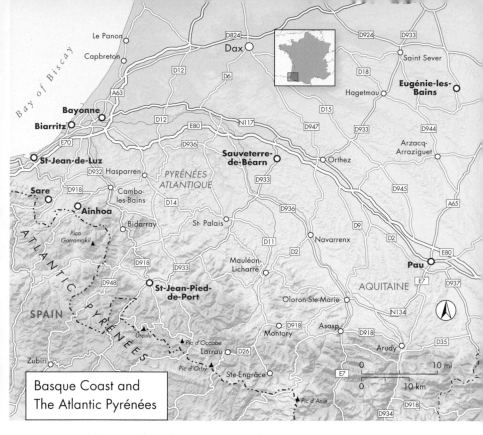

Basque Coast and
The Atlantic Pyrénées

ham (*jambon de Bayonne*) and for the annual Basque pelota world championships held in September.

GETTING HERE

SNCF connects Bayonne with Paris (4 hrs, 30 mins; €65) with four TGV trains daily. Train connections from Bayonne include St-Jean-de-Luz (22 mins, €5), St-Jean-Pied-de-Port (1 hr, 18 mins; €9.50), Toulouse (3 hrs, 21 mins; €43.50), Bordeaux (1 hr, 39 mins; €24.50), and Pau (1 hr, 7 mins; €17); trains make the short jaunt to Biarritz frequently in summer; in winter, take a bus. The Chronoplus bus network (☎ 05–59–59 –04– 61 ⊕ *www.chronoplus.eu*) connects Bayonne with towns on the French Basque Coast, notably Biarritz (15 mins, €1) and Anglet (20 mins, €1).

Visitor Information Bayonne Tourist Office ✉ *Pl. des Basques* ☎ *08–20–42– 64–64* ⊕ *www.bayonne-tourisme.com.*

EXPLORING

A small port city, Bayonne remains the capital of the Pays Basque. Even though its port is spread out along the Adour estuary some 5 km (3 miles) inland from the sea, the two rivers and five bridges lend it a definite maritime feel. The houses fronting the quay, the intimate place Pasteur, the Château-Vieux, the elegant 18th-century homes along rue des Prébendés, the 17th-century ramparts, and the cathedral are some of the town's not-to-be-missed sights. Les Halles market in the place des Halles, on the left bank of the Nive, is also a must-visit.

Cathédrale. The Cathédrale (called both Ste-Marie and Notre-Dame) was built mainly in the 13th century and is one of France's southernmost examples of Gothic architecture. Its 13th- to 14th-century cloisters are among its best features. ✉ *Pl. de la Cathédrale* ☎ *05–59–59–17–82* 🌐 *www.cathedrale-bayonne.fr* 🎫 *Free* 🕒 *Daily 7–12:30 and 3–7.*

Musée Basque. The handsomely designed and appointed Musée Basque on the right bank of the Nive offers an ethnographic history of the Basque Country and culture. ✉ *37 quai des Corsaires* ☎ *05–59–59–08–98* 🌐 *www.museebasque.com* 🎫 *€6.50; free Wed. evenings 6:30–9:30* 🕒 *July and Aug., daily 10–6:30;; Sept.–June, Tues.–Sun. 10–6:30.*

WHERE TO EAT AND STAY

For expanded hotel reviews, visit Fodors.com.

$$ BISTRO 🍴 **Bayonnais.** Next to the Musée Basque, with a dining terrace over the river Nive just short of its confluence with the Adour, this unassuming and unpretentious local favorite serves honest Basque cuisine in a traditional setting. The *agneau de lait* (suckling lamb) and the *chipirons en persillade* (cuttlefish in chopped parsley and garlic) are classics. [$] *Average main: €18* ✉ *38 quai des Corsaires* ☎ *05–59–25–61–19* 🕒 *Closed Sun., Sun. and Mon Sept.–mid-July., 2 wks in July, and 2 wks in Dec.*

$$$ FRENCH 🍴 **L'Auberge du Cheval Blanc.** Run by the Tellechea family since 1715, this former stagecoach inn in the Petit Bayonne quarter serves a combination of *cuisine du terroir* (home-style regional cooking) and original recipes in contemporary surroundings. Jean-Claude Tellechea showcases fresh fish as well as upland specialties from the Basque hills, sometimes joining the two in dishes such as the *merlu rôti aux oignons et jus de volaille* (hake roasted in onions with essence of poultry). ■ **TIP→ The Irouléguy wines offer the best value on the wine list. Be sure to be there on time: lunch ends at 1:30.** [$] *Average main: €30* ✉ *68 rue Bourgneuf* ☎ *05–59–59–01–33* 🌐 *www.cheval-blanc-bayonne.com* 🕒 *Closed Mon., 1 wk in Nov., 2 wks in Feb. or Mar., and 1st wk in July. No lunch Sat., no dinner Sun.*

$$ HOTEL 🏨 **Le Grand Hôtel.** Just down the street from the Château-Vieux, this central spot has quirky but comfortable rooms with an Old World feel, in the heart of a lovely provincial town. **Pros:** location; traditional French vibe; relaxed spirit. **Cons:** a little too relaxed; worn around the edges; hefty fees for everything, from parking to breakfast. [$] *Rooms from: €120* ✉ *21 rue Thiers* ☎ *05–59–59–62–00* 🌐 *www.bw-legrandhotel.com* 🛏 *57 rooms.*

BIARRITZ

8 km (5 miles) south of Bayonne; 190 km (118 miles) southwest of Bordeaux; 50 km (31 miles) north of San Sebastián, Spain; 115 km (69 miles) west of Pau.

Fodor's Choice ★ Biarritz may no longer lay claim to the title "the resort of kings and the king of resorts"; however, today there's no shortage of deluxe hotel rooms or bow-tied gamblers ambling over to the casino. The old, down-to-earth charm of the former fishing village has been thoroughly

Continued on page 771

BASQUE SPOKEN HERE

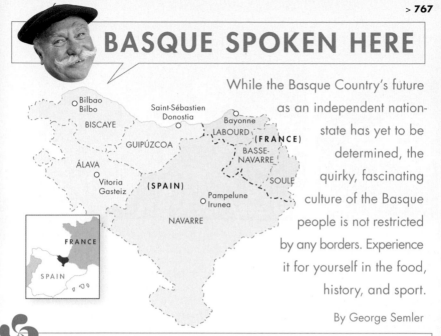

While the Basque Country's future as an independent nation-state has yet to be determined, the quirky, fascinating culture of the Basque people is not restricted by any borders. Experience it for yourself in the food, history, and sport.

By George Semler

Basque solar cross

The cultural footprints of this tiny corner of Europe, which straddle the Atlantic end of the border between France and Spain, have already touched down all over the globe. The sport of jai-alai has come to America. International magazines give an ecstatic thumbs-up to Basque cooking. Historians are pointing to Basque fishermen as the true discoverers of North America. And bestsellers, not without irony, proclaim *The Basque History of the World*. As in the ancient 4 + 3 = 1 graffiti equation, the three French (Labourd, Basse Navarre, and Soule) and the four Spanish (Guipúzcoa, Vizcaya, Alava, and Navarra) Basque provinces add up to a single people with a shared history. Although nationless, Basques have been Basques since Paleolithic times.

Stretching across the Pyrénées from Bayonne in France to Bilbao in Spain, the New Hampshire-sized Basque region retains a distinct culture, neither expressly French nor Spanish,

fiercely guarded by its three million inhabitants. Fables stubbornly connect them with Adam and Eve, Noah's Ark, and the lost city of Atlantis, but a leading genealogical theory points to common bloodlines with the Celts. The most tenable theory is that the Basques are descended from aboriginal Iberian peoples who successfully defended their unique cultural identity from the influences of Roman and Moorish domination.

It was only in 1876 that Sabino Arana—a virulent anti-Spanish fanatic—proposed the ideal of a "pure" Basque independent state. That dream was crushed by Franco's dictatorial reign (1939–75, during which many Spanish Basques emigrated to France) and was immortalized in Pablo Picasso's *Guernica*. This famous painting, which depicts the catastrophic Nazi bombing of the Basque town of Gernika stands not only as a searing indictment of all wars but as a reminder of history's brutal assault upon Basque identity.

"THE BEST FOOD YOU'VE NEVER HEARD OF"

(left) Zurrukutuna, garlic soup with codfish. (right) Preparing canapes.

So says *Food & Wine* magazine. It's time to get filled in.

An old saying has it that every soccer team needs a Basque goaltender and every restaurant a Basque chef. Traditional Basque cuisine combines the fresh fish of the Atlantic and upland vegetables, beef, and lamb with a love of sauces that is rare south of the Pyrénées. Today, the *nueva cocina vasca* (new Basque cooking) movement has made Basque food less rustic and much more nouvelle. And now that pintxos (the Basque equivalent of tapas) have become the rage from Barcelona to New York City, Basque cuisine is being championed by foodies everywhere. Even superchef Michel Guérard up in Eugénie-les-Bains has, though not himself a Basque, influenced and been influenced by the master cookery of the Pays Basque.

WHO'S THE BEST CHEF?

Basques are so naturally competitive that meals often turn into comparative rants over who is better: Basque chefs based in France or in Spain. Some vote for Bayonne's Jean-Claude Tellechea (his L'Auberge du Cheval Blanc is famed for groundbreaking surf-and-turf dishes like hake roasted in onions with essence of poultry) or St-Jean-Pied-de-Port's Firmin Arrambide (based at his elegant Les Pyrénées inn). Others prefer the postmodern lobster salads found over the border in San Sebastián and Bilbao, created by master chefs Juan Mari Arzak, Pedro Subijana, and Martin Berasategui, with wunderkind Andoni Aduriz and the Arbelaitz family nipping at their culinary heels.

SIX GREAT DISHES

Angulas. Baby eels, cooked in olive oil and garlic with a few slices of guindilla pepper.

Bacalao al pil-pil. Cod cooked at a low temperature in an emulsion of olive oil and fish juices, which makes a unique pinging sound as it sizzles.

Besugo. Sea bream, or besugo, is so revered that it is a traditional Christmas dish. Enjoy it with sagardo, the signature Basque apple cider.

Marmitako. This tuna stew with potatoes and pimientos is a satisfying winter favorite.

Ttoro. Typical of Labourd fishing villages such as St-Jean-de-Luz, this peppery Basque bouillabaisse is known as *sopa de pescado* (fish soup) south of the French border.

Txuleta de buey. The signature Basque meat is ox steaks marinated in parsley and garlic and cooked over coals.

BASQUE SPORTS: JAI-ALAI TO OXCART-LIFTING

Sports are core to Basque society, and virtually no one is immune to the Basque passion for competing, betting, and playing.

Over the centuries, the rugged physical environment of the Basque hills and the rough Cantabrian sea traditionally made physical prowess and bravery valued attributes. Since Basque mythology often involved feats of strength, it's easy to see why today's Basques are such rabid sports fans.

PELOTA

A Basque village without a frontón (pelota court) is as unimaginable as an American town without a baseball diamond. "The fastest game in the world," pelota is called *jai-alai* in Basque (and translated officially as "merry festival"). With rubber balls flung from hooked wicker gloves at speeds up to 150 mph—the impact of the ball is like a machine-gun bullet—jai-alai is mesmerizing. It is played on a three-walled court 175 feet long and 56 feet wide with 40-foot side walls.

Whether singles or doubles, the object is to angle the ball along or off of the side wall so that it cannot be returned. Betting is very much part of pelota and courtside wagers are brokered by bet makers as play proceeds. While pelota is the word for "ball," it also refers to the game. There was even a recent movie in Spain entitled *La Pelota Vasca*, used metaphorically to refer to the greater "ball game" of life and death.

HERRIKIROLAK

Herrikirolak (rural sports) are based on farming and seafaring. Stone lifters (*harrijasotzaileak* in Euskera) heft weights up to 700 pounds. *Aizkolari* (axe men) chop wood in various contests, *Gizon proba* (man trial) pits three-man teams moving weighted sleds; while *estropadak* are whaleboat rowers who compete in spectacular regattas (culminating in the September competition off La Concha beach in San Sebastián). *Sokatira* is tug of war, and *segalariak* is a scything competition. Other events include oxcart-lifting, milk-can carrying, and ram fights.

SOCCER

When it comes to soccer, Basque goaltenders have developed special fame in Spain, where Bilbao's Athletic Club and San Sebastián's Real Sociedad have won national championships with budgets far inferior to those of Real Madrid or FC Barcelona. Across the border, Bayonne's rugby team is a force in the French national competition; the French Basque capital is also home to the annual French pelota championship.

PARLEZ-VOUS EUSKERA?

Although the Basque people speak French north of the border and Spanish south of the border, they consider Euskera their first language and identify themselves as the *Euskaldunak* (the "Basque speakers"). Euskera remains one of the great enigmas of linguistic scholarship. Theories connect it with everything from Sanskrit to Japanese to Finnish.

What is certain is where Euskera did not come from, namely the Indo-European family of languages that includes the Germanic, Italic, and Hellenic language groups.

Currently used by about a million people in northern Spain and southwestern France, Euskera sounds like a consonant-ridden version of Spanish, with its five pure vowels, rolled "r," and palatal "n" and "l." Basque has survived two millennia of cultural and political pressure and is the only remaining language of those spoken in southwestern Europe before the Roman conquest.

The Euskaldunak celebrate their heritage during a Basque folk dancing festival.

A BASQUE GLOSSARY

Aurresku: The high-kicking *espata danza* or sword dance typically performed on the day of Corpus Christi in the Spanish Basque Country.

Akelarre: A gathering of witches that provoked witch trials in the Pyrénées. Even today it is believed that *jentilak* (magic elves) inhabit the woods and the Olentzaro (the evil Basque Santa Claus) comes down chimneys to wreak havoc—a fire is kept burning to keep him out.

Boina: The Basque beret or *txapela,* thought to have developed as the perfect protection from the siri-miri, the perennial "Scotch mist" that soaks the moist Basque Country.

Eguzki: The sun worship was at the center of the pagan religion that, in the Basque Country, gave way only slowly to Christianity. The Basque solar cross is typically carved into the east-facing facades of ancient *caserios* or farmhouses.

Espadrilles: Rope-soled canvas Basque shoes, also claimed by the Catalans, developed in the Pyrénées and traditionally attached by laces or ribbons wrapped up the ankle.

Etxekoandre: The woman who commands all matters spiritual, culinary, and practical in a traditional Basque farmhouse. Basque matriarchal inheritance laws remain key.

Fueros: Special Basque rights and laws (including exemption from serving in the army except to defend the Basque Country) originally conceded by the ancient Romans and abolished at the end of the Carlist Wars in 1876 after centuries of Castilian kings had sworn to protect Basque rights at the Tree of Guernika.

 Ikurriña: The Basque flag, designed by the founder of Basque nationalism, Sabino Arana, composed of green and white crosses over a red background and said to have been based on the British Union Jack.

Lauburu: Resembling a four-leaf clover, lau (four) buru (head) is the Basque symbol.

Twenty: Basques favor counting in units of twenty (*veinte duros*—20 nickels—is a common way of saying a hundred pesetas, for example).

Txakolí: A slightly fizzy young wine made from grapes grown around the Bay of Biscay, this fresh, acidic brew happily accompanies tapas and fish.

trumped by Biarritz's glitzy Second Empire 19th-century aura, and you won't find the bathing beauties and high rollers here complaining. Though nowhere near as drop-dead stylish as it once was, the town is making a comeback as a swank surfing capital with its new casino and convention center.

GETTING HERE AND AROUND

TGV trains connect Paris and Biarritz (5 hrs, 15 mins; €88) six times daily. Biarritz's La Négresse train station has rail connections with St-Jean-de-Luz (11 mins, €3.25), Bordeaux (1 hr, 50 mins; €25), and many other places, including San Sebastián, Spain via Hendaye (50 mins, €7.50). Up to 10 trains also arrive from Bayonne daily (10 mins, €3). The station is 3 km (2 miles) southeast of the city core, so catch bus No. 2 to reach the centrally located Hôtel de Ville (town hall), near the main beach. From Bayonne airport, bus No. 6 runs hourly to the Biarritz city center from 6 am to 7 pm. Most buses to Bayonne and Anglet run from the Chronoplus (formerly STAB) bus booth (rue Louis Barthous), near the main tourist office. Tickets cost €1 for a single ride, €8 for a 10-ride card. The ATCRB bus has regular service to other Basque towns, including St-Jean-de-Luz.

Visitor Information Biarritz Tourist Office ⊠ *1 sq. d'Ixelles* ☎ *05–59–22–37–10* ⊕ *www.biarritz.fr.*

EXPLORING

Once a favorite resort of Charlie Chaplin, Coco Chanel, and exiled Russian royals, Biarritz first rose to prominence when rich and royal Carlist exiles from Spain set up shop here in 1838. Unable to visit San Sebastián—just across the border on the Basque Coast—they sought a summer watering spot as close as possible to their old stomping ground. Among the exiles was Eugénie de Montijo, destined to become empress of France. As a child, she vacationed here with her family, fell in love with the place, and then set about building her own palace once she married Napoléon III. During the 14 summers she spent here, half the crowned heads of Europe (including Queen Victoria and Edward VII) were guests in Eugénie's villa: a gigantic wedding-cake edifice, now the **Hôtel du Palais,** on the main sea promenade of town, the **quai de la Grande Plage,** where the fashionable set used to stroll in Worth gowns and picture hats. Whether you consider Napoléon III's bombastic architectural legacies an eyesore or an eyeful, they at least have the courage of their convictions.

If you want to rediscover yesteryear Biarritz, start by exploring the narrow streets around the cozy 16th-century church of **St-Martin.** Adjacent to the Grand Plage are the set pieces of the Hôtel du Palais and the **Église Orthodoxe Russe,** a Byzantine-style church built by the White Russian community that considered Biarritz their 19th-century Yalta-by-the-Atlantic. The duchesses often repaired to the terraced restaurants of the festive **place Ste-Eugénie,** still considered the social center of town. A lorgnette view away is the harbor of the **Port des Pêcheurs** (Fishing Port), which provides a tantalizing glimpse of the Biarritz of old. Biarritz's beaches attract crowds—particularly the fine, sandy beaches of **La Grande Plage** and the neighboring **plage Miramar,** both set amid craggy natural beauty. A walk along the beach promenades gives a view of the foaming breakers that beat constantly upon the sands, giving the name Côte d'Argent (Silver Coast) to the length of this part of the French Basque Coast.

La Chapelle Impériale. If you wish to pay your respects to the Empress Eugénie, visit La Chapelle Impériale, which she had built in 1864 to venerate a figure of a Mexican Black Virgin from Guadalupe (and perhaps to expiate her sins for furthering her husband's tragic folly of putting Emperor Maximilian and Empress Carlotta on the "throne" of Mexico). The style is a charming hybrid of Roman-Byzantine and Hispano-Mauresque. ✉ *Rue Pellot* ☎ *05–59–22–37–10* 🕒 *July and Aug., Tues., Thurs., and Sat. 3–7; call for updated hrs Sept.–June.*

WHERE TO EAT AND STAY

For expanded hotel reviews, visit Fodors.com.

$$ SEAFOOD 🍴 **Chez Albert.** In summer, it's nearly impossible to find a place on the terrace of this popular, easygoing seafood restaurant. Views of the port and salty harborside aromas make the hearty fish and seafood offerings all the more irresistible. But beware, it is definitely on the tourist radar. [$] *Average main: €22* ✉ *Port des Pêcheurs s/n* ☎ *05–59–24–43–84* 🌐 *www.chezalbert.fr* 🕒 *Closed Nov. 28–Dec. 12, Jan. 4–Feb. 9, and Wed. except in July and Aug.*

$$$ FRENCH 🍴 **L'Atelier.** Alexandre Bousquet and Isabelle Caulier have been a big success since moving to Biarritz from Aveyron. Their hot restaurant in the Quartier Saint-Charles, a few steps from the Grande Plage, is the *dernier cri* in a town surrounded by, but not known for, great cuisine. In an artful *cadre* (scene) expect artful plates like tuna *tartare et croustillant* (raw and crunchy) in a mustard sauce, as well as specialties like *pigeonneau* (wood pigeon). The wine list includes selections from Bordeaux and Spain's Ribera de Duero. ■ **TIP→ The lunch menu is one of the best bargains in Biarritz—but culinary experiment is the catchword here, so traditionalists may prefer the crêpes and pizza elsewhere.** [$] *Average main: €28* ✉ *18 rue Bergerie* ☎ *05–59–22–09–37* 🌐 *www.latelierbiarritz.com* 🕒 *Closed 3 wks in Jan. and Mon., except in July and Aug. No lunch Sat., no dinner Sun.*

$$$$ HOTEL 🏨 **Château de Brindos.** Take Jazz Age glamour, Renaissance stonework, and the most luxe of guest rooms, add fine dining, and you have this Pays Basque Xanadu—a large, rambling, white-stone manor topped with a Spanish belvedere tower set 4 km (2½ miles) east of Biarritz in Anglet. **Pros:** flawless performance by staff; excellent dining; ultimate comfort. **Cons:** fitness facilities limited; addictively grande luxe; difficult to leave. [$] *Rooms from: €350* ✉ *1 allée du Château* ☎ *05–59–23–89–80* 🌐 *www.chateaudebrindos.com* 🛏 *24 rooms, 7 suites* 🕒 *Closed 2 wks in Feb./Mar.*

$$$$ HOTEL 🏨 **Hôtel du Palais.** Set on the beach, this majestic, colonnaded redbrick hotel with an immense driveway, lawns, and a grand semicircular dining room, still exudes an opulent, aristocratic air, no doubt imparted by Empress Eugénie when she built it in 1855 as her Biarritz palace. **Pros:** historic grounds; gastronomical nirvana; perfect location. **Cons:** staff obsessed with hotel rules; slightly stuffy; magisterially expensive.

[$] *Rooms from: €500* ✉ *1 av. de l'Impératrice* ☎ *05–59–41–64–00* 🌐 *www.hotel-du-palais.com* 🛏 *122 rooms, 30 suites.*

$ HOTEL 🏨 **Maïtagaria.** This typical Basque town house 400 yards from the beach is a handy and comfortable family operation that makes you feel more like a guest in a private home than a hotel client. **Pros:** value; location; intimacy; leafy garden. **Cons:** somewhat cramped quarters; limited soundproofing (and thus privacy). [$] *Rooms from: €95* ✉ *34 av. Carnot* ☎ *05–59–24–26–65* 🌐 *www.hotel-maitagaria.com* 🛏 *15 rooms* 🕒 *Closed Dec. 1–15.*

$$ HOTEL 🏨 **Windsor.** Built in the 1920s, close to the casino, and overlooking the Grand Plage beach, this hotel has guest rooms that are modern and spiffy: those called Classique are done in cheery oranges and reds, while those named Harmonie will make fans of minimal grays and off-whites happy. **Pros:** central beachfront location; sea views if you can get them; excellent restaurant. **Cons:** '80s decor; sea views cost double. [$] *Rooms from: €140* ✉ *19 bd. du Général-de-Gaulle* ☎ *05–59–24–08–52* 🌐 *www.hotelwindsorbiarritz.com* 🛏 *48 rooms.*

15

NIGHTLIFE AND THE ARTS

Casino de Biarritz. At the Casino de Biarritz you can play the slots or blackjack, or just channel James Bond and chill. ✉ *1 av. Edouard-VII* ☎ *05–59–22–77–77* 🌐 *www.lucienbarriere.com* 🕒 *Sun.–Fri. 8 pm–3 am, Sat. 8 pm–4 am.*

L'Arena Café. L'Arena Café, in a pretty spot at the edge of the beach, serves fine dinners and morphs into a late-night dance club around 11 pm. ✉ *Esplanade du Port Vieux* ☎ *05–59–24–88–98* 🌐 *www.arenacafe-biarritz.com.*

Le Carré Coast. Le Carré Coast serves cocktails and plays soul, jazz, and house in a glamorous design setting close to the surf. ✉ *24 av. Édouard-VII* ☎ *05–59–24–64–64* 🌐 *www.lecarrecoast.com.*

Le Playboy. Le Playboy fills with the surfing crowd in season. ✉ *15 Pl. Georges Clémenceau* ☎ *05–59–24–38–46.*

Le Temps d'Aimer. In September the three-week Le Temps d'Aimer festival presents dance performances, from classical to hip-hop, in a range of venues throughout the city. They're often at the Théâtre Gare du Midi, a renovated railway station. Troupes such as the Ballets Biarritz, Les Ballets de Monte-Carlo, and leading *étoiles* from other companies take to the stage in an ambitious schedule of events, with admission generally costing about €20. 🌐 *www.letempsdaimer.com.*

Newquay. Newquay is a midtown Irish pub popular with surfers. ✉ *20 pl. Georges Clemenceau* ☎ *05–59–22–19–90.*

SPORTS AND THE OUTDOORS

Golf de Biarritz. Golf de Biarritz has an 18-hole, par-69 course, with green fees beginning at €72 in the height of the summer season. ✉ *2 av. Edith-Cavell* ☎ *05–59–03–71–80* 🌐 *www.golfbiarritz.com.*

Parc des Sports d'Aguilera. This is the fiefdom of the champion rugby club Biarritz Olympique, winner of the 2012 European Challenge. Call for information on scheduled matches. ☎ *05–59–43–71–38* 🌐 *www.bo-pb.com.*

Le Surfing

The area around Biarritz has become Europe's hot-cool surfing center. The season kicks off big-time every summer with the Roxy Jam longboard world women's championship (usually held July 1–8 ⊕ www.roxy.com). For more action, head to the coast north of Biarritz and the towns of Anglet and Hossegor. La Barre beach in the north doubles as the hangout for dedicated surfers who live out of their vans. On the southern end (by the Anglet-Biarritz border) are surf shops, snack bars, and one boulangerie.

These give the main beach drag, Chambre d'Amour, a decidedly California flair. If you're coming by train, get off in Bayonne or Biarritz and transfer to a Chronoplus bus bound for Anglet. The main tourist office (⊠ 1 av. de la Chambre d'Amour ☎ 05–59–03–77–01 ⊕ www.ville-anglet.fr) is closed off-season. Hossegor, 20 km (12 miles) north of Bayonne, hosts the Rip Curl Pro and the ASO Junior Surf Tour Championships every August as well as the ASP World Tour competition in September.

Pelote Basque: Biarritz Athletic-club. Pelote Basque: Biarritz Athletic-club offers instruction in every type of Basque pelota including *main nue* (bare-handed), *pala* (paddle), *chistera* (with a basketlike racquet), and *cesta punta* (another game played with the same curved basket). ⊠ *Parc des Sports d'Aguilera, Fronton Euskal Jai* ☎ *05–59–23–91–09* ⊕ *www. pelotebasque.net.*

Roxy Jam Long Board. France's Atlantic Coast has become one of the hottest surfing destinations in the world. The "Endless Summer" arrives in Biarritz every year in late July for the Roxy Jam Long Board championships and concludes with other events in August.

ST-JEAN-DE-LUZ

23 km (16 miles) southwest of Bayonne; 54 km (32 miles) northwest of St-Jean-Pied-de-Port.

Fodor's Choice Back in 1660, Louis XIV chose this tiny fishing village as the place to ★ marry the Infanta Maria Teresa of Spain. Ever since, travelers have journeyed here to enjoy the unique charms of St-Jean. Along the coast between Biarritz and the Spanish border, it remains memorable for its colorful harbor, old streets, curious church, and elegant beach. Its iconic port shares a harbor with its sister town Ciboure, on the other side of the Nivelle River. The glorious days of whaling and cod fishing are long gone, but some historic multihued houses around the docks are evocative enough.

GETTING HERE

The train station (⊠ *Av. de Verdun*) has frequent service to Biarritz (11 mins, €3.50) and Bayonne (28 mins, €5). Regional ATCRB buses leave from place Maréchal Foch by the tourist office. They're slower but cheaper than the train, and give you more beach-town options, including Bayonne (40 mins, €4) and Biarritz (35 mins, €4).

Visitor Information St-Jean-de-Luz Tourist Office ⊠ *Pl. Foch* ☎ *05–59–26–03–16* ⊕ *www.saint-jean-de-luz.com.*

EXPLORING

Maison de l'Infante (*Princess's House*). The Louis XIII–style Maison de l'Infante, between the harbor and the bay, is where Maria Teresa of Spain, accompanied by her mother, Queen Anne of Austria, and a healthy entourage of courtiers, stayed prior to her marriage to Louis XIV. ⊠ *Quai de l'Infante* ⛱ *€3* ⊙ *June–Sept. 15 and Oct. 25–Nov. 11, Tues.–Sat. 11–12:30 and 2:30–6:30.*

Maison Louis-XIV. Take a tour of the twin-tower Maison Louis-XIV. Built as the Château Lohobiague, it housed the French king during his nuptials and is austerely decorated in 17th-century Basque fashion. ⊠ *Pl. Louis XIV* ☎ *05–59–26–27–58* ⊕ *www.maison-louis-xiv.fr* ⛱ *€6* ⊙ *July and Aug., daily 10:30–12:30 and 2:30–6:30; Sept.,Oct., Apr., and May, visits at 11, 3, and 4; closed Nov.–Mar.*

Place Louis-XIV. The tree-lined place Louis-XIV, alongside the Hôtel de Ville (Town Hall), with its dainty statue of Louis XIV on horseback, is the hub of the town. In summer, concerts are offered on the square, as well as the famous "Toro de fuego" festival, which honors the bull with a parade and a papier-mâché beast.

St-Jean-Baptiste. The marriage of the Sun King and the Infanta took place in 1660 in the church of St-Jean-Baptiste. The marriage tied the knot, so to speak, on the Pyrénées Treaty signed by French chief minister Mazarin on November 7, 1659, ending Spanish hegemony in Europe. Note the church's unusual wooden galleries lining the walls, creating a theaterlike effect. Fittingly, St-Jean-Baptiste hosts a "Musique en Côte Basque" festival of early and Baroque music during the first two weeks of September. ⊠ *Pl. des Corsaires* ⊙ *Daily 9–noon and 3–6.*

WHERE TO EAT AND STAY

For expanded hotel reviews, visit Fodors.com.

$$ ✕**Chez Pablo.** The catch of the day determines the offering here. Long
SEAFOOD tables covered with red-and-white tablecloths, benches, and plaster walls give off a casual vibe, but the dishes are often excellent. $ *Average main: €22* ⊠ *Rue Mme. Etxeto* ☎ *05–59–26–37–81* ▬ *No credit cards* ⊙ *Closed Sun.*

$$ ✕**La Taverne Basque.** This well-known midtown standard is one of the
BISTRO old-faithful dining emporiums, specializing in Basque cuisine with a pronounced maritime emphasis. Try the *ttoro* (a rich fish, crustacean, potato, and vegetable soup). Perhaps the best stamp of approval is that locals eat here often. $ *Average main: €21* ⊠ *5 rue République* ☎ *05–59–26–01–26* ⊕ *www.latavernebasque.com* ⊙ *Closed Mon. No dinner Sun.*

$$$$ ⌂ **Le Grand Hôtel.** Traditionally famed as St-Jean-de-Luz's premier hotel,
HOTEL this elegant Belle Époque classic originally built in the 1920s offers panoramic ocean views, intimacy, and a sense of being where the action is; redesigned rooms in pastels, wood, and marble, and the unbeatable location at the northern end of the St-Jean-de-Luz beach seal the deal. **Pros:** views; comforts; action center. **Cons:** expensive; not too relaxing

Biarritz's main beach, the Grande Plage, is the town's focal point, especially for those who don't have money to lose in the resort casinos.

unless your pockets are *très* deep; slightly self-absorbed staff. $ *Rooms from: €345* ⊠ *43 bd. Thiers* ☎ *05–59–26–35–36* ⊕ *www.luzgrandhotel. fr* ⤴ *49 rooms, 3 suites* ⊘ *Closed 1 wk around Jan 1.*

THE ATLANTIC AND HAUTES-PYRÉNÉES

The Atlantic Pyrénées extend eastward from the Atlantic to the Col du Pourtalet, and encompass Béarn and the mountainous part of the Basque Country. Watching the Pyrénées grow from rolling green foothills in the west to jagged limestone peaks in the Béarn to glacier-studded granite massifs in the Hautes-Pyrénées makes for a dramatic progression of scenery. The Atlantic Pyrénées' first major height is at La Rhune (2,969 feet), known as the Balcon du Côte Basque (Balcony of the Basque Coast). The highest Basque peak is at Orhi (6,617 feet); the Béarn's highest is Pic d'Anie (8,510 feet). Not until Balaïtous (10,375 feet) and Vignemale (10,883 feet), in the Hautes-Pyrénées, does the altitude surpass the 10,000-foot mark. Starting east from St-Jean-de-Luz up the Nivelle River, a series of villages—including Ascain, Sare, Ainhoa, and Bidarrai—are picturesque stepping stones leading up to St-Jean-Pied-de-Port and on into the Hautes-Pyrénées.

This journey ends in Pau, in the Béarn region, far from the Pays Basque. The Béarn is akin in temperament to the larger region that enfolds it, Gascony. Gascony may be purse-poor, but it is certainly rich in scenery and lore. Its proud and touchy temperament is typified in literature by the character d'Artagnan in Dumas's *The Three Musketeers*, and in history by the lords of the château of Pau. An inscription over the château's entrance, *Touchez-y, si tu l'oses*—"Touch this if you dare"—was left by the golden-haired Gaston Phoebus (1331–91), 11th count of Foix and viscount of Béarn, a volatile arts lover with a nasty temper who murdered his brother and his only son.

Farther east, past Lourdes, the Hautes-Pyrénées include the highest and most spectacular natural wonders in the cordillera: the legendary Cirque de Gavarnie (natural mountain amphitheater), the Vignemale and Balaïtous peaks, and the Brèche de Roland are the star attractions. Trans-Pyrenean hikers (and drivers) generally prefer moving from west to east for a number of reasons, especially the excellent light prevailing in the late afternoon and evening during the prime months of May to October.

SARE

14 km (8 miles) southeast of St-Jean-de-Luz, 9 km (5½ miles) southwest of Ainhoa on D118.

15

The much-prized and picturesque village of Sare, described by author Pierre Loti in his *Ramuntxo* as a virtually autonomous Eden, is built around a large fronton, or backboard, where a permanent pelota game rages around the clock. Not surprisingly, the Hôtel de Ville offers a permanent exhibition on Pelote Basque (⊙ *July and Aug., daily 9–1 and 2–6:30; Sept.–June, daily 3–6*). Sare was a busy smuggling hub throughout the 19th century, but today's visitors are drawn by lovely sights, not illicit activities: chief among them are the colorful wood-beam and whitewashed Basque houses, the 16th-century late-Romanesque church with its triple-decker interior, and the **Ospitale Zaharra** pilgrim's hospice behind the church.

GETTING HERE

Buses leave from the train station in St-Jean-de-Luz and go to Sare (30 mins, €3.50) and neighboring villages.

Visitor Information Sare Tourist Office ✉ *Mairie* ☎ *05–59–54–20–14* ⊕ *www. sare.fr.*

EXPLORING

Église Saint-Martin se Sare. The Église Saint-Martin se Sare, one of the Labourd province's prettiest churches, was built in the 16th century and enlarged in the 17th with a triple-decker set of galleries. Parish priest Pierre Axular was one of the great early authors in the Basque language. His tomb is under the bell tower with an epitaph by Prince Bonaparte: "Every hour wounds; the last sends you to your tomb."

Grottes de Sare. Up the Sare Valley are the panoramic Col de Lizarrieta and the Grottes de Sare. Just outside these huge caves, you can study up on Basque culture and millennia-long history at the **Musée Ethnographique** (Ethnographic Museum), then take a guided tour (in five languages) for 1 km (½ mile) underground and see a son-et-lumière (sound-and-light) show. ☎ *05–59–54–21–88* ⊕ *www.grottesdesare.fr* ✉ *€8* ⊙ *Nov.–Mar., daily 2–5; Apr.–July. and Sept., daily 10–6; Aug., daily 10–7, Oct., daily 10–5.*

CLOSE UP

Getting On Top of Things

Supping on hearty regional cuisine makes perfect sense after a day of hiking the Pyrénées, which are best explored on foot. Day trips to La Rhune overlooking Biarritz and the Basque Coast or the walk up to Biriatou from the beach at Hendaye are great ways to get to know the countryside. Hiking the Pyrénées end-to-end is a 43-day trip. The GR (Grande Randonnée) 10, a trail signed by discreet red-and-white paint markings, runs from the Atlantic at Hendaye to Banyuls-sur-Mer on the Mediterranean, through villages and mountains, with refuges along the way.

The HRP (Haute Randonnée Pyrénéenne, or High Pyrenean Hike) follows terrain in France and Spain irrespective of borders. Local trails are well indicated, with blue or yellow markings. Some classic walks in the Pyrénées include the Iparla Ridge walk between Bidarrai and St-Étienne-de-Baïgorry, the Santiago de Compostela Trail's dramatic St-Jean-Pied-de-Port to Roncesvalles walk over the Pyrénées, and the Holçarté Gorge walk between Larrau and Ste-Engrâce. Get trail maps at local tourist offices.

Musée du Gâteau Basque. The Musée du Gâteau Basque, tracing the evolution of the most famous of Basque pastries, is another Sare treat. ✉ *Maison Haranea, Quartier Lehenbiscay* ☎ *05–59–54–22–09* 🌐 *www.legateaubasque.com* 🎫 *€7.50* ⏲ *Daily 9–1 and 2–6:30.*

Ortillopitz. Don't miss the typical Basque house Ortillopitz, a 16th-century country manor offering farmhouse charm and scenic vistas. ☎ *05–59–85–91–92* 🌐 *www.ortillopitz.com* 🎫 *€8* ⏲ *Apr.–Oct., Sun.–Fri.*

Ospitale Zaharra. Ospitale Zaharra is the pilgrims' way station on the chemin de St-Jacques, the famed pilgrimage route to the tomb of Saint James in northwestern Spain's Santiago de Compostela.

FAMILY Fodor's Choice ★ **Petit Train de la Rhune.** The Petit Train de la Rhune, a tiny wood-panel cogwheel train (one of only three in France), hits the less-than-dizzying speed of 5 mph while climbing up La Rhune peak. The views of the Bay of Biscay, the Pyrénées, and the grassy hills of the Basque farmland are wonderful. Trips depart west of Sare at the Col de St-Ignace, reached on D4. ☎ *05–59–54–20–26* 🌐 *www.rhune.com* 🎫 *€18* ⏲ *July and Aug., daily 8:30–5:30; Sept.–June, daily 9:30–11:30 and 2–4 (departures every 35 mins).*

WHERE TO STAY

For expanded hotel reviews, visit Fodors.com.

$$ B&B/INN 🏨 **Baratxartea.** This little inn 1 km (½ mile) from the center of Sare in one of the town's prettiest and most ancient *quartiers* is a beauty—a 16th-century town house complete with exposed wood-beam framework. **Pros:** upland location 20 minutes from beach; personalized family service; splendid dining. **Cons:** can get steamy in the August *canicule*; annex rooms are less charming and rustic; open windows in farm country attract insects. [$] *Rooms from: €100* ✉ *Quartier Ihalar* ☎ *05–*

59–54–20–48 🌐 www.hotel-baratxartea.com 🛏 14 rooms ⏲ Closed mid-Nov.–mid-Mar. 🍴 Some meals.

AINHOA

9 km (5½ miles) east of Sare; 23 km (14 miles) southeast of St-Jean-de-Luz; 31 km (19 miles) northwest of St-Jean-Pied-de-Port.

Fodor's Choice ★ The Basque village of Ainhoa, officially selected by the national tourist ministry as one of the prettiest in France, is a showcase for the Labourd region. Established in the 13th century, its little streets are lined with pretty 16th- to 18th-century houses featuring whitewashed walls, flower-filled balconies, brightly painted shutters, and carved master beams. Also of note: the Romanesque church of **Notre-Dame de l'Assomption**, which has a traditional Basque three-tier wooden interior with carved railings and ancient oak stairs. Exploring Ainhoa on foot is a pleasure, but you'll need your own wheels to get to here.

15

WHERE TO STAY

For expanded hotel reviews, visit Fodors.com.

$$$ HOTEL **Fodor's Choice ★** 🏨 **Ithurria.** A registered historic monument, this 17th-century Basque-style building was once a staging post on the fabled medieval pilgrims' route to Santiago de Compostela and today makes a fitting resting spot if you're doing a modern version of the pilgrims' journey or just need a delicious stopover on your way deeper into the mountains. **Pros:** spotless; rustic charm; cheery and friendly family service. **Cons:** you'll understand why they call it luggage while hauling your gear from car to room; some room decor undistinguished. [$] *Rooms from: €158 ✉ Rue Principale ☎ 05–59–29–92–11 🌐 www.ithurria.com 🛏 28 rooms ⏲ Closed Nov.–Apr.*

$$ B&B/INN 🏨 **Oppoca.** This 17th-century *relais,* or stagecoach relay station, on Ainhoa's main square and pelota court is one of the loveliest Basque houses in town, with small but adequate guest rooms. **Pros:** helpful service; superb fare; historic site. **Cons:** cramped spaces in some rooms; center of town can be noisy on weekends and holiday eves. [$] *Rooms from: €179 ✉ Pl. du Fronton ☎ 05–59–29–90–72 🌐 www.oppoca.com 🛏 10 rooms ⏲ Closed mid-Nov.–Feb.*

ST-JEAN-PIED-DE-PORT

54 km (33 miles) east of Biarritz, 46 km (28 miles) west of Larrau.

St-Jean-Pied-de-Port, a fortified town on the Nive River, got its name from its position at the foot (*pied*) of the mountain pass (*port*) of Roncevaux (Roncesvalles). The pass was the setting for *La Chanson de Roland* (*The Song of Roland*), the anonymous 11th-century epic poem considered the true beginning of French literature. The bustling town center, a major stop for pilgrims en route to Santiago de Compostela, seems, after a tour through the Soule, like a frenzied metropolitan center—even in winter. In summer, especially around the time of Pamplona's San Fermin blowout (the running of the bulls, July 7–14), the place is filled to the gills and is somewhere between exciting and unbearable.

GETTING HERE

SNCF trains between Bayonne and St-Jean-Pied-de-Port (1 hr, 26 mins; €9.50) depart six times daily in each direction.

Visitor Information **St-Jean-Pied-de-Port Tourist Office** ✉ *14 pl. Charles-de-Gaulle* ☎ *05–59–37–03–57* 🌐 *www.stjeanpieddeport-paysbasque-tourisme.com.*

EXPLORING

Citadelle. Continue up along rue de la Citadelle to get to the Citadelle, a classic Vauban fortress, now occupied by a school. The views from it, complete with maps identifying the surrounding heights and valleys, are panoramic.

Notre-Dame-du-Bout-du-Pont (*Our Lady of the End of the Bridge*). Walk into the old section of St-Jean-Pied-de-Port through the Porte de France, just behind and to the left of the tourist office; climb the steps on the left up to the walkway circling the ramparts, and walk around to the stone stairway down to the rue de l'Église. The church of Notre-Dame-du-Bout-du-Pont, known for its magnificent doorway, is at the bottom of this cobbled street. The church is a characteristically Basque three-tier structure, designed for women to sit on the ground floor, men to be in the first balcony, and the choir in the loft above.

Pont Notre-Dame (*Notre-Dame Bridge*). From the Pont Notre-Dame you can watch the wild trout in the Nive (also an Atlantic salmon stream) as they pluck mayflies off the surface. Note that fishing is forbidden in town. Upstream, along the left bank, is another wooden bridge. Cross it and then walk around and back through town, crossing back to the left bank on the main road.

Rue de la Citadelle. On rue de la Citadelle are several sights of interest: the **Maison Arcanzola** (Arcanzola House), at No. 32 (1510); the **Maison des Évêques** (Bishops' House), at No. 39; and the famous **Prison des Évêques** (Bishops' Prison), next door to it.

WHERE TO EAT AND STAY

For expanded hotel reviews, visit Fodors.com.

$$$$
FRENCH
Fodor's Choice ★

🍴 **Les Pyrénées.** A former stagecoach inn on the route to Santiago de Compostela now houses the best restaurant in the Pyrénées, directed by renowned master chef Firmin Arrambide and his son Philippe. Characterized by refined interpretations of Pays Basque cooking based on local Pyrenean delicacies, this four-handed team has developed a devout following on both sides of the Franco-Spanish border. An hour from the port in Bayonne, the Arrambides offer superlative fish and seafood along with trout from the Nive, as well as anadromous sea trout and Atlantic salmon in season. Other dishes feature wood pigeon, langoustines, or truffles—and, for dessert, the elder Arrambide's recipe for gâteau Basque has circled the world. **■TIP→ After dining, you can bed down in one of the 14 rooms and 4 suites (€65–€275) at the inn; needless to say, you'll want to invest in one of the board plans!** [$] *Average main: €46* ✉ *19 pl. Charles-de-Gaulle* ☎ *05–59–37–01–01* 🌐 *www.hotel-les-pyrenees.com* ✍ *Reservations essential* ⏲ *Closed Jan. 5–28 and Nov. 20–Dec. 22* 🍽 *All meals.*

$$
\begin{array}{l}
\textbf{\$\$} \\
\textsc{hotel}
\end{array}
$$

$$ 🛏 **Central Hôtel.** This family-run hotel and restaurant over the Nive is a
HOTEL   vintage venue (note the 200-year-old oak staircase)—it's also the best
value in town. **Pros:** location is central, as suggested by the name; personal family service; river sounds and views. **Cons:** creaky bedsprings; can be hot in midsummer; village life starts early and you're at the heart of it. $ *Rooms from: €88* ⊠ *1 pl. Charles-de-Gaulle* 🕾 *05–59–37–00–22* 🔊 *14 rooms* ☽ *Closed Dec.–Feb.*

SAUVETERRE-DE-BÉARN

Fodor's Choice   *39 km (23 miles) northeast of St-Jean-Pied-de-Port.*
★   **Visitor Information Sauveterre-de-Béarn Tourist Office** ⊠ *Mairie* 🕾 *05–59–38–32–86* ⊕ *www.tourisme-bearn-gaves.com.*

EXPLORING

The enchanting Romanesque-turning-into-Gothic church here crowns a hill from which unfolds a storybook vista. A postcard-perfect group of buildings—the Gave d'Oloron, the fortified 12th-century drawbridge, the lovely Montréal Tower—fill the foreground, while the Pyrénées rise romantically in the distance. You cannot come to this region and miss this town.

Vieux Pont (*Old Bridge*). The bridge, known both as the Vieux Pont and the Pont de la Légende (Bridge of the Legend), is associated with the legend of Sancie, widow of Gaston V de Béarn. Accused of murdering a child after her husband's death in 1170, Sancie was subjected to the "Judgment of God" and thrown, bound hand and foot, from the bridge by order of her brother, the king of Navarre. When the river carried her safely to the bank, she was deemed exonerated of all charges.

EUGÉNIE-LES-BAINS

92 km (53 miles) northeast of Sauveterre-de-Béarn; 56 km (34 miles) north of Pau; 140 km (87 miles) south of Bordeaux.

Empress Eugénie popularized the region's thermal baths at the end of the 19th century, and in return the villagers named this town after her. Then, in 1973, Michel and Christine Guérard made the village world-famous by putting together one of France's most fashionable thermal retreats, which became one of the birthplaces of nouvelle cuisine, thanks to the great talents of chef Michel.

GETTING HERE

For transport to Eugénie-les-Bains from Pau, CITRAM Pyrénées (🕾 *05–59–27–22–22* ⊕ *www.annuaire-des-autocaristes.com*) dispatches three daily buses from Pau to the town of Aire-sur-l'Adour (1 hr, 15 mins; €15). For transport from Aire-sur-l'Adour to Eugénie-les-Bains, R.D.T.L (🕾 *05–58–56–80–80* ⊕ *www.rdtl.fr*) offers regular bus connections (20 mins, €8). For transport to Eugénie-les-Bains via Dax (71 km [44 miles]), SNCF (⊕ *www.sncf.com*) offers 20 trains daily from Bayonne to Dax (41 mins, €10). For transport from Dax to Eugénie-les-Bains, contact R.D.T.L *(above)*. The Dax to Hagetmau bus connects with the

15

Hagetmau to Aire-sur-l'Adour line, which stops in Eugénie-les-Bains (1 hr, 30 mins; €16).

EXPLORING

The little kingdom of Michel and Christine Guérard now includes restaurants serving three types of cuisine (*minceur, gourmand, and terroir*), four separate lodging arrangements, a cooking school, and a spa. Therapeutic treatments address everything from weight loss to rheumatism, while the French Ministry of Health certifies two springs—L'Impératrice and Christine-Marie— whose 39°C (102°F) waters come from nearly 1,300 feet below the surface.

WHERE TO STAY

For expanded hotel reviews, visit Fodors.com.

$$$ HOTEL **La Maison Rose.** A (relatively) low-cost, low-calorie alternative to famed Les Prés d'Eugénie, Michel and Christine Guérard's "Pink House" spa beckons with a renovated, super-stylish 18th-century farmhouse adorned with old paintings hung with ribbons, rustic antiques, and Pays Basque handicrafts—the kind of retreat that would have delighted Louis XIV's sober Madame de Maintenon. **Pros:** much easier on the plastic; a sybaritically simple spa approach; more relaxed; superb dining without stuffing. **Cons:** cravings for the foie-gras treatment next door. [$] *Rooms from: €200* ✉ *Place de l'Impératrice, Eugénie-les-Bains* ☎ *05–58–05–06–07* 🌐 *www.michelguerard.com* 🛏 *26 rooms, 5 suites.*

$$$$ HOTEL Fodor's Choice ★ **Les Prés d'Eugénie.** Ever since Michel Guérard's restaurant fired the first shots of the nouvelle revolution in the late 1970s, the excellence of this suave culinary landmark has been a given (so much so that the breakfast here outdoes dinner at most other places) and this hotel-restaurant remains an important notch on any gourmand's belt. **Pros:** Guérard in full; magical cuisine; intelligent and attentive service. **Cons:** too beautiful to close your eyes and go to sleep (fortunately, Bacchus comes to your rescue). [$] *Rooms from: €270* ✉ *Place de l'Impératrice, Eugénie-les-Bains* ☎ *05–58–05–06–07, 05–58–05–05–05 restaurant reservations* 🌐 *www.michelguerard.com* 🛏 *22 rooms, 6 suites.*

PAU

66 km (36 miles) south of Eugénie-les-Bains, 106 km (63 miles) southeast of Bayonne and Biarritz.

The stunning views, mild climate, and elegance of Pau—the historic capital of Béarn, a state annexed to France in 1620—make it a lovely place to visit and a convenient gateway to the Pyrénées. The birthplace of King Henri IV, Pau was "discovered" in 1815 by British officers returning from the Peninsular War in Spain, and it soon became a prominent winter resort town. Fifty years later English-speaking inhabitants made up one-third of Pau's population, many of them believing in the medicinal benefits of mountain air (later shifting their loyalties to Biarritz for the sea air). They started the Pont-Long Steeplechase, still one of the most challenging in Europe, in 1841; created France's first golf course here in 1856; introduced fox hunting to the region; and

The Hautes-Pyrénées have some of the best hiking trails in Europe, especially those found on the way to the Cirque de Gavarnie.

founded a famous British tea shop where students now smoke strong cigarettes while drinking black coffee.

GETTING HERE

Twelve kilometers (7 miles) north of Pau, the Pau-Pyrénées airport (⊠ *Aéroport Pau-Pyrénées, Uzein* ☎ *05–59–33–33–00* ⊕ *www.pau. aeroport.fr*) receives daily flights from Paris, London, Lyon, and Amsterdam, among other points. SNCF connects Pau with Paris (5 hrs, 34 mins; €67.50) with four trains daily. Overnight sleeper trains (7 hrs, 45 mins; €107) run via Bayonne or Toulouse. Trains connect with Biarritz (1½ hrs, €19) five times daily. In addition, you can take the train to Lourdes (29 mins, €8), Bayonne (1 hr, 33 mins; €17), and Toulouse (2 hrs, 52 mins; €30.50). Chronoplus VéoliaSTAB buses (☎ *05–59–59–04–61* ⊕ *www.chronoplus.eu/*) connect Pau with Bayonne and Toulouse. To reach the center of Pau from the train station on avenue Gaston-Lacoste, cross the street and take the funicular up the hill to place Royale.

Visitor Information Pau Tourist Office ⊠ *Pl. Royale* ☎ *05–59–27–27–08* ⊕ *www.pau-pyreenees.com.*

EXPLORING

Musée des Beaux-Arts. For some man-made splendors, head to the Musée des Beaux-Arts and feast on works by El Greco, Degas, Sorolla, and Rodin. ⊠ *Rue Mathieu-Lalanne* ☎ *05–59–27–33–02* 🎟 *€5* ⊙ *Weekdays 10–noon and 2–6, weekends 10–12:30.*

Fodor'sChoice **Musée National du Château de Pau.** Pau's regal past is commemorated
★ at its Musée National du Château de Pau, begun in the 14th century

by Gaston Phoebus, the flamboyant count of Béarn. The building was transformed into a Renaissance palace in the 16th century by Marguerite d'Angoulême, sister of François I. A woman of diverse gifts, she wrote pastorals, many performed in the château's sumptuous gardens. Her bawdy *Heptameron*—written at age 60—furnishes as much sly merriment today as it did when read by her doting kingly brother. Marguerite's grandson, the future king of France Henri IV, was born in the château in 1553. Exhibits connected to Henri's life and times are displayed regularly, along with portraits of the most significant of his alleged 57 lovers and mistresses. His cradle, a giant turtle shell, is on exhibit in his bedroom, one of the sumptuous, tapestry-lined royal apartments. ✉ *Rue du Château* ☎ *05–59–82–38–00* 🌐 *www.musee-chateau-pau.fr* 🎟 *2€* 🕒 *Mid-June–mid-Sept., daily 9:30–12:30 and 1:30–6:45; mid-Sept.–mid-June, daily 9:30–11:45 and 2–5.*

TOUT SWEET

Confiserie Francis Miot. While in Pau, enjoy some treats at Confiserie Francis Miot. Try one of the signature delicacies, "Les Coucougnettes du Vert Galant"—small, red, tender bonbons made from almond paste. ✉ *48 rue Joffre* ☎ *05–59–27–69–51.*

Musée des Arts Sucrés. At the gates of Pau in the village of Uzos, Miot has his own Musée des Arts Sucrés, with displays extolling chocolate, sugar, and confectionary creations. ✉ *Rte. de Nay, Uzos* ☎ *05–59–35–05–56* 🌐 *www.feerie-gourmande.com* 🎟 *€5.50* 🕒 *Mon.–Sat. 10–noon and 2–6.*

Sentiers du Roy. To continue on your royal path, follow the **Sentiers du Roy** (King's Paths), a marked trail just below the boulevard des Pyrénées. When you reach the top, look for the large map showing the Pyrenean peaks in the distance. Line the map sights up with the mountains and you can identify the main peaks in the Hautes Pyrénées.

WHERE TO EAT AND STAY

For expanded hotel reviews, visit Fodors.com.

$$ FRENCH 🍴 **Henri IV.** On a quiet pedestrian street near the château, this dining room with its open fire is a cozy find for a cold, wet night in winter, while the terrace is a shady place to cool off in summer. Traditional Béarn cooking here stars *magret de canard* cooked over coals and *cuisses de grenouille* (frogs' legs), sautéed dry and crispy in parsley and garlic. This is a good table for hearty local dishes, but don't expect anything extra-extraordinary from the kitchen. [$] *Average main: €18* ✉ *18 rue Henri IV* ☎ *05–59–27–54–43* 🕒 *Closed Wed. and Thurs.*

$ HOTEL 🏨 **Hôtel de Gramont.** At this 17th-century stagecoach stop ask for one of the *chambres mansardées* (dormered bedrooms) under the eaves overlooking the Vallée du Hédas, Pau's midtown gorge, for these are the coziest rooms. **Pros:** a short walk from the Château de Pau and overlooking the oldest part of town; relaxing and unpretentious; easy on the wallet. **Cons:** breakfast (at extra charge) is to be avoided; small rooms. [$] *Rooms from: €88* ✉ *3 pl. de Gramont* ☎ *05–59–27–84–04* 🌐 *www.hotelgramont.com* 🛏 *32 rooms, 3 suites.*

NIGHTLIFE AND THE ARTS

Casino. The streets around Pau's imposing château are sprinkled with cozy pubs and dining spots, although the casino offers racier entertainment. ⊠ *Parc Beaumont* ☎ *05–59–27–06–92.*

Festival de Pau. During the Festival de Pau, theatrical and musical events take place almost every evening from mid-July to late August, nearly all of them gratis. The Tango Festival erupts in mid-September. Nightlife in Pau revolves around the central Triangle area (surrounded by rue Lespy, rue Émile Garet, and rue Castetnau). ⊕ *www.festivaltangopau.com.*

LOURDES

41 km (27 miles) southeast of Pau, 19 km (12 miles) southwest of Tarbes.

The mountain town of Lourdes is probably the most famous Catholic pilgrimage site (and sight) in the world. Some 5 million visitors come each year from every corner of the globe, many of them not Christians, with most in quest of a miraculous cure for sickness or disability.

15

GETTING HERE AND AROUND

With direct rail service from Pau (28 mins, €8), Bayonne (1 hr, 44 mins; €24), and Toulouse (2 hrs, 4 mins; €26.50), Lourdes's train station on the avenue de la Gare is one of the busiest in the country. In fact, so many pilgrim trains arrive between Easter and October that the station has a separate entrance to accommodate them; and dedicated local buses transport anxious passengers to the grotto every 20 minutes. Regional **T.P.R.** and **SNCF**-run TER buses also serve the area.

Visitor Information Lourdes Tourist Office ⊠ *Pl. Peyramale* ☎ *05–62–42–77–40* ⊕ *www.lourdes-france.com.*

EXPLORING

Basilique Souterraine St-Pie X. Lourdes celebrated the centenary of Bernadette Soubirous's visions by building the world's largest underground church, the Basilique Souterraine St-Pie X, with space for 20,000 people—more than the town's permanent population. The Basilique Supérieure (1871), tall and white, hulks nearby.

Cachot. The cachot, a tiny room where, in extreme poverty, Bernadette and her family took refuge in 1856, can also be visited. ⊠ *15 rue des Petits-Fossés* ☎ *05–62–94–51–30* ⊡ *Free* ☉ *Easter–mid-Oct., daily 9:30–11:45 and 2:30–5:30; mid-Oct.–Easter, daily 2:30–5:30.*

Grotte de Massabielle. What is now a huge pilgrimage site (and a big business) has humble origins. In February 1858 Bernadette Soubirous, a 14-year-old miller's daughter, claimed she saw the Virgin Mary in the Grotte de Massabielle, near the Gave de Pau (in all, she had 18 visions). Bernadette dug in the grotto, releasing a gush of water from a spot where no spring had flowed before. From then on, pilgrims thronged the Massabielle rock for the water's supposed healing powers, though church authorities reacted skeptically. It took four years for the miracle to be authenticated by Rome and a sanctuary erected over the grotto. In 1864 the first organized procession was held. Today there are six official annual pilgrimages between Easter and All Saints' Day, the most

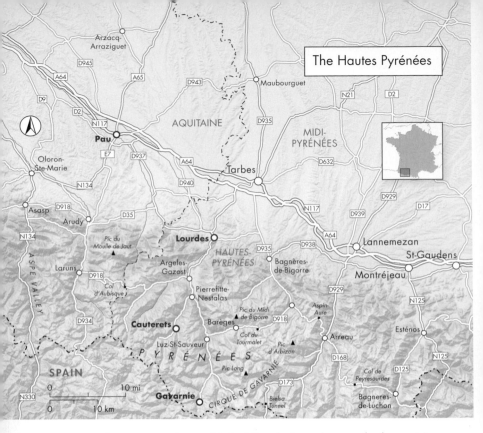

The Hautes Pyrénées

important on August 15. In fall and winter there are far fewer visitors, but that will be a plus for those in search of peace and tranquillity.

Moulin de Boly (*Boly Mill*). Across the river is the Moulin de Boly, where Bernadette was born on January 7, 1844. ⊠ *12 rue Bernadette-Soubirous* ⌷ *Free* ⊙ *Easter–mid-Oct., daily 9:30–11:45 and 2:30–5:45.*

Fodor's Choice ★ **Musée Pyrénéen.** The **château** on the hill above town can be reached by escalator, by 131 steps, or by the ramp up from rue du Bourg (from which a small Basque cemetery with ancient discoidal stones can be seen). Once a prison, the castle now contains the Musée Pyrénéen, one of France's best provincial museums, devoted to the popular customs, arts, and history of the Pyrénées. ⊠ *25 rue du Fort* ☎ *05–62–94–02–04* ⊕ *www.lourdes-visite.com* ⌷ *€6* ⊙ *Apr.–Sept., daily 9–noon and 1:30–6:30; Oct.–Mar., daily 9–noon and 2–6.*

Pavillon Notre-Dame (*Museum of Stained-Glass Mosaic Religious Art*). The Pavillon Notre-Dame, across from St-Pie X, houses the **Musée Bernadette**, with mementos of Bernadette's life and an illustrated history of the pilgrimages. In the basement is a collection devoted to religious gem-work relics. ⊠ *72 rue de la Grotte* ☎ *05–62–94–13–15* ⌷ *Free* ⊙ *July–Nov., daily 9:30–11:45 and 2:30–6:15; Dec.–June, Wed.–Mon. 9:30–11:45 and 2:30–5:45.*

WHERE TO STAY

For expanded hotel reviews, visit Fodors.com.

$$$ HOTEL 🏨 **Hôtel Gallia et Londres.** A feel of traditional France in the Louis XVI furniture and the general ambience of the place makes the pretty Gallia, not far from the sanctuaries and the grotto, something of a retreat within a retreat. **Pros:** traditional French hotel; near the sanctuaries; maintains a certain dignity in the midst of the prevailing commercial vibe of Lourdes. **Cons:** some rooms are on the small side; closed during the winter; breakfast is extra. [$] *Rooms from: €155* ✉ *26 av. B. Soubirous* ☎ *05–62–94–35–44* 🌐 *www.hotelgallialondres.com* 🛏 *88 rooms, 3 suites* 🕓 *Closed Oct. 20–Apr. 11.*

CAUTERETS

30 km (19 miles) south of Lourdes, 49 km (30 miles) south of Tarbes.

15

GETTING HERE

Unless you're coming to Cauterets from a hiking path, only one road leads into town. SNCF buses travel to and from Lourdes on it seven times a day (1 hr, €7).

Visitor Information Cauterets Tourist Office ✉ *Pl. Foch* ☎ *05–62–92–50–50.*

EXPLORING

Cauterets—which derives from the word for hot springs in the local *bigourdan* dialect—is a spa resort town (for long-term treatments) set high in the Pyrénées. It has been revered since Roman times for thermal baths thought to cure maladies ranging from back pain to infertility. Novelist Victor Hugo (1802–85) womanized here, and Lady Aurore Dudevant—better known as the writer George Sand (1804–76)—is said to have discovered her feminism here. Other famous visitors include Chateaubriand, Sarah Bernhardt, King Edward VII of England, and Spain's King Alfonso XIII.

GAVARNIE

30 km (19 miles) south of Cauterets on D921, 50 km (31 miles) south of Lourdes.

Geologists point to the natural wonder that is the Cirque de Gavarnie as one of the world's most formidable examples of the effects of glacial erosion; the cliffs were worn away by the advancing and retreating ice sheets of the Pleistocene epoch. Seeing it, one can understand its irresistible appeal for mountain climbers—it is only fitting that there is a statue of one of the first of them, Lord Russell, in the village.

GETTING HERE

From Lourdes SNCF buses connect to Luz-St-Sauveur (34 mins, €5); Gavarnie is 20 km (12 miles) south of Luz-St-Sauveur by taxi or Capou bus (30 mins, €5).

Visitor Information Gavarnie Tourist Office. Check with the Gavarnie Tourist Office for weather reports and for information about guided tours at Brèche de Roland. ✉ *Pl. de la Bergère, in center of village* ☎ *05–62–92–49–10* 🌐 *www.gavarnie.com.*

EXPLORING

Fodor's Choice ★ **Brèche de Roland.** Another dramatic sight is 12 km (7 miles) west of the village of Gavarnie. Take D921 up to the Col de Boucharo, where you can park and walk five hours up to the Brèche de Roland glacier (you cross it during the last two hours of the hike). For a taste of mountain life, have lunch high up at the Club Alpin Français's **Refuge de Sarradets ou de la Brèche.** This is a serious climb, only feasible from mid-June to mid-September, for which you need (at least) good hiking shoes and sound physical conditioning. Crampons and ice axes are available for rent in Gavarnie.

Fodor's Choice ★ **Cirque de Gavarnie.** A spectacular natural amphitheater, the Cirque de Gavarnie has been dubbed the "Colosseum of Nature" and inspired many writers, including Victor Hugo. At its foot is the village of Gavarnie, a good base for exploring the mountains in the region. The Cirque is a Cinerama wall of peaks that is one of the world's most remarkable examples of glacial erosion and a daunting challenge to mountaineers. Horses and donkeys, rented in the village, are the traditional way to reach the head of the valley (though walking is preferable), where the Hôtel du Cirque has hosted six generations of visitors. When the upper snows melt, numerous streams tumble down from the cliffs to form spectacular waterfalls; the greatest of them, Europe's highest, is the **Grande Cascade,** dropping nearly 1,400 feet.

WHERE TO EAT AND STAY

For expanded hotel reviews, visit Fodors.com.

$$
FRENCH **✕ Hôtel du Cirque.** With its legendary views of the Cirque de Gavarnie, this spot is magical at sunset. Despite its name, the hôtel is a restaurant, but not just any old one: the *garbure* here is as delicious as the sunset is grand. Seventh-generation owner Pierre Vergez claims his recipe using water from the Cirque and *cocos de Tarbes,* or *haricots tarbais* (Tarbes broad beans) is unique. Ⓢ *Average main: €16* ✉ *1-hr walk above village of Gavarnie* ☎ *05–62–92–48–02* ⓧ *Closed mid-Sept.–mid-June.*

$$$
HOTEL **Hotel Vignemale.** Behind an imposing granite facade with steep rooflines reflecting the towering Hautes Pyrénées to the south, the ample and sunny guest rooms in this spacious château-like hotel built in 1902 overlook the rushing Gave (river) de Gavarnie. **Pros:** rushing water music provided by the stream; a sense of space; a small hotel's personalized service. **Cons:** small balconies; decor somewhat dated; bathrooms not as splendid as the facade might suggest. Ⓢ *Rooms from: €170* ✉ *Village de Gavarnie* ☎ *05–62–92–40–00* ⊕ *www.hotel-vignemale.com* ⤴ *24 rooms* ⓧ *Closed mid-Oct–mid-May.*

NIGHTLIFE AND THE ARTS

La Fête des Pyrénées. Every July Gavarnie holds an outdoor ballet and music performance, La Fête des Pyrénées, using the Cirque de Gavarnie as a backdrop; showtime is at sunset. For information contact the tourist office. ☎ *05–62–92–49–10 information.*

BORDEAUX AND THE WINE COUNTRY

WELCOME TO BORDEAUX AND THE WINE COUNTRY

TOP REASONS TO GO

★ **La Route de Médoc:** With eight *appellations* (districts) in this small area alone, and names like Rothschild, Latour, and Margaux on its bottles, the route will fulfill your grape expectations.

★ **Bordeaux:** 18th-century wine merchants endowed this city with an almost regal elegance—for proof, see their gracious mansions and the city's sublime squares.

★ **The Rothschild legacy:** Although the family's Château Lafite is often locked, oenophiles will be welcomed with open arms at Château Mouton-Rothschild's visitor center and museum.

★ **St-Émilion:** With its 13th-century ramparts, cobblestone streets, and rock-face hermitage, this hilltop town presides over one of the region's richest wine districts.

★ **Bordeaux bacchanal:** Wine-themed festivals— most notably the Fête du Vin extravaganza, held in Bordeaux's biggest place at the end of June— keep corks popping.

1 Bordeaux. Dominated geographically by the nearby Atlantic Ocean and historically by great wine merchants and shippers, Bordeaux has long ranked among France's largest cities. There is considerable, if concentrated, affluence, which hides behind 18th-century facades. Showing off may not be a regional trait but, happily, the city fathers did provide a bevy of cultural riches to discover, including the spectacular place de la Bourse, the Grand Théâtre, and the Musée des Beaux-Arts.

2 The Médoc. Northwest of Bordeaux, this triangulated peninsula extends from the Garonne River to the Atlantic coast. Dutch engineers drained its marshy landscape in the 18th century to expose the gravelly soil that is excellent for growing grapes, and today the Médoc is home to several of the *grands crus classés*, including Château Margaux, Château Latour, Château Lafite-Rothschild, and Château Mouton-Rothschild. Public buses run here but stops are sometimes in the middle of nowhere—a car, bike, or guided tour may be the best option.

3 The Libournais. On the right bank of the Dordogne, this region was put on the map by two great wine districts—St-Émilion and Pomerol. Crowds head here because the town of St-Émilion looks as delicious as its wines taste: a UNESCO World Heritage Site, this open-air museum was constructed out of a limestone plateau honeycombed with vast caves and passageways, the source for the golden stonework of its 19th-century houses and steep streets. During summer, the small town is often swamped with visitors, so plan your parking and hotels carefully.

GETTING ORIENTED

Along with Burgundy and Champagne, Bordeaux is one of the great wine regions of France. As the capital of the Gironde *département* and of the historic province of Aquitaine, the city of Bordeaux is both the commercial and cultural center of southwest France and an important transportation hub. It is smack-dab in the middle of one of the finest winegrowing areas in the world: Sauternes lies to the south, flat and dusty Médoc to the northwest, and Pomerol and St-Émilion to the east.

16

Royan
Cozes
D730
Gironde
Route du Médoc
Lesparre-Médoc
Château de Loudenne
Mirambeau
St-Ciers-sur-Gironde
D730
D2
2
Montendre
Château Mouton Rotschild
Pauillac
Montlieu-la-Garde
POITOU CHARENTES
D1215
Blaye
D137
N10
Margaux
Bourg
Isle
AQUITAINE
Ste-Hélène
D2
D18
D215
D1
Banquefort
A89
N89
A10
Libourne
Pomerol
3
Bordeaux
St-Émilion
Pessac
1
D936
Gradignan
D10
Léognan
A63
Langoiran
Labrède
Haut-Bénauge
A62
Cadillac
Barsac
Loupiac
Sauternes
Langon

VISITING THE VINEYARDS

Touring a region with more than six hundred square miles of wine-growing country, 5,000 châteaux, and 100,000 vineyards producing around 70 million gallons of wine annually, you'll find it hard to resist sampling Bordeaux's liquid bounty—but where to start?

Château Smith Haut Lafitte is a famous name in Bordeaux *(above)*; the tower of Château Latour *(right, above)*; Château Margaux has Bordeaux's greatest house *(right, bottom)*.

The best bet is to head north for the Route de Médoc (also called the Route des Châteaux or the Route des Grands-Crus), armed with maps and pointers from Bordeaux's helpful Office of Tourism (the *tourisme de viticole* desk is the place for this)—it's at 12 cours du XXX-Juillet in the city center of Bordeaux. Or check out the "Wine Tours" section of the official Bordeaux tourism website before you travel: ⊕ *www.bordeaux-tourisme.com*. A map is essential, as signage is poor and many "châteaux" are small manors hidden in the hills. Three main wine regions surround the city: Médoc to the northwest, St-Émilion to the east, and Graves-Sauternes to the south. Each boasts big-name vineyards, but remember that Baron Philippe de Rothschild, owner of Mouton-Rothschild, drank *vin ordinaire* at most meals.

I HEARD IT THROUGH THE GRAPEVINE

For more tips go to the Forums at www.fodors. com. "Remember that almost all châteaux are closed from noon to 2 pm for lunch." —at. "We had a 3-hour private tour at Latour, with a movie, a tour, and a tasting. Everything was first class—especially the wine! We also made same-day reservations at beautiful Pichon-Longeville." —oforparis!

BY APPOINTMENT ONLY

If you're planning on visiting any of the famous growers (or some of the lesser known ones for that matter), make sure to contact them ahead of time to arrange a *dégustation* (wine tasting)—many of the labels are "by appointment only" because they're too small to have full-time guides. Even the famous Château Mouton-Rothschild—visited by thousands—requires reservations, at least a week in advance for a regular tour and several weeks for a tour that includes the cellars. Conveniently, you can create your agenda online by booking your visits through the tourism office's website—it also supplies you with a printable map for your personalized itinerary.

VINEYARD TOURS

The staff at Bordeaux's tourism office is very helpful, and because many vineyards are inaccessible without a car or bike, the easiest way to reach those of the Route de Médoc and Gironde is to join one of the nearly daily bus tours it sponsors.

Here's the main scoop: These tours depart from (and return to) the Office de Tourisme at 12 cours XXX-Juillet. In the off-season, same-day reservations can be had; in high season, make them in advance. There are daylong trips and also half-day versions (the latter usually from 2 to 6 in the afternoon).

In high season there's a tour every day; otherwise a few run per week. Most tours stop at two châteaux only—for instance, in the Médoc, you can visit the Château Palmer (Troisième Cru Classé) and the Château Lanessan (Cru Bourgeois)—but there are so many diverse tours that you could go on a different one each day for a week and not see the same domains. Tours are offered in several languages, including English, and usually a bus holds 40 participants.

You can view information regarding each tour (including availability) at ⊕ *www.bordeaux-tourisme.com*; then book your choice online.

THE GRAPE ESCAPE

Want to play *vigneron* (vintner) for a night? Some great vineyards welcome guests: here are two top options.

The 14th-century estate of Château Smith Haut Lafitte (☎ *05–57–83–11–22* ⊕ *www.smith-haut-lafitte.com*) now also houses the very successful Les Sources de Caudalie hotel and spa (wine-based treatments; ☎ *05–57–83–83–83* ⊕ *www. sources-caudalie.com*).

Wine king Bernard Magrez has two rooms available at his 17th-century Château Fombrauge; book through his big Luxury Wine Tourism company (⊕ *www.luxurywinetourism.com*).

16

Updated by
Avery Sumner

When travelers arrive here, Bordeaux's countryside enchants them without their quite knowing why: what the French call *la douceur de vivre* (the sweetness of living) may have something to do with it.

To the east, extending their lush green rows to the rising sun, the renowned vineyards of the Route de Médoc entice visitors to discover magical medieval wine towns like St-Émilion. To the north, the Atlantic coast offers elite enclaves with white-sand beaches. In between is the metropolis of Bordeaux, replete with 18th-century landmarks and 20-year-old college students. Some complain that Bordeaux is like Paris without the good stuff, but if you're a wine lover it's still the doorway to paradise.

From the grandest *premiers grands crus*—the Lafite-Rothschilds, the Margaux—to the modest *supérieur* in your picnic basket, Bordeaux wines command respect around the world. So much so that fans and oenophiles by the thousands come here to pay homage: to gaze at the noble symmetries of estate châteaux, whose rows of green-and-black vineyards radiate in every direction; to lower a nose deep into a well-swirled glass, inhaling the heady vapors of oak and almond and leather; and, finally, to reverently pack a few bloodline labels into a trunk or a suitcase for home.

The history, economy, and culture of Bordeaux have always been linked to the production and marketing of wine. The birth of the first Bordeaux winery is said to have occurred between AD 37 and 68, when the Romans called this land Burdigala. By the Middle Ages a steady flow of Bordeaux wines was headed to England, where it's still dubbed "claret," after *clairet*, a light red version from earlier days. During these centuries the region was also put on the tourist radar because it had become a major stopping-off point on the fabled Santiago de Compostela pilgrimage road. With all these allurements, it's no wonder the English fought for it so determinedly throughout the Hundred Years' War. This coveted corner of France became home to Eleanor of Aquitaine, and when she left her first husband, France's Louis VII, to marry Henry II of Normandy (later king of England), both she and the land came under English rule. Henry Plantagenet was, after all, a great-grandson of William the Conqueror, and the Franco-English ambiguity of the age exploded in a war that defined much of modern France and changed its face forever. Southwestern France was the stage upon which much of the war was conducted—hence the region's many castles and no end of sturdy churches dedicated to the noble families' cause.

What they sought, the world still seeks. The wines of Bordeaux set the standard against which other wines are measured, and to truly savor them you should drink them on-site—from the mouthful of golden Graves that eases the oysters down to the syrupy sip of Sauternes that civilizes the smooth gaminess of the foie gras to the last glass of Médoc paired with the salt-marsh lamb that leads to pulling the cork on a Pauillac—because there is the cheese tray yet to come. With a smorgasbord of 57 wine appellations to choose from, the revitalized city of Bordeaux, and the wine country that surrounds it with a veritable army of varietals, the entire region is intoxicating.

PLANNER

16

WHEN TO GO

Southwestern France can have bad storms even during the summer because of the nearby Atlantic. Happily, inclement weather doesn't hang around for long. French people usually vacation within their own national borders, so that means mid-July to the end of August is when you'll have company—lots of it—especially in the more famous destinations. Spring and fall are the best times to visit, when there aren't as many tourists and the weather is still pleasant. The *vendanges* (grape harvests) usually begin about mid-September in the Bordeaux region (though you can't visit the wineries at this time), and two weeks later in the Cognac region, to the north.

PLANNING YOUR TIME

How to find the best vineyards (also referred to as *crus, clos,* and *domaines*) if you're based in Bordeaux? Easy—just head in any direction. The city is at the hub of a patchwork of vineyards: the Médoc peninsula to the northwest; Bourg and Blaye across the estuary; St-Émilion inland to the east; then, as you wheel around clockwise, Entre-Deux-Mers, Sauternes, and Graves.

The nearest vineyard to Bordeaux itself is one of the best: Haut-Brion, on the western outskirts of the city, and one of the five châteaux to be officially recognized as a *premier cru*, or first growth. There are only five premiers crus in all, and Haut-Brion is the only one not in the Médoc (Château Mouton-Rothschild, Château Margaux, Château Latour, and Château Lafite-Rothschild complete the list). The Médoc is subdivided into various appellations, or wine-growing districts, with their own specific characteristics and taste. Pauillac and Margaux host premiers crus; St-Julien and St-Estèphe possess many domaines of almost equal quality, followed by Listrac and Moulis; wines not quite so good are classed as Haut-Médoc or, as you move farther north, Médoc, pure and simple.

The Médoc wine region begins at the meeting point of the Dordogne and Garonne rivers, just north of the city. The D2 (aka the Route des Châteaux) cuts northwest through the majority of the wine country along the Gironde all the way to Talais, and the D1215 farther west runs through the other side of the region entering appellations like Listrac and Moulis.

Eastward lies the Libournais and St-Émilion regions, with Libourne being the main transportation (train) hub if you're heading to the stunning Vieille Ville (Old Town) of St-Émilion, which deserves at least a day, if not two. The surrounding vineyards see the merlot grape in control, and wines here often have more immediate appeal than those of the Médoc. There are several small appellations apart from St-Émilion itself, the most famous being Pomerol, whose Château Pétrus is the world's most expensive wine. South of St-Émilion is the region known as Entre-Deux-Mers ("between two seas"—actually two rivers, the Dordogne and Garonne), whose dry white wine is particularly flavorsome. This region is famed for its sweet wines, including the world's best, which hail from legendary Sauternes.

GETTING HERE AND AROUND

Bordeaux is one of France's main transportation hubs. However, once you get out into the surrounding Gironde—the "Wine Country"—you may find its seven regions (divided according to geography and the types of wine produced) difficult to reach without a car. Public buses run frequently through the countryside, but they don't necessarily stop in convenient places. The comprehensive English version of the Conseil Général's transportation website (⊕ *transgironde.gironde.fr*) outlines your options. If you have access to a car, you'll find life much easier, particularly if you purchase a Michelin map; Map No. 234 covers a large portion of the southwest. Another option is to go on a bus tour organized by the Bordeaux tourism office.

AIR TRAVEL

Frequent daily flights on Air France link Bordeaux and the domestic airport at Limoges with Paris. Easyjet has seven direct flights a week from London to Bordeaux and Ryanair also flies direct from Edinburgh as well as into Pau and Biarritz farther south.

Airport Information Aéroport de Bordeaux-Mérignac ☎ *05–56–34–50-50* ⊕ *www.bordeaux.aeroport.fr.*

BUS TRAVEL

The Conseil Général's TransGironde network of buses includes regional operators like Citram Aquitaine, Keolis Gironde, and Cars André; these cover towns in the wine country and beach areas not well served by rail. The main Gare Routière (bus terminal) in Bordeaux is on allées de Chartres (by esplanade des Quinconces), near the Garonne River and Stalingrad square.

Contacts TransGironde ✉ *Bordeaux* ☎ *0974–500-033* ⊕ *transgironde.gironde.fr.*

CAR TRAVEL

As the capital of southwest France, Bordeaux has superb highway links with Paris, Spain, and even the Mediterranean (A62 expressway via Toulouse links up with the A61 to Narbonne). The A10 is the Paris–Bordeaux expressway and the A63 south brings you past Bayonne. The A20 south is the main route from Paris to just before Cahors, but it's an hour quicker to go south on the A10 through Tours and Poitiers.

TRAIN TRAVEL

The superfast TGV Atlantique service links Paris Gare Montparnasse to Bordeaux, 585 km (364 miles) away, in 3½ hours. Trains link Bordeaux to Lyon (6½ hrs) and Nice (9 hrs) via Marseille. At least a dozen trains leave most days from Bordeaux for St-Émilion, taking anything from 30 to 55 minutes. If you're heading north to Pauillac there are at least a dozen trains (around 80 mins) a day from Bordeaux.

Contacts Gare de Bordeaux ✉ *Rue Charles Domercq, Bordeaux* ☎ *05–47–47– 10–00.* **SNCF** ☎ *36–35* ⊕ *www.sncf.fr.*

RESTAURANTS

Although countryside Médoc eateries are few, the city of Bordeaux is jammed with restaurants, especially around place du Parlement; plus it has many cafés (notably in the Quartier St-Pierre) and bars (place de la Victoire and cours de la Somme). Not surprisingly, the wines of the region are often used as a base for regional food specialties. Lamprey, a good local fish, is often served in a red wine sauce as *lamproie à la Bordelaise*, and sturgeon cooked in a white wine sauce, as *esturgeon à la Libournaise* (Libourne-style). As for meat, the lamb from Pauillac and the beef from Bazas and Aquitaine are rightly famous, as is the wood pigeon (*palombe*). And Bordeaux has spectacular desserts, such as *fanchonnette bordelaise* (puff pastry in custard covered with meringue), *cannelé de Bordeaux* (small cakes, made in fluted molds, that can only be found here), and the famed macaroons from St-Émilion, invented there by the town's Ursuline nuns in the 17th century.

Prices in the reviews are the average cost of a main course at dinner or, if dinner is not served, at lunch.

HOTELS

Countryside hotels can be gorgeous—not to mention convenient for touring the region's famed vineyards—but basing yourself in Bordeaux city is definitely worth considering, because pickings for rural inns can be slim in summer months and nonexistent in winter, when most of them close. And don't fret about missing the vineyards. Many of the city hotels can create wine-country tours for you, as Gradyghost notes on Fodor's Talk Forum: "The concierge at the Hotel Burdigala arranged individual guided tours at First Growth vineyards like Lafite, Mouton-Rothschild, and Château Margaux. Needless to say, those were memorable experiences."

Prices in the reviews are the lowest cost of a standard double room in high season.

16

VISITOR INFORMATION

The Office de Tourisme in Bordeaux is the first place to head for further information on local and regional sights, including wine tours and tastings; a round-the-clock phone service in English is available. The office also organizes coach tours of the surrounding vineyards every day in high season and nearly every Wednesday and weekends in the off-season. The office also has branch offices at the Gare de Bordeaux train station and the airport.

Contact Office of Tourism of Bordeaux ✉ *12 cours du XXX-Juillet, Bordeaux–Cedex* ☎ *05–56–00–66–00* ⊕ *www.bordeaux-tourisme.com.*

BORDEAUX: CITY OF WINE

Bordeaux as a whole, rather than any particular points within it, is what you'll want to visit in order to understand why Victor Hugo described it as Versailles plus Antwerp, and why the painter Francisco de Goya, when exiled from his native Spain, chose it as his last home (he died here in 1828). The capital of southwest France and the region's largest city, Bordeaux remains synonymous with the wine trade: wine shippers have long maintained their headquarters along the banks of the Garonne, while buyers from around the world arrive for the huge biennial Vinexpo show (held in odd-number years). Today, much in the city is spanking new, courtesy of France's former prime minister, Alain Juppé, who became mayor of the city several years ago. As the gateway to marvelous Margaux and superlative Sauternes, Bordeaux—best entered from the south by the river—is 585 km (364 miles) southwest of Paris, 240 km (150 miles) northwest of Toulouse, and 190 km (118 miles) north of Biarritz.

GETTING HERE

If you arrive by air, the Aéroport de Bordeaux-Mérignac (☎ *05–56–34–50–50* ⊕ *www.bordeaux.aeroport.fr*) sits 10 km (7 miles) west of the city in Mérignac; the airport's Jet'Bus loops between it and the city center every 45 minutes for €7 one way, €12 return. You can also come by rail from Paris, with TGVs (⊕ *www.tgv.com*) making the 3½-hour trip at least 16 times a day; the train deposits you at one of the country's major hubs, the Gare de Bordeaux, St-Jean (☎ *36–35* ⊕ *www.ter-sncf.com*), about 3 km (2 miles) from downtown. Bordeaux's urban TBC buses (Nos. 7 and 8) will take you from the train station into the city center for less than €1.50 one way; while other buses, augmented by a multibillion-euro tramway system (completed in 2008) will help you get around the city itself with ease. The TransGironde network of regional buses (☎ *0974–500–033* ⊕ *transgironde.gironde.fr*) goes farther afield in the Gironde, and even to other nearby *départements* (provinces).

Visitor Information Office of Tourism of Bordeaux ✉ *12 cours du XXX-Juillet* ☎ *05–56–00–66–00* ⊕ *www.bordeaux-tourisme.com.*

Red Gold: The Wines of Bordeaux

Everyone in Bordeaux celebrated the 2000 vintage as the "crop of the century," a wine that comes along once in a lifetime. But bringing everything down to earth are some new sour grapes: the increasingly loud whispers that Bordeaux may be "over."

In this world of nouvelle cuisine and uncellared wines, some critics feel the world has moved away from pricey, rich, red wines and more people are opting for younger choices from other lands. Be that as it may, if you have any aspirations to being a wine connoisseur, Bordeaux will always remain the bedrock of French viticulture.

It has been considered so ever since the credentials of Bordeaux wines were traditionally established in 1787. That year, Thomas Jefferson went down to the region from Paris and splurged on bottles of 1784 Château d'Yquem and Château Margaux, for prices that were, he reported, "indeed dear." Jefferson knew his wines: in 1855, both Yquem and Margaux were officially classified among Bordeaux's top five. And two centuries later, some of his very bottles (the authenticity of their provenance has since been disputed, as well as documented in the controversial book *The Billionaire's Vinegar*) fetched upward of $50,000 when offered in a high-flying auction in New York City.

As it turns out, Bordeaux's reputation dates from the Middle Ages. From 1152 to 1453, along with much of what is now western France, Bordeaux belonged to England. The light red wine then produced was known as *clairet,* the origin of our word "claret." Today no other part of France has such a concentration of top-class vineyards.

The versatile Bordeaux region yields sweet and dry whites and fruity or full-bodied reds from a huge domain extending on either side of the Gironde (Blaye and Bourg to the north, Médoc and Graves to the south) and inland along the Garonne (Sauternes) and Dordogne (St-Émilion, Fronsac, Pomerol) or in between these two rivers (Entre-Deux-Mers).

At the top of the government-supervised scale—which ranks, from highest to lowest, as Appellation d'Origine Contrôlée (often abbreviated AOC); Vin Délimité de Qualité Supérieur (VDQS); Vins de Pays; and Vin de Table—are the fabled vintages of Bordeaux, leading off with Margaux. Sadly, the vineyards of Margaux are among the ugliest in France, lost amid the flat, dusty plains of Médoc.

Bordeaux is better represented at historic St-Émilion, with its cascading cobbled streets, or at Sauternes. Nothing in that grubby village would suggest the mind-boggling wealth lurking amid the picturesque vine-laden slopes and hollows. The village has a wineshop where bottles gather dust on rickety shelves, next to handwritten price tags demanding small fortunes.

Making Sauternes is a tricky business. Autumn mists steal up the valleys to promote *Botrytis cinerea*, a fungus known as *pourriture noble* or noble rot, which sucks moisture out of the grapes, leaving a high proportion of sugar. Sauternes's liquid gold is harvested in *vendanges* beginning in September and lasting to December. *Santé!*

16

EXPLORING

Bordeaux is a less exuberant city than many others in France but lively and stylish elements are making a dent in the city's conservative veneer. The cleaned-up riverfront is said by some, after a bottle or two, to exude an elegance reminiscent of St. Petersburg, and that stylish aura of 18th-century élan also permeates the historic downtown sector—"le vieux Bordeaux"—where fine shops invite exploration. To the south of the city center are old docklands undergoing renewal—one train station has now been transformed into a big multiplex movie theater—but the area is still a bit shady. To get a feel for the historic port of Bordeaux, take the 90-minute boat trip that leaves quai Louis-XVIII every weekday afternoon, or the regular passenger ferry that plies the Garonne between quai Richelieu and the Pont d'Aquitaine in summer. A nice time to stroll around the city center is the first Sunday of the month, when it's pedestrian-only and vehicles are banned.

> ## BORDEAUX'S BIG WINE BLOWOUT
>
> The four-day Fête du Vin (Wine Festival) at the end of June sees glass-clinking merriment along the banks of the Garonne. The city's grandest square gets packed with workshops, booths, and thousands of wine lovers. Log on to ⊕ www.bordeaux-fete-le-vin.com for all the heady details.

TOP ATTRACTIONS

Cathédrale St-André. This may not be one of France's finer Gothic cathedrals but the intricate 14th-century chancel makes an interesting contrast with the earlier nave. Excellent stone carvings adorn the facade of this hefty edifice. You can climb the 15th-century, 160-foot **Tour Pey-Berland** for a stunning view of the city; it's open Tuesday–Sunday 10–noon and 2–5. ⊠ *Pl. Pey-Berland* ☎ *05–56–81–26–25* ⊒ *€5 tower.*

Ecole du Vin de Bordeaux. On tree-lined cours du XXX-Juillet, not far from the banks of the Garonne and the main artery of the esplanade des Quinconces, you'll find the Ecole du Vin, right across the street from the city tourist office. This school—run by the CIVB (Conseil Interprofessionnel des Vins de Bordeaux), the headquarters of the Bordeaux wine trade—organizes wine initiation and tasting classes. At the same address you'll find Le Bar à Vin, which is a good place to sample reds (like Pauillac or St-Émilion), dry whites (like an Entre-Deux-Mers, Graves, or Côtes de Blaye), and sweet whites (like Sauternes or Loupiac); this can be particularly useful when trying to decide which of the 57 wine appellations to focus on in your exploration. The wine-oriented tourist office can then put you on the right path with itineraries and tour details. You can also make purchases at the **Vinothèque** opposite. ⊠ *8 cours du XXX-Juillet* ☎ *05–56–00–22–85* ⊕ *www.la-vinotheque.com* ☽ *Bar, Mon.–Sat. 11–10.*

Grand Théâtre. One block south of the Ecole du Vin is the city's leading 18th-century monument: the Grand Théâtre, designed by Victor Louis and built between 1773 and 1780. It's the pride of the city, with an elegant exterior ringed by graceful Corinthian columns and a dazzling

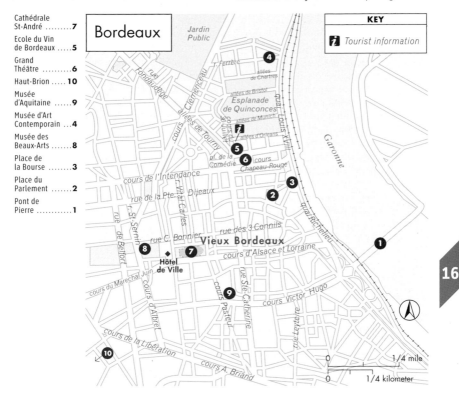

foyer with a two-winged staircase and a cupola. The theater hall has a frescoed ceiling with a shimmering chandelier composed of 14,000 Bohemian crystals. Contact the Bordeaux tourist office to learn about guided tours. ⊠ *Pl. de la Comédie* ☎ *05–56–00–85–95* ⊕ *www.opera-bordeaux.com.*

Haut-Brion. One of the region's most famous wine-producing châteaux is actually within the city limits: follow N250 southwest from central Bordeaux for 3 km (2 miles) to the district of Pessac, home to Haut-Brion, producer of the only non-Médoc wine to be ranked a *premier cru* (the most elite wine classification). It's claimed the very buildings surrounding the vineyards create their own microclimate, protecting the precious grapes and allowing them to ripen earlier. The white château looks out over the celebrated pebbly soil. The wines produced at **La Mission–Haut Brion (Domaine Clarence Dillon),** across the road, are almost as sought-after. ⊠ *135 av. Jean-Jaurès, Pessac* ☎ *05–56–00–29–30* ⊕ *www.haut-brion.com* 🎫 *Free 1-hr visits by appointment, weekdays only, with tasting* ⊙ *Closed mid-July–mid-Aug.*

Musée d'Aquitaine. Two blocks south of the Cathédrale St-André, this excellent museum takes you on a trip through Bordeaux's history, with emphasis on Roman, medieval, Renaissance, port-harbor, colonial, and 20th-century daily life. The detailed prehistoric section almost saves you a trip to Lascaux II, which is reproduced here in part. ✉ *20 cours Pasteur* ☎ *05–56–01–51–00* 🌐 *www.musee-aquitane-bordeaux.fr* 🎫 *Free* 🕒 *Tues.–Sun. 11–6.*

Musée des Beaux-Arts. One of 15 cities in France chosen by Napoléon to showcase his war-acquired works (most notably from Italy) as well as bits of existing royal art, Bordeaux houses a fetching collection in its Museé des Beaux-Arts. Pieces, which span the 15th century to present, include important paintings by Paolo Veronese (*St. Dorothy*), Camille Corot (*Bath of Diana*), and Odilon Redon (*Apollo's Chariot*), plus sculptures by Auguste Rodin. Not far from the Cathédrale St-André, this museum adorns tidy gardens behind the ornate Hôtel de Ville (town hall). ✉ *20 cours d'Albret* ☎ *05–56–10–20–56* 🎫 *Free* 🕒 *Wed.–Sun. 11–6.*

Place de la Bourse. The centerpiece of the left bank is this open square built in 1729–33. Ringed with large-windowed buildings, it was beautifully designed by the era's most esteemed architect, Jacques Gabriel, father of Jacques-Ange Gabriel (who went on to remodel Paris's place de la Concorde).

Place du Parlement. A few blocks to the southeast of place de la Bourse, place du Parlement is also ringed by elegant 18th-century structures and packed with lively outdoor cafés.

WORTH NOTING

Musée d'Art Contemporain (*Contemporary Art Center*). Just north of the esplanade des Quinconces (a sprawling square), this two-story museum is imaginatively housed in a converted 19th-century spice warehouse—the Entrepôt Lainé. Many expositions here showcase cutting-edge artists who invariably festoon the huge expanse of the square with hanging ropes, ladders, and large video screens. ✉ *7 rue Ferrère* ☎ *05–56–00–81–50* 🎫 *5€* 🕒 *Tues. and Thurs.–Sun. 11–6, Wed. 11–8.*

Pont de Pierre. For a view of the picturesque quayside, stroll across the Garonne on this bridge, built on the orders of Napoléon between 1810 and 1821, and until 1965 the only bridge across the river.

WHERE TO EAT

$$ FRENCH 🍴 **Baud et Millet.** With a cellar full of fromage—and a vast wine stock that you peruse in lieu of a list—this is a good place to get acquainted with some of the 246 different French cheeses that Charles de Gaulle famously blamed for making this such a complex, and thus difficult, country to govern. You must buzz to gain entry, and that's just the first element of the unique experience here. Order from the cheese buffet and serve yourself from the downstairs cellar, or start with a cherry tomato and Roquefort *clafoutis*, then move on to Camembert flambéed in Calvados. For €45 you can try a *dégustation* of nine cooked cheese dishes. ■ **TIP→ Genuine stinky-cheese lovers should know some cheeses here aren't as potent as can be had elsewhere in France.** [$] *Average main: €20* ✉ *19 rue Huguerie* ☎ *05–56–79–05–77* 🌐 *www.baudetmillet.fr* 🕒 *Closed late Dec.–early Jan.*

At the end of June, Bordeaux becomes one big party thanks to the four-day Fête du Vin (Wine Festival).

$ BRASSERIE 🍴 **Café Français.** Situated on a *grande place* in the Vielle Ville, with cathedral views and a traditional menu of solid sustenance, this venerable bistro attracts those looking for an all-day mixture of café and restaurant. It's the quintessential place to people-watch over a coffee or meal. ■ **TIP→ Try for a table on the terrace. The view over place Pey-Berland is never less than diverting; however, some say you end up paying for the place more than the plate.** [$] *Average main: €17* ✉ *5–6 pl. Pey-Berland* ☎ *05–56–52–96–69.*

$$$ FRENCH 🍴 **La Tupina.** Under the eye of flamboyant owner Jean-Pierre Xiradakis, *cuisine de terroir* is served up at this classic restaurant (the name means "kettle") on one of Bordeaux's oldest streets. Dried herbs hang from the ceiling, a Provençal grandfather clock ticks off the minutes, and an antique fireplace sports a grill bearing sizzling morsels of duck and chicken. Like the room itself, the menu aspires to *nostalgie*, and it succeeds. On the same street (No. 34) is the owner's fetching—and cheaper—Bar Cave de la Monnaie. You can also dine or shop at his *épicerie*, Le Comestible (No. 3), which is lined with bistro tables and jars of foie gras, cassoulet, and other regional sundries. ■ **TIP→ Copies of this business-savvy chef's southwestern cuisine cookbook are sold at the épicerie.** [$] *Average main: €31* ✉ *6 rue Porte-de-la-Monnaie* ☎ *05–56–91–56–37* 🌐 *www.latupina.com* ✍ *Reservations essential.*

$$$$ FRENCH Fodor's Choice ★ 🍴 **Le Chapon-Fin.** Some say you haven't really been to Bordeaux if you haven't been to Le Chapon Fin—an epicurean indulgence, housed in one of Bordeaux's most historically esteemed establishments, where guests once included wealthy wine merchants, elite transatlantic travelers, and cultural icons such as Sarah Bernhardt and Toulouse-Lautrec. Founded in 1825, this was one of the first 33 restaurants crowned by Michelin

Bordeaux doesn't have many grand châteaux-hotels, but the Grand Barrail Château Hôtel & Spa is a winner.

in 1933. Reopened in 1987, guests are now served from Thierry Marx–trained chef Nicolas Frion's refined modern menu in the extraordinary, original Rococo grotto *salle* (room). Expect offerings like panfried fillet of beef with eggplant cannelloni in an onion-tomato compote or lobster in chestnut cream with chanterelle ravioli. You should also prepare yourself for sommeliers boasting the region's best vintages. $ *Average main: €38* ⊠ *5 rue Montesquieu* ☎ *05–56–79–10–10* ⊕ *www.chapon-fin.com* ⌕ *Reservations essential* ⊘ *Closed Sun., Mon., and Aug.*

$$$
MODERN FRENCH

✕ **L'Estacade.** *Le tout Bordeaux* comes to this trendy glass-encased restaurant, which hangs spectacularly over the Garonne River, for its privileged views of Bordeaux proper and the 18th-century place de la Bourse on the opposite bank. The setting is sleek modern with a casual, sometimes noisy crowd. The cuisine is creative but not edgy (imagine sesame-and-soy-marinated veal, or mullet tartare with cream and fish eggs), while the wine list focuses on young Bordeaux. ■**TIP**➜ **The city's lights make views better at night.** $ *Average main: €29* ⊠ *Quai de Queyries* ☎ *05–57–54–02–50* ⊕ *www.lestacade.com.*

$
CAFÉ

✕ **L'Oiseau Cabosse.** This straight-up organic restaurant and coffee bar is a good option for a light meal. With its kind and spunky service, chic outside terrace, and interesting location in the bourgeois bohemian Quartier de la Grosse Cloche (Big Clock neighborhood), it's a welcome find in the city. Try the duck confit parmentier, curry and leek quiche, or a fresh baked dessert. ■**TIP**➜ **Don't miss the organic, artisanal cola or 100% pure cocoa hot chocolate.** $ *Average main: €12* ⊠ *30 rue Sainte Colombe* ☎ *05–57–14–02–07* ⊘ *Closed Mon. No dinner Tues. and Sun.*

WHERE TO STAY

For expanded hotel reviews, visit Fodors.com.

$ HOTEL **Acanthe Hotel.** Just steps from the place de la Bourse, this budget hotel is extremely convenient for a less grand stay in the city, and recent renovations have provided rooms with air-conditioning, double-paned windows, environmentally friendly paint on the walls, and freshened bathrooms—top-floor rooms are the best, with views over the neighboring rooftops (otherwise it can feel a bit claustrophobic). **Pros:** friendly staff; organic breakfast option. **Cons:** gets a lot of street noise. [$] *Rooms from: €75* ✉ *12 rue Saint Remi* ☎ *05–56–81–66–58* 🌐 *www.acanthe-hotel-bordeaux.com* 🛏 *20 rooms.*

$$$$ HOTEL **Grand Hôtel de Bordeaux & Spa.** Festooned in luxury fabrics and 18th-century furnishings, this posh extravaganza, designed by France's über-chic Jacque Garcia, put Bordeaux back on the world scene with its veritable army of restaurants and bars along with a swanky Roman bath–inspired spa—all just steps from the city's Golden Triangle shopping district. **Pros:** marble bathrooms and loads of in-room amenities; deluxe service; superb central location. **Cons:** some rooms lack natural light; superior rooms are small (but executive rooms let you sprawl out). [$] *Rooms from: €525* ✉ *2–5 pl. de la Comédie* ☎ *05–57–30–44–44* 🌐 *www.ghbordeaux.com* 🛏 *128 rooms, 22 suites.*

16

$$$ HOTEL **La Maison Bord'eaux.** Northwest of the city center, the street-front door of this inconspicuous boutique hotel opens onto a quiet courtyard that once served as a relay stable for carriages and today provides a welcome respite for modern travelers seeking urban tranquillity. **Pros:** nicely situated to enjoy both city center and a quiet retreat. **Cons:** modern style may not ring every traveler's bells. [$] *Rooms from: €175* ✉ *113 rue Dr. Albert Barraud* ☎ *05–56–44–00–45* 🌐 *www.lamaisonbordeaux.com* 🛏 *14.*

$$ HOTEL **Quality Hôtel Bordeaux Centre.** At the heart of Bordeaux's pedestrian center, this fully modernized hotel—in a 19th-century building in the old part of town—has compact, deep-toned rooms, and a helpful reception staff; it's the place to stay if you want businesslike contemporary comfort without original character. **Pros:** convenient location beside the Grand Théâtre; functional rooms. **Cons:** somewhat generic furnishings; parking is five minutes away. [$] *Rooms from: €135* ✉ *27 rue du Parlement-Ste-Catherine* ☎ *05–56–81–95–12* 🌐 *www.qualityhotelbordeauxcentre.com* 🛏 *84 rooms.*

NIGHTLIFE AND THE ARTS

Aux Quatre Coins du Vin. This sleek, modern wine and tapas bar has dispensing machines that allow you to taste as many wines as you want in a single sitting. ✉ *8 rue de la Devise* ☎ *05–57–34–37–29.*

Comptoir du Jazz. Near the station, this is the place not only for jazz, but also blues, soul, and funk. Log on to their website for the latest line-up. ✉ *58–59 quai Paludate* ☎ *05–56–49–15–55* 🌐 *www.leportdelalune.com.*

Grand Théâtre. Arguably one of the most beautiful historic theaters in Europe, the Grand Théâtre puts on performances of French plays and, occasionally, operas. The venue (which can be visited on guided tours) is an 18th-century showpiece studded with marble muses. ⊠ *Pl. de la Comédie* ☎ *05–56–00–85–95* ⊕ *www.opera-bordeaux.com.*

l'Apollo. A casual, friendly pub with several choices of draft beer, l'Apollo comes to life around aperitif hour—and there's almost always a billiards game underway. ⊠ *19 pl. Fernand-Lafargue* ☎ *05–56–01–25–05.*

Le Bistrot. *The* all-night club for hip-hop, disco, and theme nights like "mother funk-in" and "prohibition"—but come dressed up, as there's no admittance without a *tenue correcte* (avoid running shoes). ⊠ *50 quai de Paludate.*

SHOPPING

Between the cathedral and the Grand Théâtre are numerous pedestrian streets (rue Ste-Catherine being the biggest) where stylish shops and clothing boutiques abound—Bordeaux may favor understatement, but there's no lack of elegance in and around its Golden Triangle shopping district.

Bear in mind that the *soldes* (sales) start in France at the height of summer, especially just before Bastille (July 14) weekend.

Baillardran. With five stores in Bordeaux alone, Baillardran is going to be hard to walk by without at least looking in its windows at those indigenous sweet delights, *Bordelais cannelés!* Much like a Doric column in miniature, these small indented, caramelized cakes, made with vanilla and a dash of rum, are a delicious regional specialty. ⊠ *55 cours de l'Intendance* ☎ *05–56–52–92–64* ⊕ *www.baillardran.com.*

Fromagerie Deruelle. For a grand selection of cheeses—along with raw milk, smoked-sea-salt butter, bulk honey, and all things creamy and tasty—stop in at Elodie Deruelle's shop, Fromagerie Deruelle. ⊠ *66 rue du Pas-Saint-Georges* ☎ *05–57–83–04–15.*

Grand Déballage de Brocante. Within the shadow of the church of Saint Michel, a few blocks south of the Pont de Pierre and just off the river, one of the country's largest flea markets operates every second Sunday during the months of March, June, September, and December—all day long. Year-round, a weekly Sunday flea market is also held here, which is just the ticket if you're looking for real bargains away from the storefronts or need a nice excuse to explore the historic St-Michel quarter. ⊠ *Pl. St-Michel.*

Jean d'Alos Fromager-Affineur. For an exceptional selection of cheeses, go to Jean d'Alos Fromager-Affineur. ⊠ *4 rue Montesquieu* ☎ *05–56–44–29–66.*

La Fabrique Pains et Bricoles. Want Bordeaux's best bread to go with your cheese? Get in line. Apparently, the word's out about La Fabrique Pains et Bricoles because the queue is out the door at this fine bakery—and that's always a good sign. ⊠ *47 rue du Pas-Saint-Georges* ☎ *05–56–44–84–26.*

Vinothèque. The Vinothèque sells top-ranked Bordeaux wines. ⊠ *8 cours du XXX-Juillet* ☎ *05–57–10–41–41* ⊕ *www.vinotheque-bordeaux.com.*

ROUTE DU MÉDOC AND THE WINE COUNTRY

All along the western side of the Gironde estuary south, until you hit the meeting point of the Dordogne and Garonne rivers just north of Bordeaux city, you will encounter the almost mythical Médoc wine region. Farthest north is the Médoc appellation itself. To the south of this, the Paulliac appellation surrounds the Saint-Estéphe and Saint Julien appellations, which lie nearer to the estuary. Closer to Bordeaux, and just south of the Paulliac region, is the conglomeration of the Listrac, Moulis, Margaux, and (nearest to the city along the Garonne) the Haut-Médoc appellations.

Above the city, the D2—or Route des Châteaux—veers northwest through most of the wine country along the Gironde all the way to Talais, and the D1215 (farther west) runs through the other side of the region, giving access to appellations like Listrac and Moulis, which the D2 bypasses.

Wines from the Médoc are made predominantly from the Cabernet Sauvignon grape, and can taste dry, even austere, when young. The better ones often need 15 to 25 years before "opening up" to reveal their full spectrum of complex flavors. More celebrated vintages are found 35 km (21 miles) to the east of the city in the medieval region of St-Émilion. Here, vineyards that are family owned and relatively small—on average, just 17 acres each— are divided into two appellations, St-Émilion and St-Émilion Grand Cru. At the region's heart lies the beautiful wine town of St-Émilion.

16

GETTING HERE

If you're heading north, you'll have to make your way to or through Pauillac (try to ignore the oil refinery). TransGironde buses (☏ *0974–500–033* ⊕ *transgironde.gironde.fr*) operate in this area, making the Bordeaux–Pauillac trip in about 50 minutes. They connect Bordeaux with Margaux (90 mins) as well, and travel as far north as Pointe de Grave (2 hrs, 30 mins). At least 12 trains daily travel to Pauillac from Bordeaux, dropping you off at the Gare de Pauillac on 2 bis place Verdun. You can also ride the rails around four times a day as far as Soulac, which is 9 km (5½ miles) below Pointe de Grave, by changing at Lesparre for about €15 one way. If you want to get into the Médoc from Bordeaux by car make sure to get off the road that encircles Bordeaux (the "Rocade") using Sortie (Exit) 7.

Visitor Information Pauillac Tourist Office ⊠ *La Verrerie, Pauillac* ☏ *05–56–59–03–08* ⊕ *www.pauillac-medoc.com.*

MARGAUX

Château Margaux. Château Margaux, housed in a magnificent Neoclassical building from 1810, is recognized as a producer of premiers crus, and its wine ranks with Graves's Haut-Brion as one of Bordeaux's top five reds. As with most of the top Bordeaux châteaux, visits to Château Margaux are by appointment only. ☏ *05–57–88–83–83* ⊕ *www.chateau-margaux.com.*

Lascombes. The well-informed, English-speaking staff at the tourist office can direct you to other châteaux such as **Lascombes** and **Palmer,** which

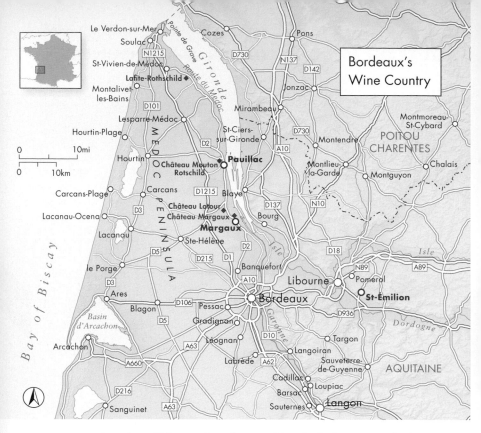

have beautiful grounds and reasonably priced wines. In nearby Cussac, visit the winery and carriage museum at **Château Lanessan.** ☎ *05–57– 88–70–66* ⊕ *www.chateau-lascombes.com.*

PAUILLAC

Some 90 km (56 miles) north of Bordeaux on highway D2 is Pauillac, home to the three wineries—Lafite-Rothschild, Latour, and Mouton-Rothschild—that produce Médoc's other top reds. If the posh prices of these *grands crus* are not for you, ask about bike rentals at the town's tourist office and pedal off to visit any of the slightly less expensive wineries nearby. ⊠ *La Verrerie* ☎ *05–56–59–03–08* ⊕ *www.pauillac-medoc.com.*

Château Lafite-Rothschild. Lafite-Rothschild is among the most resonant names in the wine world. Even by the giddy standards of the Médoc, Lafite—owned by the Rothschild family since 1868 and a recorded producer since 1234—is a temple of wine making at its most memorable. Prices may be sky-high, but no one fortunate enough to sample one of the château's classic vintages will forget the experience in a hurry. Too bad you can't visit the family château on the grounds—its rooms are the defining examples of *le style Rothschild,* one of the most opulent styles of 19th-century interior decoration. ☎ *05–56–59–26–83* ⊕ *www.*

lafite.com ✉ *Free* ⊙ *By appointment only at 2 and 3:30, reserve at least 2 wks in advance; closed Aug.–Oct.*

Château Latour. Tastings and tours at the renowned Château Latour are typically free, but very selective—you have to be a serious taster, accompanied by a guide or professional in the wine trade, and you will be expected to make a purchase. Reservations are also required, and these must sometimes be made a month in advance. If you don't make the cut, Pauillac is still worth seeing. Of all the towns and villages in the Médoc, it is the prettiest, so you may want to stroll along the riverfront and stop for refreshments at one of its restaurants. A train line connects Pauillac to Bordeaux, running several times daily in summer. ✉ *Saint-Lambert* ☎ *05–56–73–19–80* ⊕ *www.chateau-latour.com.*

Château Mouton-Rothschild. Most of the great vineyards in this area are strictly private, although the owners are usually receptive to inquiries about visits from bona fide wine connoisseurs. One, however, has long boasted a welcoming visitor center: Mouton-Rothschild, whose eponymous wine was brought to perfection in the 1930s by that flamboyant figure Baron Philippe de Rothschild. The baron's daughter, Philippine, continues to lavish money and love on this growth, so wine fans flock here for either the one-hour visit, which includes a tour of the cellars, *chai* (wine warehouse), and museum, or the slightly longer version that's topped off with a tasting. ✉ *Le Pouyalet* ☎ *05–56–73–21–29* ⊕ *www.bpdr.com* ✉ *€6.50; with tasting, €16* ⊙ *Mon.–Thurs. 9:30–11 and 2–4, Fri. 9:30–11 and 2–3, by appointment only; reserve at least 2 wks in advance.*

WHERE TO STAY

For expanded hotel reviews, visit Fodors.com.

$$$
HOTEL

Château Cordeillan-Bages. Though the clean-lined, contemporary interior of this 17th-century, stone-faced, wine-producing mansion may not call out to everyone, the vines growing right up to the property, the luxury rooms, the sommelier's dream of a wine cellar (with more than 200 different Champagnes alone), and the much celebrated restaurant are definite inducements. **Pros:** lovely marble building; location breathes tranquillity; top chef in residence; expert wine-tasting and discovery courses offered. **Cons:** somewhat faded modern decor; remote with airport 45 km (27 miles) away—but you could ask to use the chateau's helipad. $ *Rooms from: €203* ✉ *Rte. des Châteaux, 1½ km (1 mile) south of town* ☎ *05–56–59–24–24* ⊕ *www.cordeillanbages.com* ⊅ *24 rooms, 4 suites* ⊙ *Closed late Dec.–mid-Mar.*

$
HOTEL

France & Angleterre. Occupying a low-slung, 19th-century building that overlooks the quaint waterfront and Gironde estuary, this low-key spot is a convenient choice if you wish to explore Pauillac's winding streets. **Pros:** central location; estuary views. **Cons:** small, generic rooms; budget furnishings. $ *Rooms from: €75* ✉ *3 quai Albert-Pichon* ☎ *05–56–59–01–20* ⊕ *www.hoteldefrance-angleterre.com* ⊅ *28 rooms* ⊙ *Closed mid-Dec.–mid-Jan.*

16

A Fodor's.com member, t56gf, captured the medieval beauty of cobblestoned St-Émilion in this photo.

ST-ÉMILION

74 km (41 miles) southeast of Pauillac, 35 km (23 miles) east of Bordeaux.

Fodor's Choice
★

Suddenly the sun-fired flatlands of Pomerol break into hills and send you tumbling into St-Émilion. This jewel of a town has old buildings of golden stone, ruined town walls, well-kept ramparts offering magical views, and a church hewn into a cliff. Sloping vineyards invade from all sides, and thousands of tourists invade down the middle, many thirsting for the red wine and macaroons that bear the town's name. The medieval streets, delightfully cobblestone (though often very steep), are filled with craft shops, bakeries, cafés, restaurants, and—of course—wine stores (St-Émilion reaches maturity earlier than other Bordeaux reds and is often better value for the money than Médoc or Graves). For the best export prices try Ets Martin (✉ *25 rue Guadet* ⊕ *www.martinvins. com*), or climb the stairs to the *cremant* (sparkling wine) specialist and its *bar a bulles* (bubbles bar) Les Cordaliers (⊕ *www.lescordeliers.com*), where you can buy a glass or bottle of Bordeaux's bubbly to sip in a lovely courtyard beneath 13th-century cloister ruins.

GETTING HERE

To take a train to St-Émilion you first need to head to Libourne—a 10-minute cab or bus ride away. There are six trains from Paris to Libourne and another six that connect with Angoulême to Libourne. TER trains from Bordeaux run at least a dozen times a day during the week for about €9 and six times a day on weekends and holidays. It will cost you €2.50 if you opt to take a TransGironde bus (☎ *0974–500–033*

🌐 *transgironde.gironde.fr*) from Bordeaux to St-Émilion, the trip being a two-pronged affair with a changeover in Libourne and a total travel time of about an hour.

Visitor Information St-Émilion Tourist Office ✉ *Pl. des Cremeaux* ☎ *05–57–55–28–28* 🌐 *www.saint-emilion-tourisme.com.*

MÉDOC MARATHON

The Médoc Marathon (🌐 *www.marathondumedoc.com*), on the first or second Saturday of September, is more than just a 42-km (26-mile) race through the vineyards: 52 other events appear along the way, with at least 90% of the runners in disguise indulging in no fewer than 21 giant buffets of local fare, and at 22 refreshment stands en route. Speed is not exactly of the essence for most taking part in the competition; 2014 marks the 30th anniversary of this hybrid athletic-alcoholic event. Log on to the website to see entertaining videos from previous years.

16

EXPLORING

Château Angelus. The town's Office de Tourisme rents bikes (€15 per day) and organizes tours of the pretty local vineyards—the fabled **Château Angelus** and **Château Belair,** among others—which include wine tastings and train rides through the vineyards. It's best to hit the road on a weekday, when more châteaux are open.

Château Ausone. Just south of the town walls, Château Ausone is an estate that is ranked with Château Angelus as a producer of St-Émilion's finest wines.

Château du Roi (*King's Castle*). A stroll along the 13th-century ramparts takes you to the Château du Roi. To this day nobody knows whether it was Henry III of England or King Louis VIII of France who chose the site and ordered its building.

Église Monolithe (*Monolithic Church*). One of Europe's largest underground churches, the Église Monolithe was hewn out of the rock face between the 9th and 12th century by monks faithful to the memory of St-Émilion, an 8th-century hermit and miracle worker. Its spire-top *clocher* (bell tower) rises out of the bedrock, dominating the center of town. ✉ *Pl. du Marché* 🎫 *€ 7* 🕒 *Tours leave from tourist office daily.*

Place du Marché. From the castle ramparts, cobbled steps lead down to place du Marché, a leafy square where cafés remain open late into the balmy summer night. Beware of the inflated prices charged at the café tables.

WHERE TO EAT

$ BISTRO 🍴 **Chai Pascal.** Chai Pascal is a cozy yet stylish restaurant and wine bar that's popular with locals in the wine trade. Wood tables, lounge chairs and understated artwork on the original stone walls give it a casual, intellectual vibe. The menu is limited, but made fresh and very good value compared to the generally elevated prices of St-Émilion. [$] *Average main: €17* ✉ *37 rue Guadet* ☎ *05–57–24–52–45* 🌐 *www.chai-pascal.com* ☞ *Free Wi-Fi.*

$ BRASSERIE 🍴 **Chez Germaine.** Family cooking and regional dishes are the focus at this central St-Émilion eatery, which serves lunch only. The candlelit upstairs dining room and the terrace are both pleasant places to enjoy the reasonably priced set menus. Grilled meats and fish are house specialties; for dessert, order the almond macaroons. $ *Average main: €16* ⊠ *13 pl. du Clocher* ☎ *05–57–74–49–34* ⊘ *Closed mid-Nov.–mid Feb. No dinner.*

WHERE TO STAY

For expanded hotel reviews, visit Fodors.com.

$ **Auberge de la Commanderie.** Close to the ramparts, this 19th-century
HOTEL   two-story hotel has a gorgeous, white-shuttered facade that blends in beautifully with St-Émilion's stonework—public rooms overlook some vineyards, and guest rooms range from tiny and barebones to large and decorated with colorful prints; some have exposed historic stonework. **Pros:** free parking; some good deals available; inside the village. **Cons:** rooms vary widely; modern French decor. $ *Rooms from: €90* ⊠ *Rue des Cordeliers* ☎ *05–57–24–70–19* ⊕ *www.aubergedelacommanderie. com* ⤳ *17 rooms* ⊘ *Closed mid-Dec.–mid-Feb.*

$$$$ **Grand Barrail Château Hôtel & Spa.** Presiding over the picturesque
HOTEL   vineyards encircling StÉmilion, this fairy-tale Belle Époque château
Fodor's Choice has gorgeous guest rooms that are at once classic and contemporary
★   (for the full storybook experience, ask for one in the main 19th-century building rather than the modern luxury annex).**Pros:** expansive vineyard views; special spa packages; golf and hot-air balloon rides nearby. **Cons:** pricey; ambience so fairy-tale-esque it borders on unoriginal. $ *Rooms from: €320* ⊠ *Rte. de Libourne, 4 km (2½ miles) northwest of St-Émilion on D243* ☎ *05–57–55–37–00* ⊕ *www.grand-barrail.com* ⤳ *41 rooms, 5 suites.*

$$$ **La Thuilière.** It's easy to feel as though industrial-age design, modern
B&B/INN   creature comforts, and a jazz sound track have always set the scene at
Fodor's Choice La Thuilière, but this lovely castellated structure is mostly the result of
★   a spectacular renovation wrought by a hip couple who have managed to underscore the *mystère* of the late 19th-century Tudor-style château with vintage designer lighting, sleek mod furniture, and an ultrapolished black, gray, and deep-brown color scheme. **Pros:** beautiful renovation; personal service; setting equidistant for top sights. **Cons:** remote enough that a car is essential (owners can set up transportation); no other restaurants nearby. $ *Rooms from: €150* ⊠ *60 km (37 miles) northeast of St-Émilion, Saint Front de Pradoux* ☎ *06–45–35–36–82* ⊕ *www. lathuiliere.net* ⤳ *5 suites.*

$$$$ **L'Hostellerie de Plaisance.** Flaunting a unique interior design master-
HOTEL   minded by Alberto Pinto and an elite location in the upper part of
Fodor's Choice town, just across the way from the famous Église Monolithe, this stun-
★   ningly elegant Italianate mansion has long been considered the top hotel in St-Émilion. **Pros:** superstar style; ideally located in St-Émilion proper. **Cons:** certain rooms are small; pricey (breakfast alone is €30 per person). $ *Rooms from: €425* ⊠ *3 pl. du Clocher* ☎ *05–57–55–07–55* ⊕ *www.hostellerie-plaisance.com* ⤳ *14 rooms, 3 suites* ⊘ *Closed mid-Dec.–Feb.*

THE DORDOGNE

WELCOME TO THE DORDOGNE

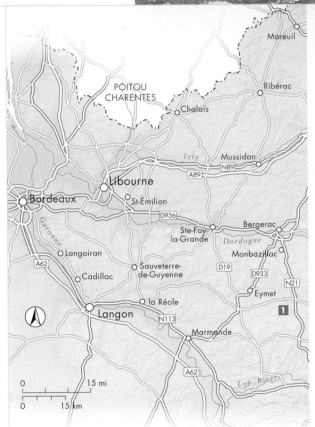

TOP REASONS TO GO

★ **Fantastic food:** Périgord truffles, foie gras, walnuts, plums, and myriad species of mushrooms jostle for attention on restaurant menus here— and the goose-liver pâté is as good as it gets.

★ **Rock stars:** Lascaux is the "Louvre" of Paleolithic man and millions have witnessed prehistory writ large on its spectacularly painted cave walls.

★ **Religious Rocamadour:** Climb toward heaven up the towering cliff to place St-Amadour's seven chapels and you might be transported to a better place.

★ **Sarlat's Cité Médiévale:** Feast your eyes on Sarlat's honey-color houses and 16th-century streets and then just feast at the hundred or so wine and foie-gras shops.

★ **Versailles in the sky:** A dizzying 400 feet above the Dordogne River, the ancestral garden of the Château de Marqueyssac is a 3-km (2-mile) maze of topiaries, parterres, and hedges.

1 **Western Dordogne to Rocamadour.** The Western Dordogne countryside is studded with Renaissance castles, like those at Monbazillac and Biron. Surrounded by lands cultivated by peasant farmers for centuries, *bastide* towns such as Monpazier were once heavily fortified. Heading southeast, the Lot Valley welcomes travelers with the lively town of Cahors, noted for its Romanesque cathedral in the Aquitaine dome style, and St-Cirq-Lapopie, a Renaissance-era time machine. Have your camera ready for Rocamadour's sky-touching Cité Religieuse, one of France's most famous pilgrimage shrines.

GETTING ORIENTED

Just northeast of Bordeaux, the region of Périgord is famed for its prehistoric art, truffle-rich cuisine, and once-upon-a-time villages. The best of these delights are found in the beloved *département* (province) called the Dordogne. Part of the Aquitaine region, this living postcard is threaded by the Dordogne River, which, after its descent from the mountainous Massif Central, weaves westward past prehistoric sites like Lascaux. Astounding, too, are the medieval cliff-hewn villages like Rocamadour—provided that you manage to peer through the crowds in high season.

17

2 Eastern Périgord to Brantôme. You'll have a tough time figuring out which sector of the Dordogne is the most beautiful, but many give the prize to the Périgord Noir. Immerse yourself in the past at Sarlat-la-Canéda, a regional capital so beautifully preserved that film crews flock here for its 16th- and 17th-century turrets and towers. Nearby are the riverside village of La Roque-Gageac and the hilltop castle at Beynac. To the north is the Vézère Valley, the prehistoric capital of France, home to fabled Lascaux. Beyond lies the thriving city of Périgueux.

EATING AND DRINKING WELL IN THE DORDOGNE

The Dordogne, or as the French like to call it, the Périgord, is considered by those in the know to have one of the best regional cuisines in the country. Local chefs celebrate the area's abundant natural bounty in epicurean preparations and simple peasant dishes alike.

The best pâté de fois gras comes from the Dordogne *(above)*; this region is truffle heaven *(right, top)*; top wines hail from Cahors.

The rich resources of the Périgord are legendary: forests and fields are alive with wild game feasting on the nuts and leaves of chestnut, walnut, and oak trees, which encourages the growth of rare mushrooms and coveted truffles. The picturesque, winding rivers are home to trout and crayfish. Rolling fields are filled with grains and vegetables, running alongside orchards of stone fruit.

Few regions in France can boast such a wide selection of local meats (particularly the famed Dordogne foie gras and equally famous pork, duck, and goose dishes); cheeses like Cabécou, Cujassous, Dubjac, Thieviers, and Échougnac; and distinctive wines, liqueurs, and brandies. This amazing variety of ingredients enables chefs here to create nearly everything from local products.

REGIONAL SPECIALTIES

Many well-known French meat dishes are named after surrounding villages and towns. Don't miss steak *à la Sarladaise* (stuffed with pâté de foie gras) or chicken *à la mode de Sorges* (stuffed with a mixture of chicken liver, mustard, bacon, and herbs). And for a sure dose of truffles, try any dish with *sauce Périgueux* or *à la périgourdine* in its name.

FOIE GRAS

Goose liver may not sound too enticing, but once you've had it there's no denying this delicious delicacy. The region has numerous farms with advertisements for foie gras everywhere you go, in shop-windows and on road signs, portraying plump geese and ducks happily meandering toward you. At any food shop, you'll find containers of fresh and frozen foie gras, and it is an ever-present restaurant offering, prepared *pôelé* (pan-fried, usually accompanied by a sweet side), in a terrine (pâté), or otherwise added to your salads and main courses.

WALNUTS

Walnuts, or *noix* in French, are ubiquitous. They mature throughout the summer and usually start falling from the trees in October. The importance of walnuts in the Dordogne—and the rest of this country—cannot be overstated because the walnut is *the* nut here (the translation of noix is simply "nut"). The French make walnut oil for cooking and drizzling on salads, incorporate walnut meat into savory and sweet dishes, and even make alcoholic beverages infused with walnut flavor. In fact, the aperitif of choice in the Dordogne is a sweet dark wine made from green walnuts picked in summer. The immature nuts impart a unique flavor to the wine.

TRUFFLES

During the months of October and November, and sometimes into December, the region's black gold—a fungus called *tuber melanosporum*—is unearthed and sold for exorbitant prices.

Found at the roots of oak trees by trained dogs and pigs, truffles contribute to the local economy, and to the region's celebrated cuisine. Their earthy perfume and delicate flavor have inspired countless dishes prepared by home cooks and restaurant chefs alike.

WINE AND LIQUOR

If you are dining on the region's fabulous bounty, the best accompaniment is a local wine, liqueur, or brandy.

Bergerac is known for its white wines made from Sémillon and Sauvignon Blanc grapes, and for its reds made from Merlot, Cabernet Sauvignon, and Cabernet Franc varieties. The area also produces excellent white dessert wines from the Sémillon grape.

The *fait maison*, or homemade, liqueurs are made from many fruits, including plum, quince, and black currant.

Fruit is also favored here for distilling brandies, with some of the best known made from cherries, grapes, pears, and plums.

17

Updated
by Jennifer
Ditsler-Ladonne

Want to smile happily ever after? Linger in a fantasyland full of castles, cliff-top châteaux, and storybook villages? Join the club. Since the 1990s the Dordogne region has become one of the hottest destinations in France. Formerly one of those off-the-beaten-path areas, it's now in danger of getting four-starred, boutiqued, and postcarded to death, but scratch the surface and you can still find one of the most authentic and appealing regions of rural France.

What's more—and unlike the Loire Valley, for example, where attractions are often far apart—you can discover romantic riverside château after château with each kilometer traveled. Then factor in four troglodyte villages, numerous natural *gouffres* (chasms), the sky-kissing village of Rocamadour, and the most famous prehistoric sights in the world, and you can see why all these attractions have not gone unnoticed: in July and August even the smallest village is often packed with sightseers.

The Dordogne *département* (province) is in the Aquitaine region of southwest France, where, above the river valleys, oak and chestnut forests crowd in on about 1,200 châteaux, most from the 13th and 14th centuries. The area is marked by rich, luxuriant valleys, through which flow clear-water rivers such as the Dordogne, Isle, Dronne, Vézére, and Lot. Separating the valleys are rugged plateaux of granite and limestone, sharp outcroppings of rock, and steep, sheer cliffs. Happily, the 10-km (6-mile) stretch of the Dordogne River from Montfort to Beynac is easily accessible by car, bike, canoe, or on foot, and shouldn't be missed—especially when fields of sunflowers line the banks in season. Offering a nice contrast to the region's rugged physiognomy and *nature sauvage* (wilderness) are hyperpicturesque villages such as La Roque-Gageac, wedged between rocky cliffs and the Dordogne River.

The region is centered on Sarlat, and its impeccably restored medieval buildings make it a great place to use as a base. Even better, the area around this town is honeycombed with dozens of *grottes* (caves) filled with Paleolithic drawings, etchings, and carvings. Just north of Sarlat is Lascaux, the "Louvre" of Cro-Magnon man and perhaps the most notable prehistoric sight.

Fast-forward 30,000 years. The modern era dawns as the region comes under Merovingian rule in the 9th century. Subsequently divided up by the dukes of Aquitaine, the region later came under English rule and was returned to the French crown around 1370. The crown complicated matters further by giving the area to the Spanish house of Bourbon in 1574, which meant Henry of Navarre inherited it . . . but in 1589 Henry became Henry IV, king of France, so the region returned to the French crown once again. Well, history is repeating itself, at least from an English perspective, as over the last several decades the British have moved back here in droves. They see the Dordogne as the quintessential French escape—and now the rest of the world is following in their footsteps.

PLANNER

WHEN TO GO

The Dordogne has a temperate climate, but it's not Provence. Local differences in climate abound, due to the fact that this is the third-largest *département* in France, with winds blowing in from the Atlantic along the western borders and varying topography and continental weather in the eastern and northern areas. Sarlat, in the southeast of the region, tends to get a lot more winter sun than other areas—perfect if you are planning to head to the film festival there in November (⊕ *www.ville-sarlat.fr/festival*). As you move westward toward the Atlantic conditions get foggier, cloudier, and colder. However, in summer the southwest area of the Dordogne is sunnier than the rest of the region, so expect good weather for Riberac's three-day Festival Le Grand Souk in mid-July (⊕ *www.legrandsouk.com*), when the cafés and streets are full of music and musicians. All in all, spring and autumn are the best times to visit since there aren't as many tourists around, and the weather is still pleasant.

PLANNING YOUR TIME

From a practical perspective, staying in Sarlat or thereabouts would be your best plan for getting to really appreciate this diverse and wonderful region. Not only is this historic town a great place to enjoy, it's also near the caves: Lascaux and Montignac to its north; Les Eyzies de Tayac to its west; Beynac-et-Cazenac, La Roque-Gageac, and Domme immediately to its south. Rocamadour is just a little farther to the southeast. Also, Sarlat is just off the A20 highway, which brings you right into Cahors to the south, and north to the regional airport in Brive La Gaillarde (the Bergerac airport to the east on the D703/D660 is a little bit farther afield).

After getting yourself situated, the first thing to do is eat, because even before enjoying those awe-inspiring views from Rocamadour and La Roque-Gageac, there's the important task of savoring foie gras and truffles. After all, scenery and history are not the only things the Dordogne is famous for! If you prefer solitude, you won't have any trouble finding it in the vast, sparsely populated spaces stretching inland and

17

eastward in the rolling countryside. The best bet is to get out of the overpopulated places such as Périgueux and Bergerac and head for the hills, literally. The cathedral in Périgueux is something to see, but the châteaux and villages that sprinkle this region like so much historical and cultural confetti (in places such as Biron, Hautefort, Beynac, and Rocamadour) are sites you'll kick yourself for not seeing before the attractions of the big towns.

VISITING THE PREHISTORIC WONDERS

Perhaps the most famous cultural sights in the Dordogne are the prehistoric caves and grottos, such as Lascaux II, Grotte du Pech-Merle, the Domme grottoes, and Grotte du Grand-Roc. Lascaux can accept up to 2,000 people a day, but others—such as the Grotte des Combarelles in Les Eyzies-de-Tayac—only take 6 people on a tour at any given time (guaranteeing an intimate look). Either because demand far outstrips supply, or because tickets are so limited, it's recommended you call or email to prebook tickets. For places like Lascaux book as far in advance as possible (up to a year). For less popular sights, a couple of days ahead of time should do, or you can sign up for a tour as early in the morning as possible.

The main tourist offices in the region, such as the one at Les Eyzies-de-Tayac, have the lowdown on all the caves and prehistoric sights in the area. If you were not able to call ahead for tickets, it's worth stopping by the cave of your choice even if the office says tickets are sold out—space often opens up. Be forewarned: you might get signed onto a tour that starts in a couple of hours, leaving you with time to kill, so have a game plan handy for other places to visit nearby.

Reaching Lascaux II is a major production without a car. If driving from Sarlat, head to Montignac, 26 km (16 miles) north on route D704; Lascaux II is 1 km (½ mile) south of Montignac on route D704. If using public transportation, get yourself to Montignac by bus from Sarlat, the nearest town with a train station (on the Bordeaux-Brive line). Sarlat has early-morning buses (7 and 9 am), which leave from place de la Petite Rigandie. In Montignac you can buy tickets for Lascaux II next to the tourist office on place Bertran.

GETTING HERE AND AROUND

AIR TRAVEL

Frequent daily flights on Air France link Bordeaux and the domestic airport at Limoges with Paris (from several provincial airports), but if you're not interested in making the trip from Bordeaux there's also Bergerac airport, which has about 23 flights a week from such diverse English airports as Southampton, Leeds Bradford, Edinburgh, Exeter, and Birmingham on Flybe and London Stansted, East Midlands, and Liverpool on Ryanair. Also, there's the regional supplier, Airlinair, which flies from Paris into nearby Brive La Gaillarde three times a day during the week and once on Sunday.

Airlines and Contacts Air France ☎ 09–69–39–02–15 ⊕ www.airfrance.com. **Airlinair** ☎ 0825/808228 ⊕ www.airlinair.com. **Flybe** ☎ 0044/1392–268513 ⊕ www.flybe.com. **Ryanair** ☎ 0044–871/246–0002 (international calls; in English) ⊕ www.ryanair.com.

Airport Information Aéroport de Bergerac-Périgord-Dordogne ☎ *05–53–22–25–25* ⊕ *www.bergerac.aeroport.fr.* **Aéroport de Bordeaux-Mérignac** ☎ *05–56–34–50–50* ⊕ *www.bordeaux.aeroport.fr.*

BIKE TRAVEL

The Dordogne is prime biking territory. In particular, the hour-long ride between Rocamadour and the Gouffre de Padirac might just be one of your most memorable experiences in France. And let's not forget daylong bike trips through the neighboring Célé Valley and the 35-km (22-mile) trip to the prehistoric Grotte du Pech Merle outside the town of Cabrerets. Happily, Cahors has plenty of places for bike rentals and picnic fixings (head for the town's covered and outdoor markets).

Contacts Atout Loc. Rents out regular bicycles and electric bikes, too. ⊠ *26 rte. du Lot, Sarlat* ☎ *05–53–28–18–33.* **Bike Bus** ⊠ *Castelnaud La Chapelle* ☎ *06–08–94–42–01* ⊕ *www.bike-bus.com.*

BOAT TRAVEL

One popular way to see the Dordogne's landscape is by canoe or kayak. Rental depots spring up frequently along the rivers of the region, especially near campgrounds. The curving and winding Vézère River is a very boat-friendly stretch, while the valley of the Lot River is famous for its dreamy dawn mists. Single-person boats go for about €10 to €20 an hour, about double that for two-person boats. Some rental companies will take you by car to a departure point upstream, and some will even provide tents and waterproof casings for overnight trips. For more information, pick up boating brochures at any tourist office in the region.

BUS TRAVEL

The regional bus operator in the Dordogne is the Trans-Périgord network. It connects the main towns in the region with 14 bus lines, operated by eight different outfits. The maximum fare is €2, and there are reduced rates if you buy 10 passes (€14), so traveling by bus in the Dorgdogne could save you a lot of money. The Périgueux to Angoulême route is operated by C.F.T.A. Périgueux and the Périgueux to Hautefort route by Périgord Voyages/Cheze. For urban transport in Périgueux town use Peribus, and in Bergerac use TUB (Transports Urbains Bergeracois).

Bus Information C.F.T.A. Périgueux ⊠ *Gare Routière, 19 rue Denis-Papin, Périgueux* ☎ *05–53–08–43–13.* **Peribus** ⊠ *Pl. Montaigne Périgueux, Périgueux* ☎ *05–53–53–30–37.* **Périgord Voyages** ⊠ *Lafeuillade, Carsac* ☎ *05–53–59–01–48.* **Trans-Périgord** ⊠ *33 rue Front, Périgueux* ☎ *05–53–02–20–85.***TUB** (*Transports Urbains Bergeracois*). ⊠ *Bergerac* ☎ *05–53–63–96–97.*

CAR TRAVEL

As the capital of southwest France, Bordeaux has superb transportation links with Paris, Spain, and even the Mediterranean (A62 expressway via Toulouse links up with the A61 to Narbonne). The A20 is the main route from Paris to just before Cahors. It connects with the N21 at Limoges, which brings you down into Périgueux and Bergerac.

A89 links Bordeaux to Périgueux and D936 runs along the Dordogne Valley from Libourne to Bergerac continuing as D660 toward Sarlat.

17

TRAIN TRAVEL

The superfast TGV Atlantique service links Paris (Gare Montparnasse) to Bordeaux—covering 585 km (365 miles) in 3½ hours—with stops at Poitiers and Angoulême. Trains link Bordeaux to Lyon (6½ hrs) and Nice (8½ hrs) via Toulouse. Twenty trains daily make the 3½-hour, 400-km (250-mile) trip from Paris to Limoges.

Bordeaux is the region's major train hub. Trains run regularly from Bordeaux to Bergerac (80 mins), with occasional stops at St-Émilion, and six times daily to Sarlat (nearly 3 hrs). At least 12 trains daily make the 90-minute journey from Bordeaux to Périgueux. A handy hint is to go to the SNCF website (⊕ *www.voyages-sncf.fr*) that specifically caters to booking trains and determining departure times *(the standard SNCF site has become a lot more efficient in recent years but is still not as good as the one mentioned above).*

Train Information SNCF ☎ *36–35* ⊕ *voyages-sncf.fr.*

RESTAURANTS

If you're traveling in the Dordogne between October and March, it's essential to call restaurants ahead of time to avoid disappointment, as some close for the slow season. Closing times, too, can be variable. When you do snag your table, home in on the menu's listing for dishes *à la périgourdine,* which usually mean you're about to enjoy truffles or foie gras, or, heaven forbid, both!

Prices in the reviews are the average cost of a main course at dinner or, if dinner is not served, at lunch.

HOTELS

Advance booking is recommended in the highly popular Dordogne, where hotels fill up quickly, particularly in midsummer. Many country or small-town hotels expect you to have at least one dinner with them, and if you have two meals a day with your lodging and stay several nights, you can save money. Prices off-season (October to May) often drop as much as 20%, but note that a number of hotels are closed from the end of October through March.

Prices in the reviews are the lowest cost of a standard double room in high season.

VISITOR INFORMATION

The main tourist office for the region, the **Comité Départemental du Tourisme de la Dordogne,** is in Perigueux. It has separate websites for different languages that will help you find what you need. Your best bet is to get information before you leave home, as in the small villages a lot of the tourist offices have unusual opening hours. Indeed, many of these information centers are not called tourist offices at all, but Syndicats d'Initiatives, communal tourist outposts with infrequent hours. If you're coming from or via London, you can visit the official French Tourist Board office there: ⊕ *www.enjoydordogne.co.uk.*

Contacts Comité Départemental du Tourisme de la Dordogne ✉ *25 rue Wilson, Périgueux* ☎ *05-53-35-50-24.*

TOUR OPTIONS

The Office de Tourisme in Sarlat offers general guided tours (€5.50) of the town in English every Wednesday from mid-May to mid-October at 11 am. The guided tours in French are much more frequent.

If it's truffles you're after, you should go on a guided tour of the truffle groves in Sorges (a picturesque village to the northeast of Périgueux). These run every Tuesday and Thursday in July and August.

Sorges Truffle Museum. In July and August, tours of the truffle groves, lasting around an hour, can be arranged at the Sorges Truffle Museum (L'écomusée de la Truffe, €5 per person); they leave from here on Tuesday and Thursday at 3:30 pm. The rest of the year, guided tours are only available, by reservation, for groups of more than 20 people. ⊠ *Le Bourg, Sorges* ☎ *05–53–05–90–11* ⊕ *www.ecomusee-truffe-sorges.com* ☻ *June and Sept., daily 9:30–12:30 and 2:30–6:30; July and Aug., daily 9:30–6:30; Oct.–June, daily 10–noon and 2–5.*

Contact Office de Tourisme ⊠ *L'écomusée de la Truffe, Sorges* ☎ *05–53–05–90–11.*

WESTERN DORDOGNE TO ROCAMADOUR

From a bird's-eye perspective the geographic area in this chapter is known in France by four colors: the Périgord Noir, Blanc, Pourpre, and Vert. Sarlat and its environs are known as the Périgord Noir, or Black Périgord; Périgueux to the north is based in the Périgord Blanc (white) region; Bergerac to the southwest is the Périgord Pourpre (purple); and Brantôme in the far north is in the Périgord Vert (green) region. With more than 2 million visitors every year, the Périgord Noir is the most frequented. But the entire Dordogne relies heavily on travelers, so the local tourist offices have plenty of informative guides and maps to help you enjoy whatever "color" you choose. Many first opt for "purple," since Bergerac is the main hub for flights (after Bordeaux). Thus we kick things off in Western Dordogne and then head southwest down to the lovely Lot Valley, where dramatic Rocamadour lures throngs of tourists and pilgrims annually.

17

BERGERAC

57 km (36 miles) east of St-Émilion via D936, 88 km (55 miles) east of Bordeaux.

Yes, this is the Bergerac of Cyrano de Bergerac fame—but not exactly. The real satirist and playwright Cyrano (1619–55) who inspired Edmond Rostand's long-nosed swashbuckler was born in Paris and never set foot anywhere near this town. That hasn't prevented his legend from being preempted by the town fathers, who have plastered his schnoz all over Bergerac's promotional materials.

GETTING HERE

About 5 km (8 miles) south of town, Aéroport Bergerac-Perigord-Dordogne (☎ *05–53–22–25–25* ⊕ *www.bergerac.aeroport.fr*) has more than 20 Ryanair, Flybe, and Airlinair flights a week. There is no airport

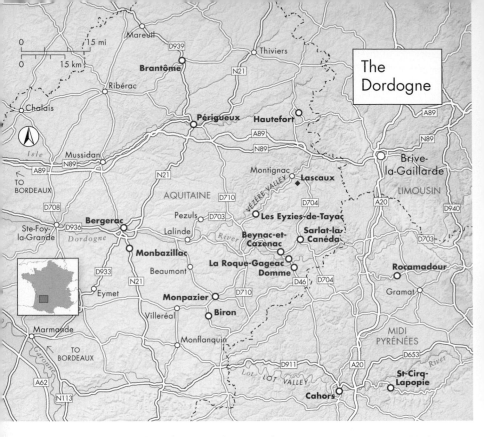

train or bus yet, so you have to take a taxi (☎ 05–53–23–32–32) into the town center. TUB (☎ 05–53–63–96–97) is the urban bus service and tickets cost € 1. Three bus operators leave the town for the surrounding region, Les Cars Bleus (☎ 05–53–23–81–92) going to Eymet on two alternating routes through Sigoules or Issigeac; Boullet (☎ 05–53–61–00–46) heading to Lalinde; and C.F.T.A. Perigueux (☎ 05–53–08–43–13) traveling to Bergerac. Every trip costs €2. Bordeaux has 13 train services daily (taking anywhere from 1 hr, 15 mins to nearly 2 hrs) that run through Bergerac and hook up with Sarlat (1 hr, 15 mins); the train station (☎ 05–53–63–53–80) is on avenue du 108e.

Visitor Information Bergerac Tourist Office ✉ *97 rue Neuve d'Argenson* ☎ *05-53-57-03-11* ⊕ *www.bergerac-tourisme.com.*

EXPLORING

They needn't have bothered erecting an exceedingly ugly statue of Cyrano in the middle of this town. Bergerac's gorgeous old half-timber houses, narrow alleys, riverside setting, and gastronomic specialties are more than enough to attract tourists staying in Bordeaux or Sarlat, both less than 100 km (62 miles) away. In the 14th century the English moved in, but in 1450 the French took over and, in time, Bergerac became a Protestant bastion. Today it's a lively farm-trade town with colorful markets held Wednesday and Saturday (the latter being the larger of the two).

Cloître des Récollets. This former convent is now in the wine business, and its stone-and-brick buildings, dating from the 12th to the 15th century, include galleries, a large vaulted cellar, and a cloister where the **Maison des Vins** (Wine Center) provides information on—and samples of—local vintages of sweet whites and fruity young reds. ✉ *1 rue des Récollets* ☎ *05–53–63–57–55* 🎟 *Free* 🕐 *Feb.–Apr., and Oct.–Dec, Tues.–Sat. 10:30–12:30 and 2–6; May, June, and Sept., Tues.–Sat. 10–12:30 and 2–7; July and Aug., daily 10–7.*

WORD OF MOUTH

"I am going back to the Dordogne again this fall (and I can't wait). Why? Because it is so beautiful around there—and all of it is steeped in history and they all speak French (and tolerate my efforts at it). I don't think any place of historical standing calls to me quite so strongly. It is like living in a novel or better."

—JoeCal

Périgord Gabarres. There are also hour-long cruises along the Dordogne (Easter–Oct., daily 11–6; €8) in old wooden sailboats, operated by Périgord Gabarres. ☎ *05–53–24–58–80.*

Vieille Ville. Guided walking tours (in English) of the Vieille Ville (Old Town) depart from the tourist office at 11 am on Wednesday in July and August. Tours last 75–90 minutes and cost €4.70.

17

WHERE TO EAT AND STAY

For expanded hotel reviews, visit Fodors.com.

$$ FRENCH FUSION 🍴 **L'Imparfait.** In the heart of old Bergerac, this characterful restaurant has beamed ceilings, openwork stone and brick walls, large lamps, and tall, cane-back chairs. The lunch and dinner menu, which changes with the seasons, is good value, considering you can start with such delights as warm oysters with saffron or a skewer of langoustine with honey and rosemary, and then move on, perhaps, to ravioli in a citron sauce. [$] *Average main: €23* ✉ *8–10 rue des Fontaines* ☎ *05–53–57–47–92* 🌐 *www.imparfait.com.*

$ HOTEL 🏨 **Bordeaux.** Although it's been in business since 1855 and has occasionally played host to some famous guests (Francis Bacon and François Mitterand among them), the Bordeaux of today has contemporary furnishings and simple, tidy rooms—the best of which look out on the garden courtyard. **Pros:** good location close to the Friday market, the old town, and the train station. **Cons:** rooms are a little too understated and are in need of some updating. [$] *Rooms from: €76* ✉ *38 pl. Gambetta* ☎ *05–53–57–12–83* 🌐 *www.hotel-bordeaux-bergerac.com* 🛏 *40 rooms* 🍽 *All meals.*

MONBAZILLAC

6 km (4 miles) south of Bergerac via D13.

From the hilltop village of Monbazillac are spectacular views of the sweet-wine–producing vineyards tumbling toward the Dordogne River.

Château de Monbazillac. The storybook corner towers of the beautifully proportioned, 16th-century, gray-stone château pay tribute to the fortress tradition of the Middle Ages, but the large windows and sloping roofs reveal a Renaissance influence. Regional furniture and an ornate early-17th-century bedchamber enliven the interior. A wine tasting is included to tempt you into buying a case or two of the famous but expensive bottles. ☎ *05–53–63–65–00 weekdays, 05–53–61–52–52 weekends* 🌐 *www.chateau-monbazillac.com* 🎟 *€7.50* ⏲ *June–Sept., daily 10–7; May and Oct., daily 10–12:30 and 2–6; Nov., Dec.,Feb., and Mar., Tues.–Sun. 10–noon and 2–5; Apr., daily 10–noon and 2–6. Closed Jan.*

MONPAZIER

45 km (28 miles) southeast of Bergerac via D660.

Fodor's Choice ★ Monpazier, on the tiny Dropt River, is one of France's best-preserved and most photographed *bastide* (fortified) towns. It was built in ocher-color stone by English king Edward I in 1284 to protect the southern flank of his French possessions. It has three stone gateways (of an original six), a large central square, and the church of **St-Dominique,** housing 35 carved-wood choir stalls and a purported relic of the True Cross.

Maison du Chapître (*Chapter House*). Opposite the church, this chapter house is the finest medieval building in town. Once used as a barn for storing grain, its wood-beam roof is constructed of chestnut to repel insects.

WHERE TO STAY

For expanded hotel reviews, visit Fodors.com.

$ HOTEL 🏨 **Hôtel de France.** Once an outbuilding on the estates of the Château de Biron, the Hôtel de France has never capitalized on its 13th-century heritage but today remains a small, modest family-run hotel that caters less to tourists than to locals—especially at its bar and restaurant (average main, $18), which serves rich regional food. **Pros:** central location; great restaurant; helpful staff. **Cons:** rooms are not nearly as impressive as the restaurant; no Internet service. [$] *Rooms from: €60* ✉ *21 rue St-Jacques* ☎ *05–53–22–66–01* 🌐 *www.hoteldefrancemonpazier.fr* 🛏 *10 rooms* ⏲ *Closed Nov.–Mar.* 🍴 *Some meals.*

BIRON

8 km (5 miles) south of Monpazier via D2/D53.

Château de Biron. Stop in Biron to see its massive hilltop castle, the highlights of which include a keep, square tower, and chapel, dating from the Renaissance, and monumental staircases. In addition to the period apartments and the kitchen, with its huge stone-slab floor, there's a gigantic dungeon, complete with a collection of scarifying torture instruments. The classical buildings were completed in 1760. The Gontaut-Biron family—whose ancestors invented great typefaces centuries ago—has lived here for 14 generations. ✉ *Bourg, Biron* ☎ *05–53–05–65–65* 🎟 *€7* ⏲ *Feb. 11.–Apr. 7, Tues.–Sun. 10–5; Apr. 8–July 7*

*and Sept.–Nov. 7, daily 10–6; July 8 –Aug., daily 10–7; Nov. 8–Dec.,
Tues.–Sun. 10–5. Closed Jan.–mid-Feb.*

CAHORS

60 km (38 miles) southeast of Monpazier via D811.

Less touristy and populated than most of the Dordogne, the Lot Valley
has a subtler charm. The cluster of towns along the Lot River and the
smaller rivers that cut through the dry, vineyard-covered plateau has a
magical, abandoned feel.

Regional information center. Just an hour north of southwestern France's
main city, Toulouse, Cahors is the Lot area's largest town. It hosts the
helpful regional information center, and makes a fine base from which
to explore the Lot River valley, a 50-km (31-mile) gorge punctuated by
medieval villages. ✉ *107 quai Cavaignac* ☎ *05–65–35–07–09* ⊕ *www.
tourisme-lot.com.*

Here and on other routes—notably the GR46, which spans the interior
of the Lot region, with breathtaking views of the limestone plateaux
and quiet valleys between Rocamadour and St-Cirq-Lapopie—*cyclotourisme* (biking) rules supreme.

GETTING HERE

Trains from Paris Gare d'Austerlitz take about five hours to reach
the Cahors station on place Jouinot Gambetta (☎ *08–36–35–35–35*).
Trains also run frequently between Toulouse and Cahors. A shuttle
(€5) between Toulouse airport and the city's bus station (next door to
the train station) runs every 20 minutes; so if you are coming by air
consider flying into Toulouse—as opposed to Bergerac, from which it
is difficult to access Cahors—or even into the regional airport of Brive
La Gaillarde and then heading south to Cahors. Buses, as in the rest of
the Dordogne, can be erratic, but they cost only €2 a trip.

Visitor Information Cahors Tourist Office ✉ *Pl. François-Mitterand* ☎ *05–65–
53–20–65* ⊕ *www.tourisme-cahors.com.*

EXPLORING

Modern Cahors encircles its *Ville Antique* (Old Town), which dates
from 1 BC. Once an opulent Gallo-Roman town, Cahors, sitting snugly
within a loop of the Lot River, is famous for its vin de Cahors, a tannic
red wine known to the Romans as "black wine." It was the Romans
who introduced wine to Cahors, and Caesar is said to have brought
Cahors wine back to Rome, but perhaps the region's biggest booster
was the local bishop who went on to become Pope John XXII. This
second Avignon pope of the 14th century made sure his hometown wine
became the communion wine of the Avignon church. Malbec is the most
common grape used, which produces, according to recent studies, one
of the most potent anticarcinogenic and heart-healthy wines on the
planet—Madiran. There's also a sizable amount of Merlot in the region,
with other vintners specializing in the local Jurançon Noir grape. Many
of the small estates in the area offer tastings, and the town tourist office
on place François-Mitterrand can point you in the direction of some of

17

the more notable vineyards, including the Domaine de Lagrezette (in Caillac) and the Domaine de St-Didier (in Parnac).

Cahors was also an early episcopal see and the capital of the old region of Quercy. Ruled by bishops until the 14th century, the university here was founded by Pope John XXII in 1322. The old parts of the town are interesting from an architectural perspective.

Cathédrale St-Étienne. The fortresslike cathedral is in Byzantine style and its cloisters connect to the courtyard of the archdeaconry, awash with Renaissance decoration and thronged with townsfolk who come to view art exhibits. ⊠ *Off rue du Maréchal-Joffre.*

Fodor's Choice ★ **Pont Valentré.** The town's finest sight is this 14th-century bridge, its three elegant towers constituting a spellbinding feat of medieval engineering.

WHERE TO STAY

For expanded hotel reviews, visit Fodors.com.

$$$$
HOTEL 🖼 **Château de Mercuès.** Set on a rocky spur just outside town, the former home of the count-bishops of Cahors has older rooms in baronial splendor (ask for one of these), as well as unappealing modern ones (which tend to attract midges); others have a mix of French Moderne and medieval-esque furniture that can be jarring, but the ambitious restaurant and great views make up for a lot of sins. **Pros:** unbeatable view; great pool. **Cons:** odd mix of furnishings. Ⓢ *Rooms from: €380* ⊠ *8 km (5 miles) northwest of Cahors on road to Villeneuve-sur-Lot, Mercuès* ☎ *05–65–20–00–01* ⊕ *www.chateaudemercues.com* ⤴ *24 rooms, 6 suites* ☉ *Closed mid-Nov.–Easter* ⦿ *Some meals.*

ST-CIRQ-LAPOPIE

32 km (20 miles) east of Cahors via D653, D662, and D40.

Fodor's Choice ★ Perched on the edge of a cliff 330 feet up, the beautiful 13th-century village of St-Cirq (pronounced san-*sare*) looks as though it could slide right into the Lot River. Filled with artisan workshops and not yet renovated à la Disney, the town has so many dramatic views you may end up spending several hours here. Traversing steep paths and alleyways among flower-filled balconies, you'll realize it deserves its description as one of the most beautiful villages in France.

GETTING HERE

The easiest way to access St-Cirq-Lapopie from Cahors's train station is to take the SNCF bus bound for Figeac (20 mins); St-Cirq is a 25-minute walk from where the bus drops you. From the Tour de Faure bus stop, go back to the D181 (sign says "St-Cirq 2 km"), cross the bridge, and walk uphill. It's a haul, but worth the hike.

Visitor Information St-Cirq-Lapopie Tourist Office ⊠ *Pl. du Sombral* ☎ *05– 65–31–31–31* ⊕ *www.saint-cirqlapopie.com.*

EXPLORING

Residents happily still outnumber travelers here, but there is a welcoming tourist office in the center of town, where you can get tips for your trip, including how to find the mostly ruined 13th-century château that can be reached by a stiff walk along the path that starts near the Hôtel

CLOSE UP

Dordogne's Indulgent Eats

The Dordogne is a land of foie gras and cognac, so travelers get to eat (and quaff) like the royals who once disputed this coveted corner, staking it out with châteaux-forts and blessing it with Romanesque churches.

Begin by following the winding sprawl of the Dordogne River into duck country. This is the land of the *gavée* goose, force-fed extravagantly to plump its liver into one of the world's most renowned delicacies.

Duck or goose fat glistens on potatoes, on salty confits, and on *rillettes d'oie,* a spread of potted duck that melts on the tongue as no mere butter ever could.

Wild mushrooms and truffles (referred to locally as "black diamonds") weave their musky perfume through dense game pâtés.

Although truffle production is nothing like it used to be, this subterranean edible fungus continues to beguile chefs and foodies.

The truffle forms a symbiotic relationship with the roots of certain trees and plants (in the Périgord region they are mainly found growing from green oaks) to form a part that is technically known as the *ascoma,* the fruiting body of a fungus.

Mysteriously appearing anytime from November to February in the forests of Périgord (and other areas of Western Europe), the more famous *truffes* (truffles) are black, but there are also white varieties—hundreds of species in all.

Truffles are savory, zesty, and extremely aromatic, and because of this they have been glorified as a delicacy in recipes for thousands of years (if we are to believe old Greek and Roman writings on the subject). They can be canned for export and are often infused into oils.

Traditionally, pigs were used to hunt for truffles; but nowadays dogs are more commonly employed because canines can be taught to point for truffles and, unlike the avaricious piglets, don't want to eat them when they find them.

Cultivation of the famous fungus by way of inoculating the roots of a host plant seedling with fungal spores has had success, although the manufactured truffles are still thought to taste inferior to the ones naturally found in the forests.

To stand up to such an onslaught of earthy textures and flavors, the best Dordogne wines—like Bergerac and Cahors—have traditionally been known as coarser brews.

However, since the 1970s the winegrowers around Cahors have succeeded in mellowing those coarser edges.

And to round it all off? A snifter of amber cognac—de rigueur for the digestion.

Dining thus, in a vine-covered stone *ferme auberge* (farmhouse inn) deep in the green wilds of the Dordogne, replete with a feast of pâtés, truffles, and cognacs, you begin to see what the 13th-century Plantagenet invaders from England were fighting for.

17

Draped on a cliff 1,500 feet over the Alzou River gorge, Rocamadour is one of the most spectacular towns of the Dordogne.

de Ville. Morning hikes in the misty gorges in the valley are beyond beautiful.

Grotte du Pech Merle. Discovered in 1922, the Grotte du Pech Merle displays 4,000 square feet of prehistoric drawings and carvings. Particularly known for its peculiar polka-dot horses, impressions of the human hand, and footprints, this is the most impressive "real-thing" prehistoric cave that is open to the public in France. The admission charge includes a 20-minute film, an hour-long tour, and a visit to the adjacent museum. Take a great bike ride here from St-Cirq-Lapopie or the SNCF bus from Cahors—getting off at Conduché (before St-Cirq) and walking the 7 km (4 miles) along D41. Alternately, you can just drive from Cahors, taking D653 for 7 km (4 miles) to the right turn by Vers. Tickets are at a premium, with a daily limit of 700 visitors, so for peak summer days book at least one week in advance. ✉ *10 km (6 miles) north of St-Cirq-Lapopie, 3 km (2 miles) west of Cabrerets* ☎ *05–65–31–27–05* 🌐 *www.pechmerle.com* 🎫 *€9* 🕑 *Early Apr.–early Nov., daily 9:30–5.*

WHERE TO STAY

For expanded hotel reviews, visit Fodors.com.

$ B&B/INN 🏨 **L'Auberge du Sombral.** If location and views are what you're after then you've found the right place. **Pros:** can't beat the location. **Cons:** things could be spiffed up a bit. [$] *Rooms from: €75* ✉ *46330 Saint Cirq Lapopie* ☎ *05–65–31–26–08* 🌐 *www.lesombral.com* 🛏 *8 rooms* 🕑 *Closed Nov. 15–Apr. 1* 🍴 *Some meals.*

ROCAMADOUR

72 km (45 miles) north of St-Cirq via Labastide-Murat.

A medieval village that seems to defy the laws of gravity, Rocamadour surges out of a cliff 1,500 feet above the Alzou River gorge—an awe-inspiring sight that makes this one of the most-visited tourist spots in France.

GETTING HERE

Bergerac airport is a bit far from this famous village, so it might be easier to take regional carrier Airlinair (⊕ *www.hop.fr/en*) to nearby Brive La Gaillarde (flights, costing as little as €60 one way, depart Paris twice a day during the week and once on Sunday); flying into Toulouse airport is an alternative. If you're getting here by train, direct connections are available to Toulouse (3½ hrs, €31) and Brive (40 mins, €8.80); keep in mind, however, that the Rocamadour–Padirac train station (shared with the neighboring village of Padirac) is 4 km (3 miles) outside the village. Walking takes about an hour, biking 15 minutes, or you can call Taxi Pascal Herbert (☎ *05–65–50–14–82, 06–81–60–14–60 cell*).

Visitor Information Rocamadour Tourist Office ✉ *Maison du Tourisme* ☎ *05–65–33–22–00* ⊕ *www.rocamadour.com.*

> ### GOD'S VIEW
>
> On the uppermost plateau of the Cité Réligieuse stands the Château de Rocamadour, a private residence of the church fathers. Open to the public for an admission fee, its ramparts have spectacular views of the gorge. But you can enjoy the same views for free just by walking the chemin de la Croix up to the castle.

EXPLORING

Rocamadour got its name after the discovery in 1166 of the thousand-year-old body of St. Amadour "quite whole." The body was moved to the cathedral, where it began to work miracles. Legend has it that the saint was actually a publican named Zacheus, who had the honor of entertaining Jesus in his home and, after the crucifixion, came to Gaul, where he established a private chapel in the cliff here. Pilgrims have long flocked to the site, climbing the 216 steps to the church on their knees. Making the climb on foot is a sufficient reminder of the medieval penchant for agonizing penance; today two elevators lift weary souls. Unfortunately, the summer influx of a million tourists has brought its own blight, judging by the dozens of tacky souvenir shops. Cars are not allowed; park in the lot below the town.

Fodor's Choice ★ **Cité Religieuse.** The Basse Ville's rue Piétonne, the main pedestrian street, is crammed with crêperies, tea salons, and hundreds of tourists, many of whom are heading heavenward by taking the **Grand Escalier** (staircase) or elevator (€2.40) from place de la Carreta up to the Cité Religieuse, set halfway up the cliff. If you walk, pause at the landing 141 steps up to admire the fort. Once up, you can see tiny place St-Amadour and its seven chapels: the basilica of **St-Sauveur** opposite the staircase; the **St-Amadour crypt** beneath the basilica; the chapel of **Notre-Dame,** with its statue of the Black Madonna, to the left; the chapels of **John the Baptist,**

17

St-Blaise, and **Ste-Anne** to the right; and the Romanesque chapel of **St-Michel** built into an overhanging cliff. St-Michel's two 12th-century frescoes—depicting the Annunciation and the Visitation—have survived in superb condition.

Hôtel de Ville. The town is split into four levels joined by steep steps. The lowest level is occupied by the village of Rocamadour itself, and mainly accessed through the centuries-old Porte du Figuier (Fig Tree Gate). Past this portal, the **Cité Médiévale,** also known as the **Basse Ville,** though in parts grotesquely touristy, is full of beautifully restored structures, such as the 15th-century Hôtel de Ville, near the Porte Salmon, which houses the **tourist office** and an excellent collection of tapestries. ☎ 05–65–33–22–00 🖾 €2.50 ⏱ July and Aug., daily 9:30–7; Jan., Feb., Nov., and Dec., daily 2–5; Mar.–June, Sept., and Oct., daily 10:30–noon and 2–6.

WHERE TO STAY

For expanded hotel reviews, visit Fodors.com.

$$$
HOTEL
Fodor's Choice
★

Château de la Treyne. Certainly the most spectacular château-hotel in the Dordogne, this Relais & Châteaux outpost sits amid Baroque gardens perched over the Dordogne River. **Pros:** the château has been sparklingly renovated; modern amenities like Jacuzzis and minibars. **Cons:** breakfast and dinner (*sans* wine) included, but rates are pricey. $ *Rooms from: €200* ✉ *15 km (9 miles) northwest of Rocamadour and 5 km (3 miles) from Lacave, Lacave* ☎ *05–65–27–60–60* ⊕ *www. chateaudelatreyne.com* ↘ *12 rooms, 5 suites* ⏱ *Closed Nov. 15–Dec. 23 and Jan. 3–Mar. 23* ⏍ *Some meals.*

$
HOTEL

Lion d'Or. In the center of Rocamadour, this simple, bargain-price, family-run hotel has a restaurant with panoramic views of the valley, where genial owners Emmanuel and Sally Vernillet serve up delicious truffle omelets and homemade foie gras au Noilly. **Pros:** location in the Old Town; amazing views from restaurant. **Cons:** rooms have floral wallpaper and linens that might not be to everyone's taste. $ *Rooms from: €57* ✉ *Cité Médiévale* ☎ *05–65–33–62–04* ⊕ *www.liondor-rocamadour.com* ↘ *36 rooms* ⏱ *Closed Jan.–Mar.* ⏍ *All meals.*

EASTERN PERIGORD TO BRANTÔME

Entering the Perigord Noir, a trifecta of top Dordogne sights awaits: the cliff-face village of La Roque-Gageac, the prehistoric grottoes of Domme, and the storybook castle at Beynac. Just eastward lies Sarlat, the regional center and a town famed for its half-timber medieval vibe. Northward lies the Vézère Valley, the prehistoric capital of France, celebrated for locales, such as Lascaux, which were settled by primitive man. Continuing north, you arrive at the bustling city of Périgueux and numerous riverside towns, including historic Brantôme. For three centuries during the Middle Ages, this entire region was a battlefield in the wars between the French and the English. Of the châteaux dotting the area, those at Hautefort and Beynac are among the most spectacular. Robust Romanesque architecture is more characteristically found in this area than the airy Gothic style on view elsewhere in France, and can be admired at Périgueux Cathedral and in countless village churches.

LA ROQUE-GAGEAC

55 km (36 miles) west of Rocamadour via Payrac, 10 km (6 miles) southwest of Sarlat via D703.

Fodor's Choice ★ Across the Dordogne from Domme, in the direction of Beynac, romantically huddled beneath a cliff, is strikingly attractive La Roque-Gageac, one of the best-restored villages in the valley. Crafts shops line its narrow streets, dominated by the outlines of the 19th-century mock-medieval Château de Malartrie and the Manoir de Tarde, with its cylindrical turret. If you leave the main road and climb one of the steep cobblestone paths, you can check out the medieval houses on their natural perches and even hike up the mountain for a magnificently photogenic view down to the village.

WHERE TO STAY

For expanded hotel reviews, visit Fodors.com.

$$ B&B/INN **La Plume d'Oie.** Famed for its eatery—the panfried fois gras is ever popular—this small inn overlooking the river and limestone cliffs welcomes weary guests with rooms that flaunt some fabulous views. **Pros:** great view; top eatery. **Cons:** hotel is noisy; no Internet service. [$] *Rooms from: €75* ☎ *05–53–29–57–05* 🌐 *www.aubergelaplumedoie.com* 🛏 *4 rooms* 🕒 *Closed late Nov.–early Mar.* 🍴 *Some meals.*

DOMME

5 km (3 miles) east of La Roque-Gageac.

Grottoes. The historic cliff-top village of Domme is famous for its grottoes, where prehistoric bison and rhinoceros bones have been discovered. You can visit the 500-yard-long illuminated galleries, which are lined with stalactites. ✉ *Pl. de la Halle* ☎ *05–53–31–71–00* 🎟 *€8.20* 🕒 *Feb. and Mar.–mid.-Nov., daily at 11, 2:30, 3:30, 4:30; Apr. and May., daily 10:15–noon and 2:30–5:30; June–Sept., daily 10:15–12 and 2:15–6.*

BEYNAC-ET-CAZENAC

11 km (7 miles) west of La Roque-Gageac via D703.

Visitor Information Beynac-et-Cazenac Tourist Office ✉ *La Balme* ☎ *05–53–29–43–08* 🌐 *www.cc-perigord-noir.fr.*

EXPLORING

One of the most picturesque sights in the Dordogne is the medieval castle that sits atop the wonderfully restored town of Beynac.

Castelnaud. With a fabulous mountaintop setting, the now-ruined castle of Castelnaud, containing a large collection of medieval arms, is just upstream from Beynac across the Dordogne. Make sure to give yourself at least an hour to visit. In summer the castle comes to life with demonstrations, reenactments, and opportunities to try out some of the medieval weapons yourself. ☎ *05–53–31–30–00* 🎟 *€8.40* 🕒 *Apr.–June, and Sept., daily 10–7; July and Aug., daily 9–8; mid-Nov.–Jan., daily 2–5 (10–5 during Christmas holidays); Oct., Feb., and Mar., daily 10–6.*

Château de Beynac. Perched above a sheer cliff face beside an abrupt bend in the Dordogne River, the muscular 13th-century Château de Beynac has unforgettable views from its battlements. Thanks to its camera-ready qualities, it frequently doubles as a film set. During the Hundred Years' War, this castle often faced off with forces massed directly across the way at the fort of Castelnaud. ☎ *05–53–29–50–40* 🎟 *€7.50* ⏲ *Mar.–May, daily 10–6; June–Sept., daily, 10–6:30; Oct. and Nov., daily 10–sunset; Dec.–Feb., daily 11–sunset.*

Fodor's Choice ★ **Château de Marqueyssac.** For Périgord Noir at its most enchanting, head to the heavenly heights of the hilltop garden at this château in Vézac, about 3 km (1½ miles) south of Beynac-et-Cazenac. The park was founded in 1682, and its design, including a parterre of topiaries, was greatly influenced by the designs of André le Nôtre, the "green geometer" of Versailles. Shaded paths bordered by 150,000 hand-pruned boxwoods are graced with breathtaking viewpoints, rock gardens, waterfalls, and verdant glades. From the belvedere 400 feet above the river, there's an exceptional view of the Dordogne Valley. For a unique and romantic perspective, in July and August, the garden is open Thursday night under candlelight. A tea salon is open from March to mid-November and is just the place to drink in the panoramic views from the parterre terrace. To get a dazzling preview, log on to the website. ✉ *Belvédère de la Dordogne, Vézac, 9 km (5 miles) southwest of Sarlat* ☎ *05–53–31–36–36* 🌐 *www.marqueyssac.com* 🎟 *€7.60* ⏲ *July and Aug., daily 9–8 (also 7–midnight Thurs. by separate ticket); Feb., Mar., and Oct.–mid-Nov., daily 10–6; mid-Nov.–Jan., daily 2–5; Apr.–June and Sept., daily 10–7.*

Château des Milandes. Five kilometers (3 miles) northwest from Castelnaud, the turreted Château des Milandes was built around 1489 in Renaissance style, and has lovely terraces and gardens. It was once owned by the American-born cabaret star of Roaring '20s Paris, Josephine Baker, and it was here that she housed her "rainbow family"—a large group of adopted children from many countries. An on-site museum is devoted to her memory. Falconry displays (April to October) are another attraction. From here D53 (via Belvès) leads southwest to Monpazier. ☎ *05–53–59–31–21* 🌐 *www.milandes.com* 🎟 *€9* ⏲ *Apr. and May, daily 10–6:30; June–mid-July. and Sept., daily 10–7; mid-July–Aug., daily 9:30–7:30; Oct., daily 10–6:15; closed Nov.–Mar.*

WHERE TO STAY

For expanded hotel reviews, visit Fodors.com.

$ HOTEL 🏨 **Pontet.** A few blocks from the Dordogne River and within the shadow of cliff-top Château de Beynac, this is one of the hotel mainstays of the adorably Dordognesque town of Beynac, with sweet and simple guest rooms upstairs plus a highly regarded riverside restaurant just a short hike away. **Pros:** charming old stone house surrounded by winding, historic streets. **Cons:** parking not provided. [$] *Rooms from: €60* ✉ *Beynac-et-Cazenac* ☎ *05–53–29–50–06* 🌐 *www.hostelleriemaleville.com* 🛏 *12 rooms* ⏲ *Closed Jan.* 🍴 *Some meals.*

SARLAT-LA-CANÉDA

10 km (6 miles) northeast of Beynac via D57, 74 km (46 miles) east of Bergerac.

Fodor's Choice
★

Sarlat-la-Canéda defines enchantment. If you're planning a trip to the many prehistoric caves and amazing perched villages near this gorgeous town, then the capital of the Périgord Noir is the place to stay. Sarlat (as it's usually called) is ideally located, with Les Eyzies-de-Tayac, Montignac, and Lascaux to its north and Beynac-et-Cazenac, Domme, and La Roque-Gageac just to its south. Even Rocamadour, to the southeast on the D704, which connects with the D673, isn't all that far from here, and Cahors is a straight shot south on the A20 *péage* (toll road) or the more scenic (and longer) N20.

GETTING HERE

Flying here usually means coming into Bergerac airport; but Airlinair (⊕ *www.hop.fr/en*)—the low-cost regional carrier—also flies from Paris to nearby Brive La Gaillarde, twice daily during the week and once on Sunday.

Sarlat train station. A half-hour walk out of town, Sarlat train station, on the northeast side of town, links you up with the rest of the Dordogne. ⊠ *2 rue Stade.*

For the four trains from Les Eyzies (1 hr) and the seven from Périgueux (1 hr, 40 mins) you'll need to change at Le Buisson. There are trains to Sarlat from Bordeaux six times a day. To get from Paris you have to change at Souillac, and the trip takes 5½ hours (about €88).

Effia Transports Belmon. Buses are operated by Effia Transports Belmon on the Souillac route. ☎ *05–56–33–03–80.*

Périgord Voyages/Cheze. Buses are operated by Périgord Voyages/Cheze on the Périgueux route. However, Sarlat proper does have the claim to fame (for a town of less than 10,000 people) of having three bus lines (Sarlat Bus). Don't get off at the train station, but at the stops at place Pasteur or rue de la République. ☎ *05–53–59–01–48.*

Visitor Information Sarlat-la-Canéda Tourist Office ⊠ *3 rue Tourny* ☎ *05–53–31–45–45* ⊕ *www.sarlat-tourisme.com.*

EXPLORING

Tucked among hills adorned with corn and wheat, Sarlat is a beautiful, well-preserved medieval town that, despite attracting huge numbers of visitors, has managed to retain some of its true character. Its evocative **Cité Médiévale** is filled most days with tour groups, and is particularly hectic on Saturday, market day: all the geese on sale are proof of the local addiction to foie gras. To do justice to Sarlat, meander through its medieval streets in the late afternoon or early evening, aided by the tourist office's walking map. The tourist office also organizes English-language walking tours every Wednesday at 11 from mid-May to mid-October (€5.50), which give you an in-depth look at the town's architecture.

The end of the Hundred Years' War (1453) led to the construction of beautiful urban buildings in the Dordogne, but Sarlat was especially

17

favored: when the English handed the region back to the French king, he rewarded loyal townspeople here with royal privileges. Before long, a new merchant class sprang up, building sublime stone mansions in the latest French Renaissance style. It's no surprise to learn that only Nice and Paris have had more films shot in their locales than Sarlat; Lasse Hallstrom's *Chocolat* (2000) and Luc Besson's *The Messenger* (1999) are only 2 of the more than 45 movies that have used the town as a backdrop. Sarlat even has its own annual film festival (in November), when comedians, film stars, producers, and film technicians arrive to host an informational get-together for 500 students. In addition, there's a theater festival here from mid-July to the end of August.

Cathédrale St-Sacerdos. The elaborate turreted tower of the Cathédrale St-Sacerdos, begun in the 12th century, is the oldest part of the building and, along with the choir, all that remains of the original Romanesque structure. ✉ *Pl. du Peyrou.*

Jardin des Enfers. The sloping garden behind the cathedral, the Jardin des Enfers, contains a strange, conical tower known as the Lanterne des Morts (Lantern of the Dead), which was occasionally used as a funeral chapel.

Place du Peyrou. Sarlat's Cité Médiévale has many beautiful photo ops. Of particular note is rue de la Liberté, which leads to place du Peyrou, anchored on one corner by the steep-gabled Renaissance house where writer-orator Étienne de la Boétie (1530–63) was born.

Rue des Consuls. The church of Ste-Marie points the way to Sarlat's most interesting street, rue des Consuls. Among its medieval buildings are the Hôtel Plamon, with broad windows that resemble those of a Gothic church, and, opposite, the 15th-century Hôtel de Vassal.

Rue Montaigne. Running the length of the Enfer gardens is the rue Montaigne, where the great 16th-century philosopher Michel de Montaigne once lived. Some of the half-timber houses that line it cast a fairy-tale spell. Rue d'Albusse (adjoining the garden behind the cathedral) and rue de la Salamandre are narrow, twisty streets that head to place de la Liberté and the 18th-century Hôtel de Ville.

WHERE TO STAY

For expanded hotel reviews, visit Fodors.com.

$ HOTEL 🏨 **Hostellerie La Couleuvrine.** Sarlat is not overly blessed with beautiful historic hotels, so this one stands out—literally—thanks to its massive crenellated tower (an imposing structure that held off besieging forces during the Wars of Religion) and an interior that includes a magically medieval restaurant. **Pros:** like a Relais & Chateaux property at one-quarter the price. **Cons:** a few blocks east of the Cité Médiévale. [$] *Rooms from: €70* ✉ *1 pl. de la Bouquerie* ☎ *05–53–59–27–80* 🌐 *www.la-couleuvrine.com* 🛏 *25 rooms, 3 suites* 🍴 *Some meals.*

$$ HOTEL 🏨 **Hôtel de la Madeleine.** Constructed in stone during the 19th-century, this sturdy building, just to the north of the Old Town, has been extensively renovated by owners Monsieur and Madame Florent, who added on great extras such as a swimming pool, hamam, and spa, in addition to upgrading bedrooms. **Pros:** lovely, spacious lounge is a great place to read and relax. **Cons:** very hard to find parking near the hotel. [$] *Rooms* *from: €125 ⊠ 1 pl. de la Petite-Rigaudie ☎ 05–53–59–10–41 ⊕ www. hoteldelamadeleine-sarlat.com ⤹ 39 rooms* ⦶⦶ *Some meals.*

LES EYZIES-DE-TAYAC

21 km (13 miles) northwest of Sarlat via D47.

Visitor Information **Eyzies-de-Tayac Tourist Office** ⊠ *19 rue de la Préhistoire* ☎ *05–53–06–97–05* ⊕ *www.tourisme-vezere.com.*

EXPLORING

Sitting comfortably under a limestone cliff, Les Eyzies is the doorway to the prehistoric capital of France. Early *Homo sapiens* (the species to which we humans belong) lived about 40,000 years ago and skeletal remains and other artifacts of this Aurignacian culture were first found here in 1868. Many signs of Cro-Magnon man have been discovered in this vicinity; a number of excavated caves and grottoes, some with wall paintings, are open for public viewing, including the Grotte-Font-de-Gamme, just south of the town, with very faint drawings to be seen on a tour, and the Grotte des Combarelles. Stop by the town tourist office for the lowdown on all the caves in the area—the office also sells tickets for most sites and you should reserve here because a surprising number of tours sell out in advance (sometimes only six people are allowed in a cave at any one time).

Grotte du Grand-Roc. Amid the dimness of the Grotte du Grand-Roc you can view weirdly shaped crystalline stalactites and stalagmites—not for the claustrophobic. At the nearby **Abri Préhistorique de Laugerie,** you can visit caves that were once home to prehistoric man. ⊠ *Rte. du Périgueux* ☎ *05–53–05–65–60* 🖃 *€7.20* ⊙ *Early July–Aug., daily 10–7; Sept.–early Nov., daily 10–6; early Nov.–Dec. and early Feb.–early Apr., Sun.–Thurs. 10–noon and 2–5; early Apr.–early July, daily 10–12:30 and 2–6. Closed Jan.–early Feb.*

Fodor's Choice ★ **La Madeleine.** Want to discover the "Brigadoon" of the Dordogne? As you head north from Les Eyzies-de-Tayac toward Lascaux, stop off 7 km (4 miles) north of Les Eyzies near the village of Tursac to discover the mysterious troglodyte "lost village" of La Madeleine, found hidden in the Valley of Vézère at the foot of a ruined castle and overlooking the Vézère River. Human settlement here dates to 15,000 BC, but what is most eye-catching today is its picturesque cliff-face chapel; seemingly half Cro-Magnon, half Gothic, it was

---

ARE YOU NUTTY?

Eco-Musée de la Noix. If you're nuts about nuts, Sarlat is your town—the Périgord is the second-biggest producer of walnuts in France, and those from the Sarladais region are prized. The nuts are sold in the markets in October and November and walnut wood (often preferred here to oak) is used to make beautiful furniture. Visit the Eco-Musée de la Noix, just south of Sarlat in Castelnaud-la-Chapelle, to learn more. ⊠ *La Ferme de Vielcroze, 12 km (7 miles) southwest of Sarlat via D57, Castelnaud-la-Chapelle* ☎ *05–53–59–69–63* ⊕ *www. ecomuseedelanoix.voila.net* 🖃 *€4* ⊙ *Easter–Oct., daily 10–7.*

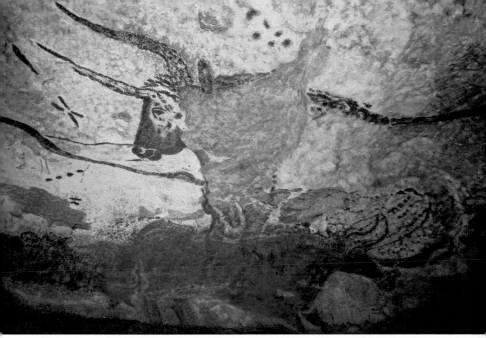

The Raphaels, Leonardos, and Picassos of prehistoric art are on view in the amazing caves of Lascaux II.

constructed during the Middle Ages. The site was abandoned in the 1920s; now guided visits tour it (call ahead, English available). ⊠ *7 km (4 miles) north of Les Eyzies-de-Tayac, Tursac* 🕾 *05–53–46–36–88* 🖃 *€5.50* ⊙ *Easter–June, Sept., and Oct., daily 10–6, July and Aug., daily 9:30–8; Nov.–mid-Feb., daily 11–5.*

Musée National de Préhistoire (*National Museum of Prehistory*). To truly enhance your understanding of the paintings at Lascaux and other caves in the Dordogne, visit the Musée National de Préhistoire, which attracts large crowds to its renowned collection of prehistoric artifacts, including primitive sculpture, furniture, and tools. You can also get ideas at the museum about excavation sites to visit in the region. ⊠ *1 rue du Musée* 🕾 *05–53–06–45–45* ⊕ *www.musee-prehistoire-eyzies.fr* 🖃 *€5* ⊙ *June and Sept., Wed.–Mon. 9:30–6; July and Aug., daily 9:30–6:30; Oct.–May, Wed.–Mon. 9:30–12:30 and 2–5:30.*

Pole International de la Prehistoire (*Prehistory Welcome Center*). After several years in the making, this well-equipped welcome center opened in 2011 to provide a solid introduction to the region's important prehistoric sites. With exhibits, slideshows, and timelines (all free of charge), the center is an excellent way to wrap your brain around the immensity of the archaeological riches in the Dordogne. ⊠ *30 rue du Moulin* 🕾 *05–53–06–06–97* ⊕ *www.pole-prehistoire.com* 🖃 *Free* ⊙ *Mid-May–Sept., daily 10–6; Oct.–Dec. and Feb.–mid-May, Sun.–Fri. 10–5; closed Jan.*

WHERE TO STAY
For expanded hotel reviews, visit Fodors.com.

$$$ 🍽 **Le Vieux Logis.** Built around the most gorgeous dining room in the
HOTEL Dordogne, this vine-clad manor house in Trémolat remains one of the

region's top hotels. **Pros:** breathtaking grounds; Le Bistrot d'en Face offers a value version of the restaurant's delectable food. **Cons:** swimming pool is small. ⓢ *Rooms from: €195* ✉ *24 km (15 miles) west of Les Eyzies, Le Bourg, Trémolat* ☎ *05–53–22–80–06* ⊕ *www.vieux-logis.com* ⤳ *17 rooms, 9 suites* ⑩*Some meals.*

LASCAUX

27 km (17 miles) northeast of Les Eyzies via D706.

For information on visiting, see the Visiting The Prehistoric Wonders section at the front of this chapter.

Visitor Information Lascaux Tourist Office ✉ *Pl. Bertran-de-Born* ☎ *05–53–51–82–60* ⊕ *www.tourisme-vezere.com.*

EXPLORING

Fodor'sChoice ★ **Grotte de Lascaux** (*Lascaux Caves*). Just south of Montignac, the famous Grotte de Lascaux contain hundreds of prehistoric wall paintings between 15,000 and 20,000 years old. The horses, cow, black bulls, and unicorn on their walls were discovered by chance by four schoolkids looking for their dog in 1940. Over time, the original Lascaux cave paintings began to deteriorate due to the carbon dioxide exhaled by thousands of visitors. To make the colorful mosaic of animals accessible to the general public, the French authorities built Lascaux II, a formidable feat in itself. They spent 12 years perfecting the facsimile, duplicating every aspect of two of the main caves to such a degree that the result is equally awesome. Painted in black, purple, red, and yellow, the powerful images of stags, bison, and oxen are brought to life by the curve of the stone walls; many of them appear pregnant, and historians think these caves were shrines to fertility rather than living quarters—no tools or implements were ever found. Unlike caves marked with authentic prehistoric art, Lascaux II is completely geared toward visitors, and you can watch a fancy presentation about cave art or take a 40-minute tour in the language of your choice. This is one of the most visited sites in the Dordogne and, in summer, tickets can be at a premium. To be sure of admittance, arrive early, as tickets can sell out by midday. During the winter season, you are permitted to purchase tickets at the site, but from April to October tickets are available only at a booth beside the tourist office in Montignac (place Bertran-de-Born). Even better, make reservations via email as soon as you know you're heading to the Dordogne. ✉ *Rte. de la Grotte de Lascaux* ☎ *05–53–05–65–60* ⊕ *www.semitour. com* ▣ *€9.70* ⊗ *Mid-Feb.–early Apr. and mid-Nov.–Dec., Tues.–Sun. 10–12:30 and 2–5:30; mid-Apr.–early July and Sept.–mid-Nov., daily 9:30–6; early July–Aug., daily 9–8.*

WHERE TO STAY

For expanded hotel reviews, visit Fodors.com.

$ RENTAL 🏠 **Manoir d'Hautegente.** Originally a forge, this old, ivy-covered manor enjoys a pastoral nook by the Coly River—a lovely vista to enjoy from your guest room or the impressive restaurant. **Pros:** cozy family feel; close to Sarlat. **Cons:** bathrooms need updating; rooms suffer somewhat from an attack of French Moderne style. ⓢ *Rooms from: €95* ✉ *12*

km (7 miles) east of Lascaux, Haute Gente, Coly ☎ *05–53–51–68–03*
⊕ *www.manoir-hautegente.com* ⤳ *11 rooms, 6 suites* ☽ *Closed mid-Oct.–Apr.* ⊙ *Some meals.*

HAUTEFORT

25 km (15½ miles) north of Lascaux via D704.

The reason to come to Hautefort is its castle, which presents a forbiddingly arrogant face to the world.

Château de Hautefort. The silhouette of the Château de Hautefort bristles with high roofs, domes, chimneys, and cupolas. The square-line Renaissance left wing clashes with the muscular, round towers of the right wing, and the only surviving section of the original medieval castle—the gateway and drawbridge—plays referee in the middle. Adorning the inside are 17th-century furniture and tapestries. ☎ *05–53–50–51–23* ⊕ *www.chateau-hautefort.com* ✉ *€8.50* ☽ *Apr. and May, daily 10–12:30 and 2–6:30; June–Aug., daily 9:30–7; Sept., daily 10–6; Mar. and Oct., daily 2–6; Nov. 1–11, weekends 2–6.*

PÉRIGUEUX

46 km (27 miles) west of Hautefort via D5, 120 km (75 miles) north-east of Bordeaux.

For anyone tired of the bucolic delights of the Périgord, even a short visit to this thriving hub may prove a welcome re-immersion in classy city ways.

GETTING HERE

Instead of using the Bergerac airport, fly on regional carrier Airlinair (⊕ *www.hop.fr/en*) to Brive la Gaillarde, west of Périgueux (low-price flights depart Paris twice a day during the week, once on Sunday). The bus station on rue Denis Papin houses C.F.T.A. Périgueux (☎ *05–53–08–43–13*), which is part of the Trans-Périgord bus system. Bus lines (1, 1A, 2, 3, 9, 10) leave here for Angoulême, Brantôme, Hautefort, and Bergerac (€2 per trip). Peribus (☎ *05–53–53–30–37*) on place Montaigne is where you can catch a city bus. The train station is also on rue Denis Papin. It takes 4½ hours to get here from Paris's Gare d'Austerlitz (connecting in Bordeaux) and a ticket costs around €71. If you're training it to Cahors from Perigueux you'll have to travel the 50 minutes east first to Brive La Gaillard and then head south to Cahors, which is another hour, all for around €28 one way. It'll take you less time to get to Bergerac (70 mins) to the southeast, but you'll still have to connect at Le Buisson.

Visitor Information Périgueux Tourist Office ✉ *26 pl. Francheville* ☎ *05–53–53–10–63* ⊕ *www.tourisme-perigueux.fr..*

EXPLORING

Périgueux (the capital of the Périgord) is a commercial center for the region, so the shops here are stylish and sophisticated—some consider them the best reason for visiting this thriving town. Specialty-food shops proliferate (pâtés are the town's chief export), as do elegant fashion

17

haunts. Don't forget the open-air markets in the heart of the medieval city, though. Farmers' markets are held daily on the place du Coderc from 8 am to 1 pm. Every Wednesday and Saturday you can catch the big markets, which spill over from the place du Coderc to the front of the Mairie (Town Hall). And if you love your *gras* (fat) as the locals do, then you'll want to witness one of the many *marchés* (markets) *de gras* (November through March, Wednesday and Saturday).

Cathédrale St-Front. Périgueux's history reaches back more than 2,000 years, yet the community is best known for this odd-looking church, which was associated with the routes to Santiago de Compostela. Finished in 1173 and fancifully restored in the 19th century, Cathédrale St-Front seems like it might be on loan from Istanbul, given its shallow-scale domes and the elongated conical cupolas sprouting from the roof like baby minarets. You may be struck by similarities between it and the Byzantine-style Sacré-Coeur in Paris; that's no coincidence—architect Paul Abadie (1812–84) had a hand in the design of both. After a mandatory visit to the cathedral, you can make for the cluster of tiny pedestrian-only streets that run through the heart of Périgueux.

BRANTÔME

Fodor's Choice

★

27 km (17 miles) north of Périgueux via D939.

Visitor Information Brantôme Tourist Office ⊠ *Bd. Charlemagne* ☎ *05–53–05–80–63* ⊕ *www.perigord-dronne-belle.fr.*

EXPLORING

When the reclusive monks of the abbey of Brantôme decided the inhabitants of the village were getting too inquisitive, they dug a canal between themselves and the villagers, setting the *brantômois* adrift on an island in the middle of the River Dronne. How happy for them, or at least for us. Brantôme has been unable to outgrow its small-town status and remains one of the prettiest villages in France. Today it touts itself as the "Venice of Périgord." Enjoy a walk along the river or through the old, narrow streets. The meandering river follows you wherever you stroll. Cafés and small shops abound.

Abbaye Bénédictine. At night the Abbaye Bénédictine is romantically floodlighted. Possibly founded by Charlemagne in the 8th century, it has none of its original buildings left, but its bell tower has been hanging on since the 11th century (the secret of its success is that it's attached to the cliff rather than the abbey, and so withstood waves of invaders). Fifth-century hermits carved out much of the abbey and some rooms have sculpted reliefs of the Last Judgment. Also here is a small museum devoted to the 19th-century painter Fernand-Desmoulin. ⊠ *Bd. Charlemagne* ☎ *05–53–05–80–63* ☞ *€4.50* ⊙ *July and Aug., Wed.–Mon. 10–7; Apr.–June and Sept., Wed.–Mon. 10–6; Oct.–Dec., Feb., and Mar., Wed.–Mon. 10–noon and 2–5.*

FRENCH VOCABULARY

One of the trickiest French sounds to pronounce is the nasal final *n* sound (whether or not the n is actually the last letter of the word). You should try to pronounce it as a sort of nasal grunt—as in "huh." The vowel that precedes the *n* will govern the vowel sound of the word, and in this list we precede the final *n* with an *h* to remind you to be nasal.

Another problem sound is the ubiquitous but untransliterable eu, as in bleu (blue) or deux (two), and the very similar sound in je (I), ce (this), and de (of). The closest equivalent might be the vowel sound in "put," but rounded. The famous rolled *r* is a glottal sound. Consonants at the ends of words are usually silent; when the following word begins with a vowel, however, the two are run together by sounding the consonant. There are two forms of "you" in French: vous (formal and plural) and tu (a singular, personal form). When addressing an adult you don't know, vous is always best.

ENGLISH	FRENCH	PRONUNCIATION
BASICS		
Yes/no	Oui/non	wee/nohn
Please	S'il vous plaît	seel voo play
Thank you	Merci	mair-**see**
You're welcome	De rien	deh ree-**ehn**
Excuse me, sorry	Pardon	pahr-**don**
Good morning/afternoon	Bonjour	bohn-**zhoor**
Good evening	Bonsoir	bohn-**swahr**
Good-bye	Au revoir	o ruh-**vwahr**
Mr. (Sir)	Monsieur	muh-**syuh**
Mrs. (Ma'am)	Madame	ma-**dam**
Miss	Mademoiselle	mad-mwa-**zel**
Pleased to meet you	Enchanté(e)	ohn-shahn-**tay**
How are you?	Comment allez-vous?	kuh-mahn- tahl-ay **voo**
Very well, thanks	Très bien, merci	tray bee-ehn, mair-**see**
And you?	Et vous?	ay voo?
NUMBERS		
one	un	uhn
two	deux	deuh
three	trois	twah

ENGLISH	FRENCH	PRONUNCIATION
four	quatre	**kaht**-ruh
five	cinq	sank
six	six	seess
seven	sept	set
eight	huit	wheat
nine	neuf	nuf
ten	dix	deess
eleven	onze	ohnz
twelve	douze	dooz
thirteen	treize	trehz
fourteen	quatorze	kah-torz
fifteen	quinze	kanz
sixteen	seize	sez
seventeen	dix-sept	deez-**set**
eighteen	dix-huit	deez-**wheat**
nineteen	dix-neuf	deez-**nuf**
twenty	vingt	vehn
twenty-one	vingt-et-un	vehnt-ay-**uhn**
thirty	trente	trahnt
forty	quarante	ka-**rahnt**
fifty	cinquante	sang-**kahnt**
sixty	soixante	swa-**sahnt**
seventy	soixante-dix	swa-sahnt-**deess**
eighty	quatre-vingts	kaht-ruh-**vehn**
ninety	quatre-vingt-dix	kaht-ruh-vehn-**deess**
one hundred	cent	sahn
one thousand	mille	meel

COLORS

black	noir	nwahr
blue	bleu	bleuh

ENGLISH	FRENCH	PRONUNCIATION
brown	brun/marron	bruhn/mar-**rohn**
green	vert	vair
orange	orange	o-**rahnj**
pink	rose	rose
red	rouge	rouge
violet	violette	vee-o-**let**
white	blanc	blahnk
yellow	jaune	zhone

DAYS OF THE WEEK

Sunday	dimanche	dee-**mahnsh**
Monday	lundi	luhn-**dee**
Tuesday	mardi	mahr-**dee**
Wednesday	mercredi	mair-kruh-**dee**
Thursday	jeudi	zhuh-**dee**
Friday	vendredi	vawn-druh-**dee**
Saturday	samedi	sahm-**dee**

MONTHS

January	janvier	zhahn-vee-**ay**
February	février	feh-vree-**ay**
March	mars	marce
April	avril	a-**vreel**
May	mai	meh
June	juin	zhwehn
July	juillet	zhwee-**ay**
August	août	ah-**oo**
September	septembre	sep-**tahm**-bruh
October	octobre	awk-**to**-bruh
November	novembre	no-**vahm**-bruh
December	décembre	day-**sahm**-bruh

	ENGLISH	FRENCH	PRONUNCIATION

USEFUL PHRASES

ENGLISH	FRENCH	PRONUNCIATION
Do you speak English?	Parlez-vous anglais?	par-lay **voo ahn**-glay
I don't speak . . .	Je ne parle pas . . .	zhuh nuh parl pah
French	français	frahn-**say**
I don't understand.	Je ne comprends pas.	zhuh nuh kohm-**prahn** pah
I understand.	Je comprends.	zhuh kohm-**prahn**
I don't know.	Je ne sais pas.	zhuh nuh say **pah**
I'm American/ British.	Je suis américain/ anglais.	a-may-ree-**kehn**/ ahn-**glay**
What's your name?	Comment vous ap pelez-vous?	ko-mahn voo za-pell-ay-**voo**
My name is . . .	Je m'appelle . . .	zhuh ma-**pell** . . .
What time is it?	Quelle heure est-il?	kel air eh-**teel**
How?	Comment?	ko-**mahn**
When?	Quand?	kahn
Yesterday	Hier	yair
Today	Aujourd'hui	o-zhoor-**dwee**
Tomorrow	Demain	duh-**mehn**
Tonight	Ce soir	suh **swahr**
What?	Quoi?	kwah
What is it?	Qu'est-ce que c'est?	kess-kuh-**say**
Why?	Pourquoi?	**poor**-kwa
Who?	Qui?	kee
Where is . . .	Où est . . .	oo ay
the train station?	la gare?	la gar
the subway station?	la station de métro?	la sta-**syon** duh may-**tro**
the bus stop?	l'arrêt de bus?	la-**ray** duh **booss**
the post office?	la poste?	la post
the bank?	la banque?	la bahnk
the . . . hotel?	l'hôtel . . .?	lo-**tel**

ENGLISH	FRENCH	PRONUNCIATION
the store?	le magasin?	luh ma-ga-**zehn**
the cashier?	la caisse?	la **kess**
the . . . museum?	le musée . . .?	luh mew-**zay**
the hospital?	l'hôpital?	lo-pee-**tahl**
the elevator?	l'ascenseur?	la-sahn-**seuhr**
the telephone?	le téléphone?	luh tay-lay-**phone**
Where are the restrooms?	Où sont les toilettes?	oo sohn lay twah-**let**
(men/women)	(hommes/femmes)	(**oh**-mm/**fah**-mm)
Here/there	Ici/là	ee-**see**/la
Left/right	A gauche/à droite	a goash/a draht
Straight ahead	Tout droit	too drwah
Is it near/far?	C'est près/loin?	say pray/lwehn
I'd like . . .	Je voudrais . . .	zhuh voo-**dray**
a room	une chambre	ewn **shahm**-bruh
the key	la clé	la clay
a newspaper	un journal	uhn zhoor-**nahl**
a stamp	un timbre	uhn **tam**-bruh
I'd like to buy . . .	Je voudrais acheter . . .	zhuh voo-**dray** **ahsh**-tay
cigarettes	des cigarettes	day see-ga-**ret**
matches	des allumettes	days a-loo-**met**
soap	du savon	dew sah-**vohn**
city map	un plan de ville	uhn plahn de **veel**
road map	une carte routière	ewn cart roo-tee-**air**
magazine	une revue	ewn reh-**vu**
envelopes	des enveloppes	dayz ahn-veh-**lope**
writing paper	du papier à lettres	dew pa-pee-**ay** a **let**-ruh
postcard	une carte postale	ewn cart pos-**tal**
How much is it?	C'est combien?	say comb-bee-**ehn**

ENGLISH	FRENCH	PRONUNCIATION
A little/a lot	Un peu/beaucoup	uhn peuh/bo-**koo**
More/less	Plus/moins	plu/mwehn
Enough/too (much)	Assez/trop	a-say/tro
I am ill/sick.	Je suis malade.	zhuh swee ma-**lahd**
Call a . . .	Appelez un . . .	a-play uhn
doctor	Docteur	dohk-**tehr**
Help!	Au secours!	o suh-**koor**
Stop!	Arrêtez!	a-reh-**tay**
Fire!	Au feu!	o fuh
Caution!/Look out!	Attention!	a-tahn-see-**ohn**

DINING OUT

A bottle of . . .	une bouteille de . . .	ewn boo-**tay** duh
A cup of . . .	une tasse de . . .	ewn tass duh
A glass of . . .	un verre de . . .	uhn vair duh
Bill/check	l'addition	la-dee-see-**ohn**
Bread	du pain	dew pan
Breakfast	le petit-déjeuner	luh puh-**tee** day-zhuh-**nay**
Butter	du beurre	dew burr
Cheers!	A votre santé!	ah vo-truh sahn-**tay**
Cocktail/aperitif	un apéritif	uhn ah-pay-ree-**teef**
Dinner	le dîner	luh dee-**nay**
Dish of the day	le plat du jour	luh plah dew **zhoor**
Enjoy!	Bon appétit!	bohn a-pay-**tee**
Fixed-price menu	le menu	luh may-**new**
Fork	une fourchette	ewn four-**shet**
I am diabetic.	Je suis diabétique.	zhuh swee dee-ah- bay-**teek**
I am vegetarian.	Je suis végétarien(ne).	zhuh swee vay-zhay-ta-ree-**en**
I cannot eat . . .	Je ne peux pas manger de . . .	zhuh nuh **puh** pah mahn-**jay** deh

ENGLISH	FRENCH	PRONUNCIATION
I'd like to order.	Je voudrais commander.	zhuh voo-**dray** ko-mahn-**day**
Is service/the tip included?	Est-ce que le service est compris?	ess kuh luh sair-**veess** ay comb-**pree**
It's good/bad.	C'est bon/mauvais.	say bohn/mo-**vay**
It's hot/cold.	C'est chaud/froid.	Say sho/frwah
Knife	un couteau	uhn koo-**toe**
Lunch	le déjeuner	luh day-zhuh-**nay**
Menu	la carte	la cart
Napkin	une serviette	ewn sair-vee-**et**
Pepper	du poivre	dew **pwah**-vruh
Plate	une assiette	ewn a-see-**et**
Please give me . . .	Donnez-moi . . .	doe-nay-**mwah**
Salt	du sel	dew sell
Spoon	une cuillère	ewn kwee-air
Sugar	du sucre	dew **sook**-ruh
Waiter!/Waitress!	Monsieur!/ Mademoiselle!	muh-**syuh**/ mad-mwa-**zel**
Wine list	la carte des vins	la cart day vehn

MENU GUIDE

FRENCH	ENGLISH

GENERAL DINING

Entrée	Appetizer/Starter
Garniture au choix	Choice of vegetable side
Plat du jour	Dish of the day
Selon arrivage	When available
Supplément/En sus	Extra charge
Sur commande	Made to order

PETIT DÉJEUNER (BREAKFAST)

Confiture	Jam
Miel	Honey

FRENCH	ENGLISH
Oeuf à la coque	Boiled egg
Oeufs sur le plat	Fried eggs
Oeufs brouillés	Scrambled eggs
Tartine	Bread with butter

POISSONS/FRUITS DE MER (FISH/SEAFOOD)

Anchois	Anchovies
Bar	Bass
Brandade de morue	Creamed salt cod
Brochet	Pike
Cabillaud/Morue	Fresh cod
Calmar	Squid
Coquilles St-Jacques	Scallops
Crevettes	Shrimp
Daurade	Sea bream
Ecrevisses	Prawns/Crayfish
Harengs	Herring
Homard	Lobster
Huîtres	Oysters
Langoustine	Prawn/Lobster
Lotte	Monkfish
Moules	Mussels
Palourdes	Clams
Saumon	Salmon
Thon	Tuna
Truite	Trout

VIANDE (MEAT)

Agneau	Lamb
Boeuf	Beef
Boudin	Sausage
Boulettes de viande	Meatballs

FRENCH	ENGLISH
Brochettes	Kebabs
Cassoulet	Casserole of white beans, meat
Cervelle	Brains
Chateaubriand	Double fillet steak
Choucroute garnie	Sausages with sauerkraut
Côtelettes	Chops
Côte/Côte de boeuf	Rib/T-bone steak
Cuisses de grenouilles	Frogs' legs
Entrecôte	Rib or rib-eye steak
Épaule	Shoulder
Escalope	Cutlet
Foie	Liver
Gigot	Leg
Porc	Pork
Ris de veau	Veal sweetbreads
Rognons	Kidneys
Saucisses	Sausages
Selle	Saddle
Tournedos	Tenderloin of T-bone steak
Veau	Veal

METHODS OF PREPARATION

A point	Medium
A l'étouffée	Stewed
Au four	Baked
Ballotine	Boned, stuffed, and rolled
Bien cuit	Well-done
Bleu	Very rare
Frit	Fried
Grillé	Grilled

FRENCH	ENGLISH
Rôti	Roast
Saignant	Rare

VOLAILLES/GIBIER (POULTRY/GAME)

Blanc de volaille	Chicken breast
Canard/Caneton	Duck/Duckling
Cerf/Chevreuil	Venison (red/roe)
Coq au vin	Chicken stewed in red wine
Dinde/Dindonneau	Turkey/Young turkey
Faisan	Pheasant
Lapin/Lièvre	Rabbit/Wild hare
Oie	Goose
Pintade/Pintadeau	Guinea fowl/Young guinea fowl
Poulet/Poussin	Chicken/Spring chicken

LÉGUMES (VEGETABLES)

Artichaut	Artichoke
Asperge	Asparagus
Aubergine	Eggplant
Carottes	Carrots
Champignons	Mushrooms
Chou-fleur	Cauliflower
Chou (rouge)	Cabbage (red)
Laitue	Lettuce
Oignons	Onions
Petits pois	Peas
Pomme de terre	Potato
Tomates	Tomatoes

TRAVEL SMART
FRANCE

GETTING HERE AND AROUND

◼ AIR TRAVEL

Flying time to Paris is 7½ hours from New York, 9 hours from Chicago, 11 hours from Los Angeles, and 1 hour from London. Flying time between Paris and Nice is 1 hour.

As one of the world's most popular destinations, Paris is served by many international carriers. Air France, the French flag carrier, offers many flights between Paris's Charles de Gaulle Airport and Newark, New Jersey; New York City's JFK Airport; and Washington's Dulles Airport; as well as Atlanta, Boston, Chicago, Cincinnati, Detroit, Houston, Los Angeles, Miami, Philadelphia, and San Francisco. Most other North American cities are served through Air France partnerships with Delta, with flights to Paris from Atlanta, Chicago, Cincinnati, Detroit, Minneapolis, New York City's JFK, Philadelphia, Pittsburg, Salt Lake City, and Seattle. Another popular carrier is United, with nonstop flights to Paris from Chicago, Cleveland, Denver, Houston, Los Angeles, Newark, San Francisco, and Washington, D.C. American Airlines offers daily nonstop flights to Charles de Gaulle Airport from numerous cities, including Boston, Chicago, Dallas/Fort Worth, Miami, and New York City's JFK.

Airline Contacts Air France ☎ *800/237-2747 in U.S., 36-54 in France [€0.34 per min]* ⊕ *www.airfrance.com.* **American Airlines** ☎ *800/433-7300 in U.S., 08-26-46-09-50 in France [€.04 per min]* ⊕ *www.aa.com.* **Delta Airlines** ☎ *800/221-1212 for U.S. reservations, 800/241-4141 for international reservations, 08-92-70-26-09 in France [€.34 per min]* ⊕ *www.delta.com.* **United Airlines** ☎ *800/864-8331 for reservations, 08-10-72-72-72 in France [€.06 per min]* ⊕ *www.united.com.*

Within Europe EasyJet ☎ *0843-104-1000 in U.K. [£.05 per min], 08-20-42-03-15 in France [at least €.12 per call]* ⊕ *www.easyjet.com.* **Ryan Air** ☎ *0871-246-0000 in U.K. [£0.10 per min], 08-92-78-02-10 in France [€0.34 per min]* ⊕ *www.ryanair.com.*

Airlines and Airports Airline and Airport Links.com. Airline and Airport Links.com has links to many of the world's airlines and airports. ⊕ *www.airlineandairportlinks.com.*

Airline Security Issues Transportation Security Administration. The Transportation Security Administration has answers for almost every security question that might come up. ⊕ *www.tsa.gov.*

AIRPORTS

There are two major gateway airports to France, both just outside the capital: Orly, 16 km (10 miles) south of Paris, and Charles de Gaulle, 26 km (16 miles) northeast of the city. Orly mostly handles flights to and from destinations within France and the rest of Europe, while Charles de Gaulle is France's major international gateway. The smaller Beauvais Airport, 75 km (46 miles) north of Paris, is used by European budget airlines. At Charles de Gaulle, also known as Roissy, there's a TGV station at Terminal 2, where you can connect to trains going all over the country. Many airlines have flights to Lyon, Lourdes, Perpignan, Biarritz, Nantes, Nice, Marseille, Bordeaux, and Toulouse.

Airport Information Charles de Gaulle/ Roissy ☎ *39-50 in France [€.34 per min]* ⊕ *www.aeroportsdeparis.fr.* **Orly** ☎ *39-50 in France [€.04 per min]* ⊕ *www. aeroportsdeparis.fr.*

GROUND TRANSPORTATION

From Charles de Gaulle, the fastest and least expensive way to get into Paris is on the RER-B line, the suburban express train, which runs daily from 5 am to 11:30 pm. The free CDGVal lightrail connects each terminal (except 2G) to the Roissypôle RER station in less than eight minutes, running daily nonstop 24/7. For Terminal 2G, take the free N2 "navette" shuttle bus outside Terminal 2F. There are other shuttle buses connecting the remaining terminals with the RER station, though CDGVal is much quicker. Trains to central Paris (Gare du Nord, Les Halles, St-Michel, Luxembourg) depart every 15 minutes. The fare (including métro connection) is €9.25, and journey time is about 30 minutes.

The Air France Cars, or coach service, is a comfortable option to get to and from the city—you don't need to have flown the carrier to use it. The coaches cost €17 if you pay onboard or €15.50 if you buy your ticket online. Line 2 goes from the airport to Paris's Charles de Gaulle Étoile and Porte Maillot from 5:45 am to 11 pm. Buses leave every 15 minutes. Line 4 goes to Montparnasse and the Gare de Lyon from 6 am to 10 pm. Buses run every 30 minutes.

Passengers arriving in Terminal 1 should use Exit 32 on the Arrivals level; Terminals 2A and 2C, Exit C2; 2B and 2D, Exit B1; Terminals 2E and 2F, Exit E8; Terminal 2G, take the N2 shuttle bus to Terminal 2F, then use Exit 3. Another option is to take Roissybus, operated by the Paris Transit Authority, which runs between Charles de Gaulle and the Opéra every 15 to 20 minutes from 5:45 am to 11 pm; the cost is €10 and you can pay onboard. The trip takes about 45 minutes in regular traffic, about 90 minutes in rush-hour traffic.

Taxis are your least desirable mode of transportation into the city. If you're traveling at peak times, you may have to stand in a long line with many other disgruntled travelers. Journey times, and, as a consequence, prices are therefore unpredictable. At best, the trip takes 30 minutes, but it can take as long as 90 minutes during rush hour. Count on a €50 to €70 fare, plus €1 for a second bag in the trunk.

SuperShuttle Paris and Parishuttle are two van companies that serve both Charles de Gaulle and Orly airports. Prices are set, so it costs the same no matter how long the journey takes. To make a reservation, call or email your flight details several days in advance (check the website) to the shuttle company and an air-conditioned van with a bilingual chauffeur will be waiting for you on your arrival. Note that these shuttle vans pick up and drop off other passengers, which can add significant time to the journey.

From Orly, the most economical way to get into Paris is to take the RER-C or Orlyrail line. Catch the shuttle bus from the terminal to the Pont de Rungis train station. Trains to Paris leave every 15 minutes. Passengers arriving in South Terminal use Exit F; for West Terminal use Exit G on the Arrivals level. The total fare is €6.45, and journey time is about 35 minutes. Another option is to take the monorail service, Orlyval, which runs between the Antony RER-B station and Orly Airport daily every four to eight minutes from 6 am to 11 pm. Passengers arriving in the South Terminal should look for Exit K, those arriving in the West Terminal, Exit A, Departures level. The fare to central Paris is €10.90.

You can also take Air France Cars, or coach service, Line 1 from Orly to Les Invalides, Montparnasse, and Etoile; Line 1 runs run every 15 minutes from 6 am to 11 pm. (You need not have flown on Air France to use this service.) The fare is €12 if you pay onboard, €11 if you buy your ticket online. The trip takes between 30 and 45 minutes, depending on traffic. Those arriving in Orly South need to look for Exit L; those arriving in Orly West, Exit D. The Paris Transit Authority's Orlybus is yet another option; buses leave every 15 minutes for the Denfert-Rochereau métro station; the cost is €7.20. You can economize further by using RATP Bus 183, which shuttles you from the South Terminal to Line 7, métro Porte de Choisy station, for €1.90. It operates daily from 6 am to 9:30 pm from the Orly Sud terminal.

Contacts **Air France Cars** ☎ 08-92-35-08-20 in France [€.34 per min] ⊕ www.lescarsairfrance.com. **Parishuttle** ☎ 08-92-69-69-00 in France [€.34 per min] ⊕ www.parishuttle.com. **RATP (including Roissybus, Orlybus, Orlyval)** ☎ 32-46 in France [€0.34 per min] ⊕ www.ratp.fr. **SuperShuttle** ☎ 08-11-70-78-12 in France [at least €.06 per min] ⊕ www.supershuttle.fr.

▌ BARGE AND YACHT TRAVEL

Canal and river trips are popular in France, particularly along the picturesque waterways in Brittany, Burgundy, and the Midi. For further information, ask for a "Tourisme Fluvial" brochure at any French tourist office. It's also possible to rent a barge or crewed sailboat to travel around the coast of France, particularly the Côte d'Azur.

Barge Companies Abercrombie & Kent ☎ 800/554-7016 ⊕ www.abercrombiekent.com. **En-Bateau** ☎ 04-67-13-19-62 ⊕ www.en-bateau.com. **European Waterways** ☎ 877/879-8808 in U.S., 877/574-3404 in Canada ⊕ www.gobarging.com. **French Country Waterways** ☎ 781/934-2454 in U.S., 800/222-1236 in U.S. (toll-free) ⊕ www.fcwl.com. **Maine Anjou Rivières** ☎ 02-41-95-10-83 ⊕ www.maine-anjou-rivieres.com. **Viking River Cruises** ☎ 800/304-9616 in U.S. (toll-free) ⊕ www.rivercruises.com.

▌ BOAT TRAVEL

A number of ferry and hovercraft routes link the United Kingdom and France. Fares depend on the length of the journey and the number of people traveling. Driving distances from the French ports to Paris are as follows: from Calais, 290 km (180 miles); from Cherbourg, 358 km (222 miles); from Caen, 233 km (145 miles); from St-Malo, 404 km (250 miles). Trains also connect these ports with Paris; the journey times to and from Caen and Calais, the closest, are about four hours.

Dover-Calais DFDS Seaways. Ferry service between Dover and Dunkirk or Calais operates at least a dozen times each day. ☎ 0871/574-7235 in U.K. ⊕ www.dfdsseaways.co.uk. **P&O European Ferries.** P&O European Ferries has up to 25 sailings a day; the crossing takes 90 minutes. ☎ 08-25-12-01-56 in France [€.15 per min] ⊕ www.poferries.com.

Portsmouth and Poole-Cherbourg, Caen and St-Malo Brittany Ferries. Brittany Ferries has three sailings per day between Caen and Portsmouth, two crossings daily between Portsmouth and Cherbourg, two crossings daily between St-Malo and Portsmouth, and one crossing daily between Poole and Cherbourg. ☎ 0871-244-0744 in U.K. ⊕ www.brittany-ferries.co.uk.

▌ BUS TRAVEL

If you're traveling to or from another country, train service can be just as economical as bus travel, if not more so. The largest international bus operator is Eurolines France, whose main terminal is in the Parisian suburb of Bagnolet (a half-hour métro ride from central Paris, at the end of métro Line 3). Eurolines runs many international routes to scores of European destinations, with fares that vary greatly depending on where and when you travel, including a route from London to Paris (8 hrs, €60). Other Eurolines routes include: Amsterdam (7 hrs, €80); Barcelona (15 hrs, €150); and Berlin (14 hrs, €140). There are economical passes to be had—15-day passes are €180–€350, a 30-day pass will cost €245–€460. These passes offer unlimited coach travel to all Eurolines European destinations.

France's excellent train service means that long-distance bus routes in France are rare; regional buses are found mainly where train service is spotty. In rural areas the service can be unreliable, and schedules can be incomprehensible for those who don't speak French. Your best bet is to contact local tourism offices.

Bus Information Eurolines France ☎ *08–92–89–90–91 in France [€0.34 per min]* ⊕ *www. eurolines.fr.*

▌ CAR TRAVEL

An International Driver's Permit is not required but can be useful in emergencies, particularly when a foreign language is involved. Drivers in France must be over 18 years old to drive, but there is no top age limit (if your faculties are intact).

If you're driving from the United Kingdom to the Continent, you have a choice of the Channel Tunnel or ferry services. Reservations are essential at peak times.

GASOLINE

Gas is expensive, especially on expressways and in rural areas. When possible, buy gas before you get on the expressway and keep an eye on pump prices as you go. These vary—anywhere from €1.50 to €1.80 per liter. The cheapest gas can be found at *hypermarchés* (large supermarkets). Credit cards are accepted everywhere. In rural areas it's possible to go for miles without passing a gas station, so don't let your tank get too low.

PARKING

Parking is a nightmare in Paris and many other metropolitan areas. "Pay and display" metered parking is usually limited to two hours in city centers. Parking is free on Sunday and national holidays. Parking meters showing a dense yellow circle indicate a free parking zone during the month of August. In smaller towns, parking may be permitted on one side of the street only—alternating every two weeks—so pay attention to signs. In France, illegally parked cars are likely to be impounded, especially those blocking entrances or fire exits. Parking tickets start at €17, topping out at €175 in a handicapped zone, for a first offense, and there's no shortage of the blue-uniformed parking police. Parking lots, indicated by a blue sign with a white "P," are usually underground and are generally expensive.

ROAD CONDITIONS

France has 8,000 km (5,000 miles) of expressway and 808,000 km (502,000 miles) of main roads. For the fastest route between two points, look for roads marked *autoroute*. A *péage* (toll) must be paid on most expressways: the rate varies but can be steep. The N (*route nationale*) roads—which are sometimes divided highways—and D (*route départementale*) roads are usually also wide and fast.

There are excellent links between Paris and most French cities, but poor ones between the provinces (the principal exceptions are A26 from Calais to Reims, A62 between Bordeaux and Toulouse, and A9/A8 the length of the Mediterranean coast).

Though routes are numbered, the French generally guide themselves from city to city and town to town by destination name. When reading a map, keep one eye on the next big city toward your destination as well as the next small town; most snap decisions will have to be based on town names, not road numbers.

ROADSIDE EMERGENCIES

If you have car trouble on an expressway, go to a roadside emergency telephone. If you have a breakdown anywhere else, find the nearest garage or contact the police. There are also 24-hour assistance hotlines valid throughout France (available through rental agencies and supplied to you when you rent the car), but don't hesitate to call the police in case of any roadside emergency; they're quick and reliable, and the phone call is free. There are special phones for this purpose on all highways; you'll see them every few kilometers—just pick up the bright orange phone and dial 17. The French equivalent of the AAA is the Club Automobile de l'Ile de France, but it only takes care of its members and is of little use to international travelers.

Emergency Services Police ☎ *17.*

RULES OF THE ROAD

Drive on the right and yield to drivers coming from streets to the right. However, this rule does not necessarily apply at traffic circles, where you should watch out for just about everyone. There are no right turns allowed at red lights unless you have a blinking arrow. Every person in the car must wear a seat belt, and children under 12 may not travel in the front seat. Speed limits are 130 kph (80 mph) on expressways (*autoroutes*), 110 kph (70 mph) on N highways (*routes nationales*), 90 kph (55 mph) on other roads (*routes*), 50 kph (30 mph) in cities and towns (*villes* and *villages*). French drivers break these limits all the time, and police dish out hefty on-the-spot fines with equal abandon. Do not expect to find traffic lights in the center of the road, as French lights are usually on the right- and left-hand sides.

You might be asked by the Police National to pull over at busy intersections. You will have to show your papers (*papiers*)—including car insurance—and may be submitted to an *alcootest* (you guessed it, a Breathalyzer test). The rules in France have become stringent because of the high incidence of accidents on the roads; anything above 0.5 grams of alcohol in the blood—which, according to your size, could simply mean two to three glasses of wine—and you are over the limit. This does not necessarily mean a night in the clinker, but your driving privileges in France will be revoked on the spot and you will pay a hefty fine. Don't drink and drive, even if you're just crossing town to the sleepy little inn on the river. Local police are notorious for their vigilance.

Some important traffic terms and signs to note: *sortie* (exit); *sens unique* (one way); *stationnement interdite* (no parking); and *impasse* (dead end). Blue rectangular signs indicate a highway; green rectangular signs indicate a major direction; triangles carry illustrations of a particular traffic hazard; speed limits are indicated in a circle with the maximum limit circled in red

❚ TRAIN TRAVEL

The French national train agency, the Sociète Nationale de Chemins de Fer, or SNCF, is fast, punctual, comfortable, and comprehensive. Traveling across France, you have various options: local trains, overnight trains with sleeping accommodations, and the high-speed Trains à Grande Vitesse, known as the TGV.

TGVs average 255 kph (160 mph) on the Lyon–southeast line and 300 kph (190 mph) on the Lille and Bordeaux–southwest lines and are the best and the fastest domestic trains. They operate between Paris and Lille/Calais, Paris and Brussels, Paris and Amsterdam, Paris and Lyon–Switzerland–Provence, Paris and Angers–Nantes, Paris–Avignon and Tours–Poitiers–Bordeaux. As with other main-line trains, a small supplement may be assessed at peak hours.

It's usually fast and easy to cross France without traveling overnight, especially on TGVs, which are generally affordable and efficient. Be aware that trains fill fast on weekends and holidays, so purchase tickets well in advance at these times. Otherwise, you can take a slow overnight train, which often costs more than a TGV. There's a choice between high-price *wagons-lit* (sleeping cars) and slightly more affordable *couchettes* (bunks, six to a compartment in second class, four to a compartment in first, or private cabins).

In Paris there are six international rail stations: Gare du Nord (northern France, northern Europe, and England via Calais or Boulogne); Gare St-Lazare (Normandy and England via Dieppe); Gare de l'Est (Strasbourg, Luxembourg, Basel, and central Europe); Gare de Lyon (Lyon, Marseille, Provence, Geneva, and Italy); Gare d'Austerlitz (Loire Valley, southwest France, and Spain); and Gare Montparnasse (southwest France).

BOOKING AND BUYING TICKETS

There are two classes of train service in France; first (*première*) or second (*deux-ième*). First-class seats offer more leg-room, plusher upholstery, private reading lamps, and computer plugs on the TGV, not to mention the hush-hush environment for those who want to sleep. The price can be nearly double, though there are often deals online.

It is best—and in many cases, essential—to prebook your train tickets. This requires making a reservation (which carries an additional charge of about €10 a person) online, by phone, or at the train station. Rail Europe does an excellent job providing train tickets to those in the United States. It offers a service and the prices reflect that. If you want to save money, however, booking with the SNCF is cheaper.

BUYING SNCF TICKETS ONLINE

For service in English, go to ⊕ *www.voyages-sncf.com* and click on the U.K. flag—this takes you to Rail Europe, SNCF's U.K. partner. Next, enter your destination and dates of travel to find fare options quoted in British pounds (these can be converted to dollars using ⊕ *www.xe.com*). You may print tickets yourself (the better option) or pick them up at a station. Do not have them sent by mail. If you choose to pick up the tickets, you will receive an email with a six-letter reference code, which you enter at one of the self-service machines in the station. (Print out the email with the confirmation code in case there is a problem with the machines and you have to queue at the station ticket window. Be sure to leave extra time for this option as lines can be long.) You can book 90 days in advance for the TGV.

RAIL PASSES TO CHOOSE FROM

There are two kinds of rail passes: those you must purchase at home (including the France Rail Pass and Eurail Pass) and those available in France from SNCF.

France is one of 24 countries in which you can use the Eurail Global Pass. Providing unlimited rail travel in all participating countries for the duration of the pass, it's a good bet if you plan to really rack up the miles. The Global Pass is available for various time periods from 10 days (about $900 first class) to up to three months (about $2,100 first class). A special "Saver" version gives a discount for two or more people traveling together first class; while the "Youth" option provides discounts for those under age 26 who are traveling second class. If your plans call for only limited train travel between France and one other bordering country (say Italy or Spain), consider a less expensive Eurail Regional Pass. Whichever pass you choose, remember that you must buy it before leaving for France.

SNCF passes are available at any train station in France. Your rail pass does not guarantee a seat, however. You need to book ahead even if you're using an SNCF rail pass.

You can get a reduced fare if you're a senior citizen (over 60). The Carte Senior is a good option if you're planning on spending a lot of time traveling; it costs €65, is valid for one year, and entitles you to up to a 50% reduction on most trains with a guaranteed minimum reduction of 25%. It also entitles you to a 30% discount on trips outside of France. With the Prix Découverte Senior option, all you have to do is show a valid ID with your age and you're entitled to up to a 25% reduction in fares in first and second class. With the Carte Enfant Plus, for €75, children 4–12 years old accompanying adults can get up to 50% off most trains for an unlimited number of trips. This card, valid for a year, is perfect if you're planning to spend a lot of time traveling in France with your children. You can also opt for the Prix Découverte Enfant Plus: when you buy your ticket, simply show a valid ID with your child's age and you can get a significant discount

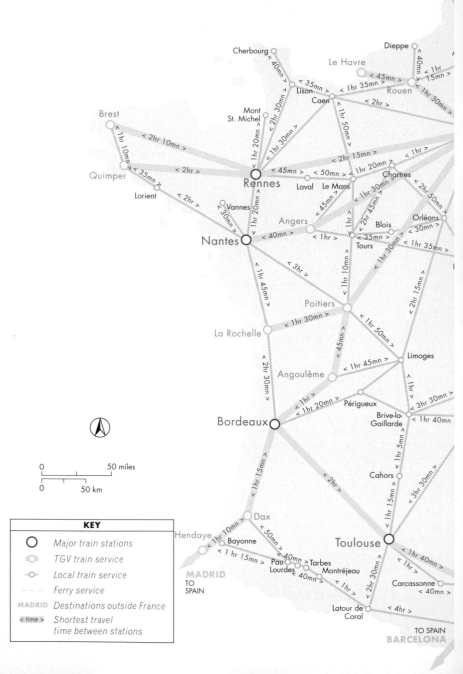

Boulogne

Dieppe

Cherbourg

Le Havre

< 40mn >

< 1hr 15mn >

< 35mn >

< 1hr 35mn >

Rouen

< 1hr 30mn >

Lison

Caen

< 2hr >

Mont
St. Michel

< 2hr 30mn >

< 1hr 30mn >

< 1hr 20mn >

< 1hr 50mn >

< 2hr 15mn >

< 1hr >

Brest

< 2hr 10mn >

Chartres

< 2hr 50mn >

< 1hr 10mn >

< 2hr >

< 45mn >

< 50mn >

< 1hr 20mn >

Quimper

< 35mn >

Rennes

Laval

Le Mans

Lorient

< 2hr >

< 1hr 20mn >

< 45mn >

< 1hr 30mn >

Orléans

Vannes

< 30mn >

Angers

< 1hr >

Blois

< 30mn >

< 1hr 35mn >

Nantes

< 40mn >

< 1hr >

Tours

< 35mn >

< 2hr 45mn >

< 1hr 10mn >

< 1hr 30mn >

< 3hr >

< 2hr 15mn >

Poitiers

< 1hr 45mn >

< 1hr 50mn >

La Rochelle

< 1hr 30mn >

Limoges

< 45mn >

< 1hr >

< 2hr 30mn >

Angoulême

< 1hr 45mn >

< 3hr 30mn >

< 1hr >

Périgueux

< 1hr 20mn >

Brive-la-
Gaillarde

< 1hr 40mn >

Bordeaux

< 1hr 5mn >

Cahors

< 3hr 30mn >

< 1hr 15mn >

< 2hr >

< 1hr 15mn >

Dax

< 1hr 10mn >

< 50mn >

Toulouse

< 1hr 40mn >

Hendaye

Bayonne

< 40mn >

Tarbes

< 1hr >

< 1 hr 15mn >

Pau

Lourdes

< 40mn >

Montréjeau

< 2hr 30mn >

Carcassonne

< 40mn >

MADRID
TO
SPAIN

< 1hr >

Latour de
Coral

< 4hr >

TO SPAIN
BARCELONA

KEY

○	Major train stations
◐	TGV train service
⊸○⊸	Local train service
- - -	Ferry service
MADRID	Destinations outside France
< time >	Shortest travel time between stations

0   50 miles

0   50 km

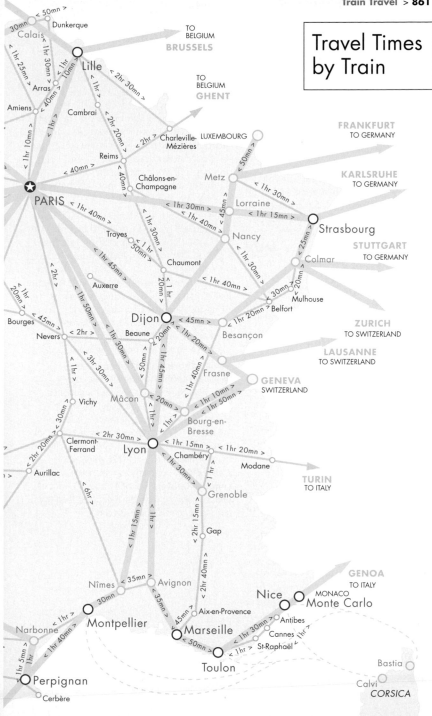

Travel Times by Train

for your child and a 25% reduction for up to four accompanying adults.

If you purchase an individual ticket from SNCF in France and you're under 26, you automatically get a 25% reduction when you flash a valid ID. If you're under 26 and plan to ride the train quite a bit, consider buying the Carte 12–25 (€50), which offers unlimited 50% reductions for one year.

If you don't benefit from any of these reductions and if you plan on traveling at least 200 km (132 miles) round-trip and don't mind staying over a Saturday night, look into the Prix Découverte Séjour. This ticket gives you a 25% reduction.

With an advance arrangement, SNCF will pick up and deliver your luggage at a given time. For instance, if you're planning on spending a weekend in Nice, SNCF will pick up your luggage at your hotel in Paris in the morning before checkout and deliver it to your hotel in Nice, where it will be awaiting your arrival. The cost is €35 for the first bag, and €17 per additional bag, with a maximum of three bags per person.

BOARDING THE TRAIN

Get to the station a half hour before departure to ensure you'll have a good seat. If you're taking a TGV, your seat is reserved by car and seat number. Before boarding, you must punch your ticket (*composter le billet*) in one of the orange machines at the entrance to the platforms (*quais*), or else you risk a €10–€25 fine (*amende*). Tickets printed by the SNCF must be validated; Eurail Passes and tickets printed at home don't need validation. If you board your train on the run and don't have time to punch it, look for a conductor (*contrôleur*) as soon as possible and get him to sign it. Once you're aboard, note that smoking is forbidden on all public transportation in France. Even lighting up in the bathrooms or connecting compartments will land you an on-the-spot fine of €68.

TO AND FROM THE UNITED KINGDOM

When you factor in travel time to and from the airport, not to mention flight delays, taking the Channel Tunnel is the fastest and easiest way between France and the United Kingdom. It'll take you two hours and 15 minutes on the high-speed Eurostar train from Paris' Gare du Nord to London's St. Pancras Station; if you wish to drive most of the route, you can put your car on the train for the Chunnel crossing, 35 minutes between Folkestone and Calais.

Britain's National Rail also has daily departures from London that link up with the Dover–Calais–Boulogne ferry services through to Paris. There's also an overnight service on the Newhaven–Dieppe ferry. Journey time is about eight hours. There's a vast range of prices for Eurostar—round-trip tickets range from €600 for first class to €88 for second class depending on when and where you travel and how far in advance you book.

Information Britain's National Rail ☎ 0845–748–4950 in the U.K., 44–0207–278–5240 from the U.S. ⊕ www.nationalrail. co.uk. **Eurail** ⊕ www.eurail.com. **Eurostar** ☎ 0843–218–6186 in U.K., 08–92–35–35–39 in France [€0.34 per min] ⊕ www.eurostar.com. **Rail Europe** ☎ 800/622–8600 in U.S. (toll-free) ⊕ www.raileurope.com. **SNCF** ☎ 36–35 in France [€0.34 per min] ⊕ www.sncf.com. **SNCF Luggage Delivery Service** ☎ 36–35 from any phone in France then say "bagages" [bah-gahj] [€0.34 per min] ⊕ www.sncf.com.

ESSENTIALS

■ ACCOMMODATIONS

Most hotels and other lodgings require you to give your credit-card details before they will confirm your reservation. If you don't feel comfortable emailing this information, ask if you can fax it. However you book, get confirmation in writing and have a copy of it handy when you check in.

Be sure you understand the hotel's cancellation policy. Some places allow you to cancel without any kind of penalty—even if you prepaid to secure a discounted rate—provided you cancel at least 24 hours in advance. Others require you to cancel a week in advance or penalize you the cost of one night. Small inns and B&Bs are most likely to require you to cancel far in advance. Most hotels allow children under a certain age to stay in their parents' room at no extra charge, but others charge for them as extra adults; find out the cutoff age for discounts.

APARTMENT AND HOUSE RENTALS

Individual tourist offices often publish lists of *locations meublés* (furnished rentals) that have been inspected and rated. Usually they're booked directly through the property owner, which generally requires some knowledge of French. Rentals that are not classified or rated by the tourist office should be undertaken with trepidation, as they can fall well below your minimum standard of comfort.

Vacation rentals in France typically book from Saturday to Saturday. Always check on policies regarding pets and children and specify if you need an enclosed garden for toddlers, a washing machine, a fireplace, and so on. If you plan to have overnight guests during your stay, let the owner know; there may be additional charges (insurance restrictions prohibit loading in guests beyond the specified capacity). Occasionally, further fees apply: these might include an end-of-stay cleaning, or even bed linen and towel rentals because vacationing French folks tend to bring their own. Be sure to plan early: apartment and house rentals are quite popular.

Contacts At Home Abroad ☎ 212/421–9165 in U.S. ⊕ www.athomeabroadinc.com. **Barclay International Group** ☎ 516/364–0064 in U.S., 800/845–6636 in U.S. (toll-free) ⊕ www.barclayweb.com. **Drawbridge to Europe** ☎ 541/482–7778 in U.S. ⊕ www.drawbridgetoeurope.com. **Fédération Nationale des Gîtes de France** ☎ 01–49–70–75–75 ⊕ www.gites-de-france.com. **Tourism In France.** (⇨ Visitor Information, below) **HomeAway** ⊕ www.homeaway.com. **Hosted Villas** ☎ 416/920–1873 in U.S., 800/374–6637 in U.S. (toll-free) ⊕ www.hostedvillas.com. **Interhome** ☎ 954/791–8282 in U.S., 800/882–6864 in U.S. (toll-free) ⊕ www.interhomeusa.com. **RentaVilla** ☎ 206/417–3444 in U.S., 877/250–4366 in U.S. (toll-free) ⊕ www.rentavilla.com. **Villas & Apartments Abroad** ☎ 212/213–6435 in U.S. ⊕ www.vaanyc.com. **Villas International** ☎ 415/499–9490 in U.S., 800/221–2260 in U.S. (toll-free) ⊕ www.villasintl.com. **Villas of Distinction** ☎ 800/289–0900 in U.S. (toll-free) ⊕ www.villasofdistinction.com. **Wimco** ☎ 800/449–1553 in U.S. (toll-free), 0870-850-1144 in U.K. ⊕ www.wimco.com.

BED-AND-BREAKFASTS

Reservation Services Bed & Breakfast.com. Bed & Breakfast.com also sends out an online newsletter. ☎ 512/322–2710 in U.S., 800/462–2632 in U.S. (toll-free) ⊕ www.bedandbreakfast.com. **Bed & Breakfast Inns Online** ☎ 800/215–7365 in U.S. (toll-free) ⊕ www.bbonline.com. **Chambres Hôtes France** ⊕ www.chambres-hotes-france.org. **Gîtes de France** ⊕ www.gitesdefrance.fr. **Hôtes Qualité Paris** ⊕ en.parisinfo.com/paris-hotels/bed-breakfast-chambres-d-hotes.

HOME EXCHANGES

With a direct home exchange you stay in someone else's home while they stay in yours. Some outfits also deal with vacation homes, so you're not actually staying in someone's full-time residence, just their vacant weekend place.

Exchange Clubs Home Exchange.com. The charge is $95.40 for a one-year membership, or $35.85 for three months. ☎ 800/877–8723 in U.S. (toll-free) ⊕ www.homeexchange.com. **HomeLink International.** The cost is $119 for a one-year membership. ☎ 800/638–3841 ⊕ www.homelink.org. **Intervac U.S.** The charge is $99 for annual membership. ☎ 800/756–4663 in U.S. (toll-free) ⊕ www.intervacus.com.

HOTELS

The quality of accommodations, particularly in older properties and even in luxury hotels, can vary greatly from room to room; if you don't like the room you're given, ask to see another.

Meal plans, which are usually an option offered in addition to the basic room plan, are generally only available with a minimum two- or three-night stay and are, of course, more expensive than the basic room rate. Inquire about meal plans when making reservations; details and prices are often stated on hotel websites.

It's always a good idea to make hotel reservations in Paris and other major tourist destinations as far in advance as possible, especially in late spring, summer, or fall. Most hotels allow you to book online. If you wish to communicate further, email is the easiest way to proceed—the hotel staff is probably more likely to read English than to understand it spoken over the phone long-distance. Whether by email, phone, or fax you should notify your hotel of a possible late check-in (to prevent your room from being given away) and to make any special requests (such as the location or the size of the room you want). Ask that the hotel provide written confirmation of your reservation and requests.

If you arrive without a reservation, the tourist offices in major train stations and most towns can probably help you find a room.

Many hotels in France are small, family-run establishments. Some are affiliated with hotel groups, such as Logis de France (⊕ www.logis-de-france.fr), which can be relied on for comfort, character, and regional cuisine. Two prestigious international groups with numerous converted châteaux and manor houses among their members are Relais & Châteaux (⊕ www.relaischateaux.com) and Small Luxury Hotels of the World (⊕ www.slh.com): check the websites for property listings. France also has numerous hotel chains. Examples in the upper price bracket are Frantel, Novotel, and Sofitel as well as InterContinental, Marriott, Hilton, Hyatt, Westin, and Sheraton. The Best Western, Campanile, Climat de France, Ibis, and Timhotel chains are more moderate. If you simply need a place to crash for one night (and aren't claustrophobic), the ubiquitous Hotel FI brand fits the bill. Typically, chains offer a consistently acceptable standard of comfort (modern bathrooms, TVs, etc.) but tend to lack atmosphere. One notable exception is Best Western: its properties are independently owned and most try to maintain the local character.

■ COMMUNICATIONS

INTERNET

Most hotels have in-room broadband connections or wireless access, although some only offer wireless access in the lobby or ground-floor rooms; if being connected from your room is important, be sure to confirm in advance. Also, if you need to spend a lot of time online, make sure to ask when you book if there's a charge for the service. Remember to bring an adapter for European-style plugs.

Wi-Fi hotspots can be found at many of the cafés and public libraries in Paris and other metropolitan areas. In smaller towns ask at the local tourism office where you can get connected. Note that if you capture a wireless network called "Free," don't be misled: it's the name of the carrier used in France and is not free of charge.

PHONES

The country code for France is 33. The first two digits of French numbers are a prefix determined by zone: Paris and Ile-de-France, 01; the northwest, 02; the northeast, 03; the southeast, 04; and the southwest, 05. Numbers that begin with 06 are for mobile phones (and are notoriously expensive). Pay close attention to numbers beginning with 08; 08 followed by 00 is a toll-free number, but 08–36 numbers can be costly (usually €0.34 per minute but sometimes €1 and up).

Note that when dialing France from abroad, drop the initial 0 from the number. For instance, to call a telephone number in Paris from the United States, dial 011–33 plus the phone number minus the initial 0 (phone numbers *in this book* are listed with the full 10 digits, which you use to make local calls).

CALLING WITHIN FRANCE

The French are very fond of their mobile phones (*portables*), meaning that telephone booths are more scarce than ever. Look for public phones in airports, post offices, train stations, on the street, and subway stations. You can use your own credit card, but keep in mind that you will be charged a €20 minimum, and you'll have 30 days after the first call to use up the credit. Alternately, you can pick up a discounted calling card (*carte téléphonique*) at newsstands, cafés with a tabac sign, or post offices. There are two types of cards: one can be used on any phone, the other has a microchip (*puce*) that works only on public phones (*les cabines*). Insert your card and follow directions on the screen (it should give you the option to read in English). Or dial the toll-free number on the back of the card, enter the identification number from the back of the card, and follow the instructions in English.

CALLING OUTSIDE FRANCE

To make a direct international call out of France, dial 00, then the country code (1 for the United States), the area code, and number.

Telephone rates have decreased recently in France now that the French Telecom monopoly finally has some competition. As in most countries, the priciest calls are between 8 am and 7 pm; you can expect to pay €0.28 per minute for a call to the United States, Canada, or some of the closer European countries such as Great Britain, Belgium, Italy, and Germany. Rates are slashed in half when you make that same call between 7 pm and 8 am, at just €0.13 per minute. Calling home with the help of international directory assistance costs a hefty €3 per call; if this doesn't dissuade you, dial ☎*118–700* and a bilingual operator will come on the line and ask which country you are calling.

Major carriers offer good rates on international calls with their calling cards (⇨ *for access numbers from France, see below*). You can also save money by using an international phone card (*télécarte international*), which you can find at the same places as a local calling card. The cards cost about €13.50 for 50 units or €22 for 120 units. Under no circumstances should you place an international call directly from your hotel room—the charges can be astronomical.

Access Codes AT&T Direct ☎ *08–00–99–00–11 in France, 800/222–0300 for information in U.S. (toll-free).* **MCI WorldPhone** ☎ *08–00–99–00–19 in France, 800/444–4444 for information in U.S. (toll-free).* **Sprint International Access** ☎ *08–00–99–00–87 in France, 888/226–7212 for information in U.S. (toll-free).*

MOBILE PHONES

If you have a multiband phone (some countries use different frequencies from what's used in the United States) and your service provider uses the world-standard GSM network (as do T-Mobile, AT&T, and Verizon), you can probably use your phone abroad. But be warned: this is often the most expensive calling option, with hefty toll charges on incoming and outgoing calls, sometimes as high as $4 per. Roaming fees can be steep, too: 99¢ a minute is considered reasonable. Sending an international text message is usually a cheaper option, but be aware that fees abroad vary greatly (from 15¢ to 50¢ and up), and there's usually a charge for incoming messages.

If you just want to make local calls, consider buying a local SIM card for about €30 (note that your provider may have to unlock your phone for you to use a different SIM card) or a cheap pay-as-you-go phone (*sans abonnement*) found at any post office or phone shop. You can then have a local number and make local calls at local rates. If your trip is extensive, you could also simply buy a new cell phone in your destination, as the initial cost will be offset over time.

■TIP➔ If you travel internationally frequently, save one of your old mobile phones or buy a cheap one online; ask your cell phone company to unlock it for you, and take it with you as a travel phone, buying a new SIM card with pay-as-you-go service in each destination.

SKYPE

Another option is to use Skype (⊕ *www.skype.com*), which allows you to make calls over the Internet. After downloading software, you can place no- or low-cost calls anywhere in the world with an Internet connection from your computer.

Contacts Cellular Abroad. Cellular Abroad rents and sells GMS phones and sells SIM cards that work in many countries with inexpensive per-minute rates. ☎ *800/287–5072 in U.S. (toll-free)* ⊕ *www.cellularabroad.com.* **Mobal.** Mobal rents mobiles and sells GSM phones (starting at $29) that will operate in 170 countries. Per-call rates are competitive but each sms (text messages) costs 80¢ to send. ☎ *888/888–9162 in U.S. (toll-free)* ⊕ *www.mobalrental.com.* **Planet Fone.** Planet Fone rents cell phones, but the per-minute rates are expensive. ☎ *888/988–4777 in U.S. (toll-free)* ⊕ *www.planetfone.com.*

▎EATING OUT

All establishments must post their menus outside, so take a look before you enter. Most restaurants have two basic types of menu: à la carte and fixed-price (prix-fixe or *un menu*). The prix-fixe menu is usually the best value, though choices are more limited. Most menus begin with a first course (*une entrée*), often subdivided into cold and hot starters, followed by fish and poultry, then meat; it's rare today that anyone orders something from all three.

A few pointers on French dining etiquette: diners in France rarely negotiate their orders, so don't expect serene smiles when you ask for sauce on the side. Order your coffee after dessert, not with it. When you're ready for the check, ask for it: no professional waiter would dare put a bill on your table while you're still enjoying the last sip of coffee. And don't ask for a doggy bag—it's just not done. The French usually drink wine or mineral water (not soda or coffee) with their food. You may ask for a carafe of tap water if you don't want to order wine or pay for bottled water.

FAST FOOD, FRENCH STYLE

Many say that bistros served the world's first fast food. After the fall of Napoléon, the Russian soldiers who occupied Paris were known to bang on zinc-top café bars, crying *"bistro"*—"quickly"—in Russian. In the past, bistros were simple places with minimal decor and service. Although nowadays many are quite upscale, most remain cozy establishments serving straightforward, frequently gutsy cooking.

Brasseries—ideal places for quick, one-dish meals—originated when Alsatians fleeing German occupiers after the Franco-Prussian War came to Paris and opened restaurants serving specialties from home. Pork-based dishes, *choucroute* (sauerkraut), and beer (*brasserie* also means brewery) were, and still are, mainstays here. The typical brasserie is convivial and keeps late hours. Some are open 24 hours a day, a good thing to know since many restaurants stop serving at 10 or 10:30 pm.

Like bistros and brasseries, cafés come in a confusing variety. Often informal neighborhood hangouts, cafés may also be veritable showplaces attracting chic, well-heeled crowds. At most cafés the regulars congregate at the bar, where coffee and drinks are cheaper than at tables. At lunch tables are set, and a limited menu is served. Sandwiches, usually with *jambon* (ham), *fromage* (cheese), or *mixte* (ham and cheese), are served throughout the day. Sometimes snacks are also for sale. Cafés are for lingering, for people-watching, and for daydreaming. If none of these options fit the bill, head to the nearest *traiteur* (deli) for picnic fixings.

See the Menu Guide at the end of the book for guidance with menu items that appear frequently on French menus and throughout the reviews in this book.

Breakfast is usually served from 7:30 am to 10 pm, lunch from noon to 2 pm, and dinner from 8 pm to 10 pm. Restaurants in Paris usually serve dinner until 10:30 pm.

PAYING

By French law, prices must include tax and tip (*service compris* or *prix nets*), but pocket change left on the table in basic places, or an additional 5% in better restaurants, is always appreciated. Beware of bills stamped *service not included* in English. The prices given in this book are per person for a main course at dinner, including tax (5%) and service; note that if a restaurant offers only prix-fixe (set-price) meals, it is given a price category that reflects the full prix-fixe price.

■ ELECTRICITY

The electrical current in France is 220 volts, 50 cycles alternating current (AC); wall outlets take Continental-type plugs, with two round prongs. Consider making a small investment in a universal adapter, which has several types of plugs in one lightweight, compact unit.

Most laptops and mobile phone chargers are dual voltage (i.e., they operate equally well on 110 and 220 volts), so require only an adapter, as do small appliances like hair dryers. Always check labels and manufacturer instructions to be sure. You may need to buy a converter if you wish to use appliances that do not work with 220 volts. Don't use 110-volt outlets marked for shavers only for high-wattage appliances such as hair dryers.

Contacts Adaptelec. Adaptelec has information on electrical and telephone plugs around the world (search for "France" on the site for detailed info). ⊕ *www.adaptelec.com.*

■ EMERGENCIES

France's emergency services are conveniently streamlined. Every town and village has a *médecin de garde* (on-duty doctor) for flus, sprains, tetanus shots, and similar problems. Larger cities have a remarkable house-call service called "SOS Médecins" (SOS Doctors, or "SOS Dentistes" for dental emergencies); dial ☎ *3624.* The cost is minimal, compared to the United States—about €70 for a house call. If you need an X-ray or emergency treatment, call an ambulance (dial ☏ 15).

Most hotels will be able to help you find assistance in the event of a medical emergency. Note that outside Paris it may be difficult to find English-speaking doctors.

Pharmacies can be helpful with minor health problems and come equipped with blood-pressure machines and first-aid kits. They also can be consulted for a list of practicing doctors in the area, nearby hospitals, private clinics, or health centers.

On the street the French phrases that may be needed in an emergency are: *Au secours!* (Help!), *urgence* (emergency), *samu* (ambulance), *pompiers* (firefighters), *préfecture de police* (police station), *médecin* (doctor), and *hôpital* (hospital).

▌ HOLIDAYS

With 11 national *jours feriés* (holidays) and at least five weeks of paid vacation, the French have their share of repose. In May there's a holiday nearly every week, so be prepared for stores, banks, and museums to shut their doors for days at a time. Be sure to call museums, restaurants, and hotels in advance to make sure they'll be open.

Note that these dates are for the calendar year 2014: January 1 (New Year's Day); April 20 and 21 (Easter Sunday and Monday); May 1 (Labor Day); May 8 (V.E. Day); May 9 (Ascension); June 8 (Pentecost Sunday); July 14 (Bastille Day); August 15 (Assumption); November 1 (All Saints); November 11 (Armistice); December 25 (Christmas).

▌ MAIL

Post offices, or PTT, are found in every town and are recognizable by a yellow La Poste sign. They're usually open weekdays 8 am to 7 pm, Saturday 8–noon. The main Paris post office is open daily, from 7:30 am until 6 am (closed for an hour and a half for cleaning). ✉ *52 rue du Louvre, Paris* ⊕ *www.laposte.com.*

SHIPPING PACKAGES

Letters and postcards to the United States and Canada cost €0.95 for 20 grams. Letters and postcards within France cost €0.63. Stamps can be bought in post offices and in cafés displaying a red tabac sign outside. It takes, on the average, three days for letters to arrive in Europe, and five days to reach the United States.

If you're uncertain where you'll be staying, have mail sent to the local post office, addressed as poste restante. The French postal service has a €0.58 per item service charge.

Sending overnight mail from major cities in France is relatively easy. Besides DHL, Federal Express, and UPS, the French post office has overnight mail service, called Chronopost, which is much cheaper for small packages. Keep in mind that certain things cannot be shipped from France to the United States, such as perfume and any meat products.

Express Services DHL ☏ *08–20–20–25–25 [€.09 per min]* ⊕ *www.dhl.com.* **Federal Express** ☏ *01–40–85–56–60 in Paris, 08–20–12–38–00 for information from all over France [€.12 per min]* ⊕ *www.fedex.com.* **UPS** ☏ *08–21–23–38–77 for information from all over France* ⊕ *www.ups.com.*

▌ MONEY

The following prices are for Paris; other areas are often cheaper (with the notable exception of the Côte d'Azur). Keep in mind that it's less expensive to eat or drink standing at a café or bar counter than to sit at a table. Two prices are listed, *au comptoir* (at the counter) and *à salle* (at a table). Sometimes orders cost even more if you're seated at a terrace table. Coffee in a bar: €1–€2.50 (standing), €1.50–€6 (seated); beer in a bar: €2.50 (standing), €3–€8 (seated); Coca-Cola: €2–€4.50 a bottle; ham sandwich: €3–€5; 2-km (1-mile) taxi ride: €6; movie-theater seat: €10.90 (morning shows are always cheaper); foreign newspaper: €1.50–€5.

Prices throughout this guide are given for adults. Substantially reduced fees are almost always available for children, students, and senior citizens.

ATMS AND BANKS

Your own bank will probably charge a fee for using ATMs abroad; the foreign bank you use may also charge a fee. Nevertheless, you can usually get a better rate of exchange at an ATM than you will at a currency-exchange office or even when changing money in a bank. And extracting funds as you need them is a safer option than carrying around a large amount of cash.

■**TIP→** PINs with more than four digits are not recognized at ATMs in many countries. If yours has five or more, remember to change it before you leave.

Readily found throughout France, ATMs are one of the easiest ways to get euros.

Note that the ATM machine will give you two chances to enter your correct PIN number; if you make a mistake on the third try, your card will be held, and you'll have to go into the bank to retrieve it (this may mean returning during opening hours). Some ATMs will accept a credit or debit card that is also a Visa or MasterCard, but not an unaffiliated bank card.

CREDIT CARDS

France is a debit-card society. Debit cards are used for just about everything, from the automatic gas pumps, to the tolls on highways, payment machines in underground parking lots, stamps at the post office, and even the most minor purchases in the larger department stores. A restaurant or shop would either have to be extremely small or remote not to have some credit-card or debit-card capability. However, some of the smaller restaurants and stores do have a credit-card minimum, usually around €15, which normally should be clearly indicated; to be safe, ask before you order. Do not forget to take your credit-card receipt,

as fraudulent use of credit-card numbers taken from receipts is on the rise. Note that while MasterCard and Visa are usually welcomed, American Express isn't always accepted.

It's a good idea to inform your credit-card company before you leave home, especially if you don't travel internationally very often. Otherwise, they might put a hold on your card because of unusual activity—not a good thing halfway through your trip. Record all your credit-card numbers—as well as the phone numbers to call if your cards are lost or stolen—in a safe place, so you're prepared should something go wrong. MasterCard and Visa have general numbers you can call (collect if you're abroad) if your card is lost, but you're better off calling the number of your issuing bank, since MasterCard and Visa usually just transfer you to your bank anyway; your bank's number is usually printed on your card.

If you plan to use your credit card for cash advances, you'll need to apply for a PIN at least two weeks before your trip. Although it's usually cheaper (and safer) to use a credit card abroad for large purchases (so you can cancel payments or be reimbursed if there's a problem), note that some credit-card companies *and* the banks that issue them add substantial percentages to all foreign transactions, whether they're in a foreign currency or not. Check on these fees before leaving home, so there won't be any surprises when you get the bill.

Reporting Lost Cards American Express
☎ 800/528–4800 in U.S. (toll-free), 01–47–77–70–00 in Paris ⊕ www.americanexpress.com. **Diners Club** ☎ 800/234–6377 in U.S. (toll-free), 514/877–1577 emergency from abroad (call collect) ⊕ www.dinersclub.com. **Discover** ☎ 800/347–2683 in U.S. (toll-free), 801/902–3100 from abroad (call collect) ⊕ www.discovercard.com. **MasterCard** ☎ 800/627–8372 in U.S. (toll-free), 636/722–7111 from abroad (call collect) ⊕ www.mastercard.com. **Visa** ☎ 800/847–2911 in U.S. (toll-free), 08–00–90–11–79 in France ⊕ www.visa.com.

CURRENCY AND EXCHANGE

The advent of the euro makes any whirlwind European tour all the easier. From France you can glide across the borders of Austria, Germany, Italy, Spain, Holland, Ireland, Greece, Belgium, Finland, Luxembourg, and Portugal with no pressing need to run to the local exchange booth to change to yet another currency before you even had the time to become familiar with the last. You'll be able to do what drives many tourists crazy—to assess the value of a purchase (for example, to realize that eating a three-course meal in a small restaurant in Lisbon is cheaper than that ham sandwich you bought on the Champs Élysées).

At this writing, one euro equals U.S. $1.30. These days, the easiest way to get euros is through ATMs; you can find them in airports, train stations, and throughout cities and towns. ATM rates are excellent because they're based on wholesale rates offered only by major banks. Remember, though, that you may be charged an added exchange fee when withdrawing euros from your account. It's a good idea to bring some euros with you from home and always to have some cash on hand as backup.

Currency Conversion Oanda.com ⊕ *www. oanda.com.* **XE.com** ⊕ *www.xe.com.* **X-Rates** ⊕ *www.x-rates.com.*

▌ PASSPORTS

All Canadian, U.K., and U.S. citizens, even infants, need only a valid passport to enter France for stays of up to 90 days.

You must apply in person if you're getting a passport for the first time; if your previous passport was lost, stolen, or damaged; or if your previous passport has expired and was issued more than 15 years ago or when you were under 16. All children under 18 must appear in person to apply for or renew a passport. Both parents must accompany any child under 14 (or send a notarized statement with

WORD OF MOUTH

"Where to go? I believe I could stick a map of France on the wall, throw a dart, and be very happy wherever it landed!"

—Nikki

their permission) and provide proof of their relationship to the child.

There are 13 regional passport offices, as well as 7,000 passport acceptance facilities in post offices, public libraries, and other governmental offices. If you're renewing a passport, you can do so by mail. Forms are available at passport acceptance facilities and online. The cost to apply for a new passport is $110 for adults, $80 for children under 16. Allow six weeks for processing, both for first-time passports and renewals. For an expediting fee of $60 you can reduce this time to about two weeks. If your trip is less than two weeks away, you can get a passport even more rapidly by going to a passport office with the necessary documentation. Before your trip, make two copies of your passport's data page (one for someone at home and another for you to carry separately). Or scan the page and email it to someone at home and/or yourself.

U.S. Passport Information U.S. Department of State ☎ *877/487–2778 toll-free* ⊕ *travel. state.gov/passport/.*

▌ SAFETY

Beware of petty theft—purse snatching, pickpocketing, and the like—throughout France, particularly in Paris and along the Côte d'Azur. Use common sense: avoid pulling out a lot of money in public; wear a handbag with long straps that you can sling across your body, bandolier style, with a zippered compartment for your money and passport. Men should keep their wallets up front. When withdrawing money from cash machines, be especially aware of your surroundings and anyone standing too close. If you feel uneasy, press the cancel button (*annuler*) and walk to an area where you feel more comfortable. Incidents of credit-card fraud are on the rise in France, especially in urban areas; be sure to collect your receipts, as these have recently been used by thieves to make purchases over the Internet. Car break-ins, especially in isolated parking lots where hikers set off for the day, are on the rise. It makes sense to take valuables with you or leave your luggage at your hotel.

Note one cultural difference: a friendly smile or steady eye contact is often seen as an invitation to further contact; so, unfortunately, you should avoid being overly friendly with strangers—unless you feel perfectly safe.

■**TIP→** Distribute your cash, credit cards, IDs, and other valuables between a deep front pocket, an inside jacket or vest pocket, and a hidden money pouch. Don't reach for the money pouch once you're in public.

■ TAXES

The initials TTC (*toutes taxes comprises*—taxes included) sometimes appear on price lists but, strictly speaking, they're superfluous because, in France, all taxes must be included in posted prices. As of January 2014, the V.A.T. (value-added tax, known here as TVA) will be applied at a base rate of 20%, with some items being taxed at higher or lower rates. By law, hotel prices must include the 20% tax; restaurant prices must include 5% for food (10% if it's take-out) but the full 20% for alcohol. Note that a 33% tax is charged on luxury goods. If taxes show up as extra charges, complain.

The good news is that many shops offer V.A.T. refunds to foreign shoppers. Non-EU residents (including Americans and Canadians) can claim a refund (less a 3% administrative fee) for any goods totaling € 175.01 purchased in the same store on a single day. Request a *détaxe* form in the store. You will be asked to show your passport. At the airport or border crossing, present the form, plus receipts for the goods purchased, to customs officials, who will issue a stamp. Proceed to the cash refund office. You may also return the form by mail.

Global Blue has refund counters at major airports and border crossings. The service issues refunds in the form of cash, check, or credit-card adjustment.

V.A.T. Refunds Detaxe TaxFree ☎ *01–42–60–29–29 in France* ⊕ *www.detaxe.com.* **Global Blue** ⊕ *www.global-blue.com.*

■ TIME

The time difference between New York and Paris is six hours (so when it's 1 pm in New York, it's 7 pm in Paris). France, like the rest of Europe, uses the 24-hour clock, which means that after noon you continue counting forward: 13h00 is 1 pm, 22h30 is 10:30 pm. The European format for abbreviating dates is day/month/year, so 7/5/13 means May 7, not July 5.

Time Zones Timeanddate.com. Timeanddate.com, The World Clock, can help you figure out the correct time anywhere in the world. ⊕ *www.timeanddate.com/worldclock.*

■ TIPPING

The French have a clear idea of when they should be tipped. Bills in bars and restaurants include a service charge incorporated into the prices, but it's customary to round out your bill with some small change unless you're dissatisfied. The amount varies: anywhere from €0.50, if you've merely bought a beer, to €1–€3 (or more) after a meal. Tip taxi drivers and hair stylists about 10%. In some theaters and hotels, coat-check attendants may expect nothing (if there's a sign saying "*pourboire interdit*"—tips forbidden); otherwise give them €0.50–€1. Washroom attendants usually get €0.50, though the sum is often posted.

If you stay in a hotel for more than two or three days, it's customary to leave something for the chambermaid—€1–€2 per day. In expensive hotels you may well use the services of a parking valet, doorman, bellhop, and concierge. All expect a tip: plan on about €1.50 per item for the bellhop and €10–€20 for a particularly helpful concierge. The other tips will depend on how much you've used a person's services—common sense must guide you here. In hotels that provide room service, give €1–€2 to the waiter (this does not apply to breakfast served in your room). If the chambermaid does some pressing, give her €1–€2 on top of the charge made.

Museum guides should get €1–€1.50 after a tour. For other kinds of tours, tip the guide or excursion leader 10% of the tour cost; it's standard practice to tip long-distance bus drivers about €2 after an excursion, too.

▌ VISITOR INFORMATION

All major cities and most small towns have tourism offices that can provide information on accommodation and sightseeing as well as maps.

France Tourism Information

France Guide. France Guide is the official website of the national Tourist Office. ⊕ *us.franceguide.com.*

Tourism Websites Tourism in France. Tourism in France has links to 3,500 tourist offices. ⊕ *www.tourisme.fr.*

ONLINE TRAVEL TOOLS

All About France Centre des Monuments Nationaux. The Centre des Monuments Nationaux runs 200 monuments—from the Arc de Triomphe to Chambord—and is chock-full of information. ⊕ *www.monum.fr.* **Chateaux and Country.** If you're château hopping, Chateaux and Country has a brief overview of hundreds of châteaux all over France. ⊕ *www. chateauxandcountry.com.* **French Ministry of Culture.** The French Ministry of Culture provides a portal to all the cultural happenings and institutions throughout France. ⊕ *www. culture.fr.* **French National Museums.** French National Museums is the main site for the Réunion des musées nationaux, which administers some of the country's largest museums. ⊕ *www.rmn.fr.*

INDEX

PHOTO CREDITS

Front cover: Hemis/awl-images [Description: Château de Versailles, Yvelines].1, Lane Clark, Fodors. com member. 3, iStockphoto. 4, alohaspirit/iStockphoto Chapter 1: Experience France: 8-9, Jon Arnold/Agency Jon Arnold Images/age fotostock. 10, Lisa Ferguson, Fodors.com member. 11(left), Michael Gwyther-Jones/Flickr. 11 (right), Betty H, Fodors.com member. 12, (left), Leigh, Fodors.com member. 12 (right), Bob Lawson, Fodors.com member. 13, Doug Pearson/Agency Jon Arnold Images/ age fotostock. 14 (left), Chris Christensen, Fodors.com member. 14 (right), AJ Kersten, Fodors.com member. 15 (left), SGM/age fotostock. 15 (right), Peter Allen, Fodors.com member. 20 (left), Pete Labrozzi, Fodors.com member. 20 (center), Tiffany Weir, Fodors.com member. 20 (bottom), Claudio Giovanni Colombo/Shutterstock. 20 (right), elaine, Fodors.com member. 21 (left), Elena Elisseeva/Shutterstock. 21 (center), Holly McKee, Fodors.com member. 21 (bottom), Tangata, Fodors.com member. 21 (right), james incorvaia, Fodors.com member. 22, basingstoke2, Fodors.com member. 23 (left), smugman, Fodors.com member. 23 (right), Judy J. Potrzeba, Fodors.com member. 24, SuperStock/age fotostock. 25, Anna McClain, Fodors.com member. 26, Le Buerehiesel. 27 (left), GLong2027, Fodors. com member. 27 (right), dthomasdupont, Fodors.com member. 28, Shannon McShane, Fodors.com member. 29 (left and right), Robert Fisher. 30, Zyankarlo/Shutterstock. 31 (left), LadyofHats/wikipedia.org. 31 (right), Elizabeth A. Miller, Fodors.com member. 32, dspiel, Fodors.com member. 33 (left), nfldbeothuk, Fodors.com member. 33 (right), schlegal1, Fodors.com member. 36, Juan Carlos Muñoz/ age fotostock. 37, von Essen Hotels. 38, James Dunn, Fodors.com member. Chapter 2: Paris: 39, ajkarlin, Fodors.com member. 40, equiles28, Fodors.com member. 41 (left), Andrea Schwab, Fodors.com member. 41 (right), Ann Forcier, Fodors.com member. 42, christinaaparis, Fodors.com member. 53, fabio chironi/age fotostock. 56, P. Narayan/age fotostock. 59, (c) Shoutforhumanity Dreamstime.com. 60, Fabien1309/wikipedia.org. 61, Renaud Visage/age fotostock. 62 (left), Frank Peterschroeder / Bilderberg/Aurora Photos. 62 (right), ostill/Shutterstock. 68, Directphoto.org / Alamy. 69, Directphoto. org / Alamy. 73, wikipedia.org. 77, Kevin George / Alamy. 82, Marisa Allegra Williams/iStockphoto. 89, ImageGap / Alamy. 93 (top), Picnic by the Seine by Gideon http://www.flickr.com/photos/ malias/2565972790/Attribution License. 93 (bottom), SuperStock/age fotostock. 94 (left), Renaud Visage/age fotostock. 94 (right), Ivan Vdovin/Shutterstock. 95 (top left), Stevan Stratford/iStockphoto. 95 (bottom), Picnic by the Seine by Gideon http://www.flickr.com/photos/malias/2565972790/Attribution License. 95 (top right), Robert Haines / Alamy. 96 (left), © Renaud Visage/age fotostock. 96 (right), Carsten Madsen/iStockphoto. 97 (top left), xc/Shutterstock. 97 (top right), Corbis. 97 (bottom), Mehdi Chebil / Alamy. 98, Elena Elisseeva/Shutterstock. 102, rfx/Shutterstock. 114, P. Narayan/age fotostock. 121, Roger Salz/Flickr. 136 (top), Richard Bryant/arcaid.co.uk/The Dorchester Collection. 136 (bottom), Shangri-La International Hotel Management Ltd. 141 (top), Jaime Ardiles-Arce/Four Seasons Hotels and Resorts. 141 (bottom), Dorchester Collection. 146, L F File/Shutterstock. 151, Paradis Latin Cabaret. 157, Cezary Piwowarski/wikipedia.org. 160, Elizabeth A. Miller, Fodors.com member. Chapter 3: Ile-de-France: 167, Wojtek Buss/age fotostock. 168, Judith Nelson, Fodors.com member. 169 (top), elaine, Fodors.com member. 169 (bottom), TravelChic10, Fodors.com member. 170, Ivan Bastien/iStockphoto. 178-79, AM Corporation / Alamy. 180 (first), Elias H. Debbas II/Shutterstock. 180 (second), Jason Cosburn/Shutterstock. 180 (third), Public Domain. 180 (fourth), Michael Booth / Alamy. 180 (fifth), Michael Booth / Alamy. 181 (left), Jens Preshaw/age fotostock. 181 (top right), Public Domain. 181 (bottom right), The Print Collector / Alamy. 182 (top), michel mory/iStockphoto. 182 (center), Mike Booth/Alamy. 182 (bottom), Tommaso di Girolamo/age fotostock. 183, Hemis/Alamy. 184 (first), Public Domain. 184 (second), Jason Cosburn/Shutterstock. 184 (third), Guy Thouvenin/age fotostock. 184 (fourth), Visual Arts Library (London) / Alamy. 185 (top), Guy Thouvenin/age fotostock. 185 (bottom), Public Domain. 186, Jim Tardio/iStockphoto. 191, Jose Ignacio Soto/Shutterstock. 194, ShutterbugBill, Fodors.com member. 205, bobyfume/wikipedia.org. 208, Jean-Luc Bohin / age fotostock. Chapter 4: The Loire Valley: 215, Kevin Galvin/age fotostock. 216, P. Narayan/age fotostock. 217 (top left), P. Narayan/age fotostock. 217 (top right), Michael McClain, Fodors.com member. 217 (bottom), Connie28, Fodors.com member. 218, Per Karlsson - BKWine.com / Alamy. 219 (left), J.Bilic/age fotostock. 219 (right), Kelly Cline/iStockphoto. 220, caspermoller/Flickr. 230, © vittorio sciosia / age fotostock. 232 (top), SuperStock/age fotostock. 232 (bottom), David Lyons / Alamy. 234 (top left), P. Narayan/age fotostock. 234 (top right), Public Domain. 234 (bottom), P. Narayan/age fotostock. 235 (top left), Duncan Gilbert/iStockphoto. 235 (bottom left), Public Domain. 235 (top right), S. Greg Panosian/iStockphoto. 235 (bottom center), Public Domain. 235 (bottom right), Visual Arts Library (London) / Alamy. 236 (bottom left), Images Etc Ltd / Alamy. 236 (top left), Marc Dantan. 236 (bottom right), vittorio sciosia / Alamy. 236 (top right), Sylvain Grandadam/age fotostock. 242-43, © Travel Pix Collection / age fotostock. 246, Château de Colliers. 253, Edyta Pawlowska/Shutterstock. 259, PHB.cz (Richard Semik)/Shutterstock. Chapter 5: Normandy: 267, San Rostro/age fotostock. 268,

NOTES

NOTES

NOTES

NOTES

ABOUT OUR WRITERS

When writer-editor **Jennifer Ditsler-Ladonne** decided it was time to leave her longtime home, Manhattan, there was only one place to go: Paris. If you're looking for rare medieval arcana or Paris's wild edible mushrooms, she's the person to call. Author of our "France Today" section of this edition's Experience France chapter, Jennifer keeps up with all aspects of the French scene, thanks to her frequent articles for *France Today*. For this edition, the Fodor's Paris restaurant and shopping critic also updated our Ile de France, Lyon, and Dordogne chapters.

Nancy Heslin has been editor of the English-language *Riviera Reporter* magazine (*rivierareporter.com*) and a travel writer since 2001, when she swapped Canada for the Côte d'Azur. A "go-to" authority, she has been interviewed by the likes of CBS News and APF (along with taking the TGV with Tom Cruise to Marseille, lunching with Prince Albert in Monaco, and sipping champagne with Paris Hilton in St-Tropez as a staffer for some leading glossies). A self-professed fois gras junkie, Nancy loves to drive the unchartered roads of Provence in quest of the ultimate village vista or undiscovered *bonne* table. For this edition, she updated our Provence and French Riviera chapters.

Christopher Mooney's articles have appeared in *Elle* and *Condé Nast Traveler*, and he is coeditor of *Paris Ritz Magazine* and *Plaza-Athénée Magazine*. Together with **Jack Vermee**, a Paris-based freelance writer, Chris updated our chapters on Brittany, Normandy, and the Loire Valley and also wrote our photo feature on Burgundy wines.

British travel writer and editor **Lyn Parry** has lived in France for almost 20 years. In Britain her Masters in Hotel and Catering Management, and a stint in a luxury four star hotel, gave her a taste for fine French food and wine. After working for the wine trade in London her nose led her to Bordeaux. Since then she has lived near Paris, and latterly in the Rhône Valley.

Lyn loves to drive off, either solo or sharing her travel adventures with her teenage son, to explore the fascinating regions throughout France. For this edition for France, she updated the Alsace-Lorraine chapter, the Burgundy chapter, and the Champagne Country chapter.

In 2007, **Avery Sumner** sold her café in the Florida Everglades and moved to France. Since then she's walked and cycled across the country perfecting the art of "slow travel," in part by leading gourmet cycling trips through Provence and Burgundy with Boston-based Duvine Adventures and more recently with her own active travel company, Slow Travel France: Real travel in the real South of France (*www.slowtravelfrance.com*). Avery also leads France yoga and writing retreats with British author Rosemary Bailey (*www.francewritingretreat.com*), but what she loves most is introducing travelers to the olive oil producers, winemakers, goat farmers and locavores in her home region of Roussillon. For this edition, Avery updated our Languedoc-Roussillon, Midi-Pyrénées, Bordeaux, and Basque, Gascony and Hautes Pyrénées chapters.

Paris-based writer and globetrotter **Victoria Tang** has lived and worked abroad for nearly 15 years. She left the corporate world to dedicate herself to travel writing, fiction, journalism, photography, and global communications. Author of guidebooks *Paris for Kids* and *France for Kids* by Marquee Publishing, she is the founder of Paris Child (*www.ParisChild.com*), an online information resource for parents. Her commercial portfolio features multiple assignments with Fodor's Travel. For this edition, Victoria updated the Corsica chapter.

Updating our Paris chapter were our team of crack writers from *Fodor's Paris 2014*: **Jennifer Ditsler-Ladonne, Linda Hervieux, Bryan Pirolli**, and **Victoria Tang**.

Linda Hervieux also updated the Travel Smart chapter.

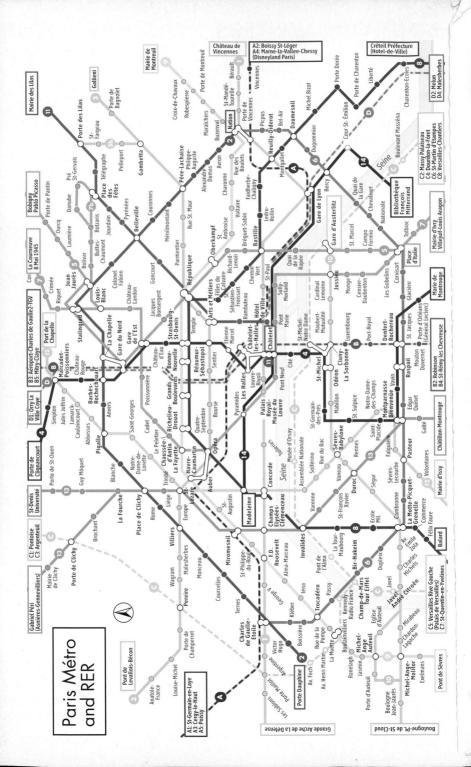

Paris Métro and RER